THE OXFORD HANDBC

LEIBNIZ

THE OXFORD HANDBOOK OF

LEIBNIZ

Edited by

MARIA ROSA ANTOGNAZZA

OXFORD

UNIVERSITY PRESS

OXFORD
UNIVERSITY PRESS

Oxford University Press is a department of the University of Oxford. It furthers
the University's objective of excellence in research, scholarship, and education
by publishing worldwide. Oxford is a registered trade mark of Oxford University
Press in the UK and certain other countries.

Published in the United States of America by Oxford University Press
198 Madison Avenue, New York, NY 10016, United States of America.

© Oxford University Press 2018

First issued as an Oxford University Press paperback, 2021

CIP data is on file at the Library of Congress
ISBN 978–0–19–974472–5 (hardback); ISBN 978–0–19–762092–2 (paperback)

To
Sophia Antognazza Hotson
31 May 1999 – 7 March 2018
loving, brave, wise

Contents

PART V SCIENTIFIC AND TECHNICAL WORK

PART VI SCIENTIFIC ORGANIZATIONS, CULTURAL NETWORKING, AND SCHOLARSHIP

PART VII ETHICS, JURISPRUDENCE, AND POLITICS

PART VIII NATURAL AND REVEALED RELIGION

List of Contributors

Maria Rosa Antognazza is Professor of Philosophy at King's College London

Richard T. W. Arthur is Professor of Philosophy at McMaster University

Alberto Artosi is Professor of Legal Theory, Legal Logic and Legal Argumentation in the Faculty of Law, University of Bologna

Philip Beeley is Research Fellow in the History Faculty, University of Oxford

Friedrich Beiderbeck is one of the editors of the political writings of Leibniz at the Leibniz-Editionsstelle of Potsdam (Berlin-Brandenburgische Akademie der Wissenschaften)

Domenico Bertoloni Meli is Provost Professor of History and Philosophy of Science and Medicine at Indiana University, Bloomington

Martha Bolton is Professor of Philosophy at Rutgers University

Gregory Brown is Professor of Philosophy at the University of Houston

James Cussens is Senior Lecturer in the Department of Computer Science, University of York

Vincenzo De Risi is CNRS Research Fellow in Paris (research group "SPHère — Science, Historie, Philosophie")

Stefano Di Bella is Associate Professor of the History of Philosophy at the University of Milan

François Duchesneau is Emeritus Professor of Philosophy at the Université de Montréal

Daniel Garber is the A. Watson Armour III University Professor of Philosophy at Princeton University

Jürgen Gottschalk is a member of the Zentrum für Geschichte der Naturwissenschaft und Technik at the University of Hamburg

Adam Harmer is Assistant Professor of Philosophy at the University of California, Riverside

Hartmut Hecht is the former director of the Leibniz-Editionsstelle of Berlin (Berlin-Brandenburgische Akademie der Wissenschaften), where Leibniz's scientific, technical and medical writings are edited

Howard Hotson is Professor of Early Modern Intellectual History at the University of Oxford

Matthew L. Jones is the James R. Barker Professor of Contemporary Civilization at Columbia University

Eberhard Knobloch is Professor of History of Science and Technology at the Technische Universität Berlin (TUB)

Brandon C. Look is University Research Professor at the University of Kentucky

Jeffrey K. McDonough is Professor of Philosophy at Harvard University

Massimo Mugnai is Emeritus Professor of Logic and Philosophy of Science at the Scuola Normale Superiore of Pisa

Margherita Palumbo is a former curator at the Biblioteca Casanatense (Rome)

Arnaud Pelletier is Professor of Philosophy at the Université Libre de Bruxelles (ULB)

Siegmund Probst is one of the editors of the mathematical writings of Leibniz at the Leibniz-Forschungsstelle / Leibniz-Archiv Hannover (Akademie der Wissenschaften zu Göttingen)

Paul Rateau is Assistant Professor at Pantheon-Sorbonne University, Paris

Anne-Lise Rey is Maître de Conferences at the University of Lille

Gonzalo Rodriguez-Pereyra is Professor of Metaphysics at the University of Oxford

Hartmut Rudolph is the former director of the Leibniz-Editionsstelle of Potsdam (Berlin-Brandenburgische Akademie der Wissenschaften), where Leibniz's political writings are edited

Donald Rutherford is Professor of Philosophy at the University of California, San Diego

Giovanni Sartor is Professor of Legal Informatics and Legal Theory at the European University Institute of Florence and at the University of Bologna

Heinrich Schepers is the former director of the Leibniz-Forschungsstelle of Münster (University of Münster and Akademie der Wissenschaften zu Göttingen), where Leibniz's philosophical writings are edited

Justin E. H. Smith is Professor of the History and Philosophy of Science at the University of Paris 7, Denis Diderot

Tzuchien Tho is Lecturer in Philosophy at the University of Bristol

Andre Wakefield is Professor of History at Pitzer College, Claremont Colleges

Stephan Waldhoff is one of the editors of the political writings of Leibniz at the Leibniz-Editionsstelle of Potsdam (Berlin-Brandenburgische Akademie der Wissenschaften)

ABBREVIATIONS

EDITIONS

A	Leibniz, G. W. *Sämtliche Schriften und Briefe*. Edited by the Academy of Sciences of Berlin. Series I–VIII. Darmstadt/Leipzig/Berlin, 1923 ff. Cited by series, volume, and page. "N." followed by an Arabic numeral indicates the number assigned to the text by the editors. The superscript "2" after the volume number indicates the second edition of the volume.
C	Leibniz, G. W. *Opuscules et fragments inédits*. Edited by Louis Couturat. Paris: F. Alcan 1903. Reprint, Hildesheim: Olms, 1988.
Deutsche Schriften	Leibniz, G. W. *Deutsche Schriften*. Edited by G. E. Guhrauer. 2 vols. Berlin, 1840.
Dutens	Leibniz, G. W. *Opera omnia, nunc primum collecta, in classes distributa, praefationibus et indicibus exornata*. Edited by L. Dutens. 6 vols. Geneva: De Tournes, 1768. Cited by volume, part (if relevant), and page.
Erdmann	Leibniz, G. W. *Opera philosophica quae extant Latina Gallica Germanica omnia*. Edited by J. E. Erdmann. Berlin, 1839–1840.
FC	*Nouvelles lettres et opuscules inédits de Leibniz*. Edited by Foucher de Careil. Paris: Auguste Durand, 1857.
FC, Oeuvres	*Oeuvres de Leibniz*. Edited by A. Foucher de Careil. 7 vols. Paris: Firmin Didot frères, 1861–1875 (vols. I and II have also appeared in second edition: Paris: Firmin Didot frères, 1867–69; unless otherwise stated, references are to the first edition).
Feller	Feller, Joachim Friedrich. *Otium Hanoveranum sive Miscellanea ex ore et schedis Illustris Viri, piae memoriae Godofr. Guilielmi Leibnitii*. Leipzig: Impensis J. C. Martini, 1718.
GB	*Der Briefwechsel von Gottfried Wilhelm Leibniz mit Mathematikern*. Edited by C. I. Gerhardt. Berlin: Mayer & Müller, 1899.

GLW   *Briefwechsel zwischen Leibniz und Christian Wolff.* Edited by C. I. Gerhardt. Halle: H. W. Schmidt, 1860.

GM   Leibniz, G. W. *Mathematische Schriften.* 7 vols. Edited by C. I. Gerhardt. Berlin/Halle: A. Asher/H. W. Schmidt, 1849–1863. Cited by volume and page.

GP   Leibniz, G. W. *Die Philosophischen Schriften.* Edited by C. I. Gerhardt. 7 vols. Berlin: Weidmannsche Buchhandlung, 1875–1890. Reprint, Hildesheim: Olms, 1960–1961. Cited by volume and page.

Grua   Leibniz, G. W. *Textes inédits d'après les manuscrits de la Bibliothèque Provinciale de Hanovre.* Edited by G. Grua. 2 vols. Paris: PUF, 1948.

Klopp   Leibniz, G. W. *Die Werke.* Edited by O. Klopp. 11 vols. Hanover: Klindworth, 1864–84. Cited by volume and page.

Pertz   Leibniz, G. W. *Gesammelte Werke.* Edited by Georg Heinrich Pertz. 4 vols. Hanover: Hahnschen Hof-Buchhandlung, 1843–47. Reprint, Hildesheim: Olms, 1966.

MANUSCRIPTS AND BIBLIOGRAPHIES

Bodemann, Briefwechsel   Bodemann, Eduard. *Der Briefwechsel des Gottfried Wilhelm Leibniz.* Hanover, 1889. Reprint, Hildesheim: Olms, 1966.

Bodemann, Handschriften   Bodemann, Eduard. *Die Leibniz-Handschriften der Königlichen öffentlichen Bibliothek zu Hannover.* Hanover/Leipzig, 1895. Reprint, Hildesheim: Olms, 1966.

LBr   Leibniz-Briefwechsel. Hanover: Niedersächsische Landesbibliothek/Gottfried Wilhelm Leibniz Bibliothek.

LH   Leibniz-Handschriften. Hanover: Niedersächsische Landesbibliothek/Gottfried Wilhelm Leibniz Bibliothek.

Ravier   *Bibliographie des oeuvres de Leibniz.* Edited by Émile Ravier. Paris: F. Alcan, 1937. Reprint, Hildesheim: Olms, 1966. Cited by the number assigned to editions.

English Translations

AG	Leibniz, G. W. *Philosophical Essays*. Edited and translated by R. Ariew and D. Garber, Indianapolis: Hackett, 1989.
Arthur	Leibniz, G. W. *The Labyrinth of the Continuum: Writings on the Continuum Problem, 1672–1686*. Translated, edited, and with an introduction by R. T. W. Arthur. New Haven: Yale University Press, 2001.
Child	Child, J. M. *The Early Mathematical Manuscripts of Leibniz*. Chicago and London: Open Court, 1920. Reprint, Mineola: Dover, 2005.
H	Leibniz, G. W. *Theodicy: Essays on the Goodness of God, the Freedom of Man, and the Origin of Evil*. Translated by E. M. Huggard. LaSalle, Ill.: Open Court, 1985.
L	Leibniz, G. W. *Philosophical Papers and Letters*. Edited and translated by Leroy E. Loemker. 2nd ed. Dordrecht/Boston: Reidel, 1969.
LA	*The Leibniz-Arnauld Correspondence*. Edited and translated by H. T. Mason. Manchester: Manchester University Press, 1967; New York: Garland, 1985.
Lodge	*The Leibniz-De Volder Correspondence. With Selections from the Correspondence Between Leibniz and Johann Bernoulli*. Translated, edited, and with an introduction by Paul Lodge. New Haven/London: Yale University Press, 2013.
Look-Rutherford	*The Leibniz-Des Bosses Correspondence*. Translated, edited, and with an introduction by Brandon C. Look and Donald Rutherford. New Haven/London: Yale University Press, 2007.
MP	Leibniz, G. W. *Philosophical Writings*. Edited by G. H. R. Parkinson and translated by Mary Morris and G. H. R. Parkinson. London: J. M. Dent & Sons, 1973.
NE	Leibniz, G. W. *New Essays on Human Understanding*. Edited and translated by Peter Remnant and Jonathan Bennett. Cambridge: Cambridge University Press, 1981.
Parkinson	Leibniz, G. W. *De summa rerum: metaphysical papers, 1675–1676*. Translated with an introduction and notes by G. H. R. Parkinson. New Haven/London: Yale University Press, 1992.
PW	*The Political Writings of Leibniz*. Translated and edited with an introduction by Patrick Riley. Cambridge: Cambridge University Press, 1972.

Sleigh   Leibniz, G. W. *Confessio Philosophi: Papers Concerning the Problem of Evil, 1671–1678*. Translated, edited, and with an introduction by Robert C. Sleigh, Jr.; with contributions from Brandon Look and James Stam. New Haven: Yale University Press, 2005.

Strickland *The Shorter Leibniz Texts*. Translated by Lloyd Strickland. London/New York: Continuum, 2006.

WFN   *Leibniz's New System and Associated Contemporary Texts*. Translated and edited by R. S. Woolhouse and Richard Francks. Oxford: Clarendon Press, 1997.

WFP   Leibniz, G. W. *Philosophical Texts*. Edited and translated by R. S. Woolhouse and Richard Francks. Oxford: Oxford University Press, 1998.

Dating

N. S.   New Style.

O. S.   Old Style.

All dates are given in the New (Gregorian) Style unless otherwise indicated.

Introduction

MARIA ROSA ANTOGNAZZA

G. W. Leibniz (1646–1716) is one of the towering figures of early modern thought. A giant of modern philosophy, comparable to philosophers of the greatest magnitude, he also made original contributions to an extraordinary variety of other fields, ranging from physics and mathematics to geology, physiology and technology, from history and librarianship to jurisprudence, politics and theology. Since the "re-discovery" of him in the early twentieth century following the publication of previously unknown logical papers, and the inception of the on-going critical edition of his works and correspondence, Leibniz has generated constantly increasing interest. Sustained traditions of intensive study of his thought continue to flourish in many countries, including Germany, France, Italy, Spain, and England but it is perhaps the North American world that has seen the most impressive surge of interest in recent decades. At the same time, international scholarship on Leibniz has constantly expanded to include not only historians of philosophy but also analytic philosophers, historians of science and mathematics, political theorists and theologians.

Amidst the current profusion of publications on Leibniz, this volume aims to provide a uniquely comprehensive, systematic, and up-to-date appraisal of Leibniz's thought thematically organized around its diverse but interrelated aspects. More specifically, this volume has a much broader scope, and is addressed to a more advanced readership, than introductory overviews focused only on his philosophical thought. Given Leibniz's firm place in the philosophical canon, the greater part of the *Handbook* is of course devoted to chapters on various aspects of his philosophy: his logic, metaphysics, philosophy of nature, ethics, and so on. At the same time, however, the volume's ambition is to give a more rounded picture of Leibniz's thought and activity than is normally done in an exclusively philosophical collection of essays. This is necessary not least because Leibniz's strictly philosophical development and the commitments arising from it often only become fully intelligible when placed within the context of his extra-philosophical commitments, activities and objectives. The volume contains contributions, for instance, on Leibniz as a mathematician (including not only his calculus but also the analysis situs, the dyadic, his work as a statistician, etc.); on Leibniz as a scientist (physics but also geology etc.); on his technical innovations; on his work as an "intelligencer" and cultural operator, as a jurist, and as a historian, editor of sources and librarian; on his views on Europe's political future and on religious toleration, ecclesiastical reunification, the advancement of medicine, and so on. In brief, the volume also intends to serve as a cross-disciplinary point of contact for the many domains to which he contributed.

With regard to the handbook's structure, it has often been noted that in Leibniz's thought everything is connected to everything or – as he put it himself – that the principles of his system "are such that they can hardly be separated one from another. Whoever knows one well, knows them all." (Leibniz to Des Bosses, November 7, 1710). Accordingly, there are many legitimate ways of organizing his doctrines for expositive purposes, various starting points from which to reconstruct his system, and different perspectives with which to look at the whole. Leibniz's thought is more aptly described as a net of mutually supporting doctrines than as a hierarchical, linear system in which doctrines become more and more peripheral as one moves down in the chain of deduction. The order of sections in the volume therefore does not reflect the order of importance of certain aspects over others, but the necessary introduction of an order of discussion which is to some extent unavoidably artificial.

The exposition starts from the Platonic element in Leibniz's thought, that is, from essences, truths, and possible worlds as eternal thoughts in the mind of God (Chapter 1). This provides the realist grounding in an otherwise conceptualist-nominalist ontology of logic, as well as the ontological setting for what follows: namely, key aspects of Leibniz's logic, metaphysics, and theory of knowledge and language. Given the exceptionally strong link in Leibniz between logic and mathematics and his attempts at a mathematization of logic, the section on mathematics follows the chapter on the *characteristica universalis*, logical calculus, and language. From mathematics, the volume moves to its central part: that is, the cluster of chapters on the physical world and its metaphysical grounding, on scientific and technical work, and on scientific organization and cultural networking. The exploration of Leibniz as creator of and a key player in scientific and learned networks is followed by a discussion of his scholarly work as a librarian and historian, both of which involve the organization of scholarly endeavor more generally. The last two sections are devoted to ethics, jurisprudence, politics, and religion—a cluster designed to re-emphasize, in conclusion, the fact that the order of sections of this book does not reflect the order of their importance for Leibniz. In sum, the volume starts with God and ends with God and the moral-religious order which was fundamental to Leibniz's overall intellectual vision. His exceptionally innovative contributions to the variety of fields explored in the body of the volume were for him all part of a comprehensive plan of development of all the sciences in the context of a stable and peaceful political order. His overarching aim was the improvement of the human condition and the celebration, thereby, of the glory of God in his creation.

Unavoidably in an exposition of Leibniz's thought, there is a certain amount of overlap between chapters: to name only a few examples, the discussion of freedom and contingency (Chapter 5) is relevant to Leibniz's theodicy (Chapter 6), and the notion of force (Chapter 17) is inseparable from a discussion of corporeal substances and monads (Chapters 18, 19, and 20). This revisiting of some topics in more than one place will instructively expose the reader to complementary views of the doctrine in question as well as to different interpretations of it (for instance, on the relationship between Leibniz's philosophy of nature and his monadology).

This leads to the international cast of contributors whose ground-breaking work on different aspects of Leibniz's thought has been assembled in this volume. Such cosmopolitanism is of paramount importance in creating a cutting-edge handbook for Leibniz. Alongside outstanding Anglo-American students of Leibniz, there are long established traditions of intensive study of Leibniz in many countries. The volume offers a distinctive and authoritative outlook on Leibniz also by tapping into the best scholarship on Leibniz world-wide. The list of authors includes very well-known and highly regarded Leibniz specialists as well as researchers from the new generation who have opened fresh lines of inquiry.

Thanks are due to Michael Misiewicz, Lucy Sheaf, and John Hotson for their help in editing some of the chapters, and to Francesca Hotson, who has helped out in her own inimitable way. Finally, I am especially grateful to leading Leibniz scholars who have commented on the structure of the volume and suggested contributors, in particular Daniel Garber, Massimo Mugnai, and Donald Rutherford.

Maria Rosa Antognazza
King's College London

LIFE AND WORKS

MARIA ROSA ANTOGNAZZA

THERE is no *Summa* of Leibniz's thought. By any standard, he was prolific: his writings will eventually encompass some 120 folio volumes of the ongoing critical edition of his works and correspondence. Yet the one thing he never wrote was a single book outlining his whole system between two covers. Instead, his views need to be patiently pieced together from a sprawling corpus of often fragmentary and occasional writings, the vast majority of which remained unpublished during his lifetime. To complicate matters further, some of the most lucid and penetrating expositions of his thought are to be found in the massive correspondence that connected him with some 1300 individuals all over Europe and as far afield as China.[1] Among them, the presence and importance of women is remarkable. Although Leibniz never married and never showed a romantic attachment, some of his closest friends and intellectually most perceptive partners were women, notably, the duchess and then electoral princess Sophie of Hanover, her daughter and Prussian queen Sophie Charlotte, and her daughter-in-law and princess of Wales Caroline.[2]

Born on July 1, 1646, in Leipzig (Saxony), Leibniz grew up in a family of staunch Lutherans belonging to the academic and juridical intelligentsia of his home town. His father, Friedrich Leubnitz (or Leibnütz), held the chair of moral philosophy at the thriving University of Leipzig, where he also served as dean of the faculty and university notary. His mother, Catharina Schmuck, was the daughter of a well-established Leipzig jurist and law professor. Left fatherless at the age of six, the young Gottfried Wilhelm attended the Leipzig Nikolaischule (one of the best preparatory schools in Saxony) from July 1653 to Easter 1661. In April 1661, he started his studies at the University of Leipzig, gaining a Bachelor's degree in philosophy with the thesis *Disputatio metaphysica de Principio Individui*, defended on June 9, 1663.[3] On June 20, 1663 he enrolled for the

---

[1] Particularly important philosophical correspondences include his epistolary exchanges with Antoine Arnauld, Burchard de Volder, Christian Wolff, Bartholomew Des Bosses, and Samuel Clarke.

[2] For a full discussion of Leibniz's life and works, see Maria Rosa Antognazza, *Leibniz: An Intellectual Biography* (Cambridge: Cambridge University Press, 2009).

[3] A VI i N. 1.

summer semester at the University of Jena (Saxony), returning to the University of Leipzig in October 1663. In 1664, he was awarded a Master's degree in philosophy with the thesis *Specimen Quaestionum Philosophicarum ex Jure collectarum*.[4] In 1665, he defended a law dissertation on conditional judgements (*De Conditionibus*),[5] gaining a Bachelor's degree in law. In 1666 Leibniz wrote one of his key early works, the *Dissertatio de Arte Combinatoria*,[6] the first part of which was defended on March 17, 1666 (under the title of *Disputatio arithmetica de Complexionibus*) for his habilitation in the faculty of philosophy. Wishing to obtain his licence and doctorate in law sooner than the University of Leipzig would allow, the precocious law student enrolled on October 4, 1666 at the University of Altdorf, near Nuremberg. Shortly after his twentieth birthday, on November 15, 1666 he defended a thesis for the licence and the doctorate in law (*Disputatio de Casibus perplexis in Jure*)[7].

Upon concluding his university studies, the young Leibniz tried his hand at a paid job as secretary of an alchemical society in Nuremberg. It was not long, however, before he departed, in the autumn of 1667, for a European grand tour via the Rhine and Holland. In the event, he did not go further than Frankfurt and the nearby Catholic Archbishopric of Mainz. By the end of the same year, another key early work of Leibniz, the *Nova Methodus discendae docendaeque Jurisprudentiae*,[8] was hastily published in Frankfurt. The following year, the talented young jurist entered the employ of the elector and prince-archbishop of Mainz, Johann Philipp von Schönborn, whose inner circle included Johann Christian von Boineburg. A Catholic convert from Lutheranism, Baron Boineburg soon became the young Leibniz's chief patron. It was during his years in Mainz under Boineburg's patronage that Leibniz conceived a comprehensive plan of *Demonstrationes Catholicae*[9] – effectively a first version of the all-embracing plan of reform and advancement of all the sciences which was to provide a leitmotif for his entire intellectual life. A host of other programmatic and innovative early writings heralded the extraordinary variety of fields which would exercise his exceptional intellectual creativity over the years, from the foundations of ethics and jurisprudence to physics,[10] from language and the ontology of logic to medicine and the creation of learned societies.[11]

It was thanks to Boineburg that in March 1672 Leibniz embarked on a four-year trip to Paris which was to prove transformative. In the French capital, he met some of the

---

[4] A VI i N. 4.

[5] A VI i N. 5-6.

[6] A VI i N. 8.

[7] A VI i N. 9.

[8] A VI i N. 10.

[9] *Demonstrationum Catholicarum Conspectus* (1668-9; A VI i N. 14).

[10] See, respectively, *Elementa Juris naturalis* (1669-71; A VI i N. 12) and the two physics treatises of 1670-1 (*Theoria motus abstracti* and *Hypothesis physica nova*; A VI ii N. 41 and N. 40).

[11] Cf. the preliminary dissertation premised by Leibniz to his new edition of Mario Nizolio's *Antibarbarus* (1670; A VI ii N. 54), *Directiones ad rem Medicam pertinentes* (published by Fritz Hartmann and Matthias Krüger in "*Directiones ad rem Medicam pertinentes*. Ein Manuskript G. W. Leibnizens aus den Jahren 1671/72 über die Medizin," in *Studia Leibnitiana* 8/1 [1976], pp. 40–68), and *Grundriß eines Bedenckens von aufrichtung einer Societät in Teütschland zu auffnehmen der Künste und Wißenschaften* (1671; A IV i N. 43).

best mathematicians and scientists of the age, including Christiaan Huygens. Huygens's guidance was invaluable in steering the young German toward ground-breaking mathematical work. Not many tutors could have been more assured of time well spent in bringing their tutees up to speed: by October 1675, Huygens's German protégé had invented the infinitesimal calculus. Before achieving such an astonishing break-through, between January and February 1673, Leibniz visited London and mingled with the fellows of the Royal Society. Among other things, he took the opportunity to demonstrate the calculating machine on which he was working. The machine was far from perfect, but the fellows were sufficiently impressed by Leibniz's acumen that they elected him to a fellowship on April 19, 1673. Back in Paris, he continued the mathematical work which eventually led him to the calculus, while also pursuing his interests in philosophy and physics.[12] Notably, in a seminal paper penned in the summer of 1676 (*De Arcanis Motus*), he first introduced the principle of equivalence between full cause and entire effect.

On October 4, 1676, having exhausted all prospects of a more permanent stay in Paris, Leibniz left the French capital to take up a position as librarian and court counselor in Hanover. The labyrinthine route by which he made his way back to his native country was a measure of his lack of enthusiasm at the prospective of settling as a middle-ranking employee in the provincial ducal residence of a cadet line of the Guelf family. After a second visit to London (October 18-29, 1676), he went to Holland where he enjoyed extended conversations with Baruch Spinoza in The Hague. In mid-December 1676 he finally arrived in Hanover, the town which was to become his primary residence for the remaining 40 years of his life.

Never dampened for long, his enthusiasm was soon revived in a flurry of proposals to the local duke. In Johann Friedrich of Hanover, Leibniz had found a congenial patron who could appreciate his grander schemes. In fact, 1678-9 marked a pivotal moment in his intellectual life: he relaunched the encyclopaedic plan of the *Demonstrationes Catholicae* in a key letter to the duke[13]; developed the notions of a *scientia generalis* and of a demonstrative or inventive encyclopaedia; quantified force as the product of mass (*m*) and the square of speed (v^2) in a ground-breaking study on the notion of force (*De corporum concursu*, January 1678)[14]; conceived the projects of a *characteristica geometrica* or *analysis situs* and of a dyadic or binary arithmetic[15]; drafted a set of logical

---

[12] The most important body of metaphysical texts of this period is a collection of writings known as *De Summa Rerum* (see A VI iii). Another key philosophical text of the Parisian period is the *Confessio Philosophi* (A VI iii N. 7), a sort of proto-theodicy composed by Leibniz between 1672 and 1673.

[13] Leibniz to Duke Johann Friedrich, autumn 1679. There are two versions of the letter (see A II i N. 213 and A I ii N. 187).

[14] Published in Michel Fichant, *G. W. Leibniz. La Réforme de la dynamique. De Corporum concursu (1678), et autres texts inédits* (Paris: Vrin, 1994).

[15] On the *characteristica geometrica* see, for instance, GM V 141-68 and A III ii N. 346 and N. 347; on the dyadic see, for instance, *De progressione dyadica*, March 25, 1679 (Couturat, 574); *De organo sive arte magna cogitandi*, March–April 1679 (A VI iv N. 50, esp. p. 158); *Summum Calculi Analytici Fastigium*, December 1679 (in Hans J. Zacher, *Die Hauptschriften zur Dyadik von G. W. Leibniz* (Frankfurt a. M.: Klostermann, 1973), pp. 218–24).

papers pioneering a logical calculus (April 1679)[16]; laid the basis for a philosophy of probability (*De incerti aestimatione*, September 1678)[17]; and renewed his proposals for the creation of scientific and learned societies.[18]

Unfortunately, however, his hopes of strong ducal support were short-lived. In December 1679 Johann Friedrich died unexpectedly, leaving the duchy in the hands of his younger brother, Ernst August, married to Sophie von der Pfalz. Unlike his wife, Ernst August had no time for Leibniz's expansive mind and expensive schemes of scientific development and all-embracing reform. Instead, the new duke was intrigued by the prospect of increasing income from the ducal silver mines that Leibniz was promising to modernize with some fancy technical innovations. Between 1680 and 1686, the self-styled mining engineer was heavily involved in the Harz mines. Although time-consuming, this technical venture did not prevent him from doing some remarkable theoretical work on the side, including proving Fermat's little theorem and inventing determinants. In October 1684, he presented his infinitesimal calculus for the first time through the publication in the *Acta Eruditorum* of the *Nova Methodus pro Maximis et Minimis*, complemented in July 1686 by *De Geometria Recondita*.[19] In November 1684, he published a key paper on the theory of knowledge (*Meditationes de Cognitione, Veritate et Ideis*).[20]

This ground-breaking mathematical and philosophical work was not matched, however, by equal breakthroughs under ground. By April 1685 it became clear that Leibniz's technical innovations were not going to flood the duke with silver. Never short of clever ideas, Leibniz changed tack, convincing Ernst August to entrust him with the task of writing the history of the duke's extended family, the Guelf dynasty. Such an enterprise was far from frivolous even in the eye of the un-scholarly Ernst August, nor was it of purely antiquarian value: on the contrary, the demonstration of a suitably distinguished pedigree was the precondition of raising the Hanoverians to electoral status – the most elevated rank within the Holy Roman Empire beneath the emperor himself. The duke was quick to see the point and, eventually, released Leibniz for archival research. Before departing in October 1687 for a journey through southern Europe which stretched the initially planned few months into more than two-and-half years, Leibniz used his last months in the solitude of the Harz mountains for extraordinarily creative intellectual work. In 1686, he wrote four key texts spanning physics, metaphysics, theology, and logic: the *Brevis demonstratio erroris memorabilis Cartesii et aliorum circa legem naturae*,[21] the *Discours de Métaphysique*,[22] the *Examen Religionis Christianae*,[23] and the *Generales Inquisitiones de Analysi Notionum et Veritatum*.[24]

---

[16] See A VI iv N. 56-64.
[17] A VI iv N. 34.
[18] See in particular two proposals of the autumn of 1678 (A IV iii N. 130 and N. 131).
[19] See, respectively, GM V 220-6 and 226-33.
[20] A VI iv N. 141.
[21] A VI iv N. 369.
[22] A VI iv N. 306.
[23] A VI iv N. 420.
[24] A VI iv N. 165.

His trip to southern Europe (November 1687-June 1690) and, in particular, his extended stay in Italy from March 1689 to March 1690, also proved fruitful. During this period, he developed a new branch of physics focused on the study of forces (for which he chose the name of "dynamics")[25] and proposed his own cosmological system.[26] At the same time, he did not neglect to pursue his main item of business namely, the discovery of the exact connection between the Este and Guelf houses (February 10, 1690). By mid-June 1690 he was finally back in Hanover, where he tried to quell the understandable annoyance of his employer at such a long, unforeseen absence by producing several outlines of the Guelf history. His plan was to complete this work by 1693. Meanwhile, in March 1692, Hanover was elevated to the status of electorate, not least thanks to Leibniz's painstaking work in assembling the historical and legal documentation supporting the case.

The mid-1690s were marked by the publication of some key papers and by important developments in the establishment of his distinctive philosophical vocabulary. In March 1694, there appeared in the *Acta Eruditorum* a brief account of his innovative theory of substance, in which the notion of force took central stage (*De Primae Philosophiae Emendatione, et de Notione Substantiae*). The core ideas of his *Dynamica* were publically presented in the first part of the *Specimen Dynamicum* included in the *Acta Eruditorum* of April 1695. In turn, the June and July issues of the *Journal des Sçavans* carried his *Système nouveau de la nature et de la communication des substances, aussi bien que l'union qu'il y a entre l'âme et le corps*. Later in 1695, he used for the first time the expression "pre-established harmony" as a short-hand for his theory.[27] Finally, the first distinctively Leibnizian use of the term "monad" to indicate "a real unity" was recorded in an unfinished letter of July 22, 1695, to the Marquis de L'Hôpital.[28] Around the same time, Leibniz also began to speak increasingly of "simple" substances.

Other notable writings of the 1690s included the *Mémoire pour des Personnes éclairées et de bonne intention* (c. 1692),[29] the *Codex Juris Gentium Diplomaticus* (published in 1693), the *Protogaea* (finished by the end of 1694 but unpublished in Leibniz's lifetime), the *Unvorgreiffliche Gedancken betreffend die Ausübung und Verbesserung der Teutschen Sprache* (1696-7),[30] the *Novissima Sinica* (published in 1697), *De rerum originatione radicali* (November 23, 1697),[31] and *De ipsa natura* (included in the *Acta Eruditorum* of September 1698).

The death of Ernst August on February 2, 1698, and the installation of his oldest son, Georg Ludwig, as the new duke and elector of Hanover, coincided with a period

---

[25] See in particular the *Phoranomus seu de potentia et legibus naturae* of July 1689, and the *Dynamica de Potentia et Legibus Naturae Corporeae* of 1689-90.

[26] See *Tentamen de Motuum caelestium Causis* (published in February 1689 in the *Acta Eruditorum*) and the *Tentamen de Physicis Motuum Coelestium Rationibus* (spring-autumn 1689).

[27] See GP IV 496; WFN 51.

[28] See GM II 295.

[29] A IV iv N. 123.

[30] *Collectanea Etymologica*, Hanover 1717, second part, pp. 255–314.

[31] GP VII 302-8.

of renewed ecumenical efforts for Leibniz. In close collaboration with Gerhard Wolter Molanus (the supervisor of Hanoverian church affairs with whom, in earlier years, Leibniz had explored the reunification between Lutherans and Roman Catholics),[32] he penned an extensive document discussing a possible union between the Lutheran Church of Hanover and the Reformed Church of the powerful Electorate of Brandenburg-Prussia.[33] Between November 1698 and February 1705, Leibniz spent extended periods of time in Berlin, where he enjoyed an exceptionally close friendship with Georg Ludwig's sister, the electress of Brandenburg and (from 1701) queen in Prussia, Sophie Charlotte. In addition to Berlin, other regular places of Leibniz's (often unauthorized) wanderings away from Hanover were Wolfenbüttel, Brunswick (Braunschweig), Celle, and, last but not least, Vienna.

The year 1700 saw his election as a foreign member of the Parisian Académie Royale des Sciences and his nomination as President of the newly created Berlin Society of Sciences. The latter was the first major realization of decades of proposals by Leibniz aimed at the establishment of academies of sciences. As captured by the motto chosen for the Berlin Society—*Theoria cum Praxi*—its regulative ideal was to foster scientific progress for the practical aim of improving the human condition.

Between the summer of 1703 and the summer of 1705, Leibniz penned his *Nouveaux Essais* in reply to Locke's *Essay Concerning Human Understanding*. Although complete, the *Nouveaux Essais* remained unpublished in his lifetime, apparently due to Leibniz's loss of interest in seeing through the press his voluminous manuscript after the death of Locke on November 8, 1704, and of Sophie Charlotte on February 1, 1705. The unexpected demise of his patroness and close friend greatly distressed Leibniz to the point of fearing for his own health. It was only after "a long interruption" in his correspondence and intellectual work that Leibniz "finally returned to [himself] and [his] friends."[34]

The enduring presence of Sophie Charlotte was felt in the other major philosophical book written by Leibniz in this period. The *Essais de Theodicée sur la bonté de Dieu, la liberté de l'homme et l'origine du mal*, published in Amsterdam in 1710, had been stimulated at least in part by conversations with Sophie Charlotte and her entourage in Lützenburg (the queen's palace outside Berlin) during the summer of 1702. Also in 1710 there appeared the first volume of the official publication of the Berlin Society of Sciences, the *Miscellanea Berolinensia ad Incrementum Scientiarum*, collecting sixty papers (of which twelve were by Leibniz himself).

---

[32] Cf. in particular the Hanoverian negotiations of 1683 led by Molanus (on the Lutheran side) and by Bishop Cristobal de Rojas y Spinola (on the Catholic side).

[33] *Unvorgreiffliches Bedencken über eine Schrifft genandt Kurtze Vorstellung*, early 1698 - early 1699, A IV vii N. 79. See also *Tentamen Expositionis irenicae trium potissimarum inter protestante controversiarum*, October-December 1698, A IV vii N. 62. In turn, Leibniz's commentary on article 17 of Gilbert Burnet's *Exposition of the Thirty-Nine Articles of the Church of England* was related to his hopes for an inter-protestant mediation by the Anglican Church. The commentary is edited, translated, and introduced by Michael J. Murray in G. W. Leibniz, *Dissertation on Predestination and Grace* (New Haven: Yale University Press, 2011).

[34] See Leibniz's letter of July 10, 1705 to Lady Masham (Klopp X 287-8 and GP III 366-7).

Far less gratifying for Leibniz was the appearance in the same year of the Royal Society's *Philosophical Transactions* for 1708. The volume included a paper by the Scottish mathematician John Keill openly accusing Leibniz of having plagiarized the "method of fluxions" discovered by Newton roughly a decade before Leibniz's invention of his calculus.[35] A more veiled charge of having built on Newton's work without proper acknowledgment went back at least to 1691, when the Swiss mathematician Nicolas Fatio de Duillier had raised the suspicion in a letter to Huygens and then again, in 1699, in a mathematical treatise.[36] Keill's accusation, however, escalated the issue to a new level.

Leibniz wrote to the Royal Society's secretary, Hans Sloane, demanding an apology.[37] Impartiality, however, was by now impossible: the incumbent President of the Society was none other than Newton himself. Rather than apologizing, Keill was invited to give a fuller account of his charges. Next came a review of the available documentation by a committee appointed by the Royal Society. A final report, composed by Newton and treating Leibniz as a plagiarist, was approved by the Society and published in January 1713 with supporting documents, once again carefully edited by Newton to uphold his side of the story.[38]

At the time, Leibniz was in Vienna on an unauthorized visit which lasted almost two years (from mid-December 1712 to early September 1714). Reached by news of the volume published by the Royal Society, in September 1713 he composed anonymously a so-called *Charta Volans* which reversed the charge of plagiarism onto Newton. Later attempts at mediation fell through. Although manuscript evidence has now substantiated Leibniz's claim that his discovery was independent of Newton, events spiralled into one of the most acrimonious and high-profile priority controversies in the history of mathematics.

However unpleasant, the sorry affair luckily did not absorb Leibniz full-time. While in the imperial capital, he wrote for Prince Eugene of Savoy a short pamphlet expounding the core ideas of his theory of monads (*Principes de la nature et de la grâce fondés en raison*, completed by August 1714) and worked at a companion pamphlet published after his death under the title of *Monadologie*. On June 8, 1714, the dowager Electress Sophie passed away, making Hanover an even more unattractive place for Leibniz. It was only the death of Queen Anne of Great Britain and Ireland, and the accession to the throne of the Hanoverian elector, Georg Ludwig (as George I), that finally convinced Leibniz to pack his bags and leave Vienna. He arrived back in Hanover on September 14, 1714 only to discover that the elector and his court had left for London three days earlier. Having played a not insignificant part in ensuring the Hanoverian succession, Leibniz was eager

[35] See John Keill, "Epistola . . . de Legibus Virium Centripetarum," in *Philosophical Transactions* 26 (1708), p. 185.

[36] See Fatio de Duillier to Christiaan Huygens, December 28, 1691, in Christiaan Huygens, *Oeuvres complètes*, 22 vols (The Hague, 1888–1950), vol. 10, p. 214 and Nicolas Fatio de Duillier, *Lineae Brevissimi Descensus Investigatio Geometrica Duplex* (London: Typis R. Everingham, 1699), p. 18.

[37] March 4, 1711 (see LBr 871, Bl. 25).

[38] *Commercium epistolicum D. Joannis Collins et aliorum de analysi promota* (London, 1712). The date of publication followed the Julian calendar, still in use in England.

to follow, but Georg Ludwig's displeasure at his prolonged absences, not to mention the delays in producing the Guelf history, proved an unsurmountable obstacle on the path to England.

Left in no doubt that permission to cross the Channel would not be forthcoming until his historiographical task was complete, Leibniz settled back in Hanover, feeling even more acutely the lack of intellectual stimulation and companionship which had often made him wander away with or without the agreement of his employer. On October 12, 1714, Leibniz's last precious friend in Hanover, Caroline, left for London to take up her new role as princess of Wales. Leibniz maintained close contacts via correspondence —a correspondence which included, between November 1715 and October 1716, a key exchange mediated by Caroline with the Newtonian Samuel Clarke.[39]

Musings about moving to Vienna or Paris came to nothing while Leibniz continued his work at the Guelf history. In the meantime, some other remarkable writings (which in all likelihood would have failed to impress George I) spilled out of his pen, including a text discussing the *Apokatastasis pantōn*, or "restitution of all things."[40] As late as the summer of 1716, Leibniz was still able to meet in Bad Pyrmont (Lower Saxony) with the Russian Czar, Peter the Great, whose patronage he had tried to secure in later years. His last dated letter, written on November 3, 1716, recorded his hopes for the flourishing of the Society of Sciences of Berlin. A few days later, on November 6, gout and arthritis forced the seventy-year-old man to bed in his Hanoverian lodgings in Schmiedestraße. Leibniz died in Hanover on the evening of November 14, 1716, with only his amanuensis and his coachman at his bedside.

[39] Published in Klopp XI and GP VII, 352-440.
[40] Published in G. W. Leibniz, *De l'horizon de la doctrine humaine*, edited by Michel Fichant (Paris: Vrin, 1991).

PART I

GOD, POSSIBLE WORLDS, AND THE ACTUAL WORLD

CHAPTER 1

···

ESSENCES, IDEAS, AND TRUTHS IN GOD'S MIND AND IN THE HUMAN MIND

···

MASSIMO MUGNAI

ESSENCES ARE LIKE NUMBERS

···

At the end of his *Metaphysical Disputation on the Principle of Individuation* (1663), Leibniz states that the "essences of things are like numbers" and that they may be considered eternal only because they "are in God" (A VI i 19; GP IV 26). What Leibniz here calls "essences (*essentiae*)," are the models of all things, possible and actual, in God's understanding; according to the scholastic tradition, he attributes to them a nature in many respects analogous to that of Plato's ideas.

Very early in Western culture, at the time of Augustine, an analogy emerged between the behavior of an architect and that of God creating the world. As an architect builds a house on the basis of a blueprint, so God, to call a particular world into existence, first conceives a model of it in his mind. Moreover, he must consider a collection of models from which to choose that which corresponds to the world that he intends to create.[1] During the Middle Ages, on the basis of this analogy and under the influence of a text entitled *On Ideas* [*De ideis*] attributed to Augustine, Plato's theory of ideas was revived, even though the revival primarily concerned the ideas in God's mind and although Plato's works in their entirety remained almost completely unknown.[2] At the same time, however, the obvious problem arose of how to avoid the risk of a dualism between a realm of ideas eternal and immutable, on the one hand, and God himself, in his turn eternal and unchanging, on the other. A related problem was how to reconcile the

---

[1] The analogy was lively expressed even by Seneca, cf. *Ad Lucilium,* VII, 65, 7.

[2] Cf. V. Boland OP, *Ideas in God According to Saint Thomas Aquinas* (Leiden/New York, Koeln: Brill, 1996), pp. 27–32.

simplicity of God's essence with the multiplicity of ideas in his mind. These issues were discussed at length by medieval philosophers; far from being settled, in the seventeenth century, they continued to be of some importance, as is shown in a letter that Leibniz wrote in 1671 to Magnus Wedderkopf, a jurisconsult in Kiel:

> For God wills the things which he understands to be best and most harmonious and selects them, as it were, from an infinite number of all possibilities. What then is the reason for the divine intellect? The harmony of things. What the reason for the harmony of things? Nothing. For example, no reason can be given for the ratio of 2 to 4 being the same as that of 4 to 8, not even in the divine will. This depends on the essence itself, or the idea of things. For the essences of things are numbers, as it were, and contain the possibility of beings which God does not make as he does existence, since these possibilities or ideas of things coincide rather with God himself.
>
> (L 146; A VI ii 117).

In this passage, written eight years after the *Disputation on the Principle of Individuation*, Leibniz continues to compare the essences of things with numbers, stating that what he calls "essences" are ideas in God's understanding and claiming that these ideas, being mere possibilities, "coincide" with God himself. Another important claim of the letter is that God has no power at all over ideas: if 2 is the ratio of 4, then this very fact cannot be altered or changed even by him because it depends only on the intrinsic nature of the ideas corresponding to 2 and 4.[3]

Thus, that there exists a realm of ideas which are unchangeable and eternal, independent even from God's will, is one of the oldest and firmest claims made by Leibniz in the development of his philosophy. We find this claim in the *New Essays* (1704), as well:

> The Scholastics hotly debated *de constantia subjecti*, as they put it, i.e. how a proposition about a subject can have a real truth if the subject does not exist. The answer is that truth is a merely conditional one which says that if the subject ever does exist it will be found to be thus and so. But it will be further asked what the ground is for the connection, since there is a reality in it which does not mislead. The reply is that it is grounded in the linking together of ideas. In response to this it will be asked where these ideas would be if there were no mind, and what would then become of the real foundation of this certainty of eternal truths. This question brings us at last to the ultimate foundation of truth, namely to that Supreme and Universal Mind who cannot fail to exist and whose understanding is indeed the domain of eternal truths. St. Augustine knew this and expresses it pretty forcefully. And lest you should think that it is unnecessary to have recourse to this Mind, it should be borne in mind that

---

[3] As noted by Mondadori; see F. Mondadori, "'Quid sit essentia creaturae, priusquam a Deo producatur': Leibniz's view", in A. Lamarra and R. Palaia (eds.), *Unità e molteplicità nel pensiero filosofico e scientifico di Leibniz* (Firenze: Leo S. Olschki, 2000), pp. 185–223, Leibniz's claim concerning the nature of ideas in God's understanding strongly reminds one of analogous positions held by Duns Scotus (cf. *Ordinatio*, I, *dist.* 36, *quaestio unica*).

these necessary truths contain the determining reason and regulating principle of existent things—the laws of the universe, in short. Therefore, since these necessary truths are prior to the existence of contingent beings, they must be grounded in the existence of a necessary substance.

(NE 448)

One may observe, however, that in the *New Essays*, in comparison with what Leibniz wrote in the letter to Wedderkopf, the emphasis is put on truths more than on ideas. But Leibniz considered ideas the buildings blocks of truths, and it is the intimate nature of ideas that enter into a proposition and determine its truth, as Leibniz explains in a short essay dated 1677:

Natures and truths are modes. The reason why a necessary proposition is true when no one is thinking must be objectively in some subject. The cause why the aforesaid proposition about the circle and the square is true is not in the nature of the circle alone nor in the nature of the square alone, but also in other natures that enter into it—for instance, of the equal and of the perimeter. The proximate cause of one thing is singular. And its cause must be in something. Therefore it must be in that in which is found the nature of the circle, the square, and the other things; that is, in the subject of ideas, or God.

(Strickland 183; A VI iv 17)

That "natures" (i.e., ideas) and truths are *modes* means that they are not substances and that, to exist, they need some subject or substantial being to which they are "attached." As Leibniz specifies in a previous essay, "modes are usually nothing but the relations of a thing to the understanding, or phenomenal capacities" (A VI ii 417; L 126). The red of an apple, for example, is a mode of being (an accidental property, in this case) of the apple and cannot exist separately from it.[4]

Attributing the status of modes to ideas and truths in God's understanding, Leibniz distances himself from a strong form of Platonism: ideas and truths are not objects existing by themselves, in a separate world of some kind. Leibniz is quite explicit on this point: "one must not say, with some Scotists, that the eternal truths would exist even though there were no understanding, not even that of God" (H 247; GP VI 226). Ideas and truths cannot exist, as it were, suspended in the void: they need the existence of an intelligent and eternal being with whom they eternally coexist. Leibniz is careful to emphasize that *God is not the author* of ideas and eternal truths, in the sense that he has not created them: "For it is, in my judgment, the divine understanding which gives reality to the eternal truths, albeit God's will have no part therein" (H 247; GP VI 226). As we read in the *Theodicy*, God has not produced ideas "by an act of his will

[4] In the *Theodicy*, Leibniz seems to accept the thesis that "there is an actual distinction between the substance and its modification or accidents" (H 145; GP VI 121). This thesis, however, does not imply that the accidents can exist independently of the substance.

any more than he thus produced numbers and figures, and all possible essences which one must regard as eternal and necessary"; and they are situated "in the ideal region of the possibles, that is, in the divine understanding" (H 330; GP VI 314). In this sense, as Leibniz writes in the letter to Wedderkopf, possibilities or ideas of things *coincide* with God himself.

There is another short text, also of 1677, in which Leibniz argues in the same vein from the objective and eternal existence of truths to the necessary existence of a being (God), which must constitute a kind of ontological support for these truths. The text is remarkable not only for its clarity, but also because it fixes some thoughts that remained present in the last years of Leibniz's life:

> It is true, or rather it is necessary, that a circle is the most capacious of isoperimetric shapes, even if no circle really exists. Likewise if neither I nor you nor anyone else of us exists.
>
> Likewise even if none of those things exist which are contingent, or in which no necessity is understood, such as is the visible world and other similar things.
>
> Therefore because this truth does not depend on our thinking, it is necessary that there is something real in it. And because that truth is eternal or necessary, this reality that is in it independent of our thinking will also exist from eternity.
>
> This reality is a certain existence in actuality. For this actual truth always subsists in actuality objectively.
>
> Therefore a necessary being exists, or one from whose essence there is existence.
>
> To put it more briefly: the truth of necessary propositions is eternal. Truth is a certain reality independent of our thinking. Certainly some eternal reality always exists. That is, the truth of necessary propositions always exists. Therefore some necessary being exists.
>
> (Strickland 181; A VI iv 18)

Another important point that emerges from this text is Leibniz's remark that some propositions are true independently of the existence of the things or state of affairs to which they refer. This claim is strongly related to a problem on the nature of truth that was raised by Hobbes and was a cause for concern to Leibniz for many years: from his edition of Nizolius's work (1670) onward.

A Puzzle About Language and Truth

Marius Nizolius (1488–1567) was the author of a book inspired by the strong reaction against scholasticism typical of many humanists and Renaissance thinkers. The title of the book, published in 1553, was *On the First Principles and the True Philosophy against Pseudo-Philosophers*, with the "pseudo-philosophers" to whom it alludes being the scholastic thinkers in general and, in particular, scholastic logicians.[5] In the book, Nizolius moves a set of quite standard accusations against medieval philosophers: prominent among them is the charge of having coined abstruse words that have muddied the waters of philosophical inquiry. Like many other humanists, Nizolius firmly believes that rhetoric is the leading discipline of philosophy and that the greater part of problems pertaining to logic may be solved easily with grammar. Having to do with persuasion, rhetoric is near to the real lives and social behavior of human beings, and, for this reason, it constitutes a strong antidote to the abstractness and abstruseness of scholastic philosophy. According to Nizolius, everyone who wants to study philosophy must first become familiar with Latin and Greek and then read the works of ancient philosophers directly in the languages in which they have been written. Nizolius believes that the Latin language reached its perfect form with Cicero and that philosophy, to free itself from any kind of sophisms and to regain a proper sense of reality, must be expressed in Ciceronian language. This emphasis on language drove him to embrace a nominalistic point of view that is quite remarkable for its rigorous intransigence.

In 1670, on Boineburg's advice, Leibniz re-edited Nizolius's book, adding a long preface that is of great interest to us for "his discussion of language, particularly philosophical language, his theory of the relation of logic to rhetoric and metaphysics, his theory of induction, and his evaluation of Scholasticism and nominalism" (L 121). When discussing Nizolius's nominalism, Leibniz defines nominalists as "those who believe that all things except individual substances are mere names" and "deny the reality of abstract terms and universals forthright" (L 128; A VI ii 427). Leibniz seems to be quite in agreement with the "nominalist sect," which he considers "the most profound of all the Scholastics, and the most consistent with the spirit of our modern philosophy" (L 127; A VI ii 427). This agreement becomes particularly evident when he, after a sketch of the history of nominalism, introduces the general rule invoked by nominalists: *entities must not be multiplied beyond necessity*. This rule, according to Leibniz, frequently misunderstood by people who consider it a violation of "the divine opulence," may be rephrased as stating that *the simpler a hypothesis is, the better it is* or that "in accounting for the causes of phenomena, that hypothesis is the most successful which makes the fewest gratuitous assumptions" (L 128; A VI ii 428). The rule, interpreted in this way, so writes Leibniz, states that whoever chooses a more complex explanation over a simpler one when giving an account of natural phenomena, by this very fact, "accuses nature, or rather God, its author, of an unfitting superfluity":

> The hypothesis of any astronomer who can explain the celestial phenomena with few presuppositions, namely, with simple motions only, is certainly to be preferred to that of one who needs many orbs variously intertwined to explain the heavens.
>
> (L 128; A VI ii 428)

---

[5] Cf. M. Nizolio, *De veris principiis et vera ratione philosophandi contra pseudophilosophos*, libri IV (Roma: Fratelli Bocca Editori, vols. 1–2, 1956).

From this rule, nominalists deduced another principle according to which "every-thing in the world can be explained without any reference to universals and real forms." Leibniz's comment on this principle seems to leave little doubt about the fact that he endorses it: "Nothing is truer than this opinion, and nothing is more worthy of a philos-opher of our own time" (L 128; A VI ii 428).

To properly understand the further developments of Leibniz's philosophy, it is impor-tant to note that he represents nominalism as a point of view suggesting a method rather than as a doctrine concerning ontology (i.e., what there is). Leibniz does not say that a nominalist has to abstain from referring to universals and real forms because nothing real corresponds to them, but because it is possible to have a simpler explanation of phe-nomena without employing them.

When preparing his new edition of Nizolius's text, Leibniz wrote some marginal remarks on a previous copy of it in which he confirms his acceptance of a form of mod-erate nominalism. Commenting on a passage in which Nizolius states that universality pertains to names, for example, he writes with approval: "Therefore, it is said cor-rectly: to be universal are names, not things" (A VI ii 450). In another marginal note, however, he criticizes Nizolius and recognizes that there are propositions that are true even though the individuals they refer to do not exist at all:

> Here [Nizolius] is wrong: if every singular thing were destroyed, some universal proposition would still be true in the realm of possibilities. If, indeed, all the ele-phants were killed, this proposition would continue to be true: "Every elephant is an animal," actually being equivalent to this conditional: "If there is some elephant (ei-ther it exists or not), it is an animal."
>
> (A VI ii 448)

An analogous claim is repeated a little later. If all human beings were annihilated, so argues Leibniz, there would still be many propositions that were true, as, for instance, the following: "If there is a man (even though at present no one exists) necessarily it is an animal" (A VI ii 451).

As emerges from these marginal notes, Leibniz has two aims: the first is to secure the independence of truth from language, and the second is to guarantee the possibility of science without committing himself to the existence of real universals. Concerning this last point, Leibniz remarks that objects of science are not only the existing things, but also the *possible* ones, so that he may conclude that science "does not regard real universals, but all singular things, including those that are possible" (A VI ii 461). Denying ontological reality to universals while at the same time attributing it to possible individuals may certainly appear a strange kind of nominalism: the act of dismissing the existence of entities (universals) seems to be largely compensated by the acceptance of another kind of beings endowed with more determinate nature (possible individuals). Leibniz, however, does not explicitly consider this objection: according to his own defi-nition of nominalism, he seems content in establishing that only individual things exist and not worried with the acceptance of possible individuals.

The other concern that Leibniz raises in his Preface to Nizolius involves an argument he attributes to Hobbes. The argument may be reconstructed as follows:

1. To be true or false are sentences (of a given language);
2. The meaning of a sentence depends on the meanings that we human beings attribute to the words composing the sentence;
3. Therefore, truth depends on the way we define terms;
4. But any definition depends on the human will;
5. Therefore, truth depends on the human will.

In a more contracted way, in Leibniz's own words: "Truth depends on the definitions of terms, and definitions depend on the human will": thus, truth is arbitrary (L 128; A VI ii 528–29).

Leibniz considers this argument of the utmost importance. If accepted, it undermines the possibility of science and of knowledge itself. It tends to reduce concepts and ideas to words, and its danger consists mainly in its offering a radical interpretation of a point of view that Leibniz sees as particularly fit for the new science born with Galileo and Descartes. As he writes, the "reformers of philosophy" of his time are almost all nominalist: some of them, however, go too far and are in danger of becoming "super-nominalist," thus sharing the same conclusion as Hobbes concerning truth. In this sense, Nizolius's extreme nominalism has a character of exemplarity that, according to Leibniz, justifies the new edition of his book. Thus, in his Preface, Leibniz takes the occasion to represent Hobbes's point of view and then to criticize it:

> I confess that Hobbes seems to me to be a super-nominalist. For not content like the nominalists, to reduce universals to names, he says that the truth of things itself consists in names and what is more, that it depends on the human will, because truth allegedly depends on the definition of terms, and definitions depend on the human will. This is the opinion of a man recognized as among the most profound of our century, and as I said, nothing can be more nominalistic than it.
>
> (L 128; A VI ii 428–29)

Leibniz's criticism rests essentially on the remark that truth, as clearly shown by mathematics and other abstract sciences (logic, for instance), does not change "when notation is changed":

> In arithmetic, and in other disciplines as well, truths remain the same even if notation is changed, and it does not matter whether a decimal or a duodecimal number system is used.
>
> (L 128; A VI ii 429)

Thus, a tension emerges very early in Leibniz's philosophy between a propensity to some kind of moderate nominalism and the need to accept a realm of truths and ideas that exist, or subsist, independently of any language, the existence of the actual world, and even all human beings. To understand how Leibniz attempts to resolve this issue, it is convenient to discuss separately his account of concepts and ideas in the human mind and that of ideas in God's understanding.

CONCEPTS AND IDEAS IN THE HUMAN MIND

In an essay written in 1675, during his stay in Paris, Leibniz discusses at some length the relationship among words, signs, and ideas. Obviously, the discussion concerns human knowledge as opposed to divine knowledge since God does not need signs and words to think. The main content of the essay may be summarized in five points (A VI iii 462–63):

1. Ideas must be sharply distinguished from *images* and, in general, from any kind of representation that may be associated with them during the activity of thinking;
2. The conceptual content of any thought has to be distinguished from the *expression* of this very thought;
3. Human beings cannot think without the aid of signs or symbols of some sort;
4. In addition to a certain level of complexity, human beings cannot have a *direct* and fully determined knowledge of a complex idea. They may know a complex idea only by taking recourse to an analysis operating on signs and deconstructing it into its constituent parts, thus attempting to grasp the logical connections that link them;
5. No complex idea is composed of ideas which imply a contradiction: contradictory ideas simply do not exist. We may certainly have (and we do have) names or images associated with clusters of ideas giving rise to a contradiction, but no single, individual idea corresponds to the linguistic expressions or to the images. Thus, for instance, if we think of the "round square," we fix our mind on the name, as it were, and juxtapose the idea of a square to that of being round, but these two ideas never "coalesce" to form a new, distinct idea. As Leibniz writes: "The number of all numbers is contradictory, i.e. without a corresponding idea." (A VI iii 463)

In the essay we are considering, Leibniz develops these points with a clear concern for the a priori proof of the existence of God. When we are thinking of something of which nothing greater can be thought, we have separately the idea of something, the idea of what we call "greater," and that of what we call "thinking," and we connect the *words* corresponding to each idea. But from the fact that we have the ideas corresponding to the words entering a given definition, it does not follow that we have the idea of the object defined. Again: we may use one word to designate a complex made of several ideas, but this does not imply that there is an idea corresponding to such a word.[6] To ascertain that this idea exists, we need to perform an analysis of its component ideas and thus check their logical compatibility. Yet we cannot carry out such an analysis without employing signs or images as surrogates for ideas. When human beings are thinking, we are in a position similar to that of a traveler who must cross a bridge during the night: to avoid falling in the void, he needs a railing to guide his hands. The characters we usually employ when thinking constitute the hand-rail necessary to secure our steps.

The characters, as Leibniz writes in a letter to Tschirnhaus dated 1678, instead of leading us away "from the things themselves," lead us "into the interior of things":

> No one should fear that the contemplation of characters will lead us away from the things themselves; on the contrary, it leads us into the interior of things. For we often have confused notions today because the characters we use are badly arranged; but then, with the aid of characters, we will easily have the most distinct notions, for we will have at hand a mechanical thread of meditation, as it were, with whose aid we can very easily resolve any idea whatever into those of which it is composed. In fact, if the character expressing any concept is considered attentively, the simpler concepts into which it is resolvable will at once come to mind. Since the analysis of concepts thus corresponds exactly to the analysis of a character, we need merely to see the characters in order to have adequate notions brought to our mind freely and without effort. We can hope for no greater aid than this in the perfection of the mind.
>
> (L 193; GM IV 461)

It is exactly because we *cannot* think without characters that Leibniz devises his project for the constitution of a universal characteristic. Once the characteristic was created, every thought and sentence would be written with great clarity, according to precise rules and employing symbols endowed with univocal meaning. Thus, Leibniz thinks of the universal characteristic as a device that should strengthen our mind, much as the telescope or the microscope does for our eyes: the "universal characteristic is supposed to do for us in mathematics and logic what the telescope does for the naked eye in perception."[7] To use this device, we need only transcribe symbols on paper or some other surface and then combine them without necessarily tending to their meaning. Leibniz usually compares the characteristic art to the thread that Ariadnes

---

[6] In this case as well, Leibniz's claim resembles Duns Scotus's position, cf. *Reportatio*, I A, dist. 5. q. 1: "To fictions and contradictions . . . do not correspond ideas in God, but only parts of ideas and these parts together do not give rise to a unitary whole, either in reality or in the understanding."

[7] Tieszen, p. 135.

gave to Theseus to find his way out of the Minotaur's labyrinth. The characteristic art transforms a weakness, as it were, of the human beings into a virtue. Because we cannot think without taking recourse to the external senses, it is precisely through the senses (our own bodily resources) that the characteristic art should offer to the human mind a reliable guide for developing our most complex and intricate thoughts.

Thus, Leibniz claims simultaneously that human beings cannot think without the aid of words or images *and* that concepts and ideas have some kind of existence independent of words and images.

The relationship between characters and ideas is further investigated in two short papers written in 1677 and 1678, respectively. The first paper has the form of a dialogue, probably inspired by Plato, between two speakers designated by the letters "A" and "B" who abruptly start discussing the nature of truth with respect to language and our psychological acts of thought. The second (*What Is an Idea*) makes important distinctions concerning the nature of ideas and introduces the notion of *expression*, which plays a crucial role in Leibniz's philosophy. In the *Dialogue* [*Dialogus*], the main target continues to be Hobbes who claims, "that truth arises from the human will and from names or characters"(L 183; A VI iv 22). Leibniz, after having conceded "that if there were no characters, we could neither think of anything distinctly nor reason about it," insists that truths, even though presupposing some characters, are independent of those characters (L 184; A VI iv 23). A remarkable aspect of the *Dialogue*, however, is that in it Leibniz argues that truths are independent of language *without* explicitly appealing to the existence of an autonomous realm of ideas. The two characters of the dialogue, indeed, agree that there are propositions that are true even though nobody is actually thinking of them. This means that "truth is a quality of propositions or thought, but of possible thoughts, so that what is certain is only that if anyone should think in this way or in the opposite way, his thought would be true or false" (L 183; A VI iv 23). In other words, truth and falsity do not depend on the psychological act of thinking some (true or false) proposition. As Leibniz observes, in the case of two islands, one circular and the other square, that the circular one contains more land is true even if nobody considers it; moreover, *it was true* "even before the geometricians had proved it or men observed it" (L 182; A VI iv 20). In the *Dialogue*, however, Leibniz seems to be more interested in explaining why different people belonging to different linguistic universes agree on the same truths than to point out the reason for which certain truths are independent of our will and even of the existence of the actual world.

To explain the nonarbitrariness of truths, Leibniz claims that even though "truths necessarily presuppose some characters," they are grounded not on what is arbitrary in these characters but "in the permanent element in them, namely, in their relation to things (L 185; A VI iv 25). He does not go into more detail, however, concerning the relationship that characters have to "things," and he limits himself to speak of "something of non arbitrary" in the use and connection of characters, corresponding to "a definite analogy between characters and things":

For although characters are arbitrary, their use and connection have something which is not arbitrary, namely a definite analogy between characters and things, and the relations which different characters expressing the same thing have to each other. This analogy or relation is the basis of truth. For the result is that whether we apply one set of characters or another, the products will be the same or equivalent or correspond analogously.

(L 184; A VI iv 24)

Leibniz's conclusion is that "if characters can be used for ratiocination, there is in them a kind of complex mutual relation [*situs*], or order which fits the things; if not in the single words at least in their combination and inflection, although it is even better if found in the single words themselves" (L 184; A VI iv 24). Here, Leibniz seems to attribute to the language (properly: to characters) a kind of pictorial power: a natural capability of representing the main features of the things or state of affairs about which one is speaking. The picture, however, will not necessarily be the same in different languages: usually, in different languages, we will have different descriptions and representations of the same things or state of affairs. But, according to Leibniz, it is precisely *because* two different systems of characters represent the same things that they may "communicate" between them in some correspondence.[8]

HUMAN AND DIVINE IDEAS

Leibniz again tackles the problem of the nature of ideas in the human mind in the short text entitled *What Is an Idea*, probably written soon after the *Dialogue* (L 207–208; A VI iv 1370–71). Here, Leibniz states that ideas have two distinct features: (1) they are something that is in our mind, not in the brain, and (2) they are dispositions. An idea consists not in an act of our mind "*but in the faculty of thinking*" (L 207; A VI iv 1370). Clearly, only ideas in the human mind may have the nature of dispositions: for in God, everything is actual and nothing is in a state of mere potentiality, which would amount to a condition of imperfection. Later on, in the *Discourse of Metaphysics* (1686), Leibniz distinguishes, in the case of human beings, an *idea* as a mere disposition from this same idea insofar as it is "grasped" with a psychological act of thought, and he uses the words *concept* and *notion* to denote this latter. In the *New Essays*, the distinction between *idea* and *concept* will be paralleled with that between *ideas* and *truths* on one hand and *concepts* and *thoughts* on the other. Ideas and truths in our soul are like the veins in a block of marble that mark out "the shape of Hercules rather than other shapes"; they

8 On Leibniz's theory of expression, cf. M. A. Kulstad, "Leibniz's conception of expression," in *Studia Leibnitiana* 9 (1977), pp. 55–76; C. Swoyer, "Leibnizian expression," in *Journal of the History of Philosophy* 33 (1995), pp. 65–99.

are "innate in us—as inclinations, dispositions, tendencies, or natural potentialities, and not as actions." Concepts and thoughts, instead, are these dispositions made actual: they are the veins of the marble brought to light (A VI vi 52).

In *What Is an Idea?* Leibniz points out that we may claim to possess or "grasp" an idea only when we are able to *express* its content, and, as a general law, he gives that something "is said to express a thing in which there are relations [*habitudines*] which correspond to the relations of the thing expressed" (L 207; A VI iv 1370). As Leibniz recognizes, there are various kinds of expressions: the model of a machine, for example, expresses the machine itself, "the projective delineation on a plane expresses a solid, speech expresses thoughts and truths, characters express numbers, and an algebraic equation expresses a circle or some other figure." What all these expressions have in common is that "we can pass from a consideration of the relations in the expression to a knowledge of the corresponding properties of the thing expressed" (L 207; A VI iv 1370). Thus, in *What Is an Idea?* Leibniz sketches a doctrine of expression that attempts to offer a more general solution to the problem raised in the *Dialogue*: how can it be that human beings employing different languages may recognize the same truths?

In a letter to Antoine Arnauld, written approximately in the same period (1687) as *What Is an Idea?* Leibniz concerns himself with the concept of *expression*: "One thing expresses another, in my usage, when there is a constant and regular relation between what can be said about one and about the other." He then remarks that expression "is common to all the forms and is a genus of which natural perception, animal feeling, and intellectual knowledge are species" (L 339). For Leibniz, ideas in the human minds are not *images* or *pictures* of some sort: they have a definite and autonomous content that God has put in perfect correspondence with the objects (when they exist) of the actual world:

> That ideas of things are in us means therefore nothing but that God, the creator alike of the things and of the mind, has impressed a power of thinking upon the mind so that it can by its own operations derive what corresponds perfectly to the nature of things. Although, therefore, the idea of a circle is not similar to the circle, truths can be derived from it which would be confirmed beyond doubt by investigating a real circle.
>
> (L 208; A VI iv 1371)

In the *New Essays*, coming back to Hobbes's thesis about the arbitrariness of truth, Leibniz emphasized once more that truth is independent of language:

> It would be better to assign truth to the relationships amongst the objects of the ideas, by virtue of which one idea is or is not included within another. That does not depend on languages, and is something we have in common with God and the angels. And when God displays a truth to us, we come to possess the truth which is in his understanding, for although his ideas are infinitely more perfect and extensive than ours they still have the same relationship that ours do. So it is to these

relationships that truth should be assigned; and we can distinguish *truths*, which are independent of our good pleasure, from *expressions*, which we invent as we see fit. (NE 296)

To Philalethes-Locke asking whether "an idea is the object of thinking," Theophilus-Leibniz answers that it is, but that it is necessary to add to that definition that an idea is "an immediate inner object, and that this object expresses the nature or qualities of things":

> If it were the *form* of the thought, it would come into and go out of existence with the actual thoughts which correspond to it, but since it is the *object* of thought it can exist before and after the thoughts. Sensible outer objects are only *mediate*, because they cannot act immediately on the soul.
>
> (NE 109)

Calculus Versus Meditation: The Role of Intuitive Knowledge

As we have seen, according to Leibniz, human beings cannot perform long inferences or analyze sufficiently complex concepts without employing something connected with their imagination and with their "external" senses. Even *mathematics* and *geometry* are subject to the faculty of *imagination*: "And these clear and distinct ideas, subject to imagination, are the objects of the mathematical sciences, namely arithmetic and geometry, which are pure mathematical sciences."

Writing to Walter Tschirnhaus in 1679, Leibniz once again stresses that "in very composite matters a calculus is necessary" and that a calculus is "nothing but operation through characters." (L 194; GM IV 462). Yet, if "in very composite matters" (i.e., when we have to deal with very complex thoughts) "a calculus" or "operation through characters" is necessary, there are even cases when a more direct approach is possible, an approach that even liberates us from using "pen and paper." In the same letter to Tschirnhaus, Leibniz calls "meditation" the mental process through which we think, relying exclusively on internal acts of reflection without taking recourse to any kind of external medium:

> Meanwhile I have a very high regard for such problems as can be solved by mental powers alone insofar as this is possible, without a prolonged calculation, that is, without paper and pen. For such problems depend as little as possible on external circumstances, being within the power even of a captive who is denied a pen and whose hands are tied. Therefore we ought to practice both in calculating and in meditating, and when we have reached certain results by calculation, we ought to

try afterward to demonstrate them by meditation alone, which has in my experience often been successful.

(L 194; GM IV 462)

If we consider that Leibniz conceives the universal characteristic as composed of two main ingredients: a set of symbols constituting a language and a set of rules specifying how to combine the symbols in order to draw inferences, it becomes clear that the characteristic should belong to what he calls the "external circumstances" that make possible our activity of thinking/calculating. As we have seen, Leibniz indeed compares the discovery of the universal characteristic to the discovery of the telescope, as an artifact that extends the power of our body:

> Once the characteristic numbers for most concepts have been set up, however, the human race will have a new kind of instrument which will increase the power of the mind much more than optical lenses strengthen the eyes and which will be as far superior to microscopes or telescopes as reason is superior to sight. The magnetic needle has brought no more help to sailors than this lodestar will bring to those who navigate the sea of experiments.

(L 224; GP VII 184–89)[9]

Even though *senses and imagination* are necessary for developing mathematics, they are *not sufficient*, however, to explain how mathematics and geometry acquire universality and demonstrative power. To reach such an explanation, we need to postulate the existence of "something higher, something that understanding alone can provide":

> Therefore, there are objects of still another nature which are not in any way included in what we notice among the objects of either the particular senses or common sense, and which, consequently, are not objects of the imagination, either. Thus, besides the sensible and the imaginable, there is that which is only intelligible, the object of the understanding alone.

(AG 188)

As Leibniz writes to Princess Sophie Charlotte, it is thanks to that "something" situated "besides the sensible and the imaginable" that we reach, by means of a merely conceptual analysis, some basic metaphysical notions:

> The thought of myself, who perceives sensible objects, and the thought of the action of mine that results from it, adds something to the objects of the senses. To think of some color and to consider that one thinks of it are two very different thoughts, just as much as color itself differs from the "I" who thinks of it. And since I conceive that other beings can also have the right to say "I," or that it can be said for them, it is

---

[9] On the metaphor of the telescope in Husserl and Gödel, cf. Tieszen, p. 134 ff.

through this that I conceive what is called substance in general. It is also the consideration of myself that provides me with other notions of metaphysics, such as cause, effect, action, similarity, etc., and even those of logic and ethics. Thus it can be said that there is nothing in the understanding that did not come from the senses, except the understanding itself, or that which understands.

(AG 188)

This passage demonstrates that from 1678 (the year of his letter to Tschirnaus mentioned earlier) to 1702, when he wrote to Sophie Charlotte, Leibniz never abandoned the idea that in addition to the mechanical procedure connected with the use of the characteristic art and with our thinking/calculating employing symbols, we dispose of another more powerful tool based on "meditation" (i.e., on reflection directed toward our acts of thought themselves). It is reflecting on our internal activity of thought, on our different levels of awareness, and on the way we relate ourselves to the objects of knowledge that we may attain some basic, primitive notions of metaphysics. Clearly, when reasoning *about* these notions, we cannot avoid the use of symbols (imagined or spoken in a kind of internal monologue). But because they are "distinct, primitive concepts," we may grasp them only by means of an act of intuition. This point is well established in the *Meditations on Knowledge, Truth and Ideas*, one of the few philosophical papers personally published by Leibniz:

Such thinking I usually call *blind* or *symbolic*; we use it in algebra and in arithmetic, and indeed almost everywhere. When a concept is very complex, we certainly cannot think simultaneously of all the concepts which compose it. But when this is possible, or at least insofar as it is possible, I call the knowledge *intuitive*. There is no other knowledge than intuitive of a distinct primitive concept, while for the most part we have only symbolic thought of composites.

(L 292; GP 4 423)

Here, Leibniz admits that, in some limited cases, we have such *intuitive knowledge* not only of simple, primitive concepts, but also of complex ones. This means, at least under certain circumstances, that we may avoid the use of symbols, and have direct access to what Leibniz calls "the realm of possibles," thus eluding the constraints usually imposed on the human mind by the necessity of employing symbols when thinking.

REFERENCES

Adams, Robert Merriew. 1994. *Leibniz: Determinist, Theist, Idealist*. Oxford: Oxford University Press.

Boland, Vivian OP. 1996. *Ideas in God according to Saint Thomas Aquinas*. Leiden/New York, Koeln: Brill.

Kauppi, Raili. 1960. *Ueber die Leibnizschen Logik*. Acta Philosophica Fennica, XII, Helsinki.

Kulstad, Mark. A. 1977. "Leibniz's Conception of Expression." *Studia Leibnitiana* 9: 55–76.

Mates, Benson. 1986. *The Philosophy of Leibniz. Metaphysics and Language*. Oxford: Oxford University Press.

Mondadori, Fabrizio. 2000. "'Quid sit essentia creaturae, priusquam a Deo producatur': Leibniz's view." In A. Lamarra and R. Palaia (ed.), *Unità e molteplicità nel pensiero filosofico e scientifico di Leibniz*. Firenze: Leo S. Olschki, pp. 185–223.

Nizolio, Mario. 1956. *De veris principiis et vera ratione philosophandi contra pseudophilosophos*, libri IV, vols. 1–2. Roma: Fratelli Bocca Editori.

Swoyer, Chris. 1995. "Leibnizian Expression." *Journal of the History of Philosophy 33*: 65–99.

Tieszen, Richard. 2011. *After Goedel. Platonism and Rationalism in Mathematics and Logic*, Oxford: Oxford University Press.

CHAPTER 2

....

THEORY OF RELATIONS
AND UNIVERSAL HARMONY

....

MASSIMO MUGNAI

THE SCHOLASTIC BACKGROUND

....

IN the fourteenth century, among the doctrines concerning the ontology of relations, the one proposed by Walter Burley (1275–1344) was considered "realistic." According to Burley, in order to have a binary relation between two real things (i.e., two things in the "external" world), five ingredients are necessary: two individuals (the *subject* and the *term* of the relation), two properties grounded each in the individuals (the *foundations* of the relation), and the relation itself. Thus, for instance, if Socrates is similar to Plato, Socrates is the subject, Plato the term of the relation of similarity, and, in both Socrates and Plato there must be a different individual instance of the same property, such as being white or being a philosopher (the same, as the schoolmen used to say, not individually, but "according to the species").[1] This theory was considered "realistic" both because it assumes as real the two fundamental properties on which the relation rests and because it attributes some kind of reality, albeit very thin, to the relation itself. On the other front, that of the nominalists, Ockham for example considered the expression "foundation of a relation" to be not very philosophical and not to be in agreement with the teachings of Aristotle. He offers, however, a very clear account of the traditional *realistic* doctrine about relations:

> On that view every relation is a thing really distinct from its foundation, so that the similarity by which white Socrates is white like Plato is a thing really and totally distinct from both Socrates and the white which grounds the similarity. The same sort of account holds in the case of paternity, filiation, and all the other things that are

....

[1] W. Burleigh, *De Relativis*, edited by H. Shapiro and M. J. Kiteley, in *Franciscan Studies* 22 (1962), p. 165.

placed in the genus of relation. Thus, although "foundation of a relation" is not a piece of Aristotle's philosophical jargon, proponents of this view claim that every relation has both a foundation and a term and that it is really distinct from both.[2]

In the seventeenth century, however, the doctrine so neatly summed up by Ockham became the prevailing view concerning relations, and it was mainly on the basis of this view that the different ontological commitments were articulated.

An important feature of the traditional doctrine of relations is the claim that the properties on which the relation is founded (the *foundations* [*fundamenta*]) are absolute, nonrelational properties. A clear sign of how widespread this doctrine was in Leibniz's times is offered by the two following passages from standard introductory books on logic written, respectively, by the French philosopher Pierre Du Moulin (1586–1658) and by Caspar Bartholinus (1585–1629), a Swedish physician who taught medicine for eleven years at the University of Copenhagen:

> Every relation belonging to this predicament is grounded on some absolute accidents by means of which it inheres in the substance: thus a thing is said to be small or big by quantity; a friend is a friend in virtue of a quality (for instance: benevolence); father and son are predicated in virtue of generation, left and right in virtue of place. We call absolute all those accidents which are not related and which can be known by themselves without the help of any accident: such an absolute accident is the foundation of the relation.[3]

Five things are needed to have a relation belonging to the predicaments [*relatio praedicamentalis*]:

I.   The Subject (some call it the remote foundation, others the extreme), which in the most cases is a substance, the subject of any accident.

II. The Foundation, which is the reason and the cause according to which a relation obtains: it is an absolute accident, a Quantity or a Quality. . . .

III. The Reason which explains why a foundation is a foundation (that someone calls "the nearest foundation [*fundamentum proximum*]"): it constitutes a single thing with the foundation itself. . . .

IV. The Term, which is said to be where the relation ends and rests. Thus, the son is the term of fatherhood and the father of sonhood. Terms are correlatives . . . The one is called *ad quem*, the other *a quo*, or better *in quo*. A relation as, for instance, fatherhood, is in a term (the father) insofar as this latter is the subject of the inherence. . . . A single accident, indeed, is only in one subject, not in several ones. . . .

---

[2] W. Ockham, *Summa Logicae*, in *Opera Philosophica et Theologica: Opera Philosophica I* (New York: St Bonaventure, 1974), pp. 177–178 (English translation from: *Ockham's Theory of Terms. Part I of the* Summa Logica, translated and introduced by Michael J. Loux [South Bend, Ind.: St. Augustine's Press, 1998], p. 176).

[3] Petrus Molineus, *Elementa Logica* (Paris, 1618), pp. 28–29.

V. The Relation itself, which is a disposition or an order between correlated things, according to which the one refers to the other.[4]

Bartholinus's account (in the second text just quoted) is slightly different from the one presented by Burley because it mentions, in addition to the *foundation*, "the reason" of the foundation. The appeal to the reason of the foundation, however, was not very common among medieval thinkers and simply attests to the difficulties one has to face when attempting to explain the nature of relations on the basis of an Aristotelian ontology. According to another author surely known by Leibniz, Johann Christopher Hundeshagen (1635–81), an example of reason of the foundation, in the case of the relation of paternity, is *generation* "which must exist between Abraham and Isaac, if Abraham has to be the father and Isaac the son."[5]

Another very important remark contained in Bartholinus's text is that "a single accident . . . is only in one subject, not in several ones." This is a time-honored principle that medieval thinkers inherited from the Aristotelian tradition: it automatically precludes the possibility that a real property in "the outside world" corresponds to a polyadic term of the natural language, inhering in several subjects. Thus, for example, the similarity relation between Socrates and Plato cannot be a property that, like a bridge, really subsists in both Socrates and Plato.[6] The principle was clearly stated by Thomas Aquinas (the same accident "never extends beyond its subject"[7]) and constituted a kind of ontological dogma for the vast majority of philosophers up until Leibniz's time, as we have seen, and beyond.

A consequence of this principle was that each binary relation[8] was split into two relational accidents, each inhering in one (and only one) of the related subjects. Thus, the relation of paternity between Abraham and Isaac, for example, was thought of as "composed" of two parts: fatherhood in Abraham and sonhood in Isaac. The case of a symmetrical relation was analogous. The similarity subsisting between Socrates and Plato, for example, was usually thought to be composed of the similarity of Socrates to Plato and the similarity of Plato to Socrates. Obviously, this kind of analysis was viable for those people who took seriously the notion of *inherence* (of a property in a substance). A nominalist like Ockham, for example, who considered this notion highly suspicious and reduced it to predication, could afford a very different explanation of the ontological nature of relations. At the same time, the principle in question did not imply a refusal of

---

[4] Caspar Bartholin, *Enchiridion logicum ex Aristotele [. . .]* (Argentorati, 1608), pp. 162–166.

[5] Johannes Christophorus Hundeshagen, *Logica, tabulis succinctis inclusa* (Jenae, 1674), p. 22.

[6] Cf. Peter Aureol's *Scriptum super Primum Sententiarum*, fols. 318ᵛa–b (translation in G. Brown, *Medieval Theories of Relations*, "The Stanford Encyclopaedia of Philosophy"): "It appears that a single thing, which must be imagined as some sort of interval (*intervallum*) existing between two things, cannot exist in extramental reality."

[7] "[A]ccidens enim non extendit se ultra suum subiectum": Thomas, *In quatuor libros Sententiarum*, II, d. 27, q. 1, ar. 6. For another version of the same principle, cf. II, d. 42, q. 1, ar. 1: "[U]num accidens non potest in diversis subiectis esse [the same accident cannot be in different subiects]."

[8] Scholastic and late-scholastic thinkers usually ignored relations with more than two subjects.

polyadicity: as Peter Aureol (1280–1322) argued in the fourteenth century, even though no real property in the "external world" corresponds to polyadic terms, they may denote *mental entities*.[9]

Relations as "Ideal" Entities

Coming now to Leibniz, we find that he develops his theory of relations according to the framework implicit in the prevailing view so clearly summarized by Bartholinus and Du Moulin. In a text written from 1664, for example, Leibniz admits that a relation needs a foundation, and, in the same vein as Bartholinus, he distinguishes between the *foundation* on which the relation rests and the *reason of inhering* (*ratio fundandi*):

> The *foundation of a relation* is that in virtue of which the relation inheres in the subject, whereas the *reason of inhering* is that in virtue of which the relation is made actual.
>
> (A VI i 95)

Later on, in 1706, in a marginal remark about a book written by the Jesuit Aloys Temmik, Leibniz states that the property on which a relation is founded is an *absolute* one (it is not relational): "The foundation of the relation belonging to the predicaments is an absolute accident."[10]

And, in one of the most frequently quoted and commented passages from his fifth letter to Clarke (1715), he summarizes with great clarity the same doctrine, which was held by many other thinkers of his time. In that passage, Leibniz considers the case of two lines, *L* and *M* with *L* being greater than *M*, and argues as follows:

> The ratio or proportion between two lines *L* and *M* may be conceived three several ways: as a ratio of the greater *L* to the lesser *M*, as a ratio of the lesser *M* to the greater *L*, and, lastly, as something abstracted from both, that is, the ratio between *L* and *M* without considering which is the antecedent or which the consequent, which the subject and which the object. And thus it is that proportions are considered in music. In the first way of considering them, *L* the greater, in the second, *M* the lesser, is the subject of *that accident which philosophers call "relation."* But which of them will be the subject in the third way of considering them? It cannot be said that both of them, *L* and *M* together, are the subject of such an accident; for, if so, we should have an accident in two subjects, with one leg in one and the other in the other, which is contrary to the notion of accidents. Therefore we must say that *this relation, in this third way of considering it,* is indeed out of the subjects; but being neither a substance nor

---

[9] Cf. Peter Aureol's *Scriptum super Primum Sententiarum*, fols. 318ᵛa–b.

[10] M. Mugnai, *Leibniz's Theory of Relations*, Studia Leibnitiana Supplementa 28 (Stuttgart: Franz Steiner Verlag, 1992), p. 161: "Fundamentum relationis praedicamentalis est accidens absolutum."

an accident, it must be a mere ideal thing, the consideration of which is nevertheless useful.

(L 704; *Correspondance* 144–45)

A central claim of this text is the well-known scholastic principle that the same accident cannot be in two subjects. From this, Leibniz infers that polyadic predicates cannot denote real entities "in the world." At the same time, however, echoing Peter Aureol's doctrine, he recognizes the mental nature of relations and admits that the consideration of these mental entities is useful (clearly alluding to their importance for the sciences, physics, and mathematics in the first place). Another important point is the distinction between the relation in the proper sense, conceived as a "mere ideal thing," and "that accident which philosophers call relation" (i.e., the relational accident inhering in only one of the related subjects). In the case of the lines L and M of the example, the *relational accidents* are the properties denoted by the words "greater" and "lesser," and they are supposed to inhere, respectively, in the line L and in the line M. Analogously, given the relation of paternity subsisting between David and Solomon, Leibniz distinguishes the two relational accidents corresponding to the words "paternity" and "sonship" from the relation of paternity understood as some property inhering in both, Solomon and David:

I do not believe that you will admit an accident that is in two subjects at the same time. My judgement about relation is that paternity in David is one thing, sonship in Solomon another, but that the relation common to both is a merely mental thing whose foundation is the modifications of the individuals.

(GP II 486)

Leibniz, indeed, admits that, in addition to individual substances and their individual modifications, there is a third kind of attribute that is "common to many subjects." As we read in a paper written some years after 1700, this third kind of attribute includes numbers, order, time, place, and, obviously, relations:

A being is either a *substance*, and in that case it can be only a subject, or it is an *attribute*, and in that case it constitutes the predicate of another being. So learning is just what gives rise to the fact that someone is learned; action that someone acts. But we may ask whether there is a third possibility, since time and place, for instance, are not subsistent things nor are their attributes. The same applies to the number and to order: so "ten" is not an attribute of anything. In fact one cannot predicate "ten" of a single aggregate or of singular things. The same applies to a relation, which is common to many subjects, such as the similarity between two things. So there are attributes which are inherent in several subjects at once. Of that kind are, for example, order, time, and place.[11]

---

[11] LH IV, 7c, Bl 75–78. For a commentary to this text, cf. M. Mugnai, "*Alia est rerum alia terminorum divisio*: about an unpublished manuscript of Leibniz," in A. Lamarra and A. Palaia (eds.), *Unità e molteplicità nel pensiero filosofico di Leibniz* (Firenze: Leo S. Olschki, 2000), pp. 257–269.

According to Leibniz, multiple inherence, which is characteristic of relations considered "outside of the subjects," is a mark of their merely mental nature because, if they were real, an argument would apply to them that would produce an infinite regress. The argument, later attributed to Bradley, was well known to medieval thinkers who attempted to refute the reality of relations and was employed by Leibniz in a short text written during the period of his stay in Paris:

> It is no wonder that the number of all numbers, all possibilities, all relations or reflections are not clearly understood, because they are imaginary beings to which nothing does correspond in the real world. Suppose, for example, that there is a relation between *a* and *b*, and call it *c*; then, consider a new relation between *a* and *c*: call it *d*, and so forth to the infinite. It seems that we do not have to say that all these relations are a kind of true and real ideas. Perhaps they are only mere intelligible things, which may be produced, i.e. that are or will be produced.

(A VI iii 399)

To explicitly characterize the "mental" nature of relations, Leibniz coins the Latin word *concogitabilitas* [*co-thinkability*]: a relation emerges as soon as several things are thought of simultaneously. As he writes in a draft probably composed in late 1690, a relation is something that results or *supervenes* without involving any change in the related subjects (A VI iv 866). Leibniz uses the scholastic notion of *supervenience* to stress that it is the simultaneous presence of a plurality of things in a single act of thinking to determine the emerging of a relation, without any intervention of the will.

THE NATURE OF "RELATIONAL PREDICATES"

If Leibniz is quite clear concerning the nature of relations "outside of the subjects," he is not so explicit about relational predicates. Given the relation of paternity that subsists between David and Solomon, he claims, as we have seen, that it is a merely ideal thing whose foundations are the modifications of the individuals, and he neatly distinguishes paternity and sonship, which are, respectively, *in* David and *in* Solomon, taking for granted that they are *individual accidents*. If they are individual accidents, however, they raise some problems concerning their ontological nature. They cannot be, indeed, the foundations of the relation "outside of the subjects" because the foundations of a relation, according to the standard doctrine of relations at the time, must be only absolute, nonrelational accidents. Moreover, insofar as they are relational, they themselves need a foundation.

That, for Leibniz, relational predicates—as contrasted with relations "outside of the subjects"—have to be considered as individual accidents of some sort seems to be confirmed by the following passage, belonging to the fifth letter to Clarke:

And here it may not be amiss to consider the difference between place and the relation of situation which is in the body that fills up the place. For the place of *A* and *B*
is the same, whereas the relation of *A* to fixed bodies is not precisely and individually the same as the relation which *B* (that comes into its place) will have to the fixed
bodies; but these relations agree only. For two different subjects, such as *A* and *B*,
cannot have precisely the same individual affection, it being impossible that the same
individual accident should be in two subjects or pass from one subject to another.

(L 704; *Correspondance* 144)

Here, Leibniz proposes to Clarke that he imagines a situation where a given body
A, being at a certain distance from a group of fixed bodies *D, E, F, G*, is replaced by a
different body *B*. Leibniz claims that *A* and *B* maintain *the same place* with respect to
the fixed bodies, but that *the relation that the body A has with these latter bodies* is "not
precisely and individually the same as the relation which *B* (that comes into its place)
will have" to them. In Leibniz's words, this amounts to distinguishing the *place* from
the "relation of situation which is in the body that fills up the place." Clearly, this raises
the question of how a *relation of situation* can inhere in a subject, according to the traditional scholastic ontology shared in great part by Leibniz.

As Thomas Aquinas points out, in each relation, two different aspects are involved: the
esse-in [*to be-in*] and the *esse-ad* [*to be-toward*]. The *esse-in* corresponds to the "accidental being" of the relation, whereas the *esse-ad* expresses the specific nature (the *ratio*)
of the relation as a distinct category.[12] Thus, whereas "other categories, such as quantity
and quality, by their own *ratio* signify something inhering in something," the category of
relation, characterized by "being toward something [*esse ad aliud*]," signifies by its own
ratio only a respect toward another.[13] The *ratio*, however, does not preclude the possibility of inherence. As we read in a book belonging to the Thomist tradition: "There are
two ways of looking at a relation: first insofar as it is a relation; second insofar as it is an
accident, i.e. considering the property on which is grounded."[14] In other words, to inhere in the subject is properly *the foundation* of the relation. Thomas Aquinas expresses
this in a paradoxical way in his *On Power* [*De potentia*], where he writes that a relation
"is something which inheres, even if it does not have that property [i.e., of inhering] by
the simple fact of being a relation."[15] Therefore, what Leibniz writes in the fifth letter to
Clarke concerning the two bodies put in the same place amounts to saying that the relation of situation cannot be the same because the *foundation* on which the relation rests is
not individually *the same*.

That Leibniz cannot consider the *situs* or the *relation of situation* as a property *inhering*
in a given subject in the same sense according to which one says that the accident *white*

---

[12] Cf. Mark G. Henninger, *Relations. Medieval Theories 1250–1325* (Oxford: Clarendon Press, 1989),
pp. 15–16.

[13] Thomas Aquinas, *Summa Theol.* I, q. 28, a. 1.

[14] The text is from the *Clipeus Thomistarum* [*Shield of Thomas' followers*] II, q. 38 (Venetiis, 1481),
quoted in A. Krempel, *La doctrine de la relation chez Saint Thomas* (Paris: Vrin, 1952), p. 269.

[15] Thomas Aquinas, *Quaestio de potentia*, q. 7, a. 9, r. 7.

inheres in the wall may be inferred from the definitions of *situs* he gives on several occasions: "the situation [*situs*] contains two conditions: that some points are given with a certain position, i.e. perceived . . ., and that they are simultaneously perceived" (A VI iv 174); ". . . if one assumes that something is not only thought but also perceived, then from this very fact situation and extension are generated" (A VI iv 382). Here, in agreement with the general definition of a relation as resulting from the thinking together of several things, *situs* is connected to the condition of *simultaneously perceiving*. In other occasions, however, Leibniz gives a less "subjective" definition of *situs*, appealing to *simultaneous existence* and not to perception (cf., for instance, what Leibniz writes in A VI iv 637: "What is extended implies a position, which is called a *situs*, of things simultaneously coexisting and having parts"). At any rate, in both cases, a situation involving the necessary reference to more than one single thing can hardly be conceived as a property inhering in a subject.

Hence, to understand what kind of reality Leibniz attributes to relational properties, we have to examine how, according to him, a relational attribute is linked to its foundation.

RELATIONAL PROPERTIES AND THEIR FOUNDATIONS

In Leibniz's times, the philosophical dispute concerning the ontology of relations (relational properties) took place against the background of the traditional doctrine attributed earlier to Walter Burley. The dispute between "realists" and "nominalists," for instance, mainly took the form of a question concerning the nature of the relationship between a relation and its foundation. To mention only the two extreme theses, we may recall that the realists held that a relation was *really* distinguished from the property on which it was grounded (its *foundation*), whereas the nominalists claimed that it was identical with the foundation. A range of intermediate positions, however, were possible, such as, for instance, the position of those who claimed that the relation was *distinguishable* from its foundation but only by an act of the understanding. Concerning Leibniz, in the texts edited up until now, there is no explicit discussion of this issue. One of the few passages in which he indirectly tackles the problem is in a paper written at the end of his life and containing precious remarks about the nature of relations in general.[16] Here, Leibniz distinguishes two classes of predicates: those "that add something to a subject" and those that do not. *Rationality*, for instance, or the *capability of wondering*, once added to a man belong to the first class, whereas the predicate of *being*

---

[16] The date of composition is assumed on the basis of the watermarks, which indicate a period between the end of 1715 and 1716, the year of Leibniz's death (cf. Mugnai, *Leibniz's Theory of Relations*, p. 154).

learned belongs to the second. The concept of man, indeed, under which an individual man falls, logically implies rationality, but it does not necessarily include the predicate of being learned (there are nonlearned men or, at least, such men are possible). Next, he considers *paternity* and poses the question of whether it "adds something to Philip." His answer is as follows:

> If individuals are considered as complete notions, it doesn't add anything. One may say that contingent properties are essential to the individuals, because the notion of an individual is such that it contains all contingent attributes. . . . As the point doesn't increase the line, thus a relation doesn't increase the subject.[17]

At first glance, Leibniz's words seem to contain a plain contradiction: *contingent* properties, indeed, are said to be *essential* to individuals. This is, however, an obvious consequence of his doctrine of the *complete concept*. In the *Discourse on Metaphysics*, Leibniz claims that, corresponding to each individual substance, there is a concept "so complete that it is sufficient to make us understand and deduce from it all the predicates of the subject to which the concept is attributed" (L 307; A VI iv 1450). Thus, the complete concept is an exhaustive description of the individual substance subordinate to it, and that description contains both kinds of predicates: the necessary and the contingent ones. If we assume, as Leibniz does, that the complete concept determines the identity of a given individual, it follows from this assumption that the least change, even in a contingent predicate, implies a change in the identity of the individual. In this sense, as Leibniz states, all contingent properties are *essential* to the individuals.[18] But then, from the point of view of an individual such as, for example, Philip or David, who is supposed to be a father, the relational predicate of being father does not add anything to him (to his complete concept). It seems that what Leibniz is saying here about relational predicates is not of much use in determining his ontological attitude. In the last sentence of the passage just quoted, however, Leibniz claims that as "the point doesn't increase the line, thus a relation doesn't increase the subject," and the fact that a relational accident doesn't increase its subject means that it does not add any further reality to it. The analogy based on the two pairs, *point/relation* and *line/subject*, is particularly revealing. If one considers that, for Leibniz, points neither compose the line nor are parts of it, then Leibniz here states that relations (relational accidents) neither compose nor are part of the subject on which they are founded. In more traditional terms, relational accidents are not really distinguished from the absolute properties (*fundamenta* [foundations]) on which they are based. Therefore, when Leibniz says that paternity or the relation of situation inheres in a given subject, he means properly that to inhere is the absolute property on which paternity or the relation of situation is founded. In the case of paternity,

---

[17] Mugnai, *Leibniz's Theory of Relations*, pp. 156–157.
[18] On this point, cf. F. Mondadori, "On some disputed questions in Leibniz's metaphysics," in *Studia Leibnitiana* 25 (1993), pp. 153–173.

for example, the absolute property on which it inheres was usually indicated in the phys-iological power of generating a child.

RELATIONS AND EXTRINSIC DENOMINATIONS

In the scholastic tradition inherited by Leibniz, a standard argument was employed to show that, although a change of an accident or, in general, of a property of a given subject implies a change in the subject itself, a relation may change without involving a change in *all* related subjects. This argument can be traced back to Aristotle, who made recourse to it in order to prove that a relation cannot have the same reality as a monadic (absolute) property (Arist. *Phys.* V ii 225b:10–13): later on, however, nominalists (and conceptualists) used it to motivate their denial of ontological reality to relations. The argument runs as follows: suppose that someone who, living in the East Indies, becomes a widower because his wife dies in Europe. Clearly, whereas the wife undergoes a change as soon as she dies, her passing from life to death does not directly affect her husband, who becomes a widower without any change occurring in him. Similar examples are present in many authors: a man who lives in France becomes a father as soon as a child is born to him in the East Indies without any change occurring in him; if a white thing is now in Spain, the emerging of a new white thing in the East Indies will produce the rela-tion of similarity of the two things without exerting any influence on the thing that is in Spain.[19] Leibniz, in his turn, seems to be well acquainted with this tradition, as witnessed by the fact that he repeats some of these examples in his writings.[20]

The possibility of arising and perishing without causing a real change in all the subjects to which a given predicate refers was considered by the scholastic tradi-tion at Leibniz's times to be typical of a class of predicates that were called *extrinsic denominations*. A denomination of a given subject was said to be *intrinsic* if it was naming an intrinsic property of the subject itself and *extrinsic* if it named a property referring to something extrinsic to it. The "denomination" *father*, for instance, is ex-trinsic because it refers to someone *external* to the subject playing the role of a father (i.e., a child). A widely accepted claim among scholastic and late-scholastic thinkers was that extrinsic denominations do not inhere properly in the subject of which they are denominated.[21]

---

[19] For the latter example, cf. Juan Sanchez Sedeno, *Quaestiones ad Universam Aristotelis Logicam*, Tomus II (Moguntiae, 1615), p. 153. The other examples are very common among scholastic authors.

[20] Cf., for instance, A VI iv 1503, where Leibniz mentions the case of a man who, being in India, is left a widower by the death of his wife in Europe.

[21] This is clearly stated by Christopher Hundeshagen, *Logica*: "*What is denominated* is the subject of that which denominates, i.e. the subject of which the predicate is *accidentally* predicated: for instance, the body in respect to blackness, the snow in respect to whiteness. And the form which denominates sometimes inheres and sometimes does not inhere in the denominated subject. Thus, from this

With respect to this traditional doctrine, Leibniz displays an attitude that, at first glance, may seem quite puzzling: in some texts, he clearly endorses it without reservations, whereas in others he explicitly refuses it. This, however, is neither the symptom of a sharp change of opinion nor of a plain contradiction. Leibniz claims that the traditional doctrine is true only if we limit ourselves to considering what happens at a superficial level: at a deeper, metaphysical level, any change in an extrinsic denomination *implies a change in all the subjects involved in the denomination*. It is typical of Leibniz to frame his discussion of certain texts in traditional terms, without advertising the fact that, when speaking with metaphysical rigor, these traditional terms need to be reinterpreted in ways that significantly depart from traditional understanding.

The following passage is a clear example of the first attitude. Here, Leibniz not only considers relations like *father* as *extrinsic denominations*, but he also says, faithful to the orthodox doctrine, that, in the case of extrinsic denominations, the relation may change without causing a change in correlated subjects:

> Therefore, all the extrinsic denominations, i.e. those denominations which arise and perish without any change of the subject, simply because something changes in something else, seem to belong to relations. Thus, a father becomes father as soon as his child is born, even though he, who happens to be in the East Indies, does not undergo any change. Thus, the similarity, which I share with someone else, is born and comes to light without any change in myself, but with a change in the other.
>
> (A VI iv 308)

At the same time, in other texts, Leibniz plainly admits that, from a rigorous metaphysical point of view, there are no genuinely extrinsic denominations: if a relation or an extrinsic denomination changes, this implies a change *in all* the related subjects. This clearly emerges from the *New Essays*, in which, according to the received view, Philaletes-Locke states that "a change of relation can occur without there having been any change in the subject": Titius, who is today a father "ceases to be so tomorrow, only by the death of his son, without any alteration made in himself." To Philaletes-Locke, Leibniz replies by means of his alter ego Theophilus:

> That can be very well be said if we are guided by the things of which we are aware; but in metaphysical strictness there is no wholly extrinsic denomination (*denominatio pure extrinseca*), because of the real connection amongst all things.
>
> (NE 227)

It is worth noting that Leibniz in his reply says that to produce the change *in* the subject to which the extrinsic denomination applies is "the real connection amongst all

originates a twofold denomination: *intrinsic* and *extrinsic*; for instance: if I say, 'the wall is white', then we have an intrinsic denomination, whereas if I say, 'the man is just before God' we have an extrinsic denomination."

things," *not* the acquisition (or loss) of the denomination itself (a classical thesis of the ontological realism about relations). Many other texts confirm that, for Leibniz, "in metaphysical strictness" there are "no wholly extrinsic denominations":

> [T]here are no extrinsic denominations, and no one becomes a widower in India by the death of his wife in Europe unless a real change occurs in him. For every predicate is in fact contained in the nature of a subject.[22]

It follows further that *there are no purely extrinsic denominations* that have no foundation at all in the denominated thing itself because the concept of the denominated subject necessarily involves the concept of the predicate. Likewise, whenever the denomination of a thing is changed, some variation has to occur in the thing itself.[23]

In the last passage, from a short essay written in 1689, Leibniz says that *whenever the denomination of a thing is changed, some variation has to occur in the thing itself because every extrinsic denomination has a basis in the denominated thing.* This implies that such a basis contains, in some sense, the reason or reasons for the attribution or loss of the denomination and that, if the extrinsic denomination changes, then the reason or reasons themselves have to change. Leibniz's conclusion is that "there is no extrinsic denomination at all in complete things":

> There is no extrinsic denomination at all in complete things; and nothing can be known or seen without being affected and undergoing a real change by this very fact, and this is typical of all intrinsic denominations. In abstract matters, however, we have recourse to this distinction of denominations just when we name something according to a change, which we are attributing to it, without noticing the intrinsic changes that from this very fact follow in all the remaining things. A good example is that of *motion*: when we mean a true and actual motion and we are considering it from the mathematical point of view, we recognize a change denominating the distance in both things of which the distance is changed. We recognize, however, a real change only in that body which is the true subject of motion, whereas the other is at rest.[24]

Leibniz is so fond of the principle according to which there are no extrinsic denominations that he even blurs the long-honored scholastic distinction between *real relations* and *relations of reason.* According to the scholastic tradition, the relation that, for instance, subsists between me and the object of my thought when I am thinking of the Emperor of China is a typical *relation of reason* (*relatio rationis*). The paternity relation between David and Solomon, instead, is a *real relation*. Leibniz, however, considers

---

[22] L 365 (A VI iv 1503): the passage is from a text probably written between 1683 and 1686.

[23] L 268 (translation slightly modified; A VI iv 1645–46).

[24] LH IV iii 5a–e; Bl 15. The entire text has been published, and translated into English, for the first time (with a short commentary) in *The Leibniz Review 19* (2009), pp. 64–66.

both as cases of extrinsic denominations and says that, in both cases, a change in the relation implies a change *in all the related subjects*:

> On my view, all extrinsic denominations are grounded in intrinsic denominations, and a thing that is seen really differs from one which is not seen: for the rays, which are reflected by the thing that is seen, bring about a change in the thing itself. What is more, in virtue of the universal connection of things, the Emperor of China as known by me differs in intrinsic qualities from himself as not yet known by me. Further, there is no doubt that each thing undergoes a change at the very same time, and it is needed time, in order for him, once not known by me to become known by me.
>
> (M. Mugnai, *Leibniz's Theory of Relations*, 53)

Leibniz here seems to say that a change occurs in the object of thought (on the obvious condition that it is a real object of our world) *because* this latter has acquired the new denomination of *being thought* (or being known) by me. What he claims, however, is that *it is because of the universal connection of things* that "the Emperor of China as known by me differs in intrinsic qualities from himself as not yet known by me." But then, the problem arises as to how Leibniz may be entitled to speak of "the universal connection of things" if relations between two or more substances are merely mental things. This question drives us to the core of Leibniz's metaphysics—that is, to the idea itself of *harmony*.

HARMONY

First of all, we have to distinguish the general notion of *harmony* from the more specialized notion of *pre-established* harmony: the former concerns the actual world in its entirety and involves all kind of creatures; the latter is a solution to the specific problem of the relationship between soul and body raised by the Cartesian dualism and eminently concerns human beings (even though Leibniz extends it to all kinds of living beings). With what he calls "the hypothesis of pre-established harmony," Leibniz assumes the existence of a mutual dependence between the soul and the body of every living being of our world, according to which the body depends on the soul ideally, "in so far as the reason of that which is done in the one can be furnished by that which is in the other" (H 162; GP VI 138). This harmonious dependence is "pre-established" because God has determined it for all time just prior to creation, as soon as he chose the ideal model of the actual world. "According to the System of Pre-established Harmony" (so writes Leibniz) "the soul finds in itself, and in its ideal nature anterior to existence, the reasons for its determinations, adjusted to all that shall surround it. That way it was determined from all eternity in its state of mere possibility to act freely, as it does, when it attains to existence" (H 325; GP VI 308). The more general harmony that rules our world, instead, states that the realm of efficient causes and that of final causes are parallel to each other; that God has no less the quality of the best monarch than that of the greatest architect; that matter is so disposed that the laws of motion serve as the best guidance for spirits; and that consequently it will prove that he has attained the utmost good possible, provided one reckon the metaphysical, physical and moral goods together.

(H 282; GP VI 264)

In the final version of his philosophy, Leibniz offers a picture of the actual world as an aggregate of individual substances, each with its (own) intrinsic modifications and without physical contact or direct influence on one another. The intrinsic modifications consist of representations and a continuous passage from representation to representation. In this world of isolated individual substances, it is God who, once for all in the instant of creation, accommodates the internal states of each substance to those of the others:

For God, comparing two simple substances, finds the reasons in each which oblige him to adapt the other to it. . . . Now this mutual connection or accommodation of all created things to each other and of each to all the rest causes each simple substance to have relations which express all the others and consequently to be a perpetual living mirror of the universe.

(L 648; GP VI 615)

Thus, the harmonious behavior of all substances in the actual world is due to God; and it is God who, accommodating the internal states of the substances, gives rise to relations. This notion of "accommodation," however, has to be explained with some care. First, Leibniz's God, when constructing the various possible worlds, proceeds "by stages" according to a *priority of nature* only, not a priority of time:

The infinity of possibles, however great it may be, is no greater than that of the wisdom of God, who knows all possibles. One may even say that if this wisdom does not exceed the possibles extensively, since the objects of the understanding cannot go beyond the possible, which in a sense is alone intelligible, it exceeds them intensively, by reason of the infinitely infinite combinations it makes thereof, and its many deliberations concerning them. The wisdom of God, not content with embracing all the possibles, penetrates them, compares them, weighs them one against the other, to estimate their degrees of perfection or imperfection, the strong and the weak, the good and the evil. It goes even beyond the finite combinations, it makes of them an infinity of infinites, that is to say, an infinity of possible sequences of the universe, each of which contains an infinity of creatures. By this means the divine Wisdom distributes all the possibles it had already contemplated separately, into so many universal systems which it further compares the one with the other. The result of all these comparisons and deliberations is the choice of the best from among all these possible systems, which wisdom makes in order to satisfy goodness completely; and such is precisely the plan of the universe as it is. Moreover, all these operations of the divine understanding, although they have among them an order and a priority of nature, always take place together, no priority of time existing among them.

(H 271; GP VI 252)

Moreover, God produces the infinity of possible worlds (and, consequently, the infinity of complete concepts that belong to each possible world) merely by combining the ideas or *essences* that he has in his mind. But God has no power over these ideas or essences other than the ability to combine them on the basis of the law of logic *and* to call into existence the world corresponding to the *best model*. As we read in the *Theodicy*: "God is . . . not the author of essences in so far as they are only possibilities. But there is nothing actual to which he has not decreed and given existence" (H 328; GP VI 314). When God compares two complete concepts or two possible substances, he finds the reasons in each that oblige him to adapt the other to it; obviously, he may even find the reasons in each that oblige him to separate the one from the other. At any rate, to guarantee a full understanding of Leibniz's words, it is important to emphasize that "obligation" in this case means properly *moral obligation or moral necessity*, not metaphysical necessity.[25]

This point is made clear by what Leibniz writes in the *New Essays* when tackling the problem of whether the same representation, internal to a given substance, could be produced by "two different constitutions" (two different individuals or phenomena):

As for what is inner: although every outer appearance is grounded in the inner constitution, it can nevertheless happen that two different constitutions result in the same appearance; yet there will be something in common, and that is what philosophers call the "immediate formal cause."

(NE 309)

This means that God, in some circumstances, can coordinate the same internal perception of a substance with two different "external objects." God's choice, however, is not "absolutely free": it is determined by the principle of the "best"; that is, by the moral obligation of choosing the best of possible worlds. In principle, if God chooses otherwise, no contradiction of any sort would follow: this, however, would be contrary to God's wisdom. Thus, God's accommodation consists mainly in something analogous to putting the pieces of a puzzle in the right places. Without God's activity, there would be no puzzle at all, but each piece has a feature that is largely independent of God's will.

Once God has created the world, as Leibniz emphasizes, relations simply result from the existence of the individual substances with their modifications:

---

[25] Cf. Jan A. Cover's review of Plaisted, *Extrinsic Denominations*, in *The Leibniz Review* 14 (2004), pp. 103–104: " 'taller than Simmias' is a fine predicate to which no *taller than Simmias* accident corresponds, there being none. . . . There are the mind-like substances and the intrinsic monadic qualitative states and God's 'arrangement' . . ., and that's it, full stop."

In addition to the substances, which are the last subjects, there are the modifications of the substances, which are subject to creation and destruction in their own right. And finally, there are the relations, which are not created in their own right but result from the creation of other things.

(*Notationes quaedam ad Aloysii Temmik Philosophiam*, in Mugnai, *Leibniz's Theory of Relations*, 155)

This passage continues with some remarkable claims that explain the nature of relations according to Leibniz:

Their reality [of relations] does not depend on our understanding—they inhere without anyone being required to think them. Their reality comes from the divine understanding, without which nothing would be true. Thus there are two things which only the divine understanding can realise: all the eternal truths and, of the contingent ones, those which are relational [*respectivae*].

(*Notationes quaedam ad Aloysii Temmik Philosophiam*, in Mugnai, *Leibniz's Theory of Relations*, 155)

Clearly, the reality of relations does not depend on the *human* understanding: it depends on the divine understanding, and relations "inhere" even though nobody thinks of them because they *supervene* to the existence of the individual substances with their intrinsic modifications (the foundations of the relations). Inhering, in the proper sense of the word, are only *the conditions* for the existence of the relations (i.e., the *foundations* on which any relation rests). That God "realizes" among the contingent truths (only) the relational ones means that as soon as he creates the individuals of a given world with their internal states (perceptions), then instantly all the relations between them are created. This is clearly expressed in a passage from a text written after 1690:

I believe that a mode is properly an accident which determines, or adds certain limits to what is perpetual and undergoes modification. But I would not attribute this property to the relation and indiscriminately to all accidents. The relation results in fact from the substances and the modes, without producing any change of itself but only in virtue of a *consequence*. In a certain sense, the relation may be defined as an *ens rationis*, which yet is real at the same time: all things in fact are constituted by virtue of the divine understanding . . . which is the cause of the eternity of possibilities and truths, even though nothing exists. . . . [T]hus, relations and orders are not imaginary . . . since they are founded in truths.[26]

---

[26] LH IV 3 5c; Bl 2 r: "Modum putem proprie esse accidens determinans seu limites quosdam adiiciens ei quod perpetuum est et modificatur. Relationi autem adeoque omni accidenti nolim hoc tribuere. Relatio autem ex substantia et modis resultat nulla propria mutatione, sed consequentia tantum, et aliquo modo Ens rationis dici potest, et si simul reale sit, quia ipsae res omnes vi summi intellecti constituuntur, quae causa quoque est ut possibilitates et veritates sint aeternae, etiam cum existentia absest."

According to Bertrand Russell, Leibniz's position about relations leads to "a special absurdity, namely, that the relational propositions, which God is supposed to know, must be strictly meaningless."[27] Leibniz, however, simply puts things the other way around: it is because God has created the individual substances and has put them together in a world that relations *result*, and the harmonious order between all the substances of the world is determined by the mutual coordination, operated by God, of the "representational" states internal to each substance with those internal to any other substance belonging to the same world.[28] As Leibniz explicitly admits: "I trace the reality of each relation back to a relationship with the divine intellect."[29]

Hence, taken at face value, Leibniz's theory of relations presents itself as an odd mixture of nominalistic-conceptualistic and realistic elements at the same time. It is nominalistic-conceptualist insofar as it denies that relations have a reality in the "external" world; it has "realistic" consequences insofar as Leibniz assumes the principle according to which the least change of denomination in a subject is correlated to a change *in the internal properties* of all things in the universe. Determining this situation are two different commitments: on one hand to nominalism-conceptualism and on the other hand to the neo-platonic claim, renewed by Renaissance philosophers, that every individual reproduces or reflects in itself the entire universe.[30]

REFERENCES

Bartholin, Caspar. 1608. *Enchiridion logicum ex Aristotele [. . .]*. Argentorati.
Brown, Jeffrey. *Medieval Theories of Relations*. "The Stanford Encyclopaedia of Philosophy." <http://plato.stanford.edu/entries/relations-medieval/>
Burleigh, Walter. 1962. "*De Relativis*, ed. H. Shapiro and M. J. Kiteley." *Franciscan Studies* 22: 155–171.
Cover, Jan A. 1995. "Review of Mugnai, *Leibniz's Theory of Relations*." *Leibniz Society Review* 5: 1–10.
Cover, Jan A. 2004. "Review of Plaisted 2002." *The Leibniz Review* 14: 103–104.
Henninger, Mark G. 1989. *Relations. Medieval Theories 1250–1325*. Oxford: Clarendon Press.
Hundeshagen, Johann C. 1674. *Logica, tabulis succinctis inclusa*. Jena.
Krempel, Thomas. 1952. *La doctrine de la relation chez Saint Thomas*. Paris: Vrin.

[27] B. Russell, *A Critical Exposition of the Philosophy of Leibniz* (Cambridge: 1900), p. 14.

[28] Cf. Jan A. Cover, review of Plaisted 2002, *The Leibniz Review* 14 (2004), pp. 103–104.

[29] "Leibniz's marginal notes and remarks to Temmik's text," in Mugnai, *Leibniz's Theory of Relations*, p. 161.

[30] Suarez, in the *Metaphysical Disputations*, listing the various opinions concerning the change of relation, mentions a position that strongly recalls that of Leibniz. Suarez, indeed, mentions some unspecified authors [*aliqui*] who claim "that, because of the acquisition of a new relation, a true, real modification takes place in the very related things, not by means of an action internal to the subject itself, but in virtue of a kind of intrinsic propagation [*per intrinsecam dimanationem*]"; Francisco Suarez, *Disputationes Metaphysicae*, 2 vols. (Paris, 1866 [Hildesheim: Olms, 1965]), vol. 2, p. 790b. Suarez considers this thesis very implausible and gets rid of it by observing that there exists no experiment or even a single piece of evidence to confirm it.

Molineus, Petrus (Du Moulin, Pierre). 1618. *Elementa Logica*. Paris.

Mondadori, Fabrizio. 1993. "On some disputed questions in Leibniz's metaphysics." *Studia Leibnitiana* 25: 153–173.

Mugnai, Massimo. 1992. *Leibniz's Theory of Relations*. Studia Leibnitiana Supplementa, 28. Stuttgart: Franz Steiner Verlag.

Mugnai, Massimo. 2000. "*Alia es trerum alia terminorum divisio:* about an unpublished manuscript of Leibniz." In A. Lamarra and A. Palaia (eds.), *Unità e molteplicità nel pensiero filosofico di Leibniz*. Firenze: Leo S. Olschki: 257–270.

Plaisted, Dennis. 2002. *Leibniz on Purely Extrinsic Denominations*. Rochester: University of Rochester Press.

Russell, Bertrand. 1990. *A Critical Exposition of the Philosophy of Leibniz*. Cambridge.

Sanchez Sedeno, Juan. 1615. *Quaestiones ad Universam Aristotelis Logicam*. Moguntiae.

Suarez, Francisco. 1866/1965. *Disputationes Metaphysicae,* 2 vols., Paris, 1866/Hildesheim: Olms, 1965.

CHAPTER 3

....

THE PRINCIPLES
OF CONTRADICTION,
SUFFICIENT REASON,
AND IDENTITY OF
INDISCERNIBLES

....

GONZALO RODRIGUEZ-PEREYRA

LEIBNIZ was a philosopher of principles: the Principles of Contradiction, of Sufficient Reason, of Identity of Indiscernibles, of Plenitude, of the Best, and of Continuity are among the most famous Leibnizian principles.[1] In this article, I shall focus on the first three principles; I shall discuss various formulations of the principles (sec. 1), what it means for these theses to have the status of principles or axioms in Leibniz's philosophy (sec. 2), the fundamental character of the Principles of Contradiction and Sufficient Reason (sec. 3), some attempts to demonstrate the Principles of Contradiction and Sufficient Reason (sec. 4), and one attempt to demonstrate the Principle of Identity of Indiscernibles (sec. 5). The main results of the chapter are summarized in a short conclusion (sec. 6).

FORMULATIONS OF THE PRINCIPLES OF
CONTRADICTION, SUFFICIENT REASON, AND
IDENTITY OF INDISCERNIBLES

Leibniz gives several different formulations of the Principle of Contradiction, among them the following ones:

---

[1] According to Ortega y Gasset, Leibniz is both the philosopher who used the greatest number of maximally general principles and the philosopher who introduced the greatest number of new principles (1979: 12).

PC1: For any two contradictory propositions p and q, one is true and the other is false (GP VI 413).[2]

PC2: For any proposition p, p is either true or false (A 6 4 670/MP 93; GP VII 299/ L225; GP VII 420/LC 96; A 6 6 362/NE 362).[3]

PC3: For any proposition p, p is not both true and false (GP VII 299/L 225; GP VII 355/LC 15).

PC4: For any proposition p, if p implies a contradiction, then p is false (GP VI 612/ L 646; A 6 4 1445/AG 19; GP VII 199).

PC5: For any proposition p, if p is false, then not-p is true (GP VI 612/L 646).

PC6: For any proposition p, if p is an identical proposition, then p is true (A 6 4 1616/MP 75).[4]

An identical proposition, or identity, is an affirmative proposition in which the predicate is explicitly included in the subject, or a negative proposition in which the non-inclusion of the predicate in the subject is explicit—for instance, truths of the form "A is A", "A is not non-A" (A 6 4 1644/AG 30–31), "AB is B" (C 11) and, surely, "AB is not non-B".[5]

The six principles above are different. Some of them can be derived from others. For instance, as noted by Sleigh (1983: 196), PC6 can be derived from PC4 and PC5 plus the idea that the opposite of an identical proposition is a contradiction. I do not know, however, of any text in which Leibniz proposes such a derivation.

One might think that the fact that Leibniz referred to such a variety of principles as the Principle of Contradiction does not necessarily suggest confusion on his part, since in at least one text he formulates several principles having to do with truth and falsity, including PC2 and PC3, and says that all of them are usually included in one designation, "Principle of Contradiction" (GP VII 299/L225). Thus, one might think that he used the phrase "Principle of Contradiction" as a collective noun. But note that this text would strongly support only the claim that he thought of PC2 and PC3 as being included in the referent of a collective noun "Principle of Contradiction"; it would support that he saw the other versions of the principle as possible referents of such a collective noun much less strongly. But, overall, there is little evidence for this collective noun hypothesis. The

[2] At A 2 1 387, Leibniz formulates the Principle of Contradiction as "two contradictories cannot be", which I take to mean something like "it is impossible that two contradictory propositions be true". It is reasonable to think, given his commitment to PC2, that Leibniz took this to mean that, necessarily, of two contradictory propositions, one is true and the other false.

[3] "MP" abbreviates *Philosophical Writings*, edited by G. H. R. Parkinson, translated by M. Morris and G. H. R. Parkinson (London: Dent, 1973). "LC" abbreviates *The Leibniz–Clarke Correspondence*, edited by H. G. Alexander (Manchester and New York: Manchester University Press, 1956).

[4] PC2–PC6 appear in Sleigh 1983: 196; I have supplied references to PC2 and PC4, which are missing from Sleigh's text, and I have omitted some of the textual references given by Sleigh. Note that sometimes Leibniz conjoins PC4 and PC6 into a single principle (A 6 4 124). Mates gives a slightly different list of Principles of Contradiction for Leibniz (Mates 1986: 153).

[5] Sometimes Leibniz gives a different characterization of identities, as propositions whose opposites contain an explicit contradiction (GP VI 612/AG 217).

texts suggest that on different occasions he used "Principle of Contradiction" to refer to different principles. This is puzzling, given the subtlety and power of Leibniz's mind, for it suggests that he did not really distinguish between the different versions of the principle.

A hypothesis that would save Leibniz's clarity of mind with respect to the distinction between these principles is that he thought of "Principle of Contradiction" as a name of whatever principle played a certain function in his theory—roughly, a principle that, in his view, excluded true contradictions and served to ground mathematical and necessary truths in general. According to this hypothesis, the meaning of "Principle of Contradiction" is relatively constant throughout Leibniz's work, but in different texts he proposes different principles as playing that role. Thus calling these different principles "Principle of Contradiction" is consistent with him having noticed that they are different. I think this hypothesis is more likely than the collective noun one, but it needs to be properly established and developed. The fact that Leibniz included so many different principles under the label "Principle of Contradiction" will, until properly explained, remain a puzzling one.

In any case, Leibniz did see some of these principles as more fundamental than others. For instance, in the *New Essays* he says that the Principle of Contradiction, stated as PC2 above, contains two assertions, which correspond to PC1 and PC3 above (A 6 6 362/NE 362). And in his second letter to Clarke, Leibniz seems to equate PC3 and PC6:

> The great foundation of mathematics is the principle of contradiction, or identity, that is, that a proposition cannot be true and false at the same time; and in this way A is A, and cannot be not A (GP VII 355/LC 15).

Here Leibniz seems to equate PC3 with the proposition that *A is A*. Now, Leibniz thinks that *L* and *L is true* are coincident propositions, that is, that they can be substituted for one another without loss of truth (A 6 4 748/LP 54).[6] Therefore, *A is A* is coincident with *A is A is true*, and in general, every identity is coincident with a proposition saying that it is true. But then, by universal generalization, one obtains PC6. However, I am not aware that Leibniz ever proposed such a derivation of PC6. Furthermore, it is not clear that PC3 and PC6 are equivalent, and Leibniz does not explain why this is supposed to be so.[7]

---

[6] "LP" abbreviates Leibniz, *Logical Papers*, edited and translated by G. H. R. Parkinson (Oxford: Oxford University Press, 1966).

[7] Note that I have altered Clarke's translation of Leibniz's. Where I have "in this way", Clarke had "therefore". In this passage, "ainsi" does not seem to have the meaning of "therefore". It should also be noted that translating "ainsi" as "therefore" would not have been more charitable to Leibniz, since it is not clear, and Leibniz does not explain how it is supposed to be, that the truth of *A is A* follows from PC3 alone.

Let us discuss the formulation of the Principle of Sufficient Reason. The essence of this principle is that there are no brute facts or truths, that is, there are no facts or truths for which no explanation can be given. Leibniz also gives various formulations of this principle, formulations that are not equivalent—at least not without presupposing further Leibnizian ideas. Here are three such formulations:

> PSR1: Nothing occurs without a sufficient reason why it is so and not otherwise (A 2 2 65; A 6 4 1616/MP 75; A 6 4 1645/AG 31; A 6 6 179/NE 179; GP VI 127/H 147; GP VI 602/AG 210; GP VI 612/AG 217; GP VII 356/LC 16).
> PSR2: Nothing occurs without a cause (A 6 4 1616/MP 75; A 6 4 1645/AG 31; GP V 127/H 147).
> PSR3: Every truth has an a priori proof (A 2 2 65).[8]

Note that the scope of PSR1 is as wide as possible. "Nothing" there ranges over facts (GP VI 612/AG 217), events (GP VII 393/LC 60) and true propositions (GP VI 612/AG 217). I am not suggesting that Leibniz made a precise distinction between facts and events—he did not, as far as I know. My point is that Leibniz wanted to apply the Principle of Sufficient Reason both to true propositions and whatever in the world corresponds to them. Leibniz also assimilates causes and reasons (A 6 6 475/NE 475), which makes PSR1 and PSR2 closer to each other than one would otherwise think.[9]

By an a priori proof, Leibniz understands a proof that reduces what is to be demonstrated to an identity (A 6 4 1645/AG 31). Thus, an a priori proof of a proposition p shows that its predicate is implicitly contained in its subject. Since identities have their predicate explicitly included in their subjects, there are no a priori proofs of them. There is a further exception to PSR3, since Leibniz developed a theory of contingency according to which contingent truths are those that cannot be analyzed into an identity in a finite number of steps, and for Leibniz the notion of a proof or demonstration is the notion of a finite analysis (A 6 4 1650). Taking note of this, Sleigh argues that Leibniz rejected PSR3 and replaced it by something like *Every truth has a proof sequence* (Sleigh 1983: 200–201). A proof sequence is like an a priori proof except that either it terminates in an identical proposition (like an a priori proof) or it merely converges on one (Sleigh 1983: 200).

---

[8] Note that at A 6 4 1616/MP 75, Leibniz restricts PSR3 to truths that are not self-evident ("per se notae"), and he says that identities are the only self-evident truths. Thus, according to A 6 4 1616/MP 75, all truths except identities have an a priori proof.

[9] For a discussion of this assimilation in the context of a discussion of the Principle of Sufficient Reason see Frankel 1986: 330–32. But texts like GP VI 127/H 147, quoted below, seem to distinguish between causes and reasons.

Even if not every proposition has a proof, according to Leibniz the predicate of every true proposition is either implicitly or explicitly contained in its subject. In this sense, every truth is analytic in Leibniz's system. This has led some commentators to identify the Principle of Sufficient Reason with the claim that *every true proposition is analytic* (Couturat 1901: 214–15, Rescher 1967: 25).

One might also attempt here the hypothesis that "Principle of Sufficient Reason" designates whatever principle plays a certain role in Leibniz's philosophy. But since there is at least one passage in which PSR1, PSR2, and PSR3 are run together as equivalent versions of the same principle, there is here more of case for thinking that Leibniz identified these principles:

> . . . a principle of the need for giving a reason, to the effect that every true proposition which is not known *per se* has an a priori proof, or, that a reason can be given for every truth, or as is commonly said, that nothing happens without a cause. (A 6 4 1616/ MP 75)[10]

The Principle of Identity of Indiscernibles is also formulated in different ways. Typically, Leibniz formulates it in these ways:

> PII1: No two beings are perfectly similar (GP IV 514/AG 164; GP VII 372/LC 36).
> PII2: There cannot be two perfectly similar beings (A 6 4 554; A 2 2 48/AG 73; A 6 4 1645/AG 32).

These formulations differ with respect to their modal force: PII2 states that the absence of perfect similarity is necessary, while PII1 simply states that there is no perfect similarity. Sometimes Leibniz declares that there are, or can be, no perfectly similar substances, or bodies, minds, or states (A 6 4 1541/AG 41–42; GP II 264/L 534–35; A 6 6 110/NE 110; A 6 6 305/NE 305; GP II 225/L 524; GP II 249/AG 174; GP VI 608/AG 214; A 6 4 554; A 6 4 1639; A 6 6 308/NE 308; GP VII 364/LC 26), but I take these to be specific instances of the Principle of Identity of Indiscernibles rather than different formulations of it. Most commentators take the Principle of Identity of Indiscernibles to be necessary (Russell 1992: 65, Parkinson 1965: 134, Rescher 1967: 48, Adams 1979: 11–12). Although formulating it without modal force, like PII1, does not necessarily mean Leibniz took the principle to be contingent, in some passages of the correspondence with Clarke, Leibniz appears to have taken it as contingent (GP VII 394–95/LC 61–62).[11]

---

[10] Lois Frankel (1986) argues extensively for the claim that Leibniz thought of the Principle of Sufficient Reason as a single principle, and she cites this passage in support of her interpretation (1986: 323).

[11] See Chernoff (1981), Cover and O'Leary-Hawthorne (1999: 204–9), and Jauernig (2008) for discussion of the modal force of the Identity of Indiscernibles. I do not mean to suggest that there are no interesting issues about the modal force of the Principle of Contradiction and the Principle of Sufficient

It is important to note that the principle means, according to Leibniz, that things must differ intrinsically. A mere relational difference is not sufficient (C 8/MP 133; A 6 6 110/NE 110). Furthermore, for Leibniz things that differ must differ qualitatively. That is, numerically different things must differ with respect to how they are intrinsically, and not with respect to *which* ones they are. Thus, if *a* and *b* are different but their difference is simply due to the fact that one of them is *a* and the other is *b*, *a* and *b* will differ *solo numero*, and this would be a violation of the Identity of Indiscernibles. For *a* and *b* to satisfy the Identity of Indiscernibles, they must differ qualitatively—they must differ more than numerically, in the sense that their difference must be grounded in a difference in their intrinsic qualities (A 6 6 57/NE 57).

Another way to see that this is the case is to understand that for Leibniz there are no purely extrinsic denominations (A 6 4 1645/AG 32). Thus, all denominations of a thing must be founded on intrinsic denominations. But the intrinsic denominations of a thing are those that can be known by inspecting the thing in itself and on its own. But, according to Leibniz, what can be known of a thing by inspecting it on its own are its qualities (GM V 180/L 255, GM VII 19/L 667). Thus, all the denominations of a thing must be founded on its qualities, and therefore the difference between two things must be a qualitative difference.

The Axiomatic Status of the Principles of Contradiction, Sufficient Reason, and Identity of Indiscernibles

It is common for Leibniz's scholars to speak of the *Principle* of Contradiction, the *Principle* of Sufficient Reason, and the *Principle* of Identity of Indiscernibles. Leibniz himself typically calls each of them *principles* (GP VI 127/H 147; GP VI 612/AG 217; GP VII 372/L IV, 5). He also calls them *axioms* (GP I 382; A 6 4 671/MP 94; A 6 4 1645/AG 31; GP VII 301/L 227; GP IV 514/AG 164; GP II 249/AG 175).[12] In one passage, Leibniz equates first principles and identical axioms (A 6 6 101).

A principle is normally understood in the sense of a *first* principle, that is, a proposition that is not derived or demonstrated from any other in a system of propositions. This permits speaking of *derived* principles, that is, propositions that are relatively high in the system of propositions in question, in the sense that although they derive from some other propositions, they figure prominently in the derivation or demonstration of other propositions. But the word *axiom* is normally used with a meaning

Reason. However, these issues do not come to the fore, when considering the formulations of those principles, as immediately as they do in the case of the Principle of Identity of Indiscernibles.

[12] Note that at GP I 382, Leibniz refers to the Principle of Contradiction, directly, as a *principle* but, by implication, implicitly calls it an *axiom*.

of ultimate priority that makes it contradictory to speak of derived or demonstrated axioms.

However, Leibniz had a conception of axioms on which it was possible to demonstrate and prove an axiom; indeed, in the *Critical Thoughts on the General Part of the Principles of Descartes*, he insists that demonstrating axioms and principles is good for the perfection of science and even as a defense from skepticism about the sciences (GP IV 355/L 383–84).[13]

Now, this is a non-technical use of the word "axiom", even with regard to Leibniz's use of the word. For Leibniz himself had a technical use of the word according to which an axiom is a necessary and indemonstrable proposition. And he adds that the true and indemonstrable axioms are identical propositions (C 186).[14] That this is a technical use of the word "axiom" is clear from the fact that in the very same text Leibniz speaks of a method that will not leave any axiom without proof, except definitions and identical propositions (C 187). So, as Couturat explains, Leibniz distinguished between identical and non-identical axioms, and the latter are the ones to be demonstrated (Couturat 1901: 201).

Thus, to the extent that Leibniz considered the Identity of Indiscernibles to be an axiom, he considered it to be a non-identical axiom, since he attempted to prove it (A 6 4 1541; A 6 4 1645; GP VII 393/LC 61). But it is interesting to note that in section 9 of the *Discourse on Metaphysics* Leibniz calls the Identity of Indiscernibles a *paradox* (A 6 4 1541). So the Identity of Indiscernibles is both an axiom and a paradox. This is paradoxical in itself! But this paradox has an easy resolution. For, as pointed out by Martinello (2006: 47), Leibniz has a conception of paradoxes as those propositions that must be proved in order to be believed (A 6 4 90).[15] Thus the Identity of Indiscernibles can be both an axiom and a paradox.

---

[13] The idea that axioms are demonstrable is not original to Leibniz: he refers to Apollonius, Proclus, and Roberval as geometers who attempted to prove axioms (GP IV 355/L 383). Undoubtedly, the idea of indemonstrability associated with axioms was also present at Leibniz's time. Two of Leibniz's correspondents, Hermann Conring and Johann Bernoulli, expressed amazement at Leibniz's claim that axioms needed to be demonstrated (A 2 1 596; GM II 316). And Leibniz mentions that Roberval was laughed at in Paris because he wanted to demonstrate Euclid's axioms (A 6 6 107). Leibniz does not identify those who mocked Roberval, but Olaso thinks Pascal might have been one of them (Olaso 1974: 164).

[14] Compare C 186 with the following: a letter to Conring in which Leibniz says that only identical propositions are indemonstrable, and that axioms are demonstrable (A 2 1 602); *On Universal Synthesis and Analysis*, where Leibniz says that identical propositions are the true axioms and what are popularly called axioms can be reduced to identities by means of analysis (A 6 4 543/L 231–32); a letter to Bernoulli in which Leibniz says that identical propositions are indemonstrable axioms and the rest are demonstrable ones (GM II 321); the *New Essays*, where Leibniz calls *secondary* axioms those that are demonstrable and *primitive* those that are not (A 6 6 407–8/ NE 408); and the *Monadology*, where Leibniz says that there are axioms or primitive principles, which cannot and need not be proved, and these are identical propositions (GP VI 612/AG 217).

[15] See also GP I 385, GP VII 294/L230, where Leibniz calls *paradoxical properties* those whose possibility can be doubted.

THE FUNDAMENTAL CHARACTER OF THE PRINCIPLES OF CONTRADICTION AND SUFFICIENT REASON

Leibniz's fundamental principles are the Principle of Contradiction and Principle of Sufficient Reason. Consider the following passages, from *Theodicy* §44 and *Monadology* §31–32, respectively:

> There are two great principles of our arguments. The one is the principle of contradiction, stating that of two contradictory propositions the one is true, the other false; the other principle is that of the determinant reason: it states that nothing ever comes to pass without there being a cause or at least a reason determining it, that is, something to give an *a priori* reason why it is existent rather than non-existent, and in this wise rather than in any other (GP VI 127/H 147).
>
> Our reasonings are based on two great principles, that of contradiction, in virtue of which we judge that which involves a contradiction to be false, and that which is opposed or contradictory to the false to be true. And that of sufficient reason, by virtue of which we consider that we can find no true or existent fact, no true assertion, without there being a sufficient reason why it is thus and not otherwise, although most of the time these reasons cannot be known to us (GP VI 612/AG 217).[16]

Although these passages do not explicitly assert it, and do not entail it either, the natural reading of them is that these two principles are equally basic and fundamental. Indeed in the correspondence with Arnauld, Leibniz says that both principles are primitive truths (A 2 2 65).[17]

There are passages where Leibniz says that some truths must be presupposed, otherwise there could be no demonstration, since proofs cannot proceed to infinity. And he says he will assume or presuppose the Principle of Contradiction (GP I 382). Why assume the Principle of Contradiction rather than other truths? Because, Leibniz says, one presupposes the Principle of Contradiction by writing and reasoning; otherwise, one would be able to defend the opposite of what one is saying (GP I 382). Leibniz thinks that in the absence of the Principle of Contradiction, all belief, affirmation, and negation would be pointless (A 66 498/NE 498). In other words, every meaningful assertion presupposes the Principle of Contradiction.[18] Thus this is a sort of Aristotelian

---

[16] For a similar statement see A 6 4 1616/MP 75.

[17] But there are texts that suggest that only one of the principles is fundamental in one way or another. Thus C 11 and A 6 4B 1379 call the Principle of Sufficient Reason the fundamental principle of reasoning, in A 6 4 543/L 232 Leibniz says that the scholastics correctly noted that all axioms (except identities) reduce to the Principle of Contradiction, in A 6 6 364/NE 364 he calls the Principle of Contradiction the only primitive principle, and in C 514/MP8 he says that the Principle of Sufficient Reason has, *after* the Principle of Contradiction, the greatest use in all sciences.

[18] Cf. A 6 6 364/NE 364, where Leibniz says that the Principle of Contradiction assumes nothing.

transcendental justification of the Principle of Contradiction: it is justified because it is a necessary presupposition of rational discourse and thought in general.

It is interesting to note that Leibniz sometimes makes what might be seen as a similar move with respect to the Principle of Sufficient Reason. At the end of his fifth letter to Clarke, Leibniz considers whether the Principle of Sufficient Reason needs to be proved, and he says that without it one cannot prove the existence of God, nor give a reason for many other important truths (GP VII 419/LC 95). Here one might see Leibniz as making the point that the Principle of Sufficient Reason is a necessary presupposition of a certain type of inquiry. But Leibniz's short remark is not sufficient to support this interesting interpretation. Furthermore, he only uses the Principle of Sufficient Reason in his cosmological argument for God's existence, not in his ontological argument.

Leibniz tends to assign different domains to these two principles. The domain of necessary truths and mathematical truths is assigned to the Principle of Contradiction, while the domain of contingent truths and truths from natural philosophy is assigned to the Principle of Sufficient Reason (A 6 4 1616/MP 75; GP VII 355–56/LC 15–16).[19] This suggests that each principle reigns over a definite and distinct area, and neither principle is prior to the other: they are like two kings each with his own territory. But the situation is more complicated. For the Principle of Sufficient Reason also applies in the domain of necessary truths (A 6 4 1650; GP VI 414; see also Broad 1975: 12, 34, and Martin 1964: 15–16),[20] and therefore the two principles share some territory. And since not even contingent truths violate the Principle of Contradiction, the Principle of Contradiction also applies in the domain of contingent truths (GP VI 414). Thus they have exactly the same territory: the domain of all truths.

But not only do they share their territory: they are in each other's territory. For the Principle of Contradiction is a necessary truth, and so the Principle of Sufficient Reason has the Principle of Contradiction in its domain. Furthermore, since the Principle of Sufficient Reason, too, is a necessary truth (GP VI 414; see also Russell 1992: 36), the Principle of Contradiction has the Principle of Sufficient Reason in its domain. This would be a problem if the propositions in the domain in which the principles applied depended for their grounding on those principles, for in that case the Principle of Contradiction and the Principle of Sufficient Reason would circularly ground each other. But that a principle applies in a certain domain simply means that all the propositions in that domain satisfy it, not that they are grounded in it.[21]

---

[19] Sometimes the Principle of Sufficient Reason is referred to the domain of metaphysics (GP VI 602/AG 209), and indeed, on more than one occasion Leibniz says that without the Principle of Sufficient Reason one would not be able to prove the existence of God (A 6 6 179/NE 179; GP VII 419/LC 95), which is clearly a metaphysical truth.

[20] Note that sometimes Leibniz suggests that identities do not satisfy the Principle of Sufficient Reason (GP III 506).

[21] This distinction seems to be what Sleigh is getting at when he points to a distinction between the domain in which a principle holds and the realm of propositions that depend on that principle (1983: 195), but Sleigh does not explain the nature of the distinction.

And when Leibniz refers to what these principles ground, he typically claims that the Principle of Contradiction grounds mathematical and necessary truths and the Principle of Sufficient Reason grounds contingent truths from natural philosophy and science (A 6 4 1616/MP 75; A 6 4 1649/AG 28; GP VII 355–56/LC 15–16). Thus, since the Principle of Sufficient Reason is a necessary truth, it should be grounded, if grounded at all, on the Principle of Contradiction.

Some Attempts to Demonstrate the Principles of Contradiction and Sufficient Reason

As I have said, Leibniz often says that these two principles are fundamental, ungrounded grounders. But sometimes he attempts to prove them—and given his conception of axioms, this should not be odd. Indeed, one should expect him to attempt to prove the Principle of Sufficient Reason, since it does not seem to be an identity: its opposite, on any of its versions PSR1–3, is not an explicit contradiction.

And neither is the Principle of Contradiction, on any of its versions PC1–6, an identical proposition. This creates a problem for Leibniz, for sometimes he says that the Principle of Contradiction is indemonstrable (A 6 4 124, A 6 4 670/MP 93), and it is clear that it should be so for him. For the Principle of Contradiction, at least when understood as PC6, is presupposed in every demonstration. For a demonstration, according to Leibniz, is a reduction to identities, and this would not be what a demonstration is if identities were not true.

But consider, for instance, PC3, which might seem to be an identity. That principle is not an identity, however. It does not say that for any true proposition p, p is not not-true. It says that for any proposition p, p is not both true and false. But this is not an identity. It is, however, reducible to an identity via the definition of *false* as *not-true* (A 6 4 749/LP 54). But this shows that the Principle of Contradiction, if formulated as PC3, is demonstrable, since it is reducible to an identity by means of definitions. At A 2 1 387, Leibniz says that the Principle of Contradiction is an identical axiom, and he formulates it as "two contradictories cannot be", which I interpret as a version of PC1 (see footnote 2). But this principle is not an identity either.

Thus it seems that the Principle of Contradiction should be demonstrable. And indeed, Leibniz attempted to give a demonstration of it, understood as PC2, from the definition of *false* as *not-true* and of *true* as *not-false* (A 6 4 749–50/LP 54–55), and PC6 can be reduced to an identity by means of the thesis that every true proposition is or is resolvable into an identity. In any case, if Leibniz had formulated PC3 as *For any proposition p, p is not both true and not-true*, then the Principle of Contradiction, understood in this way, would have been an identity, and therefore indemonstrable, according to Leibniz. But the point remains that the principles Leibniz typically refers to as the

Principle of Contradiction, although necessary, are not identities, and so he should not have thought of any of them as indemonstrable.

Let us go back to the Principle of Sufficient Reason. In several texts, most notably the *Demonstratio Propositionum Primarum* (A 6 2 483), he tries to prove the Principle of Sufficient Reason on the basis of definitions of *sufficient reason* and *requisite*. A requisite is, roughly, a necessary condition, while a sufficient reason is a sufficient condition. Leibniz says that no thing can exist without all its requisites. He then asserts that given all the requisites of a thing, it must exist, and that therefore all its requisites are its sufficient reason, and so there must be a sufficient reason for everything that exists. This argument is clearly invalid, and has been thought to be question-begging (Sleigh 1983: 204, Look 2011: 204). Since I have nothing more to add about it, I shall not discuss it further.

In the *Theodicy*, Leibniz claims that the Principles of Contradiction and Sufficient Reason are contained in the definition of the true and the false. What might this mean? According to Leibniz, an affirmative proposition is true if and only if the predicate or consequent is in the subject or antecedent, or equivalently, if and only if the concept of the predicate or consequent is in the concept of the subject or antecedent (A 6 4 1644/ AG 31, A 2 2 49; A 2 2 80; A 6 4 671/MP 93–94; GP VII 300/L 226). This theory is known as the Predicate-in-Notion, or Concept-Containment, theory of truth. As Sleigh notes, the texts suggest that the idea that the concept of the predicate is included in the concept of the subject is an analysis of the idea that the predicate is included in the subject (Sleigh 1983: 198). In any case, for present purposes, I shall formulate the theory in this way:

> PIN (Predicate-in-Notion): For any proposition *p*, *p* is true if and only if the predicate is in the subject, that is, if and only if *p* is or is resolvable into an identity (A 6 4 1644/AG 31).[22]

It is easy to see how the Principle of Contradiction, understood as PC6 above, follows from PIN, for in identical propositions the predicate is explicitly included in the subject (A 6 4 1644/AG 31). Furthermore, in *Primary Truths* Leibniz argues that the Principle of Sufficient Reason follows from PIN, because, for any true proposition *p*, that the predicate is included in the subject is a reason why *p* is true. "Otherwise", Leibniz says, "there would be a truth . . . which could not be resolved into identities" (A 6 4 1645/AG 31). So this is the sense in which the Principle of Contradiction and the Principle of Sufficient Reason are contained in the definition of the true.[23]

---

[22] But note that, as formulated, PIN makes no reference to any notions or concepts, and so "PIN" is a slightly misleading label. Some, like Couturat (1901: 208–18), seem to maintain that Leibniz accepted PIN because he accepted the Principle of Sufficient Reason. Sleigh disagrees, and suggests that PIN provided Leibniz with some tools to formulate what he regarded as a deep analysis of the Principle of Sufficient Reason (Sleigh 1982: 234).

[23] And the definition of the false? Perhaps Leibniz thought that PIN was an implicit definition of falsehood, since he defined false as not-true (A 6 4 749/LP 54). In any case, it should be noted that there are commentators who oppose the primacy of PIN. Baruch Brody, for instance, argues that Leibniz's fundamental principle is the Principle of Sufficient Reason, understood as PSR1 as applied to truths, and that from this principle Leibniz adopts PIN, for if PIN is true, the demand for a sufficient reason is

Primary Truths is a very interesting text in this connection because in it are present the Principle of Contradiction, understood as PC6 above, PIN, and the Principle of Sufficient Reason. Leibniz explicitly states PIN and the Principle of Sufficient Reason in *Primary Truths*. But it should be clear that he is implicitly committed to PC6 in this text, since he says that "primary truths are those which assert the same thing of itself, or deny the opposite of its opposite. For example, 'A is A', 'A is not not-A'" (A 6 4 1644/AG 30). What Leibniz is saying here is that identities are primary truths, and therefore he is implicitly committed to the idea that identities are truths, which is what PC6 asserts.

But although in *Primary Truths* Leibniz derives the Principle of Sufficient Reason from PIN, he does not derive the Principle of Contradiction from PIN. He states something that commits him to the Principle of Contradiction, then he states PIN, and then he states the Principle of Sufficient Reason and derives it from PIN (AG 30–31). It must also be stressed that in *Primary Truths*, Leibniz does not use the Principle of Contradiction to derive the Principle of Sufficient Reason. This is a point that needs stressing, for one would expect the Principle of Sufficient Reason, given that it is a necessary truth, to be founded on the Principle of Contradiction, which is the principle of necessary truths. Leibniz says:

> the received axiom that *nothing is without reason* . . . directly follows from these considerations; otherwise there would be a truth which could not be proved a priori, that is, a truth which could not be resolved into identities (A 6 4 1645/AG 31).

Thus, Leibniz argues that if the Principle of Sufficient Reason did not hold, there would be a truth that neither is an identity nor resolves into one. The implication is that the existence of a truth that neither is nor resolves into an identity would be absurd—and it would be absurd because it would violate the idea that for every *p*, if *p* is true, *p* is an identity or is resolvable into one. But this is only half of PIN, and it is the half that is closer to the converse of PC6 than to PC6 itself. Thus, the Principle of Contradiction is not used in the derivation of the Principle of Sufficient Reason.[24]

What does "these considerations" ("ex his", A 6 4 1645) refer to, then? It might be thought that we should take the use of the plural expression seriously, and that therefore there must be more than one consideration at play, and that the Principle of Contradiction, implicit at the beginning of the text, is an obvious candidate as one of the referents. But even taking the use of the plural seriously, given that he does not use the Principle of Contradiction in its derivation of the Principle of Sufficient Reason, there

thereby satisfied. Thus, according to Brody, when Leibniz says that the Principle of Sufficient Reason is a corollary of PIN, all he means is that the predicate's being contained in the subject is the way the Principle of Sufficient Reason is satisfied (Brody 1994: 94).

[24] My reading of *Primary Truths* thus differs from Look's, who suggests that Leibniz derives the Principle of Sufficient Reason from the Principle of Contradiction together with PIN (Look 2011: 205, 207–8, 208–9).

is a more plausible interpretation of the referents of "these considerations". This is how Leibniz introduces PIN in *Primary Truths*:

> Therefore, the predicate or consequent is always in the subject or antecedent, and the nature of truth in general or the connection between the terms of a statement, consists in this very thing, as Aristotle also observed. The connection and inclusion of the predicate is explicit in identities, but in all other propositions is implicit and must be shown through the analysis of notions; a priori demonstration rests on this (A 6 4 1644/AG 31).

There are two ideas here that are used in Leibniz's derivation of the Principle of Sufficient Reason. One is that for every *p*, if *p* is true, *p* is an identity or is resolvable into one. The other is that such resolution into identities is what a priori demonstration consists in. These are the referents of "these considerations".

We saw first that, given the way Leibniz derives the Principle of Sufficient Reason, there is no need to make the Principle of Contradiction one of the referents of "these considerations". We have now seen that not doing so is consistent with the plural phrase having a plurality of referents. This is evidence that Leibniz did not intend to use the Principle of Contradiction in the derivation of the Principle of Sufficient Reason.[25]

The other text I would like to comment on is a paragraph at the end of Leibniz's fifth letter to Clarke. Clarke asked for a justification of (Leibniz's understanding of) the Principle of Sufficient Reason. Leibniz responds that no one has ever provided a counterexample to the Principle of Sufficient Reason, and there are infinitely many positive instances of the principle that make one judge reasonably that the principle is satisfied in other cases as well, "according to the method of experimental philosophy, which proceeds *a posteriori*" (GP VII 420/LC 96). This is an inductive justification of the principle. This is not the kind of justification of the Principle of Sufficient Reason one would expect from a "rationalist" philosopher like Leibniz, and furthermore, this method of establishing the Principle of Sufficient Reason would not establish its necessity. But Leibniz is not rejecting the possibility of an a priori justification of the Principle of Sufficient Reason in this passage. All he is saying is that there is a posteriori justification for the Principle of Sufficient Reason, justification that is independent from any a priori justification. Indeed Leibniz says, after stating the inductive justification of the principle, that this would be enough to justify it even if the principle were not otherwise justified on the basis of pure reason or a priori (GP VII 420/LC 96), which indicates that Leibniz thought, in that letter, that the principle is also justified a priori.[26]

---

[25] It is interesting to compare *Primary Truths* with the text at GP VII 209–301. In this text, Leibniz states both PIN and the Principle of Contradiction. Unlike *Primary Truths*, Leibniz there explicitly states the Principle of Contradiction, though not as PC6, but as PC2 and PC3. But there the Principle of Sufficient Reason is not derived from the Principle of Contradiction but from the idea, which derives from PIN, that every true proposition that is not identical can be proved a priori (GP VII 300/L 226), which is, again, not the Principle of Contradiction in any of its guises.

[26] It is interesting to note that many years before, in *On Contingency*, Leibniz had anticipated the idea of an empirical justification of the Principle of Sufficient Reason, and he also claimed that it has

Note that this inductive justification of the Principle of Sufficient Reason contradicts Leibniz's skepticism about knowledge based purely on induction. In the *New Essays*, Leibniz says that "however often one experienced instances of a universal truth, one could never know ('asseurer') inductively that it would always hold unless one knew through reason that it was *necessary*" (A 6 6 80/NE 80, my italics). It is not that Leibniz thinks that induction never gives reasonable grounds for a universal judgment. In some cases, when we have had sufficiently many experiences, it does. But without knowing the reason why our experiences are what they are, Leibniz says in *On What Is Independent of Sense and of Matter*, one would never have absolute certainty of the corresponding universal generalization (GP VI 505/L 550).

In a marginal note to *An Introduction to a Secret Encyclopedia*, Leibniz says that what is confirmed by many indications, and which can hardly concur except in the truth, is morally certain, as opposed to metaphysically certain. And he added that morally certain is that which is incomparably more probable than its opposite (C 515/MP 9). Perhaps Leibniz, at the end of his fifth letter to Clarke, was simply trying to establish the moral certainty, as opposed to the metaphysical certainty, of the Principle of Sufficient Reason?

This seems to contradict other texts. For instance, on the same page where he explains what moral certainty is, Leibniz classifies the Principle of Sufficient Reason, stated simply as "Nothing is without reason", as a metaphysically certain principle (C 515/MP 9). And in the *Preface to an Edition of Nizolius,* Leibniz says that without reasons not based on induction, induction does not even produce moral certainty (A 6 2 432/L 129–30).

Note that in these texts, Leibniz is saying that without knowledge of the reason why our experiences are as they are, we cannot have knowledge of the corresponding universal generalization. Now, according to the passage from the fifth letter to Clarke, for every observed fact or event, there is a reason why it occurs. The corresponding universal generalization is that every fact or event has a reason why it occurs. But the only reason why, for every observed fact or event, there is a reason why it occurs, that would support inferring that every fact or event has a reason why it occurs, is that every fact or event *must* have a reason why it occurs, and this is how Leibniz understood the Principle of Sufficient Reason in that letter to Clarke (he formulated it as "le principe du besoin d'une raison suffisante", which Clarke translated as "the principle of the want of a sufficient reason": GP VII 393, 419/LC 60, 95). So trying to combine the justification of the Principle of Sufficient Reason Leibniz suggests in the fifth letter to Clarke with what he says in the passages quoted from *On What Is Independent of Sense and of Matter* and the

---

a justification based on reason. Indeed he said that the Principle of Sufficient Reason is "confirmed ('firmatur') both by reason and experience" (A 6 4 1651/AG 29). Note that the sense in which experience confirms the Principle of Sufficient Reason cannot be that of a mere corroboration, since it must be the same sense as that in which it is confirmed by reason. My interpretation is that "confirmed", in this text, must be understood in the sense of "established."

Preface to an Edition of Nizolius would lead to a circular justification of the Principle of Sufficient Reason.

Thus, it would seem as if what Leibniz says in his fifth letter to Clarke represents a change of mind with respect to induction. According to Paul Lodge, in his later years Leibniz became preoccupied with the metaphysical structure of the actual world, and as a result, he had to give experience a justificatory role in relation to some of his metaphysical principles (Lodge 2010: 24–25). The passage of Leibniz's fifth letter to Clarke might be seen as an instance of the argumentative strategy Lodge sees in Leibniz's later philosophy. But such an argumentative strategy might fail in this case. For in the correspondence with Clarke and many other texts, Leibniz applies the Principle of Sufficient Reason to the will of God, and he says that this principle dictates that the bare will of God is not a sufficient reason for God to act in one way or another, but that the will of God must be determined by some prior motive. Indeed, for Leibniz the notion of will requires a determining reason (GP VII 371–72, 392/LC 36, 59). But there is no *empirical* evidence whether the world was created by a will. Furthermore, in *Monadology* §32 Leibniz says that although there is always a sufficient reason, most of the time these reasons cannot be known by us. Thus that there must be a sufficient reason cannot be established by experience.[27]

An Attempt to Demonstrate the Principle of Identity of Indiscernibles

Although on one occasion Leibniz calls the Principle of Identity of Indiscernibles a most obvious ("manifestissimum") axiom and expresses amazement at the fact that people have not used it (GP II 249/AG 175), his demonstrations of the principle use controversial Leibnizian theses. He had two main argumentative strategies to demonstrate it. The first main strategy is exemplified in three related texts from the 1680s: *Notationes Generales* (1683–85), *Discourse on Metaphysics* (1686), and *Primary Truths* (1689). What is common to these texts is that in all three of them Leibniz argues, in one way or another, for the Principle of Identity of Indiscernibles from his theory of truth, according to which in every true affirmative proposition the predicate is included in the subject, or the concept of the predicate is included in the concept of the subject. It is also common to them, therefore, that they seem to support the necessary version of the Identity of Indiscernibles.

---

[27] I owe the point about the *Monadology* to Maria Rosa Antognazza.

Although sometimes these texts are seen as presenting the same argument (Jauernig 2008: 200, 201 n. 32), they do not present exactly the same argument. Here are three interesting differences: (a) in *Primary Truths* the Principle of Identity of Indiscernibles derives from the Principle of Sufficient Reason, but this is not so in *Notationes Generales* or the *Discourse;*[28] (b) though in both *Primary Truths* and *Notationes Generales* Leibniz states the Principle of Identity of Indiscernibles as applying to all individuals, in the *Discourse on Metaphysics* his conclusion is that no substances are perfectly similar; (c) in *Primary Truths* and *Notationes Generales* the Principle of Identity of Indiscernibles is presented as necessary, but in the final version of the *Discourse on Metaphysics* the corresponding claim about substances is not presented as necessary.[29]

The second main strategy appears in the correspondence with Clarke. There Leibniz derives the Principle of Identity of Indiscernibles from the Principle of Sufficient Reason as applied to God. The argument is, in a nutshell, that if there were indiscernibles, God would have preferred the actual world to an indiscernible world, but having a preference for one of two indiscernible worlds would be to violate the Principle of Sufficient Reason, and therefore there are no indiscernibles (GP VII 393/LC 61).

For reasons of space, I shall here discuss only what Leibniz says in the *Discourse*, the most important of these four texts.[30] In section 8 of the *Discourse*, he states that in a true proposition the subject term must contain the predicate term, so that one who understands perfectly the notion of the subject would also know that the predicate belongs to it. Since this is so, Leibniz claims, the nature of an individual substance or complete being is to have a notion so complete that it is sufficient to contain and to allow us to deduce from it all the predicates of the subject to which this notion is attributed. But from this idea that an individual substance has a complete concept, Leibniz says in section 9, several paradoxes follow; in particular it follows that it is not true that two substances resemble each other completely and differ only in number (A 6 4 1541/AG 41–42).[31]

---

[28] But note that Leibniz comes close, in section 8 of the *Discourse*, where he formulates the elements from which he will deduce the Principle of Identity of Indiscernibles in section 9, to stating PSR3, when he says that God, seeing Alexander's individual notion, sees in it the reason for all of his predicates, and that God knows a priori those predicates (A 6 4 1540–41/AG 41). Nevertheless, this is short of formulating the Principle of Sufficient Reason.

[29] Note that originally Leibniz had written that it was not possible that two substances resemble each other entirely and differ *solo numero*. He then deleted it, and wrote that it is not true that two substances resemble each other entirely and differ *solo numero* (A 6 4 1541).

[30] I discuss Leibniz's arguments in the correspondence with Clarke and *Primary Truths* in my 1999 and 2004, respectively. But I have changed my mind about some of the issues; I develop my new views in my 2014. And although what follows on the Principle of identity of Indiscernibles in the *Discourse* is roughly what I say in my 2014, that book contains a much more developed, precise, and exact explanation of my thoughts.

[31] Two interesting things to note: (a) in another text from roughly the same time, *De mundo praesenti*, Leibniz claims that individual substances are unique (which I take to be an expression of the Identity of Indiscernibles applied to substances) because their concepts are complete (A 6 4 1507), but in this text there is no mention of the theory of truth, and (b) although the Identity of Indiscernibles features in the *Remarks on Arnauld's letter* (A 2 2 48), at the end of this text Leibniz states the consequences of the proposition that the notion of a substance involves everything that happens to it, but he does not include the Principle of Identity of Indiscernibles in that list, while in the *Discourse*, in section 9, it is the first consequence to be mentioned.

Leibniz does not explain how the Principle of Identity of Indiscernibles is supposed to follow from the idea that substances have complete individual concepts. The impression the *Discourse* gives is that he seems to have thought that the Identity of Indiscernibles follows more or less immediately from the idea that substances have complete individual concepts. Does it?

That substances have complete individual concepts means that a substance's individual concept includes everything that is true of it. The Identity of Indiscernibles means that no two substances resemble each other perfectly. Prima facie, the former thesis does not entail the latter. For why couldn't A and B, two different substances, have the same complete concept? Nothing in the doctrine of complete individual concepts seems to exclude such a possibility. But if A and B have the same complete concept, they are perfectly similar.

But, it might be claimed, there is something that excludes such a possibility. For if a substance's concept contains everything that is true of it, then substance A's concept includes the concept of *being identical to A*. If so, no other substance can share its concept with A. So, it would seem, Leibniz is in a position to guarantee that every concept picks one and only one substance. And it seems to follow from this that the Principle of Identity of Indiscernibles is true and therefore that two substances do not resemble each other perfectly.

But there is a problem with this line of thought. For either being identical with a certain substance consists in having certain qualitative intrinsic features, or being identical with a certain substance is something additional to having any qualitative intrinsic features.

Suppose being identical with a certain substance consists in something additional to having certain qualitative intrinsic features. Then, even if concepts like *being identical to A* are included in the individual concepts of substances, that such concepts include everything that is true of substances does not entail the Identity of Indiscernibles. For that A and B differ with respect to *being identical to A* (and other identity related conditions like *being numerically different from B, being intelligent and identical to A*, etc.) does not mean that A and B do not perfectly resemble each other. Two things that differed only with respect to identity conditions like those just mentioned would be only numerically different and therefore perfectly similar. For, according to Leibniz, similarity is sharing of qualities, and qualities are what can be known about a thing by inspecting it by itself, without comparing it to other things (GM VII 19/L 667; GM V 180/L 255). But, unless being identical to A reduces to having certain qualitative intrinsic features, one cannot know that a substance is identical to A by inspecting it on its own. And so, unless being identical to A reduces to having certain qualitative intrinsic features, if A and B differ only with respect to being identical to A (and other identity-related conditions), A and B do not differ with respect to any qualities and are therefore perfectly similar.

Thus, including such conditions like *being identical to A* in individual concepts might deliver a version of the Identity of Indiscernibles according to which there are no two things that satisfy exactly the same predicates or concepts, but this is not Leibniz's Identity of Indiscernibles. Indeed, why couldn't the individual concept of A include the concept of *being perfectly similar to B*? Thus, if being identical to a certain substance is something additional to having qualitative intrinsic features, then if substances' complete concepts allow one to deduce everything that is true of a substance, then every individual concept picks out only one substance. But this is not sufficient to deliver the thesis that no two substances resemble each other completely.

Now, if being identical to a certain substance consists in having some qualitative intrinsic features, then of course no two things are perfectly qualitatively intrinsically similar. For in that case, *being identical to A* would be to be qualitatively intrinsically thus-and-so. And if there cannot be two things that are perfectly qualitatively intrinsically alike, Leibniz's Identity of Indiscernibles is true. I believe that Leibniz thought that identity was reducible to qualitative intrinsic character, that is, that he thought that being identical to a certain substance consists in having some intrinsic features. For reasons of space, I cannot argue for such a claim in this article.[32]

Thus, Leibniz claims to derive the Identity of Indiscernibles from his thesis that substances have complete individual concepts. But he can only establish the Identity of Indiscernibles if he assumes a thesis (that identity reduces to intrinsic qualitative character) that establishes by itself the Identity of Indiscernibles.

But note that if Leibniz assumes that identity reduces to intrinsic qualitative character, then not only can he derive the Identity of Indiscernibles, he can derive it from the thesis that substances have complete concepts. For if identity reduces to intrinsic qualitative character, individual concepts are purely qualitative. On this understanding of complete concepts the Identity of Indiscernibles follows, pretty much directly, from the thesis that substances have complete concepts.

Thus, Leibniz's argument for the Identity of Indiscernibles is a simple one. The argument is that individual substances have complete concepts that permit to deduce everything that is true of them. Since they permit to deduce everything about them, they permit to deduce facts about the identity of substances. But those complete concepts are purely qualitative. Therefore, there cannot be two substances that resemble each other perfectly. This is, I think, a valid argument, but with very controversial premises.[33]

---

[32] Adams (1979: 9–11) also makes the claim and offers a longer discussion.

[33] Broad (1975: 40) thought that the Identity of Indiscernibles does not follow from the thesis that substances have complete individual concepts (a thesis he called, rather inaccurately, the *Predicate-in-Notion Principle*, see Broad 1975: 6). But he did not argue for this; he just asserted it. Mates says, in reference to the *Discourse*, that the Principle of Identity of Indiscernibles follows from the fact that every individual concept is complete '[m]aybe via the Principle of Sufficient Reason, which itself is said to follow from the fact that every individual concept is complete', and that perhaps 'the point is that if individuals A and B express the universe in different ways, they can't fall under all the same concepts' (Mates 1986: 134–5, fn. 56). It is not clear to me how Mates understands the derivation, for if A and B are indiscernible they should express the universe in the same way. And it is not clear what role is the Principle of Sufficient Reason playing here. But, in any case, nowhere in the *Discourse* does Leibniz mention or suggest the Principle of Sufficient Reason as the bridge between the idea that individuals have complete concepts and the Identity of Indiscernibles. Rutherford denies that the

CONCLUSION

We have seen that Leibniz gave different formulations of these three important principles, and that sometimes the relation between those different formulations is not clear. Although the Principle of Contradiction and the Principle of Sufficient Reason are fundamental principles for Leibniz, to the extent that these principles are not identities, he should not have thought of them as indemonstrable. He attempted some demonstrations of them. I have briefly described some of these attempts and examined in more detail the derivation of the Principle of Sufficient Reason in *Primary Truths*, about which I have argued that Leibniz does not use the Principle of Contradiction in that derivation. I have also discussed an interesting attempt, in the correspondence with Clarke, to prove the Principle of Sufficient Reason empirically. This attempted demonstration is, given what Leibniz says in other texts, problematic. Finally, I have examined the argument for the Principle of Identity of Indiscernibles in the *Discourse*, and concluded that it is valid but with very controversial premises.

I am grateful to Maria Rosa Antognazza and Brandon Look for comments on a previous version of this article.

REFERENCES

Adams, R. M. 1979. "Primitive thisness and primitive identity." *Journal of Philosophy* 76 (1): 5–26.

Broad, C. D. 1975. *Leibniz: An introduction*. Cambridge: Cambridge University Press.

Brody, B. 1994. "Leibniz's metaphysical logic." In R. Woolhouse (ed.), *Gottfried Wilhelm Leibniz. Critical Assessments*. London and New York: Routledge, pp. 82–96.

Chernoff, F. 1981. "Leibniz's Principle of the Identity of Indiscernibles." *Philosophical Quarterly* 31 (123): 126–38.

Cover, J., and J. O'Leary-Hawthorne. 1999. *Substance and Individuation in Leibniz*. Cambridge: Cambridge University Press.

Couturat, L. 1901. *La Logique de Leibniz d'après des documents inédits*. Paris: Presses Universitaires de France.

Frankel, L. 1986. "From a metaphysical point of view: Leibniz and the Principle of Sufficient reason." *Southern Journal of Philosophy* 24 (3): 321–34.

Identity of Indiscernibles as applied to substances follows from the thesis that substances have complete individual concepts; for him it depends on an independent commitment to the Principle of Identity of Indiscernibles understood as 'the principle that for any two numerically non-identical things, there must be some discernible difference between them' (Rutherford 1995: 142). Perhaps so, but this does not help us to make sense of the argument in the *Discourse* since the only version of the Identity of Indiscernibles that Leibniz mentions in the *Discourse* is the one about substances, and so there is no indication that Leibniz is making his claim about substances differing more than numerically depend on a claim about things in general differing more than numerically.

Jauernig, A. 2008. "The modal strength of Leibniz's Principle of the Identity of Indiscernibles." In D. Garber and S. Nadler (eds.), *Oxford Studies in Early Modern Philosophy*, 4:191–225.

Lodge, P. 2010. "The empirical grounds for Leibniz's "Real Metaphysics." *Leibniz Review* 20: 13–36.

Look, B. 2011. "Grounding the Principle of Sufficient Reason: Leibnizian Rationalism and the Humean Challenge." In C. Fraenkel et al. (eds.), *The Rationalists: Between Tradition and Innovation*. Springer: Dordrecht, pp. 201–19.

Martin, G. 1964. *Leibniz: Logic and Metaphysics*. Trans. K. J. Northcott and P. G. Lucas. Manchester: Manchester University Press.

Martinello, F. 2006. *L'identità degli indiscernibili in Leibniz*. Edizione Albo Versorio: Milan.

Mates, B. 1986. *The Philosophy of Leibniz: Metaphysics and Language*. Oxford: Oxford University Press.

Olaso, E. de. 1974. "Elogio y sarcasmo de la demostración de axiomas." *International Studies in Philosophy* 6: 163–65.

Ortega y Gasset, J. 1979. *La Idea de Principio en Leibniz y la Evolución de la Teoría Deductiva*. Madrid: Alianza Editorial.

Parkinson, G. H. R. 1965. *Logic and Reality in Leibniz's Metaphysics*. Oxford: Clarendon Press.

Rodriguez-Pereyra, G. 1999. "Leibniz's argument for the Identity of Indiscernibles in his correspondence with Clarke." *Australasian Journal of Philosophy* 77 (4): 429–38.

Rodriguez-Pereyra, G. 2004. "Leibniz's argument for the Principle of Identity of Indiscernibles in Primary Truths." In M. Carrara, A. M. Nunziante, and G. Tomasi (eds.), *Individuals, Minds and Bodies: Themes from Leibniz*. Studia Leibnitiana Supplementa 32. Stuttgart: Franz Steiner, pp. 49–59.

Rodriguez-Pereyra, G. 2014. *Leibniz's Principle of Identity of Indiscernibles*. Oxford: Oxford University Press.

Rescher, N. 1967. *The Philosophy of Leibniz*. Englewood Cliffs, N.J.: Prentice-Hall.

Russell, B. 1992. *A Critical Exposition of the Philosophy of Leibniz*. London: Routledge.

Rutherford, D. 1995. *Leibniz and the Rational Order of Nature*. Cambridge: Cambridge University Press.

Sleigh, R. C., Jr. 1982. "Truth and sufficient reason in the philosophy of Leibniz." In M. Hooker (ed.), *Leibniz: Critical and Interpretive Essays*. Manchester: Manchester University Press, pp. 209–42.

Sleigh, R. C., Jr. 1983. "Leibniz on the two great principles of all our reasonings." *Midwest Studies in Philosophy* 8 (1): 193–216.

CHAPTER 4

....

THE ACTUAL WORLD

....

DONALD RUTHERFORD

THE contrast between the actual and the possible is one of the most important distinctions in Leibniz's philosophy. On it rests the central thesis of his theodicy (that the actual world is the best of all possible worlds), as well as other key doctrines, including his solution to the problem of the "labyrinth of the continuum." The same distinction, though, is also the source of long-standing interpretive problems. Among these are the ontological status of the possible, the circumstances under which possibles become actual, the "incompossibility" of possibles, and the continued dependence of actual things on God.

That the possible possesses a form of reality is a foundational tenet for Leibniz. If this were not the case, he believes, there would be no basis for the eternal truths of mathematics and metaphysics or for true propositions about the essences of things. The reality of the possible is also the starting point for Leibniz's account of the "ultimate origination of things": if the possible were not real, there would be no ground for the existence of actual things.[1] Leibniz's thinking on this topic is guided by the principle of sufficient reason: "that nothing happens without it being possible for someone who knows enough to give a reason sufficient to determine why it is so and not otherwise." Assuming this principle, he writes, "the first question we have the right to ask will be, *why is there something rather than nothing*? For nothing is simpler and easier than something." Then, supposing that some things exist, "we must be able to give a reason for *why they must exist in this way*, and not otherwise."[2]

The two most basic questions of metaphysics are thus: Why is there something rather than nothing? And, why do certain things exist while other equally possible things do not? Leibniz's response to these questions begins from the assumption that answers to them cannot be found within the things that make up the universe because it is the universe itself—the series of all actual things—that stands in need of explanation. Such an

---

[1] See, in particular, the essay "On the Ultimate Origination of Things," dated November 23, 1697 (GP VII 302–308/AG 149–155).

[2] "Principles of Nature and of Grace" (hereafter: PNG), §7 (GP VI 602/AG 210).

explanation, therefore, can only be found in an "extramundane" reason: a substance "outside the series of contingent things," which is "a necessary being, carrying the reason for its existence within itself. Otherwise, we would not yet have a sufficient reason where one could end the series. And this ultimate reason for things is called *God*" (PNG 8; GP VI 602/AG 210).

Leibniz's assertion that God is the ultimate ground of the existence of the actual world is unremarkable. It records his conviction that the explanatory regress set up by the principle of sufficient reason must terminate in a necessary being that is the ground of its own existence. Yet Leibniz's certainty on this point gives new force to the two questions with which we began. If God is a necessary being, sufficient unto himself, why does a created world exist at all? Why not the "simpler" alternative of nothing? And supposing that something exists, why just the assorted contents of the world we take to be actual rather than the manifold possibilities of things that do not exist? Leibniz's answers to these questions are the topic of this chapter. The first section, "From Possibility to Actuality," addresses his answer to the first question, focusing on his claim that every possible has a propensity to exist proportional to its degree of perfection and the consistency of this claim with the dogma that God creates contingent things *ex nihilo* through the exercise of his free will. The next sections, "Compossibility" and "The Cosmological Account," examine Leibniz's answer to the second question from the perspective of his doctrine that not all possibles are compossible and, hence, that God is limited to creating the possible world that contains the greatest total perfection. The section "The Best of All Possible Worlds" considers in more detail how Leibniz conceives of the best possible world and his efforts to reconcile a variety of distinguishable criteria of goodness. The final section, "Creation, Conservation, Concurrence," takes up his account of the continual dependence of the actual world on God and his defense of the traditional doctrine of God's concurrence in all the actions of created things.

FROM POSSIBILITY TO ACTUALITY

Leibniz affirms the theologically orthodox view that, with the exception of God, whatever exists does so because it is has been created by God. He also accepts that God creates by a free choice of his will, suggesting that the absence of a created world is a possible state of affairs.[3] Yet he immediately follows this with the assertion that this is not a state of affairs that would be realized by God or that is consistent with a correct understanding of God's nature. God's will, he says, is in no way indifferent or indeterminate: "his will is always decided, and it can only be decided by the best" (T 337; GP VI 315/H 328). Leibniz's justification for this claim is that the perfection realized in created things is a reason for God to create them. By virtue of its goodness, God's will aims at

---

[3] *Theodicy* (hereafter: T), §336 (GP VI 314/H 327).

"communicating himself" (T 228; GP VI 253/H 269); that is, it has as an end the production of perfection. Thus, antecedently, God wills the existence of all things in proportion
to their degree of perfection, but his consequent or decisive will is to create the *best*: the
greatest perfection that can be realized.[4]

Such is Leibniz's official account of the "ultimate origination of things" as it appears in
the *Theodicy*. In unpublished essays from the 1680s and 1690s, we encounter a somewhat
different story, one that some commentators have seen as pointing to a less orthodox
position.[5] In these works, Leibniz emphasizes as the ground of existence the inherent
"demand" (*exigentia*), "claim" (*praetensio*), or "tendency" (*tendentia*) of any possible to
exist (GP VII 303–305). Given this "demand" or "tendency" to exist, present in varying
degrees in all possibles, there is a competition among them. On the assumption that
the existence of some precludes the existence of others, not all can exist. Consequently,
there is a process of selection whereby the greatest collection of "compossibles"—those
possibles that can coexist—reaches actuality, leaving the rest in a condition of mere possibility (A VI iv 1442–1443).

Because this account is found primarily in Leibniz's private writings, it is tempting
to see it as an expression of his deep or "esoteric" metaphysics, which is in tension with
more orthodox, public presentations of his views. Such a reading, however, is untenable.
Leibniz alludes to the account in *Theodicy* and stresses that it is based on a figurative way
of speaking:

> One may say that as soon as God has decreed to create something there is a struggle
> among all the possibles, all of them laying claim [*pretendans*] to existence, and that
> those which, being united, produce most reality, most perfection, most intelligibility
> carry the day. It is true that all this struggle can only be ideal, that is to say, it can only
> be a conflict of reasons in the most perfect understanding, which cannot fail to act in
> the most perfect way, and consequently to choose the best.
>
> (T 201; GP VI 236/H 253)

The "demand" or "claim" that possibles make for existence refers strictly to the magnitude of the reason they offer God to create them. Possibles have a greater "tendency" to

---

[4] T 22–23. To Des Bosses, Leibniz writes: "In my judgment, unless there were a best series, God clearly
would have created nothing, since he cannot act without a reason, or prefer the less perfect to the more
perfect alternative" (Look-Rutherford 212–213). Leibniz defines "perfection" (or "metaphysical good") as
"the magnitude of positive reality considered as such" ("Monadology" [hereafter: Mon], §41; GP VI 614/
AG 218), or the "quantity of essence" (GP VII 303). Thus, in creating the greatest total perfection, God
creates the world in which "there is in actuality as much reality as possible" (GP VII 306).

[5] See David Blumenfeld, "Leibniz's theory of the striving possibles," in *Studia Leibnitiana* 5 (1973), pp.
163–177. The main texts (with dates assigned by A) include: "On First Truths," 1680 (A VI iv 1442–1443);
"General Notions," ca. 1683–85 (A VI iv 550–557); "On the Reason Why These Things Should Exist
Rather Than Any Others," 1689 (A VI iv 1634–1635); "On the Ultimate Origination of Things," 1697 (GP
VII 302–308). See also the undated summary at C 533–535/GP VII 289–291, translated as "A Résumé of
Metaphysics," in MP 145–147.

exist, to the extent that they represent a greater degree of perfection; thus, other things being equal, God has a greater reason to create them.

Reflection on the principles of Leibniz's metaphysics confirms that this is the only position he could take. "Striving" or "tendency" is a manifestation of the power of primary created beings: substances. Mere possibles have no power because they are not actual. Hence, the images of possibles "striving" in the mind of God for creation can only be a metaphor referring to the weight of the reasons they offer for creation. With the exception of God, possibles do not exist of themselves; their reality is limited to that which they possess as objects of divine ideas. To become actual or existent, things corresponding to those ideas must be created by God.[6]

COMPOSSIBILITY

No finite thing exists unless created by God, but, according to Leibniz, God does not create all possible things. Although all possibles present God with reasons to create them, some of these reasons must prevail over others because not all possibles are *compossible*. Thus, God must make a choice of some over others, opting for that collection of compossibles that is, overall, the best.

Leibniz crafted his position as a response to Spinoza's metaphysics. It is Spinoza's view that every finite thing that can exist does exist as a necessary expression of God's infinite power.[7] Leibniz rejects this view as inconsistent with an understanding of God as a supremely perfect being whose actions evidence a fundamental justice with respect to creation. A creator who merits being worshipped, whose character is appropriate for emulation by human beings, must be one who acts for the greatest reason, choosing the best *because* it is the best. As Leibniz sees it, an impersonal, all-powerful God, such as Spinoza describes, severs the essential connection between theology and morality. Our moral compass takes its direction from the justice God exercises in creation, the rightness of his action consisting in its being a free choice of the best from among a set of mutually exclusive alternatives.[8]

[6] Leibniz makes this clear in one of the private texts: "And every possible involves not only possibility but also an actual endeavor of existing [*conatum actu existendi*], not as though those things which do not exist have endeavor [*conatum*], but because in this way the ideas of essences in God demand to be actually existing; thereafter, God freely decides to choose whatever is most perfect.... From this, it is obvious that the essences of things depend on the divine nature, existences on the divine will; for nothing can obtain existence by its own force, but only by the decree of God" (A VI iv 557).

[7] Spinoza, *Ethics*, Part I, Prop. 16.

[8] He records the following in December 1676, during his most intense engagement with Spinoza's views: "If all possibles were to exist, there would be no need of a reason for existing, and mere possibility would be enough. So there would not be a God, except in so far as he is possible. But a God of the kind in whom the pious believe would not be possible, if the opinion of those who believe that all possibles exist were true" (A VI iii 582/Parkinson 105). See also "Discourse on Metaphysics" (hereafter: DM), §2; T 173–174.

Although Leibniz is satisfied to assert this conception of God against Spinoza's, he also seeks confirmation of it through his account of the ultimate origination of things. Principally, this comes through the doctrine that a choice is forced upon God by the fact that not all possibles are compossible.[9] If God's intellect represents a set of possibles as "incompossible," then God cannot, in a single act, render those possibles actual. Leibniz finds in this explanation a basis for his rejection of Spinoza's metaphysics. If possibles, by virtue of what they are, organize themselves into mutually exclusive sets of compossibles—"possible worlds"—then God is limited to creating one from among those sets: that which is the best. By reframing the problem in this way, Leibniz raises the hope of a noncircular argument against Spinoza's conception of God.

This argument obviously hinges on Leibniz's ability to delineate the sense in which possibles may be incompossible. He was aware of the difficulty he faced in this regard. If the most basic forms of possibility are simple absolute essences represented by "purely positive terms," then there is no basis for incompossibility: all such terms, and any conjunctions of them, are consistent with each other.[10]

In later writings, Leibniz takes himself to have found a solution to this problem, an account of incompossibility that blocks the inference to the existence of all possible things. Central to his account is the idea that the possibles that segregate themselves into compossible sets are possible *substances*, represented by complete concepts. Thus, possible worlds can be understood, minimally, as consistent sets of complete concepts. Still, Leibniz's formulation of this doctrine is far from clear, and his unclarity has spawned an extensive debate in the literature. On one side of the debate, defenders of the "logical interpretation" construe the relation of compossibility in terms of logical consistency: possible substances are compossible if and only if the supposition of their joint existence is logically consistent. On the other side, defenders of the "lawful interpretation" hold that possible substances are compossible if and only if they can be conceived as connected under some set of suitable natural laws.[11]

Both sides in the debate highlight plausible aspects of Leibniz's position, but, in the end, neither makes a compelling case for its reading. The strength of the logical interpretation is that it identifies incompossibility with a strict limitation on the exercise of God's power. If two complete concepts are incompossible, then the supposition of their joint existence is inconsistent and both cannot be actualized. If some complete concepts are incompossible in this sense, then God cannot, consistent with his own rationality, determine the existence of all possible things. It is doubtful, though, whether defenders of the

---

[9] For a late statement of the position, see his letter to Bourguet of December 1714 (GP III 573/L 662).

[10] He acknowledges the problem in the 1680 essay "On First Truths": "to this point, people have been ignorant of the source of the incompossibility of different things, or of what could make it the case that different essences conflict with each other, since all purely positive terms seem to be compatible with each other" (A VI iv 1443).

[11] For an overview of the debate, see James Messina and Donald Rutherford, "Leibniz's theory of compossibility," in *Philosophy Compass* 4 (2009), pp. 962–969; Margaret Wilson, "Compossibility and law," in S. Nadler (ed.), *Causation in Early Modern Philosophy* (University Park: Pennsylvania State University Press, 1993), pp. 119–133.

logical interpretation succeed in showing that any complete concepts are incompossible in this sense.[12] Much is made of the idea that there is an implicational relation among the complete concepts of substances belonging to the same world, such that the existence of one substance entails the existence of all its worldmates and the nonexistence of any substances not belonging to that world. At bottom, however, this implication rests on the assumption that the substances belonging to the same world "express" each other, meaning that there is a lawful relation between what can be said about one and the other, and that they fail to express the substances belonging to other worlds. Given this, a failure of compossibility does not amount to logical inconsistency, but only to a lack of order or lawfulness.[13]

If this is correct, then the logical interpretation of compossibility does not differ materially from the lawful interpretation. The crux of the latter reading is that, with respect to God's absolute power, the supposition of the joint existence of any two substances is logically consistent. However, it does not follow from this that any two substances are compossible because compossibility requires in addition that their states be related by some set of suitable laws.[14] The qualification of these laws as "suitable" is necessary because Leibniz asserts that a rule can be devised to fit any set of data; in this sense, any set of substances can be related by some law.[15] Yet such a law would not have the generality he associates with the exercise of God's reason. Any law by which substances are rendered compossible must be a law defined in terms of general properties of the substances and not merely brute facts determined by their particular existences.[16]

On this understanding of Leibniz's position, incompossibility does not track a logical restriction on the exercise of God's power. With respect to his absolute power,

[12] A single text, dated ca. 1687–96, supports the reading of incompossibility as logical inconsistency: "The *compossible* is that which, with another, does not imply a contradiction" (A VI iv 867/Grua 325). More frequently, Leibniz explicates incompossibility in terms of things being "incompatible" (*incompatibilia*) with respect to spatiotemporal or causal order. See C 534/MP 145–146, and the discussion in the section "The Cosmological Account."

[13] The role of the doctrine of expression is acknowledged by defenders of the logical interpretation. See Benson Mates, *The Philosophy of Leibniz: Metaphysics and Philosophy of Language* (New York: Oxford University Press, 1986), pp. 76–78, 220; Nicholas Rescher, *Leibniz: An Introduction to His Philosophy* (Lanham, Md.: University Press of America, 1979), pp. 49–50. According to Leibniz, "it suffices for the expression of one thing in another that there be some constant law of relations, by which particulars in one can be referred to corresponding particulars in the other" (C 15/MP 176–177). Cf. A II ii 240/LA 144.

[14] For an early statement of this reading, see Bertrand Russell, *A Critical Exposition of the Philosophy of Leibniz*, 2nd ed. (London: George Allen and Unwin, 1937), p. 67; for a more elaborate development, see Gregory Brown, "Compossibility, harmony, and perfection in Leibniz," in *The Philosophical Review 96* (1987), pp. 173–203.

[15] DM 6. Compare J. A. Cover and John O'Leary–Hawthorne, *Substance and Individuation in Leibniz* (Cambridge: Cambridge University Press, 1999), pp. 134, 137.

[16] "God can never have a primitive particular will, that is, independent of laws or general acts of will; such a thing would be unreasonable. He cannot determine upon Adam, Peter, Judas or any individual without there being a reason for this determination; and this reason leads of necessity to some general proposition. The wise mind always acts *according to principles*; always *according to rules*" (T 337; GP VI 315/H 328).

God could create a single substance by itself or a collection of substances whose states were disordered with respect to each other.[17] Nevertheless, compossibility does reflect constraints that God's reason imposes on the exercise of his power; specifically, it registers the fact that any actual or possible act of divine will is in conformity with the principle of order.[18] Compossible complete concepts are those that God conceives as ordered in ways necessary to make a world; incompossible complete concepts are those that fail to meet this condition. Even if God *could*, logically, create the latter, his will would not tend toward that end because of the absence of the requisite order.

The difficult question is how to understand the constraints that order places on the representation of substances as compossible or capable of joint realization in a world. For proponents of the lawful interpretation, this comes down to the fact that the substances meet some general condition, such as that their states express each other, that they are connected by suitable laws, or that they harmonize with each other.[19] A set of substances will be compossible, and hence will comprise a possible world, if and only if they meet this condition. The problem with such approaches is that they remain overly general. Each of the aforementioned concepts—expression, lawfulness, harmony—is suggestive of Leibniz's view that compossible substances instantiate a distinctive order with respect to each other. Yet there has been no convincing demonstration that any of these concepts by itself is sufficient to define the notion of compossibility.

Interpretations that follow this approach fail because they turn Leibniz's doctrine of compossibility on its head. In no text does he argue that substances are compossible— and hence belong to the same world—just in case they express one another, are lawfully related, or harmonize in their perceptions. Rather, in explicating the idea of compossibility, Leibniz is guided by a substantive conception of the order definitive of a *world*. This order is based on the spatiotemporal and causal relations that any substances must stand in if they are to be members of the same world. Giving priority in this way to the formal structure of a world forms the basis of a third approach to the problem of compossibility: the cosmological account.[20]

---

[17] See Leibniz's comment to Des Bosses in his letter of April 29, 1715 (Look-Rutherford 337–339).

[18] Possible acts of divine will are those that figure in God's knowledge of worlds he may (but, with the exception of one, does not) create. Adams notes the relevance for Leibniz of the medieval distinction between God's *potentia absoluta* and *potentia ordinata*, the former referring to God's power considered in abstraction from his other attributes; see Robert M. Adams, *Leibniz: Determinist, Theist, Idealist* (New York: Oxford University Press, 1994), p. 106, n. 36. For Leibniz, any actual or possible act of divine will is a general volition, subject to the condition of order. This means that any object of God's will is represented as "distinctly thinkable" in accordance with general principles (C 535/MP 146).

[19] Representative of the first approach are Cover and O'Leary-Hawthorne, *Substance and Individuation in Leibniz*; of the second, Russell, *Critical Exposition*; of the third, Olli Koistinen and Arto Repo, "Compossibility and being in the same world in Leibniz's metaphysics," in *Studia Leibnitiana 31* (1999), pp. 196–214.

[20] See Rutherford, *Leibniz and the Rational Order of Nature*, pp. 188–197; Messina and Rutherford, "Leibniz on compossibility."

THE COSMOLOGICAL ACCOUNT

That any compossible substances must have a specific order with respect to each other and that this order places constraints on which things can exist in a world comes out clearly in Leibniz's comparison of God to an architect who seeks to fill a given space with the most varied and elegant collection of rooms or a tiler who lays down pieces "so as to contain as many as possible in a given area" (GP VII 304/AG 151). On these scenarios, the limitations on coexistence are defined not just by logical consistency, but also by the geometry of space: how different shapes can be arranged with respect to each other in a given area. The implication of the analogy is that, just as not all tiles can be combined on a given surface, so not all possible substances can be combined in a given world; certain possibles are precluded from standing in the requisite relations to others.

In "On the Ultimate Origination of Things," Leibniz develops this line of thought in ways that suggest it is, in fact, more than an analogy. The "divine mathematics" that God employs in creation is a method for maximizing the amount of perfection, or reality, that can be contained within the "capacity of space and time," which he identifies with "the capacity of the order of possible existence" (GP VII 304/AG 151). Space and time, he writes, define the "receptivity or capacity of a world" (GP VII 303/AG 150). This means that any things conceived to exist in the same world must be understood to have well-defined spatial and temporal relations to each other; there must be a determinate answer to the question of "where" and "when" they are with respect to each other. Consequently, for God, the problem of creation does not involve maximizing the "quantity of reality" absolutely, but relative to the constraints of spatial and temporal order.[21]

Considerable evidence supports the link between these orders and Leibniz's conception of compossibility. Representative is his comment in a late reply to Pierre Bayle: "Space and time taken together constitute the order of possibilities of one entire world, so that these orders—space and time, that is—relate not only to what actually is but also to anything that could be put in its place" (GP IV 568/L 583).[22] For any possible world, there is a single world-space (or order of coexistence) and a single world-time (or order of succession) that delimit which substances can be members of that world. How exactly this is to be understood on Leibniz's mature metaphysics is a point to which we will return in the next section. For the moment, it is enough to note that Leibniz's considered view of compossibility rests on the idea of a common spatiotemporal order, a point he illustrates with the example of fictional worlds such as that of More's *Utopia*.

---

[21] For a different reading of the passages from "On the Ultimate Origination of Things," see Jeffrey K. McDonough, "Leibniz and the puzzle of compossibility: The packing strategy," in *Philosophical Review* 119 (2010), pp. 135–163. McDonough distances himself from the cosmological account at pp. 141–142, n. 12.

[22] See also T 8, T 201, and *Causa Dei*, §15: "it is useless to invent a plurality of actual worlds, since one [world] comprehends for us the totality of created things in all times and places; and it is in this sense that we use the term 'world' [*mundi*]" (GP VI 440).

Although the worlds described in such works are possible in themselves, they could not be part of our world because their inhabitants lack a spatiotemporal relation to us.[23]

For a set of possible substances to be compossible, then, it is necessary that they be related via a common spatiotemporal order. This, though, is not sufficient. Leibniz also requires that the members of the world be "connected" to one another. In the *Theodicy*, he states this as a condition that applies to any possible world:

> For it must be known that all things are *connected* [tout est *lié*] in each one of the possible worlds: the universe, whatever it may be, is all of one piece, like an ocean: the least movement extends its effect there to any distance whatsoever, even though this effect becomes less perceptible in proportion to the distance.
>
> (T 9; GP VI 107/H 128)

By the "universal connection" of things, Leibniz means a mutual dependence among the states of substances, such that a change in any one substance is reflected in a corresponding change in every other. Although he denies that substances exert a real, or "metaphysical," influence on one another, he holds that the members of a world condition each others' existence, in the sense that they are causally related under a set of contingent laws.[24]

This aspect of Leibniz's position is endorsed by the lawful interpretation; however, that account goes only part of the way in reconstructing the order of a world and the attendant idea of compossibility. The lawful interpretation highlights the dimension of order realized in the mutual causal dependence of created things, but it does not acknowledge the significance of the spatiotemporal order that defines the "capacity" of a world and provides a framework for representing the causal relations of things. According to the cosmological account, any possible world possesses a distinctive form of unity that is determined by God's representation of the spatiotemporal order and causal connection that its members would have were that world to exist. Any two things are compossible, or members of the same possible world, just in case they are conceived by God as related in these ways.

For Leibniz, then, a world is not merely a set or collection of substances; it is a unified whole that has a spatiotemporal and causal order analogous to those that unify the totality of actual things. Any possible world shares a formal structure with the actual world, and this structure conditions which things can coexist within it. A pressing question for this account is whether it is consistent with Leibniz's thesis of the maximization of perfection. If all possibles have a "claim" to exist proportional to their degree of perfection, why should we see God's creation as restricted to worlds in this sense? If God's consequent will is to produce the best, the greatest perfection or reality, why are spatiotemporal order and causal connection plausible constraints on the realization of

---

[23] A VI iv 1653–1654/AG 94; GP II 181; GP III 572/L 661.
[24] A VI iv 1646–1647/AG 33; GP IV 510/AG 161; Mon 51–52.

that end? If it is possible for God to create more reality by abandoning these constraints, why wouldn't God do so?

On behalf of Leibniz, we can reply, first, that we know that God *has* decided to create a world—existences ordered by space, time, and causation—because such a world exists; hence, the creation of a world (in this sense) is an end for God, and we may suppose that his ultimate deliberation concerns how best to realize that end. Consistent with this, Leibniz maintains that God wills the creation of the world through a single volition that comprehends "the whole order of the universe"; the object of his will is a unified series of things, not a set of independent events or existences.[25] Thus, although it would have been possible for God to have created more things realizing more total reality without the systematic order of a world, those things would fail to form a suitable object of God's will.

To this, the critic may reply that even if there exists this sort of limitation on the composition of a world, nothing prevents God from creating more than one world. Logically, the existence of one world-system does not preclude the existence of another. Why, then, does God not render all possible worlds actual? Although not all possibles can be created by God as one world, there is no logical restriction on the existence of a plurality of worlds. Thus, if God wanted to create all possible worlds, and hence the greatest possible reality, it seems that God could have done so.[26]

This scenario can be blocked if we suppose that God has a unique will to create and that, consequently, anything he creates must form part of a single comprehensive plan. Since different worlds reflect different plans, God would not will the existence of a plurality of actual worlds.[27]

This response falls short of a demonstration of the impossibility of the existence of all possible things and of the falsity of Spinoza's conception of God. In fact, following his initial engagement with Spinoza's metaphysics in 1676–77, Leibniz appears to have given little thought to the hypothesis of a plurality of actual worlds. He accepts that God

[25] See T 84 and his letter to Ernst Hesse-Rheinfels for Arnauld of April 12, 1686 ("in order to proceed exactly, it is necessary to consider in God a certain most general and most comprehensive volition that he has with regard to the whole order of the universe, since the universe is like a whole that God penetrates in a single view") (A II ii 18–19/LA 15).

[26] This concern is raised by Kointinen and Repo, "Compossibility," 213–214. Kulstad interprets Leibniz as exploring this line of thought, inspired by Spinoza, in the paper *De Formis Simplicibus*, dated April 1676 (A VI iii 522–523/Parkinson 83–85). See Mark Kulstad, "Leibniz, Spinoza and Tschirnhaus: Multiple worlds, possible worlds," in S. Brown (ed.), *The Young Leibniz and His Philosophy* (Dordrecht: Kluwer, 1999), pp. 243–262, at 256–258. Several other texts from the period find Leibniz arguing against the idea of a plurality of actual worlds: A VI iii 511/Parkinson 65; A VI iii 581/Parkinson 103–105; A VI iv 1349–1350.

[27] Compare his letter to Des Bosses of mid-October 1708 (Look-Rutherford 112–113) and his letter to Arnauld of July 16, 1686: "I think there was an infinity of possible ways of creating the world, according to the different designs which God could form, and that each possible world depends on certain principal designs or ends of God which are proper to it, that is, certain primitive free decrees (conceived *sub ratione possibilitatis*) or certain laws of the *general order* of that possible universe with which they are in accord and whose concept they determine, as they do also the concepts of all the individual substances which must enter into this same universe" (A II ii 73/L 333).

creates one from among an infinity of possible worlds because only in this way can he make sense of the belief that God acts as a just creator. The challenge for Leibniz is to reconcile this understanding of God with his modal metaphysics. If there were a presumption in favor of the actuality of many worlds, he would face a serious problem. However, if he can shift the burden of proof through a coherent account of compossibility, the most plausible creation scenario remains for him one in which God creates a single world from among an infinity of possible worlds.

THE BEST OF ALL POSSIBLE WORLDS

Leibniz's view of the actual world as the "best of all possible worlds" is based on the perfection or reality realized in it: it is the world in which "there is in actuality as much reality as possible" (GP VII 306/AG 152). Yet the thesis is not simply a claim about the maximization of a scalar quantity of "reality." Leibniz defines the possible, or whatever "expresses essence or possible reality" (GP VII 303/AG 150), as "what is distinctly thinkable [*distincte cogitabile*] without contradiction" (A VI iv 558). Thus, essences, or possible realities, are distinguished only insofar as they can be conceived as distinct by reason, from which it follows for Leibniz that a maximization of reality involves a maximization of different *forms* of reality.[28]

Leibniz's commitment to the coextension of the real and the "distinctly thinkable" entails that the world containing the greatest reality is the world in which there is the greatest "intelligibility," or the most to be understood (T 201). When asked by Wolff to explain his notion of perfection, Leibniz answers that it is "the degree of positive reality, or what comes to the same thing, the degree of affirmative intelligibility, so that something more perfect is something in which more things worthy of being observed are found" (GLW 161/AG 230). The intelligibility of the world is also a function of the order found within it, for order is simply the "distinct thinkability" (*distincta cogitabilitas*) of many things in relation to each other. Things stand in such relations insofar as they are conceived by God as instances of general rules or principles (C 535/MP 146). Leibniz claims that "nothing is more regular than the divine intellect, which is the source of all rules, and produces the most regular, that is, the most perfect system of the world, the system that is as harmonious as possible" (GLW 171/AG 233). Consequently, the world of greatest perfection is also the world of greatest "order and regularity," which produces

---

[28] "There exists, therefore, that which is the most perfect, since *perfection* is simply quantity of reality. Further, perfection . . . is to be located in form or variety" (C 534/MP 146). Some of these forms are instantiated in individual substances, others in properties of things. With regard to the former, Leibniz asserts that no two substances "can resemble each other completely and differ only in number and that what Saint Thomas asserts on this point about angels or intelligences (that here every individual is a lowest species [*species infima*]) is true of all substances" (DM 9; A VI iv 1541/AG 42).

the greatest "agreement in variety" and the richest object of intellectual contemplation. In short, Leibniz declares:

> *Perfection* is the harmony of things, or the state where everything is worthy of being observed, that is, the state of agreement or identity in variety; you can even say that it is the degree of contemplatibility [*considerabilitas*]. Indeed, order, regularity, and harmony come to the same thing.
>
> (GLW 172/AG 233–234)[29]

Such is the formal basis of Leibniz's theory of the best of all possible worlds. God creates the richest collection of beings, united by the greatest order, leading to the greatest harmony and the greatest range of opportunities for intellectual contemplation. Clearly, this is a very abstract way of representing God's ends in creation, and it does little to illuminate the connection between those ends and Leibniz's metaphysics of the created world. Within Leibniz's metaphysics, the formal attributes of perfection, which are the basis of God's choice of the best, are translated into a set of specific theses about elements of structure, design, purpose, and multiple levels of harmony that God realizes in creation. Above all, Leibniz aims to reconcile the idea that God creates the best possible world—the world of greatest perfection and harmony—with the idea that God has a particular concern to maximize the happiness of rational beings who form the most important part of creation by virtue of their fellowship with God.[30] This is a complicated topic that encompasses almost all of Leibniz's philosophy. Here, I can touch on only two central points: the contrast between instantiations of order in the physical world and at the level of substances and the contrast between order as realized in the world and order as understood and reproduced by minds.[31]

Many of Leibniz's claims about the order of the created world refer to properties of physical laws. Most prominently, he argues that the laws of motion are contingent truths that cannot be explained on the basis of the concepts of space, time, and matter alone, but instead require appeal to God's selection of the laws as the "most fitting" for a world:

> God's supreme wisdom has led him, above all, to choose *laws of motion* that are best adjusted and most suitable with respect to abstract or metaphysical reasons. The same quantity of total and absolute force, or of action, is preserved, the same quantity of respective force, or of reaction; and finally, the same quantity of directive force. . . . [T]hese laws do not depend upon the *principle of necessity*, as do logical,

---

[29] Compare his comment to Bourguet: "To be possible, intelligibility suffices; but for existence there must be a prevalence of intelligibility or order; for there is order to the extent that there is more to observe in a multitude" (GP III 558).

[30] On God's multiple goals in creation, see DM 36; "On the Ultimate Origination of Things" (GP VII 306/AG 152–153); see also PNG 10; T 119, 124, 222.

[31] For more on these issues, see Rutherford, *Leibniz and the Rational Order of Nature*.

arithmetical, and geometrical truths, but upon the *principle of fitness*, that is, upon the choice of wisdom.

(PNG 11; GP VI 603/AG 210–211)

Along with the laws of motion, Leibniz cites the laws of optics and the structure of matter (its infinite division and conformity to the principle of continuity) as examples of the order that supports God's choice of this world as the best.[32]

Depending on how one construes the ontological status of the physical in Leibniz's philosophy, one may take these as first-order claims about the order God selects for the created world or as claims that point to a deeper account of order and harmony at the level of soul-like substances or monads. On the latter reading, Leibniz's account of the "fitness" of the laws of nature concerns the order of a phenomenal universe that is the common object of the representations of perceiving substances. As early as the "Discourse on Metaphysics," Leibniz describes God as creating a world of substances by actualizing an infinity of distinct "perspectives" on a single system of phenomena (DM 14). Producing substances in this way, God creates, as it were, an infinity of "different universes, which are, nevertheless, only perspectives on a single one, corresponding to the different points of view of each monad." "And this is the way of obtaining as much variety as possible, but with the greatest order possible, that is, it is the way of obtaining as much perfection as possible" (Mon 57–58; GP VI 616/AG 220).

Leibniz's description of the world as consisting of an infinity of perceiving substances, each expressing the same universe of phenomena from a unique point of view, fits neatly with his account of the formal attributes of perfection. It is a way of maximizing variety and the total quantity of reality because it entails an infinity of points of view, each realized in a substance with unique perceptual powers, and it is a way of optimizing order because the perceptions of each substance are variations on a single template. The combination of maximal variety and optimal order makes it, by definition, the world of greatest harmony.

A further point is worth noting about this scheme. In Leibniz's view, each monad is not just a perceiver *of* a phenomenal physical universe; it is also located *in* that universe by virtue of its relation to an organic body, which it represents as its own. Even if this body has no reality beyond its being the physical point of view of the monad, a trio of important conclusions follows. First, the states of every monad are spatiotemporally locatable relative to those of every other monad via their representations of their respective bodies.[33] Second, every monad is "confusedly omniscient," registering everything that happens in the universe via its representation of its body and the causal connection of every other body to it.[34] Third, there are monads everywhere "in" matter because

---

[32] DM 19–22; GP IV 568/WF 123.

[33] C 14–15/MP 175–176; GP II 253/AG 178.

[34] C 10; PNG 13; Mon 62.

every organic body uncovered in the infinite division of matter is the point of view of some monad.[35]

Although the correct interpretation of these theses is subject to debate, together they reinforce the connection between Leibniz's account of the order of the physical world and the order realized in the harmonious perceptions of monads. The basis of this connection is his conviction that, in considering which substances to create, God conceives of them as "little worlds [*ses petits Mondes*]" (GP IV 557/L 576) that mirror in a limited form an archetype of the phenomenal universe represented in God.[36] This, in turn, allows us to give a more precise statement of the cosmological account of compossibility. Suppose, first, that the original conception of a world is that of a *cosmos*: a closed system of spatiotemporally and causally related bodies. Next, suppose that each of those bodies is identified as the point of view of a monad or is composed of bodies each of which is identified as the point of view of a monad. Then, any set of monads will be compossible just in case they are locatable in the same world: they represent themselves as parts of the same cosmos, with the result that there are determinate spatiotemporal and causal relations among any changes that occur in the contents of their perceptual states.

To this account of the organization of a world, Leibniz adds a further critical claim about the place of rational beings in it. All created substances contribute to the perfection of the world through their own perfection and through the harmonious relations in which they stand to one another. Individually, rational beings contribute far more perfection than any other type of substance (Leibniz sometimes says "infinitely" more), but they also contribute perfection in a fundamentally different way, insofar as they mirror intellectually God's own understanding of the perfection and order of things.[37] In short, whereas other beings contribute to the perfection of the universe merely by being parts of it, rational beings contribute by beings parts that are capable of understanding how all the parts, including themselves, are ordered in the universe. More than this, based on their understanding of order, rational beings are able to replicate that order through additions they make to the perfection of the universe. Thus, they understand, they plan, they construct—with all of this order-creating activity being conceived by God as part of what makes this the best of all possible worlds. Finally, and most importantly, rational beings have the capacity to understand the special place they occupy in creation—as citizens of the "city of God"—and how their role replicates the role that God plays with

---

[35] Mon 66; Look-Rutherford 24–25. For Leibniz, the last claim does not imply that matter is ultimately anything over and above monads or that monads are literally spatially proximate to each other (cf. Look-Rutherford 227, 255). For discussion of these points, see Donald Rutherford, "Leibniz as idealist," in *Oxford Studies in Early Modern Philosophy 4* (2008), pp. 141–190.

[36] "God contains the universe eminently, and the soul or unity contains it actually, being a living mirror, though active and vital, so to speak. Indeed, we can say that each soul is a world apart, but that all these worlds agree, and represent a different relation to the same phenomena. And this is the most perfect way of multiplying beings as far as possible, and in the best way possible" (GP III 72/WFN 132). Cf. DM 9.

[37] DM 35; Mon 83.

respect to creation as a whole.[38] That is, they are able to grasp reflectively that they are beings who understand order and have the capacity to produce order in the universe, just as God has brought into existence the world in which the greatest diversity of things is ordered in the most fitting manner.

The last two points highlight an essential feature of Leibniz's doctrine of the best of all possible worlds. It is mistake to think of this title as earned on the basis of the present state of the world or indeed of any finite state of it. The claim of this world to be the best rests in large part on its potential to grow in perfection indefinitely, through the intellectual and moral development of minds and the additional order and harmony they introduce into the world. With this comes the possibility of unending increases in human happiness.[39] The potential for progress of this sort is what gives Leibniz the greatest confidence in affirming this as the best of all possible worlds in the face of innumerable examples of ignorance, weakness, and cruelty that seem to count against this description.

CREATION, CONSERVATION, CONCURRENCE

God's involvement in the actual world does not end with creation. God's plan for the world embraces the totality of its history. Beyond this, though, Leibniz argues that God is directly implicated, as cause, in the continuation of the world's existence from the moment of its creation. The omnipotence that is necessary to bring things into existence is equally necessary to sustain their existence. In the "Principles of Nature and of Grace," Leibniz writes: "The reason that made things exist through [God], makes them still depend on him while they exist and bring about their effects; and they continually receive from him that which causes them to have any perfection at all" (PNG 9; GP VI 603/AG 210).

Suggested in this passage are three central theological doctrines: (i) God *conserves* the things he creates, sustaining them in existence; (ii) this conservation amounts to a *continual creation*, whereby things receive from God throughout their existence whatever perfection is in them; and (iii) the dependence of created things on God extends to all the effects brought about by them, with the result that nothing happens in the world without God's *concurrence* in the production of those effects. Leibniz aims to show that these doctrines are consistent both with the main claims of his theodicy and with his metaphysics, according to which the primary existing things, substances, are genuine secondary causes—indeed, spontaneous causes of all the changes in their own states.[40]

[38] GP VI 507/AG 192; PNG 14–15; Mon 84–86.
[39] See "On the Ultimate Origination of Things" (GP VII 307–308/AG 154–155). The contributions minds make to this progress is also the source of their greatest happiness (PNG 18).
[40] For treatments of these issues, see Robert C. Sleigh, Jr., *Leibniz and Arnauld: A Commentary on Their Correspondence* (New Haven: Yale University Press, 1990); Robert M. Adams, *Leibniz: Theist, Determinist, Idealist*; Sukjae Lee, "Leibniz on divine concurrence," in *The Philosophical Review* 113 (2004),

The first doctrine is embraced by all seventeenth-century philosophers. No finite thing is a *causa sui*; it does not exist of itself. It exists only because it has been created by God, and the fact that it exists now in no way diminishes its dependence on God for the continuation of its existence. Rather, God must actively conserve its existence (T 385).

According to the second doctrine, this dependence consists in a thing's receiving from God, throughout its existence, whatever perfection is in it. For Leibniz, this is what it means for a thing to be continually created. It is crucial to Leibniz's theodicy that God is responsible only for the *perfection* of a thing—whatever is positive, real, or good in its nature—and not for its imperfection, which is the source of error and sin. Only in this way can he defend the dogma that God is blameless with regard to the existence of sin and that all blame lies with the sinner. For some, this may seem to let God off the hook too quickly. Sin, or moral evil, is a fact about the world, a property of the actions of every (non-blessed) human will. So, why is God, on whom all created things depend, not responsible for the existence of sin and foolishness as much as for the existence of good and wise deeds?

Although sins are plentiful in the world, Leibniz follows Augustine in denying that they reflect any positive reality in the agent. They are ascribed not to an agent's perfection, but to his lack of perfection, the basis of his inability to recognize and will the good. Given this, Leibniz argues, God bears no responsibility for sin. God continually produces whatever is perfect in a created being. But no created being contains unlimited perfection; it is limited by nature. And it is this limitation—unwilled by God but contained in God's eternal idea of the thing—that explains why it fails to act rightly.[41]

Leibniz identifies the perfections received from God with the divine attributes of power, knowledge, and will. The perfection of power is the capacity to do or produce; the perfection of knowledge, the capacity to represent and comprehend; the perfection of will, the capacity to bring about "changes or products in accordance with the principle of the best." In created substances, these perfections correspond, respectively, to "the subject or the basis [*le sujet ou la Base*]," the "perceptive faculty," and the "appetitive faculty" (Mon 48; GP VI 615/AG 219). The association of power with the "subject or basis" supports the assumption that the capacity to produce change is essential to the nature of a created substance. Leibniz reiterates this point in the *Theodicy*:

> In my system every simple substance (that is, every true substance) must be the true immediate cause of all its actions and inward passions; and, speaking strictly in a metaphysical sense, it has none other than those which it produces. Those who hold a different opinion, and who make God the sole agent . . . unquestionably offend against reason.
>
> (T 400; GP VI 354/H 362–363)

pp. 203–248; Jeffrey K. McDonough, "Leibniz: Creation and conservation and concurrence," in *The Leibniz Review 17* (2007), pp. 31–60.

[41] Cf. Mon 47; T 377–380.

In making every created substance a genuine cause of changes in its states, Leibniz draws a sharp line between his metaphysics and the occasionalism of Malebranche, as well as the monism of Spinoza, which he believes occasionalism tends toward.[42] Still, one might wonder at the charge that occasionalists, in making God the only agent of change, "offend against reason." On the face of it, occasionalism has an easier time of explaining the dependence of all finite creatures on God: they are dependent both for their existence and for all the effects that are ascribed to them. None of these is due to the actions of created substances, for only God acts. In rejecting this view and upholding created substances as genuine causes while also affirming their continual dependence on God, Leibniz sets himself a more difficult explanatory task: how to make created things at once independent of and wholly dependent on God.

In his defense of the third theological doctrine, divine concurrence, Leibniz explores several ways of accommodating this division of causal responsibility. One way is to argue that God's role as the creator and conserver of the power of a finite substance is consistent with that power being exercised by the substance in the production of new modifications. Power, recall, is the "subject or basis" of a substance; if a substance is anything, it is a power to act and produce effects, even if that power itself remains dependent on God for its existence.[43] A second strategy goes beyond this to claim that not just the power but its characteristic effects remain dependent on God. Leibniz argues that successive modifications do not follow necessarily in a created substance, but only contingently, subject to the will of God. Thus, were God not to concur in the actions of a substance, willing that nature follow the same order, those modifications would not exist.[44]

Both of these theses highlight God's role in sustaining the activity of created substances: substances have no power to act unless it is continually given to them by God, and the effects that follow from their actions follow only on the condition that God wills those effects to be the lawful consequences of their causes. Neither thesis, however, fully captures Leibniz's understanding of the depth of God's involvement in the actions of created substances. In *Causa Dei*, the Latin summary of the *Theodicy*, he writes:

> God's *concurrence* . . . is at the same time immediate and special. It is *immediate* since the effect depends upon God not only by virtue of the fact that its cause originates

---

[42] T 393; GP IV 508–509/AG 160–161.

[43] "Neither does it seem to me that we have to deny action or power to created things on the grounds that if they produced modifications they would be creators. For it is God who conserves and continually creates their power, that is to say, the *source* of *modifications* within a created thing, or a state of that thing from which it can be seen that there will be a change of modifications. Otherwise, it seems to me . . . that God would have produced nothing, and there would be no substances other than God—which would bring back all the absurdities of the God of Spinoza" (GP IV 567–568/WFN 122).

[44] "When I speak of the force and the actions of creatures, I understand that each creature is presently great with its future state, and that it naturally follows a certain course, if nothing prevents it. . . . But I do not say because of this that the future state of the creature follows from its present state without the concourse of God, and I am rather of the sentiment that conservation is a continual creation with a change conforming to order" (GP III 566).

in God, but also because God concurs no less nor more indirectly in producing the effect itself than in producing its cause. The concurrence is *special* because it is directed not only at the existence of the thing and its actions, but also at the mode and qualities of existing insofar as there is in them something of perfection, which always flows from God, the father of light and dispenser of all good.

(GP VI 440)

As Leibniz sees it, God's concurrence involves more than just his conservation of a substance's causal power and his willing that such-and-such actions have such-and-such effects. It extends to his willing that such-and-such effects *should* occur "insofar as there is in them something of perfection." Consequently, even if the exercise of the power received from God is the operation of a created substance, which produces changes in its own modifications, God retains a significant role in the occurrence of those effects. Again, this raises the question of God's putative responsibility for sinful acts. Leibniz denies this with the qualification that God wills the effects in question only "insofar as there is in them something of perfection." God wills the effects that follow from a thing's actions to the extent that those effects follow from the *perfection* God has given it, but God does not affirm the effects (or concur with the action) to the extent that they follow from an imperfection in the thing (T 377; T 392).

An obvious response to Leibniz is that it is difficult to see how anything can be produced through a mere absence or privation of perfection. The power that eventuates in a change of modifications is owed to God, who wills the effects that follow from that power. The distinctive contribution of the creature, the part that is independent of God, is limited to what follows from the *absence* of power or perfection. But how is that consistent with there being any genuine causal role for the creature or for its assuming responsibility for the outcome of its actions?

Leibniz's most informative answer to this question falls back on the distinction between the form and matter of a substance. The form of a created substance is what is positive, real and perfect in it: its active power and capacities for distinct representation and striving in accordance with the principle of the best. The primary matter of a created substance is whatever resists, or limits, the actions of its form.[45] In principle, one might take Leibniz's position to be that, strictly speaking, *nothing* resists the actions of its form because nothing has power except form. In practice, under the influence of his work in dynamics, he adopts a dualistic conception of substantial power. Paired with the primitive active power of a substance is a primitive passive power, or primary matter. Although Leibniz identifies the latter with the confusion or lack of distinctness

---

[45] Leibniz relies on this distinction in his image of a heavy boat moved by the current of a river: "Let us now compare the force which the current exercises on boats, and communicates to them, with the action of God, who produces and conserves whatever is positive in creatures, and gives them perfection, being and force: let us compare, I say, the inertia of matter with the natural imperfection of creatures, and the slowness of the laden boat with the defect to be found in the qualities and in the action of the creature" (T 30; GP VI 120/H 141). Cf. T 31–33; GP VI 347–350.

in a monad's perceptions,[46] suggesting again a mere absence of perfection, there is reason to think that his account goes beyond this. We need only note that a monad's primary matter or perceptual confusion is associated with its representation of itself as an embodied creature, existing in a world of other bodies, where those bodies (its own and others) offer resistance to its efforts to will in accordance with the principle of the best (T 124, 130). Those, like Leibniz, of a Platonic disposition may think of facts of embodiment as imperfections in a created substance—ways in which it falls short of the infinite perfection of God. But, for all that, a monad's representation of itself as embodied is a positive fact about the contents of its perceptions that defines its existence as finite and explains its tendency toward sin. This fact certainly seems grounded in something rather than nothing, and it pushes against Leibniz's claim that everything real and positive in a created substance is good or perfect.[47]

CONCLUSION

Our examination of Leibniz's theory of the actual world has drawn together many parts of his philosophy. Leibniz identifies the possible with what is distinctly thinkable, and he insists that nothing possible becomes actual except through the exercise of God's power. God is disposed to create things in proportion to the perfection they are represented as having. To this extent, God has an antecedent will to create all possible things. However, Leibniz claims that God does not render all possibles actual; instead, God's wisdom and justice are expressed in his selecting for creation only the best world from among an infinity of possible worlds.

As part of his critique of Spinoza's metaphysics, Leibniz argues that God must make a choice among possible worlds because not all possibles are "compossible." A considerable literature has debated the meaning of this doctrine. I have proposed that it is best understood as the claim that not all possibles can be conceived as united within the structure of a single world, ordered by spatiotemporal and causal relations. Combined with the idea that God has a unique will to create and that this will has as its object the

---

[46] "Furthermore, since all monads (except the primitive one) are subject to passions, they are not pure forces; they are the foundation not only of actions but of resistance and passivity, and their passions are found in their confused perceptions. It is in this that matter or the numerically infinite is involved" (GP III 636/L 659).

[47] Regarding his own analogy of the laden boat, Leibniz comments in T 380: "I have used it to advantage in this work, in order to have a comparison such as should illustrate how the original imperfection of the creature sets bounds to the action of the Creator, which tends toward good. But as matter [i.e., "secondary matter"] is itself of God's creation, it only furnishes a comparison and an example, and cannot be the very source of evil and of imperfection. I have already shown that this source lies in the forms or ideas of the possibles, for it must be eternal, and matter is not so" (GP VI 341/H 353). Contrast, though, T 392: "But when one includes limitations and privations among the 'realities,' one may say that secondary causes cooperate in the production of that which is limited; otherwise God would be the cause of sin, and even the sole cause" (GP VI 349–350/H 359).

unitary order of a world, the cosmological account supports the conclusion that God creates only one world, leaving the rest as mere possibilities.

Leibniz's fundamental conception of the best of all possible worlds is that it is the world containing the greatest perfection or reality, the greatest intelligibility and order, and, consequently, the greatest harmony. This abstract representation of the optimality of the actual world is fleshed out in the theories of Leibniz's metaphysics. Among the most important claims that elaborate the view is the distinction he draws between the perfection contributed to the world by any substance and the superior perfection introduced by minds that understand and replicate order, imitating God's role within the created world. It is principally on the basis of this perfection-enhancing capacity of minds, which offers each the possibility of an indefinite increase in perfection and pleasure, that Leibniz is confident of this as the best of all possible worlds.

Throughout his writings, Leibniz emphasizes the spontaneity of created substances as agents of change in the world. This holds especially for minds, whose spontaneity takes the form of freedom, wherein they knowingly act for the sake of the best. Leibniz's insistence on the causal independence of created substances is balanced by his affirmation of their continual dependence on God for all there is of perfection in them, both insofar as they exist and insofar as they act. In reconciling these two commitments, the greatest challenge Leibniz faces is explaining not how substances get things right when they act in concord with God, but how they get things wrong when they are left to act (somehow) on their own.

References

Adams, Robert M. 1994. *Leibniz: Determinist, Theist, Idealist.* New York: Oxford University Press.

Blumenfeld, David. 1973. "Leibniz's theory of the striving possibles." *Studia Leibnitiana* 5: 163–177.

Brown, Gregory. 1987. "Compossibility, harmony, and perfection in Leibniz." *The Philosophical Review* 96: 173–203.

Cover, J. A., and John O'Leary–Hawthorne. 1999. *Substance and Individuation in Leibniz.* Cambridge: Cambridge University Press.

Koistinen, Olli, and Arto Repo. 1999. "Compossibility and being in the same world in Leibniz's metaphysics." *Studia Leibnitiana* 31: 196–214.

Kulstad, Mark. 1999. "Leibniz, Spinoza and Tschirnhaus: Multiple worlds, possible worlds." In S. Brown (ed.), *The Young Leibniz and His Philosophy.* Dordrecht: Kluwer, pp. 243–262.

Lee, Sukjae. 2004. "Leibniz on divine concurrence." *The Philosophical Review* 113: 203–248.

Mates, Benson. 1986. *The Philosophy of Leibniz: Metaphysics and Philosophy of Language.* New York: Oxford University Press.

McDonough, Jeffrey K. 2007. "Leibniz: Creation and conservation and concurrence." *The Leibniz Review* 17: 31–60.

McDonough, Jeffrey K. 2010. "Leibniz and the puzzle of incompossibility: The packing strategy." *The Philosophical Review* 119: 135–163.

Messina, James, and Donald Rutherford. 2009. "Leibniz on compossibility." *Philosophy Compass 4*: 962–977.

Rescher, Nicholas. 1979. *Leibniz: An Introduction to His Philosophy*. Lanham, Md.: University Press of America.

Russell, Bertrand. 1937. *A Critical Exposition of the Philosophy of Leibniz*. 2nd ed. London: George Allen and Unwin.

Rutherford, Donald. 1995. *Leibniz and the Rational Order of Nature*. Cambridge: Cambridge University Press.

Rutherford, Donald. 2008. "Leibniz as idealist." *Oxford Studies in Early Modern Philosophy 4*: 141–190.

Sleigh, Robert C., Jr. 1990. *Leibniz and Arnauld: A Commentary on Their Correspondence*. New Haven: Yale University Press.

Wilson, Margaret. 1993. "Compossibility and law." In S. Nadler (ed.), *Causation in Early Modern Philosophy*. University Park: Pennsylvania State University Press, pp. 119–133.

CHAPTER 5

....

FREEDOM AND
CONTINGENCY

....

JEFFREY K. MCDONOUGH

INTRODUCTION

....

BUILDERS build. Farmers farm. But what do philosophers do? One answer to this embarrassingly difficult question is that philosophers engage in conceptual engineering.[1] They hone, shape, and construct concepts that are above all useful. In doing so, they are constrained on two sides. On the one side, they are beholden to common thought and language. One could, for example, shape a concept of an omnipotent being that barks and delivers pizza but it is not clear what would be the point; introducing such a concept would only invite confusion. On the other side, philosophers are beholden to the goals of improvement and consistency. A philosopher carving out a concept of justice aims to provide insight and coherence. She fails in her task if she only tells us what every lexicographer knows or if her account proves self-contradictory.

The concepts of freedom and contingency, as they are used in ordinary language, are ripe for conceptual engineering. Our workaday understanding of freedom has many connotations but no precise and fixed meaning. It is associated, for example, with the ability to make decisions, determine courses of action, and with being responsible. It is also intertwined with the intuitive, if elusive, conviction that things could have gone otherwise. The question of how the various connotations associated with freedom should be fit together into a coherent whole is a good job for the conceptual engineer—a job that to this day remains unfinished. Much the same is true for the concept of contingency. It also has many connotations but no precise and fixed meaning. It overlaps

---

[1] For various developments of this thought, see Blackburn (1999), Brandom (2001), Burgess and Plunkett (2013a, 2013b), Chalmers (2011) and Eklund (2015). I owe special thanks to Sam Levey for helpful discussion of the relationship between Leibniz and conceptual engineering.

with our workaday understanding of freedom, especially in the thought that things could have gone otherwise. But it also has its own distinct family of connotations. It is linked, for example, to our understanding of notions such as determinism and chance. It is constrained by our willingness to make transitions among a family of modal notions; for example, by our willingness to infer from something's being contingent that it is not necessary.

Leibniz's work on freedom and contingency is, I think, best understood as an exercise in conceptual engineering.[2] Leibniz has a sense of what he thinks these concepts are good for—of how they can and should be used. Paramount in this regard are the roles that freedom and contingency play in making sense of divine and human responsibility. God is to be praised for his creation, but in order to be praiseworthy, God must be free and his creation—so it might seem—must be contingent. We are to be rewarded and punished for our voluntary actions, but in order to be worthy of reward and punishment, we must be free and our actions—so it might seem—must be contingent. Although Leibniz shapes concepts of freedom and contingency that he thinks are useful to his ends, nonetheless he does not carve with an utterly free hand. He is eager to show that his concepts of freedom and contingency are at least continuous with everyday usage and the understanding of his predecessors. Leibniz wants to improve our concepts of freedom and contingency; he does not wish to simply discard them and start wholly anew. The next section will explore Leibniz's conception of freedom. Subsequent sections will turn to Leibniz's understanding of contingency.

Freedom

Leibniz's understanding of freedom is anchored in three necessary conditions (GP VI 288–290/H 302–304). The first condition is *intelligence*, which Leibniz calls the "soul of freedom." Rational agents alone enjoy intelligence and so, for Leibniz, rational agents alone enjoy freedom in the fullest sense. But why is intelligence so important? Leibniz tells us that intelligence "involves a clear knowledge of the object of deliberation" and that it "occurs in the actual use of reason" (GP VII 288/H 303). His thought seems to

---

[2] In a letter to Gerhard Wolter Molanus of February 1698, Leibniz says as much himself:

> But the more I consider the matter, the more manifestly I seem to myself to see that the error was not so much in realities as in formulas, on account of assumed definitions of freedom, necessity, will, and right that are not only less philosophical, and less familiar, but also less suited to edification. . . . What if therefore, as I am almost persuaded, by merely developing definitions all that harshness could be softened, and it is permitted to remove the controversy about which people have sounded so tragic; do you think this should be neglected?
>
> (Schrecker, 1934, 84; cited and translated in Adams, 1994, 30).

be that intelligence allows us—at least in principle—to understand the actual good in objects of choice. It thus puts us in a position to weigh the true value of the options we confront and to choose accordingly. In doing so, it places us in a deliberative position not unlike God's deliberative position. For God, of course, chooses under conditions of perfect comprehension. The rational ability to determine our actions in light of the true value of the potential outcomes of our actions is thus, Leibniz suggests, the very heart of freedom in its fullest sense.

Leibniz nonetheless allows that in our current state we seldom, if ever, choose under conditions of perfect intellectual clarity. Our senses bombard us with confused thoughts, and we constantly make decisions on the basis of imperfect assessments of the value of the potential outcomes of our actions. To this extent we are, according to Leibniz, "the slaves of passion" and we seem to differ little from unintelligent beasts. Leibniz maintains that even under such circumstances, however, we may enjoy a sort of second-rate freedom, the "freedom of a slave" (GP VI 288/H 303). Leibniz's thought here is that even when we are not in a position to weigh the true value of the options we confront, we may nonetheless determine our actions by the apparent value of the options we face. Even where we are not free in the fullest sense of the term, we may nonetheless be free insofar as we may pursue ends that seem best to us at a particular time. Being determined by what seems best to us—whether it actually is or not—thus seems central to Leibniz's understanding of freedom in a somewhat broader, perhaps more realistic sense.

The second necessary condition for freedom Leibniz calls *spontaneity*: in order to be free, one must be an immediate causal source of one's own actions (GP VI 289–290/H 303–304). A baseball thrown through the air is not free, in part because it does not causally determine its own trajectory. Likewise, I am not free when I am pushed out of an airplane because, when pushed, I do not causally determine my exit. When I jump out of a plane myself, however, I am free since I do causally determine my exit. Leibniz's commitment to the condition of spontaneity is closely related to his critique of occasionalism—that is, the doctrine that God is the only genuine cause in the world (GP VI 292–293/H 306–307). Leibniz maintains that the doctrine of occasionalism would undermine all creaturely independence since, if occasionalism were true, no creature could be a genuine causal source of his or her own actions. By Leibniz's lights, the truth of occasionalism would mean that no creature could be spontaneous, and, thus, no creature could be free.

According to Leibniz's own mature metaphysics, all substances satisfy the condition of spontaneity (GP VI 289/H 304). For according to Leibniz's mature metaphysics, each genuine creature is not only causally isolated from every other genuine creature but is furthermore the immediate causal source of all its activities. Apparent causal interactions between creatures are, on Leibniz's view, the result of synchronized endogenous changes. When it looks like someone pushes me out of a plane, what really happens, according to Leibniz, is that the pusher does what she does as a result of her own causal power, while I do what I do as a result of my own causal power. The condition of spontaneity thus seems to be very easily satisfied. Indeed, perhaps too easily satisfied. If every creaturely action is causally driven from within, a common resource for distinguishing between voluntary and involuntary actions is lost. We can no longer appeal to a distinction between external and internal causes in order to distinguish between my being involuntarily pushed out of a plane and my voluntarily jumping out of a plane (see GP IV 517–524/WFN 79–86; for discussion, see Rutherford, 2005, and McDonough, 2016).

A third necessary condition for freedom is *contingency*: for an action to be free it must be contingent (GP VI 288/H 303; GP VI 296–297/H 310). If it is absolutely necessary that I eat an ice cream sundae, then I cannot eat an ice cream sundae freely. More centrally to Leibniz's concerns, if it is absolutely necessary that (say) Judas sins, then Judas cannot sin freely.

One might wonder how personally committed Leibniz is to the condition of contingency. In early works, he sometimes suggests that God's creation is both free and necessary (see, for example, A VI iii 122/Sleigh 45; A II i 117–118/Sleigh 3–5). Furthermore, throughout his career, Leibniz subscribes to compatibilism; that is to say, throughout his career, Leibniz maintains that freedom is consistent with causal determinism. He thus allows that I may jump out of a plane freely even if I am causally determined to jump out of a plane. He allows that Judas may sin freely even if Judas is causally determined to sin. Compatibilism, however, might make the condition of contingency seem less urgent. If I can jump out of a plane freely in spite of being causally determined, why should it matter whether or not there are other possible worlds in which I don't jump out of a plane? If Judas can sin freely in spite of being causally determined to sin, why should it matter whether or not his sinning is contingent?

Whatever his personal convictions may have been, Leibniz nonetheless repeatedly and publicly endorses contingency as a necessary condition for freedom, especially in his *Theodicy* (see, e.g., GP VI 37/H 61, GP VI 288/H 303, GP VI 296–297/H 310). It is possible that, in spite of his early wavering, he came to share the intuition that one cannot sin freely if one's sinning is not in some sense contingent. It is also possible that Leibniz privately rejected the condition of contingency even while publicly endorsing it, perhaps with the aim of currying favor or educating a wary public (see GP III 66–67/WFN 127; for discussion, see Whipple, 2015). Or, finally, it is possible—and this seems most likely to me—that Leibniz, the conceptual engineer, saw a tension between what he took to be the demands of utility and the demands of common usage. Perhaps he was never deeply convinced that a useful concept of freedom must make reference to contingency. But perhaps he also came to recognize that any concept of freedom that does not presuppose contingency threatens a dangerous rupture with ordinary usage. If that's right, Leibniz must have been alarmed that various features of his philosophical system might seem to rule out contingency altogether. The next section will therefore explore some of the ways in which Leibniz's philosophical system might seem to commit him to the view that all truths are necessary. Subsequent sections will look at Leibniz's attempts to resist the threat of necessitarianism.

NECESSITARIANISM?

Necessitarianism is the view that there are no contingent truths—that everything that is actually the case is necessarily the case. According to necessitarianism, its being sunny in Leipzig on the first of July 1646 is, if true, every bit as necessary as its being the case that triangles have three sides. According to necessitarianism, Judas's betraying Christ for thirty silver coins is, if true, every bit as necessary as two plus two equaling four. Many philosophers have been eager to deny necessitarianism. They suggest that it is simply implausible to suppose, for example, that my taking a sip of coffee is every bit as necessary as, say, the Pythagorean Theorem. They suggest that necessitarianism would run roughshod over important philosophical distinctions, that it would, for example, ruin the crucial distinction between essential and accidental properties. Leibniz's understanding of freedom, however, gives him a very specific reason for rejecting necessitarianism. As we've seen, Leibniz maintains that freedom and responsibility presuppose contingency and, thus, presuppose the denial of necessitarianism.

At least three commitments of Leibniz's philosophical system nonetheless seem to drive him toward necessitarianism. The first such commitment is the principle of sufficient reason. Put baldly, the principle of sufficient reason states that nothing happens without a sufficient reason. If there is a flash of lightning, there must be a sufficient reason for the flash of lightning. If I rob a bank, there must be a sufficient reason for my robbing a bank. Contingency, however, might seem to require that things could have gone otherwise: that there might not have been a flash of lightning; that I might not have committed a crime. But how could things have gone otherwise given the principle of sufficient reason? Perhaps a current event could have gone otherwise if a previous event had gone otherwise. But how could a previous event have gone otherwise? Perhaps a previous event could have gone otherwise if a still earlier event had gone otherwise. But how could a still earlier event have gone otherwise? A regress obviously rears its head. Some have thought, with David Hume, that such a regress is acceptable—that a regress of sufficient reasons might go back forever, one reason being sufficient for the next without any reason being necessary (Hume, 1998, 56). Leibniz, however, does not share Hume's sanguinity. He insists that any chain of sufficient reasons must ultimately terminate in a necessary reason (G VII 302–308/L 486). But if any chain of sufficient reasons must terminate in a necessary reason, it is hard to see how any of those reasons might be counted as contingent. If a prior reason is necessary and is sufficient for a subsequent reason, it is hard to see how that subsequent reason could be anything other than necessary as well.

Leibniz is also driven toward necessitarianism by a family of widely held theological views. Like most of his contemporaries, Leibniz believes that God is omnipotent and wholly good. But if God is omnipotent, it seems he must be able to bring about whatever he wills, and if he is omnibenevolent, it seems he must will the best. If, say, a flash of lightning would be for the best, it seems that God must will it, and if God wills it, it seems that it must come to pass. But how then could things have gone otherwise? How could the flash of lightning—or any other event—be contingent? Likewise, Leibniz believes that God is omniscient. But God's omniscience implies that God knows everything that will ever happen. He is ignorant of nothing, not even future events. But if God knows everything that will ever happen, how can anything happen otherwise (see, for example, A VI i 539/Sleigh 9)? If God knows that I will rob a bank, how can it be possible that I won't rob a bank? How can my robbing a bank be contingent?

A third commitment pushing Leibniz toward necessitarianism is his understanding of truth and logic. Leibniz accepts a somewhat idiosyncratic account of truth, a clear statement of which is given in a short piece dated to the mid-1680s:

> Therefore, the predicate or consequent is always in the subject or antecedent, and the nature of truth in general or the connection between the terms of a statement, consists in this very thing. . . . The connection and inclusion of the predicate in the subject is explicit in identities, but in all other propositions it is implicit. (A VI iv 1644/AG 31)

The core idea here is that, in a true statement, the statement's predicate must be contained in its subject. If, for example, the statement "Betty is tall" is true, the predicate expressed by ". . . is tall" must be contained in the concept of Betty. This is a radical view of truth. It presupposes that all statements can be put in subject–predicate form, and it says nothing about how propositions relate to the world. Nonetheless, it is not entirely implausible as an account of analytic truths. Perhaps the statement "Tricycles have three wheels" is true because the concept expressed by ". . . has three wheels" is somehow contained in the subject expressed by "tricycles." As part of his views on logic, Leibniz further maintains that for every genuine subject there is a complete concept containing every predicate that will ever be true of that subject (A VI iv 1540/AG 41). So, for example, Leibniz maintains that there must be a complete concept corresponding to Julius Caesar, and that that complete concept must contain every predicate true of Caesar. If Caesar crossed the Rubicon, Caesar's complete concept must contain the predicate expressed by ". . . crossed the Rubicon." If Caesar was stabbed by Brutus, Caesar's complete concept must contain the predicate expressed by ". . . stabbed by Brutus."

Taken together, Leibniz's views on truth and logic might seem to imply that every true statement is analytic in the sense that it is true simply in virtue of the concepts it expresses. The statement "Caesar crossed the Rubicon," for example, appears to be true simply because the predicate expressed by ". . . crossed the Rubicon" is contained in the concept expressed by "Caesar." Likewise for the statement "Betty is tall" or "Bill is handsome." Statements that are analytic in this sense, however, are commonly thought to express necessary truths. If, for example, "All tricycles have three wheels" expresses a proposition that is true simply in virtue of the concepts it involves, how then could that proposition possibly be false? How could that proposition be contingent? But if all truths for Leibniz are analytic truths, and all analytic truths are indeed necessary, how could there be any contingent truths? Leibniz's views on truth and logic thus seem to push him once again into the arms of necessitarianism. The next two sections will explore Leibniz's attempts to avoid its allegedly chilly embrace.

PER SE CONTINGENCY

Rather than abandoning either his conception of freedom or his philosophical commitments, Leibniz responds to the threat of necessitarianism by trying to refine our concept of contingency itself. His theory of per se contingency represents his first effort in this regard (see, in particular, A VI iii 116–149/Sleigh 26–109). At the heart of Leibniz's theory of per se contingency is the thought that something might be contingent considered per se, that is, considered by itself, even if it is necessary in light of God's goodness or will. Perhaps God's will entails that he creates the best of all possible worlds. And perhaps the existence of the best of all possible worlds entails that Judas exists, and, that if Judas exists, that Judas sins. If that is right, we might say that Judas's existing is hypothetically necessary; that is to say, necessary on the hypothesis of God's will. Does that mean that Judas's existence is in no sense contingent? Maybe not. Leibniz suggests that considered per se—that is, considered in isolation—Judas might or might not have existed, and, if he had not existed, he would not have sinned. Leibniz concludes that even if Judas's existence and sinning are hypothetically necessary, they are nonetheless contingent per se. Necessitarianism may be avoided—and freedom preserved—since there is, after all, a sense in which at least some truths are contingent.

It is tempting to object that Leibniz's theory of per se contingency is nothing more than sophistry—that per se contingency is not genuine contingency and that Leibniz has tried to avoid the threat of necessitarianism by simply redefining words. If we take seriously the role of conceptual engineering in Leibniz's philosophy, however, this objection—at least flatly stated—loses, I think, much of its force. Confronting a tension between his account of freedom and his broader philosophical commitments, why shouldn't Leibniz refine our admittedly hazy conception of contingency in a way that suits his needs? Why shouldn't he offer us a concept of contingency intentionally shaped to be consistent with other things he believes to be true? Having whittled a round hole, why not whittle a round peg?

Even granting a role for conceptual engineering, however, Leibniz's theory of per se contingency faces a number of serious objections. One objection suggests that Leibniz's proposed emendation of our concept of contingency simply goes too far. The following modal entailment principle is widely accepted and seems deeply entrenched in our ordinary ways of thinking: if an antecedent entails a consequent, and the antecedent is necessary, then the consequent is necessary as well; that is, if p entails q, and it is necessary that p, then it is necessary that q. Leibniz's theory of per se contingency offers him a way to reject that modal principle. It allows him to say, as he does, "that it is false that whatever follows from something <per se> necessary is itself necessary <per se>" (A VI iii 127/Sleigh 55). By the rules of the conceptual engineer, this is, in a sense, fair enough. Conceptual engineering is surely an art rather than a science, and it may be impossible to sharply separate a concept's "fixed points" from its negotiable features (see Eklund, 2015). Nonetheless, not all proposed revisions are equal, and not all must be accepted. If Leibniz is free to shape concepts to suit his purposes, we are also free to reject his proposals as suits our purposes. If it is fair enough for Leibniz to propose rejecting the modal entailment principle presented earlier, it is also fair enough for us to insist upon it.

Another objection to Leibniz's per se theory of contingency draws on a very different set of intuitions. As we've seen, Leibniz's interest in contingency is intimately related to his thinking about freedom and responsibility. Is Leibniz's theory of per se contingency sufficient for meeting the demands of divine and creaturely responsibility? Leibniz had grounds for thinking so. In thinking about divine responsibility, Leibniz seems to have been concerned above all to show that God's will plays an essential role in determining the existence of creatures since, as Leibniz puts it, "it is not at all to be thought that all things follow from God's nature without any intervention of the will" (A VI iii 364). Leibniz's per se theory of contingency notably preserves just such a role for the divine will. If we bracket the divine will, Judas's existence is merely per se possible. It is only hypothetically necessary in light of God's "will or understanding of the good" (G I 150/L 205). Relatedly, Leibniz's theory of per se contingency does nothing to threaten the thought that Judas's actions flow from his own will—that his actions are the immediate results of his own volitions. Leibniz's theory of per se contingency might therefore meet Leibniz's own standards for responsibility. But, again, we might demur. One might think that divine and creaturely freedom require a more robust sense of contingency. One might think that if God creates on the hypothesis of his necessary goodness, then God does not create freely. Divine freedom requires not just alternatives but alternatives that God could act on. One might think that if Judas sins on the hypothesis that he exists, then similarly Judas does not sin freely. Human freedom requires more than bare contingency: it requires alternatives that an agent could realize.

FORMAL CONTINGENCY

It is a testament to Leibniz's ingenuity that he offers not one, but two theories of contingency. With his second theory of contingency, Leibniz suggests that the distinction between necessary and contingent propositions can be drawn in logical terms. So, for example, in his *De Contingentia*, tentatively dated to 1689, Leibniz writes:

> And with this secret the distinction between necessary and contingent truths is revealed, something not easily understood unless one has some acquaintance with mathematics. For in necessary propositions, when the analysis is continued indefinitely, one arrives at an identical equation by means of an analysis continued to a

certain point; this is what it is to demonstrate a truth with geometrical rigor. But in contingent propositions one continues the analysis to infinity through reasons for reasons, so that one never has a complete demonstration, though there is always, underneath, a reason for the truth, but the reason is understood completely only by God, who alone traverses the infinite series in one stroke of mind. (A VI iv 1650/AG 28, translation modified)

In this and similar passages, Leibniz seems to point toward a logical or formal theory of contingency. In the case of necessary truths, logical analysis is supposed to yield finite demonstrations. Starting with only definitions and armed with the laws of logic, we can demonstrate necessary truths. In the case of contingent propositions, logical analysis does not yield finite demonstrations. Starting with only definitions and armed with the laws of logic, we cannot demonstrate contingent truths.

It is again tempting to object that Leibniz's theory of formal contingency is more sophistry than substance. That is to say, it is tempting to object that he is introducing a conception of contingency that has little to do with our everyday notions of contingency (see, e.g., Bennett, 2001, 329). In replying, Leibniz could once again take some refuge in his role as a conceptual engineer. The conceptual engineer is free—within limits—to prefer utility to common usage. But Leibniz could also emphasize that his theory of formal contingency in fact has deep roots in our ordinary ways of thinking. In philosophical discussions of contingency, it is easy to focus—as we have thus far—on intuitions concerning freedom, responsibility, and counterfactual alternatives. But the distinction between necessary and contingent truths is also intimately related to well-entrenched epistemological intuitions. It is natural to suppose that necessary truths can, at least in principle, be demonstrated a priori. If we are to know that $2 + 2 = 4$ or that the Pythagorean Theorem is true, logical demonstration seems to be the right, indeed only, approach. Contingent truths, in contrast, cannot be logically demonstrated a priori. Contingent truths such as that it was sunny last Tuesday or that Leibniz was born in 1646 are the wrong sort of truths altogether to be given a logical demonstration from definitions alone. In order to know facts about the weather and birthdays, we have to touch base with experience somewhere.

In explicating Leibniz's formal theory of contingency, commentators have generally supposed that Leibniz is drawing a distinction between propositions that have and propositions that do not have finite proofs. On this approach, necessary truths are knowable (by us) by logical demonstration because there are finite proofs of necessary truths. Demonstrating a necessary truth is akin to serially summing a finite series of numbers. Contingent truths, in contrast, are not knowable (by us) by logical demonstration because there are no finite proofs of contingent truths. Demonstrating a contingent truth would be like serially summing an infinite series of numbers. No wonder then that we can know necessary truths by logical demonstration but contingent truths only with the aid of experience.

The thought that Leibniz's formal theory of contingency is driven by a distinction between truths that have finite proofs and truths that do not is a reasonable one that can find some basis in Leibniz's texts. Nonetheless, it runs into a now well-known difficulty first articulated by Robert Adams. In reference to the proposition *Peter is a denier of Christ*, he writes:

> Even if infinitely many properties and events are contained in the complete concept of Peter, at least one of them will be proved in the first step of any analysis. Why couldn't it be Peter's denial? Why couldn't we begin to analyze Peter's concept by saying, "Peter is a denier of Christ and . . ."? (1994, 34)

The difficulty articulated by Adams, known as the Problem of the Lucky Proof, has deep roots in Leibniz's understanding of language and logic. Given Leibniz's understanding of the nature of propositions, of truth, and of demonstration, it is hard to see how there couldn't be finite proofs of contingent truths. Indeed, it is hard to see how there couldn't be very short proofs for all contingent truths.

Two main strategies have emerged for responding to the problem of the Lucky Proof. The first strategy suggests that, for Leibniz, something extra-logical must constrain the order of the steps in a logical demonstration (see, e.g., Adams, 1994, 34; Hawthorne and Cover, 2000; Merlo, 2012). So, for example, on one way of developing this general strategy, it has been suggested that a demonstration of a truth about Peter would have to proceed in the same order as the causal unfolding of Peter's intrinsic states (Hawthorne and Cover, 2000). Before one could prove that Peter is a denier, one would have to prove that Peter was a disciple. Before one could prove that Peter is a disciple, one would have to prove that Peter was a fisherman, and so on. On the plausible assumption that the series of states preceding Peter's denial is infinite, one could secure the result that no finite proof could reach the conclusion that Peter is a denier. The Problem of the Lucky Proof would thus be blocked.

Although intuitive and tempting, this first strategy for addressing the Problem of the Lucky Proof faces well-known difficulties. The causal version just sketched implies that Peter's initial state is necessary while all his subsequent states are contingent. That is, it implies, for example, that if Peter is created with brown hair, his having brown hair is necessary at the moment of his creation but contingent a minute later. An odd consequence at the least. More worrisome, however, this first strategy threatens to undermine Leibniz's sophisticated understanding of deductive proof. Unlike most of his contemporaries, Leibniz had a profound appreciation of proof as a formal procedure—that is, of proof as a procedure that depends on the form of inference, not on the meaning of the terms involved. He recognized that the validity of inferences from premises such as "if p then q" and "p" to the conclusion "q" does not depend on what "p" and "q" represent. The inference is valid regardless of whether p and q stand for dogs, cats, or parakeets. By tying logical inference to extra-logical considerations, this first strategy for responding to the Problem of the Lucky Proof threatens to undermine the very foundations of Leibniz's sophisticated understanding of logic.

A second strategy for responding to the Problem of the Lucky Proof is inspired by Leibniz's thinking about the ontological argument for God's existence (see, e.g., Maher, 1980, 238–239; Hawthorne and Cover, 2000, 153–156; and Rodriguez-Pereyra and Lodge,

2011). Leibniz famously maintains that an a priori demonstration of God's existence would require two steps. First, a demonstration that the concept of a necessary being is consistent. Second, a demonstration that such a being exists. Perhaps then a demonstration of any truth should similarly involve two steps. First, a check to show that the subject-concept is consistent. Second, a demonstration to show that the relevant predicate is contained in the subject-concept (A VI iii 582–583/Parkinson 105–107). If all that were the case, one might hope that the Problem of the Lucky Proof could be addressed by the first step. In general, for Leibniz, contingent propositions involve subject-concepts that are infinitely complex. Demonstrating that such concepts are consistent would therefore seem to require infinitely many steps. While there might be a "lucky proof" that a particular predicate is contained in a particular subject, the point would be moot. Even if one were lucky enough to demonstrate that a particular predicate is contained in a particular subject, one would still have to prove that the subject-concept itself is consistent—an infinite task.

This second strategy for blocking the Problem of the Lucky Proof is ingenious and can find some basis in Leibniz's thought. It also, however, faces well-known difficulties. Most importantly, it implies that any proposition involving an infinitely complex subject-concept will be contingent. But not all of the propositions that Leibniz thinks involve infinitely complex subject-concepts seem to be contingent. In particular, Leibniz himself suggests that all explicit identity statements must be necessary. He tells us, for example, that "An animal is an animal" is true in itself (A VI iv 292/P 42) and that "identical propositions are necessary without any understanding or resolution of the terms, for I know that A is A regardless of what is understood by A" (G I 194/L 187). By the lights of the second strategy for blocking the Problem of the Lucky Proof, however, the propositions expressed by "An animal is an animal" and "Peter is Peter" should be counted as contingent—a result inconsistent not only with contemporary convictions but also with Leibniz's own explicit remarks.

Leibniz's work on ideal languages and algorithmic machines might suggest a rather different strategy for making sense of his formal theory of contingency (see McDonough and Soysal, 2016, forthcoming). Drawing inspiration from figures such as Johann Heinrich Alsted, Johann Heinrich Bisterfeld, Jan Amos Comenius, Athanasius Kircher, and Raymond Lull, Leibniz hoped to discover an ideal language consisting of primitive simple concepts, complex concepts composed from those simple concepts, and valid rules of inference and substitution (for discussion and texts, see Antognazza, 2009, 62–63; Arthur, 2014, 29–32; Hotson, 2000, 39–50, 82–94, 150, 163–177). Leibniz maintains that users of such a language could carry out inferences algorithmically and solve arguments with mathematical certainty. Indeed, in a crucial analogy, Leibniz suggests that primitive concepts could be designated with prime numbers, complex concepts with non-prime numbers, and inferential rules could be modeled on the rules of algebra. Armed with such a language, even philosophical interlocutors could resolve their disputes with no more difficulty than calculating a bill. Even diametrically opposed parties could resolve their disputes by declaring, in Leibniz's words, "let us calculate!" (A VI iv 964; see also A VI iv 913).

Leibniz's work on ideal languages is closely related to his groundbreaking work on algorithmic machines. With stunning insight, Leibniz recognized that it should be possible for even a machine to carry out genuinely formal operations. If a logic or language could be manipulated without understanding the terms involved, then even a machine operating "blindly" ought to be able to successfully follow its rules. In the late 1670s, Leibniz famously brought that insight to fruition, inventing the first machine capable of carrying out all four algebraic operations of addition, subtraction, multiplication, and division. Leibniz's "Step Reckoner" surpassed Blaise Pascal's earlier calculating machine, the "Pascaline," precisely in its ability to solve, in an algorithmic fashion, problems not only of addition and subtraction, but also of multiplication and division.

Leibniz's work on ideal languages and algorithmic machines reveals his deep interest not only in formal systems and demonstrations per se, but also in the reach and limitations of formal systems. Perhaps then his theory of formal contingency is rooted most deeply not in whether or not, in the abstract, there exist finite proofs for contingent truths, but rather in whether or not there is a "blind" formal procedure that one might follow for demonstrating those truths from definitions in an ideal language. Put differently, perhaps his formal theory of contingency is rooted in the thought that necessary truths—like the truths of algebra—can be algorithmically decided from definitions alone, while contingent truths—truths about the weather and birthdays—cannot be so decided from definitions alone. To settle disputes about necessary truths, we need only avail ourselves of definitions and logical analysis. Turn the crank enough times, and we are guaranteed an answer. To settle disputes about contingent truths, we must reach beyond a priori definitions. To settle disputes about the weather and birthdays we must appeal, at some point, to experience. Turn the crank forever, and we might still never find an answer. In short: necessary truths are "decidable" a priori; contingent truths are not. Because it appeals not just to proofs but to properties about proofs, such an interpretation might be a called a *meta-logical interpretation*.

The prospects of a meta-logical interpretation of Leibniz's formal theory of contingency have been less fully explored than those of other interpretations. Some will no doubt object that such an interpretation does not block the possibility of a lucky proof. If a proof is understood as nothing more than a string of transformations starting with definitions and yielding an explicit identity statement, then the objection—as far as it goes—is surely correct. But there are clear avenues of response to explore. Leibniz could, for example, demand that a proof is not just a string of formal manipulations that one chances upon, but rather a string that can be systematically derived, a string that is generated by an algorithmic procedure or rule. Others may object that a meta-logical interpretation requires resources beyond Leibniz's ken. And, indeed, it should be granted that the formal notions that it relies on were not worked out in full rigor before the early twentieth century and are unlikely at any rate to fully vindicate Leibniz's position. Nonetheless, it is undeniable that Leibniz was almost eerily prescient concerning related mathematical and logical matters, and it is no stretch at all to suppose that he might have had at least an intuitive grasp of the technical notions presupposed by a meta-logical interpretation. Even if Leibniz wasn't in a position to work out all the technical details himself, it is hard not to admire the ingenuity of his formal theory of contingency. It is hard not to appreciate his insight that our concept of contingency has roots extending beyond its implications for freedom and necessitarianism. It is hard not to respect his willingness to revisit even those further implications in the search for a useful conception of contingency.

CONCLUSION

Leibniz's work on freedom and contingency is striking, challenging, and deep. Where other philosophers might be content to explicate our everyday intuitions concerning freedom and contingency, Leibniz presses further. He asks not just what our concepts of freedom and contingency are, but what they should be. He aims to reshape our understanding of what it means for an agent to be free and for something to be contingent in the hopes of improving our overall philosophical outlook. The results can be jarring. We are tempted to object that Leibniz's freedom is no freedom at all. That his contingency is contingency in name only. But Leibniz's thoughts on this topic, as on so many others, repay careful attention. Even if we are not won over, seeing how Leibniz proposes to shape concepts of freedom and contingency to suit his purposes may lead us to wonder how well our concepts are suited to our purposes. Witnessing Leibniz's efforts to reengineer concepts of freedom and contingency may embolden us to do the same.

REFERENCES

Adams, Robert M. 1994. *Leibniz: Determinist, Theist, Idealist.* New York: Oxford University Press.

Antognazza, Maria Rosa. 2009. *Leibniz: An Intellectual Biography.* Cambridge: Cambridge University Press.

Arthur, Richard T. 2014. *Leibniz.* Malden, Mass.: Polity Press.

Bennett, Jonathan. 2001. *Learning from Six Philosophers: Descartes, Spinoza, Leibniz.* Oxford: Oxford University Press.

Blackburn, Simon. 1999. *Think.* New York: Oxford University Press.

Brandom, Robert. 2001. "Modality, normativity, and intentionality." *Philosophy and Phenomenological Research* 63: 587–609.

Burgess, Alexis, and David Plunkett. 2013a. "Conceptual ethics I." *Philosophy Compass* 8: 1091–1101.

Burgess, Alexis, and David Plunkett. 2013b. "Conceptual ethics II." *Philosophy Compass* 8: 1102–1110.

Chalmers, David. 2011. "Verbal disputes." *Philosophical Review* 120: 515–566.

Eklund, Matti. 2015. "Intuitions, conceptual engineering, and conceptual fixed points." In Chris Daly (ed.), *The Palgrave Handbook of Philosophical Methods.* London: Palgrave Macmillan, pp. 363–385.

Hawthorne, John, and Jan Cover. 2000. "Infinite analysis and the Problem of the Lucky Proof." *Studia Leibnitiana* 32: 151–165.

Hotson, Howard. 2000. *John Heinrich Alsted 1588–1638: Between Renaissance, Reformation, and Universal Reform*. Oxford: Clarendon.

Hume. 1998. *Dialogues Concerning Natural Religion*, 2nd edition. Richard Popkin (ed.). (Indianapolis, Ind.: Hackett).

Maher, Patrick. 1980. "Leibniz on contingency." *Studia Leibnitiana* 12: 236–242.

Merlo, Giovanni. 2012. "Complexity, existence and infinite analysis," *Leibniz Review* 22: 9–36.

McDonough, Jeffrey K. 2016. "Leibniz on monadic agency and optimal form." In Arnauld Pelletier (ed.), *Studia Leibnitiana Sonderheft, Leibniz and Experience*. Stuttgart: Franz Steiner Verlag, pp. 93–118.

McDonough, Jeffrey K., and Zeynep Soysal. Forthcoming. "Leibniz's Formal Theory of Contingency." In Katherine Dunlop and Samuel Levey (eds.), *Logical Analysis and History of Philosophy: From Leibniz to Kant*.

McDonough, Jeffrey K., and Zeynep Soysal. 2016. "Leibniz's formal theory of contingency developed." In Ute Beckmann, et al. (eds.), *Internationaler Leibniz-Kongress X Vorträge*, vol. 1, eds. New York: Georg Olms Verlag, pp. 451–466.

Rodriguez-Pereyra, Gonzalo, and Paul Lodge. 2011. "Infinite analysis, lucky proof, and guaranteed proof in Leibniz." *Archiv für Geschichte der Philosophie* 93: 222–236.

Rutherford, Donald. 2005. "Leibniz on Spontaneity." In D. Rutherford and J. Cover (eds.), *Leibniz: Nature and Freedom*. Oxford: Oxford University Press, pp. 156–180.

Schrecker, Paul. 1934. *G. W. Leibniz: Lettres et Fragments Inédits*. Paris: Librairie Félix Alcan.

Wipple, John. 2015. "Leibniz and the art of exoteric writing." *Philosophers' Imprint* 15: 35.

CHAPTER 6

··

THE PROBLEM OF EVIL AND THE JUSTICE OF GOD

··

PAUL RATEAU

THE way Leibniz tackles the problem of evil is original, as it is explicitly connected with the theme of justice[1]. The first question evil raises is not "Why does it exist?" or the traditional "Where does it come from?" (*Unde malum?*), but rather "Who is responsible for it?" The issue is first moral and juridical, because it is the question of imputation that is at stake. Obviously, the metaphysical aspects and implications of the problem are not overlooked, but they are considered subsequently, when the inquiry has led to the origin of evil and to its essence or nature. Why does Leibniz adopt this juridical approach? It is well known that he was a jurist. One might say that Leibniz pleads God's cause as an advocate would do in a human trial. Clearly the rules of controversy that are explained and applied in the Preliminary Dissertation[2], on the occasion of the discussion of the conformity of faith with reason, are inspired by the judicial debate.

However, I think that Leibniz adopts a juridical point of view for a more fundamental reason: because he considers *injustice* to be the real evil. Injustice is all that violates the law (natural or positive): the injustice committed (sin) as well as the injustice suffered (physical pain and moral grief when not deserved). For Leibniz evil is not a scandal in itself. It becomes shocking when it seems to be unjustly allocated, when pain befalls one who did not deserve it, when sin is not followed by any punishment and is even profitable to the sinner. The existence of suffering, misfortunes, calamities, and the fact that there are wicked people in the world would not be so problematic if this suffering, these misfortunes and calamities, happened only to the wicked. Evil would be easily justified in this case, as it would appear to be natural castigation for their sins. What raises a problem is that the right order of things seems to have been turned upside down. We

---

[1] See for example: *Von der Allmacht*, A VI, 1, §§ 1–3, 537; *Confessio Philosophi*, A VI, 3, 116; in *De libertate, fato, gratia Dei*, A VI, 4-B, 1596–97, the demonstration of the proposition: "God is not the cause of evil or sin" directly follows the demonstration of the proposition: "God is supremely just."

[2] See in particular § 58 and § 72 to § 79.

thus see that the good are persecuted and suffer, that criminals commit their crimes with impunity and even seem to be rewarded by the happiness they get. Leibniz stresses this blatant contradiction between *fact* and *right*, which is felt to be intolerable under a God who is said to be good, wise, and almighty[3].

Evil challenges the justice of God in the two senses of it, as it refers to *law* and to *perfection*. On the one hand, divine justice is the rule according to which God governs the whole universe and in particular the Republic of spirits, giving rewards and punishments to each according to his merit. On the other hand, it means holiness, which Leibniz defines as the highest degree of goodness[4]. In accordance with his holiness, God always wills what is good. The apparent disorder of things (for example the prosperity of some evil men and the misfortune of numerous good people) calls in question divine justice taken in the first sense and seems to overthrow the idea of *Providence* in the world. God's physical and moral concourse to evil (physical as well as moral evil) seems to be incompatible with justice taken in the second sense, as perfection. Every creature and every action owe their being and reality to divine omnipotence and continue to exist thanks to it (conservation is a continued creation). Consequently God contributes to sins by his will and power, insofar as nothing would happen unless he made it happen and willed or permitted it. The problem raised here is the problem of *Predestination* and of human liberty. The punishment of the "sinner" does not appear to be legitimate any more, if he could not do otherwise (because his action would be completely predetermined) and if in fact the sin were ultimately imputable to God, as the primary cause of all things.

This close link between evil and justice (taken in its two senses) explains why Leibniz has chosen to write a *theo-dicy*[5]. Considering the terms in which the problem of evil is formulated, the solution can be given only by a doctrine of divine justice. This doctrine aims to prove God's innocence and holiness, and to make known the rules of his action towards his creatures in the world. I am not sure whether commentators have really understood the originality of the solution Leibniz puts forward. In this paper, I would like to question two common interpretations of his theodicy.

The first interpretation considers that, after all, most of the arguments Leibniz uses are traditional[6], as we already found them in Platonism, Stoicism, Neo-Platonism, and Augustine's tradition: the definition of evil as privation, the aesthetic comparisons that reduce it to a dissonance in a nice music or to a shadow in a beautiful painting, the thesis according to which evil is permitted by God only to obtain a greater good, etc. It is true that some arguments belong to this theological and philosophical tradition. Nevertheless I believe Leibniz reinterprets them and gives them a completely new sense.

---

[3] See for instance *Von der Allmacht* (§ 2, 537), "how divine predestination can exist in conjunction with the present misery of the pious and the good fortune of the malicious" (Sleigh 5).

[4] See *Theodicy* § 151; *Causa Dei* § 50.

[5] As it is well known, Leibniz created the neologism *Théodicée* from two Greek words: *théos* (God) and *dike* (justice).

[6] See for instance G. Grua: *Jurisprudence universelle et théodicée selon Leibniz* (Paris: PUF, 1953), 370.

The second interpretation maintains that Leibniz's conception of evil and justification of God are roughly fixed since the *Confessio Philosophi*, which some commentators regard as a juvenile or "first theodicy"[7]. According to that reading, later texts dealing with the same matter would broadly repeat the same arguments or set forth various versions of the same fundamental thesis. In *La question du mal chez Leibniz: fondements et élaboration de la Théodicée*[8], I have emphasized that the long reflection on evil and divine justice that starts in early texts and leads to the *Essays of Theodicy* reveals an important evolution. Without denying some continuity, I have identified significant revisions in the conception of God and of his relations (moral and physical concourse) to the action of his creatures, as well as in the comprehension of the nature of evil, its origin and the reason of its permission. I would like here to draw the main stages of this evolution.

CRITICISM OF TRADITION AND LEIBNIZ'S EARLY NECESSITARIANISM (UNTIL 1673)

Leibniz underlines that he was interested in questions concerning evil, divine justice, human liberty, and predestination since his first readings, when he was young and "flitted from book to book" in his father's library[9]. In a letter to Jablonski (January 23, 1700), he even says that for a long time he had been thinking of writing a theodicy "to defend the goodness, the wisdom and the justice of God, as well as his supreme power and his irresistible influence"[10]. The plan of the great theological and apologetic project of *Demonstrationes Catholicae* (1668–1669) announced in Part III chapters on the liberty of spirits (c. 16), God's law and the mutual obligations of God and his creatures (c. 17), and the cause of sin (c. 21). The title of chapter 18 even asserts: "God is not at all the cause of the evil of guilt, but only the cause by accident of the evil of punishment"[11]. However, the text entitled *Von der Allmacht und Allwissenheit Gottes und der Freiheit des Menschen* (1670–1671)[12] is the first known attempt of Leibniz to solve the problem of evil.

This draft written in German constitutes a significant indication of the state of his reflections at that time. Leibniz claims that objections against divine justice and providence are based on two main sophisms. After having easily disproved the first (which is a variant of the sophism of lazy reason), he sets out to refute the second. The second sophism asserts that God is the genuine author of sin, since he does not just permit it,

---

[7] See Y. Belaval: *Confessio Philosophi* (Paris: Vrin, 1970), "Présentation" 25–26; Grua, « Avertissement », vii; R. Sleigh speaks of "Leibniz's First Theodicy" (Noûs 30 (supplement), 1999: 481–99) but underlines significant differences with the future *Theodicy*.

[8] Paris: Honoré Champion, 2008.

[9] *Theodicy*, preface.

[10] See GP VI, 3.

[11] A VI, 1, 496.

[12] A VI, 1, 537–46.

but actually creates all the occasions that lead to it and even incites the man to commit it, whereas he could have prevented it or suspended its causes and consequences. Leibniz's first reply refers to a juridical and moral argument: "Punishment belongs to the evil will—no matter whence it comes. Otherwise, no misdeed would be punished. There is always a cause of the will outside of the willing subject, and yet it is the will that makes us human beings and persons—sinners, blessed, damned".[13]

Two reasons are here put forward. Firstly, the rule of justice demands that every sin be punished and every good action be rewarded. Secondly, in law, the imputation must fall only on the immediate cause (the will of man) and not on remote causes (even if they were determinant), nor *a fortiori* on God, the ultimate cause of things. Otherwise no sinner would be responsible for his sin and punishable for it. He would always have an excuse, and justice would never be applied.

Even if these arguments are valuable and sufficient from a juridical and moral point of view, the question of God's participation in sin still remains at the metaphysical level. Now Leibniz's position in *Von der Allmacht* may sound surprising in comparison with later texts. Probably still influenced by Luther, he maintains that God does not only permit sin, but *wants* its existence[14], because he considers that it is for the best. God is the author of sin, as he is the origin of all chains of causes. One may reply that if he *morally* concurs to sin with his will, he does not *physically* concur to it with his power, because, as Augustine and Thomas Aquinas said, evil is nothing in itself. God is the cause of all that is real, positive, and perfect in creatures, but not of their defects and imperfections, which are mere privations or negations.

Leibniz finds the argument theoretically hard to support and practically dangerous. It amounts to dividing what is in fact absolutely indivisible: on one hand being (that comes from God) and on the other hand its limits and defects (that come only from the creature). This separation is impossible as the limits and imperfections of the creature partake of its essence and define its nature. Everything, being and negation, perfection and imperfection, the *physical* and the *moral*, must then be imputable to God. Trying to clear him of the responsibility of sin by arguing that he produces only the "physical" reality of the act, but is not responsible for its "moral" quality (which makes it into a sin), is as absurd as claiming that a bad musician is the cause of only the movements of his bow but not the cause of the dissonance that comes as a result[15]. Moreover such argument would also be valid in the case of anyone who commits a sin.

This absurd division of physical concourse logically leads to the conception of evil as nil. From the moment it is distinguished from the act itself, evil becomes *nothingness* and thus needs no cause. Traditional definition of evil as non-being leads to the following consequence: nothing and nobody concur to it and neither man nor God is responsible for it. Leibniz ends on this point with a severe judgment: "Now

[13] § 13' (Sleigh 17). Cf. *Theodicy* § 264.
[14] See § 16 (Sleigh 21).
[15] See § 18 (Sleigh 23).

these are the lovely lawyers of divine justice, who will at the same time make all sinners unpunishable. And it surprises me that the profound Descartes stumbled here too"[16].

I think Leibniz has never gone back over this criticism of the reduction of evil to nothingness and of God's partial physical concourse[17]. About moral concourse, the letter to Magnus Wedderkopf (May 1671) affirms that the distinction in God between positive will and mere permission is groundless[18]. The letter puts forward another important thesis that was not explicit in *Von der Allmacht*: a *necessitarianism* that conciliates liberty with necessity without challenging the legitimacy of punishments and rewards. Everything (act and event) is necessary; God himself is necessitated by the consideration of the best: "For it is the highest form of freedom to be forced to the best by right reason [. . .] whatever has happened, is happening, or will happen is the best and, accordingly, necessary. But, [. . .] it has a necessity that takes nothing away from freedom because it takes nothing away from the will and the use of reason"[19].

Leibniz still maintains this necessitarianism[20] in the *Confessio Philosophi*, while introducing an important distinction between being the *reason* and being the *author*. The principle of reason implies that God is the ultimate cause of evil as well as of all things. This does not mean that God *wills* sin. He is the reason of it[21], as he is the first link in the series of things that exist, but he is not the author of it by his will, which aims only at the good. Hence this paradoxical explanation of evil: evil is because God *exists* and not because God *wills* it. The real origin of evil is actually in God's understanding (which contains the uncreated universal harmony) and not in his will[22], so that he is innocent of it. He physically but not morally concurs to it.

This justification of God is problematic as it makes evil necessary. The sin as any event or act in the world is necessary because its suppression would actually suppose another world[23] and then another first cause, another God (which is impossible). Even God could not remove that sin. His relation to the created world is a relation of reciprocal dependence: each term of the series (even the first: God) is attached and connected to each other, so that no term can be changed without changing all the others. If God is supposed, this universe wherein sin is exists by exclusion of any other universe. Now if this universe wherein sin is were modified, or if just one of its events were deleted, God himself would be modified or deleted. The relation is similar to a logical relation in a hypothetical proposition: if A (God) exists, B (the world) will

---

[16] Ibid.

[17] See for instance *L'auteur du péché*, A VI, 3, 150–51. See part 3 of this paper.

[18] A II, 1, 187.

[19] Sleigh 3–5.

[20] On this necessitarianism and its specific features in comparison with Hobbes, see Rateau (2008) 125–34.

[21] "All the requisites of sin come from God" (*Confessio Philosophi*, Sleigh 39).

[22] Sleigh 41–45.

[23] The possibility of other worlds is not excluded in itself, even if these worlds are *in fact* impossible, because of their incompatibility with the existence of God.

exist, and by contraposition: if B (the world) does not exist[24], A (God) will not exist either[25].

In that context, the role of divine will seems to fade off. Our world does not exist because God wills it, but just because he is. God appears more like a physical cause (the first motor) than like a genuine moral cause (the author) of the world. What then really does distinguish this God from Nature, Necessity, or Fate, which is indifferent to good and evil? And consequently how can we help but conclude that there is no supreme intelligence governing the world? At the time of the *Confessio Philosophi*, divine will is not this positive power choosing among the infinity of possibles. Will is defined as a pleasure taken in the existence of a thing[26]. It seems therefore to be a passive endorsement of what exists and derives from divine existence, as if it came only after creation to approve of it and be delighted with it, rather than an effort that made the possible world come to existence. So what about the evils that are in our world? God does not will them (although he is the final reason of them), that is to say he cannot be delighted with their existences considered in themselves, separately. He only *permits* them, insofar as they take part in the most beautiful harmony, wherein they are counterbalanced by greater goods.

The notion of permission, which Leibniz rejected in *Von der Allmacht*, is restored but takes a specific sense. Sin is permitted insofar as it is linked with the best series of things. Permitting it is neither willing nor not willing it, because if God did not will sin, it would mean that he could not do what he willed and that therefore he was not omnipotent, since sin exists. Permission is a sort of suspension of the will: it is a matter of knowledge, not of will[27]. Permitting evil is not being delighted or in pain with its existence. It means understanding its existence as inseparable from the universal harmony.

The *Confessio Philosophi* clearly differs from the future *Theodicy*, wherein permission will be reinterpreted within the framework of the distinction between antecedent and consequent wills[28]. Moreover I think it is a mistake to consider that Leibniz attenuates his necessitarianism in the *Confessio Philosophi* by introducing the distinction between absolute and hypothetical necessity. First, we have to remember that this use of scholastic distinctions is described by Leibniz himself as "superfluous and by no means obligatory or sophistical"[29]. In other terms he does not completely assume and accept this terminology. Second, the two necessities actually amount to the distinction between what exists by itself and what exists by an extrinsic cause. Things that have their reason of being in themselves (God and mathematical truths) are absolutely necessary, whereas things that have the reason of their existence from something external are hypothetically necessary, that is to say they are necessary under the condition that their causes be supposed. This is why all that follows from the absolute necessary Being is not absolutely necessary[30].

[24] We could add this specification: "as it is and not otherwise."
[25] Sleigh 47.
[26] Cf. Sleigh 55.
[27] Cf. ibid.
[28] On other differences between the two texts, see Rateau (2008) 183–95.
[29] Sleigh 53.
[30] Sleigh 55–57.

The distinction of the two sorts of necessity aims at showing in which sense sins can be said to be necessary, namely *ex hypothesi* or *per accidens* alone. Nevertheless it is applied in the context of a theology that makes the entire series of things into a consequence of divine existence and considers that only one world (ours) is possible *ex hypothesi*, i.e. in fact possible. Why? Because another world would have supposed another God—a hypothesis that is absolutely impossible, as God cannot be other than he is. The consideration of other possible creatures and events appears purely fictive, as the existence of these creatures and events is actually incompatible with the existence of God, so that the difference between what is impossible *per accidens* and what is *absolutely* impossible fades or becomes artificial.

To really establish the contingency of the world, Leibniz will have to revise some of his theses. God is no longer to be considered the first term of the entire series of things but must be said to be outside and independent of it. Thus it will be possible to assert that God might have created another world without ceasing to be God. These theological and metaphysical changes imply to revise the notion of possible (which cannot be reduced to a pure and unrealizable fiction), and the role of the divine will so as to define it as a real positive power of choosing.

Theological and metaphysical revisions (from 1675–1676 onward)

From 1675–1676 onward, some important theoretical revisions led to a new conception of God (1.), a new explanation of his physical concourse and of the origin of evil (2.) and a new definition of his permission of sin (3.).

1. As he may fear too close a proximity with Spinoza, Leibniz stresses after the *Confessio Philosophi* that God is different from Fate, Nature, and necessity, because he is a person, a spirit endowed with understanding and will[31]. God is no more the first link in the series of created things but the external reason for its existence. He is *supramundus* and independent so that the world could have been different without his being changed. Therefore other universes are not only possible in themselves, but now also *realizable* by God. In connection with this theological revision, Leibniz redefines two key concepts: those of *possible* and of *will*.

The possible is not a pure fiction or chimera. It is real insofar as it refers to a thing (*res*) that is independent of our present thought[32]. All possibles are contained in the divine understanding where they are "realized"[33]. Since 1677–

---

[31] See A VI, 3, 474–75.
[32] See letter to Foucher (1675), A II, 1, 387–88.
[33] "Realisentur" cf. *De rerum originatione radicali*, GP VII, 305.

1678[34], Leibniz even attaches a certain "pretension to existence" to them. This pretension is proportional to their degrees of perfection: the more perfect they are or the greater quantity of essence they have, the more powerful is their propensity to exist. Thus a possible is not characterized only by its logical property of non-contradiction and by its metaphysical property of potentiality (by contrast with actuality), but now also by its dynamic property: every possible involves an effort (*conatus*)[35] towards existence.

In God's mind, all possibles are combined in different and incompatible worlds. The best possible universe prevails over the other possible series of things. However it needs the intervention of an external power to come to existence. Our world then requires a God, who understands all the possibles, wills the best among them, and makes it exist by his power. The relation between understanding and will is also completely revalued. It actually supposes that the possible that tends to exist in God's mind becomes an inclination in his will. Leibniz departs from the classical pattern wherein will is merely subordinated to understanding. Will appears as the immediate translation of mental representation into effort, instead of following upon a judgment by the intellect, by submitting to it and approving it. So will and understanding are the two expressions of the same and unique effort (*conatus*), that is the divine omnipotence that must be regarded not as a pure and blind power acting without rules (*potentia absoluta*), but as the capacity of realizing what understanding represents as the most perfect, and what will finds to be the best (*potentia ordinata*).

We thus observe the same conflict in the will as in the mind between particular volitions (called "antecedent"), each of which aims at obtaining some good and avoiding some evil. As these volitions cannot all be satisfied (as well as not all the possibles can be realized), some of them are hindered—for instance: the volition of saving all men. Just as the thought of the best possible world derives from the combination of possibles, the will called "consequent" or "final" for the best—wherein the greater quantity of good and perfection is obtained for the minimum of evil—results from the composition of volitions.

2. Concerning God's physical concourse to evil, Leibniz criticizes both those who assert that God cooperates only partly[36] or indirectly (by his *concursus generalis*)[37] with the creatures' acts, and those[38] who claim that God contributes completely to sin taken

---

[34]   See *Elementa vera pietatis, sive de amore Dei super omnia*, A VI, 4-B, 1363: « ad existendum propensio »; *Dialogue entre Théophile et Polidore* (1679?), A VI, 4-C, 2232: « pretension [. . .] à l'existence ».

[35]   The use of this term appears in the years 1683–1685 (A VI, 4-A, 557).

[36]   Like Ockham, *in Sententiarum*, lib. II, q. 4–5, lib. IV, q. 8–9 E; Erasmus, *De libero arbitrio*, III, c 4, c 6, c 12, IV, 8; Molina, *Concordia*, disp. XXVI; or Suarez, *De gratia*, lib. III, cap. 46, 18.

[37]   Durand de Saint-Pourçain denies an immediate concourse of God to the actions of the creatures (*In Sententias theologicas*, lib. II, dist. 37, q. 1). Among supporters of this general and mediate concourse, Leibniz also cites Pierre Auriol, Pelagius, Louis de Dole, François Bernier (*Theodicy* § 27), and Nicolas Taurellus (ibid. § 381).

[38]   Following Thomas Aquinas, *Summa theologica*, Ia, IIae Pars, 79, 2.

in its positive reality, while evil is to be imputed to the sinner. He underlines that a partial concourse amounts to dividing the act in two parts and attributing one to God and the other to man. Even if this division were possible to draw, it would imply a new division because man's "part" should also be regarded as an act that would require God's concourse. To stop an infinite division (the part belonging to man decreasing more and more), it would be better to admit straightaway that God does the entire act[39].

Now, for supporters of an integral concourse, the division is to be drawn between the *physical* reality and the *moral* qualification of the act. God, as the ultimate cause of everything, produces sin totally without being responsible for this evil, which must be ascribed to man (considered as the moral cause of it). In *Von der Allmacht* (by the comparison with the bad musician) as well as in *L'auteur du péché* (by the comparison with the two paintings[40]), Leibniz emphasizes the impossibility of separating the act itself (the *material*) from the evil (the *formal*) inside the sin. A good action does not differ solely from a bad action for this reason that the former is conformable to virtue whereas the latter is not. Good and evil do not consist of a simple external relation (the relation to law) but refer to a difference in the nature of things. A virtuous act contains more perfection and being than a vicious act. Leibniz opposes those who, following Augustine, abstract evil from its ontological basis in order to reduce it to a negation without any reality. As nothingness needs no author, this thesis actually leads to proving that not only God but also the sinner himself is innocent!

An act forms an indivisible whole. Evil is *something* because it is inseparable from the being it limits or corrupts. God thus concurs integrally to the production of evil. The sin is said to be a "creature" produced by God[41]. Does not God's physical concourse seriously challenge his justice and the creature's responsibility? The answer actually lies in the notion of "original imperfection" (which seems to be used for the first time around 1680–1685[42]). Because of their essential limitations, creatures restrain the whole being, force, and perfection they receive from God. Their fundamental, inherent imperfection (which precedes original sin) makes them liable to fail without making their sin necessary.

The thesis according to which the origin of evil consists of the limitation of created spirits may appear traditional in a way. Nevertheless Leibniz's position differs from tradition insofar as this original imperfection does not mean only a lack of being, a

---

[39] Cf. *Conversatio cum Stenonio de libertate* (1677), A VI, 4-B, 1382.

[40] See A VI, 3, 151: "A painter creates two paintings, one of which is large so that it may be used as a model for a tapestry, while the other is only a miniature. Consider the miniature. Let us say that there are only two things to consider with respect to it, first its positive and real aspect, which is the table, the background, the colors, the lines; and then its privative aspect, which is the disproportion which respect to the large painting, in other words, its smallness. Now it would be a joke to say that the painter is the author of everything that is real in the two paintings without, nevertheless, being the author of the privative aspect, i.e., the disproportion between the large one and the small one" (Sleigh 111).

[41] Cf. *Conversatio cum Stenonio de libertate* (1677), A VI, 4-B, 1382: "Peccatum est creatura, omnis creatura a Deo continue creatur, ergo et peccatum."

[42] "Defectus originalis" (A VI, 4-C, 2577); "imperfectio rerum originalis" (A VI, 4-A, 557).

negation inherent to creatures, but also an impediment to more being, a brake on more reality and perfection. It is a sort of negative effort, a resistance to any *plus ultra* (being, good, divine grace) that Leibniz has compared to inertia or "tardivity" in physical bodies since 1685–1686[43]. Without dividing the act itself, it is therefore possible to assert that all that is real, positive, perfect in sin comes from God, whereas its limitations and defects are solely attributable to the creature.

3. Concerning God's moral concourse to evil, Leibniz's doctrine of *permission* was not completely fixed prior to his resuming the scholastic distinction between *antecedent* and *consequent* will at the time he was writing the *Theodicy* or just before[44]. Two opposite conceptions are successively upheld, then abandoned. According to the first, permission does not concern the will: it is nothing but knowing without acting (cf. *Confessio Philosophi*). The second consists of reducing permission to a positive will that is only accidental (a will *per accidens*), like in the *Conversation with Steno* (1677)[45], at the risk of making God into an accomplice or even an author of sin.

The solution that emerges consists of thinking of permission as the result of an internal self-limitation of the will. God wills all the goods, does not will the evils, and even wills to remove them *as far as* it is possible, that is to say as far as universal harmony permits it. His will "changes" when it ascends to the universal viewpoint instead of confining itself to partial ones. There is no contradiction in God, but a shift from a positive will to prevent evil (taken in isolation) to a sort of negative will not to prevent it (as it is now considered with other things and with their consequences).

Permission is the effect in the part of a choice that concerns the whole universe. It cannot be justified outside of this universal context. As nothing can be isolated from the world to which it belongs as a part, asking why God did not prevent a particular crime or did not give the grace Adam needed to resist temptation amounts to asking why he did not choose another world. The unity of the world and the interdependence of all its elements suppose the unity of the decree by which God chooses it and makes it to exist. There are no detached particular wills in God. The permission of sin is contained in a "more general, more comprehensive will"[46] that does not focus on Adam's case alone but considers the whole world in which he takes part.

God's justification is finally based on two main arguments. (1) As he is not the creator of essences, God does not decide anything about the contents of a world. He does not decide if Adam sins, but if this series of things that contains Adam the sinner is preferable to others[47]. (2) His choice of creating the world is a single and global decree[48]. It does not

---

[43] See A VI, 4-B, 1521.
[44] See Grua 468, 474. The distinction until then was limited within the context of theological issues (Grua 445, 449).
[45] A VI, 4-B, 1382.
[46] Letter to the Landgrave (April 12, 1686), GP II, 19.
[47] See for instance *Specimen inventorum* [. . .], A VI, 4-B, 1619.
[48] *Conversation sur la liberté et le destin*, Grua 482.

imply that he *absolutely* and *positively* wills all that this decree includes, in particular the sin that he only permits.

The redefinition of the notions of possible, will, permission, the assertion that God is a spirit endowed with an understanding and a will (against Spinoza), the idea that the origin of evil is located in the essence of things, and the doctrine of the unique and universal decree led to a new conceptual framework. Founded on these theoretical changes, the *Essays of Theodicy* give a complete metaphysical explanation of divine justice and of the existence of evil, which indeed goes beyond a detailed answer to Bayle's objections.

The problem of evil in the *Theodicy* (1710)

In this part, I shall focus on the way Leibniz deals with difficulties concerning the "conduct of God" and his participation in evil[49]. The solution comes within the context of a theological discourse on divine perfections and the explanation of his choice of our world instead of another possible world. Leibniz links to the conception of God he had revised after 1675, the doctrine of the infinity of possible worlds. God has an infinite wisdom that comprehends all the possibles and their combinations, a perfect good will that cannot but choose the best, and an omnipotence that makes it exist (§ 7 to § 8). Evil participates to the best so that its omission would imply the creation of a worse world. Moreover it contributes to the realization of the best as a condition *sine qua non* of greater good (in the case of moral evil), indeed even as a positive means to obtain it (in the case of metaphysical and physical evils).

The general explanation of God's moral concourse is based on the distinction of antecedent and consequent wills (§ 22 to § 25). God wills *antecedently* each good and wills to repel each evil, but wills *consequently* the best that entails his rejecting some goods and his permitting some evils. Three main reasons explain why the best is not just equivalent to the sum of all goods. (1) All goods cannot be realized together as they are not all compatible. (2) Some goods cannot be obtained unless particular evils are admitted as conditions, means, or inevitable consequences. (3) The laws of harmony demand difference, variety, and inequality in creatures. The excess of good would be a defect, as it would produce homogeneity and uniformity that would be opposed to the rules of perfection and beauty[50]. Consequent will results from the conflict and composition of all antecedent wills so as to form the most perfect whole.

Thus evil only happens "by concomitance"[51], because of consequent will. Evil is always linked to a good (its counterpart) even if we are unable to identify it. Does it mean that

---

[49] Cf. *Theodicy* § 1.
[50] Ibid. § 124.
[51] Ibid. § 209.

God wills evil consequently although he does not will it antecedently? God's relation to evil is actually different depending on the nature of it (metaphysical, physical, or moral). God may and sometimes must will *physical* evil (suffering), as the punishment of sin and also "as a means to an end, that is, to prevent greater evils or to obtain greater goods"[52]. Evil is never willed as evil. God wills (and does not only permit) suffering *relatively*: as a legitimate pain in accordance with the laws of justice[53], or as a positive means (and not only as a mere negative condition) that leads to physical and moral perfections[54], or that allows the avoidance of greater evils. Suffering is evil for who supports it, but it becomes what Leibniz calls a "subsidiary good"[55] considering these juridical, moral, and metaphysical issues. It proves to be "good" relatively speaking and thus becomes a legitimate object of God's consequent will.

Metaphysical evil can also be regarded as a "subsidiary good." In general, it means any imperfection. God inevitably wills it when he decides to create something. To create is to create finite, limited beings (the absolute perfect, God, is uncreated). Metaphysical evil is an intrinsic characteristic of creation and also the reason for its variety, diversity, and thus beauty. The various sorts of creatures (from the plainest monad to the most perfect angel) and the various degrees of reality within each sort are so many different ways of limiting being and perfection. In a particular sense, metaphysical evil means the imperfection that concerns non-rational beings. Monsters, cataclysms, earthquakes, and apparent disorders in Nature are examples of this type of evil[56]. They must be considered at a global level, as their utility and benefits may appear over a long period. The study of geology actually proves that "we owe to them [deluges, inundations, telluric disruptions] our riches and comforts, and that through their agency this globe became fit for cultivation by us. These disorders passed into order"[57].

Moral evil (sin) is a particular case. God can neither will it antecedently, consequently, absolutely, nor even relatively, unless he would contradict himself (as he would approve what he forbids). Sin can never become a subsidiary good. It still remains hateful and forbidden in itself, even when it is the occasion of a greater good. Saint Paul's rule that forbids committing evil to the end of obtaining a good is applicable to everyone, God included, and admits of no exception[58]. God's moral concourse to sin requires a doctrine of permission. Only a very powerful motive can induce God to admit sin, because only "a supreme necessity may constrain one to comply with evil"[59]. This necessity is

---

[52] Ibid. § 23. See also *Causa Dei* § 39.

[53] Pain does not always or necessarily aim at utility (the amendment of the sinner and the example for others), because it must be applied even if it is not profitable to the sinner or to anyone. Leibniz admits vindictive justice beyond just corrective justice (*Theodicy* § 73).

[54] The ordeal leads just people to felicity (ibid. § 241). See also *De rerum originatione radicali*, GP VII, 307–08.

[55] *Causa Dei* § 35; GP III, 32.

[56] *Theodicy* § 241 and § 244.

[57] Ibid. § 245.

[58] Ibid. § 25. See Paul: *Romans*, 3, 8.

[59] *Theodicy* § 121.

moral. What we cannot omit without failing in our duty is morally necessary[60]. God could have prevented sin (logical possibility) but he should not (moral impossibility), because preventing it would have meant sinning himself, acting against his perfect wisdom and goodness. Permission is justified as a result of the prevalence of a duty over another less powerful. Hence this paradox: God would have committed a sin if he had not permitted sin, as he would have created another world, necessarily worse than ours (the best). The greatest evil is not the evil committed by creatures but the evil God would have committed if he had prevented sin:

> If God chose what would not be the best absolutely and in all, that would be a greater evil than all the individual evils that he could prevent by this means. This wrong choice would destroy his wisdom and his goodness[61].

God's sin would annihilate his own divinity[62]. Evil exists because God is God and cannot but act in accordance with the best.

Metaphysical and physical evils may be willed consequently, not as ends but as means in relation to good ends. Moral evil is never willed even as a means, but only permitted as a condition *sine qua non* of the best. A means is a positive instrument that serves a good end (hence the expression of "subsidiary good"), whereas a condition *sine qua non* is a negative datum that cannot be avoided *ex hypothesi*, a circumstance that refers less to what it positively allows than to what it would hinder (the best) if it were removed. Sin enters divine ends, God turns it to the best account, but it always remains what it is: an irreducible evil. On this point, I think a tension persists in Leibniz's *Theodicy* between two different approaches to evil.

On one hand, Leibniz seems sometimes to relativize evil by reducing it to a lower degree of the good, indeed by considering it as a mere appearance that the complete view of universal harmony should eliminate. On the other hand, he stresses the effective role of evil, as it allows obtaining greater goods that it would be impossible to get without it. According to the first approach, there is no absolute irregularity or real defect in the world, but only appearances of irregularity and defect in relation to our perception. Evil is the consequence of the partial and limited vision of a creature who does not see that what seems to her to be a disorder in fact takes part in the most perfect universal order. She is like someone who stands too close to a painting and criticizes the painter's art, for she just sees a confused mix of colors and shapes without apparent order.

According now to the second approach, evil is not unreal or illusory. What would be the use of a doctrine of divine concourse and permission and the sense of a theology of Redemption, if sins and sufferings were finally only apparent? The dynamics of the universal harmony and the pleasure its contemplation provides are based on the compensation for a *genuine* evil. The appropriate metaphor can be taken from music. The

---

[60] See the example of the officer on guard at an important post (ibid. § 24).
[61] Ibid. § 129.
[62] Ibid. § 131.

good composition supposes dissonances. The listener really hears the unpleasant sound and looks for its resolution in harmony. In the case of the painting, the right viewpoint allows correcting the initial incomplete perception, whereas in the case of the music, listening to the whole piece does not change the nature of the dissonance, which remains a real and irreducible defect in itself (even if it is compensated).

It is actually hard to conciliate these two points of view that express different demands. As a mathematician Leibniz is inclined to consider that evil is like apparent irregularities in mathematics. There is no line or series of numbers that does not come under the law of an equation, even if this equation is complicated. As a jurist and a theologian, although he knows sins and sufferings go into the general arrangement of the world, Leibniz is rather inclined to regard them in accordance with justice, respectively as a positive violation of the order, and as the merited castigation of the sinner.

Apparent or real, evil is "something" as it is linked to an ontological basis (an action, a being). Leibniz maintains that God's physical concourse to evil is integral, continuous, immediate, and particular. God produces all that is real and perfect in creatures and in their actions. His cooperation is specific as it is exactly appropriate to the nature and the particular state of the creature, because "the conservation of a man standing is different from the conservation of a man seated"[63]. The good man and the bad man do not require the same quantity of divine power to exist and to persist in existence. Their moral difference is related to an ontological difference, insofar as the former has more perfection and partakes to more being than the latter.

God only produces "what is good in evil"[64], that is to say the positive reality of it. But what may be called the evil of evil (what is evil in evil) comes from the original imperfection of creatures. Without challenging God's integral concourse and the indivisible unity of act and being, it is possible to distinguish in them what belongs to God (perfection, being, force) and what belongs to the creature (limitation, restriction, inertia). Sin is not reduced to a mere moral determination (non-conformity to the law) but is imputable to the sinner in its *physical reality*. The sinner is guilty not only because he violates God's will (at the moral level) but because he also modifies the being, alters the perfection, and resists the grace he receives from God (at the physical level).

So evil is not nothingness but a privation of being. It cannot be abstracted or separated from the substance it affects. Such separation would be as absurd as imagining a limit apart from what is limited. Evil is neither a substance nor a pure negation without any attribute or quality[65]. It is a defect of perfection, an alteration of being that does not abolish it. Therefore it does not need an efficient cause but a *deficient* cause. This thesis may appear classical. It is in fact original as Leibniz links privation to the notions of capacity and receptivity of the creature. The nature of a thing defines both an ability to realize a certain quantity of perfection and a resistance to more perfection. It is positively

---

[63] Ibid. § 27.
[64] *Causa Dei* § 68.
[65] However, unlike Thomas Aquinas (*Summa theologica*, Ia, 48, 2 and 5), Leibniz does not make a clear distinction between privation and negation. On that point see Rateau (2008) 577–83.

the determination of a particular reality and negatively this *non plus ultra* that prevents any greater development (the creature cannot exceed the limits of its own essence). While it blocks the reception of more being, this limitation is similar to the inertia that Kepler and Descartes had observed in bodies[66]. The creature resists perfection as matter does the movement it receives. Privation is then not only a lack or an absence of being, but also an opposition, a reluctance to be and to be more. This again is why evil is not nil at the ontological level. If it were nothing, it would not hinder the perfecting of the creature.

As inertia, this reluctance due to original imperfection does not derive from a positive power. It is neither the negation of force (otherwise nothing would oppose God's physical concourse) nor the result of a real antagonist force (since the Manichean hypothesis is excluded). It comes from the *passive power* of the being. It is a sort of *anti-conatus*, a brake rather than a positive adverse effort. This *anti-conatus* explains our errors and malice. Error is a feature of a spirit that does not go beyond perception by the senses and does not pursue the examination of things further[67], while malice indicates a weak will that "is limited to the pleasures of the senses or to other pleasures to the detriment of greater good, as of health, virtue, union with God, felicity [...]"[68]. Error and malice result from inertia of the intellect and will. They consist of this stop, this rest, this privation of further reflection or aspiration.

Leibniz gives a rational justification of God that conciliates his omnipotence, his holiness, the existence of evil, and the freedom of man. The rehearsing of some theses from the tradition is apparent only insofar as they are completely reinterpreted. Leibniz revised his first necessitarianism but never abandoned his early criticism of those who maintain God's partial concourse and regard evil as nil. God is neither the author of sin by his will nor by his power. He only permits it and produces "what is good in evil." However, it may be said that evil exists because of God for two reasons: evil is contained in the best possible world he conceives in his infinite understanding (which comprehends the entire nature of things); he could not fail to choose the best, otherwise he would not have been God. This last position does not amount to Leibniz's early necessitarianism, as this necessity of choosing the best is only *moral*[69].

God is the source of being, reality and perfection. Evil does not refer to a positive antagonist force, but consists of privation and reluctance. It can only produce action *per*

---

[66] *Theodicy* § 30. Leibniz does not just draw here a simple analogy between metaphysics and physics, as he regards the "natural inertia of bodies" as "a perfect image and even as a *sample* of the original limitation of creatures" (my emphasis).

[67] Ibid. § 32.

[68] Ibid. § 33. See also *Causa Dei* § 73.

[69] I disagree here with Robert M. Adams, who maintains that it is logically (and not only morally) necessary, that God does what is best (see *Leibniz. Determinist, Theist, Idealist*, New York, OUP, 1994, in particular I. 1. 2.). For the discussion of this point, see Paul Rateau: "The Theoretical Foundations of the Leibnizian Theodicy and its Apologetic Aim", in Samuel Newlands, Larry M. Jorgensen (eds.), *New Essays on Leibniz's Theodicy*, Oxford University Press, 2014.

accidens, as the water in freezing is able to break a gun-barrel wherein it is confined[70]. It comes ultimately from the original imperfection of creatures. This connatural limitation makes failure *possible* but does not *necessitate* man to commit sin[71]. To make it actual, liberty is required. Man is thus totally responsible for sin. It is up to him to accept God's gifts and ends or to resist them, reduce the good effect of his concourse, and abuse the force he received from him.

[70] *Theodicy* § 153: "Evil itself comes only from privation; the positive enters therein only by concomitance, as the active enters by concomitance into cold […] Evil comes from privation; the positive and action spring from it by accident, as force springs from cold."
[71] See *Causa Dei*, § 69: "the foundation of evil is necessary, but its production is however contingent, i.e. it is necessary that evils are possible, but it is contingent that evils are actual […]."

PART II

CONCEPTS, KNOWLEDGE, AND LANGUAGE

CHAPTER 7

THE COMPLETE CONCEPT OF AN INDIVIDUAL SUBSTANCE

STEFANO DI BELLA

A PUZZLING CONCEPT

The Individual as a Subject of Predication

The doctrine of the individual/complete concept, presented by Leibniz during the 1680s as the very heart of his metaphysics of substance, lies at the intersection of three great layers of thought: (a) a logically minded unified theory of concepts and truth; (b) an ontological intuition of what is considered a "complete being"—that is, a concrete particular—where this intuition is rooted in some metaphysical insights and corroborated by a philosophical analysis of language, which, in turn, is influenced by nominalistic semantics; and (c) a reflection on individual history and destiny, within the framework of theodicean problems.

In order to disentangle these trains of thought, let me start with the presentation of this complex of ideas as they are found in the 1686 *Discourse of Metaphysics* (DM). In this text, the doctrine of individual concept is introduced in a paragraph that deals initially with the debated issue regarding the activity of creatures. Having established that "actions belong to their *supposita*," that is, to individual substances, Leibniz tackles the definition of the latter concept. His first tentative characterization is the most traditional one of "ultimate subject." With this move he reaffirms two basic aspects of the Aristotelian *Categories* that were far from taken for granted in the substance theories of his age: first, the centrality of the individual, or the fact that concrete particulars are the "primary substances"; second, the link with predication, hence a logico-linguistic approach, different from the Cartesian "way of ideas."

According to Leibniz, however, so far we are left only with a "nominal definition." In order to grant it a true content, he focuses on the concept of predication. *True* predication is interpreted as *conceptual* containment, according to the theory of truth he worked out in his early Hanoverian years: a proposition is true if the concept of the predicate is contained in the concept of the subject.[1] By applying this theory to the case of singular proposition and its ultimate subject, the result is the notion of individual concept. This is presented as the key to individual substance itself. In turn, conceptual containment is taken as the explanans of the "*inesse*" of inherence, that is, of the ontological relation between the substance and its accidents.

Completeness

The decisive feature of the individual concept is completeness: "we can say it is the nature of an individual substance or complete being[2] to have a concept so complete that it is sufficient to make us understand and deduce from it all the predicates of the subject to which the concept is attributed."[3] Leibniz's convoluted presentation suggests a dualism between the concept itself as a logical subject and an ontological meaning of "subject." This remark is related to the following problem: completeness—that is, the property of containing and giving an account of *all* the possible predicates of a concept—can certainly be a necessary condition for being (the concept of) an individual substance, but it hardly seems to be a sufficient one, insofar as *all* propositions are subject to the containment theory, even those having a general concept as their subject. As a consequence, all concepts in principle must "contain" all their possible predicates:[4] "Can one deny that every thing (whether genus, species or individual) has a complete concept, according to which God, who conceives of everything perfectly, conceives of it, that is to say a concept which contains or includes everything that can be said of the thing . . . ?"[5] Leibniz goes as far as to draw a terminological distinction between a "full concept" (*notio plena*), which is assumed to be an abstract or general one, and a "complete concept" (*notio completa*), which corresponds to an individual.[6] Beyond the "logical" criterion of containment, which applies to *all* concepts and truths, he is then bound to give us an ontological criterion for completeness, in order to circumscribe the set of individual concepts.

---

[1] The same idea is expressed in many private drafts of the 1680s, the best known of which is perhaps what is known as the *Primae Veritates* (c. 1689). The piece, now labeled *Principia logico-metaphysica* (A VI.4, 1643–1649), was cherished by Couturat, who took it as paradigmatic for his "logical" interpretation of Leibniz's metaphysics. See Couturat 1902. For further discussion of the containment principle see Mates 1986.

[2] It is worth noting that the qualification of "complete" first appears in DM 8 referring to a "being" [*être*], and only later to the corresponding "concept."

[3] A VI.4, 1540 (GP IV 433; L 307).

[4] This point has been clearly illustrated in Rutherford 1988.

[5] GP II 131 (Mason 73).

[6] "A full concept includes all predicates of a thing e.g. of heat; a complete concept includes all predicates of the subject, e.g. of this hot thing. They coincide in the case of individual substances." GP II 49, note.

Individual Essence and the Paradoxes of Identity

At the crucial juncture where he introduces his theory of the individual concept, Leibniz makes a significant step beyond the boundaries of the Aristotelian paradigm. The latter, in fact, while taking individuals as the building blocks of the ontological framework, left them in principle out of the scope of scientific enterprise. In the epistemological tradition shaped by Aristotelianism, science concerns general essences, while the individual, being "ineffabile," escapes our conceptual knowledge. Leibniz, instead, attempts to think of an "individual *concept*," expressing, as such, the true "principle of individuation" of the corresponding individual: "God. . . [is] seeing the individual notion or 'haecceity' of Alexander."[7] As a consequence, he draws from this view some theses about identity that he labels "paradoxes." The first "paradox" is the Identity of Indiscernibles (IdInd), taken in a strong sense, according to which two distinct individuals must always differ for their *monadic* properties (relational properties being parasitic on the former).

To introduce the second "paradox," it is useful to consider that individual substance in the *Categories* was labeled a "power for contraries," which means, first and foremost, its capacity to assume opposite predicates (A and not-A) successively, by remaining the same. But alternative possibilities could also be conceived as simultaneous, typically with respect to the decisions of rational free agents or to contingent causes in general.

Now, sameness through change has a prominent role in Leibniz's view of individual substance. For him, however, the a posteriori testimony of self-knowledge is not enough to justify the claim that the same "self" who was in Paris is now in Germany: one needs an a priori proof, which relies on the fact that both phases belong to the same individual concept.[8]

The same concept that grounds diachronic identity, however, does exclude the possibility of a "branching." Leibniz does not hesitate to state that, given that all properties and events in the life of an individual are included in the individual's concept (the statement that shocked Arnauld), therefore, "had something different happened in his or her life, he or she would have been not the same, but quite another individual."[9] Thus, the denial of counterfactual identity and the endorsement of the transtemporal one—the latter coherent with the Aristotelian and ordinary view, the former contradictory to it—are tightly bound in Leibniz's view, both standing or falling together with the complete concept view.

---

[7] DM 8, A VI.4, 1540 (GP IV 433; L 308). It should be noted that according to Leibniz, only God can fully grasp such concepts. Reference is made here, with 'haecceity' to Scotistic terminology, despite the severe criticism of Scotus's notion of "haecceity" in Leibniz's youthful *Disputatio de principio individui* (1663).

[8] See Correspondence with Arnauld, GP II 53 (L 335).

[9] Ibid.

Logic and Ontology of a Complete Concept

Things and Forms: The Genesis of a Complete Being

Let me first consider the notion of ontological completeness implicitly assumed in DM 8, that is, Leibniz's idea of what counts as a thing, or a "complete being." I cannot reconstruct here the complex genesis of this idea. I will focus briefly only on a text of the early Hanoverian period, the *De Cogitationum Analysi*, that in its final part addresses the ontological structure of subject and properties: "I can well conceive of a circle as something which is possible in and of itself. . . if I wish to know, however, whether a circle does now exist, and if I wish to know this a priori, I am bound to assume many other items beyond that essence, and among them the first one I should take into account. . . is nothing but the subject of the circle. . . . There are, in fact, some differences that are not drawn from forms, such as the difference between a big and a small circle, or whether there is one circle alone or many."[10] Already in some earlier drafts, Leibniz was prepared to stress the ontological distinction between "forms" (i.e. properties) and the "thing" or "subject." Some aspects of things, however, connoting their existence as individuals, are "not drawn from forms"; in present-day metaphysical jargon, they are irreducible to "suchnesses"[11] or general properties. Moreover, all these aspects are explicitly connected to the "subject." This "subject," however, is far from working as a "bare substratum." On the contrary, it is presented as an explanatory principle: "an individual is that whose intelligibility involves the intelligibility of the existence of things."[12] Here the terminology of "complete being" (taken as synonym of "substance") appears: "From all this it clearly follows that every ultimate subject is a complete being, which involves the whole of nature: that is to say, from its perfect understanding—i.e. if we understand all features by which it can be distinguished from everything else—one could infer, which possible things do exist."[13] The draft makes the idea of a complete being explicit, which the *Discourse* somehow presupposed; but it seems in turn to assume the reference to a complete knowledge, such as will be expressed by the complete concept itself.

---

[10] A VI.4, 2770.

[11] The terminology is borrowed from Adams 1979.

[12] *De Cogitationum analysi*, A VI.4, 2770.

[13] Ibid. But already in a draft from late 1676 we find the following: "In my view a substance, or a complete being, is that which by itself involves all things, or, for the perfect understanding of which the understanding of nothing else is required." A VI.3, 400. For a more comprehensive reconstruction of the genesis of the idea of the complete being and its junction with the complete concept, see Di Bella 2005.

From Abstract to Complete Terms: Language and Logic

The ontological asymmetry of subject and properties, or their one-many relationship, reappears in semantic guise in a series of drafts of linguistic-philosophical analysis (*characteristica verbalis*) of the 1680s, usually starting with the study of abstract talk. In tune with his constant antirealistic ontological commitments, Leibniz is eager to systematically avoid abstract reference. Several of these drafts start with this abstract/concrete polarity, in order to further pursue the search for substance terms. But how is one to circumscribe them among the concrete ones? The substantive/adjective distinction does not capture the decisive divide.[14] The only relevant distinction turns out to be between general terms and terms for individuals.

The analysis of ordinary language is no longer sufficient, however, to characterize the concept corresponding to a proper name. To do this, Leibniz maximizes the plurality of attributes that refer to the same subject, following the logic of predication. Once again this operation is guided by the intuitive idea of a concrete particular thing: "In order to inquire into the nature of a substance, or a subsisting thing, one should consider that, if many different attributes are said of the subject, then none of them is something subsistent; so 'hot' and 'bright,' and 'located here, or today' are said of this one and the same fire. The concept of a subsisting thing, however, e.g. of this fire, is that which includes all attributes *that can be said of the same subject, of which itself can be said.* Therefore, a subsisting thing is nothing but a complete term, that is a concept in which all properties inhere, which can be attributed to it or to the subject to which itself can be attributed."[15] Analogously, one can find the following in the *Notationes generales*, an important draft very close to the *Discourse*: "If the same thing is B, and is also C, D and so on, because it is A; in other words, if the concept A involves all concepts B, C, D etc. which can be said of the selfsame thing; then the concept A will express a singular substance. This amounts to saying that the concept of a singular substance is a complete concept, which includes all that can be said of the substance."[16] As a matter of fact, we cannot grasp any complete concept of an individual substance. Yet we are assured of its possibility, otherwise we could not account for the possibility of truths concerning concrete particulars: "Now, it is clear that *there is such a kind of concept,* according to the definition of a true proposition which I have explained. When we utter 'Alexander is strong,' indeed, we do not mean anything but that 'strong' is contained in the concept of Alexander, and the same

---

[14] Sometimes, however, Leibniz gives more relevance to the intermediate step of substantive (general) terms: "A term expressing substance is a concrete substantive. . . like 'Man.'" A few lines later, Leibniz distinguishes from this a "term expressing a singular substance, involving all predicates of its subject, i.e. a complete term." (*De abstracto, concreto, substantia, accidente*, A VI.4, 571–572).

[15] *Definitiones. Aliquid, Nihil*, A VI.4, 306. The presence of the two distinct dimensions of subject (ontological and predicative), and their link, can be clearly recognized here, despite some inaccuracy in expression, blurring "term" and "thing."

[16] A VI.4, 553.

for all predicates."[17] Of course, the "concept" we are dealing with is no longer within the scope of human semantics. It is, instead, something like an idea in God's mind.

The *Generales Inquisitiones* present a formal definition of completeness: "Take BY, and let any indefinite Y be superfluous; i.e. 'a certain Alexander the Great' and 'Alexander the Great' be the same; then, B is an individual concept. If BA is a concept, and B is an individual, A will be redundant, i.e. if BA = C, then B = C."[18] Every real addition to such a concept would imply a contradiction. How to construe a corresponding concept? Although Leibniz does not make it explicit, the underlying idea seems to be that of a procedure in which, of each pair of contradictory predicates, A and not-A, one and only one is taken. In other words, a "complete being" is an object for which the law of the excluded middle holds without restriction. But the problem remains: how can one define the stock of predicates that are presupposed? According to the general metaphysical background of Leibniz's logic, it is commonly held that the ingredients employed to construct a complete concept are, ultimately, simple concepts that are combined by the logical operation of conjunction. These conceptual tools, however—the only ones made available by Leibniz's algebra of concepts—are far from adequate for this task. In order to be used to construct an individual concept, they have to go through several transformations and be combined in complex ways.

Ingredients for a Complete Concept

Leibniz insisted on the peculiar features of his complete concepts, in contrast to the "incomplete" (i.e. general and abstract). Let me consider them briefly.

(a) *Infinite complexity.* The most obvious feature is the larger complexity of such a concept, which reflects the full determination of a concrete being. More precisely, this complexity is labeled as *infinite*, where infinity becomes the mark of individuality. This is connected, on the one hand, with Leibniz's cosmological view of a holistic world of infinitely divided matter, where "tout est lié"[19]; on the other, with his fascinating attempt, inspired by mathematical suggestions, at giving an account of contingency through the notion of infinite analysis, within his unified theory of truth. While a necessary truth can be proved in a finite number of steps, it is an impossible task to give a proof of a contingent truth, since the required analysis involves an infinite series of steps.[20] God

---

[17] A VI.4, 553.

[18] GI, Section 72, AVI.4, 762 (C 375). The definition makes use of the indefinite letters, used in this work to express a rudimentary quantification.

[19] See, for this aspect, Carriero 1993–1995.

[20] The idea of infinite analysis, with the analogy between contingent truths and irrational numbers, does not appear in the *Discourse* or in the discussion with Arnauld, while is presented as the solution to the contingency problem in other coeval or slightly later texts. See *Generales Inquisitiones*, secs. 62–67, 131–36; *De libertate*, A VI.4, 1655–1658; *De natura veritatis, contingentiae etc.*, A VI.4, 1516; *Origo veritatum contingentium*, A VI.4, 1659–1664; *De illatione et veritate*, A VI.4, 863.

as well does not achieve the analysis; rather God intuitively "sees" the inclusion of the predicate in the subject also in the case of contingent truths.[21]

(b) *Temporal order.* In DM, Leibniz's discussion shifts from "predicates" to "events" or "happenings." Better, an individual accident[22] corresponds to the whole "state" of a substance. The different states form a series, insofar as they are both causally and temporally connected. The experience of time was originally presupposed by Leibniz's idea of individual substance, which is rooted also in his philosophy of mind;[23] but, now, time is somehow included in the individual concept itself. Consider this passage in the *Notationes*, which illustrates the a priori foundation of transtemporal identity claimed in the Arnauld correspondence: "a thing can remain the same, though changed, if from its very nature it follows that the same thing must pass successively through different states. I myself am said, indeed, to be the same as I was before, because my substance involves all my past, present and future states. And it does not matter that in this way contradictory properties are predicated of me; the nature of time, in fact, amounts just to the fact that contradictory predicates can be true of one and the same thing, according to different times."[24] The last lines allude to Leibniz's "logical" interpretation of time as a way of neutralizing the contradiction lurking in the attribution of A and not-A to the same thing. Other drafts show how temporal succession depends on the causal order, the latter being in turn conceptually interpreted through the notion of the "order of nature."

(c) *Relational import.* Time is a relational order: "all propositions that involve existence and time, by this very fact involve the whole series of things; neither the 'now' or the 'here,' in fact, can be understood unless through a relation to the other things."[25] The reference to a wider context—more precisely, a *world*, to which it belongs—is a final decisive feature for this type of concept. Already for the *De Cogitationum* the reference to "all existing things" was the mark of individuality. Predicative maximality corresponds to the maximality of compossibility relations within a system of concepts. Something more than compossibility as noncontradiction, however, seems required for individual concepts belonging to a common system. Their mutual relation is qualified as "expression," and counted among the "paradoxical" consequences of the complete concept view. By the same move, the denial of intersubstantial causation follows: if a substance

---

[21] This "vision" should not be assimilated, however, to a kind of "empirical" or a posteriori knowledge. Leibniz is eager to insist on the fact that God knows a priori the *reasons* of contingent truths. Thus, it is possible in principle to give a reason for them, although it is not possible to give a demonstrative proof. Neither is it possible, at least for the human mind, to grasp a rule governing the progression. Here also the mathematical analogy breaks down.

[22] It is worth distinguishing the *concept* of a predicate, included in the complete concept, and the corresponding *accident* inhering in the individual. We can leave here further questioning about the reality of accidents within Leibniz's ontological reflection.

[23] See for instance the important draft *De Affectibus* (1679), where a psychological study on the *series cogitationum* yields a logical model of the series of states of a substance. See on this Schepers 2003.

[24] A VI.4, 556.

[25] *De natura veritatis etc.*, A VI.4, 1517.

already involves its world in its own depth, there is no need to postulate any real external interaction.

This "internalization" of world connection is often expressed by Leibniz in terms of the need for the grounding of relational predicates on the "intrinsic" ones. At least since Russell's criticism, a lot of ink has been spilled over Leibniz's alleged "reduction of relations." I cannot enter here into the intricacies of this debate.[26] It is important, however, to distinguish between conceptual containment and inherence. While individual accidents inhere in one individual substance only, concepts do include relations. Better yet, the content itself of individual accidents—independently of their ontological status, which is firmly rooted in their substance—expresses the other individuals belonging to their world.[27] Consider that they are presented as complex *perceptual* states. Thus, the "connectedness" with a world is a fundamental feature of the individual concept. Leibniz stresses that Adam's concept is not determined enough, as long as it contains only the general reference to "a woman" or "a garden" without referring to "Eve" and "the Eden."[28]

Features (a–c), taken together, confirm that the individual concept is modeled on a presupposed view of concrete individuals. It is the type of concept that matches existing things; more exactly, both actually and *possibly* existing things. A possible individual exhibits a certain internal structure and involves a certain type of predicates: "in this complete concept of Peter *as possible*. . . I concede that not only essential or necessary properties are included, *flowing from incomplete or specific notions*. . . but also existential [*existentialia*], so to speak, or contingent ones."[29]

The Individual as "Species Infima"

In vindicating the peculiar features (a–c) of his complete concept, Leibniz always contrasts it with specific notions in general, and mathematical ones in particular—the opposition being exemplified by the contrast between a mathematical concept (the sphere) and a particular, material instance of it (the sphere on Archimedes's tomb).

In apparent contrast with this, he presents his IdInd as the thesis that the individual is truly the lowest species. This equivalence is illustrated by two further comparisons: (a) Aquinas's thesis on angelic individuation, according to which each angel is like a lowest species;[30] and (b) the "sense of geometers," according to which two figures specifically

---

[26] See Mugnai 1992.

[27] Mugnai 1992 tries to capture this aspect by the distinction between "intermonadic" and "intramonadic" relations.

[28] See GP II 42, Mason 45.

[29] A VI.4, 1601 (italics mine). The term *existentialia* is coined precisely to capture those predicates that—though having no proper existential import—do refer to (possible) existence.

[30] It was not considered in the 1663 *Disputatio*, due to its limited scope (but it was criticized in Thomasius's *Preface*), whereas it is now endorsed and extended to all beings.

differ insofar as their difference can be conceptually expressed, thus allowing one to derive different properties.

Even when assimilating his individual concept with a lowest species, however, Leibniz is eager to distinguish the latter from (a) a biological species, for instance "dog," which is too vague, and (b) "universal concepts" in general, which are built up from a finite number of elements.[31] Thus, the complete concept distinguishes itself from two types of essentialist views: the old Aristotelian one, modeled on biological species or "natural kinds," and the Cartesian view, modeled on mathematical objects. It is worth noting that a finite number of ingredients gives the possibility of achieving the analysis of a concept, hence *demonstrating* its properties. This allows Leibniz to circumscribe a subset of properties within the complete concept, that can be "demonstrated," that is, are necessary.[32] Still, in metaphysical rigor, *all* constituents of the concept are "intrinsic," and any change would compromise the identity of the concept and the corresponding individual. To try to capture the sense of this intrinsicalness—the crucial one for his denial of counterfactual identity—it is worth considering a double polarity in Leibniz's presentation of the complete concept: one concerning its inner structure, and the other its link to the corresponding individual.

Sum of Predicates or Principle of Deduction?

There is a standard view (A) of the complete concept, according to which it would be nothing but an (infinite) list of predicates simply built up by the logical operators of conjunction and negation—or better, according to the foregoing remarks, an ordered series of states.

Leibniz's texts, however, do not fail to suggest a slightly different view (B), according to which the individual concept would not consist properly in the sum, or in the series of its predicates, but in a unitary principle of deduction, *over and above* the series and capable to account for it. The *De cogitationum Analysi* already gestured in this direction, and the texts that construe the complete concept in the *Notationes* style present a similar view: something is B, C, D, and so on *because* it is A. In his *Remarques* for a letter to Arnauld, then, Leibniz circumscribes a set of basic properties as the proper content of an individual concept.[33] Reading (B) has never been made fully explicit, nor

---

[31] For these distinctions, see *Notationes Generales*, A VI.4 553–554.

[32] E.g., the properties corresponding to the general concept "man," like "rationality." From a terminological point of view, Leibniz is often willing to reserve the label "essential" for this core. This has to be accurately distinguished, of course, from the meaning of "essential" relevant to "super-essentialism": the thesis (equivalent to the denial of counterfactual identity) that all properties are somehow essential to the individual. See for this controversial label Mondadori 1973, 1975, and his later clarifications.

[33] "The predicates of Adam depend or do not depend upon other predicates of the same Adam. Setting aside, therefore, those which depend upon others, one has only to consider together all the primitive predicates in order to form the complete concept of Adam adequate to deduce from it everything that is ever to happen to him, as much as is necessary to be able to account for it." (GP II 44, Mason 48) The passage was omitted in the final version of the letter actually sent.

was completely articulated by Leibniz, and many other passages tend to encourage the "standard view" (A). Still, version (B) seems to be the more natural way of making sense of the robust metaphysical import Leibniz attributes to his concept.

Concept and Thing: Embodiment

Far from being extrinsically linked to an individual thing, the concept is "embodied" within it. In other terms, it expresses a form-like nature that involves change. This is why Leibniz can connect it to his attempt at rehabilitating the Aristotelian notion of "nature" ("physis") as a principle of change.[34] And this gives its proper sense to the "intrinsicalness" of properties. In Leibniz's view, only the continuity that results from this inner capacity to master change provides an adequate account for sameness. This complex of ideas might provide a plausible ground for making sense of his puzzling denial of counterfactual identity.[35]

The "embodiment" of the concept and the related involvement of the individual's future career are often expressed by Leibniz in nomological terms. In the example of the "moy," the future predicates are transformed into "laws" already contained within their subject. The complete concept itself is equated with the "law" of the development of an individual, which reflects that of its whole world. As a corollary, a substance is said to contain in its present states the marks of its future states, as well as the traces of the past ones: an idea that could hardly be captured by a model of "complete concept" extrinsic to the thing.[36]

INDIVIDUAL HISTORY AND DESTINY: A THEODICY OF COMPLETE CONCEPTS

Individual Histories and the Concerns of Theodicy

According to DM 8, in seeing Alexander's "haecceity" God perceives the content of his "soul," with the "marks and traces" of his history, which are unknown to us and were mainly unknown even to Alexander himself.[37] Leibniz's usual examples of individual

---

[34] See *De natura sive analogo animae*, A VI.4, 1505. It is worth noting that the complete concept includes also miracles; hence its content exceeds another restricted (more epistemological) sense of "nature."

[35] This layer of Leibniz's thought has been emphasized by Adams 1985 and Sleigh 1990.

[36] See on this last remark Woolhouse 1982.

[37] Interestingly enough, in the redaction of the *Discourse*, Leibniz's first example was a material object—Gyges's or Polycrates's ring—but then it was skipped and replaced with "Alexander." See DM 8, A VI.4, 1540, and the remarks in Fichant 2004.

substances are historical figures, often considered at some crucial junctures of their careers; their complete concepts are mainly copies of their histories. Though being forced into a "logical" scheme, their matrix is basically a narrative one. It is important to remember that a favorite Leibnizian argument on behalf of possible (and unrealized) individuals is taken from literary novels and their characters.[38]

But the choice of examples and the focus on the individual's history largely obey concerns of theodicy. So far, I have considered the complete concept as a limiting notion in Leibniz's logic of concepts, or the key to his substance ontology. Most of all, however, it is used in the context of his metaphysics of creation and theodicy. Creation, indeed, is conceived of as the divine choice of one among many possible worlds in God's intellect, whose building blocks are complete concepts. In the 1680s, Leibniz has already firmly established the main lines of his theodicy project and is ready to articulate them in terms of his complete concept view.

Theological Foundation, Future Contingents, and Possible Decrees

The individual histories included in the concepts are usually considered from the perspective of divine knowledge. We already know that only God can possess complete concepts. Sometimes this theological anchorage is emphasized, as if it were the only foundation for the possibility and reality of them. Thus, at a first stage of his discussion with Arnauld, Leibniz tries to shift the burden of his theory onto the theological side, as if the complete concept were simply equivalent to the perfect knowledge God possesses of each individual.[39]

In this context, the topic of the complete concept tends to be translated into the venerable one of contingent futures: admittedly a highly controversial issue, but also one with which no theologian committed to divine omniscience could help but dealing. This way, the difficulties imputed to his own theory would at worst be shared by the standard accepted theological view. This move, however, is not simply a tactical one, given that the link with contingent futures is also documented in many unpublished Leibnizian drafts.

---

[38] I am thinking of the so-called novel argument. This idea of alternative "series of things" inspired by imaginary stories and situated nowhere seems to be a distinct source of the Leibnizian idea of "possible worlds." I have used the expression "possible individual"; interpreters have correctly stressed that unactualized worlds are populated by concepts—their ontological status being that of objects of divine understanding. Still, I think it is possible in principle to distinguish, also for these unactualized concepts, a "haecceitistic" element or core property from the set/series of their derived properties/states.

[39] See Leibniz's April letter and Arnauld's admission that he had not understood that the complete concept was referred to divine knowledge (GP II 28; Mason 27). As a matter of fact, the move was unhappy, insofar as Arnauld firmly contrasted every attempt at univocally treating divine and human ideas, and blurring respective knowledge (see GP II 31). In his following reply, Leibniz comes back to justify the complete concept even independently of God. Anyway, concepts "are represented in the divine understanding as they are in themselves" (GP II 48–49).

In the *First Truths*, the complete concept is introduced on the basis of the present determination of future statements—the latter having in turn a double ground: the theological one of foreknowledge and the purely logical one of bivalence.[40] In a theodicy draft of this period, the complete concept is presented exactly as the "objective reality of all truths" about a certain individual: "I well concede that there is something that exists before Peter's existence, and from which it infallibly follows that he will deny: I mean, there is his perfect possible notion or idea, that consists in the objective reality of all truths about Peter. . . and the reality of that possible notion of Peter does subsist from eternity in God."[41] The question still remains as to what makes these statements true. It could be the divine idea itself, and this seems to capture Leibniz's intuition in the best possible way.[42] Interestingly, this solution was traditionally felt to be unsatisfactory, insofar as it seemed to leave out God's will as well as to imply the necessity of the related truth.[43]

In Leibniz's mind, however, relying on a divine idea does not exclude the consideration of divine will. His last resource both in private reflection and discussion, in fact, is the appeal for the inclusion of God's "*possible decrees*" within the complete concept.[44] This strategy has usually been taken by interpreters as the quasi-desperate move of a philosopher forced into a corner. I do not think so. The notion of a possible decree, indeed, does reflect Leibniz's deep insight concerning the peculiar inner structure of the complete concept, embodying connections both causal and contingent.[45]

The problem with this strategy is that by weakening the internal connections of the concept, it seems to make talk about conceptual containment ultimately vacuous. Moreover, it runs afoul of another strategy Leibniz wants to apply in theodicy contexts.

Compactness as a Theodicy Strategy and "World-Bound Individuals"

As a matter of fact, the "compactness" of the complete concept, the main source of Arnauld's worries, played a relevant role in its theodicean usage by Leibniz. Provided that the concept, which is the object of divine will, is something which has to be taken

---

[40] *Principia logico-metaphysica*, A VI.4, 1646.

[41] *De libertate fato gratia Dei*, A VI.4, 1598.

[42] In this case, the objective reality itself would work as a truth-maker, more than as a truth-bearer.

[43] This point is made e.g. by Scotus in *Ordinatio* 1, dist. 38.2–39.

[44] To escape Arnauld's dilemma (either a predicate is included in the concept, hence is necessary, or is contingent, but then is not included in the concept), Leibniz stresses how "God's free decrees, considered as possible, enter into the concept of the possible Adam, while the same decrees, once they became actual, were the cause of the actual Adam" (GP II 51; Mason 56). For some other occurrences of the strategy, see e.g. *De natura veritatis etc.*, A VI.4, 1522–1523; *De libertate fato etc.*, A VI.4, 1646, *Specimen inventorum*, A VI.4, 1619, *Principia logico-metaphysica*, A VI.4, 1646.

[45] "The possibilities of individuals or of contingent truths contain within their notion the possibility of their causes, that is to say of God's free decrees; and in this they differ from the possibilities of species or eternal truths" (GP II 51; Mason).

or left *en bloc*, then God does not properly decree that "Judas will betray" but only that Judas will exist, accompanied by the actions and circumstances that belong to his concept.[46] Such a shift is made more plausible by the technical trick of translating *tertii adjecti* propositions ("Petrus est abnegans") into *secundi adjecti* ones ("Petrus-abnegans est"). But clearly the move is a relevant one, only if there is some metaphysical ground for privileging the "en bloc" reading, that is, if there is an internal connection that God himself cannot help changing; and this is precisely what the possible decrees strategy attempts to avoid. I do not see a way out of this predicament. The two strategies seem to reflect two opposite interpretations of the inner structure of the complete concept; nevertheless, Leibniz is poised to invoke them in the same paragraph.

The "en bloc" shift is applied to man's point of view, in order to eliminate any ground for lamenting one's destiny. The desire to change one's own choices and circumstances is equated to the absurd desire to change one's identity: "But someone else may say, how does it come about that this man will certainly commit this sin? The reply is easy; it is that *otherwise he would not be this man*."[47] The connection of this theodicean strategy to the denial of counterfactual identity is immediate. Far from being considered problematic, this denial is therefore introduced by Leibniz as the key for a solution.

It has been aptly observed that in this context he probably did not intend to use his possible worlds' machinery to define modal notions. Still, in a similar framework one might make sense of contingency for a world-bound individual by pointing to that individual's nonexistence in all worlds with the exception of one.[48] Properly speaking, therefore, the only contingent property of an individual would be her or his existence. Supporters of this interpretation, however, try to account for the intuitive modal distinctions within the predicates by taking Leibniz's talk about "possible Adams" or "possible Sextuses" as a counterpart-theoretical account *ante litteram*.[49] Leibniz, in any event, is prepared to handle also contingent statements having merely possible individuals as their subjects.

Making Sense of Counterfactual Talk: Counterparts and Individuals *Sub Ratione Generalitatis*

Given the close link between the complete concept and the notion of world-bound individuals, it is no surprise that Leibniz is adamant that no counterfactual statement having a proper name as its subject can be interpreted literally: "Most

---

[46] See for instance *Principia log.-met.*, A VI.4, 1646; *Specimen inventorum*, A VI.4, 1619; *De libertate fato etc.*, A VI.4, 1603; *De libertate*, A VI.4, 1657; *De natura veritatis etc.*, A VI.4, 1451.

[47] *Discourse*, sec. 30, A VI.4, 1576; L 322.

[48] See Mondadori 1975.

[49] Compare David Lewis's metaphysical interpretation of modal discourse, according to which no individual belongs to more than one world (i.e. they are "world-bound"), and modal assertions concerning her/him are interpreted via her or his "counterparts"—that is to say, the individuals most resembling her or him in the other worlds.

future conditional statements have antecedent conditions which are inconsistent. When I ask, in fact, what would have happened, if Peter had not denied Christ, I am asking what would happen, if Peter were not Peter. His denial is contained, indeed, in the complete concept of Peter."[50] Nevertheless, Leibniz's theory of individual concepts seems also to provide a promising framework for a reasonable evaluation of counterfactuals; or at least to allow for a more liberal usage of proper names. Different approaches are contemplated.

(a) Once it is admitted that talk about "possible Adams" or "possible Sextuses" is deprived of metaphysical strength, it can be permitted as a loose usage, suitable to express *our* finite point of view. The name "Adam" in this sense does not stand for a complete concept, but for an incomplete one, or better, for a family of concepts conceived with a certain degree of vagueness.

The complete concept has been contrasted earlier with the common types of general concepts—traditional universals or abstract mathematical objects. Now it is opposed to a notion that, while still general, is located at a lower level than the specific one: the "individual *sub ratione generalitatis*,"[51] which is capable of being further determined in more than one way. It can be captured by a definite description, able to univocally identify its reference in our actual world, but not among all possible worlds and individuals, for example, when "Adam" stands for "the first man."

Leibniz seems not to be particularly interested in using the members of this "resemblance family" to make sense of *de re* modal discourse. Rather, he simply insists on their nonidentity: a "Caesar" who does not cross the Rubicon cannot be our Caesar.

(b) When Leibniz is really concerned with giving a truth value to counterfactual talk, he has to focus on this or that member of the family, with a more constructivist attitude. In the selfsame piece where he rejects the possibility of a "Peter-who-does-not-deny," he shows how to construe a corresponding concept (say, P'): "by the name 'Peter' [in this derived sense] all the properties are intended, that are implied by the conditions from which the denial does not follow."[52] The concept at hand is, again, an incomplete one, which is construed, however, in a precise and controlled way. When making sense of *our* counterfactual discourse, Leibniz does not think of mates picked out in other worlds on the basis of their resemblance; rather, he has in mind

---

[50] Grua 358. The passage is taken from Leibniz's notes to a book by Twisse on middle knowledge. A parallel passage commenting the standard biblical reference for middle knowledge—the oracle given to David about what would the inhabitant of Keilah do, if he were to remain in their town—presents, however, a significant oscillation: after saying, according to his usual stance, that those Keilites would *not* be "ours," Leibniz corrects himself in the margin, saying that they *would be* the same, given that their notion contains their contingent free actions. See his notes to L. de Dole's book, A VI.4, 1789–1790. This can also be seen as a document of the persistent tension between a "compact view" of the complete concept and another making room for inner contingency.

[51] See the seminal occurrences in GP II 42, 54: "I did not consider Adam as a determinate individual, but as some person conceived *sub ratione generalitatis*, under some circumstances which seem to determine him to individuality, but do not determine him enough."

[52] Grua 358.

a determinate variation procedure starting with characters of our world. Only, he is always eager to insist that there is no identity here.

A couple of texts go so far as to envisage the translation of one individual into a different set of circumstances,[53] by emphasizing the "inner" difference among individual substances and the distinction between this inner core and the properties deriving from the relation with their respective world.[54]

(c) In the mind of God, unactualized individuals in unactualized worlds do have their *complete* concepts, which provide a basis for *God's* knowledge of what would have (contingently) happened if God had decided to actualize one of those worlds instead of ours. This topic was objectively connected with the wide debate on "middle knowledge," namely God's knowledge of "conditional futures." The final tale of the *Theodicy* discloses to us in narrative fashion this type of knowledge; moreover, it attributes to those unactualized individuals the value of a truth-maker for counterfactuals: in *seeing* the different "Sextuses," each inhabiting one apartment in the Palace of Destiny, one can see the alternative careers our Sextus could have embraced.[55] This time, a true complete concept is supposed to correspond to each of them, in order to provide determinate answers to our questions. Our vague or partial concept of an individual *sub ratione generalitatis* resolves itself into a set of perfectly determinate and disjunctively possible concepts.

I point out here only one feature of these alleged "Leibnizian counterparts"—one among several differences from the Lewisian-style counterparts with which we are familiar. Leibniz is eager to emphasize that in metaphysical rigor it is impossible that there are two individuals sharing the same history up to a certain point before branching. And this is because of a strong causal constraint, according to which each state is deterministically connected to the antecedent and following ones. Thus, we are faced with "some similar Sextuses, *having all you already know about the true Sextus, but not all that is already within him without being consciously perceived,* and therefore, not all that will happen to him in the future."[56]

Besides its holistic character, the divine knowledge of alternative histories differs from our own because it appears as a knowledge by acquaintance. Concepts are not construed, but contemplated "in the mirror" of divine understanding. The contrast,

---

[53] In a draft on middle knowledge (*Scientia Media*, 1677), Leibniz imagines Peter and Paul put into a perfectly similar setting. Their different choices will depend on their inner constitution, that is to say from "Paulinity" and "Petrinity." See A VI.4, 1374. In any case, the reference to haecceities is not "haecceitistic" in the present-day sense, insofar as they are supposed to have a qualitative and descriptive content, from which certain properties follow.

[54] This point is explicitly made in *Mentes ipsae per se dissimiles sunt inter se*. These passages might be used (incorrectly, in my view) to support the attribution to Leibniz of a kind of "transworld identity" view, allowing for one and the same individual being in two or more different worlds. However, Leibniz normally conceives the relationship of an individual with its world in a more intimate way.

[55] See *Essais de Théodicée*, GP VI 362–365.

[56] GP VI, 363. Notice the reference to the "mark and traces" thesis.

however, might not be so decisive. Leibniz's critical reflections on middle knowledge show that for him divine knowledge can never be an "empirical" one, nor can it simply record connections without a reason. Alternative histories always represent causal chains unfolding according to a rule.[57]

THE COMPLETE CONCEPT AFTER 1686

In the following decades, other approaches to substance are privileged, like the dynamical and monadological ones. One might suspect that the central focus on the individual concept is an important, but relatively circumscribed episode. I do not think so. First, this approach to individual substance provides a very general and abstract logico-ontological characterization, liable to be further specified in different ways.

Second, as a matter of fact Leibniz never rejects the complete concept view. This emerges unmistakably as a deep underlying layer of his thought in passages written until the last period of his life. Clear allusions to this view are contained in the exchanges after the "*New System*" and in the important de Volder correspondence.[58] In the last years of Leibniz's life, some more or less direct hints can be found—besides the narrative illustration of the final tale of the *Theodicy*—in private writings, such as the *Notes* to Temmik (a dense text on ontological topics),[59] or the intriguing *Apokatastasis* fragment, where combinatorial logic mixes with a philosophical meditation on human history. This gives occasion to consider the application of the logic of complete concepts to historical thought. Referring to an imaginary historical library Leibniz, the chronicler, takes into account the description of human history at different levels. The more and more detail contained within the pages and lines recalls the image of the books in the Palace of

---

[57] Moreover, also in the divine mind the identification of the world relevant for the evaluation of a counterfactual is presented as the result of a determinate variation procedure. See the comparison with the geometrical *locus* in *Theodicy*, § 414 (GP VI 362–363).

[58] See for instance these passages from a letter to de Volder: "I know that the Cartesians have felt otherwise [namely about the concept of substance]. . . but I know also that this resulted from a lack of adequate analysis, the touchstone of which is a demonstration of predicates from the subject" (GP II 239; L 526); "Matter is an incomplete being, lacking in a source for its actions. . . . Things are quite different for the soul or the mind. Since the latter is a true substance or a *complete being*, which is the source of its actions. . ." (GP II 249; L 528–529); "Singular beings do involve infinity, while by framing universal concepts we take into account only certain aspects, and leave aside innumerable others. Thus only in the case of singular things do we have a *complete concept*, which involves also changes" (GP II 277).

[59] "If individuals are understood as complete concepts, then [a predicate, or a relation] does not add anything. One might say that contingent properties are essential to the individuals, given that it is proper of individual concepts to contain all contingent predicates. Actually, however, contingent properties are not essential with respect to all predicates of the individual which do not exhaust her or his whole content and power." Mugnai draws attention to this passage of the "Notes to Temmik" edited by him. See Mugnai 1992, app. 4, 156–157, translation mine.

Destiny in Sextus's tale, where a line is prodigiously scaled up to show the extreme detail of the life of an individual. In the *Apokathastasis*, this descent into infinite detail turns out to be decisive in order to escape the cyclical closure to which the combinatorial logic (on the assumption of a finite set of elements) seemed to commit human history itself. That *infinite* detail, indeed, is bound to be made explicit in the unfolding of time, and to always open new horizons to our mind. Thus it is not by chance that the last lines of the draft focus on the *infinite* task of our empirical science in approaching individuality. The example is no longer Alexander's soul, but the much humbler one of a common insect. Still, it is enough to suggest the infinite depth of individual reality: "If we consider a fly, as well as a circle, as subject matter for science, it will be clear that the definition of fly, which exhibits its structure, is enormously more complicated than the definition of a circle. As a consequence, theorems concerning the fly will be very complex, and all the more those concerning this or that species of fly, not to speak of individuals that are subject to that quasi-science [*cuidam semiscientiae*] we need when passing from theory to praxis."[60] The reference to a "quasi science" sounds as a suggestive allusion to that desired science of the individual that Leibniz so often contemplated at the point where two of his most deeply entrenched ideas intersected: the idea of an all-embracing conceptual knowledge and the intuition that all that is real is individual.

REFERENCES

R. M. Adams. "Primitive Thisness and Primitive Identity." *Journal of Philosophy 76*, 1979, pp. 5–26.

R. M. Adams. "Predication, Truth and Trans-world Identity in Leibniz." In J. Bogen and E. McGuire, eds., *How Things Are*. Dordrecht: Reidel, 1985, 235–283.

R. M. Adams. *Leibniz: Determinist, Theist, Idealist*. Oxford: Oxford University Press, 1994.

C. D. Broad. "Leibniz's Predicate-in-Notion Principle and Some of Its Alleged Consequences." *Theoria XV* (1949), 54–70.

J. Carriero. "Leibniz on Infinite Resolution and Intra-mundane Contingency." Pts. 1 and 2. *Studia Leibnitiana 25* (1993), 1–26; *27*, 1995, 1–30.

L. Couturat. "Sur la métaphysique de Leibniz." *Revue de métaphysique et de morale 10* (1902), 1–25. Translated as *On Leibniz's Metaphysics*, in Frankfurt 1972.

J. Cover and J. Hawthorne. *Substance and Individuation in Leibniz*. Cambridge: Cambridge University Press, 1998.

S. Di Bella. *The Science of the Individual: Leibniz's Ontology of Individual Substance*. Berlin: Springer, 2005.

G. W. Leibniz. *L'horizon de la doctrine humaine. La Restitution universelle*. Edited and translated by M. Fichant. Paris: Vrin, 1991.

M. Fichant. "L'invention métaphysique." Introduction to *G. W. Leibniz: Discours de métaphysique. Monadologie*. Paris: Gallimard, 2004.

---

[60] Fichant 1991, 76.

H. Frankfurt, ed. *Leibniz: A Collection of Critical Essays.* Garden City, N.Y.: Doubleday Anchor, 1972.

M. Hooker, ed. *Leibniz: Critical and Interpretative Essays.* Minneapolis: University of Minnesota Press, 1982.

B. Mates. "Individuals and Modality in the Philosophy of Leibniz." *Studia Leibnitiana 4* (1972), 81–118.

B. Mates. *The Philosophy of Leibniz: Metaphysics and Philosophy of Language.* Oxford: Oxford University Press, 1986.

F. Mondadori. "Reference, essentialism and modality in Leibniz's Metaphysics." *Studia Leibnitiana 5* (1973), 73–101.

F. Mondandori. "Leibniz and the Doctrine of Inter-World Identity." *Studia Leibnitiana 7* (1975), 22–57.

M. Mugnai. *Leibniz's Theory of Relations.* Stuttgart: Steiner, 1992.

M. Mugnai. "Leibniz on Individuation: From the Early Years to the Discourse and Beyond." *Studia Leibnitiana 33* (2001), 35–64.

B. Russell. *A Critical Exposition of the Philosophy of Leibniz.* London: Allen and Unwin, 1900. 2nd ed. 1937.

D. Rutherford. "Truth, Predication and the Complete Concept of an Individual Substance." In A. Heinekamp, ed., *Leibniz: Questions de logique.* Studia Leibnitiana Sonderheft 15. Wiesbaden: Steiner, 1988, 130–144.

H. Schepers. "*De affectibus.* Leibniz an der Schwelle zur Monadologie: Seine Vorarbeiten zur logischen Aufbau der möglichen Welten." *Studia Leibnitiana 35* (2003), 133–161.

R. Sleigh. *Leibniz and Arnauld: A Commentary on Their Correspondence.* New Haven: Yale University Press, 1990.

P. F. Strawson. *Individuals.* London: Methuen, 1959.

R. Woolhouse. "The Nature of an Individual Substance." In Hooker 1982, 45–64.

R. Yost. *Leibniz and Philosophical Analysis.* Berkeley: University of California Press, 1954; reprint, New York: Garland, 1987.

CHAPTER 8

THEORY OF KNOWLEDGE

Mathematical and Natural Science

MARTHA BOLTON

LEIBNIZ is less interested in precise definitions of knowledge and certainty than in the conditions that enable human beings to acquire them. That it is possible for us to have propositional knowledge is not in question, still the various openings to skepticism afforded by different areas of inquiry do need to be addressed.[1] To Leibniz's mind, the epistemic merit of assent must be rated with reference to specific topics: "Only that degree of certainty is to be had which a given matter admits. But even when defined most rigorously, certainty is nothing but the clearness of truth."[2] He does recognize three general standards of certainty; the last two admit grades and are not mutually exclusive. The highest is "Evidence [which] is luminous certitude, that is, where we have no doubt because of the way we can see the ideas linked to be linked together" (NE 445). "Ideas" here refers to the concepts contained in a proposition. Beyond that: "*Certainty* might be taken to be knowledge of a truth such that to doubt it in a practical way would be insane, and sometimes it is taken more broadly, to cover cases where doubt would be very blameworthy" (NE 445). The third standard is probability. It is well known that Leibniz envisages probability as a general measure of the uncertainty of a proposition but found no way to calculate its value.[3] Still, he uses a scalable notion of objective probability to rank hypotheses. More generally, strategies for imposing rational structure on uncertain propositions are of the utmost importance for him. They allow human beings to establish propositions on which all rational parties can agree, to end disputes, to secure pegs and platforms for further reasoning. As for Descartes's way of proceeding: "[The] dictum that everything in which there is the least uncertainty is to be doubted might

---

[1] On Leibniz's complex response to skepticism in its various guises, see E. de Olaso (1997).

[2] "Preface to an Edition of Nizolius" 1670; A VI ii 409; L 122.

[3] He did devise mathematical means of determining several sorts of uncertain matters, such as the value of life annuities, as well as applying mathematics to issues of public interest, such as the correct rebate on borrowed money; much of this work is in G. W. Leibniz 2000; also G. W. Leibniz 1995.

have been more exactly formulated in the precept that we must consider the degree of assent or dissent which a matter deserves, or more simply, that we must look into the reasons for every doctrine."[4]

Leibniz investigates a question that is Aristotelian in spirit: what are the conditions that make it possible for human beings to assemble reasons for assent in various areas of concern and with appropriate assurances of truth? In Leibniz's hands, this takes into account a wide range of factors: human cognitive faculties, the nature of reality and general features of the actual world, as well as methods for the collection of data, ways of organizing such data that are apt for the discovery of causes and solution of problems, and ways of exhibiting the results as reasons for propositional assent. In the late seventeenth century, geometry and other branches of mathematics were thought to exemplify the highest degree of certainty human beings have attained. Accordingly, the demonstration of geometrical truths is the starting point of Leibniz's theory. The model is then adapted to demonstration in the natural sciences. This chapter is limited to Leibniz's theory of demonstration in mathematics and the natural sciences, but the model applies, with adjustments, to metaphysics, law, morality, and all other sciences (i.e., areas in which we can aspire to explain many truths on the basis of a few).[5] Other important parts of his theory of knowledge are not discussed for lack of space, including certainty about the existence of sensible things[6] and the grounds of assent to singular truths.

Several metaphysical doctrines shape the epistemic doctrines. One is that a human soul is a simple immaterial substance with an intrinsic disposition and tendency to obtain knowledge.[7] Constantly striving to improve the quality and extent of what it knows, a soul incorporates a causal apparatus sufficient for realizing more and more of its cognitive potential,[8] but does so haltingly, gradually, and over an indefinitely long period of time. For Leibniz, as for Aristotle, cognition is naturally connected with action: "[P]erception . . . consists in a certain action" (1710?).[9] Certainty sufficient for acting is thus a constant primary goal of a human being; progress in this matter is inherently pleasing. Something like this is true, in an abstract way, of all non-rational simple substances (monads), although their perceptions range downward over increasing degrees of confusion. A second important metaphysical doctrine

---

[4] "Critical Thoughts on the General Part of the Principles of Descartes" 1692, 1.1; GP IV 334–335; L 383.
[5] A VI vi 454; NE 454.
[6] On this, see "On the Method of Distinguishing Real from Imaginary Phenomena," A VI iv 1499–1504; L 363; also NE 374–375.
[7] In this chapter, "human mind" and "human soul" are used interchangeably; a human mind is a rational soul, or spirit, according to Leibniz.
[8] All created substances are subject to the pre-established harmony. They are causally isolated from each other but exquisitely harmonized in all their perceptions and actions. Leibniz offers a rudimentary metaphysical-cognitive-psychological theory of the operational constitution of a human soul meant to explain its cognitive performance; see Bolton 2011.
[9] "On the Souls of Men and Beasts," GP VII 328; Strickland 63. The following is entered in a long list of definitions: "Appetite is conatus arising from cognition." (Table of Definitions 1702–04, C 491); also "On the Present World" 1684–85/6?; A VI iv 1508; Arthur, 382–397.

proclaims the thoroughgoing intelligibility of reality. God, who is essentially rational, is at once the metaphysical ground of all possibilities, all truths and in possession of perfect knowledge of them. This humanly unattainable standard of certainty is not ancillary to Leibniz's theory of knowledge. Human beings may, on rare occasions, attain a certainty close to that enjoyed by God but, for the most part, manage with representations of reality that are more or less confused or incomplete but improvable.

DEMONSTRATION OF NECESSARY TRUTHS

In seventeenth-century philosophy, the term "demonstration" is generally used to mean reasoning that shows that a proposition necessarily follows from suppositions that are certain. As Leibniz says, "demonstration is reasoning by which some proposition is made certain" (to Conring, March 19, 1678; GP 1.193–99; L 187). According to the common view, a science demonstrates theorems or general laws from a small number of "first principles" that are primary in respect of certainty. But a very early essay "On the Demonstration of Primary Propositions," claims that first principles can themselves be demonstrated. Putting it differently, "no proposition is to be accepted without proof . . . that is, as long as delaying inquiry can be borne."[10] This is not innocent. First principles are precisely premises, not conclusions. Moreover, it was widely understood that, on the assumption that no proposition can be affirmed without proof, the proof of any proposition avoids reasoning in a circle only if it runs to infinity. The essay defies the skeptical threat. The controversial claim is not made with regard to truths of sense or facts about things that exist but only with regard to "propositions of reason." They "derive from ideas alone"; consequently, they are conditional and necessary—that is, eternal truths such as the abstract propositions of geometry and arithmetic. That necessary propositions are true independently of everything that exists contingently is taken for granted, and the aim is to explain how it is possible for humans to assent to such propositions for reasons that preclude doubt.

According to this early essay, first principles of reason "originate in definitions." They "follow solely from a precise and distinct explanation [of words], that is definitions" (A VI ii 479; Dascal 1987, 148). If a demonstration is nothing but a train of definitions, Leibniz supposes, a first principle can be justified without the problematic assumption that some further proposition is true. The essay stresses the advantage for satisfying a skeptic. According to an alternative view, not uncommon among scholastics, first principles receive no proof because they are *per se notae*, known by themselves from scrutiny of their terms or manifest character.[11] Leibniz contends that this is unstable. A proposition deemed to be

---

10 "On the Demonstration of Primary Propositions," A VI ii 479; Dascal 1987, 147–159.

11 Conring contends that the certainty of all reasoning comes only from the necessity of first principles. Leibniz asks what the certainty of their truth comes from; he argues that it is not from induction and thus must be from the principles themselves: "i.e. from their terms, which happens when the same is said of itself (e.g. A is A . . .) or when [it comes] only from the signification of terms, or

known per se at one time is liable to be proved later on; some propositions that are axioms for Euclid have subsequently been deduced as theorems. Moreover, for all its being known per se, the necessity that a whole is greater than its part—the foundation of the science of quantity according to Hobbes and Leibniz—is outright denied in the case of the tangent to the curve by Gregory of St. Vincent.[12] Other notions of immediate self-evidence, notably Cartesian clarity and distinctness, are equally unsustainable.[13] In the absence of an objectively accessible criterion of truth, all propositions are perpetually up for debate.[14]

By contrast, Leibniz claims, the most radical skeptic must be convinced by a demonstration containing nothing but definitions. A definition declares the speaker's intention of using a word with a certain meaning. Definitions are said to be made either by combining concepts and giving the result a name—that is, stipulating what a word is to mean—or by distilling the main ways a word in the language is ordinarily used.[15] In either case, not having a truth value, a definition is not subject to doubt. What is more, speech is impossible without agreement about the meanings of words.[16] As for propositions, there is only one case in which they are known absolutely, "when something is asserted of itself, by means of identical words, or by means of different words having the same meaning, either through universal agreement or through the will of the speaker" ("On the Demonstration of Primary Propositions," A VI ii 480; Dascal 1987, 148). Leibniz's thought seems to be this. If it is understood that the definition of n is a thing that is such-and-such and that x is an n, then the proposition that x is such-and-such is known independently of any other proposition. In correspondence with Herman Conring a few years later, Leibniz explicitly acknowledges that a demonstration contains a proposition, so, as he now says, a demonstration consists of nothing but definitions and identical propositions that instantiate the form "A is A."[17] Elsewhere, Leibniz identifies agreement

what is the same, from the understood definition the truth of the proposition is apparent" (To Conring, January 3, 1678; GP I 188), quoted in Blank 2009, 162).

[12] Olaso (1997, 102–105), suggests that the demonstration of axioms is one of several measures Leibniz takes to forestall the opening to skepticism about human reason which might otherwise be provided by paradoxes of the infinite.

[13] For example, "Meditations on Knowledge, Truth and Ideas"; A VI iv 590; AG 26–27; for more florid criticism, see, e.g., "Reflexions sur la second replique de Locke"; A VI vi 29; GP IV 328.

[14] "It is all the more urgent to offer some empirical and tangible criterion by which true demonstrations can be unquestionably shown, truth discerned from falsity and something certain established even in the sciences which are separated from imagination, finally to contain the license of exuberant spirits. For it is undignified that during the thousands of years that philosophy has flourished, we are still arrested at the principles, and nothing is established with certainty and stability" ("Elementa Rationis"; A VI iv 725).

[15] For example, "Interpretation and Argumentation in Law"; A VI iv 2782–2791; Leibniz 2006, 84. The latter is especially suited to ethics and natural law but useful elsewhere as well; see Blank 2004.

[16] Leibniz comments on his demonstration that belief cannot be coerced: "Nothing can be objected to this demonstration if the definitions I have given are followed. If, however, someone does not admit them, the dispute ends, for [the opponent] thereby declares he employs the words . . . in a sense different from the one I attribute to them." "Can there be an obligation to believe?" 1677; A VI iv 2149–2155; Leibniz 2006, 46, note 8.

[17] Letter to Conring, March 19, 1678; GP I 193 199; L 187; see Couturat 1985, 186–187.

on the meanings of words and adherence to the principle of noncontradiction (law of identity) as basic necessary preconditions for the use of language; without them, "speech would be in vain."[18] So, those who refuse to accept a demonstration from definitions are not qualified for discourse.

Still, Leibniz feels the need to defend the procedure against the objection that a definition cannot procure knowledge because it produces nothing new in one's mind: "Aren't in fact the 'new' propositions merely the old ones expressed in another way? And what is the use of proving a theorem, if I already know all about it, except for the words?" (A VI ii 480; Dascal 1987, 149). A more pressing objection might be that definitions are too easy to come by bear the weight of grounding a science. This is, in fact, Leibniz's concern. His response begins "Those who put forth such objections have not yet understood the mysteries of science, and of ideas, and of what Plato called 'reminiscence'" (A VI ii 481; Dascal 1987, 149). It is because reality is already in some way known that apt definitions can possibly assign meanings to words in such a way that they signify real things. In this context, the question is how definitions of words can be tools for organizing inchoate native knowledge, putting it in a form that can be a constituent of a proposition subject to canons of logic. Leibniz's answer is that language is indispensable for human beings to hold on to thoughts, which are elusive and fleeting. Without language, a person may on occasion realize that, say, two multiplied by two is four, but she has no way to hold on to it long enough to relate it to other multiples of two and other operations on numbers that one must learn in order to do arithmetic. Human beings cannot think of anything complex without the aid of symbols that stand in for some elements of the complex ensemble so as to abbreviate it.[19] The use of words or other sensible characters as compendious substitutes for an immediate grasp of complex intentional content is ubiquitous: "We could not think even about thought if we did not think about something else, i.e. about the particular facts which the senses provide" A VI vi 212; (NE 212). Leibniz calls this "blind" thought. The reference to Plato indicates that some form of innate knowledge is a requirement for knowledge of necessary truths that have ground in reality. The full complement of such requirements spans theories with regard to the relations between language and thought, and thought and reality, and psychological doctrines of the sort just mentioned.

The requisite ground in reality is sketched in a letter to Magnus Wedderkopf also written in 1671. It explains that there is a reason for God's creating a world in which there are sinful acts, namely, that it is most harmonious. But there is no reason in God's will for necessary truths:

> For example, no reason can be given for the ratio of 2 to 4 being the same as that of 4 to 8, not even in the divine will. This depends on the essence itself, or the ideas of

---

[18] "On the Elements of Thinking," (1676); A VI iii 503–507; Parkinson, 52–57; also "Excerpts from Notes on Science and Metaphysics," March 22, 1676; A VI iii 396–397; Parkinson, 49.

[19] See "On Mind, the Universe, and God" 1675; A VI iii 461; Parkinson, 3. Also Marcello Dascal, "Signs and Thoughts in Leibniz's Paris Notes," in Dascal 1987, 47–60; also Dascal 1978.

things. For the essences of things are numbers, as it were, and contain the possibility of beings which God does not make as he does existence, since these possibilities or ideas of things coincide with God himself.

(Letter to Wedderkopf, May 1671; A II i 117–8; L 146)

This foreshadows an argument for the existence of God premised on the fact of necessary truths. Leibniz reasons that, although necessary truths are eternal, they are not substantial beings but rather modes that "exist in" a subject as intentional objects of knowledge. The subject must be a necessary being, and, because a true proposition has many elements, some of which are elements of other truths, all these elements must exist in the same necessary being. Leibniz takes this being to be God.[20] Now he supposes that there is an independent argument for the existence of God based on nothing but Descartes's definition of an infinite being as a being with all perfections; it is sound he maintains, provided such a being is possible (as he presumes). So the argument from necessary truths can be seen as offering to explain why such truths are genuinely necessary on the basis of an independently demonstrated truth. The real ground of necessary truths is, then, essences, or possibilities, or ideas that are in God. Definitions suitable for demonstrating necessary truths purport to assign meanings to words in virtue of which they signify one or more of the essences.

Leibniz needs to say more about how names signify the realities they do. The issue is already in view in the Preface to an edition of Nizolius, *De veris principiis*, which Leibniz edited in 1671. Nizolius urges a nominalist theory, and Leibniz allows that all things except individual substances are mere names. As we would expect, he favors a moderate nominalist account of the signification of general names, one on which the meanings of general names in a language are determined by concepts which are natural names (signifiers) of essences. In Leibniz's view, Nizolius's nominalist account of the signification of general names is not sufficiently different from the unsupportable super-nominalist theory of Thomas Hobbes. Hobbes, as Leibniz reads him, holds that sentences in a language are the only bearers of truth and falsity, to the exclusion of thoughts of relations among essences; but, of even deeper concern, he maintains that definitions depend on nothing but human will, and because truths depend on the definitions given to linguistic names, it follows that truth depends on human will. In the Preface, Leibniz is content to raise the objection that different languages express the same geometrical truths.[21] But the Hobbesian argument needs to be defused. How can truth be independent of language in view of the fact that the meanings of words are fixed by conventions of linguistic use?

This is explained in a short piece given the title *Dialogue* (1677), which argues, briefly, as follows. We find that we can sometimes learn truths about a thing by examining a sensible character that is in view when we think of the thing (e.g., a figure which is not a real geometrical object). This is because there is an order in the character that is also in

---

[20] "On necessary or eternal truths" 1677; A VI iv 17; Strickland 182–183; also 181; "Monadology," 43–44; GP VI 614; AG 218. For discussion of the argument, see Adams 1994, 177–183.

[21] Preface to Nizolius, A VI ii 427; L 128.

the thing—not a similarity of basic elements, but of their combination (i.e., an analogy or similarity of structure). So there must be "a definite analogy between characters and things, and the relation which characters expressing the same thing have to each other. *This analogy or relation is the basis of truth*" (A VI iv 24: L 184; emphasis added). At this point, it remains to explain how it is possible for human beings to construct definitions that uphold this analogy. This brings Leibniz back to innatism. A short essay, "What Is an Idea?" (1678) states that there are ideas in *human* minds. In this instance, an idea is not knowledge of a thing (as it is in God) but the ability to think of it, an active potentiality. More exactly, ideas of things in a human being are tendencies to assemble "expressions" of these things from available elements: according to Leibniz one thing "expresses" another just in case they are analogous in structure. Here, the epistemic value of analogy is emphasized: "we can pass from a consideration of the relations in the expression to a knowledge of the corresponding properties of the thing expressed." This is the case provided only that a certain analogy is maintained. The essay concludes that ideas in a human mind are God-given powers by which the mind operating by itself can derive "what corresponds perfectly to the nature of things. Although . . . the idea of a circle is not similar to a circle, truths can be derived from it which would be confirmed beyond doubt by investigating a real circle" ("What Is an Idea?," A VI iv 1371; L 208).

One can see in this a version of Aristotle's doctrine that the soul comes to know a thing by taking on a similarity to it. But the essay is not clear about just what there is in a human soul that is analogous to essences, or ideas, in God. Elsewhere, Leibniz explains that ideas are active tendencies always present in a human mind,[22] but when a person thinks of, say, a circle she brings to mind some concept of it. The concept involves a sensible assembly—an image, diagram, verbal definition, or character that is structurally analogous to all possible circles. So there are many concepts, even many definitions, corresponding to the innate idea of a circle.[23]

The theory of demonstration culminates in the 1680s in accounts such as this:

> The primary truths [of reason] are those which assert the same thing of itself or deny the opposite of its opposite. . . Although they themselves have their degrees of priority, nonetheless they can all be included under the name "identities." Moreover, all remaining truths are reduced to identities with the help of definitions, that is, through the resolution of notions [concepts]; in this consists a priori proof, proof independent of experience.
>
> ("Primary Truths" 1689?; A VI iv 644; AG 30–31)

The resolution of subject and predicate terms contained in a proposition consists in replacing a term with its definition and doing the same for the terms of the definition

---

[22] NE 52, 83–84.
[23] See *Discourse on Metaphysics* 27, A VI iv 1572; NE 430. Also Mugnai 1990; Bolton 2012; Leduc (2012).

until an identity is exhibited.[24] Definitions are publicly announced, and propositions that are instances of the law of identity are expressed by formulae that are readily identifiable: "*A* is *A*," "*AB* is *A*," and the like. An objective criterion is at hand: "this is the only, and the highest, criterion of truth in abstract things, that is, things which do not depend on experience—that it must either be an identity or reducible to identities."[25] The reduction to an identity might, but in some cases need not, go all the way back to simple concepts. Leibniz's oft-repeated demonstration that a whole is greater than its part does not. Yet the fact is that relatively few demonstrations by definitions and identities can be found in the texts. The reason for this is not clear.[26]

In practice, rather than grounding reasoning on principles demonstrated in the foregoing way, Leibniz often reasons on the basis of propositions that are less certain. As he sees it, this is what Euclid did: he lacked demonstrations of his axioms and postulates but went ahead with the business of deriving conclusions from them. To be sure, Leibniz commends efforts to demonstrate the axioms by definitions and identities. But Euclid did well not to wait for that. He proved that a great many things follow from a small number of hypotheses. Reasoning is to be accepted, according to Leibniz, only if it instantiates a sensible form that is known to preserve truth or correctness.[27] The logical connections between axioms (perhaps also postulates) and derived theorems are expressed by conditional propositions which have valid intersubjectively verifiable proofs. Although the theorems are not thereby shown to be true, they have proved useful in practice. Moreover, we know what needs to be done to make them entirely certain. This exemplifies Leibniz's main strategy for leveraging uncertainty to obtain something certain.[28] Even if A and B are uncertain, we may have a valid proof that if A, then B on which we can build with good effect.

REAL AND NOMINAL DEFINITIONS

Definitions of words explicate concepts of essences, or possible things. From at least the early 1680s on, Leibniz classifies concepts on the basis of two properties: what he calls their "clarity," by contrast with "obscurity," and their "distinctness," by contrast with "confusion." These are measures of the epistemic value of a concept. In "Meditations on Knowledge Truth and Ideas" (hereafter MKTI), an article published in 1684, the

---

[24] Substitution of one term for another is not allowed if either term is "reduplicative"; see, e.g., A VI i 89; MP, 95.

[25] "On Universal Analysis and Syntheses, etc." 1683–85; A VI iv 543; L 232.

[26] See Rutherford 1996; Lodge 2010.

[27] "[A] sound demonstration is one that follows the form prescribed by logic. Not that we always need syllogisms ordered in the manner of the schools . . . , but at the very least the argument must reach its conclusion by virtue of its form. Any correct calculation can also be considered as an example of such an argument conceived in proper form" ("Meditations on Knowledge, Truth and Ideas"; A VI iv 591; AG 27; also A VI vi 479, 360; NE 479 and 360).

[28] For example, "Critical Thoughts on Descartes"; GP IV 355; L 384; A VI vi 450–451; NE 450–451.

classification covers a range of intellectual abilities up to and including those of God. In the article, concepts are considered in a dual light: as intentional contents that both contain expressions with epistemic value and have logical structure. The logical structure of concepts is compositional; Leibniz argues in 1679 that if there are concepts at all, then there are simple ones with no conceptual components: all other concepts are composed of simple ones.[29] The epistemic classification of concepts can be summarized as follows. I will be brief, because it is discussed in detail in many other places. A concept is "clear" just in case the person who has it can reliably identify its instances; a concept is "distinct" provided that either a person who has it can define it (i.e. state a necessary and sufficient condition of its object) or it is a simple concept that is not susceptible to definition. The classification can be schematized as follows: (1) a concept is either obscure or clear.[30] (2) A clear concept is either confused or distinct; (3) a distinct concept has a definition that either contains one or more confused concepts or contains nothing but simple concepts that cannot be defined. In the latter case, the concept is adequate. Finally, (4) an adequate concept is either grasped by the mind with the aid of sensible characters, or it is grasped intuitively, directly, and all at once. Leibniz waivers between saying that human beings have no adequate concepts and that some of our concepts of small numbers are of this sort. Intuitive knowledge of concepts other than those composed of a very few simple concepts seems not to be within the natural power of human beings.

With the largely hidden composition of the concepts we commonly use out on the table, MKTI observes that we often engage in blind thinking, we often use words or symbols to stand in thought for complex concepts. For all its convenience, this runs a risk. A person can construct a definition that conceals a contradiction because she understands the words singly, or at least supposes she does, and doesn't stop to consider what they might signify together; to take a simple example, "the number of numbers" implies a contradiction. If a definition of this sort is used in reasoning, contrary things follow from it, so it is necessary to take precautions. With this in view, Leibniz calls upon the distinction between nominal and real definitions, which was abroad in scholastic philosophy and can be traced back to Aristotle, *Posterior Analytics* (ch. 2, sect.10). Aristotle's text is exceedingly difficult to interpret, but, on a first attempt, it says roughly this. A definition is any account of what a thing is. One kind of definition explains the signification of the name. If, but only if, we are aware that such a thing exists, we can seek to know why. A second type of definition explains what a thing is.[31] This is apparently intended to mark a difference that is somehow crucial to Aristotle's account of the justificatory order among propositions in which the defined terms occur. Propositions with subject or predicate terms that are definitions of what a thing is are more basic in justification than those whose terms explain the name of a thing.

---

[29] "De Organo sive Arte Magna Cogitandi" 1679?; A VI iv 156–57; MP 1–4.

[30] In (1) through (4) above, "or" stands for an exclusive and exhaustive division of the class in question; e.g., a concept is obscure if and only if it is not clear.

[31] I base this on the translation by E. S. Forster in the Loeb Library edition of the *Posterior Analytics*.

According to MKTI, a definition is any necessary and sufficient condition of a thing, but knowledge of the possibility of the thing is needed for further inquiry. One kind of definition, called "nominal," leaves this question open. A second kind, called a "real definition," shows the possibility of the thing. This possibility can be known either a priori or a posteriori as Leibniz observes. If the definition is an adequate concept, then its logical consistency (inconsistency) is transparent. But, as mentioned, human beings have few, if any, adequate concepts. The text mentions a second case in which the possibility of the thing defined is known a priori (i.e., from its cause[32]); this defines a thing on the basis of a possible way of generating it. We may know, independently of experience, that such a procedure is possible if we know that the specified elements and arrangement are possible. Alternatively, the possibility of the thing defined is known a posteriori if we observe actual things that conform to the definition or we infer their possibility from other experiences. In MKTI, the distinction between types of definitions is called upon for nothing more than to guard against inconsistency. The priority of real defintions in the order of justification among propositions is considered below.

But causal definitions have a special utility. In "On Universal Analysis and Synthesis," a study paper mentioned earlier, the difference between a nominal and a real, causal definition is illustrated by the following pair. If some thing is defined as a curved line such that for any segment of the curve and any point on the curve, the angle between the point and the ends of the segment is equal, it can be doubted that such a thing is possible. Yet the figure is a circle. Compare this with Euclid's definition: a circle is the figure described by the motion of a straight line in a plane round a fixed point.[33] This describes a way of generating a thing, and, in this instance, the possibility of the generative process is plainly known from the experience of drawing. The specified mode of producing a thing might be known to be possible independently of experience. In the absence of an adequate concept, it might be inferred from truths reduced to identities, but it seems there are not many of these. So it is important that Leibniz explicitly says on more than one occasion that the possibility of what a definition purports to define can be presumed; that is, it can be regarded as possible until shown not to be so.[34] It is on this basis that he credits the ontological argument based on Descartes' defintion of God.[35]

New Essays explicates the notion of a real causal definition of a natural (non-mathematical) sort of thing as follows The essence of gold is said to be:

> what constitutes it and gives it the sensible qualities which let us recognize it and which make its nominal definition; whereas if we could explain this structure or inner constitution we would possess the real and causal definition. However in our

---

[32] See later discussion.
[33] "On Universal Analysis and Synthesis" A VI iv 541; L 230.
[34] For example, A Vi vi 438; NE 438; on the notion of presumption, 457.
[35] MKTI, A VI iv 589; AG 26; also NE 438.

present case the nominal definition is also real, not in itself (since it does not show us a priori the possibility of this body, and its mode of origin) but through experience, in that we find that there is a body in which these qualities occur together. (A VI vi 294; NE 294)

This may further clarify the notion of a causal definition; it specifies a mode of "generation" in the sense of assembling a thing's component parts in the right order. In describing a way to produce a thing, it describes the elements of its constitution.

The following passage brings out the full import of the two types of definition:

> Few people have given a good explanation of what the difference of these two definitions consists in, which must also allow us to discern essence and property. In my view this difference is that the real definition shows the possibility of the thing defined and the nominal definition does not. For instance, the definition of two parallel straight lines as "lines in the same plane which do not meet even if extended to infinity" is only nominal, for one could at first question whether that is possible. But once we understand that we can draw a straight line in a plane parallel to a given straight line by ensuring that the point of the stylus drawing the parallel line remains at the same distance from the given line, we can see at once that the thing is possible and why the lines have the property of never meeting, which is their nominal definition. (A VI vi 295; NE 295)

The passage must be read carefully. A real, causal definition of parallel lines specifies a constitution (locus of points) on the basis of which we understand why a thing with this constitution has certain properties—in particular, why it satisfies the nominal definition of parallel lines. In addition, the definition, being real, shows that the constitution it describes is possible. There is no doubt that, in the present case, this is made known by experience using a pen, or hearing about it, or the like. Accordingly, real causal definitions in general are said to be "a priori" only in the traditional sense of making an effect known from its cause (as indicated earlier). Typically, inquiry about a thing begins with a nominal definition and sets as a task finding a real causal definition for it (see A Vi vi 346; NE 346).

There are four important points to be taken from this passage. (1) The essence of a kind has (one or more) real causal definitions and one or more nominal definitions, but they define it from different perspectives. The nominal ones define it on the basis of one or more of its "properties" in a technical sense; a "property" is an attribute that belongs to all members of the kind and, strictly taken, only to them. A real causal definition specifies the constitution of the essence. (2) This constitution allows us to understand why the essence has the property specified in the nominal definition. We anticipate that this property can be deduced from a set of premises in some of which the real definition occurs as a term. (3) The constitution is known to be possible, at least in the present case, on the basis of experience. (4) Finally, a real causal definition *shows* the possibility of the thing defined *by the nominal definition*. This is perfectly plain in the text. This yields the following scheme:

Nominal definition of essence E: E is a thing that has property P. (The possibility of such a thing is not known from this defintion.)

Real causal definition of E: E has constitution C. (That C is possible is either known a priori, or presumed, or, perhaps more often, known on the basis of experience—even in the case of geometrical definitions.)

Anticipated explanatory argument: A conjunction of premises in some of which the concepts of E and C occur as terms that implies that E has P. (The completed argument shows that the object of the nominal definition is a possible being, i.e. an essence.)

If there is independent reason to assent to the premises, this argument, provides knowledge of a property of an object from its cause. In general, a reason is a known truth that makes us assent to a less well known truth; but, Leibniz explains, it is "a reason . . . *par excellence*, if it is the cause not only of our judgment but also of the truth itself—which makes it what is known as an a priori reason" (A VI vi 474; NE 474). If the premises of the argument have been demonstrated (i.e., either reduced to identities or deduced from premises of which this is true), the argument provides the highest attainable certainty in matters of pure mathematics.

But suppose the premises of the argument have not been demonstrated, and the conclusions derived from them are independently found to be true. Does the explanatory purport of the argument provide any reason to think the premises specify the true cause of the properties of the thing? Leibniz's correspondent Herman Conring argues that it is fallacious to suppose they do because true propositions can be deduced from false ones. Although Leibniz agrees with the logical point, he qualifies its implication: we can conclude the supposition is true if there is a valid argument from the effect back to the cause. This is the case if "we make use in our reasoning of . . . propositions which are convertible or whose subject and predicate are equally inclusive"; put differently, the subject and predicate concepts used throughout the proof must have extensions such that all and only possible things included in one are included in each of the others.[36] The "only if" direction of argument confers a high degree of certainty on the explanatory premises. Even though the principles of such biconditional arguments have not been demonstrated, as we suppose, Leibniz is willing to allow that they may not be in doubt.[37] Yet, if they were reduced to identities, then things that follow from them would be known, if not with more certainty at least in a better way—that is, from what is prior in nature and the ultimate cause of their truth, the principle of identity.[38]

---

[36] Letter to Conring, March 19, 1678; GP I 193–199; L 188.

[37] A VI vi 415; NE 415; see also to Bernoulli, August 29, 1696; GM III 316. I owe these references to Wilson 1999, 360.

[38] A VI vi 411–413; NE 411–413. Reduction of the axioms to identities is also said to be useful for analysis; e.g., "Critical Thoughts, on Descartes," 1.1; GP IV 354; L 382.

The same letter goes on to say that when known natural phenomena are deduced from a physical hypotheses, it does not prove that the hypotheses is true unless the argument can be reversed as we just said. "This [philosophers] have not done, nor perhaps, have they wanted or been able to do it. Yet it must be admitted that a hypothesis becomes the more probable . . . the greater the number of phenomena that can be explained by it and the fewer the assumptions."[39] This is the topic of the next section.

Knowledge of Contingent General Truths: Demonstration in Natural Science

Leibniz explicitly recognizes that there are contingent general truths. They present special problems for his theory of knowledge. Unlike general necessary truths, they have existential import.[40] But, like all universal truths, a mere review of their instances provides little reason to assent to them. Not only is there a logical gap between "some" and "all," but general truths are in some way necessary, as Leibniz sees it.[41] The (nonlogical) necessity would not be revealed even if all the instances were inspected.

Contingency gets a good bit of attention in Leibniz's metaphysics because he is anxious to avoid Spinoza's doctrine that everything that exists is strictly necessary. Leibniz vacillates over whether God's perfection makes it necessary that he create what is best, but he seems inclined to say it does. Yet he aims to show that God's choice of worlds to make actual is in some respect contingent. He relies mainly on two solutions.[42] In this connection, what is most relevant to Leibniz's theory of knowledge of general contingent truths is his contention that there is a formal property that distinguishes necessary and contingent truths. By definition, a necessarily true proposition can be "demonstrated with geometrical rigor"; its denial is a contradiction. Leibniz sometimes argues as follows. Assume that the proposition "every truth and only a truth has the greater reason" or "God always acts with the highest wisdom" is necessarily true:

> [F]rom this one cannot demonstrate the proposition "contingent proposition A has greater reason [for being true]" or "contingent proposition A is in conformity with

[39] To Conring, GP I 195–196; L 188.

[40] Although some texts suggest that all necessary truths are essential and all contingent truths are existential (e.g., "Necessary and Contingent Truths" in MP 98), this is not strictly correct because Leibniz sometimes says that it is contingent which possible world is the best; also see NE 446 on the presumption that definitions describe possible things.

[41] NE 447.

[42] See Adams 1994, 10–22.

divine wisdom." And therefore it does not follow that contingent proposition A is necessary. So although one can concede that it is necessary for God to choose the best, or that the best is necessary, it does not follow that what is chosen is necessary, since there is no demonstration that it is the best.

(De contingentia 1689?; A VI iv 1650; AG 30)

As the passage explains, this relates to the difference between the necessity of a conditional proposition (necessarily, if there is a greater reason for *A*, then *A*) and the necessity of the consequent of the proposition (necessarily *A*). By assumption, the former is true, yet if the antecedent is not necessary (not necessary that *A* has the greater reason), then neither is the consequent. Logically speaking, this is clear. But the problem for Leibniz is to say how *A*'s contingency can be accommodated by his commitment to the so-called "predicate-in-notion" theory of truth; as stated in this essay, "every true universal affirmative proposition, either necessary or contingent, has some connection between subject and predicate. In identities, this connection is self-evident; in other propositions it must appear through the analysis of terms." (*De contingentia* (1689?); A IV iv 1650; AG 30) The logical and metaphysical basis of contingency is said to consist in the distinctive formal character of the analysis:

> For in necessary propositions, when the analysis is continued indefinitely, it arrives at an equation that is an identity; . . . But in contingent propositions one continues the analysis to infinity through reasons for reasons, so that one never has a complete demonstration, though there is always underneath a reason for the truth, but the reason is understood completely only by God, who alone traverses the infinite series in one stroke of mind.
>
> (De contingentia 1689?; A VI iv 1651; AG 30)

Unlike a necessary truth, which can be demonstrated by definitional analyses of its terms ending in an explicit identity, a contingent truth has an analysis that is infinite. An analysis that terminates exhibits a reason for a necessary truth, whereas the reason for a contingent truth cannot be exhibited because it comprises an endless series of reasons. To be sure, God cannot reach the end of the infinite series, but, Leibniz maintains, he understands what it contains inasmuch as he understands the reason for the series' proceeding as it does. This is not possible for a human being.

General contingent truths are singled out for attention in this text from the mid-1680s:

> But it must not be thought that only particular propositions are contingent . . . For from the first essential laws of the series—true without exception, and containing the entire purpose of God in choosing the universe, and so including even miracles— there can be derived subordinate laws of nature, which have only physical necessity and which are not repealed except by a miracle, . . . [F]rom these there are inferred others whose universality is still less; and God can reveal even to creatures the

demonstrations of universal propositions of this kind . . . of which a part constitutes physical science.

> (De natura veritatis, contingentiae et indifferentia, etc. 1685–86?, A VI iv 1514–1523; MP 100)

When God conceives the world, he conceives items of two sorts: a series of particular things and general principles or laws. Contingent laws that have no exceptions govern everything in the world, including miracles. They are "essential to the series," as the passage explains: "when [God] chose this series of things, by that very act he decreed that he would observe them as the specific properties of just this chosen series" (*De natura veritaties, contingentiae et indfferentia, etc.* (1685-86?), A VI iv 1514–1523; MP 100). The laws are not geometrically necessary, but it is necessary that, if this series exists, these laws obtain.[43] Subordinate laws of nature and the laws of the natural sciences can be inferred from the strictly universal laws of the universe. They have a necessity, called "physical," which is subject to suspension so that the full purpose of God's creative act may be realized.

The most extensive general discussion of the rational basis for acceptance of laws in physical science is, to my knowledge, in *New Essays* (1702–04). In the dialogue carried on by Leibniz and a follower of John Locke, the latter character is skeptical about the possibility of attaining a "science of body," that is, a science of various kinds of material things. Although Leibniz concedes that we will never have a complete natural science, he undertakes to show that it is possible to make progress. What is required is a practical procedure that has a chance of yielding reasonable certainty about general principles and laws that can explain the phenomena by which we differentiate natural kinds of sensible things.[44]

New Essays on Human Understanding traces Locke's skepticism about the possibility of natural science to his rejection of innate knowledge. The Preface purports to expose the poverty of a theory of cognition such as Locke's by posing a contrast between what human beings can do, on the one hand, and what those he calls "simple empirics" do, on the other hand. In effect, it contrasts two modes of inductive inference. Simple empirics are assimilated to lower animals that act on the basis of likeness of appearance. More exactly, simple empiricism is the view that knowledge of general truths can only be gained by simple generalization over some number of similar instances (A VI vi 49; NE 49). We know that this is not reliable. A precise account of the reason for the fallibility of simple

---

[43] The text just quoted continues: "It should not disturb anyone that I have just said that there are certain essential laws for this series of things, though I said above that these same laws are not necessary and essential, but are contingent and existential. For since the fact that the series itself exists is contingent and depends on the free decrees of God, its laws also will be contingent in the absolute sense; but they will be hypothetically necessary and will only be essential given the series" *De natura veritatis, contingentiae et indifferentiae, etc.* 1685–86?; A VI iv 1514–1523; MP 100.

[44] The procedures described in *New Essays* are general, but work of François Duchesneau shows that they can be found in Leibniz's scientific works; see Duchesneau 1973.

empiricism, as Leibniz sees it, can be found in a letter to Johann Bernoulli written in 1703.[45] Leibniz intends to explain why the empirical method of calculating the probability of events is problematic. Suppose that a number of observed events can be plotted as points on a graph; Leibniz reports that he can demonstrate that there is a regular curve (i.e., a curve defined by a general formula) that runs through them all. For any subsequent data point not on this curve, there is a regular curve that passes through all the previous points and the additional one, but a different curve.[46] So, the results of the simple empirical method are just as changeable as successive phenomena are variable. It yields nothing stable on the basis of which probability can be judged.

New Essays suggests there is a better way to ground inductive generalization. Even minimal inquiry into the reason for a recurring connection among similar things enables human beings to form rules that avoid common errors. This is put in evidence of innate knowledge: "For if some events can be foreseen before any test has been made of them it is obvious that we contribute something from our side" (A VI vi 49; NE 49).

> [O]nly reason is capable of establishing reliable rules, of making up the deficiencies of those which have proved unreliable by allowing exceptions to them, and lastly of finding unbreakable links in the cogency of necessary inferences. This last often provides a way of foreseeing events without having to experience sensible links between images. (A VI iv 51; NE 51)

The remark "only reason is capable of establishing reliable rules" does not clearly exclude empirical input in the formation of rules, but it clearly assigns reason an essential role.[47]

---

[45] "When we estimate probabilities empirically, on the basis of observations, you ask whether this method allows us to obtain a perfect estimate. The inherent difficulty of doing this seems to me to be that contingent things or those which depend upon infinite circumstances cannot be determined from finite experiences. Nature has its habits, connected to the recurrence of causes, but only for the most part. Thus who can say whether subsequent experiences are not about to deviate from the law of all the antecedent experiences, on account of variations in nature itself? New diseases inundate humankind; consequently if you had as many experiences of mortality as you want, it is not so many that it is possible to assign limits to nature such that she cannot vary what follows. When we seek the trajectory of a comet based on some given number of points, we suppose that the trajectory belongs to some family of conic sections or some other more simple curves. But some number of points being given, one can find an infinity of curves passing through them. I demonstrate this as follows. I suppose (I have a demonstration of this) that some number of points being given, one can find a regular curve which joins them. Suppose that we have found it; call it A. Add to the given points another point but external to the curve and we make a curve this time which passes through the points initially given and through the new point; this is possible according to the preceding hypothesis. That curve is necessarily different from the first, even though it passes through the same points. And as this point can vary to infinity, an infinity of curves each different from the others is possible. One can compare observed cases and regular lines to rules or estimates from which cases are to be reckoned. But although it is not possible to have a perfect estimate empirically, empirical estimation is not the less useful and sufficient in practice" (to Johan Bernoulli, December 19, 1703; GM III 83–84; author's translation with assistance from Leibniz 1995, 29–30).

[46] Parmentier (1995) notes that the curves may be of infinite degree.

[47] I am grateful to Mark Kulstad for calling my attention to how difficult it is to interpret this stretch of the Preface; see Kulstad 2006 and 2011.

However, *New Essays* may give the impression that there are truths of exactly two mutually exclusive sorts: truths of reason and truths of fact. This might seem to be implied by a well-known passage on primary truths—first principles, or foundations of reasoning.[48] Primary truths of reason are said to be identities, which "derive from the law of non-contradiction" or "disparities" such as "Warmth is not the same as color." Truths of this sort are necessary and known a priori. As for the primary truths of fact, they include "I think, therefore I am," "I think various thoughts," "I think about *A*," and the like. Truths in this class are contingent and a posteriori. In general, a proposition qualifies as a first truth in virtue of two properties: it is immediately known, and it cannot be proved by anything more certain than it. Primary truths of reason are "immediate" in that nothing mediates between the subject and predicate concepts. In the case of first truths of fact, the thing known is immediately present to the awareness of the knower. Leibniz's thought seems to be that, in such cases, erroneous assent to what is in view could have no natural explanation but lack of attention.[49] This apparently provides something by way of (nonevidential) assurance of truth in his view. Beyond that, assent to primary truths, as Leibniz characterizes them, is said to be a necessary condition of human knowledge.[50]

In this division of sorts of primary truths, there is no place for contingent general truths of reason. No contingent truths are truths of reason, and no truths of reason have existential import. *New Essays* does mention mixed propositions, "which derive from premises some of which come from facts and observations while others are necessary truths" (A VI vi 446; NE 446). Although nothing but singular propositions are explicitly said to fit this profile, *New Essays* propounds several contingent universal propositions that belong to reason inasmuch as they are given proofs independent of experience. Here are two examples:[51]

> (a) As for the good pleasure of our Maker, it should be said that he conducts himself in accordance with the nature of things, in such a way that he produces and conserves in them only what is suitable to them and can be explained through their natures . . . If on the other hand . . . we could not even conceive of a general explanation for the relations between soul and body, and if, finally, God gave things accidental powers which were not rooted in their natures and were therefore out of reach of reason in general; that would be a back door through which to readmit over-occult qualities which no mind can understand, along with inexplicable "faculties" . . . helpful goblins which come forward like gods on the stage. . . to do on demand anything that a philosopher wants of them, without ways or means. But to attribute their origin to God's good pleasure—that appears hardly worthy of him who is the supreme reason, and with whom everything is orderly and connected. (A IV iv 382; NE 382)

---

[48] A VI vi 361–362; NE 361–363.

[49] This is not explicit in any text of which I know, but it is suggested by NE 238.

[50] The treatment of the argument *ad vertiginem* at NE 491 is relevant; de Olaso (1997, 113) notes that Leibniz initially called this the argument *ad scepticismum*.

[51] Also NE 220, 151, 60, 382, 68, 379; "Quelques remarques sur l'Essay," A VI vi 7.

(b) [I]t must be said that [a certain work of Robert Boyle] does spend rather too long on drawing from countless fine experiments no conclusion except one which he could have adopted as a principle, namely that everything in nature takes place mechanically—a principle which can be made certain only by reason, and never by experiments, however many of them one conducts. (A VI iv 455; NE 455)

The argument in (a) is indirect. The gist is this: assuming it is false that all the causal powers of things can be explained by their natures, then things have powers that cannot be explained at all; they are without ground in the thing and enter and leave it for no reason; they supposedly produce effects which can, in fact, only be due directly to God. An argument for (b) can be gathered from other passages.[52] Leibniz contends that, given the nature of bodies, all changes that happen to them are changes of motion. The nature of bodies can explain mechanical causes of motion, but the natures of souls cannot. So, unless everything that happens in body takes place mechanically, there are effects produced in bodies by inexplicable powers. The consequences of that are sketched in (a). Although these arguments are drawn from reason, they have minimal probative force. They have the form: If not P, then Q; so P. It is invalid; a *reductio* argument is valid only if it has an additional premise, *not-Q*.[53] Yet the reasoning simply does not show that Q is false. If someone is inclined to accept the conclusion, it may be psychologically explained, but not proved, by her native disposition to assent to what she somehow already knows.[54]

Theodicy provides a context for filling the arguments out:

Truths of reason are of two sorts. Some are those which one calls eternal truths, which are absolutely necessary in the sense that their contrary implies a contradiction: these are the truths whose necessity is that of logic, metaphysics, or geometry, and which one cannot deny without being led to absurdity. There are others which one can call positive, since they are the laws which it has pleased God to give nature, or which depend on him. We learn them either through experience, that is a posteriori, or by reason, and a priori, that is through considerations of the suitability which made them chosen. This fitness of things has also its rules and reasons, but it is the free choice of God, and not a geometric necessity, which causes preference for what is fitting and brings it into existence. Thus we can say that physical necessity is grounded on moral necessity, that is, on the choice of the wise, worthy of his wisdom,

[52] For example, A VI vi 380; NE 380.

[53] One might argue that it is not valid even then because it assumes that every genuine proposition is either true or false, but since this is a doctrine Leibniz holds (e.g., A VI vi 362; NE 362), this is no objection to its validity in his eyes.

[54] We might nowadays wonder whether Leibniz's version of innate knowledge taken in connection with the metaphysical doctrines that make human knowledge of necessary truths possible, in effect, provides a sort of external warrant something like assent due to a truth-conducive cause. Leibniz vigorously denies that innateness is a proof of truth (A VI vi 74–75; NE 74–75), but this may not decide his attitude on the question of entitlement to assent.

and both should be distinguished from geometric necessity. The physical necessity is that which makes up the order of nature.

(Discours Preliminaire, 2; GP VI 50, H 74)

Here, the class of truths of reason includes propositions that are not geometrically necessary but for which a priori proof can be found by considering their suitability to be preferred by God. The perfection and wisdom of God put him under the necessity of choosing what is best,[55] where goodness pertains to both the moral and natural orders. The laws of nature are, then, "physically necessary." The argument drawn from reason here is roughly that certain laws are suited to satisfy this demand. The statement that these positive laws are learned "either a priori or a posteriori" might seem to say that each mode of proof is complete, that it provides a level of certainty which cannot be increased by evidence drawn from the other. But a purely empirical proof is ruled out by Leibniz's critique of simple empiricism. As we will see, neither does Leibniz hold that a proof independent of experience may be so complete that its certainty cannot be raised by experiential input.

The a priori proofs of contingent general propositions offered in *New Essays* can be made to fit the mold of the a priori knowledge of positive laws of nature outlined in the quote from *Theodicy*. It says that we can know these laws by reasoning a priori from the (demonstrable) truth that the world God chooses to create is morally necessary. As Leibniz explains elsewhere, a morally necessary truth is "determined in such a way that its contrary would imply imperfection or moral absurdity."[56] This being assumed, it authorizes an argument of the following form: If *not-P*, then *Q*; *Q* is morally (physically) absurd; so *Q* is false; so *P*. The proof that all powers are explicable by the natures of things in which they inhere, supplemented by the premise that floating accidents and the like are physically absurd, is valid under this license. But an argument for the added premise is nowhere in sight. Physical absurdity is seen only by grasping the comparative perfection of infinite *possiblia*. The reason that a certain world is the best has three parts: a fixed exhaustive set of possible basic constituents of possible worlds (essences), their mutual relations of compossibility (possibility of existing in the same possible world) and in-compossibility, and their respective values. There are infinitely many possible worlds to be compared.[57]

By contrast, the indirect proofs offered in *New Essays* compare the natural value of a principle with that of its denial, to the advantage of the principle. This shows the principle has some degree of natural value. Yet in the determination of the best possible world, what counts is the value of a law and the other things it admits. In the end,

---

[55] Adams (1994, 22) notes that Leibniz used logical necessity to define the basic moral modalities: the "morally impossible" is that which "it is not possible to do without committing sin." According to Adams, "when Leibniz says that God's choice of the best is morally necessary, we must take him to mean that it is necessary that if God did not choose the best, God would not be perfectly good."

[56] "On the Radical Origination of Things" (1687), GP VII 304; L 792–793.

[57] But see the finite model of the argument in "De Veritatibus primis" (mid to late 1680), A VI iv 1442–1443; Strickland 29–30.

a comparison of combinations of positively characterized mutually compossible laws is decisive, whereas the diminutive proof compares a positive situation and its denial without taking account of the positive possibilities that situation precludes. Construing the *New Essays* arguments as attempts to prove that certain principles satisfy the demands of the moral necessity of the world hardly increases their epistemic weight.

Still, some texts may seem to suggest that a more acute argument premised on the known nature of God might be conclusive.[58] Why couldn't someone who is intellectually gifted deduce that some general principles have such a high degree of perfection that God has decisive reason to make them true without needing to take the series of things with which it is compossible into account?[59] It is because, granting that this would have some probative value, it would inevitably be deficient relative to *the* reason for the truth of these principles (if they are true). Because their truth would be more certain for God, who distinctly knows the entire reason, the certainty provided by the finite proof is, at least in theory, susceptible to enhancement. In practice, experience is always available for this purpose. Contingent laws of nature are logically tied to the actual series of things: necessarily, if this series exists, the laws are true of it. For human minds, the logical relevance of evidence from experience cannot be outrun. So if the a priori proofs found in *New Essays* are thin, it is because they are offered as a stage in a longer process by which laws of nature can be known.

The account of this inductive procedure given in *New Essays* calls upon the distinction between nominal and real definitions. Let me start with a simple empiric, a person who accepts generalizations based on similarities in the appearances of many particular things.[60] To begin inquiry about the reason for such a regularity, she needs to find nominal definitions of the kind(s) of things over which to generalize, such as the definition of gold outlined in *New Essays*, p. 294 (quoted above). One may have several such definitions, although there is, so far, no assurance that they define the same kind. Nominal definitions of the sort in question are intended to specify kinds of things that are not just possible but that actually exist. Now Locke contends that the observable qualities of things are caused by insensible inner constitutions that we are unable to know in any detail; for that reason, we cannot define kinds of sensible things that align with natural divisions or even know that there are such divisions; similar combinations of qualities might very well be caused by dissimilar inner constitutions. But where Locke sees ignorance, Leibniz sees uncertainty, which he proposes to manage by proceeding on the basis of presumptions and taking nominal definitions to be provisional, or revisable. The presumptions are not unreasonable, as he argues, and we cannot advance in natural science without them.

---

[58] Garber (2009, 247–250) gives this interpretation to "Conspectus libelli elementorum physicae" 1678–9?; (A VI iv 1998–1999; L 283) and some later texts.

[59] The following might seem to be an example: "Damnation of the innocent is a thing possible in itself or not implying a contradiction, but it is not possible for God. . . . It is not by estimating the whole harmony of things that we know that God will not eternally damn the innocent" ("De libertate a necessitate in eligendo" 1680–84; A VI iv 1453; quoted in Adams 1994, 28).

[60] At this stage, we have reason to assent to propositions to the effect that such-and-such things exist outside of us and that certain combinations of sensible qualities belong to the same thing.

One presumption is that every combination of qualities combined in the same thing corresponds to an essence which belongs to a thing just in case it has these qualities.[61] As mentioned, nominal definitions of natural kinds are open to revision in light of further information. For instance, Leibniz counts the definition of gold as "the heaviest known metal" as a nominal definition. If a heavier metal were discovered, the definition would need to be revised. Again, we might discover an alloy that satisfies our nominal definition of gold but has a considerable number of qualities which the familiar samples lack; it would then be reasonable either to alter the definition of gold to exclude the newly discovered metal or to elevate gold to a genus and find nominal definitions of its two known species.[62] In this way, the hurdles in the way of stating nominal definitions of essences can be overcome well enough to get on with the construction of real causal definitions.[63]

The aim is to specify inner constitutions that we think may explain why the nominal definition is true of the kind in question. This is the work of the inventive part of reason: "The art of deciphering the causes of phenomena, or genuine hypotheses, is like that of deciphering: an inspired guess often provides a generous short-cut" (A VI vi 454; NE 454). A condition on the possibility of constructing such a definition is that the inventor take account of what is known so far about bodies; this involves using concepts drawn from experience and experience-evidenced generalizations, whatever laws of nature we have additional reason to accept, and known truths of mathematics. It is plain enough that the mechanist principle, that everything in nature can be explained mechanistically, should frame the search. As we saw, it has the status of a principle, rather than a simple empirical generalization of the sort inferred by Boyle because it comports with an a priori assessment of what is physically more perfect than the known alternatives. This is the case with other general rules of order (or "architectonic" principles), such as the law of continuity and the principle that everything in nature happens in the most determinate way. A properly framed real causal definition of gold thus stands a chance of being subsumed under mathematical truths and mechanist laws of cause and effect.

All of these things are pulled together in a hypothesis. Under the aegis of a priori laws of order, it comprises a number of real causal definitions conjoined with mathematical truths and mechanist causal laws that connect the specified constitutions with various effects they will produce under various conditions. The hypothesis as a whole is contingent and uncertain. Nevertheless, Leibniz maintains, reasoning on the basis of such hypotheses is the only means by which we can hope to make progress in natural science:

> [E]ven principles which are not completely certain can have their uses, if we build on them purely demonstratively. You see, even though all our conclusions from them would then be merely conditional, and would be worth having only if the principle in question were true, nevertheless the very fact that this connection holds would

---

[61] NE 305–309.

[62] NE 401–2; this is discussed in Leduc 2010.

[63] The disagreement between Leibniz and Locke on essences, natural kinds, and the definitions of natural kinds of sensible things is discussed in Bolton 2017.

have been demonstrated, as would those conditional assertions . . . *This same method has another use*, namely to verify assumptions or hypotheses, in cases where many conclusions flow from them which are known on other grounds to be true . . . [I]n natural science [even though the reverse reasoning is not possible] it still yields great likelihood, when the hypothesis easily explains many phenomena which would otherwise by puzzling and which are quite independent of one another. (A VI iv 450-1; NE 450–1, emphasis added)

What promises to advance knowledge about natural kinds is the willingness to assume less than certain hypotheses in order to derive conclusions about observable things whose truth (falsity) can be independently known by experience or experiment. The results may confer some degree of probability on the hypothesis; the larger the variety of observed phenomena it can explain and the more puzzling they otherwise seem, the greater the probability.

More than twenty years prior to drafting *New Essays*, Leibniz writes to Conring:

[a physical hypothesis] is the more probable . . . the greater number of phenomena that it can explain and the fewer the assumptions. . . . [I]t can be taken as physically certain if, namely, it completely satisfies all the phenomena, as does the key to a cryptograph.

(To Conring; GP I 185–86; L 188, partly quoted earlier)

The code analogy suggests a notion of probability on which it is unlikely that a theory would account for all elements in a complex set of data by accident.[64] Again, the quotation may suggest that probability is measured pragmatically, by its predictive success. But the process of hypothesis construction urged in *New Essays*, with its diminutive a priori proofs and intimations of physical value, suggests a notion of probability as eligibility to be created, that is, degree of perfection understood as relative (nonlogical) possibility.[65] An interpretation of Leibniz's notion of probability along these lines is proposed in the literature.[66] The idea cannot be pursued as it should be here, but a rough suggestion follows.[67]

Proper inductive procedure is analogous to God's choice of a world to create. The investigator reviews the finite set of presently conceivable ordering principles, evaluates them, and selects the best, whereas God canvasses the infinite set of possible worlds and chooses the best. The inquirer's choice permeates the rest of a hypothesis in which it is

---

[64] Couturat (1985, 268–269).

[65] See "On the Radical Origination of Things" (GP VII 304; L 792–793; Strickland 31–38; also "On First Truths" (mid to late 1680s), A VI iv 18–19; Strickland 2006, 29–30; also "On the Reason Why These Things Exist Rather than Others" (1689), A VI iv 1634–1635; Strickland 30–31.

[66] Krüger (1981), which refines and develops Hacking (1971). The notion of probability sketched in this chapter owes a great deal to the former article.

[67] For a different but not inconsistent analysis of the difference between the early view of probability in the letters to Conring and the more robust account in *New Essays*, see Duchesneau 2006.

included because it regulates the definitions of natural kinds, the laws that govern them, and thus the consequences deducible from them. We can say that a hypothesis together with the observational data it explains are a finite model of the world; in this model, the only contingent truths are those comprised in the hypothesis and its verified causal implications. It seems that its probability, in Leibniz's view, is not based solely on the proportion of the data it accounts for, but also in some way on the value of the principles it posits. Lorenz Krüger points to why that can be considered a basis of probability understood as metaphysical (nonlogical) possibility:

> Given [the difference between God's certain knowledge and our conjectural judgment], the reason why we can at all believe [ourselves] to be possibly right (and Leibniz is, of course, no skeptic) derives from the fact that in our conjectures we, as it were, imitate God in thinking about possibilities and degrees of perfection.
>
> (Krüger 1981, 54)

Otherwise, why suppose our inductive inferences have any basis in the structure of the world rather than just having some fortunate consequences? In a finite model, there is a source of value in addition to the ordering principles it posits, one that is an analogue of God's consideration of the series of things contained in possible worlds. The actual series is, after all, part of the best possible world; for us, the portion of the series that we observe must stand in for this component of the actual world. That is, the greater the proportion of the observed phenomena a finite model includes, the greater the analogy between the model and the world of God's choice. This is true whether or not we tend to think of explanatory prowess as physically good, although of course we do value it for our own purposes. Leibniz can see it as a second source of value by which different finite models are to be compared and thereby assigned more or less probability. But even if this rough-and-ready sketch is granted, the two sources of value need to be weighted somehow. If model A has better ordering principles than model B, and B includes a greater proportion of the observed data than does A, how are the two to be ranked? Because the texts we are considering emphasize the latter consideration, we might speculate that unless a hypothesis contains the best principles we can presently conceive, it has no probability at all. This would leave explanatory power as the sole measure of probability.

The fact is that Leibniz's notion of the probability of hypotheses is open to several interpretations—predictive success, explanatory prowess, degree of perfection understood as a measure of (nonlogical) possibility. All of these considerations give some entitlement to assent, in Leibniz's view. But we are in a position to see that the notion that reaches to the deepest level of his metaphysics underlies his general theory of demonstration in the sciences. It is hardly less true in mathematics than physical science that we make progress by reasoning on the basis of definitions and propositions that are unreliable or uncertain precisely because they are limited representations of the more complex, indeed infinite, reality that is the metaphysical ground of all truths. Leibniz's theory of knowledge purports to identify the conditions that make this possible.

References

Adams, R. 1994. *Leibniz: Determinist, Theist, Idealist*. Oxford: Oxford University Press.

Blank, A. 2004. "Definitions, sorities arguments and Leibniz's *Méditation sur la notion commune de la justice.*" *Leibniz Review* 14: 153–166.

Blank, A. 2009. "Ramus and Leibniz on analysis." In M. Dascal (ed.), *Leibniz: What kind of rationalist?* Springer, pp. 155–166.

Bolton, M. 2011. "Leibniz's theory of cognition." In B. Look (ed.), *Companion to Leibniz*. London: Continuum International, pp. 136–158.

Bolton, M. 2012. "Metaphysics and psychology in Leibniz's theory of ideas." In H. Berger, J. Herbst and S. Erdner (eds.), *IX. Internationaler Leibniz-Kongress, Natur und Subjekt*. Hannover: Akademie Verlag Berlin, pp. 10–19.

Bolton, M. 2017. "*Essay and Nouveaux Essais*: competing theories of universals." In Stefano Di Bella and Tad Schmaltx (eds.), *Collection on seventeenth century theories of universals*. Oxford: Oxford University Press.

Couturat, L. 1985. *La Logique de Leibniz*. Hildesheim: Olms.

Dascal, M. 1978. *La Semiologie de Leibniz*. Paris: Aubier.

Dascal, M. 1987. *Leibniz: Language, signs and thought*. Amsterdam: John Benjamins.

Dascal, M. 2006. *Gottfried Wilhelm Leibniz: The Art of Controversies*. Dordrecht: Springer.

Duchesneau, F. 1973. *Leibniz et la méthod des sciences*. Paris: PUF.

Duchesneau, F. 2006. "Leibniz et la Méthod des Hypothèses." In F. Duchesneau and J. Griard (eds.), *Leibniz selon les Nouveaux Essais sur l'entendement humain*. Montreal: Vrin, pp. 99–112.

Garber, D. 2009. *Leibniz: Body, substance, monad*. Oxford: Oxford University Press.

Hacking, I. 1971. "The Leibniz-Carnap program for inductive logic." *Journal of Philosophy* 68: 597–610.

Krüger, L. 1981. "Probability in Leibniz." *Archiv für Geschicte der Philosophie* 63: 47–60.

Kulstad, M. 2006. "Is Leibniz the anti-Hume? A comparative study of foreseeing the future in the *Nouveaux Essais*." In F. Duchesneau and J. Griard (eds.), *Leibniz selon les Nouveaux Essais sur l'entendement humain*. Montreal: Vrin, pp. 59–72.

Kulstad, M. 2011. "Leibniz on the possibility of scientific prediction." In J. Antonio Nicolas and S. Toledo (eds.), *Leibniz y las ciencias empiricas Leibniz and the empirical sciences*. Granada: Editorial Comares, pp. 287–314.

Leibniz, G. W. 1995. *L'estime des apparences: 21 manuscrits de Leibniz sur les probabilités, la théorie des jeux, l'espérance de vie,*. Ed. and trans. Marc. Parmentier. Paris: Vrin.

Leibniz, G. W. 2000. *Hauptschriften zur Versicherungs- und Finanzmathematik*, E. Knobloch and J.- M. Graf von der Sculenburg (eds.). Berlin: Akademie Verlag.

Leibniz, G. W. 2006. *The art of controversies*. M. Dascal (ed.). Netherlands: Springer.

Leduc, C. 2010. "Leibniz and sensible qualities." *British Journal for the History of Philosophy* 18: 797–819.

Leduc, C. 2012. "La doctrine leibnizienne de l'idée." In H. Berger, J. Herbst and S. Erdner (eds.), *IX. Internationaler Leibniz-Kongress, Natur und Subjekt*, Hannover: Akadmie Verlag Berlin, pp. 582–590.

Lodge, P. 2010. "The empirical grounds for Leibniz's 'real metaphysics.'" *Leibniz Review* 20: 13–38.

Mugnai, M. 1990. "Leibniz's nominalism and the reality of ideas in the mind of God." In A. Heinekamp, W. Lenzen, and M. Schneider (eds.), *Mathesis rationis*. Münster: Nodus, pp. 153–167.

de Olaso, E. 1997. "Leibniz and Scepticism". In R. H. Popkin, ed. *Scepticism in the Enlightenment*. Netherlands: Kluwer, pp. 99–130.

Rutherford, D. 1996. "Demonstration and reconciliation: The eclipse of the geometrical method in Leibniz's philosophy." In R. S. Woolhouse (ed.), *Leibniz "New System" 1695*. Florence: Olschki, pp. 181–201.

Wilson, M. 1999. 'Leibniz and Locke on "first truths." In Margaret Wilson (ed.), *Ideas and mechanism*. Princeton, NJ: Princeton University Press, p. 360.

CHAPTER 9

···

THE *SCIENTIA GENERALIS* AND THE ENCYCLOPAEDIA

···

ARNAUD PELLETIER

THE NAME "*SCIENTIA GENERALIS*": TWO PROBLEMS

···

THROUGHOUT his entire life, Leibniz never abandoned the project of establishing a new form of encyclopaedia that would be not simply a collection of all available knowledge, but also a true instrument for discovering and demonstrating new knowledge. Many authors before Leibniz had already thought of turning the old compilations of knowledge—similar to that contained in Gregor Reisch's first published encyclopaedia in German countries (*Margarita Philosophica*, 1504)—into instruments for learning the sciences in a way accessible for beginners. For instance, among the many Ramist textbooks that flourished in the Reformed German countries at the beginning of the seventeenth century, Johann Heinrich Alsted published an influential seven-volume *Encyclopaedia* in 1630, prefaced with *praecognita* (i.e., all preliminary knowledge needed before undertaking the study of any subject);[1] among the Lullist tradition, Kaspar Schott published a popular encyclopaedia of all mathematical disciplines (*Cursus Mathematicus*, 1661) prefaced with some exhortations (*paraeneses*) to the candidates in mathematics.[2] Leibniz praised these pedagogical reforms of the encyclopaedic pattern but also intended to give them a more heuristic and demonstrative form. As early as

---

[1] See Leibniz's notes on Alsted's *Encyclopaedia*, in which he mentions previous encyclopaedist thinkers (A VI iv 1122).

[2] See H. Hotson, *Johann Heinrich Alsted 1588–1638: Between Renaissance, Reformation, and Universal Reform* (Oxford: Clarendon Press, 2000); *Commonplace Learning: Ramism and Its German Ramifications, 1543–1630* (Oxford: Oxford University Press, 2007); and on Schott, see E. Knobloch, "Kaspar Schott's 'encyclopaedia of all mathematical sciences,'" in *Poeiesis & Praxis 7/4* (June 2011), pp. 225–247.

1668, he conceived of the project of encyclopaedic prolegomena that should gather the elements and principles for some "catholic [i.e., universal] demonstrations."[3] Right until the end of his life, he continued to refer to his hampered intention "to put the whole of philosophy into demonstrations"[4] and thus avoid pointless disputations, for Leibniz had always been firmly convinced that "what is soundly philosophical stays out of controversy."[5] All this is well known and matches rather well the image of a universal genius versed in all the sciences that Fontenelle depicted for the first time in his *Éloge*.

However, Leibniz never realized his encyclopaedic ambitions, even though he wrote many plans, prefaces, and preparatory drafts for the "demonstrative" encyclopaedia. He had, indeed, identified two problems concerning its feasibility. On the one hand, it would require many collaborators, if only in order to collect all available knowledge and thereby set up, not the encyclopaedia itself, but its material propedeutic. Leibniz often mentions this difficulty in his numerous requests for funding addressed to possible patrons.[6] Another difficulty is mentioned in his private papers, namely, that such a demonstrative or inventive encyclopaedia—one that would eventually contribute to mankind's happiness and probably be its most valuable treasure—could only be conceived as the result of a series of projects and, in particular, the project of a *Scientia Generalis* (General Science).[7] Thus, as early as the winter of 1678, Leibniz presents the *Scientia Generalis* as an instrument for the encyclopaedia:

> It is important for the happiness of mankind to establish some encyclopaedia or an orderly collection of truths, to the extent that it will be useful to all things and thus to deduce all sufficient truths. It will be a kind of public treasure, to which will be brought all things which have been admirably discovered and observed. But since this immense labor is still very far from being achieved, especially regarding civil and natural history, we need meanwhile some *Scientia Generalis*, which contains the principles of reason and the first experiences that everybody should know.[8]

---

[3] A VI i 494 (*Demonstrationum Catholicarum Conspectus*, 1668–69): "The Prolegomena will contain the Elements of Philosophy, namely the first principles of Metaphysics (on being), of Logic (on mind), of Mathematics (on space), of Physics (on bodies) and of Practical Philosophy (on *civitas*)."

[4] Leibniz to Biber, unpublished letter, after March 1716 (LBr 64, f. 4): "Il n'y a que mon grand ouvrage Historique qui m'empeche d'executer la pensée que j'ay de mettre la philosophie en demonstrations. J'espere de l'achever dans cette année; et si Dieu me donne encor quelque vigueur apres cela, je tacheray de me decharger de quelques idées que j'ay encor pour l'avancement des connoissances."

[5] Leibniz to Hansch, July 25, 1707: Kortholt, *Godefridi Guilielmi epistolae ad diversos*, III, 70.

[6] See, e.g., A VI iv 691 (*Nouvelles ouvertures*, 1686).

[7] Following Leibniz's principal usage, we use capital letters to denote the specific project of a General Science.

[8] A VI iv 135–38 (*Studia ad felicitatem dirigenda*, hiver 1678–79): "Hinc sequitur interesse ad foelicitatem humani generis, ut condatur Encyclopaedia quaedam, seu ordinata collectio Veritatum, quad ejus fieri potest ad omnia utilia inde deducenda sufficientum. Eaque erit instar aerarii publici, cui omnia praeclare inventa atque observata inferri possint. Sed quia maximae molis futura esset, praesertim pro his quae ad historiam civilem ac naturalem pertinent, interea opus est Scientia quadam Generali, qua principia rationis atque experientiae primaria continenatur quae virum praestantem nosse decet."

Here, for the first time, Leibniz uses a positive notion of *Scientia Generalis*; he had already, with this term, criticized the Lullian idea of an *Ars Magna* or universal organon of thought.[9] However, determining the concept, the object, and even the purpose of such a *Scientia Generalis* within the Leibnizian corpus proves to be particularly problematic.

Leibniz's statements regarding the specific issue of a *Scientia Generalis* are indeed relatively rare, programmatic, and not identical in their meaning. Although the project of a *Scientia Generalis* is mentioned in about twenty drafts, none of these drafts offers a sample of it. This situation has presented scholars, first of all, with an editorial problem: because the *Scientia Generalis* is explicitly the name of a project, the question arises as to which other texts from the Leibnizian corpus could be related to this program—either as an implicit explanation or even as a partial achievement of it.[10] Commentators have been quite generous in the identification of an implicit corpus of texts thought to be thematically related or close to the *Scientia Generalis*. Louis Couturat, for instance, in his monograph *La logique de Leibniz*, devotes a whole chapter to the topic in which he actually addresses the whole Leibnizian theory of knowledge, embracing all developments on ideas, definitions, probability, principles, experimental method, and induction, as well as the *ars inveniendi* (the art of inventing; i.e., the art of finding new truths).[11] Although they do not share Couturat's interpretation, the editors of the Academy Edition have nevertheless regarded more than two hundred drafts from the period 1677–90 to be related to the *Scientia Generalis*. Some scholars even suggest that the countless notes of Leibniz's immense *Nachlass* were nothing but preparatory notes to the *Scientia Generalis*.[12] The first problem related to this editorial and interpretative issue is thus to determine the proper object of the *Scientia Generalis*.

There is, however, a second editorial problem, which may be even more significant than the first, namely, that the vast majority of explicit references to a *Scientia Generalis* belong to the "middle-years," the decade 1678–88. After Leibniz's departure for Italy in 1688, one finds only five occurrences of the phrase in the texts known thus far, four

---

[9] A VI i 193 (*De arte combinatoria*, 1666).

[10] See H. Schepers, "Scientia Generalis. Ein Problem der Leibniz-Edition," in *Tradition und Aktualität. V. internationaler Leibniz-Kongress* (Hannover, Leibniz-Gesellschaft, 1988), p. 356.

[11] L. Couturat, *La logique de Leibniz* (Paris: Alcan, 1901), chapter VI. The *ars inveniendi*, usually translated by 'art of invention' or 'art of discovery' in the secondary literature, echoes one of the two parts of Ramist logic (see Pierre de la Ramée, *Dialectique* [Paris, André Wechel, 1555], pp. 4–5: "Les parties de la Dialectique sont deux: l'invention et le Jugement," where invention refers to the analysis of the "principes, éléments, termes, moyens, raisons, preuves, arguments") and also one of the four parts of Baconian logic, namely "the art of enquiry or invention (*ars inquisitionis seu inventionis*)" and especially "the art of inventing and discovering the sciences [which] remains hitherto unknown (*ars inveniendi et perlustrandi scientias [quae] hactenus ignoretur*" (Francis Bacon, *De dignitate et augmentis scientiarum* [London, 1623]; translated by Gilbert Wats as *Of the Advancement and Proficience of Learning* (London, 1640), V, chapter II). In order to avoid the modern meaning of the term *invention*, I will refer alternatively to the *ars inveniendi*, the *art of inventing* or the *art of discovering*.

[12] Cf. Hans Poser, "Langzeitvorhaben in der Akademie. Die Geschichte der Leibniz- Edition zwischen Kaiserreich und geteiltem Deutschland," in *Die Preussische Akademie der Wissenschaften zu Berlin 1914–1945* (Berlin, Akademie Verlag, 2000), p. 376.

of which do not refer to the unrevealed project of the 1680s but clearly serve as another name for metaphysics itself. To put it briefly, there remains only one unfinished draft, probably written in the mid-1690s and not completely in line with the pieces of the former decade, that promises a new intellectual dawn under the title *Aurora or the Foundations of the Scientia Generalis*.[13] After 1688, the *Scientia Generalis* seems to disappear from the Leibnizian corpus, although Leibniz never abandoned the project of a new encyclopaedia.

Is there, then, a link between the fate of the *Scientia Generalis* in Leibniz's works and the difficulty in identifying its object? The most distinguished commentators have assumed that the disappearance of its name does not affect the understanding of its object. For instance, Heinrich Schepers, and after him Maria Rosa Antognazza, defend the overall continuity of a broad and ambitious "project," "vision," or "dream" that Leibniz never abandoned, but which took different shapes, from the early *Catholic demonstrations*, already mentioned, up to his last months.[14] Others, on the other hand, interpret this lexical disappearance as proof of the philosophical inconsistency of a project that Leibniz could not achieve as such.[15] There are good arguments for both views, but none would be relevant if one fails to recall first that Leibniz had given at least three clearly distinct characterizations of the *Scientia Generalis*, namely:

1. As an *art of inventing (and judging) in general*—as can be found in about fifteen texts written between 1679 and 1688
2. As *a science of what is thinkable in general in so far as it is such*—in a single text dating from 1686, according to which the art of inventing is only one of its constituents
3. As *metaphysics* itself—from 1688 onward[16]

Most commentators have tried to reconstruct a unified and permanent concept of *Scientia Generalis* assuming that these characterizations display only different aspects of a core concept, namely, that of Logic. Indeed, there are passages where each characterization is also directly associated with Logic, such that the *Scientia Generalis* might thus be indirectly identified with it: (1) "the art of inventing and judging" is sometimes called a "secret logic"; (2) "the science of what is thinkable in general" is said to replace the old logic; and, eventually, (3) "Metaphysics is hardly different from the true Logic, that is

[13] *Aurora seu Initia Scientiae Generalis*, LH IV, 7a, f. 11–12 (partly published in GP VII, 54–56). The word *initia* can also be translated by *beginnings* or *elements*, but its grounding function is better translated by *foundations* as will be noticed in the section "*Initia* and *Specimina*: The Structure of the *Scientia Generalis*."

[14] See H. Schepers, op. cit., p. 357 and M. R. Antognazza, *Leibniz. An Intellectual Biography* (Cambridge University Press, 2009), p. 90.

[15] See A. Drago, "The modern fulfilment of Leibniz's program for a Scientia Generalis," in *Leibniz und Europa* (Hannover, Leibniz-Gesellschaft, 1994), pp. 185–195.

[16] Respectively, A II, 1², 669 (Leibniz to Gallois, December 19, 1678); A VI iv 527 (*Introductio ad encyclopaediam arcanam*, 1683–85); A VI iv 980 (*Paraenesis de Scientia Generali*, 1688).

to say from the art of inventing in general."[17] This series of semantic equivalences finds some support in the fact that both parts of the traditional Ramist logic, namely the arts of inventing and judging, are constitutive of this *Scientia Generalis*, as well as in the fact that "Logic itself is a *scientia generalis*."[18] In my view, however, this series of equivalences merely amounts to an anachronistic anadiplosis that suppresses the conceptual and chronological differences between the three characterizations and leaves aside the true problems of the object and fate of the *Scientia Generalis*. We shall thus address these two problems anew by carefully examining how the different blueprints for a *Scientia Generalis* fulfill its original purpose, that of being a preparation for a "demonstrative encyclopaedia."[19]

The Starting Point: From Characteristic to Wisdom

In the first texts that mention the project of a *Scientia Generalis*, dating from the winter of 1678, Leibniz does not fully clarify its object but rather determines its place and function within a series of projects, each one conceived as the precondition for the next. In the passage quoted earlier, Leibniz refers only to "a collection of principles of reason and first experiences" that should establish a well-ordered and inventive encyclopaedia. But in a letter from the same period—wherein we find the sole public mention of the project—he refers to something seemingly different, namely an *ars inveniendi* that should be made possible by a new formal language or Characteristic:

> I will add something about Combinations, and the *ars inveniendi* in general. For I know that you appreciate these universal considerations, and that you yourself have important observations about them. I am more and more convinced of the usefulness and reality of this general science, and I see that few people have understood its scope. But to make it easier and, so to speak, sensible, I intend to make use of the Characteristic, of which I have spoken with you on occasion, and of which Algebra and Mathematics are merely samples. This Characteristic consists of a certain writing or language (since he who has the one can have the other) which perfectly matches the relations of our thoughts.[20]

---

[17] Respectively, A VI iv 972 (*Paraenesis de scientia generali*), A VI iv 527 (*Introductio ad encyclopaediam arcanam*), A II, 1², 662 (Leibniz to Elisabeth, November 1678). See also A VI iv 2458 (*De religione magnorum virorum*): "We will thus begin by a more general science, which is called Logic or Metaphysics."

[18] A VI iv 511 (*De artis combinatoriae usu in scientia generali*, 1683).

[19] A VI iv 708 (*Recommandations pour instituer la science générale*, 1686).

[20] A II, 1², 669 (Leibniz to Gallois, December 19, 1678).

Neither passage presents the conceptual content of the *Scientia Generalis*. Instead, they outline its material conditions and ultimate purposes: the Characteristic facilitates the *Scientia Generalis*, which in turn establishes the encyclopaedia, which finally serves mankind's happiness. Given this framework, which clearly goes from theoretical devices to practical purposes, one understands the sense in which it is legitimate to relate the *Scientia Generalis* to other Leibnizian projects. It is clear, however, that one also needs to understand how the *Scientia Generalis* relates to both Characteristic and Wisdom, almost as a middle term between them.

It is appropriate to start with wisdom, since Leibniz's first reflections on the *Scientia Generalis* originate in his Parisian notes on wisdom. Whereas the characterization of wisdom as the science of happiness (*sapientia est scientia felicitatis*) recurs often after the early texts on natural law,[21] the relation of knowledge to wisdom dates back to 1676, when Leibniz discovered and commented on Descartes's writings in Paris. The last of the six drafts known under the common title *De vita beata* is particularly significant:

> Wisdom is a perfect knowledge of the principles of all sciences (a) and of the art of applying them (b). I call *Principles* all fundamental truths, which are sufficient for drawing all conclusions (c) with, if needed, a bit of application and some exercise (d). . . . The art of applying these principles to occurrences contains in itself the art of judging well or reasoning (e), the art of discovering unknown truths (f), and finally, the art of remembering (g) what one knows at the right time and when needed.[22]

Wisdom is thus characterized by two kinds of knowledge: a theoretical knowledge of the principles of all sciences—called "fundamental truths"—and a practical knowledge of their application, a part of which is the art of discovering. This twofold aspect of wisdom, as characterized in 1676, matches perfectly what Leibniz says about the *Scientia Generalis* itself some ten years later—at a time when the *Scientia Generalis* is subordinated to wisdom:

> By *Scientia Generalis*, I understand the science containing the principles of all other sciences (a), and the method for using these principles (b), so that anyone venturing into particular things, even if endowed with an ordinary mind, would be able to understand the most difficult things (c) by means of an easy meditation or a short experiment (d), and would be able to discover the most beautiful truths and the most useful applications, as much as one can do from given data. Thus, the *Scientia Generalis* must deal both with the art of thinking correctly (e), that is to say, the art of discovering (f), judging, directing the will, retaining and remembering (g), and must also deal with the search for the Elements of the Encyclopaedia and the search for the

---

21 A VI i 457 (*Elementa juris naturalis*, around 1669–70).
22 A VI iii 669 (*De la sagesse*, 1676). The addition of letters (a), (b), (c), etc., here and in the following quotation is mine.

Highest Good, which is the ultimate cause of all meditation, for wisdom is actually nothing other than the science of happiness.[23]

According to this note, the *Scientia Generalis* cannot be taken for a merely formal instrument or a general methodology whose material achievement should be the encyclopaedia: the difficulty in grasping its object lies precisely in its constitutive twofold nature. Indeed, it embraces a twofold content (the knowledge of the *principles* of all the sciences and the knowledge of their *use*); it has a twofold task (to *understand* the first and to *discover* by means of the second); and also a twofold purpose (to search for the *elements* of the encyclopaedia and to search for the *ways* of thinking about them correctly). The specificity of this science is that it gradually discovers its own objects and that its objects gradually become its means of further discoveries. That is, the search for the elements of the encyclopaedia requires the use of already available principles and methods, but the outcome of this research is to expand the set of principles and methods that will be available for the discovery of further elements. Under "the principles of the sciences" here referred to, one should include not only formal principles but also all that lies at their foundations and constitutes their elements. In this regard, Leibniz writes in a blueprint for this new encyclopaedia that "the principles [of sciences] are either definitions or axioms or hypotheses or phenomena,"[24] and he calls "elements of eternal truth" that which constitute the grounding of truths and demonstrations in all sciences.[25] Strictly speaking, the *Scientia Generalis* does not comprehend two distinct parts—formal and material—but relies on elements having a twofold function because they can be successively considered as belonging to either its object-matter or to its instrumental part. Thus understood, the elements are also referred to as the principles (*principia*) or foundations (*initia*) of the *Scientia Generalis*.

Given this twofold function, which guarantees a systematic expansion of both the *Scientia Generalis* itself and the particular sciences, it now becomes clear how the art of discovering and judging can be, at the same time, referred to as the object ("the art of thinking correctly": *modo bene cogitandi*), the means ("containing the principles of all sciences and the method for using these principles": *principia modumque principiis utendi*), and the purpose ("to understand and discover": *intelligere et invenire*) of the *Scientia Generalis*. It is then no longer surprising that Leibniz should mention the *ars*

[23] A VI iv 532 (*Definitio brevis Scientiae Generalis*, 1683–1685): "Scientiam Generalem intelligo, quae caeterarum omnium principia continet, modumque principiis ita utendi, ut quisque mediocri licet ingenio praeditus ubi ad specialia quaecunque descenderit, facili meditatione et brevi experientia, difficillima etiam intelligere, et pulcherrimas veritates, utilissimasque praxes, quantum ex datis homini possibile est, invenire possit. Tractare ergo debet tum de modo bene cogitandi, hoc est inveniendi, judicandi, affectus regendi, retinendi ac reminiscendi, tum vero de totius Encyclopaediae Elementis, et Summi Boni investigatione, cujus causa omnis meditatio suscipitur, est enim nihil aliud sapientia, quam scientia felicitatis."
[24] A VI iv 341 (*Consilium de Encyclopaedia nova*, 1679).
[25] A VI iv 445; 675; and 972: "Vérités absolument premières ou indémontrables par nature."

inveniendi sometimes as the whole and sometimes as a part or condition of the *Scientia Generalis.*[26]

This twofold character also applies to the relation between the *Scientia Generalis* and the Characteristic; that is, to the symbolic expression of the relations between thoughts: by expressing them, the Characteristic allows the discovery of the *Scientia Generalis* itself. That is, "to make it [i.e., the *Scientia Generalis*] easier and, so to speak, sensible."[27] It is, again, no longer paradoxical that the Characteristic is thus mentioned sometimes as a condition, sometimes as a part, and sometimes even as the whole of the *Scientia Generalis.* Leibniz will explicitly address this particular structure of the *Scientia Generalis* under the distinction between its foundations (*initia*) and its examples (*specimina*).

INITIA AND *SPECIMINA*: THE STRUCTURE OF THE *SCIENTIA GENERALIS*

Leibniz's plan implies, first, the constitution or heuristic discovery of the *Scientia Generalis* itself out of the *demonstrated elements* of all the particular sciences[28] and, second, the establishment of a *demonstrative* encyclopaedia; that is to say, the development of new samples of science. The cornerstone of the plan thus relies on the possibility of transferring the principles and elements from a local science to another local science through the *Scientia Generalis.*

In some drafts written within a short period between 1679 and 1683, Leibniz introduces the distinction—taken from Jurisprudence—between the foundations (*initia*) and the samples (*specimina*) that are to be established in all sciences.[29] The foundations comprise the art of judging and inventing, the "elements of eternal truth" and the plan of the encyclopaedia. The samples comprise Geometry, Mechanics, universal Jurisprudence,[30] sometimes Mathematics and Physics,[31] and even the "Logic of Life"—namely, the logic of probabilities[32]—but should, eventually, gather together all the possible samples of all the possible sciences.[33] As expected, once applied, the *initia* would generate new *specimina* or new *applicata.*[34] Two tasks are required for this. The

[26] See, e.g., A VI iv 370; 532.

[27] A II, 1², 669.

[28] This could be compared to Jungius's heuristica: "Et Heuretica non tantum alias scientias auget, sed etiam seipsam" (Leibniz, *Vorausedition zur Reihe VI in der Ausgabe der Akademie der Wissenschaften der DDR*, Münster, fascicle 7, 1988, p. 1618).

[29] See A VI iv 359–64 (*Initia et specimina scientiae generalis*, 1679); A VI iv 443 (*Initia et specimina scientiae novae generalis*, 1682).

[30] A VI iv 359–61 (*Initia et specimina Scientiae Generalis*, 1679).

[31] A VI iv 363.

[32] A VI iv 364.

[33] A VI iv 443 (*Initia et specimina scientiae novae generalis*, 1682).

[34] A VI iv 362.

first is to explain the principles by means of which all truths have been discovered and demonstrated thus far:[35] the secret of the art of discovery—*arcanum artis inveniendi* or the secret logic—consists precisely in leaving nothing secret as regards the process of discovering, from the very idea of discovery to the different stages of the demonstration.[36] Those foundations are deemed to be even more explicit than Euclid's Elements, which display a mathematical order but not the order of discovery.[37] The second task is to set the samples and doctrines in an order that might allow new discoveries[38] (i.e., that might allow the extension and transfer of the principles' use):

> Excellent men produce everywhere outstanding samples in all areas even if they lack this unity or coordination (*conspiratio coordinatioque*) by which alone a doctrine can be transferred (*transferre posset*) to greater purposes for mankind. It is thus proposed by us to follow this *Scientia Generalis*, which makes the mind penetrate into all things and which teaches to judge what is discovered, to discover what is sought, to order everything, and which finally establishes the first principles (*prima principia constituit*) and opens the way to the ultimate causes of things (*ad summam rerum causas supremas aperit viam*).[39]

Here, Leibniz distinguishes three pathways from *initia* to *specimina* and vice versa. The first leads from the established *specimina* to the identification of their respective *initia*; the second leads from the *initia* to the first principles or the ultimate causes of things—which recalls the object of the Aristotelian first philosophy[40]—and the third way leads from the *initia* again to new *specimina* or to what he often calls "new openings."[41] Leibniz does not specify further the conditions of this extension or transposition of principles, except that it would require a great coordination of scholars and even, as he writes elsewhere, several years of coordinated work.[42] The transposition of principles does not necessarily mean exporting principles from one domain to an altogether foreign domain; it

---

[35] See A VI iv 370 (*Introductio ad scientiam generalem*, 1679): "Scientiam generalem intelligo quae modum docet omnes alias scientias ex datis sufficientibus inveniendi et demonstrandi."

[36] A VI iv 442 (*Initia et specimina scientiae novae generalis*, 1682). Those principles which build up the very secret of the art of inventing, this *arcanum artis inveniendi* which should replace Descartes's *praecipuum artis secretum* mentioned in the *Regulae ad directionem ingenii* (AT X, 381).

[37] See A VI iv 341 (*Project of a New Encyclopaedia to be written following the method of invention*, June 25, 1679), translated in M. Dascal, Q. Racionero, *Gottfried Wilhelm Leibniz: The Art of Controversies* (New York: Springer, 2008), p. 130.

[38] A VI iv 340 (ibid.): "*The essence of the project* consists in the ordering of available human knowledge that is most important and useful for life in a way *proper for discovery*. . . . Once the discoveries in any field are correctly ordered in a table, the way of continuing these discoveries will appear, i.e., the mode of discovering new things will be much easier than if one would try to discover them one by one and as if beside its own series." Those considerations are to be found as soon as 1678: A VI iv 83 (*De usu artis combinatoriae praestantissimo qui est scribere encylopaediam*, 1678); A VI iv 86 (*Atlas universalis*, 1678).

[39] A VI iv 978 (*Paraenesis de Scientia Generali tradenda*, 1688).

[40] A VI iv 980.

[41] See A VI iv 690 (*Nouvelles ouvertures*, 1686).

[42] See A VI i 4, 972.

means discovering the greatest scope of their application: Leibniz mentions examples of such successful transpositions within mathematics.[43] But whether it be a domestic or a foreign transposition, whether it be in mathematics, medicine, jurisprudence or in any other science, there is no other way to guarantee its possibility than to try it: there is no predetermined way to decide *de jure* that such a transfer or extension is legitimate or not—just as there is no other way to determine prime numbers than to try to divide them.[44]

The distinction between the *initia* and the *specimina* thus reveals that the *Scientia Generalis* cannot be understood as a universal science in the sense of a calculus or a single method that could be applied to all sciences. Its unity is not given by the uniqueness of an *organon*—as it was sought in the Ramist tradition—but by the plurality of elements and principles whose domains of validity are to be determined through the collective progress of the sciences. A remarkable feature of the structure of the *Scientia Generalis* is that it does not presuppose a priori first principles but, on the contrary, intends to discover progressively the first principles that would "open the way to the ultimate causes of things" and—as one can already guess—to wisdom. But those explicit echoes of the Aristotelian characterization of first philosophy raise a new problem for the understanding of Leibniz's *Scientia Generalis*: should it replace Metaphysics itself?

METAPHYSICS AND *SCIENTIA GENERALIS*

Because the *Scientia Generalis* takes over a foundational function regarding the sciences, Leibniz did not fail to present it as the true Metaphysics or as the fulfillment of the program attributed to Aristotle, one pursued, in a particular manner, within German Reformed scholasticism. This occurs explicitly as the project of a book entitled *Introduction to a secret encyclopaedia, or foundations and examples of the Scientia Generalis, about the renewal and growth of the sciences and the way of perfecting the mind and making discoveries for the benefit of public happiness*, presumptively dated 1686:

> The *Scientia Generalis* is nothing but the science of what is thinkable in general in so far as it is such. This includes not only what has hitherto been regarded as logic, but also the *ars inveniendi*, along with the method or the means of arrangement, synthesis and analysis, didactics or the science of teaching, the so-called Gnostology, Noology, the art of reminiscence or mnemonics, the art of characters or of symbols, the Art of Combinations, the Art of Subtlety, and philosophical grammar; the Art of Llull, the Cabbala of the wise, and natural magic. Perhaps it also includes Ontology,

---

[43] Cf. A VI iv 425 (*De arte combinatoria scribenda*, 1680).

[44] A VI iii 436 (*Sur les premières propositions et les premiers termes*, 1676). For a more detailed account of the unity of logic, see my "*Logica est Scientia generalis*: l'unité de la logique selon Leibniz," *Archives de Philosophie*, 2013/2, pp. 271–294.

or the science of something and nothing, of being and not being, of the thing and its mode, and of substance and accident. It does not make much difference how you divide the Sciences, for they are one continuous body, like the ocean.[45]

The text is often mentioned as containing the sole uncorrected mention of the word "ontology" known so far in Leibniz's papers. But although the word had emerged within Reformed scholasticism (said to have been used for the first time by Jacob Lorhard in his 1606 *Ogdoas Scholastica*), and although, to be precise, Leibniz refers here to the Timplerian characterizations of Metaphysics as the "science of what is thinkable in general in so far as it is such" or as the "science of something and nothing,"[46] it remains the case that the object of Leibniz's *Scientia Generalis* contrasts with the object of Timpler's Metaphysics.

The Calvinist Clemens Timpler (1564–1624) had defined the object of metaphysics as that which is *intelligible as such*: this supertranscendental term (*intelligibile, cogitabile*) applies both to real, extant objects and to fictional, nonexistent objects, such that the domain of the intelligible as such can be divided into something (*aliquid*) and nothing (*nihil*).[47] For Timpler, to deal with the intelligible is to deal with all that can be an object of thought as an object of thought (i.e., without considering the content [or matter] of thought), which is the object of all the other sciences.[48] By dealing with the most common, most general, and (super-)transcendental attributes of being, not only can metaphysics truly be called "a catholic or universal science" (*Metaphysica est scientia catholica seu universalis*), but it can also be sharply distinguished from Logic, understood as a practical art without a proper subject matter (*subjectum*): "The end of metaphysics is to explain all that is intelligible in as much as it falls under a manner of considering (*modus considerandi*) proper to this art; the end of Logic is to explain the manner of knowing (*modus sciendi*) well and reasoning well." In other words, metaphysics is characterized by a specific manner of considering the intelligible—namely, by ignoring the content (or "matter")—and this manner constitutes the intelligible as a *subjectum*; logic ignores any *subjectum* and deals only with our ways of knowing.

It thus becomes manifest that the passage just quoted explicitly rejects the Timplerian identification of the *science of the intelligible* with a mere *science of something and nothing*. Leibniz's "science of what is thinkable in general in so far as it is such" goes far beyond Timpler's *science of the intelligible* by embracing all the "ways of knowing" that were excluded from it.[49] The list of disciplines that Leibniz gives does not cover

---

[45] A VI iv 527 (*Introductio ad encyclopaediam arcanam*, 1686), trans. by M. Dascal, *The Art of Controversies*, op. cit., p. 220.

[46] See W. Hübener, "Scientia de Aliquo et Nihilo. Die historischen Voraussetzungen von Leibniz' Ontologiebegriff," in A. Schwan (ed.), *Denken im Schatten des Nihilismus* (Darmstadt: Wissenschaftliche Buchgesellschaft, 1975).

[47] Timpler, *Metaphysicae systema methodicum* (Hanau, 1606); Lib I, Cap. I, Qu. V., and Cap. II.

[48] Ibid., Lib I, Cap. I, Qu. V.

[49] Leibniz adds in the margin (A VI iv 528): "We consider many things not in themselves but according to the mode by which we perceive them and how they affect us."

comprehensively the content of the *Scientia Generalis* but refers to that which was excluded from the intelligible according to the Reformed metaphysics, although it is essential for discovering new intelligible things. Among others, Leibniz refers to Abraham Calov's Gnostology and Noology (which were thought to be an epistemological grounding for Metaphysics),[50] to Alsted's *praecognita* of the *Encyclopaedia* (at least to the didactics),[51] and even to Giambattista della Porta's *Magia Naturalis* (Naples, 1558), the famous treatise about the similarities among empirical things—for similarities may express some secret (i.e., so far unnoticed) regularities.[52] And it is not without irony that the *science of something and nothing* is said to be "perhaps also" (*et forte etiam*) part of the *science of the thinkable*, the point being that the latter is probably not the most fruitful way of achieving the former or of "making discoveries for the benefit of public happiness."

The outcome of this dismantlement of Timpler's concept of Metaphysics is straightforward: what had been brought under this term as a science of the intelligible was far from fulfilling its ambitious program and should thus be replaced by a new *Scientia Generalis*. This turn is made explicit in the *Exhortation to the Scientia Generalis*, written in Vienna in 1688 and dedicated to a "benevolent monarch"—probably the emperor—which seems to be Leibniz's last detailed word on the project.[53] Remarkably, the text displays three successive characterizations of the *Scientia Generalis*:

1. "There is a *Scientia Generalis*, or some secret logic, by which all things may be judged and invented out of given data within a few years.... The *Scientia Generalis* consists in judgment and invention, or in the Analytics and the Topics, that is to say, in the marks of truth and in the thread of invention."

2. "Wisdom is nothing else than the science of happiness or human perfection, and it belongs to this most general science, or Architectonic, to show how men might tend to the perfection they are capable of by nature."

3. "We thus understand that the first, or *Scientia Generalis*, that we plan to deal with is the theory of wisdom, for wisdom is the practice of this first science. I believe that this science is the one Aristotle called the sought-after science (τὴν ζητουμένην), and it seems that what he himself wrote in his *Metaphysics* is just a prolegomena for seeking it."[54]

---

[50] See A. Calov(ius), *Scripta philosophica*, Lübeck, 1651, including: I. Gnostologia; II. Noologia seu habitus intelligentiae; III. Metaphysicae divinae pars generalis; IV. Metaphysicae divinae pars specialis; V. Encyclopaedia Mathematica; VI. Methodologia; VII. Ideae encyclopaedias disciplinarum realium ... repraesentantes.

[51] See Leibniz's notes (A VI iv 1123; dated 1682) mentioning the four *praecognita*: *Hexilogia, Technologia, Archelogia, Didactica*. On the *praecognita*, see Hotson (2007), p. 177.

[52] Leibniz calls *Homoeographia* the science of similar things within one species (A VI iv 347).

[53] A VI iv 971 (*Paraenesis de Scientia Generali*—title given by the editors, 1688). In the mid-1690s, there will be only one other synopsis for a book: *Guilielmi Pacidii Lubentiani* AURORA *seu* INITIA *Scientiae* GENERALIS *a Divina Luce ad humanam felicitatem* (LH 4, 7a, f. 11–12; partly published in GP VII, 54–56).

[54] Respectively A VI, i 4, 972, 975, and 980. Couturat published only the first part of the text (C 222) and thus left aside the last two characterizations that may have challenged his interpretation.

A certain *secret logic*, an *Architectonic*, and a *theory of wisdom* with the aim of achieving Aristotle's intention: these characterizations do not refer to three incompatible objects of the *Scientia Generalis* but rather to its three simultaneous aspects resulting from its particular structure. Their unity is not the result of a closed system but of the never-ending task of identifying the principles of all knowledge. In the text just quoted, the *Scientia Generalis* is referred to by Leibniz as an "*Architectonic*"—in the sense (used only once) of a science of principles (*archai*). These may be understood as the principles of all disciplines and so remind us of Alsted's *Archelogia*, which embraced both the general principles of all disciplines and the particular principles of particular disciplines.[55] One should notice, however, that for Leibniz the distinction between the general and local principles of truths does not apply here and that his prolegomena to wisdom should already deal with the causes of things themselves:

> This *Scientia Generalis*, which deals with the causes of things, the harmony of the universe, the principles, and the arrangement of truths, is absolutely necessary to Wisdom.[56]

As is common in his writing, Leibniz conveys his own philosophical insights through a subversive interpretation of traditional notions. Here, the *Scientia Generalis* takes up some features of the Aristotelian first philosophy: it is a science in as much as it deals with causes and principles, but it is not a *first* science because, in that case, it would deal with a specific kind of beings or principles. This explains why Leibniz writes in the 1694 article on *The emendation of first philosophy* that the science τήν ζητουμένην is still desired (GP IV, 468). For dealing with "the *causes* of things and the *principles* of truths" means, on the one hand, paying no attention to the object of metaphysics as conceived within the Reformed tradition (namely, being *qua* intelligible), and, on the other hand, paying no attention to half of the definition of *philosophia prima* proposed by the Jesuit Francisco Suárez (namely, "Scientia qua de primis rerum causis et principis, et *de rebus dignissimis* considerat").[57] In other words, the *Scientia Generalis* does not relate a general ontology to a theology (or to a supreme being) but instead deals with the first principles of knowledge-and-things, among which the principles of theology do not have a special status. The *Scientia Generalis* as such is thus deprived of a specific theological dimension, but it can also, in a certain sense, be equated with theology for "the knowledge of principles is the best possible theology."[58] It is in no way surprising, then, that Leibniz uses the names "*Scientia Generalis*" and "metaphysics" in order to subvert their common meaning. This is made explicit in his notes on the Socinian author Christoph Stegmann, written after 1708:

[55] J. H. Alsted, *Scientiarum omnium Encyclopaediae Tomus primus* (Lyon, 1649), Sciagraphia, p. 4.
[56] A VI iv 980 (*Paraenesis de Scientia Generali*, 1688).
[57] F. Suarez, *Disputationes Metaphysicae*, 1, 2, 10.
[58] A II, 1², 662 (Letter to Elisabeth, November 1678).

I think that metaphysics is the science which treats of the causes of things, using the principle that nothing happens without reason, and that thus the reason of existence is to be taken in the prevalence of essences, whose reality is grounded in some primitive substance existing per se. So, simultaneously, the nature of monads or simple substances emerges. But everything in that general science, which some call metaphysics, that is worthy to be called science, belongs to logic, that is to say, to the science that uses only the principle of contradiction.[59]

Here, Leibniz clearly distinguishes a metaphysics dealing with the causes of things, the reasons of existence, the nature of the substances, and the first principles or truths, on the one hand, and what is also called metaphysics or general science, on the other hand. In the first draft of the passage, Leibniz identifies the latter with "ontology," namely, with a logical division of that which is thinkable (*cogitabile*) in terms of *ens* and *non-ens* according to the principle of contradiction. In other words, one should not confuse the division of things (or *real metaphysics*) and the distinction of terms (as is usual in the scholastic meaning of metaphysics as a *scientia communis*): in the *Nouveaux essais*, Leibniz will sharply depart from a conception of metaphysics as "a science of being in general and its principles," which in fact teaches "nothing but words."[60]

CONCLUSION: *SCIENTIA GENERALIS* OR REFORMING METAPHYSICS AND THE *ENCYCLOPAEDIA*

With the projects of a *Scientia Generalis* and a demonstrative *Encyclopaedia*, Leibniz aimed at nothing less than contributing to the wisdom or happiness of humankind. This overwhelming task is often rephrased in terms of cultural progress: the *Encyclopaedia* should promote a new kind of education; it should bring about new intellectual dispositions and new cognitive methods by fostering the development of the sciences; it should naturally be as didactical as the first projects of the Herborn Encyclopaedists.[61] But it should not be a mere inventory of the sciences nor a "real dictionary." These are in fact only a material propedeutic for it. When Leibniz lists the seventeen sciences that should be part of the *Encyclopaedia*, he explicitly orders them according to the thread of discoveries made possible by transferring the principles of each one to the next.[62] The

---

[59] LH IV, 1, 9, f. 1–7; edited by N. Jolley: "An unpublished Leibniz MS on metaphysics," in *Studia Leibnitiana* 7/2 (1975), p. 179.

[60] *Nouveaux Essais* IV, 8, 9. Leibniz refers to the Aristotelian characterization of first philosophy (*Metaphysics*, Γ 1, 1003a21).

[61] See my "Leibniz und das Problem der Kultur," in W. Li (ed.), *Leibniz und die Aufklärungskultur* (Hannover: Wehrhahn, 2013), pp. 55–77. See also A IV iv 615 (*Mémoire pour des personnes éclairées et de bonne intention*, 1692).

[62] A VI iv 343 (*Consilium de Encyclopaedia nova conscribenda methodo inventoria*, 1679).

whole *Encyclopaedia* makes up the Elements of the *Scientia Generalis*, which, in turn, provides for "new openings" or new *specimina*. The project of a *Scientia Generalis* has not failed because each newly demonstrated truth counts as one of its achievements. Because of its twofold structure, the *Scientia Generalis* lies between Metaphysics (as the science of all intelligible and sensible principles) and the *Encyclopaedia*, or, rather, it is identified with both Metaphysics on one side and the *Encyclopaedia* on the other. We may find a hypothetical explanation for the gradual disappearance of the label "*Scientia Generalis*" in the fact that Leibniz's metaphysics departs sharply not only from its Aristotelian and Suarezian acceptions, but also from the scholastic *scientia communis* or *gemeinliche Wissenschaft* and even from a *philosophia prima* understood as *theology*. This is another example of Leibniz's all encompassing way of thinking: the reform of the *Encyclopaedia* needs a reform of Metaphysics understood as the new *Scientia Generalis*.

ACKNOWLEDGMENT

This study was possible thanks to the support of the Alexander von Humboldt-Foundation (Bonn) and the Research Foundation Flanders (FWO, Pegasus Marie Curie Program).

CHAPTER 10

ARS CHARACTERISTICA, LOGICAL CALCULUS, AND NATURAL LANGUAGES

MASSIMO MUGNAI

UNIVERSAL LANGUAGE AND "CHARACTERISTIC ART"

AMONG the many philosophical projects that Leibniz conceived during his lifetime, the development of a universal language was, at the same time, the most precocious and the most persistent. We find, indeed, a clear exposition of it in the *Dissertation on Combinatorial Art*, published in 1666, when Leibniz was only twenty years old. Here, Leibniz suggests that if one resolves, by means of definitions, any term into its composing parts and then each part again into parts, one reaches in the end the simplest parts (i.e., some indefinable terms). As Leibniz remarks, these last terms are "better understood not by means of a definition, but by means of an analogy" (A VI i 195). Once all the primitive terms have been found, "they should be placed in one class, and designated by certain symbols." Leibniz's proposal is to employ numbers (A VI i 195), but this is not essential to the general aim of the project. The central point is that if we designate each primitive term with some elementary symbol of a given alphabet, then we may represent each complex term as a combination of those symbols, thus giving rise to a kind of "pictorial language" that makes clear the intimate structure of any term.

At the time when Leibniz wrote the *Dissertation on Combinatorial Art*, he thought that the simple concepts were possible to attain. Because he implicitly assumed that the simple concepts and the rules for their composition were the same for everyone, it follows that, in order to have a universal language, once the analysis and synthesis of concepts has been brought to a successful end, all we need is to agree on the alphabet.

In writings composed after the *Dissertation on Combinatorial Art*, however, Leibniz raises doubts about the possibility that human beings could ever attain the primitive concepts, and he even shows some uncertainty about the question of whether they are finite or infinite in number. He suggests, nonetheless, that we could stop at some terms that are primitive *for us*, insofar as we are not able to pursue the analysis any further (A VI iv 964).

Thus, to sum up, Leibniz's project for a universal language, as it emerges from the *Dissertation on Combinatorial Art*, is centered around the realization of three phases: (1) development of an *analysis* of concepts, so as to arrive at a set of primitive concepts from which all the others originate; (2) attribution of appropriate signs or characters to the primitive concepts; and (3) construction of a mechanism that allows one to go from simple concepts to the complex ones by reconstructing all concepts through a *synthetic* process.

During the years of his stay in Paris (1672–76), Leibniz became increasingly aware that the universal language could be realized only if other projects, on which it would substantially depend, were first achieved. Thus, he conceived a more ambitious project that joins that for the creation of such a language: the project for the so-called *characteristica universalis* ("universal characteristic"). Leibniz uses the Latin word *character* ("mark," "mould") to designate any sign that can be employed to symbolize words and thoughts traced on any kind of material (paper, wood, stone, etc.). Consequently, he calls *ars characteristica* ("characteristic art") "the art of forming and arranging the characters in such a way that they agree with the thoughts, i.e. so that they have amongst them the same relation that subsists amongst thoughts" (A VI iv 916). Even though Leibniz sometimes seems to identify universal language and characteristic art, they must be carefully distinguished. The difference emerges if we consider the structure of what Leibniz calls *General Science*; that is, the science on which the construction of the *characteristic art* is based.

According to Leibniz, the two essential parts into which General Science is divided are *analysis* and *synthesis*. At the same time, *analysis* and *synthesis* play a fundamental role for the constitution of a universal language. Conceived as a tool for the construction of a universal language, *analysis* has a narrow scope: it is a procedure that, roughly speaking, decomposes a concept into its parts, whereas *synthesis* is the process that goes in the "opposite" direction, from the parts to the whole. Insofar as they belong to the General Science, however, analysis and synthesis assume a more technical meaning, inspired by mathematics:

> We have the synthesis when, moving on from the principles and examining in an orderly way the truths, we grasp some progressions and then we construct tables or even, sometimes, general formulae in which, later on, we may find the answers to what is required. Analysis, instead, traces back till to the principles, from which the individual problem that has been proposed originates.

> (A VI iv 544)

Analysis concerns heuristic methods employed to solve problems, whereas synthesis has to do with proofs; that is, with methods employed to deduce theorems from the axioms. In this respect, analysis corresponds to what the tradition called an *art of discovery* (*ars inveniendi*) and synthesis to what was called an *art of judgement* (*ars judicandi*).

The *Encyclopaedia* and the Academy of Sciences

Leibniz, however, recognized that, in order to apply analysis and synthesis to the entire body of human knowledge, the construction of an encyclopedia was needed. Thus, he added to the projects for the constitution of the characteristic art that for the creation of an encyclopedia containing the entire knowledge gathered by human beings in every scientific and practical field. Just a few years after the *Dissertation on Combinatorial Art* (between autumn 1669 and the beginning of 1671), Leibniz outlines the project of an encyclopedia divided into two parts: one intended to contain all the *theoretical* acquisitions and discoveries; the other intended for storing *empirical* observations and historical information. This structure reflects the distinction between sentences stating theorems and sentences concerning empirical facts that Leibniz presented in the *Dissertation* of 1666 and which foreshadows the later distinction between *truths of reason* and *truths of fact* (A VI i 199).

Later on, Leibniz elaborated several projects and encyclopedia sketches based on different criteria, ranging from the simple alphabetical ordering of all notions to a structuring of disciplinary fields associated with a deductive type of presentation within each field (from principles and general concepts down to particular statements). Leibniz also insists on the necessity of including information gathered from the world of manual labor and the activity of craftsmen (A VI iv 960).

In the case of General Science, as for the encyclopedia, Leibniz displays projects that have little hope of being realized. Usually, he limits himself to delineating in a hasty way the general features of analysis and synthesis without entering into much detail and to writing plans at different moments that sometimes are not consistent with one another. The same holds for the encyclopedia, of which he never attempted to give a concrete example, continuing instead to propose mere lists of topics to be further developed.

In time, as he realizes that a single person cannot carry out the entire plan for the construction of the *characteristic art*, Leibniz thought of assigning the task to a pool of scientists. These would belong to an Academy inspired by the French Academy of the Sciences and by the Royal Society. Hence, to the phases necessary to the realization of the *characteristic art*, Leibniz adds the constitution of an Academy, which will be one of his major concerns during the last part of his life (actually culminating in the foundation of the Academy of the Sciences in Berlin).[1]

A major problem, however, for the constitution of the characteristic art was Leibniz's basic indecision concerning the nature of the universal language: whether it would have a structure similar to that of natural spoken and written languages or rather that of a merely conceptual ideography, as foreshadowed in the *Dissertation on Combinatorial Art*. Leibniz, indeed, seems to hesitate between these two models and devotes himself to two different kinds of investigations: on the one hand, he attempts to isolate the formal structures underlying the grammar of natural languages; on the other, he develops some specimens of logical calculus aiming to capture the rules that give rise to correct inferences. Leibniz's studies on the grammar of natural languages have a prevailingly normative character and are conceived as preparatory for the constitution of the so-called *rational grammar*. Leibniz thinks of the rational grammar as an instrument that would help to express in a standard form every sentence of the universal language once it was constructed. Even in this case, however, as in that of the encyclopedia, all we are left with are manuscripts of various length containing treatises that are, for the most part, unfinished, along with personal notes and scattered remarks.

The Rational Grammar

In his investigations on grammar, Leibniz aims to make explicit the general features common to all natural languages. To find these features, he analyzes the fragment of Latin currently employed by scientists and philosophers of his time, occasionally taking into account other languages like German, French, and Italian as well. The choice of Latin is not by chance: Leibniz observes that mankind has produced a variety of languages and that, with the passing of time, almost all these languages have developed a certain capacity for understanding and transmitting some piece of science. Therefore, "it is enough to assume only one [language], because any people whatsoever may find and teach the sciences"; but since Latin is the language used by the vast majority of scientists, Leibniz argues that, if one wants to have an idea of what a grammar is, it is Latin that must be preferred to other languages (A VI iv 117).

Leibniz's first purpose is to identify the various categories of words constituting a natural language: proper and common names, adjectives, particles, verbs, and the like, according to the classification used by grammarians. Next, he attempts to carry out a drastic reduction of the number of these categories with the purpose of constructing a grammar without redundancies. Implicitly applying Ockham's razor, Leibniz writes that, in the rational grammar, everything should be reduced to what is absolutely

---

[1] On Leibniz's various attempts to found an academy of the sciences, it is still useful to consult L. Couturat, *La logique de Leibniz* (Paris: Presses Universitaires de France [Hildesheim: Olms], 1901), pp. 501–528.

necessary to express the sentences conceived by our understanding (cf. A VI iv 71). The following two passages, belonging to texts written respectively in September 1678 and autumn 1688, clearly show the austerity of Leibniz's idea of rational grammar:

> Thus, we may avoid the use of adverbs, of the most part of conjunctions, of all the interjections and even of all cases, and of times and persons as well. This is the analysis of grammar, in virtue of which we understand the force and the properties of everything that is general in a given language.
>
> (A VI iv 104)

> Everything in the discourse may be analysed into the substantive name *being* or *thing*, the copula i.e. the substantive verb *is*, the adjective names and the formal particles.
>
> (A VI iv 886)

Leibniz considers the entire class of terms that constitute the vocabulary of a natural language as divided into two subclasses: words and particles. "Words supply the matter and particles the form of the discourse" (A VI iv 882): words (i.e., names, verbs, and adverbs) refer to an infinite variety of things and are as numerous as our notions or concepts; particles, on the other hand (i.e., prepositions, conjunctions, pronouns, and auxiliary verbs), determine the *logical form* of the discourse. Leibniz traces back all suffixes and prefixes to the particles, along with all kinds of inflections, as well as terms that modify the words. In accordance with the scholastic (and Aristotelian) tradition, he conceives the verb as composed of the corresponding participle and an occurrence of the copula. As such, he considers the Latin sentence *Petrus scribit* to be grammatically equivalent to *Petrus est scribens* (A VI iv 70). Concerning the copula, he says that it is part of the predicate, and, moving away from the scholastic (and ancient) tradition, he states that all sentences imply a reference to time: "The copula always includes some time as every proposition or sentence do, and this is the reason why grammarians say that words are connoting time." Otherwise, the same sentence could be true *and* false at different times (A VI iv 882).

In Latin, words are connected to other words by means of *cases*. Thus, taking one of Leibniz's favorite examples, the Latin word *ensis* ("sword") may be connected with the proper name *Evander* by means of the genitive case of the proper name itself, giving rise to the expression: *ensis Evandri* ("Evander's sword") (A VI iv 884). Other languages, such as, for instance, French and Italian, use particles to express cases (in French, a way of expressing the genitive is through the particle *de*). Leibniz concludes that particles and cases may be considered interchangeable in the rational grammar and that, therefore, "in the philosophical language, once we have prepositions, we do not need cases, and if we have cases we may avoid prepositions" (A VI iv 883–84). Even the "multitude of declensions and conjugations is superfluous":

> The multitude of declensions and conjugations is superfluous. It is superfluous to have inflexions in adjectives, for it is enough to have them in the substantive to which

the adjective is attached. In the same way, number is unnecessary in the verb, for this is sufficiently understood from the noun to which it is attached.

(G. W. Leibniz, *Logical Papers*, translated by G. H. R. PARKINSON (Oxford: Clarendon Press, 1966). Hereafter LP. 16; A VI iv 907)

At the same time, Leibniz conceives the possibility of extending the tense to other parts of the discourse in addition to the verbs: "Not only verbs, but also nouns can have tense and place. . . . Indeed, adverbs also can have a tense" (A VI iv 883–84).

The universal language should also have particles possessing different degrees of generality. There could be, for instance, particles denoting that some term maintains a specific relation with some other term or particles simultaneously denoting two different relations, as in the case of the compound particle "with-in" [*cum*-in] (A VI iv 742), and there could also be other particles employed as types to represent the behavior of several particular relations at once.

In view of constructing the universal language, Leibniz proposes a distinction between terms that are "basic" and expressions that play an auxiliary role (*servilia*). If we say, for example, "John is more learned than someone who is Paul," then "John," "Paul," and "learned" are basic terms whereas "more . . . than someone who" is an auxiliary expression (A VI iv 643). To these latter belong all those terms that in the scholastic tradition were called "syncategorematic," such as, for instance, conjunctions, prepositions, adverbs, and the like, which all require other expressions to form a meaningful unit. In writings on rational grammar, Leibniz often employs auxiliary expressions like "insofar as" [*quatenus*] "and just for that" [*et eo ipso*]—known by scholastic thinkers as "reduplicative terms"—to offer an analysis of relational sentences like "Paris loves Helen" (A VI iv 114–15), "David is the father of Solomon" (A VI vi 479), "Titius is killed by Caius" (A VI iv 651), "Titius is more learned than Caius" (A VI iv 658), and "Caesar is similar to Alexander" (A VI iv 741). In a text entitled *Grammatical Thoughts*, probably written in the autumn 1678, for instance, Leibniz proposes the following analysis of the sentence "Paris loves Helen":

a) "Paris is a lover, and by that very fact [*et eo ipso*] Helen is a loved one" (A VI iv 114–15)

Analogously, in the case of "Caius is killed by Titus":

b) "Insofar as Titius is murdering, therefore Caius is murdered" (A VI iv 651)

In general, given a sentence stating that a certain relation, say "R," holds between two subjects "a" and "b," giving rise to a sentence of the form "aRb," Leibniz reduces it to another sentence in which an auxiliary expression ("insofar as," "by that very fact," etc.) connects two sentences of the form, respectively, "a is P" and "b is Q," with "P" and "Q" each indicating one of a pair of correlated terms, such as *lover-beloved, murdering-murdered,* and so forth. The two sentences a) and b), however, are *not logically equivalent* to the sentences that they are supposed to analyze: a), for example, could be true without "Paris loves Helen" being true (if, for instance, there is a situation according to which Paris loves Venus and Helen is beloved by Agamemnon).[2] Yet, what Leibniz attempts to convey with these analyses is the idea that a relation is not a property really inhering in several subjects, but rather a result that obtains as a consequence of the fact that two or more subjects in the world have some internal properties.

Leibniz is well aware that there are different types of relations and that the above-mentioned analyses apply mainly to *asymmetrical* relations: he therefore proposes slightly different treatments for other kinds of relations. Given, for instance, a sentence of the general form "*a* is similar to *b*," with "*a*" and "*b*" being names for individuals, he suggests that it should be analyzed as "*a* is *P*" and "*b* is *P*," with "*P*" designating a property common to both *a* and *b*. In this case, too, the truth of "*a* is *P*" and "*b* is *P*" is a necessary condition for the truth of "*a* is similar to *b*," but this latter assertion is not logically equivalent to the conjunction of the first two sentences.

In the introductory pages of the *General Inquiries about the Analysis of Concepts and of Truths* (1686), however, Leibniz suggests that every term like "lover," "father," "similar," and the like that he considers "incomplete," should enter the logical calculus only if "completed." Given the sentence "Caesar is similar to Alexander," he suggests transforming it into "Caesar is similar to *A*, which is Alexander":

> Some general signs of things or terms will therefore be needed; so if we wish always to use in our symbolism integral terms alone, we must say, not "Caesar is similar to Alexander," but "Caesar is similar to the *A*, which is Alexander," or "similar to the thing which is Alexander." So our term will be, not "similar," but "similar to the *A*."
>
> (LP 48; A VI iv 741)

At any rate, it is important to emphasize that Leibniz's inquiries on rational grammar are, in large part, provisional. From these, we may have only a glimpse of the main features that Leibniz intended to give to the universal language. The universal language had to be composed of *concrete categorematic terms* (nouns and adjectives) like "man," "dog," "table," "soul," "white," and so forth; of *syncategorematic* terms, like "not," "if . . . then . . .," "and," "or," "insofar as," "because," and the like; and of the copula and of the words "thing" [*res*] or "being" [*ens*]. Syncategorematic terms could be simple or composite, thus giving rise to auxiliary expressions; these latter expressions, in turn, should be structured in such a way as to guarantee the full transparency of the relationships subsisting between the terms or sentences that they connect. Thus, for example, given a sentence like "Titius is more learned than Caius," Leibniz wishes that it would assume a form from which everyone could infer the converse: "Caius is less learned than Titius" (A VI iv 658).

---

[2] Leibniz seems to interpret the connectives "and by this very fact" (*et eo ipso*) and "insofar as" (*quatenus*) as a kind of "very strong" conditionals, but he does not elaborate this point.

LOGIC AND MATHEMATICS: INTENSION
AND EXTENSION

In antiquity and during the Middle Ages, logic and mathematics developed as two quite independent disciplines, with very weak reciprocal interaction. In late antiquity, a logical tradition established itself based on Aristotelian logic, enriched with some Stoic materials, that was considered by philosophers to dictate the standard of mathematical proofs. Mathematicians, however, when discussing the proof of a theorem, in general avoided any *explicit* appeal to logical rules or principles belonging to this logical tradition.

To find an attempt to connect logic and mathematics in Western culture, we have to wait until the first half of the sixteenth century, when two different processes took place: on the one hand, some logicians raised the problem of whether traditional logic was suitable for expressing mathematical proofs; on the other hand, the idea began to circulate that the activity of reasoning was identical with that of performing a calculation. That the activity of reasoning is the same as that of computing was firmly stated by Thomas Hobbes, and it is difficult to underestimate the novelty of this claim if we consider that, for centuries, *thinking* and *computing* were sharply distinguished.

In the *Dissertation on Combinatorial Art*, Leibniz sympathetically quotes Hobbes's claim and foreshadows the essential features of a logical calculus in which the copula plays the twofold role played in algebra by the two operations usually represented by the signs "+" and "-":

> That most profound searcher-out of the principles of all things, Thomas Hobbes, has rightly contended that every work of the human mind consists in computation, but on this understanding, that it is effected either by *adding up* a sum or *subtracting* a difference. (*The Elements of Philosophy*, Part 1, *On Body*, Chapter 1, Article 2) Accordingly, just as there are two primitive signs used by Algebraists and Analysts, + and −, so there are, as it were, two copulae, *is* and *is not*: with the former the mind puts things together, with the latter it takes them apart. In this sense, *is* is not strictly a copula, but part of a predicate, and the copulae are two: one that is named *not*, and another that is unnamed, but included in the *is* whenever *not* is not added to it. This is how *is* has come to stand for a copula. I could use for this purpose the word *really*. For example, Man is *really* an animal. Man is *not* a stone.
>
> (LP 3–4; A VI i 194)

As we have seen, Leibniz considers every elementary sentence (i.e., a sentence that cannot be analyzed into further sentences) as having the general form: "subject + copula

+ predicate." As for the copula, Leibniz thinks that it expresses a relation of *inherence* that may be read in two different ways. Given, for example, the sentence "Every man is mortal," the copula says that:

(1) Every individual falling under the concept of *man* belongs to the collection (aggregate, set, or class) of the individuals falling under the concept *being mortal*; and

(2) The concept associated with the word "man" has among its component parts the concept associated with the word "animal."

The two different approaches are represented as follows in the *New Essays*:

> This manner of statement deserves respect; for indeed the predicate is in the subject, or rather the idea of the predicate in included in the idea of the subject. . . . The common manner of statement concerns individuals, whereas Aristotle's refers rather to ideas or universals. For when I say *Every man is an animal* I mean that all the men are included amongst all the animals; but at the same time I mean that the idea of animal is included in the idea of man. "Animal" comprises more individuals than "man" does, but "man" comprises more ideas or more attributes: one has more instances, the other more degrees of reality; one has the greater extension, the other the greater intension.
>
> (NE 486)[3]

Leibniz firmly claims that, of the two points of view—that according to the extension and that according to the intension—he prefers the second. Very early, indeed, in 1679, he writes:

> Two terms which contain each other but do not coincide are commonly called "genus" and "species." These, in so far as they compose concepts or terms (which is how I regard them here) differ as part and whole, in such a way that the concept of the genus is a part and that of the species is a whole, since it is composed of genus and differentia. For example, the concept of gold and the concept of metal differ as part and whole; for in the concept of gold there is contained the concept of metal and something else—e.g. the concept of the heaviest amongst metals. Consequently, the concept of gold is greater than the concept of metal.
>
> . . . The Scholastics speak differently; for they consider, not concepts, but instances which are brought under universal concepts. So they say that metal is wider than gold, since it contains more species than gold, and if we wish to enumerate the individuals made of gold on the one hand and those made of metal on the other, the latter will be more than the former, which will therefore be contained in the latter as a part in the whole. By the use of this observation, and with suitable symbols, we

---

[3] Arnauld and Nicole, in their *Logic* (A. Arnauld and P. Nicole, *La Logique ou l'Art de penser*, edited by P. Clair and F. Girbal [Paris: Vrin, 1981], p. 59) made an analogous distinction employing the French word *comprehension* to denote what Leibniz here calls *intension*.

could prove all the rules of logic by a calculus somewhat different from the present one—that is, simply by a kind of inversion of it. However, I have preferred to consider universal concepts, i.e. ideas, and their combinations, as they do not depend on the existence of individuals.

(LP 20; A VI iv 199–200)

Here, the adoption of the *intensional* point of view is justified by appealing to the fact that it does not "depend on the existence of the individuals": Leibniz aims to construct a logical calculus of "pure concepts," in which logical consistency is the sole criterion for admissibility. Another important claim contained in this text is that by operating a "kind of inversion," a logical calculus based on the extensions of concepts can be made logically equivalent to a calculus based on intensions.[4] Leibniz, however, does not explain (either here or elsewhere) how the "inversion" ought to be understood properly: he limits himself to assuming that the two approaches are in some sense reciprocal to one another (A VI iv 839; LP 136).

The Logical Calculus: General Inquiries on the Analysis of Concepts and of Truths

Leibniz's essays on logical calculus belong to three main periods: 1679–80, 1686, and 1687–90. In the first period, he delineates the *elements* of the calculus (*Elementa calculi*) and proposes to employ numbers to test the validity of logical arguments. He suggests that we may choose prime numbers to designate primitive concepts, thus associating each complex concept with the number obtained by multiplying the numbers of its parts. In an essay of this period, Leibniz considers each term as composed of two parts: one positive and the other negative, and he characterizes the first with a positive and the second with a negative integer. He then proceeds to give the rules that determine whether a given sentence is true under such a numerical interpretation. If a positive part of the subject and a negative part of the predicate of the sentence have a common divisor, this means that the sentence implies a contradiction. For instance, given a sentence of the general form "*S* is *P*," suppose that the subject *S* is composed of the pair of

---

[4] On the relationship between extensional and intensional point of views in Leibniz's logic, in addition to the classical L. Couturat, *La logique*, pp. 335–385, cf. R. Kauppi, *Über die Leibnizschen Logik, in Acta Philosophica Fennica 12* (Helsinki: Societas Philosophica, 1960), pp. 243–256; N. Rescher, "Leibniz's interpretation of his logical calculi," in *The Journal of Symbolic Logic 19* (1954), pp. 1–13; M. Dummett, "Review of Rescher 'Leibniz's interpretation,'" in *Journal of Symbolic Logic 21* (1956), pp. 197–199; C. Swoyer, "Leibniz on intension and extension," in *Nous 29/1* (1995), pp. 96–114; and W. Lenzen, "Zur extensionalen und 'intensionalen' Interpretation der Leibnizschen Logik," in *Studia Leibnitiana 15* (1983), pp. 129–148.

characteristic numbers $< +10, -3>$ and the predicate P of the couple $< +14, -5>$. In this case, as Leibniz remarks, it is evident

> that the terms $+10$ (i.e. *two times* 5) and -5 are incompatible: they mean, indeed, things that are contradictory. At the same time, it is immediately clear from their characteristic numbers, that the proposition to which these very numbers belong is false according to the terms [*in terminis*] and that its contradictory is true on the basis of the same terms [*ex terminis*].
>
> (A VI iv 226)

Leibniz thinks of generalizing this method to all kinds of sentences and logical arguments: "making recourse to numbers, we may prove and examine all the consequences, all figures, all syllogistic moods that have been accepted till now, together with several other, more complex, arguments which are usually employed in everyday life" (A VI iv 234–35). In an essay belonging to the same period (1679), Leibniz elaborates a general rule for testing the validity of a syllogistic argument in virtue of its logical form (the test, however, may be easily generalized to any kind of argument):

> If we want to know whether some figure is valid in virtue of its form [*vi formae*], we have to see whether the contradictory of the conclusion is compatible with the premises, i.e. whether we may find numbers that can satisfy [*satisfacientes*] at the same time the premises and the contradictory of the conclusion. If we cannot find such numbers, the argument will conclude in virtue of its form.
>
> (A VI iv 256)

A remarkable achievement of the essays of the first period is the attempt to express the sentences of the logical calculus as algebraic equations. Given a sentence like "Every man is mortal," Leibniz proposes first to drop the quantifier "Every," thus reducing it to "man is a mortal." Leibniz's assumption is that the general term "man" must be interpreted as referring to *every* man. Then he proposes to substitute "man" and "mortal" each with a different letter of the Latin alphabet, thus giving rise to a formula similar to the following (with "m" for "man" and "n" for "mortal"): "a) m is n."

To give a) the form of an algebraic equation, however, Leibniz needs to tackle the problem of expressing the copula by means of the identity relation. Indeed, the copula in a sentence does not usually mean that the predicate is identical with the subject: "Every man is a mortal," for instance, does not mean that man is identical with mortal. Leibniz solves this problem by taking recourse to "indefinite letters." That is, he transforms a) into "b) $m = xn$," where the letter x designates a concept that, when juxtaposed to the concept designated by n produces a further specification of this latter. Thus, continuing with this example, if "m is n" is a symbolic transcription of "(Every) man is a mortal," then b) means that the set of all men is equal to the set of all rational animals *and*, conversely, that the concept "man" is identical to that of "rational animal." Under this interpretation, b) offers to Leibniz a very simple way of expressing those categorical sentences that are universal and affirmative. Incidentally, b) is the same formula that George Boole later adopted in his 1847 *The Mathematical Analysis of Logic* to express universal affirmative propositions.[5] Leibniz, however, finds some difficulties when attempting to transform the three remaining categorical sentences: the two particulars (affirmative and negative) and the negative universal. The difficulties are mainly determined by the intensional approach, which he favors with respect to the extensional one.

The most important essays of the second period are the *General Inquiries on the Analysis of Concepts and of Truths* (A VI iv 739–88), written in 1686, the same year of the beginning of the correspondence with Arnauld, and the composition of the *Discourse on Metaphysics*. It is the longest essay on logic ever written by Leibniz and was clearly devised for publication, even though it remained unpublished until 1903.[6]

In the *General Inquiries*, as in the other essays on logic, Leibniz uses the Latin expression corresponding to the English word "term" in a quite loose way, sometimes referring to the concept associated with a given word, sometimes referring to the linguistic item itself, and sometimes, finally, meaning the complex made of a word *and* a concept. In the *General Inquiries*, he employs the first letters (capital or small) of the Latin alphabet to denote concepts (terms) *and* propositions, and he uses the last letters (x, y, z) as variables. Concerning the use of variables, he recommends that no letter that has been used before should be employed at a determinate stage of a proof, so as to avoid confusion (cf. A VI iv 752; LP 56): "so that confusion does not arise").

The twofold meaning that Leibniz attributes to the variables (as terms and propositions) is determined by the aim of unifying the entire logic on the basis of a calculus of terms (classes). Leibniz considers this idea to be "a discovery of the utmost importance." If all conditional sentences could be reduced to categorical ones, given that the truth (or falsity) of a categorical sentence is determined by the relation of inclusion (intensional or extensional) between the concept of the subject and that of the predicate, then it would be possible to ground the entire logic of propositions on a general theory of containment between terms. To realize this project, Leibniz first needed a method to systematically transform each conditional proposition into a categorical one. To this purpose, he worked out a new kind of abstract terms that he called *logical abstracts* (*abstracta logica*), which he contrasted with the *real abstracts* of the Scholastic

---

[5] Cf. G. Boole, *The Mathematical Analysis of Logic* ([Cambridge: Macmillan 1847]/ New York: Philosophical Library, 1948), pp. 20–21.

[6] The essay was published for the first time in C 356–99. In 1982, Franz Schupp prepared a new, more reliable edition of it, along with a German translation and an extensive commentary to the text (G. W. Leibniz, *Generales Inquisitiones de Analysi Notionum and Veritatum. Allgemeine Untersuchungen über die Analyse der Begriffe und Wahrheiten* [Hamburg: Meiner Verlag, 1982]). Another useful commentary to this work with French translation and the original Latin text (based mainly on the Couturat edition but taking account of many improvements from the Schupp edition) is offered by G. W. Leibniz, *Recherches générales sur l'analyse des notions et des vérités. 24 thèses métaphysiques et autres textes logiques et métaphysiques*. Introduction and notes by J. -B. Rauzy (Paris: Presses Universitaires de France, 1998), pp. 200–320. Another useful English translation, in addition to that included in LP 47–87, is G. W. Leibniz, *General Investigations Concerning the Analysis of Concepts and Truths. A Translation and an Evaluation* by W. H. O'Briant (Athens: University of Georgia Press, 1968).

tradition. Whereas the *real abstracts* were considered by the Scholastics as something really composing the subjects, Leibniz conceived the *logical abstracts* as "posterior" to the subjects (A VI iv 992). A logical abstract term is the result of contracting an elementary proposition like "A is B" to the single term "A's being B." Because Leibniz considers the latter equivalent to "the B-ness of A," this explains the name of "abstract" that he attributes to these kinds of terms.[7] Given a conditional proposition of the general form "If A is B, then C is D," Leibniz reduces in turn its antecedent and consequent to a single term and then considers the two terms so obtained as, respectively, subject and predicate of a new categorical proposition. Thus, the proposition "If A is B, then C is D" first gives rise to two distinct terms: "A's being B" and "C's being D"; then, from these two terms, putting "A's being B" as subject and "C's being D" as predicate, we may have the single categorical proposition "A's being B is C's being D." In Leibniz's own words:

> If the proposition "A is B" is treated as a term, as we have explained that it can, there arises an abstract term, namely "A's being B," and if from the proposition "A is B" the proposition "C is D" follows, then from this there is made a new proposition of the kind: "A's being B is, or contains, C's being D"; i.e. "The B-ness of A contains the D-ness of C," i.e. "The B-ness of A is the D-ness of C."
>
> (LP 78; A VI iv 777)

As a consequence of the transformation suggested by Leibniz, class inclusion becomes the general criterion for the truth of any proposition, and thus the logic of propositions is based in the last instance on the logic of terms (of classes). To find a systematic application of this idea, we have to wait almost two centuries, until the second half of the nineteenth century, when George Boole, Sanders C. Peirce, and Ernst Schroeder promoted that branch of the newborn mathematical logic known as the "algebra of logic."[8]

Because the letters of logical calculus may be interpreted as terms *and* propositions, Leibniz is careful to distinguish two separate meanings of the equality symbol "=." When terms are involved, the equality symbol should be interpreted as the relation of identity; when propositions are involved, it means *logical equivalence*:

> "A coincides with B" if the one can be substituted in place of the other without loss of truth, or if, on analysing each of the two by substitution of their values (i.e. of their definitions) in place of the terms, the same terms appear on both sides: the same, I mean, formally—for example, if L, M and N appear on both sides. . . .
>
> I say that propositions "coincide" if one can be substituted for the other without loss of truth, or, if they imply each other reciprocally.
>
> (LP 53–54; A VI iv 746–48)

---

[7] Cf. LP 78 (A VI iv 777): "In general, if it is said that something is B, then this 'something's being B' is simply 'B-ness.' Thus, 'something being animal' is simply 'animality', whereas 'man's being an animal' is 'the animality of man.'"

[8] Cf. E. Schroeder, *Vorlesungen über die Algebra der Logik* (Leipzig: Teubner 1891), vol. *II*, pp. 1–9.

As we see, Leibniz defines "coincidence" (for terms and for propositions as well) by means of the principle of "substitutivity *salva veritate*." The principle is assumed here (and in other texts) as one of the basic tools of the logical calculus and is presented in two slightly different versions in a short remark probably written in the same year as the *General Inquiries* were composed (A VI iv 829). In this remark, Leibniz observes that, when formulating the principle, we have to distinguish *uniform substitution* (i.e., in every occurrence of a term) from a substitution limited to only some occurrences. As Leibniz explains, given the proposition:

(1) "A may be substituted where we want [*ubivis*] at the place of B" it is possible to infer from it:

(2) "B may be substituted where we want [*ubivis*] at the place of A" taking recourse to the axiom

(3) "B may be substituted where we want [*ubivis*] at the place of B."

The inference, instead, fails in the case (1) is formulated as:

(4) "A may be substituted everywhere [*ubique*] at the place of B."[9]

Moreover, as the *General Inquiries* show, Leibniz is well aware that there are contexts in which the principle of substitutivity does not work. At paragraph 19 of the *General Inquiries*, indeed, after having remarked that "coincidentals can be substituted for one another," Leibniz points out:

> Except in the case of propositions which you could call formal, where one of the coincidentals is assumed formally in such a way that it is distinguished from the others; but these are reflexive, and do not so much speak about a thing, as about our way of conceiving it—where there is a distinction between these.
>
> (LP 56; A VI iv 752)

Another interesting aspect of the *General Inquiries* is the fact that it contains Leibniz's attempts to use a symbolism made up of a combination of straight lines (which play the role of parentheses) and numbers, aiming to codify all the information needed to make the syntactic structure of any given proposition explicit. Leibniz displays the structure of a proposition in the form of a tree, with terms at the root and the entire proposition at the top. Moving from the root to the top, one may see how the proposition is progressively built up and how the single parts contribute to the constitution of the whole.

Three further issues, however, in the *General Inquiries* are worth mentioning: the attempt to distinguish *necessary* from *contingent* propositions, the use of what Leibniz calls *indefinite letters* (the last letters of the Latin alphabet: x, y, z, employed as variables)

---

[9] Cf. R. Kauppi, *Über die Leibnizsche Logik*, pp. 72–73.

to express the quantity of the terms (classes) involved in the logical calculus, and the use of *diagrams* as a general method for testing the validity of syllogistic inferences.

Having adopted the predicate in the subject principle as fundamental criterion for the truth of a proposition, Leibniz automatically assumes that, if true, both kinds of propositions—necessary and contingent—must be analytically true. And this, in its turn, means that a proposition may be analytically true without being necessarily true. Hence, the problem arises as to how to justify the fact that a proposition can be at the same time both contingent and analytically true. Now, it is precisely in the *General Inquiries* that Leibniz outlines for the first time his solution to this problem, basing it on an analogy with the calculus. In letters and writings not meant for publication, which were written *after* 1686, Leibniz points to this solution as his final answer to the problem of contingency. In the body of the *Theodicy*, however, where it would have found its most appropriate place, there is no mention of it.[10] This is probably due to the fact that, as Leibniz himself recognizes, to understand this solution properly one needs to have "some acquaintance with mathematics" (A VI iv 1650; AG 28). The solution, indeed, rests on the two concepts of *proof* and *infinity*. Leibniz thinks that we may have a *proof* of the truth of a proposition, once it has been reduced to the appropriate subject-predicate form, if we succeed in showing *in a finite number of steps* that the concept of the predicate is included in that of the subject. If the process does not end, the proposition is not proved, even though it is true. If proved, a proposition is *necessarily true*, whereas, if it is true and the inherence of the predicate in the subject cannot be proved, it is *contingently true*. Thus, "All men are rational" is necessary because the property of being rational can be derived *in a finite number of steps* from the concept of man. "Caesar crossed the Rubicon," instead, is contingent because, even though the predicate corresponding to "having crossed the Rubicon" does inhere in the complete concept of "Caesar," it is impossible to prove this very fact in a finite number of steps.[11]

As we have seen, in the logical writings composed before the *General Inquiries*, Leibniz employs what he calls *indefinite letters* to express in the form of algebraic equivalences the four categorical sentences of the Aristotelian-scholastic tradition. Given a sentence like "All men are animals," he transforms it into an equation of the form: "$m = xa$," where "m" means "man," "n" animal, and "x" denotes a concept that, juxtaposed to the concept of animal, increases the *intension* of this latter concept, thus further decreasing its

---

[10] A hint at it appears, however, in one of the papers that constitute the appendix to *Theodicy*, cf. GP VI 414.

[11] Some years later, in a short essay on freedom, Leibniz claims: "But in contingent truths, even though the predicate is in the subject, this can never be demonstrated, nor can a proposition ever be reduced [*revocari*] to an equality or to an identity, but the resolution proceeds to infinity, God alone seeing, not the end of the resolution, of course, which does not exist, but the connection of the terms or the containment of the predicate in the subject, since he sees whatever is in the series" (AG 96; A VI iv 1656). On this point, cf. F. Mondadori, "Reference, essentialism, and modality in Leibniz's metaphysics," in *Studia Leibnitiana* 5 (1973), pp. 73–101; "On some disputed questions in Leibniz's metaphysics," in *Studia Leibnitiana* 25 (1993), 153–173; B. Mates, *The Philosophy of Leibniz. Metaphysics and Language* (Oxford: Oxford University Press, 1986), pp. 104–121.

extension.[12]It is Leibniz himself who remarks in the *General Inquiries* that the letter "*x*" in this case plays the role of the particular quantifier "some."[13] In the *General Inquiries*, Leibniz extends the use of the "indefinite letters," clearly devising the possibility of employing them even as a kind of *universal* quantifier.[14]

Leibniz's use of diagrams is strictly connected with the purpose, conceived as an integral part of the characteristic art, of providing the human mind with what he calls "an *Ariadne's thread*," a concrete, tangible device for checking the validity of the inferences. Leibniz, indeed, assimilates the collection of points that belong to a segment or to the area of a circle to the collection of individuals that fall under a concept and thus represents the relationships among concepts as relationships among segments or circles in the plane. In addition to segments, straight lines, and circles, he also employs ellipses to represents terms and concepts, and he attempts to represent both approaches with the same diagrams: the intensional and the extensional one. Later, some years after the composition of the *General Inquiries*, Leibniz wrote a long essay entirely devoted to exploring the use of diagrams to test the validity of the traditional syllogistic figures.[15]

REAL ADDITION AND "MEREOLOGY"

After the *General Inquiries*, Leibniz composed a series of essays based on what he calls "real addition," in which the logical operation of negation is absent and the inverse operation of subtraction is systematically employed. Leibniz uses the symbol "$\oplus$" to denote the "real addition" that he sharply distinguishes from the ordinary addition of arithmetic. Whereas real addition is *idempotent*, ordinary addition is not. If we use the

[12] Cf. C 235: "The method based on notions is the contrary of that based on individuals, i.e. if all men are part of all animals, reciprocally the notion of being an animal will be in the notion of being a man. And if there are several animals besides men, we have to add something to the idea of being an animal to have the idea of man. In other words: increasing the conditions, we diminish the number."

[13] As the following remark clearly shows, Leibniz was well aware that the letter "*x*" in b) plays a role analogous to that of a quantifier: "Thus, we have to observe that, as in every equation or proposition which may be converted *simpliciter*, a letter alone, with no other addition, means a term taken universally ('*n*' for instance means 'every snow'), thus a letter multiplied by an unknown as for instance *s* in '*sm*' will mean a term with a particularity sign added, as in '*some meteorological phenomenon*'" (A VI iv 209). On Leibniz's use of indefinite letters to express quantification, cf. H. Burkhardt, *Logik und Semiotik in der Philosophie von Leibniz* (München: Philosophia Verlag, 1980), pp. 122–123, and, for an extensive treatment of this issue, W. Lenzen, "'Unbestimmte Begriffe' bei Leibniz," in *Studia Leibnitiana* *16* (1984), pp. 1–26.

[14] A VI iv 765 (LP 67: "It must be seen whether it is possible to do without indefinite terms [*infinitis*]. Certainly, not-A seems to be the same as that which is not A, i.e. the subject of a negative proposition whose predicate is A, or everything which is not A"). Leibniz uses the indefinite letter "Y" with a line superscript to mean "anything" ("*quilibet*").

[15] The essay was given its title by Couturat: *De formae logicae comprobatione per linearum ductus* [*On the proof of logical form by the drawing of lines*], according to the first sentence of the manuscript (C 292–321).

symbol "⊕" to denote "real" addition and "A" to denote a letter of the calculus, we have (a) $A \oplus A = A$. With ordinary addition, instead, we have the obvious: (b) $A + A = 2A$. In these essays, Leibniz proposes a very general account of the logical calculus:

> As general algebra [*speciosa generalis*] is merely the representation and treatment of combinations by signs, and as various laws of combination can be discovered, the result of this is that various methods of computation arise. Here, however, no account is taken of the variation which consists in a change of order alone, and AB is the same for us as BA. Next, no account is taken here of repetition; i.e. AA is the same for us as A. Consequently, whenever these laws are observed, the present calculus can be applied.
>
> (LP 142; A VI iv 834)

Here, Leibniz characterizes "real addition" through the properties of *idempotence* and *commutativity* and is clearly thinking of an uninterpreted calculus that is susceptible to being applied to any domain of things in which the sum operation may be performed and these two properties hold. This explains, for example, why he does not speak at all of "terms" or "propositions" in the essays based on "real addition": the letters employed in these essays stand, indeed, for any such "things" whatsoever that obey the rules of the calculus.[16] The generality of the calculus is made even clearer in a text written in 1693–94, from which the following passage has been extracted:

> The art of combinations . . . for me . . . signifies purely the science of forms or formulas, or even of variations in general. In a word, it is the universal specious arithmetic or characteristic. As such it deals with the identical and the diverse, the similar and the dissimilar, the absolute and the relative, just as ordinary mathematics deals with the one and the many, the large and the small, the whole and the part. One can even say that calculation with letters, or more precisely algebra, is in a certain sense subordinate to it, because one employs many signs which at the beginning of the calculus can be exchanged and mutually substituted without doing any arm to the reasoning. For this the letters of the alphabet are highly suitable. And when these letters or signs signify magnitudes or numbers in general, the result is algebra. . . . In this way, the greatest benefits of algebra are simply examples of the art of characters, whose usage is by no means limited to numbers and magnitudes. Then, if these letters were to signify points (as this is effectively practised by geometricians) one would be able thereby to create a certain *calculus* or sort of operation which would be quite different from algebra and which would not cease to have the same advantages as it has. . . . When these letters signify terms or concepts, as in Aristotle, this gives us that part of logic which deals with figures and modes. . . . Finally, when the letters or other characters signify true letters of the alphabet, or of the language, then the art of combinations together with consideration of the languages gives us cryptography.[17]

---

[16] Leibniz, indeed, uses the Latin neuter plural to designate the things that the letters are referring to.

[17] G. W. Leibniz, "On the Calculability of the Number of all Possible Truths," translated and edited by Philip Beeley, in *The Leibniz Review 13* (2003), pp. 99–100.

In the essays on "real addition," Leibniz sketches a kind of mereology based on the two relations of *part-whole* and *contained-container*. To the part-whole relation, Leibniz imposes the condition that the part must be homogeneous with the whole.[18] Therefore, the relation between contained and container is more general than that of part-whole, given that the former may hold even between things that are not homogeneous. One of Leibniz's favorite examples of something that inheres in something else, without being homogeneous to it (and thus not being part of it), is that of the point inhering in the line. In the more general calculus based on the relation of containment, the "real addition" is nonrestricted:

> *Postulate 2.* Any plurality of things, such as A and B, can be taken together to compose one thing, A ⊕ B, i.e. L.

(LP 132; A VI iv 834)

> [O]ur general construction depends upon postulate 2, in which is contained the proposition that any thing can be compounded with any thing. Thus God, soul, body, point and heat compose an aggregate of these five things.

(LP 139; A VI iv 842)

Leibniz's logical calculi, as they are developed in the *General Inquiries* and in the essays written in the years after 1686, are all based on few logical ingredients: negation, inclusion, and intensional juxtaposition. The operation of juxtaposition employed in the *General Inquiries* and the *real addition* of the essays on plus-minus calculus amount to the same operation performed by joining together two or more concepts: from the extensional point of view, it corresponds to the logical product (to set-theoretic intersection).[19] Oddly enough, disjunction is conspicuously absent from Leibniz's logical calculus; this is particularly puzzling in view of the following facts: (1) Leibniz was well-acquainted with the so-called De Morgan laws;[20] (2) he proposed employing the symbol "v" for logical disjunction, showing that he wanted to represent disjunction in

---

[18] In a text collecting several definitions, for instance, he writes: "In a more strict sense, the whole is taken as being homogeneous with the parts" (C 476). On the differences between "real addition" and the arithmetical operation of sum in Leibniz, cf. W. Lenzen, "Arithmetical vs 'real' addition—A case study of the relation between logic, mathematics and metaphysics in Leibniz," in *Leibnizian Inquiries—A Group of Essays*, edited by N. Rescher. Proceedings of the 5th Annual Conference in Philosophy of Science (Lanham, Md.: University of America Press, 1989), pp. 149–157.

[19] For instance, putting together the two concepts corresponding to "man" and "wise," we obtain the concept corresponding to "wise man"; that is, a concept with more conceptual content but less *extension* than that of each of its component parts. Cf. J. Venn, *Symbolic Logic*, 2nd edn. (London: MacMillan, 1894), p. 461: "To indicate a class by adding attributes together, is to confine ourselves to such a group of objects as possess both sets of characteristics."

[20] The name of the logician and mathematician Augustus De Morgan (1806–71) usually is employed to indicate two logical rules according to which from the negation of the conjunction of two or more sentences is validly inferred the disjunction of the same sentences negated (from "not: *p* and *q*" one may infer "not *p* or not *q*") and vice versa: from "not: *p* or *q*" is inferred "not *p* and not *q*." These rules were well

the calculus;[21] and (3) he explicitly recognized *idempotence* as a characteristic property of (nonexclusive) disjunction. Here is some evidence of facts (2) and (3):

> As "+" is a conjunctive sign, i.e. a sign of juxtaposition, and corresponds to "and," so that "a+b" is a and b simultaneously, there is a disjunctive sign as well, i.e. a sign that means an alternative, corresponding to [the Latin] "vel." Thus, for me "a v b" means "a or b."
>
> (GM VII, 57)

> Not all formulae mean quantity and one may find an infinity of ways to perform the calculus: in the case of a calculus based on disjunction, for instance, if one says that x is abc, one may understand that x is a or b or c. . . . In this calculus, indeed, a and aa are equivalent, and any combination of a letter with itself has no importance.
>
> (A VI iv 511–12)

Thus, even though Leibniz possesses some of the most important ingredients necessary to build a structure equivalent to what we now call a "Boolean algebra," it would be anachronistic to attribute the discovery of this structure to him because he never put all these ingredients together into a coherent whole.[22] To support this claim, it suffices to remark that Leibniz, his knowledge of De Morgan's laws notwithstanding, does not recognize as a general property of the calculus the duality that subsists between conjunction and disjunction, nor does he seem to be aware of the importance of the distributive laws that in a Boolean algebra usually connect these two logical operations.

To sum up, we may say that Leibniz aimed to construct two very general kinds of calculus: the first based on the part-whole relation and the second on the relation between *content* and *contained*. As we read in the *New Essays*:

> So it can truthfully be said that the whole theory of syllogism could be demonstrated from the theory *de continente et contento*, of container and contained. The latter is different from that of whole and part, for the whole is always greater than the part, but the container and the contained are sometimes equal, as happens with reciprocal propositions.
>
> (NE 486)

---

known long before De Morgan (by the medieval logicians, for instance), and they were associated with his name because he made a systematic use of them.

[21] Peano took the symbol "v" (the first letter of the Latin word "*vel*") to express (inclusive) disjunction from volume 7 of Leibniz's mathematical writings edited by Gerhardt (GM VII 57).

[22] For Leibniz as a "forerunner" of George Boole, cf. W. Lenzen, "Leibniz und die Boolesche Algebra," in *Studia Leibnitiana* 16 (1984), pp. 187–203. To be precise, Leibniz has all the elements sufficient for building a lattice based on the operations of meet and classical complementation. Cf. Marko Malink and Anubav Vasudevan, "The Logic of Leibniz's Generales inquisitiones de analysi notionum et veritatum," in *The Review of Symbolic Logic* 9 (2016), pp. 686–751.

Thus, the doctrine of syllogism and even traditional logic in its entirety would depend on a more abstract and general calculus, which Leibniz conceives as a tool susceptible of a plurality of applications. He thinks, for instance, of using it for the study of the so-called *analysis of situation* [*analysis situs*]. In this case, the calculus operates on collections of points of the plane having the same geometrical property: each point *x* that has a given property *X* determines a corresponding collection (X), and, in turn, each point belonging to (X) has the property *X*. Two collections (X) and (Y) *coincide* if and only if all points belonging to (X) also belong to (Y), and all points belonging to (Y) belong also to (X). Even though Leibniz does not carefully distinguish the relation of *belonging to a given collection* from *inclusion between two collections,* he clearly attempts to reduce the analysis of the situation to a calculus based on the notions of container and contained.[23]

Finally, concerning the general features of the characteristic art, one point in particular needs to be stressed. Usually, the great majority of the interpreters who attempt to give an account of Leibniz's universal characteristic tend to center it exclusively on the deductive part of logic. This, however, is quite a one-sided representation. As Leibniz explicitly says, the characteristic art should include all kinds of inferences and thus it should not only concern the study of deductive arguments, but also that of inferences based on induction and on premises that are merely probable. In a paper devoted to the characteristic art (1688), for instance, after having observed that the art applies in the first place to subjects fully determined by the data "as it happens with the problems of geometry," Leibniz emphasizes that the art finds its application even for subjects based on conjectures. The characteristic art, which is a "kind of very powerful improvement of the human reason" due to the use of certain symbols, may be applied to investigations concerning history, the "examination of natural bodies," medicine, law, and, in general, to any activity involving reason and any kind of decision making as well:

> Therefore, when the solution is neither determined nor expressible by the data, by means of this analysis we will reach one of these two results: either we will approximate the solution with an infinite process, or, in the case that we have to act on the basis of conjectures, we will determine the probability degree of the solution which may be obtained from the data.

(A VI iv 913)

---

[23] The essay referred to (*Circa Geometrica Generalia* [*About General Geometrical Concepts*]) has been published for the first time in *Leibniz's Theory of Relations,* edited by M. Mugnai (Stuttgart: Franz Steiner Verlag, 1992), pp. 139–140. For Leibniz's idea of a general calculus based on the notions of container and contained, cf. W. Lenzen, "Zur Einbettung der Syllogistik in Leibnizens 'Allgemeinen Kalkül,'" in *Studia Leibnitiana Sonderheft 15* (1988), pp. 38–71.

Natural Language and Artificial or Universal Language: "Affectus," Cases, and Circumstances

According to a tradition that was still flourishing in Leibniz's times, the primordial language of human beings was said to have arisen at the moment when God allowed Adam to give a name to the animals, plants, and everything that existed in the earthly paradise. Later on, however, so the story goes, as a consequence of the destruction of the Tower of Babel, this language was altered and hidden under the surface of the different languages that replaced it among human beings. In the seventeenth century, the German mystic and philosopher Jakob Boehme in his *Mysterium Magnum* (1623) revived the idea of an Adamic language that, because it was near the beginning of a world not yet contaminated by sin, contained many truths that later, in the course of time, were lost. At Leibniz's time, furthermore, the idea was quite widespread that the Hebrew language was, if not the Adamic one, at least its closest relative, and several authors sought to document the existence of traces of the primordial language in historical languages. This kind of inquiry, which today may appear naïve, strongly contributed to the development of scientifically based studies of natural languages and consequently of comparative linguistics.[24]

Leibniz takes part in the debate about the origins of natural languages by expressing his own skepticism about the existence of an Adamic language in the proper sense. He claims, instead, that one should not consider a particular historical language as "primitive," but rather that each natural language has elements that witness its remote origins. The historical languages (Hebrew, Greek, Latin, German, etc.) did not arise from the corruption of a unique primordial language: in each of them it is possible to retrace words that are testament to an archaic phase. Each language is the fruit of an evolution that can be reconstructed through the study of etymology and by comparison with other languages.

Leibniz's explanation of the nature and origin of historical languages is based on the concepts of *affect, onomatopoeia*, and *cases and circumstances*. By *affect* (Latin, *affectus*) Leibniz designates an emotional reaction of an animated being confronted with a thing or an event. In a list of definitions, he asserts that the *affectus* is to the soul what the impetus is to a body: just as the latter is a kind of disposition that a body has to being moved in a certain direction, so the *affectus* is a disposition of a rational agent's soul to pass

---

[24] Cf. H. Aarsleff, *From Locke to Saussure: Essays on the Study of Language and Intellectual History* (London: Athlone, 1982).

from thought to thought. In the case of the *affectus*, the disposition becomes actual by means of a connection with experience.[25]

At first sight, Leibniz's notion of *affectus* is reminiscent of the *passion of the soul* that one finds in the first chapter of Aristotle's *On Interpretation*: the similarity, however, is very superficial. In late antiquity and during the medieval period, the *passions of the soul* became the *concepts of the mind* (*animi conceptus*) mentioned by scholastic logicians (i.e., something that exclusively pertains to the understanding). For Leibniz, instead, *affectus* are not the same as *concepts* or *ideas*: they *involve concepts and ideas*, but are not identical with them. *Affectus* are essentially mingled with a nonrational element, with something that has to do with emotions and feelings. When we perceive an object or an event of the external world, the perception (a mixture of sensible and intelligible aspects) gives rise to a representation that, in turn, produces an *affectus* (i.e., a reaction of our mind triggered by perception; NE 584). If, for example, I see a dog in the street, the act of perceiving (of seeing) the dog produces in me a representation that causes a feeling. This feeling may be of happiness, fear, or indifference, but, in any case, according to Leibniz, in human beings it implies a judgment: "All affects seem to be a kind of judgements" (A VI iv 890). Therefore, hunger and thirst are not *affectus* because they do not imply a judgment of sort (A VI iv 1414), and the absence of a judgement in these latter cases is due to the fact that hunger, thirst, and similar affections do not refer to a particular object.

Another important aspect that distances Leibniz's notion of *affectus* from the traditional theory of concepts is that *affectus* are not the same for all human beings. Different people may have (and usually do have) different *affectus* depending on the circumstances of place and time in which they are living and on the constitution of the organs devised for speech.

Affectus play an essential role in Leibniz's theory of natural languages because they contribute to determining the "imposition" of words to things. Leibniz, indeed, thinks that the first words uttered in any language are expressions of some *affectus* caused by viewing or experiencing some thing or fact:

> Every language has a kind of natural origin due to the agreement of the sounds with the affects provoked in the mind by the act of seeing things. And I think that this origin took place not only in the primordial language, but also in all other languages that emerged partly from the primordial one, partly from a new usage [of the words] introduced by the human beings scattered in the world.
>
> (A VI iv 59)

These attributions of names, however, have certainly corresponded to a conditioning in the historical and natural circumstances in which people found themselves

---

[25] Cf. A. Heinekamp, "Ars characteristica und natürliche Sprache bei Leibniz," in *Tijdschrift voor Filosofie* 34 (1972), pp. 446–488; "Natürliche Sprache und Allgemeine Charakteristik bei Leibniz," in *Studia Leibnitiana Supplementa* 15 (1975), pp. 257–286.

living. The environment of those who live in cold and deserted regions is different from that of those who live in tropical forests; analogously, their social life will be different and so will the objects that make up the daily life of the individuals. Thus, the *cases and circumstances* in which the first attribution of names will have come about and inaugurated the first linguistic communication had an important role for the constitution of a given language:

> Indeed, the different people who first imposed the names, attributed different words to the same things, according to the different qualities by which they were struck, to the different circumstances and relations in which they were situated, to their own affects, to the occasions, and to their proper advantage. . . . Certainly, therefore, it is true that names are not attributed in a natural way to things; nevertheless it is also true that they are only rarely constituted on the basis of people's deliberation.
>
> (G. W. Leibniz, *Epistolaris de Historia Etymologica Dissertatio,* in S. Gensini, *Il naturale e il simbolico* (Roma: Bulzoni, 1991), pp. 201–271. Hereafter EP 215–16)

When an object struck their senses, the first human beings attributed a name to it on the basis of the reaction that it had produced in them, or on the basis of a certain property that had struck their imagination. According to Leibniz (who repeats here a commonplace of medieval linguistics), the first words expressed by humans were *interjections*: "it is quite reasonable to think that human beings . . . as soon as they began to forge some words, adapted the nouns to their perceptions and to their *affectus*; that at the beginning they employed interjections and short particles to express their own *affectus* and that from these interjections as from some seeds all languages were progressively developed" (EP 216). Because the beginnings of any natural language reside in the interjections produced by the *affectus*, in particular by *affectus* connected to sensations of pain, fear, or sudden pleasure, and because we find in nonrational animals as well these particular kind of interjections, Leibniz is driven to attribute some kind of *affectus* to nonrational animals as well (A VI iv 889).

NATURAL AND CONVENTIONAL SOURCES IN THE FORMATION OF NATURAL LANGUAGES

Concerning natural languages, Leibniz makes two claims that seem to go in opposite directions:

(1) It is not possible to find a clearly determined link based on natural grounds (and, therefore, the same for all human beings) between words and "things";

(2) There must be some nonarbitrary, natural connection that associates words with the things they are supposed to signify (A VI iv 59).

As on other occasions, when facing a time-honored philosophical problem, Leibniz attempts to mediate between two opposite claims. In the *Dissertation in Form of a Letter Concerning the History of Etymologies*, one of his last essays (1712, left unfinished), Leibniz traces the thesis of the arbitrary nature of language back to Aristotle who, he says, in this case was more inclined to contradict the truth than he was to pursue it.[26] To Plato, instead, he attributes the opposite opinion: "in his *Cratylus* Plato too began to philosophize about nouns and he found in them some concealed natural reasons." Clearly, Leibniz's sympathies are with "Ammonius and other Greek interpreters, who attempted to reconcile Aristotle with Plato" (EP 215).[27] In the same work, however, Leibniz more correctly attributes to Plato himself the "middle path" between the two extreme opinions about language:

> One needs, therefore, to take a middle path, as was also the opinion of Plato, and [to maintain] that words have a foundation in nature, even though many accidental things contributed [to their formation].
>
> (EP 215)

The same conciliatory attitude is witnessed by the *New Essays*:

> I know that the Scholastics and everyone else are given to saying that the meanings of words are arbitrary (*ex instituto*), and it is true they are not settled by natural necessity; but they are settled by reasons—sometimes natural ones in which chance plays some part, sometimes moral ones which involve choice.
>
> (NE 278)

Leibniz considers the choice of words made by the first human beings to be arbitrary because, as we have seen, it depends on contingent matters like the circumstances of where one is born or is living, circumstances that usually vary from one individual to another. The "natural side" in the constitution of a language instead relies on the constancy of some conditions that determine the attribution of a meaning to words:

> But granted that our languages are derivative so far as origins are concerned, nevertheless considered in themselves they have something primitive about them. This has come to them along the way, in connection with new root words created in our

---

[26] Leibniz wrote various different versions of the *Dissertation* clearly aiming at publishing it. A manuscript (presumably the last one), prepared by a copyist and containing several corrections and remarks in Leibniz's hand, has been transcribed and edited by Stefano Gensini as an appendix to his *Il naturale e il simbolico. Saggio su Leibniz* (Rome: Bulzoni Editore, 1991), pp. 201–271. Even though the transcription of the text presents some mistakes, this is the only existing printed version of this very interesting and important work by Leibniz on the nature and origins of historical languages. All passages from Leibniz's *Dissertation* stem from Gensini's edition.

[27] As argued by Francesco Ademollo in *The* Cratilus *of Plato. A Commentary* (Cambridge: Cambridge University Press, 2011), pp. 310–314, the *Cratylus* probably exerted a strong influence on Leibniz's ideas concerning the origins of natural languages.

languages by chance but for reasons which are grounded in reality. Examples of this are provided by words which signify the sounds of animals or are derived from them. Thus the Latin *coaxare*, applied to frogs, corresponds to the German *couaquen* or *quaken*. It would seem that the noise these animals make is the primordial root of other words in the Germanic language.

(NE 281–82)

Seeing and hearing a frog, for example, the first human beings that attributed names to things designated it by a name that reproduced its croak: the same word *"frog"* in English recalls the sound emitted by the animal to which it refers. Those words that tend to reproduce certain sounds of the objects they denote (such as "rumble," "buzz," "roar," "whisper," etc.) are called *onomatopoeic*. As Leibniz emphasizes, "languages have a kind of natural origin, deriving from the agreement of the sounds with the affects that the sight of the things excited in the mind." And this agreement is determined in the first place through the use of *onomatopoeia*:

And I would maintain that such origins occurred not only in the primordial languages, but also in the languages which were born as a result, partly from the primordial languages and partly by a new usage taking root among people dispersed over
the earth. Indubitably onomatopoeia often imitates nature in an obvious way, such as
when we attribute a *croak* to a frog, when we say "shh!" to admonish someone to be
silent or quiet, when we use *"r"* to signify running, *"hahaha"* to signify laughter, and
"alas!" to signify sadness.

(NE 59)

That for Leibniz onomatopoeic words have a natural origin is confirmed, indirectly, by his theory of *expression*. As Leibniz writes in a letter to Arnauld, the notion of expression is at the core of his entire philosophy (L 339–40; GP II 112); and, as he explains in an-
other text centered on this very notion, among the different types of expressions, those based on *similarity* are the most natural.[28] Hence, because onomatopoeic words are conceived with the aim of imitating the noises associated with the objects they refer to, they are, among all words, the most "natural" ones. In the *Dissertation* of 1712, Leibniz goes even further and says that the letters of the alphabet as well are some kind of images or signs with which human beings attempt to reproduce the disposition of the organs of speech [*organa loquendi*] when they are pronouncing a vowel or a consonant. Such is the case, for instance, of the letter "K" of the German alphabet, which corresponds to some uses of the letter "C" in Latin and that is pronounced half opening the mouth, with the latter assuming the form of a cavity and emitting a guttural sound (EP 259–60).

---

[28] Cf. L 208 (A VI iv 1371): "It is also clear that some expressions have a basis in nature, while others are arbitrary, at least in part, such as the expressions which consist of words or characters. Those which are founded in nature either require some similarity, such as that between a large and a small circle or that between a geographic region and a map of the region." Cf. D. Rutherford, "Philosophy and Language in Leibniz", in *The Cambridge Companion to Leibniz*, edited by N. Jolley (New York: Cambridge University Press, 1995), pp. 224–269.

In the *New Essays*, the conception of the onomatopoeic origin of names comes to be developed directly in relation to the *sounds* that correspond to the single letters of the alphabet:

> Now, just as the letter *R* naturally signifies a violent motion, the letter *L* signifies a gentler one. Thus we see that children and others who find *R* too harsh and diffi-cult to pronounce replace it with the letter *L*—and ask their palish pliest to play for them [*comme disant par example "mon lévélend pèle"*]. This gentle motion appears in *leben* (to live); *laben* (to comfort or give life to); . . . *lentus* (slow); *lieben* (to love); *lauffen* (to glide swiftly, like water flowing); *labi* (to glide). . . . I could mention any number of similar terms which prove that there is something natural in the origin of words—something which reveals a relationship between things and the sounds and motions of the vocal organs. This is also the reason why adding the letter *L* to other names produces diminutives in Latin, semi-Latin and High German. I cannot claim that this principle applies universally, however, since the lion, the lynx, and the leopard are anything but gentle. But perhaps people seized upon another of their characteristics, namely their speed (*lauf*), which makes them feared or which compels flight, as if anyone who saw such an animal would shout to the others: *lauf!* (run!).
>
> (NE 283)

Thus, when Leibniz speaks of *root words* (*mots radicaux*) that constitute the primitive nucleus of the vocabulary of a given language, he really means those words in which the "nearness to things" expressed by means of onomatopoeia is more evident.

A peculiarity of Leibniz's remarks on natural languages is constituted by the claim that all names—even proper names—originally had a *general character*. In fact, the property of being applied to a plurality of objects and not just to one is intrinsic to the use of names. A child who, beginning to speak, attributed a name to each object that claimed its attention would never be able to *think*. A distinctive characteristic of thought is that it refers to many things simultaneously by abstracting from their in-dividual traits and acquiring a degree of generality that situates them above examples and singular cases. The child, when it comes to learn the name "Mama," makes a ge-neric use of it to indicate other women similar to their mother, and the names of fa-mous personages from the past, like Cicero, through etymology, reveal their character of common names:

> *Proper names are ordinarily appellative*, or rather general, in their origin. . . . In fact we know that the original Brutus got this name on account of his apparent stupidity; that Caesar was the name of a baby extracted by an incision from its mother's womb; that Augustus was a name expressing veneration; that Capitone means bighead, as does Bucephalus; that Lentulo, Piso and Cicero were names initially given to those who grew certain types of vegetables. . . . It can therefore be said that the names of individuals were the names of species of things that were given to the individuals on account of their excellence or for some other reason, as the name *Grossatesta* was

given to the person who had the biggest head in the city . . . and so also that the names
of genera were given to species that were contained in them, that is to say, names of a
more general or vaguer term, were given to designate more particular species, when
one didn't care about the difference.

(NE 288–89)

This means that, for Leibniz, proper names do not have an individuating character
per se: they take on such a character only insofar as each of them comes to be associated
with a complete concept.

FROM THE CONCRETE TO THE ABSTRACT: THE ROLE OF RHETORICAL TROPES

Once the lexicon has been consolidated and has acquired the use of particles that express relations (prepositions and conjunctions and all *syncategorematic* terms), the language will have assumed a primary structure, albeit a somewhat rough one. Starting
from this base, the language will have begun to designate not just concrete objects but
also abstract ones, such as the spirit, the mind, fear, virtue, and the like. This passage
from the denotation of the concrete to that of the abstract takes place by recourse to rhetorical figures such as *metaphor, metonymy, analogy*, and the like. Having to translate,
for example, into the Hottentot language the prayer of the *Credo*, Leibniz observes that
the missionaries rendered the name of the Holy Spirit by means of a word that signifies,
among the Hottentots, "a benign and gentle puff of wind" and the same thing "happens
in relation to most other words, and we do not always notice it because most of the time
the etymology is lost." In such a case, *metaphor, metonymy, synecdoche, analogy*—which
means the classical *tropes* of traditional rhetoric—function as the instruments that, in a
certain sense, expand and dilate the original linguistic store composed of words "near to
things" and to nature, thus creating new words by designating abstractions and immaterial entities.[29]

In the case of prepositions, Leibniz thinks that they have their origins in *spatial* experience. He therefore implicitly presupposes a constancy of such experiences among
people even though the "cases and circumstances" among them varies. Prepositions
are of greatest importance for language inasmuch as "they link not only the parts of
discourse composed of the proposition and the parts of the proposition composed of
the idea, but also the parts of the idea composed in more ways by the combination of

---

[29] Cf. A. Heinekamp, "Sprache und Wirklichkeit nach Leibniz," in *History of Linguistic Thought and
Contemporary Linguistics*, edited by H. Parret (Berlin-New York: Walter de Gruyter, 1976), pp. 518–570.

other ideas." Leibniz's conviction is that prepositions such as "to, with, from, in front of, through, on" and the like "are all derived from place, distance and motion and subsequently transferred to all kind of changes, orders, sequences, differences and conformities":

> "*To*" signifies approach, as when we say "I am going *to* Rome." But also, to tie something down we make it approach the thing we want to join it to, and so we say that one thing is tied *to* another. Furthermore, since there is an immaterial tie, so to speak, when one thing follows from another according to moral reasons, we say that what results from someone's movements or decisions belongs or attaches *to* him, as if tended to cling to and go along with him. One body is *with* another when they are in the same place; but we also say that one thing is *with* whatever occurs at the same time, or belongs to the same ordering or part of an ordering, or co-operate in one and the same action.
>
> (NE 277)

The expressions "to," "with," and "between" refer from the beginning to the disposition of objects in space. Leibniz distinguishes two types of spatial reference: *a simple local relation* (*respectus localis*) and *local relation* containing local motion:

> A local relation, instead, is either simple or contains local motion. A simple local relation is found in these prepositions: *with, without, at, about (around), between.*
>
> (A VI iv 647)

> A relation of place with respect to motion is found in the following prepositions: *to, across (through), towards.*
>
> (A VI iv 649)

This is the reason why a given object *A* is *at* an object *B* (*apud B*)

> if the places of *A* and *B* are contiguous, from which one can infer that if *A* is *at B*, then *B* is also *at A.*
>
> (A VI iv 648)

In a long essay entitled *Analysis particularum* (*An Analysis of Particles*), Leibniz uses charts to illustrate the spatial situations that correspond to the various uses of prepositions (A VI iv 648). Also in the case of prepositions, it is through the use of a metaphor that people come to employ expressions that originally indicated spatial relations to designate relations among concepts:

> It is not surprising that, when forming prepositions, people took into account only place, since in the beginning they would have turned their attention only to sensible

and corporeal things; and from these, consequently, they would have transferred the words to invisible things by means of tropes.

(A VI iv 649)

If, for example, in everyday experience, we see that one object is always accompanied by another and that the first is moved together with the second, being contained in the space occupied by the latter, we say that the first is *in* the second. Consequently, if we see that a certain property is always accompanied by another one in such a way that when the second is removed the first goes along with it, we say that the first is *in* the second, or *is part* of it: it is in this sense that the concept "to be rational" is contained *in* the concept of man.

The idea that the behavior of the first human beings was mainly guided by the senses rather than by the intellect belongs to the Epicurean tradition that was revived in the fifteenth century by the rediscovery of Lucretius' poem *On the Nature of Things*. Leibniz, indeed, who seems to be well acquainted with Lucretius' work,[30] gives an account of the origins of natural languages quite similar to that presented in book V (vv. 1040–90) of *On the Nature of Things*.[31] Here, Lucretius writes that the first human beings began to associate words with things according to the different sensations that they produced on them. As we have seen, however, Leibniz prefers to speak of *affectus* instead of *sensations*. Sensations are necessary conditions for producing *affectus*, and an *affectus* is a reaction of our soul to a given sensation or complex of sensations. In an *affectus* not just mere sensations are involved but concepts as well. As Leibniz writes in a short paper of 1684 and repeats later in the *New Essays*: "there is nothing in our understanding which does not come from the senses, with the exception of the understanding itself" (NE 111). For Leibniz, indeed, there is a kind of continuity between sensations on one hand and concepts and ideas on the other: a sort of continuity that, as we read in a letter to the Princess Sophie, is largely due to the faculty of *imagination* (GP VI 500–503).

Even though the imagination reduces the gap between sensations and concepts, it does not contribute significantly to attenuating the apparent divergence between natural and universal language. The first is built starting from sensations and *affectus*, whereas the latter is strongly linked to concepts; the first tolerates ambiguities and lack of precision, and, for this reason, it is particularly suitable to expressing vague thoughts, emotions, and feelings. The second, instead, is devised as a tool aiming at securing clarity and avoiding any kind of vagueness of meaning. The two languages properly belong to

---

[30] In *Theodicy*, for instance, Leibniz quotes several verses from it (GP VI 307; H 323–24). Quite remarkably, the quoted verses are from Alessandro Marchetti's Italian translation of *On the Nature of Things*. Consider that Marchetti's translation circulated at Leibniz's times in manuscript form only (it was edited for the first time at London in 1717).

[31] "Postremo quid in hac mirabile tantoperest re,/ si genus humanum, cui vox et lingua vigeret,/ pro vario sensu varia res voce notaret?" (1056–1058).

two different domains of human culture. The natural language pertains to the domain of everyday life and of emotions, which involves the sphere of the so-called liberal arts; the universal language, instead, belongs to the realm of the exact sciences and of scientific enquiry. Even though few texts clearly suggest that the artificial language can be used to compose verses and poetical works, Leibniz never says explicitly that the artificial language, once realized, must substitute the natural one. On the contrary, Leibniz's latest views concerning the nature of monads fit quite well with the idea that the two kinds of languages each correspond to a specific feature of the human soul. According to the metaphysical hypothesis of monads, a human monad is endowed with the two faculties of *appetite* (*appetitus*) and understanding, and whereas the natural language may find its roots in the appetite, the universal language is clearly at home with the faculty of the intellect.

References

Aarsleff, Hans. 1982. *From Locke to Saussure: Essays on the Study of Language and Intellectual History*. London: Athlone.

Ademollo, Francesco. 2011. *The Cratilus of Plato. A Commentary*. Cambridge: Cambridge University Press.

Arnauld, Antoine and Nicole, Pierre. 1981. *La Logique ou l'Art de penser*. Edition critique par P. Clair-F. Girbal, Paris: Vrin.

Boole, George. 1948. *The Mathematical Analysis of Logic*. [Cambridge: Macmillan 1847.] New York: Philosophical Library.

Burkhardt, Hans. 1980. *Logik und Semiotik in der Philosophie von Leibniz*. München: Philosophia Verlag.

Couturat, Louis. 1901. *La logique de Leibniz, d'après des documents inédits*. Paris: Alcan.

Dummett, Michael. 1956. "Review of Rescher "Leibniz's Interpretation." *Journal of Symbolic Logic* 21: 197–99.

Heinekamp, Albert. 1972. "Ars characteristica und natürliche Sprache bei Leibniz." *Tijdschrift voor Filosofie 34*: 446–488.

Heinekamp, Albert. 1975. "Natürliche Sprache und Allgemeine Characteristik bei Leibniz." *Studia Leibnitiana Supplementa 15*: 257–286.

Heinekamp, Albert. 1976. "Sprache und Wirklichkeit nach Leibniz." In H. Parret (ed.), *History of Linguistic Thought and Contemporary Linguistics*. Berlin/New York: Walter de Gruyter, pp. 518–570.

Kauppi, Raili. 1960. *Über die Leibnizschen Logik*. Acta Philosophica Fennica, XII, Helsinki: Societas Philosophica.

Leibniz, G.W. *Logical Papers*. Translated by G. H. R. Parkinson. Oxford: Clarendon Press, 1966. Abbreviation: LP.

Leibniz, G. W. 1982. *Generales Inquisitiones de Analysi Notionum et Veritatum. Allgemeine Untersuchungen über die Analyse der Begriffe und Wahrheiten*. Edited by F. Schupp. Hamburg: Meiner Verlag.

Leibniz, G. W. 1968. *General Investigations Concerning the Analysis of Concepts and Truths*. A Translation and an Evaluation by W. H. O'Briant. Athens: University of Georgia Press.

Leibniz, G. W. 1991. *Epistolaris de Historia Etymologica Dissertatio*. In Stefano Gensini, *Il naturale e il simbolico. Saggio su Leibniz*. Roma: Bulzoni Editore, 1991, pp. 201–271. Abbreviation: EP.

Leibniz, G. W. 1998. *Recherches générales sur l'analyse des notions et des vérités. 24 thèses métaphysiques et autres textes logiques et métaphysiques*. Introduction et notes par J. -B. Rauzy. Paris: Presses Universitaires de France, pp. 200–320.

Leibniz, G. W. 1992. *Circa Geometrica Generalia [About General Geometrical Concepts])*. In M. Mugnai (ed.), *Leibniz's Theory of Relations*. Stuttgart: Franz Steiner Verlag, pp. 139–140.

Leibniz, G. W. 2003. "On the calculability of the number of all possible truths," transl. and edited by Philip Beeley. *Leibniz Review 13*: 99–100.

Lenzen, Wolfgang. 1983. "Zur extensionalen und 'intensionalen' Interpretation der Leibnizschen Logik." *Studia Leibnitiana 15*: 129–148.

Lenzen, Wolfgang. 1984. "'Unbestimmte Begriffe' bei Leibniz." *Studia Leibnitiana 16*: 1–26.

Lenzen, Wolfgang. 1984. "Leibniz und die Boolesche Algebra." *Studia Leibnitiana 16*: 187–203.

Lenzen, Wolfgang. 1988. "Zur Einbettung der Syllogistik in Leibnizens 'Allgemeinen Kalkül.'" *Studia Leibnitiana Sonderheft 15*: 38–71.

Lenzen, Wolfgang. 1989. *Arithmetical vs "Real" Addition—A Case Study of the Relation between Logic, Mathematics and Metaphysics in Leibniz*. In *Leibnizian Inquiries—A Group of Essays*, edited by N. Rescher (Proceedings of the 5th Annual Conference in Philosophy of Science). Lanham: University of America Press, pp. 149–157.

Lenzen, Wolfgang. 2004. "Leibniz's Logic." In Dov M. Gabbay and John Woods (eds.), *Handbook of the History of Logic. The Rise of Modern Logic: From Leibniz to Frege*, Vol. 3. Amsterdam: Elsevier-North Holland, pp. 1–82.

Malink, Marko and Vasudevan, Abumav. 2016. "The Logic of Leibniz's Generales Inquisitiones de analysi notionum et veritatum." *The Review of Symbolic Logic 9/4*: 686–751.

Mates, Benson. 1986. *The Philosophy of Leibniz. Metaphysics and Language*. Oxford: Oxford University Press, pp. 104–21.

Mondadori, Fabrizio. 1973. "Reference, essentialism, and modality in Leibniz's metaphysics." *Studia Leibnitiana 5*: 73–101.

Mondadori, Fabrizio. 1993. "On some disputed questions in Leibniz's metaphysics." *Studia Leibnitiana 25*: 153–173.

Rescher, Nicholas. 1954. "Leibniz's interpretation of his logical calculi." *Journal of Symbolic Logic 19*: 1–13.

Rutherford, Donald. 1995. "Philosophy and Language in Leibniz." In Nicholas Jolley (ed.), *The Cambridge Companion to Leibniz*. New York: Cambridge University Press, pp. 224–269.

Schroeder, Ernst. 1891. *Vorlesungen über die Algebra der Logik*, Leipzig: Teubner, vol. *II*, 1–9.

Swoyer, Christopher. 1994. "Leibniz's calculus of real addition." *Studia Leibnitiana 36*: 1–30.

Swoyer, Christopher. 1995. "Leibniz on intension and extension." *Nous 29*(1): 96–114.

Venn, J. 1894. *Symbolic Logic*. Second edn. London: MacMillan.

PART III

MATHEMATICS

CHAPTER 11

....

THE CALCULUS

....

SIEGMUND PROBST

INTRODUCTION

....

WHILE Leibniz's research and results in several other areas of mathematics were often unknown to his contemporaries or met with only small interest (see Chapters 12 and 13), differential and integral calculus is the mathematical field that achieved the greatest effect during his lifetime as well as in posterity. In the early years after the first publication of the method, contemporaries still responded cautiously; but then, in the 1690s, the new calculus spread increasingly quickly through the work and publications of the brothers Jacob and Johann Bernoulli and the Marquis de L'Hospital. The extent to which the so-called priority dispute with Newton and some of his followers grew in the last years of Leibniz's life reflects the importance attributed to the calculus by the scientific community since 1700. Initially competing with the cumbersome Newtonian method of fluxions, the concise and elegant formalism developed by Leibniz ultimately prevailed, with the result that, for example, the symbols d and $\int$ introduced by him are still in use today.

The (infinitesimal) calculus is a mathematical method in which two procedures with opposite orientation—differentiation and integration—are united in a common formalism so that the one operation is the inversion of the other. Historically, they are based on originally separated classes of methods: one for the determination of tangents of a curve (or a tangential surface on a curved surface), the other for the determination of areas under curves (or the volumes of bodies with curved surface), as well as for the arc lengths of curves (or the areas of curved surfaces of bodies). When Leibniz turned to this field of mathematics, a number of methods were known for determining tangents to a curve. For curves that could be characterized by an algebraic equation, there were already algorithmic procedures available; for certain other curves, such as the cycloids, there were geometric methods. The determination of areas under curves, the so-called quadrature, was more difficult to solve, but, in the case of common as well as higher parabolas and hyperbolas, the results were already well known. In addition to the traditional methods of ancient mathematics, especially the method of exhaustion, the mathematicians of the seventeenth century used above all the geometry of indivisibles or infinitesimal methods.

The Leibnizian calculus originally emerged from his studies in the summing of infinite number series and the quadrature of curves, which he systematically pursued since his arrival in Paris. After initial successes in 1672, notably the summation of reciprocal figurate numbers, and in 1673, notably the circle series, he proceeded to develop his formalism with the symbols d and $\int$, in essence from the end of October 1675 onward. Beginning in 1684, he published details of his methods and results in a series of articles in contemporary scientific journals. However, Leibniz probably never wrote a coherent account of his calculus; the project of a book on the *Scientia infiniti* did not materialize. As far as is known from his manuscripts today, only the beginnings of such a work were ever written (Gerhardt 1876). For an adequate reconstruction of his research and results in this field, one is therefore mainly dependent on three different types of sources: first, on the articles published by Leibniz himself in scientific journals such as the *Journal des sçavans* and the *Acta Eruditorum*; second, on his scientific correspondence; and finally on the mathematical manuscripts which remained unpublished during his lifetime. The scope of these sources is very different. All the mathematical articles published by Leibniz, most of them treating the calculus,[1] can be collected into a single volume. The correspondence concerning the calculus is more extensive, but his manuscript studies and notes on this subject will probably fill around fifteen printed volumes of the *Academy Edition*. It is only for the period covering the origins of his calculus before the end of 1676 that all the sources are available in published form. Of the studies pertaining to the discovery of the calculus, Leibniz published nothing himself, and only a few important letters on the topic appeared in print during his lifetime. In the middle and late nineteenth century C. I. Gerhardt published some important manuscripts from this period (especially in GM and GB; most of these were translated into English by Child). But only in recent years have all the texts concerning the discovery of the calculus in the collection of his manuscripts been edited. In addition to the letters (published mainly in A III i), four volumes of writings are available (A VII iii–vi). From the time of 1677–1716, there is a series of essays that Leibniz published himself. In contrast, only a small selection of manuscripts from this period have been printed from the collection (primarily in GM V and GM VII), and only a few of the still unpublished manuscripts have been the subject of scholarly investigation.

The content of most of these calculus manuscripts is therefore not yet precisely known. This amounts to a bulk of texts corresponding at least to the extent of ten volumes of the *Academy Edition* in print. Therefore, the following discussion is based mainly on the published correspondence (especially GM; GB; A III ii–viii) and the aforementioned articles in scientific journals. Until all of the relevant mathematical

---

[1] See Leibniz, *La naissance du calcul différentiel*, and Leibniz, *Die mathematischen Zeitschriftenartikel*.

manuscripts and letters of Leibniz have been published, only a preliminary and in-complete picture of what has been achieved by him in the field of calculus can be presented.

The Invention of Leibniz's Calculus, 1672–1676

During his student times in Leipzig, Jena, and Altdorf (1663–1667), Leibniz had very little contact with contemporary mathematical research. An exception was the field of combinatorics. This changed only gradually during his stay in Frankfurt am Main and in Mainz (1667–1672), when Leibniz started to study articles from the *Philosophical Transactions* (1665ff) and the collected edition of Hobbes's *Opera philosophica* (1668). At this time, his main interest was the theory of motion (see Chapter 16). Although Leibniz believed already in 1671 that he had given a theoret-ical justification of the geometry of indivisibles in his *Theoria motus abstracti* (A VI ii n. 41), he didn't succeed in applying the method and obviously abandoned an attempt undertaken to square or to rectify the hyperbola (A VII iv n. 4). Leibniz received new incentives for mathematical research when he moved to Paris in the spring of 1672. His careful reading of Blaise Pascal's *Traité du triangle arithmétique* (1665) led him not only to continue his studies on combinatorics, but also to begin an in-depth in-vestigation of numerical sequences (A VII iii n. 3–4). In the same year, starting from a problem that Huygens had posed to him, he succeeded in the summation of the reciprocal figurate numbers (A VII iii n. 1–2; A III i n. 2). Methodologically, he relied on the proposition that for a monotone sequence $(a_n | n = 1,2,...N), N \in \{1,2,...,\infty\}$, the following equation holds:

$$a_1 - a_N = \sum_{n=1}^{N} (a_n - a_{n+1}),$$

wherein $\pm \infty$ may arise as result of the sum. In Leibniz's words: "In every continuously augmented or diminished series the difference between any extremal terms is equal to the sum of the differences between all intermediate terms" (A VII iii 74; see also A III i 22–24). The summation of a series $\sum_1^N b_n$ can therefore always be effected if $b_n = a_n - a_{n+1}$ holds and the monotone sequence $(a_n | n = 1,2,...)$ is known. Leibniz extended this con-sideration to iterated differences and developed difference schemes analogous to the summations of Pascal's Triangle. Later, he denoted the difference scheme obtained from the iterated differences of the harmonic sequence $(\frac{1}{n} | n = 1,2,...)$ "harmonic triangle" (A VII iii 336). Apparently, Leibniz already at this early stage of his studies sought to square the circle by examining regular polygons for the circle approximation in order to form sequences (A VII i n. 3, 6; A VII iii n. 6). During his short stay in London, in early 1673, the mathematical research in England came into his focus; especially the two solutions for the problem of squaring the hyperbola achieved using infinite series, by William Brouncker and by Nicolaus Mercator, had a strong influence on him. After returning to Paris, and guided by Huygens, Leibniz worked through the relevant research literature.[2]

Studying Pascal's *Lettres de Dettonville* (1659), Leibniz discovered the usefulness of the triangle formed from the infinitesimal elements of abscissa, ordinate, and tangent or arc of a curve. This he named "characteristic triangle," and, in the summer of 1673, when applied to the circle, it helped him to discover a large number of area transformations (A VII iv n. 26–27) that in principle could be performed for arbitrary curves. Leibniz named one of these transformations, where the section y of the ordinate axis cut off by the tangent was used (A VII iv n. 27), his "transmutation method" (A VII iv n. 36). There we have, expressed in the notation introduced later by Leibniz,

$$y = v - x\frac{dv}{dx} \text{ and } \int v\,dx = \frac{1}{2}(vx + \int y\,dx).$$ In the case of the circle given by the equation

$v = \sqrt{2x - x^2}$, this section $y = \dfrac{x}{\sqrt{2x - x^2}}$ is equal to the tangent of the half angle. In this way, Leibniz found that he was able to obtain the difference of area between a suitably chosen segment of a circle and the circumscribed rectangle by calculating the area under the curve $x = \dfrac{2y^2}{1+y^2}$. Applying Mercator's method of series expansion for fractions resulted in $\dfrac{y^2}{1+y^2} = y^2 - y^4 + y^6 - y^8$ etc. In the autumn of 1673, this result led him to the discovery of the series $\dfrac{1}{3} - \dfrac{1}{5} + \dfrac{1}{7} - \dfrac{1}{9}$ etc. being equal to the area between the quadrant of a circle with unit radius and the circumscribed square on the radius (A VII iv n. 42). By August 1673, Leibniz had already reached basic insight in the relations of the quadrature and rectification of curves on the one side and the determination of differences or tangents on the other side, and he had sketched the beginnings of a quadrature method with recursively defined difference series, which in fact represent simple forms of the Taylor series (A VII iv n. 40). He also introduced the concept of "functio" for designating a geometric magnitude depending on the relationship between the abscissa and ordinate of a curve (e.g., the tangent, normal, etc.; A VII iv n. 27, 28, 35, 40).

After an interruption of several months, Leibniz continued, in mid-1674, his research on general methods of squaring curves. Initially, at the suggestion of Huygens, he tried to reverse Descartes's method for the determination of normals to a curve (A VII v n. 3–4, 7–9, 14, 17, 20–21, 27). But, after several months, he realized the futility of this approach. Then, in December 1674, he succeeded in solving an inverse tangent problem, corresponding to the solution of the differential equation $\dfrac{dy}{dx} = \dfrac{c}{y}$ (where c is constant), by applying the characteristic triangle (A VII v n. 17).

Perhaps stimulated by discussions with Tschirnhaus, who had arrived in Paris in late September 1675, Leibniz returned to his own methods and to the investigation of centers of gravity and static moments (on which he had worked since the spring of 1673) by

---

[2] His main sources were the works of Honoré Fabri, Christiaan Huygens, Nicolaus Mercator, Blaise Pascal, René Descartes, John Wallis, and James Gregory.

employing the methods found in the works of Fabri, Huygens, and Pascal (A VII iv passim). In this way, in October and November 1675, he reached the decisive break-through to the calculus (A VII v n. 38, 40, 44, 46; Child § 5–8), introducing the symbols d and $\int$ for the inverse operations of differentiation and summation, thereby replacing the Cavalerian term "omnes": "It will be useful to write $\int$ for omn., so that $\int l = \text{omn.} l$, or the sum of the l's." (A VII v 292; Child 80).[3] Leibniz quickly realized that he could use his approach to perform a new type of general calculus that, among other things, included his method of transmutation. He examined the conditions under which the result of squaring an algebraic curve was again an algebraic curve, considering differ-entiation and integration immediately as linear operations (A VII v n. 40). Moreover, Leibniz was able to interpret the expression $\int y\, dx$ as the sum of the rectangles formed by the ordinates and the infinitesimal differences of the abscissas, thus obtaining the area between the abscissa and the arc of the curve or as the static moments of the differences of the abscissas with respect to the axis of ordinates. This allowed him to transfer well-known theorems on static moments into the calculus; for example, $\int y\, dy = \dfrac{y^2}{2}$ (A VII v n. 46; Child § 8).

Starting from the equation resulting from the decomposition of a circumscribed rec-tangle into two areas by the arc of the curve (in his new notation: $xy = \int y\, dx + \int x\, dy$, today known as the *theorem of partial integration*), he soon gave the formula for the product rule of differentiation: $d(xy) = y\, dx + x\, dy$ (A VII v n. 51; Child § 9). A few months later, he established the quotient rule of differentiation (A VII v n. 70, 89). In his treatise *De quadratura arithmetica circuli*, completed in the summer of 1676 and intended for publi-cation, Leibniz treated the squaring of the curves of the form $y = x^e (e \neq -1)$, designated by him as "simple analytical curves," but still without using the symbols of the calculus (A VII vi n. 51, prop. XV–XXV).[4] He compiled an overview containing the general rules $d(x^e) = e \cdot x^{e-1}$ for differentiation and $\int x^e = \dfrac{x^{e+1}}{e+1} (e \neq -1)$ for summation of these curves and drew up a list of examples with rational and negative exponents e in November 1676 (A VII v n. 96; Child § 14).

WORK ON THE CALCULUS'S RULES AND FIRST PUBLICATIONS, 1677–1686

One of the main goals of Leibniz in the field of mathematics was the perfection of geometry by means of a continuation of research in the Archimedean tradition, pursuing the measurement of lengths, areas, and volumes of geometric figures that had been missing in the Cartesian approach. Already in 1673, he objected to Descartes's

[3] Only later, the term "sum" was replaced by "integral" following a suggestion of Johann Bernoulli.
[4] In this treatise, Leibniz worked out a rigorous foundation of his method of transmutation based on infinitesimals. See Knobloch (2002) and Rabouin (2015).

restriction of geometry to curves defined by polynomial equations (A VII iv 594–597), which, since his early years in Hanover, he had been accustomed to call "algebraic" (e.g., A III ii 925). Leibniz considered sums of infinite series as exact solutions, and he introduced nonalgebraic curves, which he called "transcendental," as legitimate tools of geometry (A VII iii 266–267). In the beginning, the calculus was for Leibniz the main tool for pursuing this goal, but it was not yet considered a mathematical subject matter in its own right. The fact that the calculus was for him not yet an independent discipline with its own theoretical objects becomes apparent in the changes that the concept of function underwent. When Leibniz started to use the term in mathematics, in 1673 (A VII iv 500, 504, etc.), he assumed that a "functio" was determined by the relation of a variable geometric magnitude, such as the ordinate, abscissa, tangent, normal, subtangent, and such of a given curve to a chosen axis. Even two decades later, he still expressed the same view: "I call *function* the portion of a line, which is cut off by straight lines drawn only with the help of a fixed point and the point of the curve given with its curvature" (*Nova calculi differentialis applicatio et usus*, 1694, GM V 306). However, already at this time, Leibniz wanted to transform geometry into a pure doctrine of magnitudes without any direct relation to geometric objects (GM V 264, 307). Only in the subsequent period did functions receive the status of independent mathematical objects.

For Leibniz, transcendental curves provided solutions for quadratures and rectifications of certain algebraic curves like the circle or the hyperbola, on the one side, while, on the other side, they required new algorithms for the calculation of integrals and differentials, which could not be gained directly from the general rules for differentiation and integration and the well-known algorithms for algebraic curves. In his early years in Hanover, Leibniz pursued this project further, managing to work out more general rules, such as the chain rule of differentiation, and some rules for the differentiation of the simpler transcendental curves and the differentiation of curves defined by an implicit equation. He also developed formulas for the integration of most rational and some irrational and transcendental curves.

Leibniz published his new results only gradually and in small portions. In his response to Newton's *Epistola posterior* of July 1677 (A III ii n. 54), he explained his differential calculus in considerable detail, but there were still some mistakes in the examples he gave. In his first two publications that included solutions of quadratures, first of a segment of the cycloid (*La Quadrature d'une portion de la roulette*, 1678; GM V 116–117) and then of the circle by an infinite series (*De vera proportione circuli ad quadratum*, 1682; GM V 118–122), Leibniz divulged nothing of his methods. In his next article (*De dimensionibus figurarum*, 1684; GM V 123–126), he pointed out that he was in possession of a method that allowed him to find a "quadratrix" (in modern terms, a primitive function) in certain cases of algebraic curves using an arbitrary polynomial equation with undetermined coefficients. He published the main rules of differential calculus, including the chain rule, without proof in the *Nova methodus pro maximis et minimis* in 1684 (GM V 220–226). Leibniz also gave several examples of the application of his calculus and finally the solution of the famous inverse tangent problem which Florimond de Beaune had posed to Descartes in 1638.[5] The first examples of integral calculus and general considerations for the embedding of quadratures (integration) into the more general method of solving inverse tangent problems (by solving differential equations) followed in *De geometria recondita*, published in 1686 (GM V 226–233).

THE MATHEMATICAL CHALLENGES AND OTHER PUBLICATIONS ON THE CALCULUS, 1687–1696

At the beginning, Leibniz had met with little understanding for his calculus from his friends Christiaan Huygens and E. W. von Tschirnhaus, both of whom remained largely skeptical toward it. Representatives of the older generation, such as John Wallis or Vincenzo Viviani, who received information on the new method late in their lives, shared this skeptical attitude. It was only through the publication of the *Nova methodus* and subsequent articles in the *Acta Eruditorum* that a younger generation of mathematicians became aware of the calculus and showed themselves open to its use. Jacob and Johann Bernoulli, along with John Craig, were the first to react positively. Most continental mathematicians who worked on the early development of the calculus were taught directly or indirectly by the brothers Bernoulli.

During the following years, Leibniz and his followers adopted the strategy of posing thorny mathematical problems publicly to the scholarly community and then publishing their correct solutions. In this way, they sought to demonstrate that by using the calculus they had been able to tackle those problems that had remained insolvable within the realm of Cartesian geometry. Moreover, they were able to show that the new method could be applied successfully to problems in mechanics.[6] In fact, apart from Huygens, only mathematicians who were familiar with the calculus (either according to Leibniz's method or to Isaac Newton's method of fluxions) had the necessary tools available for solving these problems. The solutions published by the authors of the challenges, along with their other journal articles, made it apparent that more and more methods for solving differential equations were now available to them.[7] Ever

---

[5] Leibniz had found the solution already in 1676 (A VII v 598–605); for a comprehensive treatment see Scriba (1964).

[6] See Heß (2005), *Leibniz auf dem Höhepunkt*, 53–54.

[7] E.g., the solution of linear differential equations by separation of variables and using an iterative process, later named after Cauchy-Picard, is addressed by Leibniz in a letter to Johann Bernoulli (A III vii 241; GM III 352).

more demanding problems in the fields of differential geometry, exponential curves, series expansions, and the treatment of families of curves could be solved using the new methods. Leibniz himself started a series of challenges in 1687 with the task of determining the isochrone curve (i.e., the curve on which a heavy body moves downward without acceleration; *De linea isochrona*; GM V 234–237). With the investigation and solution of the problem of the catenary, published in 1691 (*De linea in quam flexile se pondere proprio curvat*; GM V 243–247), he laid the foundation for a new field of research, later to be developed into the calculus of variations. It was the immediate application to problems of mechanics, and gradually to other areas of physics, that was to exemplify and determine the success of the calculus over the course of the following hundred years.

In addition, there were new developments in the infinitesimal calculus, some of which were communicated to the scholarly public. Noteworthy examples of such developments are differentiation according to the parameter in the investigation of families of curves (*De linea ex lineis*; GM V 266–269) or the introduction of exponential equations (*Nouvelles Remarques touchant l'analise des transcendantes*; GM V 278–279), both of which were published in 1692, while other advances were discussed only in mutual correspondence with L'Hospital or Johann Bernoulli, such as the question of the possibility of fractional differentiation (A III vi 510, 528). Another new approach was using the method of undetermined coefficients with infinite series characterizing transcendent curves in finding solutions to certain inhomogeneous differential equations (*Supplementum geometriae practicae*; GM V 285–288).

These developments were so rapid that Leibniz himself was only able to stay in the front line of research for a few years before the role of chief protagonist was transferred step by step first to Jacob Bernoulli and then to Johann Bernoulli. With the publication of L'Hospital's *Analyse des infiniment petits*, based on lectures he had received from Johann Bernoulli, a textbook for differential calculus became available, providing the basis for the widespread distribution of the Leibnizian calculus from 1696 onward.

DISCUSSIONS ON FOUNDATIONS, THE PRIORITY DISPUTE, AND FINAL PUBLICATIONS ON THE CALCULUS, 1696–1716

Public success in the propagation of the calculus soon brought critics onto the scene. The final twenty years of Leibniz's life were overshadowed by discussions over the foundations of the calculus and, above all, by the escalating dispute over priority in discovery and associated charges of plagiarism. Since 1694, critical views on the status of the infinitesimal quantities employed in the calculus were formulated by Bernard Nieuwentijt, who published a textbook of his own method in 1695. Nieuwentijt's criticism was rejected first by Leibniz himself (*Responsio ad nonnullas difficultates*; GM V 320–326) and later by Jacob Hermann. However, soon other opponents were to be found. Around the turn of the century, a new controversy about the foundations of the calculus came about. This time, it was driven from inside the Académie des Sciences, mainly by Michel Rolle. Leibniz tried to support his French followers L'Hospital and Varignon by sending letters to Paris destined for publication.[8] But his undogmatic approach, which argued at two different levels of discourse, metaphysical and mathematical, thereby allowing for different interpretations of the infinitesimal magnitudes, did not meet with approval either on the part of his followers or his adversaries. Moreover, this defense delivered the starting point for further lively discussions about Leibniz's conception of the foundations of the calculus which continue today (see later discussion).

After the publication by John Wallis, in the third volume of his *Opera mathematica* (1699), of some important scientific letters exchanged between Leibniz, Newton, Henry Oldenburg, and other members of the Royal Society, allegations were made that Leibniz had based his method on information gleaned from manuscripts and letters he had received or seen during his first visit to London. These allegations came from Fatio de Duillier, a friend of Newton, who had made clear his views on Leibniz already in 1691 in his correspondence with Christiaan Huygens (HO X 214). After Leibniz had established that Fatio did not have the backing of the Royal Society, he replied publicly (*Responsio ad Dn. Nic. Fatii Duillerii imputationes*; GM V 340–349). There was no further attack by Fatio, so that to Leibniz everything would now have seemed calm and the latest problem to have been overcome.

It would take ten years before the next publication appeared in print, in which the accusation of plagiarism was repeated. The author this time was John Keill, who set out his attack in an article in the *Philosophical Transactions*.[9] Although Leibniz protested, he did so without success. Newton made Keill's accusation his own, and, as president of the Royal Society, formed a committee which was tasked with passing judgment on Leibniz. In order to justify a ruling against Leibniz, he compiled a set of texts, the *Commercium epistolicum*, drawn chiefly from early correspondence and papers in the Royal Society to which Leibniz had had access. This compilation was published by order of the Royal Society at the beginning of 1713.[10]

Leibniz reacted immediately by means of a series of articles, initially anonymously, but later under his own name, in which he not only defended the independence of his discovery, but also began directing the charge of plagiarism against Newton himself.[11] Newton

---

[8] *Memoire de Mr. Leibnitz touchant son sentiment sur le calcul differentiel*; GM IV, 95–96; GM V 350; A I 20 493–494; *Extrait d'une lettre de M. Leibnitz à M. Varignon*; GM IV 91–95; L 881–885.

[9] John Keill, "Epistola . . . de legibus virium centripetarum," *Philosophical Transactions* 26 (1708/9, published 1710), 174–187.

[10] *Commercium epistolicum D. Johannis Collins et aliorum de analysi promota*, London, 1712 (published 1713).

[11] *Epistola qua probatur Analyticam Artem primum a L. fuisse editam et post complures demum annos a N. Calculum fluxionum fuisse productum* (GM V 411–413); *Remarques sur le different entre M. de Leibnitz,*

proceeded to repeat his attacks in an anonymous review of the *Commercium epistolicum*,[12] which was later added to the second edition of the book, published in 1722. It was not possible for the dispute to be resolved before the death of Leibniz, and it continued to poison relations between the supporters of the two opposing camps for decades to come.

Despite the developing priority dispute during the last twenty years of his life, Leibniz still published a number of articles in which he developed further the infinitesimal calculus. Among these articles we find in particular his studies on reducing the integration of rational curves into a few basic integrals (*Specimen novum analyseos pro scientia infiniti* and *Continuatio analyseos quadraturarum rationalium*; GM V 350–366). In contrast to Johann Bernoulli, he was unable to recognize that the presupposition of the quadratures of the circle and the hyperbola was sufficient to achieve this because he considered erroneously the decomposition of the integrand $\dfrac{1}{x^4+a^4}$ (where a is constant) to be impossible in real numbers. Further publications dealt with rolling curves, evolutes and envelopes, tangents to the curve described by the center of gravity of a given curve, or the question of the sum of an infinite sequence with two limit points.[13] In his paper *Symbolismus memorabilis calculi algebraici et infinitesimalis* (GM V 377–382), Leibniz establishes the formal analogy between a binomial $x + y$ raised to the e-th power and the e-th derivative of a product xy in general formulas:

$$p^e\left(x+y\right)=1\,p^e xp^0 y+\frac{e}{1}\,p^{e-1}xp^1 y+\frac{e.e-1}{1.2}\,p^{e-2}xp^2 y$$
$$+\frac{e.e-1.e-2}{1.2.3}\,p^{e-3}xp^3 y+\frac{e.e-1.e-2.e-3}{1.2.3.4}\,p^{e-4}xp^4 y+\&c.$$

$$d^e\left(xy\right)=1\,d^e xd^0 y+\frac{e}{1}\,d^{e-1}xd^1 y+\frac{e.e-1}{1.2}\,d^{e-2}xd^2 y+\frac{e.e-1.e-2}{1.2.3}\,d^{e-3}xd^3 y+\&c.$$

Recent Discussions on Leibniz's Calculus

Dissatisfaction with the foundations of the calculus increased further in the course of the eighteenth century and led Lagrange to initiate a prize question on the part of the Prussian Academy of Sciences in order to solve this problem. His efforts were to no

---

et M. Newton (GM V 414–416); *Lettre sur le livre intitulé Commercium Epistolicum, Brunsvik le 28. Oct. 1714* (Dutens III 441–442).

[12] Isaac Newton, "An account of the book entituled commercium epistolicum Collini et aliorum, de analysi promota," *Philosophical transactions* 29 (1714), 173–224.

[13] *De lineae super linea incessu* (GM VII 339–344); *Constructio problematis ducendi rectas quae tangunt Lineas Centrorum Gravitatis* (Dutens III 426–427); *Epistola G.G. L. ad V. Cl. Christianum Wolfium* (GM V 382–387).

avail. Although the calculus was now increasingly based on the concept of limit, only in the following century, through the establishment of a finite approach associated with the names of Cauchy and Weierstrass, was it possible for the infinitesimal method to be eliminated successively. This development appeared to have settled the question until nonstandard analysis emerged in the second half of the twentieth century. The work of figures such as Laugwitz, Schmieden, Robinson, and Nelson brought a turn-around in the understanding of fundamental questions: infinitesimals once again became legitimate objects of recognized mathematical theories. To some extent, nonstandard analysis rehabilitated procedures that Newton, Leibniz, and their successors had employed. With regard to research on Leibniz, this has led to an ongoing debate focused on interpreting his conception of the infinitesimal quantities. As mentioned earlier, Leibniz himself presented several ways of understanding these quantities in his letter to Varignon. Specifically, he argued "that it is unnecessary . . . to make sure that there are lines in nature which are infinitely small in a rigorous sense in contrast to our ordinary lines" and that it was sufficient "to explain the infinite through the incomparable." Moreover, he suggested that these incomparable magnitudes were variable and could be taken as small as necessary. The mathematician could use the infinitesimal magnitudes "as ideal concepts which shorten his reasoning" in a similar way to imaginary roots, but this would not mean that the science of the infinite was reduced to "fictions, for there always remains a 'syncategorematic' infinite" (L 881–883). For us, the question is whether Leibniz based his metaphysical foundation of the calculus wholly on the concept of the syncategorematic infinite or whether he pursued also an alternative approach of accepting infinitesimals similar to what is done in modern nonstandard analysis.[14]

References

Arthur, R. 2008. "Leery bedfellows: Newton and Leibniz on the status of infinitesimals." In U. Goldenbaum and D. Jesseph (eds.), *Infinitesimal Differences: Controversies between Leibniz and His Contemporaries*. Berlin: de Gruyter, pp. 7–30.

Arthur, R. 2009. "Actual infinitesimals in Leibniz's early thought." In M. Kulstad and M. Laerke (eds.), *The Philosophy of the Young Leibniz*. Stuttgart: Steiner, pp. 11–28.

Arthur, R. 2013. "Leibniz's syncategorematic infinitesimals." *Archive for History of Exact Sciences* 67(5): 553–593.

Arthur, R. 2015. "Leibniz's actual infinite in relation to his analysis of matter." In N. Goethe, P. Beeley, and D. Rabouin (eds.), *G. W. Leibniz, Interrelations between Mathematics and Philosophy*. Dordrecht: Springer, pp. 137–156.

Bascelli, T., P. Błaszczyk, V. Kanovei, K. U. Katz, M. G. Katz, D. M. Schaps, and D. Sherry. 2016. "Leibniz versus Ishiguro: Closing a quarter century of syncategoremania." *HOPOS: The Journal of the International Society for the History of Philosophy of Science* 6 (1): 117–147.

[14] Opposing views are stated in, e.g., Arthur (2013), *Leibniz's syncategorematic infinitesimals*; Sherry and Katz (2012), *Infinitesimals, imaginaries, ideals, and fictions*. Thanks are due to Philip Beeley for his help with a draft of this chapter.

Blåsjö, V. 2012. "The rectification of quadratures as a central foundational problem for the early Leibnizian calculus." *Historia Mathematica* 39: 405–431.

Blåsjö, V. 2016. *Transcendental Curves in the Leibnizian Calculus*. Dissertation. Utrecht University.

Blåsjö, V. 2017. "On what has been called Leibniz's rigorous foundation of infinitesimal geometry by means of Riemannian sums." *Historia Mathematica* 44(2): 134–149.

Bos, H. J. M. 1974. "Differentials, higher-order differentials and the derivative in the Leibnizian calculus." *Archive for History of Exact Sciences* 14(1): 1–90.

Bos, H. J. M. 1978. "The influence of Huygens on the formation of Leibniz' ideas." In *Leibniz à Paris; vol. 1: Les sciences.* Wiesbaden: Steiner, pp. 59–68.

Bos, H. J. M. 1980. "Newton, Leibniz and the Leibnizian tradition." In I. Grattan-Guinness (ed.), *From the Calculus to Set Theory, 1630–1910: An Introductory History.* London: Duckworth, pp. 49–93.

Bos, H. J. M. 1982. "L'élaboration du calcul infinitésimal: Huygens entre Pascal et Leibniz." In R. Taton (ed.), *Huygens et la France.* Paris: Vrin, pp. 115–121.

Bos, H. J. M. 1987. "Fundamental concepts of the Leibnizian calculus." In A. Heinekamp (ed.), *300 Jahre "Nova methodus" von G. W. Leibniz: (1684–1984).* Stuttgart: Steiner, pp. 103–118. Reprinted in 1983 as "The fundamental concepts of the Leibnizian calculus." In H. J. M. Bos (ed.), *Lectures in the history of mathematics.* Providence: American Mathematical Society, pp. 83–99.

Bos, H. J. M. 1988. "Tractional motion and the legitimation of transcendental curves." *Centaurus* 31: 9–62.

Breger, H. 2017. "On the grain of sand and heaven's infinity." In L. von Wenchao et al. (eds.), *'Für unser Glück oder das Glück anderer.' Vorträge des X. Internationalen Leibniz-Kongresses Hannover, 18.–23. Juli 2016,* vol. 6. Hildesheim: Olms, pp. 63–79.

Burscheid, H. J., and H. Struve. 2001. "Die Differentialrechnung nach Leibniz: eine Rekonstruktion." *Studia Leibnitiana* 33(2): 163–193.

Burscheid, H. J., and H. Struve. 2002. "Die Integralrechnung von Leibniz: eine Rekonstruktion." *Studia Leibnitiana* 34(2): 127–160.

Child, J. M. 1920. *The Early Mathematical Manuscripts of Leibniz.* Chicago and London: Open Court (Reprint: Mineola: Dover, 2005).

Ferraro, G. 2000. "True and fictitious quantities in Leibniz's theory of series." *Studia Leibnitiana* 32(1): 21–67.

Ferraro, G. 2001. "Analytical symbols and geometrical figures in eighteenth-century calculus." *Studies in History and Philosophy of Science* 32(3): 535–555.

Gerhardt, C. I. 1876. "Zum zweihundertjährigen Jubiläum der Entdeckung des Algorithmus der höheren Analysis durch Leibniz." *Monatsberichte der Königlich Preußischen Akademie der Wissenschaften 1875*: 595–608.

Goldenbaum, U., and D. Jesseph (eds.). 2008. *Infinitesimal Differences: Controversies between Leibniz and His Contemporaries.* Berlin: de Gruyter.

Guicciardini, N. 2003. "Newtons 'method' and Leibniz' 'calculus.'" In H. N. Jahnke (ed.), *A History of Analysis.* Providence, RI: American Mathematical Society, pp. 73–103.

Hall, A. R. 1980. *Philosophers at War: the Quarrel between Newton and Leibniz.* Cambridge: Cambridge University Press.

Heß, H.-J. 1987. "Zur Vorgeschichte der 'Nova Methodus' 1676–1684." In A. Heinekamp (ed.), *300 Jahre "Nova methodus" von G. W. Leibniz: (1684–1984).* Stuttgart: Steiner, pp. 64–102.

Heß, H.-J. 1991. "Maturing in retirement: The unknown period of the Leibnizian calculus between Paris and publication." In M. Galuzzi (ed.), *Giornate di storia della matematica. Cetraro (Cosenza), Settembre 1988.* Commenda di Rende: EditEl, pp. 247–288.

Heß, H.-J. 2000. "Invention of Infinitesimal calculus." In K. Popp et al. (eds.), *Gottfried Wilhelm Leibniz: the Work of the Great Universal Scholar as Philosopher, Mathematician, Physicist, Engineer*. Hannover: Schlüter, pp. 47–54.

Heß, H.-J. 2001. "Ausbau und Verlust der leibnizschen Führungsposition in der kontinentalen Infinitesimalrechnung." In H. Poser et al. (eds.), *Nihil sine ratione*. Hannover: Gottfried-Wilhelm-Leibniz-Gesellschaft, pp. 502–509.

Heß, H.-J. 2005. "Leibniz auf dem Höhepunkt seines mathematischen Ruhms." *Studia Leibnitiana* 37(1): 48–67.

Hofmann, J. E. 1974. *Leibniz in Paris 1672–1676: His Growth to Mathematical Maturity*. Cambridge: Cambridge University Press (Reprint: 2008).

Huygens, C. 1888–1950. *Oeuvres complètes*. 22 vols. The Hague: Nijhoff.

Jahnke, H. N. (ed.). 2003. *A History of Analysis*. Providence, RI: American Mathematical Society/London Mathematical Society.

Jesseph, D. 2015. "Leibniz on the elimination of infinitesimals." In N. Goethe, P. Beeley, and D. Rabouin (eds.), *G. W. Leibniz, Interrelations between Mathematics and Philosophy*. Dordrecht: Springer, pp. 189–205.

Katz, M. G. and D. Sherry. 2012. "Leibniz's laws of continuity and homogeneity." *Notices of the American Mathematical Society* 59(11): 1550–1558.

Katz, M. G. and D. Sherry. 2013. "Leibniz's infinitesimals: their fictionality, their modern implementations, and their foes from Berkeley to Russell and beyond." *Erkenntnis* 78(3): 571–625.

Knobloch, E. 2002. "Leibniz's rigorous foundation of infinitesimal geometry by means of Riemannian sums." *Synthese* 133: 59–73.

Knobloch, E. 2006. "Beyond Cartesian limits: Leibniz's passage from algebraic to 'transcendental' mathematics." *Historia Mathematica* 33: 113–131.

Knobloch, E. 2008. "Generality and infinitely small quantities in Leibniz's mathematics—The case of his arithmetical quadrature of conic sections and related curves." In U. Goldenbaum and D. Jesseph (eds.), *Infinitesimal Differences: Controversies between Leibniz and His Contemporaries*. Berlin: Walter de Gruyter, pp. 171–184.

Krömer, R. 2006. "Johann Bernoullis problema alterum von 1697 und die Lösungen von Leibniz, Newton und anderen." In H. Breger, J. Herbst, and S. Erdner (eds.), *Einheit in der Vielheit*. Hannover: Gottfried-Wilhelm-Leibniz-Gesellschaft, pp. 398–405.

Levey, S. 2008. "Archimedes, infinitesimals and the law of continuity: On Leibniz's fictionalism." In U. Goldenbaum and D. Jesseph (eds.), *Infinitesimal differences: Controversies between Leibniz and his Contemporaries*. Berlin: de Gruyter, pp. 107–133.

Mayer, U. 2006. "Mündliche Kommunikation und schriftliche Überlieferung: die Gesprächsaufzeichnungen von Leibniz und Tschirnhaus zur Infinitesimalrechnung aus der Pariser Zeit." In H. Breger, J. Herbst, and S. Erdner (eds.), *Einheit in der Vielheit*. Hannover: Gottfried-Wilhelm-Leibniz-Gesellschaft, pp. 588–594.

Nauenberg, M. 2010. "The early application of the calculus to the inverse square force problem." *Archive for History of Exact Sciences* 64: 269–300.

Probst, S. 2006. "Differenzen, Folgen und Reihen bei Leibniz (1672–1676)." In M. Hyksŏva and U. Reich (eds.), *Wanderschaft in der Mathematik*. Augsburg: Rauner, pp. 164–173.

Probst, S. 2006. "Zur Datierung von Leibniz' Entdeckung der Kreisreihe." In H. Breger, J. Herbst, and S. Erdner (eds.), *Einheit in der Vielheit*. Hannover: Gottfried-Wilhelm-Leibniz-Gesellschaft, pp. 813–817.

Probst, S. 2008. "Indivisibles and infinitesimals in early mathematical texts of Leibniz." In U. Goldenbaum and D. Jesseph (eds.), *Infinitesimal Differences: Controversies between Leibniz and His Contemporaries*. Berlin: Walter de Gruyter, pp. 95–106.

Probst, S. 2015. "Leibniz as reader and second inventor: The cases of Barrow and Mengoli." In N. B. Goethe, P. Beeley, and D. Rabouin (eds.), *G. W. Leibniz, Interrelations between Mathematics and Philosophy*. Dordrecht: Springer, pp. 111–134.

Rabouin, D. 2015. "Leibniz's rigorous foundations of the method of indivisibles: or how to reason with impossible notions." In V. Jullien (ed.), *Seventeenth-century indivisibles revisited*. Cham: Birkhäuser, pp. 347–364.

Renteln, M. von. 2006. "Leibniz' Publikation über Enveloppen (AE 1694) als Ausgangspunkt für die Theorie der singulären Lösungen bei Differentialgleichungen." In H. Breger, J. Herbst, and S. Erdner (eds.), *Einheit in der Vielheit*. Hannover: Gottfried-Wilhelm-Leibniz-Gesellschaft, pp. 836–844.

Roero, C. S. 2005. "Gottfried Wilhelm Leibniz: First three papers on the calculus (1684, 1686, 1693)." In I. Grattan-Guinness (ed.), *Landmark Writings in Western Mathematics: 1640–1940*. Amsterdam: Elsevier, pp. 46–58.

Roero, C. S. 2006. "Johann Bernoulli's and Leibniz's solutions to the 1703 problem on the transformation of algebraic curves." In H. Breger, J. Herbst, and S. Erdner (eds.), *Einheit in der Vielheit*. Hannover: Gottfried-Wilhelm-Leibniz-Gesellschaft, pp. 848–855.

Scriba, C. J. 1964. "The inverse method of tangents: A dialogue between Leibniz and Newton (1675–1677)." *Archive for History of Exact Sciences* 2: 113–137.

Sefrin-Weis, H. 2006. "Leibniz and the brachystochrone." In H. Breger, J. Herbst, and S. Erdner (eds.), *Einheit in der Vielheit*. Hannover: Gottfried-Wilhelm-Leibniz-Gesellschaft, pp. 964–971.

Sherry, D., and M. G. Katz. 2012. "Infinitesimals, imaginaries, ideals, and fictions." *Studia Leibnitiana* 44(2): 166–192.

Sonar, T. 2016. *Die Geschichte des Prioritätsstreits zwischen Leibniz und Newton*. Berlin: Springer.

Struve, H., and I. Witzke. 2008. "Eine wissenschaftstheoretische Analyse des Leibniz'schen calculus: das Beispiel des Krümmungsradius." *Studia Leibnitiana* 40(1): 29–47.

Tho, T. 2011. *Leibniz's Laboratory of Concepts: The Status and Structure of Infinitesimals as Metaphysical Laboratory*. Dissertation. University of Georgia, Athens.

Tournès, D. 2003. "L' intégration graphique des équations différentielles ordinaires," *Historia Mathematica* 30: 457–493.

Wahl, C. 2016. "'Ich schätze Freunde mehr als mathematische Entdeckungen': zum Prioritätsstreit zwischen Leibniz und Newton." In M. Kempe (ed.), *1716—Leibniz' letztes Lebensjahr: Unbekanntes zu einem bekannten Universalgelehrten*. Hannover: Gottfried Wilhelm Leibniz Bibliothek, pp. 111–143.

Witzke, I. 2008. "Leibniz and the radius of curvature: A case study for mathematical development." In I. Witzke (ed.), *Mathematical Practice & Development throughout History: 18th Novembertagung on the History, Philosophy & Didactics of Mathematics*. Berlin: Logos, pp. 41–65.

Witzke, I. 2009. *Die Entwicklung des Leibnizschen Calculus: eine Fallstudie zur Theorieentwicklung in der Mathematik*. Hildesheim: Franzbecker.

Youschkevitch, A. P. 1978. "Comparaison des conceptions de Leibniz et de Newton sur le calcul infinitésimal." In *Leibniz à Paris; vol. 1: Les sciences*. Wiesbaden: Steiner, pp. 69–80.

CHAPTER 12

··

DETERMINANT THEORY, SYMMETRIC FUNCTIONS, AND DYADIC

EBERHARD KNOBLOCH

··

DETERMINANT THEORY

··

The Fundamental Ideas

Leibniz's great interest in determinants was directly connected with his paramount interest in three disciplines that he spent his entire life trying to perfect and organize: the *ars characteristica*, that is, the art of inventing suitable characters and signs; the *ars combinatoria*, that is, the art of forms or of similar and dissimilar (A III, 2, 449); the *ars inveniendi*, that is, the art of inventing new theorems, new results, new methods.

These arts are strongly correlated with each other. The combinatorial art, being by far more than combinatorics in the strict sense of the word, teaches how to combine signs and characters. As a general science, it comprehended algebra. The art of inventing suitable signs supports the art of inventing that was the main aim of all Leibnizian scientific, especially mathematical, activities.

There are two important, famous examples for the usefulness and success of Leibniz's invention of suitable signs in order to foster mathematical development: the differential and integral calculus, and determinant theory. The second example is the subject that will be dealt with in the following section. What did the three arts contribute to the determinant theory? The art of inventing suitable characters led to numerical double indices. The combinatorial art helped to represent a determinant as a sum.

In order to avoid any misunderstanding, it might be useful to remember the modern definition of a determinant: Let A be a square matrix of order n, d(A) its determinant:

$$d(A) := \Sigma \, \text{sign}(s) a_{1s(1)} \ldots a_{ns(n)}$$

the sum is taken over all $s \in S_n$

In other words: Let be given n^2 numerical elements arranged in n rows and n columns. Their determinant consists of $1.2.3 \ldots n = n!$ terms of a sum. Every such term consists of n factors whereby always exactly one element is taken from one row and one column. The sign is calculated according to a certain sign rule.

Thanks to the art of inventing, Leibniz became the founder of determinant theory. It was intensely elaborated and investigated during the eighteenth and nineteenth centuries, especially because of its useful applications to physics. In fact, the literature on the history of science mentions a variety of different authors as the founders of that theory, depending on what criteria were employed to justify the choice: Gauss (who coined the name *determinans* [namely, numerus]), Cauchy (who derived a system of theorems to form a new mathematical discipline), Cayley (who introduced symbols, the vertical determinant lines or rules), Weierstrass (who established the axiomatic approach: the determinant is a linear, alternating, normal mapping), and so on (Knobloch 1994).

Apart from those of Weierstrass, Leibniz had already met all these criteria in full (Knobloch 2000, 58): he talked about *resultans* (namely, *aequatio*); he formulated a series of general theorems concerning the combinatorial aggregates, which he called "resultants," without however proving them; he invented symbols for the resultants and used a very clever subscript notation that was capable of being generalized; he discovered important results in the theory of systems of linear equations and elimination theory, which he expressed in the language of determinants.

In a deliberate departure from the tradition of Viète, Leibniz used fictitious numbers as simple, double, and multiple subscripts, since numbers have a threefold advantage: they can be checked at any stage of the calculation; they can express the various arrangements, orders, positions, and relationships between the quantities and characters; and they serve mathematical progress since they allow us to recognize laws of formation and harmonics.

In January 1675, he explicitly emphasized the greatest advantage of his method, that is, to use numbers without using a numerical calculation (A VII, 1, 530). He invented well over fifty different notations for algebraic and differential equations. A larger selection of these notations is explained in Knobloch (1982 and 2010). Only three particularly important descriptions can be included here.

From June 1678 at the latest, he used double indices for systems of linear equations:

$$10 + 11x + 12y = 0, \; 20 + 21x + 22y = 0$$

where today we write: $a_{10} + a_{11}x + a_{12}y = 0, a_{20} + a_{21}x + a_{22}y = 0$.

The numbers on the left indicate that they relate to the equation, those on the right to the variables. This index notation was used by him in his letter to the

Marquis de l'Hospital dated May 8, 1693, which was published in 1850 for the first time (GM II, 236–241). Leibniz himself never published this index notation during his lifetime. This is not true of the way of writing several polynomials with a common unknown:

$$10x^2 + 11x + 12,\; 20x^2 + 21x + 22 \text{ or } 10 + 11y + 12y^2,\; 20 + 21y + 22y^2,$$

where today we write

$$a_{10}x^2 + a_{11}x + a_{12},\; a_{20}x^2 + a_{21}x + a_{22} \text{ or } a_{10} + a_{11}y + a_{12}y^2,\; a_{20} + a_{21}y + a_{22}y^2.$$

The numbers on the left again refer to the equation, while those on the right either, together with the exponents of the related variable power, give the degree of the polynomial or agree with the exponent of the variable power. The first possibility was published by him in 1700 and in 1710 (GM V, 340–349; GM VII, 218–223). Apart from Charles Reyneau in 1708 and by Karl Friedrich Hindenburg from 1779 onward (Knobloch 2000, 57) nobody paid attention to Leibniz's explanations in this respect.

In the most important study on systems of linear equations of January 22, 1684, Leibniz developed a shorthand on the basis of the solutions or results he had obtained (Knobloch 1972). His procedure might be described as follows:

$$10 + 11a = 0,\; 20 + 21a = 0.$$

In order to eliminate a, the first equation is multiplied by 21, the second equation by -11. The sum of the two multiplied equations is

$$\frac{10.21}{-11.20} = 0$$

The rising (equation) numbers on the left do not change their order. They can be written smaller:

$$\frac{10.21}{-11.20} = 0$$

or they can be even left out since they can be added again at any time:

$$\frac{+0.1}{-1.0} = 0$$

and eventually $\overline{0.1} = 0$

Leibniz's notation $\overline{0.1}$ is equivalent to the modern term $\begin{vmatrix} 10 & 20 \\ 11 & 21 \end{vmatrix}$. In other words, Leibniz represents a determinant by the product of the elements of its main diagonal and that for up to five-row determinants. In principle $\overline{1.2.3...n}$ denotes the same system of coefficients as

$$\begin{vmatrix} a_{11} & \cdots & a_{1n} \\ \cdot & & \cdot \\ \cdot & & \cdot \\ a_{n1} & \cdots & a_{nn} \end{vmatrix}$$

When Leibniz calculated the resultant of n + 1 equations with n unknowns, his horizontal lines had to be modified accordingly. His equation

$$\overline{0.1.22} - \overline{0.2.21} + \overline{1.2.20} = 0$$

results from a development of a three-row determinant $\overline{0.1.2}$ after the second row. In the two-row determinants $\overline{0.1}, \overline{0.2},$ and $\overline{1.2},$ those numbers on the left that do not appear in the right-hand factor 22, 21, and 20 need to be added in their natural order in the solution. Now $\overline{0.1},$ for example, stands for $10.31 - 30.11.$

Leibniz talked about an "aequatio resultativa," "aequatio resultans," or simply "resultans," just as Etienne Bézout in 1764 spoke of "équations résultantes," terminology that Laplace, Binet, and Cauchy followed later on (Bézout 1764).

Inhomogeneous Systems of Linear Equations: Motivation, Rules of Signs, General Theorems

Motivation

Why was Leibniz so interested in determinants? Leibniz was convinced that the quintic equation can be algorithmically solved. His calculations led him to believe that the problem could be reduced to the solution of systems of linear equations (Knobloch 2006, 115).

Rules of Sign

At present, we know six sign rules formulated by Leibniz for the terms of determinants after June 1678. But the first four were derived from special examples, they could not be generalized. Only on January 12 (O.S.) (22 [N.S.]), 1684, he solved the sign problem in the study *De sublatione literarum ex aequationibus seu de reductione plurium aequationum ad unam* (On the elimination of letters from equations or on the reduction of several equations to one equation) (Knobloch 1972). On the margin of the manuscript he added this remark: "In this attempt I solved the problem, whereas earlier I always got stuck at some point. What is done here is an eminent example of the combinatorial art."

First of all, he formulated a recursion rule (Knobloch 1972, 176): "Two terms that differ from each other only by two corresponding coefficients (so that *nm kl* is replaced by *nl km*) of the same two equations have opposite signs." It is worth mentioning that in 1729 MacLaurin gave exactly the same rule (MacLaurin 1748, 81–85): "Opposite signs are assigned to combinations which contain the products of two opposite coefficients."

Moreover, Leibniz himself communicated a complicated version of this recursion rule to L'Hospital on April 28 (O.S.) (May 8 [N.S.]), 1693 (GM II, 240): "Eae combinationes opposita habent signa, si in eodem aequationis prodeuntis latere ponantur, quae habent tot coefficientes communes, quot sunt unitates in numero quantitatum tollendarum unitate minuto; caetera habent eadem signa." (Those combinations have opposite signs provided that they are set on the same side of the resulting equation, which have as many common coefficients as there are units in the number of quantities that have to be eliminated, whereby this number was diminished by one. The others have the same signs.)

If there are (n + 1) equations, n unknowns, it is a matter of (n - 1) common coefficients or of two different factors. In other words, Leibniz consciously concealed his knowledge by communicating an unnecessarily complicated version of the recursion rule.

Nearly immediately after the recursion rule, Leibniz writes down the general, correct sign rule (Knobloch 1972, 176-177): "Two terms that differ from each other only by an odd number of transpositions of left or right figures have opposite signs. Those that differ from each other by an even number have the same sign."

This sign rule is indeed equivalent with the rule given by Gabriel Cramer in 1750 (Cramer 1750, 658): "Qu'on compte, pour chaque terme, le nombre des dérangements: s'il est pair ou nul, le terme aura le même signe +; s'il est impair, le terme aura le signe -." (One has to count, for every term, the number of inversions: if it is even or zero, the term will have the same sign +; if it is odd, the term will have the sign -.)

While Leibniz used the notion of transposition, Cramer used the notion of inversion. A permutation is called even or odd if it contains an even or odd number of inversions, respectively. Now, a permutation is even or odd if and only if it can be generated by an even or odd number of transpositions that in general is smaller than that of its inversions. In other words, Leibniz's last sign rule and Cramer's rule are equivalent.

General Theorems

Without demonstrating them, Leibniz added three general theorems in this decisive paper dated the end of May 1684 (Knobloch 1972):

(1) Diagonalizing around the main diagonal

The same laws of arrangement and signs result if one uses the left-hand numbers 1, 2, 3, and so on instead of the right-hand numbers, and instead of 0, 1, 2, 3 the numbers 1, 2, 3, 4. In modern terms: for the formation of the determinant the rows and columns of the matrix A are interchangeable.

(2) Interchanging rows or columns

If we interchange two rows (columns), then the value of the determinant changes its sign. If we bring the rows 1, 2, . . ., n (columns) of A into a sequence $k_1, k_2, \ldots, k_n$, then the determinant is multiplied by the sign of this permutation:

$$\overline{2.1.3} = -\overline{1.2.3}, \; \overline{3.1.2} = \overline{1.2.3}$$

(3) Expanding determinants according to Laplace:

The equation $\overline{0.1.2.3} = 0$ can be written in the following four ways:

$$\overline{0.1.2.}^{4}3 - \overline{0.1.3.}^{4}2 + \overline{0.2.3.}^{4}1 - \overline{1.2.3.}^{4}0 = 0$$

$$\overline{0.1.2.}^{3}3 - \overline{0.1.3.}^{3}2 + \overline{0.2.3.}^{3}1 - \overline{1.2.3.}^{3}1 = 0$$

$$\overline{0.1.2.}^{2}3 - \overline{0.1.3.}^{2}2 + \overline{0.2.3.}^{2}1 - \overline{1.2.3.}^{2}0 = 0$$

$$\overline{0.1.2.}^{1}3 - \overline{0.1.3.}^{1}2 + \overline{0.2.3.}^{1}1 - \overline{1.2.3.}^{1}0 = 0$$

Leibniz started with the system of four (n) linear equations:

$$10 + 11a + 12b + 13c = 0,$$
$$20 + 21a + 22b + 23c = 0,$$
$$30 + 31a + 32b + 33c = 0,$$
$$40 + 41a + 42b + 43c = 0.$$

He expanded the resultant according to the coefficients of the fourth, third, second, and first rows. His determinants $\overline{0.1.2}$, $\overline{0.1.3}$, and so on are minors $d_{ik}(A)$ of (n - 1)th order, but no adjoints. In modern terms we get:

$$\det(A) = d_{i3}(A)a_{i3} - d_{i2}(A)a_{i2} + d_{i1}(A)a_{i1} - d_{i0}(A)a_{i0}, \; i = 1,2,3,4.$$

The minors $d_{ik}(A)$ are not multiplied by $(-1)^{i+k-1}$, that is, Leibniz did not introduce adjoints. The exponent reads (i + k – 1) instead of (i + k) because Leibniz began the indexation with 0. Provided that Leibniz expanded the determinant according to the (4 – i)th row, i = 0, 1, 2, 3, the value of the determinant is multiplied by $(-1)^{i}$. This difference between his own expansion and that according to Laplace's expansion does not matter in the case of resultants because the resultant must be equal to zero.

Elimination of a Common Variable

Another important application of Leibniz's determinant theory concerned the resultant of two polynomials from the ring R[x] of polynomials with coefficients in an integral domain R and the elimination of a common unknown from algebraic equations with two and more variables. He thus anticipated methods and results that were attributed to James Joseph Sylvester, Etienne Bézout, and Leonhard Euler later on.

Sylvester's Dialytic Method

In the years 1679–1681, Leibniz explained in the essay *De tollendis incognitis* (On the elimination of unknowns) (Knobloch 1980, n. 36) how the two initial equations

$$a + bx + cx^2 + dx^3 + ex^4 \text{etc.} = 0,$$
$$1 + mx + nx^2 + px^3 + qx^4 \text{etc.} = 0$$

can be multiplied by gradually increasing powers of x. If we set the coefficient determinant

$$\begin{vmatrix} a & b & c & d & e & . & . & . \\ . & a & b & c & d & e & . & . \\ . & . & a & b & c & d & e & . \\ . & . & . & a & b & c & d & e \\ 1 & m & n & p & q & . & . & . \\ . & 1 & m & n & p & q & . & . \\ . & . & 1 & m & n & p & q & . \\ . & . & . & 1 & m & n & p & q \end{vmatrix}$$

to zero, then we obtain the so-called Sylvester determinant and thus the resultant of the two polynomials. The English mathematician Sylvester published this solution in 1840. Later on, it became known as the "dialytic method" (Sylvester 1840).

Bézout's Method and Euler's Second Method

Around 1683/84, Leibniz in several studies developed a method of reducing the problem of calculating resultants to the solution of a system of algebraic equations that he was already able to determine in an elegant fashion at that time: "Let two polynomials of e-th and f-th degree be given, then these are multiplied together with auxiliary polynomials of the (f - 1)-th and (e - 1)-th degree, respectively. The product polynomials are added and the coefficients of each power of the unknowns are set equal to zero. One gets a system of linear equations that is a sufficient number of equations to determine the auxiliary variables" (Knobloch 1980, ns. 16, 50, 54).

This rule was formulated by Leibniz in its complete general form. The procedure appears in Euler (1766) and Bézout (1767).

Rules of Formation and Sign Rule of the Resultant

Around 1692/93 Leibniz had found the most important dimensional and homogeneity properties of the resultant. Two essays are especially interesting in this respect: *De tollendis literis* (On the elimination of unknowns) and *De tollenda litera ex duabus aequationibus* (On the elimination of an unknown from two equations) (Knobloch 1980, ns. 54, 56):

Let two polynomials of e-th and f-th degree be given. The resultant will have the following properties:

(1) It is homogeneous of degree f in the coefficients of the first polynomial and of degree e in the coefficients of the second polynomial (law of
homogeneity).
(2) Each of its terms consists of e + f factors.
(3) The sum of the right-hand subscripts is ef.

Leibniz's Explication Theory—Euler's First Method

Around 1693/94, Leibniz developed a type of "explication theory" of the resultant calculation (Knobloch 1974), that was explained and used by Euler in three publications
(Euler 1748, vol. 2, 269; 1750; 1766).

Let two polynomials be given:

$$10x^3 + 11x^2 + 12x + 13 = 0,$$
$$20x^3 + 21x^2 + 22x + 23 = 0.$$

Using twice a crosswise multiplication and subtraction procedure, Leibniz produced
two equations of second degree:

$$10.23x^2 + 11.23x + 12.23 = 0, \quad 10.21x^2 + 10.22x + 10.23 = 0,$$
$$-13.20 \quad -13.21 \quad -13.22 \qquad -11.20 \quad -12.20 \quad -13.20$$
$$\text{or } (10)x^2 + (11)x + (12) = 0, \quad (20)x^2 + (21)x + (22) = 0.$$

The coefficients within brackets are "explicated" by the differences between the products,
for example: 20 is explicated by 10.21 – 11.20, 21 is explicated by 10.22 – 12.20, and so on.

This procedure has to be repeated until the elimination of x from two linear
equations yields the resultant. The degree of the resultant is of course too high
this way. Yet Leibniz became interested in the law of formation of the terms
produced by repeated explications. By concentrating his efforts on the explication of the coefficient of the second equation he elaborated a "dichotomic tree,"
as he called it:

and so on.

If these substitutions (explications) are really carried out, one gets:

20,

$10.21 - 11.20,$

$10^2.22 - 10.12.20 - 10.11.21 + 11^2.20.$

$10^3.23 - 10^2.13.20 - 10^2.12.21 + 10.11.12.20 - 10^2.11.22 + 10.11.12.20 + 10.11^2.21 - 11^3.20$

In order to inquire into the structure of these rows, Leibniz denoted certain domains, that is, the second half of all terms of a row by A, the second quarter of all terms of a row by B, the second eighth of all terms of a row by C, and so on.

The capitals within brackets like (A), (B), (C) denote the sequence of first terms of a sequence of further bisections:

(A) means: we have to consider the second half (the domain). Then we have to take the first term of the second half, the first term of the second quarter, the first term of the second eighth, etc.

(B) AB means: we have to consider the second quarter of the second half of the second quarter (the domain). There we have to take the first term of the second half, the first term of the second quarter, etc.

Let us consider the aforementioned fourth row as an example. We are looking for the sequence (A):

A denotes the second half of the row that is $-10^2.11.22 + 10.11.12.20 + 10.11^2.21 - 11^3.20$.

The first term of the second half of this partial row is $10.11^2.21$.

The first term of the second quarter of this partial row is $10.11.12.20$. There is only one term. There are no further possible bisections. Hence we get: (A) = $10.11^2.21 + 10.11.12.20$.

Leibniz did not mention a non-trivial theorem that is obviously true: Any permutation of the letters of such a combination of letters leads to the same sum.

For example: (A)BB = (B)AB = (B)BA, and so on. The brackets do not matter. It is worth mentioning, however, that Leibniz deduced thirty-four corollaries regarding the formation of the terms of a row and their relations with each other.

SYMMETRIC FUNCTIONS

Motivation

Why was Leibniz so interested in symmetric functions? He inevitably came across them when he tried to solve algebraic equations of higher degree. Like his contemporaries, Leibniz was convinced that such equations could be algorithmically solved. At the end of May or the beginning of June 1678, he wrote to his friend Ehrenfried Walther von Tschirnhaus (A III, 2, 428): "Observaveram jam olim et fortasse primus radices irrationales altiores exemplo Cardanicarum inveniri posse." (Already long ago I had observed and maybe as the first that the higher irrational roots can be found according to the example of the Cardanic [roots].) In other words, Leibniz generalized the Cardanic approach by using a "section of the root" (*sectio radicis*), that is, he represented the root being sought as a sum of terms.

In about 1680/82 he wrote (Leibniz 1976, 201): "Assumo jam instar hypotheseos, quod radix quaesita aequationis x, sit polynomium, seu x = l + m etc. quae l, m, etc. sunt quantitates irrationales, posito aequationem carere termino secundo." (I assume just as a hypothesis, that the sought root x of the equation is a polynomium or x = l + m etc. These l, m, etc. are irrational quantities on condition that the second term of the equation is lacking.)

If the equation reads

$$x^n + qx^{n-1} + \ldots + t = 0$$

$$x = a + b + c + \ldots$$

there are n − 1 terms of the sum.

Hence Leibniz had to calculate the different powers of x thus dealing with expressions like

$$y = ab + ac + bc + \text{etc.} =: \underset{..}{ab}, \quad z = abc + abd + bcd + \text{etc.} =: \underset{..}{abc}, \quad \omega$$
$$= abcd + abde + \text{etc.} =: \underset{..}{abcd}$$

and so on. These are the elementary symmetric functions or "formae simplices." The two dots under a term indicate that it represents a symmetric function.

$$f = a^n + b^n + c^n \text{etc.} =: \underset{.}{a^n}:$$

These are the power sums or "potentiae combinatoriae Polynomiorum."

$$g = \underset{.}{a^n b^n}, \quad h = \underset{.}{a^n b^n c^n} \text{etc.}:$$

These are the multiform symmetric functions.

The third power of x = a + b + c reads in this notation:

$$x^3 = \underset{.}{a^3} + 3\underset{..}{a^2 b} + 6\underset{...}{abc} = \left(a^3 + b^3 + c^3\right) + 3\left(a^2 b + ab^2 + a^2 c + ac^2 + b^2 c + bc^2\right) + 6abc.$$

In general a function is called symmetric if the permutation of two variables leads to the same expression. For example, x = a + b is a symmetric function; x = a − b is not.

Tables for the Numbers of Terms in Any Symmetric Function

Around 1677/1680, he wrote in the treatise *De formis omnibus ad solas formas simplices reducendis deque aequationum radicibus novissima methodus* (On the reduction of all symmetric functions to exclusively elementary symmetric functions and a newest method of regarding the roots of equations) (Leibniz 1976, 55): "Usus formarum praeter pulchritudinem et generalitatem contemplationis in eo consistit, ut ope earum inveniamus radicem generalem aequationis affectae cujuscunque gradus." (Apart from the beauty and generality of the idea, the use of symmetric functions consists in finding the general root of a nonpure equation of an arbitrary degree.)

To that end, Leibniz had to find out the number of terms of a symmetric polynomial.

Let $l^h m^r n^s \ldots$ be a symmetric polynomial, $p = h + r + s + \ldots$ its degree, k the number of variables of a single term, v the number of admitted variables, d the number of pairwise different exponents.

What is interesting here is the number k of variables that enter a single term of the function. It does not matter whether the exponents are small or great. Only the frequency of their occurrence matters, only the type of their repetition in order to calculate the number of terms of a certain symmetric function.

The symmetric functions $l^4 m^4 n^3 o$ or $l^3 m^2 n o$ belong to the same type of repetition: one exponent (4 or 1, respectively) occurs exactly twice, two exponents occur once at a time (3, 1 or 3, 2, respectively). Such a type of repetition can be described by means of a number-theoretical partition of k (the number of variables of a single term), as follows.

In our case $k = 4$ or $4 = 2 + 1 + 1 = 2.1 + 1.2 = 2r_2 + 1r_1$

Hence there are three steps:

(1) Consider the different exponents.
(2) Determine the frequency of their occurrence.
(3) Describe the type of repetition by a (number-theoretical) partition.

Let $l^3 m^3 n^2 o^2 p$ be given as an example. Hence $k = 5$; let v be 6.

(1) There are $\binom{6}{5}$ possibilities to select a combination of five elements.
(2) Every such combination like lmnop admits $\binom{5}{2}$ terms of the type $l^3 m^3 nop$. In the whole there are $6.10 = 60$ such terms.
(3) Every such term $l^3 m^3 nop$ admits $\binom{3}{2}$ terms of the type $l^3 m^3 n^2 o^2 p$. In the whole there are $60.3 = 180$ such terms.

Between May 1677 and May 1678, Leibniz elaborated a table for the numbers of terms in any symmetric function. At the very beginning, he emphasized its usefulness (Knobloch 1973, table after p. 248): "Numerus terminorum in qualibet forma specimen est artis combinatoriae sed usum praeterea habet maximum ad multiplicationes formarum in se invicem compendio faciendas." (The number of terms in an arbitrary symmetric function is an example of the combinatorial art, but moreover it is extremely useful in order to multiply symmetric functions by each other in a shortened way.)

Step by step, the rows refer to the different types of repetition of combinations consisting of one, two, three, four, and so on elements, while the columns refer to the number of admitted variables (one, two, three, four etc.). The example $l^3m^3n^2o^2p$ considered here belongs to the same type of repetition as $l^3m^2n^2op$. The sixteenth row ($l^3m^2n^2op$) reveals 180 (our result) in the sixth column ($v = 6$):

The type of repetition in question can be described as follows. $k = 5 = 1 + 2 + 2 = 1.1 + 2.2 = 1r_1 + 2r_2$. There are $d = r_1 + r_2 = 3$ pairwise different exponents. Now the general solution of the general case can be deduced:

$$k = k_1 + \ldots + k_{r_1} + k_{r_1+1} + \ldots + k_{r_1+r_2} + \ldots + k_{r_1+r_2+\ldots r_k}$$
$$= 1 + \ldots + 1 + 2 + \ldots + 2 + \ldots + k =$$

r_1 times r_2 times r_k times
$$= 1r_1 + 2r_2 + \ldots + kr_k$$

If r_k should occur, it must be equal to 1; all the other r_i must be equal to 0.

Let $r_1 + r_2 + \ldots + r_k = d$ be the number of pairwise different exponents, M the number of terms sought, $k = v$:

$$M = \binom{k}{k_1}\binom{k-k_1}{k_2}\binom{k-k_1-k_2}{k_3}\cdots\binom{k-k_1-k_2-\ldots-k_{d-1}}{k_d} =$$
$$= \frac{k!}{k_1!(k-k_1)!}\cdot\frac{(k-k_1)!}{k_2!(k-k_1-k_2)!}\cdots\frac{(k-k_1-k_2-\ldots-k_{d-1})!}{k_d!(k-k_1-k_2-\ldots-k_{d-1}-k_d)!} = \frac{k!}{k_1!k_2!\ldots k_d!} =$$
$$= \frac{k!}{(1!)^{r_1}(2!)^{r_2}\ldots(k!)^{r_k}}$$

according to the frequencies of 1, 2, ..., k, respectively. If v should be larger than k, M has still to be multiplied by $\binom{v}{k}$. This result admits an important interpretation: M is the number of partitions of k objects into d classes $S_1, \ldots, S_d$ that contain $k_1, \ldots, k_d$ objects.

Remark 1: The order of the classes matters even if they contain the same number of elements. It matters whether l, m or n, o have the exponent 2 or 3: $l^3m^3n^2o^2p$ is unequal to $l^2m^2n^3o^3p$. Yet both terms represent the same type of repetition $k = 5 = 1.1 + 2.2$. The different exponents individualize the classes. They are distinguishable, so to speak, by different colors.

Remark 2: If only the number of classes and their contents matter, M has still to be multiplied by $\dfrac{1}{r_1!r_2!...r_k!}$, whereby the r_i are the numbers of classes of equal size. The following example might help to clarify the situation. Four objects l, m, n, o have to be put into three classes; no class must remain empty. There is only one type of partition: $4 = 1 + 1 + 2$. We get six possibilities: $l\,|n|mo$, $l|o|mn$, $m|n|lo$, $m|o|ln$, $l|m|no$, $n|o|lm$; $m|l|no$ is no new possibility because the order of the classes does not matter. Hence $S_k^d = S_4^3 = 6$. Such numbers are called Stirling's numbers of second kind.

But if we seek the number of terms of the symmetric function represented by l^3m^2no ($v = k$ and $k = 1.2 + 2.1$), there are twelve instead of six terms. We shall come back to this question later on.

The Multiplication Tables for Symmetric Functions

Leibniz's method of looking for the algorithmic solution of algebraic equations made the multiplication of symmetric functions necessary. As we have seen, he used his table for the number of terms in any symmetric function to construct multiplication tables. Hence, in 1677 he explicitly said (Leibniz 1976, 180): "Continuanda inquisitio de multiplicationibus formarum quia in materia resolutionis aequationum primaria est." (The investigation of the multiplication of symmetric functions must be continued because it is of highest importance for the solution of equations.)

He explains his multiplication method in his letter to Tschirnhaus dated the end of May or the beginning of June 1678 (A III, 2, 435, 441). Let us assume that we have to multiply l^2m by lm on condition that there are four variables l, m, n, o. There are three steps:

(1) All terms of one symmetric function have to multiplied by one term of the other function. The table for the number of terms of any symmetric function shows which of the two functions has fewer terms than the other in view of the presupposed condition: l^2m has twelve, lm has six terms. Hence it is reasonable to enumerate the six terms of lm which are multiplied by l^2m:lm ln lo mn mo no l^2m l^3m^2 l^3mn l^3mo l^2m^2n m^2n^2o l^2mno

(2) One realizes that there are repetitions. For example, the terms l^3mn, l^3mo or the terms l^2m^2n, l^2m^2o represent the same function, respectively. Yet only those terms have to be enumerated that have different relations with l^2m, that is:

$$lm \quad ln \qquad mn \qquad no$$

The others are taken into account by a later multiplication of the coefficients.

(3) The products are multiplied by coefficients consisting of apparent fractions. In reality the denominator is always a factor of the numerator. The numerator is the number of terms of the multiplier l^2m, in our case 12. The denominator is the number of terms of the product, in our case three times 12 and once 4. Hence we get the coefficients:

$$\frac{12}{12} \ \frac{24}{12} \ \frac{24}{12} \ \frac{12}{4}$$

or $l^3m^2 + 2l^3mn + 2l^2m^2n + 3l^2mno$

The Fundamental Theorem of the Theory of Symmetric Functions

Within the area of symmetric functions, the elementary symmetric functions behave like the prime numbers within the ring of integers. This matter of fact is expressed by the fundamental theorem of the theory of symmetric functions. Leibniz had already gained this insight and dealt with this subject in many manuscripts. The title of some of these manuscripts made this clear, as in the case of the manuscript cited earlier that dated from about 1677/1680: "On the reduction of all symmetric functions to exclusively elementary symmetric functions etc." In this manuscript, he avows (Leibniz 1976, 54): "Cum ergo tam paucae sint formae simplices si compositis comparentur, patet magnum calculi circa formas compendium fore, si compositas omnes ad simplices reducere possimus. Id vero succedere posse spes magna est." (Thus because there are so few elementary symmetric functions compared with composite, it is clear that there will be a considerable abbreviation of calculation regarding the symmetric functions, if we can reduce all composite to elementary. But there is a big hope that this can happen.)

Leibniz still expresses a hope. In another manuscript dated June 4, 1678, he already realizes (Leibniz 1976, 85): "Fundamentum hujus calculi sumitur ex tabula formarum in se invicem ductarum, modum autem probandi per numeros, sumsimus ex tabula exemplorum cujuscunque formae, ponendo quodlibet exemplum 1. Hinc patet posse omnes formas resolvi in x, y, z, ω et ex his facta." (The foundation of this calculation is taken from the table of symmetric functions that are multiplied by each other. But we took the way of proving by numbers from the table of terms of an arbitrary symmetric function putting every term equal to 1. As a consequence it is clear that all symmetric functions can be reduced to x, y, z, ω and to their products.)

In other words, Leibniz formulated the fundamental theorem of the theory of symmetric functions without proving it. He just expressed a research program. It did not happen by chance that he dated this manuscript. He was well aware of the importance of his discovery. About two years later he elaborated his study *Formarum reductio ad simplices* (The reduction of symmetric functions to elementary symmetric functions).

There, he systematically and recursively calculated such reductions of certain groups of symmetric functions:

$$a^3b^20 = xyz - 1yxx + 3zx - 0\delta - 3xz + 0yy$$
$$a^3b^21 = yyx - 2zxx + 5\delta x - 5\varepsilon - 3yz + 2zy$$
$$a^3b^2c = zyx - 3\delta xx + 7\varepsilon x - 12\theta - 3zz + 4\delta y$$
$$a^3b^2cd = \delta yx - 4\varepsilon xx + 9\theta x - 21\lambda - 3\delta z + 6\varepsilon y$$

The order reveals the rule of formation for such a group of functions. Leibniz ends by saying (Leibniz 1976, 191): "Perficiendus est hic calculus, mira enim compendia, et omnino totius algebrae clavem continet." (This calculation has to be perfected because it contains wonderful abbreviations and the key to the whole of algebra.)

Girard's Formula

Leibniz saw a strong parallelism between the powers of polynomials and power sums or combinatorial powers (*potentiae combinatoriae polynomiorum*), as he called them (Leibniz 1976, 200): If $x = l + m + n +$ and so on, the power sums $l^i + m^i + n^i +$ and so on are represented by means of elementary symmetric functions of l, m, n, and so on. In 1629, Albert Girard had given the first three power sums of the second up to the fourth degree in his *Invention nouvelle en l'algèbre* (Girard 1629, p. F 2r–v) without mentioning a general law of formation. Newton's recursion formulae were published in 1707, again without any general law of formation (Newton 1707, 251). Only in 1762 did Edward Waring publish such a rule in his *Miscellanea analytica de aequationibus algebraicis, et curvarum proprietatibus* (Waring 1762, 1–3) and once more in 1770 in his *Meditationes algebraicae* (1770, 1–4).

Leibniz anticipated Waring's results by about eighty years. Around 1677/79 he elaborated a table of the first nine power sums (1976, 195). He added: "Nullam unquam tabulam numerorum vidi ex qua plura mysteria pulcherrima duxerim." (I have never seen any table of numbers from which I drew more most beautiful mysteries.)

Between 1680 and 1682, Leibniz found the general law of formation of an arbitrary term of the representation of a power sum by elementary symmetric functions (1976, 200, 207, 213). The coefficient can be found thanks to a proportionality. The combination xyz might serve as an example, as follows.

There are three factors or elementary symmetric functions. Hence the apparent dimension of the term is three. The elementary symmetric functions have the dimensions one, two, three, and so on. Hence the hidden dimension of the term is six. The proportionality reads:

number of the apparent dimension of the term (3) : number of the hidden dimension of the term (6) = number of the permutations of the elementary symmetric functions of the term (3! = 6) : coefficient sought

or: $\frac{6}{3}.3! = 12$

Let r_i be the frequency of the i-th elementary symmetric function; let $x^{r_1} y^{r_2} z^{r_3}$ and so on be the term the coefficient c of which is sought. Then $1r_1 + 2r_2 + 3r_3$ and so on is its hidden dimension; $r_1 + r_2 + r_3$ and so on is its apparent dimension. The number of permutations of the elementary symmetric functions has to be calculated by means of the formula for permutations with repetitions.

$$c = \frac{\left(1r_1 + 2r_2 = 3r_3 + \ldots\right)}{\left(r_1 + r_2 + r_3 + \ldots\right)} \cdot \frac{\left(r_1 + r_2 + r_3 + \ldots\right)!}{r_1 ! r_2 ! r_3 ! \ldots}$$

The sign rule reads:

> If the apparent and the hidden dimension of a term are odd or even at the same time, its sign is +, otherwise −.

For example (I use Leibniz's notation):

$$\int 1^6 = x^6 - 6x^4 y + 6x^3 z + 9x^2 y^2 - 6x^2 \omega - 12xyz - 2y^3 + 3zz + 6y\omega$$

These rules for the calculation of the coefficients are correct, though Leibniz did not give any justification.

The Reduction of Multiform Symmetric Functions to Uniform Symmetric Functions (Power Sums)

From 1700, Leibniz corresponded with Theobald Overbeck on the reduction of symmetric functions to elementary symmetric functions. This correspondence is especially interesting because it contains new results in this respect. Overbeck summarized the most important of them in his *Diatribe algebraica de multinomiis* (Algebraic treatise on polynomials), which was presumably written in 1714 (Knobloch 1973, 146–160). I would like to discuss two problems: the multiplication of power sums or uniform symmetric functions by each other and the reduction of multiform symmetric functions or functions of the type $\Sigma a^m b^n c^p$ and so on to power sums. For technical reasons I shall use this notation instead of Leibniz's point notation.

The Multiplication of Power Sums by Each Other

Step by step, Leibniz multiplied two, three, four, and so on power sums by each other and represented the product by symmetric functions. The product of three power sums might serve as an example (*Ascensus tertius*: third step):

$$\left(\sum a^m\right)\left(\sum a^n\right)\left(\sum a^p\right) = \sum a^{m+n+p} + \sum a^{m+n} b^p + \sum a^m b^n c^p$$
$$+ \sum a^{m+p} b^n$$
$$+ \sum a^{n+p} b^m$$

A suitable notation revealed the hidden combinatorial structure of this problem. First, Leibniz replaced the powers by the exponents. The exponents of different bases are separated from each other by a vertical line:

$$= mnp + mn|p + m|n|p$$
$$+ mp|n$$
$$+ np|m$$

Second, he replaced the groups of exponents by the number of their terms. The encircled number is a coefficient that sums partitions of the same type (I write it within brackets):

$$= 3 + (3)2.1 + 1.1.1$$

In order to find the way of calculating such coefficients, we generalize Leibniz's procedure. Let k be the number of factors. One has to look for all number-theoretical partitions of k. Let

$$k = 1r_1 + 2r_2 + \ldots + kr_k$$

be an arbitrary partition. Its factor N reads as follows:

$$N = \frac{k!}{(1!)^{r_1}(2!)^{r_2}\ldots(k!)^{r_k}\, r_1!r_2!\ldots r!_k}$$

The first k powers of the denominator are necessary because all i! permutations of exponents that are represented by i, i = 1, 2, 3, . . ., k have to be suppressed. For example, let i be 2: if there is a term like mn|p|q or 2.1.1, a new term nm|p|q cannot occur, because one cannot distinguish between a^{m+n} and a^{n+m}.

The second k factors of the denominator are necessary because all r_i! permutations that are produced by the r_i sections of the same length i of exponents have to be suppressed: if there is a term like mn|p|q or $a^{m+n}b^pc^q$, the corresponding symmetric function must include the term $a^{m+n}c^pb^q$ because of its symmetry. Hence, one cannot distinguish between mn|p|q and mn|q|p.

Obviously, this problem reminds us of the table for the number of any symmetric function. The calculation of the factor N is equivalent to the following problem:

Let X be a set of k objects, let d be the number of classes of a partition so that no class remains empty. What is the number of partitions of the type $k = 1r_1 + 2r_2 + \ldots + kr_k$ (r_i is the number of classes with i objects)?

The number sought is given by N.

The Reduction of Multiform Symmetric Functions to Power Sums

The solution of this problem is based on the preceding result:

$$\left(\sum a^m\right)\left(\sum a^n\right) = \sum a^{m+n} + \sum a^m b^n$$

The last expression of this equation is a multiform symmetric function. Hence, one immediately gets

$$\sum a^m b^n = \left(\sum a^m\right)\left(\sum a^n\right) - \sum a^{m+n} \quad (*)$$

Leibniz multiplied this equation by $\sum a^p$. Functions of two variables were eliminated by means of equation (*). In such a way, he deduced step by step the representation of an arbitrary multiform symmetric function. For example:

$$\sum a^m b^n c^p d^q = 1.1.1.1 - 2.1.1 + (2)3.1 + 2.2 - (6)4 \quad (**)$$

How can one find an arbitrary representation?

Let k be the number of variables. One has to enumerate all possible number-theoretical partitions of k. The example k = 4 given earlier leads to five partitions. Let the partition of k be represented by $k = 1r_1 + 2r_2 + \ldots\ldots + kr_k$.

Its coefficient C will be $C = \left(1!\right)^{r_2} \left(2!\right)^{r_3} \ldots \left((k-1)!\right)^{r_k}$

Let the last term of equation (**) be the example: $4 = 4.1 = kr_k$. Its coefficient $C = (3!)^1 = 6$. The sign rule reads: If there is an even number of even numbers, the sign is +. If there is an odd number of even numbers, the sign is –.

These formulae were published by Waring in 1762 and in 1770 for the first time (Waring 1762, 6–8; 1770, 7–10).

DYADIC

Motivation

Leibniz was not the first author to invent, propagate, and publish a number system with the basis 2. In 1617, John Napier published his *Arithmetica localis* (Napier 1617). He explained how to represent natural numbers by means of the powers of 2 without establishing a place value system. It remains doubtful whether Leibniz knew this book before 1682, when he had already invented his dyadic (Zacher 1973, 28). The same is true of Francis Bacon's letter system that was based on two letters (Bacon 1623).

In his *Mathesis biceps vetus et nova* that appeared in 1670, Juan Caramuel y Lobkowitz dealt with different number systems among them being a binary arithmetic (Caramuel 1670). Yet there is not the least evidence that this book influenced Leibniz's invention of the dyadic (Zacher 1973, 16, 28). Maybe Erhard Weigel's quaternary number system, what is called his *Tetractys*, published in 1673 (Weigel 1673), played a certain role in this respect. But this role remains unclear.

According to his own remarks, Leibniz was inspired to look for the simplest number system, that is, dyadic or binary arithmetic, when he studied the duodecimal number system. Such a system was described by authors like Blaise Pascal (Zacher 1973, 17, 21). Leibniz was well acquainted with Pascal's book, posthumously published in 1665 (Pascal 1665).

The Nonmathematical Context

Later on, Leibniz strengthened the importance of his dyadic for nonmathematical purposes. After May 1696, he interpreted dyadic as *imago creationis*, an image of the divine creation. He explained this idea in an enclosure in his letter to Duke Rudolf August of Wolfenbüttel dated May 18, 1696 (A I, 12, N. 66, N. 67; A I, 13, N. 75). The enclosed document was titled *Mira Numerorum omnium expressio per 1 et 0, repraesentans rerum originem ex Deo et Nihilo, seu Mysterium creationis* (Wonderful expression of all numbers by 1 and 0, representing the origin of things from God and Nothing or Mystery of creation). The binary number system should illustrate his philosophical thinking. The duke coined a seal with the Latin inscription *Unus ex nihilo omnia fecit* (One made everything out of nothing) (A I, 13, N. 78, N. 79). Leibniz even believed that dyadic could be a powerful means for the propagation of the Christian faith in China. Such thoughts are to be found in his letter of early 1697 to the Jesuit Claudio Filippo Grimaldi (A I, 13, N. 321; Antognazza 2009, 358).

Another—false—analogy regarding dyadic came into being thanks to the Jesuit Joachim Bouvet. On November 4, 1701, Bouvet wrote to Leibniz from Beijing that the sixty-four hexagrams of the ancient Chinese *I Ching* (Book of changes) could be interpreted as a binary number system (Zacher 1973, no. 10). Leibniz even mentioned this seeming analogy in his only publication on dyadic (Leibniz 1705). Yet his correspondent César Caze rightly refused this analogy: the hexagrams do not represent a number system but a binary system, a collection of possible combinations of two different lines.

Mathematical Aspects and Results

When did Leibniz invent his dyadic? According to his own remarks, this must have happened during his sojourn in Paris. There is indeed a manuscript (LH XXXV 15,4 sheet 7) that was presumably written in October 1676. Besides dyadic, it also mentions the duodecimal number system.

The earliest dated manuscript dealing with dyadic is *Summum calculi analytici fastigium per calculum algorithmicum* (Highest summit of analytical calculation by means of an algorithmic calculation), dated December 1679 (Zacher 1973, no. 1). Leibniz enthusiastically praises the mathematical fruitfulness of the new number system. He is confident thus to be able to solve algebraic problems of equation theory, to approximate irrational or transcendental quantities, and to find the periodicity of the values 0 or 1 in the columns of the series of (certain) natural numbers, saying: "Possent ista et applicari ad Dioφantea, imo ad quid non? . . . Omnia alia hac methodo solvi possunt." (This could be also applied to Diophantean problems. One might even ask: To what not? . . . All other problems can be solved by this method.)

Yet Leibniz was far too optimistic. He never achieved one of these far-reaching aims. Accordingly, the mathematical content of the manuscripts dealing with dyadic is disappointing. None of the correspondents Leibniz addressed in this respect was able or willing to realize Leibniz's mathematical hopes. One of his hopes was to find a distribution law of prime numbers.

After he was elected a member of the French Academy of Sciences, he sent an article on dyadic to its perpetual secretary, Bernhard Le Bovier de Fontenelle, on February 26, 1701 (Zacher 1973, no. 9). Yet he asked Fontenelle not to publish it and to wait for further results. The main subject of this *Essay d'une nouvelle science des nombres* were the periods within the columns of values when the natural numbers written one under the other are represented by the binary number system.

Four years later, his only publication on dyadic appeared in the journal of the French Academy (Leibniz 1705), titled "Explication de l'arithmétique binaire, qui se sert des seuls caractères o et 1, avec des remarques sur son utilité, et sur ce qu'elle donne le sens des anciennes figures chinoises de Fohy." In this very short article, Leibniz illustrates the four arithmetical operations by means of some numerical examples. The considerations of periodicities are replaced by explanations of the analogy with the Chinese hexagrams.

After 1703, Leibniz corresponded about dyadic only with the mathematician Jakob Hermann. In June 1705, he wrote the treatise *De dyadicis* (On dyadic) for Hermann (GM VII, 228–234). It again only explains the four arithmetical operations within the binary number system and touches on the similarities with the Chinese hexagrams.

Leibniz's invention was not forgotten. It "provides an essential basis for the development of modern data processing." Obviously, Leibniz anticipated the enormous potential of the binary number system. For that reason, he has rightly been called the father of cybernetics (Mackensen 2000, 92, 98). Long before Rolf Paland constructed a binary calculating machine in 1984 according to Mackensen's functional drawing, Leibniz had conceived of it.

References

Antognazza, Maria Rosa. 2009. *Leibniz: An Intellectual Biography*. Cambridge: Cambridge University Press.

Bacon, Francis. 1623. *De dignitate et augmentis scientiarum*. London: John Haviland.

Bézout, Etienne. 1767. Recherches sur le degré des équations résultantes de l'évanouissement des inconnues, et sur les moyens qu'il convient d'employer pour trouver ces équations. *Histoire de l'Académie royale des sciences, année 1764*: 288–338 (Paris 1767).

Caramuel y Lobkowitz, Juan. 1670. *Mathesis biceps vetus et nova*. Campania: Officina Episcopalis.

Cramer, Gabriel. 1750. *Introduction à l'analyse des lignes courbes algébriques*. Geneva: Frères Cramer et Cl. Philbert.

Euler, Leonhard. 1748. *Introductio in analysin infinitorum*. 2 vols. Lausanne: Marcus-Michaelis Bousquet = L. Euler, Opera omnia, ser. 1, vols. 8 and 9. Leipzig: Teubner, 1922 and 1945.

Euler, Leonhard. 1750. Démonstration sur le nombre des points où deux lignes des ordres quelconques peuvent se couper. *Mémoires de l'académie des sciences de Berlin 4* (1748): 234–248 (Berlin 1750) = L. Euler, *Opera omnia*, ser. 1, vol. 26, 46–59. Zürich: Orell Füssli, 1953.

Euler, Leonhard. 1766. Nouvelle méthode d'éliminer les quantités inconnues des équations. *Mémoires de l'Académie des sciences de Berlin 20* (1764): 91–104 (Berlin 1766) = L. Euler, *Opera omnia*, ser. 1, vol. 6, 197–211. Leipzig: Teubner, 1921.

Girard, Albert. 1629. *Invention nouvelle en l'algèbre*. Amsterdam: G. I. Blaeuw.

Knobloch, Eberhard. 1972. Die entscheidende Abhandlung von Leibniz zur Theorie linearer Gleichungssysteme. *Studia Leibnitiana 4*: 163–80.

Knobloch, Eberhard. 1973. *Die mathematischen Studien von G. W. Leibniz zur Kombinatorik, Auf Grund fast ausschließlich handschriftlicher Aufzeichnungen dargelegt und kommentiert*. Wiesbaden: Steiner = Studia Leibnitiana Supplementa 11.

Knobloch, Eberhard. 1974. Studien von Leibniz zum Determinantenkalkül. Studia Leibnitiana Supplementa 13: 37–45.

Knobloch, Eberhard. 1980. *Der Beginn der Determinantentheorie, Leibnizens nachgelassene Studien zum Determinantenkalkül*, Textband. Hildesheim: Gerstenberg Verlag.

Knobloch, Eberhard. 1982. Zur Vorgeschichte der Determinantentheorie. *Studia Leibnitiana Supplementa 22*: 96–118.

Knobloch, Eberhard. 1994. From Gauß to Weierstraß: Determinant Theory and Its Historical Evaluation. In *The Intersection of History and Mathematics*, ed. Sasaki Chikara, Sugiura Mitsuo, and Joseph W. Dauben, 51–66. Basel: Birkhäuser Verlag.

Knobloch, Eberhard. 2000. First European Theory of Determinants. In *G. W. Leibniz: The Work of the Great Universal Scholar as Philosopher, Mathematician, Physicist, Engineer*, ed. Karl Bopp and Erwin Stein, 55–64. Hannover: Schlütersche GmbH & Co, KG.

Knobloch, Eberhard. 2006. Beyond Cartesian Limits: Leibniz's Passage from Algebraic to "Transcendental" Mathematics. *Historia Mathematica 33*: 113–31.

Knobloch, Eberhard. 2010. Leibniz between Ars Characteristica and Ars Inveniendi: Unknown News about Cajori's "Master-Builder of Mathematical Notations." In *Philosophical Aspects of Symbolic Reasoning in Early Modern Mathematics*, ed. Albrecht Heefer and Maarten Van Dyck, 289–302. Milton Keynes: Lightning Source.

Leibniz, Gottfried Wilhelm. 1705. Explication de l'arithmétique binaire, qui se sert des seuls caractères 0 et 1, avec des remarques sur son utilité, et sur ce qu'elle donne le sens des anciennes figures chinoises de Fohy. *Mémoires del'Académie Royale des Sciences de Paris, 5* May 1703, 85–89 = GM VII, 223–227.

Leibniz, Gottfried Wilhelm. 1976. *Die mathematischen Studien von G. W. Leibniz zur Kombinatorik, Textband. Im Anschluß an den gleichnamigen Abhandlungband zum ersten Mal nach den Originalhandschriften herausgegeben von Eberhard Knobloch*. Wiesbaden: Steiner. = Studia Leibnitiana Supplementa 16.

Mackensen, Ludolf von. 2000. The First Decimal and Binary Calculating Machines. In *Gottfried Wilhelm Leibniz: The Work of the Great Universal Scholar as Philosopher, Mathematician, Physicist, Engineer*, ed. Karl Popp and Erwin Stein, 84–107. Hannover: Schlütersche.

MacLaurin, Colin. 1748. *Treatise of Algebra in three parts*. London: A. Millar and J. Nourse.

Napier, John. 1617. *Arithmeticae localis quae in Scacchiae abaco exercetur liber unus*. In *Ioannes Neper, Rabdologiae seu numerationis per virgulas libri duo. Cum appendice de expeditissimo multiplicationis promptuario. Quibus accessit et Arithmeticae localis liber unus*, 113–154. Edinburgh: Hart.

Newton, Isaac. 1707. *Arithmetica universalis sive de compositione et resolutione arithmetica liber.* Edited by William Whiston. Cambridge: University of Cambridge.

Pascal, Blaise. 1665. *De numeris multiplicibus ex sola characterum numericorum additione agnoscendis.* In Blaise Pascal, *Traité du triangle arithmétique avec quelques autres petits traitez sur la mesme matière. Supplément.* Paris: Guillaume Desprez = Blaise Pascal, Oeuvres... publiées par Léon Brunschvicg et Pierre Boutroux, vol. 3, 311–339. Paris: Hachette.

Sylvester, James Joseph. 1840. A Method of Determining by Mere Inspection the Derivations from Two Equations of Any Degree. *Philosophical Magazine 16:* 132–135 = *The Collected Mathematical Papers of James Joseph Sylvester*, vol. 1, 54–57. Cambridge: Cambridge University Press.

Waring, Edward. 1762. *Miscellanea analytica de aequationibus algebraicis, et curvarum proprietatibus.* Cambridge: Bentham.

Waring, Edward. 1770. *Meditationes algebraicae.* Cambridge: J. Nicholson.

Weigel, Erhard. 1673. *Tetractys, Summum tum Arithmeticae tum Philosophiae discursivae compendium, artis magnae sciendi genuina radix.* Jena: Johannes Meyer.

Zacher, Hans J. 1973. *Die Hauptschriften zur Dyadik von G. W. Leibniz: Ein Beitrag zur Geschichte des binären Zahlensystems.* Frankfurt: Vittorio Klostermann.

CHAPTER 13

··

ANALYSIS SITUS, THE FOUNDATIONS OF MATHEMATICS, AND A GEOMETRY OF SPACE

··

VINCENZO DE RISI

ANALYSIS SITUS is the name given by Leibniz to a cluster of mathematical and philosophical investigations into the foundations, development, and formalization of geometry. Leibniz devoted himself to this multifaceted project throughout his life: his earliest studies date back to the Parisian period (1672–76), and his last drafts were composed at the end of his life (1714–16). These forty years' worth of efforts yielded hundreds of essays that range from short collections of notes to complex, long, and highly developed manuscripts. None of these works, however, was published during Leibniz's lifetime. His contemporaries' dismissive attitudes toward the project, as well as Leibniz's own conviction that his new discipline had yielded nothing of great consequence for the field of geometry,[1] prevented Leibniz from seeking publication.[2] Some of his writings on *analysis situs* were printed in nineteenth-century Leibniz editions, whereas others have only been published in recent years.[3] The great bulk of

---

[1] Here, some complaints from the well-known letter to L'Hospital from December 27, 1694 (in GM II 255–62): "My metaphysics is all mathematics, so to speak, or it can become so. At the present, I dare not publish my projects on the *characteristica situs* because, unless made believable through examples of some importance, it would be regarded as just a vision. Nonetheless I see in advance that it will not fail."

[2] Leibniz was particularly influenced by Huygens's poor reception of the nascent *characteristica geometrica* in his letter of November 22, 1679 (A III ii 888–89).

[3] Leibniz's papers on *analysis situs* are mostly to be found in volumes 5 (from 1858) and 7 (from 1863) of Gerhardt's edition of the *Mathematische Schriften*, but some of them are also printed in Couturat's *Opuscules et fragments inédits*. Further publications include an important text in the appendix of M. Mugnai, "Leibniz's theory of relations," in *Studia Leibnitiana Supplementa 28* (1992); the essays published in G. W. Leibniz, *La caractéristique géométrique*, edited by J. Echeverría and M. Parmentier

Leibniz's studies on the topic, however, remains unpublished in the Hannover Library. Nevertheless, we have enough material to attempt to reconstruct—albeit partially and tentatively—the main aims, developments, and outcomes of Leibniz's endeavor in a new geometry.

A NEW FORMALISM

The concept of *situation* (*situs*) is, roughly speaking, the notion of the position of an object (or a figure) in space relative to other objects. Thus, from the very beginning of Leibniz's investigations, it is considered a relational predicate—and it also is, as it were, the first source of Leibniz's later and celebrated theory of a relational space. In Leibniz's times, the notion of situation was widely employed in metaphysics, where the concept evolved from the Aristotelian category of κεῖσθαι (i.e. *situm esse*).[4] Its mathematical genealogy is long and complex, and indeed it can be traced back (again) to Aristotle's definition of a point as a "monad with position" (θέσις; that is, *positio* or *situs*[5]). In this connection, it was found in a number of geometrical books of the Early Modern Age, remaining, however, a philosophical definition and a concept without consequences on mathematical practice.[6] The only geometrical studies that made some use of *situation* were treatises on the theory of perspective, and it is not unlikely that Leibniz was inspired by Pascal's studies on perspective geometry, which he could have read in

(Paris: Vrin, 1995); and the appendix to V. De Risi, *Geometry and Monadology. Leibniz's Analysis Situs and Philosophy of Space* (Basel: Birkhäuser, 2007).

[4] Aristotle's classical loci are *Cat.* 4, 1ᵇ27 and *Top.* A 9, 103ᵇ23. A modern and relational interpretation of the category of situation can be found, for instance, in Descartes's *Principia*, II, 15 (AT VIII, 48–49).

[5] See *Metaph.* Δ 6, 1016ᵇ24–26. The definition is in fact Pythagorean and probably predates Aristotle: see Proclus Diadochus, *In Primum Euclidis*, edited by G. Friedlein (Leipzig: Teubner, 1873), p. 95. Leibniz's correction of Euclid's definition of a point in this direction is to be found in his *In Euclidis πρῶτα*, in GM V 183: "I. 'A point is what has no parts.' One must add that it has situation. Otherwise also the temporal instant and the soul were points." An instant, for Leibniz, is endowed with *positio*, which is the basic order-relation, but not with *situs*, which is a position in a co-existent order. According to Leibniz, souls (i.e., monads) have neither situation nor position.

[6] Proclus had already reproached Aristotle for his philosophically motivated revision of the definition of a point, to which he had added the notion of situation. Proclus regards this move as useless from the mathematical standpoint: see Proclus, *In Primum Euclidis*, p. 93. Such criticisms of Aristotle were not uncommon in the Modern Age, when mathematicians could not yet envision a geometrical use for the notion of situation. See, for instance, Barrow's third lecture on mathematics, in I. Barrow, *The Mathematical Works*, edited by W. Whewell (Cambridge: Cambridge University Press, 1860), p. 62. A clumsy (but mathematical) reference to the notion of situation is also to be found in Francesco Patrizi's *Della nuova geometria* (Ferrara: Baldini, 1587), and in Campanella's unpublished writings. It is very unlikely that Leibniz might have been influenced by Patrizi's (or Campanella's) work, which he probably only read during his Italian trip (in 1690; see A VI vi 966); but, in any case, these works show that the notion of situation had penetrated to the foundational studies on geometry in the seventeenth century.

manuscript form in the 1670s, but which are now almost entirely lost.[7] The idea of a *geometria situs*, however, belongs fully to Leibniz.

The primary motivation for Leibniz's research seems to stem from the common seventeenth-century epistemological concern regarding the use—and abuse—of new algebraic methods in geometry. Most mathematicians had to admit that Descartes's new algebraic methods were incredibly fruitful for the development of geometry, and no one could deny that they were an extraordinary tool in the mathematical art of discovery.[8] Moreover, the new algebra did not need to rely on diagrammatic reasoning, thus successfully escaping the many traps of imagination in synthetic geometry. Widespread and often well-founded concerns, however, were raised about the foundations of the algebraic methods, their appropriateness to the domain of geometry, their extent and soundness in demonstration, and their simplicity in definitions and proofs. Leibniz probably praised the advantages of a *cogitatio caeca* in mathematics (and metaphysics) more than anyone else. He, too, however, worried about the foundations of such symbolic methods. Algebra is a useful tool for the geometer, but its formalism has the potential to yield unsound conclusions; that is, it proves *too much* because symbols in ordinary algebra have no straightforward geometrical interpretation and may denote magnitudes that have no meaning in (classical, Euclidean) geometrical terms (e.g., imaginary numbers or high-dimensional products[9]). It is not even clear that algebra can demonstrate all the relevant geometrical results (it might prove *too little*) because its completeness could be hindered by the purely numerical origins of its formalism, which was not originally devised to solve geometrical problems. The foundations of ordinary algebra, moreover, are mostly obscure, and its rules seem to lie (also) in some geometrical results (such as Pythagoras's theorem), which makes it impossible to rely on algebra in the context of geometrical justification.

Leibniz's proposes to assuage these concerns by eliminating algebra from geometry without eliminating symbolic reasoning. His aim is thus to construct a *characteristica geometrica propria*, a new formalism for geometry, whose constants and variables range directly over points and figures in space (instead of magnitudes and numbers), whose primary relations consist in congruence and similarity (instead of equality), and whose most important and in fact unique function (instead of addition or multiplication) is *situs*—that is, a function concerning reciprocal spatial position between geometrical

---

[7] Leibniz's reading of Pascal's writings on geometry dates to the end of the Parisian Period, 1675–76, when Leibniz also recommended that Pascal's manuscripts be published: but the edition was never done, and the papers were lost. Today, we only have Leibniz's own transcriptions of a few pages of them. On the history of Pascal's papers, see J. Mesnard, "Leibniz et les papiers de Pascal," in *Studia Leibnitiana Supplementa 17* (1978), pp. 45–58. Cf. also R. Taton (ed.), *L'oeuvre scientifique de Pascal* (Paris: PUF, 1964).

[8] On symbolic reasoning as an *ars inveniendi* in geometry, see, for instance, Leibniz's *De constructione*, in GM VII 249–60.

[9] For a survey on imaginary numbers, see, for instance, R. B. McClenon, "A contribution of Leibniz to the history of complex numbers," in *American Mathematical Monthly 30* (1923), pp. 369–374.

figures. This new formalism is therefore capable of solving all the aforementioned problems (and a few more), all of which were caused by the unnatural use of an *algebra of magnitudes* (the ordinary Cartesian algebra) in place of an *algebra of situations*.[10]

Leibniz developed this new *characteristica* up to a fairly good level of sophistication, providing new symbols for functions and undefined relations, formal definitions of elementary geometrical figures (such as a straight line, a circle, a plane, etc.), and a few basic spatial configurations (angles, parallelism), as well as a number of formal axioms concerning the situational relations themselves (e.g., reflexivity, symmetry and transitivity of congruence and similarity). He also managed to demonstrate a small number of very elementary theorems that are often remarkable for their abstract form and foundational relevance and would not unworthily feature in much more mature treatises on the foundations of geometry.[11]

Ultimately, these formal axioms also provide a characterization (indeed, an implicit definition) of the notion of *situs*, the fundamental function of the system. This turns out to be nothing more than the notion of *distance* and is mainly defined with reference to the concept of congruence: two collections of objects have the same reciprocal situations if and only if one collection is congruent with the other. For instance, the extremities of two segments of equal length, or the vertices of two triangles with equal sides, or the set of points of a circumference with respect to those of another circumference with equal radius all have the same reciprocal situation. The system of situations is thus the structure of reciprocal distances between the points of a figure.[12]

This shows that the metric relations between figures or points are in fact the main subject of Leibniz's *analysis situs*. Thus, his new geometry presents no more generality (in this respect) than does classical Euclidean geometry. It is remarkable, however, that Leibniz also seems to explore some more general mathematical structures in his first studies on a geometrical formalism. On the one hand, his formal axioms and purely combinatorial techniques of proof allow him to demonstrate a number of results that allow for different geometrical systems. Leibniz is aware, for instance, that a number of the properties of a straight line that he can deduce from his axioms and definitions apply with equal force to the great circles on a sphere—and he points out

---

[10] A very good formulation of this program can be found in Leibniz's essay on *Ars Representatoria*, in V. De Risi, "Leibniz on geometry. Two unpublished manuscripts with translation and commentary," in *The Leibniz Review* 15 (2005), pp. 127–151. Cf. also §§2–7 of the *Characteristica geometrica* (GM V 141–44) and *De analysi situs* (GM V 182–83).

[11] Many mathematicians working on the foundations of geometry in the late nineteenth century knew something about Leibniz's work on *analysis situs* (through Gerhardt's edition). Peano sent a collaborator of his to Hannover to look at the Leibnizian manuscripts, and Couturat himself became involved in the Leibniz studies in this way. Pasch's work is probably the most similar to Leibniz's. Peano, Pieri, and Veronese mention him explicitly. Hilbert's work, on the contrary, departs drastically from Leibnizian geometrical practice.

[12] Some of the most important examples thereof come from the ample *Characteristica geometrica* from 1679, in GM V 141–68; much more material can be found in the preparatory drafts of this essay, in Leibniz, *La caractéristique géométrique*.

the structural resemblances between them with respect to axioms of congruence.[13] On the other hand, Leibniz's emphasis on the importance of a number of geometrical relations in addition to congruence, especially the relevance of the notion of similarity, seems to point in a nonmetrical direction—toward something that falls just short of a true geometry of projections.[14] One should not, however, overemphasize these kinds of developments: Leibniz soon abandoned them, and they seem to be more a by-product of his combinatorial approach to geometry than a real aim to the edification of a *geometria situs*.[15]

THE FOUNDATIONS OF GEOMETRY

In fact, the development of a *characteristica geometrica* occurred mostly in the early stages of Leibniz's reflections on geometry and parallels and complements his earlier research of the late 1670s and the early 1680s on a *characteristica universalis*—although it keeps surfacing again from time to time in the mature years. Be it as it may, the subsequent elaboration of Leibniz's thoughts in geometry proceeds through a thorough study of classical elementary geometry (mainly read on Clavius's edition of the *Elements*), which dispels any leaning toward new geometries but enormously enriches Leibniz's skills in foundational analysis as well as the concreteness of his approach to the most debated problems of synthetic geometry. The *analysis situs* acquires new aims and perspectives: it becomes a tool designed to *rigorize* and *ground* the geometrical sciences. Leibniz produces a number of remarkable essays filling the gaps of the Euclidean (or Early Modern) demonstrations of some classical results, and his insistence on the need

---

[13] See GM V 146–47.

[14] Since Leibniz's geometrical writings were first published at the heyday of projective geometry, a number of mathematicians assumed that any foundational study that employed the notion of similarity had to be "projective" in some sense. There are no traces, however, of a theory of projections in Leibniz's papers on *analysis situs*, and there is also no evidence of a nonmetric geometry in the proper sense. Like Desargues and other eighteenth-century perspective geometers, Leibniz uses nonmetric-preserving transformations (like similarity) only to demonstrate *metric* results—for instance, *Elements* XII, 2 (see for the relevant texts: A VI iv 378–82; GM V 182; GM VII 24 and 76–277; Mugnai, *Leibniz's Theory of Relations*, pp. 145–56; De Risi, *Geometry and Monadology*, pp. 625–626). This is not to say that Leibniz did not also work on perspective geometry; see J. Echeverría, "Recherches inconnues de Leibniz sur la géométrie perspective," in *Studia Leibnitiana Supplementa* 23 (1983), pp. 191–202; and V. Debuiche, "Perspective in Leibniz's invention of *Characteristica Geometrica*: The problem of Desargues's influence," in *Historia Mathematica* 40 (2013), pp. 359–385.

[15] In this respect, the widespread idea that Leibniz's *analysis situs* was an anticipation of Graßmann's work on vector calculus, although deeply flawed, had the advantage of pointing toward some important metric results that Leibniz could have obtained through his combinatorics; cf. H. Grassmann, *Geometrische Analyse geknüpft an die von Leibniz erfundene geometrische Charakteristik* (Leipzig: Weidmann, 1847). The alleged connection between Leibniz's geometrical researches and topology, however, seems to derive only from the fact that this latter discipline was usually called "*analysis situs*" in the nineteenth century.

of continuity assumptions in elementary proofs, for instance, or a better foundation for the use of rigid motions and superposition marks a clear advancement in the understanding of the proof-theoretic structure of geometry.[16]

Leibniz's aims, however, are not limited to an enhancement of rigor in demonstration. He would like to be able to prove all the geometrical axioms. This desire, which may appear strange today, was in fact commonplace at the time, and Clavius himself (perhaps the most influential geometer of the Modern Age) included after the Euclidean postulates and common notions their "demonstrations." Leibniz's general idea is that the need for an axiom betrays a need for a better definition.[17] It is Euclid's infamous and obscure definition of a straight line, for example, that obliged him (or modern geometers) to provide axioms that implicitly characterize it (there is only one line between any two points) and postulates that assume its possibility (there is at least a line between any two points). But with better definitions, like the ones that Leibniz himself tried to mold, axioms and postulates are proved via an analysis of definitions. For instance, given the definition of a straight line as a self-congruent line (roughly, as an axis of rotation), it follows straightforwardly, Leibniz claims, that only one such line can be traced between two points. The result should be the foundation of geometry as a perfectly unhypothetical and analytical science—which has been regarded as Leibniz's peculiar "logicist" approach to mathematics.[18]

Of course, Leibniz was well aware that the definitions themselves call for some proof: they have become principles of demonstration, not just stipulations upon words. Indeed, he argues that all definitions should be *real*, which means that they must show the possibility of their objects. If one asks, now, on which grounds Leibniz could hope to demonstrate the real possibility of the objects of geometrical definitions, the answer points at the very concept of a *geometrical space*. This concept is, in fact, the most relevant advancement that Leibniz made in the field of geometry throughout his whole attempt to construct an *analysis situs*.

THE GEOMETRY OF SPACE

In Antiquity, the subject matter of geometry was thought to be (continuous) quantities or magnitudes, like circles, straight lines, triangles, or conic sections—not space. Anyone who went through the thirteen books of Euclid's *Elements* looking for a single reference

---

[16] See for example: A VI iv 165 and 970, and the text *Demonstratio omnimoda*, in De Risi, *Geometry and Monadology*, pp. 601–603.

[17] See *Nouveaux Essais* IV 12, §4; A VI vi 451. But also: A II ii 103; A VI iv 197.

[18] See at least: A II i 351 (= A III i 14); A II i 769–71; A II ii 490–91; A III vii 113; A VI iv 165; A VI iv 703–705; A VI iv 969–70. This project was widely discussed in L. Couturat, *La logique de Leibniz* (Paris: Alcan, 1901), which contains the first extended treatment of Leibniz's *analysis situs*. Although Leibniz's injection of logic into geometry was remarkable, one has to consider that the foundations of Leibniz's geometrical

to "space" or "place" would be sorely disappointed. The Late Antiquity did have some notions of a spatial extension endowed with quantitative properties, but these notions remained largely disconnected from mathematics. Much later, some geometers and philosophers of the late Renaissance built on these Neoplatonic conceptions and developed notions of space that could have mathematical import, but the main aims of these speculations remained purely metaphysical, and the seminal concept of a geometrical space was entirely disconnected from actual mathematical practice. Even well-known understandings of space from the Early Modern Age, from Descartes's *res extensa* to Newton's absolute space, were devoid of proper mathematical attributes and remained a sort of amorphous background that only played the role of a screen in which the geometer traces those figures and magnitudes that still are the true objects of his science.

It is very difficult to fully reconstruct the complex seventeenth- and eighteenth-century developments that gave birth to modern geometry as the science of space. This transformation required that one understands space as a structure that can be endowed with intrinsic geometrical properties and investigated with mathematical methods. This same train of thought would eventually contribute to the development of the concept of a plurality of possible spaces, which in fact make their first appearance in the late eighteenth-century studies on projective and non-Euclidean geometries.

In some sense, however, this whole evolution of geometry began with Leibniz's writings on *analysis situs*. Here, for the very first time in the history of mathematics, we find geometrical definitions of space, followed by axioms and theorems about it and the first ever demonstrations having as their object the properties of space itself.

The point of departure is Leibniz's celebrated definition of space as an *order of situations*.[19] Given the notion of *situs* as distance, the definition means that space is the system of all (possible) distances between objects. In modern terms, we would say that Leibniz's notion of space is that of an abstract metric space. The terms of the situational relations (the related objects) remain abstract elements: they are bodies in physical space, but figures and points in geometrical space.[20]

Space is thus a structure, and extension is produced by a certain order of distances between points. Leibniz can thus say that space itself is *constituted by points* ("constitui, dico, non componi"[21]). It is not *composed* of points, for obviously a number of unextended points, and even an infinite number of them, could not (considered as an

---

system are to be found in the metaphysical definition of space as a total situational order, which cannot be reduced to logic alone. A very good discussion of the relations between logic and mathematics in that era is M. Mugnai, "Logic and mathematics in the seventeenth century," in *History and Philosophy of Logic* 31 (2010), pp. 297–314.

[19] See, for instance, the *Fifth Paper to Clarke*, §104, in GP VII 415. The definition is, however, very common in Leibniz's late years.

[20] In this structural definition, a point may be any object considered simply as a situational term. Cf. a text in De Risi, *Geometry and Monadology*, p. 624. The definition is already in Pascal, *Introduction à la géométrie*, now in D. Descotes (ed.), *Géométries de Port-Royal* (Paris: Champion, 2009).

[21] GM VI 370.

aggregate or a merely quantitative whole) build up anything extended. But a set of points as situational elements, that is, a set of points with a structure, with a system of reciprocal distances—this may indeed yield extension out of situation. As we can see, this is a very modern "structuralist" way out of the *labyrinthus continui*.[22]

Starting with this definition of space, Leibniz singles out a number of properties that an abstract order of situations may or may not possess. Leibniz's definitions of these properties represent a remarkable feat in geometry because most of them were constructed for the first time by Leibniz himself, and almost all of them require a high degree of conceptual sophistication. To give the most important examples, in the writings on *analysis situs* we find a good definition of isotropy (in general and not restricted to the Euclidean metric), which Leibniz calls *uniformity*; a definition of *homogeneity* that contains as a germ the modern concept of a manifold; some studies on the notion of dimensionality; a large number of very good definitions of *continuity* taken either as the modern notion of connection or as linear completeness (with a few outcomes that are not too far from Dedekind's theory of cuts); and reflections on the properties of Euclidean metrics.[23]

From this point of view, we can reformulate Leibniz's foundational program in geometry as follows. He defines *absolute space* as the total and all-encompassing order of all possible situations. This is just our notion of a metric space (and it is unrelated to inertial properties). From this basic concept, Leibniz would like to deduce an incredible number of highly characterizing space properties. He would like to prove, in fact, that the very notion of a *total* situational order entails that this order generates an extension, that it is "uniform" and "homogeneous," necessarily "continuous," necessarily tridimensional, necessarily Euclidean, and so on. To give these proofs, he embarks on the utopian project, half philosophical and half mathematical, of demonstrating many important Euclidean theorems and axioms, taking his new geometry of space as its starting point. Especially remarkable are Leibniz's many and varied attempts to prove

---

[22] This appears to be a late discovery, and many writings on situational analysis dating to the 1670s and 1680s are still uncertain on the possibility of grounding *extensio* on *situs* (see, e.g., the texts published in Leibniz, *La caractéristique géométrique*, p. 138; and in De Risi, *Geometry and Monadology*, pp. 588 and 624). A clear presentation of Leibniz's views on the topic in his young and early mature years is offered in G. W. Leibniz, *The Labyrinth of the Continuum. Writings on the Continuum Problem, 1672–1686*, edited by R. T. W. Arthur (New Haven: Yale University Press, 2001). The editor thereof made a great deal of important contributions with respect to clarifying Leibniz's conceptions of continuity and extension; concerning the views presented here, cf. his seminal paper: R. T. W. Arthur, "On the unappreciated novelty of Leibniz's spatial relationism," in *Leibniz. Tradition und Aktualität. V Internationaler Leibniz-Kongreß* (Hannover, 1988); as well as his recent R. T. W. Arthur, "Leibniz's theory of space," in *Foundations of Science 18* (2013), pp. 499–528. On *analysis situs* and continuity, cf. also J.-P. Alcantara, *Sur le second labyrinthe de Leibniz* (Paris: L'Harmattan, 2003). For a fuller account of the relation of continuity and situation, see my essay in V. De Risi (ed.), *Leibniz and the Structure of Sciences. Modern Perspectives on the History of Logic, Mathematics, Dynamics*, forthcoming.

[23] The relevant texts are mostly to be found, and discussed, in De Risi, *Geometry and Monadology*, pp. 178–264. On the connection between *analysis situs* and the theory of space, see also the contribution of David Rabouin in T. Paquot and C. Younès (eds.), *Espace et lieu dans la pensée occidentale* (Paris: Editions La Découverte, 2012).

the Parallel Postulate, which predate the more famous (and more developed) attempts made by Saccheri, Lambert, and Legendre and are made in the context of a general theory of space that not many of those later geometers were able to envision.[24] His progress in the field is, obviously, very limited (not only regarding the Euclidean Axiom), and he was aware of the many shortcomings of his demonstrations. Thanks to these (alleged) results and these very rich geometrical properties of space itself, Leibniz could be able to prove the real possibility of all the elementary definitions of geometry. From these definitions, as we have seen, the whole classical geometry would follow. It seems that his foundational project in geometry was indeed closely linked with his new conception of space as a situational order.

The actual products of the *analysis situs* as an analysis of the concept of space are thus very poor, both because Leibniz's grand project of founding all of the principles of Euclidean geometry on the abstract concept of a metric space was clearly doomed to failure and because the actual geometrical arguments he offers are seldom worth the effort of any serious mathematician. It would be hard, however, to overestimate the significance of this project to the development of mathematics: space has indeed become a geometrical structure instead of a metaphysical amorphous extension external to geometry, and geometry itself is no longer concerned with triangles and circles but has instead attained its modern status as a *science of space*.

Geometry and Metaphysics

The remarkable, although very imperfect, fruits of Leibniz's investigations into a new geometry were reaped in later years to yield even more remarkable advancements in philosophy. In fact, from at least the 1690s, although chiefly after the turn of the century, Leibniz's writings on *analysis situs* were often integrated into more general considerations of metaphysics and the theory of knowledge, and his openly philosophical essays, in turn, bear traces of the many private experiments that Leibniz attempted in his mathematical studies.

This attitude is especially significant for the development of a theory of sensible knowledge, which Leibniz seems to have first developed around the time that he was composing *Nouveaux Essais*. The theory ultimately tends toward an epistemology of spatial perception. The main tool employed by Leibniz seems to be his earlier definition of geometrical similarity through co-perception (two objects are similar if they can only be distinguished through co-perception, but not if considered one by one),[25] which

---

[24] On Leibniz's essays on the theory of parallels, see V. De Risi, *Leibniz on the Parallel Postulate and the Foundations of Geometry* (Basel: Birkhäuser 2015).

[25] This definition is found for the first time in Leibniz's letter to Gallois from September 1677, in A II i 380; A III ii 227–28.

not only injects phenomenological elements into the foundational attempts in mathematics but also adds a geometrical twist to the theory of perception itself. The relations of co-existence and co-perceptibility that obtain between objects are clearly identified with situational relations, a notion that allows for a characterization of space as the order of co-existence or simultaneous perception (or perceptibility), a concept connected in turn to Leibniz's theory of clear and confused ideas and many other phenomenological issues. Some characterizations of the principle of the identity of indiscernibles in its perceptual form are clearly linked to the geometrical notions of congruence and similarity, and even modal concepts that touch on the theory of possible worlds find their perceptual and geometrical correlate here. In some of his latest essays,[26] where the connection between situational analysis and sensible perception is carried to its furthest extreme, Leibniz seems inclined to define space as a form of sensible perception (almost in Kantian terms) and even, to some extent, to posit a "transcendental" determination of space itself.[27]

The importance of Leibniz's studies on *analysis situs* is also apparent in his celebrated exchange with Clarke. In fact, we know that a number of drafts on the *geometria situs* were written in the very same months of that famous correspondence, and Leibniz seemed to intend to publish at least some of them in those late years. Indeed, he clearly imagined that a developed *analysis situs* might serve as mathematical support for his metaphysical position. In any case, it is certain that Leibniz's geometrical studies shed a great deal of light on his late conception of space as it is defended against Newton and Clarke. Many of the issues debated there about Leibniz's relational notion of space and motion are better understood as declinations of his new, structural approach to a geometry of space. In this connection, even the issues about the theory of inertia and absolute space seem to be just corollaries and scholia to a bigger mathematical and epistemological quarrel about the very object of geometry and its definition.

Last, I will mention the fact that Leibniz's definition of space as a structure and a system of relations paves the way for a better understanding of the much vexed question of the relationship between monads and bodies. As we have seen, one of the most notable results of Leibniz's *analysis situs* is that space can be considered as *constituted* by points, and extension can be produced by a set of unextended elements endowed with a situational structure. A cosmological picture that presented Leibnizian physical bodies as constituted by monads (thought of as point-like substances) in a system of situational relations would be too simplistic to function as a successful reading of the late

---

[26] For example, the *Initia rerum mathematicarum metaphysica* from 1715, whose original title was *De calculo situs* (GM VII 17–29). But see also the (early) §§105–108 of the *Characteristica geometrica*, which were not published by Gerhardt and can be read in Leibniz, *La caractéristique géométrique*, pp. 228–232.

[27] For a discussion of the very complex phenomenological and transcendental elements of Leibniz's project of an *analysis situs*, I cannot but refer to my *Geometry and Monadology*, pp. 297–428. The first discussion of Leibniz's geometrical ideas in relation to his theory of knowledge and metaphysics is to be found in E. Cassirer, *Leibniz' System in seinen wissenschaftlichen Grundlagen* (Marburg: Elwert, 1902), which unfortunately enjoyed no great favor in subsequent scholarship on the topic.

monadology—but could nevertheless serve to both shed light on *some* of Leibniz's later declarations about monads and corporeal substances[28] and to help us construct a reasonable chart of some of the possible outcomes of the later Wolffian and post-Wolffian *physical monadologies* (taken in a broad sense). Leibniz's own point of view (as I think) is that monads (as mind-like substances) are not situated at all—they are not in space. But we *perceive* them by *expressing* their intermonadic (nonspatial) relations as situational relations (i.e., as a spatial extension). Here, *exprimere* means something like an isomorphic image, a representation that does not preserve the inner nature but instead the order and structure of the relations involved.[29] So that, in the end, we can (more or less) faithfully represent through situational relations what happens in the supersensible realm and perceive monads as phenomena (bodies) in space. In this theory, we finally integrate all aspects of Leibniz's late epistemology of sensible perception, his metaphysical thoughts on monads and space, and his most daring mathematical results. I will not belabor the interpretation of the connection between monads and phenomena through situation because it is very complicated.[30] However, I wish to point to the fact that such a conception is entirely reliant on the mathematical notion of expression as an isomorphism and the geometrical discoveries about the structural nature of space associated with the *analysis situs*.

CONCLUSION

Leibniz's writings on *analysis situs* were lost to the mathematical and philosophical tradition of the Modern Age. His metaphysical conception of space, which played such an important role in the development of eighteenth-century philosophy, remained partial and undefended without its natural complement of geometrical investigation, and the problem of the composition of the continuum, or the relation between monads and space, was left unsolved by the Wolffian tradition.

The very idea of an *analysis situs*, however, surfaced already in the few Leibnizian works published in the eighteenth century and engendered a large debate on these topics and a quarrel between Euclidean defenders of a geometry of figures against the new geometry of space. The dream of a new geometry was pursued in Leibniz's name, and new and un-Leibnizian methods were devised to answer geometrical and philosophical questions that Leibniz had already addressed in his unpublished writings. Many

---

[28] On the issue, see D. Garber, *Leibniz: Body, Substance, Monad* (Oxford: Oxford University Press, 2009).

[29] On the concept of expression as an isomorphism, see, at least: M. A. Kulstad, "Leibniz conception of expression," in *Studia Leibnitiana 9* (1977), pp. 55–76; C. Swoyer, "Leibnizian expression," in *Journal of the History of Philosophy 33* (1995), pp. 65–99; V. Debuiche, "La notion d'expression et ses origines mathématiques," in *Studia Leibnitiana 41* (2009), pp. 88–117.

[30] See again De Risi, *Geometry and Monadology*, pp. 486–550.

scientists and philosophers claimed that they understood what Leibniz had envisaged with his studies. Wolff, Euler, Buffon, Lambert, Kant, Carnot, Graßmann, Klein, Riemann, Poincaré: all of them relied on Leibniz to illustrate their own attempts to construct a new geometry—and sometimes a new metaphysics that hinged on mathematical results. Vector calculus, projective geometry, and topology were in turn recognized as the proper *analysis situs* and ascribed to Leibniz, even though they departed greatly from Leibniz original ideas. The failed publication of Leibniz's writings, in this sense, proved to be even more effective toward the development of modern geometry, and his fragmentary suggestions and the spell of a name—*analysis situs*—produced, in the end, greater revolutions than he had expected.

CHAPTER 14

....

PROBABILITY AND STATISTICS

....

JAMES CUSSENS

INTRODUCTION

....

LEIBNIZ's role in the development of probability and statistics is aptly summarized by the following observation of Hacking (1975): "Leibniz did not contribute to probability mathematics but his conceptualization of it did have lasting impact."

The bulk of this essay will thus naturally focus on this conceptualization. However, this mathematical lacuna is something of a puzzle: why did such an outstanding mathematician (co-discoverer of the calculus, no less), and one with a deep interest in combinatorial reasoning, fail to contribute to the mathematics of probability?

The answer to this puzzle lies, I think, in how Leibniz wants to use probability. Leibniz is not especially interested in computing the sort of probabilities that arise in games of chance (see, however, Knobloch-Schulenburg 2000 for Leibniz's use of probabilities in calculating life annuities etc.), and he is surprisingly careless on the few occasions where he does so. Leibniz has far more ambitious plans for probability: his goal is that it should be no less than a "new kind of Logic" that can guide human reasoning in all circumstances, not just at the gaming table.

The first part of this essay analyzes Leibniz's attempt to construct this logic. In this part, the main thrust of Leibniz's writings on probability will be emphasized and a consistent theory of probability will emerge. However, Leibniz was not wholly consistent in his writings on probability. In addition to this probabilistic logic designed for human reasoning, there are also hints of a Leibnizian theory of probabilities as objective propensities. This theory is never explicitly formulated by Leibniz, and there is controversy concerning the degree to which he embraced such a view and its consistency with his metaphysics (Hacking 1971; Krüger 1983; Wilson 1971). An analysis of these issues will constitute the second part of this piece. Leibniz contributed to statistics and statistical inference as well as to probability; these are examined in the third section, which is followed by a brief conclusion.

LEIBNIZ'S NEW KIND OF LOGIC

The central feature of Leibniz's conception of probability is that it is intimately connected to legal reasoning. The history of this connection is given by Hacking (1975, chap. 10), who makes the telling observation that Leibniz used "probability" to measure degrees of proof in law as early as his 1665 baccalaureate essay *De conditionibus*. This was before his education in mathematical probability gained during his visit to Paris (1672–1676).

Leibniz's extensive legal studies had left him well equipped to appreciate jurists' thinking on how to justify judgments given evidence. In a typically Leibnizian approach of combining the best of old thinking with new developments, his dream was to augment established juridical thinking with the then new mathematics of probability. This was most clearly expressed in the *New Essays*:

> Jurisconsults in treating the proofs, presumptions, conjectures and indices have said a number of good things on the subject (of degrees of assent) and have entered into considerable detail. . . . there are many degrees of *conjecture* and *indices*. . . . the entire *form of juridical procedures* is in fact nothing but a species of Logic applied to questions of law. Physicians also have a number of degrees and differences in their *signs* and *indications* which may be seen among them.
>
> The Mathematicians of our day have begun to estimate chances in connection with gambling games. . . . I have more than once said that we should have a *new kind of Logic* which would treat of degrees of probability, since Aristotle in his *Topics* has done nothing less than that, and was content with putting in order certain topics which may be useful on some occasion where it is a question of amplifying a speech and giving it some semblance of truth. But he did not take the trouble to give us a necessary balance to weigh probabilities and to form solid judgements accordingly. It would be well for future investigators of this matter to pursue the examination of *games of chance*; and in general I should wish some skillful mathematician might want to write an ample work, with full details and thought out well, on all sorts of games; this would be very useful for perfecting the art of discovery, the human mind revealing itself better in games than in the most serious matters.
>
> (NE IV chap. 16)

From such a legal conception of probability a number of consequences naturally follow. First, since for Leibniz there is always a correct judgment in any legal matter and moreover, in principle, reason permits us to find it, it follows similarly that there is always a correct probability for any uncertain event relative to the evidence, and it, too, can be calculated:

> Even if it is only a question of probabilities we can always determine what is most probable on the given premises. True this part of useful logic is not yet established anywheres, but it is put to wonderful uses in practise when there are hypotheses, indications, and conjectures involved in ascertaining degrees of probability among

a number of reasons appearing on one side or another of some important deliberation. Thus when we lack sufficient data to demonstrate a certitude, the matter
yielding only probability, we can always give demonstrations at least concerning the
probability itself. I do not speak here of that probability of the *Casuists*, based on
the number and reputation of scholastic doctors, but of that probability drawn from
the nature of things in proportion to what we know of them and which we may call
likelihood.

(GP VII 167; Wiener 1951, pp. 29–88)

What is most striking to the modern reader is Leibniz's (characteristic!) optimism: not
only is there always "a probability drawn from the nature of things in proportion to what
we know of them," this probability can always be calculated. Somewhat embarrassingly
the necessary calculus is not yet established, but elsewhere Leibniz promises us that his
very own Universal Characteristic will do the job:

Our Characteristic, however, will reduce all questions to numbers, and thus present
a sort of statics by virtue of which rational evidence may be weighed. Besides, since
probabilities lie at the basis of estimation and proof, we can consequently always
estimate which event under given circumstances can be expected with the highest
probability.

(GP VII 184–189; Wiener 1951, pp. 17–25)

Leibniz never succeeded in producing such a Characteristic and thus was not able to
apply probability to real legal cases. As Franklin notes (2001, p. 365), when, in 1703,
Bernoulli asked for legal examples where posterior probabilities could be applied,
Leibniz could supply nothing. Leibniz thus represents "not only the coming together of
legal and mathematical probability, but also their divergence" (Franklin 2001).

Leibniz's aspiration for universality is in stark contrast to modern mathematical probabilistic reasoning where probabilities are only determined and can only be calculated
from other already given *probabilities*. The process is entirely deductive: for example,
given values for P(a), P(b), and P(b|a), Bayes theorem provides a value for P(a|b) with
absolute certainty. Leibniz aims to go beyond this mundane deductive reasoning, and so
it is appropriate for Hacking to call Leibniz's program *inductive logic*.

Does this inductive logic entail a subjective or objective interpretation of probability? Parmentier (1993) has argued that "legal concepts and techniques thus bestow
on Leibniz's conception of probability a 'legal objectivity' that, by avoiding a priori
probabilization and equiprobability, allowed him to escape the objective/subjective
alternative."

I think it is at least clear that Leibniz's probability is neither subjective in the sense
of de Finetti nor objective in the sense of von Mises. (The very different positions on
probability taken by de Finetti and by von Mises are ably explained by Gillies [2000].)
For Leibniz, probabilities are always conditional on what is known and are thus epistemic and so not objective properties of the world. However, we are not at liberty to

subjectively choose probability values: given any body of evidence a and any proposition b there is a unique value for P(b|a) independent of anyone's views on the matter.

As Leibniz acknowledged, a full-blown inductive logic was not yet available. Nonetheless, there were circumstances where probabilities could already be computed. Most importantly, this is the case when we have "equal hypotheses." Again, the *New Essays* provides an account of Leibniz's (1981) thinking: "The foundation on which [De Witt] built goes back to *prosthaphaeresis*, that is, to taking an arithmetical mean among several equally acceptable hypotheses, and our peasants have long used it in doing their natural mathematics. . . . [They use] the axiom of *aequalibus aequalia,* equal hypotheses must have equal weight" (NE IV chap. 16; Wiener 1951, p. 86).

The idea here is that if a set of n mutually exclusive and exhaustive hypotheses have "equal weight," then each has probability 1/n. Leibniz does not present this finding as any great discovery on his part: after all peasants have long been using a similar principle in combining estimates of the value of land. However, what Leibniz does provide is an analysis of what makes hypotheses equal. This is given in *De incerti aestimatione* (*DIA*) (A VI iv 91–101), a landmark manuscript from 1678. In addition, *DIA* explains how unequal probabilities are derived and hints at the connection between Leibniz's probability and his metaphysics. The next section analyses *DIA* in some detail.

De Incerti Aestimatione

The importance of *DIA* is flagged up by Hacking (1975). Biermann and Faak (1957) analyzed it in some detail with a focus on its mathematical content. An English translation and commentary are provided, respectively, by de Melo and Cussens (2004).

Most of *DIA* concerns the *division problem*: how to divide up the stakes in an interrupted game of chance. As previously mentioned, Leibniz's mathematical solutions to the problem are not impressive, justifying Biermann and Faak's (1957) assertion that *DIA* "did not lead to new, fruitful results for the division problem." Note that Pascal had already solved the problem in 1654. Given the focus on the division problem in *DIA* it is natural that Leibniz usually presents arguments in terms of *expected values* rather than directly in terms of probabilities. The expected value is just the probability of winning multiplied by the amount gained upon winning. Since this amount is, by assumption, fixed, the distinction between expected value and probability is not important and so will be suppressed here to more clearly focus on probability.

Unsurprisingly, given his background in jurisprudence, Leibniz is most concerned that the division be done *fairly*, and so he begins *DIA* by considering what makes a game fair: "A game is fair if there is the same proportion of hope to fear on either side" (de Melo and Cussens 2004). Then he proceeds to specify what is required for an equal proportion of hope to fear: "Axiom. If players do similar things in such a way that no distinction can be drawn between them, with the sole exception of the outcome, there is the same proportion of hope to fear" (ibid.).

Leibniz then later makes a number of crucial connections: "Probability is the degree of possibility. The hope is the probability of having. The fear is the probability of losing. The estimated value of a thing is as high as each one's claim to it" (de Melo and Cussens 2004). It follows that an equal hope:fear ratio for all the players leads to each having an equal probability of winning and this ratio is the same for all "If players do similar things in such a way that no distinction can be drawn between them." It is tempting to view the resulting probabilities as objective features of a fair game defined as one where "players do similar things," but this would be a mistake. What matters is our inability to discriminate between eventual winners and losers because "no distinction can be drawn between them." For Leibniz, there is never any objective uncertainty concerning the outcome. As he wrote elsewhere: "And even this effect of small things causes those who do not consider things correctly to imagine some things happen accidentally and are not determined by destiny, for this distinction arises not in the facts but in our understanding, just as one who does not comprehend the large number of small things belonging to every particular effect and does not recognize any cause he does not see, will then imagine that aces turn up in dice simply by chance" (Deutsche Schriften II p. 48; Wiener 1951, p. 572). In contrast to probability, fairness *is* an objective feature of a game: "If the pool is formed by common, equal contribution of the players, if each one is playing in the same way, and if for the same outcome the same prize or the same penalty is fixed, the game is fair" (de Melo and Cussens 2004); and in a truly fair game it is impossible for us (but not God) to draw a distinction between the players. Based on this (lack of) evidence, the correct epistemic probabilities have to be uniform. This inference, Leibniz claims, "can be demonstrated by metaphysics: where the appearances are the same, the same judgement can be formed about them" (de Melo and Cussens 2004). Hacking states that the metaphysics in question is Leibniz's Principle of Sufficient Reason, but it is difficult to see how this principle—nothing occurs without a sufficient reason why it is so and not otherwise—permits the given inference.

DIA also shows us what we can *do* with epistemic probabilities: why bother to derive them anyway? Leibniz can show the practical use of probability, since he views it as a *quantified right*:

> let us posit that the game is a frequent affair, so that anyone can easily find a buyer of his expectation by auction sale when he wants to. In that case we shall argue as follows: The hope is worth as much as the authority to have the thing.
>
> (de Melo and Cussens 2004)

> If the outcomes are equally easy or equally possible the authority to have the thing in one outcome compared to the authority to have the thing in every outcome is like one compared to the number of outcomes.
>
> (de Melo and Cussens 2004)

Note that in the first of these two quotes, Leibniz is careful to state that only if (1) expectations are *liquid* in the financial sense, and (2) the "game is a frequent affair" can the connection between hope and authority be made. In this case, the probability of a given player winning determines a *fair price* for that player's position, or what is the same thing, a fair share of the pot to give to the player should the game be interrupted.

This is similar, but not identical, to the attitude taken in modern decision theory. There, epistemic probabilities are used to determine optimal choice in a situation of uncertainty where, typically, that choice with highest expected utility is chosen. Leibniz is characteristically more concerned with what is just than what is advantageous.

Feasibility

Having established the conditions under which it is rational to ascribe equal probabilities, Leibniz can now consider how other probabilities might be inferred. In the *New Essays,* Leibniz (1981) takes the straightforward approach of assuming some basic equiprobability and then simply counting how many ways an event can be "made":

> [They use] the axiom of *aequalibus aequalia*, equal hypotheses must have equal weight. But when the hypotheses are unequal, we make comparisons among them. Let us suppose, for example, that with two dice one is to win if he rolls a 7 but his adversary is to win if he makes a 9; we ask what is the ratio of their probabilities of winning? I say that the latter's probability is only two thirds that of the first, for the first can make 7 in three ways (1 and 6, or 2 and 5, of 3 and 4) and the other can make 9 in only two ways (3 and 6, or 4 and 5). And all these ways are equally possible. Hence, the probabilities, which are to each other as the number of equal possibilities, will be in the ratio of 3 to 2, or as 1 to 2/3. I have more than once said that we should have a *new kind of Logic*.
>
> (NE IV chap. 16; Wiener 1951, pp. 86–87)

Apart from the unargued assumption of equal possibilities this process is deductive and uncontroversial. But in a letter to Bourguet in 1714, Leibniz explicitly claims a more general applicability for this approach. It is an important passage and has received different translations into English (Hacking 1975; Wiener 1951), so first it is quoted in the original French:

> L'art de conjecturer est fondée sur ce qui est plus ou moins facile, ou bien plus ou moins faisable, car le latin facilis derivé a faciendo veut dire faisable mot à mot: par exemple, avec deux dés, il est aussi faisable de jetter douze points, que d'en jetter onze, car l'un est l'autre ne se peut faire que d'une seule maniere; mais il est trois fois plus faisable d'en jetter sept, parce que cela se peut fair en jettant 6 et 1, 5 et 2, et 4 et 3; et une combinaison icy est aussi faisable que l'autre.
>
> (GP III 570)

My translation is as follows:

> The art of conjecture is based on what is more or less easy, or more or less feasible, for the Latin *facilis* derived from *faciendo* means feasible literally: for example, with two dice, it is as feasible to throw twelve points as to throw eleven, for both can be made in only one way; but it is three times more feasible to throw seven, because that can be made by throwing 6 and 1, 5 and 2, and 4 and 3; and one combination here is as feasible as the other.

Note that Leibniz has blundered since, as any backgammon player knows, there are two ways of making an eleven: (5,6) or (6,5) whereas (6,6) is the only throw making twelve. The probability of throwing eleven is thus 2/36 = 1/18, whereas a twelve has probability 1/36. More importantly, note that the combinatorial reasoning that can uncontroversially be used for dice scores is given as merely an *example* of a more general principle based on easiness or feasibility.

POSSIBLE WORLDS AND ACTUAL PROBABILITIES

The preceding analysis has focused on those passages consistent with Leibniz's well-documented legally inspired epistemic probability. But *DIA* and various other pieces also contain hints of a different view of probability closely connected to Leibniz's doctrine of possible worlds and his views on contingency.

For example, in *DIA*, almost parenthetically, Leibniz says that "probability is the degree of possibility" a statement Hacking (1975) identifies as "the ultimate source of the Laplacian definition of probability." (Laplace's is the best-known definition in terms of equiprobability.) Moreover, Hacking argues that this second sort of probability is nonepistemic, and thus "Leibniz had two justifications of expectation, one based on insufficient reason, and one based on physical equipossibility. He does not actually say there are two distinguishable ideas of probability but he does present two differentiated arguments" (Hacking 1975). Leibniz never provided a clear account of probability as a physical propensity, so the issue is the extent to which he embraced it and whether it is consistent with his metaphysics.

The obvious basis for a Leibnizian account of objective probability is his famous theory of possible worlds. The temptation is to move from a set of possible worlds vying for existence in the mind of God to a probability distribution over possible worlds, where the probability of any given world is determined by its degree of possibility. After all, "Probability is the degree of possibility" (de Melo and Cussens 2004).

For us, possibility is an all-or-nothing affair: something, whether a specific event or an entire world, is either possible or it is not. But for Leibniz possibility comes in degrees. We have seen that Leibniz (correctly) views *easiness/feasibility* as objective. From Leibniz's theory of *Daseinstreben* (the struggle of essences for existence) we have that degrees of *possibility* are also (metaphysically) objective: "all possible things,... tend by equal right towards existence, according to their degree of essence or reality, or according to the degree of perfection they contain, for perfection is nothing else than quality of essence" (GP VII 302–308; Wiener 1951, pp. 345–355). We have seen that Leibniz has used the objective notions of easiness/feasibility (together with a principle of indifference) to construct a theory of epistemic probability; the issue is whether he also considered using metaphysical possibilities as a basis for objective propensities.

Wilson (1971) cannot see how he can:

> As a theory of the origination of things the *Daseinstreben* presents an all-or-nothing proposition: that fully determinate possible world with the most perfection achieves existence, and all its competitors fail. Certainly to say that possible world *W* has twice the perfection of possible world *W'* is not to say that the former may be expected to occur twice as often as the latter! Neither, however, is it to say that it has twice the chance of occurring. And it is not clear what sense could be ascribed, within Leibniz's system, to the claim that one world is more makeable than another.

This is a compelling argument. The passage already quoted shows Leibniz as a strict determinist concerning the actual world, arguing that it is a mistake to "imagine aces turn up in dice simply by chance."

Leibniz (1923) does explicitly connect *contingency* to possibility:

> All contingent propositions have reasons for being as they are rather than otherwise, or (what is the same thing) they have *a priori* proofs of their truth, which render them certain, and show that the connection of subject and predicate in these propositions has its foundation in the nature of the one and the other; but they do not have demonstrations of necessity, since these reasons are only founded on the principle of contingency, or of the existence of things, i.e. on what is or appears the best among several equally possible things.
>
> (A VI iv 1529; Wiener 1951, pp. 290–345)

But as Leibniz explicitly says, contingent events (such as *Caesar crossed the Rubicon* or, presumably, *the next dice throw will render a score of seven*) are "certain," and thus presumably all have an objective probability of one.

Inductive Inference

Although possible worlds do not lead to a Leibnizian theory of objective probabilities, they do inform his views on choosing between competing hypotheses. There is the actual world in which all is determined, but only God knows the actual world completely. Human beings know the actual world only partially, but *at least they know that it is* the "best" possible world. This gives us something to go on, when reasoning with partial information. For example, we know that *simplicity* and *fecundity* will be strongly represented in the best world. "Thus we may say that in whatever manner God might have created the world, it would always have been regular and in a certain order. God, however, has chosen the most perfect, that it to say the one which is at the same time the simplest in hypotheses and the richest in phenomena" (A VI iv 1529).

This should guide us when considering which of competing hypotheses are more likely to be the case: it provides us with a (justified) *inductive bias*:

> The conjectural method a priori proceeds by hypotheses, assuming certain causes, perhaps, without proof, and showing that the things which now happen would follow from these assumptions. A hypothesis of this kind is like the key to a cryptograph, and the simpler it is, and the greater the number of events that can be explained by it, the more probable it is. But just as it is possible to write a letter intentionally so that it can be understood by means of several keys, of which only one is the true one, so the same effect can have several causes. Hence no firm demonstration can be made from the success of hypotheses. Yet I shall not deny that the number of phenomena which are happily explained by a given hypothesis may be so great that it must be taken as morally certain. Indeed hypotheses of this kind are sufficient for everyday use. Yet it is also useful to apply less perfect hypotheses as substitutes for truth until a better one occurs, that is, one which explains the same phenomena more happily or more phenomena with equal felicity. There is no danger in this if we carefully distinguish the certain from the probable.
>
> (L 280–289)

As Cohen (1989, p. 27) notes, "[Leibniz] apparently never tried to represent or elucidate these thoroughly Baconian criteria with his mathematics of chance, despite his readiness to apply the calculus of chance to other kinds of probability-judgement."

STATISTICS AND STATISTICAL INFERENCE

Leibniz was strongly in favor of the collection of all sorts of statistical data and had important things to say about what can be inferred from such data. As Hacking (1990, pp. 18–19) recounts, Leibniz advocated the establishment of a Prussian state bureau of statistics that would collect information on, among other things, the population and its density and age profile, as well as births, marriages, and deaths. Leibniz was prepared to make inferences from the already existing Prussian register of births, producing a figure for Prussia's population by multiplying the annual birthrate by the suspiciously round figure of 30 (Hacking 1990, p. 19).

Concerning statistical inference, it is interesting to trace how Leibniz's views altered over time. His writings on insurance provide an appropriate starting point. Leibniz was of the view that public companies insuring against, for example, fire, should be set up, since he was skeptical that private companies would be willing to bear the risk. There is a striking *absence* of statistical inference in these writings:

> It is interesting to notice that the brilliant scientist Leibniz, who so favoured the foundation of insurance companies, did not realize the benefit of probability theory and mortality tables for the insurance business. A possible explanation of why we do not find any of Leibniz's works on insurance that build upon the developments of probability theory and mortality is that he seems to have lost interest in insurance in 1683, years before he learned more about these new theoretical concepts.
>
> (von der Schulenburg and Thomann 2010)

But by 1703 Leibniz *was* engaged in the application of probabilities to, for example, mortality data, via his correspondence with Jakob Bernoulli concerning the estimation of probabilities from sample data. Bernoulli wanted to know "how much more probable it is for a young man of twenty years to survive an old man of sixty years than for an old man of sixty years to survive a young man of twenty years". Since this (difference in) probability cannot be deduced like those concerning dice throws, he begun "to inquire whether what is hidden from us by chance *a priori* can at least be known by us *a posteriori* from an occurrence observed many times in similar cases—i.e. from an experiment performed on many pairs of young and old men."

Using (presumably) what we now know as *Bernoulli's weak law of large numbers* (Stigler 1986, p. 66), Bernoulli reaches a positive conclusion:

> I can now determine how many trials must be set up so that it will be a hundred, a thousand, ten thousand, etc., times more probable (and finally, so that it will be morally certain) that the ratio between the numbers of possible outcomes which I obtain in this way is legitimate and genuine.
>
> (Bernoulli to Leibniz, October 3, 1703: GM III 77–78; Sung 1966)

So, Bernoulli argues, from mortality statistics probabilities can be estimated to any desired degree of accuracy. But Leibniz disagrees. Although "the estimation of probabilities is extremely useful,"

> there appears to me to be a difficulty in this conclusion: that happenings which depend upon an infinite number of cases cannot be determined by a finite number of experiments; indeed nature has her own habits, born from the return of causes, but only "in general." And so, who will say whether a subsequent experiment will not stray somewhat from the rule of all the preceding experiments, because of the very mutabilities of things?
>
> (Leibniz to Bernoulli, December 3, 1703: GM III 83–84; Sung 1966)

This is a statement of what has come to be known as the *problem of induction*, a problem famously analyzed by Hume (1739/2007, pt. 3, sec. 6). Note that Leibniz's argument was written a full eight years before Hume was born.

As both Keynes (1921, pp. 368–369) and Daston (1988, pp. 129–130) explain, the basis of the disagreement between Bernoulli and Leibniz is that Bernoulli explicitly assumes that trials are sampled from a stable population—he uses the model of drawing differently colored pebbles from an urn. Leibniz argues against the general applicability of such a model; in particular it does not apply to human diseases.

Interestingly, by 1714 Leibniz appears to have come round to Bernoulli's view on the possibility of statistical inference. The following is from a letter to Bourguet in that year.

> One may still estimate likelihoods [*vraisemblances*] a posteriori, by experience; to which one must have recourse in default of a priori reasons. For example, it is equally likely that a child should be born a boy or a girl, because the number of boys and girls is very nearly equal all over the world. One can say that what happens more or less often is more or less feasible in the present state of things, putting together all considerations that must concur in the production of a fact.
>
> (GP III 570; Hacking 1975, p. 128)

In the original French, Leibniz writes "il est egalement vraisemblable que l'enfant qui doit naistre soit garçon ou fille," which can be translated as "it is equally likely that the child due to be born is a boy or a girl." The point is that Leibniz's use of the definite article in *l'enfant* suggests that he has the likelihood of a singular event in mind: the event of some particular child turning out to be a boy or a girl. The probability in question must then be epistemic, since the event is singular and we will eventually know the child's sex—in any case Leibniz would certainly have had an epistemic interpretation in mind. If this interpretation is accepted, then Leibniz has provided an example of inferring an epistemic probability from relative frequency data, although the statistical inference is done in a cavalier way and makes no use of Bernoulli's theorem.

The final sentence of the preceding quotation suggests a generalization of arguments using feasibility. With dice, we consider the throws that produce a certain total and put them together by the simple process of counting. But more generally, we may consider the "considerations together which should concur in the production of a fact" and quantify feasibility by "putting all considerations together." This suggests there may be valid ways of combining "considerations" other than counting. (Both Hacking [1975, p. 128] and Wiener [1951, p. 88] translate *concourir à* as *concur*, but due to the ambiguity of that word a better translation is *contribute to*.)

Leibniz was of course ignorant of the various biological mechanisms that together contribute to there being roughly equal numbers of boys and girls, but nonetheless (by 1714 at least) *he was prepared to infer from statistical data that some such "considerations" must exist*. There has to be a sufficient reason for everything; this is the reason for the observed relative frequency. Moreover, these considerations determine the feasibility of births of either sex, and this objective feasibility justifies epistemic probability. Leibniz saw objective *easiness* or feasibility as the basis for epistemic probabilities. As he wrote elsewhere: "Quod facile est in re, id probabile est in mente" (A VI ii 492; Hacking 1975, p. 128).

Leibniz can legitimately view the feasibility of an event, whether the event be an observed dice score or the birth of a boy, as a *partial reason* for that particular event. "There must always be some foundation of the connection of terms in a proposition, which must be found in their notions. This is my great principle, with which I believe all philosophers must agree, and of which one of the corollaries is this vulgar axiom, that nothing happens without a reason. . . though often this reason inclines without necessitating" (GP II 56–57; Russell 1937, pp. 32–33). Interestingly, a similar approach is taken to finding reasons for human behavior without at the same time destroying freedom: "There is always a reason or greater inclination behind what we in fact choose to do; our choice may depend not only on argument, good or bad, but also on passions, habits dispositions of the organs of thought, external impressions, greater or less attention, etc. This does not destroy freedom although it inclines it" (Wiener 1951, p. 96).

Although Leibniz's principle is called his Principle of *Sufficient* Reason, note that in both of the passages just quoted he writes of "reasons" with no claim that these reasons are *sufficient* to explain the phenomena under consideration. Indeed, they surely cannot be sufficient, since the "reason inclines without necessitating."

Conclusion

What is remarkable in Leibniz's writings on probability and statistics (as in much of his other work) is the extent to which he prefigured much later thinking. Consider the following three important probabilistic and statistical ideas that Leibniz addressed. Probability as logic: although Keynes (1921) is the most prominent advocate of this interpretation, it is clear, as Hacking has argued, that this notion originated long before with Leibniz. The problem of induction: although credit for an appreciation of this problem is usually given to Hume, the basic difficulty, at least, of inductive inference was appreciated by Leibniz much earlier. Simplicity as a justified inductive bias: although attributed to the much earlier Ockham, Leibniz provides a metaphysical basis by grounding such a bias in his philosophy of the "best possible world." Leibniz is careful to balance simplicity with "fit to data": the really probable hypotheses are both simple and able to explain lots of events. In addition, there is certainly no guarantee that the simplest hypothesis consistent with data is true; Leibniz disagrees with Bernoulli that "nature follows the simplest paths."

Returning, in conclusion, to consider Hacking's claim that Leibniz's conceptualization of probability had a lasting impact, it seems impossible to deny that it did. It is true that Leibniz is not as *prominent* a philosopher of probability and statistics as the likes of Keynes, de Finetti, and Popper, but his *influence*, although underacknowledged, is substantial.

Thanks to Maria Rosa Antognazza for her critical input and to Alexandra Lanot for her advice on French translations.

REFERENCES

Biermann, Kurt-Reinhard, and Margot Faak. "G. W. Leibniz' *De incerti aestimatione.*" *Forschungen und Fortschritte* 31 (1957), 45–50.

Cohen, Jonathan L. *An Introduction to the Philosophy of Induction and Probability.* Oxford: Oxford University Press, 1989.

Daston, Lorraine. *Classical Probability in the Enlightenment.* Princeton: University Press, 1988.

de Melo, Wolfgang David Cirilo, and James Cussens. "Leibniz on Estimating the Uncertain: An English Translation of *De incerti aestimatione* with Commentary." *Leibniz Review* 14 (2004), 31–56.

Franklin, James. *The Science of Conjecture: Evidence and Probability before Pascal.* Baltimore: The Johns Hopkins University Press, 2001.

Gillies, Donald. *Philosophical Theories of Probability.* London: Routledge, 2000.

Hacking, Ian. *The Emergence of Probability.* Cambridge: Cambridge University Press, 1975.

Hacking, Ian. "The Leibniz-Carnap Program for Inductive Logic." *Journal of Philosophy* 68:19 (1971), 597–610.

Hacking, Ian. *The Taming of Chance.* Cambridge: Cambridge University Press, 1990.

Hume, David. *A Treatise of Human Nature.* Vol. 1. 1739. In *The Clarendon Edition of the Works of David Hume.* Edited by David Fate Norton and Mary J. Norton. Oxford: Clarendon Press, 2007.

Keynes, J. M. *A Treatise on Probability.* London: Macmillan, 1921.

Knobloch, E., and J.-M. Graf von der Schulenburg, eds. *G. W. Leibniz, Hauptschriften zur Versicherungs-und Finanzmathematik.* Berlin: Akademie Verlag, 2000.

Krüger, Lorenz. "Probability in Leibniz: On the Internal Coherence of a Dual Concept." *Archiv für Geschichte der Philosophie* 63 (1983), 47–60.

Parmentier, Marc. "Concepts juridiques et probabilistes chez Leibniz." *Revue d'Histoire des Sciences* 46 (1993), 439–485.

Russell, Bertrand. *A Critical Exposition of the Philosophy of Leibniz.* 2nd ed. London: Allen and Unwin, 1937.

Stigler, Stephen M. *The History of Statistics: The Measurement of Uncertainty before 1900.* Cambridge, Mass.: Harvard University Press, 1986.

Sung, Bing. *Translations from James Bernoulli.* Technical report no. 2. Cambridge, Mass.: Department of Statistics, Harvard University, 1966.

von der Schulenburg, J.-Matthias Graf, and Christian Thomann. "Gottfried Wilhelm Leibniz's Work on Insurance." In *The Appeal of Insurance.* Edited by Geoffrey Clark et al. Toronto: University of Toronto Press, 2010, chap. 2, pp. 43–51.

Wiener, Philip P., ed. *Leibniz Selections.* New York: Scribners, 1951.

Wilson, Margaret. "Probability, Propensity, and Chance: Some Doubts about the Hacking Thesis." *Journal of Philosophy* 68:19 (1971), 610–617.

PART IV

THE PHYSICAL
WORLD AND ITS
METAPHYSICAL
GROUNDING

....

CHAPTER 15

THE LABYRINTH OF
THE CONTINUUM

....

RICHARD T. W. ARTHUR

LEIBNIZ typically described his theory of substance as a solution to the difficulties of the continuum, a way out of the infamous "labyrinth of the continuum." This will seem odd if the composition of the continuum is understood as a purely mathematical problem—that of whether a line, for instance, is composed of points or infinitesimals, or perhaps neither. Natural philosophers in the seventeenth century, however, understood the problem in a much wider sense, as applying to all existing quantities and their composition: what (if any) are the first elements of things and their motions? Are there atoms or indivisible elements of substance, as Gassendi and many of his contemporaries proposed? If so, this leaves many difficulties unresolved: what is the origin of their cohesion? why does the division of matter stop at some point? Perhaps, as Galileo proposed, matter is made up of points, held together by the indivisible voids separating them, with both points and voids lacking quantity. But then how do things lacking quantity compose into something continuous? In Descartes's natural philosophy, individual bodies are distinguished by their differing motions, which actually divide them. But in order for there to be motion in the plenum, this division must proceed to infinity. How is this possible? For Hobbes, a body in motion must have at each instant an endeavour or "beginning of motion" (corresponding to a Galilean "degree of motion" or one of Cavalieri's indivisibles), and the same endeavours are the cornerstones of his materialist psychology. But can any sense be made of the composition of motions from endeavours without supposing the composition of space out of points, or time out of instants, which geometry forbids? It is this whole cluster of problems concerning infinite divisibility, the actual infinite, mathematical indivisibles, the existence of atoms of matter or substance, and the analysis of continuous space, time, and motion that constitutes Leibniz's "labyrinth of the continuum," and for which his theory of substance was intended as a solution.

In outlining his solution, Leibniz characteristically explained it by contrast with the false conceptions he believed had led others astray (and that correspond, in almost every case, to blind alleys from which he had had to extricate himself in his earlier studies). Continuous things, he stressed, cannot be composed by an aggregation of first elements: insofar as anything is continuous, its parts are indiscernible from one another, and thus indefinite. The continuum is therefore not an actually existing thing, a whole composed of determinate parts, but an abstract entity. Thus "those who compose the line from points have quite improperly sought first elements in ideal things or relations."[1] In existing things, by contrast, the parts are determinate, and units are prior to any whole aggregated from them. Matter, for example, considered abstractly, is homogeneous and continuous, consisting in a pure potentiality for division; but taken concretely it is at any instant not only infinitely divisible but actually infinitely divided by the differing motions of its parts. As a result of these continually changing motions, no part of matter, however small, remains the same for longer than a moment; even shape or figure is eva-nescent, and a body with an enduring figure is something imaginary. Similarly, there is no stretch of time, however small, in which some change does not occur.

Actual things, on the other hand, presuppose true unities. Thus, each actual part of matter presupposes something that is truly one, and from which its actuality derives. These true unities are what Leibniz calls simple substances, entities that contain an "en-telechy" or actualizing principle. Leibniz's employment of these scholastic terms reflects his deeply held belief that many Aristotelian principles, when properly interpreted, provide a sound foundation for the mechanical philosophy that is otherwise lacking. In Descartes's philosophy, material substance is essentially passive, and so does not con-tain any foundation from which its motions or capacity to do work can be derived. For Leibniz, a substance is rather essentially something that acts, and the effects of its actions will be local motions. The capacity for such action, married with a tendency to actually bring it about, is what he dubs "force": "and this force does not consist in a mere faculty, such as the Schools seem to have been content with, but instead is endowed with an endeavour or striving, such that it will attain its full effect unless it is impeded by some contrary endeavour."[2] This force is thus the foundation for the motion of any actual part of matter at any instant: "For not only is a body in a place commensurate with itself at the present moment of its motion, but it also has an endeavour or striving to change place, so that the subsequent state follows of itself from the present one, by a force of nature."[3] One sense in which this primitive force is an entelechy, something that "makes something actual," is that the differing endeavours or tendencies to motion to which it gives rise are what make actual the various parts into which matter is divided at different instants. Without some such entelechies or principles of activity, Leibniz held, the var-ious parts into which mechanical philosophers supposed matter to be divided at any instant would not even be distinguishable from one another.[4] This necessity for there to

---

[1] "Remarques sur les Objections de M. Foucher" [1695]; GP IV 491. All translations given here are my own.
[2] *Specimen Dynamicum* [1695], GM VI 235.
[3] *De ipsa Natura* [1698], §13; GP IV 513.
[4] *De ipsa Natura*, §13; GP IV 513.

be such active substances everywhere in matter is, in Leibniz's eyes, what is missed by his contemporaries such as Arnauld, De Volder, or Foucher: "those who have found that relations such as number and space (which comprise the order or relation of possible co-existent things) cannot be formed from an assemblage of points, have for the most part been mistaken in denying that substantial realities have first elements, as if there were no primitive unities in them, or as if there were no simple substances."[5] Simple substances, for Leibniz, are unities that cannot be resolved into anything more primitive: they are enduring sources of activity, from each of which emanates a series of states governed by its own individual law, each state being a representation of everything else in the universe contemporary with it. Each substance, moreover, being a primitive force or source of activity, also involves an instantaneous endeavour or striving toward a change of state, and this endeavour is what is real in motion at each instant, as manifested in the derivative active forces resulting from it.

The foregoing sketch, of course, leaves much to be explained, but it does at least indicate in general terms how Leibniz's views on substance bear on the analysis of the continuum. In order to elaborate his solution to the labyrinth in more detail, it will be convenient to sketch its historical development, beginning with Leibniz's first systematic foray into natural philosophy. It is here that the relationship between the theory of substance and the composition of the continuum is most explicit.

THE GEOMETRY OF INDIVISIBLES: THE PRESUPPOSITION ARGUMENT

When Leibniz burst on the intellectual scene in Europe in the early 1670s, it was as an enthusiast of the new mechanical philosophy. The new learned societies of London and Paris found themselves presented with a treatise on physics, *Hypothesis Physica Nova* ("A New Physical Hypothesis," hereafter *HPN*), sporting novel theories of a wide range of phenomena from the formation of the solar system to the cohesion of atoms, and founded on an intriguing theory of the continuum, given in an accompanying tract, the *Theoria Motus Abstracti* (*TMA*). The germ for this theory is the identification of substance—which for Leibniz is by definition indivisible—with the indivisibles of geometry. Here he builds on Hobbes's treatment, but where the Englishman went for an uncompromising finitist reinterpretation of indivisibles or points, Leibniz blithely substitutes an equally uncompromising commitment to the actually infinitely small. Thus Hobbes had rejected the Euclidean definition of a point as "that which has no part" in favor of "that whose part is not considered"; Leibniz rejects both in favor of "that which *has no extension*, that is, whose parts are indistant."[6] On the one hand, the bold

---

[5] "Remarques sur Foucher"; GP IV 491.
[6] *Theoria Motus Abstracti* (*TMA*); A VI 2, 264–65.

assertion that indivisibles contain parts avoided Aristotle's objection (in *Physics* 231b) that indivisibles, being partless, cannot be composed into a continuum; on the other, since Leibniz defined magnitude as "the multiplicity [*multitudo*] of its parts," Leibniz's points (unlike Galileo's *parti non quante*) could have a magnitude. Their ratio to a finite line would then be as 1 to ∞, not 0 to 1,[7] as would a partless point or minimum. The latter is rejected on geometric grounds: "a minimum cannot be supposed without it following that the whole has as many minima as the part, which implies a contradiction."[8]

In justification of this idea of points with parts but no extension, Leibniz followed Hobbes in appealing to horn angles, angles between a straight line and a curve, one of which could be bigger than another even while both are less than any rectilinear angle that can be assigned. He also appealed to the Scholastic doctrine of signs in support of the idea that even simultaneous things could have an order of priority, an ordering of parts without extension. But his strongest argument was an ingenious inversion of Zeno's dichotomy argument applied to motion. If motion is to occur, then it must have a beginning. But whatever is moving in a given interval must already have been moving in the first half of that interval, so the beginning of the motion must be contained in this interval. But what is moving in the first half must already have been moving in the first half of this half, and so on to infinity. Zeno concluded that motion could never begin; Leibniz (taking for granted the reality of motion) concluded that since the beginning of any motion cannot consist in an extended stretch of motion, this beginning must be unextended. Indeed, since this argument is applicable to any subinterval of the motion— or likewise to any subintervals of lines, bodies, or times—it entails the stronger conclusion that any subinterval whatever must contain an unextended beginning. Thus a beginning of motion, which Leibniz followed Hobbes in calling an endeavour (*conatus*), is proportional to the beginning of a line (point) covered in the beginning of an interval of time (instant). If follows that if we take two points p and q that are the beginnings of two different lines described in time T by the unequal uniform motions whose speeds are M and N, they will be proportional to the endeavours that are the beginnings of these motions, M/∞ and N/∞, respectively. Therefore, even though these points are infinitely small, they will be in the ratio M:N, that is, in the same ratio as their generating motions. An infinity of points of length MT/∞ will compose a line of length MT, just as an infinity of endeavours M/∞ will compose the motion M.

In the *HPN*, Leibniz used this theory of indivisibles of different sizes to explain the cohesion of bodies in terms of the fusing together of their boundaries. When one body impinges on another, the indivisible constituting the boundary of the impelling body is greater than that of the body with which it is colliding in proportion to the endeavours of their motions; their boundaries therefore overlap, so that the bodies are truly continuous and cohering, as opposed to being merely contiguous. By this means, Leibniz sought to explain the original cohesion of the hollow atoms, or *bullae* (literally,

---

[7] *TMA*; A VI 2, 265.
[8] *TMA*; A VI 2, 264. The argument is given below.

bubbles), that he claimed in the *HPN* were formed shortly after Creation like the little globules of glass shooting off in a glassworks.[9] The spinning motion imparted by the Sun's rays would result in concentric rings of matter made to cohere by the endeavours propagating around them.

It is the connection of endeavours with indivisibles, moreover, that carries the metaphysical weight in Leibniz's early theory. Following Hobbes's construal of endeavours as incipient desires and aversions, with the mind a kind of means for containing contrary endeavours beyond a moment, Leibniz construed bodies as "momentary minds." By this means, he boasted to Oldenburg in 1671, he could "demonstrate" the indestructibility of mind from the fact that "once two contrary endeavours in the same point of a body are compatible beyond a moment, no other bodies can slip between them, nor can they be prized apart by any force for all eternity."[10] He advertised this theory to Duke Johann Friedrich as providing a firm foundation for the Christian dogma of bodily resurrection, and as being able to circumvent the problem posed by cannibalism: the idea was that the mind, "safe and sound in its point," could lie dormant until resurrection, when its sphere of influence could expand to a full-size body again, the mind determining the identity of the individual.[11] Moreover, if the mind is contained in a mathematical point at the extremity of a pointed body, a division of the body resulting in a division of the point could produce a multiplication of minds. By this means, he claimed in a letter to Lambert van Velthuysen,[12] he could use this theory of indivisibles to explain "with as much clarity as sunshine" how "mind can multiply itself, without new creation, by traduction, with no mention of incorporeality." (Traduction is the idea that in biological generation, the soul of the offspring is not created de novo by God but instead results from a kind of budding of the parents' souls together with the genetic matter, by analogy with the grafting of trees.)

THE DIFFERENTIAL CALCULUS: INFINITESIMALS AND INFINITE WHOLES AS FICTIONS

By the time Leibniz had arrived in Paris in 1672, however, he had come to see that the distinction he had made in the *TMA* between indivisibles and minima could not be sustained. The same argument that he had given in the *TMA* against minima (partless points) could be applied to indivisibles: the points on the diagonal of a rectangle could be put into 1–1 correspondence with the points on one side, and these with the points

[9] *HPN*; A VI 2, 226.
[10] Letter to Oldenburg, 1671; A II 1, 90.
[11] Letter to Duke Johann Friedrich, May 1671; A II 1, 113.
[12] Letter to van Velthuysen, May 1671; A II 1, 97–98.

on a part of the diagonal equal in length to the side, so that there would be as many points in the part of the diagonal as in the whole, contrary to the part-whole axiom.[13] Nevertheless, Leibniz still upheld the infinitely small beginnings he had established by the dichotomy argument, provided they were regarded instead as defined by motion. Thus two lines generated in the same time by different generating motions would have at any instant infinitely small lengths proportional to those motions. Consequently, from now on Leibniz would sharply distinguish such infinitesimals from points. Points, he realized, must be mere endpoints, the boundaries of a line segment. As such, they would be of dimension 0, and thus not homogeneous with a line of dimension 1. An infinitely small part of the line, on the other hand, must be homogeneous with the whole of which it is part; it would therefore have extension, be further divisible, and would itself be bounded by endpoints.

This conception of infinitely small parts as dimensionally homogeneous with the whole they composed was a notion Leibniz found confirmed in the mathematical work of Pascal, which he was reading at this time (winter 1672–73) under Huygens's guidance. On this conception, the area under a curve could be regarded as made up of an infinity of infinitely small rectangular areas, each with the height of an ordinate and with an infinitesimal width, at least as a means of calculation. Also with Huygens's encouragement, Leibniz had quickly made great progress in his studies of infinite series, discovering a simple relationship between a series of terms and a second series whose terms are the differences of the first, his "Difference Principle." If, from a given series A, one forms a difference series B whose terms are the differences of the successive terms of A, the sum of the terms in the B series is simply the difference between the last and first terms of the original series: "the sum of the differences is the difference between the first term and the last."[14] Leibniz immediately applied this result to infinite series whose infinitieth term could be taken to be 0, yielding results for sums of infinite series such as that of the reciprocal triangular numbers: $^1/_1 + {}^1/_3 + {}^1/_6 + {}^1/_{10} + {}^1/_{15} + \ldots = 2$.

With his characteristic genius for generalization, Leibniz extended these considerations to continuous quantities, and within a mere three years was led to formulate what we now call the Fundamental Theorem of the Calculus: if dx is the infinitely small difference between the infinitely many successive values of x, the area under a curve $y = f(x)$ (its quadrature, Q) between $x = a$ and $x = b$ can be represented as an infinite sum: $Q = \int_n f(x_n)dx$. Now if one has an expression for the general term of another series $g(x_n)$, the difference between whose successive terms is $f(x)dx$, one may apply

---

[13] This argument depends for its success on Leibniz's conception of magnitude as the "multitude of its parts." So long as points are conceived as parts of the line, the multitude of points composing the diagonal will be both greater than and equal to the points composing the side, because the magnitude of the diagonal is greater than that of the side. Leibniz held onto this definition of magnitude but came to deny the composition out of indivisible points, i.e., that points were parts. Of course, that a proper part (i.e. subset) of a set can be put in 1–1 correspondence with the whole set is later taken by Dedekind and Cantor as the very definition of an infinite set. But Leibniz insisted that the part-whole axiom must apply without exception, and therefore denied that an infinite set could be regarded as a collection.

[14] A VII 3, 95.

the Difference Principle: the sum (integral) of the differences equals the difference of the first term and the last (the definite integral evaluated between first and last terms), $\int_a^b f(x)dx = [g(b) - g(a)]$.

Some of Leibniz's reasonings on the way to formulating his calculus are of special interest with regard to its foundations. Thus in a paper written in 1674, Leibniz calculated the area (ACBEM on his figure) under the hyperbola $x = 1/(1 - y)$ between the y-axis and the line y = 1 by expanding it as an infinite series of terms $x = (1 - y)^{-1} = 1 + y + y^2 + y^3 + \ldots$ and then effectively integrating term-wise to obtain ACBEM $= 1 + \frac{1}{2} + \frac{1}{3} + \frac{1}{4} + \frac{1}{5} + \ldots$, which is infinite. By a similar means, he was also able to calculate a finite area under the curve on his diagram, CFGLB, as $1 - \frac{1}{2} + \frac{1}{3} - \frac{1}{4} + \frac{1}{5} + \ldots$. But on subtracting the finite space CFGLB from the infinite space ACBEM, he obtains ACBEM $- CFGLB = (1 - 1) + (\frac{1}{2} + \frac{1}{2}) + (\frac{1}{3} - \frac{1}{3}) + (\frac{1}{4} + \frac{1}{4}) + (\frac{1}{5} - \frac{1}{5}) + \ldots = 1 + \frac{1}{2} + \frac{1}{3} + \frac{1}{4} + \frac{1}{5} + \ldots = $ ACBEM. Thus "the area of the space [ACBEM] remains the same even when the finite space [CFGLB] is subtracted from it." From this he concludes that "the infinite is not a whole, but only a fiction; for otherwise the part would be equal to the whole."[15]

Here we see the emergence of Leibniz's doctrine of the fictionality of infinite magnitudes. But the connection with infinite series is particularly revealing since, in the foregoing reasoning, treating the space ACBEM *as if* it were a whole is equivalent to treating the infinite series *as if* it had a last term; indeed this is presupposed by all his applications of the Difference Principle. This gives the all-important connection between Leibniz's doctrines of the fictionality of infinite wholes and the fictionality of infinitesimals.

By 1676, Leibniz had built these beginnings into the differential calculus, creating the notation and rules for differentiation we use today, and with explicit recognition of the inverse nature of integration (Bernoulli's term) and differentiation. He had also developed the foregoing intuitions about the fictional character of the infinite and the infinitesimal into a sophisticated foundation for the calculus based on the Archimedean axiom, which implies that no matter how small a geometric quantity is given, a smaller can be found.[16] On this conception, an infinitesimal is a *compendium* (an abbreviated expression) for a variable finite quantity that can be made as small as desired. The infinitesimal is treated *as if* it is an actual quantity in certain defined circumstances, although one that can be ignored by comparison with a finite quantity. For example, in a formula obtained by treating dx as a nonzero quantity, the neglect of expressions involving dx in comparison with x is justified by reference to the Archimedean axiom. If $y = x + dx$, where dx is an arbitrarily small variable quantity, and D is any preassigned difference between y and x, no matter how small, then dx may always be taken so small that $dx <$ D. Therefore, since dx, the difference between y and x, is smaller than any assignable,

---

[15] A VII 3, N. 38_{10}, 468 [October 1674].

[16] The axiom states: "Those magnitudes are said to have a ratio to one another which are capable, when multiplied, of exceeding one another" (Euclid, *Elements*, bk. 5, def. 4). That is, for any two geometric quantities x and y (with $y \rangle x$), a natural number n can be found such that $nx \rangle y$. It also follows that no matter how small a geometric quantity x is given, a smaller (y/n) can be found.

it is unassignable, and effectively null. Thus, a converging infinite series can be treated as if it were an infinite sum with a last (infinitely small) term, and this is justified by the fact that the difference between this and the sum of a finite series with the same first term and law of progression can be made smaller than any quantity assignable, and thus null. Similarly, the area under a curve $y = f(x)$ can be treated as if it were the sum $\int f(x)\, dx$ of rectangles of height y and width dx where the dx are infinitely small differences of (fictional) successive values of x, and this is justified by the fact that the difference between this area and the sum of the sum of a finite number of finite elements of area can be made smaller than any predetermined value. Later Leibniz would develop these ideas into his Law of Continuity: "If any continuous transition is proposed that finishes in a certain limiting case [*terminus*], then it is possible to formulate a general reasoning that includes that final limiting case."[17]

THE ACTUAL INFINITE

In keeping with this account of the infinitely small, and perhaps also stimulated by Spinoza's related views on the infinite, which he studied in early 1676, Leibniz articulated a subtle theory of the actual infinite. According to this view, it is perfectly legitimate to describe a plurality of things as actually infinite, without that committing you to there being an *infinite number* of them. To say that there are infinitely many prime numbers, for example, is to say that for any finite number you choose, there are actually (not merely potentially) more primes than this; it is *not* to say that there is a number of primes that is greater than any finite number, that is, an infinite number of them. The infinite, like the infinitely small, is thus treated as a *syncategorematic* term, one that derives its meaning from the sentence in which it occurs, but one for which there is no corresponding entity.[18]

The significance of this for Leibniz's theory of matter can be seen as follows. He had long been firmly committed to the division of matter to infinity, and as we saw, initially interpreted this division as issuing in indivisibles. But with the collapse of his earlier attempt to distinguish indivisibles from minima, Leibniz was unable to see how to avoid the conclusion that an actually infinite division of matter would issue in minima. In some of the fragments he penned in Paris that last spring of 1676, he experimented with the idea that a solid body or atom would be an infinity of such material points held together by a mind, although he no longer seemed sure how the mind could achieve this.

[17] *Historia et Origo calculi differentialis a G. G. Leibnitzio conscripta*, (ed. C. I. Gerhardt), Hanover, 1846.

[18] "It is easy to demonstrate that there is no infinite number, nor any infinite line or other infinite quantity, if these are taken as genuine wholes. The Scholastics were taking that view, or should have been, when they allowed a *syncategorematic infinite*, as they called it, but not a *categorematic* one." *Nouveaux Essais*, xvii, A VI 6, 157.

Finally, as his calculus took shape, he came to see that infinite division need not issue in points after all. If matter is infinitely divided in the syncategorematic sense, each part will be divided in such a way that, no matter how small a part is taken, it is divided further still. He found support for this in the argument in Descartes's *Principles* (or perhaps Spinoza's rendition thereof) that bodies are actually divided by the differing motions of the parts inside them. For a part of matter can be individuated by all its constituents having a motion in common, without this precluding these constituents having other motions that further divide the part. No reason could be given, he concluded, for God's "putting a stop to his handiwork" and ceasing this division at any point.[19] There is therefore no such thing as a perfect liquid, one consisting in points: "on the contrary, every liquid has some tenacity, so that although it is torn into parts, not all the parts of the parts are so torn in their turn; instead they merely take shape for some time, and are transformed; and yet in this way there is no dissolution all the way down into points, even though any point is distinguished from any other by motion."[20]

In the late 1670s and 1680s, Leibniz builds on this conception of the actual infinite division of matter to argue that body, understood as something merely material, has no more than a phenomenal unity. Taking as a premise the nominalist principle that *the reality of an aggregate derives only from the reality of its constituents*, he argues that body will have "no reality at all if each constituent being is still a being by aggregation, for whose reality we have to find some further basis."[21] If a body is the aggregate of the parts into which it is divided, then its reality consists in the parts alone, and not in their being perceived as one. But since each of these parts is further divided, the argument iterates: the body is a perceived unity and a plurality of parts, but each of these parts is also a perceived unity and a plurality of parts, and so on down. If there are no true unities, then, given infinite division, the reality of body will elude analysis, and it will exist merely as a perceived unity, a pure phenomenon. If, on the other hand, there exist true unities in the body, then the body's reality will reduce to the reality of these, while its own unity will consist only in their being perceived together. It will then be what Leibniz in his correspondence with De Volder calls a "quasi substance," a plurality of substances with no substantial unity. This returns us to a consideration of substance.

ATOMS OF SUBSTANCE AND THE PLURALITY OF FORMS

Although by the spring of 1676 Leibniz had abandoned the composition of the continuum from indivisibles, and had arrived at his interpretation of geometric

---

[19] *Pacidius Philalethi* [1676]; A VI 3, 561.
[20] *Pacidius Philalethi*; A VI 3, 555.
[21] Letter to Arnauld, April 30, 1687; GP II 96.

infinitesimals as fictional parts of the line, he was still not sure what the implications were for his theory of substance. He had strong motivations for retaining mind-containing atoms of some kind, since, as we saw, he thought he could explain the immortality of rational souls in terms of their being contained in indivisibles, and thereby also explain the propagation of souls by traduction. In addition, as we have seen, his earlier theory was motivated in part by the idea that the mechanical philosophy was incomplete without some principle of activity from which the motions of bodies would derive, and he had seized on Hobbes's endeavour as providing such a principle. Thus, as late as April 1676 Leibniz was entertaining the idea that every atom contains a mind or soul as its principle of individuation, each associated with its own vortex, and that "the soul itself activates this vortex."[22]

In the summer of 1676, however, Leibniz underwent a kind of conversion from the materialist trend of these speculations. This may have been induced by his reading of Plato's dialogues, two of which he was then translating, particularly the passage from Plato's *Phaedo* where Socrates criticizes his former teacher Anaxagoras for "introducing mind but making no use of it."[23] The idea is that Socrates's remaining on the bench in prison cannot be understood in terms of material causes, and can only be understood teleologically, that is, in terms of his mind acting according to its own end-directed laws, in step with his body acting according to the laws of mechanics. Any model of the mind such as Leibniz had previously been entertaining, where the mind acts on the matter of its own vortex, would from now on be rejected out of hand as too naive. Cementing him in this opinion would have been the Occasionalist arguments familiar to him from his discussions with Malebranche in his four years in Paris. Malebranche argued that the purely passive nature of body—conceived as mere extended substance—precludes it from having any power to "transmit to another body the power transporting it,"[24] a power that must therefore reside only in God. Although Leibniz wanted each body to contain its own principle of activity, and thus to be more than mere extended substance, he had to concede to Malebranche that there was no way to conceive how such a principle could act on anything outside itself.

Leibniz was, nevertheless, firmly committed to the mechanical philosophy. As he affirmed to Hermann Conring in January 1678, he regarded as "demonstrated" Robert Boyle's claim "that *everything in nature happens mechanically*."[25] When Conring professed alarm at this apparent endorsement of Cartesianism, Leibniz reassured him that he was very far from rejecting the substantial forms necessary for individuating parts of matter.[26] Boyle himself, of course, did not regard mechanism as incompatible

---

[22] *De unione animae et corporis* [February(?) 1676], A VI 3, 480.

[23] Plato, *Phaedo*, 97b–99c. In his *Discours de métaphysique* of 1686, Leibniz makes a marginal note to himself to insert the translation of this passage at §20, "A memorable passage by Socrates in Plato's *Phaedo*, against over-materialistic philosophers" (GP IV 446; GP II 13).

[24] Nicolas Malebranche, *The Search after Truth*, trans. T. M. Lennon and P. J. Olscamp (Columbus: Ohio State University Press, 1980), p. 660.

[25] Herman Conring in January 1678.

[26] Herman Conring in January 1678.

with an inherent teleology in created things mandated by God's providence. But he vehemently rejected substantial forms, attaching to the first edition of his *Origin of Forms* a lengthy critique of them. His main target was Daniel Sennert, who in 1636 had recommended, against the atomism of his contemporary Sébastien Basson, that substantial forms should be retained.[27] Atoms must be animated, Sennert had claimed, in order to account for such phenomena as the formation of minerals and biological generation. Now Leibniz agreed with Boyle about not employing forms to explain particular phenomena, but he could not agree that matter left to itself would have any means for self-organization, nor with Boyle's conception of teleology as simply imposed from above by divine fiat. On these points, therefore, Leibniz's sympathies would have lain with Sennert rather than Boyle. For Leibniz, as for Sennert and other Lutherans such as de Goodt, God's instruction in Genesis 1:22, "Be fruitful and multiply," could only be understood to mean that the entities created by God in the first days contained within them the capacity for propagating all their descendants. They must possess, in Leibniz's words, "a form or force . . . from which the series of phenomena will follow according to the dictate of the original command."[28]

Consequently, Leibniz appealed to the same tradition of Latin pluralism as had Sennert, advocated above all by J. C. Scaliger, in trying to resolve the problem of forms. According to this tradition, matter, prior to its being organized by a form into an organic body, does not exist as a pure potentiality (as in the orthodox Thomist tradition) but instead has its own reality. This reality has its source in the parts of a body themselves being made actual by their own subordinate forms. Boyle's sarcastic criticisms about how these mysterious forms could arise or perish are then neatly sidestepped by Leibniz's proposal "that every soul, and indeed every corporeal substance, has existed from the beginning of things."[29] Thus the forms or forces responsible for the teleology of bodies are coeval with the created world and are identified by Leibniz with the true unities presupposed by every existing body, as demanded by the infinite aggregate argument described above. Every actual part of matter is either the organic body of a substance (like an animal) or a collection of such (like a woodpile): "all bodies are either organic or collections of organic bodies."[30] The organic body is animated by a dominant form, but the parts of the body are actualized by their own subordinate forms: every organism contains within its body further subordinate organisms, and "every generation of an animal is only a transformation of an already living animal"[31]—a conception for which Leibniz saw significant empirical support in the microscopic observations

---

[27] Daniel Sennert, *Hypomnemata Physica* (Frankfurt, 1636).

[28] *De ipsa Natura*, §6; GP IV 507.

[29] From *Mira de natura substantiae corporeae*, [March 1683]; A VI 4, 1466; LoC 265). Cf. "Whatever acts cannot be destroyed, for it certainly endures as long as it acts, and will therefore endure forever" (*De origine rerum ex formis* [April 1676]; A VI 3, 521).

[30] *Ex Cordemoii tractatu*; A VI 4, 1798.

[31] Draft of a letter to Arnauld, December 8, 1686; GP II 72.

of Anton van Leeuwenhoek and Marcello Malpighi. But how do these considerations about substance relate to the continuum?

SUBSTANCE AS FORCE

According to Leibniz, the Ariadne's thread that led him out of the labyrinth was the estimation of forces. At first blush, it appears as though he must here be referring to a different labyrinth, since it is not at all clear how a specific issue in physics—namely, the correction of the Cartesian measure of force, mv ("quantity of motion"), to the Leibnizian measure, mv^2 ("living force")—could be relevant to the problem of the continuum. There is, however, a deep connection through the definition of substance as *something that acts*, a definition Leibniz takes as axiomatic. His upholding of this idea of substance is in itself an implicit criticism of Cartesianism. There must be a "this something" (Aristotle), and there must be some measure of the activity of this something at each instant. To begin with, as we saw, Leibniz saw a solution in the Hobbesian notion of endeavour, identifying this as the principle of activity of bodies. But, as he recounts in many writings, if a body consisted only in size, shape, position, and their changes, together with such an endeavour, this would have the unwelcome consequence that "the largest body at rest would be carried away by the smallest body colliding with it."[32]

This is where Leibniz's revamped notion of substance comes into play. The argument so far has been that there must be real unities in matter, and also that there must be some principles by which the differing motions in matter at any instant might be distinguished. These desiderata are both satisfied by Leibniz's conception of the unities or substances as beings capable of action, for which it is necessary for them to be repositories of *force*. On the one hand, force is "an attribute from which change follows, whose subject is substance itself";[33] on the other, it involves an endeavour or striving, and this is what the reality of motion consists in: "there is nothing real in motion but that momentaneous thing which must be constituted by a force striving toward change."[34] This force is thus the foundation for the motion of any actual part of matter at any instant. It is an *entelechy* in the sense that it remains self-identical through the changes of state that it brings into actuality: it is the real foundation at any instant for the momentary state of motion individuating the actual part of matter that constitutes its organic body, as well as for the derivative passive forces of impenetrability and resistance. Derivative force is momentaneous, and since "what is momentary in action . . . is

---

[32] *Specimen Dynamicum*, GM VI 241.

[33] Letter to De Volder, April 3, 1699; GP II 170.

[34] *Specimen Dynamicum*, GM VI 235. In Leibniz's dynamics, these primitive forces give rise to the derivative forces that manifest themselves in phenomena, the most important of which is the living force, mv^2, which is a measure of the activity of a body at an instant or its capacity to do work, anticipating the modern notions of energy and work.

accidental or changeable,"[35] it exists only as a modification of the primitive force that it presupposes.[36] The differing tendencies to motion to which the entelechies in matter give rise are what make actual the various parts into which matter is divided at different instants. Infinitely divided matter, that is, presupposes entelechies that determine its actual parts.

This bears on Leibniz's philosophy of space as follows. According to the account of the continuum that he had developed in the 1670s, space cannot be regarded as composed of points, or time of instants, without contradiction. Any finite line segment is bounded by two points, which are its modes. Between these bounds there is a continuous extension, and this may be regarded as divisible into further such segments. That is, in the abstract, a space or extension may be regarded as composed of such parts, but being continuous, it is not actually divided into them. Actual division pertains to actual entities, like extended matter, the actually divided phenomenal plenum. But extension in itself is essentially passive; in order for matter to be actually divided, there must be active entities in it, the entelechies responsible for the instantaneous motions determining the different divisions it undergoes at different instants. "The extended," Leibniz explains to De Volder in 1699, "has no unity except in the abstract, namely when we divert the mind from the internal motion of the parts by which each and every part of matter is, in turn, actually subdivided into different parts, something that plenitude does not prevent. Nor do the parts of matter differ only modally if they are divided by souls and entelechies, which always persist."[37] Now every actual part of matter has a situation relative to other bodies in the plenum, and space is the order of these situations (a kind of complex of divisions or cells); abstract space consists in the order of all possible such situations. Such a space, conceived apart from the things in it that would induce the divisions, is therefore purely ideal, consisting only in the possibility for division. It is simply an order, the order of all possible situations, and not something (*contra* Newton) that could actually exist.

MONADS AND THE CONTINUUM

We have seen that Leibniz had initially conceived his indivisibles as actually infinitely small parts of the continuum, but that this conception did not survive his rejection of geometric indivisibles in 1671–72 and his subsequent reconstrual (in 1676) of the infinitely small parts of the continuum as fictions. This went along with a reinterpretation of the actually infinite division of matter as not issuing in a last or smallest part, but as a division only into finite parts that are themselves divided into finite parts *in infinitum*. Nonetheless, as we have seen, one feature of the earlier conception remains fundamental

[35] Letter to De Volder, June 30, 1704; GP II 270.
[36] Untitled ms. [1702], GM VI 102–3.
[37] Leibniz to De Volder, April 1699; GP II 170.

for his mature philosophy: this is the idea that every part of an actually divided body *presupposes* an indivisible substance that is active, and whose instantaneous action is the foundation of the body's motion. These substances *are in* matter everywhere: "Since monads or principles of substantial unity are everywhere in matter, it follows from this that there is also an actual infinity, since there is no part, or part of a part, which does not contain monads."[38]

Thus for an entity *B* to *presuppose* entities *A* is for the *A* to *be in B*. As Leibniz writes in 1714, "we say that an entity is in [*inesse*] or is an ingredient of something, if, when we posit the latter, we must also be understood, by this very fact and immediately, without the necessity of any inference, to have posited the former as well."[39] This is the way, then, that a line can be regarded as an infinite aggregate of points, and a body as an infinite aggregate of substances: "just as there is no portion of a line in which there are not infinitely many points, so there is no portion of matter that does not contain an infinity of substances. But just as a point is not a part of a line, but a line in which there is a point is such a part, so also a soul is not a part of matter, but a body in which there is a soul is such a part of matter."[40] Although points are not parts of a line, they are presupposed in any of its parts; analogously, monads are not parts of matter, but presupposed in any of its actual parts. Moreover, being simple, they are not further resolvable, and are therefore said to be its *constitutive principles*. As Leibniz writes to Fardella:

> There are infinite simple substances or created things in any particle of matter; and matter is composed from these, not as from parts, but as from constitutive principles or immediate requisites, just as points enter into the essence of a continuum and yet not as parts, for nothing is a part unless it is homogeneous with a whole, but substance is not homogeneous with matter or body any more than a point is with a line.[41]

As explained, the *reality* of an aggregate reduces to the reality of its constituents, and the *unity* of the aggregate results from these constituents being perceived together. Monads are also presupposed by temporal phenomena, but here different considerations must apply. For the constituents of a temporally extended phenomenon cannot be perceived together at the same time. There is therefore no *unity* of temporally extended phenomena. The *reality* of a phenomenal duration, on the other hand, consists in the monadic states it presupposes, and the reality of motion in the momentaneous endeavour toward change, or appetition, existing at every instant. Likewise, the momentaneous derivative forces, being modifications of primitive forces, presuppose the existence of those enduring unities or sources of action that they modify. Here it may be objected that if monadic states are instantaneous, and according to Leibniz nothing that exists only for an instant can be said to exist, his monadology does not in the end

---

38   Letter to Des Bosses, February 14, 1706; GP II 301.
39   *Initia rerum mathematicarum metaphysica* [1714], GM VII 19.
40   Leibniz, Notes on discussions with Michel Angelo Fardella [1690], A VI 4, 1673.
41   Leibniz, for Fardella [1690], A VI 4, 1673.

escape the labyrinth. To that objection I think the best answer is this: a monadic state is a kind of ideal limit of making finer and finer discriminations of states, each of which involves a certain degree of abstraction or limitation.[42] Thus, all change presupposes a difference between two states. A continuous process is analyzable as an infinite series of infinitesimal such differences; but according to Leibniz's analysis of continuity, this is a *compendium* for the fact that finer and finer determinations of discrete states are possible, in such a way that no smallest difference (corresponding to a discontinuous change) would ever be reached.

[42] Cf. the illuminating analysis given by Donald Rutherford, "Leibniz on Infinitesimals and the Reality of Force," in *Infinitesimal Differences*, ed. Ursula Goldenbaum and Douglas Jesseph (Berlin: de Gruyter, 2008), 255–80.

CHAPTER 16

....

EARLY PHYSICS

....

PHILIP BEELEY

INSPIRATION IN BAD SCHWALBACH

....

LEIBNIZ'S introduction to physical questions came about largely by accident when, in August 1669, he accompanied his patron Johann Christian von Boineburg on his annual journey to take the waters to the spa town of Bad Schwalbach in Hesse. While Leibniz was there, he was lent a copy of the recently published April 1669 issue of the *Philosophical Transactions* by a friend of von Boineburg's, the Kiel law professor Erich Mauritius. Far removed from the meetings of the leading scientific institution in Europe, he was able to read that investigations on the true laws of motion were of central concern to members of the Royal Society of London. The April issue contained Christiaan Huygens's contribution to that debate, which had controversially been suppressed from earlier publication because the journal's editor and owner, Henry Oldenburg, had considered Huygens's laws to be largely identical with those of the English mathematician Christopher Wren.[1]

During the next two years Leibniz came to adopt quite a different approach to the laws of motion from that he had found in the *Philosophical Transactions*. Crucial to this development is a distinction he made in notes he drew up toward the end of his stay in Bad Schwalbach, to which he gave the title *De rationibus motus*. There, he asserts that motion can be handled in two different ways: "according to reason or according to the senses" (A VI ii 159). As he would later explain more fully, it was in his view necessary to distinguish between those propositions whose truth depends on the sense perception, as is the case of physical experiments or observations, and those which depend on a

---

[1] On the background to this controversy, see Oldenburg's preface to Huygens, "A summary account of the laws of nature", p. 925: "Before these Rules of Motion be here deliver'd, 'tis necessary to preface something, whereby the worthy Author of them may receive what is unquestionably due to him, yet without derogating from others, with whom in substance he agreeth." See also Duchesneau, *La dynamique de Leibniz*, pp. 36–37.

"clear and distinct imagination or ideas" (A II i² 353). Following this distinction, the laws of motion proposed by Huygens and Wren could not be genuine laws at all, but were instead to be seen as descriptions of natural phenomena. Moreover, the two approaches did not possess the same epistemic value. For, although the senses did not have the power to override the judgment of reason, the opposite was certainly true: "wherever the senses appear to contradict reason it is necessary to conclude that something exists which is not perceived except through its effect" (A VI ii 159). Based on these sentiments, Leibniz went on to produce two quite different theories of motion at the beginning of the 1670s, one a theory of abstract motion based on pure reason, which he dedicated to the Académie des sciences in Paris; the other, a theory of concrete motion seeking to provide an adequate account of all natural phenomena, which he dedicated to the Royal Society.

LEIBNIZ'S TWO THEORIES OF MOTION

Extensive surviving drafts reveal that Leibniz continued to occupy himself with topics associated with a purely rational theory of motion from the autumn of 1669 through to the beginning of 1671. In contrast, apart from notes on Honorato Fabri's *Physica* (Lyon, 1669), scarcely anything survives of his early deliberations on concrete motion. We meet the two theories for the first time in Leibniz's introductory letter to Oldenburg of July 23, 1670, which appropriately accompanied one from Boineburg, who had been a correspondent of the secretary of the Royal Society for some time.[2] In the letter, Leibniz first announces work in progress on what he called "the true theory of motion", demonstrated "in the geometrical way from the definition of terms only", before outlining his planned physical hypothesis:

> And I have other ideas by the aid of which, adopting a certain unique hypothesis of a particular universal motion in our terraquaerial globe that both Copernicus and Tycho can accept, I can give the grounds of all the motions in bodies that puzzle us with a hitherto unusual clarity, that is, of gravity, levity, of all hydrostatical paradoxes, of mechanics, the motion of projectiles, of reflections and refractions; and also (you will be astonished) of the three so called chemical principles, reduced from the ordinary state of confusion to precise definitions, and so of all solutions, reactions, precipitations; and that not by means of certain atoms nor fragments nor abstractions, but by means of a familiar and almost mechanical way of reasoning. (A II i² 95–6)

---

[2] No doubt with Boineburg's encouragement, Leibniz used the opportunity of his introductory letter to Oldenburg as a means to initiating a dialogue with Hobbes. To this end, he enclosed a letter to Hobbes, asking Oldenburg to ensure that Hobbes received it. For good reason, the secretary of the Royal Society seems to have ignored Leibniz's request. See Beeley, "Leibniz and Hobbes", pp. 46–47.

Oldenburg warmly encouraged the scientific endeavors of his fellow countryman, on a number of occasions ensuring that his letters were read to the assembled members at the Society's meetings. Having already announced his intention of dedicating the physical hypothesis to the Royal Society and repeatedly urged by Oldenburg to bring the tract to a conclusion, Leibniz sent the first parts of the still incomplete work to London in March 1671.[3] A number of members were asked to examine the work and report back on it. Only Robert Hooke, John Pell, and John Wallis seem to have carried out this request. Nothing is known of Pell's views, but Hooke's opinion was short and dismissive.[4] Wallis, on the other hand, produced an extensive appraisal in which he pointed out the substantial agreement between the young German philosopher and his own views, set out in his recently published *Mechanica, sive de motu, tractatus geometricus* (London 1670–1).[5] When Wallis subsequently read Leibniz's *Theoria motus abstracti*, which arrived with the remainder of the physical hypothesis, he was rather less impressed.[6]

It was an astute move on Leibniz's part to have framed his *Hypothesis physica nova* with the Royal Society so much in mind. Not only did he cite publications by esteemed members of the Society such as Hooke, Robert Boyle, and Wren, but he also addressed many of the experimental questions with which English virtuosi had been concerned. Leibniz's strategy proved successful. The positive report on the *Hypothesis physica nova* by Wallis, published in the *Philosophical Transactions*, played a decisive role—alongside the presentation of his then still incomplete calculating machine—in Leibniz's election to the Royal Society in April 1673.[7]

Laws of Motion in a Pure State of Nature

Leibniz's reflections on a rational theory of motion which led to the publication of his *Theoria motus abstracti* in 1671 were inspired by Thomas Hobbes, with whose work he had been acquainted since his student days in Leipzig. More recently, he had studied intensely Hobbes's *De corpore* in the copy of the English philosopher's *Opera philosophica*

---

[3] For an account of how the *Hypothesis physica nova* emerged and was conveyed to Oldenburg in London see Beeley, "A philosophical apprenticeship", pp. 54–59.

[4] As recorded in the Journal Book of the Royal Society, when Hooke returned the copy of Leibniz's "New Physical Hypothesis", at the meeting on May 11, 1671 (old style), he declared "that he was not satisfied with it". See Birch, *The History of the Royal Society of London*, II, p. 481.

[5] For Wallis's report on Leibniz's *Hypothesis physica nova*, see his letter to Oldenburg of April 7, 1671 (old style), *Correspondence of John Wallis (1616–1703)*, ed. P. Beeley and C. J. Scriba, III, pp. 442–447.

[6] Wallis's short report on the *Theoria motus abstracti* is contained in his letter to Oldenburg of June 2, 1671 (old style), *Correspondence of John Wallis (1616–1703)*, ed. P. Beeley and C. J. Scriba, III, pp. 453–454.

[7] See Birch, *The History of the Royal Society of London*, III, pp. 73, 82. See also Beeley, "A philosophical apprenticeship", pp. 68–69.

(Amsterdam 1668) purchased by Boineburg in October 1669.[8] Having credited himself with discovering the principle "Nothing is without reason" (nihil sine ratione) to be the foundation of the science of mind and motion, whereas the principle "The whole is greater than the part" (totum esse maius parte) constituted the foundation of geometry, Leibniz set out to develop his theory of abstract motion with demonstrative rigour, starting out from clear and distinct definitions. Conceiving motion like extension as a continuum, he followed Hobbes in postulating conatus to be the beginning or the end of motion, comparable to the relationship "between point and space or one and infinity" (A VI ii 265). Moreover, since each conatus was understood as being essentially vectorial in nature, having inherently a certain degree of motion as well as direction, Leibniz also considered it to be something more than a limiting concept; namely, as a homogeneous element of continuous motion, a "motion through a point in an instant of time" (A II i^2 166). For the young Leibniz, as for Hobbes, whatever is set in motion will continue to move with the same velocity and the same direction until it is hindered.[9] Consequently, the limiting case was not identified with the negation of all movement. In that moment when motion of a body ceases, the body will strive to overcome the hindrance blocking it; which is to say that the body actually begins to do this.[10]

Leibniz was required therefore to ascribe to his conatus concept different, even contradictory, determinations at the same time. Indeed, this ambivalence was a necessary prerequisite for his explanation of the mechanics of collision, especially linear nonelastic collision, in which either one of the two bodies is repulsed or when the two colliding bodies have the same velocity and bring each other to rest. Leibniz was convinced that, in such cases, at the moment of collision each body possesses contrary conatus: its own as well as that of the opposing body. A stronger movement corresponds to a stronger conatus, so that where different conatus are in play the conatus of the faster body gains the upper hand and effectively decides the outcome of the collision.[11] Since Leibniz in most of the cases assumes similar bodies, the result of the collision is determined by the simple addition or subtraction of velocities. Thus, if two bodies A and B collide linearly with velocities V_1 and V_2, respectively, then where $|V_1| > |V_2|$ the result will be that the two bodies proceed in the original direction of A and with the velocity $V = |V_1| - |V_2|$. In the case where $|V_1| = |V_2|$, however, A and B, in colliding, will bring

[8] On the background to Leibniz's early encounters with Hobbes's work see Garber, *Leibniz: Body, Substance, Monad*, pp. 14–17, and Goldenbaum, "Indivisibilia vera", especially pp. 60–62. Leibniz's annotations on Boineburg's copy of Hobbes's *Opera philosophica* are listed on pp. 80–94.

[9] In *De rationibus motus* Leibniz writes, "Whatever is moved will always be moved with the same speed in the same direction as long as it is not hindered by another contiguous body" (A VI ii 161). Cf. Hobbes, *De corpore*, p. 122.

[10] Leibniz writes, "Nor can it be denied that it continues at least to strive even when it stops; and therefore it strives or what is the same it begins to move the obstacles blocking it however large they might be even if it is overcome by these" (A VI ii 265). See also Beeley, *Kontinuität und Mechanismus*, p. 319.

[11] See Leibniz's fourth draft of the *Theoria motus abstracti* (A VI ii 171).

each other to a state of rest since their velocities cancel each other out.[12] If, on the other hand, two bodies moving in the same direction but with different velocities collide, they proceed afterward in that direction with the velocity of the faster body.[13] Only in this case is there an increase in velocity; otherwise, subtraction predominates. And since in the laws of oblique collision subtraction likewise outweighs addition, Leibniz's abstract laws of motion imply, all other things being equal, a steady reduction in the quantity of motion in the world. For this reason, he found it necessary to postulate the existence of mind as a source of motion.[14] In continuation of this idea we find that minds are located in vortices in some of the physical tracts he produced during his stay in Paris.[15] For their part, the vortices served to explain how minds or souls could be indestructible.

The laws of oblique collision rest partly on the principle "The whole is greater than the part", partly on the principle of reason. The latter applies, for example, when, seen from the collision normal, two obliquely colliding bodies move linearly and with the same velocity. In this case, according to Leibniz, the velocity of the bodies will not change, but instead the direction of their motion will change. Following collision, they will proceed together with their original velocity along the line that bisects the outer angle of collision. This choice of the middle or optimal path between the two opposites, which represents a minimal change, is seen by Leibniz as being an immediate consequence of the principle of reason, to which he probably appeals here for the first time in a physical context. He enthuses that it is "almost the pinnacle of the rationality in motion" that bodies under those conditions pursue such a path, for this result "does not come about simply from the brute subtraction of equals, but rather from the choice of a suitable third way, which can be traced to a remarkable but necessary kind of providence which without doubt is not to be found otherwise in the whole of geometry or phoronomy" (A VI ii 268). Leibniz's conclusions in this respect anticipate his later discovery that, in some cases in optics, a purely quantitative approach based on efficient causes does not suffice to explain why light takes the shorter and therefore optimal path.[16]

Employing the laws of oblique collision of two bodies moving linearly with the same velocity, Leibniz comes to reject the demonstrations of Descartes, Hobbes, and Kenelm Digby that, in optics, the angle of incidence and the angle of reflection are always equal.[17]

---

[12] Leibniz presents these results in the "Theoremata" section of the *Theoria motus abstracti* (A VI ii 269). On the addition and subtraction of conatus, see Duchesneau, *La dynamique de Leibniz*, pp. 50–52.

[13] Leibniz notes in *De conatu et motu, sensu et cogitatione* that, in this case, the speed of the antecedent body is accelerated but that there is no addition of conatus (A VI ii 281).

[14] Thus, Leibniz writes in *De materia prima* "If bodies are without mind it is impossible that motion can be eternal" (A VI ii 280). See also Garber, "Motion and metaphysics in the young Leibniz", pp. 170–171.

[15] Thus, in notes on science and metaphysics, dated March 18, 1676, he writes: "There are just as many vortices in the world as there are minds, or little worlds or perceptions" (A VI iii 393). See also *De veritatibus, de mente, de Deo, de universo* (A VI iii 509).

[16] For a more detailed discussion on the role of final causes in Leibniz's work on optics, see Hecht, "Dynamik und Optik bei Leibniz", pp. 95–99, and Beeley, "In inquirendo sunt gradus", pp. 34–35.

[17] Leibniz writes of the demonstrations of Descartes, Hobbes, and Digby that they "have more the charm of opinion that the rigour of demonstration" (A VI ii 229).

He reaches this conclusion by assuming that one of the bodies (*AB*) has as one of its sides a perfectly flat surface so that reflective motion can be considered as a special case of oblique collision. Leibniz assumes further that *AB* moves in the direction *CF*, while the other body (*E*) moves in the direction EG. The point where the two bodies meet is denoted by *D*. On the basis of the law he has elicited, the two bodies following collision will move with their original velocity along the line *DH*, which bisects the outer angle of collision or angulus divergentiae ∢ *EDC* (A VI ii 180). If the plane surface *AB* moves perpendicularly to the path *CF*, the angle of incidence ∢ *EDB*, in which *E* hits *AB* will have the magnitude ∢*EDC* – 90°. The angle of reflection ∢ *HDA*, formed by the path of *E* (and *AB*) following the collision and the plane *AB* at the moment of collision itself, will have the magnitude 90° – (∢EDC/2). From here, it follows that the angle of incidence and the angle of reflection are equal when the angulus concursus ∢*EDC* is 120°, and, that is to say, only when they are 30°. This conclusion is, he says, "sufficiently established by algebra" (A VI ii 180).[18]

THEORY OF CONCRETE MOTION

As in the case of the laws of motion proposed by Huygens and Wren, the young Leibniz does not doubt that the equivalence of the angle of incidence and the angle of reflection obtains in nature and, as such, corresponds to a true perception of a natural phenomenon. But he denies that it can be strictly proved from rational principles. Part of the task he set himself in the theory of concrete motion, to which he also gave the name *Hypothesis physica nova*, was to construct a model that explains natural phenomena, while at the same time accounting for how the divergence between the two theoretical models comes about. By providing such an account, he believed he was able to reconcile theory with scientific practice, a guiding principle in much of his thought but understood here on a more profound theoretical level.

When seeking to explain the need for his two tracts, Leibniz made a distinction between two types of motion: on the one hand, pure or private motion, such as would occur in a vacuum or resting medium, and, on the other hand, various kinds of concrete or public motion that are to be found in the world around us.[19] In the *Hypothesis physica nova*, he presents a physical system that is able to account for such concrete motion by supposing that the world consists of bodies small and large that are moved or carried by an all-encompassing element: namely, rapidly circulating ether. The concept of ether

---

[18] A detailed discussion of Leibniz's argument is to be found in Beeley, *Kontinuität und Mechanismus*, pp. 338–341.

[19] Thus, in *Leges reflexionis et refractionis*, he says that "it is necessary to know that there are two kinds of motion in the world; that some are pure or private motions and that others are public motions or such as are dependent on the system" (A VI ii 314). See also Leibniz, *La réforme de la dynamique*, pp. 38–41, and Beeley, "Mathematics and nature", pp. 134–135.

serves as a universal principle of motion on which he is able to base his mechanistic explanation of all natural phenomena. Moreover, it is by reason of the concept of ether that Leibniz is able to reconcile his abstract laws of motion with natural phenomena or, more generally, reason with experience. In a contemporary letter to Pierre de Carcavy, a leading figure in the Académie des Sciences, he writes:

> This hypothesis applies the abstract to the concrete, geometry to physics and shows that the phenomena of the world cannot be reconciled at all or only badly with the abstract laws of motion, or experience with reason, if a certain general spirit or living motion is not brought in as first carrier, which can equally be called ether or quintessence or world spirit or fine matter. (A II i^2 209)

As Leibniz concedes in his letter to Oldenburg of April 29, 1671 (old style), when bodies collide absolutely or abstracted from the conditions that obtain in the real world, the results of this collision can often appear paradoxical precisely because they diverge from phenomena. Explaining, he points out that "the one deals with the magnitude, shape and motion of the apparent body, the other with the true body" (A II i^2 166). Thus in "a free or natural state", where there are no physical constraints, "a body with as large a magnitude as one pleases can easily be moved by a body with as small a magnitude as one pleases", everything happens as if in a vacuum. In contrast, in the physical system, "so to speak in the civil state", we are dependent only on what we can see while efficient causes such as those brought about by the insensible ether go unobserved (A VI ii 227).

The cosmological model of the *Hypothesis physica nova* assumes the existence of an immobile mass of ether filling all interstitial space between the sun and the earth, the remaining planets of the solar system being ignored. Motion of the ether is brought about by the rotation of the sun. Since ether is originally immobile, it is conceived as lacking cohesion, a property of bodies that, according to his model, is brought about by motion. Indeed, it is on account of the relationship between motion and cohesion that he assumes all heavenly bodies to rotate around their centres.[20] The rotation of the sun also serves to explain the emission of its particles as light. The unavoidable consequence of this model—that at some stage the sun must become exhausted—is met by the further assumption that the sun's particles have innate rotational movements of their own.[21] In this respect, he rejects the explanatory model found in Hobbes and Torricelli that the rotational movement of the sun suffices to explain how the motion of ether comes about.

[20] Leibniz sets out his arguments for these original motions at the beginning of his *Hypothesis physica nova* (A VI ii 223). See also his letter to von Guericke of August 17, 1671 (A II i^2 241) and Garber's discussion in "Leibniz: Physics and philosophy", p. 275, where he points out the similarity to Descartes's creation account in *Le monde*.

[21] As Leibniz points out, "Therefore in order that the sun can radiate or act in all parts it is necessary that there is a certain motion in its parts which is distinct from the motion of the whole around its own centre" (A VI ii 224). A more detailed discussion of this argument is found in Beeley, *Kontinuität und Mechanismus*, pp. 147–148.

Contemporary opinion diverged as to whether light was propagated in the form of a stream of particles or as waves transmitted through a medium, with Descartes and Barrow favouring the former, Huygens and Hooke the latter. Following a general policy of evincing the agreement of his new physical hypothesis with scientific thought, while at the same time avoiding the dogmatic pursuance of a certain opinion, he leaves the question of the nature of light open. Similarly, he denies that there could be any decisive empirical proof, for much that appears rectilinear in the world is in fact curved.[22]

It is through ether penetrating the originally homogeneous mass of the earth that, according to Leibniz's physical model, the diversity of the natural world comes about. Trapped in bubbles (bullae) formed under the influence of heat or light, the ether, through its motion combined with that of the earth itself, lends these bubbles a certain consistency. These bubbles in turn are constitutive of all material nature, being described as "the seeds of things, the fabric of species, receptacles of ether, the basis of body, the causes of consistency, and the foundation of as much variety we admire in things as the impulses in motion" (A VI ii 226). Leibniz cites the chemist Joan Baptista van Helmont in this context, and, indeed, there is a clear similarity between his bubbles concept and van Helmont's thesis that individual things are generated through a process of fermentation caused by the archeus acting on water.[23]

Only part of the ether or light is considered by Leibniz to contribute to the generation of the natural world. The remaining part that does not penetrate the earth's mass circulates from east to west, thereby moving in the direction opposite to that of the earth's rotation. This circulatory movement of ether, which he postulates as resulting from a combination of motions, plays a crucial role in Leibniz's physical hypothesis. It not only serves to explain the wind and the tides as cosmically influenced phenomena, but also what he calls "the three fundamental phenomena of our earth", namely, gravitation, elasticity, and magnetism (A II i^2 211). From these three, other phenomena are to be deduced.

For Leibniz, the key to explaining both elasticity and gravitation is the innate tendency of ether to overcome hindrances to continuing its circulatory movement. Thus, the "elastic force" (vis elastica) is described as resulting from the immediate striving of the ether to divide further any more coarse matter standing in its path until "a similar degree of fineness" is reached to that possessed by the ether itself (A II i^2 167). This phenomenon occurs only in the case of bodies that offer no internal resistance to division and where, through extension or compression, an excess of a certain element is created leading to a temporary imbalance. The sometimes forceful return to the initially stable state, "which the system works towards", is identical with the restoration of the original equilibrium

[22] Thus, he writes in *Hypothesis physica nova* "This cannot be refuted by any experiments, since many movements which appear to be straight are in fact curved, but so imperceptibly so that all phenomena occur just as if they were truly straight" (A VI ii 229).

[23] See the final section of Leibniz's *Hypothesis physica nova* (A VI ii 255), and Beeley, *Kontinuität und Mechanismus*, pp. 151–152.

(A II i^2 211–12).[24] The application of this model to the phenomena of collision is apparent, but equally it applies to the case of an airgun, where the compression of air comes about through the simultaneous extension of ether, for, as Leibniz writes, "every dilation of the one is a compression of the other" (A II i^2 132). Similarly, when air is pumped out of Otto von Guericke's so-called Magdeburg hemispheres, Leibniz argues, an excess of ether comes about inside the receptacle. On the basis of the comparison of these cases, Leibniz rejects von Guericke's assertion that the force with which air re-enters the evacuated hemispheres results solely from the pressure of air, asserting rather that it results from both "the pressure and the elasticity of air" (A II i^2 237).

Employing the same model as for elasticity, Leibniz explains gravitational attraction as occurring when the movement of ether is hindered by internally cohesive bodies, be they solids or fluids. The common property of such bodies is that they strive down-ward because ether "presses" them in that direction (A VI ii 249). Leibniz's explanation again employs the concept of equilibrium. He assumes that ether circulates the earth as a homogeneous whole. In order that homogeneity be maintained, the velocity of the ether necessarily increases proportionally to the distance from the earth's surface. And because, according to Leibniz, a fast movement of ether is hindered more by bodies standing in its path than a slower movement, the tendency of the ether is to move such hindrances to "where they disturb less"; that is to say, downward (A II i^{2}165).

Finally, magnetism, too, is explained in terms of the striving of the movement of ether to maintain equilibrium. Both William Gilbert and Johannes Kepler had argued for the essential identity of magnetism and gravitation.[25] Leibniz takes up this idea and assumes that the movement of ether from east to west will be least disturbed when a body hindering it lies in north–south orientation because only in this case will the pressure of ether be distributed evenly over the body (A II i^2 165). A body that, like the needle of a magnet, can move horizontally about its center and that stands obliquely or in the same direction as the ether movement, will be pressed by the ether into north–south orientation. This phenomenon, he suggests, can be observed in many bodies, but is in none so apparent as in magnets themselves. He does not deal with the problem of declination but expresses the hope "that sometime its cause might be given by the same means" (A II i^2 212).

Scientific Validation

When Leibniz described the laws of motion set out by Huygens and Wren as "phe-nomena", he not only emphasized that, for him, these laws were based on observations

---

[24] For a detailed discussion of Leibniz's early work on elasticity, see Breger, "Elastizität als Strukturprinzip der Materie bei Leibniz", pp. 113–114.

[25] On the identity of magnetism and gravitation in Gilbert and Kepler, see Koyré, *Études galiléennes*, pp. 80, 249.

made under experimental conditions, but also their contingent nature. The laws published in the *Philosophical Transactions* in 1669 were based on elastic collision, which could only occur under the specific conditions of the natural world, in which the movement of the invisible ether constituted the true source of elasticity. Erroneously, Leibniz took "elastic" to be a property of the body and not of the collision itself; elastic collisions, where there is no loss of kinetic energy, obtain according to modern understanding on the basis of perfectly hard bodies.

Throughout the *Hypothesis physica nova*, Leibniz cites examples where his ideas, some more, some less, accord with theoretical or observational results found in contemporary scientific literature such as Boyle's experiments with the air pump in *Nova experimenta physica-mechanica* (London 1669), or Athanasius Kircher's work on magnetism *Magnes sive de arte magnetica* (Cologne 1643), or the microscopic world revealed by Hooke in his *Micrographia* (London 1667). Leibniz claims that the physical explanation set out in the *Hypothesis physica nova* is something more than a hypothesis precisely on account of this perceived agreement, whereby "it appears to combine and harmonize the various hypotheses of others" (A VI ii 257). In the same vein, he writes in a letter to Oldenburg that there is "nothing among publically known experiments" which he would not expect "with a remarkable clarity of simple harmony" to be reconcilable with it (A II i^2 204). This, in turn, is an indication of the importance he accorded to already existing experimental evidence when framing the hypothesis itself.

But most important is the implicit agreement of his physical hypothesis with reason. As Leibniz demonstrates with respect to motion, only at first blush do the phenomena differ from "the principles of reality", the account given in the *Theoria motus abstracti* (A VI ii 242–3). Showing that his hypothesis not only saves the phenomena but also agrees with reason, Leibniz believes that it can justifiably be said to approach and even reach the status of demonstrable truth, understood in the sense of rigorous deductions from clear and distinct definitions (A VI iii 3). Successful application and agreement with reason are for him the bywords of a hypothesis which aspires to truth.

Leibniz's Physics from Mainz to Paris

Following the publication of his *Hypothesis physica nova* and the *Theoria motus abstracti* in Mainz in 1671, and the republication of both of these works in London later in the same year, Leibniz continued to work on topics they had dealt with or explicitly left out. Thus, cosmological theory, which was omitted from the new physical hypothesis, was subsequently taken up within the same conceptual framework in his *Hypothesis de systemate mundi* (A VI iii, 293–9). Some of his deliberations, such as those on the composition of conatus, went into early drafts for one of his major early philosophical projects, the *Elementa de mente et corpore*. Further work on the laws of reflection and refraction also followed in which he emphasized the need for understanding accurately the differences between private and public motion, noting that "otherwise we will never harmonize the phenomena of concrete motion with the demonstrations of pure or universal phoronomy, no less independent of the senses than geometry" (A VI ii 314). He argues that it is important to recognize the different conditions that obtain when investigating reflection and refraction under these two different points of view. Above all, Leibniz set about producing a new and improved version of his physical hypothesis, to which he gave the name *Summa hypotheseos physicae novae*, in which he took account of certain criticisms raised by von Guericke, Wallis, and Adam Kochański.

Leibniz continued to investigate questions of the physical sciences after his arrival in Paris in March 1672, and especially in the light of his initial meetings with Huygens. In *Propositiones quaedam physicae*, probably written during the first six months of his stay, he develops further the idea, present already in the *Hypothesis physica nova*, that from a single phenomenon—namely, the daily circulation of light around the earth—all other phenomena can be explained. His deliberations drew partly on experimental evidence and led him to some remarkable conclusions, such as "matter does not consist in extension, but rather in motion" (A VI iii 56) and "without minds in the world no continuous motion is possible" (A VI iii 57). As a corollary to the latter, he argues that without minds as principles of motion the natural world would tend toward general "equilibrium or rest" (A VI iii 68).

The question of explanatory principles is taken up in a different manner in *Principia mechanica*, which Leibniz probably wrote sometime between 1673 and 1676. Here, following the contemporary model of reducing geometrical questions to arithmetic, he sets himself the task of similarly reducing problems of mechanics to pure geometry. The methodological justification for this approach is not only that geometry constitutes a "higher and more simple knowledge" (A VI iii 101) but also the unreliability of empirical evidence. Thus, Leibniz provides a series of arguments to show that from the phenomena of bodies changing position we are unable to judge which of the bodies has moved (A VI iii 104). At the same time, he finds that the concepts of absolute motion and absolute rest are senseless and concludes from this that different systems of the world may have equal scientific footing: "for no hypothesis could be refuted in favour of another by means of a reliable proof" (A VI iii 110).

Between the summer of 1672 and the beginning of 1675, Leibniz worked intensively and productively on a range of physical questions in the fields of pneumatics, mechanics, and optics. Among the works he excerpted and annotated were von Guericke's *Experimenta nova* (Amsterdam 1672), Wallis's *Mechanica*, and Galileo's *Discorsi* (Leiden 1638).[26] His reading of Huygens's letter to Gallois, published in the *Journal des Sçavans* in July 1672, was particularly inspirational. In that letter, the Dutch mathematician had reported on experiments with the Torricellian tube using water purged of air. When the surrounding air pressure was reduced using an air pump similar to Boyle's, Huygens found that the water column did not fall—an anomaly that could not be reconciled

---

[26] For a summary of books on the physical sciences read by Leibniz during his stay in Paris, see Kirsanov, "Leibniz in Paris", especially pp. 137–139.

with current mechanistic models. Another anomaly was that perfectly smooth parallel plates that could not be pulled apart under normal air pressure likewise adhered in a vessel from which air had been evacuated. It seemed probable that these phenomena were related, but Leibniz's investigations revealed that they did not have a common explanation: "it is therefore necessary to say that the union of the two plates in a vacuum depends on a different principle to the suspension of a fluid purged of air" (A VIII i 440).

Throughout the early 1670s, Leibniz had considered the problem of a physical vacuum, generally denying its possibility. Now, in Paris, he discussed various attempts to explain the fundamental phenomenon of the Torricellian experiment on which contemporary scholarly opinion was divided, not only with regard to the possibility of a vacuum but also as to the reason that mercury remained suspended in the inverted closed tube. Francis Line's explanation, published in his *Tractatus de corporum inseparabilitate* (London 1661), postulated the existence of a fine material thread holding up the mercury and was thus able to reconcile the phenomenon with the Roman Catholic priest's Aristotelian convictions.[27] Leibniz deliberated at length the conclusions of authors such as Blaise Pascal, Boyle, and von Guericke on the work of Evangelista Torricelli and devised an experiment capable of refuting Line's "funiculus theory" (A VIII i 326).

Since his earliest deliberations on von Guericke's experiment with the Magdeburg hemispheres and with the phenomena of collision, Leibniz had been concerned with gaining a better understanding of the nature of elasticity. Elastic collision could, in his view, only obtain in the actually existing world, and, therefore, the concept of elasticity represented for him the key to reconciling pure theory with the results of experimental investigations. In a letter to Edme Mariotte, probably written in July 1673, he describes what he calls "the great principle of elasticity" as being "the true cause of all phenomena of the collision of bodies" (A II i² 370) and, by the end of the following year, he set about developing a calculus by which elastic force could be measured.[28] Leibniz recognized that both Wallis and Mariotte had worked on the topic of elasticity, but claimed to have discovered the importance of the principle independently of those authors (A II i² 370–2). It would appear that Leibniz began a detailed study of Wallis's *Mechanica* some time toward the end of 1674. He also made extensive excerpts from the text, to which he added notes of his own (A VIII ii 64–106). His attention was drawn particularly to the seventh proposition of the first chapter, where Wallis states that effects are proportional to their sufficient causes.[29] Approvingly, he notes that for Wallis this proposition opens the gateway from mathematics to physics.[30]

---

[27] For a detailed description of Leibniz's proposed experiment for testing Line's funiculus hypothesis, see Hecht, "Das Experiment in Leibniz' frühen Pneumatica", pp. 125–126.

[28] Leibniz treats of this topic in his *Schediasma de calculo elastico* (A VIII i 505–26) and in *Calculus elasticus* (A VIII i 527–40). For a short discussion of these works, see Hess, "Die unveröffentlichten Arbeiten", pp. 192–193.

[29] See Wallis, *Mechanica*, p. 16: "Effectus sunt causis suis adaequatis proportionales."

[30] Leibniz writes, "Effectus sunt causis suis adaequatis proportionales. Hanc propositionem ait transitum aperire a mathematica ad physicam" (A VIII ii 65). See Fichant, "Les concepts fondamentaux", pp. 228–229.

A decisive step in Leibniz's reform of dynamics from the end of his stay in Paris was the recognition that a regulative principle of the equivalence, not just the proportionality, of the full cause and the complete effect would provide the means of harmonizing the empirical laws of motion with an a priori principle of conservation, as he would set out in his important tract *De corporum concursu*. By the time he departed from the French capital, he had added a new physical axiom to stand alongside those of mathematics and politics, one that would be programmatic for future work: namely, that "the whole effect is equivalent to its cause" (A VI iii 427).[31]

REFERENCES

Beeley, Philip. 1996. *Kontinuität und Mechanismus. Zur Philosophie des jungen Leibniz in ihrem ideengeschichtlichen Kontext*. Stuttgart: Steiner Verlag.

Beeley, Philip. 1999. "Mathematics and nature in Leibniz's early philosophy." In S. Brown (ed.), *The Young Leibniz and his Philosophy*. Dordrecht: Kluwer, pp. 123–145.

Beeley, Philip. 2004. "A philosophical apprenticeship: Leibniz's correspondence with the Secretary of the Royal Society, Henry Oldenburg." In P. Lodge (ed.), *Leibniz and His Correspondents*. Cambridge: Cambridge University Press, pp. 47–73.

Beeley, Philip. 2005. "In inquirendo sunt gradus—die Grenzen der Wissenschaft und wissenschaftliche Grenzen in der Leibnizschen Philosophie." *Studia Leibnitiana* 36: 22–41.

Beeley, Philip. 2011. "Leibniz and Hobbes." In B. Look (ed.), *The Continuum Companion to Leibniz*. London: Continuum, pp. 32–50.

Beeley, Philip, and Christoph J. Scriba. 2003. *The Correspondence of John Wallis (1616–1703)*. 8 vols. (four published). Oxford: Oxford University Press.

Birch, Thomas. 1756-7. *The History of the Royal Society of London for Improving of Natural Knowledge*. 4 vols. London: A. Millar.

Breger, Herbert. 1984. "Elastizität als Strukturprinzip der Materie bei Leibniz." In A. Heinekamp (ed.), *Leibniz' Dynamica*. Wiesbaden: Steiner Verlag, pp. 112–121.

Duchesneau, François. 1994. *La dynamique de Leibniz*. Paris: Vrin.

Fichant, Michel. 1978. "Les concepts fondamentaux de la mécanique selon Leibniz, en 1676." In A. Heinekamp and D. Mettler (eds.), *Leibniz à Paris (1672–1676). Tome. 1: Les sciences*, Wiesbaden: Steiner Verlag, pp. 219–232.

Garber, Daniel. 1982. "Motion and metaphysics in the young Leibniz." In M. Hooker (ed.), *Leibniz: Critical and Interpretive Essays*. Manchester: Manchester University Press, pp. 160–184.

Garber, Daniel. 1995. "Leibniz: Physics and philosophy." In N. Jolley (ed.), *The Cambridge Companion to Leibniz*. Cambridge: Cambridge University Press, pp. 270–352.

Garber, Daniel. 2009. *Leibniz: Body, Substance, Monad*. Oxford: Oxford University Press.

Goldenbaum, Ursula. 2008. "Indivisibilia vera—how Leibniz came to love mathematics." In U. Goldenbaum and D. Jesseph (eds.), *Infinitesimal Differences. Controversies between Leibniz and his contemporaries*. Berlin, New York: De Gruyter, pp. 53–94.

---

[31] Leibniz discusses this principle further in *Catena mirabilium demonstrationum de summa rerum* (A VI iii 584). See also Hess, "Die unveröffentlichten Arbeiten", pp. 190–191; Duchesneau, *La dynamique de Leibniz*, pp. 100–101.

Hecht, Hartmut. 1996. "Dynamik und Optik bei Leibniz." *Naturwissenschaften, Technik und Medizin* NF 4: 83–102.

Hecht, Hartmut. 2008. "Das Experiment in Leibniz' frühen Pneumatica." In H. Hecht, R. Mikosch, I. Schwarz, H. Siebert, and R. Werther (eds.), *Kosmos und Zahl. Beiträge zur Mathematik—und Astronomiegeschichte, zu Alexander von Humboldt und Leibniz.* Stuttgart: Steiner Verlag, pp. 123–135.

Hess, Heinz-Jürgen. 1978. "Die unveröffentlichten naturwissenschaftlichen und technischen Arbeiten von G. W. Leibniz aus der Zeit seines Parisaufenthaltes. Eine Kurzcharacteristik." In A. Heinekamp and D. Mettler (eds.), *Leibniz à Paris (1672–1676). Tome. 1: Les sciences*, Wiesbaden: Steiner Verlag, pp. 183–217.

Hobbes, Thomas. 1655. *Elementorum philosophiae sectio prima de corpore.* London: Andrew Crook.

Huygens, Christiaan. 1669. "A summary account of the laws of motion." *Philosophical Transactions* 46 (12 April 1669): 925–928.

Kirsanov, Vladimir. 2008. "Leibniz in Paris." In H. Hecht, R. Mikosch, I. Schwarz, H. Siebert, and R. Werther (eds.), *Kosmos und Zahl. Beiträge zur Mathematik—und Astronomiegeschichte, zu Alexander von Humboldt und Leibniz.* Stuttgart: Steiner Verlag, pp. 137–151.

Koyré, Alexandre. 1939. *Études galiléennes.* 3 vols (continuously paginated). Paris: Hermann.

Leibniz, G. W. 1994. *La réforme de la dynamique*, ed. M. Fichant. Paris: Vrin.

Wallis, John. 1670–71. *Mechanica, sive, de motu, tractatus geometricus.* London: Moses Pitt.

CHAPTER 17

FORCE AND DYNAMICS

DANIEL GARBER AND TZUCHIEN THO

INTRODUCTION

ALTHOUGH it was not until 1689 that Leibniz coined the term "dynamica" and invented the science of dynamics proper, the roots of the program go back many years before then.[1] Leibniz was interested in physics from his earliest years. In 1671, at the age of twenty-five, he wrote and published the *Theoria motus abstracti* (*TMA*) and *Hypothesis physica nova* (*HPN*) inspired by his reading of Hobbes and the disputes over the laws of collision in the *Philosophical Transactions*. But it was not until his in-depth study of Wallis, Pardies, Huygens, and other writings on mechanics, optics, and astronomy during his Paris period (1672–76) that a mature physical theory began to emerge. The conception of a world grounded in the notion of force—what one might call the dynamics project in the broader sense—can be traced to 1676 when Leibniz established the principle of the equipollence of cause and effect. In the next few years, he would begin to establish the foundational elements of a physical theory with writings on the principle of the conservation of force, on the relative nature of motion, and on motive force. Although the project was never brought to full completion, its maturation can be seen in the writings of 1689, when the Greek-inspired neologism "dynamica" was coined, and in the writings of the 1690s (like the "Specimen dynamicum"), when the dynamics was brought into a full dialogue with Leibniz's central metaphysical doctrines. Despite continued references to it, active progress on the dynamics ceased around 1700.

This is the story we will tell in this chapter. Beginning with Leibniz's juvenilia, we will move through the crucial periods of the emergence the dynamics itself and its

---

The author's names are listed alphabetically. They are equally responsible for the contents of the essay.

[1] On the history of the term "dynamica" in Leibniz's writings, see Michel Fichant, "Les dualités de la dynamique leibnizienne," *Lexicon Philosophicum* 4 (2016), pp. 11–41, esp. 12–16.

maturation, discussing its fundamental challenges and the important relation between physics and metaphysics that continued to motivate Leibniz throughout his career.

Leibniz's Physical Theory before 1676

The philosophical world into which Leibniz was born was in the midst of a fundamental transformation, moving away from the Aristotelian natural philosophy that had dominated the schools and toward new natural philosophies grounded in mathematics and mechanics. Appeals to substantial form were rejected in favor of the explanation of physical phenomena in terms of the size, shape, and motion of their constituent parts.[2]

In the later part of the 1660s, the young Leibniz did not yet have a broad view of the range of problems that occupied the new natural philosophers of his day. Rather, trained in philosophy and law, Leibniz first approached physics as a domain that had to be reconciled with more traditional philosophy and with religion so that it did not fall into the perceived traps of Cartesian metaphysics or, worse, materialism.[3] In his writings in 1668/9, he sought to build a conception of the world that made room for God and the substantial forms of the schoolmen while at the same time giving the moderns their due. Substantial forms, conceived of as immaterial, for example, play a significant role in his early accounts of the mysteries of faith in the context of a mechanist world, including transubstantiation and the resurrection of the body at the Second Coming.[4] The importance of immaterial forms even in a mechanist world was expressed neatly in his "Confessio naturae contra atheistas" of 1668/9:

> At the beginning I readily admitted that we must agree with those contemporary philosophers who have revived Democritus and Epicurus . . . that so far as can be done everything should be derived from the nature of body and its primary qualities—magnitude, figure, and motion. . . . But what if I should demonstrate that the origin of these very primary qualities themselves cannot be found in the essence of body? Then indeed, I hope, those naturalists will admit that body is not self-sufficient and cannot subsist without an incorporeal principle.
>
> (A VI i 289–90; L100)

[2] The classic statement of what came to be called "mechanical philosophy" is Robert Boyle, *The Origine of Formes and Qualities (According to the Corpuscular Philosophy)* (Oxford: H. Hall, 1666). For some historical background on the project, see Daniel Garber and Sophie Roux, eds. *The Mechanization of Natural Philosophy* (Dordrecht: Springer, 2013), pp. 3–26.

[3] Maria Rosa Antognazza, *Leibniz: An Intellectual Biography* (Cambridge: Cambridge University Press, 2009), pp. 106–107.

[4] On transubstantiation, see the essay "De transsubstantione" (c. 1668), A VI i 508–12; L 115–18. On the resurrection of the body, see the appendix to a letter to Johann Friedrich, May 21, 1671, "De resurrectione corporum," A II i 183–5. See also Garber, *Leibniz: Body, Substance, Monad* (Oxford: Oxford University Press, 2009), pp. 40–43. In a different (and perhaps not altogether consistent way), the mechanist interpretation of form as figure or shape is an important theme in his correspondence with his teacher Jacob Thomasius, where Leibniz attempted to argue that the new mechanist philosophies are consistent with Aristotle. See Leibniz's letter to Thomasius of April 20/30, 1669 (A II i 23–38; L 93–104).

But while immaterial substantial forms persist in his more theologically oriented writings, it is interesting that when he turns toward physics proper, they are much less in evidence.

In the summer of 1669, working on a reorganization of the legal system for the Baron von Boineburg in Mainz, Leibniz was introduced to the new work on the theory of collision by Huygens, Wren, and Wallis, recently published in the *Philosophical Transactions* of the Royal Society. This led Leibniz to begin formulating his own ideas about physics.[5]

At the heart of Leibniz's new physics was the Hobbesian idea that the only activity in bodies is motion. In a set of notes written shortly after he first became acquainted with the problem of impact, Leibniz set out an account of motion that closely resembles the principles that Hobbes had set out in his *De corpore*: "Whatever is at rest is always at rest, until it is hit by another body in motion. . . . Whatever moves always moves with the same speed and in the same direction, unless it is prevented by another contiguous body" (A VI ii 160–1).[6] From this, Leibniz drew an important conclusion, one that Hobbes also had drawn: "Rest is not the cause of anything, that is, a resting body does not give either motion, or rest, or direction, or speed to another body" (A VI ii 161).[7] And so a body at rest offers no resistance to acquiring new motion. Mentality is by no means missing in this new physics. For example, Leibniz held, at least at first, that "one cannot explain the origin of curvilinear motion unless one assumes incorporeal beings" (A VI ii 163). And, famously, in the very early physics, he held that every body is a "momentary mind."[8] But the spirit of the physics was decidedly mechanical.

Leibniz divided his early physics into two parts: an abstract theory of motion and a concrete theory of motion. The abstract theory gave the basic laws, understood in abstraction from the concrete makeup of the physical world. At the level of the abstract theory of motion, impact was central. But if motion is the only cause in the material world, then impact can only be understood in terms of the composition of velocities of the bodies in impact. For the young Leibniz, this meant that size or mass could play no role in determining the outcome of collisions. This, of course, is inconsistent with everyday experience, where size does seem to play an important role: a larger and more massive body would seem to be harder to set into motion than a smaller one. This is where the concrete physics of the *HPN* comes in. Leibniz presents a hypothesis about

---

[5] Antognazza, *Leibniz*, pp. 107–108.

[6] Cf. Hobbes, *Elementorum philosophiae sectio prima de corpore* (London: Andrew Crooke, 1655); *De Corpore*, 8.19, 9.7, trans. in Thomas Hobbes, *Elements of Philosophy, the First Section, Concerning Body* (London: Andrew Crooke, 1656), pp. 83, 90.

[7] Cf. Hobbes, *De Corpore*, 15.3: "rest does nothing at all, nor is of any efficacy; and . . . nothing but motion gives motions to such things as be at rest, and takes it from things moved."

[8] See *TMA* (A VI ii 266). On this and on mentality in general in the period, see Garber, *Leibniz*, pp. 29–40. But see Ursula Goldenbaum, "Individibilia Vera—How Leibniz came to love mathematics," in *Infinitesimal Differences*, edited by Ursula Goldenbaum and Douglas Jesseph (Berlin and New York: Walter de Gruyter, 2008), pp. 53–75, who argues that the introduction of mind into a Hobbesian materialism was a primary motivation of the physics in the Mainz period.

the state of the world that, together with the abstract laws of the *TMA*. yields something like the phenomena we experience and that are found in the Huygens/Wren laws. Writing to Henry Oldenburg on July 13/23, 1670, Leibniz claims to have shown that the Huygens/Wren laws "are not primary, not absolute, not clear but, no less than gravity, follow from a certain state of the ter-aqueous globe" (A II i 95).[9]

In 1672, Leibniz left his ambitious juridical work in Mainz for an even more ambitious diplomatic mission in France. This provided the occasion for a more serious engagement with mathematics and physics. We might characterize Leibniz's physics, until the end of his Paris period, as kinematic, concerned mainly with motion. After the *séjour Parisien*, Leibniz's work on power and force would begin to be of central concern. This path would supersede the kinematical approach developed in his youth and lead him toward the constitution of a dynamics, a project that would have consequences both for his physics and his metaphysics.

1676–89: The Axiom of Mechanics and the Measure of Force

During his time in Paris, outside of his official diplomatic work, Leibniz spent much time working on mathematics under the tutelage of Christiaan Huygens. But, in Paris, he also began studying mechanics in a consistent way. Reading Wallis, Mariotte, Pardies, and Huygens, a mathematically informed Leibniz was able to translate the traditional problems of mechanics, filtered through the Renaissance and early modern innovators, into his own philosophical project. This study of mechanics yielded something that kinematics could not: the concepts of force and power.

Leibniz continued to work on his physics in Paris. There are a number of pieces from the Paris period that involve extensions and systematizations of the earlier physics of the *TMA* and *HPN*.[10] In addition, there are numerous manuscripts from the Paris period that attest to Leibniz's curiosity about a wide variety of physical phenomena and related technical questions, including magnetism, pendula, free fall, impact, friction, and perpetual motion, among many other questions.[11]

But, probably in the summer of 1676, Leibniz wrote an essay that changed the direction of his thought about the physical world. The "De arcanis motus" stands out among his many reflections on physical questions in the period due to its attempt at setting out a new direction for his future work. In this seminal essay, Leibniz turned away from

---

[9] See also *HPN* § 23 (GM VI 29); A VI ii 231–2. On how exactly this physical hypothesis reconciled the abstract laws with experience, see Garber, *Leibniz*, pp. 20–22.

[10] See the studies collected in A VI iii 3–111, 163–8.

[11] These are collected in A VIII i and A VIII ii.

motion and toward the power that bodies in motion have to produce measurable effects as the foundation of an understanding of the physical world.

In this essay, Leibniz emphasized that, just as the "first axiom" in geometry is that a whole is the sum of its parts, the "first axiom" in mechanics is the equality (or equipollence) between full cause and entire effect:[12]

> Hence it is necessary that the cause be able to do as much as the effect and vice versa. And thus any full effect, if the opportunity offers itself, can perfectly reproduce its cause, that is, it has forces enough to bring something back into the same state that it was in previously, or into an equivalent state. (For being able to measure equivalent things, it is therefore useful that a measure be assumed, such as the force necessary to raise some heavy thing to some height.). . . . Hence it happens that a stone which falls from some height constrained by a pendulum can climb back to the same height, but no higher, if nothing interferes and it acts perfectly, and if nothing of the forces are removed, no lower either.
>
> ("De arcanis," p. 204)

A clear consequence of this is the conservation of force or power, the ability to do work. To take the example Leibniz himself uses here, the force or power possessed by a body or size m and speed v is the height to which that body could raise itself through that motion. Leibniz is careful also to state explicitly here that there can be no perpetual motion in physical systems (machines) ("De arcanis," p. 205).

One important consequence Leibniz drew from the new conservation law was the necessity to posit resistance in bodies, even bodies at rest, a radical change from the physics that he had worked out before coming to Paris. In an unnamed text thought to be from the late 1670s that we shall call "De legibus naturae," Leibniz wrote:

> There was a time when I believed that all the phenomena of motion could be explained on purely geometrical principles, assuming no metaphysical propositions, and that the laws of impact depend only on the composition of motions.
>
> (A VI iv 1976; AG 245)

This, of course, refers to his earlier views in the *TMA* and *HPN*, where Leibniz held that bodies by themselves have no resistance and that the size of bodies can play no role in the basic laws governing collisions. As noted previously, in those earlier works, the abstract

---

[12] The text of the essay is published in appendix 4, pp. 202–205, of Hans-Jürgen Hess, "Die unveröffentlichten naturwissenschaftlichen und technischen Arbeiten von G.W. Leibniz aus der Zeit seines Parisaufenthaltes. Eine Kurzcharakteristik," in Gottfried-Wilhelm-Leibniz-Gesellschaft and Centre national de la recherche scientifique (France) (eds.), *Leibniz à Paris: 1672–1676*. Wiesbaden: Steiner, 1978: vol. 1, pp. 183–217. The quotation is found at p. 203. In later references, we refer to the pagination in this publication, abbreviated as "De arcanis." The essay has recently been published in A VIII ii 133–38.

account of motion was reconciled with the phenomena through a hypothesis about the state of the world. But Leibniz reports that he came to reject that solution:

> But when I considered how, in general, we could explain what we experience everywhere, that speed is diminished through an increase in bulk [*moles*], . . . I stopped, and all my attempts having been in vain, I discovered that this, so to speak, inertia of bodies cannot be deduced from the initially assumed notion of matter and motion, where matter is understood as that which is extended or fills space, and motion is understood as change of space or place.
>
> (A VI iv 1980; AG 249)

What is important here is that it is not just in the macroscopic phenomena of everyday experience that speed is diminished through an increase in bulk, but *everywhere*, at the microscopic as well as the macroscopic level. That is because if speed were not diminished by bulk, that is, if a body in motion could move a greater body just as easily as it could move a lighter body, then the principle of equipollence would be violated at the microscopic level if not at the macroscopic. Which is to say that the principle of equipollence, the conservation of the ability to do work, requires that bodies offer resistance to being set in motion. And so, at the end of the "De arcanis motus," Leibniz wrote:

> Unless body were to resist, perpetual motion would follow, since a body resists in proportion to its bulk [*moles*], since there is no other factor that would limit it [*nulla alia ratio determinandi*]. That is to say, since there is no other factor [*ratio*] which would hinder it from rebounding to less than its [original] height, since in itself, without an extrinsic impediment through the impulse of [another] body, it would give [the other body] its whole motion, and retain it as well.
>
> ("De arcanis," p. 205)

And so, in addition to the force associated with motion that is conserved and issues in measurable effects, Leibniz proposes here another force, a passive force of resistance.

At the time he wrote the "De arcanis motus," Leibniz thought that the quantity conserved is identical with the Cartesian quantity of motion: size times speed. The next step in the development of his science of motion is found in the manuscript "De corporum concursu" (January 1678).

As the title suggests, the central issue concerns the problem of relations between bodies in collision and is clearly modeled after the correction of the Cartesian laws of motion by Wallis, Wren, and Huygens that had so inspired Leibniz back in 1669. Following this model, the treatise is meant to provide a general theory of collision based on the transformation of the distribution of a conserved quantity among two bodies with differing sizes and speeds before and after collision. The key change from his earlier studies is the concept of power and the equipollence of cause and effect discussed in the "De arcanis motus." In this manuscript, the term "force," standing for the quantity conserved in the physical system across modifications of speeds and directions between bodies, begins to be employed in a systematic and rigorous way.[13]

This document is the remarkable record of Leibniz's discovery that the proper measure of force is not size times speed ($m|v|$), as might be suggested by the Cartesian principle of the conservation of quantity of motion, but mv^2. The text is divided into a series of "*schedae*" or sheets. The first sheet begins as follows:

> In all motion the same force (*vis*) is always conserved.
>   Force is the quantity of the effect, or what follows from that, composed of the size of the body multiplied by the magnitude of the speed.
>
> ("De corporum concursu," p. 71)

Leibniz's starting place, then, is the same as Descartes's. In the text that follows, Leibniz works through the problem of impact using the Cartesian assumption but without making much progress. Finally, in the eighth sheet, Leibniz realizes where he has gone wrong:

> Force is the quantity of the effect. Hence the force of a body existing in motion should be estimated by the height to which it can ascend.
>
> ("De corporum concursu," p. 152)

But the height to which a body with a speed v can ascend is just the height from which it would acquire the speed v in free fall. From Galileo, we know that the square of the speed acquired in free fall is proportional to distance through which the body falls. And thus Leibniz concludes:

> Hence the same force remains not when the same quantity of motion, that is the sum of the products of speed and [size of] bodies remains, but when the sum of the products of speed squared and [size of] bodies [remains].
>
> ("De corporum concursu," p. 153)

That is to say, the force conserved is measured by mv^2. Leibniz then goes back through the sheets and carefully notes the numerous places where his initial assumption led him astray, beginning with the definition of force in the opening lines of the first sheet: "Error: id hinc non sequitur in nostro systemate." "Error: This doesn't follow from this in our system" ("De corporum concursu," p. 71).[14]

---

[13] "De corporum concorsu" in Leibniz (1994), Michel Fichant (ed.), *G. W. Leibniz: La réforme de la dynamique: De corporum concursu (1678) et d'autres textes inédits* (Paris: J. Vrin, 1994), pp. 71–171. This text is scheduled to appear in A VIII iii.

[14] It is important to note that, even if the literal laws of motion set out by Descartes in *Principia Philosophiae* were rejected, a magnitude very close to the Cartesian quantity of motion—the product of quantity of body and *velocity* (i.e., a vector quantity)—was interpreted by Leibniz, after the 1678 rectification, as an important quantity within his mechanics. We see such a conservation

It is quite probable that this argument was informed by Leibniz's knowledge of Christiaan Huygens's work on collision. In an extended essay, *De motu corporum ex percussione*, thought to date from after 1673, Huygens uses Galileo's law of free fall together with the idea that a body in motion with speed v can lift itself to the height h such that, were it to fall from h, it would acquire velocity v to solve problems in impact. Indeed, Huygens uses it to argue that, in collision, the product of the magnitudes and the square of their speeds is conserved.[15] Though Huygens's essay was not published until 1703, after his death, it seems quite reasonable to suppose that he and Leibniz spoke about such matters in Paris. But there is a crucial difference between Leibniz and his mentor. For Huygens, mv^2 is a mathematical magnitude without any particular physical interpretation.[16] For Leibniz, on the other hand, it is a mathematical expression of the ability a body in motion has to accomplish an effect, what he will later come to call living force (*vis viva*). Living force will become one of the basic concepts in his catalogue of forces that will define his dynamical physics and metaphysics.

All the arguments that we have been discussing so far are found in papers unpublished in Leibniz's lifetime. The central argument concerning the measure of motive force was first made public in an article that Leibniz published in the *Acta eruditorum* in March 1686: "Brevis demonstratio erroris memorabilis Cartesii" (A VI iv 2027–30; L 296–98). In this essay, Leibniz began by assuming the conservation of motive force (*vis motrix*) without demonstrating it. Nor, in the end, did he explicitly give the measure of motive force that he had derived earlier, mv^2. The focus of the essay is a demonstration, in the style of the argument drawn from Huygens and Mariotte that he had given in the "De corporum concursu," that the motive force of a body in motion is distinct from its Cartesian quantity of motion. Using the height to which a body in motion with velocity v could raise itself as a measure of its motive force, the assumption that a body can raise itself to the height such that if it fell from that height, it would naturally acquire the velocity v when it fell, and the Galilean law of free fall, in accordance with which the distance fallen is proportional to the square of the velocity acquired, Leibniz concludes:

> It must be said, therefore, that forces are proportional, jointly, to bodies (of the same specific gravity or solidity) and to the heights which produce their velocity or from which their velocities can be acquired. . . . They are not generally proportional to

quantity—treated by Leibniz as the "quantity of (common) progress," applicable to rectilinear collisions—throughout Leibniz's work on the mechanics and the eventual dynamics. On the different conservation laws Leibniz posits, see Daniel Garber "Leibniz: Physics and philosophy" in *The Cambridge Companion to Leibniz*, edited by Nicholas Jolley (Cambridge: Cambridge University Press. 1995), pp. 270–352, 316–319.

[15] See *De motu*, props. 8, 11, Christiaan Huygens, *Oeuvres* (The Hague: M. Nijhoff, 1888–1950), vol. 16, pp. 53–65 and 73–77, translated in Richard J. Blackwell, "Christian Huygens' *The Motion of Colliding Bodies*," *Isis* 68 (1977), pp. 574–597, esp. 583–588 and 590–592

[16] See Martial Gueroult, *Dynamique et métaphysique leibniziennes* (Paris: Les Belles Lettres, 1934), pp. 82–98.

their own velocities, though this may seem plausible at first view and has in fact usually been held.

(A VI iv 2030; L 298)[17]

And so, Leibniz concludes, "there is a big difference between motive force and quantity of motion, and the one cannot be calculated by the other, as we undertook to show"
(A VI iv 2029; L 297). Implied, though not stated, is the conclusion that the measure of
motive force is not $m|v|$ but mv^2 and that this quantity is conserved.

There were a number of immediate responses to this argument from defenders
of Descartes and his heritage in physics, what came to be called the *vis viva* controversy, though the term *"vis viva"* would only be coined some years later.[18] The "Brevis
demonstratio" was published in March, and, by September, there was an answer from
the Abbé Catelan, followed in 1689 by a reply from Denis Papin.[19] In both cases, the
controversies continued over a number of exchanges. Indeed, the controversy continued well into the eighteenth century, long after Leibniz's death.[20]

The "De arcanis motus" and succeeding texts are concerned with the ability a body in
motion has to accomplish an effect and its conservation. But there is another important
ingredient of Leibniz's physics in the late 1670s: his view on the relativity of motion. In
a manuscript that Leibniz wrote probably at about the same time as he wrote the "De
arcanis motus," he noted:

> from the phenomena of change of situation alone we can never have any certain
> knowledge of absolute motion and rest. But if absolute motion cannot be discerned
> from other phenomena, not even by those to whom all phenomena have been re-
> vealed, it follows that motion and rest taken absolutely is an empty name, and what-
> ever is real in them consists only in relative change.
>
> (A VI iii 110)

This is a question that interested Leibniz through much of the late 1670s. In numerous
texts of the period, Leibniz explores the idea that motion considered as change of place
is only relative. If this is all there is to motion, then we can make any hypothesis about
which of a group of bodies in relative motion is actually in motion and which is actually

---

[17] On the aims and goals of the argument in the "Brevis demonstratio," see Gregory Brown, "'Quod
Ostendendum Susceperamus': What did Leibniz undertake to show in the Brevis Demonstratio?" in
Leibniz' Dynamica, edited by Albert Heinekamp (Stuttgart: Franz Steiner Verlag, 1984), pp. 122–137.

[18] See Carolyn Iltis, "Leibniz and the vis viva controversy," *Isis* 62 (1971), pp. 21–35.

[19] See Gueroult, *Dynamique et métaphysique*, p. 65; See also, Alberto Guillermo Ranea, "The a priori
method and actio principle revised: Dynamics and metaphysics in an unpublished controversy between
Leibniz and Denis Papin," *Studia Leibnitiana* 21 (1989), pp. 42–68; See also François Duchesneau, *La
Dynamique de Leibniz* (Paris: J. Vrin, 1994), pp. 303–306.

[20] See references in Idan Shimony, "Leibniz and the vis viva controversy," in *The Practice of Reason*,
edited by Marcelo Dascal (Amsterdam/Philadelphia: John Benjamins, 2010), pp. 51–73, note 1.

at rest while saving all the appearances.[21] This view is also known as the *equivalence of hypotheses.*[22]

But the equivalence of hypotheses raises a problem for Leibniz: if motion is considered only kinematically, as change of relative position, then motion would seem not to be real:

> That matter and motion are only phenomena, or contain in themselves something imaginary, can be understood from the fact that different and contradictory hypotheses can be made about them, all of which nevertheless satisfy the phenomena perfectly, so that no reason can be devised for determining which of them should be preferred. In real things, on the other hand, every truth can be accurately discovered and demonstrated.
>
> (A VI iv 1463; Arthur 257)[23]

This is a very uncomfortable position for a mechanist to adopt: how can everything be explicable in terms of the size, shape, and motion of bodies if motion itself isn't really real? The solution that Leibniz ultimately arrives at is *force*: force can be used to distinguish true motion from rest. As Leibniz writes in another piece, likely from the late 1670s or early 1680s: "And so we attribute motion to that thing which has a force of acting [*vis agendi*]" (A VI iv 2019).[24] This force of acting is presumably to be identified with the force associated with the ability that a body in motion has to accomplish an effect, the force measured by mv^2 that is conserved in the world, in accordance with the principle of equipollence.

By the late 1670s, Leibniz had come to recognize the centrality of two kinds of force: the active force associated with bodies in motion, by virtue of which motion is grounded and distinguished from rest and by virtue of which bodies in motion can produce their effects, and the passive force of resistance by which bodies resist the acquisition of new motion. It will be another decade or so, at the end of the 1680s, before Leibniz actually coins the term "dynamics" for his new science of body and motion. But,

---

[21] See the texts cited in Garber, *Leibniz*, pp. 106. Leibniz's reflections here are almost certainly connected with his discussions with Huygens and with Huygens's texts, where he often uses the method of comparing an experiment done on a boat and observed both by the people on the boat and by those on shore to derive results. See also, Leibniz, "Principia mechanica," A VI iii 101–11.

[22] The term "aequipollentia hypothesium" is owed to Kepler's use of the concept in his consideration of the different astronomical hypotheses: Ptolemaic, Tychonic, Copernican. See Johannes Kepler, *Gesammelte Werke* vol. III, edited by Kepler-Kommission Der Bayerischen Akademie der Wissenschaften (München: C. H. Beck'sche Verlagsbuchhandlung, 1990), pp. 71–77.

[23] We agree here with Richard Arthur's dating of 1678/9 for this text.

[24] In this passage, Leibniz goes on to say: "Whence it is also obvious that those who have said that what is real and positive in motion belongs equally to both of two continuous bodies receding from one another have spoken falsely. For there can be a force of acting (and thus also the cause of the change of situation) in only one of them." First among those who have "spoken falsely" here in saying that motion belongs equally to two bodies receding from one another is Descartes. See *Principia philosophiae* II.29–30. Note that the words "change of situation" in the last sentence are conjectures by the editors.

by the end of the 1670s, though yet unnamed, the project of the dynamics, the science of force, has begun.

THE EMERGING DYNAMICAL METAPHYSICS

In the previous section, we emphasized the technical advances that Leibniz made in the 1670s: the discovery of the principle of equipollence, the discovery of the conservation of mv^2, the account of the equivalence of hypotheses, and the notions of active and passive force that are associated with those innovations. But connected with these advances were advances in the metaphysics of body. In an outline for a book consolidating these new discoveries, a text the Akademie editors have named the *Conspectus libelli elementorum physicae* (1678/9), Leibniz wrote:

> There follows now a discussion of incorporeal things. Certain things take place in body which cannot be explained from the necessity of matter alone. Such are the laws of motion, which depend upon the metaphysical principle of the equality of cause and effect. Therefore we must deal here with the soul and show that all things are animated.
>
> · (A VI iv 1988; L 278–79)[25]

At roughly the same time that he wrote the *Conspectus libelli*, Leibniz wrote to his employer, the Duke Johann Friedrich: "I reestablish substantial forms with demonstrative certainty [*démonstrativement*] and explain them intelligibly" (A I ii 225).[26]

What Leibniz suggested here is that the laws of motion, which depend on the principle of equipollence, could not be explained unless there were forms in bodies. Leibniz was somewhat cryptic about this question in the passages quoted, but it isn't difficult to figure out what he had in mind here. Earlier we discussed a piece from the late 1670s that we called "De legibus naturae," in which Leibniz argues for the necessity of resistance in bodies. Leibniz wrote:

> [O]ver and above that which is deduced from extension and its variation or modification alone, we must add and recognize in bodies certain notions or forms that are immaterial, so to speak, or independent of extension, which you can call powers [*potentiae*], by means of which speed is adjusted to magnitude. These powers consist

---

[25] Cf. A VI iv 1398–99; Arthur 245, which may be from the same period. In this quotation, we are omitting the last lines: "Without soul or form of some kind, a body would have no being, because no part of it can be designated which does not in turn consist of more parts. Thus nothing could be designated in a body which could be called 'this thing,' or a unity." These sentences gesture at another, different conception of corporeal substance, one grounded not in force but in unity. For a discussion, see the chapter "Body and corporeal substance" in this volume and especially Garber, *Leibniz*, chap. 2.

[26] Cf. A II i 754.

not in motion, indeed, not in conatus or the beginning of motion, but in the cause or in that intrinsic reason for motion, which is the law required for continuing.

(A VI iv 1980; AG 250)

Resistance, that "[power] by means of which speed is adjusted to magnitude," seems to be conceived as a kind of activity in this text. But activity cannot be derived from bare extended matter or from motion, which is just change of place: it requires something distinct from that, something from which activity can be derived. This is what Leibniz calls form, soul, or powers.

For Leibniz, then, the conservation principle entails that there must be something in body over and above extension from which resistance can arise. But so does the force that grounds the reality of motion. In the early texts where the *vis agendi* first comes up, Leibniz doesn't address this question explicitly, though we suspect that he had thought of it at the time. But a few years later, in section 18 of the *Discours de métaphysique* (1686), he writes:

> For if we consider only what motion contains precisely and formally, that is, change of place, motion is not something entirely real. . . . But the force or proximate cause of these changes is something more real, and there is sufficient basis to attribute it to one body more than to another. . . . Now, this force is something different from size, shape, and motion, and one can therefore judge that not everything conceived in body consists solely in extension and in its modifications, as our moderns have persuaded themselves. Thus we are once again obliged to reestablish some beings or forms they have banished.
>
> (A VI iv 1558–9; AG 51)

And, with this, we have a second physical argument from force for putting forms in bodies.

In both of these arguments, the assumption is that force—both the passive force of resistance or the active force (*vis agendi*)—resides in the substantial form, which Leibniz thinks of as the seat of all force or activity. By the mid-1680s, though, this metaphysics changes in a subtle way: Leibniz came to distinguish the active *vis agendi* associated with motion from the passive force of resistance; the former remains in the substantial form, whereas the latter is now put into matter.[27] In a passage from the essay "De modo distinguendi phaenomena realia ab imaginariis," now dated as between Summer 1683 and Winter 1685/6, Leibniz wrote:

> Concerning bodies I can demonstrate that not merely light, heat, color and similar qualities are apparent but also motion, figure, and extension. And that if anything is real, it is solely the force of acting and suffering [*vim agendi et patiendi*], and hence that the substance of a body consists in this (as if in matter and form). Those bodies,

---

[27] For the details of how this happens, see especially Garber, *Leibniz*, chap. 3.

however, which have no substantial form are merely phenomena or at least only aggregates of the true ones.

(A VI iv 1504; L 365)[28]

Acting and resisting each have their own kind of force, the one associated with form, the other with matter.

In this way, with the reform of physics comes the reform of metaphysics as well. Just as understanding the importance of the notion of force leads to a proper understanding of the laws of nature, it leads as well to a proper understanding of the notions of body and substance. As he wrote in the essay "De primae philosophiae emendatione, et de notione substantiae," published in 1694, after his science of dynamics was well under way, "the concept of *forces* or *powers* . . . for whose explanation I have set up a distinct science of *dynamics*, brings the strongest light to bear upon our understanding of the true concept of *substance*" (GP IV 469; L 433).

We now have the basis of the dynamical conception of body that will be developed most explicitly in the "Specimen dynamicum," as we shall see later.[29] With this, Leibniz's dynamical metaphysics of body has the beginnings of an alternative to Cartesian bare extended substance.

1689–1700: The *Phoranomus* and the *Dynamica*: the Foundations of a Science of Force

In 1687, Newton published his *Philosophiae naturalis principia mathematica*. While Leibniz claims to have read this only in Rome in the summer of 1689, recent scholarship has established quite conclusively that Leibniz likely had read at least significant parts of the work during his visit to Vienna in the autumn of 1688.[30]

---

[28] The essay continues: "Substances have metaphysical matter or passive power insofar as they express something confusedly; active, insofar as they express it distinctly." This suggests an idealistic reading of Leibniz's position, identifying active and passive force with distinct and confused expression. But it isn't obvious what this last line really means or even when exactly it was written. On this, see Garber, *Leibniz*, pp. 167–170.

[29] As noted in note 25, the dynamical conception of body is not the only one Leibniz has going at that moment: there is another conception as well, one grounded in the notion of unity and individuality: substantiality requires genuine individuals, forms, or souls united to organic bodies. While Leibniz obviously thought that dynamical conception of substantiality and that grounded in unity pick out the same things, it isn't altogether clear if they are really consistent.

[30] See Domenico Bertoloni Meli, *Equivalence and Priority: Newton versus Leibniz* (Oxford: Oxford University Press, 1993).

One immediate response to Newton was the essay, "Tentamen de motuum coelestium causis," published in the *Acta Eruditorum* in 1689, where Leibniz presents a vortex-theoretical account of planetary motion that, he argues, is capable of accounting for important parts of the phenomena that motivated Newton's theory of universal gravitation (GM VI 161–87).[31] Now, it is somewhat contested how deep an influence Newton's new book had on Leibniz's program at that moment: in the late 1680s and through much of the 1690s, Cartesian physics, broadly taken, is still Leibniz's main target.[32] There is little in the writings of 1689 and the years that immediately follow that suggests a direct engagement with the physics of Newton's masterwork.[33] But, even so, the publication of Newton's *Principia* may have stimulated Leibniz to do something more systematic than he had attempted up to that point and induced him to put together a kind of "distinct science" of force and power, as he put it in the "De primae philosophiae emendatione." This is the new science of dynamics.

The "dynamics," properly speaking, was born during Leibniz's 1689 voyage to Italy. The trip was taken ostensibly to do research for the history of the house of Guelph (his aristocratic employers), but Leibniz took the opportunity to visit the savants of these countries and to attend the meetings of the *Accademia fisico-matematica* in Rome, with whose members Leibniz had already corresponded for quite some time.[34] Alongside many other philosophical developments, it was on this trip that Leibniz wrote his lengthiest physical treatises: first, in the summer of 1689, the *Phoranomus seu de potentia et legibus naturae*, based on actual discussions he had in the *Accademia fisico-matematica*; and then, a couple of months later, the *Dynamica de potentia et legibus naturae corporeae*

[31] See translation and discussion of "Tentamen de motuum coelestium causis" in Bertoloni Meli, *Equivalence and Priority*, pp. 126–142. In 1704, Pierre Varignon pointed out a major error in the "Tentamen," namely, that Leibniz's calculation of centrifugal force was only half of its true value. This was corrected in a later version of his planetary theory, the "Illustratio tentaminis de motuum coelestium causis" (1706) (GM VI 254–76), which remained unpublished in Leibniz's lifetime. See Paolo Bussotti, *Complex Itinerary of Leibniz's Planetary Theory: Physical Convictions, Metaphysical Principles and Keplerian Inspiration* (New York: Birkhäuser, 2015), p. 21 and chap. 4.

[32] See Andrea Costa, *G. W. Leibniz: Dynamica de potentia et legibus naturae corporeae. Materiaux pour une édition critique* (Dissertation, École des Chartes, Paris, 2011), p. 41.

[33] The only apparent reference to Newton is in *Phoranomus* §21 (M 750), to someone who claims that God placed a certain attraction or gravitation in bodies. But Leibniz doesn't identify Newton by name here. Cf. also §24 (M 758), where Leibniz considers the claim that gravity may decrease in intensity as a body recedes from the earth. References to the *Phoranomus* are to the edition of Gianfranco Mormino, in Francesco Piro, ed., *Gottfried Wilhelm Leibniz: Dialoghi filosofici e scientifici* (Milan: Bompiani, 2007), pp. 680–885, which gives the Latin with Italian translation on facing pages. It is abbreviated here and below by "M." There is an earlier edition by André Robinet, *Physis* N.S. 28/2 (1991), pp. 429–541 and *Physis* N.S. 28/3 (1991), pp. 797–885. The First Dialogue is divided into numbered sections by Leibniz, though the second is not. When referring to passages in the First Dialogue, we will use Leibniz's numberings.

[34] Antognazza, *Leibniz*, 301–303.

tentamen scientiae novae. In these two writings, which remained unpublished until long after Leibniz's death, the science of dynamics was born.[35]

The *Phoranomus* was written as a dialogue in two parts. The choice of the dialogue form was in apparent homage to Galileo, whose *Discorsi* form a kind of model for Leibniz's project.

Dialogue I is structured around the distinction between dead force and living force (§ 18). Examples of dead force (also called "conatus") are gravitation and centrifugal force (§ 21), forces that give rise to motion, although they themselves don't involve actual motion. Living force, also called "impetus," on the other hand, is the force associated with a body actually in motion.[36] After the opening remarks concerning the work of the *Accademia* and its members, Leibniz begins Dialogue I with a methodological discussion, treating most notably the equipollence of cause and effect (§§ 6–9). The first extended discussion is then an account of Archimedean statics (§§ 10–18), the domain of dead force. While Archimedean statics deals with dead force and its laws, the force that most interests Leibniz is the kind of force that actually moving bodies possess, that by virtue of which they are capable of doing work. This is the domain of phoranomics proper: "living force pertains to phoranomics [*Phoranomices*]." As such, Leibniz claims, phoranomics concerns "the very laws of nature, which motive forces observe concerning the communication of motions" (§ 23). Dialogue I continues, with many nods toward Galileo, with a treatment of accelerated motion, the actual motion that arises from the continual application and repetition of a dead force like gravitation or centrifugal force (§§ 24–26). The dialogue ends with a consideration of motion with resistance (§§ 27–30) and the motion of projectiles (§§ 31–32).

In the opening sentences of Dialogue II, Leibniz informs us that, so far, we have only been in the vestibule: "now it is time to enter into the sanctuary of nature," where the "true laws of nature can be deduced" (M 782, 784). This is the function of the second dialogue.

The first question taken up is that of resistance, "whether you think . . . a large body is moved with more difficulty than a small one" (M 782).[37] The argument about resistance

---

[35] For the Italian context, see André Robinet, *Iter Italicum (mars 1689–mars 1690): La dynamique de la République des Lettres* (Florence: Leo S. Olschki, 1988).

[36] This fundamental distinction will play a visible role in the later "Specimen dynamicum" (1695), discussed in more detail later. Later, in the second dialogue of the *Phoranomus*, Leibniz argues that the source of the Cartesian law of the conservation of quantity of motion ($m|v|$) is the fact that the Cartesians, like the ancients, were aware only of statics, the domain of dead force, not living force, and so were led into their error. The idea is this. In a lever, say, the force of each weight will be the mass times the distance from the fulcrum. Because the lever constrains the motion of the weights, when they begin to move through the (dead) force of gravity, their speeds will be proportional to their distances from the fulcrum, and so their forces will be proportional to their masses and their speeds. See M 832f. See also "Specimen dynamicum" (GM VI 239; AG 122); and the post-1686 supplement to the "Brevis demonstratio" (GM VI 119–23; L 298–9), esp. p. 120.

[37] Leibniz addresses this question in much the same way as he had about a decade earlier, in the essay "De legibus naturae" discussed earlier (a strategy he will also use in the later "Specimen dynamicum"),

and the nature of body, which we have seen in Leibniz's writings since the late 1670s, is followed by another argument familiar from his earlier writings, one concerned with the nature of motion. In the *Phoranomus*, Leibniz argues that "what is real and absolute in motion doesn't consist in what is purely mathematical, such as change of neighborhood or situation, but in motive power itself" (M 800).

So far, Dialogue II of the *Phoranomus* seems quite continuous with Leibniz's earlier treatment of motion and force. The next question treated, the measure of powers (*aestimatio potentiarum*), is also a question treated in earlier texts, including the "De corporum concursu" and the "Brevis demonstratio." But the way Leibniz treats this question is rather different from anything that had gone before. Leibniz does discuss a variety of arguments concerning the proper measure of living force and its conservation based on the idea that force or power is to be measured through an effect that completely consumes that force; that is, the height to which a body moving with a given speed can raise itself. This is the strategy that Leibniz followed in the "De arcanis motus," the "De corporum concursu," and the "Brevis demonstratio." But, in the *Phoranomus*, before setting out these arguments, Leibniz approaches the question from a very different perspective, that of uniform motion considered per se. Here, the *effect* of force or power that is to be measured is simply the displacement of a body a certain distance in a certain time, an effect that does not completely consume the force in the way raising the body a certain distance does. (It should be noted here that the notion of an "effect" at issue includes *both* distance traveled *and* the time (speed) in which it takes place.) Leibniz concludes that when considering nonviolent effects (i.e., the effects that involve bodies in uniform motion moving distances at particular speeds), the force or power—the ability to produce a (nonviolent) effect—is proportional not to speed but to the square of the speed (M 800–810).[38]

The result—that force or power is proportional to mv^2—looks remarkably like the conclusion that Leibniz reached using the argument from the Galilean law of free fall.

---

with a story about the errors of his youth: "When I first wandered from the thorny brambles of the schools into the more agreeable fields of recent philosophy" (M 786). As in the earlier piece, Leibniz rehearses the earlier physics of the *TMA* and *HPN*, bodies without resistance and the difficulties that that got him into.

[38] The argument proceeds as follows. Leibniz begins with the assumption that when considering bodies moving uniformly with the same speed, the power (*potentia*) of the body is proportional to its size (M 804). He then considers a series of cases, where we are dealing with two bodies of the same size: (1) *A* travels distance 1 in time 2; (2) *B* (same size as *A*) travels distance 1 in time 1; (3) *B* travels another distance 1 in a successive time 1. Combining cases (2) and (3) we get (4): *B* travels distance 2 in time 2 (M 808). The effect of case (2) is double the effect of case (1) since the body moves the same distance in half the time. Similarly, case (3) is double the effect of case (1). Thus, case (4), which is case (2) + case (3) is four times the effect of case (1). But in case (4), a body travels the double distance in the same time as the body in case (1). That is to say, body *B* in case (4) is moving at twice the speed as *A* is in case (1) and has four times the effect. We are indebted here to Fichant, "Les dualités de la dynamique leibnizienne," pp. 35–36.

However, unlike the Galilean argument, this argument makes no assumptions about free fall. For Leibniz, as for his Cartesian antagonists, gravity was not a basic force in bodies but something due to the particular contingent configuration of the world (M 748). It obviously concerned Leibniz that his main argument against the Cartesian conservation law depended upon this contingent fact: that in bodies falling under the force of gravitation, the speed at which a body falls is proportional to the square root of the distance fallen. For that reason, no doubt, Leibniz wanted to find an a priori way of proving his conservation law. But there is something of a problem here. The kind of effect at issue in the a posteriori proof is what Leibniz calls a *violent effect*, "one for which the force has to be expended, or one in which the force has to be consumed," such as a body that lifts itself to a given height.[39] But the effect at issue in the a priori argument is an effect of a very different kind: it is simply the distance traveled during a particular time by a body in uniform motion. It is interesting that, in both cases, the effect is proportional to the square of the speed. But it is not at all clear that one is dealing with the same kind of effect or the same kind of power.

Nevertheless, in the *Phoranomus*, Leibniz saw the correspondence between the two arguments, the a priori and the a posteriori, as significant, and sought to confirm his new approach:

> And since this conclusion will soon appear true by way of indisputable *a posteriori* arguments, I don't think that there is another *a priori* argument in nature than the one presented here. And it seems to me that that argument used in the schools certainly holds here if it holds anywhere, that *if a conclusion is true, and there is no other reason for it, then this reason is true.*
>
> (M 814–16)

In this way, the a posteriori argument would seem to confirm our confidence in the a priori argument; curiously enough, in the *Phoranomus*, the a priori argument is thought not to be fully self-sufficient and to depend in some way on the more secure a posteriori argument.[40] In much of the rest of the dialogue, then, Leibniz will present various versions of the a posteriori argument, variants and developments of the arguments that he had used earlier and that depend on the Galilean law of free fall (M 826–839).

While the systematic intentions of the *Phoranomus* are clear, Leibniz allowed the manuscript to remain in a draft form and abandoned it for work on the later *Dynamica*.

The *Dynamica* was written a few months after the *Phoranomus*, between Rome and Florence, and exists in three different drafts.[41] One can trace, in fact, the progress in drafting the *Dynamica* in the correspondence between Leibniz and the Baron Rudolph

---

[39] See the discussion in "Specimen dynamicum" (GM VI 243–44; AG 127).

[40] Cf. Fichant, "Les dualités de la dynamique leibnizienne," pp. 36–37.

[41] For a study of the manuscript situation and a transcription of the entire text, see Costa, *Dynamica*. Costa's versions of the texts are scheduled to be published by Olms Verlag, with commentaries by Michel Fichant and Enrico Pasini.

Christian von Bodenhausen, who acted as a kind of editor and scientific advisor to Leibniz on the project. Indeed, it is in this correspondence that the term "dynamica" first seems to have appeared, replacing the term "*phoranomices*" that Leibniz had used in the earlier dialogue.[42] The final draft was left with Bodenhausen in Florence in November 1689, on the way back to Hanover in order to produce a fair copy and to see it through to publication. Leibniz had wanted to add some sections at the end of the treatise relating to applications of the dynamics but this was never accomplished. The treatise was never completed and never published. When Bodenhausen died roughly a decade after this in April 1698, these materials were sent back to Leibniz.

Unlike the *Phoranomus*, a pair of dialogues, the *Dynamica* is a single treatise, where the material is set out in a series of definitions, axioms, propositions, and scholia. Overall, the *Dynamica* is divided into two parts: "simple dynamics, abstracted from things, and concrete dynamics, concerning that which happens in the system of things" (GM VI 285). While this division would seem to echo the distinction between the abstract theory of motion in the *TMA* and the concrete theory of the *HPN*, it is in fact quite different since it tracks the a priori approach to force and its conservation, deriving from a consideration of bodies in uniform motion, and the earlier approach based on the Galilean law of free fall. Many of the rules and results in the *Phoranomus* are reproduced in the later *Dynamica*.[43] Hence, Leibniz's specific arguments were already in their largely final form by the time Leibniz composed the *Phoranomus*. The manuscript, however, does show transformation on the level of theoretical foundations and gives us a clue to why the earlier text may have been abandoned and a new exposition attempted.

This is especially true in part I of the *Dynamica*, where Leibniz develops his a priori account of force and its conservation.[44] In the version of the a priori argument in the *Phoranomus*, the basic notion is that of an *effect*. The effect of a uniform motion involves both the distance traveled and the time (speed) in which it is done. In the *Phoranomus*, the force or power of a body in uniform motion is proportional to its effect, understood in this way. But in the *Dynamica*, Leibniz introduces the notion of a *formal action* (*actio formalis*). Leibniz begins with a new definition of a formal effect (*effectus formalis*):

> The quantity of a formal effect in motion is that whose measure is a certain quantity of matter (with motion equally distributed) moved through a certain distance.[45]
>
> (GM VI 345)

---

[42] Fichant, "Les dualités de la dynamique leibnizienne," p. 13.

[43] Robinet provides a concordance of the two works in his edition of the *Phoranomus*, pp. 440–442.

[44] For studies of transformation of the a priori argument from the *Phoranomus* to the *Dynamica* emphasizing the importance of the introduction of the notion of *action*, see François Duchesneau, *La dynamique de Leibniz*, chap. 3, and Michel Fichant, "Les dualités de la dynamique leibnizienne." These studies supersede earlier discussions of Leibniz's a priori argument in Martial Gueroult, *Dynamique et métaphysique* and the commentary in Robinet (ed.), *Phoranomus*.

[45] A quantity of matter is said to have "motion equally distributed," roughly speaking, if all of its parts move with the same speed in the same direction. See GM VI 330, def. 1. So, for example, a rotating body does not satisfy this definition.

Leibniz then defines formal action (*actio formalis*):

> The quantity of formal action in motion is that whose measure is a certain quantity of matter moved through a certain distance (with uniform motion equally distributed) within a certain time.[46]

(GM VI 346)

In the formal effect, we are dealing simply with matter translated and the space through which the translation is made, whereas in formal action it is a question of the time or speed by which the translation is made.

The new definition of formal action allows Leibniz to redo the a priori arguments of the *Phoranomus* in a clearer way. In the *Phoranomus*, all the work is done by "effect," which is somewhat muddled insofar as the term has to include both the distance traveled by a body and the speed with which the distance is traveled. With the notion of "formal action," these two are separated: formal effect is the distance of the displacement of the mass (the body), and the action is the displacement done in time. And so Leibniz can set out his basic a priori result from the *Phoranomus* with greater precision and clarity. The demonstration, echoing a section of the *Phoranomus*, is given in a quasi-syllogistic form in the "Preliminary Specimen" to the *Dynamica*:

> An action bringing about double the effect in a single unit of time is double the action bringing about double the effect in two units of time; an action bringing about double the effect in two units of time is double the action bringing about a single effect in a single unit of time. Therefore, an action bringing about double the effect in a single unit of time is four times the action bringing about a single effect in a single unit of time, that is, in the same amount of time.

(GM VI 291; AG 110)

More generally, the formal action of a body in uniform motion is proportional to the square of its velocity.

But what is the connection here between action and force or power? Leibniz offers the following definition of absolute power (*potentia absoluta*):

> Absolute power of that which moves is a property [*affectus*] of [that thing], proportional to the quantity of action following *per se* from the state of being in motion within a certain time, that is, proportional to the quantity of formal action which a moving body exercises if the motion were to continue uniformly through a time of a given magnitude. And so, in equal times of acting, and assuming uniform formal actions, the absolute motive powers are proportional to formal actions.

(GM VI 359)

---

[46] Uniform motion here is motion with constant velocity. See GM VI 326. The formal effect just involves the distance a body moves, whether its speed is uniform or accelerated, but the formal action is defined in such a way as to require the body to be moving uniformly.

And so, Leibniz concludes, for a body moving in uniform motion, its absolute motive power will be proportional to its size and the square of its velocity; that is, proportional to mv^2 (GM VI 364).

Leibniz goes on in part II of the *Dynamica* to develop the kind of a posteriori arguments for the measure and conservation of motive power as mv^2 that we have seen in earlier texts (GM VI 457–64). But, in the *Dynamica*, the a priori demonstration is presented on its own, without any need of support from the a posteriori demonstration. Indeed, Leibniz even suggests that one can derive Galileo's law of free fall from the a priori demonstration:

> Thus, we already not only have a remarkable agreement among truths, but also a new way is opened for demonstrating Galileo's propositions about the motion of heavy bodies without the hypothesis he had to use, namely, that in their uniformly accelerated motion, heavy bodies acquire equal increments of velocity in equal times. For this very fact, as well as the lemma assumed above, can be derived from our fourth demonstration [i.e., the a priori demonstration], which does not depend on them as assumptions.
>
> (GM VI 292; AG 111)

In this way, in the *Dynamica*, the a priori argument would seem to have priority over the a posteriori.

1690–1700: FINAL DYNAMICAL ESSAYS AND THE METAPHYSICS OF THE DYNAMICS

Although the *Dynamica* of 1689 was written with the intention of publication, the manuscript never saw publication. Nonetheless, throughout the 1690s, Leibniz continued work on the dynamics in a number of texts, both unpublished and published.

The unpublished "Essai de dynamique" (1692) sets out a version of the argument for Leibniz's conservation principle, organized formally with definitions, axioms, postulates, and the like and establishing that force, and not Cartesian quantity of motion, is conserved. This essay seems to have been part of Leibniz's campaign to convince the members of the Académie royale des sciences to adopt his views.[47] Another unpublished text of note is an essay, thought to date from the late 1690s,[48] also entitled the

---

[47] The text is found in Pierre Costabel, *Leibniz and Dynamics* (Ithaca, NY: Cornell University Press, 1973), pp. 108–131. The argument that it was directed at the *Académie* is found in Costabel, *Leibniz and Dynamics*, ch. 1.

[48] On the dating, see Costabel, *Leibniz and Dynamics*, p. 30.

"Essai de dynamique."[49] The essay begins with the familiar Galilean argument, followed by the a priori argument. Intended, in all likelihood, for publication, the essay ends with the articulation of three quantities that must be conserved in collision. Consider two bodies, *a* and *b*, such that *a* moves with velocity *v* before collision and velocity *x* after, and *b* moves with velocity *y* before and *z* after. Leibniz proposes that the following three equations are satisfied:

(1)   Conservation of relative velocity: $v - y = z - x$
(2)   Conservation of common or total progress: $av + by = ax + bz$
(3)   Conservation of total absolute force or moving action: $avv + byy = axx + bzz$

(GM VI 227–28; Langley, New Essays, 667–68)

The third, of course, is the central conservation principle of Leibniz's dynamics; the other two are proved in the section of the *Dynamica* where Leibniz treats collision (see GM VI 494, prop. 10 and GM VI 496, prop. 12). Leibniz shows how, from any two of the equations, one can derive the third (GM VI 228; Langley, *New Essays*, 668). Although there is nothing substantive in the "Essai" that cannot be found in the *Dynamica*, it is an elegant summary of some of the central technical themes.[50]

There is also some material related to the dynamics project in the unpublished "Animadversiones in partem generalem Principiorum Cartesianorum," comments on parts I and II of Descartes's *Principia philosophiae* (1644). In Leibniz's comments on *Principia* II.36, where Descartes presents his conservation law, Leibniz presents a version of the Galilean argument against Descartes's principle (G IV 370–72; L 393–95). Leibniz also offers a refutation of Descartes's account of impact, both the general law (*Principia* II.40–44) and the seven specific rules Descartes proposes for the collision of two bodies in direct impact that Descartes works out following the general law (*Principia* II.45–52) (G IV 373–80; L 396–402).

The pieces Leibniz published in the 1690s, on the other hand, all go beyond the *Dynamica* in one way or another. The first of these pieces, "De primae philosophiae emendatione, et de notione substantiae," mentioned earlier, was published in the *Acta eruditorum* in March 1694. While it gives no technical details of the scientific project, this essay contains one of the very first uses of the term "dynamica" in print.[51] From its title, it is obvious that the main focus of this short essay is metaphysics. In it, Leibniz makes the claim that it is only through the notion of force that we can

---

[49]   GM VI 215–31; translation in Leibniz (1896), A. G. Langley (ed.), *New Essays Concerning Human Understanding together with an Appendix Consisting of Some of his Shorter Pieces* (New York: Macmillan, 1896), pp. 657–670.

[50]   On this essay, see Marshall Spector, "Leibniz vs. Cartesians on motion and force," *Studia Leibnitiana* 7 (1975), pp. 135–144.

[51]   G IV 469; L 433. The first occasion in which the term appears in print is found in "De causa gravitatis," (1690) GM VI 195.

understand the notion of substance. This is, in essence, the dynamical view of body that was noted earlier.

This metaphysical dimension of the dynamical program, largely missing from the *Dynamica* itself, is an especially prominent feature of the "Specimen dynamicum." Although it was written in two parts, only part I was published, in the *Acta eruditorum* of April 1695. Ostensibly a response to friends who urged Leibniz to reveal some features of his new project of dynamics, the essay gives some hints of what he was working on in the still unfinished *Dynamica*.[52]

The key distinction between active and passive forces, and, within active forces, between dead force and living force, is quite prominent in part I of the essay (GM VI 236–29; AG 119–22). As in previous writings, Leibniz attributes the errors of earlier thinkers to the fact that they only knew of dead force (GM VI 239; AG 122–3). As in earlier texts, Leibniz introduces the idea of the passive force of resistance in bodies through a cautionary tale about his own earlier views and how he came to reject them (GM VI 240–2; AG 123–5). In part I, he also offers a version of his argument that force is distinct from Cartesian quantity of motion and that it is force, not quantity of motion, that is conserved (GM VI 243–6; AG 127–30). Interestingly enough, Leibniz only offers the a posteriori argument from the Galilean law of free fall; although he mentions that there is an a priori measure of force "from a very simple consideration of space, time and action," he notes only that he shall explain that "elsewhere" (GM 243; AG 127). As a matter of fact, the a priori approach never finds its way into any of Leibniz's publications. The unpublished part II continues with some further details from the *Dynamica*. Leibniz discusses some of his views on impact and the relativity of motion, and he presents some consequences of the principle of continuity. Among those consequences is the view that all bodies are elastic, that all impact is elastic, and that "every passion of a body is of its own accord, that is, arises from an internal force, even if it is on the occasion of something external" (GM VI 251; AG 134). Connected with the principle of continuity is the critique of the Cartesian rules of impact that had been developed in greater length in his unpublished "Animadversiones" on Descartes (GM VI 250; AG 133–4). Moreover, in part II of the "Specimen dynamicum," unlike in the *Dynamica* itself, there is also a brief mention of Newton:

> I cannot agree with certain philosophical opinions of certain important mathematicians, who, beyond the fact that they admit empty space and don't seem to

---

[52] The full title of this essay is: "A Specimen of Dynamics, Toward Uncovering and Reducing to their Causes Astonishing Laws of Nature concerning the Forces of Bodies and their Actions on One Another." The full text is found in GM VI 234–46; AG 117–30 (part I) and GM VI 246–54; AG 130–8 (part II). For earlier versions, see Leibniz, *Specimen dynamicum*, Hans Günther Dosch, Glenn Most, Eno Rudolph, and Jörg Aichelin, eds. (Hamburg: Meiner, 1982), with critique in Eberhard Knobloch, "Review of G.W. Leibniz, Specimen Dynamicum," *Annals of Science* 40 (1983), pp. 501–504. On the development of Leibniz's publication, see Glenn W. Most, "Zur Entwicklung von Leibniz' *Specimen Dynamicum*," in *Leibniz' Dynamica*, Studia Leibnitiana, Sonderheft 13, ed. A. Heinekamp (Stuttgart: Steiner, 1984), pp. 148–163.

shrink from attraction, also take motion to be an absolute thing, and strive to prove this from rotation and the centrifugal force that arises from it.

(GM VI 253; AG 136)

While most of the technical details track pretty closely what can be found in the earlier *Phoranomus* and *Dynamica*, the novelty of this text consists in its elaboration of a larger metaphysical framework. In the "De primae philosophiae emendatione," Leibniz had suggested that the notion of force has great significance for metaphysics. In the "Specimen dynamicum," he makes good on that claim with a more detailed development of the dynamical conception of body. A fourfold hierarchy of forces is presented, distinguishing between active and passive, primitive and derivative (GM VI 236–39; AG 119–22):

	Active	Passive
Primitive	Form	Matter
Derivative	Living/Dead	Impenetrability/Resistance

The distinction between active and passive forces, and within those forces, between living and dead, impenetrability and resistance, is not new. But the distinction between primitive and derivative, not to be confused with activity and passivity, is relatively original with the "Specimen dynamicum." Derivative forces are just the variable forces that appear in physics (GM VI 237; AG 120). Primitive forces, on the other hand, are those which ground, in bodies, the derivative forces: "primitive [active] force . . . corresponds to the *soul* or *substantial form* . . ." ". . . the *primitive force of being acted upon* [*vis primitive patiendi*] or of *resisting* constitutes that which is called *primary matter* in the schools, if correctly interpreted" (GM VI 236–7; AG 119–20). The derivative forces seem to be the momentary spatiotemporal states of the primitive forces, which are either living or dead forces in the case of active force, or impenetrability or resistance in the case of passive.[53]

Primitive active and passive forces, form and matter, come together to produce a corporeal substance. As we noted earlier, this dynamical view of corporeal substance goes back to the late 1670s and arises at the same time as an alternative to the view of corporeal substance grounded in the notion of unity—a view which Leibniz considered

---

[53] The notion of a primitive force goes back to at least the mid-1680s. In "De mundo praesenti" of 1685/6, Leibniz writes: "*Matter* is the principle of passion, or primitive force of resisting, which is commonly called bulk or antitypy, from which flows the impenetrability of body. *Substantial form* is the principle of action, or primitive force of acting" (A VI iv 1507–8; Arthur 285–7). Similarly, in the "Specimen inventorum de admirandis naturae generalis arcanis" (1688), he writes: "And this principle of actions, or primitive force of acting, from which a series of various states results, is the form of the substance" (A VI iv 1625; Arthur 321). But the addition of a coordinate notion, that of a derivative force, seems to be new to the "Specimen dynamicum."

complementary to the dynamical view (see note 25). In the "Specimen dynamicum," however, this dynamical view of corporeal substance is completely united with the technical part of the dynamics: together they form a science of force that unifies both the physics of motion and the metaphysics of body.

The connection between the physics and metaphysics of force is emphasized again in the third major dynamical publication of the 1690s, the "De ipsa natura," "On Nature Itself, or, on the Inherent Force and Actions of Created Things, Toward Confirming and Illustrating their Dynamics," published in the September 1698 issue of the *Acta eruditorum*. The essay is focused on the metaphysical side of the program. The main argument is against the idea that bodies are completely without force or power and are inert, and the related doctrine of occasionalism, the view that the only genuine causal agent in the world is God. Leibniz argues that to take such a view is equivalent to Spinozism:

> the very substance of things consists in a force for acting and being acted upon. From this it follows that persisting things cannot be produced if no force lasting through time can be imprinted on them by the divine power. Were that so, it would follow that no created substance, no soul would remain numerically the same, and thus, nothing would be conserved by God, and consequently everything would merely be certain vanishing or unstable modifications and phantasms, so to speak, of one permanent divine substance. Or, what comes to the same thing, God would be the very nature or substance of all things, the sort of doctrine of ill repute which a recent writer, subtle indeed, though profane, either introduced to the world or revived.
>
> (GP IV 508–9; AG 159–60)

Thus, in this essay, Leibniz advances the metaphysical view that was at the center of the "Specimen dynamicum": the idea that body is made up of a "passive force of resisting" that constitutes "primary matter or bulk" and an active principle, a "primitive motive force," which is "called *the soul* in living things and *the substantial form* in other things" (GP IV 510–11; AG 161–2). At the end of the essay, Leibniz offers an ingenious argument (to which he returns a number of times later) that unless there were force and activity in bodies, over and above extension, there could be no change in the material world (GP IV 512–4; AG 163–5).

THE DYNAMICS AFTER 1700

The dynamical project was never really abandoned. In a letter to Nicolas Rémond on June 22, 1715, Leibniz wrote:

> My dynamics requires a work of its own, since I haven't yet said everything nor communicated that which I have to say about it. You are right, Monsieur, to judge that it is in good part the foundation of my system, since there one learns the difference

between truths whose necessity is brute and geometric and truths which have their source in suitability and in final causes.

(GP III 645)

Although after the "De ipsa natura" and the (later) "Essai de dynamique" there are no substantive essays on the dynamics, published or unpublished, the dynamics continues to be a subject of discussion in various other ways. It is very much present in the correspondence with de Volder.[54] Ursula Goldenbaum has also recently called attention to the importance of dynamical themes in the correspondence between Leibniz and Jacob Hermann in the early eighteenth century.[55]

But Leibniz faced a serious problem with the metaphysical side of the program, with the dynamical conception of body. The dynamical conception of body was born in the late 1670s, at the same time as the "unity" conception of corporeal substance. At this moment, Leibniz advanced the view that the ultimate constituents of the physical world were unities of substantial form and primary matter, interpreted (eventually) as primitive active force and primitive passive force. At the same time, Leibniz also held the view that the ultimate constituents of the physical world were, like us, unities of soul and body, animate beings, living things. There is every reason to believe that Leibniz thought that these two pictures were completely consistent with one another, that all the way down to tiny beings, living animals are unities of active and passive force. But in the mid-1690s, something new emerged: monads. These nonextended and mindlike unities replaced corporeal substances as the ultimate constituents of the world. This change in the metaphysics of unity raised a problem with the ontology of body: how are bodies to be integrated into the world of monads? This is a problem that Leibniz confronted mainly in his correspondences, particularly those with de Volder and Des Bosses. It is not clear that he ever came to a considered view about how to relate the two domains. But it is interesting that, throughout the discussions, he never gave up the dynamical view of bodies in terms of active and passive, primitive and derivative force. Indeed, one can see throughout the correspondence different suggestions about how these distinctions that shape the metaphysics of body in the "Specimen dynamicum" can be accommodated within a world of monads.[56] It is not clear that Leibniz ever reached a considered view on the question. In the end, like the dynamics itself, it seems like a project that was never completed.[57]

[54] See Anne-Lise Rey, "L'ambivalence de l'action," In Anne-Lise Rey (ed. and trans.), *Leibniz- de Volder Correspondance* (Paris: J. Vrin, 2016), pp. 7–83. See also Anne-Lise Rey, "L'ambivalence de la notion d'action dans la Dynamique de Leibniz," *Studia Leibnitiana* 41 (2009), pp. 47–66, 157–182.

[55] Ursula Goldenbaum, *Ein gefälschter Leibnizbrief?: Plädoyer für seine Authentizität* (Hanover: Wehrhahn Verlag, 2016).

[56] For a fuller development of this theme see Garber, "Body and Corporeal Substance" in this volume.

[57] On why the dynamics was never finished, see Stephen Howard, "Why did Leibniz fail to complete his dynamics?" *British Journal for the History of Philosophy* 25 (2017), pp. 22–40.

Acknowledgment

The authors would like to thank Maria Rosa Antognazza for her very helpful comments on an earlier draft of this essay.

References

Antognazza, Maria Rosa. 2009. *Leibniz: An Intellectual Biography*. Cambridge: Cambridge University Press.

Bertoloni Meli, Domenico. 1993. *Equivalence and Priority: Newton versus Leibniz*. Oxford: Oxford University Press.

Blackwell, Richard J. 1977. "Christian Huygens' The Motion of Colliding Bodies," *Isis* 68: 574–597.

Brown, Gregory. 1984. "'Quod Ostendendum Susceperamus': What did Leibniz undertake to show in the Brevis Demonstratio?" in Albert Heinekamp (ed.), *Leibniz' Dynamica*. Stuttgart: Franz Steiner Verlag, pp. 122–137.

Boyle, Robert. 1666. *The Origine of Formes and Qualities (According to the Corpuscular Philosophy)*. Oxford: H. Hall.

Bussotti, Paolo. 2015. *Complex Itinerary of Leibniz's Planetary Theory: Physical Convictions, Metaphysical Principles and Keplerian Inspiration*. New York: Birkhäuser.

Costa, Andrea. 2011. *G. W. Leibniz: Dynamica de potentia et legibus naturae corporeae. Materiaux pour une édition critique*. Dissertation, École des Chartes, Paris.

Costabel Pierre. 1973. *Leibniz and Dynamics*. Ithaca, NY: Cornell University Press.

Duchesneau, François. 1994. *La Dynamique de Leibniz*. Paris: J. Vrin.

Fichant, Michel. 2016. "Les dualités de la dynamique leibnizienne." *Lexicon Philosophicum* 4: 11–41.

Garber, Daniel. 1995. "Leibniz: Physics and philosophy." In Nicholas Jolley (ed.), *The Cambridge Companion to Leibniz*. Cambridge: Cambridge University Press, pp. 270–352.

Garber, Daniel. 2009. *Leibniz: Body, Substance, Monad*. Oxford: Oxford University Press.

Garber, Daniel, and Sophie Roux, eds. 2013. *The Mechanization of Natural Philosophy*. Dordrecht: Springer.

Goldenbaum, Ursula. 2008. "Individibilia Vera—How Leibniz came to love mathematics." In Ursula Goldenbaum and Douglas Jesseph (eds.), *Infinitesimal Differences*. Berlin and New York: Walter de Gruyter, pp. 53–75.

Goldenbaum, Ursula. 2016. *Ein gefälschter Leibnizbrief?: Plädoyer für seine Authentizität*. Hanover: Wehrhahn Verlag.

Gueroult, Martial. 1934. *Dynamique et métaphysique leibniziennes*. Paris: Les Belles Lettres.

Hess, Hans-Jürgen. 1978. "Die unveröffentlichten naturwissenschaftlichen und technischen Arbeiten von G. W. Leibniz aus der Zeit seines Parisaufenthaltes. Eine Kurzcharakteristik." In Gottfried-Wilhelm-Leibniz-Gesellschaft and Centre national de la recherche scientifique (France) (eds.), *Leibniz à Paris: 1672–1676*. Wiesbaden: Steiner, 1978: vol. 1, pp. 183–217.

Hobbes, Thomas. 1655. *Elementorum philosophiae sectio prima de corpore*. London: Andrew Crooke.

Hobbes, Thomas. 1656. *Elements of Philosophy, the First Section, Concerning Body*. London: Andrew Crooke.

Howard, Stephen. 2017. "Why did Leibniz fail to complete his dynamics?" *British Journal for the History of Philosophy* 25, pp. 22–40.

Huygens, Christiaan. 1888–1950. "De motu corporum ex percussione." In *Oeuvres complètes de Christiaan Huygens*. The Hague: M. Nijhoff, vol. XVI, pp. 21–91.

Iltis, Carolyn. 1971. "Leibniz and the vis viva controversy." *Isis* 62: 21–35.

Kepler, Johannes. 1990. *Gesammelte Werke* vol. III. Kepler-Kommission Der Bayerischen Akademie der Wissenschaften (ed.), München: C. H. Beck'sche Verlagsbuchhandlung.

Knobloch, Eberhard. 1983. "Review of G. W. Leibniz, Specimen Dynamicum." *Annals of Science* 40: 501–504.

Leibniz, Gottfried Wilhelm. 1896. *New Essays Concerning Human Understanding together with an Appendix Consisting of Some of his Shorter Pieces*. A. G. Langley (ed.). New York: Macmillan.

Leibniz, Gottfried Wilhelm. 1982. *Specimen dynamicum*. Hans Günther Dosch, Glenn Most, Eno Rudolph, and Jörg Aichelin (eds.). Hamburg: Meiner.

Leibniz, Gottfried Wilhelm. 1994. "De corporum concorsu." In Michel Fichant (ed.), *G. W. Leibniz: La réforme de la dynamique: De corporum concursu (1678) et autres textes inedits*. Paris: J. Vrin, pp. 71–171.

Leibniz, Gottfried Wilhelm. 2007. *Phoranomus seu de potentia et legibus naturae*. In Francesco Piro, Gianfranco Mormino, and Enrico Pasini (eds.), *Gottfried Wilhelm Leibniz: Dialoghi filosofici e scientifici*. Milan: Bompiani, pp. 680–885; 1991. Also in André Robinet (ed.), *Physis* N.S. 28/2 (1991): 429–541 and *Physis* N.S. 28/3 (1991): 797–885.

Most, Glenn W. 1984. "Zur Entwicklung von Leibniz' *Specimen Dynamicum* in Leibniz' *Dynamica*." In A. Heinekamp (ed.), *Studia Leibnitiana*, Sonderheft 13, pp. 148–163.

Ranea, Alberto Guillermo. 1989. "The *a priori* method and *actio* principle revised: Dynamics and metaphysics in an unpublished controversy between Leibniz and Denis Papin." *Studia Leibnitiana* 21: 42–68.

Rey, Anne-Lise. 2009. "L'ambivalence de la notion d'action dans la Dynamique de Leibniz." *Studia Leibnitiana* 41: 47–66, 157–182.

Rey, Anne-Lise. 2016. "L'ambivalence de l'action." In Anne-Lise Rey (ed. and trans.), *Leibniz-de Volder Correspondance*. Paris: J. Vrin, pp. 7–83.

Robinet, André. 1988. *Iter Italicum (mars 1689–mars 1690): La dynamique de la République des Lettres*. Florence: Leo S. Olschki.

Shimony, Idan. 2010. "Leibniz and the *vis viva* controversy." In Marcelo Dascal (ed.), *The Practice of Reason*. Amsterdam/Philadelphia: John Benjamins, pp. 51–73.

Spector, Marshall. 1975. "Leibniz vs. Cartesians on motion and force." *Studia Leibnitiana* 7: 135–144.

CHAPTER 18

....

BODY AND CORPOREAL
SUBSTANCE

....

DANIEL GARBER

LEIBNIZ opens his "Monadologie" with the statement that monads "are the true atoms of nature, and, in a word, the elements of things" ("Monadologie" §3, GP VI 607; AG 213). In a famous passage from the correspondence with de Volder, he writes that "considering the matter carefully, it should be said that there is nothing in things except simple substances and in them perception and appetite" (Lodge 306–7).[1] Statements like these have led commentators to ignore the realm of body and corporeal substance in Leibniz's thought altogether. Philosophers go for what is fundamental, what is metaphysically at the bottom of things, and are less interested in the derivative realms of being that are found further up the chain. In practice, historians of philosophy seem to have attributed this view to Leibniz as well. And so they have gone directly for the monadic level, assumed that that is where the philosophical action is to be found in his thought, and assumed that whatever he says about the level of the physical must, in some way, be either a shorthand for something at the monadic level or mere pandering to an audience incapable of understanding the true depth of his thought.[2] But this is an unfortunate mistake. While some contemporary physicists focus on the level of elementary particles, others work with what they call "condensed matter", that is to say medium-sized dry goods and wet goods. This level of body was of central importance to Leibniz's thought as well, from the beginning to the end.

We will begin with an account of Leibniz's earliest conception of body, very much influenced by Descartes and Hobbes. But, late in the 1670s, Leibniz came to see problems

---

[1] Lodge contains a new Latin text with English translation on facing pages. The page numbers I cite include both the Latin and the English.

[2] A younger colleague once showed me a referee's report on an article he had submitted to a philosophy journal involving Leibniz's views on body and corporeal substance. The article was rejected on the grounds that since Leibniz thought that everything was just monads, he couldn't have anything interesting to say about bodies.

with this view of body and introduced a new conception of body grounded in force, unity, and the Aristotelian notions of matter and form as Leibniz reinterpreted them. We will then trace the development of this view of body as it passes from a version of the view that corporeal substance is metaphysically basic to something rather less well-defined, when monads are introduced as the new metaphysical ground in the late 1690s.[3]

FIRST THOUGHTS ON BODY

Body and the physical world were among the things that Leibniz thought about when, in the late 1660s, he began to record his thoughts. It is too strong to say that Leibniz had a definite view on body at that time; he was clearly trying out different positions and exploring the intellectual world. Like most other young men of his time, he was educated in the Aristotelian philosophy, and one can suppose that he accepted an Aristotelian conception of body at that time. But, early on, Leibniz set that aside and adopted something of a mechanist conception of body and the explanation of phenomena in the physical world. Writing to Nicolas Rémond many years later, Leibniz notes that he "discovered Aristotle as a lad, and even the scholastics did not repel [him]." But, at a certain point, he decided to go with the moderns. He reports that he recalls:

> walking in a grove on the outskirts of Leipzig called the Rosental, at the age of fifteen, and deliberating whether to preserve substantial forms or not. Mechanism finally prevailed.
>
> (GP III 606; L 654–5)

To reject substantial forms meant, of course, to reject Aristotelian hylemorphism. And to adopt mechanism meant to sign on to a conception of the world in which body is taken to be defined in terms of its broadly geometrical properties and in which everything was to be explained in terms of size, shape, and motion.[4]

---

[3] This essay is structured around the still somewhat controversial view that monads only enter Leibniz's metaphysics some time in the mid- or late 1690s. I argue this most recently and at greatest length in Garber, *Leibniz: Body, Substance, Monad* (Oxford: Oxford University Press, 2009). Parts of this essay are drawn from that book. The main alternative view is that Leibniz accepted some version of the monadology from the late 1670s or early 1680s. For the best defense of this traditional view, see especially Robert M. Adams, *Leibniz: Determinist, Theist, Idealist* (Oxford: Oxford University Press, 1994), part III. There are now a number of other views on the question in the literature. See, e.g., Christia Mercer, *Leibniz's Metaphysics: Its Origins and Development* (Cambridge: Cambridge University Press, 2001), chap. 7; Glenn Hartz, *Leibniz's Final System: Monads, Matter and Animals* (London and New York: Routledge, 2007); Peter Loptson and Richard Arthur "Leibniz's body realism: Two interpretations," *Leibniz Review* 16 (2006), pp. 1–42; Jeffrey McDonough, "Leibniz's conciliatory account of substance," *Philosophers' Imprint* 13 (2013), pp. 1–23; Pauline Phemister, *Leibniz and the Natural World: Activity, Passivity, and Corporeal Substances in Leibniz's Philosophy* (Dordrecht: Springer, 2005).

[4] For a fuller account of the young Leibniz's engagement with mechanism and, more generally, natural philosophy, see Philip Beeley, *Kontinuität und Mechanismus: zur Philosophie des jungen Leibniz*

Even so, the young Leibniz offered a number of different versions of the mechanist conception of body in these years. One of Leibniz's earliest declarations of his adherence to the mechanical conception of nature occurs in a letter he wrote to his teacher, Jakob Thomasius on April 20/30, 1669. There, he tells his teacher that "I maintain the rule which is common to all of these renovators of philosophy, that only magnitude, figure, and motion are to be used in explaining corporeal properties" (A II i 25; L 94) Furthermore, he claims, "whether learned or ignorant, . . . men find that the nature of body consists in two things—extension and antitypy [i.e., impenetrability] together" (A II i 36/L 101). But in an interesting move, the young Leibniz argues here that this is what Aristotle actually meant all along.[5] And so, he argues, Aristotle's primary matter is just the extended substance that the mechanical philosophy recognizes, and substantial form is just shape (see A II i 26–7, 30; L 95–6, 98). Ironically enough, this version of mechanism accepts substantial forms, although interpreted in a rather mechanist way.[6]

But this is the only text I know where Leibniz takes this Aristotelian line. In a wide variety of other early texts, the young Leibniz is much more orthodox in his mechanism and advances a conception of body that is more clearly in opposition to Aristotelian hylemorphism. It is this conception of body that underlies his first serious foray into physics, the *Theoria motus abstracti* (*TMA*) and *Hypothesis physica nova* (*HPN*) of 1671. In the *HPN* he writes:

> I agree completely with the followers of those excellent gentlemen, Descartes and Gassendi, and with whomever else teaches that in the end, all variety in bodies must be explained in terms of size, shape, and motion.
>
> (*HPN* § 57; A VI ii 248; cf. A VI ii 249–50)

Bodies in this early physics offer no resistance in and of themselves. As in Hobbes's physics, all activity, including hardness and resistance, derives from motion. In some preliminary notes to the *TMA*, Leibniz writes:

> that hardness which is perceived by sense is nothing but resistance; all resistance is motion, and therefore, only those things are hard whose surface parts are so moved by

---

in ihren ideengeschichtlichen Kontext (Stuttgart: Steiner, 1996) and his chapter on Leibniz's early physics in this volume.

[5] Here, Leibniz distinguishes between the *true* Aristotle (whom he claims to follow) and the Aristotle of the schoolmen. See A II i 26; L 95.

[6] On Leibniz's general project for the reconciliation of the moderns with the Aristotelian philosophy, see Christia Mercer, "The seventeenth-century debate between the Moderns and the Aristotelians: Leibniz and Philosophia Reformata," *Studia Leibnitiana Supplementa* 27 (1990), pp. 18–29.

a strong motion in such a way that they oppose the impetus of things impelled from the outside.

(A VI ii 161)[7]

Sensible bodies are divided into bubbles, larger bubbles containing smaller bubbles to infinity (*HPN* §§ 43–44; A VI ii 241–42; Arthur 338–39; see also A VI ii 280; Arthur 344). But the coherence of the bubbles can only derive from their motion: "a body is harder to the extent that it moves more quickly around its own axis" (A VI ii 164). Because of the centrality of motion in differentiating impenetrable body from mere space, in this period, Leibniz sometimes claims that the essence of body is not extension but motion.[8] One can find the same basic view of body expressed through much of the later 1670s.[9]

At the same time that the young Leibniz is advancing a mechanist conception of *body* grounded in extension and motion, a mode of extension, one can find a somewhat different conception of *substance* in the texts. The context is theology, and Leibniz worries about issues like transubstantiation and resurrection. For transubstantiation to be possible, we must be able to understand how it is that the host can become the body of Christ when it is consecrated by the priest. And to understand how the resurrection of the body is possible at the end of days, we must be able to understand how it is possible for my body now and my body then to be the same body. Leibniz's solution is to appeal to substantial forms. In connection with transubstantiation, he writes:

> I demonstrate the numerical identity of substance from the numerical identity of substantial form, in conformity with the principles of the noblest scholastic and Aristotelian philosophers, those for whom substantial form is the principle of individuation. I define transubstantiation as change of substantial form.

(A VI i 511; L 117)

The substantial form, what he thinks of as a "concurrent mind" in these texts, together with the body in this context constitutes for Leibniz a substance (A VI i 508–9; L 115–6).

The appeal to substantial form works also to understand resurrection. Every living body, Leibniz claims, has a "kernel of substance," a very small, hard body "which is the proximate instrument and as it were the vehicle of the soul" (A II i 175–6, 185). (The soul, of course, is traditionally one kind of substantial form.) It is this kernel of substance that defines my body as mine and that ensures the continuity from my current body to the final judgment.

---

[7] Cf. Thomas Hobbes, *Elements of Philosophy, the First Section, Concerning Body* (London: Andrew Crooke, 1656), chap. 15.3: "it is therefore manifest, that rest does nothing at all, nor is of any efficacy; and that nothing but motion gives motion to such things as be at rest, and takes it from things moved."

[8] See, e.g., Leibniz to Arnauld, early November 1671, A II i 278; L 148; Leibniz to Oldenburg, October 15/25, 1671, A II i 271.

[9] See Garber, *Leibniz*, pp. 44–47.

One might see a certain tension between this theological domain, where Leibniz makes appeal to substantial form and substance in a straightforwardly Aristotelian way, and the domain of physics, where he adopts a straightforwardly mechanist conception of body that, with the exception of his sometimes "mechanized" Aristotelianism, does completely without forms. But there is no direct inconsistency, I think: in physics, it is *body* that is at issue, whereas in theology it is *substance*; in physics we can make do with body characterized in terms of extension and its modes, whereas in theology, substance and substantial forms seem to be needed. The apparent tension is resolved at the end of the 1670s, when Leibniz realizes that he needs to introduce substance and thus substantial forms into physics as well, fundamentally transforming his conceptions of both body and substance.

In a letter Leibniz wrote to his employer at Hanover in the autumn of 1679, he made an important announcement: "I reestablish substantial forms with demonstrative certainty [*démonstrativement*] and explain them intelligibly" (A I ii 225; cf. A II i 754). In another document from about the same period, the outline of a book on physics that he had contemplated writing but that he never really started—what the Akademie editors have named the "Conspectus libelli"—Leibniz offered more detail. After discussing a number of other topics in physics, Leibniz contemplates turning to substantial forms:

> There follows now a discussion of incorporeal things. Certain things take place in body which cannot be explained from the necessity of matter alone. Such are the laws of motion, which depend upon the metaphysical principle of the equality of cause and effect. Therefore we must deal here with the soul and show that all things are animated. Without soul or form of some kind, a body would have no being, because no part of it can be designated which does not in turn consist of more parts. Thus nothing could be designated in a body which could be called "this thing," or a unity.
>
> (A VI iv 1988; L 278–9; cf. A VI iv 1398–9; Arthur 245, which may be from the same period)

As we have seen, substantial forms never really left Leibniz's ontology; they were always part of his conception of substance as used in his philosophical theology. But they had been banished from his physics, the science of body. By the late 1670s, they seem to have come back.[10]

This last passage suggests that there are two motivations for returning to substantial forms. On the one hand, Leibniz alludes to arguments that derive from the behavior of body: "certain things take place in body which cannot be explained from the necessity of matter alone." But, on the other hand, there are other considerations deriving from the infinite divisibility of body: "without soul or form of some kind, a body would have

---

10 On this, see Michel Fichant, "Leibniz: Pensées sur l'instauration d'une physique nouvelle (1679)," *Philosophie* 39–40 (1993), pp. 3–26, and "Mécanisme et Métaphysique: le rétablissement des formes substantielles (1679)," *Philosophie* 39–40 (1993), pp. 27–59.

no being, because no part of it can be designated which does not in turn consist of more parts." We will take up the second consideration first.

Body and Corporeal Substance: Unity

Leibniz had been concerned with issues of unity and individuality since early in his thought.[11] But, by the 1680s, they become quite central to his notion of substance. This is a theme that is especially salient in his correspondence with Arnauld.[12] A central argument there is what might be called the *aggregate argument*. In his letter to Arnauld, April 30, 1687, Leibniz writes:

> I believe that where there are only entities through aggregation, there will not even be real entities; for every entity through aggregation presupposes entities endowed with a true unity. . . . I do not grant that there are only aggregates of substances. If there are aggregates of substances, there must also be genuine substances from which all the aggregates result. One must necessarily arrive either at mathematical points from which certain authors make up extension, or at Epicurus's and M. Cordemoy's atoms (which you, like me, dismiss), or else one must acknowledge that no reality can be found in bodies, or finally one must recognize certain substances in them that possess a true unity.
>
> (A 2.2.169; GP II 96; LA 120; see also A 2.2.82; GP II 58; LA 66; A 2.2.114–15; GP II 72; LA 88; A 2.2.186; GP II 97; LA 121; A 2.2.248; GP II 118; LA 151–2)

In an earlier draft, Leibniz makes it even clearer that it is extended bodies to which the argument applies:

> Now each extended mass can be considered as composed of two or a thousand others; there exists only an extension achieved through contiguity. Thus one will never find a body of which one can say that it is truly a substance. It will always be an aggregate of many. Or rather, it will not be a real entity, since the parts making it up are subject to the same difficulty, and since one never arrives at any real entity, because entities made up by aggregation have only as much reality as exists in their constituent parts.
>
> (A2.2.114–15; GP II 72; LA 88)

[11] On this, see Garber, *Leibniz*, 55–70.
[12] For more detailed developments of this theme in the correspondence, see Robert Sleigh, Jr., *Leibniz and Arnauld: A Commentary on their Correspondence* (New Haven: Yale University Press, 1990), chaps. 5–6; Samuel Levey, "On unity: Leibniz-Arnauld revisited," *Philosophical Topics* 31 (2003), pp. 245–275; Martha Bolton, "Leibniz to Arnauld: Platonic and Aristotelian themes on matter and corporeal substance," in *Leibniz and His Correspondents*, ed. Paul Lodge (Cambridge: Cambridge University Press, 2004), pp. 97–122; and Garber, *Leibniz*, chap. 2.

Leibniz sees here a problem with extended bodies of the kind that Descartes or Hobbes (or his own earlier philosophy) had recognized as fundamental. Insofar as they are divisible, they are made up of smaller parts. But insofar as each of the parts is itself divisible into smaller parts, there doesn't seem to be a level at which one is dealing with genuine entities, genuine individuals. And so, he argues, for extended *bodies* to be real, there must be some genuine individual *substances* in the world to ground the reality of the aggregates that are extended bodies. That is to say, physical *bodies* must be composed of *substances*, and substances must be genuine individuals in some sense.

But what does Leibniz have in mind by these "certain substances...that possess a true unity?" These are what he often calls corporeal substances. One example of a corporeal substance is us:

> man ... is an entity endowed with a genuine unity conferred on him by his soul, notwithstanding the fact that the mass of his body [*la masse de son corps*] is divided into organs, vessels, humors, spirits, and that the parts are undoubtedly full of an infinite number of other corporeal substances endowed with their own entelechies.
>
> (A II ii 251; GP II 120; LA 154)[13]

But we are not the only example of such things in the world:

> I also believe that to wish to restrict genuine unity or substance to man almost without exception is to be as limited in metaphysics as were in physics those who enclosed the world in a ball. And since genuine substances are as many expressions of the whole universe considered in a certain sense and as many duplications of the works of God; it is in keeping with the greatness and beauty of God's work, since these substances do not impede one another from making as many [substances] in this universe as possible and as higher reasons allow.
>
> (A II ii 187–8; GP II 98; LA 123)[14]

Corporeal substances, then, are souls united with bodies. But the body of a corporeal substance is, in turn, made up of smaller corporeal substances, souls and bodies, to infinity. And so, Leibniz often says, "everything is full of animate bodies" (A II ii 249; GP II 118; LA 151)

The "everything" in question is meant to include *in*animate bodies as well. In a letter from 1698, Johann Bernoulli asked Leibniz how far one had to divide a piece of inanimate matter, such as a piece of flint, before coming to a genuine substance, that is, an animate body. Leibniz answered with this:

> You ask me to divide for you a portion of mass [*massa*] into the substances of which it is composed. I respond, there are as many individual substances in it as there are

---

13 Cf. Leibniz to Malebranche, June 22/July 2, 1679, A II i 719.
14 Cf. A VI iv 1399; Arthur 245; A VI iv 1989; L 279; A VI iv 2008–9; L 289.

animals or living things or things analogous to them. And so, I divide it in the same way one divides a flock or fish pond, except that I think that the fluid [i.e., air or water] that lies between the animals of the flock, or between the fishes, and also the fluid (indeed, any remaining mass [*massa*]) contained in any fish or animal, ought to be divided again as if it were a new fish pond, and so on to infinity.

(A III vii 908 (AG 167–8); Cf. A II ii 120; GP II 76; LA 154)

Inanimate bodies, then, aren't substances, but aggregates of substances.

Individual corporeal substances are conceived of as living creatures of a certain kind, like animals. But, as these passages suggest, the body of a corporeal substance is itself made up of smaller corporeal substances as well, each of which has a soul (substantial form) and a body (matter), which, in turn, is made up of corporeal substances smaller still, and so on to infinity.[15] In this way, on Leibniz's view, as on earlier more orthodox mechanist views, bodies are infinitely divisible: inanimate bodies divisible into corporeal substances, while the corporeal substances that make up inanimate bodies are themselves composed of smaller corporeal substances to infinity, united by a single soul. But even if bodies are infinitely divisible, there is no violation of the aggregate argument: bodies are grounded in genuine unities, genuine individuals, corporeal substances. This is what we might call the Unity Conception of body and corporeal substance: on this conception, the ultimate constituents of the physical world are animate beings (corporeal substances) conceived of as genuine unities, and inanimate bodies are conceived of as aggregates of such unities.

Bodies and Corporeal Substances: Motion and Resistance

The "Conspectus libelli" suggests that there is another path to the revival of substantial forms. "Certain things take place in body which cannot be explained from the necessity of matter alone." These "certain things" lead Leibniz to posit "soul or form of some kind" in body and, like the aggregate argument, lead us to a conception of bodies in which "all things are animated."[16]

Some of those considerations arise from a consideration of the laws of motion, "which depend upon the metaphysical principle of the equality of cause and effect." What Leibniz has in mind is this. In his earlier conception of body, all activity in body is motion. From this, he concludes: "all power in bodies depends on the speed" (A VI ii 228). And so the laws of collision that he proposed in the *TMA* are basically the

---

[15] This would seem to lead directly to the doctrine of animals as "machines de la nature" that Leibniz advances in his "Système nouveau" (1995). For more on this, see François Duchesneau, "Leibniz on Physiology and Organic Bodies" in this volume and the references cited there.

[16] For a more detailed development of these arguments, see Garber, *Leibniz*, chaps. 3 and 4.

composition of velocities of the two colliding bodies.[17] As a consequence, when a body *A* in motion, however small, collides with a body *B* at rest, however large, *A* transmits to *B* all of its motion without losing any of its own, and the two move off in the direction *A* had been moving before the collision and at the speed *A* had been moving. This seems at odds with our everyday experience, of course, and Leibniz tried to devise various means of reconciling what he was convinced that theory demanded with experience.[18] In general, these strategies involved positing mechanical structures in the world such that bodies satisfying his resistance-free abstract laws of motion on the most basic physical level would *appear* to behave in such a way that bodies resisted the acquisition of motion in proportion to their size.

But even if appearances can be saved, Leibniz came to see a fundamental problem with this strategy. By the mid-1670s, Leibniz came to adopt a new basic principle in physics: that "it is necessary that the cause be able to do as much as the effect and vice versa."[19] (This is what he is referring to as the "metaphysical principle of the equality of cause and effect" in the "Conspectus libelli.") Now, on the physics of the *TMA* and *HPN*, where the laws of motion are just the laws of the composition of velocities, this principle will be violated at the most basic physical level. A body in motion is capable of producing an effect, say, raising itself a certain distance. If two bodies, *A* and *B*, moving with the same speed collide head on, the motion of both will be lost and, with it, the capability of producing any effect. Or, if a body in motion *A* collides with a body at rest *B*, then the two bodies would go off with the same velocity *A* originally had, increasing its capability of producing an effect and raising two bodies a certain distance rather than just one. Leibniz came to see that if the new conservation principle was to hold, then he must posit in bodies an inherent force of resistance to the change in the motion of a body or to its acquisition of new motion.[20] By the end of the decade, this observation led Leibniz to the view that the nature of body must be other than he (and Descartes and Hobbes) had thought it to be.[21] In the "Conspectus libelli," the suggestion is that this leads us to

[17] See A VI ii 268; L 142, §§20–4.

[18] See Garber, *Leibniz*, 16–22, 99–102.

[19] The clearest and most extensive statement of this new principle is found in an essay, "De arcanis motus," thought to have been written in 1676. The text of the essay is published on pp. 202–205 as appendix 4 to Hans-Jürgen Hess, "Die unveröffentlichten naturwissenschaftlichen und technischen Arbeiten von G. W. Leibniz aus der Zeit seines Parisaufenthaltes. Eine Kurzcharakteristik," in Gottfried-Wilhelm-Leibniz-Gesellschaft and Centre national de la recherche scientifique (France) (eds.), *Leibniz à Paris: 1672–1676*. Wiesbaden: Steiner, 1978: vol. 1, 183–217. The quotation is found at p. 203. The text has recently been published in A VIII ii 133–38.

[20] For a more careful development of this argument, see the chapter by Garber and Tho, "Force and Dynamics" in this volume.

[21] This was an argument that Leibniz repeated often. See, e.g., A VI iv 1976–80; AG 245–50; *Discours de métaphysique* §21; GP IV 464–6; GM VI 240–2; AG 123–5; "Phoranomus seu de potentia et legibus naturae," Gianfranco Mormino, ed., in Francesco Piro, ed., *Gottfried Wilhelm Leibniz: Dialoghi filosofici e scientifici* (Milan: Bompiani, 2007), pp. 680–885, at pp. 786–798. It is also rehearsed frequently in letters.

the conclusion that there must be a "soul or form of some kind" in body from which such a force of resistance might arise.

There is another argument in this period concerning the nature of body that also turns on force and motion. The question of the reality of motion is something that concerned Leibniz from early on, when he first began to think about the physical world.[22] But the problem of motion is nicely summarized in the *Discours de métaphysique* of 1686. He writes:

> if we consider only what motion contains precisely and formally, that is, change of place, motion is not something entirely real, and when several bodies change position among themselves, it is not possible to determine, merely from a consideration of these changes, to which body we should attribute motion or rest, as I could show geometrically, if I wished to stop and do this now.
>
> (*Discours de métaphysique* § 18, A VI iv 1559; AG 51)

Leibniz's point here is a familiar one: that when we consider only extension and its modes in body, when two bodies, *A* and *B* are in motion with respect to one another, there is no real difference between saying that *A* is at rest and *B* in motion or that *B* is at rest and *A* is in motion. But Leibniz does not want to conclude here that "motion is not something entirely real." Instead, he continues with a criterion for distinguishing real motion from rest:

> But the force or proximate cause of these changes is something more real, and there is sufficient basis to attribute it to one body more than to another. Also, it is only in this way that we can know to which body the motion belongs.
>
> (*Discours de métaphysique* § 18, A VI iv 1559; AG 51)

This "force or proximate cause" of change is what he elsewhere calls a "*vis agendi*" or a "force of acting" (see A VI iv 2019). This, in turn, leads him to a conclusion very similar to the conclusion of the argument to which he was led by the principle of the equality of cause and effect:

> Now, this force is something different from size, shape, and motion, and one can therefore judge that not everything conceived in body consists solely in extension and in its modifications, as our moderns have persuaded themselves. Thus we are once again obliged to reestablish some beings or forms they have banished.
>
> (*Discours de métaphysique* § 18, A VI iv 1559; AG 51)

And, once again, we are led to positing a "soul or form of some kind" in body.

How does the positing of a soul or form address the problems of resistance and motion? The position seems to be this. In order to introduce resistance into bodies

---

[22] See Garber, *Leibniz*, 106–115.

and enable them to satisfy the principle of the equality of cause and effect, we must introduce something in bodies over and above extension and motion, something from which the force of resistance can derive. And, in order to be able to distinguish between motion and rest and ground a real notion of motion in bodies, we must introduce something in bodies over and above extension and the change of place, something from which a "force of acting" can arise. In both cases, the idea is that form or soul, traditionally understood as a source of activity—in contrast with passive extended matter—will provide the activity needed to ground resistance and motion.

Throughout the 1680s, though, Leibniz's position developed and deepened. In the late 1670s, form was introduced as the ground of all activity in body. But by the mid-1680s, the position had evolved. In an important fragment from about the time of the *Discours de métaphysique*, Leibniz wrote:

> Corporeal substances have parts and species. The parts are matter and form. Matter is the principle of being acted on [*principium passionis*] that is, the primitive force of resisting, which is commonly called bulk or antitypy, from which flows the impenetrability of body. The substantial form is the principle of action or the primitive force of acting. Furthermore, there is in every substantial form a certain knowledge [*cognitio*] that is an expression or representation of external things in a certain individual thing, in accordance with which a body is *per se* one, namely in the substantial form itself. This representation is joined with a reaction or conatus or appetite which follows this thought of acting. This substantial form must be found in all corporeal substances which are *per se* one.
>
> (A VI iv 1507–8; Arthur 285–7)[23]

In this passage, Leibniz clearly distinguishes between the ground of the *vis agendi* that is necessary for the reality of motion and the ground of the force of resistance that is necessary to ensure that the equality of cause and effect is not violated. The active force is associated with form, and the passive force of resistance is associated with matter.

This view gets its canonical presentation in Leibniz's "Specimen dynamicum" (1695), the first public exposition of his new science of force, what he came to call his dynamics.[24] He writes:

> *Active force* (which might not inappropriately be called *power* [*virtus*], as some do) is twofold, that is, either *primitive*, which is inherent in every corporeal substance *per se* . . . or *derivative*, which, resulting from a limitation of primitive force through the collision of bodies with one another, for example, is found in different degrees. Indeed, primitive force (which is nothing but the first entelechy)

---

[23] Leibniz never does say exactly what the species are.
[24] On the project of Leibniz's dynamics, see the chapter by Garber and Tho, "Force and Dynamics" in this volume.

corresponds to the *soul or substantial form*.... Similarly, passive force is also two-fold, either primitive or derivative. And indeed, the *primitive force of being acted upon* [*vis primitiva patiendi*] or of *resisting* constitutes that which is called *primary matter* in the schools, if correctly interpreted. This force is that by virtue of which it happens that a body cannot be penetrated by another body, but presents an obstacle to it, and at the same time is endowed with a certain laziness, so to speak, that is, an opposition to motion, nor, further, does it allow itself to be put into motion without somewhat diminishing the force of the body acting on it. As a result, the *derivative force of being acted upon* later shows itself to different degrees in *secondary matter*.

(GM VI 236–7; AG 119–20)

There are two important distinctions here: between active and passive force and between primitive and derivative force. So, in all, there are four kinds of force: primitive and derivative active force and primitive and derivative passive force. The derivative forces, active and passive, are the familiar physical magnitudes we see in the world, the momentary states of bodies. The derivative active forces are living force, the force associated with a body in actual motion, and dead force, the momentary accelerative force in a heavy body straining on a cord preventing it from falling or in an arrow at the moment when the archer releases it from a taut bow. The derivative passive forces are impenetrability, the force by which a body resists penetration, and resistance, the force by which a body resists the acquisition of new motion. These forces are grounded in the primitive forces, active and passive, those constituents of body from which arise the derivative forces. Leibniz claims here that primitive active and passive force are what the scholastics should have meant by substantial form and primary matter. And here we seem to rejoin the Unity Conception of body and corporeal substance.

In Leibniz's dynamical writings on force, the focus is on force, active and passive, and not on individual corporeal substances and their relation with body. But the passage quoted earlier from the "Conspectus libelli" suggests that he saw the considerations of force leading to much the same place as the considerations of unity: the need to ground the laws of nature that leads him to the conclusion that "we must deal here with the soul and show that all things are animated" is directly connected in Leibniz's mind with the observation that "without soul or form of some kind . . . nothing could be designated in a body which could be called 'this thing,' or a unity." This suggests that Leibniz saw considerations of force as an alternative way of approaching the same metaphysical conclusion as he reached with the aggregate argument, that bodies are made up of corporeal substances conceived of as unities of form and matter. But these considerations of motion, conservation, and collision lead us to a different perspective on corporeal substances: individual corporeal substances are here understood as made up of primitive active and passive forces. This is what we might call the Dynamical Conception of body and corporeal substance.

BODY, CORPOREAL SUBSTANCE,
AND BEYOND

In this way, we seem to have two argumentative paths to a single conclusion: that bodies are ultimately made up of corporeal substances, conceived on the model of animate beings, unities of soul and body, form and matter, and primitive active and passive force. I don't mean to suggest that the view is unproblematic. The conception of soul in the Unity Conception fits well enough with the conception of primitive active force in Dynamical Conception, where it is simply identified with the soul. But it is not altogether clear where to put the primitive passive force, the primary matter of the Dynamical Conception of corporeal substance in the organic body of the kinds of corporeal substances that are at the center of the Unity Conception of corporeal substance prominent in the exchange with Arnauld. Since the body of a corporeal substance is made up of tinier corporeal substances, unities of soul and body, to infinity, there doesn't seem to be an obvious place for primitive passive force. But, be that as it may, there is every reason to think that, one way or another, Leibniz thought that he could reconcile these two conceptions of corporeal substance and that the two approaches to corporeal substance and the renovation of substantial forms converge on a single view.

In the 1680s and, at least, in the first part of the 1690s, when this view of body and corporeal substance is first introduced, what some call Leibniz's "Middle Years," it is important to note that this account of body and corporeal substance represents the bottom level of Leibniz's metaphysics. Corporeal substances, at this moment, at least, seem to be the ultimate and metaphysically most basic constituents of the world. But at some time in the mid-1690s, this will begin to change.[25]

In the first half of the 1690s, the Dynamical Conception of body and corporeal substance seems to be very much on Leibniz's mind. In 1693, he had written to a correspondent, Jacques L'Enfant, that "I cannot see how one can find there [i.e. in substance] anything more primitive than . . . force" (Leibniz to L'Enfant, December 5, 1693; A II ii 753). In the following year, he published the essay "De primae philosophiae emendatione" in the *Acta eruditorum*. There, he claimed that "the concept of *forces* or *powers* . . . brings the strongest light to bear upon our understanding of the true concept of *substance*" (GP IV 469L 433). In a letter to Bossuet in the same year he wrote that "I find nothing so intelligible as force" (Leibniz to Bossuet, July 2/12, 1694; A1.10.143–4;

---

[25] For a more detailed account of the changes that Leibniz's thought underwent during the mid- and late-1690s, see Garber, *Leibniz*, chap. 8, and Garber, "Monads on my mind," in Adrian Nita, ed., *Leibniz's Metaphysics and the Adoption of Substantial Forms: Between Continuity and Transformation* (Dordrecht: Springer, 2015), pp. 161–176. As more and more new texts from the 1690s are edited and published, no doubt our picture of Leibniz's intellectual development during this important period in his thought will be further enriched.

WFN 30). This seems to culminate in 1695 in the view of substance in terms of primitive active and passive forces in the "Specimen dynamicum."

But, in another text in 1695, there are indications that he had begun to find something more primitive still. At the end of the first part of his "Système nouveau," Leibniz wrote:

> There are only atoms of substance, that is, real unities absolutely destitute of parts, which are the source of actions, the first absolute principles of the composition of things, and, as it were, the final elements in the analysis of substances [*les premiers principes absolus de la composition des choses, & comme les derniers élemens de l'analise des substances*]. We could call them metaphysical points: they have something vital, a kind of perception, and mathematical points are the points of view from which they express the universe. But when corporeal substances are contracted, all their organs together constitute only a physical point relative to us. Thus physical points are indivisible only in appearance; mathematical points are exact, but they are merely modalities. Only metaphysical points or points of substance (constituted by the forms or souls [*constituez par les formes ou ames*]) are exact and real, and without them there would be nothing real, since without true unities there would be no multitude.[26]

It is clear here that Leibniz has the question of unity on his mind and that true unities are needed to ground the reality of things: it is unity and not force that is at issue here. But, Leibniz insists, the real unities that appear to ground the world are "absolutely destitute of parts" and appear to be something distinct from corporeal substances. At about the same time two new terms enter Leibniz's vocabulary: "simple substance" and "monad." In an unpublished note, probably written in 1696, a reply to a critique by Simon Foucher, Leibniz writes that "in actual substantial things, the whole is a result or coming together of simple substances" (GP IV 491; AG 146). The term "monad" appears for the first time in a letter to L'Hospital dated July 12/22, 1695: "The key to my doctrine on this subject consists in the consideration of that which is genuinely a real unity, a monad" (A III vi 451; WFN 57).[27] Now, it isn't entirely clear that these changes represent the adoption of a new doctrine. The passage from the "Système nouveau" can be read in a way that makes it consistent with the corporeal substance ontology.[28] Furthermore, it also isn't clear that, when first introduced, the term "monad" isn't just a synonym for "unity." In a letter to Johann Bernoulli from September 20/30, 1698, Leibniz writes: "What I call a complete monad or individual substance [*substantia singularis*] is not so much the soul, as it is the animal itself, or something analogous to it, endowed with a soul or form and an organic body" (A III vii 909; AG 168). This, of course, is just the corporeal substance view. But,

---

[26] Leibniz, "Système nouveau," in *Journal des sçavans* (1695), 300; AG 142. I am quoting and citing the original publication of Leibniz's essay since the text usually cited in GP IV is that of a later version.

[27] It also appears in a letter to Michelangelo Fardella September 3/13, 1696, A II iii 192–93.

[28] See Garber, *Leibniz*, 333–335.

within a few years, it is clear that we are in a different world. In a famous passage, written to Burchard de Volder on June 30, 1704, Leibniz declared:

> Indeed, considering the matter exactly carefully it should be said that there is nothing in things except simple substances and in them perception and appetite.
>
> (Lodge 306–7)

Here, it is clear that we are dealing with a world whose ultimate constituents are simple, nonextended, and mindlike substances, the familiar monads of the "Monadologie." But where in this world do bodies and corporeal substances fit? This is a very complicated question and has many dimensions. There is no definitive answer, I think, because, I would claim, Leibniz didn't arrive at one. But the texts do give us indications of some of the directions in which he was thinking.[29]

Bodies, Corporeal Substances, and Monads

A central question would seem to be the relation between bodies and corporeal substances, on the one hand, and the world of monads, on the other. And here there appear to be at least two different accounts in Leibniz's writings.

The passage from the letter to de Volder on June 30, 1704, quoted earlier, continues as follows:

> moreover, matter and motion are not so much substances or things as phenomena of perceivers, the reality of which is located in the harmony of perceivers with themselves (at difference times) and with other perceivers.
>
> (Lodge 306–7)

The suggestion here is that matter and motion in bodies is nothing more than the common perception of perceivers (monads) in harmony with one another. This suggestion is made more explicit still in certain passages in his correspondence with Des Bosses:

> It is true that the things that happen in the soul must agree with those which happen outside the soul; but for this it is sufficient that those things that happen in one soul correspond both among themselves and with those things that happen in any other soul; and there is no need to posit something outside of all souls or monads. According to this hypothesis, when we say that Socrates is sitting, nothing more is

---

[29] For a more detailed version of the reading I am offering here, see Garber, *Leibniz*, chap. 9.

signified than that those things that we understand by "Socrates" and "sitting" are appearing to us and to others for whom it is a concern.

> (Leibniz to Des Bosses June 16, 1712; Look-Rutherford 256–7)[30]

On this view, the world of bodies would seem just to be the common dream of an infinity of monads. This would make bodies phenomenal in an obvious sense: bodies would exist only insofar as they are the contents of monadic perceptions. This is what we might call the Common Dream Conception of body. On this conception, it would seem as if the world of bodies is altogether eliminated from Leibniz's world.

But in Leibniz's writings from the period after monads were introduced, there is also a rather different account of where bodies fit. On this account, bodies are conceived of as aggregates of monads. This is quite clear in the opening section of the "Principes de la nature et de la grâce" of 1714:

> A substance is a being capable of action. It is simple or composite. A simple substance is that which has no parts. A composite substance is a collection of simple substances, or monads. Monas is a Greek word signifying unity, or what is one. Composites or bodies are multitudes; and simple substances—lives, souls, and minds—are unities. There must be simple substances everywhere, because, without simples, there would be no composites.

> (GP VI 598; AG 207)[31]

This view is suggested in many other places in Leibniz's writings. In a letter to de Volder from June 20, 1703, he tells his correspondent that:

> simple things alone are true things, the rest are only beings through aggregation, and therefore phenomena, and, as Democritus used to say, exist by convention, not in reality.

> (Lodge 264–5)

The view is also suggested, for example, in a passage that Leibniz wrote to Des Bosses on March 11, 1706:

---

[30] See also Leibniz to Des Bosses, February 15, 1712, Look-Rutherford 226–7; and Leibniz to Des Bosses, May 16, 1716, Look-Rutherford 370–1. Look-Rutherford contains a new Latin text with English translation on facing pages. The page numbers I cite include both the Latin and the English.

[31] See also the text that Leibniz had originally written for Rémond in 1714 to explain his views: "I believe that the entire universe of creatures consists only in simple substances or monads, and in their aggregates. These simple substances are what we call mind in us and in spirits, and soul in animals. . . . Aggregates are what we call bodies." (GP III 622)

from many monads there results [*resultare*] secondary matter, together with derivative forces, actions, and passions, which are only beings through aggregation, and thus semi-mental things, like the rainbow and other well-founded phenomena.

(Look-Rutherford 34–5; see also Leibniz to Des Bosses, July 31, 1709, Look-Rutherford 140–1)

Here, as in the view of the Common Dream Conception, bodies are taken to be phenomenal, although in a somewhat different sense. In the case of aggregates of monads, the activity of the mind enters in binding the monads together and treating them as one thing: they are phenomenal in the sense in which inanimate bodies were phenomenal in his "middle years"; that is, aggregates of monads, which are genuine substances.[32] This is what we might call the Aggregate Conception of body.

But what of the corporeal substances of his earlier view and the idea that inanimate bodies are aggregates of corporeal substances? Here, the positions Leibniz takes get somewhat complicated. On the Common Dream Conception, it seems quite clear that there cannot be corporeal substances, properly speaking: bodies are just the intentional objects of monadic perceptions. But it isn't so clear what to say about corporeal substances on the Aggregate Conception.

Sometimes Leibniz seems to take the view that whereas monads are substances, aggregates of monads are not, strictly speaking. This seems to be the conclusion of the passage from the de Volder letter of June 20, 1703, quoted earlier:

simple things alone are true things, the rest are only beings through aggregation, and therefore phenomena, and, as Democritus used to say, exist by convention, not in reality.

(Lodge 264–5)

A year later, he wrote to de Volder that "considering the matter carefully, it should be said that there is nothing in things except simple substances and in them perception and appetite" (Lodge 306–7). Leibniz repeats this same view in a letter to Pierre Dangicourt on September 11, 1716, just weeks before his death:

I am also of the opinion that, to speak exactly, there is no need of extended substance. . . . True substances are only simple substances or what I call "monads." And I believe that there are only monads in nature, the rest being only phenomena that result from them. Each monad is a mirror of the universe according to its point of

---

[32] Cf. Leibniz to Des Bosses, February 15, 1712, where Leibniz considers one possible understanding of body: "bodies are mere phenomena, and so extension also will be only a phenomenon, and monads alone will be real, but with a union supplied by the operation of the perceiving soul on the phenomenon" (Look-Rutherford 224–7). In calling the rainbow a phenomenon here, he seems to be thinking of it as a collection of water droplets united by the perceiver who perceives them together (Cf. A VI iv 555).

view and is accompanied by a multitude of other monads which compose its organic body, of which it is the dominant monad.[33]

These passages strongly suggest that there are no complex substances over and above the simple substances or monads.

It should be noted in this connection that even when Leibniz denies that aggregates of monads can make up genuine (corporeal) substances, he doesn't necessarily give up his earlier idea that the physical world is made up of living things, that inanimate bodies are aggregates of such living things, and that the bodies of living things are collections of living things united by a single soul. In the "Monadologie," for example, Leibniz is very careful not to recognize any genuine substances over and above nonextended monads. But, even so, he writes:

> there is a world of creatures, of living beings, of animals, of entelechies, of souls in the least part of matter. Each portion of matter can be conceived as a garden full of plants, and as a pond full of fish. But each branch of a plant, each limb of an animal, each drop of its humors, is still another such garden or pond. . . . Thus we see that each living body has a dominant entelechy, which in the animal is the soul; but the limbs of this living body are full of other living beings, plants, animals, each of which also has its entelechy, or its dominant soul.
>
> ("Monadologie" §§ 66, 67, 70; GP VI 618–19; AG 222)

Although now ultimately grounded in monads, the world of bodies in the "Monadologie" has the same structure and architecture that it had when it was earlier grounded in corporeal substances.

But corporeal substances didn't altogether disappear in the later texts. Despite the apparent denial of corporeal substances in texts like the de Volder letters, there are other passages in that exchange that seem to assert that some aggregates of monads can constitute corporeal substances. In an oft-cited passage from the letter of June 20, 1703, he writes:

> I therefore distinguish: (1) the primitive entelechy, i.e., the soul; (2) matter, namely, primary matter, i.e., primitive passive power; (3) the monad completed by these two things; (4) the mass, i.e., the secondary matter, i.e., the organic machine, for which innumerable subordinate monads come together; and (5) the animal, i.e., the corporeal substance, which the monad dominating in the machine makes one.
>
> (Lodge 264–5)

---

[33] G. W. Leibniz, *Recueil de diverses pieces sur la philosophie, les mathematiques, l'histoire &c. par M. de Leibniz*, ed. Cretien Kortholt (Hamburg: Abram Vandenhoeck, 1734): 1–2. This passage is cited and discussed in Look-Rutherford 401 note 105.

Here, it seems that he recognizes corporeal substances as "organic machines" made up of monads, united by a "monad dominating the machine." (We will return to this passage later.) This view is also advanced in the "Principes de la nature et de la grâce" of 1714. In a passage quoted earlier, Leibniz compares simple and composite substances:

> A simple substance is that which has no parts. A composite substance is a collection of simple substances, or monads.
>
> (GP VI 598; AG 207)

In a later section, he writes:

> each distinct simple substance or monad, which makes up the center of a composite substance (an animal, for example) and is the principle of its unity, is surrounded by a mass composed of an infinity of other monads, which constitute the body belonging to this central monad. . . . Each monad, together with a particular body, makes up a living substance.
>
> (GP VI 598–9; AG 207–8)

Although composed of metaphysically more basic monads now, the corporeal substances in this passage look very much like the living things found in earlier texts, such as the Correspondence with Arnauld.

There is another rather different treatment of corporeal substance in Leibniz's later thought. The question of corporeal substances is the center of Leibniz's correspondence with Des Bosses, starting with the letter of February 15, 1712. The discussion centers around the famous *vinculum substantiale*, the substantial bond (or chain) that is supposed to transform a collection of monads into a genuine corporeal substance.[34] Leibniz introduces the discussion as follows:

> If corporeal substance is something real over and above monads, as a line is taken to be something over and above points, we shall have to say that corporeal substance consists in a certain union, or rather in a real unifier superadded to monads by God.
>
> (Look-Rutherford 224–5)

This substantial bond is taken to be something genuinely substantial, a something that exists over and above the monads.[35] And, for that reason, if Leibniz were to adopt it, it would clearly constitute a rejection of the view that all there are are monads. It isn't entirely clear whether Leibniz actually endorsed the existence of substantial bonds. When it is first introduced, it seems to be discussed in a very tentative and hypothetical way, a thesis apparently tailored to allow the Jesuit Des Bosses to be able to accept a Catholic

---

[34] For an excellent discussion of this question, see the extensive editors' introduction to Look-Rutherford and the references cited there.

[35] See Garber, *Leibniz*, 374–380 for a development of this point.

conception of the Eucharist within the context of a theory of monads. But, as the discussion goes on, Leibniz seems to warm up to the idea more and more, and one might make the argument that he actually comes to accept the hypothesis as his own.[36] Whether or not he does, it is certainly clear that he takes it seriously as a possible account of the place of corporeal substances in the monadology.

There is no question that, at the bottom level, metaphysically speaking, there are monads and that bodies are aggregates of monads—at least in these passages we have been examining. But these texts that we have been examining suggest that Leibniz at least contemplated the view in the context of his later metaphysics that corporeal substances constitute a kind of intermediate stage between monads and inanimate bodies. But it is also interesting to trace what becomes of the two conceptions of body and corporeal substance that we found at work in the earlier writings, before monads were introduced.

Unity finds a clear place in the later metaphysics. Monads, the "true atoms of nature and, in brief, the elements of things," as he puts it in §3 of the "Monadologie" (GP VI 607; AG 213) are the ultimate unities: simple, without parts, nonextended, and indivisible in the strongest sense. Unities constitute the ultimate ground of things both on the Common Dream and the Aggregate Conception of body. In those texts where Leibniz seems to recognize corporeal substances as well, unity also seems to enter at a second level: corporeal substances are unities composed of more fundamental unities—monads—and in turn constitute the unities that make up inanimate bodies.

But what becomes of the Dynamic Conception of body and corporeal substance? Here, the story gets more complicated still. Let us consider first the treatment in the correspondence with de Volder. In the letter of June 20, 1703, Leibniz approaches the question of body, both unity and activity:

> When I say that a substance, albeit a corporeal one, contains an infinity of machines, at the same time I think that it must be added that it includes the one machine composed from them, and that it is actuated by one entelechy, without which there would be no principle of true unity in it.
>
> (Lodge 260–1)

This is the familiar doctrine of the correspondence with Arnauld and other earlier texts. In this passage, it is corporeal substance as the unity that grounds body that seems to be at issue: though monads may be the ultimate metaphysical foundation of everything, even so, corporeal substances as unities seem to enter at an intermediate level. But the Dynamical View of body and corporeal substance in terms of primitive force has not been forgotten. Leibniz goes on to add some clarifications to his remarks to de Volder:

---

[36] See Garber, *Leibniz*, 380–382.

Properly and rigorously speaking, perhaps one will not say that the primitive entelechy impels the mass of its body, but only that it is joined with a primitive passive
power that it completes, i.e., with which it constitutes a monad.

(Lodge 260–1)

The monad, Leibniz tells us, is composed of a primitive entelechy joined with primitive
passive power. This, of course, recalls the vocabulary of the "Specimen dynamicum" and
the dynamical metaphysics of force. In the next sentence, we are told where the derivative forces are to be found:

But in the phenomena, i.e., in the resulting aggregate, everything is indeed explained
mechanically, and masses are understood to impel one another. And in these phenomena, nothing is needed except the consideration of derivative forces, once it is
agreed where they result from, namely the phenomena of aggregates from the reality
of monads.

(Lodge 260–1)

In these texts, bodies, then, seem to be aggregates of monads, and it is in these aggregates
of monads that we find the derivative forces that correspond to the primitive forces. This
view is summarized a couple of paragraphs later in the same letter:

I regard the substance itself, endowed with primitive active and passive power, like
the *I* or something similar, as the indivisible, i.e., perfect, monad, not those derivative forces that are continually found to be one way and then another. . . . The forces
that arise from mass and speed are derivative and belong to aggregates, i.e., phenomena. . . . And, indeed, derivative forces are nothing but modifications and echoes
of primitive forces.

(Lodge 262–3)

Shortly after comes a passage I quoted earlier:

I therefore distinguish: (1) the primitive entelechy, i.e., the soul; (2) matter,
namely, primary matter, i.e., primitive passive power; (3) the monad completed
by these two things; (4) the mass, i.e., the secondary matter, i.e., the organic machine, for which innumerable subordinate monads come together; and (5) the animal, i.e., the corporeal substance, which the monad dominating in the machine
makes one.

(Lodge 264–5)

In very crude terms, the view seems to be this: the ultimate constituents of the world are
now monads, nonextended and simple. Bodies are taken to be aggregates of monads.
But what of the primitive and derivative forces? Leibniz seems to put the *primitive*
forces from Dynamical Conception into the *monads* and the *derivative* forces into the

aggregates of monads. Monads can be considered as unities of primitive active and primitive passive forces, soul and primary matter. Monads then make up animals or corporeal substances, unities of a dominant monad and an "organic machine" made up out of "innumerable subordinate monads" that constitute "the animal, or corporeal substance." Inanimate bodies, then, are presumably aggregates of these animals or corporeal substances. It is to these higher level aggregates, corporeal substances and aggregates of corporeal substances, that the derivative forces pertain, both the derivative active forces associated with motion, such as living and dead force, and the derivative passive forces associated with resistance and impenetrability. In this rather intricate schema, monads, corporeal substances, and bodies come together, as do the Unity and Dynamical Conceptions.

The Dynamical Conception of body and corporeal substance enters into the discussion in the correspondence with Des Bosses as well, though in a rather different way. Very soon after introducing the *vinculum substantiale* in the letter of February 15, 1712, Leibniz turns to the status of matter and form in the corporeal substance:

> from the union of the passive powers of monads there in fact arises primary matter, which is to say, that which is required for extension and antitypy, or for diffusion and resistance. From the union of monadic entelechies, on the other hand, there arises substantial form; but that which can be generated in this way, can also be destroyed and will be destroyed with the cessation of the union, unless it is miraculously preserved by God. However, such a form then will not be a soul, which is a simple and indivisible substance.
>
> (Look-Rutherford 224–5)

The primary matter, what he had called the primitive passive force of a corporeal substance in the "Specimen dynamicum" is, presumably, a reflection of the primitive passive force of the monad, and the form, what he had called the primitive active force of a corporeal substance in the "Specimen dynamicum," is a reflection of the primitive active force of the monad, although Leibniz is careful to say that this "composite soul" is *not* a simple and indivisible substance. This is interestingly different from the view we saw in the de Volder letters. There, primitive force is in the monads and derivative force in their aggregates, which are phenomenal. But here there are primitive forces both at the monadic and at the corporeal levels: both the matter and the form are duplicated. Furthermore, in the corporeal substance, the form is not a soul—strictly speaking, not a single substance, not a dominant monad. But all this is just on the condition that there is a substantial bond. If there is no such thing, then, it seems, the Common Dream conception of body is true, and the primary matter and substantial form will just be phenomenal:

> If that substantial bond [*vinculum substantiale*] of monads were absent, then all bodies with all their qualities would be only well-founded phenomena, like a

rainbow or an image in a mirror—in a word, continuous dreams that agree perfectly
with one another; and in this alone would consist the reality of those phenomena.

(Look-Rutherford 226–7)

It seems, then, that there is primitive force, active and passive, in *both* the monad *and*
the corporeal substance, the forces in the latter arising from the forces in the former.
(Presumably there are derivative forces, too, though not mentioned here.) It is by virtue
of having the substantial bond that the corporeal substance has *real* primitive forces,
which would only be phenomenal if there were no substantial bond.

The doctrine of the substantial bond gets considerable development in the succeeding
letters between Leibniz and Des Bosses, and Leibniz's view evolves in interesting ways
over the course of the exchange. In the last letter Leibniz wrote to Des Bosses, dated May
29, 1716, he writes:

I do not say that there is a mediating bond between form and matter but, rather,
that the substantial form itself of the composite and primary matter taken in the
Scholastic sense, that is, primitive active and passive power, belongs to that bond, as
the essence of the composite.

(Look-Rutherford 366–7)

In this way, the substantial bond is now the seat of primitive active and passive force in
the composite. But, interestingly enough, it is not clear that the monads contribute anything at all to this anymore. Leibniz continues in the next sentence:

However, this substantial bond is naturally, and not essentially, a bond. For it requires
monads but does not involve them essentially, since it can exist without monads and
monads without it.

(Look-Rutherford 366–7)

If I read this right, the substantial bond is largely independent of monads. And, in a later
passage from the same letter, Leibniz seems to indicate that the composite substance is
independent as well:

Composite substance does not formally consist in monads and their subordination,
for then it would be a mere aggregate, that is, an accidental being; rather, it consists in
primitive active and passive force, from which arise the qualities and the actions and
passions of the composite, which are perceived by the senses, if they are assumed to
be more than phenomena.

(Look-Rutherford 370–1)

At this point, interestingly enough, Leibniz may be back to where he was more than
twenty years earlier in the articulation of the Dynamical Conception in the "Specimen
dynamicum." The composite substance is grounded in primitive active and passive

force, form and matter, which exists in the substantial bond. But the substantial bond exists independently of the world of monads: the substantial bond, in this way, seems to be a bond no longer. Most surprisingly, the monads seem to have dropped out. I don't want to suggest that this is Leibniz's final judgment on the matter, but, nevertheless, it is interesting that he seems to have considered it.

The positions on body and corporeal substance that Leibniz takes after introducing monads are complicated and strongly suggest that he hadn't fully worked out what he thought. In that respect, his account of body in the context of the monadological metaphysics remained a work in progress until the end. But, even so, there is a clear lesson from these texts: even after monads are introduced, body is not simply eliminated. Leibniz continues to experiment with what it is and where it goes until the end. Whatever its metaphysical status, whether it is foundational or derivative, and whatever relations it may bear to the monadological metaphysics, Leibniz's conception of body and corporeal substance, a world of living things grounded in active and passive forces, remains an important part of his philosophical project.

References

Adams, Robert M. 1994. *Leibniz: Determinist, Theist, Idealist.* New York: Oxford University Press.

Beeley, Philip. 1996. *Kontinuität und Mechanismus: zur Philosophie des jungen Leibniz in ihren ideengeschichtlichen Kontext.* Stuttgart: Steiner.

Bolton, Martha. 2004. "Leibniz to Arnauld: Platonic and Aristotelian themes on matter and corporeal substance." In Paul Lodge (ed.), *Leibniz and His Correspondents.* Cambridge: Cambridge University Press, pp. 97–122.

Fichant, Michel. 1993. "Leibniz: Pensées sur l'instauration d'une physique nouvelle (1679)." *Philosophie* 39–40: 3–26.

Fichant, Michel. 1993. "Mécanisme et Métaphysique: le rétablissement des formes substantielles (1679)." *Philosophie* 39–40: 27–59.

Garber, Daniel. 2009. *Leibniz: Body, Substance, Monad.* Oxford: Oxford University Press.

Garber, Daniel. 2015. "Monads on my mind." In Adrian Nita (ed.), *Leibniz's Metaphysics and the Adoption of Substantial Forms: Between Continuity and Transformation.* Dordrecht: Springer, pp. 161–176.

Hartz, Glenn. 2007. *Leibniz's Final System: Monads, Matter and Animals.* London and New York: Routledge.

Hess, Hans-Jürgen. 1978. "Die unveröffentlichten naturwissenschaftlichen und technischen Arbeiten von G.W. Leibniz aus der Zeit seines Parisaufenthaltes. Eine Kurzcharakteristik." In Gottfried-Wilhelm-Leibniz-Gesellschaft and Centre national de la recherche scientifique (France) (eds.), *Leibniz à Paris: 1672–1676.* Wiesbaden: Steiner, vol. 1, pp. 183–217.

Hobbes, Thomas. 1656. *Elements of Philosophy, the First Section, Concerning Body.* London: Andrew Crooke.

Leibniz, G. W. 2007. "Phoranomus seu de potentia et legibus naturae," Gianfranco Mormino, ed., in Francesco Piro, ed., *Gottfried Wilhelm Leibniz: Dialoghi filosofici e scientifici.* Milan: Bompiani, pp. 680–885.

Leibniz, G. W. 1734. *Recueil de diverses pieces sur la philosophie, les mathematiques, l'histoire &c. par M. de Leibniz*, ed. Cretien Kortholt. Hamburg: Abram Vandenhoeck.

Leibniz, G. W. 1695. "Système nouveau de la nature et de la communication des substances . . . " *Le journal des sçavans*. 27 June 1695: 294–300 and 4 July 1695: pp. 301–306.

Levey, Samuel. 2003. "On unity: Leibniz-Arnauld revisited." *Philosophical Topics* 31: 245–275.

Loptson, Peter, and Richard Arthur. 2006. "Leibniz's body realism: Two interpretations." *Leibniz Review* 16: 1–42.

McDonough, Jeffrey. 2013. "Leibniz's conciliatory account of substance." *Philosophers' Imprint* 13: 1–23.

Mercer, Christia. 1990. "The seventeenth-century debate between the Moderns and the Aristotelians: Leibniz and Philosophia Reformata." *Studia Leibnitiana Supplementa* 27: 18–29.

Mercer, Christia. 2001. *Leibniz's Metaphysics: Its Origins and Development*. Cambridge: Cambridge University Press.

Phemister, Pauline. 2005. *Leibniz and the Natural World: Activity, Passivity, and Corporeal Substances in Leibniz's Philosophy*. Dordrecht: Springer.

Sleigh, Robert, Jr. 1990. *Leibniz and Arnauld: A Commentary on their Correspondence*. New Haven: Yale University Press.

CHAPTER 19

···

MONADS

···

DONALD RUTHERFORD

THE monad is Leibniz's most brilliant piece of theorizing and an idea of enduring importance for metaphysics. Leibniz conceives of the monad as a mind-like substance, giving
it a superficial resemblance to Descartes's conception of mind as *res cogitans*, an immaterial thinking thing. Yet Leibniz develops the idea of a monad in ways that go well beyond
Descartes's theory. The monad is not just a subject of thought and volition, but a fundamental constituent of all reality. Furthermore, though all monads are endowed with
basic mental properties—perception and appetite—in most monads these properties do
not rise to the level of consciousness. Some monads are endowed with perceptual and
appetitive powers adequate for animal souls; in other, so-called "bare" monads, perception and appetite are construed in ways that have only a minimal connection to familiar
psychological functions.

According to Leibniz's final metaphysics, the created world consists only of monads
and of things whose existence and properties can be explained in terms of monads.[1]
Leibniz thus assigns to monads an explanatory role not unlike that of elementary
particles in modern physics: monads are the "true atoms" of nature.[2] Nevertheless,
there remains this important difference: the monad is not a physical entity. It does not
have parts or interact causally with other monads. It is, in Leibniz's words, a "formal

---

[1] "True substances are only simple substances, or what I call *monads*. And I believe that there are only
monads in nature, the rest being only phenomena that result from them" (1716; Dutens III 499). Related
statements are found in "Conversation of Philarète and Ariste" (ca. 1712–15; GP VI 590/AG 265); "Against
Barbaric Physics" (ca. 1710–16; GP VII 344/AG 319); and in late letters to Burcher De Volder, 1704–6
(GP II 262; GP II 270/AG 181; GP II 275–276/AG 181–182; GP II 282/AG 185); Giambattista Tolomei,
1705 (GP VII 467–468); the Electress Sophie, 1706 (Klopp III 173); Louis Bourguet, 1714 (GP III 566,
575); Nicholas Remond, 1714–15 (GP III 606/L 655; GP III 622; GP III 636/L 659); and Samuel Masson,
1716 (GP VI 625/AG 227). For defenses of this reading of Leibniz's late metaphysics, see Robert Adams,
Leibniz: Determinist, Theist, Idealist (New York: Oxford University Press, 1994); Donald Rutherford,
Leibniz and the Rational Order of Nature (Cambridge: Cambridge University Press, 1995); and
Rutherford, "Leibniz as idealist," in *Oxford Studies in Early Modern Philosophy 4* (2008), 141–190.
[2] "Monadology," §3 (hereafter cited as Mon, followed by section number, according to the text in GP
VI 607–623/AG 213–225).

atom," with properties akin to those of Aristotelian substantial forms, rather than a material atom.[3]

Leibniz's theory of monads is nothing if not audacious. For this reason, it is crucial to understand how he argues for the theory, the conclusions he draws from it, and the problems that remain in interpreting it. In the end, even if we are not persuaded by Leibniz's account, we should see it as a profound attempt to establish a comprehensive theory of nature that links the domains of the mental and the physical, grounding both in the fundamental reality of monads.

WHY MONADS?

Leibniz's most famous argument for the existence of monads is summarized in the opening sections of the "Monadology":

1. The MONAD, which we shall discuss here, is nothing but a simple substance that enters into composites—simple, that is, without parts.
2. And there must be simple substances, since there are composites; for the composite is nothing more than a collection, or *aggregate*, of simples.
3. But where there are no parts, neither extension, nor shape, nor divisiblity is possible. These monads are the true atoms of nature and, in brief, the elements of things. (GP VI 607/AG 213)

Section 1 stipulates that a monad is a "simple substance," that is, a substance lacking parts. Section 2 asserts that, given the existence of composites (things having parts), there must be simples (things lacking parts) from which composites arise as aggregates. Because simples, by definition, lack parts, they must be unextended and indivisible (section 3). Hence, these properties must belong to monads, which are the "true atoms of nature" and the "elements of things."

Leibniz's argument for monads rests on a particular understanding of the requirements of ontological grounding, that is, of which things must exist as a condition for the existence of other things.[4] As he sees it, whatever is "many" or composed of parts depends for its existence on what is essentially "one" and not composed of parts, the property in terms of which he defines the monad. Two lines of reasoning with deep roots

---

[3] See the "New System" (GP IV 478–479/AG 139), and his comment to Bierling from 1712: "Monads should not be confused with atoms. Atoms (as they are imagined) have shape. Monads no more have shape than do souls" (GP VII 503).

[4] The topic has undergone a recent revival in philosophy. See *Metaphysical Grounding: Understanding the Structure of Reality*, edited by Fabrice Correia and Benjamin Schnieder (Cambridge: Cambridge University Press, 2012).

in his thought come together in this inference.[5] First, whatever is many, or a multitude, presupposes the existence of unities, for a multitude can only come to be through the multiplication of unity.[6] Second, whatever is a composite or aggregate has a reality that is derivative from that of the things from which it is composed; hence, on pain of regress, for a composite to have any reality, its existence must be explained in terms of its composition from things whose reality is not derivative.[7] Leibniz identifies the latter class of things with that of *substance*. By definition, a substance is both a per se real being, depending on nothing for its existence except God, and a per se unity.[8] Thus, the existence of anything composite must be grounded in the existence of substances, which Leibniz identifies with monads.

Leibniz applies this conclusion to all material things. Any body consisting of extended matter is divisible into parts ad infinitum.[9] Because the division of matter never comes to an end, no principle of unity can be found in extended matter as such. Yet, if bodies are real or have a mind-independent existence, they must have a ground in some per se reality. Given this, Leibniz concludes that the reality of bodies must be located in monads: real unities that are not composed of parts. Expanding on the argument of the "Monadology," he writes to De Volder:

> I have undertaken to prove these [true and real unities] from the fact that otherwise there would be nothing in bodies. I have established the following consequences: first, those things which can be divided into many things are things consisting of many things or aggregates. Now, second, whatever are aggregates of many things are not one except by virtue of the mind, nor have they any reality except that which is derivative or which belongs to the things from which they are aggregated. Therefore, third, things which can be divided into parts have no reality unless there are in them things which cannot be divided into parts. Indeed, they have no reality except that of the unities which are in them.
>
> (GP II 261)

A thing divisible into parts is an aggregate whose unity depends on the relations among its parts. But Leibniz holds that relations are not existing things in their own right; all relations are merely mental or ideal. Hence, any aggregate owes its existence to a mind's

---

[5] For a careful analysis, see Samuel Levey, "On unity, borrowed reality and multitude in Leibniz," in *The Leibniz Review* 22 (2012), pp. 97–134.

[6] This claim is ubiquitous in Leibniz's writings. It is extensively aired, for example, in his correspondence with the Electress Sophie. See Leibniz's letters to her of September 1695 (GP VII 540); June 12, 1700 (GP VII 552–553); and November 30, 1701 (GP VII 557).

[7] This emerges as a central theme in the Arnauld correspondence. See Leibniz's letter to Arnauld of April 30, 1687 (A II ii 184–186/LA 120–122).

[8] Famously he asserts to Arnauld, "To be brief, I hold as axiomatic this identical proposition which is varied only by the emphasis: namely, that *what is not truly ONE being is not truly one BEING*" (A II ii 186).

[9] Although the argument does not depend on it, Leibniz, in fact, makes the stronger claim that any portion of matter is not just infinitely divisible, but infinitely divided, by virtue of the motion of its parts. See his letter to De Volder of June 30, 1704 (GP II 268/AG 178–179).

representation (in thought or perception) of the unity of some plurality of things.[10] At the same time, if an aggregate is real at all, its reality must be explained in terms of the *per se* reality of substance. That is the weight of the grounding argument. If matter is infinitely divisible, however, nowhere in it do we find parts that are true unities: parts that are not themselves further divisible. It is just here that Leibniz invokes the existence of monads. By his lights, *something* must ground the reality of bodies, and this can only be something that has a *per se* unity and reality. Thus, monads must exist as a condition for the existence of bodies.[11]

Leibniz advances a structurally similar argument for the existence of monads based on the need for an intrinsic principle of change. Change is observed to occur in bodies, but nowhere in extended matter do we find a ground for change—that is, a principle that explains why bodies change as they do. According to Leibniz, such a ground is supplied by substance, which by nature is an *entelechy* or principle of action: a spontaneous source of change (Mon 18). This second grounding argument reaches the same conclusion as the first: for material things to exist as they do—in this case, as things that change—they must be grounded in monads, which are both *per se* unities and intrinsic sources of change. The close relation between these arguments is observed in the draft of a 1702 letter to Pierre Bayle in which Leibniz successively asserts their conclusions:

> There must be simple beings, otherwise there would be no compound beings, or beings by aggregation, which are phenomena rather than substances, and exist (to use the language of Democritus) by *nomos* rather than *physis*, that is, notionally or conceptually, rather than physically. And if there was no change in simple things, there would be none in compound things either, for all their reality consists only in that of their simple things.
>
> (GP III 69/WFN 129–130)[12]

At bottom, then, Leibniz's arguments for the existence of monads rest on the demand for an ultimate ground for the existence and properties of bodies—a ground he claims must be sought in the *per se* reality, unity, and activity of substance.

Such grounding arguments involve a significant set of assumptions. They require that we accept that the existence of some things depends on the existence of ontologically prior things, which serve as ultimate grounds to the extent that they themselves

---

[10] Cf. *New Essays* II xii 6 (RB 146); II xxiv 1 (RB 226).

[11] Leibniz restates the argument in a subsequent letter to De Volder (GP II 267–268). The exact nature of the dependence of matter on monads remains obscure. Leibniz insists that the grounding relation is not mereological or compositional. Monads, he says, are not parts but *requisites* of matter (GP VII 503). He must say this because the spatial division of matter proceeds ad infinitum; never in the division do we arrive at indivisible monads, and, conversely, no extended matter can be built up from unextended simples. These conclusions are the basis of Leibniz's resolution of the "labyrinth of the continuum" (see Arthur, Chapter 15 in this volume). To the extent that monads serve as "requisites" or ontological grounds for the existence of matter, the grounding relation must be understood differently. I return to this point in the section "Monads and Matter."

[12] Cf. GP II 252/AG 177; GP III 67/WFN 128.

do not depend for their existence on anything else (except God). Furthermore, they assume that such grounding relations are governed by the principle of sufficient reason; thus, we can reason our way from the existence of one thing to the existence of prior things on which it depends. On Leibniz's account, we can conclude that unities must exist because only they render intelligible the existence of a multitude or aggregate. Finally, all such arguments are conditional in form. They establish that *if* anything exists or involves change, then this existence or change must be accounted for in terms of the prior existence and change of substances, for only substances are per se unities and sources of change. Arguments of this form invite the skeptical response that perhaps no composite things really exist or exhibit real change. Perhaps all composite things are merely appearances: things we take to be real but about which we are mistaken. The consequences for Leibniz's grounding arguments are clear: if there is nothing whose existence and properties stand in need of grounding, then there is no case for the existence of monads as the necessary grounds of such things.[13]

Even if we accept the soundness of Leibniz's grounding arguments, a further challenge confronts the claim that they establish the existence of monads. What these arguments prove at most, a critic may object, is the existence of *substances*: true unities that are intrinsic sources of change. The arguments do not show that these substances must be monads, substances that are simple or without parts. The basis for the critic's objection is that the same grounding arguments appear prominently in Leibniz's writings from the 1680s, particularly in his correspondence with Arnauld, where he appears to accept that the substances grounding bodies are themselves corporeal. They are "quasi-Aristotelian" hylomorphic substances: living bodies, whose substantiality is founded on the unity given to them by a soul-like substantial form.[14] In contrast to material things in general, living bodies *are* true unities capable of serving as the grounds of the reality of other material things. Consequently, the critic claims, the grounding arguments do not

---

[13] Leibniz concedes that we have only a moral certainty that bodies exist based on the presumptive wisdom God exercises in creating the world of greatest perfection (see his letter to Des Bosses of April 29, 1715; Look-Rutherford 338–339). His arguments for the existence of monads as grounds for the existence of bodies hinge on this premise. However, this qualification is less significant than it might otherwise be. As we shall see in the next section, Leibniz also holds that monads are necessary as substantial grounds for perceptual change; that is, change that occurs within us when we perceive the changing states of physical things. Thus, even if the latter were purely phenomenal, with no ground in an external reality of monads, there would have to be an internal ground for change in the soul. Summarizing these two explanatory roles of monads, Leibniz writes: "Consequently, it must be admitted that something besides matter is both the principle of perception or internal action, and of motion or external action. And such a principle we call substantial, and also primitive force, primary entelechy, and in a word, soul, since the active conjoined with the passive constitutes a complete substance" ("Reflections on the Souls of Beasts," 1710; Dutens II i 230).

[14] For an influential account, see Daniel Garber, *Leibniz: Body, Substance, Monad* (Oxford: Oxford University Press, 2009).

establish the existence of monads as against corporeal substances. Either is qualified to serve as the ultimate ground for the existence of other things.[15]

One of the most contentious issues in Leibniz scholarship over the past several decades has been when and why Leibniz abandoned a basic ontology of corporeal substances in favor of the theory of monads.[16] The term "monad" itself means simply *one* or *unity*.[17] When Leibniz begins to use the word as a technical term around 1695, he sometimes includes corporeal substances within its scope.[18] Fairly quickly, however, this usage is abandoned in favor of one that restricts the reference of the term to unextended, soul-like substances. Thus, by the early 1700s, Leibniz often speaks of "unities or simple substances," implying that he regards the terms as coextensional.[19]

What accounts for Leibniz's conversion to the view that the only true substances are monads? The matter remains controversial, but the following is one plausible explanation.[20] By Leibniz's lights, the soul or mind—an immaterial, active being—is a prime candidate for being a substance. Lacking extended parts, the soul qualifies as a true unity, and the power of volition is evidence of its capacity for spontaneous action. Thus, souls or minds by themselves count as substances, a view Leibniz appears to hold in common with Descartes.[21] Yet Leibniz's philosophical commitments are diverse. Although he recognizes the attractions of the soul-as-substance view, he also is drawn to the Aristotelian model of hylomorphic substance, exemplified by living bodies, such

---

[15] This objection has been effectively pressed by Samuel Levey, "On unity and simple substance in Leibniz," in *The Leibniz Review 17* (2007), pp. 61–107; and "On unity, borrowed reality and multitude in Leibniz," op. cit.

[16] For some commentators, the pertinent question is *whether* Leibniz abandons an ontology of corporeal substances in favor of one that ascribes an ultimate reality to monads alone. See, e.g., the readings offered by Pauline Phemister, *Leibniz and the Natural World* (Dordrecht: Springer, 2005); Peter Loptson and R. T. W. Arthur, "Leibniz's body realism: Two interpretations," in *The Leibniz Review 16* (2006), pp. 1–42; Glenn Hartz, *Leibniz's Final System* (New York: Routledge, 2007).

[17] "*Monas* is a Greek word signifying unity or what is one." "Principles of Nature and of Grace" (hereafter: PNG), §1 (GP VI 598/AG 207). In an earlier (1698) letter to Johann Bernoulli, he wrote: "By monad I understand a substance truly one, namely one which is not an aggregate of substances" (GM III 537/AG 167).

[18] The first dated occurrence of the term is in a 1695 letter to the Marquis de l'Hospital, where Leibniz identifies a monad with "what is genuinely a real unity" (A III vi 451/WFN 57). In several contemporary texts, he extends the term to embodied creatures: "What I call a complete monad or individual substance is not so much the soul as it is the animal itself, or something analogous to it, endowed with a soul or form and an organic body" (GM III 542/AG 168; cf. GM III 552/L 512). Nevertheless, in the 1695 "New System," he appears to commit himself to a monadic conception of substance: "There are only *atoms of substance*, that is, real unities absolutely destitute of parts, which are the source of actions, the first absolute principles of the composition of things, and, as it were, the final elements in the analysis of substances" (GP IV 482/AG 142). Where Gerhardt gives the final words of the sentence as "des choses substantielles" ("of substantial things"), the published version of the text reads "des substances."

[19] His writings contain many examples of similar expressions: "this simple substance, this unity of substance or this *monad*" (1700, GP VII 552); "unities or simple things" (1702, GP VI 538/L 559); "unities or simple substances" (1706, Grua 64); "unities or monads" (1714, GP III 622).

[20] For a fuller rehearsal of the argument, see Donald Rutherford, "Unity, reality and simple substances: A reply to Samuel Levey," in *The Leibniz Review 18* (2008), pp. 207–224.

[21] See, e.g., "Discourse on Metaphysics," §§32–33 (A VI iv 1581–1582/AG 64–65).

as plants and animals. This view, which holds that a soul or substantial form does not naturally exist apart from the body with which it is united, is compelling on intellectual grounds for Leibniz and an element of Catholic theology that he seeks to uphold.[22]

Problems arise when Leibniz attempts to put these views together. If the soul is a substance in its own right, as he seems to affirm in the "New System," then any corporeal substance must be a composite being, consisting of a soul or form and so-called *secondary matter*, which itself is composed of an infinite envelopment of living bodies within living bodies. Whether Leibniz was struck by the problem in quite this way, it is difficult to see how the soul could unite the matter of its body—by hypothesis, an aggregate of independently existing substances—in a per se unity. Leibniz believes that no particular matter is essential to the identity of a corporeal substance; the soul alone is the ground of its identity. Moreover, his own preferred explanation of the relation of the soul and its body is in terms of their preestablished harmony—a relation that he admits does not support an understanding of the composite as a per se unity. Consequently, when challenged by Catholic defenders of the unity of the complete human being, Leibniz falls back on the claim that he "does not deny" the real or metaphysical union of soul and body—the sort of union necessary to produce a per se unity of them—but that it must be accepted on the basis of faith rather than reason.[23]

Whatever Leibniz's final position on the union of soul and body, he was strongly drawn to the thesis that reality ultimately consists only of monads and their internal modifications. It appealed to him for reasons of ontological parsimony,[24] and it supported the intuition, on which he acknowledged his debt to Plato, that what is

---

[22] On Leibniz's understanding of corporeal substance, see Garber, Chapter 18 in this volume. Leibniz's ambivalence concerning the extension of the term "substance" (whether it includes souls or corporeal substances, or both) is apparent in works from the 1680s and early 1690s. In response to Arnauld's objection that if the soul and the body are distinct substances, then one cannot be the substantial form of the other, Leibniz says only that the body by itself is not a substance, but a being by aggregation, and then adds: "Besides, the last [Fifth] Lateran Council asserts that the soul is truly the substantial form of our body" (A II ii 119/LA 93). For a careful assessment of Leibniz's view of substance during the period, see R. C. Sleigh, Jr., *Leibniz and Arnauld: A Commentary on Their Correspondence* (New Haven: Yale University Press, 1990).

[23] Leibniz's remarks on the metaphysical union of soul and body fall into two distinct groups. In his reply to Tournemine (GP VI 595/AG 196–197) and in the *Theodicy* (Preface, GP VI 45; "Preliminary Discourse," §55, GP VI 81; Part I, §59, GP VI 135), he appears concessive. By contrast, in letters to the Electress Sophie (GP VII 555; Klopp III 174–175) and to De Volder, he challenges whether there is anything intelligible to be said beyond the doctrine of preestablished harmony: "In the schools they commonly look for things that are not so much ultramundane as utopian. Recently the clever French Jesuit Tournemine supplied me with an elegant example of this. When he had praised somewhat my preestablished harmony, which seemed to explain the agreement that we perceive between the soul and the body, he said that he still desired one thing, namely, the reason for the union, which certainly differs from the agreement. I answered that whatever that metaphysical union is that the schools add over and above agreement, it is not a phenomenon, and we do not have any notion of it or acquaintance with it. Thus I could not have intended to explain it" (GP II 281/AG 184).

[24] "Indeed, everywhere and throughout everything, I place nothing but what we all acknowledge in our souls on many occasions, namely, internal and spontaneous changes. And so, with one stroke of mind, I draw out the entirety of things" (GP II 276/AG 182).

fully real is not the world given to our senses—even the mathematically representable world of extended material things—but a world fully intelligible to the mind, which he identified with monads.[25] Monads are entities that most clearly satisfy the conditions that define a substance or per se real being: true unities that are spontaneous sources of change. If the existence of all other things can be explained in terms of monads and their properties, then Leibniz has made a strong case for the latter as a foundational ontology. Before judging his success in this regard, we must look more closely at the properties he ascribes to monads.

What Is a Monad?

Leibniz's inspiration for the monad is an immaterial soul or soul-like form. In developing this idea, however, he arrives at a conception of the monad as a theoretical entity in its own right. He categorizes both human minds and animal souls as instances of monads, but the concept itself is free of any essential dependence on Christian theology or Aristotelian metaphysics. It is the product of Leibniz's attempt to think through the notion of a substantial ground of all created existence.

As we have seen, Leibniz defines the monad as a "simple substance"—one without parts into which it can be divided—and hence a "true unity." The simplicity and indivisibility of the monad support its claim to be foundational in an ontological sense: monads are the ultimate constituents—but not ultimate parts—of all existing things. The simplicity of monads entails that they are *immaterial* beings because anything material, according to Leibniz, contains parts into which it can be divided.[26] It further implies that there is no conceivable way in which a monad can come to be or cease to be naturally: it can "only begin by creation or end by annihilation, whereas composites begin or end through their parts" (Mon 6), and there is no way of explaining how a monad can be changed internally by anything external to it because there are no parts to be rearranged, added to, or subtracted from. In Leibniz's famous phrase, monads are "without windows" through which they can be affected by external things (Mon 7).

The simplicity of monads, however, does not preclude them from having qualities in the form of a multiplicity of internal modifications. Indeed, Leibniz argues that monads must have such modifications. First, it follows from the principle of the

---

[25] See his strong statement of this position in his 1702 letter to Queen Sophie Charlotte, "On What Is Independent of Sense and Matter" (GP VI 502–503/AG 189).

[26] "I don't admit simple bodies. There is nothing simple, in my opinion, but true monads which have neither parts nor extension. Simple bodies, and even perfectly similar ones, are a consequence of the false hypothesis of the void and atoms, or of lazy philosophy, which does not sufficiently carry out the analysis of things and fancies it can attain to the first material elements of nature, because our imagination would be therewith satisfied" (Fifth Letter to Clarke, §24; GP VII 394/AG 333–334). Note the distinction between the false conception of elements (material atoms) that satisfies the imagination and the true conception (monads) to which intellectual analysis leads us.

identity of indiscernibles (and ultimately the principle of sufficient reason) that if any two monads are nonidentical, there must be a qualitative distinction between them, one founded on an "intrinsic denomination" (Mon 9). Second, if monads are to play a fundamental explanatory role, accounting for the difference and change in other things (e.g., bodies), then there must be variations in monads, which are grounds of change insofar as they are enduring subjects of a succession of states (Mon 8). To fulfill this role, it is not enough for monads to be *subject* to change; they must be sources of the changes in themselves: "The monad's natural changes come from an *internal principle*, since no external cause can influence it internally" (Mon 11). Thus, every monad must be, in the term Leibniz borrows from Aristotle, an *entelechy*: a principle of action, in which change is continually actualized in a succession of different states (Mon 18).

The picture Leibniz constructs of the monad is highly abstract. What we are presented with in the opening sections of the "Monadology" is a model of what a fundamental entity would have to be like. In every monad:

> besides the principle of change, there must be *diversity in that which changes*, which produces, so to speak, the specification and variety of simple substances. This diversity must involve a multitude in the unity or in the simple. For, since all natural change is produced by degrees, something changes and something remains. As a result, there must be a plurality of properties and relations in the simple substance, although it has no parts.

> (Mon 12–13)

Leibniz proposes this as the most basic process occurring in nature. The momentary state of every monad is characterized by a multitude of distinct modifications, with change occurring through the gradual variation of those modifications.[27]

At this point, Leibniz moves to the second stage in his development of the concept of the monad, in which he gives greater specificity to the diversity of modifications that define the monad's state. A monad does not contain just any multitude of modifications. Each of its passing states "involves and represents a multitude in the unity or simple substance," making it a state of *perception*. Leibniz defines perception, in general, as "the representation of a multitude in a unity" (GP VII 529). In making representation an essential feature of a monad's states, he commits himself to two points. First, the states of a monad have content or are information bearing. Second, by virtue of this content, monads "express" each other. Although monads are physically isolated from each other, there are well-defined relations between the contents of their states (Mon 56, 59).[28]

---

[27] It is sometimes asked how, if a monad is without parts, there can be a multitude of distinct modifications in it. Leibniz answers this by appeal to the example of the mind, in which there can be many perceptions, thoughts, and feelings simultaneously. It is also worth noting, though, the abstractness of his account: he, in effect, sketches the idea of a state description of an ideal machine or "automaton" (Mon 18).

[28] For Leibniz's technical notion of expression, see A VI iv 1370/L 207; A II ii 240/LA 144; C 15/MP 176–177; and Chris Swoyer, "Leibnizian expression," in *Journal of the History of Philosophy* 33 (1995), pp.

This supports the central claim of the doctrine of preestablished harmony: monads are programmed by God to change their states in a coordinated fashion in relation to the states of all other monads. We might think of this as the operating system of the monad, which involves its states being continually updated to reflect the contents of other monads' states. Leibniz then takes a further crucial step by specifying the basic content of a monad's states (in effect, the simulation program they all run). The multitude that every monad represents consists of the many things making up a single physical universe, which Leibniz conceives as a material plenum (there is no void; all extension is full of matter). The metaphysical theory is now in place. God creates every monad as a "concentrated universe" (GP III 575/L 663). It contains a complete representation of what we take to be the physical universe, and in each monad this representation is continually updated in coordination with the representations of every other monad to reflect the evolving history of the universe.

The details of this picture are far from intuitive, but they reflect Leibniz's efforts to think through what the fundamental constitution of reality must be like, given his conviction that matter—the divisible stuff "diffused" in extended things—does not meet the exacting standards he places on the real. If matter is not real, then the physical universe composed of material things is not real either. Yet we are convinced that we live in a material world. Leibniz ties this conviction to the confused content of our perceptions. Not satisfied to say with Descartes that our senses mislead us about the real properties of bodies, Leibniz contends that perceptual experience disposes us to misconceive reality in a more fundamental way. At the same time, he accommodates the facts of our experience by building them into the basic plan according to which we represent the world. In short, reality consists of unextended monads; but each of those monads represents a world of material things corresponding to the world we take to be real.

The move to draw Leibniz's theory closer to ordinary experience should not proceed too quickly. His underlying idea is that every monad is endowed by God with a *complete* representation of the physical universe. No created monad is, or can be, aware of all of this detail extending to the outermost reaches of space and to the beginning and end of time. But all of it is present as content in every monad's states, most of it inaccessible for the purposes of cognition. Metaphysically, this is the basic form of perception that Leibniz ascribes to all monads. There are many monads, so-called *bare monads*, in whose perceptions there is nothing "distinct," nothing "in relief and stronger in flavor." Such monads exist as though in a "stupor," meaning that they are entirely unaware of and cognitively unresponsive to the world of their representations (Mon 24). Nevertheless, the representations are there and they are continually updated to reflect the evolving state of the perceived physical universe. Leibniz ascribes this change to a monad's force of "appetition": the inherent tendency of its perceptual states to give way to new

---

63–99. As Swoyer argues, Leibniz conceives of expression as a structure-preserving mapping, whereby relations in one domain are lawfully related to relations in another. The implication is that monads express each other by virtue of functional relations between *relations* (spatiotemporal and causal relations) represented in their perceptions.

states (Mon 15). These two powers, perception and appetition, exhaust the properties of a monad. As he writes to Des Bosses in 1713, "since monads are nothing other than representations of phenomena with a transition to new phenomena, it is clear that in monads there is perception on account of the representation, and appetition on account of the transition; and there are no principles from which anything else could be sought" (Look-Rutherford, 318–319).[29]

The final stage in Leibniz's development of the concept of the monad imposes on top of this framework an account of animal and human psychology, identifying the soul or mind of complex living creatures with a superior kind of monad. "[S]ince sensation is something more than a simple perception," he writes, "I think that the general name of monad and entelechy is sufficient for simple substances which only have perceptions, and that we should only call those substances *souls* where perception is more distinct and accompanied by memory" (Mon 19; cf. PNG 4). By perceptions that are "distinct," Leibniz means ones that stand out "in relief" and affect a subject sensibly, in contrast to the soul's state during "a deep, dreamless sleep" (Mon 20). Such perceptions are characteristic of animal life, in which a creature's experience is marked by its responsiveness to representations of its body and its physical environment. In any soul, only a small portion of its perceptions are "heightened" in this way (Mon 25). These stand out against the background of the infinite detail of the universe, represented unconsciously in every monad, and become the basis of an animal's ability to learn from experience: "We observe that when animals have the perception of something which strikes them, and when they previously had a similar perception of that thing, then, through a representation in their memory, they expect that which was attached to the thing in the perception, and are led to have sensations similar to those they had before" (Mon 26).

For the most part, human minds operate like the souls of animals: "Men act like beasts insofar as the sequence of their perceptions results from the principle of memory alone. . . . We are all mere Empirics in three fourths of our actions" (Mon 28). Nevertheless, Leibniz credits minds with a fundamentally different kind of cognition than that enjoyed by lesser souls. Human minds, and those of more elevated spirits, have the capacity for reflective thought on which depends their ability to acquire rational knowledge:

> It is . . . through the knowledge of necessary truths and through their abstractions that we rise to *reflective acts*, which enable us to think of that which is called "I" and enable us to consider that this or that is in us. And thus, in thinking of ourselves, we think of being, of substance, of the simple and of the composite, of the immaterial

---

[29] Cf. Mon 17; PNG 2; GP IV 562/L 579. I pass over one significant issue regarding the form of the laws governing monadic change. Leibniz describes these as "laws of the *final causes of good and evil*" (PNG 3), reinforcing the point that the actions of a monad are teleological or end-directed. For contrasting accounts of how this should be understood, see Martha Brandt Bolton, "Change in the Monad," and Donald Rutherford, "Laws and Powers in Leibniz," both in *The Divine Order, the Human Order, and the Order of Nature: Historical Perspectives*, edited by Eric Watkins (Oxford: Oxford University Press, 2013), pp. 175–194, 149–174, respectively.

and of God himself, by conceiving that that which is limited in us is limitless in him. And these reflective acts furnish the principal objects of our reasonings.

(Mon 30; cf. PNG 5, 14)

Minds are distinguished from animal souls by their ability to grasp necessary truths and to link them in demonstrative reasoning. That minds are able to do this is ascribed to the fact that they have access to a distinct kind of cognitive content made available to them through "reflective acts." In reflective thought—thought *about* thinking and about themselves as subjects of thought—minds gain access to an inner intelligible reality. They comprehend the fundamental concepts on which Leibniz builds his metaphysics, especially the concepts of being, unity, and infinity (or God).[30] These concepts are the basis of a mind's ability to comprehend the perfection, order, and justice that define God's plan for the world and thereby to realize its own role as an autonomous subject of the "city of God": "the most perfect possible state under the most perfect of monarchs" (Mon 85).

Leibniz depicts monads as ordered in a hierarchy of perfection, defined by the distinctness of their perceptions (Mon 48, 60). At the top of the hierarchy is God, whose omniscience reflects his standing as the unique actually infinite being.[31] Below God are rational minds, capable of varying degrees of distinct intellectual knowledge; then animal souls, possessing some distinct perceptions; and finally, bare monads, whose perceptions are wholly confused and "sunk in matter." Two points should be noted in interpreting this hierarchy of perfection. First, though Leibniz undoubtedly understands God as a perfect unity, the designation of God as a "monad" is in tension with the theoretical framework developed in the "Monadology." In no meaningful sense is God's nature defined by perception and appetition in the way that Leibniz characterizes them.[32] Second, the assumption that perfection can be measured along a single dimension of perceptual distinctness obscures the difference between two kinds of cognitive content. The background condition for perception in all monads is the representation of a material manifold (i.e., the physical universe). The distinctness of perception in this sense is a function of how much of the infinite detail of the universe stands out in the perceptions of a given monad. In different monads, different aspects of the manifold appear in relief based on how their sensory organs are affected by the motions of matter. A soul whose body is responsive to auditory stimuli will perceive different features as distinct than will a soul whose body is responsive to visual stimuli (PNG 4).[33] A different sense of distinctness,

---

[30] In a 1696 letter to the Electress Sophie, Leibniz writes: "My fundamental meditations turn on two things, namely, on unity and on infinity" (GP VII 542). In a later letter to her, he includes among the concepts acquired through reflection those of "force, action, change, time, identity, one, true, good, and a thousand others" (GP VII 552).

[31] "Thus God alone is the primitive unity or the first simple substance" (Mon 47). In other texts, Leibniz explicitly refers to God as a monad (GP III 636/L 659; GP VII 502).

[32] In Mon 48, Leibniz is more careful to say that a monad's perceptual and appetitive faculties are "imitations" of the divine attributes of knowledge and will, "in proportion to the perfections they have."

[33] Understanding this statement in accordance with the doctrine of preestablished harmony: no soul is directly affected by the body.

however, comes into play in the case of rational minds, whose cognitive capacities are enhanced by their grasp of intelligible concepts. Conceptual content of this sort is more distinct to the extent that it is less confounded by perceptual representations of matter and analyzed into simpler constitutive concepts. Because different kinds of content are involved in the two cases, there is no single dimension along which monads can be ordered in terms of the distinctness of their perceptions.

In the end, Leibniz recognizes three basic types of monads: God, minds, and all other soul-like substances. Between God and all created monads there is a categorical distinction grounded in the difference between infinite and finite, creator and created. Leibniz elaborates this distinction through the doctrine that every created monad is endowed with primitive passive power or *primary matter*, manifested in its confused perceptions of matter. A monad is lower in the hierarchy of perfection to the extent that the changes in its states are ascribed to this passive, material principle rather than to its primitive active power or form manifested in distinct perceptions.[34] Leibniz also holds, however, that just as no finite increment of perfection, however great, spans the divide between God and any created being, so no finite increment of perfection spans the divide between minds and other monads. As he sometimes says, minds are "infinitely nearer" to God than all other things.[35] Whereas souls in general are "living mirrors or images of the universe of creatures," minds are also "images of the divinity itself, or of the author of nature, capable of knowing the system of the universe, and imitating something of it through their schematic representations of it, each mind being like a little divinity in its own realm" (Mon 83). Because of their intellectual capacities, minds partake of "a moral world within the natural world" (Mon 86), reflecting their ability—and obligation—to model their actions on those of God and to contribute through their endeavors to the perfection of the world.

A WORLD OF MONADS

Leibniz describes a monad's perceptions and appetitions as "intrinsic denominations," meaning that they are qualities that can be predicated of a monad independently of its relations to other created beings.[36] At the same time, he regards these qualities as the basis of a monad's relations to other monads in a world:

---

[34] Cf. GP II 252/AG 177; GP III 636/L 659; and *Theodicy* §124: "If [an intelligent creature] had only distinct thoughts it would be a God, its wisdom would be without bounds: that is one of the results of my meditations. As soon as there is a mixture of confused thoughts, there is sense, there is matter. For these confused thoughts come from the relation of all things one to the other by way of duration and extent. Thus it is that in my philosophy there is no rational creature without some organic body, and there is no created spirit entirely detached from matter" (GP VI 179/H 198).

[35] Cf. "Discourse on Metaphysics," §§35–36 (A VI iv 1584–1587/AG 66–68).

[36] See Mon 9 and C 9/MP 134: "From this it appears that two intrinsic denominations are required, a power of transition and that to which the transition is made."

In the way in which I define perception and appetite, all monads must be endowed with them. I hold *perception* to be the representation of plurality in the simple, and *appetite* to be the striving from one perception to another. But these two things occur in all monads, for otherwise a monad would have no relation to the rest of the world.

(GP III 574–575/L 662–663)

That monads exist related to other monads in a world may seem to rest uneasily with Leibniz's claims about the ontological independence of monads. On the one hand, each monad is, "as it were, a certain world of its own,"[37] with no real, or physical, dependence on any other existing thing except God; changes in a monad's perceptual states come about through its own appetitions, independently of the states of other monads. On the other hand, no monad exists separated from a world of other monads. Reinforcing this point in a 1698 letter to Gabriel Wagner, Leibniz quips: "solitary monads do not exist. They are monads, not monks" (Grua 395).

Reconciling these claims requires drawing some distinctions. According to Leibniz, no monad requires the existence of any another monad, in the sense that it is metaphysically possible for the former to exist as the individual it is without the existence of the latter. To Des Bosses he asserts that God could create a single monad—presumably any monad—and sustain its existence independently of the existence of any other monad.[38] However, this scenario of one or more isolated substances does not comport with Leibniz's understanding of possible worlds. Possible worlds are not merely consistent sets of arbitrary possible substances. Instead, Leibniz begins from the idea that any possible world is a way of being a *world*, where there are strict conditions on the kind of order that must be realized among a plurality of things for them to constitute a world. Leibniz accepts the now widely held view that any world is closed with respect to spatiotemporal and causal order. That is, for any possible world, any member of such a world must be spatiotemporally related and causally connected to every other member of that world.[39]

The challenge lies in understanding how these conditions can be met in the case of monads. Leibniz does not take worldhood to imply that monads are located in a physical space shared with bodies—either Newtonian absolute space or a material plenum—and he does not backtrack on his doctrine that monads do not affect each other through an immediate causal influence.[40] Nevertheless, he holds that the monads of a world are united through orders of coexistence and succession, identified with a generalized notion of spatiotemporal order, and through relations of *commercium* or mutual connection, which are relations of "ideal" causal dependence.[41] In defining these

---

[37] Look-Rutherford 226–227, 242–243; A VI iv 1550/AG 47.

[38] Look-Rutherford 336–339.

[39] I defend this reading in Chapter 4, "The Actual World" (Rutherford, this volume)

[40] Look-Rutherford 226–227.

[41] See, in particular, the supplementary study to his letter to Des Bosses of February 15, 1712 (Look-Rutherford 232–233). According to Leibniz, "The modifications of one monad are the ideal causes of the modifications of another monad . . . insofar as reasons appear in one monad which, from the beginning of things, prompt God to produce modifications in another monad" (Look-Rutherford 298–299; cf.

relations among monads, Leibniz makes one critical assumption: that every monad has a body that fixes its position and causal state relative to that of every other monad.[42] This thesis plays a key role in the theory of monads, as can be seen in the link Leibniz establishes between it and his explanation of the finitude of monads: "God alone is above all matter, since he is its author. But creatures free or freed from matter would at the same time be divorced from the universal connection [la liaison universelle], like deserters from the general order" (GP VI 546/L 592).[43] The thesis of the embodiment of monads is thus employed in explaining the difference between God and created monads and in explaining how monads are related in a world.

Leibniz's defense of the embodiment of monads is consistent with a realism about bodies—a position that maintains, for example, that a monad and its organic body together form a corporeal substance that possesses a per se unity. Yet the account does not require this. Leibniz's explanation of the finitude of monads and of the order and connection among them stands even if every monad has only a phenomenal body whose represented structure and relations to other bodies are the basis of the monad's having a "point of view" on the universe (Mon 57). As he explains in the "Monadology," monads are related in a common universe through representations of their particular bodies:

> Thus, although each created monad represents the whole universe, it more distinctly represents the body which is particularly affected by it, and whose entelechy it constitutes. And just as this body expresses the whole universe through the interconnection of all matter in the plenum, the soul also represents the whole universe by representing this body, which belongs to it in a particular way.
>
> (Mon 62)

Every monad represents itself as a unique body, which is spatiotemporally and causally related to every other body in the universe, including those represented by other monads as *their* bodies. On these grounds, Leibniz concludes that every monad is related to every other monad via relations of coexistence and succession and relations of mutual causal dependence. That is, there are determinate answers to the questions of where and when any monad is and of what its state of activity is relative to those of other monads.[44] The answers to these questions are given in terms of the relations among the

---

274–275). Specifically, one monad is said to *act* on another just in case it represents its body as the physical cause of changes in the body of the second monad, and that monad in turn represents its body as *acted on* by the body of the first monad (Mon 49–52; *Theodicy* §66).

[42] "My own view is that the soul always thinks and feels, is always united with some body, and indeed never suddenly and totally leaves the body with which it is united" (*New Essays* II xxiii 20; RB 221).

[43] Cf. *Theodicy* §124, quoted in note 34.

[44] GP II 253/AG 178; C 14/MP 175–176; RB 155. In his letter to Des Bosses of May 26, 1712, Leibniz writes: "monads in themselves do not even have a situation [*situm*] with respect to each other—at least one that is real, which extends beyond the order of phenomena. Each is, as it were, a certain world apart, and they correspond to each other through their phenomena, and not through any other intrinsic intercourse and connection [*nullo alio per se commercio nexuque*]" (Look-Rutherford 240–243). His

bodies that each monad represents as its own. And these answers hold independently of whether the relation between a monad and its body goes beyond its representation of that body as its physical point of view on the universe. If the latter condition is met, and if all monads represent themselves as parts of the same universe, then those monads together constitute a world.

MONADS AND MATTER

The thesis that reality ultimately consists solely of monads and their internal modifications is defended by Leibniz in many late texts.[45] This bold thesis raises numerous questions, the most pressing of which is the relation of monads to what common sense and science affirm as ontological *terra firma*: the physical world of material things, including our own and other living bodies. As Leibniz confronts this topic, it divides into two questions. First, can a relation among monads account for the supposed unity of a living body or corporeal substance? Second, does the metaphysics of monads support a plausible explanation of the reality of matter, whose properties appear categorically different from those of monads?

It is common to depict the theory of monads and the theory of corporeal substances as competing metaphysical pictures that Leibniz is forced to choose between. If the latter theory is taken to be a fundamental ontology, which treats corporeal substances as irreducible to monads, then it is incompatible with the thesis that monads are the elements into which all other things are resolved. But the later Leibniz does not think of corporeal substances in this way. Until the end of his life, he insists that matter is structured by the infinite envelopment of living bodies within living bodies (Mon 63–70). What changes as he develops the theory of monads is that he rejects the corporeal substance theory as fundamental from an ontological point of view. Although the infinite envelopment of living bodies accurately describes what we would find if we analyzed any piece of matter physically—it would consist of living bodies, each of which was composed of smaller living bodies, ad infinitum—a deeper level of reality underlies this representation of matter. At this level, matter itself is nothing but monads. We find this view stated in an important text from the final decade of Leibniz's life:

> A substance is either simple, such as a soul, which has no parts, or it is composite, such as an animal, which consists of a soul and an organic body. But an organic body, like every other body, is merely an aggregate of animals or other things which are living and therefore organic, or finally of small objects or masses; but these also are finally resolved into living things, from which it is evident that all bodies are finally

position is thus that though monads have no real situation with respect to each other, or causal influence on each other, they have *ideal* versions of these relations, based on the phenomena they represent.

[45] See note 1.

resolved into living things, and that what in the analysis of substances, exist ulti-mately are simple substances—namely, souls, or, if you prefer a more general term, *monads*, which are without parts. For even though every simple substance has an or-ganic body which corresponds to it—otherwise it would not have any kind of orderly relation to other things in the universe—yet by itself it is without parts. And because an organic body, or any other body whatsoever, can again be resolved into substances endowed with organic bodies, it is evident that in the end there are simple substances alone, and that in them are the sources of all things and of the modifications that come to things.

(C 13–14/MP 175)

On Leibniz's final view, all matter—including the organic matter of living bodies—is nothing more than monads. Living bodies, which he describes in some late writings as "composite substances," consist of a soul or dominant monad and an organic body made up of an infinite envelopment of smaller living bodies. Each of these bodies, in turn, consists of a dominant monad and a organic body similarly composed. Thus, following through the resolution of any composite substance into its constituent elements, one finds in the end only monads: a dominant monad and a mass of subordinate monads, each of which is the dominant monad of an organic body that is a component of the or-ganic body of the dominant monad.[46]

Because a composite substance is a *composite*, made up of an infinity of monads, it can only be, given the principles of Leibniz's philosophy, an *ens per aggregationem* whose unity is a function of mind-dependent relations. Strictly speaking, it cannot be a substance if a necessary condition for that is being an *unum* per se.[47] The contin-uing presence of the vocabulary of "corporeal substance" in Leibniz's late writings can be charitably interpreted along the following lines. As we have seen, the thesis of mo-nadic embodiment is a cornerstone of his metaphysics. According to this thesis, every monad represents itself as a corporeal substance: an enduring living body. Furthermore, this appearance has a ground in reality: there *are* other monads that represent them-selves as the organic bodies into which the dominant monad's body can be resolved. Nevertheless, the composite made up of the dominant monad and the mass of subor-dinate monads is only a special sort of aggregate: one in which the monads are ordered with respect to each other based on relations of ideal causation.[48]

---

[46] Cf. GP II 252/AG 177; GP VII 502; and PNG 3: "Each distinct simple substance or monad, which makes up the center of a composite substance (an animal, for example) and is the principle of its unity, is surrounded by a *mass* composed of an infinity of other monads, which constitute the *body belonging to* this central monad, through whose properties the monad represents the things outside, similarly to the way a center does" (GP VI 598/AG 207).

[47] A point Leibniz acknowledges to Des Bosses: "monads do not constitute a complete composite substance, since they do not make a per se unity, but a mere aggregate, unless some substantial bond is added" (Look-Rutherford 242–243). Cf. GP VI 628/AG 229, and, on the notion of a "substantial bond," note 50.

[48] In notes for his letter to Des Bosses of January 24, 1713, Leibniz writes: "I acknowledge no modes of monads except perceptions and appetites, or tendencies to new perceptions; and through these alone it

From the point of view of the theory of monads, this seems a wholly successful piece of reductive metaphysics. Living bodies no longer qualify as substances in the strict sense, yet Leibniz has the resources to uphold many common beliefs about the embodied life of human beings.[49] To claim more than this, he thinks, one must appeal to extra-philosophical considerations that, if not contrary to reason, are nonetheless above reason.[50]

The reduction of living bodies to monads, however, opens the door to a deeper problem. According to Leibniz's analysis, any living body consists of a soul or dominant monad and a mass of lesser monads associated with the matter of the soul's body. Yet in what sense can the latter monads be identified with the matter of the body? How do they ground or otherwise explain the body's existence? This question seems especially pressing when we consider that monads are, by definition, unextended immaterial substances. In what sense could such things account for the reality of our and other living bodies?[51]

happens that souls or monads are subordinated to one another—that is, subordinated representatively, with no real influx between them" (Look-Rutherford 302–305). Cf. Look-Rutherford 256–257.

[49] In a letter to Des Bosses of August 19, 1715, he writes, "even if bodies were not substances, nonetheless all men will be inclined to judge that bodies are substances, just as they are all inclined to judge that the Earth is at rest, even though it is really in motion" (Look-Rutherford 346–347). Leibniz agrees that sense experience corroborates the existence of corporeal substances, but he does not think that this settles the issue of their ontological status: "If bodies were mere phenomena, they would not deceive the senses on account of that. For the senses do not make known anything about metaphysical matters" (Look-Rutherford 368–369).

[50] On the distinction between "above reason" and "contrary to reason," see Maria Rosa Antognazza, "The Conformity of Faith with Reason in the 'Discours Préliminaire' of the *Theodicy*," in Paul Rateau (ed.), *Lectures et interprétations des Essais de théodicée de G. W. Leibniz* [Studia Leibnitiana Sonderhefte 40] (Stuttgart: Steiner, 2011), pp. 231–245. In response to Des Bosses's concern to uphold the reality of corporeal substance, Leibniz proposes the device of a "substantial bond" (*vinculum substantiale*) designed to supply the principle of unity that is otherwise lacking in an aggregate of monads. After exploring various ways in which this hypothesis might be defended as an extension of the theory of monads, he concludes that the arguments favoring it hinge on matters of faith, in particular, acceptance of the Catholic doctrine of transubstantiation (Look-Rutherford 224–227). As a Lutheran, Leibniz does not accept this interpretation of the Eucharist (Look-Rutherford 152–153). A stronger case can be made by appeal to the mystery of the Incarnation (Look-Rutherford 278–279). In the end, though, Leibniz appears satisfied to defend the theory of monads as adequate for a "fundamental investigation" of things within the order of nature (Look-Rutherford 254–255). As he writes in his letter of January 24, 1713: "The hypothesis of mere monads has this distinction, that, with it assumed, nothing remains unexplained, nor is anything assumed except what is proven and what must be assumed necessarily" (Look-Rutherford 306–307). For a fuller discussion of these points, see Look-Rutherford lvii–lxxv.

[51] Leibniz designates the matter whose reality is to be explained as "*secondary matter*—i.e. matter as it actually occurs, invested with its derivative qualities" (RB 222; cf. RB 378, 434), or "the complete body that results from the active and the passive" (GP II 171/AG 173). He distinguishes this both from "primary matter," or primitive passive power taken in abstraction from a complete nature, and from the Cartesian notion of matter as *res extensa*, which is an abstraction from a body's active *and* passive powers and in itself purely phenomenal.

What Leibniz has to say on this question is far from conclusive, and he in fact seems torn between several responses.[52] His most radical stance rejects the substantial reality of matter all together in favor of the view that the physical properties of bodies exist only as the contents of monadic perceptions. On this view, call it phenomenalism, there is nothing that the body is over and above the harmonious perceptions of monads. Support for this position comes from a well-known passage in a 1704 letter to De Volder:

> [C]onsidering the matter carefully, we must say that there is nothing in things but simple substances, and in them, perception and appetite. Moreover, matter and motion are not substances or things as much as they are the phenomena of perceivers, the reality of which is situated in the harmony of the perceivers with themselves (at different times) and with other perceivers.
>
> (GP II 270/AG 181)[53]

Yet Leibniz does not consistently defend this phenomenalist position even in his correspondence with De Volder. In his next letter, responding to De Volder's complaint that he (Leibniz) seems "to eliminate bodies completely and place them in appearances," Leibniz writes:

> I don't really eliminate body, but reduce it to what it is. For I show that corporeal mass, which is thought to have something over and above simple substances, is not a substance but a phenomenon resulting from simple substances, which alone have unity and absolute reality. . . . It is necessary that these simple substances exist everywhere. . . . In the *mass of extension*, or rather, of extended things, or, as I prefer, in the multitude of things, I say that there is *no unity*, but rather innumerable unities.
>
> (GP II 275/AG 181–182)

What we commonly take to be a real thing existing in its own right—extended matter—is, Leibniz suggests, a "phenomenon resulting from simple substances." As such, this phenomenon is not illusory or a mere appearance. It has a kind of reality by virtue of being grounded or "well founded" in monads. In explaining this point, Leibniz draws on the analogy of the rainbow: just as the rainbow's colored bands are the appearance to us of a multitude of water droplets refracting different wavelengths of light, so extended matter is the appearance to us of an multitude of unextended monads. The

[52] See Rutherford, "Leibniz as idealist." For a bolder thesis about Leibniz's lack of a final position on these issues, see Garber, *Leibniz: Substance, Body, Monad*, chapter 9.

[53] Similar statements appear in letters to Des Bosses: Look-Rutherford 226–229, 240–243, 254–257. See also a passage omitted from the final draft of his letter to Bourguet of March 22, 1714: "The difficulty that is raised concerning the communication of motion ceases when one considers that material things and their motions are only phenomena. Their reality lies only in the agreement of the appearances of monads. If the dreams of the same person were consistently followed, and if the dreams of all souls were in agreement, there would be no need for anything else to produce body and matter from them" (GP III 567n.).

analogy is instructive, but it can take us only so far in understanding Leibniz's position. He asserts that monads are located everywhere in matter or that everything is full of monads, a statement that is supported by his analysis of living bodies into their constituent monads.[54] Yet he also cautions that talk of spatial location or of filling extension is not to be taken literally in the case of monads. In contrast to the rainbow, where the water droplets are spatially located relative to our body and causally responsible for the bands of color we see in the sky, monads are neither parts of bodies nor the physical causes of their appearance to us.[55]

It is important to have in focus the problem as Leibniz sees it. Contrasting his metaphysics with Spinoza's, he writes in 1715: "according to Spinoza . . . there is only one substance. He would be right if there were no monads; then everything except God would be of a passing nature and would vanish into simple accidents or modifications, since there would be no substantial foundation [*base des substances*] in things, such as consists in the existence of monads" (GP III 575/L 663). What we are presented with in corporeal phenomena, Leibniz believes, is a constantly changing array of accidents. These accidents include all of a body's kinematic and dynamic properties. For such accidents to exist, they must have a ground in substance. As we have seen, extended matter as such lacks the unity definitive of substance. Hence, the accidents that mark the existence of bodies must be grounded in some other substance(s). One possibility that Leibniz rejects is Spinoza's doctrine that all accidents are modifications of a single substance: God. Against this, he defends monads as the substantial foundations for the existence of all accidents. The question is whether he provides an adequate explanation of how this might be so.

Phenomenalism offers one version of how such an explanation might go. On this view, none of a body's physical properties has a mind-independent reality, none is a formal modification of external monads, but they all have a foundation in substance as the contents of monads' perceptual states. The simplicity of this account makes it attractive to Leibniz. Furthermore, this explanatory strategy represents at least part of his position because he consistently maintains that many of a body's physical properties—extension, shape, motion—are merely phenomenal. It is only a body's dynamical properties—its active and passive force—that are real and hence arguably require an external ground in the reality of substance (and not just an internal ground in the perceiver of those phenomena).[56]

One of the critical points Leibniz makes in this connection is that the monads grounding the reality of physical forces are not elementary parts of matter. They do not, in other words, explain matter's macroscopic properties by comprising an underlying physical microstructure. When Leibniz claims that monads are "in" matter or that they

---

[54] GM III 537/AG 167; GP VII 500–502, 549; Look-Rutherford 25.

[55] Look-Rutherford 226–227, 254–255.

[56] Cf. the opening of the *Specimen dynamicum* (GM VI 234–235/AG 117–118). To Des Bosses, he writes that if there are only souls or monads, "all real extension would also vanish, not to mention motion, whose reality would be reduced to mere changes of phenomena" (Look-Rutherford 242–243).

are the "elements" of things he relies on his technical notion of substance as a "requisite" (*requisitum*) for what it grounds.[57] Roughly, to say that one thing is a requisite of another is to say that the former is a necessary condition for the existence of the latter *and* that it renders its existence intelligible (in accord with the principle of sufficient reason). On this basis, Leibniz also claims that a thing derives its reality from that of its requisites.[58] Consequently, if monads are requisites of matter, then the existence of matter presupposes the existence of monads, which supply a ground for the reality of the active and passive forces of matter.

If this is not complicated enough, Leibniz draws on two different notions of a requisite, distinguished as a *requisitum immediatum* and a *requisitum mediatum*.[59] The difference between these notions, both of which Leibniz applies to monads, is that immediate requisites are metaphysically necessary conditions for the existence of a thing. His grounding arguments establish monads as requisites in this sense: matter cannot be conceived to exist (as a multiplicity subject to change) unless it is understood in terms of monads. But Leibniz also interprets monads as grounding the properties of matter in the weaker sense of being "mediate requisites." He clarifies this claim in a letter to Des Bosses, in which he explains that the soul of a worm existing in a human body is not a "substantial part" of the body but a "mere requisite"—and not a requisite "by a metaphysical necessity, but rather because it is required in the course of nature" (Look-Rutherford, 296–297; cf. 226–227). His point is that even if it is necessary that there be monads everywhere in matter, it is not necessary that the soul of the worm be one of those monads. The worm's soul is one of the monads grounding the reality of that particular human body because the worm's body happens to be one of the components of that body. The claim that the worm's soul "is required in the course of nature" is thus a way of affirming that the appearance of the human body is well-founded or has a ground in reality in that there are monads that represent themselves as the infinitely enveloped components of that body.

Leibniz presents a similar account to Christian Wolff in explaining the ground of the dynamical properties of matter. Because physical derivative forces—"conatus and impetus, and the actions that follow from these"—are changeable accidents, they must be modifications of some "substantial active thing, or primitive force" (GLW 130). This thesis, which Leibniz defends in his 1695 *Specimen dynamicum*, remains part of his position when he adopts the theory of monads. Yet Wolff is reasonably puzzled about how the primitive force of monads—that of appetition—*could* ground the reality of physical forces. How can the forces of bodies be understood as modifications of the primitive forces of monads? In responding to Wolff, Leibniz makes it clear that he regards external monads as grounding derivative forces to the extent that those monads *represent* themselves as exerting the physical forces in question:

[57] Monads are "not parts but requisites of bodies" (GP VII 503). Cf. A VI iv 1669/AG 103; A VI iv 1673.
[58] For Leibniz's definitions, see A VI iv 650, 871, 990. I discuss the point at greater length in Rutherford, "Leibniz as idealist."
[59] A VI iv 627, 650.

You ask how primitive force is modified, for example, when the motion of heavy objects is accelerated in descent; I respond that the modification of primitive force, which is in the monad itself, cannot be better explained than by explaining how derivative force is changed in the phenomena. For what is exhibited extensively and mechanically in the phenomena is, concentratedly and vitally, in monads. . . . What is exhibited mechanically and extensively through the reaction of what resists and the restoration of what is compressed is concentrated dynamically and monadically . . . in the entelechy itself, in which there is the source of mechanism and a representation of mechanical things; for phenomena result from monads (which alone are true substances).

(GLW 138–139)[60]

Again, the pattern of explanation is that external monads supply what is "required in the course of nature" for the phenomena to be well-founded. The phenomena are not illusory or mere appearances, provided there are monads that are a substantial foundation for them. Yet the monads supply this foundation by *representing* themselves as the physical causes of the phenomena. Thus, Leibniz explains derivative forces not as formal modifications of primitive force, but only as features of the content of the perceptions of monads. The account he defends to Wolff amounts to a version of phenomenalism, augmented by the thesis that the phenomena perceived by monads are well-founded because God has chosen to create substances that represent themselves as the material constituents and physical causes of those phenomena.[61]

Leibniz's account of monads as immediate requisites of matter supports a more robust conclusion. His grounding arguments imply that, properly understood, matter *is* monads. What we took to be an extended object infinitely divisible into parts becomes intelligible from the point of view of reason as an infinity of simple substances. On this analysis, we have a firmer hold on the claim that the dynamical properties of bodies—their active and passive forces—are grounded in a substantial reality. The active and passive forces ascribed to bodies are our representations of the primitive active and passive powers of other monads. The extended mass of the body is a confused image of the diffusion of the primary matter of monads, just as the body's moving forces are a confused image of the entelechies of those monads.[62] To this extent, Leibniz's account more

---

[60] For further discussion of this exchange, see Donald Rutherford, "Idealism declined: Leibniz and Christian Wolff," in *Leibniz and His Correspondents*, edited by Paul Lodge (Cambridge: Cambridge University Press, 2004), pp. 214–237.

[61] For a development of this interpretation, see Adams, *Leibniz: Determinist, Theist, Idealist.* I take this to be the crux of Leibniz's claim that matter "results" from monads: "Accurately speaking . . . matter is not composed of these constitutive unities but results from them, since matter or extended mass is nothing but a phenomenon grounded in things, like the rainbow or the mock-sun, and all reality belongs only to unities. . . . Substantial unities are not parts but foundations of phenomena" (GP II 268/AG 179). Cf. GP II 276/AG 182; GP III 636/L 659.

[62] To De Volder, Leibniz writes: "[Extension] expresses only a certain nonsucessive . . . and simultaneous diffusion or repetition of a certain nature, or what comes to the same thing, a multitude of things of the same nature, existing together, with a certain order among themselves. It is this nature, I say, that is said to be extended or diffused. . . . Furthermore, the nature which is supposed to be diffused,

closely tracks the rainbow example. The colored bands of the rainbow are artifacts of our mode of perception, but they have a foundation in the differential refraction of light by droplets of water. Analogously, the corporeal aspects of active and passive force are artifacts of our mode of perception, but they have a foundation in the primitive active and passive powers of monads. Yet there is also a significant difference between the two accounts. In the case of the rainbow, we are able to bridge, in an informative way, the gap between the phenomenon and its ground. We can explain why light, refracted as it is, alters our retina in such a way as to produce the appearance of an array of colored bands. In the case of the matter-monad relation, we can describe no such connection between appearance and reality. Perceptually, we are presented with a world of extended material things, and intellectual analysis alone supports the conclusion that the world we perceive is really one of an infinity of simple substances. No intermediate steps fill the gap between phenomenon and ground. Instead, we must be satisfied with the distinction between two fundamentally different epistemic perspectives: the world as represented perceptually by monads and the world as comprehended by reason.

CONCLUSION

The theory of monads is Leibniz's fullest attempt to limn reality from the standpoint of reason alone. In the theory, he describes what the properties of a fundamental entity would have to be and how such entities can be conceived as related in a world. Leibniz starts from the assumption that reality is structured by relations of ontological dependence that are subject to the principle of sufficient reason. Given this, he is confident that if a multitude of things exists, and if change occurs, there must be a ground for these facts—a ground found in monads.

If this analysis can be sustained, Leibniz has shown that what we represent perceptually as extended matter, infinitely divisible into parts and subject to change, must be monads because that conception of matter alone identifies the grounds of its existence. Leibniz's explicit claims about the relation of matter and monads to some extent confound this conclusion. On the one hand, he asserts that the derivative forces of matter can exist only as modifications of the primitive force of monads. This sounds like the conclusion of his grounding arguments. However, when Leibniz explicates this claim, he falls back on a different kind of grounding relation: one that construes corporeal phenomena as "well-founded" to the extent that there are monads that represent themselves as the material substrate and physical causes of those phenomena. On this analysis, matter is not shown to *be* monads, but to be the harmonized contents of the perceptions of monads.

repeated, continued, is that which constitutes the physical body [*corpus physicum*]; it cannot be found in anything but the principle of acting and being acted upon, since nothing else is suggested to us by the phenomena" (GP II 269/AG 179). Cf. GP II 195/L 532; Look-Rutherford 364–365.

Leibniz's account of matter and its properties as "well-founded phenomena" is consistent with his ontological analysis of matter, but it responds to a different question: not what is matter, but which monads are sufficient "in the course of nature" for a phenomenon to be well-founded. The answer to the ontological question can only be *monads* because these are the "elements" of all things. Yet, beyond showing that our understanding of matter terminates in monads, Leibniz is taxed to establish a meaningful explanatory relation between the two. He is keen to build bridges between the theory of monads and the views of the world supported by sense experience and the physical sciences, but such bridges remain provisional and dependent on analogy.

In the end, Leibniz's metaphysics comes closest to that of Plato, the philosopher with whom he has the deepest sympathy. Through reason, we gain access to an "intelligible world" that cannot be fully reconciled with the manifest image of the world given in sense perception.[63] The epistemic perspective of science, no less than that of ordinary experience, is tied to the form of our perceptual representations. As such, it cannot deliver a view of reality—the world of monads—as it is in itself. But the philosopher does have access to this view, acquired through the diligent use of reason, and Leibniz takes himself to have delivered a first glimpse of it.[64]

REFERENCES

Adams, Robert M. 1994. *Leibniz: Determinist, Theist, Idealist*. New York: Oxford University Press.

Antognazza, Maria Rosa. 2011. "The conformity of faith with reason in the 'Discours Préliminaire' of the *Theodicy*." In Paul Rateau (ed.), *Lectures et interprétations des Essais de théodicée de G. W. Leibniz* [Studia Leibnitiana Sonderhefte 40]. Stuttgart: Steiner, pp. 231–245.

Bolton, Martha Brandt. 2013. "Change in the monad." In Eric Watkins (ed.), *The Divine Order, the Human Order, and the Order of Nature: Historical Perspectives*. Oxford: Oxford University Press, pp. 175–194.

Correia, Fabrice, and Benjamin Schnieder (eds.). 2012. *Metaphysical Grounding: Understanding the Structure of Reality*. Cambridge: Cambridge University Press.

Garber, Daniel. 2009. *Leibniz: Body, Substance, Monad*. Oxford: Oxford University Press.

Hartz, Glenn. 2007. *Leibniz's Final System. Monads, Matter and Animals*. London and New York: Routledge.

Levey, Samuel. 2007. "On unity and simple substance in Leibniz." *The Leibniz Review* 17: 61–107.

Levey, Samuel. 2008. "Why Simples? A reply to Donald Rutherford." *The Leibniz Review* 18: 225–247.

Levey, Samuel. 2012. "On unity, borrowed reality and multitude in Leibniz." *The Leibniz Review* 22: 97–134.

Loptson, Peter, and R. T. W. Arthur. 2006. "Leibniz's body realism: Two interpretations." *The Leibniz Review* 16: 1–42.

---

[63] *New Essays* IV iii 6 (A VI vi 378–379).

[64] My thanks to Maria Rosa Antognazza for helpful comments on an earlier draft of this chapter.

Phemister, Pauline. 2005. *Leibniz and the Natural World: Activity, Passivity and Corporeal Substances in Leibniz's Philosophy*. Dordrecht: Springer.

Rutherford, Donald. 1995. *Leibniz and the Rational Order of Nature*. Cambridge: Cambridge University Press.

Rutherford, Donald. 2004. "Idealism declined: Leibniz and Christian Wolff." In Paul Lodge (ed.), *Leibniz and His Correspondents*. Cambridge: Cambridge University Press, pp. 214–237.

Rutherford, Donald. 2008. "Unity, reality and simple substances: A reply to Samuel Levey." *The Leibniz Review* 18: 207–224.

Rutherford, Donald. 2008. "Leibniz as idealist." *Oxford Studies in Early Modern Philosophy* 4: 141–190.

Rutherford, Donald. 2013. "Laws and powers in Leibniz." In Eric Watkins (ed.), *The Divine Order, the Human Order, and the Order of Nature: Historical Perspectives*. Oxford: Oxford University Press, pp. 149–174.

Sleigh, Robert C., Jr. 1990. *Leibniz and Arnauld: A Commentary on Their Correspondence*. New Haven: Yale University Press.

Swoyer, Chris. 1995. "Leibnizian expression." *Journal of the History of Philosophy* 33: 63–99.

CHAPTER 20

....

MONADIC PERCEPTION

....

HEINRICH SCHEPERS

In Leibniz's mature metaphysics, the term "perception" has a special meaning and plays a central but hitherto insufficiently noticed role. According to Leibniz, there is nothing in reality but monads together with their perceptions and appetites. Matter and motion are merely phenomena of perceivers, and the only reality they have is to be found in perceivers and their mutual harmony. Leibniz seems to have formulated this thesis for the first time on June 30, 1704, when he wrote to Burchard de Volder:

> Indeed, when considered carefully, it may be said that there is nothing in the world but simple substances and, in them, perception and appetite; moreover, matter and motion are not so much substances or things as the phenomena of perceivers, whose reality lies in the harmony of perceivers with themselves (at different times) and with other perceivers.[1]

With perhaps the same thought in mind, he maintained as early as 1679 that there are really only spirits (*mentes*) and their perceptions.[2]

Leibniz defines a perception as the expression of multiplicity in unity—an expression, he explains, which differs completely from that of mirrors or of corporeal organs, which are not real unities.[3] In his corrections and additions for a planned new edition of the *Nova methodus discendae docendaeque Jurisprudentiae* (ca. 1695–1709), we find: "Perception is the expression of multiplicity in a unity or in a simple substance."[4]

---

[1] GP II 270. "Imo rem accurate considerando dicendum est nihil in rebus esse nisi substantias simplices et in his perceptionem atque appetitum; materiam autem et motum non tam substantias aut res quam percipientium phaenomena esse, quorum realitas sita est in percipientium secum ipsis (pro diversis temporibus) et cum caeteris percipientibus harmonia" (translated in Lodge, p. 307).

[2] A VI iv 279.14. "Ergo revera solae existunt mentes et earum perceptiones."

[3] A VI iv 1625.17–19 (1688). "Patet etiam quid perceptio sit, quae omnibus formis competit, nempe expressio multorum in uno, quae longe differt ab expressione in speculo vel organo corporeo quod vere unum non est." Translated in MP, p. 85.

[4] A VI i 286.20. "Perceptio est expressio multorum in vere uno seu in substantia simplice."

This perceived multitude is not any particular multitude, but rather the whole world as seen from the point of view of that which is "truly one," that is, the monad. Leibniz explains this by means of his town metaphor. This well-known metaphor, if correctly interpreted, describes a virtual town and its observers who, from their respective points of view, themselves produce, by dint of their perceptions, all the data from which the town is constructed—just as it is done in modern computer animation.

It is only in a metaphorical sense that a Leibnizian monad can "see" the world because its perceiving is not a passive receiving. Rather, it is an action, an action that emerges and remains inside the monad, which, Leibniz says metaphorically, has no "windows" that might allow any entrance or exit. Here, the principal difficulty of Leibniz's new metaphysics appears: there are not enough understandable terms to formulate his theses, so he is forced to modify the meaning of old terms or to use current terms in a metaphorical sense. Therefore, he insists that his definitions should be understood to have the precise meaning that he has given them.

In one of his last attempts to convince De Volder, perhaps in January 1705, we read that only simple substances can be the sources or principles and, at the same time, the subjects ("*simul et subjecta*") of the series of perceptions that unfold in them and that express the totality of phenomena in the greatest and most orderly variety.[5]

The crucial words "*simul et subjecta*" were held back in the version of the letter sent to De Volder—a sign that Leibniz did not expect his partner to have the ability to understand the core of his metaphysics. In his last letter, Leibniz tried once more to impress upon De Volder the key features of his theory but did not, in the end, dispatch the letter (perhaps because the draft was too densely written). In it we read that, in his view, arguments can prove the existence of nothing except perceivers and perceptions and what should be admitted in them: in perceivers, the transition from perception to perception while the subject remains the same; in perceptions, the harmony of perceivers.[6]

He continues by declaring that, in every perceiver, there is an active and a passive force, active when passing to a more perfect state; passive, on the contrary, when passing to a less perfect state. He adds that there are infinitely many perceivers, as many as there are simple substances or monads. Therefore, every monad is a perceiver. The order of perceivers among themselves, expressed by our phenomena, constitutes our notions of time and space. Here, Leibniz maintains that masses, as well as the passive forces of bodies, are mere idols that describe the phenomena resulting from the passions

---

[5] GP II 278. "Facile enim vides simplices substantias nihil aliud esse posse quam fontes seu principia simul et subjecta totidem perceptionis serierum sese ordine evolventium, eandem phaenomenorum universitatem maxima ordinatissimaque varietate exprimentium."

[6] GP II 281 (Febr. 6, 1706): "Nullius alterius rei, meo judicio, comprobari existentia argumentis potest quam percipientium et perceptionum, si causam communem demas, eorumque quae in his admittere oportet, quae sunt in percipiente quidem transitus de perceptione in perceptionem, eodem manente subjecto, in perceptionibus autem harmonia percipientium."

the perceivers have.[7] Leibniz closes this remark with a declaration (which in fact he deleted): "either there is no subject of perceptions or all I said I hold for demonstrated."[8]

In the same letter, Leibniz reminds De Volder that, in nature, there cannot be things other than simple substances and the aggregates resulting from them. In simple substances, we find nothing other than perceptions and reasons for perceptions. Those postulating more need to provide the marks by means of which anything further might be established and explained. Leibniz claims to have written many times already about these theses, although he grants that not everything is organized in a way that might amount to a demonstration in the eyes of others. Nonetheless, he held it as demonstrated that it is essential for a substance that its present state involves all future ones and, vice versa, that the force or reason for new perceptions should be found nowhere else but inside the monad.[9] Already in 1688, Leibniz wrote that, as a consequence, the nature of each substance consists in expressing the whole universe through its immanent operations:

> Because each thing has intercourse with all others, either mediately or immediately, consequently the existence of each substance possesses a nature such that its agency or passivity, that is, the series of its immanent operations, expresses the whole universe.[10]

These immanent operations are nothing other than a substance's perceptions and appetites, and the unity of the perceiver constitutes the connection by which consecutive perceptions may be derived from preceding perceptions: "Perception, however, is the soul's own operation, and the unity of the perceiver constitutes the connection of perceptions according to which subsequent perceptions are derived from preceding perceptions."[11]

[7] "In omni percipiente vis activa passivaque est: | activa in distincta perceptione, passiva in confusa *canc.* | activa in transitu ad perfectius, passiva in contrario; percipientia autem infinita sunt, nempe quot simplices substantiae sive Monades. Horum ordo inter se nostris phaenomenis expressus constituit temporis spatiique notiones. Quod vero ex passionibus percipientium resultat phaenomenaque ipsa circumscribit, universim sumtum, molis seu vis corporum passivae idolum facit."

[8] "Caeterum aut nullum esse subjectum perceptionum, aut competere ipsi quae dixi pro demonstrato habeo."

[9] GP II 282. "Nihil enim reale esse potest in natura quam substantiae simplices, et ex iis resultantia aggregata. In ipsis autem substantiis simplicibus nihil aliud novimus quam perceptiones aut perceptionum rationes. Qui plura postulat, opus habet notis, quibus et comprobentur et declarentur. Pro demonstrato habeo (uti aliquoties scripsi, etsi nondum omnia ita ordinare licuerit, ut aliorum oculis subjicere commode demonstrationem possim) esse substantiae essentiale, ut status ejus praesens involvat futuros, et vice versa neque aliunde Vis peti potest, aut ratio transitus ad novas perceptiones" (Lodge, p. 332).

[10] A VI iv 1625.12–15. "Cum vero omnia cum aliis mediate aut immediate commercium habeant, consequens est omnis substantiae hanc esse naturam, ut vi sua agendi aut patiendi, hoc est serie suarum operationum immanentium exprimat totum universum" (Parkinson 85).

[11] Leibniz to Des Bosses (April 1709); GP II 372. "Operatio autem animae propria est perceptio, et unitatem percipientis facit perceptionum nexus, secundum quem sequentes ex praecedentibus derivantur."

Perhaps early in 1705, Leibniz already wrote to De Volder explaining that primitive forces cannot be different from the internal tendencies of simple substances that, following the laws of their natures, move from perception to perception while they harmonize among themselves, referring to the same phenomena in their different states:

> Derivative forces I relegate to phenomena, but I judge it to be manifest that primitive forces are nothing other than the internal tendencies of simple substances, which, by means of the laws of their natures, move from perception to perception, while they harmonise among themselves, representing the same phenomena of the universe in a different way, something that necessarily originates from a common cause.[12]

Leibniz claims to have reduced all to simplicity while arriving at principles that are manifestly necessary and sufficient such that it would be not only superfluous to add any others, but also inconsistent and nonexplanatory. To ask why there are only perceptions and appetites in the monad is, for Leibniz, to ask for something ultramundane, like summoning God to explain why he wanted that we think what we think.[13]

It is commonly said that one thing is "represented" by another thing—for example, a country by its ambassador; the multitude of phenomena by a perception. Leibniz, however, goes a step further. A perception is not only earlier than the phenomena; it is itself just this multitude. Therefore we can say that the monad is, at every moment that it perceives, nothing but a representation of all simultaneous phenomena:

> And since monads are nothing other than representations of phenomena with a transition to new phenomena, it is clear that, in them, perception occurs on account of representation, and appetite occurs on account of the transition; nor there are principles from which anything else could be sought.[14]

Leibniz is convinced that there are simply no principles that allow any other conclusion. To his former secretary R. C. Wagner, he explains on June 4, 1710: "[T]he correspondence between the internal and the external or the representation of the external in the

---

[12] Leibniz to de Volder (January 25 1705), GP II 275. "Vires derivativas ad phaenomena relego, sed vires primitivas manifestum esse censeo nil aliud esse posse quam tendentias internas substantiarum simplicium, quibus certe suae naturae lege de perceptione in perceptionem transeunt, atque inter se simul conspirent, eadem universi phaenomena diverso habitu referentes, quod necesse est oriri a communi causa" (Lodge, p. 319).

[13] Leibniz to de Volder (June 30, 1704), GP II 271. "Vides quo res simplicitatis sit reducta, cum ad ipsa principia perventum sit quae necessaria et sufficientia esse manifestum est, ut adjicere aliqua non tantum superfluum, sed et inconsistens et inexplicabile videatur. Porro ultra haec progredi et quaerere cur sit in substantiis simplicibus perceptio et appetitus, est quaerere aliquid ultramundanum ut ita dicam, et Deum ad rationes vocare cur aliquid eorum esse voluerit quae a nobis concipiuntur" (Lodge, p. 309).

[14] Leibniz to Des Bosses, August 23, 1713 (GP II 481): "Et cum Monades nihil aliud sunt, quam repraesentationes phaenomenorum cum transitu ad nova phaenomena patet in iis ob repraesentationem esse perceptionem, ob transitum esse appetitionem; nec dantur principia unde aliquid aliud peti possit."

internal, of the composite in the simple, of the multitude in the unity is that which really constitutes a perception."[15] Again, in December 1714, he writes to Louis Bourguet pointing out that, otherwise, a monad would have no connection to the world: "For perception is the representation of the multitude in the single; and appetite is the tendency from one perception to another: yet these two things are in all Monads, for otherwise a Monad would not have any connection to the rest of things."[16]

In the monad, the multitude is not only represented, but also varies by being variously represented:

> Furthermore, as in us the will corresponds to the intellect, so the appetite—or the impulse to act which tends towards a new perception—corresponds to perception in every primitive Entelechy (sc. Monads). In fact, not only is the variety of the object represented in the perceiver, but also the variation of the representation itself, because even that which needs to be represented is varied.[17]

Accordingly, Leibniz defines perception as the representation of external variation in the internal.[18] In this way, he takes it for granted that every first entelechy, or monad, "possesses an internal variation, according to which external actions are varied."[19] Consistent with this, we read in the *Monadology*: "The transitory state that involves and represents a multitude within the unity, or in the simple substance, is nothing other than what one calls *perception*."[20] And, in the *Principes de la nature et de la grâce*, he defines perception as "the inner state of the monad representing external things."[21]

This formulation should not to be understood as though, at first, there exist external things—even mind-independent things—and then there are inner states corresponding to them. On the contrary, "external things" are nothing but phenomena that are actively produced by and within the monad, where they remain. This transitory state is not only the state of the perceiving monad but also the state of the whole world, and, as such, the

---

[15] GP VII 529, June 4, 1710: "[C]orresponsus interni et externi seu repraesentatio externi in interno, compositi in simplice, multitudinis in unitate revera perceptionem constituit."

[16] GP III 574 f., December 1710: "Car perception est la representation de la multitude dans le simple; et l'appetit est la tendance d'une perception à une autre: or ces deux choses sont dans toutes les Monades, car autrement une Monade n'auroit aucun rapport au reste des choses." Similarly to Nicolas Remond, only using *l'unité* as synonymous of *le simple* (GP III 622).

[17] GP VII 330 (1710). "Porro ut in nobis intellectioni respondet voluntas, ita in omni Entelechia primitiva (scil. *Monada*) perceptioni respondet appetitus, seu agendi conatus ad novam perceptionem tendens. Neque enim tantum in percipiente varietas objecti repraesentatur, sed etiam fit variatio ipsius repraesentationis, quia etiam repraesentandum variatur."

[18] GP VII 329f. "Sed perceptio nihil aliud est, quam illa ipsa repraesentatio variationis externae in interna."

[19] GP VII 329. "Nam omnis Entelechia prima habet variationem internam, secundum quam etiam variantur actiones externae."

[20] GP VI 608, §14. "L' état passager, qui enveloppe et represente une multitude dans l'unité, ou dans la substance simple, n'est autre chose que ce qu'on appelle la Perception."

[21] GP VI 600 (before September 1714): "la Perception qui est l'état interieur de la Monade representant les choses externes."

state of all monads which constitute their world and the pre-established harmony ruling therein.

Writing sometime after May 5, 1706, to Christian Wolff, Leibniz uses a simplified terminology to express the same doctrine. Instead of attributing perception and appetite to the monad, he explains that "in the soul there are these two: a state and the tendency to another state."[22]

With respect to the fact that the monad represents also its future states, Leibniz invents the term *percepturitio*—a perception that will be in the future—using this new word instead of *appetitus*. Even the force Leibniz "gives" to substances, still in 1712, means "nothing other than a state from which another state follows, if nothing prevents it."[23]

That the *perceptum* can be nothing less than the whole world is typical of Leibniz's rationalism, which cannot find a reason for a restriction on a part. But we should remember that, for Leibniz, the world is not a whole, not a substance at all; the world is nothing other than the community of all compatible monads:

> The infinite universe itself could not be a single or whole Being, in the same way that infinite Number could not be one whole, something which others have shown already.
>
> I call the World the entire collection of extant things, and all that follows from them, such that one could not at all say that several worlds might exist at a different time and different place.[24]

To understand what is meant by a world being a community of all compatible substances or monads, we must go a step further and ask what constitutes a monad as such. Perception being the only activity by which the monad operates, it is therefore exactly that which constitutes the monad as a possibility in God's mind already before Creation: "I will reply that God is the cause of all that exists outside himself, not that he is the cause of his own intellect, nor therefore of the ideas showing the essences of things."[25] The ideas that show the essences of things, namely possible individuals, we

---

[22] GLW 56. "In anima duo sunt: Status et tendentia ad alium statum."

[23] A. Robinet, *Malebranche et Leibniz, relations personnelles, présentées avec les textes complets des auteurs et de leurs correspondants revus, corrigés et inédits*, Paris, 1955, p. 420f. "Par la force que je donne aux substances, je n'entends autre chose qu'un estat duquel suit un autre estat, si rien ne l'empeche." Similarly, already in 1691, see LH IV 3,4 Bl.14. Cf. GP III 341 and GM VII 17ff. Leibniz uses the formulation "si rien ne l'empeche," or its Latin equivalent "nisi quid impediat," from as early as 1679, meaning the passive role each substance plays during its self-constitution.

[24] A VI iv 2308.20 (ca. 1685). "ipsum Universum infinitum non fore Ens unum aut totum, quemadmodum nec Numerus infinitus unum totum est, quod jam alii ostenderunt." *Theodicy* §8: "J'appelle Monde toute la suite et toute la collection de toutes les choses existantes, afin qu'on ne dise point que plusieurs mondes pouvoient exister en différent temps et différent lieux"; Cf. *Causa Dei* §15, GP VI 440.

[25] A VI iv 1362.17 (1677). "respondebo Deum esse causam omnium quae existunt extra ipsum, non vero esse causam sui intellectus nec proinde idearum essentias rerum exhibentium."

should understand as monads. At the same time, he writes to Honoré Fabri: "So not essences, but things, are created."[26]

Instead of saying that the complete notion is constituted that way, Leibniz takes the finished product as a starting point for comprehending all that occurs to a simple substance as a consequence out of its idea. This idea is nothing other than an alternative way of understanding the complete notion as constituted by the sequence of perceptions: "What happens to each one is but the consequence of its idea alone." This follows the statement: "All that can ever happen to us, are the consequences of our being."[27] Leibniz explains to Arnauld: "Every present state happens to the substance *spontaneously* [that is, without any external influence], being nothing other than the sequence out of its preceding state."[28]

In one of his earliest formulations, we find in a footnote already the full meaning of a "complete notion": it comprehends all that is in a substance and so also all external things or, in other words, the complete universe:

> A complete thing, or substance, [is that] the complete notion of which [contains] all things that are in it, whence it also contains all external things, or the whole universe.[29]

Insisting that all monads are accompanied by a *manière de corps organique*, Leibniz amplifies this claim by relating it to the perceptions of the monad. He writes to Lady Masham in May 1704: "I hold not only that all Souls or Entelechies have with them an organic bodily manner, proportioned to their perceptions."[30] This means that perceptions determine the kind of organic body that is attached to the monad, which itself is not corporeal.

For Leibniz, the most harmonious equates to the most possible and the most compatible. Therefore, compatibility is the real principle of existence and even the principle for the composition of possible worlds. Strictly speaking, this principle consists in the compatibility of simultaneous perceptions in each of the possible worlds.

Responding to Locke in his *Nouveaux Essais*, Leibniz declares that "the reality of all things other than simple substances consists only in the foundation of the perceptions or phenomena of simple substances."[31] Leibniz speaks here of "perceptions," with regard to

---

[26] A II,1² 463, Leibniz to Honorato Fabri, beginning of 1677: "neque enim essentiae sed res creantur."

[27] A VI iv 1550f. (Beginning of 1686) "Tout ce qui nous peut jamais arriver, ne sont que des suites de nostre estre." "Ce qui arrive à chacune n'est qu'une suite de son idée toute seule."

[28] A II ii 53, GP II 47. "Tout estat present d'une substance luy arrive spontainement, et n'est qu'une suite de son estat precedent." Translated by Roger Ariew and Eric Watkins in *Readings in Modern Philosophy*, vol. I (Indianapolis, Hackett, 2000), p. 264.

[29] A VI iv 631 (1685–1686). "Res completa seu substantia ejus cujus completa notione [continet] omnia quae in ipsa unde et omnia aliena seu totum universum."

[30] GP III 340 (May 1704) "[J]e tiens non seulement que ces Ames ou Entelechies ont toutes une maniere de corps organique avec elles proportionné à leur perceptions."

[31] NE II, 12 §5, A VI vi 145.18–21: "Car le premier entendement est l'origine des choses; et même la realité de toutes choses excepté les substances simples, ne consiste que dans le fondement des perceptions

the actions of the monad, and of "phenomena," with regard to the result of these actions. Given the fact that nothing enters the monad from outside, the basis of perceptions and phenomena are the perfections that emanate from God and that the monad acquires while constituting itself. It is important to consider the meaning of "emanation." The traditional concept "*causa per emanationem*" means a cause that remains in its effect. Leibniz takes this to imply an efficient cause without change of itself.[32] According to this way of speaking, we remain always in God's hand.

It is our mind that produces the phenomenon; the divine mind—or, more precisely, God's will—creates the thing. That is, it transposes the phenomena—generated by perceptions—into existence: "Our mind produces the phenomenon; the divine (mind), the thing."[33]

When Leibniz says that God, being himself the universal source of everything, has made monads the sources of their phenomena, he does not mean that God created their individuality but that the monad is intended by God to receive its phenomena from its own spontaneous or free actions; that is, precisely through the sequence of its perceptions:

> For God expresses everything perfectly, all at once, the possible and the existent, past, present and future. He is the universal source of all, and the created Monads imitate him as far as it is possible for creatures to do so: he has made them sources of their phenomena, that contain connections, more or less distinct, to all, according to the degrees of perfection of each of these substances.[34]

This is the only way in which the totality of possibilities could have constituted themselves. Each perception is born from preceding ones, following the laws of good and evil and harmonizing with all that happens in the community of compatible monads, that is, in their possible world ("It is from preceding perceptions themselves that subsequent perceptions are born, by the laws of appetites").[35] Similarly, in *Principes de la nature et de la grâce*, Leibniz declares: "the perceptions in the Monad are born out of one another according to the laws of the Appetites, or the *final causes of good and evil*."[36]

The subject or nature of the perceiver consists in that which remains the same through all the changes it undergoes. That is, the harmonious nexus of perceptions constitutes

o-u des phenomenes des substances simples." Gerhardt read wrongly *perceptions des phénomenes* (GP V 132).

[32] A VI ii 490.2 (1671–1672): "(Causa per emanationem) est causa efficiens sine mutatione sui."
[33] C 528, (perhaps about 1710): "Nostra Mens phaenomenon facit, divina Rem."
[34] GP IV 564: "Car Dieu exprime tout parfaitement à la fois, possible et existant, passé, present et futur. Il est la source universelle de tout, et les Monades creées l'imitent autant qu'il est possible que des creatures le fassent: il les a faites sources de leur phenomenes, qui contiennent des rapports à tout, mais plus ou moins distincts, selon les degrés de perfection de chacune de ces substances."
[35] GP IV 551 (1702): "Ce sont les perceptions precedentes mêmes dont naissent les suivantes par les loix des appetits."
[36] GP VI 599: "[L]es perceptions dans la Monade naissent les unes des autres par les loix des Appetits, ou des *causes finales du bien et du mal*."

the unity of the perceiver itself: "The operation proper to the soul is perception, and the nexus of perceptions, according to which subsequent perceptions are derived from preceding perceptions, forms the unity of the perceiver."[37]

Moreover, the terminology of "internal/external" should be understood as only metaphorical. In fact, there is nothing external apart from monads, which produce in the same way their world inside themselves. Furthermore, what Leibniz calls "phenomena" in fact remain inside the monad and are, in addition to the monads from which they result, the only existing things in the world ("I believe that there are only monads in nature, everything else being only the phenomena resulting from them").[38]

No monad ever stops perceiving. Even death is nothing other than a state of confused perception, a state out of which we shall emerge because our representations of the universe will not remain forever in confusion:

> The substance that has perception, being naturally representative of the whole universe according to its point of view, would never cease to represent, since the universe never ceases to act. And death is nothing other than a state of highly confused perceptions, which differs only more or less from the state in which one finds oneself when one sleeps without having dreams that one can remember, or when one is in a faint that takes away our sentience. But there are reasons to think that these confused perceptions regenerate themselves, as it happens when we awake from a slumber or lethargy: it is true that the regeneration after death does not happen so soon in simple animals, but it remains still reasonable that it happens; for that which is a representation of the universe would not remain forever in confusion.[39]

Even the "petites perceptions"—as different as they are from the monadic perceptions with which we are presently concerned—are credited with functions in the field of physics or the philosophy of nature, which Leibniz normally ascribes to metaphysics (or, as he likes to refer to this domain, Pneumatics).[40]

[37] Leibniz to Des Bosses, April 24, 1709 (GP II 372). "Operatio autem animae propria est perceptio, et unitatem percipientis facit perceptionum nexus, secundum quem sequentes ex praecedentibus derivantur."

[38] Erdmann 745 B (September 11, 1716): "Je crois qu'il n'y a que des monades dans la nature, le reste n'étant que les phenomenes qui en résultent."

[39] Draft for the letter to Hartsoeker (February 6, 1711) GP III 521: "La substance qui a de la perception, estant naturellement representative de tout l'univers suivant son point de veue, ne sauroit jamais cesser de representer, comme l'univers ne cesse jamais d'agir. Et la mort n'est autre chose que l'etat des perceptions fort confuses, qui ne differe que du plus ou moins de l'etat, où l'on se trouve quand on dort, sans avoir des songes dont on se puisse souvenir, ou lorsqu'on est dans quelque evanouissement qui nous ote le sentiment. Mais il y a lieu de juger, que ces perceptions confuses se redeveloppent, comme il arrive quand nous nous reveillons d'un assoupissement ou d'une lethargie: il est vray que le redeveloppements apres la mort n'arrivent pas si tost dans les simples animaux, mais il demeure tousjours raisonnable qu'ils arrivent; car ce qui est une representation de l'univers ne sauroit tousjours demeurer en confusion."

[40] A VI vi 57.29–30: "une bonne Pneumatique, qui comprenne la connoissance de Dieu, des ames, et des substances simples en general"; and 527.2–3: "sous le titre de Metaphysique ou Pneumatique."

In several parts of his *Nouveaux Essais sur l'entendement humain*, Leibniz tries to get Locke closer to his special Metaphysics—for example, when he explains that these insensible perceptions constitute the same individual who is characterized by the traces which these perceptions conserve from the individual's former states, thereby connecting these states with his present state. This is a process—Leibniz clarifies—that can only be understood by a higher spirit, that is, by God or perhaps by angels.[41]

This purely metaphysical explanation would surely not have been understood by Locke in ignorance of Leibniz's metaphysics, any more than the following remark that more precisely aims at Leibniz's mostly private doctrines. In it he reveals that even the pre-established harmony between soul and body is to be explained by these insensible perceptions. Clearly, this explanation could only be given by appealing to monadic perception:

> It is also by means of the insensible perceptions that I explain this wonderful pre-established harmony between soul and body, and indeed among all the monads or simple substances, which takes the place of the untenable influence of one on another.[42]

The following paragraph begins with the remark that the *petites perceptions* have a greater efficacy than people usually think. They are in fact what builds, among other things, the connection that each thing has with all the other things in the universe:

> These minute perceptions, then, are of greater efficacy than one thinks. They constitute that *je ne sais quoi*, those tastes, those images of sensible qualities, clear in the aggregate, but confused as to the parts; those impressions that surrounding bodies make on us, and which involve the infinite; that connection that each being has with all the rest of the universe.[43]

Two months before the end of his life, Leibniz described to Dangicourt in great detail what his pre-established harmony consists in. He goes back a long way. He recalls that only simple substances, which he calls "monads," are real substances. In nature, there are only monads; everything else being only phenomena resulting from monads. In the monad itself there are only perceptions and appetites, or a striving for new perceptions. Each monad is a mirror of the universe, enfolding from the beginning all its states, past

[41] A VI vi 55.8–10. "Ces perceptions insensibles marquent encore et constituent le même individu, qui est caracterisé par les traces, qu'elles conservent des estats précedens de cet individu, en faisant la connexion avec son estat present, qui se peuvent connoistre par un esprit superieur."

[42] A VI vi 55.17–19. "C'est aussi par les perceptions insensibles que j'explique cette admirable harmonie préestablie de l'ame et du corps, et même de toutes les Monades ou substances simples qui supplée à l'influence insoutenable des uns sur les autres."

[43] A VI vi 54.26–55.3. "Ces petites perceptions sont donc de plus grande efficace qu'on ne pense. Ce sont elles, qui forment ce je ne say quoy, ces gouts, ces images des qualités des sens, claires dans l'assemblage, mais confuses dans les parties; ces impressions que les corps envionnans font sur nous, et qui enveloppent l'infini; cette liaison que chaque estre a avec tout le reste de l'univers."

and future, in such a way that an omniscient being could read out of it the complete history of the monad. The monads, being mirrors of one and the same world that they represent, correspond to one another and form an infinite multiplication of the same world, even though the universe itself is a diffusion to infinity.[44]

Of course, the correspondence between body and soul, as Leibniz shows in his *Système nouveau de la nature et de la communication des substances* of 1695, is only a particular instance of his hypothesis asserting a pre-established harmony, which at that time he still called a "*Hypothèse des accords.*" The new terminology was introduced publicly in September 1696 in the *Journal des Savants* and became his preference from then onward.[45] After rejecting both theories of influence and of occasionalism, he writes there that there remains no other hypothesis but his own hypothesis of a pre-established harmony:

> Hence there remains only my Hypothesis, namely that of the harmony pre-established by divine artifice, which from the beginning formed each of these substances . . . each of which is only following its own laws, which it received with its nature, yet in accordance with the others: just as if there were a mutual influence, or as though God were always intervening beyond his general concurrence.[46]

In his *Nouveaux Essais sur l'entendement humain,* written around 1704, he refers to himself as l'*Auteur* du Systéme de l'Harmonie préétablie,[47] assuming this to be generally known in the literary world. With it, he enters into a discussion with his contemporaries although limiting his comments to the created world and avoiding references to his metaphysics of possible worlds. Nevertheless, his remarks should be understood in relation to his doctrine of possible worlds and possibilities, at least with reference to his Principle of Harlequin: *Tout comme icy.* It is God who has pre-established everything. Looking at his creation, this thesis is acceptable. But strictly speaking, or in metaphysical rigor, God finds all the possibilities already in his mind, including those that are to be created

---

[44] Erdmann 745 ff. (September 11, 1716): "Les veritables substances ne sont que les substances simples ou ce que j'appelle Monades. Et je crois qu'il n'y a que des monades dans la nature, le reste n'etant que les phénomènes qui en résultent. Chaque monade est un miroir de l'univers selon son point de vue . . . Et en elle meme il n'y a que des perceptions et tendances à des nouvelles perceptions ou appétits. . . . La monade donc enveloppe par avance en elle ses ètats passés ou futurs, en sorte qu'un omniscient l'y peut lire; et les monades s'accordent entr'elles, étant des miroirs d'un même univers à l'infini, quoique l'univers même soit d'une diffusion à l'infini. C'est en cela que consiste mon Harmonie préétablie."

[45] *Journal des Savants*, Paris, 1696, p. ix.

[46] GP IV 501 (1695). "Ainsi il ne reste que mon Hypothese, c'est à dire que la voye de l'harmonie pré-établie par un artifice divin prevenant, lequel dès le commencement a formé chacune de ces substances . . ., qu'en ne suivant que ses propres loix, qu'elle a receues avec son estre, elle s'accorde pourtant avec l'autre: tout comme s'il y avoit une influence mutuelle, ou comme si Dieu y mettoit toujours la main au delà de son concours general."

[47] See A VI vi 43.

("God is omniscient. For he knows the possibilities or essences of things from the consideration of his own intellect").[48]

Focusing his attention on created beings, Leibniz speaks of God as the author of a pre-established harmony.[49] This "pre-establishment" is to be understood as an act of God's will in creating the world that he recognized as the best among all possible worlds. Already in 1689/90, Leibniz states:

> And so coherence is the sign of truth; the will of God, on the other hand, is the cause; the formal reason is that God perceives something optimum or harmonious, or that something is pleasing to God. And so the divine delight itself is, so to speak, the existence of things.[50]

However, in view of the fact that God is not the author of the essences or possibilities that constitute the infinity of possible worlds, including our world before creation, this thesis has to be relativized. As we have seen, according to Leibniz, "God is the cause of all that exists outside himself, not . . . the cause of his own intellect, nor therefore of the ideas showing the essences of things."[51]

In sum, perception and the transition to new perceptions are the only activities of the monad, which have their origin in preceding perceptions and therefore in the monad itself, where they also remain. The sequence of these spontaneously constituted perceptions characterizes and constitutes each monad as such. The content of a monad's perception is the momentary state of the whole world or, more precisely, the state of all the monads that are compatible with that monad. In every possible world, these sequences are fully determinate. Therefore Leibniz can speak about the law of their nature. It is only this feature that allows a fair division of possibilities in possible worlds, each with its perfect history belonging to exactly one world. This is the basis on which the doctrine of pre-established harmony should be understood. This doctrine refers chiefly to the created world and only in a more restricted sense to the harmony of body and soul.

---

[48]   A VI iv 2317.9ff.(1685). "Deus est omniscius. Nam possibilitates seu essentias rerum novit ex consideratione intellectus sui."

[49]   GP IV 499 and 501: "la voye de l'harmonie pré-établie, par un artifice divin prevenant"; and still in August 1716, he wrote: "en vertu de l'harmonie que Dieu a preétablie" (GP VII 411).

[50]   A VI iv 1637.15–17 (1689–1690): "Signum veritatis itaque cohaerentia est, causa autem est voluntas Dei, formalis ratio est quod Deus percipit aliquid optimum esse seu harmonicωtaton, sive quod aliquid Deo placet. Itaque ipsa ut ita dicam voluptas divina est rerum existentia."

[51]   A VI iv 1362.17 (1677–1678): "[R]espondebo Deum esse causam omnium quae existunt extra ipsum, non vero esse causam sui intellectus nec proinde idearum essentias rerum exhibentium."

CHAPTER 21

MIND AND BODY

ADAM HARMER

INTRODUCTION

LEIBNIZ systematically distinguishes between substances and aggregates. A substance is a being that must have true unity (Leibniz calls it an *unum per se*), whereas an aggregate is merely a collection of other beings and not itself a single thing or a substance. An aggregate has merely accidental unity, which, in Leibniz's view, originates in some mind perceiving the collection together (Leibniz calls it an *unum per accidens*). Leibniz illustrates this distinction by contrasting, for example, herds and armies (aggregates) with sheep and soldiers (substances). Characterizing substance as *unum per se* fits rather nicely with the account we find in Leibniz's *Monadology* (1714); that is, that the world is constituted by the harmonious perceptions and appetites of infinitely many simple, active, mind-like substances—what he calls *monads*. A monad, insofar as it is *simple*, is not at risk of failing to meet Leibniz's strict criteria of substantial unity.

Yet for many years prior to the *Monadology*, and even in the *Monadology* itself, Leibniz appears willing to extend the term "substance" to things other than monads: *animals* and, more broadly, *living beings* are characterized as substances. But living beings are not simple substances; they are composites of a soul (or dominant monad) and an organic body, a body that is itself constituted by a mass of infinitely many other substances. Given that a substance must be an *unum per se*, can Leibniz establish that living beings are substances? Or should he conclude that the only substances are simple, mind-like monads?

One way to approach these questions is to consider Leibniz's views about the union of mind and body. The central questions I address in this chapter are:

1. Do the mind and body interact? How is interaction related to union?
2. Do mind and body together constitute an *unum per se*? If so, what is Leibniz's account of the per se unity of mind-body composites?

A few points of clarification are required concerning how we should understand the character of these questions for Leibniz. For some philosophers (Descartes, for instance), the human being is the only mind-body composite. For Leibniz, however, the problem of mind-body union is not restricted to human beings but has a broader application. *Soul*, for Leibniz, is a genus with various species falling under it: rational souls—minds—and nonrational souls—what Leibniz sometimes calls "forms." For this reason, I will characterize the central question as one of *soul-body union*, rather than *mind-body union*. Furthermore, in Leibniz's view, the soul and body are not really distinct substances in their own right (as they are for Descartes and other dualists). The human body, on Leibniz's view, is not a material substance at all, but a collection or aggregate of substances—what Leibniz often calls "second matter." (There are also difficult questions about the nature of the substances that make up these aggregates—are they composites themselves or are they mind-like simple substances?—that I will ignore at present.) Leibniz's account of the soul differs from the Cartesian one, too. In some texts, Leibniz characterizes the soul as a substance in its own right, whereas at other times he more guardedly describes the soul as only the *form* of a substance.

With all of this in mind, Leibniz's answers to our central questions can be outlined as follows, leaving the details aside to be developed later. Leibniz denies that soul and body genuinely interact, but he does not deny the *appearance* of interaction. He proposes the system of pre-established harmony to explain the apparent interaction of soul and body.[1] However, I will argue that pre-established harmony is not an explanation of the *unity* of soul-body composites, although it does account for *union* in another sense.[2] Despite this fact, there are texts in which Leibniz seems to claim that soul and body together constitute an *unum* per se.[3] Nevertheless, I will provide reason to think that Leibniz does not provide an account of soul-body unity. I will suggest that if there are any prospects in Leibniz for providing such an account, they do not rely on any relation (such as pre-established harmony) between the soul and the body but, instead, on certain *structural features* of soul-body composites.

---

[1] Pre-established harmony is also called the *hypothesis of concomitance*. See, e.g., A II ii 53.

[2] Some interpreters suggest Leibniz changed his mind on this issue. See, e.g., Daniel Garber, *Leibniz: Body, Substance, Monad* (New York: Oxford University Press, 2009), p. 80; and Donald Rutherford, *Leibniz and the Rational Order of Nature* (New York: Cambridge University Press, 1995), chapter 10.

[3] The texts in which Leibniz seems to characterize soul-body composites as per se unities are often difficult to interpret. First of all, Leibniz rarely uses the phrase "*unum per se*" explicitly, using, for example, "*Ens vere unum,*" "*veritablement un estre,*" or "*unité veritable*" instead. (I should note that I am treating all such phrases as effectively equivalent, although there might be some reason to resist this.) Second, it is often not altogether clear what the unity is being attributed to; i.e., is it being attributed the soul-body composite or simply the soul? For a representative selection, which is by no means complete, see, e.g., A VI iv 627, A VI iv 1506-1508., A VI iv 1583, A II ii 249, GP IV 395, GP IV 459, GP IV 572.

SOUL-BODY INTERACTION

Pre-established harmony is Leibniz's alternative to the extant seventeenth-century accounts of soul-body interaction. In the *New System*, after discussing the shortcomings of Descartes's and Malebranche's treatments of the problem, Leibniz writes, "I was led, little by little, to a view that surprised me, but which seems inevitable, and which, in fact, has very great advantages and rather considerable beauty."[4] He goes on to elaborate his view:

> [W]e must say that God originally created the soul (and any other real unity) in such a way that everything must arise for it from its own depths, through a perfect *spontaneity* relative to itself, and yet with a perfect *conformity* relative to external things.[5]

Although there is, strictly speaking, no causal interaction between soul and body, pre-established harmony stands in for an account of interaction, since, as Leibniz continues,

> [t]here will be a perfect agreement among all these substances, producing the same effect that would be noticed if they communicated through the transmission of species or qualities, as the common philosophers imagine they do.[6]

Although not a causal relation, pre-established harmony is nonetheless a relation between soul and body, one that explains the appearance of their interaction.

In these passages, we find two main features of pre-established harmony:

> *Spontaneity:* Everything that happens to a soul arises from its own depths. That is, for any state, x, of a soul, s, the causal ancestry of x contains only states of s.
>
> *Conformity:* The states of soul and body *agree* with each other. That is, for any state of the soul, y, there is a corresponding state of its body, y^*, such that y and y^* agree with one another, though they have no causal connection.

Taken together, spontaneity and conformity explain the appearance of interaction between soul and body. Leibniz sometimes says that the soul and body each follow their own laws (the soul the laws of final causes, the body the laws of efficient causes or mechanical laws), yet they agree perfectly with one another.[7] That is, a soul really does cause its own states, but it does not cause the states of any body. (One thing to note about these passages is that at no time is causal efficacy attributed to a body. A body, for Leibniz, is an aggregate of substances, and any causal efficacy it appears to have is ultimately explained

---

[4] GP IV 484; AG 143.
[5] GP IV 484; AG 143.
[6] GP IV 484; AG 143.
[7] GP VI 620; AG 223.

by the *forms* of the substances in the aggregate. I will not develop this any further here, though.)

It is also worth noting that pre-established harmony has both a specific and a general application. The specific application of pre-established harmony explains the appearance of interaction between soul and body. The general application explains the appearance of interaction between any two (or more) substances. One way to express this aspect of Leibniz's view is to say that he denies *intersubstantial causation*—causation between substances—but accepts *intrasubstantial causation*—causation within a substance. Neither do minds, strictly speaking, interact with bodies, nor do bodies, strictly speaking, interact with each other. As such, my soul and body not only *conform* or *agree* with each other, they agree with all other created substances as well. Thus, the notion of *harmony* has various senses for Leibniz, including soul-body harmony, intersubstantial harmony, harmony between types of explanations (i.e., mechanical and final-causal), and so on.

At this point, we might wonder: how does pre-established harmony relate to soul-body union? I will take up this question at more length in the following section. For now, let us consider the following, slightly more modest question: how does pre-established harmony even explain the connection between a particular soul and body such that they jointly make up one animal? Given that the soul and body do not, strictly speaking, interact, and furthermore that each substance harmonizes with every other substance, not only the substances contained in its body, how can Leibniz explain the privileged connection between the soul and body of an individual animal? Leibniz's account is that souls perceive their own bodies more distinctly than they perceive anything else in the world.[8] Thus, I perceive my hands, legs, and feet more distinctly than I perceive the chair I am sitting on or the table in front of me. This may sound somewhat surprising. As Antoine Arnauld plausibly objects, it seems odd to claim that I perceive, for example, the motions of lymph in my lymphatic vessels more distinctly than I perceive the motions of Saturn, since the motions of lymph in my lymphatic vessels are effectively inscrutable to me.[9] Leibniz's response to Arnauld's question is somewhat puzzling: he claims that I perceive my body more distinctly than, for example, the motions of Saturn because my body provides my soul with a particular perspective on the world.[10] That is, as Leibniz has written earlier in the correspondence with Arnauld, a particular mind "is an expression of the phenomena of all other bodies in accordance with the relationship to its own."[11] In effect, my body is the lens through which my soul sees the rest of the world. To make this slightly more palatable, it must be kept in mind that, for Leibniz, the entire physical world is interconnected such that, at any given time, my body expresses the entire universe.[12] This provides some basis for the view that I can perceive the universe

[8]   A II ii 116; GP II 74.
[9]   A II ii 221; GP II 105–106.
[10]   A II ii 240; GP II 113.
[11]   A II ii 82; GP II 58; LA 65.
[12]   GP VI 618.

beyond my body simply by perceiving my body. Ultimately, then, the distinctness of the perceptual relation explains why my body is *my body* despite the fact that my soul and body do not strictly interact and that my soul conforms with the entire universe.

Pre-established Harmony and Soul-Body Unity

Although pre-established harmony explains the apparent interaction of soul and body, I will argue that it does not explain how soul and body together constitute an *unum per se*, although it does explain *union* in another sense. Before we can address this issue, however, we must consider whether and to what extent Leibniz is committed to the unity of soul-body composites in the first place.

There is an ongoing controversy in the literature concerning Leibniz's commitment to *corporeal substances*. Daniel Garber has suggested that Leibniz's basic ontological commitments change dramatically between what he calls the "Middle Years" (roughly 1680–1700) and the "Mature Period" (roughly 1700–16).[13] (There is also controversy about where to draw the dividing lines between the different periods of Leibniz's thought, although nothing I say here turns on the particular dates I have chosen.) Garber's contention is that, in the Middle Years, Leibniz is committed to *bona fide* corporeal substances, composites of soul and body that have true, substantial unity, and that these corporeal substances are the basic constituents of reality. Later on, this commitment disappears and the fundamental constituents of reality come to be simple, partless, active substances, which Leibniz calls "monads." However, others, Robert Adams and Robert Sleigh to cite two canonical sources, argue that Leibniz's commitment to simple substances is already implicit in his views during the so-called Middle Years.[14] That the commitment to simple substances comes to take center stage does not, therefore, betray a radical change of mind on Leibniz's part, but instead is just the natural development of his implicit commitments or maybe just an original commitment being made explicit. A third option worth noting, which has been highlighted by some of the recent literature on this topic, is that, even during the Mature Period, Leibniz uses the language of corporeal (or sometimes composite) substance.[15] This suggests that the shift

---

[13] See Daniel Garber, "Leibniz and the foundations of physics: The Middle Years," in *The Natural Philosophy of Leibniz*, edited by K. Okruhlik and J. R. Brown (Dordrecht: Kluwer Academic Publishers, 1985), pp. 27–130; and Garber, *Leibniz*, p. 382.

[14] See Robert C. Sleigh Jr., *Leibniz and Arnauld: A Commentary on Their Correspondence* (New Haven: Yale University Press, 1990); and Robert M. Adams, *Leibniz: Determinist, Theist, Idealist* (New York: Oxford University Press, 1994).

[15] See, e.g., Jeff McDonough, "Leibniz's conciliatory account of substance," in *Philosopher's Imprint* 13/6 (2013), pp. 1–23; Look-Rutherford, Introduction; and Richard T. W. Arthur and Peter Lopston, "Leibniz's body realism: Two interpretations," in *The Leibniz Review 16* (2006), pp. 1–42.

between corporeal substances and monads may not be primarily a developmental shift. Perhaps a better way to understand what is going on is to think of Leibniz as wrestling with different conceptions of substance throughout his entire career. I do not aim to settle this issue here, but merely to keep it in view while considering Leibniz's engagement with the question of soul-body unity.

This dispute has clear implications for the topic of soul-body unity because, if Leibniz was always a monadologist, it is possible that he never took seriously the view that soul and body together make up an *unum per se*. If this is correct, any search for Leibniz's account of soul-body unity will be in vain. I cannot definitively rule this option out. Nevertheless, it is undeniable that there are texts in which Leibniz at least seems to characterize soul-body composites, the human being in particular, as per se unities.[16] For this reason, it seems worthwhile to look for an account.

A good place to start the search is with pre-established harmony itself. A *prima facie* reason to think pre-established harmony is a good candidate is that Leibniz often presents pre-established harmony as an account of soul-body *union*. One example is in Leibniz's *New System*, published in 1695, the full title of which is *New System of the Nature of Substances and their Communication, and of the Union which Exists between the Soul and the Body* (1695).[17] The account of union we find there is pre-established harmony. Some commentators have suggested, on this basis, that pre-established harmony should be read as an account of the *unity* of soul-body composites. Daniel Garber, for instance, writes that "since the result of a union is a unity, and a genuine unity is, for Leibniz, a substance, this suggests that the hypothesis of concomitance [i.e., pre-established harmony] is supposed to account for the fact that mind and body together constitute a substance."[18] However, there are reasons to resist this interpretation of Leibniz's view.

In an exchange with the Jesuit Father Tournemine between 1704 and 1708, Leibniz denies both that pre-established harmony provides an account of soul-body unity and that he ever intended it to do so. Tournemine had voiced concern that, although Leibniz often claims that pre-established harmony fares better than the Cartesians (by which Leibniz means the occasionalists) as an account of soul-body union, it does no better at explaining their unity.[19] Here is Leibniz's reply:

> I have to admit that I would be greatly mistaken if I objected against the Cartesians that the agreement which, according to them, God maintains immediately

---

[16] For discussion of some early texts (late 1660s) in which Leibniz explicitly upholds the unity of soul-body composites, see Maria Rosa Antognazza, "Leibniz's theory of substance and his metaphysics of the Incarnation," in *Locke and Leibniz on Substance and Identity*, edited by Paul Lodge and T. W. C. Stoneham (Abingdon/New York: Routledge, 2014). The text Antognazza discusses in some detail is "De Incarnatione Dei." See A VI.1, 532.

[17] GP IV 477–87.

[18] Garber, *Leibniz*, p. 80.

[19] For Tournemine's criticism, see René-Joseph de Tournemine, "*Conjectures sur l'Union de l'Ame et du Corps,*" *Journal de Trevoux, ou Memoires pour servir a l'histoire des sciences et des arts*, vol. III (May 1703), 869; WFN 251.

between the soul and the body, does not create a genuine unity, because most certainly my *pre-established harmony* could not do it any better. My aim was to explain naturally what they explain by perpetual miracles, and in doing so I attempted only to give an explanation of the phenomena, that is to say, of the relation we perceive between the soul and the body. But since this metaphysical union, which is added on to that, is not a phenomenon, and as we have not even been given an intelligible notion of it, I have not taken it upon myself to look for an explanation of it.[20]

In this passage, Leibniz claims that the goal of pre-established harmony is (and was) to explain "the relation we perceive between the soul and the body," by which he means their apparent interaction. He distinguishes this goal from a different more ambitious one: to explain the "metaphysical union" between soul and body. In a letter to Burcher de Volder, which Leibniz wrote after reading Tournemine's objection but before publishing his reply, Leibniz characterizes the hope for an account of metaphysical union as "utopian."[21] In this passage, Leibniz even appears dubious that the notion of metaphysical union has been given an intelligible characterization.

If we turn back to the *New System*, it is possible to see merely the aim that Leibniz suggests: an account of *interaction*. There, Leibniz characterizes pre-established harmony as a "mutual relationship, arranged in advance in each substance in the universe, which produces what we call their communication, and which alone constitutes *the union of soul and body*."[22] This brief formulation of his view, read in light of his remark to Tournemine, can be seen as further indication that by "union" Leibniz means "communication" (i.e., the deflationary sense of "interaction" developed earlier in this chapter) and nothing more. If we turn to the *Monadology*, we find Leibniz using "union" and "conformity" almost interchangeably: "these principles [i.e., the principles of pre-established harmony] have given me a way of naturally explaining the union, or rather the conformity of the soul and the organic body."[23]

If pre-established harmony was always intended to account only for interaction, there is good reason to resist the claim that pre-established harmony explains the unity of soul-body composites. Interaction and unity are importantly different. Two things can interact without thereby constituting a unity.[24] When the sense of "union" involved in pre-established harmony is understood as "interaction," the plausibility of inferring *genuine unity* from *union*, as Garber does, quickly disappears.

---

[20] GP VI 595; WFN 250.
[21] GP II 281; Lodge, p. 481.
[22] GP IV 484–85; WFN 18.
[23] GP V 620; AG 223.
[24] For further development of this view, see Rozemond "Body and Soul," pp. 152–156.

Soul-Body Unity

Despite this, it is certainly possible that Leibniz is being disingenuous in his reply to Tournemine. Perhaps he has changed his view but is attempting to save face by denying that he ever had "utopian" hopes for pre-established harmony. Perhaps Tournemine's remarks prompted Leibniz to consider more deeply something he had been taking for granted.[25] Furthermore, if we look at some texts from Leibniz's Middle Years, it seems that Leibniz does, at least during this period, believe that soul and body together make up an *unum per se*. How can this be reconciled with Leibniz's claim that anything beyond "the phenomena" is a utopian dream, one that he never set about attempting to realize?[26]

There are various passages from Leibniz's correspondence with Arnauld, in which Leibniz attributes true unity to the composite of soul and body. Consider the following:

> Supposing that there is a soul or *substantial form* in beasts or other corporeal substances, one must reason with respect to them on this point as we all reason with respect to man, who is *an entity endowed with a true unity* that his soul gives to him, not withstanding the fact that the mass of his body is divided into organs, vessels, humors, spirits, and that the parts are undoubtedly full of an infinite number of other corporeal substances endowed with their own forms.[27]

There are two aspects of this passage that I would like to highlight, although I will focus on the first for now:

1. Leibniz claims that the soul *gives true unity to the human being*. This suggests that a soul-body composite, in this case a human being, can be an *unum per se*.
2. Leibniz's phrasing is rather tentative: *we must reason* with respect to animals as *we all reason* with respect to man. It is unclear, therefore, how strong Leibniz's commitment really is here.

In another letter to Arnauld, Leibniz writes:

> [I]t is the animated substance to which the matter belongs that is *truly one being*, and the matter taken as a mass in itself is only a pure phenomenon or well-founded appearance, as also are space and time.[28]

---

[25] For development of this view, see Rutherford, *Rational Order*, pp. 273–276.

[26] This question treats the question of "metaphysical union" as equivalent to the unity of soul-body composites. There is some reason to worry about this identification, although I cannot fully engage this issue here.

[27] A II ii 250–51, n. 77; GP II 120; LA 154; emphasis added.

[28] A II ii 249; GP II 118; WFP 131; emphasis added.

In this passage, true unity is attributed to "the animated substance." Although it may be possible to understand "the animated substance" as indicating the soul, I think there is good reason to think that Leibniz means to indicate the soul-body composite. Leibniz's correspondence with Arnauld is full of language suggestive of a roughly hylomorphic conception of substance. This is displayed by Leibniz when he says, "[a]s our body is the matter, and the soul is the form of our substance, it is the same with other bodily substances."[29] So it is natural to read "the animated substance" as referring to the soul-body composite.

What are we to make of Leibniz's claim to Tournemine that he never intended to explain the "metaphysical union" of soul and body in light of these attributions (and others like them) of true unity to the soul-body composite? Some commentators have identified the exchange with Tournemine as a turning point for Leibniz's theory of substance, after which he realized that he was no longer entitled to maintain the true unity of soul-body composites.[30] However, I think it is more likely that Leibniz is being straightforward with Tournemine; that is, that Leibniz never intended pre-established harmony to account for the unity of soul-body composites. As I see it, there are two ways to maintain this view. The first is to find a basis for downplaying the importance of the passages written to Arnauld (and others like them). The second (which I favor, as will become clear) is to consider that if Leibniz did in fact think that soul-body composites were true unities, he might have thought so, not in virtue of some relation (such as pre-established harmony) between the soul and the body, but for other reasons. I will briefly consider the first option before turning, in the following section, to the second.

That all of the texts just considered are written to Arnauld provides some reason to wonder: does Leibniz equally attribute true unity to soul-body composites outside of the Arnauld correspondence? Could Leibniz's friendliness toward a roughly hylo-morphic theory of substance be explained away as a nod to Catholic orthodoxy, one which wouldn't ruffle the feathers of the Catholic Arnauld?[31] It is not altogether clear why Catholic Orthodoxy would require a commitment to corporeal substances with true unity, and none of the discussions of this possibility has provided a compelling explanation.[32]

So, although it is possible that Leibniz's willingness to use the language of *corporeal substances* is ultimately a concession to the Catholics, more evidence is needed.

One reason internal to the texts themselves and on the basis of which we might sus-pect that the commitment to corporeal substances is not very strong is that, as noted earlier, Leibniz's phrasing in some of the passages considered is rather cautious: *one*

---

[29] A II ii 250, n. 77; GP II 119; LA 153.

[30] See Rutherford *Rational Order*, pp. 273–276.

[31] For this suggestion, see R. Adams, *Leibniz*, p. 307; see also Rutherford, *Rational Order*, p. 268.

[32] One possibility derives from the decree by the Fifth Lateran Council (1512) that the soul is to be considered the substantial form of the body. For discussion, including reasons to think this does not explain why the per se unity of corporeal substance is a Catholic commitment, see Rozemond "Body and Soul," pp. 176–177.

must reason with respect to animals as *we all reason* with respect to man. Perhaps Leibniz is simply noting a way in which "we all reason" rather than expressing a genuine commitment.

Still, there might be other, deeper theological commitments driving Leibniz's commitment to corporeal substances, although not Catholic ones. In particular, Leibniz's account of the Incarnation appears to be modeled after the union between soul and body and furthermore to require a proper substantial union between different substances.[33] The Incarnation is a mystery that Leibniz, as a Lutheran, would be motivated to accommodate. It is not only Catholic Orthodoxy, then, that might push Leibniz to account for soul-body unity, but also theological commitments much closer to home.

TRUE UNITY

Despite the evidence that Leibniz is willing to characterize soul-body composites as true unities, I do not think that pre-established harmony explains the unity of soul-body composites or that Leibniz ever thought so. Instead, I suggest that the more likely candidate for an account of unity is the *structure* of soul-body composites. Although I do not think that Leibniz ever argues for the per se unity of soul-body composites on this basis, I do think that it provides a way of understanding his stated commitment to this unity.

At least as early as 1685, Leibniz expressed the view that true unity involves *having no parts*. In the following passage, Leibniz characterized the difference between substances and aggregates in terms of having and not having parts, respectively:

> But actually no entity that is really one is composed of a plurality of parts, and every substance is indivisible, and those things that have parts are not entities, but merely phenomena.[34]

This passage was written near the beginning of Leibniz's correspondence with Arnauld. It very strongly indicates that, at this time, Leibniz believed that *having no parts* is at least a necessary condition of *being a true unity*. Of course, more needs to be said about what it means to have or not have parts. I consider this further later. For now, the passage provides some insight into why and in what sense Leibniz would be willing to attribute true unity to a soul-body composite.

If we take another look at the quoted passages, the ones in which Leibniz attributes true unity to soul-body composites, we find that none of them offers a positive account

---

[33] For a very helpful discussion of Leibniz's account of the Incarnation in relation to his philosophy, see Antognazza, "Incarnation." However, and as Antognazza also notes, it is not clear whether the type of union required by the Incarnation is the same as the substantial unity required by composite substances.

[34] A VI iv 627; Arthur, pp. 272–273.

of the unity of composites. Rather, each states that composite substances (e.g., human beings) are true unities despite the fact that the bodies of such composites have parts.[35] Consider once more: "man. . . is an entity endowed with a true unity that his soul gives to him, not withstanding the fact that the mass of his body is divided into organs, vessels, humors, spirits."[36]

In my view, Leibniz's attributions of true unity to soul-body composites are, therefore, not based on pre-established harmony but instead rely on the structure of composites. At least two questions arise at this point:

1. How can Leibniz maintain that a soul-body composite such as a human being has no parts? Is it not plain that we have parts: cells, limbs, organs, and so on?
2. Why are soul and body themselves not considered *parts* of the composite substance? Even if we can establish—in light of question 1—that the complexity of the body of a substance does not entail that the substance has parts, shouldn't we still conclude that a substance is composed of (at least) two parts: a body and a soul?

The problem indicated by question 1 can be addressed by distinguishing the *body of a substance* from the *substance itself*. In this way, Leibniz can maintain that the body of a substance has parts, although the substance itself has no parts. The body of a substance is still an aggregate for Leibniz, even though it is the body of a substance. There are various passages in which Leibniz clearly distinguishes the substance from its body, one of which we have seen earlier. In these passages, Leibniz attributes unity to the substance but not to the body. He makes analogous claims about the persistence of substances. Consider the following passage from the *New Essays*:

> So we must acknowledge that organic bodies as well as others remain "the same" only in appearance, and not strictly speaking. . . . [A]s for substantial beings, *quae uno spiritu continentur* as one of the ancient jurists says, meaning that a certain indivisible spirit animates them: one can rightly say that they remain perfectly "the same individual" in virtue of this soul or spirit which makes the *I* in substances which think.[37]

"Organic bodies" is Leibniz's term for the bodies of substances. This passage claims that the body of a substance does not persist, although the substance itself does. In light of the distinction between the substance and the body of the substance, we can say that the things mentioned earlier—cells, limbs, organs—may be parts of the *body of the substance*, but they are not parts of the *substance itself*.

---

[35] For development of the view that Leibniz presumes rather than argues for the unity of the composite, see Robert C. Sleigh, *Leibniz and Arnauld*, p. 107.

[36] A II ii 251; GP II 120; LA 154.

[37] NE 231.

Leibniz faces more difficulty in attempting to respond to question 2. Why are the soul and body not parts of the composite substance? There is a preliminary response open to Leibniz in light of how he defines "part," but it faces certain difficulties, as we will see. A part is, for Leibniz, a *homogeneous requisite*.[38] Soul and body might fail to be parts of the substance, on this definition, because they are not *homogeneous*, they are not the same kind of thing as each other or as the substance they jointly constitute.

As Leibniz writes to De Volder, "substantial unities are not parts, but the foundations of phenomena."[39] To keep track of this, I will call soul and body *constituents* of composite substances (not parts). We can then distinguish two types of composition: *part-wise composition* versus *constituent-wise composition*. As we have seen in the earlier quoted texts, Leibniz is clear that part-wise composition is incompatible with per se unity. However, the presence of constituents could still be compatible with per se unity. If so, this would allow Leibniz to maintain the per se unity of the soul-body composite despite the presence of a plurality of constituents: so long as the constituents are not parts, per se unity can be maintained.

This line of response is complicated, however, by the fact that Leibniz does not give a straightforwardly hylomorphic account of substance. Unlike Aristotle, for Leibniz, soul and body are not strictly heterogeneous because a body is ultimately resolvable into a collection of soul-like monads. So, the soul is a monad, and the body is a collection of monads. In what sense, then, do the soul and body fail to be homogeneous? This line of reasoning pushes toward the conclusion that composite substances do, in fact, have parts and thus can be nothing more than mere aggregates.

Nonetheless, there may be some room for Leibniz to resist this conclusion. Despite the apparent homogeneity of the soul and body on the monadological analysis, Leibniz is explicit that monads are not parts. One way to make sense of this is to move away from relying on *homogeneity* to characterize parts and rely instead on the fact that, for Leibniz, parts are always essential to the wholes they compose. This gives a more robust way to distinguish between the parts of an aggregate and the constituents of a substance. As Leibniz writes, "what constitutes the essence of an entity through aggregation is only a state of being of its constituent entities."[40] Unlike a substance, a change to the parts of an aggregate entails a change to the identity of the aggregate. If, for example, the MacLean herd is made up of three sheep, Angus, Barclay, and Calum, and Calum leaves the herd and is replaced by Dugald, then the MacLean herd is not, strictly speaking, the same herd anymore. Calum himself, by contrast, continues to be the same sheep even if he grows, gets shorn, or has his hooves trimmed. On this characterization, monads will fail to be parts because the removal of any given monad does not affect the identity of the composite. As Leibniz writes in the *Monadology*, "all bodies are in a perpetual state of

[38] A II ii 251, n. 77; GP II 120; LA 153. See also GM VII 18–19; L 667–668 for a similar characterization with different terminology.

[39] GP II 268; Lodge 463.

[40] GP II 96–97; LA 121.

flux, like rivers, and parts are constantly coming into them and going out."[41] Substances, however, "remain perfectly 'the same individual.' "[42] This provides a way, which does not rely merely on a terminological distinction, to maintain that soul-body composites, even when understood as collections of monads, do not have parts.

But even if Leibniz thinks of soul-body composites along the lines I have suggested, as constituent-wise composites rather than part-wise composites, this does not fully answer the question of soul-body unity. At best, understanding the soul and body as constituents rather than parts of composites meets one necessary condition of substantial unity; namely, not having parts. But it seems that some account of the unity of the constituents—of soul and body—is still needed. Even granting that soul and body are constituents in the sense just elaborated, how could it be that a soul-body composite is not a *composition* in any problematic sense?

Here, we might consider two different ways to think about the structure of composite substance, formulated in terms of "form" and "matter":

1. *Actual-Constituent View*: Form and matter are entities in their own right, so related as to compose a unified composite substance.
2. *Dual-Aspect View*: Form and matter are *not* entities in their own right, but aspects of a single thing, which we can consider separately (but which cannot exist separately).

Each of these views is represented within the scholastic-Aristotelian tradition to some degree, and Leibniz would have been familiar with them both.[43] The Dual-Aspect view more nearly aligns with Aristotle himself, although Aquinas also held something like this view, with the caveat that the human soul (being immortal) can in some way *subsist* without any matter. The Actual-Constituent view appears to have been held by, for example, William Ockham and Duns Scotus.[44] Leibniz's own texts fall on both sides of this divide.

Which of these two conceptions of substance one favors has important consequences for whether and in what sense the "composition" of soul and body is compatible with true unity. On the Dual-Aspect view, one need not explain how the composition of form and matter results in a being with true unity because form and matter are not things in their own right. On this view, soul and body need not be even *constituents*, but instead something like *aspects* of the individual being. As such, no account of how they come together to form a true unity would be needed. On the Actual-Constituent view, on the other hand, some account does appear to be needed as to how these two (or more) distinct entities can compose a being with true unity. Some would deny that such an

---

[41] GP VI 619; WFP 278.
[42] NE 231.
[43] For the development and discussion of a similar distinction, see Look-Rutherford xliii.
[44] For further discussion, see Marilyn Adams, *William Ockham* (New York: Oxford University Press, 1987), pp. 633–670.

account can be given at all. Aquinas, for example, denies that more than one actual constituent can combine to form a being with true unity.[45]

Because the Dual-Aspect view seems much more congenial to the possibility of accounting for the per se unity of a composite substance, it would be nice if there was evidence that this is how Leibniz understands the structure of composite substance. But, as I mentioned, the evidence is at best divided. Some commentators have picked up on the evidence inclining toward the Dual-Aspect view and proposed that Leibniz held something like Aquinas's view.[46] There are, however, at least two reasons to resist attributing the Dual-Aspect view to Leibniz. First, even during the Middle Years, Leibniz characterizes bodies as aggregates of substances.[47] This suggests that the Actual-Constituent view is a better fit, insofar as substances are beings in their own right. Second, even by the earliest years of his Mature Period, the Dual-Aspect view seems to fit more neatly as a characterization of monads than of composite substances. Consider the following well-known passage from a 1703 letter to De Volder:

> I therefore distinguish: (1) the primitive entelechy, i.e., the soul; (2) matter, namely, primary matter, i.e., primitive passive power; (3) the monad completed by these two things; (4) the mass, i.e., the secondary matter, i.e., the organic machine, for which innumerable subordinate monads come together; and (5) the animal, i.e., the corporeal substance, which the monad dominating in the machine makes one.[48]

In this passage, Leibniz claims that the primitive entelechy (i.e., the form) combines with the primitive passive power (i.e., the matter) to complete, not the composite substance as we might expect, but the *simple substance* (i.e., the monad). The dominant monad is then distinct from and joined to its body, which is itself a mass of subordinate monads.

Given this characterization, it seems difficult to see how Leibniz could understand composite substance along the lines of the Dual-Aspect view. The composite substance is fairly clearly characterized as a collection of monads—that is, as independent beings—that bear certain relations to one another (the relevant relation here being *domination*). Consequently, it seems that he must think about composites along the lines of the Actual-Constituent view. But, given Leibniz's exacting standards of substantial unity, this seems to preclude an account of the per se unity of composite substance—Leibniz appears to be of the same mind as Aquinas on this point. (But note also that even in this passage Leibniz claims that the machine is "one.")

Despite the difficulty Leibniz faces in accounting for the per se unity of composites on the Actual-Constituent view, all hope may not be lost. Paul Lodge (2014) has recently suggested that the relation of monadic domination—articulated in (5) of the passage to

---

[45] For discussion, see M. Adams, *Ockham*, pp. 637–638.
[46] For development of this view, see R. Adams, *Leibniz*, pp. 269–274.
[47] See, e.g., GP IV 491; WFP 185.
[48] GP II 252; Lodge, p. 438.

De Volder just quoted—might ground the substantial unity of soul-body composites.[49] On Lodge's account, domination might be sufficient to ground per se unity because it provides an internal principle of unity for the collection of monads that make up the composite.[50] That this relation is internal marks a clear difference between soul-body composites and aggregates. Aggregates, such as flocks of sheep or armies, have an *external* principle of unity: some mind grouping the parts of the aggregate on the basis of relations that hold between them. For example, I think of the sheep Angus, Barclay, Calum, and Dugald as *the MacLean herd* because they are standing near one another in the same meadow. Unlike this example, the relation grounding the unity of a composite (i.e., domination) is *internal* to the collection. Furthermore, on Lodge's account, domination does not rely on the perception or grouping by some finite mind (as with the herd of sheep) but only on facts, represented by the divine mind, about the relations between the relevant monads. Thus, the domination relation, on Lodge's account, does not yield an aggregate in the way that my mental grouping of the four sheep does. For this reason, Lodge characterizes domination as a "non-aggregate relation."[51]

As Lodge himself notes, this approach faces some textual obstacles. For example, Leibniz writes to Des Bosses that "composite substance does not formally consist in monads and their subordination."[52] Although not an explicit denial that the domination relation can ground the unity of composites, this text tends in that direction. Nevertheless, as I see it, Lodge's (2013) approach has two significant virtues. First, it reckons with the places in which Leibniz characterizes soul-body composites as having per se unity. We have seen some such texts from Leibniz's correspondence with Arnauld in the 1680s; there are others stretching well into Leibniz's mature philosophy.[53] Any approach that abandons the per se unity of composites is forced to explain these texts away somehow. Second, it aligns the question of unity with the question of what sense of "composite" is at stake. Aggregates, such as bodies, are clearly composites in a certain sense. But perhaps, as Lodge suggests, not all composites are aggregates. Or, put in the terms I have elaborated earlier: not all composites have parts. If correct, Lodge's account would provide just what Leibniz, on my account, needs: a way, independent of pre-established harmony, to account for the unity of the actual constituents of a composite substance.[54]

[49] Paul Lodge, "Corporeal Substances as Monadic Composites in Leibniz's Later Philosophy," in *Leibniz's Metaphysics and Adoption of Substantial Forms*, edited by A. Nita (Springer, 2014).

[50] Lodge, "Monadic Composites."

[51] Lodge, "Monadic Composites."

[52] Look-Rutherford 371; quoted in Lodge, "Monadic Composites."

[53] Here is one from 1702: "This substance [i.e., a corporeal substance] of course, is one per se, and not a mere aggregate of many substances, for there is a great difference between an animal, for example, and a flock." GP IV 395; AG 252

[54] Despite my sympathies with Lodge's approach, I am hesitant to accept that domination grounds the per se unity of monadic composites. I see some difficulty in differentiating domination from a special case of relations of harmony, which I argued earlier in this chapter would not be sufficient for per se unity.

One problem faced by any account given, on Leibniz's behalf, of the unity of soul-body composites is that, in his late correspondence with the Jesuit Bartholomew Des Bosses, Leibniz appears to admit that something more is needed to explain the unity of composite substance. On one interpretation of this correspondence, the lack of an account of the per se unity of composite substance is what prompts Leibniz to consider the introduction of a bond—*vinculum*[55] (which later becomes the substantial bond; the *vinculum substantiale*[56])—invoked to account for transubstantiation within the theory of monads. The status of the substantial bond within Leibniz's philosophy is the subject of ongoing dispute, and I cannot engage the issue fully here. Still, one way to read the introduction of substantial bonds is to see it as Leibniz's own tacit admission that the Actual-Constituent view creates difficulty for the claim that soul and body constitute a composite with per se unity. This would square with some of the concerns I raised earlier about Leibniz's prospects for accounting for the unity of anything with more than one constituent.

CONCLUSION

One virtue of the approach I have developed is that it allows us to take Leibniz's remarks to Tournemine at face value. It also allows us to take seriously Leibniz's stated commitment to the per se unity of composite substance, at least in the Middle Years and perhaps beyond. On my interpretation, although Leibniz may have held that soul-body composites have per se unity, he did not hold that pre-established harmony was the explanation of their unity. However, my suggestions do not provide a complete account of the unity of composite substance.

Whether or not Leibniz can ultimately give an account of the per se unity of composites, one important consequence of my view is that the way in which Leibniz understands unity in the early to middle period prefigures very closely the way in which he understands simplicity later on—"simple, that is, without parts."[57] This result has a direct bearing on the status of composites in any period of Leibniz's thought. What follows, in my view, is that composites, understood in the specific sense of part-wise composites, were never part of Leibniz's fundamental ontology. Substances are always noncomposite, in this sense, for Leibniz. Perhaps Leibniz's transition to a monadological metaphysics is ultimately motivated by his inability to account for the unity of anything composite (i.e., anything with more than one part, constituent, element, ingredient, etc.). Or perhaps the transition need not abandon the unity of soul-body composites after all. A great deal hinges on what sense of "composite" is at stake. Relative to what has been achieved here, however, any conclusions on these matters must remain speculative.

[55] Look-Rutherford 23. For discussion, see Look-Rutherford lv, lviii–lix.
[56] Look-Rutherford 227. For discussion, see Look-Rutherford lxii–lxxii.
[57] GP VI 607; AG 213.

ACKNOWLEDGMENTS

I am grateful to Marleen Rozemond, Christian Barth, Maria Rosa Antognazza, Paul Lodge, and the participants of the Toronto-Berlin-Groningen Workshop on Medieval and Early Modern Philosophy and the History of Modern Group at the University of Toronto for comments on previous versions of this chapter.

REFERENCES

Adams, Marilyn McCord. 1987. *William Ockham*. 2 Vols. New York: Oxford University Press.

Adams, Robert M. 1994. *Leibniz: Determinist, Theist, Idealist*. Oxford: Oxford University Press.

Antognazza, Maria Rosa. 2014. "Leibniz's theory of substance and his metaphysics of the Incarnation," in Paul Lodge and T. W. C. Stoneham (eds.), *Locke and Leibniz on Substance and Identity*. Abingdon/New York: Routledge.

Arthur, Richard T. W., and Peter Lopston. 2006. "Leibniz's body realism: Two interpretations." *The Leibniz Review* 16: 1–42.

Garber, Daniel. 1985. "Leibniz and the foundations of physics: The Middle Years," in K. Okruhlik and J. Brown (eds.), *The Natural Philosophy of Leibniz*. Dordrecht: Kluwer Academic Publishers, pp. 27–130.

Garber, Daniel. 2009. *Body, Substance, Monad*. Oxford: Oxford University Press.

Lodge, Paul (ed. and trans.). 2013. *The Leibniz-De Volder Correspondence*. New Haven: Yale University Press.

Lodge, Paul. 2014. "Corporeal substances as monadic composites in Leibniz's later philosophy," in A. Nita (ed.), *Leibniz's Metaphysics and Adoption of Substantial Forms*. Springer.

McDonough, Jeff. 2013. "Leibniz's conciliatory account of substance." *Philosopher's Imprint* 13(6): 1–23.

Rozemond, Marleen. 1997. "Leibniz on the union of body and soul." *Archiv für Geschichte der Philosophie* 79: 150–78.

Rutherford, Donald. 1995. *Leibniz and the Rational Order of Nature*. New York: Cambridge University Press.

Sleigh, Robert C. Jr. 1990. *Leibniz and Arnauld: A Commentary on Their Correspondence*. New Haven: Yale University Press.

CHAPTER 22

....

SPACE AND TIME

....

HEINRICH SCHEPERS

Leibniz's theory of space and time does not belong to his (or any) theory of knowledge; it belongs instead to his metaphysics. Like St. Augustine, Leibniz puts the question in the following terms: "What, then, is time?"[1]

Let us leave aside for the moment the diachronic development of Leibniz's revolutionary theory about space in its very different stages to instead concentrate synchronically on its rational construction. Leibniz's first approach to the determination of the nature of time and space begins with the assumption that anything free from contradiction exists and—to be precise—exists earlier, simultaneous, or later than another thing, either according to its own nature or according to time.[2]

When according to its own nature something is earlier than something else, the former is the source of the latter. The consequence of this approach is that time and space are nothing other than orders governing these things, independently of whether such things really exist or are merely possibilities.

Beings within these orders constitute the totality of things that are conceivable as consistent beings. Those beings that are compatible with one another belong to the same world. Within that world, they change their state, that is, the totality of their predicates, moving with each change to a contrary state but without losing their identity or their compatibility with the other things in their world. Within every possible world there is a complete interdependence between the bearers of these states. Each state provides the reason for the following state or, to be precise, for all subsequent states; conversely, each state has its reason—*nihil sine ratione*.

Instead of referring—as Wittgenstein does—to the logical space which contains all that is the case (i.e., facts or extant states of affairs), Leibniz speaks of all things that are conceivable, the totality of possibilities, which he situates in God's intellect, the classic

---

[1] A. Augustinus, *Confessiones*, "*Quid ergo est tempus? Si nemo ex me quaerat, scio; si querenti explicare velim nescio*" XI, 14 (17).

[2] This reflects the traditional distinction of "*prius natura vs. prius tempore.*"

regio idearum. For Leibniz, "possibilities" are not "facts" but conceivable "things." God thinks all possible things before his will decides to create some of them.[3]

What does it mean to say that God thinks every possibility? He thinks of all possibilities not merely abstractly, as truths about facts, but as different subjects, as simple substances with all their attributes contained in their complete notions. When Leibniz says that God creates a substance that expresses the whole universe as viewed from one perspective among others, and knowing that it belongs to the best of all possible worlds, he does not have in mind the "creation by God" in any ordinary sense. Already before Creation, all simple substances were possibilities striving to exist, a process that took place in God's mind. This process should be regarded as having come to completion at the point at which God "surveyed" his intellect to decide which of the possible worlds is the best. Every possibility, that is, every simple substance, has constituted itself spontaneously:

> For God turns—so to speak—on all sides and in all ways the general system of phenomena that he finds it fit to produce so as to manifest his glory and, inspecting all the faces of the world in every possible way, since there is not a single connection that escapes his omniscience, the result of each view of the universe as seen from a certain place, is a substance that expresses the universe in conformity with that point of view, should God find it fit to render his thought effective and produce that substance.[4]

God's mind encompasses the totality of necessary truths as well as the totality of possibilities. This may be understood as a form of "superconceptualism": God's thought follows precisely the necessary truths, and he thinks only—and all—the possibilities because there is nothing else to be conceived. Both determine the form and content of his mind. The possibilities are thought by God to be substances in constant development, which warrant their own individuality from their own spontaneous actions. Acting in this way, substances have no effect on each other, but Leibniz must show how activity and passivity are located in the internal operations of each monad. As creatures, all monads are limited, and each has some degree of passivity in proportion to the degree of confusion of its consciousness. God alone is pure activity.

All his life, Leibniz kept the core of his metaphysics highly private. This is true also of his theory of time and space. One reason for this secrecy may have been that his opinions were not yet sufficiently elaborated. A more forceful reason was the fear of being laughed at by people who could not understand his sophisticated theories, which

---

[3] Leibniz to Arnauld, July 14 1686, A II ii 71: "les circonstances individuelles du temps, du lieu et autres . . . les essences sont dans l'entendement de Dieu avant la consideration de la volonté."

[4] A VI iv 1549.19–1550.5 (beginning of 1686): "Car Dieu tournant—pour ainsi dire—de tous costés et de toutes façons le systeme general des phenomenes qu'il trouve bon de produire pour manifester sa gloire et regardant toutes les faces du monde de toutes manieres possibles, puisqu'il n'y a point de rapport qui échappe à son omniscience, le resultat de chaque vue de l'univers comme regardé d'un certain endroit, est une substance qui exprime l'univers conformement à cette vue, si Dieu trouve bon de rendre sa pensée effective, et de produire cette substance." Translated in L 311 ff.

might have endangered his great project, the *Scientia Generalis*, for which support from high authorities was needed. Perhaps Leibniz wanted to avoid the risk of having his writings condemned by the Roman Curia to the Index of prohibited books, as in fact happened in 1745.[5] He developed his opinions regarding time and space in several stages and recorded them in various forms, most of them reserved for his own private use. On several occasions, he inserted short notes in his letters, presenting different levels of explanation according to the expected ability of his correspondent to grasp what he meant.

A note from 1685 tails off: "these things are more difficult to explain since they force us to take into consideration the divine nature."[6] Similarly, he closes an account offered to Antoine Arnauld with the following words: "Every notion we have about time and space is grounded in this accord [i.e., what Leibniz later calls a 'pre-established harmony'] but I would never be finished if I had to give a thorough explanation of all which is connected with this subject."[7] Some time earlier, Simon Foucher received this advice: "considerations of this kind are not suited for all people, and uneducated persons will understand nothing before their mind is rightly prepared."[8] Leaving London at the end of 1676, Leibniz closes his dialogue *Pacidius Philaleti* with the confession that he did not report all discussions because not all people were worthy of learning the whole matter, and, to be sure, only some were ripe and prepared enough for it.[9]

Drawing on compelling evidence, I will try to present chronologically what this "difficult explanation"—which Leibniz himself never explicitly wrote down on paper—might have looked like. In particular, I will draw attention to the genesis of possibilities.

Let us start from April 1679, his month of glory, in which he discovered the dyadics (the basis of modern digitization), his calculus for the universal characteristics, and the logico-ontological relations explored in a series of texts entitled *De affectibus* (where he defined for the first time the rational sequence of his logical definitions). In these reflections Leibniz also identifies the elements of his theory of space and time, including the notion of simultaneity, the various ways of saying earlier and later, the logical sequence growing to ontological reason, and the modal logic of compatibility. At the same time, he discovered the far-reaching consequences of the little word "now" (*nunc*). He explained that each time we say "now," we actually refer to the whole world and the

---

[5] Margherita Palumbo, "Die römische Zensur des Briefwechsels Leibniz-Clarke oder 'Leibniz im Abriss," in H. Breger, J. Herbst and S. Erdner (eds), *Akten des IX. Internationalen Leibniz-Kongresses, "Natur und Subjekt". Hannover, 26. September bis 1. Oktober 2011*, Nachtragsband Hannover 2012, pp. 72–86, esp. n. 38.

[6] A VI iv 629.19: "Sed haec omnia difficilioris explicationis sunt, coguntque nos venire ad divinae naturae considerationem."

[7] A II ii 245.11–13 (October 9, 1687): "Toute la notion que nous avons du temps et de l'espace est fondée sur cet accord, mais je n'aurois jamais fait, si je devois expliquer à fonds tout ce qui est lié avec nostre sujet." Translated in L 341.

[8] A II ii 202.15–17 (May 23, 1687): "mais ces sortes des considerations ne sont pas propres à estre vues de tout le monde, et le vulgaire n'y sçauroit rien comprendre avant que d'avoir l'esprit preparé."

[9] A VI iii 571.8–10 (November 9–10, 1676): "(quaedam enim dicta erant ultro citroque quae huc transferri non possunt, quod non omnes iis digni, aut certe pauci maturi atque praeparati videantur)."

whole of time. Moreover, when we utter a factual sentence containing the little word "is," we include the whole world (by saying "It is cold," we mean "it is cold here and now").[10]

Already in November 1676, he had indicated that it would be worth the trouble to consider that in which the harmony between time and motion consists.[11] Shortly before this, he had tried to define time as a certain continuum, with respect to which anything can be said to have duration. But he immediately added that a clearer explanation would be to attribute to time a nature by which a plurality of things can be grasped simultaneously.[12]

Together with this pair of definitions, we find some further remarks on time and space beginning with the difference between duration and time and ending with the realization that, for an explanation of these matters, a more profound meditation would be necessary. Leibniz distinguishes time from duration just as he distinguishes space from collocation. According to him, it is silly to say that a day has duration. On the other hand, we say that a mayfly lasts just one day. It would be clearer to attribute to the nature of time the fact that many things can be understood as existing simultaneously than to conceive time as a continuum in which something persists. Leibniz then tries to define what simultaneity is. Things are simultaneous when they can be perceived by a single act of the mind. But such an action takes time. Therefore, it would be better to define simultaneity abstractly—in a more basic way—as the situation in which the existence of one thing entails the existence of the other, too, and in which it is not possible to grasp the one without grasping the other. Surely, Leibniz says, if we possessed perfect wisdom—if we were gods—then we would understand that all that seems to us (due to our ignorance) to be simultaneous by chance is in fact following its own nature and that they coexist as a consequence of the necessity of God's intellect. Here Leibniz pauses: all this should be more accurately discussed since it is based on first notions that are not explicable on account of their being simple and to their being conceived per se. The crucial point of Leibniz's theory of time lies in this definition of simultaneity dating from this time until the end of his reflections.[13]

[10]   H. Schepers, "*De affectibus*. Leibniz an der Schwelle zur Monadologie. Seine Vorarbeiten zum logischen Aufbau der möglichen Welten," in *Studia Leibnitiana*, 35(2), 2003, pp. 133–61.

[11]   A VI iii 563.21: "Sed operae pretium erit considerare materiae temporis et motus harmoniam."

[12]   A VI iii 484.3: "Tempus est continuum quoddam secundum quod aliquid intelligitur durare. Sed ut rem clarius explicem, cogitandum est eam potissimum tempori naturam tribui, ut plura simul esse intelligantur."

[13]   See A VI iii 484 (spring of 1676): "Duratio est existendi continuitas. Tempus non est duratio, non magis quam spatium collocatio. Et ineptum foret dicere, diem esse durationem. Cum contra Hemerobia per diem durare dicamus. Tempus est continuum quoddam secundum quod aliquid intelligitur durare. Sed ut rem clarius explicem, cogitan dum est eam potissimum tempori naturam tribui, ut plura simul esse intelligantur. Simul autem sunt quae una mentis actione sentiri possunt. Sed quoniam ipsa, Mentis actio habet tractum, videndum an non ea simul esse dicamus, quorum si unum existit, existit et alterum. Atque illud sane in confesso est, si duo sint eiusmodi, ut impossibile sit alterum sine altero intelligi, ea simul esse. Et certe si perfecte sapientes essemus id est Dii, facile videremus quae nobis per accidens simul esse nunc videntur ob ignorantiam nostram, coexistere ipsa natura, id est Divini intellectus necessitate. Sed haec accuratius discutienda. Sunt enim ultimae denique horum notionum inexplicabiles, vel ideo quia per se intelliguntur simplicesque sunt."

Leibniz explains further that if one thinks of time as homogeneous, then eternity is endless time; understood, however, as an attribute of the eternal being—namely, God (as Leibniz does)—then eternity amounts to duration through endless time. But the real origin and intrinsic nature of eternity is the necessity of existence, which does not imply any succession but brings it about that the eternal co-exists with all things.[14]

Leibniz insists that space differs from body just as time differs from an existent thing. A few lines earlier in the same paper, Leibniz defines simultaneous things as being *suppositione connecessaria*, that is, as necessary once God has created the series of things (i.e., the world).[15]

Simultaneity of beings may seem trivial, but it is fundamental to understand that for Leibniz it is the simultaneity of existing things and not the simultaneity of moments or facts. Therefore we read: "What exists in act, exists simultaneously," which means, "Given any existent, any other must be earlier, later or simultaneous."[16]

Already in April 1679, Leibniz remarked that the notion of time includes the entire series of things, as well as the will of God and that of all free beings.[17]

That means, first, that the notion of time involves the will of all free beings insofar as they act freely in striving to exist and, second, that it involves the will of God, who selects from among these strivers those which together constitute maximum perfection. Therefore, it is the totality of possible beings along with their orders of simultaneity and succession, which they themselves have created, that makes it even possible for us to think the notions of space and time. This order concerns only facts, including all contingent facts coming into existence, as well as those that remain mere possibilities. By *involvere* ("to involve"), Leibniz means that, from the existence of a thing, one can infer the existence of the involved thing; on the other hand, "to be involved," means that from the existence of a thing that is involved in something else, it is possible to infer the existence of the involving thing.[18]

---

[14] See A VI iii 484.15–27: "Aeternitas si ut aliquid tempori homogeneum concipiatur, erit tempus interminatum; sin ut attributum alicuius aeterni, erit duratio per tempus interminatum. Sed vera origo atque intima aeternitatis natura est ipsa existendi necessitas, quae nullam per se dicit successionem, etsi fiat ut omnibus coexistat, quod aeternum est. Ut in duratione, ita in Extensione est forma quaedam simplex per se intelligibilis, cuius idea est praesens menti, quaeque adeo est inexplicabilis. Id ergo secundum quod res dicuntur extensae, cui extensio sola per se competit, in ordine tamen ad ea quae aliud quiddam praeterea continent, dicitur Locus, et absolute, Spatium, et secundum spatium res concipimus sitas, et simul sensibiles, et invicem distantes, et figuratas. Sed ad haec explicanda profundiore opus meditatione. Illud interea notare suffecerit Immensitatem respondere aeternitati, utque aeternitas per se non dicit successionem, ita nec immensitatem dicere extensionem sive partes. Deinde notabimus, tam differe locum a corpore, quam tempus a re existente."
[15] A VI iv 393.12–14 (1680–85): "Simul sunt, quae suppositione connecessaria sunt, suppositione, inquam, id est posita serie rerum."
[16] A VI iv 393.12–14 (1680–85): "Quaecumque actu existunt, simul existunt. Seu quaecumque existentiam habent, datum unum, alio vel prius est vel posterius vel simul."
[17] A VI iv 1441.11 (April 1679): "Temporis autem conceptus involvit totam seriem rerum et voluntatem Dei ac rerum aliarum liberarum." Cf. A VI iv 1517.25 (end of 1685 until middle of 1686).
[18] A VI iv 1439 (April 20, 1679): "Involvitur in aliquo cujus existentia ex alicujus existentia concludi potest. Involvit aliquid id ex cujus existentia aliquid concludi potest."

Of course, the collection of metaphysico-logical definitions from mid-1685 is not short of remarks concerning time and space.[19] Simultaneity is defined in terms of one thing being the condition of its coexistent; it follows that if there is no such condition, then that other thing must be earlier or later. To be earlier is to be simultaneous with the cause; to be later, simultaneous with the effect. By the same token, to be earlier is to be simpler or that which is the requisite of the other; that is to say, that which is its necessary condition.[20]

The *measurement* of time and space requires a fixed point on which one has come to an agreement; clocks, however, do not make time—they only show it. It is the same with the motion of celestial bodies. The *root of time* is the first cause (i.e., God) who contains virtually the successions of all things. All that is real is in space and time, that is to say, in God. At this point, Leibniz interrupts his meditation, declaring this to be a matter in need of a more difficult explanation because it requires a consideration of the divine nature, which is to go even deeper into metaphysics.[21]

When Leibniz understands time to be an imaginary thing—like space, qualities, and many other things—he means that time is not real but only a *relation*.[22] When he says that the "root of time" lies in God as in the first cause, this should be taken to point toward God's will, which brings into existence that which his intellect has recognized as the best. It does not at all mean that God created the possibilities from which he could choose for existence. That would contradict Leibniz's earlier view, repeated many times, that substances are spontaneous or free acting, with their principle of action within themselves.[23]

[19] A VI iv 624–630.

[20] See A VI iv 628.25–629.2: "Simul sunt quorum unum absolute alterius conditio est. Sin unum alterius conditio est interveniente mutatione, tunc unum est prius, alterum posterius. Illud autem intelligitur prius quod simul est cum causa, posterius quod simul est cum effectu. Vel prius intelligitur quod est simplicius vel quod est alterius requisitum. Requisitum autem definivi conditionem natura simpliciorem eo cujus conditio est. Si A sit B, et A non sit B, dicitur A esse mutatum, seu verum esse de diverso tempore."

[21] See A VI iv 629.2–20 (mid-1685): "Metimur autem tempus uniformi quadam mutatione ad partes rei permanentis applicata ita ut prius sit quod applicatur parti minus distanti a termino assumto. Illud est fundamentum mensurandae rerum durationis, quod assumtis diversis motibus uniformibus (tanquam diversis horologiis exactis) habetur consensus; adeoque quaecunque fiunt aut sunt simul, aut aliquo priora aut posteriora. Tempore prius est quod cum aliquo positione incompatibile est, et eo simplicius est. Alterum autem dicitur posterius. Simul sunt, quae suppositione connecessaria sunt, suppositione inquam id est posita serie rerum. Tempus est Ens imaginarium, quemadmodum, locus, qualitates, aliaque multa. Cognoscimus uniformi aliqua mutatione, utrum aliquod sit prius, an posterius, sed quia diversae uniformes mutationes sunt simul, est aliqua causa hujus simultaneitatis et prioritatis; nam horologia non efficiunt sed indicant tantum prioritatem et posterioritatem. Idem est de motu coeli neque enim a motu horologii differt, quam ut majus et minus. Radix autem temporis est in causa prima, successiones rerum virtute in se continente, quae facit, ut omnia sint simul, aut priora vel posteria. Idem est de Loco nam efficit causa prima ut omnia distantiam quandam habeant. Quicquid ergo reale est in spatio et tempore, id est in Deo omnia complectente. Sed haec omnia difficilioris explicationis sunt, coguntque nos venire ad divinae naturae considerationem."

[22] GP II 515: "spatium absolutum aliquid imaginarium est, et nihil ei reale inest, quam distantia corporum; verbo, sunt ordines, non res."

[23] A VI i 508.14 (1668): "Substantia est ens per se subsistens, quod habet principium actionis in se."

But what brings it about that something is earlier or later? As we have seen, Leibniz certainly rejects the measurement of time as an answer: "Clocks cause nothing, but only show that something is earlier or later than another."[24] According to Leibniz, to be earlier in time depends on being earlier in nature, which is in turn indicated by a corresponding ease in the cognition of its possibility. Given two states that contradict one another, the one earlier in time is the one earlier in nature because the earlier contains the reason for the later.[25]

Of course, all these views are based on Leibniz's rationalist credo that our thinking is composed of simple, irreducible terms (even if these simple elements remain to be known) and that the ontological nature of things corresponds exactly to this logical structure. More precisely, Leibniz explains that one thing is earlier or later than another, having posited that both exist, when the one thing goes together with another thing that is incompatible with the other.[26]

In appealing to incompatibility—or incompossibility—Leibniz invokes his theory of possible worlds. A possible world is a unit consisting of individual possibilities that are at every moment compatible. The *incompatibilia* just cited are those possibilities that may belong to the same world only because they differ in time; they exist earlier or later but never simultaneously. That they belong to the same world follows from the assumption that both (when there are two) "exist," as Leibniz puts it—a kind of existence that, to be sure, is not limited to only our world.

According to Leibniz, we recognize what time is when something remains the same despite undergoing variations; that is, when it follows from its nature that it has successively distinct states. I will be said to be the same as before because my substance involves all my previous, present, and future states. The nature of time consists precisely in the possibility of contradictory things being true of the same thing or person at different times.[27]

It is remarkable that the notion of order does not appear in the definitions of space and time until 1685/86. A footnote to a text dating from June 1685–March 1686 (added

---

[24] A VI iv 629.13: "Horologia non efficiunt, sed indicant tantum prioritatem et posterioritatem."

[25] A VI iv 181.1–3 (spring–summer 1679): "Et proinde Natura prius est, cujus possibilitas facilius demonstratur, seu quod facilius intelligitur. Ex duobus statibus quorum alter alteri contradicit, is est tempore prior qui est prior natura"; A VI iv 563.9–11 (summer 1683–beginning of 1685): "Porro ex duobus statibus contradictoriis ejusdem rei, is prior tempore est, qui natura prior est, seu qui alterius rationem involvit, vel quod eodem redit, qui facilius intelligitur."

[26] A VI iv 390.3 (July 1680–March 1685): "Si duo incompatibilia existant, tempore different, illud eorum tempore prius (posterius) erit, quod est natura prius (posterius). Illud quoque prius vel posterius alio est (positis ambobus existentibus) quod simul est cum incomponibili alterius"; A VI iv 629.2–20 (mid-1685): "Tempore prius est quod cum aliquo positione incompatibile est, et eo simplicius est. Alterum autem dicitur posterius."

[27] A VI iv N.131 556.19 (July 1683–February 1685): "Res eadem manere potest, licet mutetur, si ex ipsa ejus natura sequitur idem debere successive diversos status habere. Nimirum idem dicor esse qui ante, quia substantia mea omnes status meos praeteritos praesentes futurosque involvit, nec obstat quod ita de me contradictoria dicantur; haec ipsa enim natura est temporis, ut secundum diversum tempus possint contradictoria esse vera de eodem."

perhaps some time later) captures this idea for the first time: "Place [is] the order of coexistents, time the order of changes."[28]

In his final year in Italy, Leibniz penned a short remark in which he asserted that the foundation of these relations is to be found in God, especially in his magnitude, eternity, and immensity. Although the reasons he gives for this are not repeated in other texts, they are consistent with his views. If striving ("*conatus*") or, in short, action is added to space or quantity, Leibniz writes, then something substantial is added, which can only be in God, the primary One. This real space should be an indivisible and unchangeable unity. It contains not only existent things but also possibilities. Lacking appetite, space is indifferent to any kind of change. From this perspective, there can be no difference. With the addition of appetite, striving toward new perceptions, existing substances were made and so matter or the aggregate of infinite unities.[29]

Insofar as space really corresponds to God's omnipresence, space is unlimited, indivisible, and devoid of any kind of change.[30] Elsewhere, Leibniz says that to think of time as composed of discrete moments is as absurd as thinking of a line as composed of points.[31]

In the second part of his *Specimen Dynamicum*, dating from April 1695, we read the following: the first thing to know is that space, time, and motion have something of an *ens rationis*; they are true and real not per se but insofar as they involve the divine attributes, immensity, eternity, and activity (or the force of created substances).[32]

Some time later, Leibniz proposed a more precise definition, which became his favorite until the end of his life. Emphasizing first of all continuity and then the importance of both existing and merely possible individuals, he defines time and space as

---

[28] A VI iv N.148 630.28 fn. 10 (June 1685–March 1686): "Locus ordo coexistendi, Tempus ordo mutationum."

[29] A VI iv 1641.12–19 (March 1689–March 1690): "Tempus et Locus, seu duratio et spatium sunt Relationes reales, seu existendi ordines. Earum fundamentum in re est Divina magnitudo, aeternitas scilicet et immensitas. Nam si spatio seu magnitudini addatur appetitus vel quod eodem redit conatus, adeoque et Actio, jam aliquid substantiale introducitur, quod non in alio est quam in Deo, seu Uno primario. Spatium scilicet reale per se aliquid Unum est indivisibile, immutabile; nec tantum continet existentias sed et modos. Appetitus vero spatio accedit, facit substantias existentes atque adeo materiam seu aggregatum infinitarum Unitatum."

[30] A VI iv 990.16–18 (September–December 1688): "spatii et creaturae extensio differunt quod spatii extensio per se absoluta est, interminata, impartibilis, omnis mutationis expers; breviter quicquid in spatio reale est, est ipsa omnipraesentia Dei."

[31] A VI iv 562.22 (summer 1683–beginning of 1685): "Tempus autem ex momentis componi aeque absurdum est quam linea componi ex punctis."

[32] GM VI 247: "Sciendum est ante omnia . . . spatium, tempus et motum habere aliquid de Ente rationis, nec per se sed quatenus Divina attributa, immensitatem, aeternitatem, operationem aut substantiarum creatarum vim involvunt, vera et realia esse." See also A VI vi 227.1–3: "Les relations et les ordres ont quelque chose de l'etre de raison, quoiqu'ils ayent leur fondement dans les choses. Car on peut dire que leur réalité, comme celle des verités eternelles, et des possibilités, vient de la supreme raison"; A VI vi 155.6–8: "Il [Dieu] est la source des possibilités comme des existences, des unes par son essence, des autres par sa volonté. Ainsi l'espace comme le temps n'ont leur realité que de luy."

follows: "Time is the continuous order of existing things in accordance with their variations. Space is the continuous order of simultaneously existing things."[33]

To the Cartesian De Volder, he wrote that Descartes's extension seems to be no more than a continuous order of coexistence, just as time is a continuous order of successive existence. Therefore, neither time nor space should be regarded as a substance; only those things that exist in these orders are to be regarded as such.[34]

In June 1704, he added: "Space is nothing other than the order of simultaneously existing possibilities, just as time is the order of successively existing possibilities."[35]

Also around 1704, in his *Nouveaux Essais*, Leibniz stated more precisely that time and space are mere relations, not only between existing things, but also between possibilities as though they existed. It would be correct to say that God is the fountain-head of this order. Note that here he withholds from Locke his conceptualistic view of God's mind consisting of all possibilities.[36]

Nevertheless, they are ideal entities, as are numbers and other relations, insofar as their reality consists in being looked at, not only by God, but also by rational monads such as we.

The apparent triviality of the relation of order soon turns into complexity if we answer the question "what is it that really made the order?" in the way that Augustine did.[37] For Leibniz, it is the totality of possibilities that have constituted themselves by their spontaneous actions. But, in a simpler way, he also says to Locke that space and time, far from being themselves substances, depend on the things which they contain: "place or time, far from being determinants by themselves, need themselves to be determined by the things they contain."[38]

The logical and, as such, non-tensed definition, "Possible are all things that are thinkable, free of contradiction,"[39] when applied to beings, indicates all that is simultaneously conceivable as free of contradiction. That implies, strictly speaking, the distinct conceivability of every simple substance, which in turn implies that its order be in correlation with every other simple substance. Leibniz offers a formulation that imitates the traditional dictum "*Forma dat esse rei.*" According to this formulation, it is distinct conceivability that gives order to things: "*Distincta cogitabilitas dat ordinem rei.*"[40]

---

[33] C 479 and 480 (1702–04): "Tempus est ordo continuus existentium secundum mutationes.... Locus est ordo continuus existentium eodem tempore."

[34] GP II 221.24, 31 (December 1700): "extensio mihi nihil aliud esse videtur, quam continuus ordo coexistendi, ut tempus continuus ordo existendi successive. Unde non unum magis quam alterum pro substantia habere, sed ipsa quae sic existunt."

[35] GP II 269 (June 30, 1704): "Spatium nihil aliud est quam ordo existendi simul possibilium, uti tempus est ordo existendi successive possibilium."

[36] A VI vi 154 (1703–05): "temps et l'espace sont de la nature des verités eternelles, qui regardent egalement le possible et l'existant."

[37] A. Augustinus, *Confessiones, Videant itaque nullum tempus esse posse sine creatura*, XI, 30 (40).

[38] A VI vi 289.28: "le lieu ou le temps bien loin de determiner d'eux mèmes, ont besoin eux memes d'estre determinés par les choses qu'ils contiennent."

[39] A VI iv 1352.13 (perhaps 1677).

[40] GP VII 289–91 and C 535 (c. 1703).

This conceivability is not restricted to being conceived by God but applies to the ability to be conceived at all; that is, the ability to be. It concerns the logical aspect of every substance, its *notio completa*, which contains its relations to all singular substances contained in its world.

Leibniz pursues his analysis of time to the roots, defining the notion of change—which he characterizes as an aggregate between contradictory states—as so elementary as to involve nothing more than the direct transition from a state into its contradictory.[41]

Speaking about existent things, we can say contradictory things about the same thing; whence there is time and change.[42] In order to grasp the nature of time, one has to consider the primitive change or contradictory predicates of some one thing in different respects—these different respects being precisely the consideration of time. Space and time are not things (i.e., substances); they are real relations. Since there is no principle that allows an identification of the subject of motion, neither is there absolute place nor absolute motion. Therefore, motion is relative.[43] This primitive change—that is, this transition to a contradictory state—happens directly, without any mediation or gap.[44]

This transition is, first and foremost, the action of a singular individual and has a direct effect on every other individual. Leibniz gives an example: "When I say 'Peter denies' and correlate this with a certain time, then I presuppose the nature of time, which includes all that exists just at that time."[45]

Abstractly speaking, this means that the whole series of things—the series of all things in a possible world—is included in every sentence involving existence and time. Neither "now" nor "here" could be understood without reference to every other thing in the world.[46] This change can only be caused by the action that every simple substance brings about in accordance with its own individual law.[47]

---

[41] A VI iv 1411.10 (April 1679): "Mutatio est aggregatum ex duobus statibus contradictoriis."

[42] A VI iv N.97 393.12 (July 1680–March 1685): "mutatio, duratio, duo status contradictorii ejusdem, hinc diversitas temporis, tempore prius, tempore posterius et simul. Quaecunque actu existunt simul existunt. Seu quaecunque existentiam habent, datum unum alio vel prius est, vel posterius, vel simul. Et quidem si prius est et posterius, aestimari potest quanto, seu ex alicujus mutationis uniformis vestigio"; A VI iv N.196 931.2 (August 1688–January 1689): "possunt enim cum de existentia agitur, contradictoria dici de eodem, unde tempus et mutatio."

[43] A VI iv N.312 1621.22 fn. 3 (1688): "Ad temporis naturam intelligendam requiretur ut consideretur mutatio seu contradictoria praedicata de eodem, diverso respectu, qui respectus nihil aliud est quam consideratio temporis. Spatium et tempus non sunt Res, sed relationes reales. Nullus est locus absolutus, nec motus, quia nulla sunt principia determinandi subjectum motus."

[44] A VI iv N.76 307.25 (January–September 1679): "revera mutatio sit aggregatum duorum statuum oppositorum in uno temporis tractu, nullo existente momento mutationis. "

[45] A VI iv N.165 763.20 (April–December 1686): "Si dico 'Petrus abnegat', intelligendo de certo tempore, utique praesupponitur etiam illius temporis natura, quae utique involvit et omnia in illo tempore existentia."

[46] A VI iv 1517.25 (end of 1685–mid-1686): "Hinc omnes propositiones quas ingreditur existentia et tempus, eas ingreditur eo ipso tota series rerum; neque enim τὸ *nunc* vel *hic* nisi relatione ad caetera intelligi potest."

[47] A VI iv 1411.16 (April 1679): "Actio est mutationis causa."

Space and time are orders. But how do these orders come into being? Following Leibniz, it can be said that God created them, but only inasmuch as God decreed that the best of possible worlds should exist. This answer does not take into account Leibniz's conviction that all substances are endowed with a primitive force that enables them to act spontaneously and strive to exist. Hence, the orders constitute space and time, not as things apart from the substances themselves but as relations among substances, which in turn belong to the same world in virtue of their compatibility with one another. Time requires subjects to retain their identity and their compatibility forever. Leibniz speaks of "the mystery of the duration of substances," something "unknown to Aristotle."[48]

For Leibniz, the duration of substances is given by the fact that they come into existence only by creation and can end only by annihilation.[49]

In April 1679, Leibniz already held that action—by which he means "spontaneous action"—is the cause of change. In 1696, after having asserted in his published *Système nouveau* that his hypothesis of spontaneity is possible, he asks rhetorically: "For why could God not give to a substance at the outset a nature or internal force which could produce in it in an orderly way . . . everything that is going to happen to it, that is to say, all the appearances or expressions it is going to have, and all without the help of any created thing?"[50]

Leibniz goes on to point out that this should in fact be more than a hypothesis because it would be impossible to explain the matter in a better, more intelligible way than in relation to the notion of action as he defines it.[51] This action is guided by final causes insofar as it follows the principle of the best.[52] Leibniz claims that, in a "marvelous" way, he arrived a priori at an estimation of forces from the inner nature of action and power.[53]

Later he insisted to De Volder: "If nothing is active from its own nature, then nothing at all will be active. After all, what reason is there for activity, if it is not in a thing's nature?" Every action requires change; therefore, substances have a tendency toward internal change, and it can be said that temporality follows from a thing's nature. Leibniz

---

[48] Leibniz to Foucher, May 23, 1687; A II ii 202,12: "Aristote . . . n'ayant pas sçeu le mystere de la durée des substances."

[49] GP VI 152 (1710); cf. A VI iv 1624.6 (perhaps 1688): "Je tiens que les Ames et generalement les substances simples ne sauroient commencer que par la creation, ny finir que par l'annihilation."

[50] GP IV 485, WFN 18f (1685): "Cette hypothese est tres possible. Car pourquoy Dieu ne pourroit il pas donner d'abord à la substance une nature ou force interne qui luy puisse produire par ordre (comme dans une Automate spirituel ou formel, mais libre en celle qui la raison partage) tout ce qui luy arrivera, c'est à dire, toutes les apparences ou expressions qu'elle aura, et cela sans le secours d'aucune creature?"

[51] GP IV 486 and 487, WFN 20: "Outre tous ces avantages qui rendent cette Hypothese recommendable, on peut dire que c'est quelque chose de plus qu'une Hypothese, puisqu'il ne paroist gueres possible d'expliquer les choses d'une autre maniere intelligible . . . estant conforme à la notion de l'Action, que nous venons d'etablir."

[52] GP VI 599 (1714): "Et les perceptions dans la Monade naissent les unes des autres par les loix des Appetits, ou des causes finales du bien et du mal."

[53] See Leibniz to De Volder, GP II 158 (December 27, 1698): "Eandem virium aestimationem aliis adhuc demonstrationibus a priori seu ex intima natura actionis et potentiae mirabiliter concludo, quae nunc omitto vitandae prolixitatis." Translated in Lodge, p. 37.

concluded this remark with the words: "From universals there follow eternal things; from individuals there follow temporal things as well."[54]

All individual things are successive; that is, subject to succession. Leibniz therefore asks himself: what is permanent in the nature of a substance? His answer is: "the very law that involves continued succession, which in individual things corresponds to the law that is in the whole universe."[55]

Leibniz opts for the simpler idiom of *lex ipsa* over the more complicated account of self-constitution by which the act of creation quasi-codified the sequence of changes achieved by each simple substance as its own law prior to being selected for existence. He expanded in his letter to De Volder dated January 21, 1704: "I say that the fact that there is a certain persisting law, which involves the future states of that which we conceive of as the same, is the very thing that constitutes the same substance."[56]

In 1716, the last year of Leibniz's life, the question of space and time arose in the course of his discussion with Samuel Clarke. Although Leibniz's answers had by now matured, they were not enough to convince his adversary to abandon the position of his master Isaac Newton, a position based on the view that space and time were absolute entities. Leibniz's metaphysical theory, totally unknown to Clarke could as such be no match against the physical theses of Newton, which also had the advantage of being nearer to common opinion. In fact, Leibniz and Clarke were speaking at cross purposes. In his last letter to Clarke, dated from the middle of August 1716, Leibniz offered some central hints (especially in paragraphs 83–89) to which Clarke could not reply other than with the words, "All This, I acknowledge, I understand not at all."[57] Leibniz did not introduce new arguments aside from those he needed to refute Newton's main thesis setting space as *sensorium Dei*.

One year earlier, Leibniz had presented the core of his revolutionary theory of space and time quasi-axiomatically in his *Initia rerum mathematicarum metaphysica*,[58] a paper that remained unpublished in his lifetime but was certainly sent to Christian Wolff, who took over the content but trivialized it in ignorance of Leibniz's private metaphysical papers. Therefore, Leibniz's theory remained without *Wirkungsgeschichte* despite the efforts of Wolff[59] and A. G. Baumgarten.[60]

[54] GP II 263 (January 21, 1704): "Si nihil sua natura activum est, nihil omnino activum erit; quae enim tandem ratio actionis si non in natura rei? . . . Sed cum omnis actio mutationem contineat, ergo habemus . . . tendentiam ad mutationem internam, et temporale sequens ex rei natura. . . . Ex universalibus aeterna, ex singularibus et temporalia consequuntur" (Lodge, p. 289).

[55] GP II 263 (January 21, 1704): "Sed omnes res singulares sunt successivae . . . Nec mihi aliud in eis est permanens quam lex ipsa quae involvit continuatam successionem, in singulis consentiens ei quae est in toto universo" (Lodge, p. 289).

[56] GP II 264: "Legem quandam esse persistentem, quae involvat futuros ejus quod ut idem concipimus status, id ipsum est quod substantiam eandem constituere dico" (Lodge, p. 291).

[57] *Correspondance Leibniz-Clarke présentée d'après les manuscrites originaux des bibliothèques de Hanovre et de Londres*, edited by A. Robinet (Paris, 1957).

[58] GM VII 17–19.

[59] Cf. Chr. Wolff, *Deutsche Metaphysik* (1720) §94–101 and *Ontologia* (1728) §572; there, he quotes from the 1717 printed letter of Leibniz to Nicolas Remond from March 14, 1714 (GP III 612, L 655 ff).

[60] A. G. Baumgarten, *Metaphysica* (1739) §239.

Whereas Descartes took it to be evident that time is discontinuous and that no moment is connected to a prior moment and that, therefore, no state of anything can be a sufficient reason for that thing's state at a later time, Leibniz asserts—metaphorically—that every monad is big with the future and keeps traces of the past and that all that happens has its sufficient reason in former causal states and in the final causality of future states: *Nihil sine ratione*. As he wrote to Des Bosses in his last letter, the fact that matter naturally requires extension means that its parts naturally require an order of co-existence among themselves.[61]

To understand Leibniz's assumptions and their consequences, we need to enter deeply into his metaphysics, as he himself reminds us several times. Without acknowledgment of his new notion of possibility, necessary for the constitution of the infinite totality of possible beings that, as free-acting subjects, constitute themselves, and without recognizing that all things remain in harmonious connection, never acting against one another, in short, without the acknowledgment of pre-established harmony, it is not possible to understand what Leibniz means when he defines something as earlier than another in terms of the former being the reason of the latter or even the reason of all beings later than it. Only in this metaphysical context can one accept Leibniz's theory about space and time.

This theory is paradigmatically modern in making not only existent things the conditions for knowing what time is, as Augustine did,[62] but also the actions by which actual and possible beings constitute themselves with the sequence of their perceptions. Things do not act in space and time but constitute the orders that we can recognize as space and time. This requires a Copernican turn for our thinking, as Leibniz himself was aware.[63] Leibniz's universal assumption that former states involve everything that comes later is not easy for us to accept. Nevertheless, many scientific findings of today are specifications of this assumption. Although Leibniz accepts that infinitely many hypotheses could satisfy the aspects of phenomena that can be grasped by mathematics, he would surely never favor any other over his *metaphysical* thesis that space and time have their reason in the actions of simple substances.

---

[61] GP II 515 (May 29, 1716): "Materiam naturaliter exigere extensionem, est partes ejus naturaliter exigere inter se ordinem coexistendi."

[62] A. Augustinus, *Confessiones, Videant itaque nullum tempus esse posse sine creatura.*

[63] Cf. GP VII 543 and C 486.

PART V

SCIENTIFIC AND TECHNICAL WORK

CHAPTER 23

....

OPTICS

....

JEFFREY K. MCDONOUGH

ALTHOUGH often overlooked today, optics thrived in the early modern era as a science of first rank engaging many of the best minds of the period and producing some of its most dramatic scientific results.[1] This essay attempts to shed light on Leibniz's efforts to contribute to the development of early modern optics by focusing on his derivations of the laws of reflection and refraction.[2] The first three sections examine his attempts to derive the central laws of geometrical optics in works drawn from his early, middle, and later optical studies.[3] The fourth section briefly considers the broader significance of his sophisticated approach to the laws of optics. Connections to more familiar themes from Leibniz's philosophy are drawn along the way.

Leges Reflexionis et Refractionis Demonstratae, 1671*

Leibniz's earliest studies in optics take place against the background of his first systematic theory of the natural world, as presented in his twin studies of 1671, the *Theoria motus abstracti* (TMA) and the *Hypothesis physica nova* (HPN, also known as the *Theoria motus concreti*) (A VI.ii.261–276, 221–257). The first of these works presents a rather surprising

---

[1] For general studies of seventeenth-century optics, see Vasco Ronchi, *The Nature of Light*, trans. V. Barocas (Cambridge, Mass.: Harvard University Press, 1970); A. I. Sabra, *Theories of Light from Descartes to Newton* (New York: Cambridge University Press, 1981).

[2] This essay overlaps in parts with three longer and more detailed studies by the author: Jeffrey K. McDonough, "Leibniz's Two Realms Revisited," *Noûs* 42, no. 4 (2008), 673–696; "Leibniz on Natural Teleology and the Laws of Optics," *Philosophy and Phenomenological Research* 78, no. 3 (2009), 505–544; "Leibniz's Optics and Contingency in Nature," *Perspectives on Science* 18, no. 4 (2010), 432–455.

[3] Many of Leibniz's optical studies are catalogued in LH 37.2. A collection of helpful, if not always reliable, transcriptions of Leibniz's optical writings is available in Ernst Gerland, *Leibnizens Nachgelassene Schriften Physikalischen, Mechanischen und Technischen Inhalts* (Leipzig: Teubner, 1906). The definitive edition of Leibniz's optical works will appear (primarily) in series 8 of the Akademie edition of Leibniz's writings, the first volume of which is now available and contains several intriguing early studies.

account of the fundamental or "private" laws of the natural world, according to which the motions of bodies are determined solely by their *conatus* with no role assigned to their respective sizes or masses. The second work presents Leibniz's attempt to reconcile these supposed fundamental laws of nature with the dictates of idealized experience, and in particular with the laws of impact then recently made public by Huygens and Wren. Leibniz is explicit both in the HPN and in other early writings that the laws of optics are to be counted among the derived or "public" laws of nature (A.VI.ii.228–231, 312).

In the first of a series of three pieces dated by the Akademie editors to the same period as the TMA and HPN, Leibniz offers a succinct derivation of the law of reflection (A.VI. ii.309–310). Referring to the figure below, he proposes to let A be a body traveling along a straight line from point a striking the plane bc at point d.

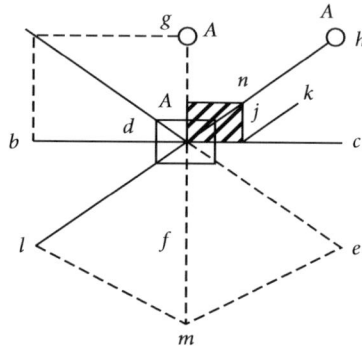

g   A   A
       h
n   k
A   j
b   d   c
l   f   e
m

Leibniz argues that at point d, the body A will "try to continue its motion with the same speed in the same direction from d to e" (A.VI.ii.309–310). He maintains, however, that the motion from d to e "can be understood to be composed from two *conatus* [one] from d to c and [one] from d to f, in such a way that the *conatus* toward c would be as much stronger than the *conatus* toward f as the straight line dc is greater than the straight line df" (A.VI.ii.310). From this result, Leibniz is able to demonstrate the core dictate of the law of reflection, namely, that the angle of incidence (adb) must be equal to the angle of reflection (hdc) (A.VI.ii.310).

A similarly elegant derivation of the law of refraction, however, is conspicuously absent from the *Leges Reflexionis et Refractiones*. In the first of the three pieces, Leibniz proposes to prove that "If the incident [ray] penetrates a resisting [medium] from a more resisting [medium] it is refracted from the perpendicular; if from a less resisting [medium], toward the perpendicular" (A.VI.ii.312). The derivation that follows begins as one might expect, with Leibniz imagining, in reference to figure 1 here, that body A travels along the straight line hd striking the surface bdc. Having suggested that the impetus of the striking body will be diminished (or increased) in proportion to the resistance of the refracting medium, however, the proof quickly trails off. In the second piece, Leibniz affirms proportionality between on the one hand the ratio of the sine of the angle of incidence and the sine of the angle of refraction and on the other hand the ratio of the resistances of the relevant mediums (A.VI.ii.313, 318). Having come that far, however, Leibniz's derivation ultimately breaks off abruptly, literally in midsentence (A.VI.ii.320–322). The third piece takes up once again the topic of refraction, but makes no attempt to derive the law of refraction itself (A.VI.ii.322–323).

It seems likely that Leibniz's failure to produce an elegant derivation of the law of refraction in the *Leges Reflexionis et Refractiones* is due to his appreciation of the deep difficulties of constructing a proof within the confines of an austere mechanism. It was well known, for example, that a ray of light traveling from one medium to another medium may be refracted either away from a perpendicular drawn at the point of impact (with the ray bending, as it were, in the counterclockwise direction) or toward such a perpendicular (with the ray bending, as it were, in the clockwise direction). Strict mechanists, like Descartes, had a relatively easy time accounting for the case of refraction away from the perpendicular. For in that case, they could suppose that the direction of the refracted ray is determined crucially by the vertical tendency of the ray being reduced by the refracting medium. The case of refraction toward the perpendicular, however, was thought to present a greater difficulty. For in that case, it was harder to imagine a plausible mechanical cause for what, by parallel reasoning, would appear to be an increase in the vertical tendency of the ray as it entered into the refracting medium.

In the *Leges Reflexionis et Refractiones*, Leibniz attempts to address this worry through the postulation of an "elastic force" (*vi Elastica*) (A.VI.ii.314). The rough idea is that the elastic force of a medium may lend an additional downward tendency to a projectile or ray of light moving from one medium to another and thereby act as the cause of the observed phenomenon of refraction toward the perpendicular. Leibniz maintains that elastic forces are similarly necessary for explaining how the vertical component of the tendency of a ray of light may be reversed in cases of reflection, and he insists that in recognizing the elasticity of reflecting bodies he is able to explain what had been simply taken for granted by his predecessors (A.VI.iv.1404). Because in his early writings Leibniz takes elastic forces themselves to be explained by his distinction between fundamental and derived laws of nature, he could see his earliest system of the world, as sketched in the TMA and HPN, as both lending support to and, in turn, being supported by his earliest accounts of the laws of reflection and refraction (A.VI.ii.228–231).[4]

Unicum Opticae, Catoptricae et Dioptricae Principium, 1682

Although the *Leges Reflexionis et Refractiones* are dominated by a broadly mechanistic approach to the laws of optics, Leibniz's writings from mid-1670s on also reveal a deep and abiding interest in a radically different approach to deriving the laws of reflection

---

[4] For discussion of the place of elasticity in Leibniz's early thought, as well as in the problems discussed hereafter, see Herbert Breger, "Elastizität als Strukturprinzip der Materie bei Leibniz," *Studia Leibnitiana Sonderheft 13* (1982), 113–121.

and refraction. That approach is clearly on display in one of Leibniz's most significant scientific writings, the *Unicum Opticae, Catoptricae et Dioptricae Principium*, published in the 1682 edition of the *Acta Eruditorum* (Dutens 3.145–150). In it, Leibniz introduces as "the first principle" of optics, catoptrics, and dioptrics the rule that "Light radiating from a point reaches an illuminated point by the easiest path" and shows how this "unitary principle" may be used to derive both the laws of reflection and refraction.[5]

In his derivation of the law of reflection, Leibniz argues, in reference to the figure below, that "in simple optics, the ray directed from the radiating point C to the illuminated point E arrives by the shortest direct path, in the same medium, that is, by the straight line CE":

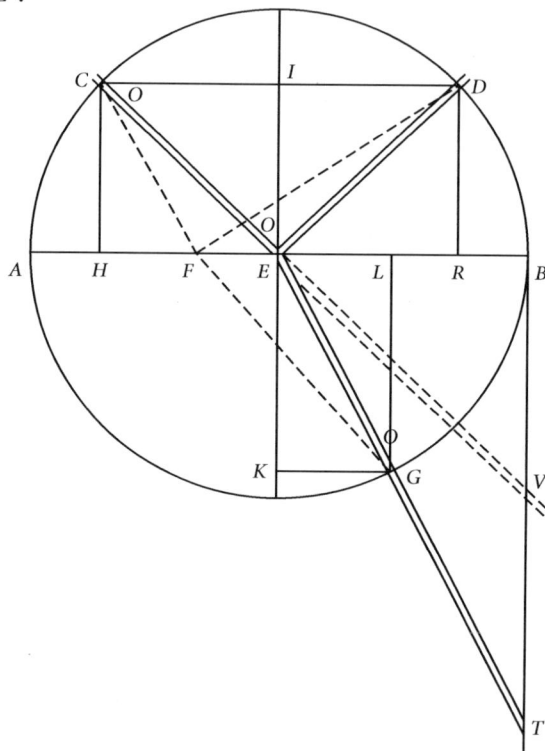

The accompanying proof of the law of reflection is geometric and elegant. Leibniz reasons that under the given conditions, "the whole path CE + ED becomes the least of all . . . if E is taken to be such that as a result the angles CEA and DEB are equal, as is evident from geometry" (Dutens 3.145). In a related piece, however, Leibniz hints at a more tantalizing set of metaphysical or "architectonic" considerations that almost certainly helped to motivate his approach to the laws of optics in the *Unicum Opticae, Catoptricae et Dioptricae Principium*. In his *Metaphysical Definitions and Reflections*, he suggests

---

[5] Leibniz's 1682 paper is also discussed in Gerd Buchdahl, *Metaphysics and the Philosophy of Science. The Classical Origins: Descartes to Kant* (Oxford: Blackwell, 1969), 425–434; Hartmut Hecht, "Dynamik und Optik bei Leibniz," *NTM International Journal of History and Ethics of Natural Sciences, Technology and Medicine* 4, no. 1 (1996), 83–102.

that since nature always chooses the "optimal means . . . there ought to be a reason only for a long or short journey," drawing, in effect, the conclusion that a ray of light reflected from C to D must pass through the point E on the grounds that (1) there would have to be a reason for its passing through any point, and (2) there could be no reason for its passing through some point other than E (A.VI.iv.1405).

Leibniz's derivation of the law of refraction in the *Unicum Opticae, Catoptricae et Dioptricae Principium* is necessarily more involved than his derivation of the law of reflection. Whereas the paths of reflected rays of light typically coincide with shortest reflected paths between two points, this evidently cannot be the case with refracted rays (since refracted rays typically follow bent rather than straight paths). Leibniz's solution to this difficulty is to suppose that a refracted ray must always follow the "easiest" path—rather than the shortest path—from one point to another, where the "ease" of a path is a measurable quantity that can be computed by multiplying the distance of the path by its resistance. With this strategy in mind, Leibniz argues, in essence, that the actual refracted path from C to T will be CET, provided that the quantity determined by the length of CE times the resistance of the medium IE plus the length of ET times the resistance of the medium EK is less than the quantity similarly determined from the sum of any other two paths CF and FT.

In casting his proof in terms of "ease" rather than speed, Leibniz hoped to resolve a dispute that had pitted Descartes and his defenders against the great mathematician Pierre Fermat. The nub of the dispute concerned the question of whether light travels faster in denser materials, such as water, or faster in rarer materials, such as air. Fermat took the perhaps more intuitive view that light travels faster in rarer materials and was thus able to argue that a ray of light, such as CET in figure 2, may follow a quickest path by traveling a greater distance through air (IE) and a shorter distance in water (EK). Cartesians objected. On theoretical grounds, they argued that rays of light must travel faster in denser materials. Descartes, for example, suggests that air acts like a soft body absorbing the motion of a ray of light, while water acts more like a hard body that preserves (even while redirecting) a ray's motion.[6] Cartesians consequently maintained that a path such as CET could not represent the quickest path from C to T and that Fermat's principle must therefore be false. By introducing the notion of "ease," Leibniz hoped to strike a conciliatory middle position between these two opponents, one that would allow him to side with the letter of the Cartesian view that light travels faster in denser materials while nonetheless preserving the spirit of Fermat's position by insisting that CET is after all a minimal path with respect to ease if not with respect to speed.

The technical innovation represented by Leibniz's introduction of the quantity of "ease" reflects a general conciliatory attitude on his part toward what may be thought of as mechanistic and optimality approaches to deriving the laws of optics. Whereas Descartes, Fermat, and later Cartesians saw two irreconcilable methods for discovering the laws of optics, Leibniz saw two complementary routes to scientific discovery. In keeping with this view, Leibniz affirmed throughout his career that it must be possible to derive the laws of optics from broadly mechanistic considerations, and he manifestly

---

[6] *Oeuvres de Descartes*, Ed. by C. Adam and P. Tannery. Paris: L. Cerf, 1997-1913, volume VI, p. 103.

believed that such a derivation was readily available in the case of the law of reflection. He also insisted, however, from at least the late 1670s on, that the laws of optics may also be derived from considerations of optimality. He thus insists throughout his mature career that "Both methods are good, [and that] both can be useful not only for admiring the skill of the great workman but also for making useful discoveries" (GP IV 447–448).

Tentamen Anagogicum. Essay Anagogicum dans la recherche des causes, 1696*

For all the innovation it represents, Leibniz's 1682 essay makes no significant advance on at least one difficulty that had separated proponents of mechanistic and optimality approaches to the laws of optics. That difficulty is perhaps most apparent in cases of reflection involving concave mirrors: in reflecting off of a concave mirror, a ray of light may travel along a path that is in fact longer, slower, and "harder" than other merely possible paths that would involve the ray reflecting off one of the mirror's "upturned" sides. Fermat and Leibniz had maintained that in such cases a ray of light should be viewed as being optimized with respect to a tangent drawn at the point of reflection, and even in later writings Leibniz continues to insist that "Order demands that curved lines and surfaces be treated as composed of straight lines and planes, [so that] . . . a ray is determined by the plane on which it falls, which is considered as forming the curved surface at that point" (GP VII 274/L 479). Opponents of the optimization approach to the laws of optics, however, understandably demurred. They saw such appeals to tangent planes as an ad hoc response to a family of clear counterexamples to the proposal that rays of light always follow optimal paths regardless of whether those paths are taken to be shortest, quickest, or easiest paths.

Leibniz's derivations of the laws of optics in the *Tentamen Anagogicum* address this technical problem head on and in the process display the full sophistication of his mature work in optics. The proofs may be thought of as being developed in three steps.[7] In the first step, Leibniz considers, with respect to the figure below, "a curve AB, concave or convex, and an axis ST to which the ordinates of the curve are referred:"

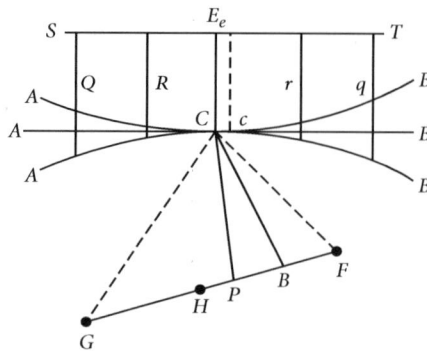

---

[7] For discussion of Leibniz's proofs in the *Tentamen Anagogicum*, see also François Duchesneau, *Leibniz et la Méthode de la Science* (Paris: Presses universitaires de France, 1993), 284–310.

Stating the problem in terms of finding the point C that is unique with respect to its ordinate (i.e. y-axis) value, Leibniz characterizes C as the only point on AB that does not have a corresponding point of the same ordinate value a finite distance away, that is, as the only point on AB whose "twin" with respect to ST would have to be "infinitely close." As Leibniz shows, it is therefore possible to find C by taking the derivative of an equation describing the line AB and setting it equal to zero. With good justification, Leibniz maintains that this now standard operation for determining local maxima and minima greatly simplifies the calculations employed in his derivations of the laws of reflection and refraction.

In the second step, Leibniz shows how the law of reflection may be derived from the principle that "a ray is directed in the most determined or unique path, even in relation to curves" (GP VII 274/L 479). In reference once again to figure 3, Leibniz considers a ray of light traveling between the fixed points F and G being reflected off a mirror ACB, which might be planar, concave, or convex. Tacitly assuming that the medium through which the light travels is everywhere the same, Leibniz reduces the problem of finding the path unique with respect to "ease" to the problem of finding the point C such that the path FCG is unique with respect to its length. Using the technique set out in the first step, and elementary trigonometry, Leibniz is able to show that for such a path the angle of incidence FCA must be equal to the angle of reflection GCB. Because his derivation is fully applicable to standard cases involving concave and convex mirrors, Leibniz could see his derivation of the law of reflection in the *Tentamen Anagogicum* as a response to the family of counterexamples just highlighted.

In the third step, Leibniz uses essentially the same strategy in order to derive the law of refraction. In reference to the figure below, Leibniz considers a refracting surface ACB that, again, might be planar, concave, or convex, and lets F and G represent illuminating and absorption points for a ray of light (so that the refracted ray of light is represented by FCG):

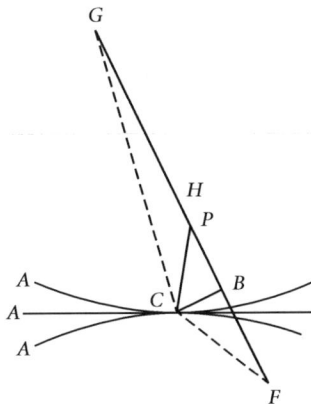

Here once again Leibniz reduces the problem of finding the path unique with respect to ease to the problem of finding the point C such that the path FCG is unique with respect to its length. Employing the same technique as above and using elementary trigonometry, Leibniz is able to show in this case that (1) the ratio of the sine of incidence to the sine of refraction is inversely proportional to the ratio of incident velocity to the refractive velocity, and (2) the ratio between the sine of the angle at which a ray of light strikes a refractive surface and the sine of the angle at which the ray is refracted is a constant determined by the mediums involved. Here as well, since Leibniz's proof is fully applicable to standard cases involving concave and convex surfaces, he could see his derivation of the law of refraction as a response to standard counterexamples that had been raised against Fermat's approach.

In the *Tentamen Anagogicum*, Leibniz explicitly ties his optimization approach to the laws of optics to his defense of divine teleology. Going in one direction, he maintains that the laws of optics lend support to the belief in a providential creator. The laws of optics, he suggests, cannot plausibly be viewed as being either absolutely necessary or wholly contingent. He concludes that they must therefore "originate in the wisdom of their Author or in the principle of greatest perfection, which has led to their choice" (GP VII.272/L 478). Going in the other direction, he maintains that his optimization approach to the laws of optics shows how reflection on God's ends can yield tangible advancements in the study of nature. Indeed, he goes so far as to suggest that the law of refraction must have first been discovered by considering final causes and that Descartes, the first to publish the law of refraction, must therefore have appropriated his results from the work of Willebrord Snell and his disciples while living in Holland (GP VII.274/L 480). Although the charge of plagiarism may well have been unfair to Descartes, the laws of optics nonetheless arguably provide Leibniz with his best example of how he sees the laws of nature as supporting his commitment to the providential design of the world, as well as his best response to Descartes's proposal to "banish from our philosophy the search for final causes."[8]

Optics and Optimal Form

Leibniz's sophisticated derivations of the laws of reflection and refraction take on a broader significance when viewed against the backdrop of his general interest in what he terms the "Method of Optimal Forms" (*Methode de Formis Optimis*) (GP VII:272/L 478). In the simplest of terms, an optimal form is a structure that admits of a locally unique minimum or maximum value, and that may therefore, at least in principle, be treated using the same mathematical techniques that Leibniz helped to pioneer in his sophisticated derivations of the laws of optics.[9] While it had long been recognized that natural

---

[8] *Oeuvres de Descartes*, Ed. by C. Adam and P. Tannery. Paris: L. Cerf, 1997-1913, volume VIIA, p. 15. For discussion of the connection between Leibniz's optics and teleology see: François Duchesneau, "Hypothèses et Finalité dans la Science Leibnizienne," *Studia Leibnitiana* 12 (1980), 161–178; George Gale, "Did Leibniz Have a Practical Philosophy of Science? Or, Does 'Least-Work' Work?," in *Akten des II. Internationalen Leibniz-Kongress, Studia Leibnitiana*, supp. 13 (Wiesbaden: F. Steiner Verlag, 1974); George Gale, "Leibniz' Force: Where Physics and Metaphysics Collide," in *Studia Leibnitiana, Sonderheft* 13 (Stuttgart: F. Steiner Verlag, 1984); David Hirschmann, "The Kingdom of Wisdom and the Kingdom of Power in Leibniz," *Proceedings of the Aristotelian Society* 88 (1988), 147–159.

[9] For discussion of the notion of optimal form and its history, see Don S. Lemons, *Perfect Form: Variational Principles, Methods, and Applications in Elementary Physics* (Princeton, N.J.: Princeton

phenomena often appear to instantiate optimal forms, the development of the calculus, as well as a growing appreciation of the limitations of strict Cartesian mechanism, led in Leibniz's time to an increased interest in a handful of special problems involving optimal form. A brief survey of three of those problems may help to give a sense of the larger implications of Leibniz's sophisticated approach to the laws of optics.

A first special problem is treated in Leibniz's "*Demonstrationes Novae de Resistentia Solidorum*" (New proofs concerning the resistance of solids), published in the July 1684 edition of the *Acta eruditorum* (Dutens 3.161–166). It concerns a difficulty introduced by Galileo, namely, the problem of determining the resistance of solid beams to bending under the force of applied weights. Drawing on Hooke's spring law, as well as on Mariotte's assertion that all bodies are flexible to some degree, Leibniz argues that Galileo's proposed formula for the resistance of a beam should be replaced by a new formula that crucially takes into account variations in resistance over the cross-section of a beam as well as over its length.[10] In doing so, he helps to show how weighted beams may be viewed as instances of optimal form. Just as rays of light may be viewed as minimizing speed, distance, or ease, bending beams may be viewed as minimizing overall stress energy.[11] With his *Demonstrationes Novae de Resistentia Solidorum*, Leibniz not only made an important advance with respect to the first of Galileo's "two new sciences" but also showed in convincing fashion how attention to optimal form may bear fruit well outside the domain of optics.

A second special problem was introduced by James Bernoulli in the 1690 May edition of the *Acta eruditorum*, when he challenged his fellow mathematicians and natural philosophers to "find the curve assumed by a loose string hung freely from two fixed points . . . [assuming] the string is a line which is easily flexible in all parts." At the close of the contest, three correct solutions had been received: one from Johann Bernoulli, James's younger brother and perpetual rival; one from Huygens, who coined the term "catenary" to name the resulting curves; and one from Leibniz, who reportedly replied with a solution on the day he received the challenge. The solutions collectively showed that catenaries, like rays of light and bending beams, may also be treated as instances of optimal form. Just as rays of light take optimal paths and bent beams assume optimal configurations, hanging chains take on an optimal shape that, in Leibniz's terms,

University Press, 1997); Robert Woodhouse, *A Treatise on Isoperimetrical Problems, and the Calculus of Variations* (New York: Chelsea Publishing Company, 1810); Wolfgang Yourgrau and Stanley Mandelstam, *Variational Principles in Dynamics and Quantum Theory*, 3rd ed. (London: Sir Isaac Pitman, 1968).

[10]   More specifically, he argues that, with respect to a cubical beam, the Galilean formula $P_b = 1/2\,P_t$ should be replaced by the formula $P_b = 1/3 P_t$, where P_b is the breaking force in bending by terminal load and P_t is the breaking force in tension. For a historical and technical discussion, see C. Truesdell, *The Rational Mechanics of Flexible or Elastic Bodies, 1638–1788*, vol. 11, pt. 2, *Leonhardi Euleri Opera Omnia* (Turici: Orell Füssli, 1960), 38–42, 59–64.

[11]   On this point, see especially, Mark Wilson, "From the Bending of Beams to the Problem of Free Will," *A Priori 4* (2010). See also Hartmut Hecht, *Mathematik und Naturwissenschaften im Paradigma der Metaphysik* (Stuttgart: Teubner, 1992), 100–104.

maximizes descent or, in modern parlance, minimizes potential energy. As is made especially clear in a letter he wrote to Huygens dated September 14, 1694, Leibniz's efforts to respond to Bernoulli's challenge served to show once again that the notion of an optimal form, championed in his optical studies, can be utilized to make novel discoveries well outside the domain of optics.[12]

A third special problem was introduced in the June 1696 edition of the *Acta eruditorum* when Johann Bernoulli dared "the most acute mathematicians flourishing in the whole world" to find the path of quickest descent between two points in the vertical plane for a freely falling body. Taking advantage of his calculus, Leibniz was again able to solve the problem of the brachistochrone, as it came to be called, on the day he received it. Of the four other solutions submitted—one from each of the Bernoulli brothers, one from Newton, and one from L'Hopital, two merit special mention. Johann Bernoulli's solution was remarkable for showing how the quickest path of descent could be found by treating a descending body as a ray of light passing through increasingly dense media so that the path of quickest descent could be found by exploiting the already known laws of refraction. James Bernoulli's solution, although perhaps less imaginative, was equally remarkable. It highlighted the fact that any portion of a path of quickest descent must itself be a path of quickest descent, and that consequently any larger path can be thought of as a path that is such that any of its subpaths is unique with respect to quickest descent. This important property of optimal forms, noted explicitly by Leibniz in his *Tentamen Anagogicum*, would prove to be crucial to the later development of what has become known as the calculus of variations proper (GP 7: 272/L 478).

Special problems such as those involving bending beams, the catenary, and the brachistochrone set the stage for later developments that further extended the spirit of Leibniz's approach to the laws of reflection and refraction. Spurred by Leibniz's treatment of bending beams, James Bernoulli, for example, would take up in greater detail problems of "elastica" and produce the first general equations in the theory of elasticity.[13] Prompted by the debate treated in Leibniz's 1682 paper, Maupertuis would develop his famous, general "principle of least action," according to which "in all the changes that take place in the universe, the sum of the products of each body multiplied by the distance it moves and by the speed with which it moves is the least possible."[14]

---

[12] Christiaan Huygens, *Oeuvres complètes de Huygens*, vol. 10 (La Haye: M. Niijhoff, 1888), 679. See also GM VII 370–372.

[13] C. Truesdell, *The Rational Mechanics of Flexible or Elastic Bodies, 1638–1788*. In Leonhardi Euleri, *Opera Omnia*, ser. 2, vol. 11, pt. 2. Edited by Joachim Otto Fleckenstein. Turici: Orell Füssli, 1957: 63, 88–109.

[14] P. Maupertuis, *Oeuvres de Maupertuis* (Lyons: Jean-Marie Bruyset, 1698–1759), vol. 4, p. 20, vol. 2, p. 274. For related discussion, see François Duchesneau, "L'Épistémologie de Maupertuis entre Leibniz et Newton: Physique et Physiologie," *Revue de synthèse 113–114* (1984), 7–36; Martial Gueroult, *Leibniz, Dynamique et Métaphysique, suivi d'une Note sur le Principe de la Moindre Action Chez Maupertuis* (Paris: Aubier-Montaigne, 1967); Hartmut Hecht, "La Quantité de la Force et Quantité d'action: Dynamique et Métaphysicque Chez Leibniz et Maupertuis," in *La Notion de Nature Chez Leibniz: Studia Leibnitiana, Sonderheft 24*, ed. Martine de Gaudemar (Stuttgart: Franz Steiner

Such results would later be refined and extended by the next half generation of natural philosophers, resulting in the full flourishing of what would become known as the rational mechanics of the eighteenth century. Thus, Euler, for example, would offer systematic treatments of the special problems just discussed in the process of drawing out the full implications of Newton's second law and arriving at his definitive statement of the principle of linear motion.[15] Lagrange would pick up the intellectual thread present in the notion of an optimal form and produce the first general variational method for dynamics, publishing his results in his *Mechanique Analytic* in 1811.[16] In light of these developments, one might reasonably conclude that although in surveys of the history and philosophy of science Leibniz is most often associated with his role in the *vis viva* controversy and his exchange of letters with Samuel Clark, his most enduring scientific legacy might well be his influence on the development of modern rational mechanics, whose founding proponents were, in effect, drawing out and extending many of the implications already present in his relatively accessible optical studies.

CONCLUSION

Although necessarily incomplete, even the brief discussion offered here of Leibniz's derivations of the laws of optics should be sufficient to suggest three general conclusions: First, his interest in optics spanned the entire breadth of his career, running from studies concurrent with his earliest systematic treatments of physics to mature studies as represented most famously by his *Tentamen Anagogicum*. Second, within that long span, he continued work on and refined his earlier efforts, at first more radically when his views on the physical world shifted dramatically around the time of his years in Paris, and then more cautiously as his physical and metaphysical views continued to ferment. Third, his thinking about optics intertwines in interesting and often surprising ways with other threads associated with his thought, from the nature of material bodies and divine choice to the implications of his calculus and related scientific techniques. One may reasonably hope that more of Leibniz's interests in the study of optics and optical phenomena, as well as their broader implications for his widely ranging pursuits, will come to light as the Akademie editors continue their important task of bringing his scientific, medical, and technical writings to print.

Verlag, 1995); Hartmut Hecht, "Leibniz' Concept of Possible Worlds and the Analysis of Motion in Eighteenth Century Physics," in *Between Leibniz, Newton, and Kant*, ed. W. Lefevre (Dordrecht: Kluwer, 2001), 27–45.

[15] See Leonhardi Euleri, "Découverte d'un Nouveau Principe de Mécanique," *Mémoires de l'académie des sciences de Berlin 6* (1752), 185–217; reprinted in Leonhardi Euleri, *Opera Omnia*, ser. 2, vol. 5, ed. Joachim Otto Fleckenstein (Turici: Orell Füssli, 1957), 81–108.

[16] C. Truesdell, "A Program toward Rediscovering the Rational Mechanics of the Age of Reason," *Archive for History of Exact Sciences 1* (1960), 33.

REFERENCES

Breger, Herbert. "Elastizität als Strukturprinzip der Materie bei Leibniz." *Studia Leibnitiana Sonderheft 13* (1982), 113–121.

Buchdahl, Gerd. *Metaphysics and the Philosophy of Science. The Classical Origins: Descartes to Kant.* Oxford: Blackwell, 1969.

Duchesneau, François. "Hypothèses et Finalité dans la Science Leibnizienne." *Studia Leibnitiana 12* (1980), 161–178.

Duchesneau, François. *Leibniz et la Méthode de la Science.* Paris: Presses Universitaires de France, 1993.

Leonhardi Euleri. "Décuverte d'un Nouveau Principe de Mécanique," *Mémoires de l'Académie des Sciences de Berlin 6* (1752), 185–217.

Leonhardi Euleri. *Opera Omnia.* Edited by Joachim Otto Fleckenstein. Turici: Orell Füssli, 1957, ser. 2.

Gale, George. "Did Leibniz Have a Practical Philosophy of Science? Or, Does 'Least-Work' Work?" In *Akten Des II. Internationalen Leibniz-Kongress, Studia Leibnitiana,* supp. 13, 151–160. Wiesbaden: F. Steiner Verlag, 1974.

Gale, George. "Leibniz' Force: Where Physics and Metaphysics Collide." In *Studia Leibnitiana, Sonderheft 13,* 62–70. Stuttgart: F. Steiner Verlag, 1984.

Gerland, Ernst. *Leibnizens Nachgelassene Schriften Physikalischen, Mechanischen und Technischen Inhalts.* Leipzig: B. G. Teubner, 1906.

Gueroult, Martial. *Leibniz, Dynamique et Métaphysique, suivi d'une Note sur le Principe de la Moindre Action Chez Maupertuis.* Paris: Aubier-Montaigne, 1967.

Hecht, Hartmut. "Dynamik und Optik bei Leibniz." *NTM International Journal of History and Ethics of Natural Sciences, Technology and Medicine 4,* no. 1 (1996), 83–102.

Hecht, Hartmut. "La Quantité de la Force et Quantité d'action: Dynamique et Métaphysicque Chez Leibniz et Maupertuis." In *La Notion de Nature Chez Leibniz: Studia Leibnitiana,* Sonderheft 24, edited by Martine de Gaudemar. Stuttgart: Franz Steiner Verlag, 1995, 59–66.

Hecht, Hartmut. "Leibniz' Concept of Possible Worlds and the Analysis of Motion in Eighteenth Century Physics." In *Between Leibniz, Newton, and Kant,* edited by W. Lefevre. Dordrecht: Kluwer, 2001, 27–45.

Hecht, Hartmut. *Mathematik und Naturwissenschaften im Paradigma der Metaphysik.* Stuttgart: Teubner, 1992.

Hirschmann, David. "The Kingdom of Wisdom and the Kingdom of Power in Leibniz." *Proceedings of the Aristotelian Society 88* (1988), 147–159.

Huygens, Christiaan. *Oeuvres completes de Huygens,* vol. 10 (La Haye: M. Niijhoff, 1888).

Lemons, Don S. *Perfect Form: Variational Principles, Methods, and Applications in Elementary Physics.* Princeton, N.J.: Princeton University Press, 1997.

Maupertuis, P. *Oeuvres de Maupertuis* (Lyons: Jean-Marie Bruyset, 1698–1759).

McDonough, Jeffrey K. "Leibniz on Natural Teleology and the Laws of Optics." *Philosophy and Phenomenological Research 78,* no. 3 (2009), 505–544.

McDonough, Jeffrey K. "Leibniz's Optics and Contingency in Nature." *Perspectives on Science 18,* no. 4 (2010), 432–455.

McDonough, Jeffrey K. "Leibniz's Two Realms Revisited." *Noûs 42,* no. 4 (2008), 673–696.

Ronchi, Vasco. *The Nature of Light.* Translated by V. Barocas. Cambridge, Mass.: Harvard University Press, 1970.

Sabra, A. I. *Theories of Light from Descartes to Newton*. New York: Cambridge University Press, 1981.

Truesdell, C. "A Program toward Rediscovering the Rational Mechanics of the Age of Reason." *Archive for History of Exact Sciences 1* (1960), 1–36.

Truesdell, C. *The Rational Mechanics of Flexible or Elastic Bodies, 1638–1788*. In Leonhardi Euleri, *Opera Omnia*, ser. 2, vol. 11, pt. 2. Edited by Joachim Otto Fleckenstein. Turici: Orell Füssli, 1957: 11–416.

Wilson, Mark. "From the Bending of Beams to the Problem of Free Will." *A Priori 4* (2010).

Woodhouse, Robert. *A Treatise on Isoperimetrical Problems, and the Calculus of Variations*. New York: Chelsea Publishing Company, 1810.

Yourgrau, Wolfgang, and Stanley Mandelstam. *Variational Principles in Dynamics and Quantum Theory*. 3rd ed. London: Sir Isaac Pitman, 1968.

CHAPTER 24

···

COSMOLOGY

···

DOMENICO BERTOLONI MELI

COSMOLOGY, or a discourse about the universe and its physico-mathematical structure and laws, presented several interrelated dimensions in the late seventeenth and early eighteenth centuries. The condemnation of Galileo in 1633 was still fresh in the mind of European intellectuals of Leibniz's generation and was the subject of reflections and debates: the title of the book in question, *Dialogue Concerning the Two Chief World Systems, Ptolemaic and Copernican* (Florence, 1632) provides us with the first relevant meaning of cosmology, one that was close to Leibniz's concerns over several decades. Around the time of his Italian journey, he composed several memoranda in which he sought to show the equivalence among different world systems and the practical superiority of Copernicus's and to argue that there was no contradiction between the Copernican system and Scripture. The mid-1690s saw a reconfiguration of Leibniz's priorities, with a notable shift of emphasis toward reunification of the Protestant churches and with a consequent decline in his efforts to have the ban against Copernicus lifted by the Catholic Church.

At the time the issue of the world system was being reshaped by recent astronomical, mathematical, and physical findings. Leibniz became especially concerned with these problems in the immediate aftermath of the publication of Newton's *Philosophiae naturalis principia mathematica* (London, 1687), which raised key issues at the intersection between the mathematical and physical treatment of forces and vortices. The *Tentamen de motuum coelestium causis* of 1689 and a number of related published and unpublished drafts and treatises are the key relevant texts in which Leibniz sought to forge an original alternative interpretation to Newton's. Leibniz's main creative period in this area was at the end of the 1680s: after that time, he tinkered with various aspects and corrected some inaccuracies in his previous formulations without altering its basic framework.

Finally, at the end of his life, Leibniz tied more strongly his reflections on cosmology to the notion of conservation, theological concerns about God's intervention in the world, and a deeper analysis of the notions of space and time. The *locus classicus* of these elaborations is the *Leibniz-Clarke Correspondence*, which was part of a larger exchange including Caroline, Princess of Wales. In addition, Leibniz relied extensively on his *Essais de Théodicée* (Amsterdam, 1710), which was one of Caroline's favorite texts. His main targets were Newton's *Principia*, which was challenged here from a different perspective, and the queries to the *Opticks*, which raised a number of general issues to do with God's intervention and role in the world, thus going well beyond strictly optical concerns.

In the rest of this contribution, I shall examine these issues in turn. As we are going to see, Leibniz's interest in cosmology was tied to some of his other concerns, such as freedom in philosophizing and the abolition of censorship, the reunion of the churches, and God's role in the universe.

WORLD SYSTEMS

Debates about the world systems were part of a student's education and of the knowledge and concerns of the learned community in the second half of the seventeenth century. In his *Hypothesis physica nova* or *Theoria motus concreti* (Mainz, 1671), Leibniz presented views consistent with the followers of both Tycho and of Copernicus; indeed, he advertised his views in the very title. From early on, Leibniz saw the advantages of the Copernican system but had reservations in calling it "true" in a strict philosophical sense because the issue was tied to complex notions, such as the nature of motion, space, and time, not to mention the entanglement with his project for the reunion of the churches.[1]

Leibniz identified the issue of Copernicanism as especially significant in the 1680s in the correspondence with Landgraf Ernst von Hessen-Rheinfels, who was one of his closest confidants. In 1652, Ernst had converted from Calvinism to Catholicism and was both promoting church reunion and proselytizing. In the correspondence, Leibniz went as far as to grant infallibility to the Catholic Church on all points of faith. In addition to major doctrinal points, however, Leibniz raised the issue of the world system, relying on an adroit analogy that had already been mentioned by Copernicus in the dedication to Pope Paul III in *De revolutionus orbium caelestium*: he argued that Church Fathers—notably Lactantius, who was not mentioned by name, however—claimed that the Earth was flat and that they denied the existence of inhabitants of the antipodes; similarly, in his own times, the Catholic Church denied and even banned the Copernican system. However, Leibniz argued, these are matters depending on facts and reason rather than faith, and therefore the Church should not interfere with them. Nor, argued Leibniz, should one dissimulate one's beliefs because these are matters of great importance in philosophy.[2] Thus, Leibniz singled out a cosmological problem, namely the system of

---

[1] The title reads: *Hypothesis Physica Nova, Quâ Phænomenorum Naturæ plerorumque causæ ab unicum quodam universali motu, in globo nostro supposito, neque Tychonicis, neque Copernicanis aspernando, repetuntur.*

[2] A I iv, N. 285. Antognazza, *Leibniz*, 218–219.

the world, as a notable obstacle—together with other issues—to a hypothetical conversion to Catholicism and to freedom in philosophizing.

Leibniz returned to the problem of the world system and the anti-Copernican ban in his exchange with Landgraf Ernst. In a letter written from Vienna at the beginning of Summer 1688, Leibniz referred to a key passage in Scripture by Joshua, in which he ordered the sun to stand still, thus prolonging the length of the day:[3]

> If Joshua had been a disciple of Aristarchus or Copernicus, he would not have changed the way he expressed himself, otherwise he would have shocked the people present as well as common sense. All Copernicans, in their ordinary speech and even among themselves, when the issue is not science, will always say that the sun has risen or set, and will never say it of the earth.

Here, Leibniz seemingly endorses a view that can be characterized as "accommodation," according to which the language of Scripture accommodates itself to the beliefs of common people. Similar views were expressed by several others, including Galileo in the letter to Grand Duchess Christina, for example.[4]

During his Italian journey and in its aftermath, Leibniz showed cautious optimism about the state of the Catholic Church and drafted some documents intended for high-ranking prelates and aimed at having the anti-Copernican ban lifted; indeed, while in Italy and especially in Rome, he established contacts with the most open wing of the Catholic hierarchy on the subject. Although in those documents he still emphasized the importance of freedom in philosophizing, significant aspects of his rhetorical strategy changed, and he frequently emphasized the honor of Italy and the need to reverse its intellectual decline, a clear sign that he was addressing an Italian audience.[5] The key texts are a memorandum in all probability addressed to Father Antonio Baldigiani SJ, with the incipit *Praeclarum Ciceronis dictum est*, and one for other prelates in Rome, *Cum geometricis demonstrationibus*, both likely dating from 1689. In those texts, Leibniz modified and refined his hermeneutical stance on Scripture, going back on his previous strategy. For example, in *Cum geometricis demonstrationibus*, he states:[6]

> [I]t is correct to say that in this place [Joshua's intimation to the sun] Holy Scripture spoke in a way that serves both the truth and the proper meaning of the words; it is less correct to say that it accommodates itself in the beliefs people have than to say that

---

[3] A, I v, N. 183, pp. 185–186.

[4] McMullin, "Galileo on Science and Scripture." Funkenstein, *Theology and the Scientific Imagination*, 213–222.

[5] Robinet, *Iter italicum*, 96–118 and 231–3. Bertoloni Meli, "Leibniz on the Censorship." Antognazza, *Leibniz*, 301–302.

[6] The essay was incorrectly identified by Couturat. Robinet, *Iter italicum*, 111–114, at 112, translated in Leibniz, *Philosophical Essays*, 90–94, quotation at 92. Robinet seems to think those two texts were different versions of the same document, an opinion not supported by paleographic evidence and not taken up by the Akademie Ausgabe. Bertoloni Meli, "Leibniz on the Censorship," 25.

it transmits the greatest hidden treasures of wisdom of all kinds, for this is something more worthy of its author, God.

Leibniz's change of stance is both explicit and remarkable here; especially noteworthy is his rejection of the verb "to accommodate" in favor of a stronger adherence to the text. Similarly, in the memorandum probably intended for Baldigiani, Leibniz went as far as to endorse the application of censorship to those holding views rather close to Galileo's in the letter to Grand Duchess Christina:[7]

> In the meantime censorship has been rightly applied to the audacity of those who seemed to judge Holy Scripture less reverently, that is, as if it had not spoken accurately, with the pretext that its aim is to teach the way to salvation, not philosophy. In fact, it is more respectful and truer to acknowledge that in the holy texts are also hidden all the recondite treasures of the sciences, and that absolutely correct things are said not less about astronomical matters than about all the others, which can be stated without damage to the new system. In fact the holy authors could not express the thoughts of their mind in a different way without absurdity, even if a new true system were posed a thousand times.

The key to this shift of hermeneutical stance with regard to Scripture was relativity of motion. Because space without matter is something purely imaginary, Leibniz argued, motion is only a mutual change of position among bodies; therefore, any body can be considered to be at rest or in motion. Ultimately, the choice of world system turns out to be a matter of intelligibility. Leibniz often employed the simile of architectural drawings showing a building from different perspectives: although they are all legitimate, depending on the problem at hand, some may be more appropriate than others, and in some circumstances some may be inadequate.[8]

There are two problems associated with relativity of motion or, as Leibniz often called it, the "equivalence of all hypotheses," meaning that, in a system of bodies, anyone of them can be taken to be at rest or in motion. The first is that in cases of rectilinear uniform translation, two systems can be seen to be indistinguishable— this principle is generally known as *Galilean invariance*. When rotations are involved, however, as Newton pointed out in the scholium to the eighth definition in *Principia mathematica*, two systems can no longer be taken as equivalent because real rotations engender forces to escape along the tangent. Leibniz's response was that all curvilinear motions consist of combinations of—at times infinitesimal— rectilinear motion and because relativity of motion holds for rectilinear ones, it must hold for curvilinear motions as well; hence, nothing violates the equivalence of hypotheses.[9]

---

[7] A VI, 4C, N. 377, 2071.

[8] Leibniz, *Philosophical Essays*, 91.

[9] Leibniz, *Philosophical Essays*, 91. Newton, *The Principia*, 412–413. In the following section, we are going to see an example of Leibniz's approach to curves.

The second problem stems from views internal to Leibniz's system; while holding space, time, and motion to be relative, Leibniz also believed force to be absolute. The privileged expression for force was mv^2 or *living force*; namely, mass times the square of velocity. Leibniz was prepared to state that this expression was conserved for all types of impacts regardless of the nature of the bodies, arguing that the portion of living force that appeared missing in some types of collisions was in fact absorbed by the internal components of the colliding bodies. The notion that living force would be absolute seems to imply that velocity would be absolute, too; a significant factor, however, would be that, although the absolute value of the velocity is determined, its direction would not. Even so, there remains a tension between the absolute nature of force and the relative nature of motion, especially when different observers in relative uniform motion with each other are concerned. From a strictly phenomenological standpoint, however, Leibniz endorsed relativity of motion.[10]

In conclusion, Leibniz presented lack of freedom concerning the world system as an important factor against the Roman Church. During his Italian journey, he shifted from an accommodationist interpretation—according to which Scripture speaks following the traditional or even naïve views of common people of the time—to a stricter reading according to which Scripture speaks the truth about all matters. This truth, however, may not emerge from a first literal reading of Scripture but may result from a more sophisticated interpretation going hand in hand with the most advanced natural investigations. Leibniz's diplomatic and intellectual objective was to convince the Catholic hierarchy to lift the ban against Copernicus, which in his view did serious damage to freedom of philosophizing. Indeed, in later writings, such as the *Nouveax essais sur l'entendement humain*, he unhesitatingly argued that the lack of philosophical freedom and the anti-Copernican ban seriously affected the progress of the sciences.[11]

THE PHYSICAL AND MATHEMATICAL STRUCTURE OF THE WORLD

Leibniz's early conceptions about the structure of the world and its physico-mathematical properties followed mainstream views and involved vortices carrying the planets around the sun, satellites around the primary planets, and comets across vortices, in line with what Descartes had presented in the *Principia philosophiae* (1644). Newton, too, broadly adhered to such views until the time of composition of the

---

[10] Bertoloni Meli, "Leibniz on the Censorship of the Copernican System," 25–26. See also the following section.

[11] A VI vi 515. Similar views apply to the debates on the formation of the Earth and the interpretation of *Genesis*. See Leibniz, *Essais de Théodicée*, para. 244–245; Antognazza, *Leibniz*, 327.

Principia in the mid-1680s. Leibniz's sustained engagement with these matters came in the aftermath of Newton's *Principia mathematica* in 1687.

Newton's views, however, underwent a major transformation in the mid-1680s, when, helped by a series of experiments on motion in resisting media and astronomical data combined with shrewd reasoning, he challenged the existence of an interplanetary fluid responsible for carrying planets, satellites, and comets. Rather, he came to believe that such a fluid would hinder their motions; therefore, their regularity over exceedingly long times ruled out the existence of any vortex. Although Newton had left the explanation of gravity ostensibly open, in practice, by denying the existence of a medium responsible for it, he had raised the specter of occult forces acting at a distance and nonmechanical actions. Newton was also able to prove mathematically a large number of theorems; notable among them was that the areas described by bodies moving around a center of force are proportional to the times, and, conversely, for bodies moving in a curved line in a plane, if a radius drawn to a point describes areas proportional to the times, the bodies are urged by a centripetal force toward that point. These propositions accounted for and generalized Kepler's second law of planetary motion, according to which the areas swept out by the radius from a planet to the sun are proportional to the times. In addition, Newton presented mathematical treatments of a staggering number of phenomena, such as the motions of planets, satellites—especially the Moon—and comets, tides, the precession of the equinoxes, and the shape of the Earth. Together with these brilliant technical results came conceptual reflections and analyses on key notions, such as mass, space, time, and motion. Many of Leibniz's subsequent reflections on cosmology came in response to Newton; therefore, their views have to be seen together.[12] At times, Newton led readers to believe that he was drawing a distinction between a mathematical and physical treatment of motion in which physical impact plays a role: at the beginning of section 11 in book I, for example, he referred to attractions, qualifying his usage of this term by stating that, in the language of physics, they may be more properly called impulses. However, large portions of the rest of the book tried to argue that the interplanetary space is virtually if not rigorously a void, leaving Leibniz to wonder whence those impulses would originate because there was no impelling matter.[13]

Leibniz responded with a number of papers inspired by Christoph Pfautz's review of Newton's *Principia* that appeared in the *Acta Eruditorum* and especially by the treatise itself. The most important of his papers was the *Tentamen de motuum coelestium causis*, published in the same journal for February 1689. In a related piece published in the *Acta Eruditorum* for January 1689 (*De lineis opticis*), Leibniz intimated that he had reached his results about planetary motion long before—possibly in Paris—and that Pfautz's review had merely stimulated him to publish them, thus affirming both that before writing the *Tentamen* he had seen only the review rather than the book itself

[12] Wilson, "The Newtonian Achievement in Astronomy." Janiak, *Newton as Philosopher.* Bertoloni Meli, *Thinking with Objects,* chapter 9. Guicciardini, *Reading the "Principia,"* chapters 3–4.
[13] Bertoloni Meli, *Equivalence and Priority,* 164. Newton, *The Principia,* 561.

and, moreover, that his theory was independent of Newton's *Principia* and preceded his own reading of the review anyway; both claims appear to be in contrast with the manuscript evidence. Indeed, we lack a suitable paper trail on the topic of planetary motion before 1688, and the actual manuscript evidence shows that the preparatory manuscripts for the *Tentamen* stem directly from Leibniz's annotations on the *Principia* itself rather than Pfautz's review. In all likelihood, it was his initial success in attaining genuinely novel and important results that prompted Leibniz to claim both precedence for his theory and independence from Pfautz's review and from Newton's treatise: by so doing, he implicitly highlighted the originality and significance of his contributions, which may have been obscured and overlooked had he stated his reliance on Newton. But whereas his motivations may be a matter for speculation, the actual path he followed can be carefully documented through an extensive set of manuscripts.[14]

In a few months, Leibniz attained remarkable results in retrieving crucial propositions in the *Principia* from a very different and, for him, acceptable physical and philosophical standpoint; moreover, Leibniz's results appeared promising in attaining even more. After a brief historical introduction, Leibniz's *Tentamen* wasted no time in setting out in the first paragraph the key principles of his theory in deductive fashion:[15]

> (1) To tackle the matter itself, then, it can first of all be demonstrated that according to the laws of nature *all bodies that describe a curved line in a fluid are driven by the motion of the fluid.* For all bodies describing a curve endeavour to recede from it along the tangent (because of the nature of motion), it is therefore necessary that something should constrain them. There is, however, nothing contiguous except for the fluid (by hypothesis), and no conatus is constrained except by something contiguous in motion (because of the nature of body), therefore it is necessary that the fluid itself be in motion.

Writing almost in syllogistic form, Leibniz spelled out the laws and conditions enabling him to state in the second paragraph that "(2) Hence it follows that *planets are moved by their aether*, namely they have fluid orbs that are deferent or moving."

It is worth examining in some detail the nature of Leibniz's results. Whereas Newton had posited the existence of central forces and had then derived a striking number of propositions from them, Leibniz was able to retrieve some of Newton's crucial achievements by positing a vortex carrying the planets and moving around

---

[14] Bertoloni Meli, *Equivalence and Priority*, especially General Introduction, chapter 5, and appendix 1. Guicciardini, *Reading the "Principia,"* chapter 6, especially 149–152. Antognazza, *Leibniz*, 296. Putting in print a short paper on planetary motion nearly two years after Newton had published a 500-page tome on the subject and claiming not to have seen it is a strange way of proceeding in many respects by seventeenth-century standards as well.

[15] Bertoloni Meli, *Equivalence and Priority*, 128–129.

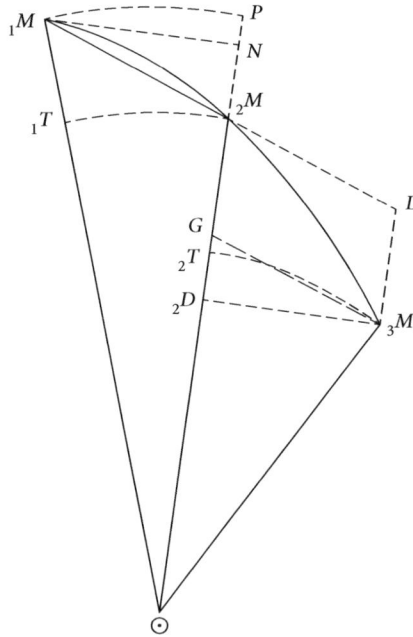

FIGURE 24.1 Leibniz's representation of orbital motion in the *Tentamen*

a center—occupied by the Sun in ☉—with a speed whose component perpendicular to the radius was inversely proportional to the distance from that center. In this way, mechanical actions were restored (see Figure 24.1, which is my faithful rendering of the relevant portion of Leibniz's more elaborate diagram); $_1M_2M_3M$ is an infinitesimal arc of the trajectory of the planet, which can be decomposed into the circular motions $_1MP$ or $_1T_2M$ and $_2T_3M$ around the center and radial motions toward or away from the center $_1M_1T$ or $_2M_2T$, as if on a rotating ruler. The same motion $_1M_2M_3M$ can be also represented in a different way, as a rectilinear uniform motion $_1M_2ML$ and a deviation L_3M parallel to the radius P_2M☉; this would be Leibniz's rendering of Newton's trajectory, composed of the tangent to the curve in $_2M$ and the action of gravity L_3M. Notice that, generally for Leibniz—although not for Newton—the tangent is the prolongation of the chord $_1M_2M$, and all curves can be seen as polygons with infinitesimal sides. Making this choice is legitimate and leads to the same result as taking the tangent in the traditional way because the arcs $_1M_2M$ and $_2M_3M$ are infinitesimal; although, if one makes this choice, the motion along the segment L_3M has to be taken as uniform rather than uniformly accelerated because the curvature is not continuous.[16]

---

[16] Leibniz initially committed a mistake by a factor of 2 due to the different representation from Newton's, but this was not especially significant and was later corrected. Bertoloni Meli, *Equivalence and Priority*, 187–189.

The two different decompositions of the trajectory have profound physical and philosophical implications: in one account, the orbiting body would simply move with a rectilinear uniform motion $_2ML$ combined with a deflection L_3M towards the center $\odot$ due to the action of gravity. When the arcs $_1M_2M$ and $_2M_3M$ shrink in size, one would approximate a continuous curve with a continuous action of gravity. The physical framework for this representation would involve an unhindered motion in a void and action at a distance. Alternatively, the orbiting body would move along circular arcs $_1T_2M$ and $_2T_3M$ with a speed that, at each point, is inversely proportional to the radius, and it would also move along the radius with what Leibniz called a "paracentric motion" resulting from a combination of a centrifugal force due to the rotation and an action of gravity toward the center. Leibniz was able to calculate those tendencies and to determine that the former is inversely proportional to the third power of the radius, the latter inversely to the square of the radius. The physical framework here is different because the circular motion would be due to a vortex rotating with the same speed as the planet in what Leibniz called a "harmonic circulation" (in which the circular speed is inversely as the radius), and the center-seeking component of radial motion would also be due to the action of a fluid—albeit one that seems more ad hoc since its mechanism of action was not explained.[17]

Leibniz's solution had its problems, however: although it accounted for the area law, it seemed at odds with Kepler's so-called *harmonic law*, according to which the square of the period of revolution is proportional to the third power of the semi-major axis of the ellipse. This law had been recently shown by Giandomenico Cassini to hold not only for planets but also for the satellites of Jupiter and Saturn; thus, it had a strong empirical basis. With simple manipulations, one could see that the third law required the square of the speed of orbiting bodies—as opposed to the simple speed—to be inversely proportional to the radius. Indeed, in the last paragraph of the *Tentamen*, Leibniz pointed out the mechanism for gravity and Kepler's third law as the main outstanding problems of his theory. One may add here that both relations hold and are compatible: one for the individual orbiting body, the other comparing orbiting bodies among themselves. That the circular component of the speed is inversely proportional to the radius captures the conservation of angular momentum. Paradoxically, Leibniz's equations became significant in the mid-eighteenth century not in relation to a vortex but as abstract relation.[18] Moreover, although planets move approximately on a plane and in the same direction, comets moved in all directions and at all angles with respect to the plane of the ecliptic, thus raising serious issues about the claim that they were carried by a vortex: how could a vortex move in so many directions? Leibniz was never able fully to address these objections: he tinkered with a number of ad hoc solutions to the first problem, at times positing an implausible second vortex rotating with a speed appropriate to satisfy

---

[17] Bertoloni Meli, *Equivalence and Priority*, 121–122. In his calculations, Leibniz relied on the figure, where $_1MN$ and $_3M_2D$ are perpendicular to the radius PO, and $_3MG$ is parallel $_2ML$.

[18] Bertoloni Meli, *Equivalence and Priority*, 142. Bertoloni Meli, "The emergence of reference Frames."

Kepler's third law, and he argued that the motion of comets was not sufficiently known to warrant conclusions, a position he maintained as late as the *Essais de Théodicée* in spite of Newton's and Edmond Halley's work showing that they move in conic sections.[19]

Around 1689–90, Leibniz planned a new edition of the *Tentamen*, called by Gerhardt "zweite Bearbeitung," in which he introduced a fluid emitted from the center—thus separate from the rotating vortex—responsible for gravity; furthermore, he sought to present his theory in a form acceptable to the Catholic Church. To this end, he deftly deleted references to Copernicus and Epicurus, for example, and emphasized in the strongest way relativity of motion, stating that not even an angel could determine with metaphysical certainty anything about absolute motion and that even acting force would be unhelpful in this regard. Thus, the "zweite Bearbeitung" ties nicely together the cosmological concerns of the previous and the present sections.[20]

In conclusion, in the fall of 1688, Leibniz drafted the *Tentamen*, which, despite some largely mathematical imperfections, contained important results and looked overall like a promising starting point. Although Leibniz was able to fix those imperfections by the beginning of the eighteenth century, his theory never overcame the substantive physical problems he had encountered early on, notably the conflict between Kepler's second and third laws, the mechanism explaining gravity, and the motion of comets. Paradoxically, Leibniz's mathematical formulation resurfaced in the mid-eighteenth century as a fertile mathematical technique encompassing the conservation of angular momentum, without any connection to the vortex that had been his original motivation.

God's Rules and Conservation

In the early 1710s, Leibniz's priorities and concerns shifted from the physico-mathematical study of the motion of celestial bodies to a physico-philosophical analysis of key notions. Around the turn of the century, the priority dispute over the invention of calculus soured the relations among Leibniz, Newton, and their allies, a situation that deteriorated until Leibniz's death and continued even thereafter. Both in the *Essais de Théodicée* and in the correspondence with Caroline, Princess of Wales, and Samuel Clarke, Leibniz raised a number of issues relevant to cosmology in response to Newton's views. Although such issues were mainly philosophical and theological and are therefore irrelevant to the fine mathematical points of the priority dispute, it is worth bearing in mind that the dispute provided a backdrop for those exchanges. Partly for this reason, before examining Leibniz's views, we need to sketch very briefly Newton's positions. The topics that concern us here can be grouped in three categories: the nature of gravity and

[19] Leibniz, *Essais de Théodicée*, para. 245.
[20] GM VI 161–87. Bertoloni Meli, "Leibniz on the Censorship of the Copernican System," 36–40; *Equivalence and Priority*, 155–161. De Risi, *Geometry and Monadology*, 538n70.

action at a distance; absolute space, time, and motion; and the decrease of motion in the universe with the consequent need for God's intervention "to wind up his clock."

Newton's views on gravity and the existence of an ether underwent some changes from the first to the later editions of the *Principia* (1687, 1713, and 1726, respectively) and the editions and translations of the *Opticks* (1704, 1706 in Latin, 1717/18 for the second English edition): in those years Newton oscillated between a nonmaterial cause for gravity—namely God—and a material one in the form of an ether. Recent works have emphasized that Newton conceived the action of the ether as being fundamentally different from that of a Cartesian vortex: the latter would act mechanically on the surface of bodies; the former would act in such a way that mass and distance would be the key variables, not surface, and therefore, in a technical or rigorous sense, would not be mechanical from his perspective. Because at least some of the speculations on the ether appeared after Leibniz's death, Leibniz took Newton to subscribe to action at a distance through a void.[21]

In the *Essais de Théodicée*, Leibniz attacked Newton's notions of universal gravity and action at a distance from a theological standpoint, tying his analysis to an examination of the doctrine of the Eucharist. Briefly put, he argued that, according to Lutheran theologians, it is possible not only that a body may act immediately on many other bodies distant from it and among themselves, but also that that body can be present to those distant ones and can be received by them in a way that does not involve distances and spatial dimensions. The primary context Leibniz is referring to here is the body of Christ being received in holy communion. However, in a striking semantic shift, he referred to Newton's notion of gravity and action at a distance as well, relying on the analogy between immediate operation and presence because, in his view, possibly one notion depends on the other. The upshot of this reasoning was that, in the same way as God acts on those who partake of the body and blood of Christ in the Eucharist, so a grain of sand could act on the sun at a distance without any intervening medium. This symmetry, however, presents problems; in the Lutheran interpretation, as Leibniz reminded Caroline, the Eucharist is a miracle, but this is legitimate because the Eucharist is a divine mystery. In the same way, gravity, too, would be miraculous—indeed a perpetual miracle—but this is not legitimate because miracles should not be invoked to explain natural things. He further added that the Newtonians—he had especially John Locke in mind here—were wrong in denying the Lutheran doctrine of the Eucharist while at the same time endorsing action at a distance: paradoxically, they were denying a legitimate

[21] Janiak, *Newton as Philosopher*, 74–80. A word is in order about the queries. The first edition of the *Opticks* (1704) had sixteen; the Latin edition *Optice* (1706) had seven additional queries; in the second English edition (1717/18, thus published after Leibniz's death), there appeared eight further queries, numbered 17–24, dealing extensively with an ethereal medium, whereas the seven queries from 1706 were shifted and renumbered as 25–31. Although it is customary to refer to the numbering of the 1717/ 18 edition, it is worth bearing in mind that Leibniz was not reading the same edition and that our own readings of Newton in the twentieth and twenty-first centuries is colored by the editions of his manuscripts and correspondence and may differ considerably from the readings by Leibniz and his contemporaries.

miracle in a matter of faith while endorsing a perpetual miracle in explaining natural events. The defense of the Lutheran religion was a key feature of Leibniz's correspondence with Caroline; hence, his gambit seems especially adroit. Here, too, as in the analysis of Joshua's intimation to the sun to stand still, Leibniz joined theological debates, scriptural hermeneutics, philosophy, and cosmology.[22]

Newton's views on absolute space, time, and motion were presented in the scholium to the eighth definition in the *Principia* accompanied by thought and real experiments that attracted Leibniz's attention from his first reading of Newton's work. At first, Leibniz doubted whether Newton's rotating bucket experiment had been performed accurately, thus focusing on an empirical aspect; later, in the correspondence with Clarke, however, he deployed more powerful arguments in the form of what we may call "cosmological thought experiments" joined with the principles of sufficient reason and of the identity of the indiscernibles: his analysis has profound implications for cosmology that have attracted the interest of philosophers and physicists to the present day. For example, in Leibniz's fourth paper to Clarke we read:[23]

> To say that God can cause the whole universe to move forward in a right line, or in any other line, without making otherwise any alteration in it; is another chimerical supposition. For, two states indiscernible from each other, are the same state. . . . It is a like fiction, (that is) an impossible one, to suppose that God might have created the world some millions of years sooner. They who run into such kinds of fictions, can give no answer to one that should argue for the eternity of the world.

In other words, if two situations were in principle indiscernible from each other in all respects, God would lack a sufficient reason to prefer one over the other, and therefore they would not be two; thus, two hypothetical situations that are in principle indiscernible cannot be truly so but must be one and the same. Therefore, because space and time are uniform, Leibniz could argue that they are not absolute and independent of the bodies in them, but, rather, they are "certain orders of things," as he put it, because there cannot be any reason to prefer a specific place or a specific instant over another place or instant in view of their uniformity. Thus, Leibniz used cosmological examples about bodies in space and time—together with other forms of reasoning—to draw conclusions about space and time.

The third topic points to important differences between Newton's and Leibniz's worldviews and cosmology. Overall, conservation principles played only a minor role for Newton—for example, in the conservation of quantity of motion (taking direction into account or, as we would say, vectorially)—but even this important proposition is

---

[22] Leibniz, *Théodicée*, preliminary dissertation, para. 18–19. Cohen, "Newton's Copy of Leibniz's *Théodicée*." Bertoloni Meli, "Caroline, Leibniz, and Clarke," 474–480. On Leibniz's scriptural hermeneutics see the essays by Maria Rosa Antognazza in this volume.

[23] Newton, *The Principia*, 408–416. Bertoloni Meli, *Equivalence and Priority*, 99–100. Leibniz and Clarke, *Correspondence*, 38–39. Vailati, *Leibniz & Clarke*, provides a comprehensive analysis of this major exchange. See also the essays by Vincenzo De Risi and Heinrich Schepers in this volume.

presented merely as a corollary to the third law of motion stating the equality of action and reaction. By contrast, conservation played a central role for Leibniz, not so much for quantity of motion as for living force especially and its different manifestations; by living force, he meant mass times the square of speed or equivalent formulations. For example, in Query 31 of the *Opticks*, Newton argued: "from the various Composition of two motions, 'tis very certain that there is not always the same quantity of Motion in the World," and further: "by reason of the Tenacity of Fluids, and Attrition of their Parts, and the Weakness of Elasticity in Solids, Motion is much more apt to be lost than got, and is always upon the Decay." To obviate this state of affairs, Newton envisaged the existence of active principles, such as the cause of gravity and of fermentation. This is already a major distinction with Leibniz's cosmological views: Newton seems to consider and attach a physical significant meaning to quantity of motion in a Cartesian sense, thus without direction, which indeed can increase or decrease.[24] But even active principles are not enough because "blind fate" could not make planets and comets overcome the perturbations and irregularities arising from their mutual actions; therefore "this System wants a Reformation." This was likely the passage Leibniz seized on in claiming that, according to Newton, God's intervention would be needed "to wind up his clock" in his first letter to Samuel Clarke and that was discussed at length in the subsequent exchanges in relation to conservation principles and God's planning. The issue of the stability of the solar system in the presence of perturbations resulting from the mutual attraction of bodies remained a challenging task in the history of celestial mechanics.[25]

Thus, between 1710 and 1716, Leibniz's interests in cosmology were reshaped. He now focused especially on the nature of gravity and action at a distance, space, time, motion; the decrease of motion in the universe; and God's intervention: all these topics stem from Newton's worldview and highlight its significance to Leibniz's thought and to the intellectual world at the time.

CONCLUSION

Leibniz had a sustained interest in cosmological matters throughout his career. His reflections took different forms in different periods, ranging across debates on Copernicanism and the world system, the structure of the world and its physical and mathematical properties, conservation principles, and God's role in the universe. Cosmology had a distinctive empirical and mathematical dimension tied to physical and mathematical astronomy, mechanics, and natural philosophy. Despite Leibniz's deep engagement with all these aspects, however, his interests were never restricted to them; as in many other domains, he saw his cosmological reflections as part of a larger

---

[24] Newton, *Opticks*, 397–399, quotations at 397 and 398. Bertoloni Meli, *Thinking with Objects*, 298.
[25] Newton, *Opticks*, 401. Leibniz and Clarke, *Correspondence*, 11. Funkenstein, *Theology and the Scientific Imagination*, 192–201.

picture in which church reunion, biblical hermeneutics, theological concerns, and philosophical matters played a key role.

Scholars have long realized that both Leibniz's thought on the physical and mathematical structure of the world and his cosmological reflections on God's rules and conservation principles are closely tied to Newton's work so that the two are profitably studied and understood together. Recent works on Newton have focused not only on his contributions to physico-mathematics, but also more specifically on their philosophical implications, seeing him as a philosopher in his own right. These works provide an especially promising standpoint from which to re-examine Leibniz's own positions, thus further strengthening the flourishing Leibnizian scholarship in these areas.[26]

REFERENCES

Aiton, Eric J. 1972. *The Vortex Theory of Planetary Motion*. London/New York: Macdonald/American Elsevier.

Antognazza, Maria Rosa. 2009. *Leibniz: An Intellectual Biography*. Cambridge: Cambridge University Press.

Bertoloni Meli, Domenico. 1999 "Caroline, Leibniz, and Clarke." *Journal of the History of Ideas* 60: 469–486.

Bertoloni Meli, Domenico. 1988. "Leibniz on the Censorship of the Copernican System." *Studia Leibnitiana* 20: 19–42.

Bertoloni Meli, Domenico. (1993) "The Emergence of Reference Frames and the Transformation of Mechanics in the Enlightenment." *Historical Studies in the Physical and Biological Sciences* 23(2): 301–335.

Bertoloni Meli, Domenico. 1993. *Equivalence and Priority: Newton versus Leibniz. Including Leibniz's Unpublished Manuscripts on the "Principia."* Oxford: Oxford University Press.

Bertoloni Meli, Domenico. 2006. *Thinking with Objects. The Transformation of Mechanics in the Seventeenth Century*. Baltimore: Johns Hopkins University Press.

Cohen, I. Bernard. "Newton's Copy of Leibniz's Théodicée." *Isis* 73: 410–414.

De Risi, Vincenzo. 2007. *Geometry and Monadology. Leibniz's "Analysis Situs" and Philosophy of Space*. Basel: Birkhäuser.

Funkenstein, Amos. 1986. *Theology and the Scientific Imagination from the Middle Ages to the Seventeenth Century*. Princeton, NJ: Princeton University Press.

Guicciardini, Niccolò. 1999. *Reading the "Principia." The Debate on Newton's Mathematical Methods for Natural Philosophy from 1687 to 1736*. Cambridge: Cambridge University Press.

Janiak, Andrew. 2008. *Newton as Philosopher*. Cambridge: Cambridge University Press.

Leibniz, Gottfried Wilhelm. 1989. *Philosophical Essays*. Translated by Roger Ariew and Daniel Garber. Indianapolis, IN: Hackett.

Leibniz, Gottfried Wilhelm, and Samuel Clarke. 1956. *The Leibniz-Clarke Correspondence*, edited by H. G. Alexander. Manchester: Manchester University Press.

---

[26] Among the most historically sensitive works in this area, see, e.g., Janiak, *Newton as Philosopher*; McMullin, "The Impact of Newton's *Principia* on the Philosophy of Science"; Smith, "The Methodology of the *Principia*."

McMullin, Ernan. 1998. "Galileo on Science and Scripture," in Peter Machamer (ed.), *The Cambridge Companion to Galileo*. Cambridge: Cambridge University Press, pp. 271–347.

McMullin, Ernan. 2001. "The Impact of Newton's *Principia* on the Philosophy of Science." *Philosophy of Science 68*: 279–310.

Newton, Isaac. 1952. *Opticks*. New York: Dover (based on the fourth edition, London, 1730; first published London, 1704).

Newton, Isaac. 1999. *The Principia. Mathematical Principles of Natural Philosophy*. A New Translation by I. Bernard Cohen and Anne Whitman assisted by Julia Budenz. Berkeley: University of California Press.

Robinet, André. 1988. *G. W. Leibniz. Iter italicum*. Florence: Olschki.

Smith, George. 2002. "The Methodology of the *Principia*," in I Bernard Cohen and George Smith (eds.), *The Cambridge Companion to Newton*. Cambridge: Cambridge University Press, pp. 138–173.

Vailati, Ezio. 1997. *Leibniz & Clarke. A Study of Their Correspondence*. Oxford: Oxford University Press.

Wilson, Curtis. 1989. "The Newtonian Achievement in Astronomy," in René Taton and Curtis Wilson (eds.), *Planetary Astronomy from the Renaissance to the Birth of Astrophysics*. Cambridge: Cambridge University Press, pp. 233–274.

CHAPTER 25

THE ORIGINS AND HISTORY OF THE EARTH

ANDRE WAKEFIELD

LEIBNIZ has long played a significant if somewhat secondary role in the history of geology. He sometimes features as a Cartesian cosmogonist who endeavored to trace the origins of the earth according to mechanical principles; elsewhere he appears as a direct disciple of Nicolas Steno, the father of stratigraphy; others emphasize his association with Thomas Burnet, whose *Sacred History of the Earth* (1684) attempted to weave Descartes's conjectural history of the earth together with the narrative scheme of Genesis. In truth, Leibniz was all and none of these things.

Our troubles begin with the term "geology." During Leibniz's lifetime, there were cosmographers, dowsers, mineralogists, smelters, subterranean geometers, cameralists, and geognosts. There were *not* however geologists or paleontologists.[1] That may seem obvious, but it is important, because Leibniz's work on the origins of the earth has most often been interpreted within a historiographical tradition that projects these modern sciences back onto the past, seeking there the seeds of future discovery. Karl von Zittel, for example, felt that Leibniz's cosmogony suffered because of "the author's conscientious effort to present a historical account of the earth's surface that should be in harmony with the Mosaic genesis."[2] Archibald Geikie praised Leibniz's theory of the earth for anticipating aspects of modern physics.[3] Horace Woodward appreciated Leibniz's efforts to distinguish sedimentary from igneous rocks but complained that Leibniz's catastrophist view of sudden and violent change rendered his views incompatible "with the modern doctrines of geology."[4] For Gabriel Gohau, only Steno's work was really "of

---

[1] See Ernst P. Hamm, "Knowledge from Underground: Leibniz Mines the Enlightenment," *Earth Sciences History* 16 (1997): 77–99, on 78; Warren Dym, *Divining Science: Treasure Hunting and Earth Science in Early Modern Europe* (Leiden: Brill, 2010).

[2] Karl von Zittel, *History of Geology and Palaeontology to the End of the Nineteenth Century*, translated by Maria M. Ogilvie-Gordon (London: Walter Scott, 1901), 28.

[3] Archibald Geikie, *The Founders of Geology*, 2nd ed. (London: Macmillan, 1905), 81.

[4] Horace B. Woodward, *History of Geology* (London: Watts., 1911), 13.

direct and immediate interest to geologists," while Leibniz's approach had more to do with paleontology.[5] More recently, Richard Fortey inspected Leibniz's earth-history for anticipations of modern geology and found it wanting. "Why then did Leibniz's shrewd observations fail to move geology significantly towards becoming a mature science? For all its insights, *Protogaea* does not seem to a modern geologist like the natural ancestor of Lyell's *Principles of Geology*. The missing ingredient is an awareness of geological time."[6]

But there have also been dissenting voices. For Martin Rudwick, *Protogaea* was important because it "provided a model of Earth-history that allowed for the organic origin of fossils, preserved Steno's and Woodward's understanding of strata as sequential deposits, and was conformable to both scripture and reason."[7] Paolo Rossi saw significance in the Leibnizian attempt to bridge human and natural history.[8] And Ernst Hamm has emphasized how the mining and chemical traditions that permeate Leibniz's writings about the origins of the planet distinguish his work from other contemporary "physical cosmogonies."[9]

The most important of Leibniz's writings about the earth—really the only important one—was *Protogaea*, which explored fossils, the origins of the earth, and the natural history of the planet. It was intended as a preface to his history of the House of Brunswick.[10] The only surviving manuscript copy of *Protogaea* in Leibniz's own hand is

[5] Gabriel Gohau, *A History of Geology*, rev. and translated by Albert V. Carozzi and Marguerite Carozzi (New Brunswick, N.J.: Rutgers University Press, 1990), 61.

[6] Richard Fortey, "In Retrospect: Leibniz's Protogaea," *Nature 455*, 4 (2008): 35.

[7] Martin J. R. Rudwick, *The Meaning of Fossils: Episodes in the History of Palaeontology* (London: Macdonald, 1972), 91.

[8] Paolo Rossi, *The Dark Abyss of Time: The History of the Earth and the History of Nations from Hooke to Vico*, translated by Lydia G. Cochrane (Chicago: University of Chicago Press, 1984), 56.

[9] Hamm, "Knowledge from Underground," 79–80; Rachel Laudan, *From Mineralogy to Geology: The Foundations of a Science, 1650–1830* (Chicago: University of Chicago Press, 1987), 45, 68.

[10] The close connection between Leibniz's history of the Guelfs and *Protogaea* is clearly articulated in a manuscript from 1690, "Entwurf der Welfischen Geschichte." Other material generated by Leibniz appeared in the *Origines Guelficae*, published after his death between 1750 and 1780. The *Origines Guelficae* represented the collective efforts of successive court historians and librarians in Hannover, among them Leibniz, Johann Georg Eckhart, Johann Daniel Gruber, and Christian Ludwig Scheidt. A complete edition of Leibniz's history of the House of Brunswick, the *Annales Imperii Occidentis Brunsvicenses*, did not appear until the nineteenth century, when Georg Heinrich Pertz produced an edition of it. See G. W. Leibniz, "Entwurf der Welfischen Geschichte," vol. 4, 240–254, and *Annales Imperii Occidentis Brunsvicenses*, vols. 1–3, in G. W. Leibniz, *Gesammelte Werke*, edited by Georg Heinrich Pertz, 4 vols. (Hannover: Hanschen Hof-Buchhandlung, 1843-1847; reprint, Hildesheim: Olms, 1966); Gottfried Wilhelm Leibniz,, Johann Georg von Eckhart, Johann Daniel Gruber, Christian Ludwig Scheidt, and Johann Heinrich Jung, *Origines Guelficae*, edited by Christian Ludwig Scheidt (Hannover: H. E. C. Schleuter, 5 vols., 1750–1780); Alois Schmidt, "Der Herkunft der Welfen in der bayerischen Landeshistoriographie des 17. Jahrhunderts und bei Gottfried Wilhelm Leibniz," in Herbert Breger and Friedrich Niewohner, eds., *Leibniz und Niedersachsen: Tagung anläßlich des 350. Geburtstages von G. W. Leibniz*. Studia Leibnitiana Sonderhefte 28 (Wolfenbüttel: F. Steiner, 1996), 127–147; Maria Rosa Antognazza, *Leibniz: An Intellectual Biography* (Cambridge: Cambridge University Press, 2009), 329, 524–525, 531; and David Oldroyd, "The Genesis of Historical Research on the History of Geology, with Thoughts about Kirwan, de Luc, and Whiggery," in *A Master of Science History: Essays in Honor of Charles Coulston Gillispie* (Dordrecht: Springer, 2012), 167–177.

a mess, but generations of editors have worked diligently to clean it up, so that the work now appears more coherent and polished than it actually was.[11] The original manuscript reveals a series of fragments that drift from topic to topic. Nevertheless, several discrete and interconnected narratives emerge out of these fragments. These include a conjectural history of the earth from its earliest beginnings, an account of fossils that treats them as the vestiges of real animals (and *not* mere "games of nature") and a new science of "Natural Geography" rooted in the conviction that one could "read" the earth's history, layer by layer.

FOSSIL OBJECTS: *LUSUS NATURAE* OR THE REMAINS OF REAL ANIMALS?

Leibniz drafted *Protogaea* between 1691 and 1693, but it languished in Hannover's Royal Library for over fifty years, until Christian Ludwig Scheidt saved it from the "moths and dust" and published it in 1749.[12] This does not mean that the work had no influence before its publication: excerpts and descriptions circulated among Leibniz's wide circle of correspondents at the end of the seventeenth century. Moreover, he prepared several shorter articles based on *Protogaea*. An outline of the work appeared in the *Acta Eruditorum* during 1693; and in 1710 Leibniz penned a commentary about a fossil crocodile discovered near Eisenach. He also submitted articles based on the *Protogaea* to the Royal Society of London (1697) and the Academy of Sciences in Paris (1706). Neither of these appeared in print, but the latter piece was read by Bernard de Fontenelle to the Academy on September 4, 1706.[13]

This last paper, the one delivered by Fontenelle, sounded one of the central themes from *Protogaea*: fossil shells and fish were the remains of real animals and not mere "games of nature" (*lusus naturae*). Leibniz's argument was far from original: Steno and John Woodward, especially, had urged the same thing. But Leibniz's considerable chemical knowledge allowed him carefully to distinguish inorganic products, such as crystallized silver salts, from the organic remains of animals and plants.[14] Though

---

[11] The surviving copy (LH: Ms. XXIII, 23a) is the basis of two edited translations with facing-page Latin text: *Protogaea*, edited and translated by W. v. Engelhardt (Stuttgart: Kohlhammer, 1949), and *Protogaea*, edited and translated, with an introduction, by Claudine Cohen and Andre Wakefield (Chicago: University of Chicago Press, 2008). Unless otherwise noted, references to *Protogaea* are from the Cohen and Wakefield edition.

[12] *Protogaea, sive, De prima facie telluris et antiquissimae historiae vestigiis in ipsis naturae monumentis dissertatio*, edited by Christian Ludwig Scheidt (Göttingen, 1749), v–vi.

[13] Rhoda Rappaport, "Leibniz on Geology: A Newly Discovered Text," *Studia Leibnitiana* 29, 1 (1997): 6–11. G. W. Leibniz, "Protogaea," *Acta Eruditorum* (January 1693), 40–43; G. W. Leibniz, "Epistola," *Miscellanea Berolinensia I* (1710): 118–120. A full transcription of what Fontenelle read before the Paris Academy of Sciences appears in Rhoda Rappaport's article.

[14] See Hamm, "Knowledge from Underground," 80.

it may seem clear that fossil fish are the remains of real fish, it was not at all obvious three centuries ago. If fossils were the remains of real, dead, past animals, then how could one explain their presence on the tops of the highest mountains? And how could one explain all the strange-looking fossils, such as "Ammon's horns" (ammonites), that resembled no living creature? Most contemporaries could not accept the implications of the claim that such "fossil objects" were the vestiges of a lost world, one that differed greatly from the present. Though Leibniz himself never spelled out those implications, others would. The most notorious example was Benôit de Maillet's sensational *Telliamed*, which probably drew inspiration from *Protogaea*. In it, Maillet imagined the gradual retreat of the oceans, an earth of unfathomable age, and the transformation of species.[15]

Leibniz himself had once rejected the idea that fossils might be the remains of ancient plants and animals. In an early manuscript, written around 1678, he sided with Athanasius Kircher, arguing that the "petrifications" (fossils) one found buried in the earth were mere "sports of nature" and not the remains of real animals.[16]

> I find it difficult to believe that the bones one sometimes finds in the fields, or that one discovers by digging in the earth, are the remains of real giants; similarly, that the Maltese stones commonly called serpent teeth are parts of fish. . . . If that were true, perhaps the earth would have to be much older than is reported by the holy scriptures. But I don't want to stop there, and we need to give natural reasons here. Thus, I believe that these forms of bones of animals and shells are often only games of nature which have been formed apart without having come from animals. . . . stones grow and take on a thousand strange forms, as testify the stones that the reverend father Kircher has amassed in his Subterraneous World.[17]

During the early 1670s Leibniz thus embraced the notion that all fossils were mere games of nature. But then he changed his mind completely, probably because of his 1678 encounter with Steno, whose *Prodromus* (1669) is quoted at length in *Protogaea*.[18] In any case, by the 1690s Leibniz had rejected the idea that fossil fish and shells could have been produced by some formative power of the earth. In *Protogaea*, for example, he ridiculed the notion that mere games of nature could account for the detailed imprints of fish in slates or of shells in stone. Those who clung to *lusus naturae*, he now argued, were "seduced by the fairy tales of Kircher or Becher, and of other credulous or vain writers

---

[15] For the argument about *Protogaea*'s relationship to *Telliamed*, see Claudine Cohen, "Leibniz et Benôit de Maillet: De la Protogée au Telliamed," in Francine Markovits, ed., *Telliamed* (Paris: Université de Paris Ouest–Nanterre–La Défense, 2011), 55–78.

[16] Claudine Cohen, "Un manuscrit inédit de Leibniz (1646–1716) sur la nature des 'objets fossiles,'" *Bulletin de la Société Géologique de France* 169, 1 (1998): 137–142. Athanasius Kircher, *Mundus subterraneus*, 2 vols. (Amsterdam, 1664–1665).

[17] Ibid., 140. See also Roger Ariew, "Leibniz on the Unicorn and Various Other Curiosities," *Early Science and Medicine* 3 (1998): 267–288, on 283, n. 46.

[18] Cohen, "Un manuscrit inédit de Leibniz," 138.

of this sort, who describe the wonderful games of nature and its formative power, all embellished with a great display of words."[19]

This criticism of words unhinged from experience cuts to the heart of *Protogaea*. It explains why the work is filled with detailed and extensive descriptions of trochites, asterias, glossopetrae, amber, osteocolla, belemnites, Ammon's horns, and many other "fossil objects." Historians of geology especially have tended to ignore this part of *Protogaea*, focusing instead on the earlier sections, which describe the first formation of the earth. For Leibniz, however, careful analysis and description of fossil objects was absolutely crucial, because it allowed "arguments of the eyes" to overcome fantasies of the imagination. He thus worked closely with Nicolaus Seelander, official engraver for the Royal Library in Hannover, to produce a series of illustrations that would accompany the text. (Christian Ludwig Scheidt later appended these engravings to the 1749 edition of *Protogaea*.) In a striking passage, Leibniz identified the purpose of these illustrations: "It is better to look upon the thing itself, and to recognize the obvious arguments of a buried animal."[20]

Even the careful illustrations of Seelander, however, failed to do justice to the full-blooded, tactile experience of handling actual fossils. Many of the fish and shells depicted in *Protogaea* came from the natural history cabinet (*Naturalienkabinett*) of Friedrich Lachmund, a physician from Hildesheim. Leibniz viewed Lachmund's collection in November 1687, and he also made great use of the ducal collection (*Kunstkammer*) in Kassel.[21] He particularly sought out specimens that captured the past in vivid, living detail. "I have here in my hands," he wrote, "a barbel, a perch, a bleak, sculpted in stone. Not long ago an immense pike was dug out of a quarry, its body bent and its mouth open, as if it had been caught alive and turned to stone by the power of the Gorgon. I have also seen sea fish like the ray, the herring, and the lamprey, the last one sometimes lying crosswise with a herring."[22] For Leibniz, these fossils provided self-evident arguments for their own reality. The anatomical details preserved in them, down to fins and scales, were so precise that he found it impossible to accept that some playful "sport of nature" could have produced them accidentally. Especially good specimens, like those in Lachmund's collection, captured life in action, as if the past had been frozen in stone for the benefit of future generations. Leibniz was also aware, however, that natural history cabinets separated fossils from their surroundings, thereby obliterating the context of discovery. From his experiences with mines and caves and well digging, Leibniz knew that fossil fish and shells tended to cluster together, usually in a single layer of earth. This pointed to a historical explanation: some catastrophic event, like an earthquake, had filled the waters with earth long ago. Fossil fish were thus documents of nature waiting

---

[19] Leibniz, *Protogaea*, 72–73 (§ 24). Leibniz refers here to Johann Joachim Becher (1635–1682), well-known chymist, cameralist, and projector.

[20] Leibniz, *Protogaea*, 58–59 (§ 23).

[21] Horst Bredekamp, *Die Fenster der Monade: Gottfried Wilhem Leibniz' Theater der Natur und Kunst* (Berlin: Akademie, 2004), 29.

[22] Leibniz, *Protogaea*, 44–45 (§ 18).

to be deciphered; the natural historian, drawing on these archives of nature, had to re-construct a narrative of past events.

Reconstruction of the distant past using the documents of nature demanded imagi-nation, and Leibniz certainly used hypotheses and possible pasts to construct a conjec-tural history of the earth. Like Burnet's *Sacred History of the Earth*, Leibniz's *Protogaea* drew upon the archives of nature to reconstruct the terrestrial past. For many, it went too far. Even Leibniz's editor, Christian Ludwig Scheidt, suggested that it would have been better to follow Augustine's example, admitting the ignorance of men and taking the sacred texts as primary evidence, rather than hazarding guesses about prehistory.[23] As he created an imagined past for the earth, however, Leibniz derided what he regarded as perversions of the imagination in the service of ignorance and superstition. "One blindly believes the stories of people who have accustomed themselves, through their own credulity and that of others, to deceiving and being deceived—people who see homunculi and Plutonic monks nearby while they work underground, and who search the earth for hidden treasures with divining rods."[24] Because of his extensive experi-ence in the Harz mines, Leibniz knew a great deal about miners and their beliefs, most of which he dismissed. Miners in St. Andreasberg had discovered a depiction of Jesus on the cross, all in silver; elsewhere miners found a "finger-sized miner of silver" fully dressed in his uniform and carrying a basket of precious metals; and clever merchants liked to prepare mandragora from bryony root as a way to fool gullible customers. But Leibniz regarded all of these examples as "products of the imagination, not the eyes."[25] Miner superstitions and Kircher's philosophical excurses on *lusus naturae* thus stemmed from the same source: the corrupted imagination.

In addition to visiting natural history cabinets, Leibniz was a reluctant spelunker who collected fossils underground. *Protogaea* contains firsthand accounts of his visits to the Scharzfeld and Baumann caves. He was so taken with the *Baumannshöhle* that he had an engraving of it prepared to accompany the narrative of his tour—the illus-tration included a cross-section of the cave together with images of the fossil objects that he discovered there.[26] After spending the night in the mining town of Elbingerode, Leibniz and his companions moved on to the little village of Rübeland, entering the cave in the evening. After squeezing himself through a narrow passage and straddling a large rock, Leibniz entered a series of caverns, where he witnessed the many "wonders" of the cave: Moses with two horns, the ascension of Christ stamped in a rock, the figure of a

---

[23] Christian Ludwig Scheidt, introduction to G. W. Leibniz, *Protogaea, sive, De prima facie telluris et antiquissimae historiae vestigiis in ipsis naturae monumentis dissertatio* (Göttingen, 1749), 1–26.

[24] Leibniz, *Protogaea*, 26–27 (§ 9).

[25] Leibniz, *Protogaea*, 74–75 (§ 24).

[26] The engraving was partly based on an earlier illustration that appeared in Hermann van der Hardt, "Descriptio speluncae ad sylvam harcyniam in agro Brunsuicensi," *Acta eruditorum* (1702): 305–308. Stephan Kempe, "The Baumann's Cave at Rübeland/Harz, Germany: One of the Caves Noted in Early Science History for Its Cave Bear and Cave Hyena Bone Deposits," *Scientific Annals, School of Geology, Aristotle University of Thessaloniki*, special vol. 98 (2006): 213–220. My thanks to Daniel Garber for pointing this out.

monk in one of the columns, "something that looks like an oven, an organ, a forest, and who knows what else." All of this provided Leibniz with more evidence that Kircher's thesis was mistaken, because "the games of nature presented in these caves demand the support of the imagination." The Baumann Cave also provided Leibniz with confirmation of Steno's thesis about "solids enclosed in solids."

> I found it especially noteworthy that there is a rock enclosed in another rock, which is clearly bounded by a thin, dark yellow crust that is even now still forming as water drips onto the stone. This crust is then covered by a new coat of rock, identical to the first. . . . But what pleased me most was a piece I found and then had broken off. For there is a piece of bone enclosed in it, and, on the basis of its texture, its surface, its color, and finally its taste, no observer can doubt that it came from an animal.[27]

It would be a mistake however to view Leibniz as some proto-paleontologist. He was probably more like a well-educated amateur spelunker. Already by the mid-seventeenth century, the Baumann Cave was a popular destination for naturalists, tourists, and travelers. Matthaeus Merian's *Topographia* (1654) included a description that paralleled Leibniz's account. Merian recommended that visitors hire an experienced guide; and he urged those without guides to use a thread, Ariadne-like, as insurance, "because if one gets lost in the countless caverns, it is impossible to find one's way back out again, as evidenced by the dead bodies or skeletons that one finds inside, so that one must stay, die, and rot in there."[28] Leibniz's account of his visit to the Scharzfeld Cave, where he encountered a narrow passage underground, suggests that he may have taken Merian's advice to heart. "I did not want to go any farther, because the guides said there was not much more to see."[29]

Leibniz's interest in caves was probably piqued by the discovery of a fossil "unicorn" near Quedlinburg. *Protogaea* includes a description of the discovery, together with an engraving depicting the animal. (Othenio Abel called it the first attempt to reconstruct a vertebrate in the history of paleontology.)[30] Otto von Guericke, inventor of the air pump and mayor of Magdeburg, described the find in his *Experimenta nova* (1672), and Leibniz relied on the credibility of his witness as evidence for the existence of the unicorn. And a strange beast it was, more odd monstrosity than elegant mythical creature, "with a raised head and carrying on its forehead an extended horn about five yards long; the horn was the width of a human leg and tapered gradually."[31] As Roger Ariew has

---

[27] Leibniz, *Protogaea*, 108–113 (§ 38).

[28] Matthaeus Merian, ed., *Topographia und Eigentliche Beschreibung der Vornembsten Stäte, Schlösser auch anderer Plätze und Örter in denen Herzogthümern Braunschweig und Lüneburg* (Frankfurt, 1654). Also Daniel Garber, "De ortu et antiquissimis fontibus Protogaeae Leibnizianae dissertatio: Observation, Exploration, and Natural Philosophy," in J.A. Nicolás and S. Toledo, eds., *Leibniz y las ciencias empíricas/ Leibniz and the Empirical Sciences* (Editorial Comares: Granada, 2011), 65–85, and Kempe, "Baumann's Cave at Rübeland/Harz."

[29] Leibniz, *Protogaea*, 104–105 (§ 36).

[30] Othenio Abel, *Geschichte und Methode der Rekonstruktion vorzeitlicher Wirbeltiere* (Jena: G. Fischer, 1925).

[31] Leibniz, *Protogaea*, 100–103 (§ 35).

argued, however, it was really Leibniz's commitment to naturalism, his turn away from *lusus naturae* and nature's formative force, that led him to accept Guericke's unicorn. For him, the remains of the unicorn in Quedlinburg were not the vestiges of some mythical, magical creature; rather, like Glossopetrae or Ammon's horns, the unicorn represented one of many fossil objects requiring careful explanation and demystification.[32]

Human History and Natural History

Even as Leibniz collected and analyzed the documents of nature to build a history of the earth, he was traveling through Italy and the German lands collecting documents to support the dynastic claims of the House of Braunschweig-Lüneburg.[33] After the final failure of his mining venture in the Harz during the spring of 1685, Leibniz had agreed to write a dynastic history, a project that would take him through the lands of southern Germany and all the way to Italy in search of evidence linking the Italian house of Este to the Guelfs.[34] Recall that *Protogaea* was intended as a preface to this dynastic history, a fact that emerges clearly throughout the later sections of the work. As Hannover's de facto court historiographer, Leibniz combed dynastic archives, medieval chronicles, and ancient histories in search of genealogical clues. Along the way, he developed an acute sense for changes in the land, a conviction that the constant "struggles between sea and land" had completely changed the face of the planet since ancient times. In general, Leibniz explained, "you can be sure how much change time has wrought by comparing the present face of things to what history describes."[35] For example, the domain of Este, former seat of the Guelfs, had witnessed dramatic changes in its physical geography; the Adriatic Sea near Venice had receded and marshes had been drained, so that the coastline appeared completely different from ancient times. Elsewhere, in Frisia and the Low Countries, whole forests buried deep in the earth bore witness to some ancient catastrophe. "This is why men believe that in a time before all reported history, the boiling ocean, raging from the northeastern and northwestern winds that still attack these coasts today, burst onto the land with great force."[36]

The connection between natural and human history, between *Protogaea* and the dynastic history of the Guelfs, helps to explain why Leibniz closed his earth-history with descriptions of well digging. Under Modena, "present seat of the princes of Este," was a "vast lake hidden in the earth," so that one could sink a well anywhere in the whole city

[32] Ariew, "Leibniz on the Unicorn," 282–285.
[33] Günter Scheel, "Leibniz als Historiker des Welfenhauses," in Wilhelm Totok and Carl Haase, eds., *Leibniz: Sein Leben, sein Wirken, seine Welt* (Hannover: Verlag für Literatur und Zeitgeschehen, 1966), 227–276.
[34] Maria Rosa Antognazza, *Leibniz: An Intellectual Biography* (Cambridge: Cambridge University Press, 2009), 230–231.
[35] Leibniz, *Protogaea*, 120–121 (§ 41).
[36] Leibniz, *Protogaea*, 138–139 (§ 47).

at a depth of seventy feet. Leibniz carefully observed the well diggers of Modena, and he charted the layers of earth that they uncovered as they sunk their wells. First they hit debris from the old city, "the paving stones of forgotten avenues and other vestiges of antiquity." Next one encountered earth and then more debris, "as if the city had been destroyed more than once." Below that the well diggers came upon a thick layer of clay, and then a rotten earth composed of leaves and roots and tree trunks, followed by more clay, until one finally struck the water.[37] Similarly, Leibniz enumerated the layers of earth uncovered by Amsterdam well diggers in excruciating detail: "seven feet of garden earth, nine of peat, nine of clay, eight of sand, four of earth, ten of clay, another four of earth, ten feet of sand upon which houses there are anchored, two of clay, four of white sand, five of dry earth, one of mud, fourteen of sand, three of sandy clay, five of sand mixed with clay, four of sand mixed with seashells."[38] From these layers Leibniz brought the past to life, imagining the repeated "floods and catastrophes" that had deposited so many layers of clay and sand during the interminable struggle between sea and land.

Read as a stand-alone work, *Protogaea* seems to end with a whimper, providing lists of the earth's layers from different regions of Europe. As a preface to Leibniz's dynastic history of the Guelfs, however, the approach makes more sense. By watching the well diggers, one could trace the transition from natural to human history, as the ruined forests of prehistory gave way to the ruins of ancient cities. For Leibniz the historian, nature thus provided its own documents to compensate for the absence of human chronicles. "For us, nature thus stands in place of history. But our written history repays nature's grace, so that her brilliant works, which still lie open before us, will not be ignored by posterity."[39]

A New Science of "Natural Geography"

Given Leibniz's predilection for ventures—from academies to mining machines—it should come as no surprise that an ambitious intellectual project lay at the heart of *Protogaea*, for he proposed an entirely new science called "natural geography," which would trace the history of the earth from its origins to the present. As we have seen, fossils and earth strata constituted two essential evidential sources for this new science; moving farther back in time, however, Leibniz understood that he could rely only on scripture, reason, and the most general laws of nature to reconstruct the past. These elements formed the heart of his account about the first formation of the earth.

In the beginning, the earth was a molten globe. Upon cooling, it formed a crust or "slag that covered the molten earth mass, as if in a blast furnace, eventually hardening after fusion."[40] Vaporized by the original heat, water eventually condensed on the

---

[37] Leibniz, *Protogaea*, 122–125 (§ 42).
[38] Leibniz, *Protogaea*, 138–139 (§ 48).
[39] Leibniz, *Protogaea*, 140–141 (§48).
[40] Leibniz, *Protogaea*, 6–7 (§ 3).

surface of the cooling globe, washing over the crust and absorbing ashes and fixed salts to form the salty seas. Shrinking as it cooled, the earth formed great "bubbles" of air and water. These great rock blisters then weakened and collapsed, forming great mountains and unleashing massive floods. The floods, in turn, left behind sediments. After this initial period of great violence, the hard rock of the young earth "was divided and kneaded into little particles" until "the action of salts was added to the force of the heat, thereby eroding the hard rocks to a fertile soil, which could nourish plants and animals."[41] Leibniz would reprise this theme in *Theodicy*, arguing that the apparent disorders of the primordial earth had eventually rendered it habitable.[42]

Leibniz's terrestrial history drew heavily on the methods of Descartes, the writings of Burnet, and the chemical traditions of German mines and laboratories. Descartes's *Le Monde* (1633) and *Principia philosophiae* (1644) had endeavored to explain the formation of the earth in mechanical terms. Burnet, weaving this Cartesian approach together with the narrative scheme of Genesis, depicted the earth as a ruin, the product of catastrophe and primordial chaos.[43] Like Burnet, Leibniz used evidence from both sacred and natural history in his effort to reconstruct the deep past, but he rejected both the geometrical abstraction of Descartes and the vision of original chaos espoused by Burnet. "God," he explained, "makes nothing without order."[44] Jagged mountains and raging seas were not the marks of a fallen earth; rather, everything had its purpose.[45]

Though it would be anachronistic to call *Protogaea* a work of geology or paleontology, one could argue that it helped create the conditions for the possibility of those disciplines. Leibniz himself was certainly looking to the future as he imagined his new science of natural geography: "our descendants will be able to explain everything better when human curiosity will have advanced far enough to describe the kinds and layers of the earth that extend through the various territories."[46] From the caves of the Harz to the wells of Modena, Leibniz had begun, in his own small way, to do that painstaking descriptive work in the ancestral and dynastic lands of the Guelfs. But he knew that his vision demanded a grand cooperative venture that would collect and organize local knowledge from around the globe to build a universal history of the planet. *Protogaea* was thus only an example, a prod, and a suggestion. Leibniz acknowledged these limitations on the very first page: "But if we do not completely achieve our goal, then we will at least have a model, for when everyone contributes curiosity locally, it will be easier to recognize universal origins."[47]

John Woodward's *Essay toward a Natural History of the Earth* (1695), which combined an organic interpretation of fossils with Burnet's catastrophic vision of the biblical

[41] Hamm, "Knowledge from Underground," 79–80.

[42] G. W. Leibniz, *Essais de Theodicee*, in GP VI, 262–63.

[43] Rossi, *Dark Abyss of Time*, 36–37.

[44] Leibniz, *Protogaea*, 2–3 (§ 2).

[45] Pascal Richet, *A Natural History of Time*, translated by John Venerella (Chicago: University of Chicago Press, 2007), 119–120; Cohen and Wakefield, introduction to Leibniz, *Protogaea*, xix–xx.

[46] Leibniz, *Protogaea*, 10–11 (§ 5).

[47] Leibniz, *Protogaea*, 2–3 (§ 1).

flood, has long been regarded as a foundational text in the history of geology. *Protogaea* was equally pathbreaking. Though it remained unpublished until 1749, a short version appeared in 1693 in the *Acta Eruditorum*, two years before the appearance of Woodward's *Essay*; moreover, the work circulated widely in manuscript form after 1695. Leibniz's theory of the earth thus "made it possible for fossils to become evidence for the history of life."[48] In other words, it helped create the possibility for the modern disciplines of geology and paleontology. Almost a century later, Georges Buffon, the most prominent naturalist of the eighteenth century, would use *Protogaea* as a foundation for his *Epochs of Nature* (1778). This, too, stands as testimony to the lasting impact of *Protogaea*.

BIBLIOGRAPHY

Abel, Othenio. *Geschichte und Methode der Rekonstruktion vorzeitlicher Wirbeltiere.* Jena: G. Fischer, 1925.

Antognazza, Maria Rosa. *Leibniz: An Intellectual Biography.* Cambridge: Cambridge University Press, 2009.

Ariew, Roger. "Leibniz on the Unicorn and Various Other Curiosities." *Early Science and Medicine 3* (1998): 267–288.

———. "Protogaea." In *Leibniz: Tradition und Aktualität.* V. Internationaler Leibniz-Kongress. Hannover: Gottfried-Wilhelm-Leibniz Gesellschaft, 1988.

Bredekamp, Horst. *Die Fenster der Monade: Gottfried Wilhelm Leibniz' Theater der Natur und Kunst.* Berlin: Akademie, 2004.

Buffon, Georges-Louis Leclerc, comte de. *Les Époques de la nature.* Edited by Jacques Roger. Reprint: Paris: Editions du Muséum National d´Histoire Naturelle, 1988.

Burnet, Thomas. *The Sacred Theory of the Earth: Containing an Account of the Original of the Earth and of All General Changes Which It Hath Already Undergone or Is to Undergo 'till the Consummation of All Things.* London, 1684.

"A Carcharadon-Head Dissected." In Gustav Scherz, ed., *Geological Papers,* trans. Alex J. Pollock (Odense: Odense University Press, 1969), 72–117.

Cohen, Claudine. "Leibniz's Protogaea: Patronage, Mining, and Evidence for a History of the Earth." In Suzanne Marchand and Elizabeth Lundbeck, eds., *Proof and Persuasion: Essays on Authority, Objectivity, and Evidence,* 125–143. Turnhout: Brepols, 1996.

———. "Un manuscrit inédit de Leibniz (1646–1716) sur la nature des 'objets fossiles.'" *Bulletin de la Société Géologique de France 169,* 1 (1998): 137–142.

———. "Leibniz et Benoît de Maillet: De la Protogée au Telliamed." In Francine Markovits, ed., *Telliamed,* 55–78. Paris: Université de Paris Ouest–Nanterre–La Défense, 2011.

Descartes, René. *Le Monde, ou, Traité de la lumière.* Translated, with an introduction, by Michael Sean Mahoney. New York: Abaris Books, 1979.

———. *Principles of Philosophy.* Translated by Valentine Rodger Miller and Reese P. Miller. New York: Dordrecht, 1983.

Dym, Warren. *Divining Science: Treasure Hunting and Earth Science in Early Modern Europe.* Leiden: Brill, 2010.

---

[48] Rudwick, *Meaning of Fossils,* 91.

Fortey, Richard. "In Retrospect: Leibniz's Protogaea." *Nature 455*, 4 (2008): 35.

Garber, Daniel. "De ortu et antiquissimis fontibus Protogaeae Leibnizianae dissertatio: Observation, Exploration, and Natural Philosophy." In J.A. Nicolás and S. Toledo, eds., *Leibniz y las ciencias empíricas/Leibniz and the Empirical Sciences* (Editorial Comares: Granada, 2011), 65–85.

Geikie, Archibald. *The Founders of Geology*. 2nd ed. London: Macmillan, 1905.

Gohau, Gabriel. *A History of Geology*. Revised and translated by Albert V. Carozzi and Marguerite Carozzi. New Brunswick, N.J.: Rutgers University Press, 1990.

Gould, Stephen J. *Time's Arrow, Time's Cycle: Myth and Metaphor in the Discovery of Geological Time*. Cambridge, Mass.: Harvard University Press, 1987.

Guericke, Otto. *Experimenta nova (ut vocantur) Magdeburgica de vacuo spatio*. Amsterdam, 1672.

Hamm, Ernst P. "Knowledge from Underground: Leibniz Mines the Enlightenment." *Earth Sciences History 16* (1997): 77–99.

Hölder, Helmut. *Geologie und Paläontologie in Texten und ihrer Geschichte*. Freiburg: Alber, 1960.

Kempe, Stephan. "The Baumann's Cave at Rübeland/Harz, Germany: One of the Caves Noted in Early Science History for Its Cave Bear and Cave Hyena Bone Deposits," *Scientific Annals*, School of Geology, Aristotle University of Thessaloniki, special vol. *98* (2006): 213–20.

Kircher, Athanasius. *Mundus subterraneus*. 2 vols. Amsterdam, 1664–1665.

Laudan, Rachel. *From Mineralogy to Geology: The Foundations of a Science, 1650–1830*. Chicago: University of Chicago Press, 1987.

Leibniz, Gottfried Wilhelm. "Protogaea." *Acta Eruditorum* (January 1693): 40–42.

———. *Protogaea, sive, De prima facie telluris et antiquissimae historiae vestigiis in ipsis naturae monumentis dissertatio*. Edited, with an introduction, by Christian Ludwig Scheidt. Göttingen, 1749.

———. "Epistola." *Miscellanea Berolinensia I* (1710): 118–120.

Leibniz, Gottfried Wilhelm, Johann Georg von Eckhart, Johann Daniel Gruber, Christian Ludwig Scheidt, and Johann Heinrich Jung. *Origines Guelficae*. Edited by Christian Ludwig Scheidt. Hannover: H. E. C. Schleuter, 5 vols., 1750–1780.

———. *Protogée: Ou de la formation et des révolutions du Globe*. Edited, with an introduction and notes, by Betrand de Saint-Germain. Paris: L. Langlois, 1859.

———. *Protogaea*. Edited and translated by W. v. Engelhardt. Stuttgart: Kohlhammer, 1949.

———. *Protogaea: De l'aspect primitif de la terre et des traces d'une Histoire très ancienne que renferment les monuments mêmes de la Nature*. Translated by Bertrand de Saint-Germain. Edited with an introduction and notes by Jean-Marie Barrande. Toulouse: Presses universitaires du Mirail, 1993.

———. *Protogaea*. Edited and translated, with an introduction, by Claudine Cohen and Andre Wakefield. Chicago: University of Chicago Press, 2008.

Merian, Matthaeus, ed. *Topographia und Eigentliche Beschreibung der Vornembsten Stäte, Schlösser, auch anderer Plätze und Örter in denen Herzogthümern Braunschweig und Lüneburg*. Frankfurt, 1654.

Oldroyd, David, and J. B. Howes. "The First Published Version of Leibniz's 'Protogaea.'" *Journal of the Society for the Bibliography of Natural History 9* (1978): 56–90.

Oldroyd, David. *Thinking about the Earth: A History of Ideas about Geology*. London: Athlone, 1996.

————. "The Genesis of Historical Research on the History of Geology, with Thoughts about Kirwan, de Luc, and Whiggery." In *A Master of Science History: Essays in Honor of Charles Coulston Gillispie* (Dordrecht: Springer, 2012), 167–177.

Rappaport, Rhoda. "Leibniz on Geology: A Newly Discovered Text." *Studia Leibnitiana 29*, 1 (1997): 6–11.

————. *When Geologists Were Historians, 1665–1750.* Ithaca, N.Y.: Cornell University Press, 1997.

Richet, Pascal. *A Natural History of Time.* Translated by John Venerella. Chicago: University of Chicago Press, 2007.

Rossi, Paolo. *The Dark Abyss of Time: The History of the Earth and the History of Nations from Hooke to Vico.* Translated by Lydia G. Cochrane. Chicago: University of Chicago Press, 1984.

Rudwick, Martin J. R. *The Meaning of Fossils: Episodes in the History of Palaeontology.* London: Macdonald, 1972.

Scheel, Günter. "Leibniz als Historiker des Welfenhauses." In *Wilhelm Totok and Carl Haase,* eds., *Leibniz: Sein Leben, sein Wirken, seine Welt* (Hannover: Verlag für Literatur und Zeitgeschehen, 1966), 227–276.

Schmidt, Alois. "Der Herkunft der Welfen in der bayerischen Landeshistoriographie des 17. Jahrhunderts und bei Gottfried Wilhelm Leibniz." In Herbert Breger and Friedrich Niewohner, eds., *Leibniz und Niedersachsen: Tagung anläßlich des 350. Geburtstages von G. W. Leibniz.* Studia Leibnitiana Sonderhefte 28 (Wolfenbüttel: F. Steiner, 1996), 127–147.

Steno, Nicolaus. *De solido intra solidum naturaliter contento dissertationis prodromus.* Florence, 1669.

Wakefield, Andre. "Leibniz and the Wind Machines." *Osiris 25* (2010): 171–818.

Woodward, Horace B. *History of Geology.* London: Watts, 1911.

Woodward, John. *An Essay toward a Natural History of the Earth.* London, 1695.

Zittel, Karl von. *History of Geology and Palaeontology to the End of the Nineteenth Century.* Translated by Maria M. Ogilvie-Gordon. London: Walter Scott, 1901.

CHAPTER 26

PHYSIOLOGY AND ORGANIC BODIES

FRANÇOIS DUCHESNEAU

In his natural philosophy, Leibniz grants living beings a prominent place. More than any other savants of his epoch, he was concerned with the appropriate methods to account for the structures, functions, and modes of reproduction of organisms; and he monitored closely contemporary developments in the life sciences. On the other hand, his metaphysics contains arguments and notions that build on physiological concepts to express the condition of finite substances and the relationship between substances in the phenomenal world. For Leibniz, at least in the later stages of his career, the account of living individuals and of their properties would provide access to a well-founded representation of corporeal substances in general. Hence the importance of analyzing his physiological views, which developed concomitantly with significant stages of his metaphysics. This metaphysics on the other hand, especially in its later version as a final embodiment of "general science," fostered a reassessment of the way physiology, combining theory with experience, should deal with living bodies, which form "divine machines of nature." (Smith 2011) In this perspective, it will be relevant to trace back the meaning that Leibniz conferred, at the turn of the 18th century, to the concept of "organism," a concept physiologists were then beginning to use, but with diverse meanings. By his specific notions of "organism" and "organic body," Leibniz would counter natural philosophers who were appealing to "vital souls," "plastic natures," "hylarchic principles," and so forth to account for the production and operations of living beings—a trend that will be later identified with "vitalism." Leibniz's arguments were stated in paradigmatic form in the controversy in which he opposed Georg Ernst Stahl and the latter's anti-mechanist medical theory. This points to the revised scientific program about living beings that Leibniz would sketch for future enquiries.

THE ADOPTION OF
MICRO-MECHANIST MODELS

Very early on, Leibniz expressed views on how to develop medicine and physiology, that new science of living bodies that was emerging from microscopic anatomy (*anatomia subtilis*) in the second half of the 17th century. (Wilson 1995) In the earliest plans for an academy of science to be established in Germany, Leibniz had expressed the need to join theory with experience in order to improve the incomplete histories of vital phenomena, normal and especially pathological, and to build a "system of true aphorisms and observations." (A IV 1, 541) However, the main problem was to find means of reaching to "the internal constitution of this clock which is subject to such disorders." (A IV 1, 551) To that end, as Leibniz stated in *Directiones ad rem medicam pertinentes* (1671–72), scientists and practitioners should resort to all available means provided by physics, chemistry, and anatomy "so as to proceed mathematically in medicine." (Hartmann and Krüger 1976, p. 65; A VIII 2, 664) An original way to achieve that objective had been shown by anatomists like Lorenzo Bellini, Nicolaus Steno, or Marcello Malpighi, who had framed mechanist models based on analogies with observed microstructures to account for the sequences of actions deriving from, or affecting, organic parts. Leibniz was explicitly preoccupied with the appropriate method for introducing the "form of science" (*forma scientiae*) in the interpretation of these more complex phenomena. What he had in mind was the superposition of analogy-based demonstrative syntheses to experience-derived micro-mechanist models, so as to account for physical and chemical processes in the living. The whole procedure would consist of combining analyses of comprehensive sets of empirical data with projections of hypotheses on the inner structures and operations of organic bodies. The challenge was to conceive the inner constitution and dynamic dispositions of the least parts in animals and plants. As Leibniz told Hermann Conring, a physician, in 1678, the validity of the so-framed hypotheses would be best established if they were simple, could account for the largest number of phenomena with the fewest presuppositions, and indeed could foster sound predictions about phenomena yet to be discovered. (A II 1, 399)

From the early 1680s on, Leibniz constantly stresses the importance of systematically collating observations and framing valid explanations by applying a *mathesis physica* to inductive inferences. (Letter to F. Schrader, April 1681, A II 1, 519) However, organic bodies impose manifest constraints on our analytic means. Every real body is organic because it possesses a formal raison d'être irreducible to the physical order, which depends on a substantive principle that is conceived as an agent of life, that is to say of perception and appetition; and this principle is the true source of the unity and dynamic integration characterizing the living body. Organic bodies have a special phenomenal status owing to their capacity for expressing the formal unity and integration of actions and passions *sub modo materiali*, but this perceiving principle remains foreign to the physiological elements proper and cannot intervene for explaining phenomena in their own order. What is at stake was the possible extension of the field of physiological and pathological observations by model-building. As Leibniz argues in the *Praefatio ad libellum elementorum physicae* (1678–79):

> The discovery of causes, without which we should not expect great advancements in the most necessary part of physics, medicine, could not be hoped for from the hasty discourses of agitated minds on all topics, but only from profound and quasi-geometrical thoughts. For our body is a hydraulic and pneumatic machine, and it contains fluids which act not only by their weight and other modalities manifest to the senses, but also by secret processes, namely solutions, precipitations, evaporations, freezing, and indeed filtrations, as well as by numerous other modalities by which complex bodies are resolved into imperceptible parts. Therefore if reasons borrowed from geometry and mechanics are not provided, which apply equally well to perceptible and imperceptible realities, nature will escape us because of its subtlety; and here above all reason must supply for the lack of experience, for reason may consider some corpuscle one hundred thousand times more subtle than a grain of dust flying in the air and compare it to other corpuscles of equal subtlety with no lesser facility that the playing ball one holds in one's hand. (A VI 4, 1998)

At the initial stage, the method rests on empirical connections for which the analogy of a common structure is to be sought. A second stage consists of building explanatory models on this extended empirical base: it implies transposing the observable or analogically inferred properties into physical or chemical properties that may represent the inner structure of organic bodies. The key to this procedure resides in analyzing relevant empirical properties down to their presumed determining micro-structural conditions. The analysis is deemed sufficient if it enables the investigator to figure out how the emerging effect may result from as exact a combination of micro-structural efficient causes as possible.

In a period of intense philosophical invention that will culminate with the *Système nouveau de la nature et de la communication des substances* (1695), Leibniz proceeds to a review of contemporary physiological notions to sketch a theoretical framework for the mechanist interpretation of vital phenomena. The result is the recently edited set of manuscript pieces about the "animal machine." (Pasini 1996)

In particular, the text entitled *Corpus hominis et uniuscujusque animalis machina est quaedam*, which dates back to the early 1680s, represents probably Leibniz's best effort to characterize from a micro-structural perspective the concept of an organic machine in its application to the living organism. This machine may be conceived in two distinct ways. On the one hand, it should be considered as a device capable of a kind of perpetual motion: "Animal bodies are machines of perpetual motion, or expressed more clearly, they have been arranged so as to keep forever a cycle of perpetual motion of a determinate and special kind." (LH III, I, 2, f. 1, in Pasini 1996, p. 218) On the other hand, these bodies should be conceived as complex mechanisms implementing three orders of functions, namely vital, animal, and generative. These last ones have been added to the others, because a living individual cannot indefinitely keep its vital motion in a context of altering conditions: so nature has invented, by way of reproduction, a mode of successive perpetuation of functions from individuals to individuals. A clear equation is set between the identified function or end of the machine and the analysis of means for achieving this end. The representation of the machine's end is the starting point for explaining the mechanical dispositions involved, which in turn will be decomposed into more particular ends. The notion of a "perpetual motion machine" seems *prima facie* paradoxical, since a mechanical perpetual motion is impossible. But an organic machine, contrary to any artificial machine, would in effect imply an endogenous principle of autonomy that would restore its motile capacity to a constant level in time. While all man-built machines must have their force restored by various external means, nature has endowed its own machine: (1) with the power of repairing its used parts by assimilating food (vital functions); (2) with the power of moving itself to avoid external causes of attrition and to reach restorative nutriments; and (3) with the power of being warned of its own modifications or of those of surrounding bodies, as well as of being stimulated into reacting consequently (animal functions). (4) Furthermore, the natural machine has been given the power of preserving the species beyond the individual (generative functions), since the latter's power of preserving its integrity through change shall be ultimately checked by irremediable accidents—disease, decay, and death. The prime motor of the organic body at the basis of vital functions is to be conceived as analogous to a subtle ethereal and flammable matter, a sort of *lumen* that is transmitted to all corporeal parts wherein it provokes durable dynamic effects, namely chemical reactions. Leibniz insists on the role of blood and of its components as vectors of dynamic effects, by means of systoles and diastoles, which are amplified by the action and reaction of the cardiac muscle and echoed throughout the other organs by the vascular system. Presuming that the seat of vital effervescence is in the heart, and that from there physical and chemical effects are multiplied throughout, the physiologist will need to explain the respiratory function by a correlation of mechanisms implying an alternation of processes that later physiology will identify as "metabolic." This dynamic representation of vital processes is often evoked by means of analogies with physical phenomena of luminescence and warmth and with chemical phenomena of fermentative effervescence. Ultimately, Leibniz seems to favor the notion of an assemblage of minute organic machines characterized by elastic microstructures and capable of producing oscillations through which motive forces will be functionally maintained.

The explanation of animal functions presumes that there is an endogenous source of combustible for the "fire machine" that the living animal forms. The effervescent fluid thus produced must circulate through all organs: hence the composite constitution of the body, which is made of solid and soft parts of a general vascular type, in order to convey the dynamic agent to the various organs in which it will cause chemical reactions. The system thus provides for a functional account of animal motions by means of (material) spirits. Leibniz argues that the nerves, as vessels with enveloping membranes and appended muscles, are maximally distended by spirits resulting from an effervescence of blood. Nerves are under tension and form a dynamic equilibrium with one another, as would many inflated vesicles under a common envelope. If, for a cause either internal or external, this equilibrium is broken, a chain reaction follows to restore it. If this result cannot be easily obtained, motions of greater amplitude may occur, as those of a sudden water flow, of a released spring under tension, or of the spark-triggered deflagration of gunpowder: such motions can affect more or less extended areas of the organism in order to remove impediments to regular processes. Leibniz's objective is to figure out how dynamic effects in integrative networks can provide equivalent models for the sensitive and motile functions of the animal machine. The outstanding feature of this hypothetical machine is that, because of its integrative dynamic dispositions, "the animal force is entirely in the whole and entirely in any of its parts." (LH III, I, 2, f. 2, in Pasini 1996, p. 223) What emerges then is the notion of a force (*vis*) distinct from the motion (*motus*) it generates and which originates so to speak from within the organic body. This force is at once the central principle of action of the integrative system of organic structures and processes, and the regulative principle of the vital operations that make the individual body appear for a time to be the continuous agent of its own conservation. In this latter role, it is relayed in time by bodies of its own species that it has begotten.

Indeed, Leibniz's "reformed mechanics," founded on the principle of conservation of *vis viva* (Duchesneau 1994; Leibniz 1994), has provoked an original unfolding of the physiological model, wherein we find combined an account of organs and functional dispositions of the vital mechanics, and an account of formal principles destined to represent the causal agent whose action results in dynamic effects in the organic machine:

> For we demonstrate that one thing is force, another motion, and that motion is inherent (*inesse*) in the extended mass; motive force is inherent in a different subject which in common bodies we call substantial form, in the living, soul, in man, mind: hence it will be possible to explain with unexpected clarity the origin of sense and appetite in animals, the union of soul and body, and the mode by which the soul acts on the body or is affected by the latter. (LH III, I, 2, f. 2, in Pasini 1996, p. 223–24)

Leibniz's adhesion to a micro-structural model of vital phenomena is here particularly obvious. But at the same time, the model was starting to become more complex and encompassing. This was partly the consequence of the reformed mechanics, first formulated in *De corporum concursu* (1678), but partly also the result of inserting a metaphysical dimension, that of a principle of life, or perception and appetition, within the notion of animal machine. However this appeal to metaphysics shall not contravene to Leibniz's acceptance of the modern physiologists' micro-mechanist methodology, which aimed at conjoining the empirical enquiries of subtle anatomy with the projection of explanatory models inspired by physics or chemistry.

MACHINES OF NATURE, MONADS,
AND ORGANIC BODIES

The conception of living beings as "machines of nature" that Leibniz developed in the mature period of his philosophy set the stage for a re-evaluation of the micro-mechanist approach in physiology. Through exchanges with Arnauld and Fardella in the late 1680s, Leibniz established a conceptual framework that closely associated the finite substance with an organic body in an overarching representation of living beings as "machines of nature" distinct from "machines of the art." (Duchesneau 1982; Fichant 2003; Duchesneau 2010; Smith 2011) Machines of nature are indeed endowed with an integrative unity that unfolds in the internal organization of their parts, each of which forms in turn a machine of nature at its own level of integration, and so on indefinitely, at least for our finite minds. The combination of the dominant monad with its organic body forms a complex substance whose reality is not in question as it would be in an idealist perspective according to which the body would be only a phenomenal representation correlative of the monad's perceptual activity. But this idealist interpretation that was indeed current among specialists of Leibniz's metaphysics has been efficiently challenged in the more recent period. (Fichant 2004; Phemister 2005)

In my opinion, the decisive step toward the original conception of machines of nature took place concurrently with the formulation of the dynamics proper in the 1690s. Before, Leibniz did not diverge much from the Malpighi-inspired view of corporeal machines that the early 1680s manuscripts reflected. However, a transition was taking place toward a hypothesis about animal substances that would imply both a substantial form and a body that jointly achieved the condition of a *unum per se* (*Discours de métaphysique*, 1686, art. 34). In this transition period, a relation of equivalence had also been set between the mechanical explanation of processes and the network of intelligibility that teleology would project on organic phenomena. Hence a restoration of final causes in the phenomenal sequences takes place across the whole system of nature, but more directly in the sphere of living beings where they would assist in explaining the connection between organic structures and vital functions (*Discours de métaphysique*, 1686, art. 22). This correspondence between causal mechanisms and teleological dispositions in natural agents did not mean however that one could resort to soul-like principles in analyzing specific organic phenomena. These phenomena were supposed to be accountable for by means of mechanical processes alone.

However two factors combined to produce a major shift in Leibniz's philosophy of nature. The first was a redefinition of the notion of finite substance in the course of the correspondence with Arnauld. A question had arisen concerning the substantial standing of bodies, essentially those of man and animals. Because of doubts raised by Arnauld against the definition of substance by means of "complete notion," Leibniz finally concluded that substance should be defined as a principle of true unity, and that if this principle was to be attributed to bodies, it could only be so because of the individual form of a substance, namely the corresponding soul or entelechy. (Letter to Arnauld of April 30, 1687, A II 2, 190) Then, Leibniz developed the idea that the connection between parts in bodies, which do not possess true unity, depends on inner relationships in the substantial units of which they are composed. Leibniz acknowledges indeed that there is some kind of phenomenal unity resulting from the connection between organic parts themselves, but, at the level of formal reasons, this is not enough for identifying real units underpinning the simultaneous and successive orders displayed by those phenomena. The reality in bodies that founds their unity of structure and operation should be sought in true units that manifest themselves by animating the integrative organic parts. Leibniz recalls in this context that the organic whole formed by a soul and its body is to be viewed in turn as composed of parts, each of which is composed of further wholes ruled over by corresponding entelechies. Thus the organic body appears as a combination of substantial units under a dominant monad, although the soul of such a body could not be held for an aggregate of subordinate souls.

The letter to Arnauld of October 9, 1687, presents the notion of "corporeal substance," which deserves to be admitted since the "animated body" possesses an integrative unity resulting from the substantiality of the soul that expresses itself through it, or at least from "an entelechy which is analogous to the soul, since otherwise bodies would be only phenomena." (A II 2, 252; L, 344) From this point of view, it is important to distinguish the inferior or simpler corporeal substances from the living ones and the animals, and the latter from man as a corporeal substance ruled over by a mind. Leibniz holds that the animated or "informed" bodies occupy the least parts of the phenomenal world. Due to the infinite divisibility of matter, souls, or at least forms, have this feature in common that they constitute an infinite manifold: consequently, there is an analogical relation of infinite development in the compounds of souls and organic parts. Therefore global corporeal substances can present a corporeal mass constituted of aggregates of organic microstructures whose unity depends on animal souls, but at the same time we may conceive that the mass informed by such entelechies can be decomposed into a manifold of corporeal substances, each of which possesses its own animating principle. The Leibnizian formulation is at once significant:

> [. . .] assuming there is a soul or entelechy in beasts or in other corporeal substances, we must reason in this matter just as we all reason in regard to man. Man is a being endowed with a true unity given him by his soul, in spite of the fact that the mass of his body is divided into organs, ducts, humours, and spirits and that these parts are undoubtedly filled with an infinity of other corporeal substances endowed with their own entelechy. (A II 2, 251; L, 344)

This point is further illustrated by reference to Antoni Van Leeuwenhoek's observation that "an infinite number of small animals are present in the least drop of water." (A II 2, 254; L, 345, quoting Leeuwenhoek 1677) This argument is abstracted from its original context for the sake of justifying the persistence *post mortem* of the animal with a drastically reduced organic body. Leibniz readily acknowledges that, phrased in this way, the argument had not been put forward as such by naturalists who, especially Jan Swammerdam and Leeuwenhoek, had focused their attention on the phenomena of generation, which they had interpreted as mere transformations of organic bodies. Compared to phenomenal birth in which the animal undergoes a rather gradual transformation, death would represent a kind of violent and sudden regression of the organic body subject to corruption. And the organic reduction that occurs down to parts too small for our means of observation and analysis seems to mean, for plain living beings and animals under the human threshold, an attrition of their functional properties they may not recover from, except in some cases of apparent resuscitation from death-like lethargic states.

For his own part, Leibniz is very keen on establishing that the order of living substances follows the differences and degrees of expression of their entelechies or souls and that this scale applies as well to the structural and functional organization of the corresponding bodies. Thus he opens the door to comparative researches about a progressive differentiation in organization along the chain of beings. Following Malpighi, he especially insists on structural analogies between animal and vegetal machines of nature that foretell of similar analogies in functional processes and modes of integration, left to be unveiled.

The other main source for Leibniz's notion of organic body as machine of nature is the transformation of his revised mechanics into the dynamics proper that was achieved in the *Dynamica de potentia* (1689–90) and fostered various publications thereafter. (Duchesneau, 1994) Leibniz has set a conservation principle more general than the principle of conservation of *vis viva* in fixing the a priori conditions for a theory of formal or essential action in cases of unconstrained motion when the body, moving freely and without resistance, moves its own mass with a given speed over a given distance. We are presented with a transposition of motile action as a sort of active form, of causal agent in the body, comprising at once propensity for action and motive effect translating this propensity in duration. The action thus accomplished represents a force that would reconstitute itself integrally by a kind of inner and endogenous causality. As Leibniz explains to De Volder in 1699: "In the free formal action of the mover, when conceived as acting upon itself, we can conceive analogically a real effect that will not be the change of place (which we consider only to be a modal effect), but the mover itself preparing with a given speed for producing itself the next moment, self-generating with the same speed exerted the moment before." (GP II, 191; A II 3, 596)

The theory of compound substances as organic entities is directly affected by the tenets of the dynamics, and especially by the fourfold distinction proposed in the *Specimen dynamicum* between primitive and derivative active and passive forces. (GM VI, 236–37) The primitive active and passive forces signify the essential properties of corporeal substances pertaining to their formal element, the entelechy; the derivative active and passive forces characterize the interactions of bodies as revealed by experience. What is thrown into relief in this theoretical construction is the relation of sufficient reason and ordained expression that rules over the connection between primitive and derivative forces. The mechanical effects that occur at the phenomenal level must express the kind of determination and order that characterizes the fundamental units of force. These units show an endogenous power to act that develops as a propensity to constantly regenerate itself and as an individualized source of functional activity. Leibniz tends to grant these units an immanent architectonic power, resulting in finalized action in the structures and operations of organic bodies. These intrinsically active substances are accordingly real individuals. As mentioned in the *Système nouveau*: "it is impossible to find the principles of a true unity in matter alone or in what is merely passive." (GP IV, 478) Atoms cannot be true units of nature. One needs real active units to account for the persistence of phenomenal compound substances. These units are to be conceived as animated points, sorts of substantial atoms comprising force and action, from which complex substances of the sense-perceived world draw their dynamic properties and organization. The properties of the true units of nature, which Leibniz will designate as "monads" from 1695 on, are reflected in the intelligible features of the corresponding organic bodies that combine with them to form corporeal substances.

For Leibniz, the formal perfection of substantial units consists of primitive force as a source of continuous action and diversified effects: this force expresses itself in the organic arrangement (at once mechanical and teleological) of the physical realities deriving their integrative unity from that source. This is why Leibniz envisions in the true units of nature a sort of perception that possesses something "vital"; (GP IV 482–83) but he underlines at once that this vitality as expressed in the world of phenomena conforms to the mathematical laws and models ruling over bodies. There is no doubt that organic structures are subject to the laws regulating derivative forces. But in applying these laws as well as subordinate physical and chemical laws, we should take into account the functional and integrative order of organic effects. In the *Système nouveau*, because of the characteristics of living beings and of their specific whole-part integration, Leibniz excludes the possibility that they could be formed by mere mechanical epigenesis. He refers to the metamorphoses in organic form observed by Swammerdam, Malpighi, and Leeuwenhoek: these observations seem to justify that one may dispense with conceiving the organism as resulting from a mechanical clustering of parts. Since the organic machine exists only by the effect of its formal units, the mechanical derivation of the organizing program itself for combining and recombining the parts of the machine remains inconceivable. If the preformation hypothesis seems therefore methodologically valid to characterize the origin of living beings, or at least the continuity in organic arrangement between generations, it does not seem appropriate to suppose that the animal disappears at death as if its organizing form disintegrated. As an animal supposes a specific organization depending on a formal cause or force, organisms are constantly transforming themselves without creation or annihilation. Hence the well-known thesis:

> This led me at length to conclude that there is only one reasonable view to take—that of the conservation not only of the soul but also of the animal itself and its organic machine, even though the destruction of its grosser parts may have reduced this

machine to a size so small that it escapes our senses just as it did before birth. (GP IV, 480; L 455)

Organization then is the persisting expression of the soul, monad, or entelechy in a constantly changing corporeal structure. Hence the idea of a kind of immanent law ruling continuously over the morphological, and by implication, over the physiological transformations of the living being. The *De ipsa natura* (1698) mentions, in a similar context, the presence of a *lex insita* governing the actions and passions that successively affect corporeal substances because of their correspondence with the internal determinations of monads: this is "[. . .] an internal law from which their actions and passions follow, even if this law is mostly not understood by the creatures in which it inheres." (GP IV, 507; L 500) When Leibniz professes: "there happens only a transformation of one and the same animal, as its organs are differently folded and are more or less developed," (GP IV, 481; L 455) he in fact underlines that the organic machine is ruled over by a specific law of transformation. Of whatever size and appearance the animal, or more generally, the living being is, the organization of its body expresses, by the ordered sequence of changes it undergoes, the inner disposition and innate activity of one and the same animating principle. Along a similar approach, it appears that organic bodies develop their successive states by means of a structural predetermination (*praedelineatio*) that should be supposed to be linked to primitive forces. These forces represent the active element in corporeal substances, and they determine an identity of organization for these substances across the sequences of transformation that their organic bodies undergo. At the phenomenal level, these sequences of transformation are to be seen as processes of adjustment of structures and organic operations following interactions occurring between bodies in their common environment.

In attributing an inner law of transformation to machines of nature, Leibniz posits as their definitional feature structures and functions that develop to infinity. To this end, he argues from the "nestedness" (*emboîtement*) of organic parts in one another to infinity, each of which would form a totality at a given level of integration. This type of structural combination rests on the hierarchic integration of primordial units that correspond to the aggregate of parts in the machine and grant it a power to adapt and adjust itself so that it can be preserved through the transformations of the organic body. Whatever the animal's size, it has an organized body expressing in its inner dispositions the inherent activity of its animating principle. But this essential body is not necessarily a miniature of the observed body: it is only a pre-existing minimal organic structure, connected with the "program" of the organism to be achieved through generation. (Nachtomy 2009) Correlatively, Leibniz asserts the multi-functionality of the organic machine: he relies for that purpose on the "emboîtement" of organic parts into one another, each constituting a totality at a given level of integration. This type of structural combination grounded in the underlying formal units yields adaptive processes (indeed in a pre-Darwinian meaning), as well as a capacity for self-preservation: "We must recognize that the machines of nature have a truly infinite number of organs, and are so well equipped and so completely proof against all accidents that it is impossible to destroy them." (GP IV, 482; L 456)

In the *De ipsa natura*, Leibniz challenges the view that animating principles, such as Henry More's "hylarchic principle," or "spirit of nature," inhere in material realities and form organisms. Machines of nature do not require the same type of formative principle as man-made machines, since they actualize nature's substantive plan directly. Hence their preformation: "I consider it sufficient that the mechanism of the world is built with such wisdom that these wonderful things depend upon the progression of the machine itself, organic things particularly, as I believe, evolving by a certain predetermined order." (GP IV, 505; L 499) Leibniz resumes Robert Boyle's corpuscularian argument that a body's inner mechanism is its very nature, but with the additional condition that the laws governing mechanisms are metaphysically derived, as stated in the *Specimen dynamicum* (1695). Relying on his theory of essential or formal action, Leibniz supposes that phenomenal realities and their properties follow from the inner qualities and operations of the dynamic units they depend on. Consequently, for all physical realities, particularly the more organized ones, their series of states and processes are caused by an inherent form or force that constitutes and actualizes the law of their series, as intended in the plan of nature. In the same way, Leibniz dissociates himself from the Cartesians. He will not admit that animals are deprived of a sensitive soul, which man alone would possess. Dynamic principles apply to all physical realities, which differ only in complexity of structures and integrative processes. Hence an analogical ground for analyzing the properties and operations of living beings inferior to humans: "I believe on the contrary that it is consistent neither with the order nor with the beauty or the reason of things that there should be something vital or immanently active only in a small part of matter, when it should imply greater perfection if it were in all." (GP IV, 512; L, 504)

ORGANISM AND THE DEVELOPMENT OF PHYSIOLOGY

Once the notion of machine of nature has been acquired and the theory of monads and organic bodies is in place, Leibniz completes what we might call his metaphysics of life, as it is finally illustrated in the *Monadologie* (1714). But at the same time, he keeps assessing the current state of physiological and medical doctrines and proposing relevant strategies for their advancement. One element that came rapidly to the fore in these later discussions was the specificity of living beings qua "organisms." There may have been earlier occurrences of this word "organism" in Leibniz's manuscripts (Cheung 2006); but the dating of these and notably of the fragment entitled *Du Rapport général de toutes choses* (A VI 4, 1614–15) might be posterior to 1700. Nonetheless, A. Nunziante rightly traced back to the late 1680s significant preliminary steps in the forging of this notion (Nunziante 2002, p. 116–23). In any event, the first public use of the concept in its typical Leibnizian meaning seems to have occurred in 1704 in a letter to Lady Masham. According to R. Andrault, Georg Ernst Stahl, a major physician and professor at the University of Halle, known for having introduced "animism" as the grounding principle of his physiological and pathological theory, did use the term as early as 1684 in his *De intestinis eorumque morbis*, but my impression is that he did not give it any major and specific role previous to his *Disquisitio de mechanismi et organismi diversitate* (1706). Alternatively, the term made its way into Nehemiah Grew's *Cosmologia sacra* (1701), where it was meant to signify in the first instance those complex combinations of elementary microstructures in living bodies that are responsible for functional operations: "Organism designates at once the complex structure of an animated body compounded of several visceras, and the structure of this viscera as it is composed by the reiteration of thousands of small nested bodies and as it has a proper function that essentially results from the geometry of this composition." (Andrault 2010, p. 32) Personally, I would point to the previously unanalyzed appearance of the term in Friedrich Hoffmann's *De natura morborum medicatrice mechanica* (1699). The context here is afforded by the controversy between the philosopher Johann Christoph Sturm and the physician Günther Christoph Schelhammer about the legitimacy of equating, following Boyle's suggestion, nature with mechanism: in this controversy, the latter opposed the former's occasionalism for the sake of preserving the autonomy of action for natural (corporeal) substances according to an Aristotelian pattern. The polemics motivated Leibniz to write his *De ipsa natura*, wherein he exposed his philosophy of nature and the actual conciliation of mechanism with a law-governed phenomenal world, itself dependent upon the actions and passions of monadic individualities. Hoffmann, a professor of medicine at the University of Halle and a correspondent of Leibniz during this precise period, also reacted to the same controversy on behalf of a revised mechanistic conception of living organisms (*medicina rationalis*). The significant statement of his concerning "organism" reads: "When several material causes are so coordinated and arranged that effects follow corresponding to the idea of the craftsman who set to himself a given end, one speaks of mechanism, but a more perfect mechanism is also called by some an organism, since such a mechanism is found in organic bodies." (Hoffmann 1749, I, p. 50) Here, the notion mainly signifies such a complex organization of microstructures in organic bodies as results in the accomplishment of ends that correspond to the vital operations and constitute a special expression of nature's divine craftsmanship. We are not very far from the meaning that Leibniz gave to the notion when he stated:

> [. . .] The organism is essential to matter, but to matter arranged by a supreme wisdom. This is why I define the Organism or natural Machine, a machine every part of which is a machine; consequently its subtle contrivance goes to infinity, since nothing is small enough to be neglected, while the parts of our artificial machines are not machines. (Letter to Lady Masham, June 30, 1704, GP III, 356)

The concept of organism applies to compound substances, which monads or souls and organic bodies form jointly. As the simple substance contains an inner representative manifold stretching to infinity, so the machine of nature as a complex of organic dispositions undergoes successive phases of folding and unfolding. As the organization of its structures for the sake of filling vital functions results from an infinite craftsmanship, this machine is organic down to its innermost parts as far as analytic regress goes. By contrast with the limited teleological features of man-made machines, organism as such characterizes the structure and operation of organic bodies that imply a form of mechanism so subtly integrated that the living being stays self-sufficient and develops functional operations to infinity: "And the organism of the living is nothing else than a more divine mechanism progressing infinitely in subtlety." (C, 16) An animal is a substance composed of a soul together with its organic body. This body is conceived as an aggregate of more elementary living beings, nested in one another to infinity. The compound substance's soul is to be identified with the leading monad, which affords a principle of integration for the organic body as machine of nature: "The animal [is this] corporeal substance which the monad exerting its dominion over the machine renders one." (Letter to De Volder, June 20, 1703, GP II, 252) Organism characterizes the combination of integrative structures and functions that unfold from the inner dispositions of this corporeal substance, the dispositions of which Leibniz will equate with "preformation" to the very end of his life:

> The organism of animals is a mechanism that supposes divine preformation. What follows from it is purely natural and entirely mechanical. Whatever is performed in the body of man and any animal is no less mechanical than what is performed in a watch. The difference is only such as ought to be between a machine of divine invention and the workmanship of an artist as limited as man is. (Fifth letter to Clarke," §§115–16, GP VII, 417–18)

Therefore there was no surprise in Leibniz's opposition to Stahl's radical conceptual distinction between organism and mechanism in the *Disquisitio*, republished as an introductory essay in the *Theoria medica vera* (1708). (Stahl 1708; Stahl 1720; Duchesneau & Smith 2016) For Stahl, the soul was an active immaterial substance acting as the final and efficient cause of all vital and organic movements. It exists only in and for the body that serves as its instrument. Through its *logos*, the soul has inner knowledge of the various organs and their capacity to undergo changes according to subconscious psychological intents. The body consists of unstable chemical aggregates constantly on the verge of dissolving. The soul's main function is to oppose this tendency to corruption by preserving and adjusting the organic whole. Stahl resorts to the term "organism" to contrast the condition of the animated body with that of a mere "mechanism." Thus Stahl's organism is a heterogeneous aggregate of material compounds and structures subservient to the soul's ends. Maintaining and integrating the various physiological processes presupposes indeed that the particular mechanisms are regulated by a kind of immanent and unconscious knowledge and power to act. So, the organism would be a fragile chemical machine entirely dependent upon the organizing and vitalizing powers of the soul. Consequently, illness and death would be essentially caused by the soul suffering morbid distractions and failing to fulfill its vital duties.

Leibniz opposes Stahl's views and argues that we have no need for that kind of soul "for the reason that there is preformation and an organism to infinity." (GP VI, 544) Against Stahl, Leibniz upholds the autonomous order of physiological phenomena. The principle of sufficient reason implies that "everything that occurs in matter derives from the preceding state of matter according to the laws of change." (Dutens II 2, 131) These laws form the kingpin of all explanations by way of mechanism; and, in the phenomenal world, there is no exception to the rule of mechanism. Indeed organic phenomena and natural laws ruling over organic bodies need to be substantially and causally grounded in the theory of monads and the laws of inner change. And it is appropriate to acknowledge a principle of harmonic correspondence that correlates sequences of perceptions and appetites on the one hand with sequences of states of organic bodies on the other, in virtue of an original divine preformation. But the key to Leibniz's position stands in this statement: "[. . .] in the organic body of the living being, which is presided over by the soul as its particular ruling agent, even if the source of all action is in the soul, nothing happens contrary to the laws of the body, as well as nothing happens in the soul, if not by its own laws, even if the source of its passions comes from matter." (Dutens II 2, 133) No one is able to conceive how the body's geometrical and mechanical properties can arise from the monad's perceptions and appetites, and reciprocally. Because of original preformation alone is the correlation such that "the soul is an essential representation of the body and the body an essential instrument of the soul." (Dutens II 2, 133) The principle of expressive correspondence applies to all corporeal phenomena as well as to all monadic substrates. Therefore final or instrumental determination should not be restricted to a single type of natural entities, souls, for finality and causal efficiency are fully distributed in both spheres of reality. As a consequence, instrumental teleology does not appear anymore as the exclusive mode of production of organic phenomena by the soul, but only as one of the two ways of explaining them, the other consisting of revealing the sequences of physical and chemical processes by which vital operations are achieved. As already stated, the latter is more profound and more difficult; but teleology as applied to natural processes in their very order may serve as a provisional substitute for causal efficient derivation: "Even if the effects arise from the inner motions and structures of the machine, however, as these internal aspects are unknown to us, one can guess what they are from the ends more easily than from mechanisms." (Dutens II 2, 135) Thus it is understandable that Leibniz rejects Stahl's radical distinction between organism and mechanism. For him organism is only a higher-level mechanism, and, as a property, it characterizes the inner order of organic bodies. Organism designates a principle of composition of the structures and processes that unfold infinitely within the living machine. Even if the formal unit from which an integrated manifold arises is to be found only in an entelechy, the analysis of these structures and processes should not require our appealing to modes of explanation other than mechanist models, since "organism is nothing else formally than a mechanism, but more subtle and divine, since everything in nature occurs mechanically." (Dutens II 2, 136) Indeed the determining condition of life consists of the capacity of perception and appetition, that is to say the formal characteristics of the dominant monad associated with the organic body, but Leibniz attributes the functions of preservation, restoration, and reproduction of living beings to a vegetative force: at least this would be a consequence deduced from the material conditions of organic arrangement understood in terms of movements and micro-movements. On the other hand, Leibniz reduces the direct role of the soul in these processes, since it boils down to a mere matter of harmonic effects, without direct causation by the animating principle over the corporeal processes by which life manifests itself materially. Thus life is made into a psychological equivalent of corporeal mechanism and the latter suffices for maintaining, achieving, and reproducing such functional movements as express life organically. And these expressions of life are also to be connected through the same system of physical laws to the larger field of external physical conditions that induce constant changes in the living microstructures and micro-processes. Organism is the key feature of a world of living creatures, that is to say, of a world of organic bodies intrinsically linked to perceiving monads. It is probably right to suppose that the ultimate version of Leibniz's system in the *Principes de la nature et de la grâce* (1714) and in the *Principes de la philosophie ou Monadologie* integrates such a concept of organism, and that this concept guides the interpretation of monads by making living beings and especially animals into true analogues of real substances.

Inspired by his late theory of the living, Leibniz supports a reformed mechanist trend in physiology and medicine, as evidenced in a number of correspondences with scientists. In particular, the question that he addresses with Domenico Guglielmini and Hoffmann relates to the application of mathematical models to represent the forces involved in physiological processes. Working out appropriate micro-mechanist explanations could not take place without exact observation of the various actions that functions imply. The structural approach is indeed essential for analyzing dispositions proper to the natural machines, but this analysis would be incomplete if it could not reach to the immanent forces that unfold operations in such complex mechanisms. Leibniz insists that physiologists take into account empirical modalities of organization and of ensuing processes, as well as theoretical views on forces, which are the true causes of phenomenal sequences. Indeed, the partial and provisional hypotheses of the so-called *medicina rationalis* should ultimately rest on the theory of monads and primitive forces as a grounding requirement. But the scientific representation of machines of nature should rest more immediately on the functional interpretation of material processes along systematic analogies induced from observation and experience. And in this context, building a true physiology requires that the limitations of any mechanist representation of the living should not be lost sight of. Thus Leibniz writes to Guglielmini: "It is true that starting from the distant principles of Democritean philosophy, a transition would not appear evident to special physics (= physiology) and that the foundations of functions should rather be sought from experiments; but I feel that it also belongs to this art to deduce appropriate consequences from these." (Letter to Guglielmini of September 1697, in Cavazza 1987, p. 72; A III 7, 577) Approximately the same statement is to be found addressed to Hoffmann: "I should hope that men expert in explaining the mechanism of nature would go progressively farther and care not to reduce everything, as the Cartesians do, by a sudden leap to first principles: magnitude, figure and motion, which is impossible for us to do, but analyze gradually compounded realities into simpler ones which bring us nearer to principles." (Letter to Hoffmann of September 17, 1699, in: Hoffmann 1749, I, p. 50b; A III 8, 239)

Accordingly, Leibniz will suggest discarding or amending a priori models so that explanations better fit the immanent complexity of vital functions. The late exchanges with Johann Bernoulli, Bernardino Zendrini, and Pietro Antonio Michelotti illustrate that precise trend toward the implementation of physiology and medicine after the pattern of a *physica specialis*. The sought-for explanations ought not to be contrary to either reason or experience, since hypotheses are based at once on the observed processes and on presumed hidden physical and chemical dispositions, which are attached to microstructures and elicit appropriate dynamic interactions between elementary components (corpuscles or conspiring micro-motions). The correspondence with Bernoulli after 1710 will thus concentrate on muscular motion and on the hypothesis of vital or animal spirits as "agents of impetus" (*impetus facientia*). Leibniz will suggest suspending the attempted derivation of the phenomena involved from the pure geometrical and mechanical properties of elementary matter: instead, physiological explanation should be provisionally limited to physiological properties, such as the vital contractility of muscle fibres, which Giorgio Baglivi had just revealed at that time. Such properties are first identified from the observation of specific actions affecting various structures and microstructures. Then attempts are made at transcribing these *sui generis* functional properties into special mechanisms embodied in the microstructure of fibres. And these mechanisms are equated with special physical processes and chemical reactions. Indeed, it is important to seek the deepest possible interpretation of vital phenomena, but the idea prevails that we should limit ourselves to formalizing specific phenomenal relations after the best analogical models presently available from physics and chemistry. (Letter to Johann Bernoulli of May 6, 1712, GM III-2, 887–88)

Zendrini, for instance, was studying the dynamics of blood occasioned by the heart's systolic contractions and by their transmission along artery membranes. He submitted to Leibniz a model to account for it based on calculations relative to an equivalent inorganic machine. Though favorable to this type of approach, Leibniz underlined that Zendrini's lemma would need to be rendered far more complex to fit the corresponding vital phenomena, especially in regard to their constant restoration in time. (Letter to Zendrini of March 15, 1716, GM IV, 250) Michelotti was interested in the functions of secretion on which he will publish a major work in 1721 (Michelotti 1721). Faced with the disparity of mechanical and chemical models proposed at the time, Leibniz suggests that the analysis should take into account a complete set of factors so as to approximate the complexity of the processes involved. (Letter to Michelotti of September 17, 1715, Dutens II 2, 89–91) At the same time, he concludes that the physiological explanation might in this instance limit itself to identifying physical causes that can be strictly inferred from the correlation of phenomena; then these causes may be equated with special forces resulting from special combinations of *conatus* in the parts under investigation. Clearly, Leibniz has in mind a "special physics" that would identify vital processes from experience, link them with functional properties of organic micro-mechanisms, account for them by combinations of physical and chemical models, and insert them in a system of machines of nature endowed with integrative organization down to infinity.

***

In Leibniz's time, micro-mechanism seemed to dominate, though not exclusively, the more innovative trend in physiology, and microscopic anatomy (*anatomia subtilis*) determined the representation of living beings (Duchesneau 1998). The basic postulate was that human understanding could rely on microscopic observation and account for microstructures by framing mechanical models: along that trend, hope was to attain the real causes of physiological phenomena. The analogy with man-made machines would contribute to the analysis of functions and facilitate knowledge of nature's concealed processes. The micro-mechanists considered the whole living being as a structure composed of "minute machines" (*machinulae*) nested in one another. The way in which such elementary material components combined remained a problem. Hence a procedure of structural "schematism" that indefinitely postponed identifying a complete sufficient reason for such combinations: such was the case with Malpighi, a profound investigator on these life science issues. Natural scientists and philosophers were also faced with the question of how living beings formed and exerted vital functions: inquiries on this issue tended to be indefinitely suspended because it was presumed that such complex organizations pre-existed any generative process. Finally, it seemed more and more difficult to deny animals sensibility as a specific vital function: for a growing number of natural philosophers, the infinitely complex vital mechanisms seemed to require the operation of a soul or of some kindred principle to account for the body's autonomous and regulative functions. But on the nature of such a principle most mechanists of the later generation, like Hoffmann, Guglielmini, or Baglivi, remained utterly skeptical, while a new animist trend was soaring up from various horizons, particularly in Stahl's school. In this context, Leibniz tried to provide an architectonic theory of organic bodies that could overcome some of the difficulties of micro-mechanism without abandoning the norms of a rational inquiry. The dynamics seemed to justify attributing endogenous power to organisms, and the theory of monads, with its pattern of formal units, suggested a causal interpretation of elementary structures and processes that made for the combination and self-regulation of emergent vital operations. Leibniz promoted an enriched empiricist methodology for physiology in order to adjust mechanist models *stricto sensu* to the complex reality of organic entities. Analyzing highly complex and variable vital phenomena requires a close reading and analytic deciphering of appearances at several levels: on that basis, explanations of a necessarily provisional nature will rely on defining specific functional properties attached to specific organs. The greater part of Enlightenment physiology will promote the analysis of such properties in connection with their respective organs, down to the most elementary structural and functional units of life. While Leibniz's metaphysical system of nature provided tenets for a theory of life, the physiological science will endeavor to set up principles for a reasoned natural history of vital phenomena that would avoid the limitations of the more rigid mechanist models. Leibniz's revised mechanist approach, based on his newly defined concepts of "organism" and "organic body," aimed at submitting this analysis to the requirements of a science of well-founded phenomena. Needless to say, the various interpretations it fostered have exerted an undeniable influence on subsequent physiology up to the more recent period.

REFERENCES

Andrault (Raphaële), 2014. *La Vie selon la raison. Physiologie et métaphysique chez Spinoza et Leibniz*, Paris: Honoré Champion.

Cavazza (Marta), 1987. "La corrispondenza inedita tra Leibniz, Domenico Guglielmini, Gabriele Manfredi," in M. Cavazza (Ed.), *Rapporti di scienziati europei con lo studio bolognese fra '600 e '700, Studi e memorie per la storia dell'Università di Bologna*, Bologna: Presso l'Istituto per la storia dell'Università, pp. 51–79.

Cheung (Tobias), 2006. "From the organism of a body to the body of an organism: occurrence and meaning of the word 'organism' from the seventeenth to the nineteenth century," *British Journal for the History of Science*, 39, pp. 319–39.

Duchesneau (François), 1982. *La Physiologie des Lumières*, The Hague: Nijhoff.

Duchesneau (François), 1994. *La Dynamique de Leibniz*, Paris: Vrin.

Duchesneau (François), 1998. *Les Modèles du vivant de Descartes à Leibniz*, Paris: Vrin.

Duchesneau (François), 2010. *Leibniz. Le vivant et l'organisme*, Paris: Vrin.

Duchesneau (François) & Smith (Justin E. H.), 2016. *The Leibniz-Stahl Controversy*, New Haven: Yale University Press.

Dutens: Leibniz, G. W., 1768. *Opera omnia, nunc primum collecta, in classes distributa, praefationibus et indicibus exornata*. Ed. by L. Dutens. 6 vols. Geneva: De Tournes. Cited by volume, part (if relevant), and page.

Fichant (Michel), 2003. "Leibniz et les machines de la nature," *Studia Leibnitiana*, 35/1, pp. 1–28.

Fichant (Michel), 2004. "L'Invention métaphysique," in G.W. Leibniz, *Discours de métaphysique*, suivi de *Monadologie* et autres textes, Paris: Gallimard, pp. 7–140.

Hartmann (Fritz) & Krüger (Matthias), 1976. "Directiones ad rem medicam pertinentes. Ein Manuskript G.W. Leibnizens aus den Jahren 1671/72 über die Medizin," *Studia Leibnitiana*, 8/1, pp. 40–68.

Hoffmann (Friedrich), 1749. *Operum omnium physico-medicorum supplementum primum*, Genevae: Apud Fratres de Tournes.

Leeuwenhoek (Antoni van), 1677. "Observations concerning Little Animals Observed in Rain, Well, Sea and Snow-water," *Philosophical Transactions*, Nr. 133, March 25, pp. 821–831.

Leibniz (Gottfried Wilhelm), 1994. *La Réforme de la dynamique. De corporum concursu (1678) et autres textes inédits*, Paris: Vrin.

Michelotti (Pietro Antonio), 1721. *De separatione fluidorum in corpore animali dissertatio physico-mechanico-medica*, Venitiis: Pinellorum Aere.

Nachtomy (Ohad), 2009. "Leibniz and *The Logic of Life*," *Studia Leibnitiana*, 41/1, pp. 1–20.

Nunziante (Antonio-Maria), 2002. *Organismo come armonia. La genesi del concetto di organismo vivente in G. W. Leibniz*, Trento: Verifice.

Pasini (Enrico), 1996. *Corpo e funzioni cognitive in Leibniz*, Milano: Franco Angeli.

Phemister (Pauline), 2005. *Leibniz and the Natural World: Activity, Passivity and Corporeal Substances in Leibniz's Philosophy*, Dordrecht: Springer.

Smith (Justin E. H.), 2011. *Divine Machines: Leibniz and the Sciences of Life*, Princeton: Princeton University Press.

Stahl (Georg Ernst), 1708. *Theoria medica vera*, Halae, Literis Orphanotrophei.

Stahl (Georg Ernst), 1720. *Negotium otiosum seu Σκιαμαχία adversus positiones aliquas fundamentales Theoriae medicae verae a Viro quodam celeberrimo intentata*, Halae: Litteris et impensis Orphanotrophei.

Wilson (Catherine), 1995. *The Invisible World: Early Modern Philosophy and the Invention of the Microscope*, Princeton: Princeton University Press.

CHAPTER 27

···

MEDICINE

···

JUSTIN E. H. SMITH

THE PLACE OF MEDICINE

··

LEIBNIZ is, of course, known as a polymathic thinker, yet, for the most part, medicine
has not generally been included on the long list of fields in which Leibniz is credited
for his contribution. This absence would have disappointed Leibniz because, over the
course of his long career, he developed a number of important projects related to medicine, public health, and closely allied areas, and often spoke explicitly of his desire to
exercise influence in these. Recent scholarly work, however, is beginning to take note
of this aspect of Leibniz's work. Most important, the editors of the Academy Edition
of Leibniz's collected writings are currently editing series 8, which is to be devoted to
Leibniz's medical and natural-scientific writings and will include editions of all of the
previously unpublished manuscripts in section III on medicine of Eduard Bodemann's
catalog.[1]

It is useful to contextualize the role of medicine in Leibniz's broader intellectual project in relation to his contemporaries and immediate predecessors. As is well known,
over the course of the sixteenth and seventeenth centuries, a slow but certain revolution took place in the study of medicine thanks to a wide array of both cultural changes
and scientific discoveries. Causes of illness were becoming clearer, methods of diagnosis
were improving, and treatments were increasingly efficacious.[2] These developments
were significant enough to create a general impression in the era that medicine was
a "new" science, that there had been a sort of break between the ancients and the

---

[1] See E. Bodemann, *Die Leibniz-Handschriften der Königlichen öffentlichen Bibliothek zu Hannover*
(Hildesheim: Olms, 1895).

[2] To mention just a few of the authoritative studies of the history of early modern medicine, see Roy
Porter, *Flesh in the Age of Reason: The Modern Foundations of Body and Soul* (New York: Norton, 2003);
Charles Webster, *The Great Instauration: Science, Medicine, and Reform, 1626–1660* (Teaneck, NJ: Holmes
and Meier, 1976).

moderns that rendered the formers' medical learning largely irrelevant. Thus, in his *Animadversiones* with Georg Ernst Stahl, Leibniz himself describes medicine as being in its "adolescence."[3]

Leibniz was a nonphysician with a serious intellectual investment in the study and advancement of medicine. In this, he was representative of a broad tendency in early modern philosophy, one that might be called "medical eudaimonism," the idea that the advancement of medicine is central to and constitutive of the project of philosophy to the extent that health, well-being, and longevity are necessary for the practice and promotion of virtue. Recent scholars have characterized Descartes not so much as a philosopher who was interested in medicine but as a *medical philosopher*, that is, as a thinker who considered medicine to be largely constitutive of his overall philosophical project.[4] In fact, the medical orientation that we find in Descartes' philosophy was the rule rather than the exception among seventeenth-century philosophers. Leibniz was very much in line with this general tendency, even if he did not attribute to medicine quite the importance that his French predecessor had.

Descartes had understood medicine as the art of maintaining health, and he described health, in turn, as "undoubtedly the chief good and the foundation of all the other goods in this life."[5] Leibniz tended to characterize medicine's role in only slightly more moderate terms, holding that health is second only to virtue and that, therefore, medicine is the second most important human art after philosophical theology. Thus, Leibniz wrote to Bouvet in 1697:

> Medicine is the most necessary of the natural sciences. For just as theology is the summit of the knowledge of things pertaining to spirit, and just as it contains both good morals and good politics, one can say that medicine as well is the summit and as it were the principal fruit of our knowledge of bodies, to the extent that they are related to our own. But all of physical science and medicine itself have as their final goal the glory of God and the supreme happiness of men, for in conserving them, medicine gives them the means to work for the glory of God.[6]

This point of difference between the two philosophers may ultimately be understood as a reflection of the divergence between Descartes' pure mechanism on the one hand and Leibniz's modified or supplemented version of the mechanical philosophy on the other. In Leibniz's philosophy, the order of mechanical causes runs parallel to the order of teleology, and, in the end, bodies are but the phenomenal unfolding of the perceptions of immaterial substances.

---

[3] G. W. Leibniz, *Gothofredi Guillelmi Leibnitii Opera omnia*, edited by Louis Dutens (Geneva: Fratres de Tournes, 1768), vol. II ii, p. 148.

[4] See in particular Vincent Aucante, *La philosophie médicale de Descartes* (Paris: Presses Universitaires de France, 2006).

[5] AT VI 61–62.

[6] Feller 115. Critical edition: A I xiv N. 470.

Where an early modern philosopher places medicine in the hierarchy of human endeavors is not an afterthought, but rather it is at once a positioning of his own philosophical views. Leibniz's demotion of medicine from the supreme position in which Descartes and the Cartesian school of medical philosophy would have liked to place it is, at the same time, an announcement that not all can be accounted for in terms of the motions and impacts of bodies and that, in this respect, as Leibniz puts it in another context, Descartes remained stalled in the antechamber of philosophy.[7]

It is significant that, with respect to education and career, Leibniz, unlike so many other philosophers of his era, was not himself a physician but rather a jurist and a diplomat. We might suppose that his positioning of medicine relative to morality is also a reflection of his professional activity, where, once again, he was obliged to take an interest in intentions and designs rather than simply in the bodily effects of bodily causes to which the Cartesian school had reduced medicine. Leibniz in fact believed that his status as a nonphysician and an amateur of medicine positioned him well to promote this discipline and to assess its progress.

Leibniz often boasted of his uniquely clear-sighted—because nonprofessional—insights into medical matters. Thus, he wrote boldly in his treatise *De novo antidysenterico americano* of 1695–96 that "nothing is more precious to men than health," evidently deviating from his usual ranking of health in the number two spot. He then goes on to add: "This may be said all the more fervently by me, who is not a doctor, since I will be less suspect of seeking to advance my own usefulness."[8] Leibniz repeated this claim to nonpartisanship throughout his debate with the physician Georg Ernst Stahl in 1709–10 concerning the deeply philosophical matter of the role of the soul (if any) in the vital motions of the body.[9] Ultimately, for Leibniz, it is precisely his own sort of disinterestedness that would ideally reign as the prevailing spirit among practicing physicians as well, and thus, paradoxically, it is his own position as a nonphysician that ought in his view to serve as a model for physicians. More particularly, it is the organization of religious orders, and thus of a career devoted to morality and the love of God, that would best serve, Leibniz thinks, as a model for the organization of medicine, "for," as he writes in the *Directiones ad rem medicam pertinentes* of 1671, "members of religious orders are disinterested."[10] We will return to Leibniz's proposals for the organization of the institution of medicine in the final section.

[7] See, for example, Leibniz to Chr. Philipp, early December 1679, A I ii N. 524.

[8] Dutens II ii 111. Critical edition in A IV vi N. 84.

[9] Georg Ernst Stahl, *Georgii Ernesti Stahlii negotium otiosum: Seu Σκιαμαχια adversus positiones aliquas fundamentales Theoriae medicae verae* (Halle: Impensis Orphanotrophei, 1720); to appear as *The Leibniz-Stahl Controversy*, edited by François Duchesneau and Justin E. H. Smith (New Haven: Yale University Press, 2016). Although Stahl is identified as the sole author of this text, it in fact consists in an exchange between the Halle Pietist physician and Leibniz.

[10] See Justin E. H. Smith, *Divine Machines: Leibniz and the Sciences of Life* (Princeton: Princeton University Press, 2011), appendix 1, "Directions Pertaining to the Institution of Medicine" (1671) §50, 284. This text was previously published in German in a critical edition by Fritz Hartmann and Matthias Krüger, *Studia Leibnitiana Sonderheft 8/1* (1976), pp. 40–68.

INFLUENCES AND DEVELOPMENT

One of Leibniz's most substantive and interesting texts on medicine, the *Directiones ad rem medicam pertinentes*, was composed by Leibniz very early (in 1671), thus earlier than the great majority of his core philosophical doctrines had begun to take shape. At this time, Leibniz takes medicine very seriously, and he evidently intends to make great contributions of his own to its advancement. This early on, he is intimately familiar with the work of all of the influential medical authors of his era. In this text, he reveals his interest in Santorio Santori (Sanctorius), the Paduan author of *De statica medicina* (1637); the self-taught Dutch anatomist Lodewijk De Bils (Bilsius); Phillip von May, the author of the *Chiromantia medica* (1667); Moyse Charas, the Parisian pharmacist and author of the *Pharmacopée royale galénique et chimique* (1676); and many others besides.

The *Directiones* will be followed by several substantial texts on medical questions composed across Leibniz's entire career and at each of the many stages of the parallel development of his so-called mature philosophy. A few of these deserve particular mention, including the *De scribendis novis Medicinae elementis* of 1682 or 1683, in which Leibniz defined "medicine" as "nothing other than to prescribe a method to a given mechanic who is able to conserve the machine that has been entrusted to him, so that it will always operate correctly."[11] Roughly twelve years later, Leibniz composed a similar prescriptive letter on the advancement of medicine, which was published as an "Extrait d'une lettre sur la maniére de perfectionner la Médecine" in the *Journal des Sçavans* of 1694.[12] Soon after, we have Leibniz's major contribution to pharmacology, his 1696 report to the Leopoldine Society *De novo antidysenterico americano*,[13] which is discussed later. In 1704–05, we find a short but incisive text *De causis febrium*,[14] and, between 1708 and 1710, Leibniz composed his extensive animadversions against G. E. Stahl's *Theoria medica vera* of 1708.[15] This short list could be filled out with a great many more examples, but already it suffices to show that medicine was for Leibniz an enduring and serious interest.

One particularly important medical thinker in Leibniz's background was Franz de la Boë (Franciscus Sylvius, 1614–72), of whom at least four students went on to have significant correspondences or personal interactions with Leibniz: Burchard de Volder, Niels Stensen (Steno), Regnier De Graaf, and Jan Swammerdam. De la Boë's most significant work was the *Praxeos medicae idea nova*, published in the same year that Leibniz wrote the *Directiones*. Leibniz would follow De la Boë's account of the production of blood, preferring this over Descartes' more influential theory,[16] and he also followed the author

---

[11] Smith, *Divine Machines*, appendix 4, 299.

[12] See Dutens II ii 162–164. See A IV v N. 83; cf. A I x N. 163.

[13] See Dutens II ii 110–119.

[14] LH III v 111–112; published in a critical edition as an appendix to Enrico Pasini, *Corpo e funzioni cognitive in Leibniz* (Milan: FrancoAngeli, 1996).

[15] Stahl, *Negotium otiosum*.

[16] See Pasini, *Corpo e funzioni cognitive in Leibniz*, 110–111.

of the *Praxeos* in his sympathy toward a thoroughgoing *iatrochemistry*, that is, the view that the workings of the human body are best understood in chemical terms and that medical treatments will just as often be of a chemical as of a botanical nature. De la Boë's iatrochemistry was particularly influential in Leibniz's own views on fermentation, a chemical process thought to be responsible for a wide variety of physiological phenomena and also having a wide array of instantiations beyond the body and throughout the natural world.

Leibniz's many sources for his medical thought are too numerous to list here, and the development of his medical thought is too storied and complex to describe in its diachronic detail.[17] In many respects, his development here reflects the development of his philosophy as a whole: we see an early, fervent commitment to the explanatory promise of the mechanical philosophy followed by a gradual reintroduction of a role for teleological explanation, one that sees it as coexisting with mechanical explanation and that sees each of the two types of explanation as accounting for one and the same world at different metaphysical levels and in view of different epistemological exigencies. Leibniz's philosophical development here is well beyond the scope of the present chapter.

In the *Directiones*, Leibniz explicitly cites de la Boë's disciple Stensen, along with the Italian Lorenzo Bellini, as two figures who had made tremendous recent progress in the mathematization of medicine. He later came to see this project as only partially realizable. As Leibniz wrote to Michelotti in a letter on animal secretion of 1715:

> There may be many mechanical causes that explain secretion. I suspect however that one should sooner explain the thing in terms of physical causes. Even if in the final analysis all physical causes lead back to mechanical causes, nonetheless I am in the habit of calling "physical" those causes of which the mechanism is hidden.[18]

Here, then, "physical" contrasts with "mechanical" to the extent that the latter lends itself to immediate mathematization, given the state of our knowledge and our capacity for observation, whereas physical explanation remains avowedly hypothetical. In his treatise of the early 1680s entitled *Corpus hominis . . . est machina quaedam*, Leibniz explicitly held that "any machine . . . is best defined in terms of its final cause," so that "in the description of the parts it is . . . apparent in what way each of them is coordinated with the others for the intended use."[19] Thus, unlike Descartes, for whom treating the human body as a machine meant the radical extirpation of final-causal explanation from medicine and physiology, for Leibniz the mechanical body could suitably be explained in teleological terms, where these are understood simply as the account of the functioning of interworking organs.

---

[17]   I have offered a somewhat more detailed survey of the development of Leibniz's medical thought in Smith, *Divine Machines*, chapter 1.

[18]   Dutens II ii 91.

[19]   See Smith, *Divine Machines*, appendix 3, §1, 292. Text previously published in a critical edition as an appendix to Pasini, *Corpo et funzioni cognitive in Leibniz*.

EXPERIMENT

Leibniz coupled his commitment to mechanical teleology with a thorough-going support of medical empiricism. Indeed, medicine provides a good example of the regional character of Leibniz's theory of knowledge and of his philosophy of science. That is, Leibniz accepted that how one comes to know something will depend a great deal on the nature of the knowledge sought after. He believed that medicine had only begun to make progress in the modern era and that it had been hindered previously by a theory-ladenness that turned out, in the end, to be grounded in mere superstition. His 1671 *Directiones* may be read as a manifesto declaring the supreme importance of experiment for resolving medical questions and the importance, to speak with Bacon, of "laying one's notions by." If there is any question about the influence of the celestial bodies on human health, say, then these should be put to the test:

> [T]he difference of climates, of the soils, of the air, etc., should be precisely noted: in this way many admirable things will result. Certain people should then be contracted to make inductions and observations from these. Attention should be paid to astrological effects: whether, for example, it is true what they say, that if a woman gives birth during a (solar) eclipse, she and the child will die, and other things in this sort of tradition.[20]

Not just in testing questionable causal explanations, but also in resolving practical questions about the maintenance of health, empirical methods were promoted by Leibniz as the best course. Thus, he advised that "tests should be made to determine what would happen if a man were continually nourished with water, or with water and bread, etc."[21]

One of the most striking aspects of Leibniz's promotion of empiricism is his grasp of the importance of bodily secretions for the diagnosis of a patient's medical condition. Leibniz's views are not entirely original here; they are, indeed, in keeping with the much broader turn in experimental philosophy, particularly as spearheaded in the Baconian tradition and in the Royal Society, toward measurement of absolutely everything that can be measured. Moreover, over the course of the first half of the seventeenth century, there occurred a broad transition in the way bodily signs, particularly fluids, were "read," from a broadly divinatory to a broadly diagnostic framework. Much of this transformation went on at the level of medical practice rather than theorizing and much of this in the practice of the Paracelsian medical tradition in Germany.[22] In part

---

[20] Smith, *Divine Machines*, appendix 1, §22, 280.

[21] Smith, *Divine Machines*, appendix 1, §32, 282.

[22] See, for example, Jole Shackelford, "Paracelsian uroscopy and German chemiatric medicine in the *Medicina Pensylvania* of George de Benneville," in Jürgen Helm and Renate Wilson (eds.), *Medical Theory and Therapeutic Practice in the Eighteenth Century: A Transatlantic Perspective* (Stuttgart: Franz Steiner Verlag, 2008), pp. 13–35.

echoing these transformations, Leibniz believed that an informative "reading" can only be obtained from bodily fluids, both from natural excretions such as sweat, urine, or even hair and nails, as well as from fluids that are forced out by art, such as vomit. Thus, Leibniz wrote in the *Directiones* of 1671: "From the figure of the hair of a person all sorts of useful conclusions can without doubt be made. Of the nose and other [parts] I do not wish to say."[23] What Leibniz adds to contemporary interest in, say, measuring the viscosity of urine samples, is his own particular belief, perceptible across a broad range of his interests, that measurements of this sort can be brought together to produce a sort of meta-measurement in the form of what we now call "statistics": by compiling and comparing uroscopic data, it in turn becomes possible to obtain better diagnoses of the health condition of any one individual through an investigation of the urine. Thus, we may say that, as concerns the study of secretions, Leibniz is not entirely original, but he is particularly lucid in his understanding of the potential significance of this study.

Secretions are important, in Leibniz's view, both because they come from the inside and thus give a report on the current state of a region of the living body that would only become directly visible in the age of x-rays and because they, in contrast with the more solid parts of the body, are constantly in flux and thus presumably more susceptible to being qualitatively or chemically altered by the advent of an illness. Not only the liquids that emerge naturally, such as urine and sweat, but also those that must be forced out, such as arterial blood or vomit, as well as the relatively more solid parts that are constantly growing out from the interior, such as hair and nails: all of these should be taken as objects of study. Leibniz even advised that "one should make tests with different sorts of baths, for all baths are in a certain sense in the category of infusion through the pores."[24] For Leibniz, it was not simply that the information gathered from secretions would be diagnostically useful for the individual patient from whom they were obtained, but also that, if the results of extensive testings were systematically compiled, then this would enable physicians to establish norms and averages for the human body and thereby gain a more thorough mastery of the distinction between the healthy and the pathological than had been possible in the era of medical reliance upon anecdotes. We consider Leibniz's conception of medicine as a data-gathering enterprise shortly.

Another area of empirical investigation that Leibniz considers crucial for the advancement of medicine is experimentation on animals. Here as well, especially in an early text such as the *Directiones*, Leibniz was particularly inspired by the recent experimental work done in the Royal Society. For example, in his 1669 *Tractatus de corde*, Richard Lower advocates the use of dogs for transfusion experiments precisely because their facial expressions may reliably be read as reports on their inner states. Leibniz himself read Lower's treatise with great interest, and, in the 1671 *Directiones*, reports with evident excitement that "in England a weak horse was made strong again by the use of fresh sheep's blood,"[25] an example that came to him from Lower.

---

[23] Smith, *Divine Machines*, appendix 1, §33, 282.
[24] Smith, *Divine Machines*, appendix 1, §42, 283, 1671.
[25] Smith, *Divine Machines*, appendix 1, §42, 283, 1671.

Leibniz sees vivisection as complementary to autopsy of human cadavers: the two to-gether give us the closest possible picture of what is happening within the living human body. We can learn not just about anatomy from animals, but also about pathology and the stages of development of diseases, since, as Leibniz wrote, "we can cut them open when and how we please."[26] Leibniz goes on to note that "we can test medicines [*arzneyen*] on animals when we please, and from this make a conclusion according to its analogy [*proportione*] to human beings."[27] He adds, as if disappointed, that "we cannot make such tests on humans."[28]

Leibniz's promotion of vivisection might seem out of step with the picture of him, passed down at least since Kant's lectures on ethics, as a gentle soul, unwilling to do harm to any living creature. We learn from the lecture notes held by Kant's disciple G. L. Collins, that "Leibniz used a tiny worm for purposes of observation, and then carefully replaced it with its leaf on the tree, so that it should not come to harm through any act of his."[29] This reputation seems to have been won for Leibniz primarily in view of his nearly life-long opposition to the Cartesian animal-machine doctrine and his promo-tion of his own alternative to this doctrine, according to which animals are ensouled and are capable of a degree of perception that enables them to experience true pleasure and pain. But it is important to bear in mind that no obvious ethical consequences follow immediately from the rejection of the Cartesian theory of animals. Indeed, for some early modern vivisectionists, it was precisely *because* animals were fundamentally like human beings in their soul-based vital functions that these beings could be taken as suitable test subjects for the advancement of medicine.

It is true, anyway, that Leibniz became less interested in vivisection later in life. The latest mention I have been able to find of this interest comes from the late 1670s, in notes on Henry More's *Immortality of the Soul*, where Leibniz recalled that, at some earlier point, he had "seen with my own eyes a frog completely disembowelled, its heart, stom-ach and guts taken out of its body by a very skillful anatomist friend of mine."[30] Not only is this one of Leibniz's later expressions of interest in vivisection, it also reveals the extent and limitations of Leibniz's actual encounter with the sort of experimenta-tion he enjoyed promoting at a distance. As far as can be told, the only physiological experiment Leibniz ever performed concerned the properties of what he called "animal glutinosity": his experiment involved frying an egg,[31] which he likely would have been doing whether this served a scientific end or not. In medical and physiological experi-mentation, Leibniz remained very much an outsider, cheering on and promoting a field to which he did not contribute directly. This is something, again, that he would insist

---

[26] Smith, *Divine Machines*, appendix 1, §28, 281, 1671.

[27] Ibid.

[28] Ibid.

[29] Kant, *Vorlesungen über Ethik* 27:459, cited from Kant, *Lectures on Ethics*, translated by P. Heath and J. B. Schneewind (Cambridge: Cambridge University Press, 1997), 212–213; see also *Kritik der praktischen Vernunft* 5:160.

[30] Notes on Henry More's *Immortality of the Soul*, 1677–78(?), A VI iv 1679.

[31] A III vi 302.

gave him a uniquely clear perspective in the field, but something that may also have been a source of regret for a thinker with such great competence in so many different fields.

PHARMACEUTICS

It would be artificial to separate Leibniz's medical interests from his study of pharmaceutics. Particularly in view of his association with the iatrochemical school, for which the new, modern medicine was to be based on the treatment of diseases by chemical remedies, for Leibniz, as for his contemporaries, the study of pharmaceutics was a proper part of medicine rather than a supplement to it. It was, moreover, the part to which Leibniz made the most original contributions.

Among the manuscripts in Bodemann's LH III catalog are hundreds of pharmaceutical recipes written out in Leibniz's hand using the conventional pharmaceutical notation. Sometimes Leibniz's prioritization of pharmaceutics, among the many possible interests he was free to pursue, defies our expectations as to what Leibniz himself, as a philosopher, ought to have considered important. Thus, for example, when he is admitted in 1676 by Descartes' executor Claude Clerselier to copy out what he can of his French predecessor's *Nachlass*, Leibniz seized the opportunity to transcribe Descartes' cure for constipation.[32] This might be dismissed as merely a curious anecdote, yet, on reflection, it is extremely telling because it reveals that Leibniz was clearly working with a different understanding of the legacy of his predecessor than we have today and, moreover, that Leibniz wished to carry on this legacy through his own attention to questions of health and longevity.

Nearly twenty years later, in the midst of one of his periods of most intense philosophical innovation, Leibniz would simultaneously be working on his single most significant contribution to pharmacology: his treatise *De novo antidysenterico americano*, which he addressed in 1696 to the Imperial Leopoldine Academy (founded in 1652 as one of the earliest medical societies in Germany). Emetics had been a long-standing interest for Leibniz, from the *Directiones* of the early 1670s up until the time of this work of the mid-1690s on the ipecacuanha root, which we know better today in its commercially available form as "syrup of ipecac." Leibniz wrote *De novo antidysenterico* after reading extensively about the Brazilian plant and apparently after conducting experiments on himself with the root. Ipecacuanha had been brought back to Europe by the Dutch physician Wilhelm Piso in 1641 and had been written about extensively in his *Historia naturalis Brasiliae*, co-written with Georg Markgraf in 1648. The root was introduced to Paris in 1672 and was made famous when the physician Jean-Adrien Helvétius used

---

[32] AT XI 644.

it successfully to treat Louis XIV's dysentery. It is clear from Leibniz's study that he has a detailed knowledge of Piso's work.

It is likely that Leibniz himself had already learned of ipecacuanha's use while in Paris a quarter of a century earlier. He was aware of its widespread use among the Brazilian natives and of its more recent successes in France, but he was nonetheless the first to give an exhaustive account of its many uses, not only against dysentery, but also as an emetic, a diaphoretic (causing one to perspire), and an expectorant (causing salivation). Although Leibniz knew that Piso had written of native Brazilian knowledge of the root's emetic properties, he nonetheless claimed in his 1696 treatise that he himself introduced ipecacuanha as a purgative into the European pharmacopoeia, whereas his predecessor Helvétius had only recognized its usefulness against diarrhea.

Leibniz later wrote, in a letter to Schelhammer of 1715, of his own understanding of the importance of purgatives in medical treatment:

> I consider that purgations are often useful, not in the way that many believe, whereby the corrupt elements are ejected, but rather in quickening the lethargic nature by its own instruments, and in such a way almost that vomiting is useful in apoplexy. I submit these, my very audacious conjectures, to your judgment.[33]

Is this, now, of any philosophical relevance? It would be simplistic to suppose that there is any direct connection between Leibniz's particular philosophical model of the organic body on the one hand, which takes it to be a constant companion to the soul even as it is in perpetual flux "like a fountain," and, on the other hand, Leibniz's interest in drawing out the inner fluids of the body. A case might, however, be cautiously made.

As we have begun to see in the discussion of secretions, Leibniz was staunchly opposed to all forms of physiognomy, that is, to the "reading" of people's moral character, robustness, and future prospects from more or less permanent bodily features. As late as the *Nouveaux essais* of 1704, Leibniz continued to argue against Locke's view that membership in the human species is ultimately a matter of convention and that this is shown by the physiological proximity of some abnormal human beings to animals, that in fact there is nothing at all about the bodily conformation of a human being that bears on his or her humanness. Outward disfigurement cannot be a sign of the absence of a soul for Leibniz, for the same reason that physiognomy is of no use in medicine: "One would not," he wrote in 1704, "be able to give a reason why the . . . face that is a bit longer, or a flat nose . . . could not coexist . . . with a soul."[34] Although Leibniz's purposes are very different in the argument against Locke, his rejection of the view that permanent bodily features of an individual tell anything at all of significance about that individual may ultimately be traced back to his very early argument in favor of reading the constantly changing bodily fluids instead of the stable and unchanging bones and other macroanatomical features.

[33] Dutens II ii 73.
[34] GP V 299.

At the same time, early on, Leibniz explicitly rejected the idea that there is any permanent bodily core that preserves the identity of a being; thus, he spoke out against the Kabbalistic doctrine that there is a bone, the *luz*,[35] somewhere in the body that serves as the perpetual vehicle of the individual human spirit. Instead, Leibniz opts for a metaphysics of corporeal substance on which the soul is indeed perpetually embodied, yet this embodiment does not involve any permanent attachment to some bit of matter or other. Thus, just as the shape of the nose tells you nothing about the character or robustness of a person—whereas the analysis of her sweat does—so too, on a metaphysical level, a person (or any corporeal substance) is characterized by the fact that it always acts through some more or less fluid bodily vehicle, even though it is not rigidly fixed to some body or other. Thus, the connection between the flux model of corporeal substance on the one hand and the medical interest in bodily fluids on the other might be a real one. Indeed, in the polemic with Stahl, Leibniz explicitly stated his familiar philosophical claim that the body is akin to a river by appeal to an example drawn from physiology, indeed from the very examples of medical "readings" that he had so vigorously advocated in the *Directiones* several decades earlier: "Perpetual perspiration," he wrote, "as well as a number of indices, show that animal bodies not only must take in solid nutriments at regular intervals, but also that they are in perpetual flux like a river."[36]

The interest in *simplicia* or botanical remedies also provides a useful point of access to Leibniz's interest in global geography and in what Londa Schiebinger has aptly identified as "bioprospecting." In his 1695 *De novo antidysenterico americano*, Leibniz cited chapters 49 and 65 of Piso's *Historia naturalis Brasiliae* in their entirety. There, the Dutch explorer described indigenous Brazilian uses for both the *caa-apia* and the ipecacuanha roots. Piso reported (and Leibniz transcribed) of the latter root that "it relieves flatulence and other illnesses, counters the effect of poisons and of venoms both hidden and manifest, immediately expelling them through vomiting. Wherefore it is carefully [*religiose*] guarded by the Brazilians, who first revealed its virtues to us." [37] Leibniz complained in his treatise that "there are in fact a number of people who deny that medicines of so much proven virtue could be obtained for the illnesses of every temperament and constitutions. Some of them condemn everything that is exotic as unsuited to our bodies."[38] What is more, Leibniz's complaints about the stagnancy and inefficacy of European medicine appear to echo Piso's own derisive account of native Brazilian responses to illness. Leibniz wrote that "medicine is an uncertain art, which sustains the credulity of men, like the great dream of the philosophers' stone."[39] What works for a Brazilian body works just as well for a European, and credulity works in the one case just the same as in the other. Leibniz proceeds to point out that the root's virtue could not be peculiar to the region in which it is found because, after all, colonial bioprospecting is in

---

[35] A II i 185.
[36] Stahl, *Negotium otiosum*, 152–153.
[37] Dutens II ii 171.
[38] Ibid.
[39] Ibid.

the end only a worthwhile endeavor to the extent that the plants discovered have some use at home. As Leibniz ironically put it: "[Piso], in fact, is not writing this for the sake of practicing medicine in Brazil."[40] We see, then, that Leibniz is interested in absorbing medicinal knowledge from wherever it may come and recognizes the value of the indigenous knowledge that was beginning to make itself known in the early period of colonialism in which Leibniz lived. Here, Leibniz is fairly typical of the era: he understood that practical advances could be made, particularly in medicine, through attention to native knowledge systems while at the same time giving little credit to the rationality or abstract foundations of these systems.[41]

PUBLIC HEALTH

We have already seen that, for Leibniz, the medical care of the body is an activity that runs parallel to the spiritual care of the soul. It is in this regard not surprising to learn that, in his public health proposals, he envisions the ideal organization of medicine as one that would model it after organized religion, and in particular after religious orders. In a remarkable passage of the 1671 *Directiones*, among the lengthiest in the entire text, Leibniz spelled out a plan for a complete overhaul of the way patients go to doctors. At the heart of this plan is the suggestion that medical consultations should be as easy as going to a priest for confession, and he even referred to doctors as "Medical father confessors" (*Medicalische Beichtväter*).[42] He proposed that such "confessions" should be obligatory, but also imagines that if properly set up, citizens would go to them with pleasure. Leibniz continues:

> So that the confessions are more effective, and more general, lists of questions should be prescribed to people, just as we have confessional booklets that list a thousand different sins that could be imagined, so that no one forgets anything. There should be different times of year during which every person performs his medical confession, and says everything, and sketches out the preceding period, [including] anything that he will consider with even a little anxiety. Everyone should, however, be free to have additional confessionals. And just as in sacred matters one is free to have an additional father confessor, who is not of the [same] parish, so too the same thing should happen here, [namely,] that there be certain free doctors who are bound to no parish and so can be chosen when one wishes.[43]

---

[40] Ibid.

[41] On the European absorption of native American medicinal knowledge in the seventeenth century, see Londa Schiebinger, *Plants and Empire: Colonial Bioprospecting in the Atlantic World* (Cambridge, MA: Harvard University Press, 2004).

[42] Smith, *Divine Machines*, appendix 1, §54, 285.

[43] Ibid.

So far, we have seen Leibniz's proposals for the patient; his ideas concerning the transformation of the doctor's approach to his task in the "confessional" are no less radical. Just as priests do not only assign penance for sins committed, he argued, but also counsel how to conduct one's life better in the future, doctors should not only cure illnesses but also help patients to lead a healthy life. In this, Leibniz was plainly following not so much the prevailing sentiment of practicing physicians as the spirit of his predecessors in what might be called "medical eudaimonism," which was on display, for example, in Bacon's and Descartes' preoccupation with regime, well-being, and longevity:

> For the rules or exigencies of medical father confessors as well should consist not so much in prescriptions as in regulation of the diet, just as the rules and exigencies of the spiritual father confessor should consist more in certain prescribed useful acts, than in the praying of a certain number of Hail Marys or Our Fathers.[44]

Like their spiritual counterparts, the medical father confessors would be sworn to secrecy. This rule imposes a harsh limitation on Leibniz's firm commitment to the central importance of systematic data collection in the advancement of medicine. But there are ways to compensate for this loss. Leibniz believed that pharmacists in particular, rather than physicians, should be charged with the task of compiling the health records of the population they serve.[45] The most important form of medical record keeping in Leibniz's view is the compilation of death statistics, and, in the *Directiones*, Leibniz made his first mention of "bills of mortality," arguing that these should "be brought to the greatest possible perfection, and must not be made only in the large cities, but also everywhere in the countryside."[46] In the 1694 note "On the Method of Perfecting Medicine," Leibniz reiterated his interest in promoting this form of record-keeping, this time making the source of the idea more or less explicit by citing the phrase "bills of mortality" in English:

> I do not know whether in Paris they still keep the estates or anniversary lists of Baptisms and of Funerals in this large city, which they composed during the time I was there. This project seemed very useful, as much so as the *Bills of mortality* of London, from which able men have drawn conclusions of consequence.[47]

The source of this phrase is almost certainly the work of John Graunt and William Petty, who together introduced new methods in the demographic study of the spread of plague in England in the 1660s and, for this, are considered key figures in the development of modern epidemiology.[48] Although surely unknown to Leibniz at the time of the

[44] Ibid.
[45] Smith, *Divine Machines*, appendix 1, §57.
[46] Smith, *Divine Machines*, appendix 1, §22.
[47] Dutens II ii 162.
[48] See *The Economic Writings of Sir William Petty, together with the observations upon Bills of Mortality, More Probably by Captain John Graunt*, edited by Charles Henry Hull, 2 vols. (Cambridge: Cambridge University Press, 1899).

Directiones, by the 1690s, the Italian physician Bernardino Ramazzini (often identified as the founder of occupational medicine), came to play an important role in Leibniz's thinking about public health issues. Leibniz often praised Ramazzini as advancing beyond astrology and the other divinatory arts, or, perhaps better, for offering a sort of astrology in reverse by advocating not predictive reading from signs but rather a comprehensive *retrodictive* reading of signs: "He says he wants to make up these sorts of *Medical Calendars*, but not, as the astrologers do, at the beginning of the year, but rather when the year is over."[49] It was such comprehensive retrodiction that Leibniz believed would ultimately make possible a real predictive science of human health. Statistics would come to replace divination as the guide to the future course of events.

Leibniz's life-long interest in advancing public health is clearly of a pair with his other large-scale schemes for social improvement, including, for example, his designs for public transportation, for lighting the streets of cities, and for the establishment of scientific academies. All of these interests reveal a combination of both theoretical and very practical concerns motivating a thinker capable of working at both levels at once. Alongside the schemes for establishing academies, Leibniz's interest in public health seems to have been among his most personal and most long-standing interests. In two separate texts of 1701—the "Summary Statement concerning Medical Observations that may be constantly implemented and perpetually advanced," and the "Prescription concerning regular observations for the promotion of the Health System"—Leibniz brings together his medical and public-policy interests in order to promote a mature and well thought-out scheme for the establishment of a public health system.[50] And, well into the eighteenth century, we continue to find echoes of the same basic scheme laid out in the 1671 *Directiones*. In 1701, Leibniz wrote two separate drafts of proposals for the collection of public health data, an interest that was also echoed in the major treatise *De methodo botanica* of the same year. There, he explicitly identified the record-keeping aspect of medicine as the activity most useful to human thriving, and thus, to return to the hierarchy with which began, second only to virtue among human goods. He wrote that if "distinguished men" continue exchanging medical information and compiling observations, then

> not only shall we progress in understanding illnesses that proceed in singular and not yet investigated fashion, but a vast thesaurus of the most beautiful observations will soon be compiled, which will be of much use to the human race, so that I know nothing next to the practice of virtue that can be professed to be more pious and in agreement with Christian charity.[51]

---

[49] G. E. Guhrauer (ed.), *Leibnitz's deutsche Schriften* (Berlin, 1838), B II, 458. Critical edition: A I vi N. 56.

[50] See, for example, Leibniz's *Summarische Punctuation die medicinalische Observationes betr. so durchgehends anzustellen und beständigt fortzusetzen seyn möchten*, in Onno Klopp (ed.), *Die Werke von Leibniz* (Hanover, 1864–84), vol. 10, 346–350; also his *Verordnung betr. regelmäßige Beobachtungun zur Förderung des Sanitätswesens*, in Klopp vol. 10, 350–353.

[51] Dutens II ii 172.

Here, Leibniz is clearly expressing the view with which we began this chapter: that the advancement of medicine is second only to the promotion of virtue as a human good. In the end, for Leibniz, the entire medical project, from advancing better methods of diagnosis to the compilation of medical statistics and the establishment of a public health system, is rooted in the single most foundational concern that he had, the promotion of Christian charity.

CHAPTER 28

···

ALCHEMY AND CHEMISTRY

···

ANNE-LISE REY

ᴀʟᴄʜᴇᴍʏ ᴀɴᴅ ᴄʜᴇᴍɪꜱᴛʀʏ

Oᴠᴇʀ the past thirty years, researchers have begun to realize that alchemy once held an important place within modern science. The most notable impact of this mounting awareness has been to demonstrate the very rationality of alchemy.[1] Scholarly attention has been focused on the question of the significance of the definite article "al" in "alchemy." These two terms—alchemy and chemistry—have even been understood as orthographic variants describing one and the same field of inquiry, rather than as two aspects (irrational and rational) of the same practice. Furthermore, scholars are now seeking to bring an end to the false division between alchemy's hermeticism and chemistry's rationality. Larry Principe and William Newman have suggested using the term "chymistry"[2] to encompass both alchemy and chemistry as they were practised in the classical Age.

It would seem that if alchemy was not in fact irrational, then nothing set it apart from the chemistry of its time. Alchemy could be understood as a philosophy of nature taking chemical operations conducted in laboratories and using them to explain the constitutive principles underpinning mixed bodies in all their states. In addition to the lack of differentiation, at least with respect to the rationality (or lack thereof) at work in these practices, the idea persisted that the article "al" bestowed some kind of primacy: thus, paradoxically, alchemy was considered to be a science of established principles, whereas chemistry involved practical operations on matter.

Reflecting this, one of the aims of recent studies into the place held by alchemy in the seventeenth and eighteenth centuries—before the shift to the modern Lavoisier paradigm for classifying the elements and the supposed advent of "genuine" chemistry—has

---

[1] B. Joly, *La rationalité de l'alchimie au XVIIe siècle* (Paris: Vrin/Mathesis, 1992).
[2] William R. Newman and Lawrence Principe "Alchemy vs. chemistry: The etymological origins of a historiographic mistake," in *Early Science and Medicine* 3 (1998), pp. 32–65.

been to re-evaluate its importance in the grand, ordered narratives of the Scientific Revolution, particularly by highlighting the interdisciplinary dynamic behind it (i.e., by highlighting its links to theology, technology, artisan craft, pharmacology, and medicine).

In such a framework, it is difficult to take Leibniz's well-known membership of a secret alchemical society in Nuremberg[3] in the 1660s as a simple youthful error.[4] But neither is it possible to point to alchemy's recurrent presence in the Leibnizian corpus as incontestable proof of the hidden but fundamental influence of alchemy in the development of Leibniz's metaphysics or as a hidden key to the concept of monad.[5] Given that the boundaries between "rational" and "irrational" were not as sharply defined in the late seventeenth century as they are today, both accounts of Leibniz's relationship to alchemy are flawed.

We must therefore differentiate and link together two genres of text within the Leibnizian corpus. First, there are texts broaching subjects traditionally considered to belong to the domain of alchemy, viz. everything touching on problems related to the transmutation of metals or the search for the Philosopher's Stone, how to write in riddles, the use of codes, other methods of encrypting texts, and the like. An example of this is the *Oedipus chymicus*[6] of 1710, the title of which is a homonym of an important text by J. -J. Becher.[7] Leibniz's text combines an experimental account of the transmutation of metals and a cryptic puzzle whose solution is the term "arsenic."

[3] G. MacDonald Ross, "Leibniz and the Nuremberg Alchemical Society," in *Studia Leibnitiana* 2/6 (1974), pp. 222–248.

[4] Bernard Le Bovier de Fontenelle's "Eulogy" for Leibniz proposes a different interpretation: "Once he had been received Doctor of Law in Altorf, he went to Nuremberg to see the Savants. He learned that there was in that Town a well-hidden Society of persons working in Chemistry and seeking the Philosopher's Stone. He was at once possessed of the desire to make profit of this occasion and become a Chemist, but the difficulty was in being initiated into the Mysteries. He took Books of Chemistry, gathered together the most obscure expressions, those he had least heard used, made of them a Letter unintelligible even to himself, and sent it to the Director of the Secret Society, demanding he be admitted in light of this proof of his great Knowledge. There was no doubt that the Author of the Letter was an Adept, or close to it, [so] he was welcomed with honour into the Laboratory, and bid fill the functions of Secretary. He learned much from them all the while they believed to be learning from him, it seems he presented as knowledge gained through much endeavour those views his natural genius provided him, and in the end it seems beyond doubt that when they discovered it, they did not cast him out" (*Oeuvres*, vol. 1, Paris: Salmon, 1825, 232–259).

[5] This interpretation is variously advocated by A. J. Aiton, A. Coudert, S. Brown, A. Becco, and George MacDonald Ross. Cf. A. J. Aiton, *Leibniz. A Biography* (Bristol: Hilger, 1985), especially p. 15; Allison P. Coudert, *Leibniz and the Kabbalah* (Dordrecht: Kluwer, 1995), in particular p. 95; Stuart Brown, "Some occult influences on Leibniz's Monadology," in A. Coudert, R. Hopkin, and Gordon Weiner (eds.), *Leibniz, Mysticism and Religion* (Dordrecht: Kluwer, 1998). Cf. A. Becco, "Leibniz et François-Mercure Van Helmont: Bagatelle pour des monades," in *Studia Leibnitiana* 7 (1975), pp. 119–141; George MacDonald Ross, "Alchemy and the development of Leibniz's metaphysics," in *Studia Leibnitiana Supplementa* 22 (1982), pp. 40–45.

[6] Cf. http://www3.bbaw.de/bibliothek/digital/struktur/01-mise/

[7] J. -J. Becher, *Oedipus chimicus* (Amsterdam, 1664). In this text, however, Becher proposes an alternative division between chemistry and alchemy since he conceives alchemy as a limited part of chemistry focused on gold (for the preparation of the elixir of life) and operations on metals. (cf. 7° Section, §6 "De Methodo Chimiae studiendi").

Second, there are the texts dealing with what Leibniz himself takes to result from the practice of physics: that is, practices that render imperceptible constituents of bodies intelligible. For Leibniz, it is a question of favoring the practical bent of these "workers of matter," or chemists, and conceiving of their labors as a necessary complement to physics. In this connection, it is worth recalling a letter Leibniz most likely intended for Christian Philip. In the course of a critique of Descartes's errors, Leibniz writes: "Beyond that, Monsieur Descartes did not know Chemistry, without which it is impossible to advance the customary physics" (A II i 782).[8] In the same way, some years later, in a letter to Johann Andreas Stiesser from May 25, 1700 (Dutens II 2 129–130), Leibniz proposes a definition of chemistry as the practical side of general physics. In short, throughout the corpus of Leibniz's writings, we find a recurrent definition of chemistry as practical physics.

Whereas Leibniz manifests a genuine interest in the objects of chemistry—as shown in his letters asking about the latest progress in experiments on the transmutation of metals, his letters to Friedrich Hoffmann, the composition of a history of phosphorous (Dutens II ii 102–108), his close discussions with Bernard Le Bovier de Fontenelle[9] about Nicolas Lemery's artificial thunder, as well as other experiments conducted during public meetings at the Académie Royale des Sciences between 1700 and 1701—his significant interest in chemistry probably stems from the view that chemical experiments and discursive alchemical practices could lead to a greater understanding of nature.

How should we understand the claim that the practice of chemistry could reveal the intelligibility of the natural world even though, historically, it was the dissociation between the heuristic fertility of chemical practices and discredited chemical principles which, for a time, guaranteed interest in "chymistry" in the seventeenth century? To answer this question, one must first understand the place Leibniz accords to these practices in the procedures targeting the intelligibility of nature.

CHEMICAL PRACTICES AND INTELLIGIBILITY

The identification of chemistry with practice and its promotion for that specific reason is restated in Leibniz's *Plan de la création d'une société des arts et des sciences en Allemagne* (Plan for the creation of a Society of the Arts and Sciences in

---

[8] Leibniz adds: "what he says of salts stirs pity in those who have understanding of it and it is clear to see that he did not know their differences. Had he had less ambition toward making a sect, more patience in reasoning on perceptible things, and less of a fondness for exploring the invisible; he may perhaps have laid the foundations for true physics, for he had the praiseworthy genius to succeed in this, but having strayed from the true path, he besmirched his reputation, which will not endure so long as that of Archimedes, and all will soon be forgotten of the pretty Tale of Physics he has given us" (A II i 782).

[9] A. Birembaut, P. Costabel, S. Delorme, "La correspondance Leibniz-Fontenelle et les relations de Leibniz avec l'Académie royale des Sciences en 1700–1701," in *Revue d'histoire des sciences et de leurs applications* 2/19 (1966), pp. 115–132.

Germany)[10]: "laboratory workers, charlatans, alchemists, and other meddlers and bohemians are ordinarily folk of great skill and even experience . . . such a man knows more by experience and by the reality of nature than someone else who passes in the world for a savant, and who, having learnt what he knows from books, knows how to reproduce it with eloquence." In this passage, Leibniz confirms the lack of clear differentiation between chemistry and alchemy, ranks alchemy among other apparently disreputable practices, and, above all, depicts the knowledge on which alchemical practices are based in a most interesting light: it is knowledge that comes from experience and a grasp of "the reality of nature."

This promotion of chemistry as an experimental mode of access to the reality of nature is set out in a significant passage from his exchanges with the chemist Georg Ernst Stahl. A distinctive feature of this correspondence is the emphasis that is laid on the importance of chemistry for understanding and knowing bodies. Leibniz states that chemistry relates to all bodies: "all bodies are the concern of Chemistry, for they are treated under the aspect of physical operations, which consist in an imperceptible process, not as structure but as mass."[11] Chemistry is the science that transforms matter and thereby allows us to know it—but only according to its mass.

It is undoubtedly for this reason that Leibniz judges chemistry to be "too empirical" (a judgment he also sees fit to make in relation to medicine). He deems it necessary for this practical, indispensable knowledge to be completed with a form of inquiry that would attend to the structure of bodies and would bring this empirical knowledge into a fruitful relation with metaphysical principles. It is a matter of rendering the imperceptible constituents of bodies intelligible and thereby bringing chemistry's epistemic function to the fore. Indeed, in the *Plan de la création d'une société des arts et des sciences en Allemagne*, Leibniz indicates that knowledge of the various methods of distillation and of precipitates, fermentations, and chemical reactions opens access to "most of nature's interior functions, and principally [those of] the human body" (FC Oeuvres VII 85). He adds: "no doctor without any profound knowledge of this philosophical chemistry can observe the true method of healing." Leibniz thus underlines the epistemic and therapeutic utility of chemistry, and this leads him to promote comparative anatomy.[12] However, this endorsement of chemistry presupposes that it is consistent with the mechanical analysis of bodies that Leibniz advances—and, crucially, that Leibniz's conception of dynamics, with its focus on the concept of force, can be accommodated.

In the 1670s, Leibniz began work on a mechanical reduction of chemical operations as a condition of their intelligibility. A letter to Otto Tachenius sheds light on this

[10] FC, *Oeuvres* VII "Leibniz et les Académies," in his *Plan de la création d'une société des arts et des sciences en Allemagne*, "Réflexions sur l'établissement en Allemagne d'une Académie ou société des sciences pour faire fleurir le progrès des arts et des sciences," §19.

[11] Leibniz's twelfth doubt in the *Negotium otiosum*. Cf. Stahl, *Negotium otiosum*, Dutens 1768, II ii 131–161. Cf. F. Duchesneau and J. Smith's edition, published by Yale University Press.

[12] Justin Smith, *Divine Machines, Leibniz and the Sciences of Life* (Princeton, NJ: Princeton University Press, 2011).

endeavor: "I have reduced to manifest causes this hidden mystery of nature" (A II i 100). Similarly, Leibniz writes in an unpublished essay from the early 1670s: "I can now dare hope that I have discovered a reason to link mechanical philosophy, which reduces everything to size, shape, and motion, with chemistry, which reduces everything to certain reactions and solutions" (A VI ii 325).[13] Finally, in a letter to Henry Oldenburg written on April 29, 1671, Leibniz writes: "all reactions, fermentations, and resolutions can be generally reduced to the reaction occurring between acid and alkali, the latter depending on the elastic force" (A II i 167).

It seems that, according to Leibniz, chemical processes must be reduced to mechanical explanations in order for us to understand them clearly. Indeed, results of chemical experiments that modify bodies are presented in *Veritates physicae* (1678–80) (A VI iv, 1984–1985) as perceptible physical truths that are reached by induction. Leibniz defines the limits of these results in epistemic terms: due to their conjectural character, they do not enable identification of the cause of phenomena we observe, but they do enable the formulation of hypotheses that can aid toward understanding natural phenomena. It is to the question of how they do so that we now turn.

In his Preface to a new edition of M. Nizolius's *Antibarbarus* (A VI ii 413), Leibniz suggests that there is a striking similarity between the approach of philosophers who conceive of bodies and the qualities of bodies and the approach of chemists who, with their mixtures and solutions, produce new bodies previously unknown to doctors. He conceives of the production or identification of new bodies as an anticipation[14] of discoveries allowed, for instance, only by the use of the microscope thanks to its ability to reveal what was hitherto imperceptible. In the 1690s, a letter to Henri Justel (August 27, 1692) reaffirms the similarity between the philosopher's approach and the chemist's but goes even further by showing how chemical experiments bring us to an understanding of nature: "as well as the fire enclosed within the earth, I find an infinity of effects [which are] perfectly similar to those of the chymistry laboratories" (A I viii 413). Leibniz observes a similarity between naturally occurring changes and changes produced in chemistry laboratories; this similarity then leads him to propose an explanation for natural changes that is grounded in the chemical elements. The lexicon of chemistry is used here to make hitherto unexplained phenomena intelligible. Thus, the chemical activity of reproducing or anticipating the natural transformations of an organic body serves to render visible—or, to use a more appropriate term, intelligible—the very organization of these bodies.

With the question of the organization of bodies, we enter into the metaphysical terrain of the theory of substance. Does Leibniz make room for chemistry in the metaphysical sphere? Or, with its strict empiricism, must chemistry be confined to the domain of practical operations? There is a tradition in Leibniz studies that supports the

---

[13] See also the letter to Lambert van Velthuysen, May 5, 1671.
[14] Cf. F. Duchesneau, *Physiologie des Lumières: Empirisme, modèle et théories* (La Haye: Nijhoff, 1982), p. 90.

hypothesis of an alchemical influence behind the conceptualization of the monad. This hypothesis must now be presented and briefly discussed.

LEIBNIZ AND HERMETICISM: ALCHEMY AND THE MONAD

The aim here is to determine whether the principal, but hidden, source of the fundamental notion of Leibniz's rationalist metaphysics, viz. the notion of monad, is in fact alchemical. What are the arguments in defence of this position? The key claim is that the active or vital dimension that is so prominent in Leibniz's later metaphysics of simple substances was inspired by—or at least corresponds with—the alchemical principles developed most notably by Franciscus Mercurius Van Helmont.

The idea of this kinship is defended by several commentators and originates in an article by W. Julius Pagel dating from 1931.[15] This claim is based on three arguments: first, that there is a similarity between Van Helmont's notions of seed and seminal principle[16] and Leibniz's notion of monad, leading to an understanding of Van Helmont's principle as a sort of "proto-monad"; second, that Leibniz endeavored to "spiritualise" Henry More's physical monad; third, that the appeal in Leibniz's theory of substance to a twofold element that is both active and passive proves the influence of cabbalistic philosophy. In particular, Allison Coudert claims in *Leibniz and the Kabbalah*[17] that Leibniz's knowledge of the alchemical conceptions of matter and spirit influenced the development of his concept of monad. She finds Leibniz's attempt to combine an active and passive element particularly suggestive here. In a similar vein, in an article on the occult influences on Leibniz's monadology, Stuart Brown suggests that the Leibnizian notion of a simultaneously active and passive substance is an idea specific to Van Helmont's cabbalistic philosophy.[18] Likewise, Anne Becco[19] and George MacDonald Ross[20] both develop this idea of a Helmontian "inspiration." Becco defends the idea that Van Helmont's unity is complex without being a compound, and she claims that, in Leibniz's appropriation of Van Helmont's terms, he moves from a concrete atomism, in which

---

[15] W. Pagel, "Helmont, Leibniz, Stahl," in *Studhoffs Archiv* 24 (1931), pp. 19–59.

[16] Hiro Hirai, *Le concept de semence dans les théories de la matière à la Renaissance de Marsile Ficin à Pierre Gassendi* (Turnhout: Brepols, 2005), p. 496.

[17] Allison P. Coudert, *Leibniz and the Kabbalah* (Dordrecht: Kluwer, 1995), p. 95.

[18] Stuart Brown, "Some occult influences on Leibniz's Monadology," in A. Coudert, R. Hopkin, and G. Weiner (eds.), *Leibniz Mysticism and Religion* (Dordrecht: Kluwer, 1998). B. Orio has developed many arguments in favor of this thesis in two important papers: see Bernardino Orio, "Leibniz y los Helmontianos," part 1, in *Revista de filosofia* 19 (1998), pp. 153–182, and part 2, in *Revista de filosofia* 20 (1998), pp. 149–200.

[19] A. Becco "Leibniz et François-Mercure Van Helmont: Bagatelle pour des monades," in *Studia Leibnitiana Sonderheft* 7 (1978), pp. 121–142.

[20] G. MacDonald Ross, "Leibniz and Alchemy," in *Studia Leibnitiana Sonderheft* 7 (1978), pp. 166–180.

the principles are air and fire, to a formal atomism that turns the monad into a simple substance. She regards the spiritualization of the physical monad as Leibniz's response to the metaphysical problem of unity and suggests that Leibniz undertook to "rationalize" the cabalistic lexicon: "The veritable crux of the Helmontian question comes to the fore in the shift from the monadomagies to the monadology, that is to say that this confrontation incites Leibniz to employ a cabbalistic lexicon, the lexicon of the monad, rationalising it, creating the fundamental relationship between monad and logos."[21] For Ross, the lexical and thematic similarities between alchemical theory and Leibniz's philosophical outlook are both striking and troubling. The most notable similarities in this regard are Leibniz's insistence that everything is living, his idea of universal sympathy, the continuity he posits between different kinds of beings, the description of nature in moral and religious terms, and, of course, his refusal to radically separate spirit and matter.[22]

However, if we adopt a genetic approach to understanding the development of Leibniz's ideas, rather than looking for decisive influences or similarities, the internal logic of his thought becomes clearer.[23] Such an approach allows us to appreciate the coherence and originality of Leibniz's claim that the essence of substance is activity. The fact that, in the 1700s, this activity could be described as taking the form of a living power does not prove that Leibniz endorsed vitalism of any kind. In fact, for Leibniz, "life" must be understood in the sense of a "principle of perception." This activity—which in later texts does indeed take the form of life or organization[24]—expresses itself through beings that progressively acquire more and more perfection, more and more reality. This reality, however, is never material, for this active principle is initially identified with force, then with action, and finally with perception. It is therefore unthinkable that the monad could have been material and then, dematerializing, could have become vital. Leibniz is absolutely clear on this point. He rejects the chemical principles (which he so often dismisses as mere caprices) in order to establish the dynamic principles of substance. He states his position particularly clearly in a letter to Andreas Morell from September 29, 1698:

> I also fear that everything that is said of salt, sulphur, and mercury as principles of things are but mere metaphorical games [jeux de metaphores] . . . I would side rather with those who recognize in God as in every other spirit three properties [formalités]: force, knowledge, and will. For every action of a spirit requires *posse*,

[21] Becco, "Leibniz et François-Mercure Van Helmont," 137.

[22] MacDonald Ross leans on textual elements to prove the influence of alchemical ideas in the earliest developments of Leibniz's metaphysics, cf. the 1671 text *De resurrectione corporum* (A II i 112–116), as well as the letter to Herzog Johann Friedrich from 1671 (A II i n. 59, 177).

[23] See M. Fichant, "L'invention métaphysique," in G. W. Leibniz (ed.), *Discours de Métaphysique, suivi de Monadologie et autres textes* (Paris: Gallimard, 2004), p. 111. "The question of putative borrowings is less interesting than the question of the internal combination of meanings inherent to the genetic construction of Leibniz's concepts and lexicon."

[24] F. Duchesneau, *Leibniz, le vivant et l'organisme* (Paris: Vrin, 2010).

scire, velle. The primitive essence of every substance consists in force; and it is this force in God which means that God necessarily is, and that everything that is must emanate from him. . . . This Trinity [force, knowledge and will] is more distinct and more solid, in my opinion, than that of salt, sulphur, and mercury, which issues only from a misunderstood chemistry. (Grua I 139)

Here, Leibniz regards the Paracelsian trinity of sulfur, mercury, and salt as a "misunderstood chemistry." He rejects this trinity to endorse instead the triad *posse, scire, velle,* traditionally referred to the Holy Trinity. In so doing, Leibniz combines the idea that force is the primitive essence of all substance with the notion of real spiritual unity.

In conclusion, the relevance of chemical practices to epistemic efforts aimed at making nature intelligible is based on the view that chemists' experiments produce conjectural epistemic results that may well anticipate a fuller understanding of natural processes. In this sense, these experiments are perfectly connected to Leibniz's metaphysics. On the other hand, the alleged alchemical proximities of this metaphysics give way to a project of general science in which chemical experimentation has a well-identified function.

REFERENCES

Aiton, A. J. 1985. *Leibniz. A Biography.* Bristol: Hilger.

Becher, J. -J. 1664. *Oedipus chimicus.* Amsterdam.

Becco, A. 1975. "Leibniz et François-Mercure Van Helmont: Bagatelle pour des monades." *Studia Leibnitiana* 7: 119–141.

Birembaut, A., P. Costabel, S. Delorme. 1966. "La correspondance Leibniz-Fontenelle et les relations de Leibniz avec l'Académie royale des Sciences en 1700–1701." *Revue d'histoire des sciences et de leurs applications* 2(19): 115–132.

Brown, S. 1988. "Some occult influences on Leibniz's Monadology." In A. Coudert, R. Hopkin, and G. Weiner (eds.), *Leibniz, mysticism and religion,* ed. Dordrecht: Kluwer [International archives of the History of Ideas, 158], pp. 1–21.

Coudert, A. P. 1995. *Leibniz and the Kabbalah.* Dordrecht: Kluwer [International archives of the History of Ideas, 162].

Duchesneau, F. 1982. *Physiologie des Lumières: Empirisme, modèle et theories.* La Haye: Nijhoff.

Duchesneau, F. 2010. *Leibniz, le vivant et l'organisme.* Paris: Vrin.

Fichant, M. 2004. "L'invention métaphysique." In G. W. Leibniz (ed.), *Discours de Métaphysique, suivi de Monadologie et autres textes.* Paris: Gallimard.

de Fontenelle, B. Le Bovier. 1825. *Oeuvres: 1.* Paris: Salmon, pp. 232–259.

Hirai, H. 2005. *Le concept de semence dans les théories de la matière à la Renaissance de Marsile Ficin à Pierre Gassendi.* Turnhout: Brepols.

Joly, B. 1992. *La rationalité de l'alchimie au XVIIe siècle.* Paris: Vrin/Mathesis.

Macdonald Ross, G. 1974. "Leibniz and the Nuremberg Alchemical Society." *Studia Leibnitiana* 2(6): 222–248.

Macdonald Ross, G. 1978. "Leibniz and alchemy." *Studia Leibnitiana, Sonderheft* 7: 166–180.

Macdonald Ross, G. 1982. "Alchemy and the development of Leibniz's metaphysics." *Studia Leibnitiana Supplementa* 22: 40–45.

Newman, W. R., and Principe, L. 1998. "Alchemy vs. chemistry: The etymological origins of a historiographic mistake." *Early Science and Medicine* 3: 32–65.

Orio, B. 1998. "Leibniz y los Helmontianos," part 1. *Revista de filosofia* 19: 153–82; part 2, *Revista de filosofia* 20: 149–200.

Pagel, W. 1931. "Helmont, Leibniz, Stahl." *Studhoffs Archiv* 24: 19–59.

Smith, J. 2011. *Divine Machines, Leibniz and the Sciences of Life.* Princeton, NJ: Princeton University Press.

CHAPTER 29

....

CALCULATING MACHINE

....

MATTHEW L. JONES

[T]he arithmetical instrument that puts all the labor of the mind into wheels.[1]

— Leibniz (1676)

IN 1671, Leibniz announced to the French theologian Antoine Arnauld two machines he had envisioned: one for arithmetic, the other for geometry. The first promised to perform all four operations of arithmetic "mechanically without any work of the mind." The second promised a new way of "determining, using a machine, analytical equations and the proportions and transformations of figures without tables, calculation, or the drawing of lines." The potential of this geometric machine was massive: "If we could transform all figures into thinkable ones, I do not see what could still be desirable."[2] The transformations of the envisioned geometrical machine were realized not in any physical machine but in his new symbolic calculus that permitted just such transformations of figures.[3] In contrast Leibniz spent decades and a small fortune attempting to realize his arithmetical machine. No prototype machine was functioning adequately when he died in 1716. His failure sullied his reputation with scientific societies during his lifetime but served as a great inspiration for later inventors who typically knew only the machine's appearance and promised function (see Figure 29.1).

---

[1] "Dissertatio exoterica de usu geometriae" (August–September 1676), A VII vi 488.

[2] Leibniz to Arnauld (early November 1671), A II i 286.

[3] The remarkable manuscripts on the geometric, algebraic, and even analytical machines have not to my knowledge been studied closely. See LH 35,3A,20, ff. 1–4 (a.k.a. Cc 816); LH 35,12,1, f. 13; A6, 3:412–413; LH 35,13,1, f. 408 (Cc 1069); LH 35,13,1, f. 444–445.

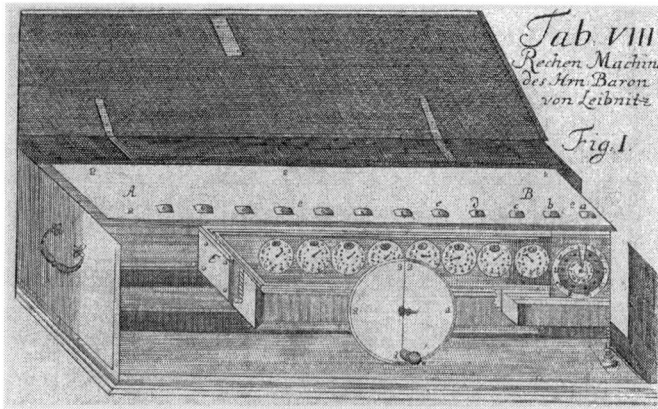

FIGURE 29.1 Diagram of Exterior of Leibniz's calculating machine.

from Jacob Leupold, *Theatrum arithmetico-geometricum: das ist: Schau-Platz der Rechen- und Meß-Kunst* (Leipzig, 1727), plate VIII. Special Collections, Columbia University Library.

To build a calculating machine in the seventeenth-century, a philosopher needed knowledge about materials; to gain any practical form of such knowledge in the early-modern era, one needed to learn about the people possessing such knowledge. This chapter sketches the challenges Leibniz faced in building a calculating machine, looks at his philosophical remarks about such machines and the skilled people needed to make them, and recounts the legacy of his failure to produce a machine understood to be adequately functional.[4]

Presenting a Multiplying Machine

In February 1672–73, Leibniz presented a model of his calculating machine to the Royal Society of London. He had been working on calculating machines for several years but only began his serious work once he arrived in Paris in 1672.[5] The records

[4] For the history of early calculating machines, see especially Michael R. Williams, *A History of Computing Technology* (Englewood Cliffs, N.J.: Prentice Hall, 1985) and Jean Marguin, *Histoire des instruments et machines à calculer: Trois siècles de mécanique pensante, 1642–1942* (Paris: Hermann, 1994); Ernst Martin, *The Calculating Machines*, trans. Peggy Aldrich Kidwell and Michael R. Williams (Cambridge, Mass.: MIT Press, 1992) (now available in an expanded and illustrated form at http://www.rechenmaschinen-illustrated.com/); much new research can be found at Stephan Weiss, "Beiträge zur Geschichte des mechanischen Rechnens," http://www.mechrech.de/.

[5] Leibniz's manuscripts on the machine, primarily in LH 42, 4 and 5, are not yet edited. For the development of Leibniz's machine, see Florin-Stefan Morar, "Reinventing machines: The transmission history of the Leibniz calculator," in *The British Journal for the History of Science* 48/1 (2014), as well as the unpublished Ludolf von Mackensen "Die Vorgeschichte und Entstehung der ersten digitalen 4-Spezies-Rechenmaschine von Gottfried Wilhelm Leibniz ...". Dr. rer. nat., Technischen Hochschule München, 1968, henceforth VM. The primary study of the development of the machine drawing upon the manuscripts is now the learned Ariane Walsdorf, "Biographie einer Rechenmaschine: Die

of the Society note that Leibniz "shewed them a new arithmetical instrument, contrived, as he said, by himself, to perform mechanically all the operations of arithmetic with certainty and expedition, and particularly, multiplication." His model of an instrument was far from finished: "He gave some proof of what he said, but acknowledged the instrument to be imperfect."[6] Before turning to Leibniz's two solutions to mechanizing multiplication, consider one way of performing multiplication by hand. If we were to multiply 4,567 × 245 by hand, we would probably write something like the following:

$$
\begin{array}{r}
4567 \\
\times \quad 245 \\
\hline
22835 \\
18268 \\
+ \ 9134 \\
\hline
1118915
\end{array}
$$

We would probably produce the intermediate stages, such as $4,567 \times 5 = 22,835$, using memorized multiplication tables for single digits: $7 \times 5 = 35$, so we write 5 and carry the 3. We could also find the intermediate stage simply by adding 4,567 five times: $4,567 \times 5 = 4,567 + 4,567 + 4,567 + 4,567 + 4,567 = 22,835$. The multiplication of multiple-digit numbers can be reduced to a series of repeated additions. Then sums of each series of additions (22,835, 18,268, 9,134) are added. Mechanizing multiplication done in this fashion requires:

1.   Mechanizing multiple additions of the same number: for example, $4,567 \times 5$, then × 4, then × 2

2.   Mechanizing the process of adding each intermediate amount to a higher decimal place; that is, the mechanization of the process of offsetting each intermediate amount one column to the left:

$$
\begin{array}{r}
22835 \\
18268 \\
+ \ 9134 \\
\hline
\end{array}
$$

Entwicklungs- und Herstellungsgeschichte der Leibniz-Rechenmaschine," in Klaus Badur, Ariane Walsdorf, Erwin Stein, and Franz Otto Kopp (eds.), *Das letzte Original. Die Leibniz-Rechenmaschine der Gottfried Wilhelm Leibniz Bibliothek* (Hannover: Gottfried Wilhelm Leibniz Bibliothek-Niedersächsische Landesbibliothek, 2014), which came to my attention just as this chapter was completed.

 [6]   Thomas Birch, *The History of the Royal Society of London for Improving of Natural Knowledge, from Its First Rise* (London 1756–57), vol. 3, p. 73.

Let's start with the first stage in the mechanization: the process of mechanizing multiple additions of the same multiplicand (4,567) for each digit of the multiplicator (245). In the machine of Leibniz's predecessor Blaise Pascal, the user has to dial each addition for each place value manually. To multiply, say, 4 × 5, the user would have to dial 4 into the machine five times (like dialing the phone number 44444 on a rotary phone). To multiply 45 × 5, the user would have to dial 5 on the first input and then 4 on the second into the machine five times: 5 then 4, 5 then 4, 5 then 4, 5 then 4, 5 then 4. Obviously, such a process quickly becomes tedious.

Leibniz sought to have the machine do the entire calculation. To automate the process of performing multiplication via repeated addition, Leibniz needed a way to input the amount to be added for each place value and then to have that amount added to result wheels as many times as necessary. In our preceding example, Leibniz needed to create a way to set the four digits to be multiplied on the machine to 4 5 6 7 and then have the machine add 4 5 6 7 four times in their respective place value columns without having to dial each digit manually multiple times. He needed what he called a "multiplying wheel" that could be set to add a given digit multiple times.

During his time in Paris, Leibniz devised two solutions to performing these additions mechanically, each of which was reinvented multiple times in the next two centuries, likely with no knowledge of Leibniz's ideas. In one solution, he envisioned a "wheel with mobile teeth," now called a variable cogwheel (upper left in Figure 29.2). In such a wheel,

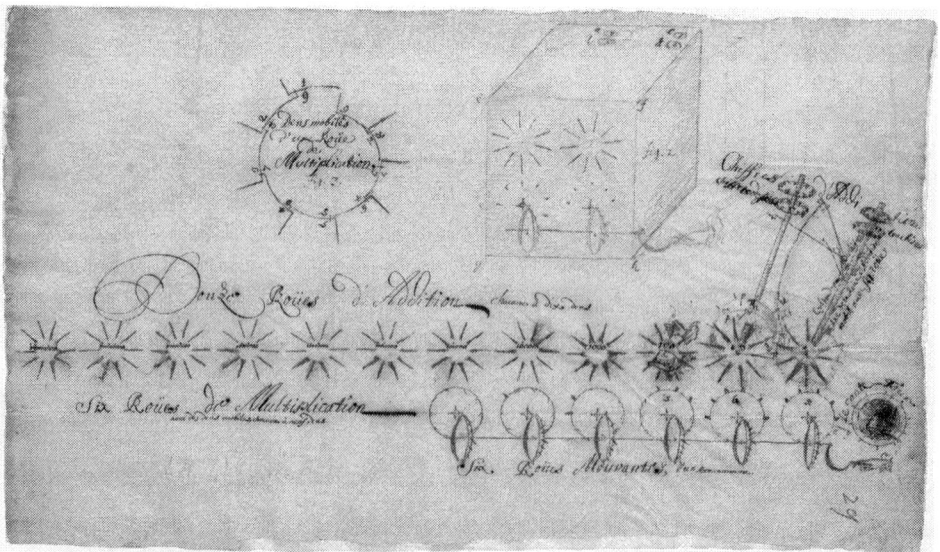

FIGURE 29.2 Manuscript drawing of Leibniz's multiplying machine, including variable cogwheel—"Dens mobiles d'une Roüe de multiplication" (upper left). c. 1673. LH 45, 5, f. 29r.
Courtesy of Gottfried Wilhelm Leibniz Bibliothek—Niedersächsische Landesbibliothek, Hanover.

FIGURE 29.3 Schematic diagram of stepped drum. Author's image, OpenSCAD.

"as many teeth" will protrude from the cogwheel as are needed to equal "the number to be multiplied."[7]

His second solution was the "wheel with unequal teeth," now called a stepped drum (Figures 29.3–29.4).[8] The stepped drum is a cylinder with nine teeth of increasing length arranged radially. A small gear moves along the axis of the drum. Depending on the position of the gear, a different number of teeth will be communicated when the stepped drum rotates 360 degrees. Setting the number 4 into the machine would move the small gear so that each full rotation of the stepped drum would move its corresponding gear four steps. The stepped drum provided the multiplying mechanism in Leibniz's machines from 1674 at the latest until his death.

Whether with variable cogwheels or stepped drums, the machine would, in principle, work similarly. Take our example of multiplying 4,567 × 245. This involves setting 4 5 6 7 into the machine and then causing all multiplying wheels to rotate five times by turning a crank (as shown being held by a hand in Figure 29.4). To multiply the next digit, 4, the user moves the entire multiplying mechanism one digit to the left and then turns the crank, causing the multiplying wheels to rotate 4 times, and so forth.

The diagrams of 1673–74 (see Figure 29.4) suggest that Leibniz showed the Royal Society the basic idea of using a multiplication carriage (in front and on the bottom)

---

[7] For Leibniz's discussion of the requirements of the "multiplying wheels," see especially "Project de la machine" (before May 24, 1673), LH 42,5, 54v; edition in VM, pp. 145–146. For the cogwheel, see also the undated LH 42,5, f. 29; N. Joachim Lehmann, "Leibniz' Ideenskizze zum 'Sprossenrad,'" in *NTM: Zeitschrift für Geschichte der Naturwissenschaft, Technik und Medizin* (1987); and Erwin Stein and Franz Otto Kopp, "Konstruktion und Theorie der Leibnizschen Rechenmaschinen im Kontext der Vorläufer, Weiterentwicklungen und Nachbauten: Mit einem Überblick zur Geschichte der Zahlensysteme und Rechenhilfsmittel," in *Studia Leibnitiana* 42/1 (2010), pp. 37–40. In his earliest papers on a calculating machine, he considers performing multiplication directly.

[8] For the stepped drum, see LH 42,5, f. 14r, in VM, pp. 168–169, which he dates to c.1672; 15.7.1677, LH 42,4, f. 7r, 8v; 8.5.1682, LH 42,4, f. 40; 7.1685, LH 42, 5, f. 11r. For the influence of the stepped drum, see Friedrich W. Kistermann, "When could anyone have seen Leibniz's stepped wheel," in *Annals of the History of Computing* 21 (1999); compare, however, Stephen Johnston, "Making the arithmometer count," in *Bulletin of the Scientific Instrument Society* 52 (1997), note 9.

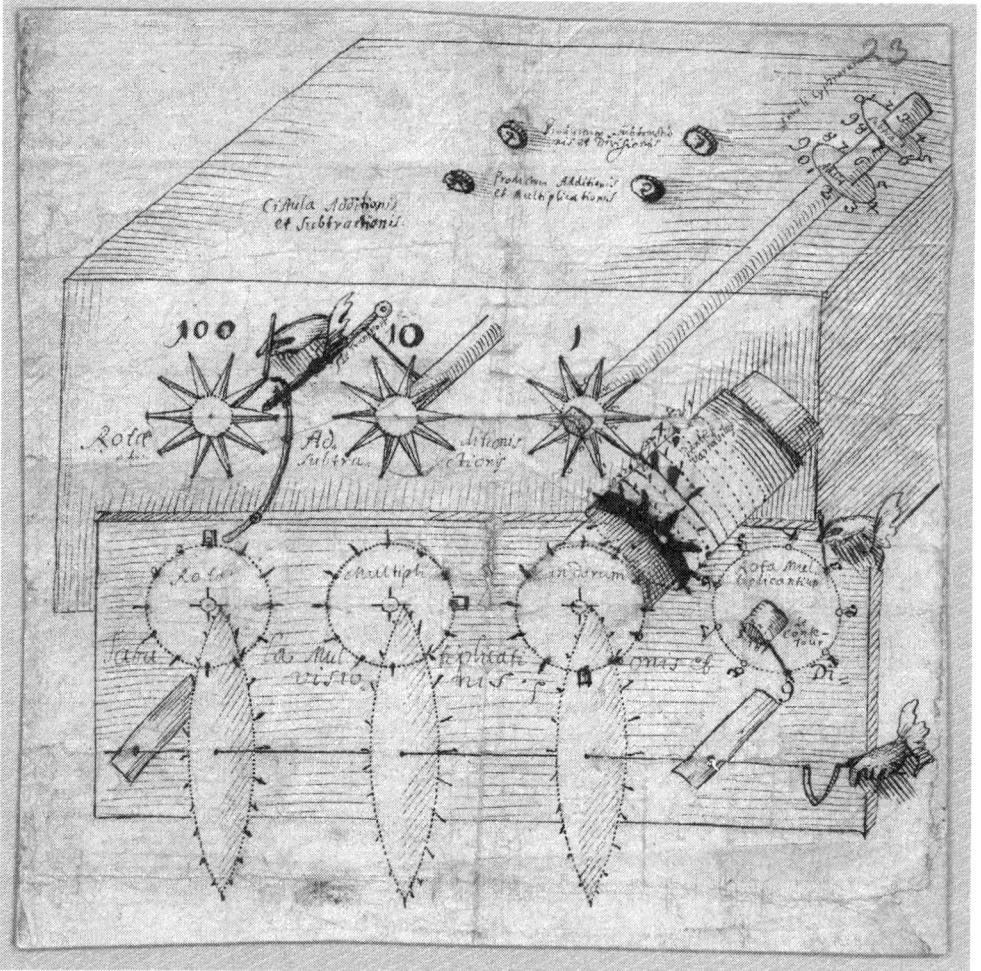

FIGURE 29.4 Manuscript drawing of Leibniz's multiplying machine, with stepped drum mechanism at right. c. 1673. LH 42, 5, f. 23r.

Courtesy of Gottfried Wilhelm Leibniz Bibliothek—Niedersächsische Landesbibliothek, Hanover.

that could freely move left and right along the primary addition apparatus (behind and on top). The diagrams of 1673–74 do not show the adding mechanism and offer little indication of how carries would be performed. Leibniz may have been protecting his current mechanism from prying eyes; more likely, the machine displayed to the Royal Society was incomplete precisely because it could not automatically perform carries. Given that any multiplication would necessarily involve sequences of additions, solutions to the mechanization of addition had to be robust, fast, and accurate. Leibniz realized quite early on that he would need to solve two major problems of carrying mechanisms: first, the sufficient-force problem (the need to propagate carries across multiple digits) and the keeping-it-digital problem (the requirement that the machine report only counting numbers, not something in between).[9] His working papers show him considering the merits of using springs versus weights in providing sufficient force.[10] These documents reveal how far Leibniz was in 1673 from a functioning mechanism: they articulate more the general requirements for a machine than an actual design of one. Bringing the carry mechanism into practice would require that Leibniz and his artisans convert all the vague, qualitative descriptions in his working papers—"a reasonable length," "enough speed"—into physical mechanisms grounded in the properties of available materials. Transforming Leibniz's calculating machine from the nonfunctional demonstration model presented to the Royal Society to something functional enough that Leibniz could sell it to the French crown and receive the approval of the learned proved far more difficult than Leibniz ever expected.[11]

FINDING ARTISANS, PINCHING
THEIR SECRETS

"Wanting to have my Arithmetical Machine made," Leibniz explained in 1673, he came "to enter into knowledge" of the artisans of Paris.[12] Paris had structural advantages allowing for such a concentration of artisans, skills, and materials. Leibniz remarked, "Manufactures, for the most part, are in the most flourishing state that could be wished for, in part because of the ingenuity of the nation, in part because of the particular care of the king, who had made the best artisans from all around come, and . . . [took] from them their secrets and their inventions." Leibniz greatly admired the French minister Jean-Baptiste Colbert's policy of attracting artisans—the great as well as the middling—and then stealing their secrets. He undertook to do it a bit himself.[13] A little cash and a little skill eased the way.

Early during his Parisian stay, Leibniz explained, "I am reduced to a voluntary hermitage, to the extent of speaking to almost no one except my two artisans." Working with them on

---

[9] See Matthew L. Jones, *Reckoning with Matter: Calculating Machines, Innovation, and Thinking about Thinking from Pascal to Babbage.* (Chicago: University of Chicago Press, 2016), pp. 26–27.

[10] See "Project de la machine" (before May 24, 1673), LH 42,5, 57r–v; in VM, p. 153.

[11] For Leibniz's efforts to gain patronage and preferment with the machines, see Matthew L. Jones, "Improvement for profit: Calculating machines and the prehistory of intellectual property," in Mario Biagioli and Jessica Riskin, eds., *Nature Engaged: Science in Practice from the Renaissance to the Present* (New York: Palgrave-MacMillan, 2012). Leibniz quickly got himself into trouble with the Royal Society; see Leibniz to Oldenburg July 15, 1674 and Oldenburg to Leibniz, August 12, 1674, in Henry Oldenburg, *The Correspondence of Henry Oldenburg,* ed. A. Rupert Hall and Marie Boas Hall, 13 vols. (Madison/London: University of Wisconsin Press/Mansell/Taylor and Frances, 1965–86), vol. 9, pp. 44 and 141.

[12] Leibniz to Christian Habbeus, May 5, 1673, A I i 417.

[13] Leibniz to Christian Habbeus, May 5, 1673, A I i 416–417.

his machine required "a man entirely."[14] Leibniz chose the Parisian clockmaker Ollivier to construct the calculating machine, explaining that he had "run all over Paris before picking this one."[15] We know little about their collective work while Leibniz remained in Paris. But once Leibniz moved from Paris to Hanover, much that would have been oral and haptic had to be written down and drawn. Moving from face-to-face to exclusively written and pictorial collaboration was difficult for Leibniz as well as Ollivier. Apparently literate but little used to written communication, Ollivier rarely managed to make his technical difficulties clear. Leibniz was better at communicating solutions in ways meaningful and helpful to Ollivier, who clearly longed to discuss things in the presence of the parts and models in question; Leibniz was poor at directing and informing his agents in Paris who managed Ollivier's work on his behalf.

In May 1677, Ollivier wrote to Leibniz, now in Hanover, to excuse his slow progress, to complain about his pay, to ask for clarification, and to promise to return to the project before long. He noted, "I still have difficulty with the carry, which cannot be made as easily as we had proposed."[16] Solving the problem was hampered by Leibniz's secrecy and distance. Leibniz sent Ollivier a remarkable "memoire" setting forth an improved design for the carry mechanism of the calculating machine. Leibniz's memoire is a testament to the difficulty of technical communication before the age of standardized written and pictorial communication practices in engineering.[17] In the memoire, as in nearly all his writings on the calculating machines, Leibniz provided few metrical specifications of the parts involved: he provided their relative relationships in space, their proposed motions, and a general sense of the proportions of the pieces to one another. Other than specifying the number of teeth of various gears, he gave no measurements of size or angles for the parts. Considerable recent work by engineers and historians attempting to reconstruct Leibniz's machine demonstrates how carefully the machine must be calibrated or tuned in order to function with any degree of accuracy.[18] So does Leibniz's later correspondence from the 1690s and early 1700s concerning the later version of

---

[14] Leibniz to Louis Ferrand (May 1672), A I i 452. See now Walsdorf, "Biographie einer Rechenmaschine," pp. 66–73.

[15] Leibniz for Académie des sciences (early 1675), LH 42,5, f. 33v; VM, p. 177.

[16] Ollivier to Leibniz (May 24, 1677), A III ii 148.

[17] Leibniz, "Memoire pour Monsieur Ollivier touchant la machine arithmetique perfectionée," July 15, 1677, LH 42,4, ff. 7–9.

[18] See, for example, N. Joachim Lehmann, "Neue Erfahrungen zur Funktionsfähigkeit von Leibniz' Rechenmaschine" in *Studia Leibnitiana* 25 (1993); Klaus Badur and Wolfgang Rottstedt, "Und sie rechnet doch richtig!: Erfahrungen beim Nachbau einer Leibniz-Rechenmaschine," idem. 36 (2004); and Erwin Stein and Franz Otto Kopp, "Konstruktion und Theorie der Leibnizschen Rechenmaschinen im Kontext der Vorläufer, Weiterentwicklungen und Nachbauten: Mit einem Überblick zur Geschichte der Zahlensysteme und Rechenhilfsmittel," idem. 42/1 (2010); Klaus Badur, "Die große dezimale Rechenmaschine und ihre Nachbauten," in Ariane Walsdorf et al., ed., *Das letzte Original. Die Leibniz-Rechenmaschine der Gottfried Wilhelm Leibniz Bibliothek* (Hannover: Gottfried Wilhelm Leibniz Bibliothek-Niedersächsische Landesbibliothek, 2014); Erwin Stein and Franz Otto Kopp, "Konstruktiv-mathematische Erforschung der Dezimalmaschine und funktionsoptimierter Hannoverscher Nachbau für vollständige Zehnerüberträge," idem.

the machine that has come down to us. Scholars of Leibniz's work on machines and mechanisms have underscored this inattention to detail as a cause of his failures as an engineer.[19]

Historians of technology have stressed that different styles of technical drawing and description imply and accompany different conceptions and organizations of intellect and labor.[20] More specified drawings aid the engineer and manager in controlling and regulating production; less specified drawings suggest the need for the discretion and competence of the producers. The indeterminate nature of Leibniz's description and drawings—the quite deliberate gaps and omissions in Leibniz's memoire—testify to the creativity and the innovative use of outside knowledge and discretion Ollivier was supposed to provide. Throughout the early development of the arithmetical machine, Leibniz depended on Ollivier for minor tweaks, connections to suppliers, knowledge of metals and lubricants, and the organization of a workforce. Ollivier was responsible for choosing among design options, such as whether to use a spring or a weight in a given place, as well the fine metrical and timing details of the design.

The artisan seems to have made a machine within Leibniz's specifications only to find it too difficult to use. Ollivier's impasse prompted Leibniz to rework his design some months later, to confront, in particular, issues of weight and timing. Leibniz's working sketches of 1679 show that he concluded that he had been too cavalier in thinking about the issues of timing and speed in the carry mechanism, particularly in cases of carries upon carries.[21] More work was needed—so much so that, several years later, Leibniz abandoned the approach to carrying tens detailed in the memoire almost completely.

With his fortunes in France fading quickly, Ollivier resolved to move to Hanover. While no hard evidence demonstrates that Ollivier traveled to Hanover, various traces suggest he did so.[22] Ollivier abruptly disappears from Leibniz's correspondence: this suggests that they had returned to face-to-face interaction, with Ollivier again becoming an invisible technician, his struggles and innovations leaving no trace in the archive. Whatever the case, some invisible artisan in Hanover appears to have continued to work on the machine. In the mid-1690s, the clockmaker Georg Heinrich Kölbing worked on the machine; a junior clockmaker, Adam Sherp did so until 1700.[23] While all apparently worked to develop Ollivier's machine, they probably did not produce Leibniz's surviving calculating machine, which was rediscovered and partially reconstructed in 1876 and

---

[19] See, e.g., Jon Elster, *Leibniz et la formation de l'esprit capitaliste* (Paris: Aubier Montaigne, 1975), p. 78.

[20] Ken Alder, *Engineering the Revolution: Arms and Enlightenment in France, 1763–1815* (Princeton: Princeton University Press, 1997), pp. 129, 136–153; Steven Lubar, "Representation and Power," in *Technology and Culture* 36 (1995), esp. pp. 70–74.

[21] See discussion of difficulties with calculating machine: August 22, 1679, LH 42,4, 1r.

[22] See A III ii 806. Leibniz to Johann Friedrich, May 1678, A I ii 175; VM, pp. 93, 117.

[23] Florin-Stefan Morar, "Leibniz's Calculating Machine and the Social Meaning of Invention in the Context of Early Modern Science" (Universität Bielefeld, 2009), pp. 21–22, citing LBr 489 and A I xvii 11.

currently resides in a vault in the Leibniz Library in Hanover.[24] This "newer" machine was built and "debugged" over many years, alongside Ollivier's "older" machine.

TRYING TO COORDINATE: HANOVER
TO HELMSTEDT TO ZEITZ

The effort to "perfect" the calculating machine continued on and off until Leibniz's death.[25] Work on the machine continued sporadically in Hanover until 1700, when Leibniz transferred supervisory responsibility to a client of his, one Rudolf Christian Wagner, "a young learned scholar and mathematician much practiced in mechanical things."[26] Leibniz helped Wagner become a professor of mathematics at the University of Helmstedt; Wagner paid Leibniz back in part by dedicating years of service to supervising the activity of a variety of artisans on the calculating machine.[27] Perfecting the carry mechanism was the central task. The progress of the work remained extremely slow. Wagner's frequent illnesses ground work to a halt, the artisans became preoccupied with other work, and Leibniz was slow to respond to queries about potential changes to the design.[28]

In 1711, Leibniz transferred the working pieces of the machine again, this time to officials within the court of Moritz-Wilhelm of Zeitz.[29] Responsibility for the machine was divided among a court official named Buchta, given overall supervision of the work; a court deacon named Gottfried Teuber, given technical supervision; and artisans, charged with implementation. Finding artisans willing to be "diligent and docile" continued to be a challenge, and Leibniz worked to bring a skilled clockmaker, Haas from

---

[24] For these nineteenth-century reconstructions, see Morar, "Reinventing Machines."

[25] Versions of the verb "to perfect" (perfecter, *perfectieren*, etc.) appear throughout the correspondence in describing the nature of this activity.

[26] Leibniz to Landgrave Karl of Hessen-Kassel, July 1, 1701, A I xix 334. The correspondence with and around Wagner, Buchta, and Teuber is available in preliminary transcriptions in series A I and A III. See Transkriptionen für die Leibniz-Akademieausgabe der Leibniz-Forschungsstelle Hannover, available at http://www.gwlb.de/Leibniz/Leibnizarchiv/Veroeffentlichungen/Transkriptionen.htm. On the Helmstedt stage, see Ernst-Eberhard Wilberg, *Die Leibniz'sche Rechenmaschine und die Julius-Universität in Helmstedt*, ed. Alfred Kuhlenkamp (Brauschweig 1977); Günter Scheel, "Helmstedt als Werkstatt für die Vervollkommnung der von Leibniz erfundenen und konstruierten Rechenmaschine," in *Braunschweigisches Jahrbüch für Landesgeschichte* 82 (2001); Morar, "Reinventing Machines," and Walsdorf, "Biographie einer Rechenmaschine," pp. 90–98. See Klaus Badur, "Die große dezimale Rechenmaschine und ihre Nachbauten," idem., ed. Ariane Walsdorf et al., pp. 139–143.

[27] See Leibniz's letters of recommendation, A I xix 108–111.

[28] Wagner to Leibniz, February 15, 1701; Wagner to Leibniz, October 22, 1706, in Transkriptionen.

[29] See Adolf Schmiedecke, "Leibniz' Beziehungen zu Zeitz" in *Studia Leibnitiana* 1/ 2 (1969) and Walsdorf, "Biographie einer Rechenmaschine," pp. 99–101. For portions of Leibniz's correspondence with Teuber, see G. W. Leibniz, *Epistolae XLVI ad Teuberum concionatorem aulae Cizensis*, ed. C. F. Nobbe (Typis impressil Staritz, 1845), to be used in conjunction with Transkriptionen and the manuscript letters in LBr 916.

Augsburg, to Zeitz. Like Ollivier, Haas protested the schemes for payment from Leibniz and his agents.[30] Real work began only in 1714.

In Zeitz, carry remained the primary concern.[31] Teuber, like Wagner, understood the basic principles of the machine and many of the particulars and was to innovate as seemed necessary.[32] Leibniz granted Teuber broad authority to change the design as needed.[33] When working with an artisan, Teuber was charged to "direct him and animate him to diligence," and an entirely new machine was begun.[34] Despite considerable effort, neither the old nor the new model of the machine was perfected at the moment of Leibniz's death in 1716.[35] To this day, scholars studying Leibniz's machine disagree on how well its different iterations functioned—or could have functioned.[36]

LEIBNIZ'S ACCOUNT OF PRACTICAL KNOWLEDGE

Leibniz greatly valued artisanal skills. Such skills were a problem for philosophical analysis and for concrete statecraft. His epistemological and practical views on artisans and their skills informed his theology and political economy alike. Late in the 1690s, Leibniz complained about the dangers of producing only raw materials and exporting them: "We work properly for foreigners, more or less like the journeymen who help artisans, who make less money although they do the hardest part of the work, since they work using force rather than cleverness, like the animals who serve us and whom we direct."[37] According to Leibniz, those states whose industries produce finished cloth deserve greater recompense: they act less through force than through skill and intelligence.

Leibniz recognized the necessity for artisans characterized by their industry and their real skill in inventing and adjusting machines. At the same time, Leibniz saw such practical artisanal capacities as decidedly inferior to theoretical knowledge as a way of knowing, however much artisanal skill surpassed theoretical understanding in knowledge about the particulars of nature and the means to manipulate it. He claimed that, in general, most skilled labor is capable only of responding in precisely defined ways

[30] Leibniz to Teuber, April 8, 1712, in Leibniz, *Epistolae XLVI ad Teuberum*, p. 23.
[31] Leibniz to Teuber, January 3, 1712, in Leibniz, *Epistolae XLVI ad Teuberum* and see Leibniz to Teuber, September 23, 1714 and October 7, 1714, in Transkriptionen.
[32] See Leibniz to Teuber, February 2, 1711, in Leibniz, *Epistolae XLVI ad Teuberum*.
[33] Leibniz to Buchta, November 15, 1713, in Transkriptionen.
[34] Leibniz to Buchta, March 3, 1714, in Transkriptionen.
[35] For the state of the machine at Leibniz's death, see Morar, "Leibniz's calculating machine," pp. 23, 29, drawing upon the letters of Teuber.
[36] For a sophisticated account of the problems of claims about whether the machine "works," see Morar, "Reinventing Machines."
[37] A I xi 168; discussed in André Robinet, *G. W. Leibniz: Le meilleur des mondes par la balance de l'Europe* (Paris: Presses Universitaires de France, 1994), p. 267.

to stimulation: "Human beings act like animals insofar as the consecutions of their perceptions are produced only from the principle of their memory." He conceded that "we are only Empirical in three quarters of our actions," even though such ways of acting do not stem from judgments of the reason and do not thus involve what defined us as human.[38] Like animals, simple empirics act as if things will always happen as they have before; they cannot register and contend with exceptions, whether in human affairs, in the human body, or in the technological world. Only a theoretically informed practice can recognize and contend with exceptions in a general way.[39] Alas, Leibniz conceded, the method of using reason is not yet perfected: the crude current state of fundamental propositional knowledge precludes contending with all problems.

Like Blaise Pascal, Leibniz distrusted inventors anchored only in theory, just as Leibniz dismissed artisans lacking any theory as mere empirics. Unlike Pascal, he recognized that skilled artisans frequently had just the blend of the practical and the theoretical necessary, given the current state of theoretical knowledge: "For an artisan who knows nothing of Latin or Euclid, when he is a skilled man, and knows the reasons for what he does, he truly has the theory of his art, and is capable of finding expedients for all sorts of events."[40] An artisan who possessed the theory of his art did not have to act like an animal or a simple empiric. Better artisans could contend with the unexpected and were capable of innovation using their theory. In searching for an artisan to produce his calculating machine, Leibniz had explicitly sought such a higher sort of craftsperson and defended the higher salary such a person required: "It is just to pay a skilled master not only for the time he has worked—without speaking of the novelty and the risk of the enterprise—but also for his industry and his skill in distinguishing himself from an utter ignoramus."[41]

Using terms likely borrowed from Pascal, Leibniz mocked philosophers and projectors who lacked the knowledge gained from practical experience with the world: "A demi-savant puffed up with an imaginary knowledge projects machines and buildings that could not succeed, for he lacks all the theory necessary. He understands perhaps the vulgar rules of movement . . ., but he does not understand that part of Mechanics I call the science of resistance or of hardness" (A VI iv 712). In a Baconian vein, Leibniz often insisted that philosophers should attempt to uncover artisanal knowledge and give it a formal expression that allowed articulation, replication, and distribution.[42] For example, the practical how-to knowledge concerning the hardness and resistance, the elasticity and springiness of materials learned through practical interaction and experience will, with time and work, be cataloged, made

---

[38] *Monadologie*, 1714, GP VI 611.

[39] *Nouveaux essais sur l'entendement humaine* (1703–04), A VI vi 50–51.

[40] "Recommandation pour instituer la science générale" (April–October, 1686(?)), A VI iv 712.

[41] Leibniz for [Académie?] (before December 15, 1676), LH 42, 5, f. 37v, 38r; in VM 172, 173.

[42] Among others, see "Discours touchant la Méthode de la Certitude" (August 1688–October 1690?), A VI iv 959–961.

recognizable, and given theoretical explanation, to become what he called "distinct" knowledge.[43]

In appreciating artisanal skill, Leibniz recognized the importance of knowledge that was neither cognized nor distinctly expressed. He praised the power and necessity of skilled modes of perceiving and acting, even as he underscored their limits and called for their replacement through techniques meant to perfect reasoning insofar as possible for fallen human beings. While praising the superior knowledge of mathematicians, Leibniz years later conceded that the skill of a "worker or engineer . . . could have this advantage above a great mathematician that could discern among them [polygons] without measuring them," like colporteurs who can eye the amount of weight they can carry—"in which they surpass the greatest expert in statics in the world." He conceded, "This empirical knowledge, acquired through long exercise, is of great use for acting quickly, as engineers often have need of." Such "confused" knowledge was still inferior to what Leibniz called "distinct" knowledge.[44] Theory may, at some future time, become a practice capable of providing quick resolutions. In the meantime, Leibniz argued, finding "a good solution to a muddled difficulty" still required "that we have the force of extraordinary genius or that we have a long practice that makes the answer come into our mind machine-like and by habit, when that answer would need to be sought through reason."[45]

Once the art of reasoning and its attendant tools were sufficiently developed to allow human beings to cognize theoretical knowledge quickly, a philosopher-engineer would always be able to devise mechanisms far more sufficiently and far more completely than any skilled artisan. Lacking sufficient theoretical knowledge and tools for abridging reasoning, inventors continued to need skilled artisans to help them foresee, recognize, and solve problems and difficulties of all kinds.

MATERIALIZING MIND IN THE SEVENTEENTH CENTURY

Commentators on Blaise Pascal's machines from the mid-seventeenth century marveled that they could perform operations previously considered an exclusive province of reason. His sister remarked, "This work was considered a new thing in nature, as it reduced into a machine a science that resides entirely in the mind, and having found the means to perform all the operations with perfect certainty, with no need for

---

[43] Leibniz's detailed studies on elasticity, during the period of the invention of the calculating machine and the early steps of the calculus, are central to the still underutilized A VIII i. More generally, see Herbert Breger, "Elastizität als Strukturprinzip der Materie bei Leibniz," in *Studia Leibnitiana Sonderheft* 13 (1984).

[44] A VI iv 262.

[45] "Recommandation pour instituer la science générale" (April–October 1686(?)), A VI iv 711.

reasoning."[46] Pascal's machine illustrated that some parts of reasoning could be done mechanically—but no one claimed that Pascal's machine made it obvious that reason might be entirely susceptible to mechanization. He noted, "The arithmetical machine produces effects that approach thinking more than anything animals do. But it does nothing about which it could be said that it has a will, as is the case with animals."[47] Reflection on calculating machines made material minds more thinkable, to be sure; just as often, such reflection delimited the scope of explanations possible within a purely mechanical philosophy.[48]

In an undated manuscript, Gottfried Wilhelm Leibniz reflected on some lessons his calculating machine could impart:

> The machine . . . shows [*faire voir*] that the human mind can find the means of transplanting itself in such a way into inanimate matter that it gives to [matter] the power of doing more than it could have done by itself: to convince via the senses those who have difficulty conceiving that \how/ the Creator could house [*loger*] the appearance of a mind a little more generally in a body, however furnished with many organs; since even brass can receive the imitation of an operation of reason which concerns a particular or determinate truth, but [also] more difficult ones, especially as the Pythagoreans believed one can distinguish a human being from an animal and to place as part of the definition [of man] the faculty of using numbers.[49]

Leibniz cast the calculating machine as a palpable intervention in the major early-modern debate about what sorts of causes were philosophically licit in explaining the creation, emergence, and ordinary phenomena of nature. The envisioned calculating machine provided tangible evidence of what matter in locomotion, acting entirely through efficient causality, could—and could not—achieve. A goal-achieving artifice, the machine illustrated that matter in motion, suitably well organized, could exhibit some mind-like behaviors. Complex organized phenomena required neither some immaterial soul nor a "plastic nature" directing the motion of matter nor the direct and particular concurrence of God himself. The machine likewise suggested that matter in motion could never be so well organized except through an initial, creative organizing activity of a rational mind, human or divine. The *appearance* of intelligence did not require the continuous activity of an intellective substance. The *creation* of the appearance of intelligence in matter, on the other hand, certainly did require the activity of an intellective substance.

---

[46] Mdm. Périer, Blaise Pascal, *Œuvres complètes*, ed. Jean Mesnard, 4 vols. (Paris: Desclée de Brouwer, 1964–), vol. 1, pp. 576–577; 608.

[47] Blaise Pascal, *Pensées*, ed. Gérard Ferreyrolles and Philippe Sellier (Paris: Livre de Poche, 2000), S617.

[48] On this, see Jones, *Reckoning with Matter*, ch. 6.

[49] LH 42,4, f. 33r. At the end of the passage, Leibniz originally wrote and then deleted "and to give the definition [of man] as an animal capable of using numbers."

AN INSPIRING FAILURE

Archimedes, Leibniz wrote, had a talent lacking in Descartes and Galileo: "He had a marvelous mind for inventing machines useful for life."[50] Leibniz offered what can only be seen as an autobiographical encomium: "We see every day that people of good sense, who have need of some artisans, after having understood the matter and reasons of practice, know how to provide openings in extraordinary cases, which the craftspeople do not perceive at all."[51] This ability to provide openings in extraordinary cases alone could lead human beings to their highest potential by inventing techniques and machines capable of overcoming the difficulties of mind and body alike. Leibniz's work on the calculating machine testified to his skill in finding such openings. Or at least it was supposed to. To convey the importance of his innovations in calculating machines and the quadrature of the circle, Leibniz sketched a commemorative medal around 1676 (see Figure 29.5).

Just before describing his machines to his future patron Johann Friedrich, he offered "to bring new inventions and curiosities from extraordinary cabinets. . . . In these matters, I have had enough lucky opportunities . . . having learned from workmen themselves many things, some curious, others important for commerce and manufacture."[52] In including his calculating machine in the list of achievements he presented to princes, he used his new technology as evidence that he could be a new kind of state counselor, essential in a cameralist age—a counselor capable of seeing the openings necessary to improve technology and polity at once. Leibniz presented himself as a superior form of projector, schooled in theory, grounded in practical knowledge, and capable of producing the improvements necessary for social order, health, economy, and morals.[53] He could convert the imperfectly understood and ill-distributed knowledge of artisans into practices essential to develop the state and its people. Leibniz wasn't able to do all this.

An early nineteenth-century history of calculating machines relayed an oft-told tale about failed genius. "Herr von Leibniz invented a calculating machine, which, however, was never perfected and reduced to practice, even though he spent more than 20,000 Thaler on its implementation."[54] Perhaps the most salient fact for the proliferation of calculating machines in the eighteenth century was Leibniz's failure to bring his calculating machine to practice.[55] Although Leibniz belatedly published an account of his machine in 1710, he did not disclose the mechanism in any meaningful way; contemporaries

---

[50] Leibniz to Malebranche, June 22, 1679, A II i 720.
[51] "Recommandation pour instituer la science générale" (April–October 1686(?)), A VI iv 712.
[52] Leibniz to Johann Friedrich, January 21, 1675, A I i 493.
[53] Compare Andre Wakefield, "Leibniz in the Mines," *Osiris* 25 (2010).
[54] Johann Paul Bischoff, *Versuch einer Geschichte der Rechenmaschine: Ansbach 1804*, ed. Stephan Weiss (München: Systhema Verlag, 1990), p. 124.
[55] See Jones, *Reckoning with Matter*, ch. 4.

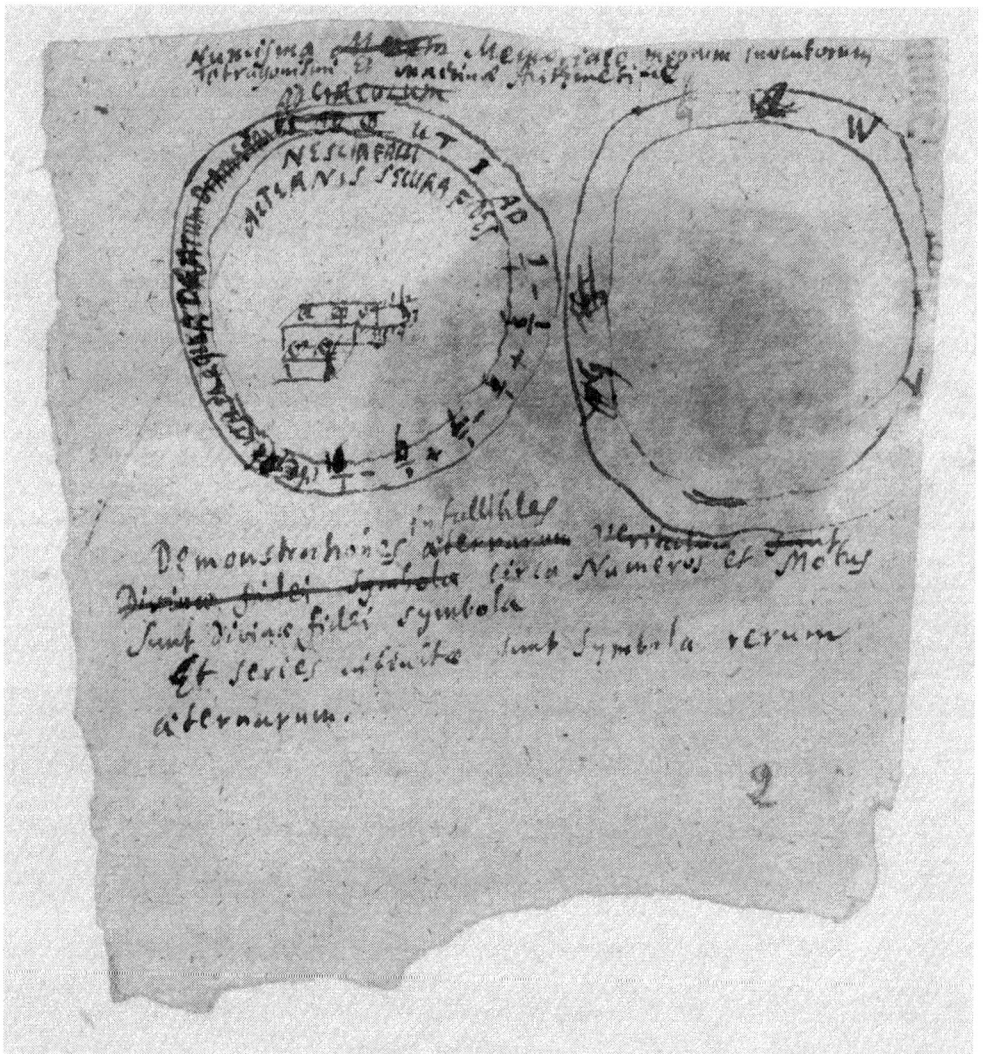

FIGURE 29.5 Leibniz, "Numisma Memoriale meorum Inventorum Tetragonismi et Machinae Arithmeticae" c. 1676, LH 35, 2,1, f. 2. Gottfried Wilhelm Leibniz Bibliothek—Niedersächsische Landesbibliothek, Hanover.

bemoaned this lack of disclosure (see Figure 29.1). An article in 1769 noted, "Neither this description nor this figure suffices in any way for forming an idea of the mechanism of this curious machine."[56] That the "universal genius" Leibniz failed to bring a machine to practice made the pursuit of a better-realized machine a tempting goal for professors,

---

[56] *Journal des Savants* (December 1776), p. 871. A description of the stepped drum, without a diagram, was printed in Johann Stephan Pütter, *Versuch einer Academischen Gelehrten-Geschichte von*

philosophers, and clockmakers alike; to produce, to repair, or even to design a potentially more perfected machine could become a tangible display of knowledge, skill, and ability useful to polities across Europe. The minister and clockmaker Philipp Hahn recounted how the edifying example of Leibniz's twenty years of work and large sums spent helped him surmount his doubts once difficulties set in: "So I was not deterred."[57] A lack of knowledge, far from hindering the creative energies of inventors, prompted them—and permitted them—to reinvent Leibniz's machine in pursuit of glory and profit alike.

der Georg-Augustus-Universität zu Göttingen (Göttingen: Wittwe Vandenhoek, 1765), pp. 243–246. See Walsdorf, "Biographie einer Rechenmaschine," pp. 103–105.

[57] Philipp Matthäus Hahn, "Beschreibung einer Rechnungs-Maschine, wodurch man ohne Mühe, durch bloße Herumführung eines Triebels, die vier gewöhnlichen Rechnungs-Arten verrichten kann," *Der Teutsche Merkur* 2.Viertelj (1779), p. 139.

CHAPTER 30

THE TECHNOLOGY OF MINING AND OTHER TECHNICAL INNOVATIONS

HARTMUT HECHT AND JÜRGEN GOTTSCHALK

LEIBNIZ's earliest reflections on technical constructions and procedures are part of a paper entitled *De longitudinibus inveniendis*. It was written between the end of 1668 and the beginning of 1669. This elaboration belongs to a series of thirteen papers on nautical themes and has been published in volume 1 of the new series VIII of the Academy Edition of Leibniz's *Sämtliche Schriften und Briefe,* devoted to Leibniz's writings on science, medicine. and technology. This paper and all the writings of series VIII are testimony to Leibniz's fundamental and lifelong interest in technology and make these contributions an essential part of his legacy—a part that is still underestimated.

In *De longitudinibus inveniendis* (A VIII, 1: N. 2) Leibniz tackled a problem that was intensively discussed in his time. He and his contemporaries were searching for the theoretical and practical solution of the question of how to determine longitude. The answer was of paramount interest for navigation, and most contemporary scholars and engineers expected the solution of the longitude problem from the construction of precision chronometers. Huygens had proposed using pendulum clocks for this purpose. Leibniz was familiar with Huygens's proposal but also knew the shortcomings and weaknesses of its practical realization. For that reason, he did not concentrate on the improvement of clocks alone, as others did, but instead proposed to make use of an apparatus that automatically transfers the route of a ship to a map. By such means, Leibniz expected that the captain of a ship would be supplied with complete information and should be able to determine the vessel's actual position from the graphically represented path. Leibniz called this apparatus *instrumentum longitudinum* or *autometron* and discussed, as was typical for him, different possibilities for improving it. Interdependencies like this are characteristic of Leibniz's approach to analyzing and solving scientific problems. In the next section, these are discussed in more detail, with the focus there on vacuum phenomena.

THE RELATIONSHIP BETWEEN SCIENCE
AND TECHNOLOGY

In 1672, Leibniz read an extract of a letter published by Christiaan Huygens (1629–95) in the *Journal des Sçavans* (Huygens 1672: 133–40). The letter dealt with anomalies appearing in vacuum experiments and stimulated Leibniz to write a large number of notes, excerpts, and drafts testifying to his early interest in experimental sciences and its instrumentation.

Among the experiments discussed by Huygens was a test with a siphon under vacuum conditions. He described how it had greatly surprised him that the siphon operated inside the vacuum receptacle in exactly the same manner as outside it. Huygens therefore concluded that the air pressure (i.e., the traditional explanation of the siphon phenomena) could not be responsible for the operation of the device. Moreover, it became clear to him that he not only had to search for a new explanation, but also for an explanation based on new experimental results.

In his response to Huygens's letter, entitled *De variis experimentis pneumaticis*, Leibniz therefore designed a similar experiment. As one can see in Figure 30.1, the apparatus consists not only of a Torricellian tube *ab* alone or of adhesive plates *ml* alone within a receptacle (as had been the case in Huygens's arrangement) but also of a pump *gh* and

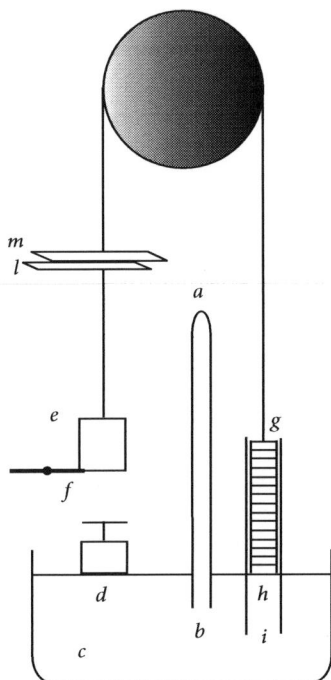

FIGURE 30.1 Experimental equipment (A VIII, 1: 350).

two adhesive plates. In this way, Leibniz enlarged the experimental basis of the vacuum experiments and combined, as parts of one and the same experiment, objects of investigation that Huygens had sharply separated from one another. It can be seen from this example that scientific problems and the development of experimental arrangements are closely connected with one another in Leibniz's approach.

In the following years, Leibniz designed a plurality of experiments to analyze the vacuum phenomena. This inspired him to contrive a large number of instruments and devices. In a paper from 1676, for instance, Leibniz discusses a new kind of clepsydra or water meter (A VIII, 1: 572–78). It is based on a siphon, which is fixed to a wooden board or other material floating on the water. In the ordinary clepsydra, time is measured by the quantity of water running out of the vessel. But, in contrast to the old water clocks, Leibniz provides for a continual outflow. Indeed, all the clepsydras before Leibniz suffered from a systematic defect: their outflow depends on the height of the water surface, which in turn varies with the quantity of water remaining. This produces a time dilatation instead of an equal flow over equal time intervals. It is clear that such a clepsydra cannot measure time exactly (i.e., with respect to an invariant unit). Leibniz's invention corrects this problem. In his construction (Figure 30.2), the water does not leave the vessel directly but rather via the floating siphon. As can be seen from the figure, the distance between the water surface and the orifice through which the water leaves the vessel remains constant. Therefore, water is allowed to flow out not only continuously,

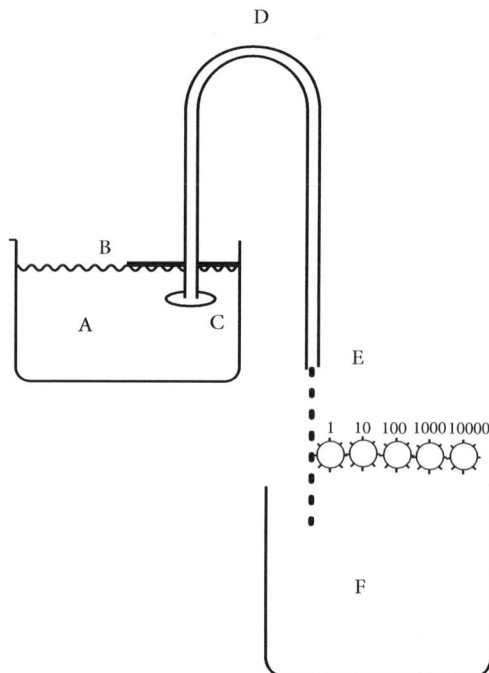

FIGURE 30.2 Clepsydra uniformiter fluens (A VIII, 1: 574).

but also in equal measures (i.e., in equal quantities over equal times). From Figure 30.2 it can also be seen that Leibniz completed his water clock with a counter that automatically registers the outflow of water (i.e., the time). It should be emphasized here that such an automation of processes is one of the guiding principles of Leibniz's endeavors in experimental sciences, as well as in technology, as shown later in more detail.

For the moment, let us concentrate on a further example concerning the so-called *instrumentum inclinationum* (A VIII, 1: 399–401). This is simply a tube filled with a certain amount of mercury and closed at the both ends. In its initial position (i.e., positioned horizontally with respect to the surface of the earth), the mercury is located at the bottom of the tube. As soon as the tube is rotated into the alternative perpendicular position, the mercury will be above the air and will compress the air inside the tube downward. Depending on the inclination of the tube, the lower surface of the mercury will reach well-defined positions within the tube. It was Leibniz's idea to find a relationship between pressure and volume with the help of this instrument—and this is indeed an appropriate device for this purpose, one still used in lectures on experimental physics to demonstrate the Boyle-Mariotte law of gases. The proof of the law lies in the observation that the distance from the mercury adhering to the supporting plane remains constant independently of the inclination of the tube (Figure 30.3).

In addition to this scientific application of his instrumentum inclinationum, Leibniz developed many other ideas for its use in practice. Among the most important fields

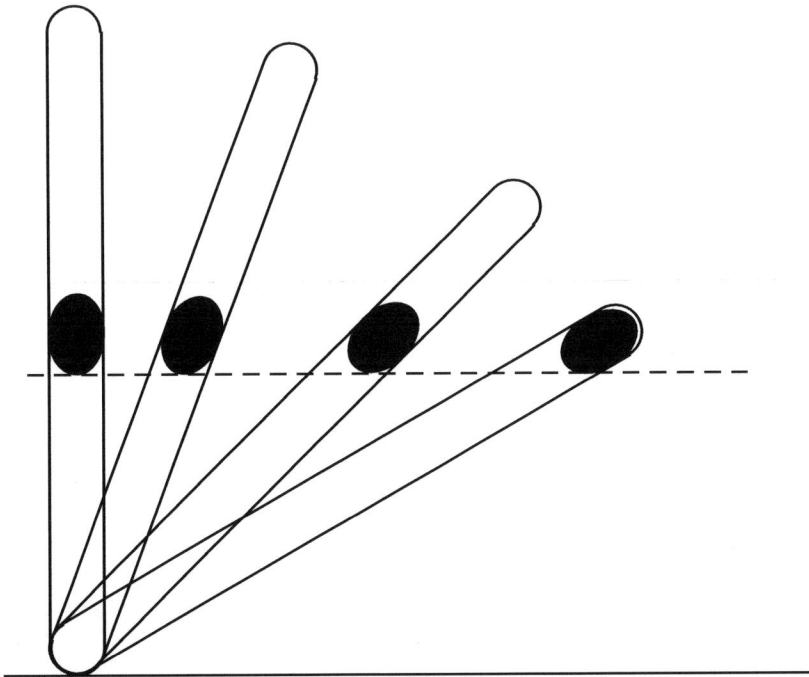

FIGURE 30.3 Instrumentum inclinationum (Drawing: H. Hecht).

of application he includes geography, navigation, hydrostatics, and architecture. These and other instruments indicate that devices and technical procedures are not only the results of scientific research, but are also means to establish and found science itself, as we now show through the example of the exclusion of the principle of a perpetuum mobile.

THE *PERPETUUM MOBILE*
AND ITS EXCLUSION

A perpetuum mobile is a machine that, once activated and only stimulated by its own motion, will run forever unless subject to an external force. In 1671, Leibniz wrote a paper presenting an example of his design for such a machine (A VIII, 1: 59). The device is outlined in very great detail, and the young Leibniz seemed to be convinced that its construction could be successful. The paper was discussed with his friend, Johann Daniel Crafft (1624–97), and an agreement was signed in which the two men undertook to inform one another about their activities and results with respect to *perpetua mobilia* (A VIII, 1: 554).

As shown by Vladimir Kirsanov in his paper "Leibniz in Paris", during his stay in Paris, Leibniz was still interested in this theme and presented two different designs. The leading idea of Leibniz's constructions is described by Kirsanov as follows: "The whole artifice of perpetual motion consists in finding the way of restoring the restoring force without using the force, which has to be restored. For that reason two forces have to be connected to each other in such a way that the restoring force acts separately whereby everything is compensated without affecting the machine" (Kirsanov 2008: 143).

A careful study of the Paris manuscripts on mechanics shows that Leibniz's thought experiments with *perpetua mobilia* end in the middle of 1674. That is exactly the time when he begins to study Mariotte's (ca. 1620–84) *Traitté de la percussion ou chocq des corps* and Wallis's (1616–1703) *Mechanica*. There is an interesting manuscript among Leibniz's Paris papers that begins with the definitions in chapter 1 of Wallis's *Mechanica* and ends with Leibniz's own reflections on motion. In the course of these reflections, he explicitly rejects the possibility of constructing a *perpetuum mobile* (A VIII, 2: 118). The decisive passage in this manuscript was repeated word for word in the manuscript that summarizes the essentials of a theory of motion at the same time (A VIII, 2: 163). Last, but not least, we find a first fruitful application of the rejection of *perpetua mobilia*.

The manuscript in question was first discussed by Kirsanov (2008: 144–46). It deals with the construction of a wind clock, which Leibniz describes as a machine that produces not a "perpetual" but a "perpetuated" motion by means of external forces like the power of wind. The fundamental difference between a *perpetuum mobile* and the perpetuated motion of the wind clock lies in the fact that a *perpetuum mobile* works

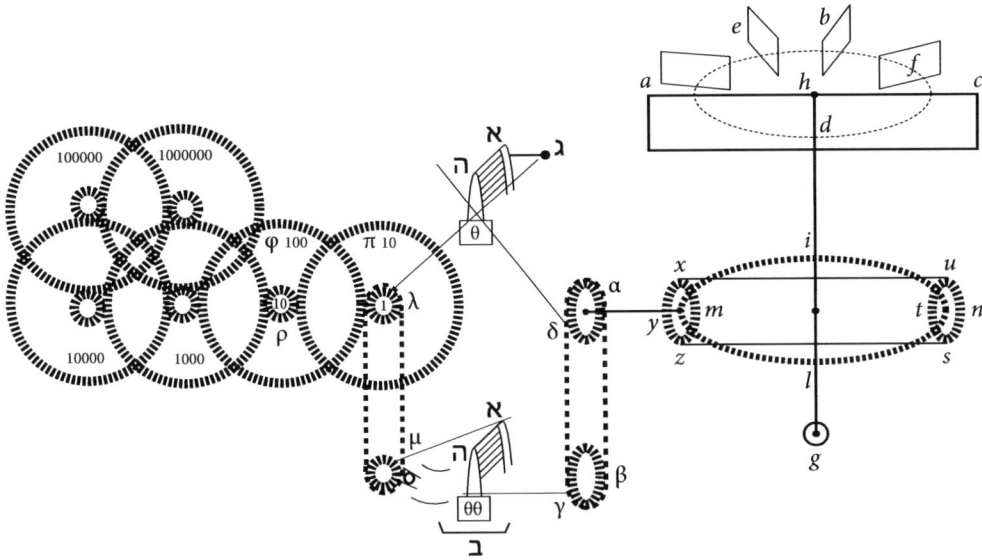

FIGURE 30.4   Horologium ventaneum perpetuum (A VIII, 2: 472).

endlessly driven only by its own internal operations, whereas the operating mode of the wind clock is perpetuated by an external source of power.

The title of the manuscript is *Motus regularis continuus a causa irregulari, discontinuata seu Horologium Ventaneum Perpetuum* (A VIII, 2: N. 94) (Figure 30.4). It briefly describes the main problem treated in the text, namely, how a regular continual motion can be generated by an irregularly and discontinuously acting external agent. For this purpose, Leibniz proposes a mechanism composed of two parts: namely, a windmill that provides the discontinuous power and a clock that indicates the time by a continuous rotation of its hands. The most interesting component of this machine is the constructional element that intertwines the two parts of the mechanism.

Kirsanov describes it as represented by two chain transmissions. The first one, Kirsanov writes, "is a part of the clock, the second—of the windmill. There are two weights; when one is sinking, another is being elevated; the exchange takes place when the first weight reaches its lower point (the depository). At this very moment the second weight reaches its upper point and happens to be suspended on a special hook. As soon as the first weight touches the depository, an elastic element (or a spring) will release the second weight from the hook and it will pass to the first chain transmission. Simultaneously the second hook will catch the weight stored in the depository and start to lift it up" (Kirsanov 2008: 146).

As can be seen in Figure 30.4, Leibniz solves the problem by transforming the discontinuous rotation of the mill sails first into a longitudinal motion of the weights. After that, the longitudinal motion is transformed into a uniform rotation of the clock's hands. The principal idea of a mechanism that transforms a linear motion into a uniform rotation had already been formulated by Leibniz in 1671 (A VIII, 1: N. 57). He now presents a new version of it, namely, a device analogous to a modern ratchet, which ensures that the transmission is allowed to move only in one direction. Otherwise, a continuous elevation and descent of the weights (i.e., the theoretical core of the whole mechanism) would not be realized.

Indeed, Leibniz applies the idea of storing power for the first time to his *horologium ventaneum*, in which the elevation of the weights is equivalent to an accumulation of power. It is power of natural origin, such as the power of wind or water, and it is successively accumulated by the elevation of the one weight and consumed by the descent of the other. In this way, a motion results that guarantees a uniform rotation of the clock's hands. However, it is not only the uniformity of motion that is based on power storage here, but a perpetual uniform motion, one caused by natural sources like wind and water.

Leibniz's wind clock from 1674, therefore, paved the way for the formulation of his concept of living force, and it is a first application of an idea that he consciously applied in the Harz project. In particular, it influenced his understanding of automatic machines.

Automatic Machines

A more general remark regarding this point is found in the *Specimen dynamicum* (April 1695), in which Leibniz emphasized that the ancients had an understanding of "dead forces" only or, in other words, a science of the five simple machines (lever, inclined plane, wedge and screw, wheel and axle, pulley) (Leibniz 1989: 439). Their main goal, he continues, was the analysis of the constraints of equilibrium in statics, whereas he would pave the way for a science of "living forces" dealing with equilibrium in dynamics. The machines that represent this new science are, therefore, of another type. They are not simple machines like the lever, wedge, and pulley but automatic ones that are able, for instance, to steer a ship into a port without any human assistance (A VIII, 1: N. 13_5). Another appropriate illustration for such a machine is the above-mentioned *horologium ventaneum*, which, as Leibniz says, does not only regulate itself but rather corrects its path in remarkable fashion in relation to the sun (A IV, 4: 69).

Central elements of automatic machines are, as can be seen from these examples, control cycles consisting of the recording of data, its comparison with a desired result, the calculation of deviations, and its self-correction through feedback. Although in Leibniz's time the understanding of these machines was still in its infancy, his insight and presentation of the problems are exceptional. Leibniz did not confine the application of these principles to machines, but transferred the idea of automatic machines to technological procedures, as well as to physical motion and biological generation. The idea of self-production and self-reproduction can even be found in the basic features of Leibniz's theory of monads.

Two passages in the *Monadology* are of greatest interest in this context. In §18, Leibniz declares that it would be possible to designate the created monads as *entelechies* because they have a certain autonomy and perfection that makes them not only sources of their internal activity but also, simultaneously, so to speak, incorporeal automata. Here, Leibniz describes the actions assigned to a metaphysical construct in terms of the technological principles of an apparatus or, in other words, he transforms technological principles in such a way that they gain a metaphysical meaning while simultaneously maintaining their principal difference.

This becomes clear when reading the preceding paragraph, in which Leibniz formulates his well-known windmill metaphor. Leibniz writes: "In imagining that there is a machine whose construction would enable it to think, to sense, and to have perceptions, one could conceive it enlarged while retaining the same proportions, so that one could enter into it, just like into a windmill. Supposing this, one should, when visiting within it, find only parts pushing one another, and never anything by which to explain a perception" (Rescher 1991: §17). In the case of a natural automaton, however, one would always find other natural automata.

The natural automaton (in contrast to an artificial machine) is still a machine in its smallest parts, ad infinitum. The difference between the two kinds of machines is not of principle but of degree because an artificial machine is also composed of smaller artificial machines; but in natural machines, this process of composition goes ad infinitum. Leibniz gives the following example to illustrate: a tooth of a brass wheel, he writes, "has parts or pieces, which to us are no longer artificial things, and no longer have something recognizably machine-like about them, reflecting the use for which the wheel is intended. But the machines of nature, namely living organisms, are still machines even in their smallest parts, *ad infinitum*" (Rescher 1991: §64).

All artificial machines are therefore based on natural machines because an engineer or craftsman has to presuppose natural materials for his activities. It is their aim to transform nature, but they cannot create it. Against this background, it becomes possible to distinguish automatic machines from mere mechanisms. A mechanism is put into operation by external forces. It stops as soon as the moving force is consumed. These are the so-called simple machines and mechanisms, such as a tackle. The mechanism of an automaton, in contrast, is based on natural processes that put it into operation (i.e., into a self-acting continuous motion). The wind clock discussed earlier is an example of an automatic machine. The ability to construct machines of this kind, as well as systems of automatic machines, is an appropriate illustration of what Leibniz had in mind when he defined man as a little god in his region (Rescher 1991: §83).

The creation of God thus has to be understood as a complex system of automatic machines ad infinitum. And, in the Harz Mountains, Leibniz demonstrated that the construction of automatic machines must not be reduced to special devices only. His activities followed the idea of advancing autonomy and perfection to overarching principles that govern whole technological processes.

LEIBNIZ AND THE CONTEXT FOR HIS INTERESTS IN TECHNOLOGY

Leibniz's intensive preoccupation with technology is primarily associated with the commissions he received from Duke Johan Friedrich (1665–79), and his successor (and later Elector) Ernst August (1679–98) of Hannover, for the improvement of the efficiency of mining in the Harz Mountains in the periods 1679–86 and 1692–96, respectively. The assignment was for the realization of his ideas and the execution of corresponding trials for alleviating water shortages during periods of drought. In the years 1666–78, extended droughts had greatly restricted the operation of the many waterwheels and brought mining operations (particularly silver mining) virtually to a standstill (A I, 2: 99–103) because the requisite quantity of water was not available to drive the waterwheels and operate the pumping machinery. Alternatives, therefore, had to be sought, and Leibniz found these in the use of wind power. At first, he converted a conventional windmill for the operation of the pumps. An appropriate construction was found for the transmission of the rotating force from the prime mover into the vertical alternating force required for the operation of pumps by means of a system of gearing with crankshafts and connecting rods to the cylinder pistons.

Unfortunately, the experiments did not lead to any long-term success because of varying strengths, directions, and frequencies of the prevailing winds. These setbacks, together with the time and effort required for the erection of a windmill at each and every mine experiencing water shortages, induced Leibniz to develop a new plan by which combined and coordinated wind and water power resources could be exploited. To this end, he undertook a personal inspection and survey of the district in question. In Leibniz's plan for a water circulation system, natural conditions relating to the capacities of ponds, such as evaporation, seepage, and losses of service water for the operation of waterwheels, were important factors to be taken into account. Furthermore, the gradients of the trenches and channels in relation to the rate of flow and the holding or volumetric capacity of the ponds, as well as differences in elevation, had to be considered. The minimal requirement for economical operation was the fulfilment of the condition that, during extended periods of drought, the water reserves in the ponds would suffice for continuous operation over a period of three months.

The optimal solution for economical and unrestricted operation was to be a water circulation system involving a moderate energy requirement combined with the properties of having minimal interference, not being accident-prone, having a reliable and passable maintenance requirement, and, as far as possible, being self-regulating. Leibniz's circulation project involved an extensive and continuous recirculation of wind and water power resources. His scheme suggests a possible inkling or premonition of future pump-storage techniques (Figure 30.5). The circulation system itself entailed a series of additional engineering innovations. Thus, he undertook a number of experiments with horizontally rotating wind machines of the kind previously known in China (LH

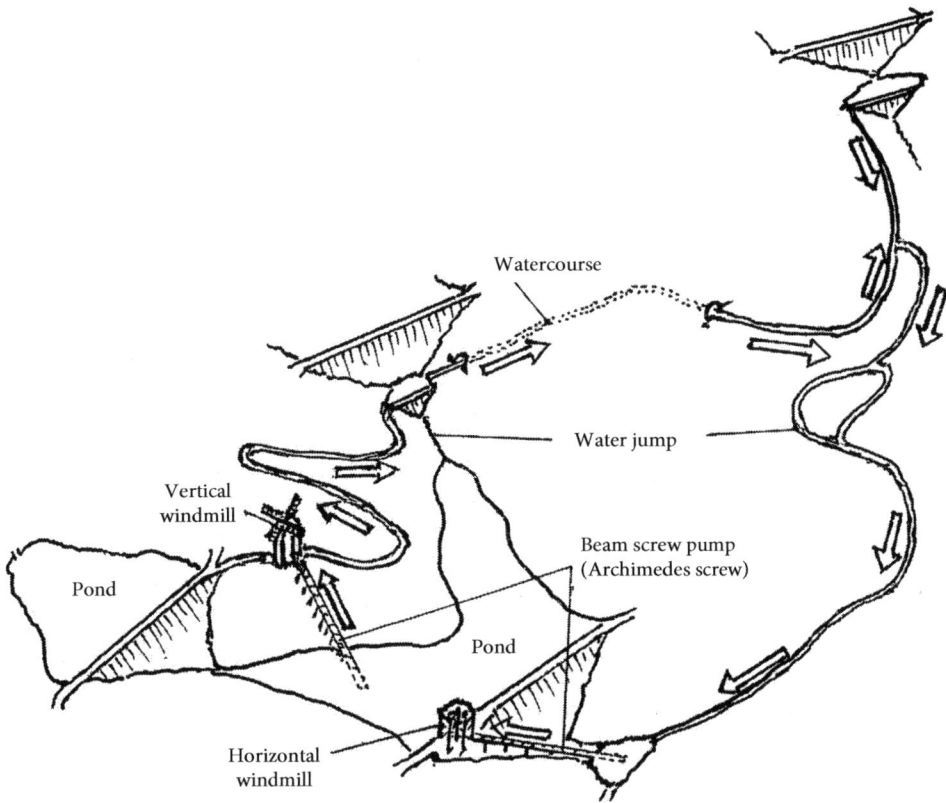

FIGURE 30.5 Water recirculation system (Drawing: J. Gottschalk).

XXXVIII Bl. 366r°), and he planned the direct or immediate application of appropriately designed windmills for the drainage of mines using multiple pumping assemblies connected in series down through the mine. These wind-powered machines were conceived as an alternative to waterwheels, being able to exploit available wind power in times of water shortages.

As part of the circulation system, water was to be raised by the power of windmills using Archimedean screw pumps of the type used in Holland placed, in a series of relatively short stages of 4 to 6 meters, into purpose-built ponds at different levels. Accordingly, by means of series of stair-step ponds, water would be continuously pumped into the uppermost pond reservoirs. From these, by virtue of the force of gravity, cascading waterfalls would power the waterwheels at the mine heads, and the spent water would be returned to the lowest collecting ponds for recirculation, as in modern pump-storage systems.

Leibniz saw another alternative in the indirect use of windmills in mining. In this case, windmills would be erected not at each and every mine head but only at certain locations where the prevailing wind conditions were favorable. The power would then be distributed to the individual mines employing a mechanical transmission system based on the use of the rod engine technology that was widely deployed in German mining districts in the sixteenth and seventeenth centuries.

Leibniz likewise introduced a series of suggestions for the improvement of winding or hoisting machinery used to raise ore from the mines. He found that the imbalance between the conveyor skip and conveyor chains or ropes in hoisting operations frequently resulted in accidents and injuries to the miners and horses used to power the winding machinery in the mines, where the pits were frequently inclined or slanting. Leibniz therefore attempted to achieve complete counterbalance in hoisting operations by introducing a balance or continuous rope following a principle similar to that of the

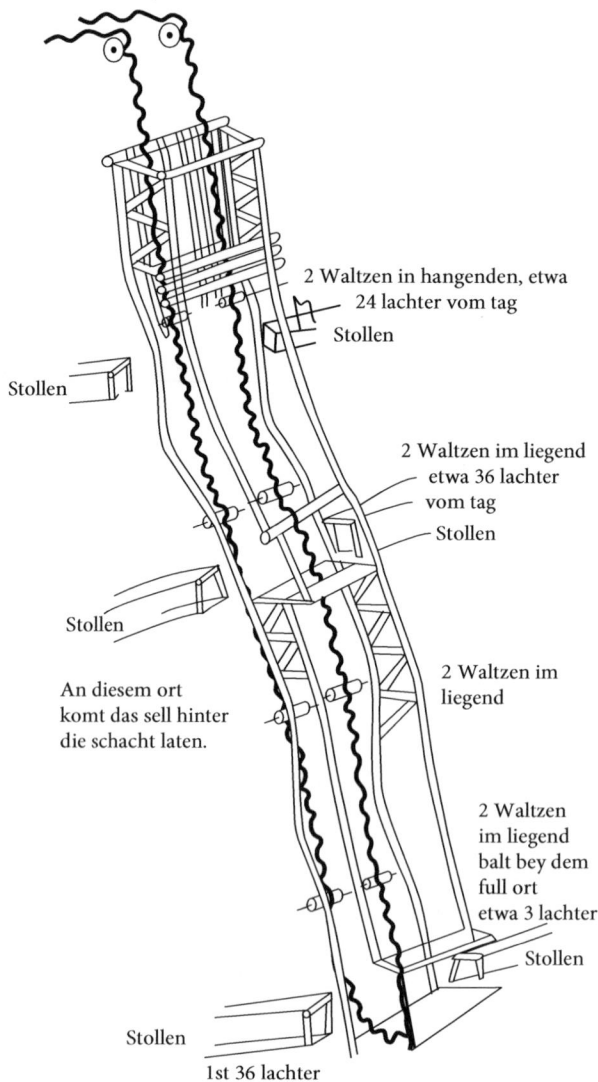

FIGURE 30.6 Endless rope (Stein, E. and Heinekamp, A. 1990: 134, drawing J. Gottschalk).

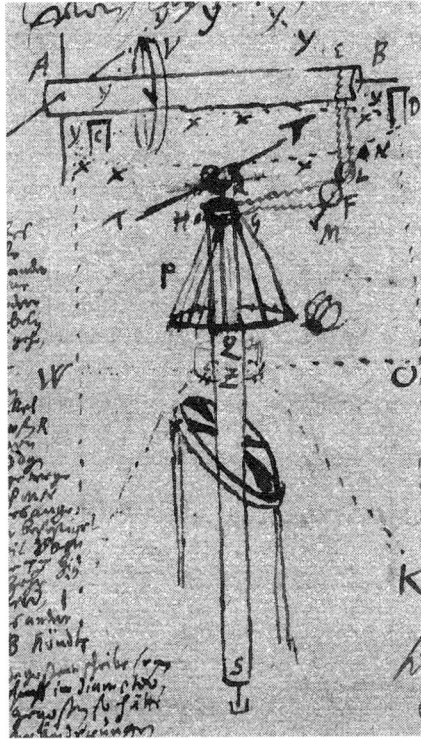

FIGURE 30.7 LH XXXVIII Bl. 68 r°.

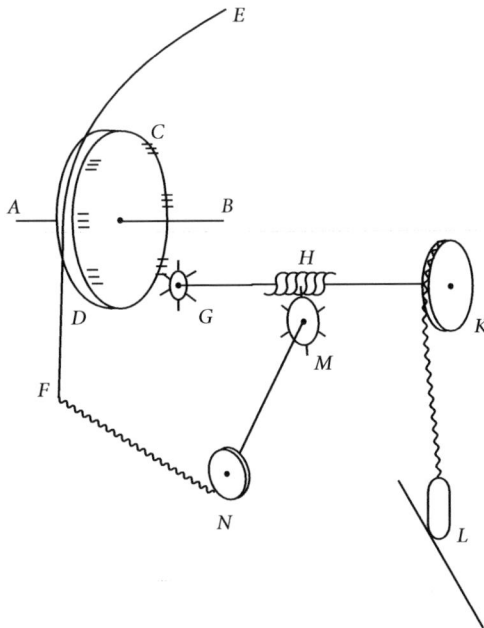

FIGURE 30.8 Inventum memorabile (Drawing: H. Hecht).

paternoster elevator. The empty skip was connected above and below to the hoisting ropes or chains to form an endless connection and provide complete counterbalance. Thus, the sole imbalance arose from the payload, the weight of the ore that was to be raised. As an alternative to this endless chain or rope connection (Figure 30.6), Leibniz also introduced a conical winding drum or bobbin to achieve counterbalance in hoisting operations (Figure 30.7). The conical winding drum or bobbin was mounted on the vertical power shaft (usually of a horse mill), and, in the course of the winding operation, compensation was achieved by virtue of the variation of the length of the lever arm along the conical drum or over the rope-layered bobbin. Leibniz obtained this idea from his observation of a spring-driven clock with its regular operating sequence.

In his desire for technical improvement and with the goal of achieving optimal, simple, and practical solutions, Leibniz wanted to be, to the greatest possible extent, free from unforeseeable disturbance factors, such as human functional failure in the timely rotation of the sails of a vertical windmill into a changed wind direction. For this reason, he conceived an automatic control mechanism to rotate the sails into the prevailing wind direction. In addition, he envisaged a mechanism, his *inventum memorabile* (Figure 30.8), for the timely and regular braking of the wind shaft to avoid excessive damaging strain on the machinery resulting from excessively rapid rotation of the sails.

Volume A VIII, 1 of the Academy Edition shows that many of the technological solutions that Leibniz presented in the context of his mining activities had already been formulated when he was a young man of about twenty-five years. An example of this remarkable precocity is the wheel mechanism outlined in A VIII, 1, N. 67. This mechanism appears also in A VIII, 1, N. 13₅, as well as in the wind clock and the windmill systems of the Harz mining project just discussed.

Moreover, Leibniz often combined procedures or technological processes that other inventors and engineers strictly divided from one another. For instance, he designed an apparatus that realizes type setting and printing as components of one and the same operation (A VIII, 1: N. 56). The same idea was applied to his project of a deciphering machine.

LEIBNIZ'S *MACHINA DECIPHRATORIA*

In 2012, Nicholas Rescher published the reconstruction of a *machina deciphratoria* (deciphering machine) on the basis of hints given by Leibniz in three notes written for his audience with Emperor Leopold I, in Vienna. These notes, Rescher stresses, provide a wealth of information about the deciphering machine, which can be summarized as follows:

1. The machine can be used like a clavichord by touching piano keys.
2. The results will immediately emerge and have only to be copied off by the user.
3. Enciphering and deciphering are inverse operations.

4. Because of a variable use of different encipherments, the code is difficult to crack.
5. The *machina deciphratoria* and the calculating machine are based on a similar principle.
6. It is a smallish machine and therefore easy to transport.

Its operating mode corresponds to that of Leibniz's arithmetical machine. And, just like the well-known calculating machine, it consists of an input mechanism and a recording instrument coupled by one of Leibniz's most fruitful technical innovations, the so-called stepped drum (*Staffelwalze*). Leibniz wished to achieve the letter input through something like a piano keyboard and the letter output by means of a display drum. These work together with the help of an activating drum that is turned to make a rotation with each keystroke and a display drum to which the output letters are attached, in similar fashion to the numbers of the so-called results mechanism (*Resultatzählwerk*) in his arithmetical machine.

The heart of the machine, however, is the already mentioned stepped drum that regulates the enciphering or deciphering processes. Rescher explains as follows: "Let the top slat read EDACFB, while the keyboard in front reads ABCDEF (this simplified six letter alphabet will serve for an example). Then the message BE A BAD BED is encoded as DF E DEC DFC. Leibniz of course, realized that this would not provide a secure encryption, and so used his stepped drum to make the encryption polyalphabetic. Hence the complex rotation of alphabets as controlled by the stepped drum.

The machine accordingly so functions that each time a key is depressed, its stepped drum (Staffelwalze) turns, say, 60 degrees (where there are six steps on the drum). After a certain number of letters are depressed (say three), the hexagonal alphabet drum turns so that another slat appears. The setting of this stepped drum determines the rotation sequence" (Rescher 2012: 40).

At the end of his description of Leibniz's *machina deciphratoria*, Rescher gives a short review of the history of cryptography and characterizes Leibniz's device as "a massive chronological anomaly. For an effective cryptological attack of his cipher machine would call for the mechanized sophistication of the 1930s in the time of the 1670s" (Rescher 2012: 43). That is exactly what we have observed in many of Leibniz's technological ideas and projects. We therefore entirely share Rescher's sentiment that Leibniz conceived projects within a mechanical tradition of thought that, under changed conditions, could be realized today. And we follow him in his understanding of Leibniz as a German Leonardo da Vinci (Rescher 2012: 35).

References

Gottfried Wilhelm Leibniz Bibliothek—Niedersächsische Landesbibliothek Hannover (LH XXXVIII Bl. 68 r°).
Huygens, C. 1672. "Extrait d'une lettre de M. Hugens de l'Academie des Sciences à l'auteur de ce journal, touchant les phenomenes de l'eau purgée d'air." *Journal des Sçavans* (1672): 133–40.

Kirsanov, V. 2008. "Leibniz in Paris." In H. Hecht et al. (eds.), *Kosmos und Zahl. Beiträge zur Mathematik- und Astronomiegeschichte, zu Alexander von Humboldt und Leibniz*. Stuttgart: Steiner.

Leibniz, G. W. 1989. *Philosophical Papers and Letters*. L. E. Loemker (ed.). Dordrecht: Kluwer Academic Publishers.

Rescher, N. 1991. *Leibniz's Monadology. An Edition for Students*. Pittsburgh: University of Pittsburgh Press.

Rescher, N. 2012. *Leibniz and Cryptography. An Account on the Occasion of the Initial Exhibition of the Reconstruction of Leibniz's Cipher Machine*. Pittsburgh: University Library System, University of Pittsburgh.

Stein, E., and A. Heinekamp (eds.). 1990. *Leibniz, Gottfried Wilhelm: Das Wirken des großen Philosophen und Universalgelehrten als Mathematiker, Physiker, Techniker*. Katalog der Erstausstellung an der Universität Hannover vom 9. bis 12. April 1990. Hannover: Schlütersche Verlagsanstalt und Druckerei.

PART VI

SCIENTIFIC ORGANIZATIONS, CULTURAL NETWORKING, AND SCHOLARSHIP

CHAPTER 31

SCIENTIFIC ORGANIZATIONS AND LEARNED SOCIETIES

HARTMUT RUDOLPH

BEFORE entering into a discussion of Leibniz's projects for scientific organizations, it should be noted that Leibniz spoke of "societies" rather than universities. The reason for this is that, like many of his contemporaries, Leibniz did not believe that universities had much potential for innovation. On the other hand, for Leibniz, an academy or society was "an open institutional form of knowledge"; it offered the possibility "to bring together research and at the same time give it a basis between science and life from which it could operate freely."[1] His preference for the term "society" rather than "academy" can be explained by the fact that, in his day, the German usage of the latter term suggested an educational establishment or an art institution rather than a learned society. Finally, Leibniz's concept of "societas" also always implied a connection with society at large.[2]

SCIENCES TO BENEFIT HUMANKIND: LEIBNIZ'S PLANS AS PART OF A STRATEGIC PROJECT

Leibniz's plans for an academy or society of sciences should in fact be understood as part of a broader project or, rather, as part of a large and strategic plan.[3] As shown by his correspondence with Duke Johann Friedrich in the fall of 1679, Leibniz had already

---

[1] Mittelstrass, 17.
[2] Sakai, 165.
[3] Here, compare Schepers, *Demonstrationes* and Antognazza, 90–92.

conceived of this "proposal laid out in universal terms"[4] when he was living in Mainz. Leibniz summarized his plan in a "Demonstrationum catholicarum conspectus" (A VI i n. 14) and offered Johann Friedrich an overview of its key themes (A II i n. 213). In this "Conspectus," issues linked to the Christian religion play a prominent role whereas the traditional disciplines of philosophy—metaphysics, logic, mathematics, physics, and practical philosophy—are merely listed in the "Prolegomena." This conception reflects Leibniz's conviction that reason not only supports the truth of Christianity but is perfected by it, leading to the recognition of the good; that is, to the recognition of what is best in general for humanity. Consequently, in these early plans for an academy, one finds already proposals for the reconciliation of the various Protestant churches with the Roman Catholic church—a task that was "to be realized before all others."[5] More generally, the early drafts show that Leibniz's plans for an academy—like his over-arching life's project—have a political direction, one aiming at establishing a *res publica* of the entire human race.

Early Ideas in Mainz

From his years in Mainz to the very end of his life, Leibniz's plans for an academy were nourished both by his scholarly endeavors and by his political activities. In Leipzig, he could already observe the work of learned societies through the activities of the *Fruchtbringende Gesellschaft* (founded in 1617) as well as the *Societas naturae curiosorum*.[6] In the winter of 1666–67, as a member of the *Nürnberger Gelehrtengesellschaft*, he encountered a society focused on chemical-alchemical experiments.[7] A first detailed picture of his plans emerges from memoranda and appeals that he drew up around 1669 to 1671 for the Elector of Mainz, Philipp von Schönborn (A I i n. 23–25; A IV iv n. 43–45). "Usefulness," as opposed to the mere repetition of scholastic knowledge or the mere satisfaction of curiosity, was the hallmark of the ideas of reform in the seventeenth century, largely inspired by Francis Bacon's *Great Instauration* (1620). The young Leibniz's conception of the "usefulness" of learned societies can be gleaned from his comments in a text from 1669: "That which is most useful for everybody is that which is most pleasing to God . . . But what is most pleasing to God is that which brings about the perfection of the universe . . . Everything which serves for the perfection of mankind leads to the perfection of the universe" (A IV i 552–553).

Leibniz's vision for how the sciences—and especially scientific societies—could benefit Germany comes to light in a number of suggestions that Leibniz started to prepare

---

[4] Schepers, *Demonstrationes*, 8. Schepers finds in this "great plan" the "enduring leitmotiv of Leibniz' creative work" (op. cit., 14).

[5] "Ante omnia efficiendum est"; A IV i n. 46.

[6] Cf. Otto, 53 with reference to Döring and A VI ii 4.

[7] These experiments seem to have struck him as foolish blustering (A IV i 574: "rodomontaden," "narrenwerck"). Cf. Otto, 54 with reference to Ross.

for the Emperor in 1668 and then directed to the Electoral Prince in Mainz. By that time, Leibniz had already made it clear that he thought that Germany was lagging behind other countries in terms of the efficiency of the sciences pursued there. Starting with the proposals he had made for a commission overseeing the entire Empire for the control, coordination, and censure of the book trade,[8] in early 1670 Leibniz proposed a society of learned persons in Germany ("societas eruditorum Germaniae"). This society was meant to cultivate an international exchange with scholars all over the world, work at the establishment of a universal library, set up universal indices, perfect medical science, foster mathematics, coordinate experimental and theoretical research, and, beyond that, regulate all manufacturing and trade. Like his later recommendations, this plan included also proposals for ways of financing the society's work, such as the suggestion of a tax on paper. In short, this plan was an attempt to transfer the regulation of almost every aspect of civic life to the sciences (A I i n. 25).

In his *Grundriß eines Bedenckens von aufrichtung einer Societät in Teütschland zu auffnehmen der Künste und Wißenschaften* (likewise originating in Mainz), Leibniz pointed to the discoveries and inventions of his century. Most of these, particularly in medicine and the natural sciences, would "have a use in human life" if they were applied in an ethically responsible way for the good of humankind. To bring this about was a matter for the "moralists," the "politicians," and the "rectors of public things." They should not simply trace the "luster of divine glory in nature" but, rather, imitate this glory ("Herrlichkeit"); that is to say, imitate the glory of God "by means of good works." God has provided for his creatures in such a way that they are in a position to "mirror" the beauty and harmony of divine creation. Here is the basis of the indissoluble connection between the unending increase of knowledge along with its application, on the one hand, and the "honor of God" ("Ehre Gottes"), on the other.[9] Such insights, be they in medicine or in mechanics, were aimed at "the happiness of the human race": to the best of one's ability, one had to work to make life tolerable; to nourish the poor; to promote justice; to sustain the public order; to advance the well-being of the fatherland; to avoid famine, pestilence, and war; and to spread true religion and piety. As early as in this *Grundriß eines Bedenckens*, Leibniz based the foremost meaning of learning (science) on the divine qualities of justice, wisdom, and goodness or love, which human beings cannot recognize, honor, and praise without further developing all branches of knowledge, applying them in a useful way for the benefit of humankind (A IV i 535): "Hence, too, that which is spent on honorable, God-fearing, and reasonable people for perfecting natural science and the scientific arts must be regarded as supporting a most pious cause, and as a donation to the inexhaustible, true honor of God" (A IV i 535).[10]

The connection between this beneficial use and the honor of God is elucidated by Leibniz a decade later in texts concerned with the significance of religious orders and

[8] Cf. Böger, *seculum*, 55–75.
[9] Cf. Totok, 294–295.
[10] Ibid.

the founding of a *societas theophilorum* (A IV iii n. 130 and 131). "No lovelier hymn can be sung" to the majesty of God than by means of research that does not limit itself to mere curiosity but is oriented toward public usefulness (*publica utilitas*, A IV iii 875). Such reform and improvement of scientific insights could only be the result of the unprejudiced exploration of the "immeasurable field of nature," as Leibniz explained in 1679 in a methodological treatise calling for the establishment of scientific societies (A IV iii 876).

Leibniz believed that the more those engaged in scientific investigation collaborated with those working in such fields as technology, medicine, and handwork, the more useful the fruits of their investigation would be. In his view, Germany had a particular advantage in this respect, and he expected that the work of such societies would not simply benefit other nations but would allow the Germans themselves to harvest the fruits of their practical and scientific abilities in greater measure than ever before.[11]

Overall, from around 1679, Leibniz's writings on this topic show that he conceived of a learned society as a quasi-religious order: a "society of the friends of God for praising God, and setting itself in opposition to the atheism which, imperceptibly, is spreading over the globe."[12] This demand was not determined by any merely apologetic interest in regard to Christianity; rather it was motivated by the need to direct the entire scientific effort toward human progress—a progress which could only be attained when scientists and scholars acted out of love of God; that is, love of the divine perfections, wisdom, and the *summum bonum*. Accordingly, the scientific and methodological advances that Leibniz envisioned for his projects were all supposed to flow ultimately from *amor dei* or charity.

On the other hand, in his early sketches, just as in later years, Leibniz explicitly distanced himself from the utopias of a Thomas More, a Tommaso Campanella, or a Francis Bacon (*Ad scientiam generalem praefatio. De insula utopica* [c. 1688], A VI iv A, n. 207). Leibniz saw in utopian thought an obstacle to the attainment of human happiness and preferred to direct his attention to what could be achieved in reality. Each person should work in line with his capacity and in his "sphaera activitatis" (i.e., according to his place in society) toward the common good. Reaching this goal did not call for extraordinary means; rather, a high degree of usefulness could be attained even with a relatively slight effort. In his view, "establishing a society, though small at the start

---

[11] Hence, Böger sees the plan to establish an Academy (A IV n. 44) as "extremely imperial-patriotic in its tone" and calls it a "testimony" to the "national mood of readiness to get going" in Germany following the Thirty Years War (*seculum*, 92–93). It should be noted that Leibniz's statements must not be read in the sense of a nationalism of the kind produced in the nineteenth and early twentieth centuries. The reference to the supposedly specific German abilities by no means detracts from the global direction of Leibniz's intentions.

[12] "Societas Theophilorum ad celebrandas laudes Dei opponenda gliscenti per orbem Atheismo" (fall 1678); A IV iii n. 131.

but nonetheless well founded, will be one of the easiest and most important means" to reach the common good (A IV i 536).

Winning the Great Princes

In an age of enlightened absolutism, Leibniz was aware that the only way to realize his goal was to enlist the support of the "great princes" and territorial rulers. Therefore, he sought to persuade those in power that they could not only win for themselves undying fame, but also derive immeasurable usefulness from such an engagement.[13] If they applied their efforts to the happiness of humankind instead of getting lost in bagatelles and seeking pleasure in games and cabals, they would in fact be working for their own fulfilment and satisfaction.

Leibniz also believed that the success of his academy projects (and, incidentally, of his economic projects) would be jeopardized if the plans were discussed in the public sphere rather than prepared in secret. For this reason, he criticized the academy proposals advanced by his teacher Erhard Weigel: "One ought to have helped a number of things along without propagating them in public before one had sought support for such initiatives at courts. For if initially such ideas have been spread among the people and have been discussed in public forums, the chance of their being realized is diminished."[14] Thus, all Leibniz's plans and projects and all his initiatives for founding scholarly societies are characterized by their having been directed to princely houses. This also hold true in the case of the academy plans that were developed during Leibniz's final years in Paris, especially the *Drôle de Pensée* (1675)—a proposal that was certainly significantly shaped by specific experiences in Paris.[15]

In brief, as long as Leibniz continued in princely service (i.e., from his Mainz period onward), we may regard him as someone who was urgently seeking to bring about the establishment of learned societies. Especially in the years in Mainz, he encountered, in the inner court circle, ideas and plans that were similar to his own conceptions or even suggested and sharpened them.[16]

---

[13] Leibniz to Johann Sebastian Haes, February 24, 1695 (a draft never sent), A III vi 304–305.

[14] Leibniz to Johann Andreas Schmidt, February 18, 1695, A I xi 297; quotation of the Latin original in Otto, 62, n. 53.

[15] Cf. in this connection the analysis of Böger, *seculum*, 96–106.

[16] For instance, in 1669, his sympathetic patron Johann Christian von Boineburg had conceived the plan of an "Universitas praecipuarum mundi scientiarum et artium . . . in Germania" inspired by the Royal Academy in Paris and the Royal Society of London (Brather, with reference to Karl Wild 1899, xix, n. 16a). Similar thoughts appeared in the project (that would eventually fail) of a "Universitas Brandenburgica gentium, scientiarum et artium" advanced by the Swedish diplomat Bengt Skytte, whom Leibniz met during his time in Frankfurt on Main in 1668.

Leibniz's Initiatives before the Establishment of a Society of Sciences in Berlin

When in 1676 Leibniz once again entered princely service in Hanover, he had the advantage of many years of practical experience of the work of academies, notably the Parisian *Académie des sciences*.[17] At the same time, he used his years in Paris to develop connections within the Royal Society (of which he became a member in 1673), having already established contact with its secretary, Heinrich Oldenburg, in Mainz in 1670.

Hanover

After moving to the court in Hanover, Leibniz discovered in Johann Friedrich von Braunschweig-Lüneburg a prince who "with his extraordinary talents and his great virtue" worked for "public welfare" ("le bien public")[18]—and for Leibniz such work was an essential precondition for the realization of his plans for an academy. Starting in 1676, Leibniz composed a number of documents and memoranda connected with the early proposals in Mainz but which were enriched by the deeper understanding he had gained in Paris. In particular, he promoted an *art of invention* which, thanks to a universal language or *characteristica universalis*, would make the entire encyclopedia of human knowledge universally available and would open up a completely new way of expanding knowledge in all areas guided by the ultimate aim of improving the human condition.[19]

In a number of letters to Johann Friedrich of 1679, Leibniz sets forth with great frankness what was new and revolutionary in his vision, vis-à-vis (for instance) Francis Bacon's *Novum Organum* and the way in which the sciences in France or England were conducted.[20] Athanasius Kircher's *polygraphie* or the *ars magna* of Ramón Lull were described as toys in comparison with the *scientia generalis* and *characteristica universalis* that Leibniz was hoping to develop. In his view, the learned society he was proposing to

---

[17] Cf. for instance Leibniz's report from December 20, 1672, to Philipp von Schönborn with its detailed information on the cultivation of the sciences by the Royal Academy there, particularly on the accomplishments of its "most famous" member, Christiaan Huygens (A I i 296–300). Leibniz was elected member of the Académie in 1699.

[18] In September 1677, to Jean Gallois (A I i 379); cf. also I. Böger, op. cit., vol. I, 115–116 and vol. II, 47. Böger shows that the plans and drafts that Leibniz produced for Johann Friedrich were an indispensable stage in Leibniz's society project; cf. Böger, *seculum*, 115–118.

[19] On this, cf. for example Heinrich Schepers, "Einleitung" to A VI iv A, l–lv.

[20] On the gradual development of this new approach, see, along with the writings from 1676 (A VI iii n. 55 and 56), those from 1679 pertaining to *scientia generalis, characteristica, calculus universalis* (A VI iv A), as well as Leibniz's correspondence with Johann Friedrich, especially in A II i 2nd ed., n. 197a.

his Prince would tower over all the academies hitherto regarded as exemplary (A II i 2nd ed., 702–703). The financing of the project was meant to be made possible through technical renovations of the Ducal mines in the Harz. However, Leibniz's hopes for the establishment of an academy were dealt a bitter blow when Johann Friedrich died at the end of 1679.

Habsburg 1688

In October 1688, Leibniz was finally granted the audience with Emperor Leopold I that he had wished for twenty years earlier (A IV iv 15, 40, 50, 79). The most detailed of his notes (A IV iv n. 8) document that all the proposals presented to the Emperor led to the recommendation to found a society of sciences or other similar "institutions and administrations." Their purpose was to gather all knowledge contributing to the good of humankind. To this effect, Leibniz had not only worked out a comprehensive series of proposals but was also busying himself in virtually all areas as an innovator (A IV iv 79). Almost all the points of the program presented to the Emperor reflected ideas that could be found in his early writings as well as proposals expounded in later memoranda and "instructions," notably those on the founding of the Brandenburg Academy. Among other things, in his communication with Emperor Leopold, Leibniz connected his project of a universal characteristic and formal language with the idea of a Christian mission in the East among the Chinese and Japanese (A IV iv 62).

The *Memoire* of 1692

In 1692, in a *Memoire pour des Personnes éclairées et de bonne intention* (A IV iv n. 123), Leibniz set out the key elements of his plan for an academy. He turned to those intellectuals and enlightened people who are of good will but let themselves be distracted by trifles and thus neglect to do what is good. Leibniz was convinced that, if capable individuals applied themselves to practical and concrete work in the public interest (*application*) and exchanged knowledge and skills (*communication*), in a mere ten years more could be achieved than in several hundred years. "As far as I am concerned," Leibniz wrote, "I put forward the great principle of metaphysics and morality," namely, that the world is governed by the most perfect intelligence and reason, a universal monarchy of an all-powerful and perfectly wise monarch. His subjects are all spirits, that is, substances that are capable of using their reason and thus forming a community with God. Everything else is nothing more than an instrument of the glory of God or an instrument of public happiness. The more spirits have good will, contributing to the glory of God, the more they will participate in this happiness (A IV iv 613–614).

A striking feature of the *Memoire* is how closely Leibniz links his conception of an academy to his metaphysics—indeed, paragraphs XXXV and XXXVI of the *Discourse de Métaphysique* are cited almost verbatim. Once again, it is clear that Leibniz's efforts were to a large extent motivated by his metaphysical insights and by his awareness of his own responsibility to advance the glory of God. This sense of responsibility prompted him to seek the swift realization of his plans. He frequently spoke of the ten years ahead of him that could not be allowed to go to waste, and he pointed out that humankind would need centuries to regain opportunities if they were lost now.[21] This sense of urgency suggests that Leibniz viewed the progress of humankind and the increased provision of common welfare as closely tied to his plans for his own life. The *Memoire* was intended to bring the best minds of his time together since any individual would always be overwhelmed by the task at hand. The most learned should communicate not only among intellectuals but also with those directly involved in mastering practical life, that is, technicians, physicians, handworkers, and farmers. This communication, whether proceeding orally or in written form, was meant to remain strictly oriented to general usefulness.

Once again, Leibniz emphasized what was new in his conception of an academy in comparison with similar projects in Europe. Other academies limited themselves to particular areas of knowledge and made no attempt to unite the various branches of knowledge. Their publications only served curiosity. They failed to focus on general usefulness and on the perfection of humankind. Leibniz expected that academies would develop the ability to promote activities that could have an impact in a short period of time, since "time is the most precious of all things."

Comments made by Leibniz in the following year betray a certain disillusion regarding princes' readiness to accept his idea of an academy. When "usefulness is not immediately to be grasped with the hands," the princes seemed unapproachable. As a result, his hopes were directed at rich sponsors without "laughing heirs." Their endowments could offer the societies secure financing, without the founders needing to exert influence on the direction of the society. Such rich private persons could thereby earn for themselves besides "divine reward in heaven . . . immortal fame on earth."[22] Leibniz was even led to consider the cultivation of silkworms as a means of securing funding for societies (A IV v n. 69). Despite all his disappointments, however, he continued to search for opportunities to gain the support of a prince for his plans.

THE SOCIETY OF SCIENCES IN BERLIN

Leibniz saw just such a chance in the fall of 1694. Following the death of Samuel Pufendorf, the Berlin court historiographer, Leibniz hoped to be recommended for the post that was now vacant. To this end, he not only presented a detailed summary of the specific duties of a court historiographer but also outlined how a prince should promote

---

[21] Cf. Leibniz to Haes (supra note 13); A III vi 304; here cf. also Otto, 59, n. 43 with further citations.
[22] Leibniz in June 1693 to Huldreich von Eyben (A I ix n. 329). See also Brather, xxiii, n. 49.

the culture of his country and increase the prosperity of his subjects.[23] Leibniz began by contrasting Germany with France and the Netherlands. These neighboring countries made efforts early on to develop trade and manufacturing; their populations had grown considerably, agriculture was progressing, and all this was attractive to capital. In Germany, people had only given thought "substantially late" to the question of what is economically necessary. This difference in attitude had led to a loss of wealth in the Empire, which had in turn resulted in a reversal in the thinking of a number of enlightened princes. The late Elector of Brandenburg, Friedrich Wilhelm, had attended to these matters most assiduously, and Leibniz listed a number of measures that had led to a notable strengthening of the economy. These measures had in turn benefited the poor and the sick and were therefore also an act of brotherly love and piety (in this connection Leibniz cited Matthew 25:40). With its universities and grammar schools, the electorate had a good educational system at its disposal, and in its extensive territory there were excellent talents. Therefore, it was time to establish a Brandenburg learned society, Leibniz argued, following the example of the royal societies in London and Paris. This society should gather together learned men from all branches of science, particularly the natural sciences and mathematics, to collect "useful ideas" by means of "inventions and experiments."

In brief, in this initiative from early 1695, Leibniz linked his proposals to the specific situation of the leading rulers in Europe at the time of the Nine Years' War (1688–97), seeing the Electoral Prince of Brandenburg as virtually the only person among the princes of Europe who could develop his country in this way for the general good.[24]

First Beginnings of a Berlin Learned Society

Leibniz's promptings in regard to the founding of a "societas Electoralis Brandenburgica" did not come in isolation from his personal ambitions. This can already be seen in his remark that he "could contribute something to the good establishment of such a plan" (A I xi n. 120). Still, the founding of a Berlin learned society did not develop directly from the proposals Leibniz himself had made in 1695. Starting in 1696, there were efforts at the Berlin court to build an observatory of the kind that had already existed for thirty years in Paris and London. The archivist of the Cabinet, Johann Jacob Chuno, and the judicial councillor, Johann Gebhard Rabener, can be described as the moving spirits behind this effort. Leibniz first heard of the plan for the construction of the observatory via Chuno in the fall of 1697, and he immediately saw in it an opportunity to promote his ongoing project of the establishment of a Berlin learned society. In the winter of 1698, the Electoral Princess Sophie Charlotte charged her court preacher, Daniel Ernst Jablonski, to contact Leibniz and to include him in preparations for erecting an observatory.[25]

---

[23] Cf. A I xi n. 120–123.

[24] See A I xi n. 122.

[25] Cf. D. E. Jablonski on March 5, 1698 (A I xv n. 268).

Once again, Leibniz responded with the proposal of expanding the project to include the founding a society of the sciences. The occasion of a visit to Hanover by the Electoral Princess gave him the additional possibility of presenting Sophie Charlotte with this request in conversation.[26] However, in August, he learned from Jablonski that even the plan for an observatory was not winning sufficient support at court and that more favorable "Conjunctiones" would have to be waited for.[27] These would not become available until the winter of 1700.

Inception and Plans

Leibniz used the occasion of the renewed discussion of calendar reform among the Protestant estates in the Empire in 1699 to propose that the observatory and learned society be financed from the proceeds from a calendar monopoly. It appears that this suggestion finally moved the Elector to agree to both proposals.

Leibniz's plan had as its goal an academy that would be unique in Europe in its combination of scientific activity and practical usefulness (i.e., in its contribution to the improvement of the general conditions of life). In his view, the two Royal Societies in Paris and London and the Accademia del Cimento in Florence could serve as a model, but only to a limited degree.[28] The way he saw it, these societies certainly had outstanding scholars at their disposal, but pursued their science "in curiosis," neglecting social usefulness in general and the increase of "comfort for human life and nourishment of the lower classes" in particular. As a decade earlier, in his proposal for the Emperor, Leibniz had already connected the idea of a mission to peoples in the Far East with the project of an academy, now he linked the all-important missionary task to the growth of the sciences and the "increase of general usefulness" in order to form an "indissoluble threefold rope" ("funiculum triplex indissolubile").

In a letter of March 26, 1700, to Jablonski (A I xviii n. 275), Leibniz accepted the office of President of the Society. A few days later he received word that the Electoral Prince had made it a condition of his support for the Society that it also devote itself to the "Kultur" of the German language.[29] With this request Friedrich III was surely following the French model, which included the cultivation of the French language among the tasks of the Paris Académie. For Leibniz this represented nothing more than the fulfilment of a long-standing desire—one attested most recently in the extensive *Unvorgreiffliche Gedancken* of 1697.[30] His immediate reaction was to send a slightly altered copy of the *Unvorgreiffliche Gedancken* to Berlin.[31] With the additional involvement of the

---

[26] Cf. Böger, 377.

[27] D. E. Jablonski on August 6, 1698, to Leibniz (A I xv n. 488); cf. also Böger, 377.

[28] See Leibniz's memorandum from March 25/26, 1700 (A IV viii n. 72).

[29] D. E. Jablonski, on March 23, 1700, to Leibniz (A I xviii 471–472).

[30] Cf. *Consultatio de Naturae cognitione* (A IV iii n. 133) and the lengthy *Unvorgreiffliche Gedancken betreffend die Ausübung und Verbesserung der teutschen Sprache* (A IV vi n. 79).

[31] Cf. correspondence between March 19 and 28 in A IV viii 406.

humanities, the planned Berlin Society would place itself in a unique position in Europe with regard to the broad range of sciences it was pledging to promote.[32]

Foundation und Construction

Finally arriving in Berlin on May 10, 1700, Leibniz was given the opportunity to clarify his vision in a number of conversations with the Electoral Prince and various court officials.[33] Probably in June 1700,[34] a memorandum surfaced in which the general purpose of the planned institution was described for the first time through the famous formula "theoria cum praxi zu vereinen" (to unite theory with practice). It is clear that Leibniz's "*theoria cum praxi* signified not only a scientific and technical principle, but also an ethical principle."[35] The two founding documents, both composed by Leibniz in July 1700,[36] mirrored this conception. Leibniz envisaged an organization of the society into "Departments"[37]: one for natural and medical investigations; one for mathematical, astronomical, and mechanical sciences; one for Germanic and historical studies; and, finally, one for literary-historical and Oriental inquiries. This arrangement marked the start of something new, namely, an organization linking theory to practice and no longer dividing the sciences according to their respective methodologies without any consideration for political and social needs (as was at the time still the case with the Académie Française).[38]

The most significant project that came to fruition during Leibniz's Presidency was the *Miscellanea Berolinensia*[39]—the periodical that was to document the work of the Society for the world of learning, following the model of the periodical publications of the Academies of Paris and London. Leibniz worked hard at this publication and contributed papers on various subjects, including mathematics and physics. After a prolonged period of gestation, the first volume appeared in 1710.

Secondary literature generally refers to the large gap between Leibniz's hopes for the Berlin project and the state in which he left it behind. The reasons for this are many and diverse, but it is clear that difficulties of an organizational nature were a significant obstacle. The plan of holding regular sessions with learned members did not succeed, and,

---

[32] Here also compare Böger, 381–385.

[33] Compare Jablonski's diary entries for the period from May 10–25, 1700. On the very day of his arrival, Jablonski showed him the square on which the observatory was to be built. In addition to the Society, the desired church union between Lutherans and Calvinists was a theme of the discussions at court; cf. Kvačala, 279–280.

[34] Cf. A IV viii 425.

[35] Mittelstrass, 17.

[36] A IV viii n. 79 and 80.

[37] Brather, 200–208.

[38] Here compare also Brather, 201 and Böger, *seculum*, 385.

[39] The complete title is: *Miscellanea Berolinensia ad incrementum scientiarum, ex scriptis Societati Regiae Scientiarum exhibitis*; cf. Brather, 279–293.

in those crucial early years, no outstanding scholars could be recruited as members. Leibniz also had limited time to devote to his duties as president because of his duties to the House of Hanover. Furthermore, the financial means required for supporting the Academy and realizing its projects were lacking precisely when these (particularly in the case of the natural sciences and technology) were supposed to serve the improvement of the conditions of life of the population. Finally, the new Prussian monarchy suffered at the time from considerable financial difficulties. The hopes related to Leibniz's demand "to unite theory with practice," remained largely unfulfilled. Nonetheless, this institution conceived by Leibniz developed in the course of the eighteenth century, above all under Friedrich II, to become one of the leading scholarly societies in Europe.

INITIATIVES AFTER THE FOUNDATION IN BERLIN

Leibniz himself would scarcely have been under any delusions regarding the extent to which his vision was being achieved in Berlin. However, this awareness did not deter him from continuing to press for the foundation of academies elsewhere. The fact that he was not blind to the conditions that were required for the realization of such a project can be seen in his relatively muted reaction to Landgraf Ernst von Hessen-Kassel's plan to found an academy.[40] As Leibniz saw it, the seat of one of the princely houses was required if an academy were to bear the global fruits that Leibniz hoped for. Accordingly, his efforts were directed toward Dresden, toward the imperial court in Vienna, and finally toward the court of the Czar, always in the hope of creating a further learned society that could be linked with all the others.

Saxony

Ever since 1695, Leibniz had been trying to attract the attention of the Electoral Prince of Saxony.[41] His visits to Sophie Charlotte enabled him to meet the envoy of Electoral Saxony, Jakob Heinrich von Flemming, who enjoyed the special favor of the Electoral Prince. For even longer, Leibniz had cultivated connections with the Jesuit Father Carlo Maurizio Vota, who was able, as the father confessor of the Polish king, to influence Augustus the Strong. In March 1704, Leibniz sent his co-worker, Johann George Eckhart, to Saxony with instructions and letters of recommendation for Flemming and Vota,[42] in the hope of getting his project moving. Among other things, Eckhart was supposed to

---

[40] Leibniz to Haes (supra note 13); cf. also Otto, 61, n. 51.
[41] Cf. here and in what follows, Otto, 62–81.
[42] A I xxiii n. 113, 114, and 116.

enquire whether Leibniz could be named president (Praeses) of the proposed academy and whether his long-standing friend and correspondent, Ehrenfried Walter von Tschirnhaus, could be established as vice-president. Leibniz had not only given Eckhart instructions that he had already drafted in March; in case Eckhart was granted an audience with the King, Leibniz had also provided detailed documents that Augustus the Strong needed only sign for the Society to come into effect.

Leibniz's proposal extended the tasks envisaged for the new Society even beyond those planned for the Berlin version.[43] The Society was to actively offer counsel on all practical areas of public administration (including statistics and a "house of intelligence"),[44] the military, schools, health matters and the world of books (including book censorship and the control of textbooks), the system of traffic, commerce, industry, mining, iron works, agriculture, and forestry. The task of developing protection against damage from the elements was also to be assigned to the Society, as it had already been in Brandenburg. One could nearly speak of an overarching institution which, entrusted with far-reaching competences, was to help shape life in Electoral-Princely Saxony in all its essential aspects.[45]

The Imperial Society of Sciences in Vienna

As already shown, earlier plans for an academy were aimed at the capital of the Habsburgs and their Empire. In 1704 (the same year in which he also started to draft proposals for the establishment of academies in Saxony and Russia),[46] Leibniz once again reiterated his ideas for an academy in a memorandum to the Emperor's brother-in-law, the Elector Johann Wilhelm von der Pfalz.[47] However, the death of Leopold I in 1705 effectively thwarted this plan. Leibniz was not able to travel again to Vienna until December 1708. Soon after arriving, he discovered that the conditions under the new emperor, Joseph I, were not unfavorable to him. Among other people, he could count on the sympathetic hearing of the Emperor's wife, Wilhelmine Amalia (daughter of Johann Friedrich of Braunschweig-Lüneburg). It was, however, the highly regarded Prince Eugene of Savoy who became Leibniz's most important friend, advocate, and champion in Vienna.

In connection with his efforts to obtain a salaried position as Imperial Aulic Councillor (*Reichshofrat*), Leibniz revived his project of a *Collegium historicum imperiale* of twenty years earlier. As shown by his proposal to the influential Cardinal

---

[43] Apart from A I xxiii n. 113, the plan also emerges from Eckhart's "Travel Journal" that begins on August 18, 1704; Bodemann, 190–198.

[44] Here compare Otto, 82, n. 168.

[45] Böger, 423; according to Böger, the project is here "unmistakably converting into the hybrid or the utopian" (ibid).

[46] See *Specimen Einiger Puncten, darinnen Moscau denen Scienzen beförderlich seyn könnte* (1704); A I xxiii n. 49 (cf. A I xxiii liv); Böger II 159, n. 120.

[47] Cf. Bergmann.

von Lamberg, archbishop of Passau, the Historical Collegium was meant to include also auxiliary sciences, suggesting that Leibniz conceived of it as conducive to the establishment of a society of science. However, it was only under Emperor Karl VI that these plans began to come to fruition. Shortly after his coronation at the beginning of 1712, Leibniz (now sixty-five) was finally assured of gaining the position of *Reichshofrat*.[48] The first audience granted to him by Karl VI was in the middle of January 1713. A month or so earlier, on December 18, Leibniz had spelled out for the Emperor his activities as a scholar and political counsellor.[49] According to his own account, he had "from his youth onwards" reflected on the way he might accomplish something notable "for the honor of God and for the very best of the human race by means of the sciences." Far more would have come about, Leibniz continued, "if I had had instead the good fortune to find a great potentate, who likewise on this point (namely the sciences) might show a special fondness in encouraging the glory of God and what is best for his subjects." "All this," he concluded, "I hope finally to find with his Imperial Majesty."

Just as in Saxony, Leibniz did not neglect to hint that he himself was available to direct such a society. Undeniably, Leibniz's efforts to gain a salaried position as *Reichshofrat* were linked to his plans for an academy since he could have hardly moved from Hanover to lead the planned academy without the assurance of a firm appointment in the Viennese court. Nevertheless, Leibniz confessed to the Dowager Empress Amalia, due to his advanced age, it was unlikely he would be able to enjoy the fruits of the project. His striving was all the same to contribute to the glory of God, to serve the Emperor and his realm, and to be useful to his neighbor[50].

As preparation for the audience with Karl VI in January 1713, Leibniz composed a number of documents, one of which—a draft in Latin for an Imperial German Society— went so far as to envisage the academy as an institution covering the entire Empire.[51] On August 14, 1713, Leibniz finally received the imperial assurance[52] of the establishment of the academy as well as the assurance that he would be named as its Director. A handsome salary of 4,000 Gulden was also promised. Just as in the case of earlier projects, Leibniz provided detailed proposals for the financing of the academy; these proposals aimed not only to ensure that it would not be a permanent drain on the imperial purse but also to allow it to generate wealth for the country. Unfortunately, however, despite the great sympathy for the project in general, Leibniz's proposals for financing the academy did not meet with the agreement of Karl VI.[53] Leaving Vienna in September 1714, Leibniz saw in the influential Eugene of Savoy a kindred spirit to whom he could entrust a letter

---

[48] Herzog Anton Ulrich to Leibniz on February 3, 1712; Transkriptionen 1712, n. 47; http://www.gwlb. de/Leibniz/Leibnizarchiv/Veroeffentlichungen/Transkriptionen1712.pdf (22.2.2015); Faak's account of Leibniz's efforts is still valuable.

[49] Idem, n. 386.

[50] Klopp, 216–217.

[51] Cf. Klopp, 187.

[52] Klopp, 241–242.

[53] Klopp, 203.

summarizing his vision for the Society and distilling the plans he had developed over decades for the establishment of academies.[54]

In the end, however, despite all the good will for the project, the uncertainty on how to finance this costly enterprise prompted the Emperor to hold back (and so it was not the case, as the eighteenth-century rumor had it, that the failure to realize this project was due to Jesuit reservations about placing a Protestant in charge of such a key institution). Until the very last days of his life, Leibniz remained very hopeful that the imperial academy would indeed be founded. Prince Eugene's victory in Peterwarde, three months before Leibniz's death, and the prospect of an imminent end to the sixth Turkish War gave further impetus to this hope. On the other hand, Leibniz knew that he would not live to see the founding of the society himself, faced as he was with rapidly deteriorating health. During the very last days of his life, Leibniz turned again to Berlin and Vienna,[55] composing letters concerned with the development of the Society in Berlin and with the steps that were necessary for the establishment of a Society in Vienna.

Russia

Leibniz saw in Peter the Great a manifestly brilliant ruler whose plans for reform held out great promise not only for his own realm but also for all of Christendom. Compared with the academic projects drafted for Germany, most of the seven proposals for the Czar, contained in a Memorandum of 1697 (A IV vi n. 40) are of a preliminary nature. According to Leibniz, Russia was still a *tabula rasa* from the point of view of the existence of scientific institutions, and so certain preparatory measures were in order for the sciences to be of benefit to the land and its ruler. Leibniz suggested that an "Établissement General pour les Sciences et Arts" be set up first of all. It should be staffed by scholars who were distinguished by the breadth of their knowledge and who would have been expected to manage a large network of correspondence. As regards financing, Leibniz stressed that time was of the essence: the sooner the project was realized, the richer its fruits would be. A delay could easily prove to be "too expensive." Among other things, he proposed a relaxation of the rules that restricted the movement of foreign scholars into the country. Next, he explained that libraries, printing establishments, cabinets of rarities, botanical gardens, and zoological collections would all be required for the dissemination of human knowledge. Moreover, the liberalization of travel as well as improvements to the transport system would allow access to the knowledge that was available abroad. An educational system also had to be built up. The aim of schools and academies should be to introduce young people to the sciences and to promote the development of the virtues. Their curricula should include history, mathematics, German, and the ancient languages (above all, Latin). Leibniz also recommended the promotion

[54] Leibniz to Eugene of Savoy (August 17, 1714). Klopp, 246–252.
[55] Leibniz to M. L. von Printzen (November 3, 1716) and to Heraeus (November 1, 1716).

of agriculture and of manufacturing, the expansion of traffic routes, and the draining of marshes.

His contacts with a number of foreign scientists in Russia—among them Heinrich van Huyssen (a teacher of the Czar's son from 1702 to 1705) and Nicolaas Witsen[56]—were not immediately fruitful. During his short stay in Dresden in early 1704, Leibniz made contact with the Russian plenipotentiary Johann Reinhold von Patkul. In a Memorandum delivered to him, Leibniz proposed that the scientific academies currently in Germany, and especially the Saxon Society, "extend their effectiveness on to Moscow." Under the Czar's protection and with his help, the Society was to carry out its observations and research projects in Russia. Leibniz also listed a series of other capitals and border cities in which research establishments should be founded. The spectrum of research areas should be extended from "astronomical-magnetic" observations to surveys of the Earth, from geology and the exploration of the animal and plant world to the history and language of the peoples of the gigantic Russian realm. For various reasons,[57] this initiative was not carried out either.

Leibniz's correspondence with Johann Christoph Urbich lasted longer. Urbich first entered service in the court of Hanover in 1683 and, from 1707 to 1712, worked as the Russian envoy in Hanover and Vienna. He rightly saw that Leibniz was favorable to the idea of Hanover drawing closer to the Czar, even though at that time the Czar was by no means uncontroversial in Europe. During his short stay in Vienna, Leibniz met with Urbich, who asked him for a memorandum for the Czar on the "Introduction of the arts and sciences" to Russia.[58] In this document, Leibniz once again pointed to the opportunities afforded by the introduction of brand new scientific institutions, especially in regard to the education of youth (considered by Leibniz as having the highest priority). The improvement of the conditions of life for humankind and the celebration of the glory of God that this would bring about were, as always, central to Leibniz's plans. The true purpose of scientific studies was, according to Leibniz, "human felicity."

Apart from details applying specifically to Russia, these proposals were essentially the same as those contained in the Memorandum for the Czar (1697) and in the drafts for the establishment of societies in Saxony and in the Habsburg lands. A report from Urbich years later indicated that the Czar in fact received the content of Leibniz's memo via Urbich. In addition to thinking highly of Leibniz on account of his learning,[59] the Czar also appreciated his efforts over the years in favor of a more friendly policy toward Russia on the part of the House of Hanover[60].

---

[56] On this and on further contacts, see Guerrier. In 1710, Huyssen became the first person in Russia admitted as an active member in the Berlin Society.

[57] Patkul ended up in a Swedish prison and was killed there in 1707. In any case, in these years, the Czar was distracted from political reforms at home by the Nordic War.

[58] Guerrier II, 95–100; here cf. Guerrier I, 68–71; translation into French in Leibniz, Le droit.

[59] Cf. the extract from a report of Urbich for the Russian chancellor Golofkin from March 5, 1712; Guerrier II, 209.

[60] Cf. Guerrier I, 93–104.

Thanks to Urbich's positive reports, Leibniz was therefore not unknown to the Czar when, at the end of October 1711, their first personal meeting took place in Torgau. The occasion was Anton Ulrich's daughter's marriage to the Czar's son. Leibniz prepared himself carefully for this meeting, drafting a number of proposals.[61] Much that was familiar from earlier drafts turned up again in these documents: the plea for the education of young people so that they could learn mathematics, the natural sciences, and a number of languages; for the introduction of a social system (e.g., pensions, insurance, health care); for the provision of sources of income by means of banks and lotteries; and for improved infrastructure, such as better routes for traffic and for the exchange of goods. There were also proposals for mines, manufacturing, and agriculture. Above all, Leibniz insisted, as ever, on the need to promote the sciences. In this regard, he saw a special task for Russia in so far as it could serve as a bridge connecting the scientific discoveries of Europe with those of China.

Leibniz's focus on mathematical and scientific research, and on astronomical observations and investigations of magnetism "from Finland to the border of Chinese Tartary," particularly matched the interests of the Czar. These investigations, combined with the research that Leibniz had already undertaken into the various languages of the peoples in Peter's vast empire, as well as their history, were meant to make Leibniz's project of an academy in Russia accessible to the Czar. His obvious interest gave hope to Leibniz that a decisive step toward the realization of his major life project could be achieved in the last years of his life. This, at least, is how a letter he wrote on January 16, 1712, can be interpreted. According to Leibniz, nothing else had been lacking to him "than a great master who is sufficiently willing to take charge of this matter." That Leibniz was not from Russia should not have been an obstacle:

> for I am not one of those devoted solely to their native land or some other particular nation; instead, I aim at the benefit of the entire human race; for I consider heaven as the fatherland and all well-disposed men as its fellow citizens, and I prefer accomplishing much good among the Russians than only a little with the Germans or other Europeans . . ., for my inclination and pleasure are aimed at the best in general. (Guerrier II, 208)

A few months before his death, Leibniz had a final opportunity to converse with Peter the Great when he was spending time in Bad Pyrmont at the spa. In the foreground of the tasks mentioned in three memoranda composed by Leibniz for the Czar in June 1716 stood the collection, in libraries, of the knowledge available to humankind. In particular, Leibniz proposed to increase its accessibility by the development of (alphabetical and systematic) indices, inventories, handbooks (these arranged as "Institutiones" by the respective scientific disciplines), and encyclopedias.

---

[61] On this, cf. the documents in Guerrier II, 168–183. A more precise version of his remarks on linguistic research and on his observations on magnetism is found, e.g., in the copious memorandum of September 23, 1712 (Guerrier II, 239–249).

The extent to which elements of the academy founded by Peter the Great in 1724 can be directly traced back to Leibniz's designs is controversial, but, at the very least, the structure and the personnel of the Academy of St. Petersburg mirrored the proposals that Leibniz had presented to the Czar—as did (more significantly) its prescribed arrangement of tasks. Above all, however, one should point to the central function of the Academy, which was understood by the Czar to be a meaningful instrument for the realization of his program of reform. The Czar himself also initiated two of the projects called for by Leibniz: the determination of the border between Asia and America (with the expedition of Vitus Jonassen Bering) and the founding of a capital for the promotion of the sciences; that is, the Academy of St. Petersburg. The observation of magnetic declinations and the collection of samples of the languages of the peoples living in the Czar's empire, both proposed by Leibniz, were also taken up at a later time (Guerrier I, 189–190).

Conclusion

From his time in Mainz until only a few weeks before his death, Leibniz made great efforts to bring to fruition his goal of establishing learning societies. Their purpose was to make available human knowledge in its entirety and to expand such knowledge optimally. In his view, the drive for new knowledge should not be provided merely by curiosity; instead, all scientific effort ought to be tied to usefulness and ultimately serve that which is best in general. Leibniz's academic projects represent a very significant element in his strategic life-long plan, with its fundamental political goal being the perfection of humankind. In pursuit of this goal, he drew attention to his experience as a political counsellor and to his outstanding scholarly achievements in a broad range of disciplines. Both the advances that were being made in his time and his own personal accomplishments suggested to him that a golden opportunity to realize this goal was being offered to humankind. Should this chance be misplaced, humankind might well have to wait centuries to attain the progress that seemed to Leibniz possible in his lifetime. Hence, with the most powerful princes of the Empire and with Czar Peter I, he made efforts not only to secure the founding of academies but also to ensure that he himself would be given the directorship of these institutions so that he could facilitate the cooperation among the various European societies that he deemed essential.

Leibniz's global perspective is illustrated particularly well by his project of advancing the sciences in Russia (a project that he saw as particularly worthwhile since he regarded Russia as the land bridge between the great cultures of humankind, Europe and China) and the beginnings of the work of the societies of Central Europe initiated by the Berlin Society. He was convinced that the gain accruing to the individual state would harmonize with the benefit to humankind as a whole and contribute to its "perfection."

Even if many elements of his plan today strike us as comparable to the utopias of the Early Enlightenment, Leibniz himself saw in his projects a rejection of the utopian. He was convinced that these projects were attainable if steady advances were made with a view to serving the general good. Indeed in all these proposed projects, Leibniz included detailed plans for financing them. For these reasons, he did not give up when confronted with temporary obstacles, above all when supportive princes were held back by wars or financial constraints from a prompt implementation of his grand plans.[62]

REFERENCES

Antognazza, M. R. 2009. *Leibniz. An Intellectual Biography.* Cambridge: Cambridge University Press.

Bergmann, J. 1855. "Leibnizens Memoriale an den Kurfürsten Johann Wilhelm von der Pfalz etc." *Sitzungsberichte der philosophisch-historischen Classe* 16: 3–23.

Bodemann, E. 1883. "Leibnizens Plan einer Societät der Wissenschaften in Sachsen." *Neues Archiv für Sächsische Geschichte und Altertumskunde* 4: 177–214.

Böger, I. 1990. "Der Spanheim-Kreis und seine Bedeutung für Leibniz' Akademiepläne." In H. Poser and A. Heinekamp (eds.), *Leibniz in Berlin, Studia Leibnitiana.* Sonderhefte 16. Stuttgart: Steiner, pp. 202–217.

Böger, I. 2002. "*Ein seculum . . . da man zu Societäten Lust hat.*" *Darstellung und Analyse der Leibnizschen Sozietätspläne vor dem Hintergrund der europäischen Akademiebewegung im 17. und frühen 18. Jahrhundert,* 2nd ed. Munich: Herbert Utz.

Brather, H.-S. 1993. *Leibniz und seine Akademie. Ausgewählte Quellen zur Geschichte der Berliner Sozietät der Wissenschaften 1697–1716.* Berlin: Akademie-Verlag.

Döring, D. 1996. *Der junge Leibniz und Leipzig: Ausstellung zum 350. Geburtstag von Gottfried Wilhelm Leibniz im Leipziger Alten Rathaus.* Berlin: Akademie-Verlag.

Faak, M. 1966. *Leibniz als Reichshofrat,* phil. diss. Berlin: Humboldt Universität.

Guerrier, W. 1873. *Leibniz in seinen Beziehungen zu Russland und Peter dem Grossen. Eine geschichtliche Darstellung dieses Verhältnisses nebst den darauf bezüglichen Briefen und Denkschriften.* Hildesheim: Gerstenberg.

Klopp, O. 1869. "Leibniz' Plan der Gründung einer Sozietät der Wissenschaften in Wien." *Archiv für österreichische Geschichte* 40: 157–255.

Kvačala, J. 1901. "Počátky Berlínské akademie." In *Český časopis historický* 7: 265–293.

Leibniz, G. W. 1994. *Le droit de la raison. Textes réunis et présentés,* René Sève (ed.). Paris: Vrin, pp. 241–246.

Mittelstrass, J. 2012. "Leibniz's World: Calculation and Integration." In *Theoria cum praxi. Aus der Welt des Gottfried Wilhelm Leibniz. Beiträge anlässlich der Ausstellung Gottfried Wilhelm Leibniz. Philosoph, Mathematiker, Physiker, Techniker 10. Juni bis 14. Oktober 2002.* Vienna: ÖAW, pp. 13–18.

Otto, R. 2000. "Leibniz' Projekt einer Sächsischen Akademie im Kontext seiner Bemühungen um die Gründung gelehrter Gesellschaften." In D. Döring and K. Nowak (eds.), *Gelehrte Gesellschaften im mitteldeutschen Raum (1650–1820),* vol. 76/2 of Abhandlungen der Sächsischen Akademie der Wissenschaften zu Leipzig. Phil.-hist. Klasse. Stuttgart/ Leipzig: Hirzel, pp. 53–94.

---

[62] My sincere thanks for the translation of the German original go to Joseph B. Dallett, Ph.D. (Ithaca, New York).

Ross, G. M. 1974. "Leibniz and the Nuremberg Alchemical Society." *Studia leibnitiana* 6: 222–248.

Sakai, K. 2008. "Sozialpolitische Leitbilder. Leibniz' Grundsätze einer gerechten Sozialpolitik." *Studia Leibnitiana* 40(2): 153–167.

Schepers, H. 2011. "*Demonstrationes Catholicae*—Leibniz' großer Plan. Ein rationales Friedensprojekt für Europa." In F. Beiderbeck and S. Waldhoff (eds.), *Pluralität der Perspektiven und Einheit der Wahrheit im Werk von G. W. Leibniz. Beiträge zu seinem philosophischen, theologischen und politischen Denken.* Berlin: Akademie-Verlag, pp. 3–14.

Totok, W. 1966. "Leibniz als Wissenschaftsorganisator." In W. Totok and C. Haase (eds.), *Leibniz. Sein Leben—Sein Wirken—Seine Welt.* Hanover: Verlag für Literatur und Zeitgeschehen, pp. 293–320.

CHAPTER 32

....

LEIBNIZ'S NETWORK

....

HOWARD HOTSON

INTRODUCTION

....

THE study of Leibniz is framed by a paradox. His system of thought is an all-embracing network of mutually dependent conceptions, each one so inextricably related to the others that changing one would alter the whole. Yet Leibniz never expressed this coherent, all-embracing system in a single, all-embracing work. Instead, his writings are a patchwork of innumerable fragments, the overwhelming majority unpublished in his lifetime.[1]

The key to resolving this paradox is the recognition that, for Leibniz, philosophy was a social activity. This point is perhaps best understood in contradistinction to that most memorable image of the seventeenth-century philosopher: Descartes immured in his stove-heated room, insulated from all external stimuli, engaged in pure introspection. Leibniz, by contrast, did not philosophize in solipsistic isolation from the world. A "modern" philosopher of the second generation, he saw intellectual reform as a collaborative enterprise, engaging a vast company of fellow citizens of the *respublica litteraria* communicating avidly through an expanding variety of media. The episodic arrival of these communications—books, journals, visitors, and letters—at a rhythm largely outside his control, injected a chaotic element into the order in which his mind and pen moved from one topic to another[2]; and these random stimuli kept his

---

[1] Eduard Bodemann, *Die Leibniz-Handschriften der Königlichen öffentlichen Bibliothek zu Hannover* (Hanover, 1889; Hildesheim: Georg Olms, 1966) groups Leibniz's 50,000 working papers under 41 headings. Emile Ravier, *Bibliographie des œuvres de Leibniz* (Paris, 1937; facs. repr. Hildesheim: Georg Olms, 1966) lists 78 works published by Leibniz himself, together with 116 articles and 58 reviews in the learned journals of his day. To these must be added 72 Leibnizian works published by his contemporaries during his lifetime, and 557 individual works first published posthumously before 1937.

[2] This chaos is immediately apparent in Kurt Müller and Gisela Krönert's indispensable reference work, *Leben und Werk von Gottfried Wilhelm Leibniz: Eine Chronik* (Frankfurt am Main: Vittorio Klostermann, 1969).

philosophical system in a state of perpetual becoming. Because his core doctrines were tightly interrelated, his views on any given topic could unexpectedly be reshaped or refined by fresh thinking on any number of other topics; so as long as fresh impulses continued to arrive, it was impossible to regard his treatment of any particular doctrine as "finished." Hence the paradoxical outcome: an extraordinarily coherent and economical intellectual system documented, not by a synthetic *opus magnum*, but by an immense profusion of literary fragments.

In the absence of his *summa philosophica*, "generations of Leibniz scholars have had to tease out an overview of his gradual and complex intellectual evolution largely from his sprawling correspondence and innumerable working papers."[3] Perhaps more than any other thinker of similar stature, Leibniz requires his students to study his thought not as a static, fixed product, but as a process of constant refinement and adjustment. Because this process is propelled by dialogue with contemporaries, discussion of the evolution of Leibniz's thought also requires the capacity to master an extraordinarily voluminous body of data on the movements, networks, activities, and perspectives of hundreds upon hundreds of contemporaries. This obviously lends a particular significance to the study of Leibniz's correspondence and correspondents. Understanding Leibniz's intellectual network is not merely a historical challenge: it is more like the precondition for fully understanding his intellectual evolution. Leibniz's network is a major subject of study in its own right, one of the most important manifestations of the *respublica litteraria* which played such a central role in European intellectual life during the sixteenth, seventeenth, and eighteenth centuries. Yet the primary justification for devoting a chapter of this *Handbook* to it is that understanding Leibniz's network is also indispensable for understanding his thought. In addition to the challenge of comprehending the ideas themselves, the student of Leibniz must somehow master the pan-European network of intellectual contacts which stimulated both the ideas and the sometimes chameleonic expressions of them.

Awareness of the centrality of his correspondence to Leibniz's philosophical *oeuvre* is, of course, not new. Since Erasmus, it was common for scholars to publish edited versions of selected letters during their lifetimes and for larger collections to be published shortly after their deaths. Although Leibniz suggested as early as 1695 that his correspondence with Arnauld might be published,[4] it was only after his death that the first such volume appeared: Samuel Clarke's

---

[3] Quoting the opening paragraph of Maria Rosa Antognazza, *Leibniz: A Very Short Introduction* (Oxford: Oxford University Press, 2016), p. xv.

[4] Leibniz to Foucher, April 6/16, 1695: Leibniz, *Die Philosophischen Schriften*, C. I. Gerhardt (ed.), 7 vols. (Berlin: Weidmannsche Buchhandlung, 1875-1890; repr., Hildesheim: Olms, 1960-1961), vol. I, p. 420. On the early history of the publication of Leibniz's letters, see the most extensive discussion of Leibniz's correspondence network to date: Nora Gädeke, "Gottfried Wilhelm Leibniz," in Christiane Berkvens-Stevelinck, Hans Bots, and Jens Häseler (eds.), *Les grands intermédiaires culturels de la République des Lettres: études de réseaux de correspondances du XVIe au XVIIIe siècles* (Paris: Champion, 2005), pp. 257–306, here pp. 266–268.

collection of letters exchanged with Leibniz in 1715–16 and published the following year.[5] Large-scale publication began almost immediately, with J. F. Feller's collection of miscellanea in 1718 and Christian Korholt's four–volume collection in 1734–42.[6] Despite the steady accumulation ever since,[7] three hundred years after his death we are still awaiting a critical edition of the complete Leibnizian epistolary: the on-going Akademie-Ausgabe still lacks the last and most active decade of Leibniz's correspondence.

The daunting scale of the problem, however, has been evident since at least 1889 and the appearance of E. Bodemann's survey of the more than 1,000 people whose letters to or from Leibniz are preserved.[8] In 1966, Georg Gerber compiled from Bodemann a statistically based overview of Leibniz's epistolary network which remains the point of departure for work on this topic.[9] During the past four decades, a handful of scholarly articles have emerged from deep within the Leibniz Archive in Hanover, surveying Leibniz's network within the broader *respublica litteraria*,[10] grounding it in the postal communications of his day,[11] and experimenting with means of bridging the vast gulf between Gerber's bare statistics and a full survey of Leibniz's correspondence as a whole.[12] No similar overviews have been attempted in English, but, meanwhile, Leibniz's correspondences with a handful of individual

[5] *A Collection of Papers, Which passed between the late Learned Mr. Leibnitz, and Dr. Clarke, In the Years 1715 and 1716. Relating to the Principles of Natural Philosophy and Religion* (London: James Knapton, 1717).

[6] Joachim Friedrich Feller (ed.), *Otium Hanoveranum sive Miscellanea ex ore et schedis . . . Leibnitii* (Leipzig: Johann Christian Martini, 1718); Christian Korholt, *Viri illustris Godefridi Guil. Leibnitii epistolae ad diversos*, 4 vols (Leipzig: Breitkopf, 1734–42).

[7] Cf. Ravier, *Bibliographie*, no. 327 ff: most of the more miscellaneous publications include correspondence; Detlef Döring, "Leibniz-Editionen in Leipzig. Der Druck der Schriften und Briefe von G. W. Leibniz in der ersten Hälfte des 18. Jahrhunderts," *Leipziger Kalender* (1998), pp. 69–95.

[8] E. Bodemann, *Briefwechsel des Gottfried Wilhelm Leibniz in der königlichen öffentlichen Bibliothek zu Hannover* (Hanover, 1889; repr. Hildesheim: Georg Olms, 1966).

[9] Georg Gerber, "Leibniz und seine Korrespondenz," in Wilhelm Totok and Carl Haase (eds.), *Leibniz. Sein Leben—sein Wirken—seine Welt* (Hanover: Verlag für Literatur und Zeitgeschehen, 1966), pp. 141–172.

[10] See especially Gerda Utermöhlen, "Der Briefwechsel des Gottfried Wilhelm Leibniz— die umfangreichste Korrespondenz des 17. Jahrhunderts und die 'république des lettres,'", in Wolfgang Frühwald et al. (eds.), *Probleme der Brief-Edition: Kolloquium der Deutschen Forschungsgemeinschaft, Schloss Tutzing am Starnberger See, 8.–11. September 1975* (Boppard: Boldt, 1977), pp. 87–104; Nora Gädeke, "Das Korrespondenzverzeichnis der Akademie-Ausgabe— Hilfsmittel oder Forschungsinstrument?," in Wenchao Li (ed.), *Komma und Kathedrale. Tradition, Bedeutung und Herausforderung der Leibniz–Edition* (Berlin: De Gruyter, 2015), pp. 81–93; Nora Gädeke, "Leibniz lässt sich informieren—Asymmetrien in seinen Korrespondenzbeziehungen," in Klaus-Dieter Herbst and Stefan Kratochwil (eds.), *Kommunikation in der Frühen Neuzeit* (Frankfurt am Main: Lang, 2009), pp. 25–46.

[11] Gerd van den Heuvel, *Leibniz im Netz. Die frühneuzeitliche Post als Kommunikationsmedium der Gelehrtenrepublik um 1700* (Hameln: C. W. Niemeyer, 2009).

[12] In the most substantial of these surveys, Nora Gädeke studied the years 1671, 1677, 1685, 1699, and 1715 as a means of plotting the evolution of Leibniz's network over time: see her "Leibniz"

philosophers have been subjected to monographic study or meticulous edition and translation in England, France, Italy, and the United States,[13] notably in the excellent "Yale Leibniz" series.[14]

Attempts have also been inaugurated recently to move beyond particular correspondences to more general patterns. In 2005, Paul Lodge published a volume of essays discussing Leibniz's epistolary exchanges with ten philosophical contemporaries and one collective: the Jesuit missionaries in China.[15] Generalizing on this latter case, a group of Italian Leibniz scholars recently organized a colloquium exploring the "subnetworks" in Leibniz's correspondence; that is to say, his contact with clusters of individuals in specific places (Berlin, London, Paris), institutions (Roman Jesuits, Helmstedt professors), disciplines (Italian physiologists, astronomers working on calendrical reform), projects (the *opus historicum*), and topics (ecclesiastical reunion, the right of resistance).[16] In between these two projects, a volume has appeared attempting to survey Leibniz's relations with the learned world around 1700.[17]

These approaches now urgently need to be complemented by a fresh assault on the task of mapping Leibniz's network as a whole. In order to understand Leibniz's letters, we need to know the people to whom they are addressed. In order to understand those people, we need to understand the networks in which they also moved. How can the evolution of Leibniz's intellectual network as a whole be rendered intelligible? How can the community of Leibniz scholars create the means for navigating the many dimensions of this intellectual network freely and easily? This problem—one of the most intractable currently obstructing the future development of Leibniz studies—is the primary focus of the text which follows. Rather than attempting a prose overview of Leibniz's network on the basis of current knowledge, this chapter will attempt to assess the various dimensions of this challenge and the means whereby it might be overcome.

(2005), pp. 271–296. The same approach is applied to 1716 in Eadem, "Leibniz" Korrespondenz im letzten Lebensjahr—Gerber reconsidered," in Michael Kempe (ed.), *1716—Leibniz' letztes Lebensjahr: Unbekanntes zu einem bekannten Universalgelehrten* (Hanover: Gottfried Wilhelm Leibniz Bibliothek, 2016), pp. 83–109.

[13] For further detail, see notes 47 to 59.

[14] Namely, of the correspondences with Des Bosses by Look and Rutherford (2007), De Volder by Lodge (2013), and Arnauld by Voss (2016). For details, see notes 45, 52, and 47, respectively.

[15] Paul Lodge (ed.), *Leibniz and his Correspondents* (Cambridge: Cambridge University Press, 2004), which examines correspondence with Thomasius, Oldenburg, Foucher, Arnauld, Fardella, De Volder, Lady Masham, Wolff, Des Bosses, and Princess Caroline of Wales.

[16] Enrico Pasini, Margherita Palumbo, Roberto Palaia, and Matteo Favaretti, "Subnetworks in Leibniz's Correspondence and Intellectual Network," colloquium held at the Herzog August Bibliothek, Wolfenbüttel, March 15–17, 2017: http://www.hab.de/files/programm_12.pdf. Cf. the pioneering discussion of "sub-networks" in Gädeke, "Leibniz" (2005), pp. 286–290.

[17] Berthold Heinecke and Ingrid Kästner (eds.), *Gottfried Wilhelm Leibniz (1646–1716) und die gelehrte Welt Europas um 1700* (Aachen: Shaker, 2013).

NUMERICAL SCALE

What, then, are the obstacles to gaining a ready overview of Leibniz's correspondence? And how might those obstacles be removed or at least reduced? The first and most obvious problem is one of sheer scale. Comparison with his intellectual predecessors and contemporaries helps appreciate the nature of the problem. For Francis Bacon, some 943 letters survive;[18] for René Descartes, just 727;[19] for Baruch Spinoza, a mere 88 have survived, and only 45 others have currently been postulated,[20] while the standard edition of *The Correspondence of John Locke* includes 3,648 letters.[21] The leading astronomers of the period corresponded in similar numbers: to and from Tycho Brahe, we possess 505 letters; for Johannes Kepler, 1,154;[22] for Galileo Galilei, 3,257;[23] for Christiaan Huygens, 3,080; for Isaac Newton, less than 1,800 letters.[24] Even more relevant are the benchmarks provided by the central brokers of intellectual exchange in the decades before the foundation of the academies of science. Marin Mersenne left behind only 1,905 letters.[25] For Nicolas-Claude Fabri de Peiresc, about 3,500 have been published, and between 5,000 and 7,000 are thought to be extant, although these may represent only half of the original number.[26] Similarly for Samuel Hartlib: the most complete enumeration of his correspondence to date lists 4,718 letters, and a careful calculation indicates that they were originally perhaps three times as many.[27] Surprisingly, the better institutionalized

[18] See "The Francis Bacon Correspondence Project," directed by Alan Stewart, with Patricia Brewerton and Andrew Gordon: http://www.livesandletters.ac.uk/projects/correspondence-francis-bacon.

[19] Descartes, *Correspondance*, published with an introduction and notes by Charles Adam and Gérard Milhaud, 8 vols (Paris: Presses Universitaires de France, 1936–63; repr. Nendeln: Kraus Reprint, 1963–1971). Very little of this survives in manuscript.

[20] *The Collected Works of Spinoza*, ed. and trans. E. Curley, 2 vols. (Princeton: Princeton University Press, 1985–2016). The letters postulated by Jeroen van de Ven are included in "The Spinoza Web": https://spinozaweb.org/letters.

[21] *The Correspondence of John Locke*, ed. E. S. De Beer, 8 vols. (Oxford: Clarendon Press, 1989).

[22] Johannes Kepler, *Gesammelte Werke*, ed. M. Caspar, et al., currently 20 vols (Munich: C. H. Beck, 1938).

[23] *Le Opere di Galileo Galilei, Edizione Nazionale*, ed. Antonio Favaro, 20 vols. (Florence: Barbera, 1890–1909; repr. 1929–39 and 1964–68).

[24] *The Correspondence of Isaac Newton*, ed. H. W. Turnbull, et al., 7 vols. (Cambridge: Published for the Royal Society at the [Cambridge] University Press, 1959–77) contains 1,552 letters in the main series, not all of them to or from Newton himself. Another 150 are printed as addenda, and a further 40 await publication. I owe these estimates to Robert Iliffe.

[25] *Correspondance du P. Marin Mersenne, Religieux Minime*, ed. Cornelis De Waard, René Pintard, Bernard Rochot, and Armand Beaulieu, 17 vols. (Paris: PUF and CNRS, 1933–88). The inventory on Early Modern Letters Online (hereafter EMLO) also contains 11 letters subsequently published by Noel Malcolm: for details see http://emlo.bodleian.ox.ac.uk/blog/?catalogue=marin-mersenne.

[26] *Lettres de Peiresc*, ed. Philippe Tamizey de Larroque, 7 vols. (Paris: Imprimerie nationale, 1888–98): an inventory of this edition, compiled by Peter N. Miller, is available on EMLO: http://emlo.bodleian.ox.ac.uk/blog/?catalogue=nicolas-claude-fabri-de-peiresc.

[27] An inventory of Hartlib's letters, compiled by Howard Hotson and Leigh T. I. Penman, is available on EMLO: http://emlo.bodleian.ox.ac.uk/blog/?catalogue=samuel-hartlib#contents. For the calculation

intelligencers of the subsequent generation did not match these figures. The standard edition of the correspondence of Henry Oldenburg numbers 3,139 letters.[28] Athanasius Kircher left behind only 2,686.[29] Pierre Bayle's extant epistles number only 1,791.[30] Leibniz's surviving correspondence is on a very different scale. In 1889, Bodemann put the number of letters at 15,300, and the current estimate is roughly 20,000 surviving letters: three to five times the number of Peiresc and Hartlib, six or seven times that of Oldenburg and Kircher, twenty to thirty times the number of Bacon or Descartes, and well over two hundred times larger than Spinoza. Among the canonical philosophers and scientists of his age, Leibniz is without parallel as a correspondent.

For this enormous disparity, there are several explanations. In the first place, the preservation rate of Leibniz's correspondence is unusually good thanks to a serene archival history both before and after his death.[31] For most of his adult life, Leibniz lived in Hanover—for the last eighteen years in the same apartments in Number 10 Schmiedestraße—steadily accumulating papers without serious disruption. On November 15, 1716—only hours after his death the previous evening—his archive was officially placed under seal.[32] His papers were then transferred *en masse* for safekeeping to the royal library where, through a seamless line of institutional descent, they have become the crown jewels of the Landesbibliothek which now bears his name. Among these papers were not only his incoming correspondence but also outlines, extracts, and copies of his outgoing letters, which today supplement the letters actually sent, preserved in libraries and archives throughout and beyond Europe.

A second and no less important explanation is that Leibniz's correspondence was not confined to "philosophy" or "science" even in the broadest construction of those terms.

---

of its original size, see Penman, "*Omnium Exposita Rapinæ*: The Afterlives of the Papers of Samuel Hartlib," in *Book History*, 19 (2016), 1–65.

[28] *The Correspondence of Henry Oldenburg*, ed. and trans. A. R. Hall and M. B. Hall, 13 vols. (Madison: University of Wisconsin Press; London: Mansel; London: Taylor & Francis, 1965–86). Over one hundred additional letters were subsequently published as addenda, and more are being prepared for publication in coming years.

[29] A catalogue of Kircher's extant letters, compiled in several phases by many hands, is available on EMLO at http://emlo.bodleian.ox.ac.uk/blog/?catalogue=athanasius-kircher.

[30] *Correspondance de Pierre Bayle*, critical edition established under the direction of Elisabeth Labrousse and Antony McKenna, with the collaboration of Wiep van Bunge, Hubert Bost, Edward James, Annie Leroux, Fabienne Vial-Bonacci, Bruno Roche, and Eric-Olivier Lochard, 15 vols. (Oxford: The Voltaire Foundation, 1999–2017). Electronic edition: http://bayle-correspondance.univ-st-etienne.fr/?lang=fr. Catalogue of correspondence: http://emlo-portal.bodleian.ox.ac.uk/collections/?catalogue=pierre-bayle#resources. Here again, the vagaries of preservation distort the picture: before October 1681, for instance, extant correspondence mentions two missing letters for every one which survives.

[31] On the archive, see James O'Hara, "'A chaos of jottings that I do not have the leisure to arrange and mark with headings': Leibniz's Manuscript Papers and their Repository," in Michael Hunter (ed.), *Archives of the Scientific Revolution: The Function and Exchange of Ideas in the Seventeenth-Century* (Woodbridge: Boydell Press, 1998), pp. 159–170; Gädeke, "Leibniz: (2005), pp. 264–266.

[32] Maria Rosa Antognazza, *Leibniz: An Intellectual Biography* (Cambridge: Cambridge University Press, 2009), p. 544.

This is hardly surprising: his official roles were not court philosopher and mathematician but court counselor, librarian, and historiographer. These duties are clearly evident in the relative size of the three series of letters being published in the Akademie Ausgabe, each of which has now reached 1705 or 1706: the second series, for the philosophical letters, contains four volumes; the third, for mathematical, scientific, and technical letters, contains nine; and the first series, for general, political, and historical letters, numbers 26 volumes.[33] In other words, the bulk of general, political, and historical correspondence surpasses that of philosophical, mathematical, scientific, and technical put together by about two to one. Leibniz's letters are more numerous partly because the business conducted within them is far more expansive than that of most other leading intellectuals of his day.

Counting correspondents rather than correspondence produces a very similar impression. Tycho Brahe exchanged surviving letters with 123 correspondents, Bacon with about 200, Descartes with just 92, Mersenne with 218, Hartlib with 327, Christiaan Huygens with 260, Kircher with an impressive 736, Bayle with 280. For Leibniz, Bodemann counted 1,063 correspondents in 1889, the standard estimate until recently has been about 1,100, and ongoing research is now likely to raise this to 1,300 or beyond.[34] At the height of his epistolary activity in the first decade of the eighteenth century, Leibniz was corresponding with nearly 200 people every year. He maintained correspondence with more than 150 of these people for a decade or more and with about 50 for more than two decades.[35] The quality of these connections is at least as impressive as the quantity. The list of Leibniz's correspondents reads like a *Who was Who* of the contemporary republic of letters, and this is no accident. As early as August 1671, in a letter to the imperial librarian and historiographer in Vienna, Peter Lambeck, the 25-year-old Leibniz boasted of his exchanges with 22 of the chief men of learning which he was already assiduously cultivating: Athanasius Kircher and Francesco de Lana in Italy, Otto von Guericke and Hermann Conring among many others in Germany, the royal librarian Pierre de Carcavi, Louis Ferrand, and others in France, Henry Oldenburg and John Wallis in England, Johann Georg Graevius and Lambert van Velthuysen in the Dutch Republic, and Vitus Bering in Denmark.[36] Not until Voltaire did one of Europe's foremost intellectuals pursue a correspondence similar in scale to that of Leibniz. This may explain the ironic fact that it was the future author of *Candide* (1759) who testified most clearly to Leibniz's centrality to the intellectual networks of his day. "There was never a more universal correspondence kept between philosophers than at this period,"

---

[33] Akademie-Ausgabe (A), Reihe I: *Allgemeiner, politischer und historischer Briefwechsel*; Reihe II: *Philosophischer Briefwechsel*; Reihe III: *Mathematischer, naturwissenschaftlicher und technischer Briefwechsel*. On the first series, see Nora Gädeke and Françoise Leloutre, "Au-delà de la philosophie: L'édition de la correspondance générale, politique et historique de Leibniz," *Les Études philosophiques*, 164 (2016), 577–595.

[34] I am grateful to Miranda Lewis for extracting these figures from EMLO.

[35] Gerber, "Leibniz und seine Korrespondenz," p. 145.

[36] A I, 1 N. 27. Cf. further early examples and an analysis of 1671 in Gädeke, "Leibniz," pp. 263–264, 274–276.

he wrote in his panegyric to the age of Louis XIV, "and Leibniz," "a man of the most universal learning in Europe," "contributed not a little to encourage it."[37] Modern experts concur.[38]

GEOGRAPHICAL SCOPE

How, then, can we gain an overview of the general shape of nearly 20,000 letters? Since a letter is a written communication between people in different places, the most basic "shape" of a correspondence is arguably cartographic. The very basic map of Leibniz correspondence reproduced as Figure 32.1 provides a point of departure for discussing the best means of visualizing such a network.

Even from such a simple map, several things are immediately evident. One is the wide geographical scope of Leibniz's network. The correspondence with China and the Far East is one of its most famous features.[39] The late exchanges with Russia are equally distinctive. Also evident is the dense concentration of this network in the Holy Roman Empire in general and in northern Germany in particular. Between these two extremes, most of the rest of Europe is embraced as well, including Poland, Sweden, Denmark, the Low Countries (north and south), England, France, Spain, Italy, and the Swiss Confederation. Enumerating the cities with which Leibniz corresponded most avidly creates a similar impression of the balance between local political contacts and more distant intellectual ones. Leibniz exchanged letters with 80 people in Berlin, Hanover, and Paris; with 62 people in London and 61 in Vienna; with 46 in Helmstedt, 40 in Wolfenbüttel, 33 in Leipzig, 30 in Hamburg, 25 in Rome, 21 in The Hague, 20 in Celle, 18 in Dresden, 17 in Jena, 16 in Halle, 15 in Venice and Clausthal-Zellerfeld, and 14 in Amsterdam. Other foreign centers with multiple correspondents were Modena (12); Florence (11); Copenhagen, Oxford, and Utrecht (7 each); and Leiden, Stockholm, and Strasbourg (6 each).[40] Without comparative maps of the correspondences of contemporary intellectuals, it is difficult to comment further with complete confidence, but very few of his intellectual contemporaries straddled the Catholic–Protestant divide of post-Reformation Europe as comfortably as Leibniz, and few intellectuals since Erasmus

[37] Voltaire, *Siècle de Louis XIV*, chapter 34, "Des Beaux-Arts en Europe du temps de Louis XIV," translated in *The Works of M. de Voltaire*, trans. T. Smollett, T. Francklin, et. al., 36 vols. (London; Printed for J. Newbery et al., 1761–65), vol. 9 (1761), pp. 161, 160.

[38] Gerda Utermöhlen, "Der Briefwechsel des Gottfried Wilhelm Leibniz—die umfangreichste Korrespondenz des 17. Jahrhunderts und der „république des lettres,"" in Wolfgang Frühwald et al. (eds), *Probleme der Briefedition* (Boppard: Boldt, 1977), pp. 87–104.

[39] R. Widmaier, *Leibniz korrespondiert mit China: der Briefwechsel mit den Jesuitenmissionaren* (Frankfurt am Main: Klostermann, 1990); H. Poser and W. Li (eds.), *Das Neueste über China: G. W. Leibnizens Novissima Sinica von 1697* (Stuttgart: Steiner, 2000); Franklin Perkins, "Leibniz's Exchange with the Jesuits in China," in Lodge (ed.), *Leibniz and His Correspondents*, pp. 141–161.

[40] Gerber, "Leibniz und seine Korrespondenz," pp. 146–148.

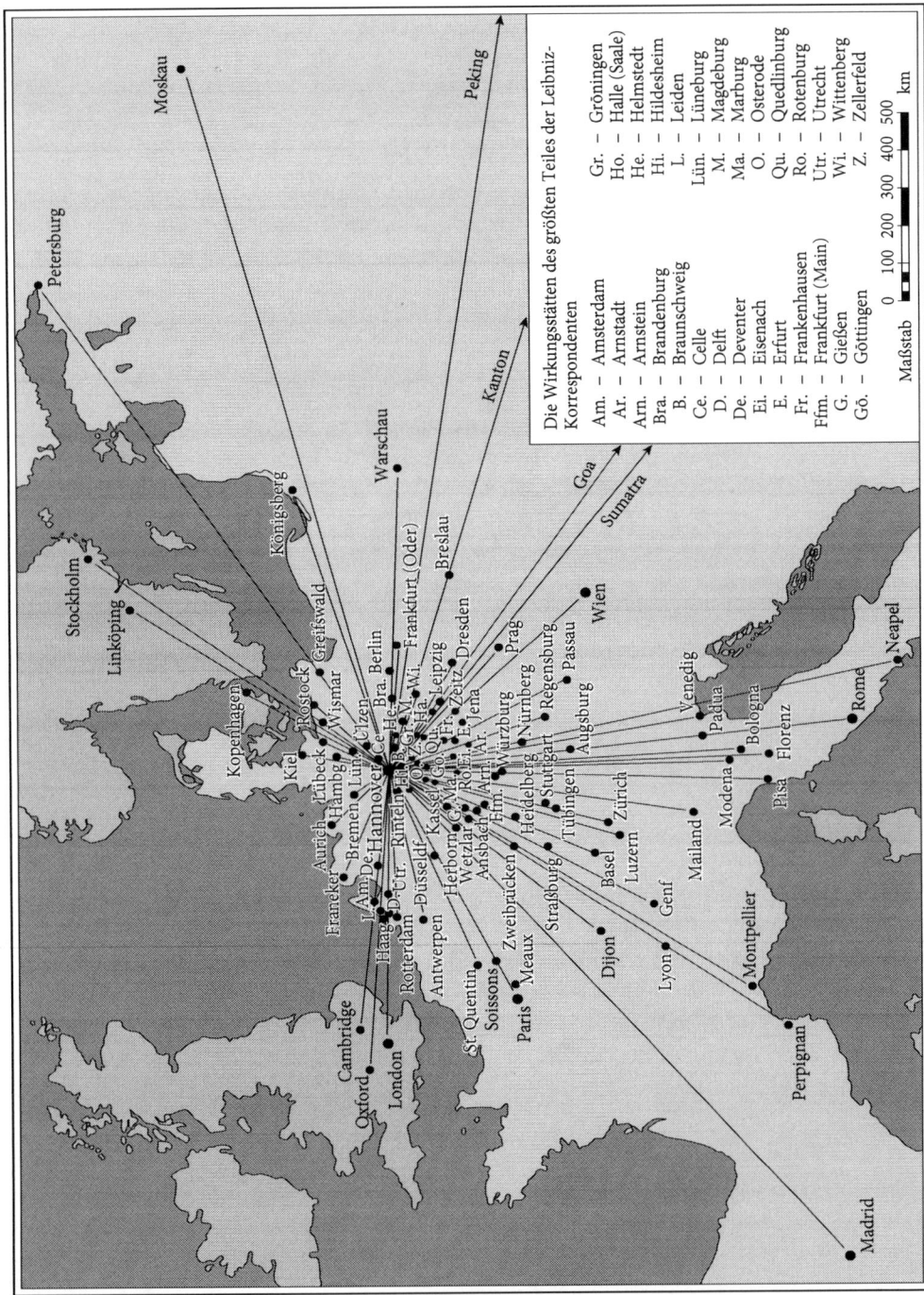

FIGURE 32.1 Main cities of residence of Leibniz's correspondents. This map, of unknown origin, was previously on the website of the Gottfried Wilhelm Leibniz-Bibliothek in Hanover. The caption and place names are still given in the German form of the original map.

appear to have communicated so routinely across a broader swathe of European regions.[41] In order to move beyond vague comparisons of this kind, we will need structured means of comparing the scope of intellectual networks with one another.

Equally evident, however, are the inadequacies of a static image of this kind for visualizing even this relatively straightforward data. For one thing, the correspondence of a lifetime is displayed as if it took place simultaneously. No allowance is given for the changing shape of Leibniz's network over time. For another, the scale of the map is an awkward compromise. The focus is too narrow to capture all the points of contact: the links with Beijing, Canton, Sumatra, and Goa are designated only by vectors pointing vaguely east. Yet the scope is much too broad to portray the rich data on the Holy Roman Empire in general and northern Germany in particular. The very regions where the contact is most intensive are thereby rendered illegible. A third problem is that no attempt is made to distinguish the places with which Leibniz corresponded intensively from those with which he exchanged a single extant letter. Resolving this third problem would only compound the second one, since the points of most frequent contact are found disproportionately within the congested north German center of this network. The conclusion is obvious: there is no prospect whatsoever of gaining an adequate overview of Leibniz's correspondence network within a single, static, two-dimensional map—at least not a map of a size capable of being reproduced on the pages of a book such as this one. To grasp even the most basic data on Leibniz's intellectual network—the places to and from which he exchanged correspondence—a dynamic, data-driven, interactive map is needed.[42]

DYNAMISM

An even more basic problem with this static image is that it portrays Leibniz himself as stationary. In order to simplify the image and its production, it assumes that the correspondence of his entire lifetime was conducted from his study in Hanover. But although often portrayed as a sedentary figure, immobilized in Hanover, Leibniz—as specialists know perfectly well—was surprisingly mobile. Before settling in Hanover at the end of 1676, he had traveled from Leipzig to Jena, Nuremberg, Frankfurt, Mainz, Paris, London, and Holland. A decade later, his historical researchers took him on a 32-month journey through southern Germany, Austria, and Italy. Throughout his years

---

[41] Cf. the maps of Erasmus's correspondence network in Christoph Kudella, "The Correspondence Network of Erasmus of Rotterdam: A Data-Driven Exploration", unpublished PhD dissertation, National University of Ireland, Cork, 2016, ch. 8.

[42] Much of the recent innovation in this field has emerged from the Humanities + Design lab in Stanford, which built on the previous work of Stanford's "Mapping the Republic of Letters" project and produced the Palladio tool for visualizing complex historical data. See further http://hdlab.stanford.edu/, http://republicofletters.stanford.edu/, and http://hdlab.stanford.edu/palladio/about/, resp.

in Hanover, he commuted regularly to the Guelf courts in Celle and Wolfenbüttel and frequently visited the mines in Clausenthal-Zellerfeld and the university in Helmstedt. In his later years, he was a repeat visitor to Berlin and paid a second extended visit to Vienna. Altogether, his travels covered an estimated 20,000 kilometers. So mobile was he, in fact, that his employers repeatedly complained that the one place he was never to be found was in Hanover.[43]

Figure 32.2 provides an indication of the complexity and range of Leibniz's itinerary. Superimposing the exchange of correspondence on top of this itinerary would provide a map both far more accurate than Figure 32.1 and also even more in need of dynamic and interactive functionality to be rendered intelligible. The first problem, that of depicting the vast number of Leibniz's letters, has now been compounded by a second one: the problem of depicting more dimensions than can be easily expressed on a printed page. Two dimensions are needed to represent the space through which Leibniz and his letters move, a third to represent the sequence of his movements in time, and each must be examined at several scales.

The purpose of these movements was to conduct business which could not easily be transacted through script or print, and this introduces another crucial mode of intellectual exchange not captured in these maps or the datasets from which they are drawn: direct, face-to-face discussion. We know from a variety of sources that many of these discussions were important for the development of Leibniz's thought and its expression on paper. To name only two famous instances, conversations with Sophie Charlotte and Prince Eugene of Savoy helped to prompt the composition of some of the most important expressions of his philosophy: respectively, the *Theodicy*, and the twin pamphlets on monads which became almost synonymous with his name after his death: the *Monadology* and *Principes de la nature et de la grâce*. Different in character are institutionalized encounters with multiple colleagues at the same time. On December 27 and 30, 1707, for instance, Leibniz presided over sittings of the Berlin Society of Sciences, which discussed a variety of projects: a history of the Brandenburg episcopate, calendar reform, the agenda of the society's mathematicians, and the plan to appoint "Stadt- und Land Physicos."[44] These verbal encounters are not typically as well documented as the epistolary ones, yet an adequate account of Leibniz's intellectual network must supplement catalogues of correspondence with location and contact histories, capable of aggregating all the tiny scraps of relevant data which survive.

The same applies, needless to say, to the location and contact histories of his 1,300 correspondents, some of whom were far more mobile even than Leibniz himself. In some instances, the same person corresponded with Leibniz from several different places on

---

[43] Cf., for instance, Antognazza, *Leibniz*, pp. 381, 466. Georg Ludwig to Sophie, October 23, 1703: Leibniz, *Gesammelte Werke*, ed. G. H. Pertz, 4 vols. (Hanover: Hahnschen Hof-Buchhandlung, 1843–1847; reprint, Hildesheim: Olms, 1966),vol. I, pt. 1, p. xiv. Sophie to Leibniz, January 22, 1709: Leibniz, *Die Werke*, ed. O. Klopp, 11 vols. (Hanover: Klindworth, 1864–1884), vol. IX, p. 294.

[44] Müller and Krönert, *Leben und Werk von Leibniz*, p. 203: *Oeuvres de Leibniz*, ed. A. Foucher de Careil, 7 vols. (Paris: Firmin Didot frères, 1861–1875), vol. vii, pp. 644–644.

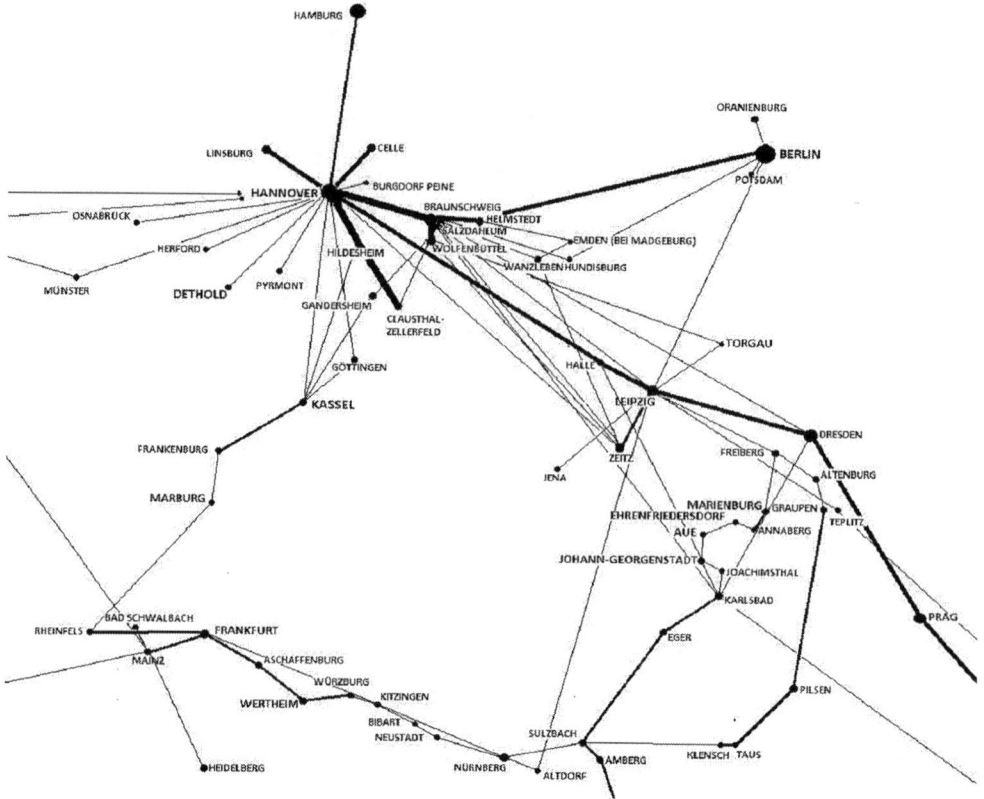

FIGURE 32.2 Leibniz's travels. This figure redraws, for greater clarity, a portion of "Leibniz' Reisen," an anonymous, hand-drawn map in the Gottfried Wilhelm Leibniz-Bibliothek in Hanover, reproduced in Albert Heinekamp and Isolde Hein, *Leibniz und Europa* (Hanover: Schlütersche Verlagsanstalt und Druckerei, 1994), p. 64. Thicker lines represent multiple voyages; larger dots represent multiple visits.

this map. In others, their movements brought travelers to Hanover, Wolfenbüttel, or Berlin, allowing days or even weeks of intensive discussions. It is enough to mention his conversations in Berlin with Toland or in Hanover with Des Bosses.[45]

Moreover, Leibniz's interlocutors were not atomic individuals. They were grouped by membership of confessions, religious orders, professions, offices, philosophical schools, national allegiances, and dynastic service, among other things. While some moved as free agents, others were displaced involuntarily as large groups. The paradigmatic example in Leibniz's day is the Huguenot diaspora (Figure 32.3). Prior to 1685, French Calvinists were densely interrelated by confession, education, and intermarriage in an archipelago of Protestant strongholds within their native land. In the years surrounding the Revocation of the Edict of Nantes, prominent members of this group were scattered

---

[45] F. H. Heinemann, "Toland and Leibniz," *The Philosophical Review* 54 (5/1945), pp. 437–457; *The Leibniz-Des Bosses Correspondence*, translated, edited, and with an introduction by Brandon C. Look and Donald Rutherford (New Haven and London: Yale University Press, 2007); Antognazza, *Leibniz*, pp. 418–421, 476–479.

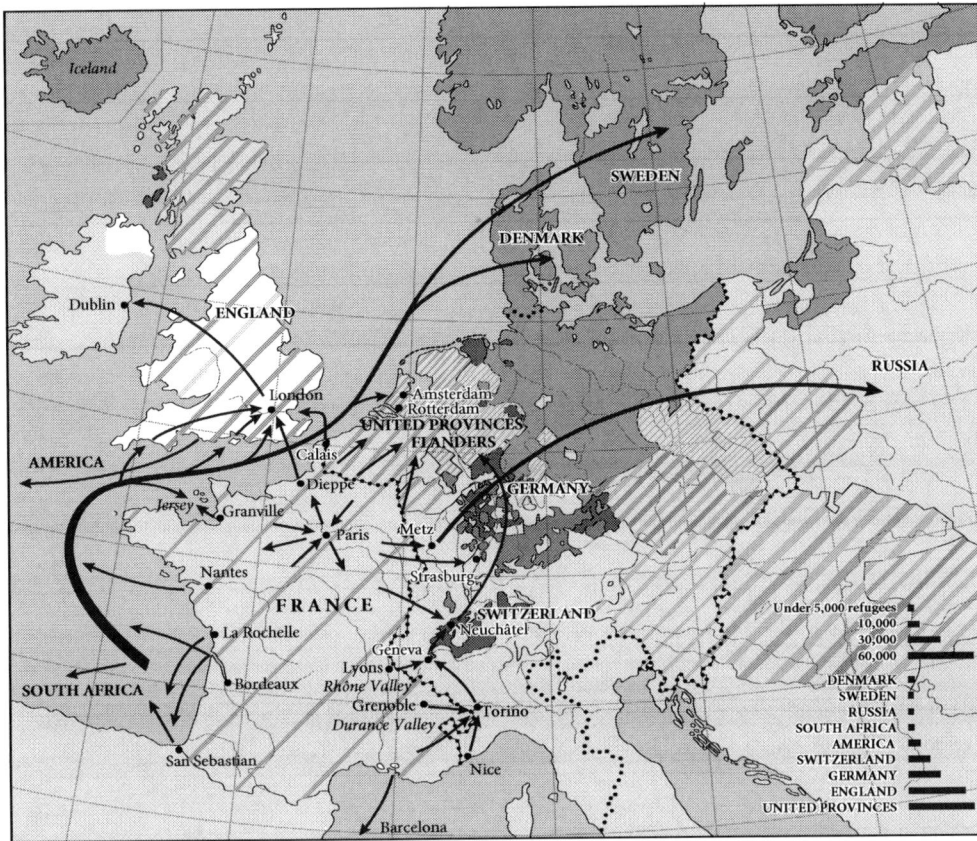

FIGURE 32.3 The Huguenot diaspora (c. 1695).

Reproduced with permission of the Musée international de la Réforme, Geneva.

across Reformed Europe—northward to the Dutch Republic, England, Scotland, and Ireland, and eastward to the Swiss Confederation and enclaves of the German Reformed tradition, now led by Brandenburg. This displacement expanded a pre-established network of prominent intellectuals across Europe, including Pierre Coste and Henri Justel in England; Jacques and Henri Basnage de Beauval, Pierre Bayle, Daniel Larroque, and Jean Le Clerc in Holland; Denis Papin in Marburg; and Isaac Jaquelot, Philippe Naude, and Alphonse des Vignoles in Berlin. Again, this example must stand for the other mobile networks of trade, diplomacy, science, and religion which knit individuals together into sometimes highly robust and well-organized networks.

SOCIAL DEPTH

The manner in which Leibniz's correspondents were bound together varied with another dimension of his network: namely, its extraordinary social depth. Socially, a correspondence could bind together very different sorts of people, including many who had never met or, indeed, would not care to mix socially; and in this respect too Leibniz's correspondence is exemplary. Of the 1,063 correspondences counted by Bodemann, only about one-quarter (c. 270) are categorized primarily as intellectuals.[46] Among these, by far the most closely studied correspondences are with some of the roughly 70 people engaged in the speculative branches of philosophy, including Arnauld,[47] Bayle, Clarke,[48] Des Bosses,[49] Fardella,[50] Foucher,[51] Landgraf Ernst von Hessen-Rheinfels, Malebranche, de Volder,[52] and Wolff.[53] Another 60 are mathematicians: the Bernoulli brothers, Bodenhausen, Conti, Fardella, Guido Grandi, Huygens, l'Hospital, Mariotte, Newton, Tschirnhaus, Varignon, and Zendrini. A similar number are engaged in physical, geographical, geological, astronomical, or chemical sciences: Fahrenheit, Foucher, Guericke, and Papin in physics; Halley and Römer in astronomy, not to mention Oldenburg.[54] Yet another 60 are educators and academics, notably his own teacher in Leipzig, Jakob Thomasius.[55] About 50 are historians,

[46] These statistics and lists derive from Gerber, "Leibniz und seine Korrespondenz," pp. 162–69. Cf. Gädeke's analysis of the social composition of Leibniz's correspondents in 1699: "Leibniz" (2005), pp. 284–286.

[47] G. Lewis, *Lettres de Leibniz à Arnauld d'aprés un manuscript inédit* (Paris: Presses Universitaires de France, 1952); Robert Sleigh, *Leibniz and Arnauld* (New Haven and London: Yale University Press, 1990); Leibniz, *Der Briefwechsel mit Antoine Arnauld*, ed. R. Finster (Hamburg: Meiner, 1997); Martha Brandt Bolton, "Leibniz to Arnauld: Platonic and Aristotelian Themes on Matter and Corporeal Substance," in Lodge (ed.), *Leibniz and His Correspondents*, pp. 97–122; *The Leibniz-Arnauld Correspondence, With Selections from the Correspondence with Ernst, Landgrave of Hessen-Rheinfels*, ed., trans. and introduced by Stephen Voss (New Haven and London: Yale University Press, 2016).

[48] Ezio Vailati, *Leibniz and Clark: A Study of their Correspondence* (Oxford: Oxford University Press, 1997).

[49] V. Mathieu, *Leibniz e des Bosses* (Turin: Facoltà di Lettere e Filosofia, 1960); Brandon Look, "On Substance and Relations in Leibniz's Correspondence with Des Bosses," in Lodge (ed.), *Leibniz and His Correspondents*, pp. 238–261; *The Leibniz-Des Bosses Correspondence*, trans. and ed. Look and Rutherford.

[50] S. Femiano, "Über den Briefwechsel zwischen Michelangelo Fardella und Leibniz," *Studia Leibnitiana*, 15 (1982), 153–183; Daniel Garber, "Leibniz and Fardella: Body, Substance and Idealism," in Lodge (ed.), *Leibniz and His Correspondents*, pp. 123–140.

[51] Stuart Brown, "The Leibniz-Foucher Alliance and Its Philosophical Bases," in Lodge (ed.), *Leibniz and His Correspondents*, pp. 74–96.

[52] Bertrand Russell, "The Correspondence between Leibniz and De Volder," *Proceedings of the Aristotelian Society*, 28 (1927), 155–176; Paul Lodge, "Leibniz's Close Encounter with Cartesianism in the Correspondence of De Volder," in Lodge (ed.), *Leibniz and His Correspondents*, pp. 162–192; *The Leibniz-De Volder Correspondence, With Selections from the Correspondence Between Leibniz and Johann Bernoulli*, translated, edited, and with an introduction by Paul Lodge (New Haven and London: Yale University Press, 2013).

[53] *Briefwechsel zwischen Leibniz und Christian Wolff*, ed. C. I. Gerhardt (Halle, 1860; repr. Hildesheim: Georg Olms, 1963); Donald Rutherford, "Idealism Declined: Leibniz and Christian Wolff," in Lodge (ed.), *Leibniz and His Correspondents*, pp. 214–237.

[54] Philip Beeley, "A Philosophical Apprenticeship: Leibniz's Correspondence with the Secretary of the Royal Society, Henry Oldenburg," in Lodge (ed.), *Leibniz and His Correspondents*, pp. 47–73.

[55] *Leibniz-Thomasius, Correspondence, 1663–1672*, texte établi, introduit, traduit, annoté et commenté par Richard Bodéüs (Paris: J. Vrin, 1993); Christia Mercer, "Leibniz and His Master: The Correspondence with Jakob Thomasius," in Lodge (ed.), *Leibniz and His Correspondents*, pp. 10–46.

antiquarians, genealogists, numismatists, or experts in heraldry (Muratori, Papebroch, Paullini, Rymer, and Tentzel), to which can be added a score of philologists and linguists, such as von der Hardt, Le Fort, Ludolf, Meier, Nicaise, and Sparfvenfelt.

To these intellectuals, however, can be added some 240 members of the learned professions. Half are members of the clerical estate: Catholics (such as Pellison and Bossuet, Rojas y Spinola, and Buchhaim), as well as Anglicans (Gilbert Burnet), Lutherans (Molanus, Spener) and Reformed (Daniel Ernst Jablonski). The other half is divided among experts in law and medicine: the former include some of the leading legal scholars and political thinkers of the day (such as Conring and Pufendorf); the latter, a large number of influential "Leibärtzte" or physicians to princes and other prominent persons.

Needless to say, these categories overlap. Historians shade off into a score of librarians and archivists, including Justel in London and Thevenot in Paris. Another 20 correspondents are book dealers, yet another 20 are scribes. Richer still is the correspondence with 50 learned artisans and technicians: mining engineers in the Harz, instrument makers involved in perfecting his calculating machine, engravers, mechanics, and printers.

It is at the opposite end of the social hierarchy, however, that Leibniz's address book is most remarkable. Nearly one-third of his correspondents (340 persons according to Gerber) derive from the political sphere: emperors and kings, princes both secular and ecclesiastical, ministers and secretaries of state, diplomats and emissaries spiraling out from Hanover to include the Guelf lands and northern Germany, the Holy Roman Empire more generally, and the whole of Europe not subject to the Ottomans. Particularly striking is Leibniz's correspondence with learned noblewomen. Between 1680 and 1714, he exchanged more than 400 letters with Sophie, Duchess and Electress of Hanover, making her the second-most frequent of all his correspondents. With her daughter, Sophie Charlotte, Electress of Brandenburg and Queen in Prussia, he exchanged another 150 letters.[56] In the final years of his life, Sophie's daughter-in-law, Caroline von Ansbach—the wife of Georg (II) August of Hanover who became Princess of Wales in 1714—played a crucial role in mediating his relations with the English court and the Newtonian spokesman, Samuel Clarke.[57] Some years earlier, Leibniz had employed a similar strategy in pursuing a correspondence with Lady Damaris Masham as a means of engaging with John Locke, who was living in her household at the time.[58] Other learned women with whom he avidly corresponded included

---

[56] Gädeke, "Leibniz lässt sich informieren," p. 12. Lloyd Strickland (ed. and trans.), *Leibniz and the Two Sophies: The Philosophical Correspondence* (Toronto: Iter, 2011) shows how much of these exchanges were devoted to philosophy.

[57] D. Bertoloni Meli, "Caroline, Leibniz, and Clarke," *Journal of the History of Ideas*, 60 (1999), 469–86; Gregory Brown, "'... et je serai tousjours la même pour vous": Personal, Political, and Philosophical Dimensions of the Leibniz–Caroline Correspondence," in Lodge (ed.), *Leibniz and His Correspondents*, pp. 262–292.

[58] Pauline Phemister, "'All the time and everywhere everything's the same as here': The Principle of Uniformity in the Correspondence between Leibniz and Lady Masham," in Lodge (ed.), *Leibniz and His Correspondents*, pp. 193–213.

*

JAMES I (1566–1625)
James VI, King of Scotland (1567–1625)
James I, 1st King of Great Britain (1603–1625)

m. 1589

Anne of Denmark
(1574–1619)

FREDERICK V (1596–1632)
"The Winter King"
Elector palantine of the Rhine (1610–1623)
King of Bohemia (1619–1620)

m. 1613

ELIZABETH STUART (1596–1662)
"The Queen of Hearts"

C
King of Engla

CHARLES II (1630–1685)
Restored to English Throne in 1660
King of England, Scotland, Ireland (1660–1685)

ELIZABETH (1618–1680)
Princess of Bohemia
Abbess of the Protestant Convent at Herford, Wesphalia
Friend and Correspondent of Descartes (1596–1650)

WILLIAM III
(1650–1702)
(Son of Mary and
William of Orange
Prince of Orange
King of England
Scotland, Ireland
(1689–1702)

m. 1677

MARY II (1662–1694)
Queen of England, Scotland,
Ireland (1689–94)

SOPHIE (1630–1714)
Duchess of Hanover (1679)
Electress of Hanover (1692–1698)
Dowager Electress of Hanover (1698–1714)
Patroness and friend of LEIBNIZ

m. 1658

Ernst August (1629–1698)
Prince-bishop of Osnabruck (1661)
Duke of Luneburg–Calenberg (Hanover) (1679)
1st Elector of Brunswick–Luneburg (Hanover) (1692–1698)
Set LEIBNIZ to work on a history of the House of Brunswick

Jo
Duke of Luner
(m. 1668 Benedi
n
Retaine

Friedrich (1657–1713)
Friedrich III, Elector of Brandenburg (1688)
Friedrich I, King of Prussia (1701–1713)
Founded Berlin Academy (1700) at urging of
LEIBNIZ who was elected president for life

m. 1684

SOPHIE CHARLOTTE (1668–1705)
Electress of Brandenburg (1688) and 1st Queen of Prussia (1701–1
Friend of LEIBNIZ, who on her deathbed wrote: " I go now to satis
curiosity about the basic causes of things, which LEIBNIZ was never
teach me about space, and the infinite, about being and nothingness;
the King my husband I prepare the drama of a funeral, which will giv
new opportunity to demonstrate his magnificence."

Friedrich Wilhelm (1688–1740)
Elector of Brandenburg (1713)
Friedrich Wilhem I, King of Prussia (1713–1740)
In 1731 he banished Christian Wolff (1679–1754)
follower of LEIBNIZ and Professor of Mathematics and
Philosophy at Halle, at 48–hour notice and "on pain of
the halter," for teaching what the King had come to be
convinced by Wolff's Pietist enemies was fatalistic
determinism

m. 1706

SOPHIE DOROTHEA (1687–1757)
Electress of Brandenburg
Queen Consort

FRIEDRICH II (1712–1786)
Known as "The Great"
King of Prussia (1740–1786)
Recalled Christian Wolff to Halle in 1740
Patron of Voltaire (1694–1778)

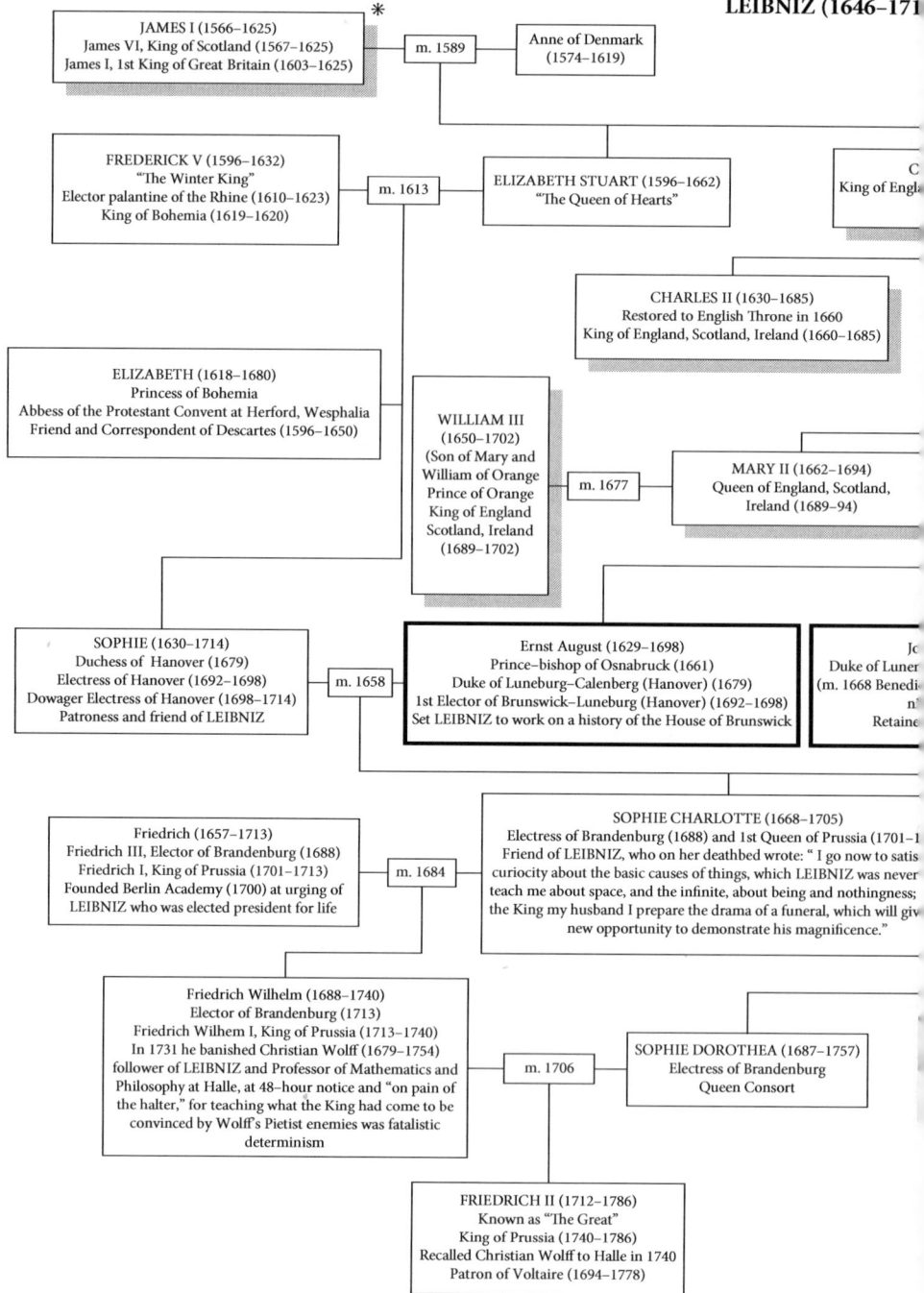

* **Note that the shadowed boxes trace the
movement of the British Crown**

FIGURE 32.4 Leibniz and the Hanoverian Succession. Shadowed boxes denote the succession ●
the British crown. Bold boxes denote Leibniz's employers.

First published as Gregory Brown, "Leibniz and Royalty," *Leibniz Society Review*, 5 (1995): fold-o
chart facing the last page in this issue. Reproduced with permissio

Georg (1582–1641)
Duke of Lûneburg–Calenberg (Hanover) (1636–1641)

m. 1617

Anna Eleonore of Hessen–Darmstadt (1601–1659)

LES I (1600–1649)
Scotland, Ireland (1625–1649)
ecuted in 1649

m. 1625

Henrietta Maria (d. 1669)
Daughter of Henry IV of France

JAMES II (1633–1701)
King of England, Scotland, Ireland (1685–1688)

MARY (1631–1660)
(m. William II, Prince of Orange)

(1) Anne Hyde
(1637–1671)

m.

(2) Mary of Madena
(1658–1718)

ANNE (1665–1714)
Queen of England, Scotland, Ireland (1702–1707)
Queen of Great Britain & Ireland (1707–1714)
[m. George of Denmark (el. 1708)]

JAMES francis
Edward Stuart
(Old Pretender)
(d.1766)

Christian Ludwig (1622–1665)
Duke of Lûneburg–Calenberg (Hanover)
(1641–1648)
Duke of Lûneburg–Celle (1648–1665)
[m.1653 (Sophie) Dorothea of Holstein–Glücksburg (1636–1689)]

n Friedrich (1625–1679)
g–Calenberg (Hanover) (1665–1679)
Ienriette of the Palatinate (1652–1730)
of Sophie and Elizabeth)
e services of LEIBNIZ in 1676

Georg Wilhelm (1624–1705)
Duke of Lunenburg–Calenberg (Hanover) (1648–1665)
Duke of Lunenburg–Celle (1665–1705)

m. 1675

Eleonore Desmiers d'Olbreuse
(1639–1722)

)
y
to
for
n a

GEORG LUDWIG (1660–1727)
Hereditary Prince of Luneburg–Calenburg (Hanover) (1679);
Electoral Prince of Hanover (1692); Elector of Hanover (1698);
George I, King of Great Britain & Ireland (1714–1727).
Left Leibniz in Hanover to work on what became his Annales Imperil
Occidentis Brunswicenses; refused Leibniz's request (made through
Caroline and Minister Bernstorff in December 1715) to be made an
historiographer of Great Britain

m. 1682
(div. 1694)

Sophie Dorothea (1666–1726)
Princess of Celle (Ahlden)

GEORG AUGUST (1683–1760)
Electoral Prince of Hanover (1698)
Prince of Wales (1714)
Elector of Hanover (1727)
eorge III, King of Great Britain and Ireland (1727–1760)

m.1705

Princess Caroline of Brandenburg–Ansbach (1683–1737)
Princess of Wales (1714)
Electress of Hanover (1727)
Queen Consort (1727–1737)
friend and pupil of LEIBNIZ
The "Caroline" of the Leibniz–Clarke Correspondence

FRIEDRICH LOUIS (1707–1751)
Prince of Wales (1728–1751)

m.1736

Augusta of Saxe–Gotha–Altenburg
(1719–1772)

GEORGE III (1738–1820)
King of Great Britain, Ireland, and Hanover (1760–1820)
The "King George" of the American Revolution

**Prepared by Gregory Brown
University of Houston
(Revised 03/17/05)**

Duchess Elisabeth Charlotte of Orléans, Empress Amalie (wife of Joseph I), Madame de Brinon, and Duchess Benedicte (wife of Johann Friedrich). Leibniz's letters to and from learned women outnumber the entire correspondences of many of his intellectual predecessors.[59]

These 1,300 correspondents are not unrelated individuals: like the displaced Huguenot scholars discussed earlier, they are bound together in multiple ways crucial for understanding the network as a whole and Leibniz's interaction with it. An illuminating illustration of the most basic social bonds comes from the very apex of the social hierarchy: namely, the links of blood and marriage which bound together the core of Leibniz's contacts among the crowned heads of Europe. At the center of Figure 32.4 is the intersection of the House of Stuart and the House of Lüneburg-Calenberg (Hanover), which resulted in the succession of the latter to the British crown. Also represented are the "Winter King and Queen of Bohemia," William III of Orange, the newly created kings of Prussia, and the royal families of Denmark and France. A fuller version would add still further rulers to Leibniz's network, capped by the Russian Czar, Peter the Great, and three successive Holy Roman Emperors, Leopold I, Joseph I, and Charles VI. These linkages were also the product of physical mobility: dynastic networks were knit together above all by daughters moving from one court to seal marriage alliances in another. In assessing Leibniz's communications with any one of these individuals, and indeed with their servants and subordinates, their place in the larger network and the histories of those networks must constantly be borne in mind.

Leibniz's network, therefore, was structured and sustained by far more than his correspondence. In order to understand these additional structural elements, we need systems capable of systematically assembling data on linkages such as these. Biographical data are needed even in order to identify people—that is, in order to disambiguate people who shared names or titles with one another or who were referred to under a variety of names and titles. Location histories are required to track movements, as Leibniz's own itinerary shows. Contact histories are needed to coordinate the innumerable scraps of data documenting nonepistolary contact between students and teachers, colleagues, members of learned societies, greetings exchanged between mutual friends, direct and indirect services, and mere co-citation within the texts of letters themselves. Typologies (which IT experts call "ontologies") are needed to assemble data on the various kinds of relationship—of blood and marriage, students and teachers, patrons and clients, nations and confessions—which structured these communities. Network analysis—a powerful tool in the sciences—must be adapted for dealing with the many peculiarities of historical data in this field. Developing a standard model for capturing and analyzing

---

[59] For an overview, see Gerda Untermöhlen, "Die gelehrte Frau im Spiegel der Leibniz-Korrespondenz," in S. Neumeister and C. Wiedemann (eds.), *Res Publica Litteraria: die Institutionen der Gelehrsamkeit in der frühen Neuzeit* (Wiesbaden: Harrassowitz, 1987), pp. 603–618.

data on citizens of the republic of letters is perhaps the most urgent desideratum in this entire field.

SPACE AND TIME

Structured prosopographical data of this kind consist of event streams, which locate a particular activity—chairing a meeting, buying a book, writing a letter—in time and space. Rigorously standardized data of this kind therefore require the ability to model space and time consistently, and this raises a series of even more fundamental issues. In Leibniz's day it was not just people, letters, and books which were in motion. The very landscape through which they moved was constantly shifting beneath their feet, and so was the way in which they measured and recorded time.

The political and ecclesiastical geography of Leibniz's day was extremely complex, above all in his beloved Holy Roman Empire, which was divided into hundreds of semi-autonomous imperial free cities, counties, and principalities, both secular and ecclesiastical. Although a modern gazetteer can easily pinpoint places on the physical landscape of Germany, it is of little use in positioning them within the hundreds of political entities which made up this complex landscape. This complexity is further compounded by constant change (Figure 32.5). The boundaries between these polities, and their political, dynastic, and confessional relations with one another, shifted continuously. The Hanoverian succession to the British crown in 1714 is a particularly pertinent example, but far from unique: the very same years saw the transfer of the southern Netherlands, Milan, Naples, and Sardinia from the Spanish to the Austrian Habsburgs. Whole kingdoms changed shape in this period as well: the armies of Louis XIV expanded the boundaries of France at the expense of the Empire, while the Austrian Habsburgs reconquered much of Hungary from the Ottoman Turks. After these and many subsequent changes, the boundaries of Leibniz's day do not coincide with the modern national boundaries employed in most gazetteers today. This poses a severe constraint on our capacity to visualize and analyze the basic data documenting Leibniz's world. Superimposing the data describing his intellectual network on a map of the shifting political borders of his lifetime is a fundamental desideratum of Leibniz scholarship, but one which surpasses the capabilities of existing scholarly infrastructure.

Time was not standing still either. Leibniz lived in a period in which Europeans were transitioning from one calendar to another, and this adds another level of complexity to his network. Pope Gregory XIII had introduced the Gregorian calendar in October 1582. By the end of the sixteenth century, it had been adopted by virtually the all Catholic polities and by virtually no Protestant ones. The Protestant estates of the Empire waited another century, finally abandoning the older Julian calendar on February 18–March 1, 1700, together with Denmark-Norway. The individual provinces of the Dutch Republic

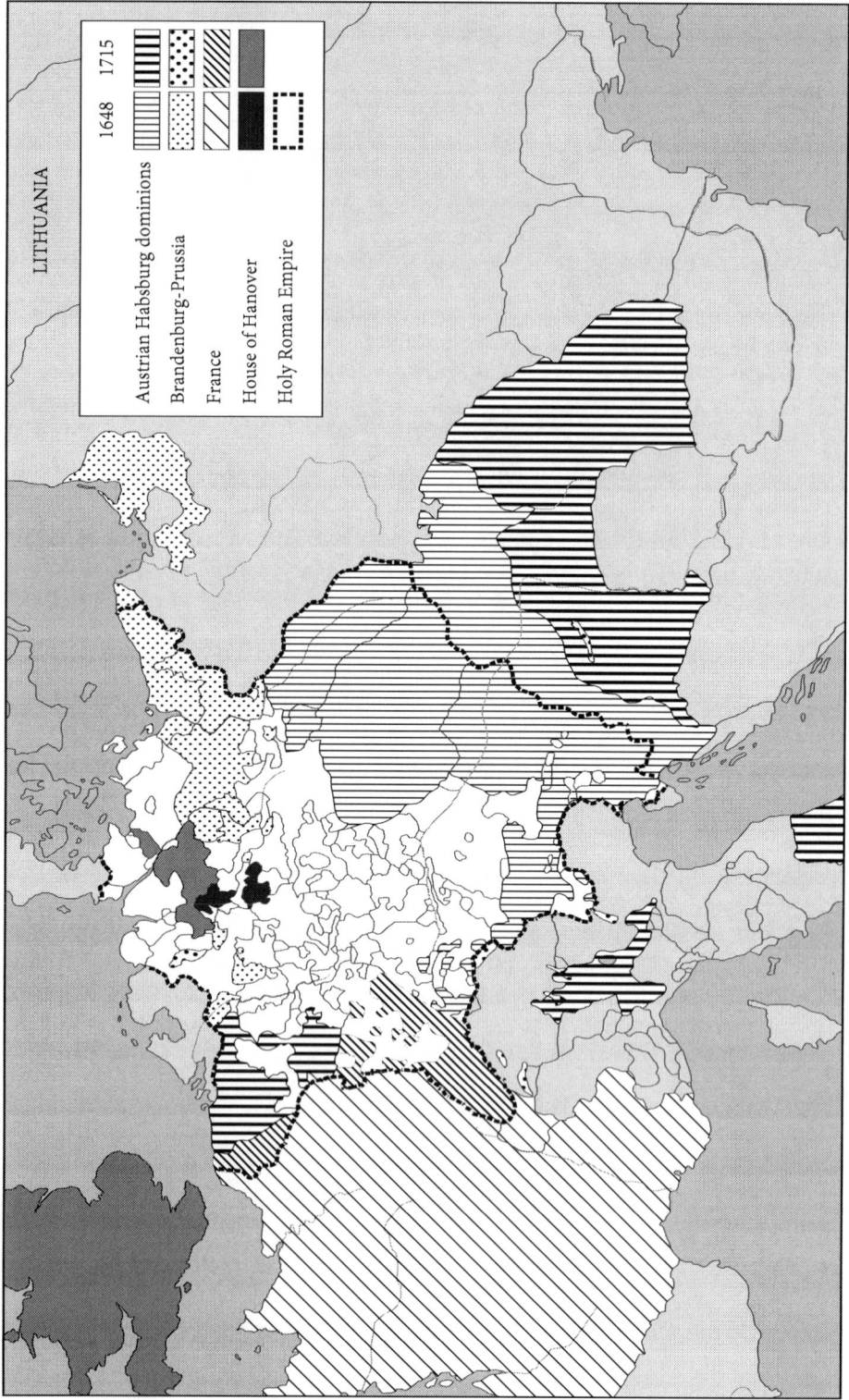

FIGURE 32.5 Major changes of borders and rulers during Leibniz's lifetime.

Map by Howard Hotson.

quickly followed their lead, as did the Protestant Swiss cantons (on December 31, 1700-January 12, 1701). But England, Wales, Scotland, and Sweden clung to the Julian calendar until 1752, while differing among themselves as to whether to begin the New Year on March 1 ("old style Julian") or January 1 (new style). Russia did not adopt the Gregorian system until 1918.[60]

Tools exist for automatically resolving competing calendrical systems, but this does not end the chronological confusion. Unsurprisingly under these circumstances, many letters to and from Leibniz are not precisely dated. Even after meticulous study, only a date range can typically be identified, and sometimes even these date ranges are highly uncertain. Any attempt to visualize correspondence networks or to analyze them computationally must develop standard means of dealing with dates which are unknown, incomplete, imprecise, uncertain, and nonstandard.

CONTENT

For the historian of philosophy or ideas, understanding the temporal, spatial, and personal dimensions of Leibniz's network will seem incomplete without equally effective means of mapping the conceptual landscape of his correspondence as well. Here again, correspondence poses particularly difficult problems. A formal treatise moves through a compact body of knowledge in a disciplined and orderly way, typically outlined in a table of contents and sometimes indexed as an additional aid to locating material on specific topics. By contrast, an individual letter can teem with heterogeneous information and leap abruptly from one topic to another. This juxtaposition of divergent material displays the pursuit of knowledge in action with the utmost immediacy but increases the difficulty of finding the material relevant to any particular inquiry. How might technology assist the researcher in locating material on specific topics within the hundreds of thousands of passages which make up Leibniz's 20,000 letters?

In addressing this challenge, a first step must be to provide a controlled vocabulary with which to map the conceptual structure of Leibniz's letters. The difficulty of doing so is partly that the most comprehensive sets of modern categories—such as the Library of Congress topical headings—do not coincide with those which would have been employed by the ducal librarian in Wolfenbüttel between 1691 and 1716. "Philosophy," to mention only the most obvious case, contained a vast disciplinary domain which today includes the social and natural sciences as well as philosophy as currently defined. Many of the subdivisions of philosophy in Leibniz's day, such as "physics," meant something different then than they do now. New disciplines were emerging as well, as Leibniz's own coinage, "dynamics," illustrates perfectly. Moreover, in Leibniz's day, there was not one,

---

[60] C. R. Cheney and Michael Jones (eds.), *A Handbook of Dates for Students of British History* [Royal Historical Society Guides and Handbooks, 4] (rev. ed., Cambridge: Cambridge University Press, 2000), pp. 236–241.

universally understood method for dividing and arranging the various compartments of learning. Instead, while some still clung to traditional Aristotelian categories, new systems were proliferating and competing with one another. To complicate matters further, the act of assigning a particular text to one category or another—whether ancient, early modern, or modern—is an act of judgment which any two scholars may perform differently. This problem is particularly acute when the topic explicitly under discussion relates to underlying issues merely implicit in the correspondence in question.

In principle, it should be possible to solve this problem by allowing different users to categorize or analyze texts in terms of multiple different ontologies. The basis for doing so would be to tag the thematic content of texts in terms of the conceptual taxonomy (or "ontology")[61] of their choice. A range of such ontologies could then be interlinked in a manner which allows a degree of flexibility in searching or sorting material in (say) a modern taxonomy which has been tagged in an Aristotelian one, and vice versa. Negotiating such a system for a correspondence as complex and comprehensive as Leibniz's would be a demanding enterprise.

Even if a structure of topics can be agreed, identifying the specific topics handled in any particular letter would pose additional challenges. Manual tagging by a trained team of expert users would be the most reliable method but also very laborious and expensive. Scholarly crowdsourcing might be employed for a first round of general and provisional topics, which could then be refined by domain experts. The high-tech solution would involve state-of-the-art topic modeling—a form of natural language processing which defines abstract "topics" in terms of clusters of words recurring with statistically defined patterns of frequency. The difficulty of applying this method is compounded by the polyglot nature of Leibniz's correspondence.[62] Topic modeling of multi-lingual corpora of learned correspondence from this period has been attempted by the ePistolarium project by the Huygens Institute of Dutch History.[63] The challenges are formidable, but, with technology developing rapidly, it would be unwise to discount the feasibility of this method in the not-too-distant future.

---

[61] The usage here derives from information science (rather than metaphysics), in which an "ontology" is a set of formal names and definitions of the types, properties, and interrelationships of the entities within a particular domain of discourse.

[62] Latin dominated Leibniz's earliest correspondence and was retained for communication with Italy, the Jesuits, and scholars from the German-speaking world. French dominated both philosophical and political correspondence from the Parisian period onward. German was used far less frequently than either, and Italian, Dutch, and English occasionally for letters to Leibniz. Precise proportions are unknown: Gerber, "Leibniz und seine Korrespondenz," pp. 148–154; Gädeke, "Leibniz," pp. 270–271.

[63] The ePistolarium is the major outcome of the project "Circulation of Knowledge and Learned Practices in the 17th-century Dutch Republic": http://ckcc.huygens.knaw.nl/. On the project, see Walter Ravenek, Charles van den Heuvel, and Guido Gerritsen, "The ePistolarium: Origins and Techniques," in Jan Odijk and Arjan van Hessen (eds.), CLARIN in the Low Countries (London: Ubiquity Press, 2017), ch. 26. DOI: https://doi.org/10.5334/bbi.

EXPLORING MULTIPLE
DIMENSIONS SIMULTANEOUSLY

Determining how to model and represent the individual dimensions of Leibniz's correspondence network does not, however, exhaust the challenges confronting the would-be cartographer of his intellectual world. A more general problem is how to explore several of these dimensions simultaneously. An excellent starting point for considering this problem is provided by Figure 32.6: a heroic attempt to represent the topical and geographical dimensions of Leibniz's network on a single hand-drawn map.

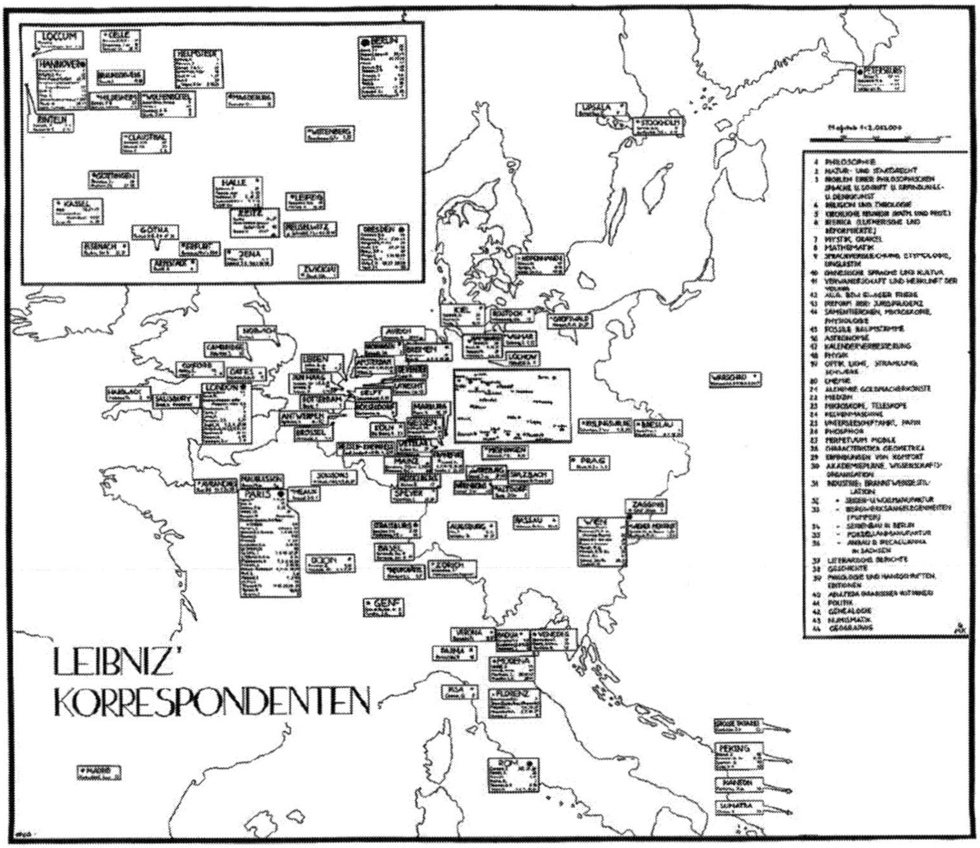

FIGURE 32.6 Topics discussed between Leibniz and his major correspondents. "Leibniz' Korrespondenten," an anonymous, hand-drawn map, previously published in Heinekamp and Hein, *Leibniz und Europa*, p. 66, and Gädeke, "Leibniz" (2005), p. 301.

Reproduced with permission of the Gottfried Wilhelm Leibniz-Bibliothek, Hanover.

The basic format of this image is once again cartographical. Each rectangle on the map locates a city significant within Leibniz's network. Within the rectangles are listed, alphabetically by surname, the principal people with whom he corresponded in each city. Each name is followed by one or more numbers, which refer to the 44 topics listed in the legend to the right. In short, this is an ingenious experiment: a novel attempt to map the intellectual geography of Leibniz's world in terms of the topics which he discussed with people in different places.

As a visualization, this map is unsuccessful in the sense that most of the information on it cannot be directly apprehended visually: it needs to be read. Comparison with Figure 32.1 suggests a network less squarely concentrated on the Empire and more orientated to western Europe—the northern and southern Low Countries, England, and France, as well as northern Italy. This may suggest that Leibniz's philosophical and scientific correspondence is orientated westward, while his general, historical, and political correspondence in concentrated in the Empire. But whether this impression is correct is impossible to say based on this presentation of the evidence, and, in every other respect, this map does not make the data on which it is based intelligible visually. This is essentially a cartographically organized index, one that allows the user to cross-reference (via the coded numbers) between people in specific places and the topics in the legend, but an alphabetically organized index would have served almost exactly the same function. In other words, the geographical distribution of topical codes does not allow the viewer to *see* the topical geography directly: one can only work it out, number by number and person by person, by laboriously cross-referencing to the legend. Nor is it possible to work the other way around: to start with the legend and then find all the cities and people who discussed a particular topic. Even though the topics chosen are rather general, the image is far too complex to be legible visually.

Yet this remarkable map is nevertheless very useful in suggesting a visual interface for exploring complex digital data. Given properly structured data, a series of enhancements could transform this interface into a very useful tool for exploring the multiple dimensions of Leibniz's network. Adding topical filters would allow users to see at a glance how individual topics and clusters of topics are distributed geographically. Adding a chronological slider could allow the user to watch the evolution of topical networks over time and to isolate specific periods for closer study. A zoom function would allow magnification of regions too dense to be visualized on a pan-European scale. Switching to a semi-cartographic layout could spread the information across the screen in more legible fashion while maintaining the rough geographical relationships between these places. Clicking on individual cities might produce a graphic indication of the relative size of the individual correspondents' exchanges with Leibniz and bar graphs showing the distribution of their letters over time. Clicking on individual correspondents could bring up graphs showing how the topical structure as well as the frequency of their letters changed over time and indicate what is known about their own movements. Ideally, the user could then click through to view the biographies, itineraries, and prosopographies of Leibniz's correspondents; the distribution of all of their known letters; and the intersection of their correspondence networks with Leibniz's. Ideally, clicking on individual topics or letters could allow the user to drill down into the texts of the letters themselves. In the best of all possible worlds, such an interface would allow the user not only actively to explore all the data on the system but also to suggest emendations, refinements, and additions to existing data, in a manner which tracks and credits contributions and also allows the policing of quality control. In short, this remarkable map provides an excellent means of beginning to think about the kind of "virtual research environment" which could transform the study of Leibniz's network in particular and the early modern republic of letters more generally while providing a platform for radically multilateral scholarly collaboration in collecting fresh data as well.

This scenario raises a final point about visualizations as a mode of understanding data of this kind. Much of the skepticism about the utility of visualizations in this field arises from a misunderstanding of how they can best be used. The purpose of a digital research environment of this kind is not to produce a single, static view of the data which makes everything clear. That may have been the primary objective when visualizations had to be laboriously created by hand and reproduced as static, black-and-white images on paper. But there are limits to the amount of information which can be conveyed by any such image, and that level is way below what is needed to understand a large-scale, highly complex dataset. The purpose of an interactive interface is precisely to overcome this inherent limitation by allowing the user to cycle easily through many different views at many different scales of many different portions of many different dimensions of the data, until the pertinent aspects of its structure become clear. Even when certain views are then selected for reproduction in hard copy, the primary utility of the interface is to facilitate the *process* of exploring complex data, not to produce a single static *product* capturing one aspect of it.

Nouvelles Ouvertures

How, then, to capture this complexity? How do we make such a large and complex mass of material legible as a whole, or as something like a whole?

In searching for an answer, the starting point is obvious. Data on intellectual networks have at least six main dimensions: the four discussed earlier (temporal duration, spatial breadth, social depth, and thematic range), as well as media of transaction and language. A sheet of paper, for all practical purposes, has only two dimensions. So ink on paper is not an adequate means of exploring the evolution of an intellectual network. Instead, what is needed is a means of analyzing each of these six dimensions individually and in combination with one another. Moreover, in order to explore a large dataset of this kind, we need to be able to filter the data, to model many of these dimensions in a variety of different ways, and to view the results at a multitude of different scales. Providing this functionality requires the development of models, tools, systems, and conventions which do not yet exist or which have not yet been adapted for ready scholarly use. It is largely for this reason that our grasp of the changing shape of Leibniz's network as a whole has not advanced very much in the half-century since the classic article by Georg Gerber in 1966.[64] Prose is not well adapted to exploring such complicated material, even when accompanied by tables, graphs, charts, and maps of the conventional kinds.

One of the most important tasks of the next decade will therefore be to develop shared solutions to a set of technical problems prerequisite to collecting and analyzing large quantities of historical data of this kind. Needless to say, this is a challenge of daunting complexity—tantamount, one might say, to mastering the complexity of Leibniz's intellectual world itself. This challenge will only be met if approached in an appropriate manner.

To begin with, the scale of this challenge requires that it must be tackled in a highly collaborative fashion. For instance, no one person is going to capture data on Leibniz's 1,300 correspondents single-handedly. This must be a collective undertaking, in which experts on particular individuals, disciplines, and regions pool their knowledge. Thankfully, precisely such collaborative efforts are currently being organized in Turin.[65]

Second, this collaborative work must be carefully coordinated. To extend the previous example, work on collecting prosopographical data on Leibniz's correspondents requires the existence of a robustly user-tested data model. If the deficiencies of a data model are revealed well after work has begun, there is the grave danger that work will have to be repeated, thus draining the project of resources, energy, and credibility. A robust prosopographical data model, capable of accommodating all the data on a diverse group such as Leibniz's correspondents, can only be developed through close and sustained collaboration between specialists in all the relevant regions, periods, and fields.

This brings us to a third crucial point: this coordinated collaboration will need to be highly interdisciplinary. Developing such a prosopographical data model will require the collaboration of experts from many different fields, involving not only philosophers but historians in all the disciplines and regions involved in Leibniz's network. Drawing up an adequate and consensual blueprint of the underlying infrastructure will require scholars from many different disciplines to sit down for structured discussions, sustained over several years, with a diverse range of specialists: librarians, archivists, experts in many different kinds of information technology, graphic designers, and intellectual property lawyers, to name a few.

---

[64] Gerber, "Leibniz und seine Korrespondenz."

[65] "LCA: G. W. Leibniz's Correspondents and Acquaintances. Intellectual networks, themes, individuals," a project coordinated by Enrico Pasini and initiated by the Italian Society of Leibnizian

Given the scale of the commitment involved, it follows that infrastructure of the requisite scale and sophistication is unlikely to be created for dealing with the network of any one historical individual—however important and intensively studied. Every single one of the problems encountered in mastering Leibniz's network also obstructs the study of all the other networks which made up the republic of letters, from before Erasmus until after Voltaire. The challenge of developing a fresh approach to Leibniz's network must therefore be incorporated into the broader attempt to reassemble and map the republic of letters more generally.[66] In any case, each of Leibniz's correspondents exchanged letters and reciprocal influences with other people as well—including with one another. It is therefore impossible to cut off the study of Leibniz's network from the broader study of the intellectual communities of his day.

Leibniz could, however, provide a natural centerpiece to that effort, since his network poses all the challenges involved on a grand scale: an unusually large extant correspondence (20,000 letters) with an unusually large number of correspondents (c. 1,300) of truly extraordinary social depth and professional diversity (from emperors to artisans), drawn from an unusually large geographical area (stretching across and beyond Europe), centered on the most complicated political and confessional geography of early modern Europe (the Holy Roman Empire), engaged in polyglot and multimedia communication on a truly encyclopedic range of contemporary topics. Leibniz is central and representative, and he also provides a uniquely challenging test case. To crack the problem of dealing with the most comprehensive intellectual network of its time is to crack the broader problem of the mapping of the republic of letters more generally.

The scale and complexity of the data needed to understand these networks has proved almost unmanageable during the age of script and print, but digital technology now holds out the promise of a collaboratively conceived, designed, built, and populated infrastructure capable of rendering these data intelligible for the first time. Ultimately, transitioning to this new infrastructure will require an academic culture shift. Institutions must learn to collaborate rather than compete, since solving such problems surpasses the resources—intellectual as well as financial—of any one institution. Funding agencies must be prepared to invest in infrastructure capable of supporting whole areas of humanistic scholarship, in addition to bespoke systems to sustain individual projects. Assessment regimes must

studies (Sodalitas Leibnitiana) in collaboration with other European societies of Leibnizian studies and supported by the fMOD Research Group of the University of Turin: http://www.leibnitiana.eu.

[66] Leadership in this enterprise has been provided between 2014 and 2018 by COST Action IS 1310: "Reassembling the Republic of Letters, 1500–1800," which aims (in the words of its project subtitle) to negotiate "a digital framework for multi-lateral collaboration on Europe's intellectual history" (http://www.republicofletters.net/). A book-length blueprint of this framework (available also as an open-access, enhanced publication) is currently being prepared by the Action chairs, Howard Hotson and Thomas Wallnig, for publication by the Göttingen University Press. This Action builds on the Mellon-funded collaborative research project in Oxford, "Cultures of Knowledge: Networking the Republic of Letters, 1550–1750," (http://www.culturesofknowledge.org/) and its flagship output, "Early Modern Letters Online" (http://emlo.bodleian.ox.ac.uk/).

expand their criteria to accommodate the full range of contributions needed to design, build, and populate as well as use such systems, which fall outside the traditional categories of academic production. In short, a transformation of many different aspects of academic culture will be required, one as wide-ranging as the print revolution still unfolding in Leibniz's day but moving at a much faster pace. The payback will be radically to enhance the ease with which we can explore the many dimensions of Leibniz's intellectual world and thereby to understand the development of his thought in greater depth and detail.[67]

[67] This chapter is particularly indebted to the work of Nora Gädeke, and has been enriched and reshaped by much valuable assistance from Maria Rosa Antognazza. While this chapter was in press, on 13 October 2017 the Personen- und Korrespondenz-Datenbank der Leibniz-Edition was opened to international research at https://leibniz.uni-goettingen.de/pages/index. This resource made available records of some 14,000 letters published and 10,807 persons mentioned within the Akademie Ausgabe to date, with more records subsequently added as further volumes are published. Among other features, these records contain links to the relevant texts within the edition, to further information and alternative name forms for correspondents, and to relevant authority files such as GND (the German national *Gemeinsame Normdatei*, also known as the *Universal Authority File*) and VIAF (*Virtual International Authority File*), indispensable for disambiguating and linking open data. Individual fields within the biographical data are also searchable, such as political titles and functions, political and territorial affiliation, religious affiliation, education, profession, and academic title. Multiple filter functions and combinations of search options can be used to generate complex queries which will greatly facilitate the exploration of this invaluable dataset. Three visualizations prepared by Nora Gädeke and Lothar Krempel suggest fruitful ways forward for the visual presentation and interrogation of the data.

CHAPTER 33

LEIBNIZ AS HISTORIAN

MARIA ROSA ANTOGNAZZA

In the summer of 1716, a few months before dying, Leibniz penned a letter to a Polish diplomat called Biber: "[I]t is only my massive historical work," he explained, "that hinders me from executing my idea of presenting philosophy demonstratively. I hope to finish [the Guelf history] this year; and if God gives me more strength thereafter, I will try to discharge myself of certain ideas I still have regarding the advancement of knowledge."[1]

Leibniz came to regard the task of writing the history of the Guelfs as a millstone around his neck, one that held him back from pursuing his true intellectual passions, not to mention preventing him from joining the newly created Hanoverian king, George I, in London. After his return from Vienna on September 14, 1714, the now elderly man tried to make haste, devoting a great part of his energies to his historical assignment. Yet he passed away on November 14, 1716, with his history still unfinished. Labor on this magnum opus, the *Annales Imperii Occidentis Brunsvicenses*, had started back in June 1685, when Leibniz had himself petitioned Duke Ernst August of Hanover to entrust him with the project. At his death in 1716, two decades were still missing before the end of the first volume of the *Annales* in the year 1024, and not a single page of them had been published.

One may be tempted to conclude that Leibniz's historical ventures were a failure, an ill-judged investment of time and efforts which had cost him dear without delivering any significant results. This conclusion, however, would be myopic. There is more to Leibniz's historiographical efforts than immediately meets the eye. To start with, his historical work in uncovering the illustrious pedigree of the cadet line of Guelfs which ruled Hanover played a significant role in their elevation to the status of electoral princes of the Empire in March 1692. Likewise, Leibniz's painstaking assembly and publication of historical legal documents strengthened the case for a Hanoverian succession to the throne of Great Britain and Ireland. By the standards of any other historian, the success

---

[1] LBr 64, Bl. 4r. Summer of 1716. Unless otherwise stated, translations are my own.

of these two major dynastic claims would have been regarded as crowning a lifetime of well-spent effort. If they are regarded as misplaced activity today, that is largely because Leibniz himself is studied primarily by philosophers and regarded as a theoretician rather than a historical actor in his own right. Leibniz's involvement with history and historiography, however, is longer and deeper than even his contributions to two dynastic turning points of early modern Europe. It goes back all the way to his years of formation in Leipzig and punctuates his life until his very last days in Hanover. The aim of this chapter is to provide a first impression of this long and deep engagement, in the hope of stimulating a more thorough exploration.[2]

Leibniz's Life-Long Engagement with History and Historiography

The edition of Leibniz's historical writings—series five of his works and correspondence—has yet to begin.[3] The true extent of Leibniz's work as historian will be fully known only once publication of this series is complete. Meanwhile, to glean some of his views and achievements in the field of history, we have to rely on an array of partial editions and on the ongoing publication of his general correspondence.[4] Among the

[2] Lewis W. Spitz concluded his discussion of "The significance of Leibniz for historiography" (*Journal of the History of Ideas* 13 (1952), pp. 333–348, here p. 348) with the following appraisal: "His own historical writing and specific historical theory were of relatively little import. But the impact of his thought on the Enlightenment and on historicism led to a diligent recovery of the past and to particular interpretations of that past. It is in this that his great significance for historiography lies." The dismissive judgment of the significance of Leibniz's thought and work specifically on history, over and above his more general philosophical impact, is shared, for instance, by Yvon Belaval, "Leibniz comme historien," in *Leibniz als Geschichtsforscher*, edited by Albert Heinekamp (Wiesbaden: Franz Steiner Verlag, 1982), pp. 30–37 (see esp. p. 37). This chapter hopes to show that such judgment is too hasty.

[3] Series V: "Historische und sprachwissenschaftliche Schriften," in G. W. Leibniz, *Sämtliche Schriften und Briefe*, edited by the Academy of Sciences of Berlin, Series I–VIII (Darmstadt—Leipzig—Berlin, 1923 ff.).

[4] See especially G. W. Leibniz, *Gesammelte Werke*. Erste Folge: "Geschichte," edited by Georg Heinrich Pertz. 4 vols. (Hanover: Hahnschen Hof-Buchhandlung, 1843–1847), including the *Annales Imperii Occidentis Brunsvicenses*; and Series I: "Allgemeiner, politischer und historischer Briefwechsel," in Leibniz, *Sämtliche Schriften und Briefe*. The best modern selection of Leibniz's historical writings and letters has been published in 2004: G. W. Leibniz, *Schriften und Briefe zur Geschichte*, edited by Malte-Ludolf Babin and Gerd van den Heuvel (Hanover: Verlag Hahnsche Buchhandlung, 2004). The most significant investigations of Leibniz as historian include the groundbreaking doctoral thesis of Louis Davillé, *Leibniz Historien. Essai sur l'activité et la méthode historique de Leibniz* (Paris: Félix Alcan, 1909); Werner Conze, "Leibniz als Historiker," instalment 6 of *Leibniz zu seinem 300. Geburtstag: 1646–1946*, edited by Erich Hochstetter (Berlin: de Gruyter, 1951), 85 pp.; Spitz, "The significance of Leibniz for historiography"; Antonio Corsano, "Leibniz e la storia," in *Giornale critico della filosofia italiana* 33 (1954), pp. 356–368; Günter Scheel, "Leibniz als Historiker des Welfenhauses," in *Leibniz. Sein Leben, sein Wirken, seine Welt*, edited by W. Totok and C. Haase (Hanover: Verlag für Literatur und Zeitgeschehen, 1966), pp. 227–276; *Leibniz als Geschichtsforscher*. On Leibniz as editor of historical sources see *Leibniz*

things we already know, however, is that Leibniz's fascination with history began very early. In one of his self-descriptions, Leibniz reported that, as a young boy, he would not put down a German historical book until he had finished reading it.[5] Soon after beginning formal schooling at the Nikolaischule at the age of seven, he progressed to Latin history books. More precisely, the *Opus Chronologicum* by Sethus Calvisius and an illustrated edition of Livy's Roman history appear to have topped the chart of his favorite readings—one of many signs of his natural precocity.[6] In one of his earliest writings, the *Nova Methodus Discendae Docendaeque Jurisprudentiae* (1667),[7] the young Leibniz assigned great importance to the study of the history of jurisprudence as an investigation of the sources of early modern law in medieval, ancient, and biblical legal systems.[8] This early emphasis on sources was to characterize the historiographical work which Leibniz himself began after his move to Hanover in 1676.

Thereafter, his gradually growing involvement in historical matters was closely (if not exclusively) bound up with his service to the Hanoverian dukes. As early as 1677, for instance, he supported with historical arguments the claim to proper international representation by the major German princes who did not enjoy electoral status, such as the Braunschweig-Lüneburg house headed by the duke of Hanover.[9] In the same year, he started to research the link between the Italian noble house of Este and the Guelf family.[10] Between 1678 and 1680, he proposed a reorganization of the ducal archives under a general director (a position he coveted for himself), aimed at optimizing the use of historical and legal sources in administrative matters.[11] As early as 1680, he suggested writing a history of the Guelfs with a focus on the more recent periods.[12] It was only after 1685, however, that this initially tangential idea snowballed into an increasingly time-consuming major task.

This development was triggered by the genealogical researches of the Venetian abbot, Teodoro Damaideno. Damaideno had constructed an ambitious Guelf genealogy covering more than 2,400 years and linking the prestigious Este family to the Braunschweig-Lüneburg house. For dynastic rather than scholarly reasons, a rigorous demonstration of this link was close to Duke Ernst August's heart since it could help propel the house of Hanover to electoral status. The duke naturally requested the opinion of his most learned employee, who was at the time heavily involved in failing schemes for the Harz

---

als Sammler und Herausgeber historischer Quellen, edited by Nora Gädeke (Wiesbaden: Harrassowitz, 2012). The paucity of Anglophone literature on Leibniz's engagement with history is striking.

[5] *Selbstschilderung* (Pertz I, 4, 166).

[6] *Selbstschilderung* (Pertz I, 4, 166).

[7] A VI ii N. 27.

[8] Cf. Scheel, "Leibniz als Historiker des Welfenhauses," p. 233.

[9] See *Caesarini Fürstenerii de Jure Suprematus ac Legationis Principum Germaniae*, A IV ii N. 1, written on the occasion of the peace conference held in Nijmegen following Louis XIV's aggression against Holland.

[10] See Leibniz to Bonaventura Nardini, August 18, 1677 (Ms XXIII, 186, H. V, Bl. 76).

[11] See for instance A I ii N. 70, N. 71, N. 72; A I iii N. 17, N. 27; and A IV iii N. 28.

[12] See A I iii 20 and A I iii 57.

mines. Leibniz replied in no uncertain terms: Damaideno's *Opus Genealogicum* fell far short of the methodological standards of a truly rigorous historical investigation.[13] His motives in doing so are not difficult to surmise: since rivers of silver were not gushing from the mines in the Harz as Leibniz had recently hoped, he may have sought to offer something of similar value to his patron. In any case, this is the conclusion which Ernst August drew from the remark, and the court counsellor was transformed from a self-styled mining engineer into a dynastic historiographer seeking to set new standards in a robust history of the deep past of the Guelfs.[14]

In the short-term, this assignment provided Leibniz with a degree of freedom from more tedious court duties (such as the chancery work expected from him) and sent him roaming across southern Europe for more than two and a half years, from November 1687 to June 1690. Needless to say, while retracing the footsteps of the Guelfs in the archives and monuments of Germany and Italy, Leibniz took the liberty of engaging in a host of other intellectual enterprises. But he also succeeded spectacularly in his main official goal: namely, the establishment of the precise relationship between the Guelf and the Este families. The key piece of the puzzle concerned the origins of the alleged common ancestor of the two families, a Northern Italian margrave named Albert (or Adalbert) Azzo II (996–1097).[15] It was toward the end of Leibniz's long voyage that the mystery was finally unveiled. In February 1690, upon visiting the tombs of the ancient Este in the Abbey of Vangadizza (Badia Polesine, Veneto), he discovered the funerary monuments of Azzo II and his wife, Kunigunde (Cunizza) von Altdorf (*c.* 1020–55). The epitaphs revealed the exact connection between the Este and Guelf houses. Azzo, whose link to the Este had been established by Leibniz through the study of a manuscript codex held in Augsburg, had married Kunigunde, an heiress of the Bavarian line of the Guelf house. Their son Welf IV (*c.* 1040–1101), created duke of Bavaria as Welf I in 1070, was the direct ancestor of the Guelf line of the Braunschweig-Lüneburg dukes.[16]

After returning in triumph to Hanover in June 1690, Leibniz was at pains to convince Ernst August that the magnitude of his historical discoveries amply justified two years and eight months of absence. All the same, he realized that it was high time to summon his historiographical skills in the production of tangible results. Between the autumn of 1690 and 1692, he drafted several outlines, including a *Brevis synopsis historiae*

---

[13] Cf. A I iv xlvi–xlvii, N. 149, N. 158, N. 415, N. 416, N. 454; and Leibniz, *Schriften und Briefe zur Geschichte*, pp. 86–93.

[14] See Niedersächsische Staatarchiv Cal. Br. 23 IV Nr. 25 Bl. 142 (quoted in Scheel, "Leibniz als Historiker des Welfenhauses," p. 244); Duke Ernst August for Leibniz, "Resolution" (A I iv N. 159); A I iv–xliv; Kurt Müller and Gisela Krönert, *Leben und Werk von Gottfried Wilhelm Leibniz. Eine Chronik* (Frankfurt am Main: Klostermann, 1969), p. 75; *Sitzungsberichte Akademie Wien, phil. hist. Kl.* 22 (1856), p. 272 (quoted in Scheel, "Leibniz als Historiker des Welfenhauses," p. 245).

[15] Scheel, "Leibniz als Historiker des Welfenhauses," pp. 245–246.

[16] See A I v 525–526, 533, 534, 636–637, 666–667; A I vi 266; A I vii 473; *Scriptores rerum Brunsvicensium*, in Leibniz, *Schriften und Briefe zur Geschichte*, pp. 252–253; *Brevis Synopsis historiae Guelficae*, in Leibniz, *Schriften und Briefe zur Geschichte*, pp. 810–811.

Guelficae.[17] In November 1695, on the occasion of the marriage of Duke Rinaldo III of Modena with the oldest daughter of the late Duke Johann Friedrich, Charlotte Felicitas, he released a thirteen-page *Lettre sur la connexion des maisons de Brunsvic et d'Este.*[18]

More generally, as he tried to explain to the duke, one key reason for his slow progress was the rigorous methodology he had adopted. His history was based on the direct consultation of the sources. As anyone who ever attempted archival research would know, that took time.[19] Leibniz was not exaggerating the extent to which he had painstakingly identified and collected a large body of documentary evidence on which to base his account. This evidence included not only historical texts and legal documents, but also, for instance, ancient coins. Some of this material found its way into a five-hundred-page volume of medieval legal documents published in 1693 under the title of *Codex Juris Gentium Diplomaticus.* The volume was followed in 1700 by a five-hundred-page sequel, entitled *Mantissa Codicis Juris Gentium Diplomatici.*[20] Although a planned supplement containing fifteenth- and sixteenth-century documents never went to press, many a historian would have regarded these massive editions of medieval texts, documenting the internal and external relations of European states and the relationship between temporal and spiritual authority in the Middle Age, as a major accomplishment well-worth one's monthly salary for a decade or more. More importantly, Leibniz's commitment of time and effort to the edition of sources manifested the seriousness with which he approached the methodology of historiography, while the range of documents he sourced provided an insight into the depth of his genuine historical interests. Although the immediate goal of his historical assignment was to provide the Braunschweig-Lüneburg house with an appropriate pedigree for their dynastical claims, Leibniz conceived this task as an opportunity to compose a universal history in which the destiny of the Guelfs was embedded within a stable and peaceful European order. A key goal of his historical work was to unearth the roots of this order, shedding light on its formation and its legal basis in a long historical tradition which had balanced for centuries two complementary supranational powers, the pope and the emperor. Leibniz's historical researches, therefore, were also designed to give a firm, empirical foundation both to his abstract views of politics and his practical activities aimed at healing both imperial politics and ecclesiastical strife.

The breadth and ambition of this historiographical project was also shown by his initial plan for a grand, multivolume edition of German historical sources under the

---

[17] See Pertz I, 4, pp. 227–239 and Leibniz, *Schriften und Briefe zur Geschichte*, pp. 800–837. The *Synopsis* underwent several revisions until it was finalized around 1695 (see Scheel, "Leibniz als Historiker des Welfenhauses," p. 250 and Leibniz, *Schriften und Briefe zur Geschichte*, pp. 800–801). Several other preparatory pieces, meant to contribute to the magnum opus, are collected in Leibniz, *Schriften und Briefe zur Geschichte*, pp. 838–906.

[18] A IV vi N. 3 and Leibniz, *Schriften und Briefe zur Geschichte*, pp. 896–906.

[19] Cf. A I vi N. 20–21.

[20] See Ravier N. 33 and N. 50. Cf. Davillé, *Leibniz Historien*, part I, chapters iv and v. Extracts from the *Codex Juris Gentium Diplomaticus* are published in Leibniz, *Schriften und Briefe zur Geschichte*, pp. 138–217.

title of *Monumenta Historiam Brunsvicensem Illustrantia*. Although the edition did not materialize in this form, three substantial volumes of medieval documents (the *Accessiones Historicae*) were published in Leipzig (the first volume) and in Hanover (volumes two and three) between 1698 and 1700.[21] In fact, Leibniz had wished to foster systematic research on German history for quite some time. Back in December 1687, during the first phases of his tour of southern Germany and Italy, he had discussed the plan of establishing a *Collegium Imperiale Historicum*, charged with the publication of chronicles of German history, the edition of documents, and the creation of a journal devoted to historical sources. The last, extensive edition of sources undertaken by Leibniz—the *Scriptores Rerum Brunsvicensium*—was directly linked to the history of the Guelfs, of which it was meant to provide the documentary underpinning. Three volumes belonging to this series and totaling more than three thousand pages appeared in Hanover between 1707 and 1711.[22] Other editions of sources included an intriguing text on the life of Pope Alexander VI, discovered among the rich holdings of the Ducal library in Wolfenbüttel, where Leibniz held the position of director since 1691—a role also closely related to his historiographical work, since it was normal in this era for custody of the greatest libraries to be entrusted to historians.[23] In sum, Leibniz's editions of documents exceeded a grand total of 6,000 pages. This number alone should give us pause, given that Leibniz is commonly regarded as having published relatively little during his lifetime.[24] That he is nevertheless casually described as a work-shy employee and a failed historian is further evidence of the extent to which his historical accomplishments remain poorly integrated into general conceptions of Leibniz.

As for the history of the Guelfs proper, the *Annales Imperii Occidentis Brunsvicenses*, Leibniz displayed in it the same breadth of conception. Explicitly rejecting a narrow-minded approach focused on minute details of family genealogy, he broadened his horizon to embrace the history of the whole Holy Roman Empire.[25] Only in this larger context, he reasoned, would the true significance of the Guelf family's destiny be fully visible. The history of the Holy Roman Empire, in turn, was inextricably interwoven with the history of Europe more generally, justifying (at least to his own satisfaction) his decision to start the *Annales* in 768, the year in which Charlemagne became King of the Franks. The plan was to proceed then year by year until 1235. Eventually, however, the magnitude of the task convinced Leibniz to end a first, free-standing volume of the

---

[21] See Ravier N. 43, N. 48, N. 49; Scheel, "Leibniz als Historiker des Welfenhauses," pp. 263–264, 273; Müller–Krönert, *Leben und Werk*, pp. 130, 153, 169; A I xi l–lii; Leibniz, *Schriften und Briefe zur Geschichte*, pp. 232–235; Davillé, *Leibniz Historien*, book I, chap. v.

[22] See Ravier N. 65, N. 66, and N. 69; and Davillé, *Leibniz Historien*, part I, chap. vi.

[23] *Specimen Historiae Arcanae sive Anecdotae de Vita Alexandri VI* (Hanover, 1696) and *Historia Arcana sive de Vita Alexandri VI* (Hanover, 1697). See Leibniz, *Schriften und Briefe zur Geschichte*, pp. 218–229.

[24] As a standard of comparison, the journal articles published by Leibniz in his lifetime total some 1,400 pages: see *Essais scientifiques et philosophiques: Les articles publiés dans les journaux savants*, collected by Antonio Lamarra and Roberto Palaia, 3 vols. (Hildesheim: Olms, 2005).

[25] Cf. Pertz I, 4, 240.

Annales with the year 1024, which marked the death of the last emperor of the Saxon dynasty, Heinrich II. This first volume would thus also have covered the beginning of the new Braunschweig line originating from Azzo II (996–1097). In this way, Leibniz explained to the Hanoverian Prime Minister in 1714, if God decided to "dispose of him" before he was able to finish the second volume, "the first one will be a complete work."[26]

As Prime Minister Bernstorff was well aware, however, the *Annales* were literally only one part of the story since Leibniz had decided that two preliminary treatises were also needed. Ranging beyond both the Empire and Europe, one was devoted to nothing less than the natural history of the earth as a whole: this is the *Protogaea*, which covered the origin of the earth in general and the origin of Lower Saxony in particular.[27] Bridging geological prehistory and the medieval past, the second treatise was devoted to an equally capacious account of human geography: a study of the origins and migrations of peoples, reaching as far as the origins of the first inhabitants of Lower Saxony. Leibniz envisaged tracking such migrations through the comparative study of languages (that is, in his own phrase, through a genetic study of "the harmony of languages"),[28] thus further expanding the scope of his historical research to linguistic studies. Unlike the *Protogaea* (which was published posthumously), a limited sample of his research on the origins of people did see the light in his lifetime.[29] Even more substantial preparatory work remained unpublished and can be traced, for instance, in his correspondence.[30]

As if such projects were not enough fully to occupy anyone, the Hanoverian dukes did not hesitate to call upon Leibniz's historical and legal skills for other matters as well, and especially for those more likely to bring immediate benefits than their historian's investigation of great migrations. One such matter concerned the lucrative neighboring duchy of Sachsen-Lauenburg. The ruling duke, Julius Franz of Sachsen-Lauenburg (1641–89), had no male heirs, and this opened the opportunity for his neighbors, the Lüneburg dukes, to make a case for their right to inherit. From 1681 onward, Leibniz took the lead in building a historical and legal case for this claim, grounded in the earlier supremacy over Sachsen-Lauenburg of the Guelf's ancestor, Heinrich der Löve (1129 or 1130–95). For such a purpose, he amassed another impressive trove of documentation.[31] The claim to Sachsen-Lauenburg was finally legalized by the emperor on April 28, 1716,[32] a few months before Leibniz's death. A moment's reflection on the monetary stakes of

---

[26] See Leibniz to Andreas Gottlieb von Bernstorff, December 8, 1714 (Klopp XI, 22–24).

[27] The *Protogaea*, already finished by the end of 1694, remained unpublished during Leibniz's lifetime and appeared for the first time in Göttingen in 1749 (*Protogaea sive de prima facie telluris et antiquissimae historiae vestigiis in ipsis naturae monumentis dissertatio*, edited by Ch. L. Scheid).

[28] See Leibniz to Duke Ernst August, mid-January 1691 (*Entwurf der Welfengeschichte*) (A I vi 23–24) and A I vi 442. See also Pertz I, 4, 240–241 and A I xi lv–lvi.

[29] See the nine-page *Dissertatio de Origine Germanorum*, published in 1697 (Ravier N. 40), and the longer *De Origine Francorum Disquisitio*, published in 1715 (Ravier N. 74).

[30] Cf. for instance Leibniz, *Schriften und Briefe zur Geschichte*, pp. 688–692.

[31] In the decade 1681–1692, there are some fifty texts linked to this inheritance claim, covering more than 200 pages of A IV iv (see N. 18–69). See also two texts of 1693 published in A IV v N. 14–15.

[32] Günter Scheel, "Leibniz als politischer Ratgeber des Welfenhauses," in *Leibniz und Niedersachsen*, edited by Herbert Breger and Friedrich Niewöhner (Stuttgart: Steiner, 1999), pp. 35–52 (here p. 42).

such a success should dispel once and for all the notion that Leibniz's tardy historical labors were an unmitigated waste of his time and his employers' money. Even more important to the Hanoverian dukes were Leibniz's historical memos connected with the elevation to electoral status in 1692 and with the long battle faced by the newly created ninth electorate to have its office fully recognized.[33]

In sum, it is clear that Leibniz's sustained engagement with history and historiography was propelled in no small measure by the demands of his salaried post. Yet the choice to go to such great lengths in fulfilling his employers' requests was his own, and this raises an obvious question. Why did Leibniz continuously expand the scope of his historical research in the face of the acute displeasure of those very employers, not to mention at the cost of his philosophical, scientific, mathematical, and other activities? There can be little doubt that one of the factors was Leibniz's own temperament; yet, at a deeper level, such an extraordinary extension of a limited historiographical assignment to cosmic dimensions cannot be simply explained by reference to the author's insatiable curiosity and characteristic tendency to leave major projects unfinished.[34] Ultimately, it was rooted in Leibniz's conception of history—a conception profoundly embedded, in turn, in his philosophical thought.[35]

LEIBNIZ'S CONCEPTION OF HISTORY

In the "Preface" to the *Accessiones Historicae* published in 1698, Leibniz gave a crisp, brief account of his view of history:

---

[33] In 1692–98, Leibniz wrote around thirty such texts (see A IV iv N. 70–77; A IV v N. 16–30; A IV vi N. 7–11; A IV vii N. 17–19). Moreover, he drafted the historical part of the speech read by Otto Grote (as Duke Ernst August's representative) at the investiture ceremony held in Vienna on December 19, 1692 (see Scheel, "Leibniz als Historiker des Welfenhauses," p. 268).

[34] This is the diagnosis of the problem offered to Leibniz's employers by Leibniz's duplicitous collaborator on the Guelf history, Johann Georg Eckhart. For instance, the very day before Leibniz's death, Eckhart wrote to Minister Bernstorff that the history of the Guelfs would never be finished "because [Leibniz] is far too much distracted; and since he wants to do everything and to be involved in everything, he can finish nothing, not even if he had angels as assistants." (In R. Doebner, "Leibnizens Briefwechsel mit dem Minister von Bernstorff," *Zeitschrift des Historischen Vereins für Niedersachsen* [1881], pp. 370–371).

[35] In his "Vorwort" to *Leibniz als Geschichtsforscher* (pp. vii–xi), Albert Heinekamp notes the existence of two opposing historiographical traditions regarding the relationship between Leibniz's historical work and his philosophy. On the one hand, Conze claims that Leibniz's philosophy of history and his philosophical thought are unified by the concept of "optima universi series" (see "Leibniz als Historiker," p. 45). On the other hand, Corsano, "Leibniz e la storia," p. 367, sees Leibniz's engagement with history and philosophy, respectively, as belonging to two completely heterogeneous orders of truth; likewise, Croce maintains that "Leibniz's monad is the exact opposite of historical individuality" (Benedetto Croce, *La storia come pensiero e come azione*, 5th ed. (Bari, 1952), p. 62 ff.). According to Spitz ("The significance of Leibniz for historiography," p. 333), "the essential connection between his philosophy and history was there, but he did not consciously elaborate its terms in any coherent fashion."

There are three things we seek in history: firstly, the pleasure of knowing individual things, then maxims which are useful first and foremost for life; and, finally, the origins of the present in the past, since all things are best known from their causes.[36]

The objects of history are, for Leibniz, individual or particular things, as opposed to the abstract, universal entities which are the objects of logic and mathematics.[37] In turn, the kind of truths investigated by history are truths of fact, as opposed to the truths of reason investigated by logic and mathematics. Truths of fact are governed by the principle of sufficient reason and have only a moral or hypothetical necessity, as opposed to the absolute necessity of truths of reason, which are directly ruled by the principle of noncontradiction. Although there is a sufficient reason for any truth of fact— that is, a sufficient reason why anything "should be thus and not otherwise"—"most often these reasons cannot be known to us."[38] All truths of fact are the result of an infinite chain of reasons which connects everything with everything else. It is precisely this infinity which prevents the finite human mind from fully discovering the sufficient reason which led to these truths. Likewise, although an infinite mind embracing the complete concepts of individual substances could know a priori all that is true of them, finite human minds can know truths of fact only a posteriori. This latter kind of knowledge, which includes the vast majority of truths involving individual substances (as opposed to the abstract objects of logic and mathematics), is the field of history:

> God, seeing the individual notion or *haecceitas* of Alexander, sees in it at the same time the foundation and the reason of all the predicates which can truly be stated of him, as for example, that he will vanquish Darius and Porus, to the point of knowing *a priori* (and not by experience) whether he died a natural death or died by poison, something we can know only through history.[39]

Coming to know such individual things, Leibniz suggested in the *Accessiones Historicae*, gives us pleasure (*"voluptas"*). Given that, according to his theory of motivation, what motivates us is the search for happiness, and happiness is, in turn, a "lasting state of pleasure,"[40] it is not surprising that Leibniz regarded the delight provided by historical knowledge, broadly conceived, as a prime motivation for engaging in historical studies.

The second, key motivation of historical studies for Leibniz is the traditional humanist one: history's major role in teaching lessons of life, in acting as *magistra vitae*. In

[36] Leibniz, *Schriften und Briefe zur Geschichte*, p. 232. Cf. *Nouveaux Essais*, Book IX, Chap. xvii, § 11 (NE 470).

[37] Cf., for instance, a fragment written after 1696: "*Philosophia est complexus Doctrinarum universalium [opponitur Historiae quae est singularium]*" (Couturat, *Opuscules*, p. 524); *Nouveaux Essays*, Book IV, Chap. xxi, § 5 (NE 524); and a memo of 1708 for Peter the Great (in Woldemar Guerrier, *Leibniz in seinen Beziehungen zu Russland und Peter dem Grossen* (St. Petersburg and Leipzig, 1873), p. 97).

[38] *Monadology* § 32; GP VI, 612.

[39] *Discourse on Metaphysics* § 8; A VI iv 1540–41.

[40] PW 83.

particular, the utility of examples of historical figures in commending or discouraging certain courses of action was strongly stressed by Leibniz, as well as routinely employed in his own writings.[41] In his view, however, it was not merely a matter of collecting edifying examples. As clarified by the *Nouveaux Essais*, by "useful lessons" he did not mean "simple moralizings, of which the *Theatrum vitae humanae* and other such anthologies are filled, but rather skills and items of knowledge which not everyone would think of when they were needed."[42] In brief, insofar as history offers guidance for our actions in a variety of complex situations, the study of history has, for Leibniz, an important moral role to play.

Finally and most importantly, history contributes to the highest kind of knowledge in its uncovering the origins of the present in the past. Leibniz stressed that the discovery, through a historical investigation, of why present matters are the way they are, is a case of knowledge from causes. Thus, although historical knowledge is par excellence a posteriori, history leads to knowledge *per causam*, that is, to a priori knowledge as traditionally understood. In other words, although the causal chain explaining truths of fact can only be investigated a posteriori through historical research, the fruit of such an investigation is a kind of a priori knowledge insofar as present matters are explained through their causes.

In turn, a text of June 1679 devoted to the project of developing a new kind of encyclopaedia gives us some insight into what is, according to Leibniz, the nature of a historical explanation at its most fundamental level. In this text, he distinguished between "simple qualities," that is, qualities "which cannot be described, but must be perceived in order to be known" (such as "light, colour, sound"), and "composite qualities," that is qualities which "can be explained by description, and thus are in a certain manner intelligible" (such as "firmness, fluidity, softness, tenacity"). To treat something *historically*, Leibniz continued, is to enumerate "in which way [simple qualities] are usually linked amongst themselves and with other intelligible qualities."[43] A historical explanation, the passage suggested, links single direct experiences to one another and to composite notions. Only when linked in this way and subsumed under composite notions (that is, abstract concepts such as "firmness," "tenacity"), can these individual experiences be described and become, therefore, intelligible ("And in truth those preceding simple qualities cannot be subjected to reasoning unless they are subsumed under these composite qualities").[44]

Such a broad conception of what counts as a historical explanation provides, in turn, the backdrop for the priority given by Leibniz to "universal history." Although history can be and often needs to be organized and studied according to a variety of different

---

[41] See, for instance, NE 470 and a text of 1695–96 in which "instructive examples" are regarded as "the true juice of history" (Leibniz, *Schriften und Briefe zur Geschichte*, p. 70). Both *Nouveaux Essais* and *Theodicy* are full of historical examples.

[42] NE 471.

[43] *Consilium de Encyclopaedia nova conscribenda methodo inventoria* (A VI iv 347).

[44] A VI iv 347.

categories, Leibniz saw these categories not as separate kinds but as aspects of a unified, all-embracing inquiry. The priority and fundamentality of this overarching approach was already firmly in place in one of the first reflections by Leibniz on history, namely in a letter of 1670 to his former history professor at the University of Jena, Johann Andreas Bose. On the one hand, Leibniz conceded that there are different "histories": the history of places or geography, the history of times or chronology, the history of lives or biography, the history of families or genealogy, the history of states, the history of the progress of the arts and sciences or *historia literaria*, and so on. But, on the other hand, he opposed Bose's sharp distinction among different species of history separated by their different objects. In Leibniz's view, different "histories" were instead parts of one universal history.[45]

The desideratum of a universal history remained on his mind throughout his life.[46] Notwithstanding its unity, however, universal history could and should be explored, for Leibniz, in its different aspects. A first, fundamental distinction drawn by Leibniz was the traditional one between natural history and civil or human history.[47] Another traditional distinction followed: between sacred and profane history,[48] or between ecclesiastical and political history. Further specific subdivisions, tracking different subjects (the history of migrations, of insignia, of rites, of funerals, of trade, of spectacles, and so on),[49] were also acknowledged. Among these specialized histories, particular importance was assigned by Leibniz to the development of a history of illnesses based on the creation of official and systematic medical annals.[50] Interestingly, he also explicitly recommended pursuing the history of material culture (such as, for instance, "the entire history of clothing and tailoring") since sifting "the materials of antiquity right down to the tiniest trifles" can bring to light important matters.[51]

As regards historical periodization, he favored a distinction between four great historical periods: the most ancient history antedating Greek history; Ancient History, covering Assyrian, Persian, Egyptian, Macedon, Greek, and Roman history until the barbaric invasions of the Roman Empire; the Middle Ages or *Historia media*, covering the period between the barbaric invasions and the parallel histories of Byzantium and of the Holy Roman Empire until Frederick III (1415–1493); and "recent history," stretching

[45] Leibniz, *Schriften und Briefe zur Geschichte*, p. 60. In his reply, Bose explicitly rejected Leibniz's proposal and repeated that there are different species of history because they have different objects. Therefore, they cannot be conceived as parts of a universal history. (Quoted in Leibniz, *Schriften und Briefe zur Geschichte*, p. 61, footnote 5).

[46] Cf. for instance, *Nouveaux Essais*, Book IV, Chap. xvi, § 11 (NE 471).

[47] Cf., for instance, *Consilium de Literis instaurandis condendaque Encyclopaedia*, autumn 1679 (A IV iii 794): "*Historia Universalis*, id est tam naturalis quam civilis"; *Memoire pour des Personnes éclairées et de bonne intention*, c. 1692 (A IV iv 616).

[48] A VI iv 953.

[49] Cf. Dutens V 212.

[50] Leibniz discussed this matter especially with the physician of the court of Modena, Bernardino Ramazzini. Cf. Maria Rosa Antognazza, *Leibniz: An Intellectual Biography* (Cambridge: Cambridge University Press, 2009), p. 336 and Davillé, *Leibniz Historien*, p. 350, note 4.

[51] NE 470.

to his present time.[52] He also envisaged a broadening of historical research to the provision of a proper world history which would embrace, for instance, Chinese and Arab history.[53]

As regards, most importantly, the existence of a general direction of history, he conceived history as both providentially guided and following an overall trajectory of progress despite apparent cyclical set-backs. "These beautiful pieces of historical knowledge," Leibniz wrote in 1686, "somehow allow us to enter into the secret of providence."[54] A few years earlier, in an unpublished text of 1682, he devoted several pages to an exploration of "the use of history for recognizing providence in the passing of empires and the permanence of the Church."[55] This providential direction followed, according to Leibniz, neither a simple cyclical path nor a straight line. Rather, it was best represented by the movement of an ascending spiral, visually combining cyclical return with unending progress: "And thus it would be agreeable that the same human being should be brought back not simply by returning to the earth but as if through a spiral or winding way, thence progressing to something greater. This is to go back to leap better forward, as at a ditch."[56] Indeed, in one of his last texts, focused on the doctrine of the *Apokatastasis pantōn* (or "restitution of all things"),[57] Leibniz ultimately rejected the pagan doctrine of eternal return in favor of the "gradual improvement and elevation" of all things:[58] "Even if a previous century returns for what concerns things which can be sensed [*quoad sensibilia*] or which can be described by books," Leibniz noted, "it will not return completely in all respects: since there will always be differences although imperceptible and such that could not be sufficiently described in any book." He concluded that for "this reason it could be the case that things gradually although imperceptibly progress for the better after the revolutions."[59]

The ascending spiral was not the only striking metaphor introduced by Leibniz to represent history. In a manuscript of 1695–96, he compared history "to the body of an animal, where there are bones which support everything, nerves which connect them, spirits which move the machine of humours that constitute, in turn, the nourishing juice, and finally the flesh, which gives accomplishment to the entire mass." "The parts of History," he continued, "corresponds to this well enough. Chronology to the bones,

---

[52] Dutens V 212. See also the distinction between "Historia Medii Aevi" and "Historia Hodiena" in the *Nova Methodus Discendae Docendaeque Jurisprudentiae*, 1667 (A VI i 321).

[53] Cf. *Nouvelles Ouvertures*, 1686, in Leibniz, *Schriften und Briefe zur Geschichte*, p. 63.

[54] *Nouvelles Ouvertures*, in Leibniz, *Schriften und Briefe zur Geschichte*, p. 64.

[55] In Leibniz, *Schriften und Briefe zur Geschichte*, pp. 540–544 (here p. 540).

[56] *Demonstrationes de Universo immenso aeternoque; de Mundis et aevis, deque rerum longiquarum et futurarum statu*, c. February–March 1701 (in G. W. Leibniz, *De l'horizon de la doctrine humaine*, edited by Michel Fichant (Paris: Vrin, 1991), pp. 56–60, here p. 58).

[57] See the two versions of this "meditation" of 1715 (entitled, respectively, Ἀποκατάστασις πάντων, and Ἀποκατάστασις) published by Fichant in Leibniz, *De l'horizon de la doctrine humaine*, pp. 60–66, 66–77. The first version can also be found in Leibniz, *Schriften und Briefe zur Geschichte*, pp. 550–560.

[58] Cf. Leibniz to Johann Wilhelm Petersen, October 15, 1706 (in Leibniz, *De l'horizon de la doctrine humaine*, p. 25) and Leibniz to Johann Fabricius, March 10, 1712 (Dutens V, 297).

[59] Ἀποκατάστασις (in Leibniz, *De l'horizon de la doctrine humaine*, p. 72).

genealogy to the nerves, hidden motives to the invisible spirits, useful examples to the juice, and the detail of circumstances to the entire mass." "However," he concluded, "the soul of all this is truth."[60] Over and above everything else, historical research should aim, Leibniz concluded, at truth. Therefore, since "History without truth is a body without life, one should try never to advance anything without foundation, and purge History bit by bit of the fables which have slipped into it."[61]

EPISTEMOLOGY OF TESTIMONY AND HISTORIOGRAPHICAL METHODS

As with any other *recherche de la vérité*, the first step on the path to (historical) truth is to establish appropriate methods. History, Leibniz was clear, is based on testimony. The epistemology of testimony is therefore central to the issue of historical credibility— a topic discussed in early modern works under the category of *fides historica*, often in the context of juridical considerations.[62] Interestingly, this category suggested that, like other accounts based on testimony, historical cognition is really a kind of faith. The degree of assent to historical claims should be proportionate to the degree of trustworthiness of the witnesses.[63] For instance, in the *Nouveaux Essais*, Locke's spokesman, Philalethes, assigned the proposition "that Julius Caesar lived" to "confident belief" under the category of judgment. Following Locke, this move placed assent to this piece of commonly endorsed historical "knowledge" two notches down from "assurance," that is, two steps below belief grounded in the highest degree of probability given by "the constant observation of our selves" and "the uniform reports of others" ("for example, that fire warms, that iron sinks in water").[64] After "assurance," the next in line is "confidence." There is "confidence," Leibniz explained summarizing Locke, when "the historians all report that so-and-so preferred his private advantage to the public. Since it has always been observed that this is the practice of most men, the assent which I give to these histories is a case of '*confidence*.'"[65] "Confident belief" is even further

---

[60] In Leibniz, *Schriften und Briefe zur Geschichte*, p. 70.

[61] In Leibniz, *Schriften und Briefe zur Geschichte*, p. 71.

[62] Cf., for instance, *De fide historica commentarius* (Helmstedt, 1679) by Johann Eisenhardt (professor of history at the University of Helmstedt), to which Christian Thomasius opposed a *Dissertatio de fide juridica* (Halle, 1699). Leibniz noted in the *Nouveaux Essais*, Book IV, Chap. xvi, § 11 (NE 469): "Jurists have written *de fide historica*, but the topic would be worth a more painstaking inquiry, and some of these gentlemen have not been demanding enough."

[63] See, in particular, the discussion "of the degrees of assent" in *Nouveaux Essais*, Book IV, Chap. xvi.

[64] *Nouveaux Essais*, Book IV, Chap. xvi, § 6 (NE 464). Cf. John Locke, *An Essay Concerning Humane Understanding* (London: Printed for Th. Basset, 1690; 2nd ed. London: Printed for Awnsham and J. Churchill, 1694). Cited from the critical ed. by P. H. Nidditch in *The Clarendon Edition of the Works of John Locke* (Oxford: Clarendon Press, 1975), Book IV, Chap. xvi, § 6, pp. 661–662.

[65] *Nouveaux Essais*, Book IV, Chap. xvi, § 7 (NE 464).

down the line: "Thirdly, when there is nothing in the nature of things for or against a fact, and it is vouched for by the testimony of people who are not suspect—for instance, that Julius Caesar lived—it is accepted with 'confident belief.'"[66] Finally, "'when testimonies . . . clash with the ordinary course of nature, or with one another', the degree of probability can 'infinitely vary'. Hence arise the degrees which 'we call *belief, conjecture, . . . doubt, wavering, distrust*.'" "There it is," Leibniz concluded, "'where . . . exactness is required, to form a right judgement, and to proportion the assent' to the degrees of probability."[67]

It should be noted that "judgement"—the epistemological category under which all of these degrees of assent were placed—was for Locke specifically different from "knowledge." "The Mind," he wrote in the *Essay*, "has two Faculties conversant about Truth and Falshood. *Firstly, Knowledge*, whereby it certainly perceives, and is undoubtedly satisfied of the Agreement or Disagreement of any *Ideas. Secondly, Judgement*, which is the putting *Ideas* together, or separating them from one another in the Mind, when their certain Agreement or Disagreement is not perceived, but *presumed* to be so; . . . And if it so unites, or separates them, as in Reality Things are, it is right *Judgement*."[68] In other words, Leibniz glossed, "judgement" meant in this context "probable belief."[69] In order to reach truth—that is, in order to achieve a "right judgment" (a true belief) in which ideas are united or separated "as in Reality things are"—the degrees of probability should be evaluated. Although, for Leibniz as for Locke, belief is not voluntary, belief is responsive to reasons. The investigation of the probability of something is nothing else than an inquiry into the reasons we have to believe or disbelieve something. Leibniz often described this investigation in juridical terms, explicitly drawing inspiration from the formalized processes employed in courts for evaluating the reliability of testimony and the strength of arguments for and against a certain claim.[70] By the same token, he seemed to place historical inquiries into a quasi-juridical framework in which the degrees of probability of alleged historical facts are evaluated on the basis of commonly acknowledged features of testimony.

Thus he noted that "scholars in the field of history have great respect for contemporary witnesses to things; though the principal claim to credence, even of a contemporary, is restricted to public events." Contemporary testimonies about, say, the hidden motives which moved someone to do something tell us at best "what various people have believed" rather than providing evidence for some historical fact.[71] Or, again, "when we have just one writer of antiquity to attest to some fact, then certainly none of those who have copied what he said have added any weight to it—indeed they should all be entirely

---

[66] *Nouveaux Essais*, Book IV, Chap. xvi, § 8 (NE 464).

[67] *Nouveaux Essais*, Book IV, Chap. xvi, § 9 (NE 464).

[68] Locke, *Essay*, Book IV, Chap. xiv, § 4, p. 653.

[69] *Nouveaux Essais*, Book IV, Chap. xiv, § 4 (NE 457).

[70] Cf. for instance NE 464–68. This formulation of his historical arguments in quasi-juridical terms is unsurprising not only given his training, but also given the direct political stakes of his historical services to the House of Hanover.

[71] *Nouveaux Essais*, Book IV, Chap. xvi, § 10 (NE 466–67).

disregarded." On the other hand, "when the histories of different nations converge, in matters where it is not likely that one has been copied from the other, that is a powerful evidence of truth."[72] More generally, Leibniz's firm awareness of the epistemic status of historical cognition based on testimony as "probable belief" with different degrees of probability manifests itself in the recurrent use, in the *Annales*, of expressions such as "it is plausible," "it seems likely," "if we accept."[73]

The fact that, from a strictly epistemological point of view, there is "faith in," rather than "knowledge of," historical "facts" should not lead, however, to skepticism. Germane to the debate on *fides historica* was the challenge brought by so-called historical Pyrrhonism. On the title-page planned for the *Annales*, Leibniz envisaged "the figure of triumphant truth *over haughty historical Pyrrhonism.*"[74] His reply to skepticism about the certainty of our cognition of historical facts was to build historical claims on a robust basis. To start with, he thought of the investigation of degrees of probability as eventually rising to the formal rigor of a new part of logic—a logic of probability of which he repeatedly lamented the lack and to which he wished to devote the last period of his life.[75] Furthermore, he recommended grounding any historical claim on clearly identified *monumenta*[76] divisible into three main categories.[77] The first category contained *monumenta* in the physical sense of buildings, objects, and other material remains providing information about past activities, habits, achievements, and so on. The second comprised written documents both from contemporary sources and from later accounts, including inscriptions (for instance) on coins and graves. The third was orally transmitted evidence: not only oral traditions but also languages themselves, the origin and development of which could shed light on a variety of historical questions.

For the discovery and study of this broad range of *monumenta*, Leibniz enlisted a number of sciences and learned disciplines. For instance, around 1692, he wrote in a *Memoire pour des Personnes éclairées*:

> Besides natural history it is also important to know human history, and the arts and sciences which depend on it. It comprehends the universal history of time, the geography of places, the recovery of antiquities and of ancient records, such as medals, inscriptions, manuscripts etc.; the knowledge of languages and what is called philology (which also includes etymological origins); I would add intellectual history [*l'Histoire Literaire*], which teaches us about the progress of our knowledge . . . I even hold that human history includes that of customs and of positive laws . . . besides

---

[72] *Nouveaux Essais*, Book IV, Chap. xvi, § 11 (NE 469).

[73] The recurrent use of these expressions as a sign of critical distance from the historical accounts presented in the *Annales* is noted in Leibniz, *Schriften und Briefe zur Geschichte*, p. 24.

[74] Niedersächsische Landesbibliothek: Ms XII 713 a Teil IV. Reproduced in Leibniz, *Schriften und Briefe zur Geschichte* (figure IV).

[75] See, for instance, A VI iv 914; A I xiii 555; NE 466.

[76] See Leibniz to Lorenzo Alessandro Zacagni, May 8, 1704 (A I xxiii 355).

[77] These three main types of *monumenta* are identified by Davillé, *Leibniz Historien*, pp. 386–387, from which I am drawing.

the fundamental laws of states, with the heraldry, genealogies and the well-known controversies or pretensions of princes, about which it is well to be informed—not so much because these things are significant in themselves, as because they cause great revolutions which envelop us and which interest the societies of which we are part.[78]

Not surprisingly, given his sustained engagement with the edition of medieval documents, he assigned the highest importance to diplomatics, followed by epigraphy and numismatics.[79] Among his correspondents, dozens of *sçavans* were antiquarians, genealogists, numismatists, experts in heraldry, philologists, and linguists (for instance, von der Hardt, Le Fort, Ludolf, Muratori, Nicaise, Papebroch, Paullini, Rymer, Sparfvenfelt, and Tentzel), whom he regularly asked for advice in relation to his historiographical work and with whom he exchanged information. In particular, he regarded linguistic studies as the key to unlocking a treasure trove of knowledge of the past. In brief, Leibniz was fully aware that the "*fides Historiae*" must be systematically grounded in sources, broadly conceived, if it was to triumph over historical Pyrrhonism.[80] What is more, he did not leave the meticulous work of unearthing and preserving such sources merely to the labors of others, but undertook himself grand editions of original documents with notable success.

Last but not least, Leibniz regarded this sort of philological-historical work on ancient sources as particularly important for establishing and defending the truth of the Christian religion. Since the history of "the true revealed religion . . . is most important for our salvation, in order to know what God has revealed or not," he wrote in the *Memoire pour des Personnes éclairées*, "one can say with reason that the greatest function of the knowledge of ancient things and of dead languages is that which one derives from them for [use in] theology, both as regards the truth of the Christian religion and the authority of the sacred books, and in order to explain these very books, eliminating one thousand difficulties; and, finally, in order to know the doctrine and practice of the Church of God, and the laws or Canons of the divine jurisprudence."[81] Undoubtedly Leibniz saw the development of philologically and historically robust biblical studies, and of a reliable ecclesiastical history, as tools which would help rather than threaten the Christian religion.[82] He acknowledged that the truth of the Christian revelation, unlike

---

[78] A IV iv 616; PW 107 (slightly modified).

[79] Leibniz, *Schriften und Briefe zur Geschichte*, p. 30.

[80] Cf., for instance, an excerpt from a letter of March 1693, printed on the verso of the title page of the *Codex Juris Gentium Diplomaticus* (Hanover, 1693): "The quality of documents itself is of great importance for historical credibility [ad Historiae fidem] and for the inner knowledge of things" (in Leibniz, *Schriften und Briefe zur Geschichte*, p. 138).

[81] A IV iv 616; partially translated in PW 107.

[82] See, for instance, a letter of October 18, 1678, to Pierre-Daniel Huet (A II i 641): "It must be demonstrated first of all that the sacred books we have are genuine and have come down to us uncorrupted in substance. No one can do this satisfactorily unless he understands the mysteries of the art of textual criticism and can explore the reliability of the manuscripts and unless he is familiar with the linguistic particularities, with the spirit of that epoch and with its chronology." Trans. by Irena Backus in *Leibniz: Protestant Theologian* (Oxford: Oxford University Press, 2016), p. 170.

the atemporal truth of natural or rational religion, must be grounded in history because Christianity's claims are centered on events which are supposed to have taken place in a certain time and space and to have been recorded in historical documents.[83] Thus, in his view, "history renders service to piety and it is from history that the truth of our religion can be demonstrated, for it is in history that it is adumbrated in no uncertain way."[84] And again, as he declared in 1686, "the History of Antiquity is of absolute necessity for the proof of the truth of religion."[85] In turn, the opening paragraph of the "Preliminary Discourse" of the *Theodicy* made clear that the epistemic status of the Christian revelation is that of testimony.[86] As in any case of testimony—Leibniz specifically mentioned here the credibility of reports about China—its trustworthiness must be investigated with the tools of historical sciences in order to warrant faith in what is claimed.

To conclude, the chief purpose of this brief discussion was to show that a comprehensive study of Leibniz as historian, superseding Davillé's monumental but dated doctoral thesis of 1909 on *Leibniz Historien*, is both worthwhile and urgently needed. Lamenting the paucity of studies which derive "the most useful things from history," Leibniz wrote in the *Nouveaux Essais*: "it is astonishing that with so many useful things still to be done, men nearly always spend their time on what has been done already."[87] Perhaps the same could be said for the overcrowding of certain areas of Leibniz's studies while large swaths of Leibniz's work still remain *terra incognita*. Underexplored territories certainly include his reflection on the nature of history and historiography and his work as an historian.[88]

References

Antognazza, Maria Rosa. 2009. *Leibniz: An Intellectual Biography*. Cambridge: Cambridge University Press.
Backus, Irena. 2016. *Leibniz: Protestant Theologian*. Oxford: Oxford University Press.

[83] Cf. Leibniz to Claude Nicaise, April 30/May 10, 1697 (A II iii 301): "the truth of revealed Religion is founded on the facts of ancient History which cannot be better proved than by the historical materials [les monumens] of antiquity."

[84] *Contemplatio de Historia Literaria Statuque Praesenti Eruditionis*, 1682 (A VI iv 468). Trans. by Backus in *Leibniz: Protestant Theologian*, p. 166.

[85] *Nouvelles Ouvertures*, in Leibniz, *Schriften und Briefe zur Geschichte*, p. 63. Cf. a letter of January 23, 1708: "History (which includes [the study of] antiquities) is useful to the proof of religion; it teaches us the origins, it instructs us through examples" (in Bodemann, Handschriften, p. 25).

[86] *Theodicy*, "Preliminary Discourse," § 1 (GP VI 49–50): "faith, as regards the motives which verify it, depends on the experience of those who have seen the miracles, on which revelation is founded, and on the Tradition worthy of credibility, which has transmitted them to us, both through the Scriptures, and through the report of those who have preserved them." Cf. also the correspondence with P. D. Huet (1678–79) and the text of 1682 published in Leibniz, *Schriften und Briefe zur Geschichte*, pp. 520–549; and Leibniz to Thomas Burnett, July 17/27, 1696 (A I xii N. 469).

[87] NE 471.

[88] Many thanks are due to Howard Hotson for his insightful comments on a draft version of this chapter.

Belaval, Yvon. 1982. "Leibniz comme historien." In Albert Heinekamp (ed.), *Leibniz als Geschichtsforscher*. Wiesbaden: Franz Steiner Verlag, pp. 30–37.

Conze, Werner. 1951. "Leibniz als Historiker." In Erich Hochstetter (ed.), instalment 6 of *Leibniz zu seinem 300. Geburtstag: 1646–1946*. Berlin: de Gruyter.

Corsano, Antonio. 1954. "Leibniz e la storia." *Giornale critico della filosofia italiana* 33: 356–368.

Croce, Benedetto. 1952. *La storia come pensiero e come azione*, 5th ed. Bari: Laterza.

Davillé, Louis. 1909. *Leibniz Historien. Essai sur l'activité et la méthode historique de Leibniz*. Paris: Félix Alcan.

Doebner, R. 1881. "Leibnizens Briefwechsel mit dem Minister von Bernstorff." *Zeitschrift des Historischen Vereins für Niedersachsen*, pp. 370–371.

Gädeke, Nora, ed. 2012. *Leibniz als Sammler und Herausgeber historischer Quellen*. Wiesbaden: Harrassowitz.

Guerrier, Woldemar. 1873. *Leibniz in seinen Beziehungen zu Russland und Peter dem Grossen*. St. Petersburg and Leipzig: Commissionäre der Kaiserlichen Akademie der Wissenschaften.

Heinekamp, Albert. 1982. "Vorwort" to *Leibniz als Geschichtsforscher*. Wiesbaden: Franz Steiner Verlag, pp. vii–xi.

Lamarra, Antonio, and Roberto Palaia, eds. 2005. *Essais scientifiques et philosophiques: Les articles publiés dans les journaux savants*, 3 vols. Hildesheim: Olms.

Leibniz, G. W. 1843–1847. *Gesammelte Werke*. Erste Folge: "Geschichte," edited by Georg Heinrich Pertz. 4 vols. Hanover: Hahnschen Hof-Buchhandlung.

Leibniz, G. W. Forthcoming. Series V: "Historische und sprachwissenschaftliche Schriften." In G. W. Leibniz, *Sämtliche Schriften und Briefe*, Series I–VIII. Darmstadt—Leipzig—Berlin: Akademie Verlag.

Leibniz, G. W. 1991. *De l'horizon de la doctrine humaine*, edited by Michel Fichant. Paris: Vrin.

Leibniz, G. W. 2004. *Schriften und Briefe zur Geschichte*, edited by Malte-Ludolf Babin and Gerd van den Heuvel. Hanover: Verlag Hahnsche Buchhandlung.

Locke, John. 1690/1694. *An Essay Concerning Humane Understanding*. London: Printed for Th. Basset; 2nd ed. London: Printed for Awnsham and J. Churchill.

Müller, Kurt and Gisela Krönert. 1969. *Leben und Werk von Gottfried Wilhelm Leibniz. Eine Chronik*. Frankfurt am Main: Klostermann.

Nidditch, P. H. 1975. *The Clarendon Edition of the Works of John Locke*. Oxford: Clarendon Press.

Scheel, Günter. 1966. "Leibniz als Historiker des Welfenhauses." In W. Totok and C. Haase (eds.), *Leibniz. Sein Leben, sein Wirken, seine Welt*. Hanover: Verlag für Literatur und Zeitgeschehen, pp. 227–276.

Scheel, Günter. 1999. "Leibniz als politischer Ratgeber des Welfenhauses." In Herber Breger and Friedrich Niewöhner (eds.), *Leibniz und Niedersachsen*. Stuttgart: Steiner, pp. 35–52.

Spitz, Lewis W. 1952. "The significance of Leibniz for historiography." *Journal of the History of Ideas* 13: 333–348.

CHAPTER 34

LEIBNIZ AS LIBRARIAN

MARGHERITA PALUMBO

A LIFE AMONG BOOKS

BOOKS served as a constant background over the course of Leibniz's life and activities and inspired his interests and studies in an extraordinary variety of fields. From childhood, he was always surrounded by books, reading with the rudimentary Latin of an eight-year-old (*dum vix latine balbutiens*)[1] the volumes of his father's library in Leipzig, a rich collection of classical, philosophical and historical works. As a young student at the Nikolaischule and later at the University of Leipzig, he visited public libraries as well as the shops of booksellers and printers. He was also an assiduous visitor of the lively book fair in his hometown. In 1668, Leibniz moved to Mainz, where he accepted the offer of the politician and bibliophile Johann Christian von Boineburg to enter his service. Thanks to his supportive patron, Leibniz met in Mainz and in Frankfurt prominent and learned persons, developed his early political and theological plans, began working out his huge and ambitious encyclopedia project, reflected on the *characteristica universalis,* gave form to a program of reform and advancement of sciences, and proposed the establishment of a German learned society. In this multifaceted and only apparently heterogeneous framework, the book continued to play its decisive and significant role as a vehicle of knowledge. It was, therefore, necessary on the one hand to organize the German book production and trade—as Leibniz outlines in numerous memoranda, first in the *Nucleus Librarius Semestralis*—and on the other to organize the libraries as privileged "storehouses" and as a "memory" of human knowledge. The extensive book collection of his prime patron presented him with the opportunity to not only reflect about its best possible arrangement but also to put into practice the subject of his reflections: Leibniz put together, in fact, the catalog of the Bibliotheca Boineburgica, with nearly ten thousand entries, according to an elaborate

---

[1] *Wilhelmus Pacidius. Entwurf einer Einleitung* (1671-1672) (A VI,2, N. 59: 510).

system of *loci communes* within comprehensive classes. Books and libraries also played an important role in his later, fruitful sojourn in Paris between 1672 and 1676. These years proved crucial not only for his strictly mathematical and philosophical reflections and the establishment of an immense network of contacts and correspondences but also for the reading of new books and for the study and transcription of manuscripts in the magnificent Bibliothèque du Roi, for meeting the librarians Pierre de Carcavy and Étienne Baluze, for the assiduous frequenting of beautiful Parisian private collections, and for the discovery and the partial purchase of a lot of small *curieux* books in the well-furnished bookshops of Paris. Leibniz also spent several months in London, and here, too, he had the opportunity of buying the "fleur des livres d'Angleterre."[2] Together with the volumes he had acquired during his formative years in Germany, these books in French and English formed the original nucleus of his private library.

At the end of his first extended stay abroad, Leibniz received from Duke Johann Friedrich of Braunschweig-Lüneburg the proposal of an appointment as counselor and librarian at the Hanover Court. From the brilliant and exciting Paris and its stimulating intellectual and scientific milieu Leibniz moved, in December 1676, to this provincial and lackluster town in Lower Saxony, remote from major cultural borders. It was the decisive choice of his existence: Leibniz was in fact keeper for life of the Hanoverian small court library, which at his arrival possessed only 3,310 printed books and 158 manuscripts. His services were retained under the successors of Johann Friedrich: the dukes Ernst August and, in 1698, Georg Ludwig, the future George I of Great Britain. In 1690, on his return from a long and intense trip through archives and libraries in southern Germany, Austria, and Italy *à la chasse* of rare printed books, ancient codices, and unknown documents for composing the history of the Guelf dynasty, the dukes of the oldest Braunschweig-Wolfenbüttel branch appointed him director of the celebrated and valuable Bibliotheca Augusta, the today called Herzog August Bibliothek. In 1676, Leibniz could perhaps scarcely have imagined that he was to remain tied to the extended Guelf house and its libraries for the rest of his life, which spanned over four decades until his death in 1716. Nor was he fully convinced—although, to borrow Wilhelm Totok's apt definition, he was unquestionably a *Mann des Buches* who always took a profound and genuine interest in the *res libraria* in a broader sense—that a job as librarian could really represent the exclusive or the more adequate context for realizing his scientific and even practical expectations and purposes. Nevertheless, it is precisely this evident sense of dissatisfaction and his perceptible inability to present himself as a traditional court librarian that constitute the deep roots of an innovative concept of the library, and of its role and its functions in a general reform of science and learning, quite aside from any possible and concrete accomplishment of projects and programs. Soon after his arrival in Hanover in mid-December 1676, Leibniz declared to Duke Johann Friedrich his intention to extend a little "the usual care of the Library, and therefore the traditional duties of a Librarian."[3] These words provide the key to understanding his significant

---

[2] Leibniz to Christian Habbeus, May 5, 1673 (A I, 1, N. 277: 417).
[3] Leibniz to Duke Johann Friedrich, January 1677 (A I, 2, N. 6: 12).

contributions in this field and the relationship between his activity as court librarian and various other facets of his work. This is a far cry from interpretations given by some scholars, who in the past have often overvalued and at the same time "restricted" the role of Leibniz as a pure theoretician of a pure library science, a discipline that can only be understood correctly if seen in terms of its close interrelations and connections with Leibniz's other broader intellectual plans and crucial aspects of his thought.

The Library as Encyclopedia

Leibniz never gave a systematic form to his reflections about the functions, the organization, and the improvement of libraries. His own private book collection included treatises devoted to this topic, such as Gabriel Naudé's widely circulated *Advis pour dresser une bibliothèque* (1627) and Louis Jacob's *Traité des plus belles bibliothèques* (1644), not to mention the even greater number of bibliographies, *historiae literariae,* and catalogs of public and private libraries. But Leibniz himself never had the intention of writing similar works, although many among his correspondents and interlocutors were convinced that he was an authority in this field, a real *bibliothèque vivante* (living library).[4] His vast correspondence testifies to the fact that he might well have accepted a perhaps more generous appointment at the Bibliotheca Regia in Paris, the Hofbibliothek in Vienna, or even the Vatican Library,[5] whose precious and fascinating manuscript collections had never left his mind. Notwithstanding the attractiveness of these offers, Leibniz remained a librarian in Lower Saxony until his death, committing these thoughts—as well as many other aspects of his kaleidoscopic activity—to private papers, letters, and memoranda for "internal consumption," written for his patrons and princes, court secretaries, officers, ministries, and administrators charged with the *Kammer* (the Treasury, which had to pay his salary and to assign funds for acquisitions), as well as for the various key actors of the book world, such as librarians, booksellers, and agents on the market. The scattered nature of these works, however, does not prevent us from being able to make a detailed reconstruction of what is really a coherent and remarkable theory. I have earlier drawn attention to Leibniz's stated intention of extending his duties as ducal librarian in an unusual or unexpected manner. The object of this "declaration of intent" is an all-encompassing vision in which the concept "library" acquires a broader sense, becoming an essential element of a general and ambitious plan for the reform of science and learning. Its keywords are *instauration, advancement, preservation* and *systematization of human knowledge,* resulting in the construction of an encyclopedia of all disciplines and the elaboration of new forms of public communication and learned collaboration and culminating in the search of the

---

4 Christian von Weselow to Leibniz, December 14 (24), 1691 (A I, 7, N. 263: 480).
5 See, for instance, Leibniz to Abbé Le Thorel, November 25 (December 5), 1698 (A I, 16, N. 195).

common good and of happiness grounded in wisdom, understood as the true goals of human beings. This is the deeply intertwined theoretical and practical background of Leibniz's activity in this field, which represents an original "extension" in comparison with the traditional image of a court librarian. It is no coincidence that between 1677 and 1679 Leibniz not only addressed to his patron a dense *promemoria* for the improvement of the ducal library, in which he underlined the importance of a careful choice of books, thanks to the *advantages* offered by a broad network of correspondence and the good use of learned journals (both of which he considered basic and effective vehicles of public communication), but also elaborated—as he had done earlier in Mainz with the *Nucleus Librarius*—the plan of the bibliographic review *Semestria Literaria*. He promoted, too, the foundation in Germany of a society of science and sketched projects devoted to the *scientia generalis,* the *characteristica universalis,* and the *encyclopedia,* all of which represented the complementary aspects of a unitary program grounded on the same principles and, though dealing with different issues, an astonishingly similar argumentative structure.

In this all-embracing vision, the library represents the result of centuries of speculation and practice, showing in a material and concrete way—through the volumes on its bookshelves—the "seeds of the evident and wonderful truths," the "new realities," the "ingenious observations," and the "remarkable considerations" offered by any field of knowledge and any kind of mechanical art, including those that were wrongly or superficially considered marginal. Since the encyclopedia ought to be a universal and exhaustive repository, a library ought to be the bibliographical mirror of universality and exhaustiveness across all disciplines. In various works, the encyclopedia is defined as a *bibliotheca contracta* or a *bibliotheca portatilis* (portable library), and in a programmatic *promemoria* addressed to Duke Ernst August dated 1680, Leibniz maintains that "a Library would be an Encyclopaedia, that is to say that one could learn from it all the matters of consequence and of practice." "This," he adds, "has always been and remains my opinion."[6] In fact, this opinion pervades his entire thought as a true leitmotiv, starting with the proposals he outlined at the beginning of his career as librarian in Hanover and extending through to a memorandum written in October 1716 to Johann Philipp von Boineburg, son of Johann Christian, who took the initiative of contacting his father's old protégé regarding the new location of the library he inherited in Erfurt, the German town where the collection is still preserved.[7] This was Leibniz's last opportunity to expound his conception of the *res libraria*, thus in a way closing the circle of a lifelong reflection that the young, promising, and hopeful collaborator of Baron von Boineburg had started in Mainz.

---

[6] Leibniz to Duke Ernst August, November 1680 (A IV, 3, N. 30: 350). See also *Semestria Literaria* (*Consilium de literis instaurandis condendaque Encyclopaedia*) (1679), "Finis universi operis elaboratio Encyclopaediae, ut aliquot voluminibus Portatilis contineatur" (A IV, 3, N. 116: 792).

[7] On this library see Leibniz's correspondence with Philipp Wilhelm Boineburg, LBr 84; see also K. Paasch, *Die Bibliothek des Johann Christian Boineburg* (Berlin, 2005).

Just as an encyclopedic inventory should offer a choice of the best and most useful knowledge and discoveries in every field, the library should be equipped with a choice of the best and most useful books across all disciplines. In this regard, a library is not a simple and accidental stock of volumes; according to Leibniz's conception it should not be "overloaded" with an infinity of books, a vain and blind mass of paper, parchment, and ink. Rather, to use Leibniz's own terminology properly, it must be a science-repository, a printed archive, a general inventory, a memory aid, a bibliographical reflection of the praiseworthy *curiosité*, a compendium of all the sciences, and a treasure of the most beautiful thoughts of the greatest men. In other words, the authentic purpose of the library is the conservation and preservation of past and present knowledge and, consequently, its transmission—precisely as an encyclopedia or universal *repertorium*—to future generations.[8] It is clear that this "ideal library," or—as Leibniz wrote from Paris to Christian Habbeus[9] —this library *à ma phantasie*, can offer the material for the construction of the encyclopedic inventory.

AN UNUSUAL COURT LIBRARIAN AND THE CRITERIA FOR SELECTING BOOKS

If the library collection must provide the material itself for the encyclopedia, it follows that the first and crucial task of a librarian is that of rigorously selecting which books should be preserved in its rooms. This task is made even more difficult due to the "awful mass of volumes" that are printed on a daily basis, including superfluous books that oppress not only the good librarians but also the true *savants*. Such books cause a dangerous and damaging confusion both within the book trade and in the advancement of knowledge.[10]

It was during the fruitful years spent in Paris that Leibniz elaborated the idea of the *bibliothèque à sa phantasie,* an ideal library—put into practice at least in his private book collection—which should only include two categories of books: first, those containing inventions, demonstrations, and experiences, and second, books of a political, historical, or geographical nature.[11] The main deficiency of most of the collections he had visited in Paris was, in fact, that they were scarcely useful at best and completely useless at worst. In spite of their unquestionable luxury, these libraries could not be regarded—in the sense of Leibniz's "beautiful libraries"—as offering a real contribution to the advancement of the sciences. Much as they were truly remarkable mirrors

---

[8]   See, for instance, Leibniz to Duke Ernst August, November 1680 (A IV, 3, N. 30: 350); *Paraenesis de scientia generali* (August–December 1688?) (A VI, 4 A, N. 206: 972); and *Discours touchant la méthode de la certitude et l'art d'inventer* (August 1688–October 1690?) (A VI, 4 A, N. 204: 956–957).

[9]   Leibniz to Christian Habbeus, May 5, 1673 (A I, 1, N. 277: 417–418).

[10]   *Préceptes pour avancer les sciences* (GP VII: 160–161).

[11]   Leibniz to Christian Habbeus, May 5, 1673 (A I, 1, N. 277: 417–418).

of social status, they remained an empty image consisting of a large number of fine and richly bound volumes, *livres de peu usage* or *livres à la mode*. While it is true that a library must be equipped with whatever is "necessary," this does not mean that the necessary is an undifferentiated "quantity." On the contrary, it is the result of a careful "choice." Astonishingly, this program guides not only the expansion of Leibniz's private library but also the extension of the ducal collections in Hanover and Wolfenbüttel, as testified by several *promemoria* and letters written during his long career. Moreover, the philosopher's program was not based on the usual guidelines of the traditional court librarian, who was usually expected to propose to his patrons the acquisition of sumptuously illuminated manuscripts or lavishly engraved volumes *in folio*. Rather, it was founded on the concepts of the usefulness and value of the books for the learned aims of the *république des lettres*. The plan is lucidly outlined in his 1677 "declaration of intent" to Johann Friedrich and finds a concrete and coherent achievement thanks to the acquisition, in 1678, of the *curieuse* collection of the Hamburger naturalist Martin Fogel. This collection included 3,600 useful and selected books, consisting mostly of small volumes with plain parchment bindings but displaying—so affirms a proud Leibniz— enlightening knowledge, beautiful discoveries, and fruitful experiments.[12] Following the sudden death of the trusted duke Johann Friedrich, Leibniz made similar proposals and appeals to his successor, Ernst August, but with limited success. Nevertheless, he wrote, over and again, a series of memoranda and notes about expanding the library through the acquisition of, first, the works of ancient authors (defined by Leibniz as *fontes* or *Brunnquellen*), and second, of the so-called *libri primarii* or *Kern-Bücher*, that is, reference books such as handbooks, bibliographies, encyclopedias, dictionaries, and other general instruments that reflect, in a comprehensive or epitomized form, the state of all knowledge at a given moment. Finally, it was necessary, according to Leibniz, for a good, beautiful, selected library to be endowed with remarkable "new" books or *libri originales*.[13]

In most cases, these plans remained a dead letter, and the only notable exception was the acquisition, in 1696, of the private collection of Melchior von Westenholz, which was particularly well endowed with historical books and proved very useful as Leibniz set forth writing the dynastic history of the Guelfs. His attempt to convince Ernst August (who was busy laying claim to the ninth electorate of the empire) of the pivotal role of a library in a broader horizon also fell on deaf ears, and the court collections enjoyed fewer and fewer financial resources.[14] Leibniz's efforts for saving the library from progressive decline failed completely under Ernst August's son, Georg Ludwig. With remarkable tenacity, Leibniz renewed his appeals for financial support, especially in 1700,

[12] See Leibniz to Duke Johann Friedrich, July 6 (16), 1678 (A I, 2, N. 46: 56–57).

[13] See, for instance, Leibniz's letter to the *Oberhofmarschalle* Friedrich Wilhelm von Görtz and Franz Ernst von Platen, October–November 1696 (A I, 13, N. 52: 67), and later the *Promemoria* for Georg Ludwig, May 22, 1702 (A I, 21, N. 10: 17–19).

[14] See W. Ohnsorge, *Zweihundert Jahre Geschichte der Königlichen Bibliothek zu Hannover (1665–1866)* (Göttingen, 1962), 30.

the year when the Society of Science of Berlin was founded, thanks to his efforts. He did not neglect the second aspect of his unitary and indefatigable activity as promoter of the advancement and communication of knowledge. He tried assiduously to explain to the new elector and to the Hanoverian ministers and officers that a library was not like a stone or metal object but resembles an animal, a living being that necessarily required constant and adequate alimentation for its survival and for showing to the whole *res publica literaria* how extensively the House of Braunschweig-Lüneburg valued and promoted the sciences.[15] When in September 1714 Georg Ludwig left Hanover for London to be crowned king of England, the library was closed for a long stretch, and financial contributions to it were almost completely suspended. This caused Leibniz's sense of intellectual isolation to become more accentuated. His declared intention of expanding the collections of this provincial library, as well as extending his duties as court librarian, ended on the River Leine in failure.

Leibniz's service at the court of Wolfenbüttel as director of the ducal library appears to have been more successful. Compared to the Hanoverian library, this library, founded by Duke August the Younger, held impressive manuscript and printed collections. The duke's sons, Rudolf August and Anton Ulrich, were well known at the time for their keen interest in the arts and letters. The former was a collector of Luther's works, while the latter was a refined lover of literature, theatre, poetry, and music. His great novel, *Die Römische Octavia*, is the visible sign of a veritable passion. Therefore, Leibniz's continuous search for enlightened and supportive patronage for his wide-ranging projects seemed to have finally reached a possible fulfillment. But in Wolfenbüttel things quickly turned for the worse, and Leibniz's plans ran into financial difficulties. In the early years following his official appointment on January 14, 1691, he was compelled to write a stream of dense letters to the dukes and their closest counselors. He had experimented with the apparatus of argumentation and the supporting rhetorical style in his attempt to win over his Hanoverian employer, and, he added, "if all these higher reasons do not have the expected effects, I'll burn my Cicero and all my rhetorical commonplaces."[16] The Bibliotheca Augusta was one of the most celebrated libraries in Europe. It was not a mere court *ornament* but an authentic treasure for the whole *res publica literaria*, and should the dukes allow the downfall of such a treasure, Leibniz argued, the entire learned community would pronounce an anathema against them. It was therefore essential to ensure a permanent and adequate acquisitions budget for the library so as to serve the preservation and the diffusion of this "public" treasure of knowledge.[17] Once more in 1701, Leibniz exhorted Duke Anton Ulrich to remember his court library, in that time *peu Auguste*.[18] It is surprising to note that also in these letters, the philosopher

[15] Leibniz to Friedrich Wilhelm von Görtz, January 26, 1706 (A I, 25, N. 326: 532).
[16] Leibniz to Lorenz Hertel, January 24 (February 3), 1697 (A I, 13, N. 90: 147).
[17] So wrote Leibniz to the court marshal in Wolfenbüttel, Friedrich von Steinberg, autumn 1696 (A I, 13, N. 54: 71).
[18] Leibniz to Duke Anton Ulrich, May 8, 1701 (A I, 19 N. 64: 103).

never takes on the usual role of a traditional court librarian. He never speaks of the library as a reflection of the prestige of a dynasty consisting of thousands upon thousands of folio volumes, possibly bound in morocco with gold tooling, or as a symbol of sovereign political power. The concept of the *bibliothèque de parade*, based on the ostentation of luxury and puissance, was always and radically extraneous to Leibniz's vision.[19]

After the death in 1705 of his brother Rudolf August, Duke Anton Ulrich decided to give a new impulse to the book collections of his house, and in order to support Leibniz (who could not always be at Wolfenbüttel) decided to add a librarian to its staff. The choice became the counselor Lorenz Hertel, who in 1716 succeeded Leibniz as director of the Augusta. Hertel and Leibniz had long corresponded with one another on topics such as politics, diplomacy, and court affairs, but from 1705 onward the central, if not exclusive, theme of their epistolary exchange became the library and its books. This correspondence represents a primary source for the history of the Augusta. It also offers a precious opportunity to evaluate Leibniz's distance from the traditional figure of the court librarian, a figure that was indeed wholly embodied by Hertel. This contrast appears already in the early stages of their collaboration, like a watermark hidden under the formality of the epistolary style of the Leibnizian age. On the occasion of the auction of the collection of the Hanoverian *Hofrat* Anton Lucius, Hertel strongly chastised Leibniz for having bought for the ducal library only small volumes rather than *livres importants*. Leibniz's reply constitutes an authentic *apologie*, a dense summary of his general vision of a library and of its functions, with little or no regard to the social status of its owners. He defends his choice with steadfast conviction and determination: "I prefer 30 small curious books to a voluminous work that contains nothing more than repetitions." He does not deny that Duke Anton Ulrich wanted to equip his library with important books but stressed that one ought to give a correct interpretation of this intention: the duke, he argues, was a truly "enlightened" prince and therefore knew all too well that the most important books were not necessarily the most "voluminous" ones. "I consider mainly," Leibniz adds, "whether the author has offered, through his book, a service to the Republic of Letters . . . and, moreover, the small curious books disappear with time and must therefore be preserved in the great libraries."[20] A traditional court librarian like Hertel could not understand these statements, and until Leibniz's death in 1716 their relationship remained quite problematic from this perspective. Hertel had misunderstood not only the practical aspect of this criterion in the choice of books but also the ethical and, at the same time, political principle underlying Leibniz's statements.[21] In fact, only a duke, an elector, a king, a tsar, or an emperor could give concrete orders and issue persuasive rules for

---

[19] See also in the quoted letter to Duke Johann Friedrich, January 1677 (A I, 2, N. 6: 15–16).

[20] Leibniz to Lorenz Hertel, April 3, 1705 (A I, 24, N. 286: 508).

[21] It is for this reason that the numerous plans and sketches about the library and its organization are included in series IV, *Political Writings*, of Leibniz's Akademie Ausgabe.

advancing the sciences. Leibniz's plan inevitably required a supportive and sympathetic patronage to serve as an institutional framework. As he wrote in the *Discours touchant la méthode de la certitude et l'art d'inventer,* one of the essential tasks, and the moral duty, of the *princes éclairés* was to promote all measures and instruments—including a library as the mirror of the beauty of human knowledge, and consequently as the "quintessence of the best books"—needed to reach this goal, in view of its highest aims: the common good and the true happiness of humankind. On the other hand, one of Leibniz's essential tasks and indeed his moral duty as a court librarian was to provide his "enlightened princes" with continuous "reminders" of the authentic goals of political power.[22]

ORDER OF BOOKS, ORDER OF KNOWLEDGE

According to Leibniz, a key task of the librarian was not only selecting books but also ordering them. Already during his youth, while in Mainz, he started reflecting about catalogs and possible arrangements of books, as illustrated in the aforementioned subject catalog of the library of his patron Johann Christian von Boineburg. When he arrived in Hanover in 1676, he found the three thousand or so volumes of the ducal library registered in a classified catalog according to a schema elaborated by his predecessor, Tobias Fleischer. After the death of Duke Johann Friedrich, who had shown himself sympathetic to the possibility of putting into place a new system for cataloging the books owned by the House of Braunschweig-Lüneburg,[23] Leibniz had to drop his project due to the lack of interest shown by Ernst August and Georg Ludwig. The lack of collaborators had also frustrated his plans. The situation was very different at the Bibliotheca Augusta, which boasted an exemplary classified catalog that facilitated access to the collections. Here, aided by the two library secretaries Reinerding and Sieverd, Leibniz could concentrate his efforts on compiling an alphabetical author catalog, or *index nominalis,* as a complementary apparatus to the systematic arrangement of that library.[24]

Leibniz also discusses the order of books in a library in some well-known pages of his *Nouveaux Essais sur l'Entendement humain,* composed between 1703 and 1705. Here he points out one of the major difficulties encountered by librarians: since "one and the same truth may have many places according to the different relations it can have, those who arrange a library very often do not know where to place certain books, being in suspense

---

[22] See *Discours touchant la méthode de la certitude et l'art d'inventer* (August 1688–October 1690?) (A VI, 4 A, N. 205: 963).

[23] See A I, 2, N. 6: 16.

[24] Leibniz had stressed the need for such a catalog since the beginning of his activity in Wolfenbüttel. See the agenda in the short paper *Bey der Bibliothec zu Wolfenbütel* (1691), "Indices zu verbessern: Index Nominalis also einzurichten daß man das begehrte buch leicht finde" (A IV, 5, N. 87: 685).

between two or three places equally suitable."[25] In this regard, Leibniz maintains that the traditional, convenient, and therefore more applied "faculty system," that is, the division based on the four university faculties of theology, jurisprudence, medicine, and philosophy, "is not to be despised." Leibniz appears to be satisfied with the "easier" solution to his problem, which was essentially the model presented by Naudé in the *Advis pour dresser une bibliothèque*. But this is only apparently so, since he never ceased to develop, modify, and refine his schemas of classification of the sciences and of books—an indefatigable effort that denotes a degree of theoretical dissatisfaction. Besides dealing with cataloging in the strict and concrete sense of the term, Leibniz also approaches this subject from an abstract or theoretical perspective. He does this in writings devoted to two further aspects of his thought, both of which—as has already been pointed out—are deeply intertwined with the general concept of the library: first, the establishment and the organization of scientific societies, and second, the development of the encyclopedia of the sciences. Thanks to the Leibniz-Edition and particularly to the volumes of Series IV (*Politische Schriften*), we have today at our disposal—besides the *Idea Leibnitiana bibliothecae ordinandae* (*fusior* and *contractior*), published by Joachim Friedrich Feller in the *Otium Hanoveranum* (1718)[26] —countless preparatory notes, sketches, schemas, and fragments regarding this crucial point. "Sed sunt tamen difficultates"[yet there are many difficulties]," Leibniz wrote in 1693.[27] And again in 1716, in the *Breve consilium de bibliotheca*, he tried to incorporate the variety of books into a coherent system that reflected the variety of sciences.[28] In the end, however, he never gave a definitive outline of the ultimate form he would have wanted to give to this order. Yet this endless continuity confirms the centrality of the *ordinatio librorum* and its fundamental role in a wide-ranging project. Often Leibniz compares the actual state of human knowledge to a shop or a storehouse that contains a multitude of precious wares but lacks both order and a proper inventory.[29] The effects of this situation are striking, as is the stylistic register used by Leibniz: humankind wanders with difficulty and confusion in the dark and chaos, without a guide or any precise direction, without a possible object, and without even knowing its present state. Real advancement, therefore, necessarily requires a *filum Ariadnaeum* to serve as a guide through the centuries of reflections, observations, and discoveries of our ancestors—a heritage that risks being erased from our memory.[30]

---

[25] *Nouveaux Essais* (A VI, 6, N. 2: 524).

[26] Later in Dutens, 5:209–214, and now in A IV, 5, N. 81: 649–655; A IV, 6, N. 72: 504–507.

[27] *De fine scientiarum* (1693) (A IV, 5, N. 70: 591). See also *De ordinanda Bibliotheca* (1693) (A IV, 5, N. 78: 626–34) and *De dispositione Bibliothecae per ordinem facultatum* (1696–1697?) (A IV, 6, N. 77: 516–519).

[28] LH XL, fols. 101–125.

[29] This is a recurring metaphor in Leibniz's writings, particularly in the plans addressed to his patrons. See, for instance, *Aufzeichnung für die Audienz bei Kaiser Leopold I*, August/September 1688 (A IV, 4, N. 6: 23).

[30] See *Précepts pour avancer les sciences* (GP VII: 157). Similar expressions are to be found in many other encyclopedic writings; see the *Consilium de literis instaurandis condendaque Encyclopaedia* in

Such an Ariadne's thread could be provided by a universal and comprehensive inventory of all knowledge. A basic precondition for this fundamental achievement—one of the hallmarks of Leibniz's entire thought—is offered by the bibliographical content of the most significant public and private libraries. The philosopher raises this point in a text he wrote in 1671, the *Grundriss eines Bedenckens von aufrichtung zu einer Societät in Teütschland zu auffnehmen der Künste und Wissenschafften*.[31] Leibniz returned to this idea in his later writings. For instance, during his tireless search for more enlightened patronage, career advancement, and better remuneration, he sketched a number of plans for Peter the Great, the tsar of Russia, proposing the modernization and the development of the sciences in the immense and "virgin" Russian territory. Expounded in typical Leibnizian succession, this program moves from scientific investigations and geographical explorations to the development of a great and well-endowed library, the institution of a learned society, and finally the construction of an encyclopedia or a *repertorium universale*, whose compilation was to be based first and foremost on the "beautiful catalogues of libraries."[32]

In this conceptual horizon, therefore, the arrangement of books according to a coherent and efficient system becomes not only an essential task of the librarian but an "ethical" one, too. The same example of a storehouse full of wares that lacks an inventory and is therefore completely useless in the end is also used by Leibniz to describe the state of a library that lacks catalogs or indices.[33] Once more, the terms and images he employs are identical, revealing two aspects of a unitary problem that he dwelled on throughout his entire life: *de ordinatione librorum* (the order of books) and *de ordinatione cognitionum* (the order of knowledge).

Semestria Literaria (A IV, 3, N. 116), and *Recommandation pour instituer la science générale* (April–October 1686?) (A VI, 4 A, N. 161: 694–713).

[31] *Grundriss eines Bedenckens von aufrichtung zu einer Societät in Teütschland zu auffnehmen der Künste und Wissenschafften* (A IV, 1, N. 43: 539).

[32] *Denkschrift über die Verbesserung der Künste und Wissenschaften im Reich Russischen*; V. Guerrier, *Leibniz in seinen Beziehungen zu Russland und Peter dem Grossen* (St. Petersburg u. Leipzig, 1873), 356.

[33] See, for instance, the letter to the dukes of Wolfenbüttel, June 7 (17), 1695 (A I, 11, N. 45: 63).

PART VII

ETHICS,
JURISPRUDENCE,
AND POLITICS

CHAPTER 35

....

HAPPINESS AND JUSTICE

....

GREGORY BROWN

SHORTLY after undertaking an intensive study of Hobbes in the winter of 1669 and the spring of 1670, Leibniz became involved in a project, under the auspices of the Elector of Mainz, to reform Roman civil law. Although this project was never completed, it provided the occasion for Leibniz to produce a series of important studies in natural law, which the editors of the Akademie edition of Leibniz's *Sämtliche Schriften und Briefe* have grouped under the heading of *Elementa juris naturalis* (1670–1671, A.VI.i.431–485; hereafter, EJN). In these studies, we find a remarkable record of Leibniz's struggles to reconcile the kind of egoism that he had encountered in his studies of Hobbes with what he took to be the demand of justice that we "have regard for the interests of another."[1] These struggles ultimately gave birth to the two central concepts of Leibniz's moral theory, those of disinterested love (*amor non mercenarius* [A.IV.v.61], *amour non mercenaire*, *pur amour, amour veritable* [GP.III.384], *verus amor* [*Mantissa*,[2] page 3 of unnumbered preface]; *amour desinteressé* [GP.II.577]), and love, or charity, of the wise (*caritas sapientis* [Dutens.IV.iii.294], *charité du sage* [M.58/PW.57][3]), the latter of which became Leibniz's standard definition of justice. These notions, in whose development Leibniz took great pride, endured virtually unchanged into the works of his maturity, thus providing the foundation for his efforts to ground the happiness of man in virtue and the good of others.

MOTIVATION: WHAT MOVES US TO ACT?

....

In the *Discours de Métaphysique*, Leibniz spoke of two free decrees of God upon which the actual world was founded: "upon the first decree of God, which inclines him always

---

[1] A.VI.i.431. All translations are my own, although I provide a reference to a standard English translation when available.

[2] "*Mantissa*" refers to G. W. Leibniz, *Mantissa codicis juris gentium diplomatici* (Hannover, 1700).

[3] "M" refers to G. Mollat (ed.), *Mittheilungen aus Leibnizens undgedruckten Schriften* (Leipzig: H. Haessel, 1893).

to do what is the most perfect, and upon the decree that God has made (on the basis of the first) with respect to human nature, which is that man will always do (although freely) what appears the best" (A.VI.iv.1548/AG.46). Thus, "the object of the will is the apparent good," which, he observed, is "a most ancient and common dogma" (A.VI. iv.1380). Consequently, a deliberate act of the will presupposes a judgment that something is good, a doctrine that was explicitly stated in his earliest systematic work in natural law, the *Nova methodus discendae docendaeque jurisprudentiae* (1669; hereafter NM): "every action of the soul is a thought, for even to will is nothing other than to reflect upon the goodness of a thing."[4] Thus, also in the *Théodicée*: "the will is never led to act except by the representation of the good, which overcomes the opposite representation" (GP.VI.128/H.148). And it becomes clear from many other passages that the good that Leibniz thought moves us to act is *our own perceived good*. To survey just a few passages from different periods of his career, in the fourth set of notes for EJN, Leibniz wrote:

> prudence cannot be separated from our own good, and whatever they may say against it is both empty and alien to the practice itself of those speaking. *There is no one who deliberately does anything except on account of his own good [Nemo est qui quicquam consulto faciat nisi sui boni causa]*, for we even seek the good of those whom we love on account of our own pleasure, which we receive from their happiness.
>
> (A.VI.i.461/L.134; emphasis added)

Later, in a set of notes that the editors of the Akademie edition of Leibniz's works tentatively date between 1680 and 1684, Leibniz wrote:

> The root of liberty in man is the divine image, whereby God certainly wills to create him free and brings it about that anything of such a nature *is moved only by consideration of its own good [non nisi a boni proprii qua talis consideratione moveretur]*, just as God in choosing is only concerned about his own glory; there is only this difference, that a man can be deceived as a result of the original imperfection of the creature, God cannot.
>
> (A.VI.iv.2577; emphasis added)

Later still, in a letter to Claude Nicaise of August 19, 1697, Leibniz wrote: "*we do everything for our good [nous faisons tout pour nostre bien]*, and *it is impossible that we should have any other feelings [et il impossible que nous ayons d'autres sentimens]*, whatever we may say about it" (A.II.iii.369/W.565; emphasis added). And, still later, in the preface

---

[4] A.VI.i.284/L.88. In a later revisionary note to this passage written some thirty years later, Leibniz wrote that "to will is nothing other than a striving from thought, i.e., to strive for something on account of its goodness perceived by thought" (A.VI.i.284 Z.4–6 D 91; cf. A.VI.iv.1412).

to the *Mantissa*, and against those who held "that it is more perfect so to abandon yourself in God that you are moved by his will alone and not by your own delight," Leibniz wrote:

> But it must be understood that this conflicts with the nature of things, for the endeavor to act [*conatus agendi*] arises from a striving [*tendendo*] for perfection, the perception of which is pleasure; otherwise there is no action or will. And even with regard to ill-advised decisions, we are moved by a certain perceived appearance of good or perfection, even if we miss the goal, or rather pay for an ill-sought, trifling good by throwing away a greater; *nor is it possible to renounce, more than verbally, the impulse to one's own good without at the same time renouncing one's own nature [neque impulsui a bono suo nisi cum natura sua renuntiare ultra verba potest]*.
>
> (*Mantissa*, page 3 of the unnumbered preface/L.424; emphasis added)

It is important to note, on the one hand, that Leibniz was a motivational hedonist, declaring in *Théodicée* (§289) that "in truth we will only what pleases us" (G.VI.289/ H.303) and in the *Nouveaux Essais* that "in substances which are capable of pleasure and pain, every action is an advance towards pleasure and every passion an advance toward pain" (A.VI.Vi.210/NE. 210). On the other hand, and despite what might be suggested by his mention of pleasure in the quotations from EJN and *Mantissa* in the preceding paragraph, Leibniz did not regard pleasure as the only intrinsic good; in fact, he did not regard it as an intrinsic good at all, if that is understood to be something that is desired for its own sake. For Leibniz, intrinsic goods are *pleasant things*, and this, as will be seen, has significant implications for an understanding of his account of disinterested love.

Leibniz defined the good in various ways. Sometimes he defined it as "what contributes to pleasure" (A.VI.iv.1358, cf. A.VI.iv.303,1412,1419,2760,2773,2810), or "what contributes more to [a creature's] joy than to its sorrow" (A.VI.iv.2761). And so in a list of definitions from ca. 1701–05, he wrote that "the *good of each thing* is what contributes to its happiness" (Grua.667). But he also defined "the good" as "what contributes to perfection" (A.VI.iv.405), the "true good" as "that which serves in the perfection of intelligent substances" (M.48/PW.50), and the "general good" as "the advance toward perfection of men" (K.X.11/PW.105). These different senses of "good" are related through Leibniz's definition of pleasure as "the perception of perfection"[5] (A.VI.iv.2803/ W.568; cf. A.VI.vi.194/NE.194; A.VI.iv.2810). Thus, what "serves in the perfection of intelligent substances" will also contribute to their pleasure. The good is what contributes to pleasure, but not all pleasant things are truly good: "unfortunately, what pleases us at present is often a real evil, which would displease us if the eyes of our understanding

---

[5] A.VI.iv.2803/W.568. "W" refers to Philip Wiener, editor and translator, *Leibniz Selections* (New York: Charles Scribner's Sons, 1951). Cf. A.VI.vi.194/NE.194; A.VI.iv.2810.

were open" (G.VI.289/H.303). In particular, bodily pleasures, or "pleasures of sense," can often produce harm (see, e.g., Grua.579–580/PW.83). Since we only will what pleases us, but it is not the case that everything that pleases us contributes to our true good (i.e., our happiness), we are often led astray; and it is the business of right reason to determine what contributes to a person's happiness:

> happiness is nothing other than lasting joy. However, we do not incline specifically to happiness, but to joy, that is say, to something present; it is reason that leads to the future and to what lasts.

> (A.VI.vi.90/NE.90)

I will return to the last point later, but, for the moment, it should be noted that Leibniz often suggests that it is our perfection—the perfection of our intellect and will in particular—that constitutes our happiness because the perfection of the mind is the stable and enduring source of our highest pleasures: "happiness consists in the perfection of mind."[6] Moreover, we shall see that, for Leibniz, the good of others, that is, their happiness or perfection, is something that can be desired in itself precisely *because* it is an *immediate* source, not just of our pleasure, but more importantly, of an increase in our own perfection, which on Leibniz's view not only produces our immediate pleasure, but also augments that which is the enduring source of our pleasure. This is the key to Leibniz's reconciliation of his egoistic psychological assumptions with his belief that we can, and morally ought to, desire the good of others for its own sake. Unlike theories with which we are perhaps more familiar, Leibniz did not hold that something desired in itself is desired independently of a concern for one's own good; for, as we have seen, it was Leibniz's view that nothing could, as a matter of natural law, be desired in *that* way. Nor, as we have also seen, was there anything that Leibniz thought could move us to act, when we act deliberately, besides the desire for our own good.

Motivation and Obligation: What Obligates Us to Act Justly?

In paragraph 14 of Part II of NM, Leibniz undertook to "elicit a sound method [for learning and teaching jurisprudence] from the definitions of things themselves" (A.VI.i.300); he proceeded, in this and the following six sections, to deduce a series of rights and obligations for all rational beings. He began by defining jurisprudence as "the science of actions insofar as they are said to be just or unjust" and added that "*justice*. . . and *injustice* are whatever is useful or harmful to the public" (A.VI.i.300). In

---

[6] A.VI.iv.1992/L.279. For a more detailed account of the relationship between pleasure, happiness, and perfection in Leibniz, see Brown (2011), especially pp. 286–303.

paragraph 14(a.) he argued that "the *morality* . . . , i.e. the Justice or Injustice of actions, arises from a quality of a person in the process of acting, having arisen from preceding actions, which is called *moral Quality*." Leibniz then qualified this by adding, "but the real Quality in the process of acting is twofold, the power of acting [*potentia agendi*] and the necessity of acting [*necessitas agendi*], so moral power is called *Right* [*Jus*] and moral necessity is called *Obligation* [*Obligatio*]" (A.VI.i.301). He went on to deduce the rights of freedom (*libertas*), faculty (*facultas*), and authority (*potestas*), as well as the corresponding obligations not to hinder the freedom, faculty, or authority of others. Leibniz's initial deduction ends with paragraph 19, where, in referring to the previous six sections, he concluded that "in this way, therefore, we have deduced the highest source of all Right" (A.VI.i.304).

Christopher Johns has recently argued that the fact that the definitions that Leibniz appeals to in deducing rights and obligations in NM do not "mention hedonism, happiness, psychological egoism, universal love, or God's will" shows that none of those notions can be what Leibniz took to be the "ground" of right and obligation, contrary to what he thinks many commentators have suggested (Johns 2013, 11). He attributes to Leibniz the view that "the moral qualities [of right and obligation] are independent of empirical causes, desires, facts, and value-free mechanisms," so that "the whole of jurisprudence may be derived from a wholly a priori foundation" (Johns 2013, 9), and he suggests that Leibniz "approaches Kant, since he bases practical philosophy upon pure reason, freedom, and self-rule" (Johns 2013, xi). He concludes that "the usual consequentialist factors constitute a descriptive moral psychology, but not the normative criteria for his practical philosophy" (Johns 2013, xi) and thus that "it is important to keep psychological *motivations* (such as pleasure, or happiness, or love) conceptually distinct from rational *justifications*" (Johns 2013, 4).

Johns suggests that Leibniz "often does not clearly distinguish the motive for action from the principle that makes the action right" (Johns 2013, 24). But this way of putting the matter, I think, may reflect a confusion of two questions that I think Johns himself fails to keep distinct, namely, the question of what is morally right and the question of what obligates an agent to do what is right. Leibniz tends to focus on the latter question—the question of what gives moral obligation normative force—and, for him, obligation cannot be disentangled from motivation. As we have seen, Leibniz believed that, as a matter of natural law, human agents are incapable of acting deliberately except on account of their own perceived good. He was also committed to the view that *ought* implies *can*, declaring that "nothing impossible is an obligation or a right" (A.VI.iv.2751; cf. A.VI.iv.2759, 2763). For Leibniz, there can be no obligation without motivation, and no motivation without concern for one's own good. Consequently, he held that no one "can be obligated except to his own good" (A.VI.i.461/L.134): a judgment about what appears to a person to be in his own best interest is integral to the decision about what he ought morally to do because such a judgment is integral to any deliberate decision to act at all. Thus, the definition of obligation as a "moral necessity" that Leibniz presents in paragraph 14(a.) of NM can at best be a nominal definition because it does not yet reveal how a moral necessity could actually move a person to act, nor, consequently, how obligation is possible; showing how obligation is possible requires showing how a rational agent might be moved to act for another's good, which can effectively be done only by providing a causal definition of obligation.[7] It is for this reason, I think, that in speaking of civil law in paragraph 18 of NM, Leibniz argues that the purpose of civil and criminal process "is enforcement, which is the actualization of moral qualities, so that he who has moral authority [*potestatem*] or necessity may also have natural authority or necessity" (A.VI.i.304). So legal enforcement provides the normative force that actualizes moral right and obligation.

The matter is much the same in the case of natural right. In paragraphs 73–75 of NM, Leibniz picked up the thread of his earlier deduction and undertook to establish the "three grades of *Natural Right*," which, ranked in increasing order of perfection, are: "*strict Right (Jus strictum), equity (aequitas), piety (pietas)*" (A.VI.i.343). For Leibniz, these three grades of right correspond to the three precepts of right (*juris precepta*) given at the beginning of Justinian's *Institutes*: "not to injure another" (*alterum non laedere*), "to give to each his own" (*suum cuique tribuere*), and "to live honorably" (*honeste vivere*) (*Institutes* I.i.3). Of particular interest here is what Leibniz says in paragraph 75, where he asserts that "piety is. . . the third grade of *Natural Right*, and it gives perfection and effect to the others" (A.VI.i.344). For "whenever strict Right and equity are without Physical bond," Leibniz argues,

> God becomes an accessory and brings it about that whatever is useful to the public, that is, to the human race and the world, is made useful to individuals. And thus every honorable thing is useful and every base thing is harmful because God has established rewards for the just and punishments for the unjust based upon his wisdom: and what the reason of omnipotence resolves to achieve, prevails.
>
> (A.VI.i.344)

Thus, piety perfects strict right and equity by providing a motive to act justly when physical bonds fail. Such bonds presumably involve fear of harm or expectation of benefit,

---

[7] Leibniz's methodology requires that definitions used in a deductive science must be shown to be consistent. Leibniz thought this could be done by analyzing the concepts contained in those definitions into their primitive components, a process that would reveal any hidden inconsistencies. But Leibniz did not believe that humans were capable of performing such exhaustive analyses, and thus no such analysis was undertaken, either in NM or in any other work. That is why, in practice, Leibniz often resorted to "causal definitions," which are real definitions because they establish possibility:

> to form a hypothesis, i.e. to explain a way of producing something, is nothing other than to demonstrate the possibility of the thing, which is useful, even if the thing adduced is often not generated in such a way. For instance, the same ellipse can be understood either as described in a plane with the aid of two foci and an encircling string, or as cut from a cone or cylinder. And when one hypothesis, i.e. one mode of generation, is found, a real definition is produced from which others can be deduced, out of which may be selected those which agree more with other things, when the way in which the thing is actually produced is sought.

(A.VI.iv.542/L.231; cf. A.VI.vi.293–294/NE.293–294, GP.II.63/LA.72)

but the conditions under which they might fail are left to be explored in later works. Still, and for the moment, it can at least be said that this passage suggests that strict right and equity require some kind of physical bond in order to have normative force, so that when those bonds are lacking, fear of punishment or hope of reward from God are required to make good the deficit and bring it about that the obligations arising from strict right and equity are absolutely binding.[8] Johns dismisses the reference to God's rewards and punishments as having to do only with motivations: "Since we tend to be motivated by self-interest, we lack that *vinculum physica* or physical bond to move us to act honorably. Therefore, God has made honor coincident with utility, for those insufficient in virtue" (Johns 2013, 20). But, as we have seen, Leibniz does not say that we merely *tend* to be motivated by self-interest but that, as a matter of natural law, we are *always* motivated by our own good when we act deliberately. Thus, I think Johns is wrong to suggest that, for Leibniz, physical bonds are necessary only "for those insufficient in virtue," as if those possessing sufficient virtue have no need of such bonds because they can act independently of any desire for their own good. On the other hand, as we shall see, it is true that, for Leibniz, the virtuous man does not act either to avoid punishment or for the sake of rewards beyond the pleasure he takes in acting for the good of others; but this obviously does not mean that the virtuous man acts independently of a concern for his own good because that is something as contrary to natural law for him as it is for those who lack virtue. It is also worth noting that Leibniz explicitly states that "it is necessary to recognize in God an infinite *power* and *goodness*; these are perfections of which the first *should obligate* [*doit obliger*, emphasis added] us to be good, and the second should make us want to be" (Grua.499; cf. Dutens.IV.iii.280/PW.72). Thus, in paragraph 75 of NM, Leibniz asserted that "the existence of the wisest and most powerful of any being, i.e. of God, is the ultimate foundation of Natural Right" (A.VI.i.344–5).

The need for a real definition of obligation is reflected in the fact that Leibniz elsewhere defined obligation [*obligatio*] as "a necessity in acting which a fear of punishment imposes" (A.VI.iv.2751; cf. A.VI.iv.2152). However, Leibniz held that "there can be *natural rewards and punishments*" (A.VI.vi.96/NE.96), and hence a "natural obligation" (*obligatio naturalis*) (Dutens.IV.iii.280/PW.71) that would bind men to their own good even in a state of nature in which there are no superiors to enforce legal requirements and even under the assumption that God does not exist,

> since certainly care for one's own preservation and benefit requires many things from men towards others, which even Hobbes has observed in part. And alliances of thieves confirm this bond of obligation [*obligationis vinculum*] by example: while

---

[8] It seems clear, then, that for Leibniz "physical bond" involves fear of punishment or loss of benefit *at the hands of men*, who punish breaches of equity and right either in a civil state or in a state of nature. But, as we shall see, the joy that the virtuous man feels in the exercise of his own moral virtue and in the good that it produces in others can also act as a physical bond. Later, I will have more to say about the conditions under which Leibniz thought these bonds might fail and hence about the need for God to reinforce them with divine rewards and punishments.

enemies to others, they are forced to cultivate a certain sense of duty toward each other, although. . . a law of nature that proceeds from this alone would be very imperfect.

(Dutens.IV.iii.280/PW.71)

Similarly, in the *Méditation sur la notion commune de la justice*, following his definition of justice as the charity of the wise, Leibniz added:

> Wisdom, which is the knowledge of our own good, brings us to justice, that is to say, to a reasonable advancement of the good of others. We have already adduced one reason for this, which is the fear that we may be harmed if we should do otherwise. But there is also the hope that others will do the same for us.

(M.58–9/PW.57; cf. M.55/PW.54)

It is not surprising, then, that in the *Méditation* Leibniz deduced the first two grades of natural right solely by appeal to a person's concern for his own good,[9] as he did as well in the preface to the *Codex juris gentium diplomaticus* (A.IV.v.61–63/PW.171–174) and in *De justitia et jure* (A.VI.iv.2778–2279). But the reason Leibniz suggests that a natural law based on "care for one's own preservation and benefit. . . would be very imperfect" if God did not exist is not because such a law would not be genuinely binding, but rather because, as he noted in the *Nouveaux Essais*,

> there are some cases in which there would be no way of demonstrating that the most honorable thing is also the most useful. It is thus only the consideration of God and immortality that makes the obligations [*obligations*] of virtue and justice absolutely binding [*indispensables*].

(A.VI.vi.201/NE.201)

There are two kinds of cases that Leibniz had in mind here: (1) those in which men could violate the demands of strict right and equity to their own advantage without fear that their misdeeds might be detected by other men (see, e.g., M.60/PW.58; Dutens.IV.iii.277/ PW.67–68) and (2) those in which honor requires a man to give up everything, even including his own life, for the sake of the public good (A.VI.i.431; Dutens.IV.iii.276–277/ PW.67–68; A.IV.v.63/PW.173). In the first kind of case, the threat of future punishment in an afterlife at the hands of a God for whom no sin goes undetected would make "the obligations of virtue and justice absolutely binding"; in the second kind of case, future rewards in an afterlife would make it possible for a person to make the most extreme sacrifices for the public good without being guilty of "magnificent folly [*splendida stultitia*]" (Dutens.IV.iii.277/PW.67). This is why Leibniz held that "the science of natural right according to Christian doctrine" is "more sublime and complete" than "an

---

[9] See M.55–59/PW.54–57. For an account of the deduction in the *Méditation*, see Brown (1995), pp. 418–419.

inferior degree of natural right, which can be valid even in the view of atheists" (Dutens. IV.iii.277/PW.67); why he argued that this theory of natural right constitutes "universal justice" (A.VI.iv.2871, M.64/PW.60) or "universal jurisprudence" (Dutens.IV.iii.278/ PW.69); why he thought that piety is the highest degree of natural right, which perfects the lower degrees of strict right and equity; and, finally, why he concluded in NM that "God is the ultimate foundation of Natural Right" (A.VI.i.345).

The fact that Leibniz says, in the passage from the *Nouveaux Essais* quoted earlier, that it is "only the consideration of God and immortality that makes the obligations of virtue and justice absolutely binding," suggests that concern for our own welfare and happiness is not only what *motivates* us to act justly, but also what *obligates* us to act justly. Earlier in that same work, he had written that "I admit that there is scarcely any precept to which one would be indispensably obligated [*seroit obligé indispensablement*] if there were not a God who leaves no crime without punishment nor any good action without reward" (A.VI.vi.96/NE.96); and elsewhere, as we have seen, he declared that "it is necessary to recognize in God an infinite *power* and *goodness*, of which the first should *obligate* [*doit obliger*, emphasis added] us to be good and the second should make us want to be."[10] The latter point, Leibniz noted,

> is not insignificant for the practice of true piety: for it is not sufficient that we be sub-missive to God in such a way that we would even yet be subject to a tyrant; nor is he to be only feared on account of his greatness, but also loved on account of his goodness, which is taught as much by holy scripture as by right reason. And to this lead the best principles of universal jurisprudence, which also agree with sound theology and bring about true virtue.
>
> (Dutens.IV.iii.280/PW.72)

DISINTERESTED LOVE: THE RECONCILIATION OF SELF- AND OTHER-REGARDING MOTIVES

The last two passages just quoted suggest that although the power of God is the source of obligation, fear of punishment or hope of reward is not the only thing that can moti-vate just action; indeed, Leibniz thought such motivations could not be the motivations of the truly just man. But, given Leibniz's theory of action, we can *want* to be good only if we perceive being good as conducive to our own welfare; how this can be done

---

[10] Although, as noted earlier, Leibniz did believe that there are "*natural rewards and punishments*" and hence a "natural obligation" that would bind men to their own good even if, *per impossibile*, God did not exist.

independently of fear of punishment or hope of external reward is what Leibniz's notion of disinterested love is supposed to explain.

In his fourth set of notes for EJN, and referring to his earlier claim that "there is no one who deliberately does anything except on account of his own good," Leibniz wondered: "But how are these views reconciled with what was said above, where we said that nothing can be desired by us except on account of our good [*boni nostri causa*], when we now deny that another's good is to be desired for the sake of our own [*propter nostrum*]?"[11] His answer was that "it is doubtless brought about by a certain principle observed by few, from which a great light can be thrown on true jurisprudence as well as theology. Without doubt this matter hinges on the nature of love" (A.VI.i.463–464/L.136). In his *Initium institutionum juris perpetui*, Leibniz observed:

> Prudence is the science of right, i.e., the science of freedom and duties, or the science of right in some proposed case or fact. I call it a science, even if practical, because all its proposition can be demonstrated from the definition of the good man alone and do not depend on induction and examples.
>
> (M.1–2)

The reason the science of right can be deduced from the definition of the good man alone is because, in the fifth and sixth set of notes for EJN, Leibniz defines the good man as "whoever loves all men" (A.VI.i.466, 481); and, after stating that "we love those whose happiness pleases us," he observes that "from this definition many very beautiful Theorems of importance in Theology and morality [*re morali*] can be demonstrated" (A.VI.i.482).

Perhaps the most important theorem that Leibniz thought could be derived from his definition of love is that we can, and ought to, seek the good of others for its own sake. In his fourth set of notes for EJN, Leibniz wrote:

> There is a twofold way of desiring the good of others; one is for the sake of our good [*propter nostrum*], the other is as if it were our good [*quasi nostrum*]. The former is that of the calculating man, the latter is that of the lover. The former is the affection of a master toward his servant, the latter of a father toward his son; the former of one in need of an instrument, the latter of a lover toward his beloved. One is desired for the sake of something other than the good of others, another for the sake of the good of others itself. But, you ask, how is it possible that another's good be the same as our own, and yet sought for its own sake? For another's good can be our own good in another way, as a means, but not an end. In truth, and on the contrary, I reply: it can be our good as an end and desired in itself when it is pleasant. Now all pleasant things are desired in themselves, and whatever is desired in itself is pleasant; other things

---

[11] For a detailed discussion of Leibniz's technical use of the terms *boni nostri causa* and *propter nostrum* [*bonum*], see Brown (2011), especially pp. 279–281.

are desired for the sake of what is pleasant, according as they produce it, preserve it, or eliminate opposing things.[12]

The reason we can desire the good of others "as if it were our good" is precisely because "it can *be* our good *as an end* and desired in itself when it is pleasant" (emphasis added). As Leibniz wrote much later, in a letter of 19 August 1697 to Claude Nicaise:

> it is evident from the notion of love. . . how we seek *at the same time* our good for ourselves and the good of the beloved object for it itself, when the good of this object is immediately, finally (*ultimato*) and in itself our end, our pleasure, *and our good* [emphasis added]—as happens in regard to all things desired because they are pleasing in themselves, and are consequently good of themselves, even if one should have no regard to consequences; these are ends and not means.
>
> (A.II.iii.369/W.565)

Because the good of those we love is also *our good*, our good and the good of those we love *together* constitute the end of our desire. To desire the good of others "in itself" does not mean for Leibniz to desire it independently of any concern for our own good, but, and on the contrary, it is to desire it because it is an *immediate* source of pleasure and not because it is a means to some further thing that we desire as a source of our own good.[13] It is important to emphasize that Leibniz does not say that it is *pleasure* that is desired in itself (whatever that might mean), but rather *pleasant things*, because they are immediate sources of pleasure. That is why Leibniz says that it is *the good* of others (i.e., their *perfection*) that is desired in itself, not the pleasure we derive from it.

Later in the fourth set of notes for EJN, Leibniz concluded that "*justice* therefore will be the habit of loving others (or seeking the good of another and delighting in another's good in itself) as long as it can be done prudently (or as long as it is not the cause of greater pain)" (A.VI.i.465/L.137), and

> in order that we may now at last reach a conclusion, the true and perfect definition of Justice is therefore the habit of loving others, or taking pleasure from the expectation of another's good whenever the occasion occurs. It is equitable to love all others whenever the occasion arises. We are obligated (we ought) to that which is equitable. It is unjust not to be delighted by the good of another whenever the occasion arises. The just (what is permitted) is whatever is not unjust. Therefore justice is not only what is equitable—to be delighted by the good of another when the occasion arises— but also whatever is not unjust—to do what you please whenever an issue does not arise. Right is the power of doing what is just.[14]

---

[12] A.VI.i.464/L.136 Loemker's translations of this and other passages in the fourth set of notes for ENJ are deeply flawed. See Brown (2011).

[13] For more on this important point about how Leibniz understood the notion of desiring something in itself or for its own sake, see Brown (2011), pp. 276–278.

[14] A/L.137. When Leibniz says that "right is the power of doing what is just," the context of the passage makes clear that the just includes both what is equitable *and* what is *permissible*; so right is simply the

Among the theorems that Leibniz eventually deduced in his fifth set of notes for EJN from his definitions of the good man and love, nearly two pages of them relate the notions of justice and love, beginning with "every just thing is understood by some case of loving all men" and ending with "whatever is not necessary for loving somebody (anybody) is not a duty" (A.VI.i.472, 473).

The love that moves us to seek the good of others for its own sake is what Leibniz came to call "disinterested love": "*to love* truly and disinterestedly is nothing other than to be led to find pleasure in the perfections or in the happiness of the object" (A.II.iii.441/W.566). This kind of love is "independent of hope, fear, and any regard for utility. Certainly the happiness of those whose happiness pleases us turns into our own happiness, since things that please us are desired for their own sake" (A.IV.v.61/PW.171). It is the kind of love that is borne toward God by him who is "the friend of God" (A.VI. iv.2804/W.569), and it is the kind of love that, borne toward men, constitutes charity (A.II.iii.368–369/W.564). Thus, it is the kind of love that is borne toward other men by those who are truly just: "a *good man*. . . is one who loves everybody, as far as reason permits" (A.IV.v.61/PW.171). On Leibniz's view, a disinterested love of all men is born from a love of God. Because God's perfections are infinite, "one cannot know God as one should without loving him above all things" (M.62/PW.59), and "one cannot love God without loving one's brother" (Grua.581/PW.84). But "since we can know [God] only in his emanations, these are two means of seeing his beauty, namely in the knowledge of eternal truths . . . and in the knowledge of the Harmony of the universe (in applying reasons to facts)" (Grua.580–581/PW.84). In coming to know the perfections of God through a contemplation of the beauty and order of the cosmos, we find pleasure in God's perfection and are moved to love God and thus to imitate his perfection. In this way, the perfections of God are transferred into us, and it is actually the perception of our *increasing* perfection that constitutes our pleasure: "pleasure is nothing other than the perception of increasing perfection. And in some way the perfection of God is transferred into us, by being understood and loved" (A.VI.iv.2871). But the wise man also comes to recognize the perfections of God in all rational souls, which, on Leibniz's

ability (i.e., the freedom) to act or refrain from acting without violating moral or legal norms, whereas obligation is the necessity to act in order not to violate moral or legal norms, or, as Leibniz put it elsewhere: "*Obligation* is necessity in acting which a fear of punishment imposes. *Right* is liberty in acting freed from fear of punishment" (A VI iv 2751; cf. Grua 181). Leibniz sometimes expressed the same idea without explicit reference to punishment as such:

> Therefore the *right* which we have of acting or not acting is a certain power, i.e., a moral freedom. *Obligation*, however, is a moral necessity, doubtless imposed on him who wishes to maintain the name of a good man.
>
> (A.VI.iv.2850)

Here again, right is simply the ability (i.e., the freedom) to either act or refrain from acting without being subject to moral censure, whereas obligation is the necessity to act if one is to avoid being subject to moral censure (i.e., if one is "to maintain the name of a good man").

view, are "images of the divinity itself . . . , capable of knowing the system of the universe, and imitating something of it through their architectonic models of it, each mind being like a little divinity in its own province" (GP.VI.621/AG.223; cf. GP.VI.604/AG.212). By imitating God, who "loves souls in proportion to the perfection which he has given to each of them" (A.VI.iv.2804/W.568), the good man is led to charity of the wise—to love all men, but only to the degree that reason permits (i.e., to the degree that each reflects the perfections of God):

> Therefore he who loves God is wise and will love everyone, but each one more the more distinct traces of divine virtue shine forth in him and in whom he will expect a keener and stronger ally in respect of the common good, or what comes to the same thing, in looking after the glory of God, who is the giver of all good things.
>
> (A.VI.iv.2863)

Thus, "it can be said that as soon as [justice] is founded upon God or the imitation of God, it becomes universal justice and contains all the virtues" (M.64/PW.60).

As with God, so with men who are loved disinterestedly—their perfections are transferred into us because we learn from them and are inspired to imitate their perfection:

> *Pleasure* is the feeling of a perfection or an excellence, whether in ourselves or in something else. For the perfection of other beings also is agreeable, such as understanding, courage, and especially beauty. . . For the image of such perfection in others, impressed upon us, causes some of this perfection to be implanted and aroused within ourselves. Thus there is no doubt that he who consorts much with excellent people or things becomes himself more excellent.
>
> (GP.VII.86/L.425; cf. Grua.582)

And love is necessary because "hatred and envy . . . impede us from taking pleasure in [the perfection of others]" (Grua.582). Unlike those lacking true virtue, who are moved to act justly only by hope of reward or fear of punishment, the *disinterested* love that the good man has for all men moves him seek their good because he finds pleasure in the very act of benefitting them:

> he who acts well, not from hope or fear of a superior, but by an inclination of his soul, is so far from not acting justly that that very one acts more justly in the best way, by a kind of human imitation of divine justice. Now he who does good from love for God or neighbor finds pleasure in the act itself (for that is the nature of love) and does not need any other incentive, or the command of a superior.
>
> (Dutens.IV.iii.280/PW.72; cf. M.60–61/PW.57–58)

Because the disinterested lover takes pleasure in the perfections of God that he perceives in those whom he loves, he is moved to preserve and augment their perfection. But he increases the perfection of his own will by exercising his moral virtue, and the perception of his increasing moral perfection is pleasing to him. The increasing perfection of those whom he benefits also produces pleasure in him because their perfection becomes his own perfection: their knowledge can become his knowledge by learning from them, their virtue can become his virtue by imitating them, thus increasing his own perfection, and he is moved to love them more and disposed to benefit them more because of it. By the same token, those who are benefitted perceive their own increasing perfection and thus are pleased; they will consequently be moved to love their benefactor and be inspired to imitate his perfection and hence disposed to benefit him in turn, as well as others whom they love, to the degree that they perceive the perfections of God within them. A community of disinterested lovers is Leibniz's moral ideal because such a community is driven continuously toward greater perfection by a feedback mechanism based on the infectious nature of perfection itself and of the love that it engenders: the perfection of each is reinforced and augmented by the perfection of all, so that the perfection of all is constitutive of the perfection of each.

The wise man knows that the happiness of others is constitutive of his own. Since the wise and truly just man finds his own good in the good of others, his natural desires align with his duty to seek the good of others for its own sake: "The moral is what right reason, or prudence, or care for one's own good makes equivalent to the natural" (Grua.721); "in fact our natural affections produce our contentment, and the more one is within the natural, the more one is led to find his pleasure in the good of others, which is the foundation of universal benevolence, of charity, of justice" (Dutens.V.44/PW.198). Like God, in whom "it is not possible to envisage... any other motive than that of perfection, or if you will, of his pleasure, assuming in accordance with my definition that pleasure is nothing other than a feeling of perfection" (M.60/PW.57; cf. Dutens.IV.iii.280–281/PW.72), the just man does not act from fear of punishment, but from love, which produces his pleasure and his contentment. Thus

> it is said that the law is not established for the just. To so great an extent is it opposed to reason that the law or constraint alone make just, although it must be granted that those whose soul does not reach that degree of perfection are obligated only by hope and fear and that it is especially in the expectation of divine vengeance, which it is not permitted to escape by death, that they can discover the absolute and universally valid necessity of observing law and equity.
>
> (Dutens.IV.iii.280/PW.72)

In a letter of May 14, 1698 to Claude Nicaise, Leibniz recalled what he had written five years earlier in the preface to his *Codex juris gentium diplomaticus*:

> I explained my definition [of love] in the preface to my *Codex diplomaticus juris gentium*. . . because I needed it in order to give the definition of justice, which in my opinion is nothing other than charity regulated by wisdom; now since charity is universal benevolence, and benevolence is a habit of loving, it was necessary to define

what love is. And since To Love is to have a feeling that finds pleasure in what accords with the happiness of the object loved, and since Wisdom (which makes the rule of justice) is nothing other than the science of happiness, I showed by this Analysis that *happiness is the foundation of justice*, and that those who would give the true Elements of jurisprudence, which I do not yet find properly written, ought to begin by establishing the science of happiness, which does not yet appear well established, although the books on moral philosophy are full of discourses on the blessedness of the sovereign good.[15]

Unlike Kant, then, Leibniz did not—and indeed, given his theory of action, could not—maintain that it is the bare rational capacity of man alone that is the foundation of the true virtue (*caritas sapientis*) characteristic of the wise and good man; for Leibniz, true virtue is instead founded on a rational concern for one's own good, which leads to a disinterested love of others and the happiness or perfection that flows from it.

Good, Pleasure, Happiness, and Perfection

We have seen that Leibniz sometimes suggests that we derive pleasure from perceiving the *perfection* of those we love and sometimes that we derive it from perceiving their *happiness*. Sometimes, too, he seems to suggest that it is *pleasure* that is our *good*, whereas at other times he suggests that it is *happiness* or *perfection* that is our *true good*. I have already indicated that, despite what his language sometimes suggests, especially in his early works, Leibniz did not ultimately hold that our true good is pleasure—which concerns only the present and may lead to future harm—but rather happiness, which is a state of *lasting joy* found in the enduring perfection of our minds (G.VII.86/L.425). Reason directs us to pursue our "true happiness," and it functions to determine what true happiness consists in, as well as the means of achieving it. Thus, for example, in the *Nouveaux Essais* Leibniz wrote:

> To speak against reason is to speak against truth, because reason is a chain of truths. It is to speak against oneself, and against one's own good, since the principal point of reason consists in knowing and pursuing the good. . . . True happiness *ought* [*devroit*]

---

[15] A.II.iii.441/W.567, emphasis added. It is significant that some twenty-six years earlier, in his fourth set of notes for EJN, Leibniz introduced his discussion of the science of right in this way:

> Now it will suffice to sow the seeds of that science which shows why individuals must yield to the good of all men *if they should want happiness, increased by reflection, to flow back upon themselves*. To have shown this is to have handed down the Elements of Law and Equity, which we now undertake to accomplish with blessings from heaven.
>
> (A.VI.i.460/L.133; emphasis added)

always to be the object of our desires, but there is reason to doubt that it is. For often we scarcely think of it, and I have here pointed out more than once that unless appetite is guided by reason, it tends toward present pleasure and not toward happiness, that is to say, toward lasting pleasure, although it does aim to make it last.

(A.VI.vi.199–200/NE.199–200; emphasis added)

And, in his *Jugement sur les oeuvres de Mr. le comte de Shaftsbury*, Leibniz argued that "reason requires... that... we devote much to our satisfaction: it commands us to strive for *happiness*, which is nothing other than a state of lasting joy; and what goes toward that is our true interest" (Dutens.V.41/PW.197). But reason *guides* desire; it does not supplant desire by providing a motive independent of the agent's good. Christopher Johns has argued that, on Leibniz's view, "reason is sufficiently motivational and normative," in part because he believes that for Leibniz freedom and rational self-rule must be independent of desire in general and desire for one's own good in particular (Johns 2013, especially 144–145, for example). But this, I think, is based on a misunderstanding of Leibniz's view of the relation between freedom, reason, and desire (on which, see Rutherford 2005, especially 168–177). Reason directs us away from the often destructive and always fleeting pleasures of sense to the rational and enduring pleasures of the mind ("one need not beware at all the pleasures which are born of the understanding or of reasons" (Grua.580/PW.83–84)); but it does not do so by opposing all desire, but rather by opposing infelicitous "appetitions with images of greater goods or evils to come" (A.VI.vi.189/NE.189).

There remains the problem of resolving Leibniz's claim that we derive pleasure from the perfection of those we love with his claim that we derive it from their happiness. This problem has led John Hostler to argue that Leibniz's definition of love as finding pleasure in the happiness of others is "misleading," and he consequently argues that "we are not dealing with the other man's happiness itself, but with the things that make him happy [that is, his perfections]: it is these that are made the objects of volition when we love him" (Hostler 1975, 49). On the other hand, Donald Rutherford has attempted to resolve the difficulty by arguing that "happiness is the external sign of perfection," and hence we find pleasure in the perfection of others, but indirectly, by finding pleasure in their happiness (Rutherford 1995, 57).

Both Hostler and Rutherford interpret Leibniz as holding that happiness is an affective state of the soul, distinct from its perfection and involving pleasure; and it is indeed the case that Leibniz sometimes speaks of happiness in just this way (see, e.g., G.VI.507/L.552). But elsewhere, Leibniz suggests a somewhat different picture. For example, in his letter of May 14, 1698 to Nicaise, Leibniz wrote that "*to love* truly or disinterestedly is nothing other than to be led to find pleasure in the perfections or in the happiness of the object, and consequently to find pain in what may be contrary to its perfections" (A.II.iii.441/W.566), which suggests that, for Leibniz, the happiness of an object is to be identified with its perfections. Again, in a tract on wisdom, Leibniz wrote:

Happiness is the state of a lasting joy.

He who is happy certainly does not feel his joy continuously. . . . But it is enough that he is *in a state* to feel joy as often as he thinks of it, and that at other times a joyousness in his conduct and his nature arises from it.

(GP.VII.86/L.425)

On this account, happiness is a state that enables one to experience pleasure at will. Similarly, again in his letter of May 14, 1698 to Nicaise, Leibniz wrote that "happiness. . . consists in a lasting state of possession of *what is necessary in order to taste pleasure*" (A.II.iii.441/W.567, emphasis added). What one must possess in order to taste pleasure on Leibniz's view, of course, is perfection, which accords with his definition of pleasure as the perception of perfection. So, for Leibniz, perfection *constitutes* the happiness of persons. We perceive the happiness of a person by perceiving the perfections of his mind. So, when Leibniz told Nicaise that "*to love* is to find pleasure in the perfections or in the happiness of the object," he was indicating that, in the case of persons, happiness simply consists in the perfections of their minds.[16] In the same letter again, he declared that "*to love* is to have a feeling which makes us find pleasure in *what conduces to the happiness of the beloved object*" (A.II.iii.441/W.567, emphasis added), and what conduces to the happiness of a person, or rather constitutes it, is his perfection. That is why Leibniz often simply identifies the happiness of minds with their perfection, saying in the *Discours de Métaphysique*, for example, that "happiness is to persons what perfection is to beings" (A.VI.iv.1587/AG.68) and declaring flatly in his *Praefatio ad libellum elementorum physicae* that "happiness consists in the perfection of the mind" (A.VI.iv.1992/L.279).

Leibniz's tendency to identify happiness with perfection of the mind—because perfections of the mind are enduring sources of pleasure and hence are constitutive of happiness—not only helps us to understand why his definition of love, as finding pleasure in the happiness of another, accords with his definition of pleasure, but also to understand why he often claims that the happiness of those we love even becomes our own happiness. Again, their happiness or perfection becomes our perfection: we increase our knowledge by learning from them and increase our virtue by imitating their virtue, and the sense of our increasing perfection is our pleasure.

References

Brown, Gregory. 1995. Leibniz's moral philosophy. In *The Cambridge Companion to Leibniz*. Edited by Nicholas Jolley. New York: Cambridge University Press.

---

[16] The identification of perfection and happiness is also suggested by the following remark from one of Leibniz's letters to Sophie: "the happiness, or the perfection of another, in giving us pleasure, enters immediately into our own happiness" (A.I.xiv.58).

Brown, Gregory. 2011. Disinterested love: Understanding Leibniz's reconciliation of self- and other-regarding motives. *British Journal for the History of Philosophy 19*: 265–303.

Hostler, John. 1975. *Leibniz's moral philosophy*. London: Duckworth.

Johns, Christopher. 2013. *The science of right in Leibniz's moral and political philosophy*. New York: Bloomsbury.

Rutherford, Donald. 1995. *Leibniz and the rational order of nature*. New York: Cambridge University Press.

Rutherford, Donald. 2005. Leibniz on spontaneity. In *Leibniz: Nature and freedom*. Edited by Donald Rutherford and J. A. Cover. New York: Oxford University Press.

CHAPTER 36

LEIBNIZ AS JURIST

ALBERTO ARTOSI AND GIOVANNI SARTOR

Leibniz's Legal Career

Leibniz's legal career has rarely attracted the attention of Leibniz scholars. To some, it could therefore come as a surprise that Leibniz enjoyed a brilliant career as a jurist, a career studded with a series of increasingly prestigious official positions: assessor (i.e., judge) to the High Court of Appeal of Mainz, in 1669, at the age of twenty-three; *Hofrat* (court counsellor) in Hanover in 1677; *Geheimer Justizrat* (privy counsellor of justice) in Hanover in 1696 and in Brandenburg in 1700; privy counselor of justice to the Russian tsar Peter the Great of Russia in 1712; and *Reichshofrat* (member of the Imperial Aulic Council, one of the two higher courts of appeal of the Empire) in 1713.

Although Leibniz's studies were initially directed toward philosophy (he enrolled in the faculty of philosophy of the University of Leipzig in 1661), he decided that becoming a lawyer was the right career for him on account of his "preference for a career in the world rather than in the academy" (Mulvaney 1994, 413). Moreover, the law played a key role in his family, especially on the maternal side. His mother was the daughter of the renowned lawyer Wilhelm Schmuck. After her father's death, she was placed under the guardianship of the distinguished law professor Quirinius Schacher. Leibniz's maternal aunt was married to the eminent jurist Johann Strauch, who would exercise a considerable influence in strengthening Leibniz's legal vocation.

In 1663, after receiving a bachelor's degree in philosophy, Leibniz joined the law faculty of Leipzig, where he started his legal apprenticeship under the guidance of Quirinius Schacher and Bartholomaeus Schwendendörffer. In 1664, he graduated as a master of philosophy, and, by the end of that year, he defended and published his second academic dissertation, *Specimen quaestionum philosophicarum ex jure collectarum* (Specimen of Philosophical Questions Collected from the Law, A VI i 69–95; hereafter

Specimen quaestionum philosophicarum),[1] which coupled his recent legal training with his philosophical interests. In September 1665, Leibniz earned a bachelor's degree in law, for which he wrote the dissertation *Disputatio juridica de conditionibus* (Juridical Disputation on Conditions, A VI i 97–150; hereafter *Disputatio de conditionibus*) under the supervision of Schwendendörffer. Immediately upon earning his habilitation in philosophy (March 17, 1666), he turned to his legal studies, working on his dissertation for the degree of doctor of law. Astonishingly, the faculty of law refused him the title under the pretext that he was too young. As a result, in October 1666, Leibniz moved to the faculty of law of the University of Altdorf (near the imperial free city of Nuremberg), where he submitted his doctoral dissertation, *Disputatio inauguralis de casibus perplexis in jure* (Inaugural Disputation on Perplexing Cases in the Law, A VI i 231–256; hereafter *Disputatio de casibus perplexis*).[2]

In February 1667, at the age of twenty-one, Leibniz obtained the doctoral degree and, having declined the offer of an academic position, he left Nuremberg entertaining the idea of traveling to Holland (Antognazza 2009, 80). On his way to Frankfurt, he wrote his first (and only) jurisprudential treatise, the *Nova methodus discendae docendaeque jurisprudentiae* (A New Method for Learning and Teaching Jurisprudence, A VI i 259–364; hereafter *Nova methodus*),[3] by which he planned to win the favor of the prince-elector of Mainz. The new work so impressed the elector that he took the young scholar into his service as assistant to his *Hofrat* Hermann Andreas Lasser, who was working to reform the electorate's legal code. In 1669, Leibniz was appointed to the highest tribunal of the electorate, this despite his Lutheran persuasion (the Mainz electoral court was Roman Catholic). In the same year, he collected his first three legal dissertations into a single volume under the title of *Specimina juris* (Specimens of Law), probably looking to organize them into a systematic treatise to be used as a companion to the *Nova methodus*. For the publication in the *Specimina juris*, the material in the *Disputatio de conditionibus* was rearranged in a more readable form under the title of *Specimen certitudinis seu demonstrationum in jure exhibitum in doctrina conditionum* (Specimen of Certainty or Demonstrations in Law Exhibited in the Doctrine of Conditions, A VI i 369–430; hereafter *Doctrina conditionum*).[4]

The plan for a rational ordering of the entire body of law lies at the heart of Leibniz's work during the Mainz period. In his famous letter to Antoine Arnauld of November 1671, he described his project on the codification of Roman law as follows:

> I am working on a Nucleus of Roman Laws, which presents – in the same words of such laws, concisely and in good order, as a new example of a new perpetual Edict—what is truly law in the entire Corpus, truly fresh (*novum*) and effective law, and

---

[1] English translation in Artosi, Pieri, and Sartor 2013, 1–48. Italian translation in Leibniz 2015, 53–104.
[2] English translation in Artosi, Pieri, and Sartor 2013, 71–131. French translation in Leibniz 2009. Italian translation in Leibniz 2014 e in Leibniz 2015, 105–152.
[3] Italian translation in Leibniz 2012. Partial English translation in Johns 2013, 149–163.
[4] German translation in Armgardt 2001. French translation in Leibniz 2002.

can have force also now. In addition, I am thinking of recapitulating the Elements of Roman Law in a short table which presents, at a single glance, the few clear rules the combination of which can solve all cases, and furthermore, new measures for abridging lawsuits. . . . In addition to these, I am planning to collect in a short book the Elements of Natural Law, from which everything will be demonstrated from definitions alone.

(A II i 173)

As Leibniz himself wrote in his 1672 letter to Louis Ferrand (A I i 181), he was working on the *Nucleus of Roman Laws* (*Nucleum legum romanarum*) as assistant to Lasser,[5] whereas the *Elements of Roman Law* (*Elementa romani juris*) and the *Elements of Natural Law* (*Elementa juris naturalis*) were his own contribution. As this letter reveals, along with other writings from this period, the codification project included a fourth part, the "Body of Roman Law," for which Lasser was responsible. As is suggested by Leibniz's 1670 letter to Thomas Hobbes, the *Elements of Roman Law* may have been the first contribution Leibniz planned to make to the project (see the later section "Roman Law and Natural Law" for the relevant quotation). The preserved drafts are from the years 1667–72 (*Elementa juris civilis*, A VI ii 35-93.; Grua 705–721). Indeed, many of those ideas were clearly anticipated in the *Nova methodus*.[6]

Codification projects were taken up again during Leibniz's stay in Hanover. Leibniz's revived interest in legal matters after his Paris period (1672–76) is documented by a number of writings from the late 1670s to the late 1690s. Most of these writings refer to a plan for a *Codex Leopoldinus* dating back to 1678. This project, too, was never realized.[7] In 1693, as a by-product of his research on the history of the House of Hanover, Leibniz published a *Codex juris gentium diplomaticus* (Diplomatic Code of the Law of Nations). Although this work is more historical and political than juridical—it is a collection of public documents and treatises chronologically ordered from the end of the eleventh century to the seventeenth century—the preface (PW 165–176) contains a refined statement of Leibniz's doctrine of natural law first expounded in the *Nova methodus* (see the section "Roman Law and Natural Law").

Even though all of Leibniz's codification projects remained only on paper, the enactment a "new body of law accurately disposed" (A VI i 307), continued to be a prominent concern of Leibniz as a legal reformer. From 1708 to the year of his death, Leibniz

---

[5] Testifying to Leibniz's collaboration with Lasser is the *Ratio corporis juris reconcinnandi* (A Method for Rearranging the Body of Law, A VI ii 93-113), a project for a systematic reformulation of Roman law published in June 1668.

[6] See Leibniz's request for a new legal corpus in *Nova methodus*, II, 21 (A VI i 307), as well as the projects for the *Elementa juris* (Elements of Law) and *Juris naturalis elementa demonstrative tradita* (Elements of Natural Law Demonstratively Delivered) included in the list of desiderata that closes the *Nova methodus* (A VI i 364).

[7] Aside from a *Praefatio novi codicis* (Preface to a New Code), written between 1680 and 1685 (Grua 624–628), what remains of the planned code is a cluster of drafts and notes dating to the second half of the 1690s (see, in particular, Grua 791–797; 819–838).

corresponded with Heinrich Ernst Kestner, who in his *De statu jurisprudentiae, necessariaque juris naturalis et civilis conjunctione* (1699) had mentioned Leibniz in support of his criticism of Roman law and his preference for natural law and traditional German law (Grua 682). Leibniz replied that although in Roman laws there is much that is "obscure, perplexing and redundant," they must be considered as the basis of the law: going back to the ancient German laws, with their innumerable traces of barbarism, would be tantamount to eating acorns after having harvested corn (*inventa fruge glandibus vesci*). At the same time, the body of Roman law could be reduced to a few general rules "in which both equity and meaning would appear in a clear light" and "all the variety of cases" would be "encompassed as if it were encircled with a net" (Leibniz to Kestner, September 5, 1708, Dutens IV iii 253). This is what Leibniz had dreamed of from the time he "first set [his] feet in the paths of jurisprudence" (Leibniz to Hobbes, July 13/23, 1670, A II i 57; L 106) and what comes up again in his last letter to Kestner as the need for a "brief, clear, sufficient new code" (Leibniz to Kestner, July 1, 1716, Dutens IV iii 269), almost exactly the words he had used in the *Nova methodus* to convey his early idea of a new legal corpus to be "written . . . in a complete, brief, ordered manner" (A VI i 307).

LEIBNIZ'S EARLY LEGAL WORKS

As already noted, Leibniz's early legal works include the following main texts, collected in the *Specimina juris* of 1669: the *Specimen quaestionum philosophicarum* of 1664, the *Disputatio de casibus perplexis* of 1666, and the new *Doctrina conditionum* (based on the *Disputatio de conditionibus* of 1666).

Three basic ideas seem to underlie Leibniz's approach to the law[8] since these very early works, published when he was just eighteen to twenty-five years old.

The first idea is that legal research and problem-solving, especially adjudication, require an *interdisciplinary dialogue*; namely, a dialogue between the law and many other disciplines, ranging from philosophy to logic, theology, mathematics, and physics.

The second idea is that the law also requires *intradisciplinary dialogue*; namely, a dialogue between different strands of legal thinking: on the one hand, the different theories of natural law—scholastic and contractarian approaches in particular—and on the other hand, the different sources and doctrines of positive laws, in particular, Roman law and the laws of the German states.

---

[8] Leibniz uses two Latin terms for "law": *jus* (*droit* in French) and *lex* (*loi* in French). *Jus* denotes usually the law as a whole, or a body of it (natural law, positive law, Roman law, etc.). *Lex* usually denotes a particular law—in the sense of a specific element of positive law, namely, a statute, regulation, rule, or fragment of the Digest—or also a set of such laws. Sometimes Leibniz also uses the term *jus* (or *droit*) to denote natural or just law as opposed to unjust positive laws, as when he says that: "The *droit* could not be unjust, it is a contradition, but the *loi* can be so" (Mollat 47, PW 50; see Armgardt 2015*b*). Here, we use the term "law" in both senses, relying on the context to disambiguate.

The third idea is that the law requires a *large toolbox of reasoning methods and cognitive tools* (see Dascal 2004, 40–41) to be selected on a *pragmatic* basis; that is, by looking at how effectively the different tools and methods can aid legal inquiry. The traditional and ambitious purpose of constructing a "universal jurisprudence" as a "science of the just and the unjust"—a science described in Ulpian (D. 1.1.10.2., *De justitia et jure*) as based on an "awareness of human and divine affairs"—requires highly innovative tools, including, but not limited to, those afforded by contemporary developments in logic and mathematics.

The first idea is boldly stated in the very first pages of *Specimen quaestionum philosophicarum*, where Leibniz mounts an attack against those jurists who assume that law should be independent from philosophy (broadly understood to include science and mathematics). He argues not only that many philosophical considerations can be found in legal sources, but also that philosophy is needed to address legal issues, for "many places in [the] law would be an inextricable labyrinth without the guidance of philosophy." Having established this point, he re-examines a variety of legal issues in an encyclopedic progression from logic to metaphysics, going through mathematics, physics, physiology, and zoology—an examination in which he canvasses such diverse questions as the nature of indefinite proposition, the allocation of the burden of proof, the location of bodies in space and the final points of movement, the parts of the human body, the pertinence of law to animals, the classification of animals as wild or tame, the existence of mythical beings, whether humans share a common nature, logical and legal paradoxes, identity and consciousness, the relation between the whole and the part, and the ontological status of moral entities and relations.

Leibniz shows that there is nowhere an unsolvable conflict between law and philosophy. In some cases—as with regard to the different ways of understanding universals either as philosophical kinds or as legal collectives (*universitates*)—the apparent conflict is shown to be merely terminological (Question I). In other cases, the differences are found to have a pragmatic foundation. For instance, the fact that the burden of proof in legal proceedings is managed differently than in the philosophical game of *Obligationes* depends on the fact that the law is aimed at achieving a fair outcome within a reasonable amount of time; for which reason the burden of legal proof has to be allocated to the party who can more easily discharge it (Question II).

Evidence of the consilience between law and science can indeed be found in the tradition of Roman law, which provides solutions that are sound and equitable in the context of the working of nature. For instance, a physical-geometrical justification supports the Digest rule that, in order to avoid damaging a neighbor's property, the distance of a ditch from the border around the property should be noninferior to the depth of the ditch (Question III). The justification of this rule pertains to physics: the water along the sides of the ditch will seep into the ground at an angle at no less than 45 degrees from the surface until it reaches the depth of the ditch, after which point it will run down perpendicularly. Thus, a distance at least equal to the depth of the ditch ensures that the water will never reach the neighbor's land and thus prevents unjust damage. This example shows how, according to Leibniz, a just rule of law can be identified by combining abstract legal axioms, such as the fundamental principle that no harm should be done to others (*neminem laedere*), with scientific knowledge of the laws of nature.

Finally, there are cases in which, by merging legal and philosophical insights, a solution can be found to apparently unsolvable dilemmas, such as the paradoxes of Protagoras and of *lex Falcidia* (which would also be taken up in the *Disputatio de casibus perplexis*).

The Protagoras case concerns a dispute between the philosopher and one of his students, who had agreed to pay the philosopher a fee if and only if he, the student, will win his first legal case. Because the student refuses to take part in any case, the philosopher brings suit to recover payment, which puts the judge in a paradoxical situation. Assume that the judge finds for the philosopher (i.e., grants the request for payment); then, he should rather find for the student (i.e., reject the request) according to the contract because the student does not win his first case. On the other hand, assume that the judge finds for the student and rejects the request for payment; then he should rather find for the philosopher (i.e., grant the request) because the student wins his first case. So the student should win if he loses and should lose if he wins. Leibniz's solution to the paradox consists in setting up a temporal frame in which the judicial decision acts as the turning point, in combination with the legal burden of proof. *Before* the decision, the philosopher cannot prove the ground of his request; namely, that the student will win his first case. Thus, the philosopher's request for payment should be rejected (i.e., the student should win). However, *after* this decision, the philosopher can sue the student a second time and should win this second case, given the student's victory in the previous (first) one. In this way, the just outcome—the payment of the philosopher for his services—would be achieved.

The *lex Falcidia* case concerns a testator who, having already bequeathed three quarters of his estate, bequeaths the remaining quarter under the necessary and sufficient condition that *lex Falcidia* does not apply (*lex Falcidia* limited valid bequests to three quarters of an estate, the remaining quarter being reserved to the testator's heirs). Now, let us assume that the last bequest is *valid*. In this case, *lex Falcidia* applies because the three-quarters threshold has been crossed; the bequest is consequently *invalid*, since the necessary condition for its validity (the nonapplication of *lex Falcidia*) fails to be satisfied. Assume, on the contrary, that the bequest is *invalid*. In that case, *lex Falcidia* does not apply because the threshold is not crossed; the bequest is therefore *valid* since the sufficient condition for its validity (the nonapplication of *lex Falcidia*) is satisfied. Thus it seems that the bequest is valid if invalid and vice versa. Leibniz's solution to the apparent paradox if twofold. According to strict law, he argues, the exceeding bequest is to be considered invalid on the basis of the contradiction between the consequence of its validity (the application of *lex Falcidia*) and the necessary precondition for its validity (the nonapplication of *lex Falcidia*). However, the bequest may be considered to be valid according to an equitable interpretation of the will (i.e., by assuming that the testator intended to prevent the application of *lex Falcidia* by having all bequests, including the last one, proportionally reduced so that their sum remains below the allowed three-quarters).

The 1666 doctoral dissertation *Disputatio de casibus perplexis* is meant to provide an overall approach for dealing with "perplexing" (i.e., hard) cases. In these cases, a conflict between two legal solutions is generated by the application of rules that are only contingently contradictory, meaning that they lead to contradictory conclusions only when applied to particular factual circumstances. In comparison with the *Specimen quaestionum philosophicarum*, the *Disputatio* has a stronger legal and academic flavor because Leibniz engages with numerous legal authorities in providing support for his arguments while also applying conceptual tools that were unusual in legal arguments, such as propositional logic and the logical features of ordering relations.

Having introduced the notion of perplexity, Leibniz surveys various traditional ways of dealing with legal uncertainties, rejecting all of them. For example, the *non-liquet* approach, where the judge abstains from taking any decision in unclear cases, is rejected as incompatible with the judge's obligation to decide every case.

Having disposed of these approaches, Leibniz argues that there is a single legally correct answer to every legal case. This Leibnitian one-right-answer thesis results from the combination of two sets of assumptions pertaining to natural law and to the burden of proof. With regard to natural law, Leibniz assumes that (1) it is directly applicable to legal issues; (2) while being limited by positive law, it is in principle complete (it can provide an answer to any legal issue not being regulated by positive law); and (3) it integrates positive law by offering solutions to all interpretive doubts. With regard to the burden of proof, Leibniz assumes that (1) the burden of proof for the grounds adduced in support of a claim falls on the claimant, and (2) this also applies to the positive laws in which the claimant grounds a claim. These two sets of assumptions enable Leibniz to argue that "everything can in effect always be decided on the basis of the mere law of nature and of nations, under which nothing is uncertain" (Artosi, Pieri, and Sartor 2013, 83). This is so for three reasons. First, even where a case is not regulated by any positive laws, there is no uncertainty because natural law applies directly. Second, where it is uncertain whether any positive laws apply, the case can be decided by relying on the burden of proof: the party grounding a claim on a positive law whose existence cannot be proved will lose, having failed to discharge his burden. And third, where a positive law does apply but there is uncertainty about its interpretation, natural law supplements positive law, pointing to the correct interpretation.

So it seems that Leibniz as a young lawyer was endorsing what can be described as a legal version of his famous principle of sufficient reason, reflecting his trust in rationality and his aversion to arbitrariness: in every legal case, the applicable law provides sufficient reasons in support of a legal solution; namely, reasons making that solution legally preferable to all available alternatives.

Having set out his perspective on legal reasoning and its sources, Leibniz takes up his examination of perplexities, distinguishing them into two main kinds: perplexing dispositions and perplexing concourse. Dispositions are clauses in acts of will (contracts, promises, testaments, etc.) having a conditional form "if *A* then *B*," so that the realization of the antecedent condition *A* generates the legal effect *B*. Different cases of perplexing dispositions are distinguished.

(a) An antecedent condition extends into the future and contradicts the effect it should generate. This may happen directly, the condition being logically inconsistent with the effect it should generate (e.g., If you will not be my heir, be my heir!), or indirectly, the inconsistency resulting from further facts entailed by the effect (e.g., the nonapplication of *lex Falcidia* generates the validity of the exceeding bequest and, consequently, the crossing of the threshold, which determines the application of *lex Falcidia*).

(b) The fulfilment of the antecedent condition presupposes the prior realization of the conditioned effect, which can only be generated by that condition (e.g., "If you have freed the slave you inherited from me, be my heir!").

(c) A disposition provides a basis for incompatible claims by different persons.

(d) Two dispositions are circular because the fulfilment of the condition of one disposition determines, as its effect, the realization or the nonrealization of the condition of the other (e.g., "If Titius will inherit, Sejus shall inherit; if Sejus will inherit, Titius shall inherit").

Leibniz's approach to perplexing dispositions consists in viewing them as invalid and, in any event, as ineffective. This also follows from the burden of proof. As the party who grounds a claim only in a perplexing disposition necessarily fails to discharge his burden of proof, the claim must be rejected.

Perplexing concourse concerns situations where several people assert a right to which they are each *prima facie* entitled, but the priorities between their claims are inconsistent. In the typical case, the inconsistency results from circular preferences, where claim A is preferred to claim B, which in turn is preferred to claim C, which in turn is preferred to A ($A > B > C > A$), as shown in Figure 36.1 (extracted from the picture on the cover of the *Disputatio*).

For instance, in Roman law, a tacit hypothec A prevailed over a subsequent express hypothec B, which prevailed over the posterior dowry C, which prevailed over the tacit hypothec A.

Leibniz observes that lawyers often address indeterminacy in rankings on the basis of transitivity: if $A > B$ and $B > C$, it must be that $A > C$. However, he argues that not all relations are transitive (e.g., fatherhood and nearness are not). Moreover, transitivity fails to solve circularities; it instead makes circular rankings (such as $A > B > C > A$) inconsistent

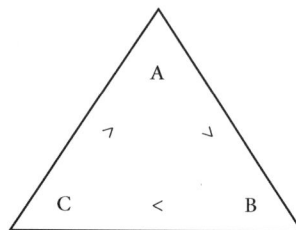

FIGURE 36.1 Circular preferences.

(because it allows us to conclude, for instance, that $A > C$, which is incompatible with $C > A$). Nor can we assume that one ranking (e.g., the one favoring the dowry) prevails in a case of uncertainty because this is a matter of law, where there cannot be uncertainty. The Leibnitian solution to circular rankings has two prongs. The first prong consists in appealing, whenever possible, to a metalevel ranking: if one ranking (say, $A > B$) is to be preferred to the others—for example, by virtue of its higher source (e.g., having been established by the prince)—then this ranking prevails and indirectly adjudicates conflicting priorities (the sequence $A > B > C$, where $A > B$ is stronger than $C > A$, overrides $C > A$).

When none of the circular transitive rankings prevails, there is parity among the conflicting claims, and this matter is to be addressed in different ways depending on whether the object of the claim is indivisible or divisible. If the object is indivisible and insusceptible of joint ownership, as is the case with benefices (livings) or guardianship, none of the competing claimants will obtain it, and so all of them will lose. If the object is divisible or susceptible of joint ownership, each claimant will be entitled to a portion of it or to its ownership pro rata. By applying these criteria—while allowing for derogations based on further legal principles, such as the preference for liberty (*favor libertatis*), under which a slave is deemed free even when there is an unresolved ranking of claims for and against his liberty—all cases can find a single legally justified solution.

The last work of the young Leibniz's legal triptych is the 1669 *Doctrina conditionum*, which results from his rewriting of the 1665 *Disputatio de conditionibus*. In the *Doctrina*, Leibniz provides the first work ever to consistently and extensively apply the logical-axiomatic methods to the law, developing an architecture of eighty definitions and seventy theorems.

The *Doctrina* starts with a range of definitions aimed at characterizing the general logical structure of conditionals (conditional propositions); namely, the connection between a conditioning proposition (*conditio*) and a conditioned one (*conditionatum*). Two kinds of conditionals are distinguished: the logical conditional (e.g., "If he is a man, then he is an animal") and the moral conditional (e.g., "If the ship arrives, Titius shall have 100 sesterces"). The moral conditional establishes a legal effect; that is, it establishes a conditional right (*jus conditionale*). Two inferential relations may be grounded in a conditional, *illatio* and *suspensio*. According to *illatio*, "If the *conditio* is true . . . the *conditionatum* is also true"; according to *suspensio*, the falsity of the *conditio* entails the falsity of the *conditionatum*. If we model the Leibnitian conditional as a material or strict conditional $A \Rightarrow B$, then *illatio* appears to be a valid inference of propositional logic: that is, *modus ponens* (from A and $A \Rightarrow B$, we derive B), whereas *suspensio* corresponds to a deductively invalid inference, the so-called *fallacy of negating the antecedent* (from $\neg A$ and $A \Rightarrow B$, we derive $\neg B$). According to Leibniz, whereas merely logical conditionals only support *illatio*, moral conditionals also enable *suspensio*: "The moral *conditio* suspends the *conditionatum*" (Theorem 5). For instance, the moral conditional just presented allows us to infer from the nonarrival of the ship the conclusion that Titius is not entitled to 100 sesterces. To justify this specifically "moral" inference, Leibniz observes that any legal effect can only exist on the basis of a specific legal ground. This justifies arguing *a contrario*. In particular, "another person can have a right only according to the will of the person to whom the right belongs originally (as nobody can be deprived of its right against his will)." Now, the person making the disposition "If *A* then *B*" has not declared that the right *B* should exist when condition *A* fails to exist. Therefore, the conditioned right only exists when the condition exists (for some considerations on the logical structure of conditional dispositions in Leibniz, see Armgardt 2014), so that the nonfulfilment of condition *A* entitles us to deny the existence of the conditioned right *B*.

Reasoning with legal conditions requires more than propositional logic because possibility and time need also to be taken into consideration. In particular, Leibniz observes that the existence of a conditional right presupposes the uncertainty of the condition ("An uncertain condition produces a conditional right"), which is removed when the condition has either taken place or become impossible. If the condition obtains, it becomes historically necessary (as "What is done cannot become undone," *Factum infectum fieri non potest*, §49), so that the disposition becomes pure (unconditioned). If the condition fails (i.e., its verification becomes impossible, §50), the disposition becomes ineffective (*vitiatur*). A full logical analysis of the patterns of reasoning identified by Leibniz in the *Doctrina conditionum* still has to be developed (see Armgardt 2015a, Magnier 2015, Rahman 2015); it would require a combination of multiple logical tools, from predicate to modal and temporal logic (Armgardt 2001), possibly extended with methods for defeasible reasoning and argumentation.

Leibniz's construction is developed mainly through definitions and theorems derived by substitution of definitional equivalents. He does admit, however, that at some points the definitions are insufficient to derive a true legal proposition, although he still calls such conclusions "theorems." For example, Theorem 27—the equal entitlement of parties having equally strong claims—is not inferred from the definitions but rather receives "some kind of demonstration that at the same time illustrates and proves (*simul illustrante et probante*, A VI i 392)" through an analogy between laws of nature (of physics) and rules of law. The equal division corresponds to the physical phenomenon in which a body at rest simultaneously impacted by two bodies incoming with the same force and from different directions will proceed in a direction that is intermediate between—and thus equally divergent from—the directions of the two impacting bodies. With regard to Theorem 49, prohibiting certain collusive agreements between an heir and a legatee working out to the disadvantage of the party being the beneficiary of the legate, Leibniz accepts that he cannot find an adequate support in strict law and thus only an appeal to equity can provide a justification.

Leibniz's acknowledgment that certain true legal propositions cannot be derived geometrically may appear to be a failure of his axiomatic-definitional approach to the law, but we could instead see it as an honest recognition of the limits of the geometrical method and of the need to complement it with further, weaker forms of reasoning, such as the appeal to analogy or to the reasoned balancing of competing claims (an aspect of his approach to the law that we address in the section "Legal Reasoning").

In 1666, one year after receiving the bachelor's degree in law, Leibniz published the *Dissertatio de arte combinatoria* (Dissertation on Combinatorial Art, A VI i 163–230), his first main contribution to logic and mathematics, where he applied his newly discovered combinatorial method to the law as well in order to construct all possible cases and thus identify gaps (possible cases that are still unregulated). For example, he argued that in Roman law a mandate can be in favor of the principal (1) and/or the agent (2) and/or a third party (3), yielding seven possible cases, each involving a different set of beneficiaries to be taken into account (1, 2, 3, 12, 13, 23, 123). One of these cases was not addressed by the Roman jurisconsults.

The Nova Methodus

Written while traveling "from a guesthouse to the other, without books" (A VI i 292), the *Nova methodus* represents Leibniz's comprehensive attempt at basing the law on a firm rational footing and providing jurisprudence with a "solid method" by which legal propositions could be derived from a basic set of definitions and precepts concisely expressed and rationally ordered. But it would be wrong to see in that work an essentially foundational endeavor. As a plan for legal education, Leibniz's "new method" was primarily aimed at training the ideal or "perfect" lawyer by equipping him with a vast array of theoretical and practical skills. According to the proposed plan, the basic legal training pertains to didactic or positive jurisprudence, in analogy with the organization of theological studies since theology and jurisprudence share an "amazing similarity" (A VI i 294). Didactic jurisprudence should be based on the geometric method, starting from definitions and precepts "in imitation of Euclid's *Elements*" (A VI i 295). In addition to didactic jurisprudence, the education of the "perfect" lawyer requires training in historical and exegetic jurisprudence, the latter involving the legal application of various disciplines: grammar, rhetoric, ethics, politics, logic, metaphysics, and physics (in which regard Leibniz refers to his *Specimen quaestionum philosophicarum* and to a future treatise on *Legal Philology and Philosophy*). Leibniz recognizes in particular the need for a legal geometry and a legal arithmetic, examples of which are, respectively, Question III of the *Specimen* (see the section "Leibniz's Early Legal Works") and the determination of the degrees of consanguinity in Problem III of *Dissertatio de arte combinatoria* (A VI i 327). Finally, the practice of law requires (still in analogy with theology) a polemic jurisprudence meant to help the lawyer steer his course in the perilous waters of legal cases, a task to be accomplished by equipping him with the "compass" of natural law (see the section "Roman Law and Natural Law").

However, the lawyer has to take into account not only natural law, which is based on reason, but also civil law, whose existence is rather based on fact—being a matter of history whether a certain custom was introduced or whether a certain law was issued by a person having the corresponding power according to fact or convention (A VI i 341). Therefore, the lawyer has to use two different "decision principles" in order to adapt the law to new cases: reason for natural law and analogy (*similitudo*) with existing laws or customs for civil law. Since the assessment of similarity of a new case with a particular positive law requires determining the reason of that law—namely, the political purpose it is meant to serve—the lawyer must also engage with "the part of politics that is called nomothetic" (i.e., legislative), from which it follows that: "the jurist sitting in the courtroom has two eyes: the science of natural law and the nomothetic science" (A VI i 342). Therefore, the jurist, while being guided by the highest norms of natural justice, has also to take into account the actual sociopolitical conditions of society, a thought that Leibniz would entertain for the rest of his life and that goes hand in hand with his insistence on the relativity of positive law as opposed to the perpetuity of natural law.

Finally, the lawyer should have access to a systematic collection of legal decisions or controversies, arranged *more mathematico* (A VI i 346), i.e., according to the mathematical order of basic legal elements (definitions and precepts). Leibniz offers no example of this. Instead, he suggests a straightforward way to apply a crude symbolic notation to various kinds of legal arguments in analogy to Isaac Barrow's symbolic treatment of Euclid's *Elements*.[9] Finally, having illustrated his plan for restructuring the study of law (a two-year program instead of the usual five-year program), Leibniz closes his book with a portrait of the graduate student who sums up all the characteristics of his ideal lawyer:

> He will settle controversies by his judgment, and, *free of tutors at last, in the turf of the sunlit campus*,[10] he will fly across the law's wide expanse, perusing the authentic law books, at first the titles and the laws most necessary, then he will gradually add other laws [. . .]. He will extract from there the laws that provide decision to various controversies, and he will craft new rules and new universal principles that others have overlooked; he will use commentaries and will penetrate into the reasons behind the laws and will gradually acquire the prudence of a legislator, if not the role. Then, having advanced through the wide sea of controversies, he will observe the customs of the courts and the judgments handed down by the forebears. He will notice those conflicts, disagreements, and dissimilarities between legal systems that are dependent on national character and on the differences among states. And he will learn to deduce, with unbroken connection, firm demonstrations from the unchanging principles of natural law and from public interest, and to cut, with the sword of unvanquished science, the empty subtleties and laughable allegations of the practitioners of law, and the tangled knots deriving from the doctors' purported authority and inappropriate use of brocards. This I will call a true philosopher of law, a priest of justice, and an expert in the law of nations and in what depends on it, and in both civil and divine law.
>
> (A VI i 362)

---

[9]   I. Barrows, *Euclidis Elementorum Libri xv breviter demonstrati*, first published in 1654. Barrow was Newton's teacher and predecessor as holder of the Lucasian Chair of Mathematics at Cambridge University.

[10]   Here, Leibniz is quoting Horace's *Ars poetica* from memory. The actual verses (161–62) read: "*Inberbis iuvenis, tandem custode remoto / gaudet equis canibusque et aprici gramine campi*" ("The beardless youth, free of tutors at last, delights / In horse and hound, and the turf of the sunlit Campus").

ROMAN LAW AND NATURAL LAW

The most important reason behind Leibniz's strong inclination for Roman law was his belief in it as the realization of the rational principles of natural law.[11] This view is clearly expressed in Leibniz's 1670 letter to Hobbes. In mentioning "a work on rational jurisprudence on which I am collaborating with a friend" (i.e., Andreas Lasser: see the first section), he writes

> I observed the unbelievable subtlety and soundness of expression with which the Roman jurisconsults gathered their answers which are preserved in the Pandects. . . . I realized that a large part of them were arrived at almost entirely by demonstration from the law of nature alone. . . When I first set my feet in the paths of jurisprudence, therefore, I began four years ago to work out a plan for compiling in the fewest words possible the elements of the law contained in the Roman Corpus (in the manner of the old Perpetual Edict), so that one could, so to speak, finally demonstrate from them its universal laws. There are many laws which will prove refractory to this method, especially in the Imperial Rescripts, because they do not belong to natural law. However, these are clearly discernible among the rest and will be counterbalanced by the multitude of the others—especially since I venture to assert that half of the Roman law is mere natural law.
>
> (A II i 56-57; L 106)

Indeed, at that time, Leibniz had already effected the assimilation of Roman law to natural law with the doctrine of natural law expounded in the *Nova methodus*. The novelty of this doctrine is that it links natural law with the three highest principles of Roman jurisprudence (A VI i 343–345). There are three degrees of natural law, Leibniz says, corresponding to the three basic principles of Roman law. The first degree, strict or pure law (*jus strictum seu merum*), "is nothing other than the law of war and peace" and has as its precept the principle *neminem laedere* ("to injure no one"). Strict law pertains to the lowest form of justice; that is, to the kind of justice which Aristotle called commutative justice. The second degree of natural law, equity "or equality, that is the ratio or proportion between two or more, consists in harmony or congruence" and has as its key precept the principle *suum cuique tribuere* ("to give everyone his due"), corresponding to Aristotle's distributive justice. Finally, the third degree of natural law, piety, has as its precept the principle *honeste vivere* ("to live honorably"). These three degrees are ordered in a hierarchy of perfection in which each degree in the hierarchy is more perfect than the previous one, confirms it, and overrides it in

[11] This was perfectly in keeping with Leibniz's view of Roman law as the law of the Empire and the legal foundation of Christendom. On the relationship between Roman law and Leibniz's political ideal, see Riley 1996, 184–185.

case of conflict. As the highest degree of natural law, piety "gives the others perfection and execution." This is to be understood in the light of two attributes of God, namely, wisdom and power:

> For God, in that he is omniscient and wise, confirms pure right and equity; in that he is omnipotent, he puts them into execution. Thus the utility of mankind, and indeed the beauty and the harmony of the world, coincide with God's will.
>
> (A VI i 344)

This, however, does not imply any voluntarism, for God's will necessarily conforms to the rational dictates of his wisdom (see also Johns 2013, 5, 18–19, 166 n.). Still, a problem does arise because, as Leibniz acknowledges, "strict right and equity lack a physical bond," with the consequence that humans may lack sufficient motivation to comply. Leibniz's solution appeals to God's intervention in a way that clearly foreshadows his later doctrine of a divinely established harmony between the two kingdoms of nature and grace:

> God by his intervention brings it about so that anything of public utility, i.e., useful for mankind and for the world, is also useful for each individually; accordingly, everything honest is useful, and everything base is harmful. Since it is evident from his wisdom that God assigned a reward to the just and a punishment to the unjust, and the reason of his omnipotence demonstrates that he will accomplish what he has assigned. Therefore, the existence of a wisest and most powerful Being, that is God, is the ultimate grounds of natural law.
>
> (A VI i 344–345)

In addition to anticipating a crucial development of Leibniz's mature metaphysics, the three-degrees doctrine of the *Nova methodus* would become central to Leibniz's later accounts of natural law. Versions of it occur in his notes on the elements of natural law from the years 1677–78 (Grua 606–612, 616–617, 618–621) and in sections XI–XIII of the Preface to the *Codex juris gentium* (PW 171–174; see Leibniz's explicit reference to his youthful work on p. 173). Leibniz once again went back to his three-degrees doctrine in the years 1695–97, when he set out to provide a systematic exposition of his lifelong work on natural law (*Elementa juris perpetui*, Grua 636, 639), also planning a second revised edition of the *Nova methodus*. More than an echo of this doctrine can also be detected in the late *Meditation on the Common Concept of Justice*, written around 1702–03 (PW 60). But it is especially in the 1695 note *Initium institutionum juris perpetui* (Beginning of the Institutions of Perpetual Law) that the identification of Roman law with natural law reached its fullest extent:

> It is clearly apparent . . . that the precepts of eternal law, which is also called "natural," are nothing other than the laws of the perfect state. . . . The precepts in question are

three . . . : *neminem laedere, suum cuique tribuere*, and *pie vivere*. The first is the precept of peace, the second is that of commodity, the third is that of salvation.

(Leibniz 1965, 195–196)

Here, as Riley (1996, 200–202) remarks, "[n]o longer are *neminem laedere, suum cuique tribuere*, and *honeste vivere* just historical residues of a concrete legal and jurisprudential system; they have become the principles of 'natural' (indeed 'eternal') justice. . . . Roman jurisprudence is now also natural, eternal, and divine. . . . The jurisprudence of the Eternal City has become eternal *stricto sensu*."

Leibniz's approach to natural law also explains his criticisms of leading contemporary philosophers, in particular, Hobbes and Pufendorf (Riley 1996, ch. 3; Armgardt 2015*b*). Leibniz's attitude to Hobbes is twofold. On the one hand, Leibniz has a deep admiration for Hobbes's method and style ("nothing is more elegant and suitable to the public use than [your] definitions," he writes in his letter to Hobbes of 1670; A II i 56; L 105). On the other hand, he rejects two key aspects of Hobbes's approach to law and politics: the reduction of justice to the arbitrary will of the sovereign (i.e., the idea that "just is whatever pleases the most powerful" [*Meditation on the Common Concept of Justice*, PW 47]) and the view that all power must be concentrated in a single person or body, that the government, "cannot be anything but unitary" (*Caesarinus Fürstenerius*, PW 118). Leibniz's opposition to Pufendorf, on the contrary, is both methodological and substantive. According to Leibniz, Pufendorf fails on both accounts: he is unable to provide a logical derivation of his conclusion from his defective principles (*The Principles of Pufendorf*, PW 65), and he makes "all juridical obligations derivative from the command of a superior" (PW 73). For Leibniz, on the contrary, "justice follows certain rules of equality and of proportion [which are] no less founded in the immutable nature of things and in the divine ideas, than are the principles of arithmetic and of geometry" (PW 71). However, the discovery of the precepts of natural law does not proceed only through logical derivations from first principles (although a derivation would be necessary for the demonstration of such precepts): aspects of natural law can also be extracted or inferred inductively from the legal sources and in particular from Roman law (Armgardt 2015*b*, 23).

DEONTIC LOGIC AND THE ELEMENTS OF NATURAL LAW

Leibniz's project of demonstrating the elements of natural law "from definitions alone" was not brought to completion. However, a number of drafts and fragments of the project remain from the years 1669–71 (*Elementa juris naturalis*, A VI i 431–485). The main idea is introduced as follows in the 1671 letter to Arnauld (see the first section of this chapter):

> For I define a good or just man (*vir bonus seu justus*) as one who loves everyone; love as pleasure taken in the happiness of others, and pain in the unhappiness of others; happiness as pleasure without pain; pleasure as the sense of harmony; pain as the sense of disharmony; sense as thought with will or with a conatus to act; harmony as diversity compensated by identity. . . . From these I deduce all the theorems of right and equity (*juris et aequi*). That is permissible (*licitum*) which is possible for a good man. That is duty (*debitum*) which is necessary for a good man. Hence it is clear that the just man, the man who loves all, necessarily strives to please all, even when he cannot do so, much as a stone strives to fall even when is suspended.
>
> (A II i 173-174; L 150)

The definition of the good or just man found in the letter just quoted clearly expresses the definition of justice in terms of love, which foreshadows his final and most famous definition of justice as the "charity of the wise." Leibniz's suggestion is that this definition, together with a few other definitions (of love, happiness, pleasure, pain, sense, and harmony), can provide the basis for working out all propositions about natural law and equity. But he does not confine himself to this claim. He also sets out to show how it can be implemented, anticipating much of modern deontic logic, as can be seen in particular from a draft dating to the first half of 1671 (A VI i 465–480).

This text begins with Leibniz's novel definition of *justice* as "the habit of loving everyone" (on the Leibnitian concept of love, see Brown 2011). The good man is correspondingly defined as being one who "loves everybody." As the sphere of what is morally and legally permissible, *jus* is characterized as "the capacity of the good man" (*potentia viri boni*), namely, as the range of possibilities that are available to the good man. Accordingly, whatever a good man could possibly do, consistently with his goodness, is thereby legitimate or permissible (*justum*). This, Leibniz observes, corresponds to the idea of Roman jurists that "what is not defined by the law should be referred to the choice of the good man."

On the basis of the definition of permissibility (*jus*) as the possibility open to the good man, Leibniz can affirm that "what Grotius calls moral qualities are nothing else that the qualities of the good man." Such moral-legal modalities (*juris modalia*) parallel alethic modalities and are likewise interdefinable, as illustrated in Table 36.1, appearing on the first page of the draft:

Using the notation of modern deontic logic, Leibniz's permissibility (*justum*) can indeed be expressed through a permission operator **P**, relativized to a person x and a proposition φ. In other words, that an act or proposition φ is *justum* for a person x means that φ is permitted for $x: Justum_x(\varphi) =_{df} \mathbf{P}_x \varphi$. The definition of the permissible as what is possible for a good man can therefore be expressed through the propositional schema $\mathbf{P}_x \varphi =_{df} \Diamond(G_x \wedge \varphi)$. According to the schema, that φ is permissible for x means that it is possible ($\Diamond$) that, at the same time, x is good and φ is the case.

Table 36.1 Moral–legal and alethic modalities

Possible	is whatever	can (potest)	happen.
Impossible		cannot (non potest)	
Necessary		cannot fail to (non potest non)	
Contingent		can fail to (potest non)	
Justum	is whatever it is	possible	for a good man to do.
Injustum		impossible	
Debitum		necessary	
Indebitum		contingent	

The impermissible (*injustum*) or prohibited can similarly be expressed through the negation ($\neg$) of permissibility: *Iniustum$_x$* $(\varphi) =_{df} \neg \mathbf{P}_x(\varphi)$. Going back to the definition of permissibility, we can also say that what is impermissible or forbidden is impossible for the good man (i.e., it cannot possibly coexist with his goodness), or equivalently, its negation is necessarily ($\square$) entailed by goodness: $\neg \mathbf{P}_x \varphi = \neg \Diamond (G_x \wedge \varphi) = \square (G_x \rightarrow \neg\varphi)$.

The obligatory (*debitum*) is what one is not permitted not to do, such that *Debitum$_x$* $(\varphi) =_{df} \neg \mathbf{P}_x \neg\varphi$, which, using the usual symbol for obligation, can also be expressed as $O_x \varphi$. Going back to the original definition of permissibility as applied to $\neg\varphi$, we get that what is obligatory for x cannot fail to coexist with x's goodness, or, equivalently, it is necessarily entailed by x's goodness, i.e., $O_x \varphi = \neg \mathbf{P}_x \neg\varphi = \neg \Diamond (G_x \wedge \neg\varphi) = \square (G_x \rightarrow \varphi)$.

Finally, the omissible (*indebitum*) for a person x is what is not obligatory for x (i.e., what he is permitted not to do), so that *Indebitum$_x$* $(\varphi) =_{df} \neg O_x \varphi = \mathbf{P}_x \neg\varphi$.

The connection between alethic and deontic modalities enables Leibniz to derive the basic principles of standard deontic logic relativized to particular individuals, as well as the principles connecting deontic and alethic modalities, without assuming any specifically deontic axiom. All the work is performed by his definition of *justum* and of the cognate terms, and by their linkage to a basic modal logic, under the assumption that human goodness is possible, $\Diamond G_x$. Thus, he can affirm that "Nothing permissible is impermissible" (*Nullum justum est injustum*), which simply appears to be the tautology $\mathbf{P}_x(\varphi) \rightarrow \neg(\neg \mathbf{P}_x(\varphi))$, if we define *injustum* as $\neg \mathbf{P}_x$. He can also affirm that "Everything obligatory is possible" (*Omne debitum possibile est*): $O_x \varphi \rightarrow \Diamond \varphi$.

A further development consists in combining the legal modalities with judgments of "easiness" (*facilitas*) Easiness is defined as "intelligibility in itself (*per se*)"; that is, as pertaining to the conceivability of a thing regardless of its connections with other things (such connection, on the contrary, would be relevant to judgments of probability). Leibniz observes that in order to conceive the possibility of a thing, we only need to consider the requirements for the existence of that thing, whereas in order to conceive the impossibility of a thing, we need to consider the requirements of both the thing at issue and of something else incompatible with it. Therefore, possibilities are "easier" (*facilior*) than impossibilities, and, in particular, permissibilities (understood as possibilities for the good man) are easier than impermissibilities (impossibilities for the good man). Accordingly, it is easier for an act to be permissible than for it to be impermissible (*Actus facilius est justus quam injustus*). Moreover, acts are presumed to be permissible (*Actus praesumitur justus*) rather than prohibited. This also applies to the permissibility of an omission (i.e., to omissibility): acts are also presumed to be omissible rather than obligatory.

Finally, by combining legal and alethic modalities with the definition of the good man as he who loves everybody, Leibniz obtains further theorems, such as "Everything permissible is possible for one who loves all" (*Omne justum possibile est amanti omnes*); "Everything obligatory is necessary for one who loves all" (*Omne debitum necessarium est amanti omnes*), and "Everything impermissible is impossible for one who loves all" (*Omne injustum impossibile est amanti omnes*).

From the vantage point of modern deontic logic, we can say that what Leibniz has developed in this extraordinary text is a reduction of deontic logic to alethic modal logic, anticipating by almost three centuries the analogous proposals by Kanger (1957/1971) and Anderson (1958).[12] From Leibniz's point of view, this analysis of deontic notions represents a major development in his lifelong search for rationality in law and ethics, from his initial "art of forming cases" to a legal-ethical science grounded in the highest form of justice, a science that he presents as follows:

> Jurisprudence is the science of the just, i.e. the science of freedom and duties, or the science of the law, given some case or fact. I call it a science, albeit practical, since all of its propositions can be demonstrated from the mere definition of the good man, and do not depend on induction and examples. . . . I call it a science of the just, i.e. of what is possible for a good man, because at the same time it shows what is impossible for him to do and what is possible for him not to omit. I call it a science of duties, i.e. of what is impossible for a good man and necessary to him, that is, impossible to omit, since the remaining actions that are not excluded, are considered just and indifferent, namely, possible and contingent.
>
> (A VI i 467)

The importance of this new approach to law is borne out by Leibniz's writings from the years 1677–78, and in particular by his second series of notes on the elements of natural law, where he seeks to combine his three-degrees theory of natural law with his good man–based system of legal modalities under his mature definition of justice as the charity of the wise (see, e.g., Grua 603–612).

---

[12] As observed by Hilpinen (2001). On Leibniz's deontic logic, see also Kalinowski and Gardies 1974 and Lenzen 2005.

LEGAL REASONING: THE BALANCE
OF REASONS

For Leibniz, the law is not a self-sufficient and closed discipline. On the one hand, it needs knowledge and methods from other domains of science and philosophy (see the preceding section "Leibniz's Early Legal Works"); on the other hand, it can contribute to the progress of other domains since it best exemplifies certain aspects of rationality (see Boucher 2008). As Leibniz states in the draft *Ad stateram juris de gradibus probationum et probabilitatum* (Towards a Balance of Law Concerning the Degrees of Proof and Probabilities, C 210–214; LH IV vi 17, 1–2),[13] written around 1676, the law excels at governing the exercise of reason under conditions of uncertainty, disagreement, conflicts of interests, and time constraints (on legal paradigms within Leibniz's theory of controversies, see Dascal 2006). Legal decision-making—although far from perfect—best exemplifies how we should proceed when addressing "the most serious deliberations on life and health, on the state, on war and peace, on the moderation of conscience, on care of eternity." The law is most advanced in the development of the master instrument of rationality, namely, the "balance" of reasons, or "logometric scales," which could determine and compare the weights of "arguments of discussants, opinions of authors, voices of advisors." Two aspects of the law are most relevant to this purpose.

The first aspect is its ability to give form to disputes, setting out rule-governed procedures for dialectical exchange and impartial adjudication, as

> ultimately, what else is a judicial process if not the form of disputing transferred from the Schools to life, purged of vacuousness and limited by public authority in such a way that it is not allowed with impunity to divagate or to evade, so that nothing is omitted that could be useful for the search of truth? (C 211)

The second aspect is the law's ability to rationally address contingent matters, as in the interpretation of public and private decisions, the assessment of past facts, and argumentation:

> As the Mathematicians have in necessary things, so the Jurists have exercised optimally logic, namely, the art of reason, in contingent things. From this exercise they have obtained many prescriptions on full and semi-full proves, on presumption, on conjecturing the meaning of laws, contracts and last wills, on indicia of crimes . . . ; and moreover the legal commonplaces of arguments, which enrich the Topics with axioms of law, commonly called maxims. (C 213)

---

[13] English translation in Dascal 2006, 35–40.

This 1676 draft is merely the preface to an envisaged work, but its ideal integration can be found in a text of 1678–79 entitled *De legum interpretatione, rationibus, applicatione, systemate* (On the Interpretation, Reasons, Application, and System of Laws, A VI iv C 2782–2791).[14] Leibniz observes that interpreting a law involves not only making sense of the words stated (*dictum*) by the legislator but also determining the view (*sententia*) the legislator intended to express (i.e., what he thought or would have thought had he been asked). To establish the legislator's intention, we have to consider his reasons rather than his affections, even though the legislator's irrational affections may determine what reasons he selected and prioritized. Therefore, interpreters should adopt a pragmatic-contextual approach, sticking to those reasons that effectively moved the legislator, even when they do not have a universal significance, because they correspond to the partic-ular affections of the legislator or to the specific needs of his state. The interpreter may disregard the principles endorsed by the legislator only when such principles are man-ifestly absurd or contrary to reason. This limitation of the interpretive space is inspired by both institutional and cognitive considerations: interpreters should not usurp the legislator's place, and they are also subject to affections and mistakes.

As concerns argumentation in matters of law, Leibniz distinguishes two basic kinds of legal inference: the *proof* (*probatio*) of a law, where the interpretation of a law is a con-clusion to be justified according to reasons, and the consequence (*consequentia*) of a law, where the (interpreted) law is a premise for a determination concerning a particular case. He also distinguishes two kinds of correct (*recta*) legal inference: deductive infer-ence, or *demonstration*, and presumptive inference, or *topic*. Both have faulty (*vitiosae*) counterparts; namely, paralogism and sophism, respectively. An inference that fails to meet the standard of *demonstration*—and would indeed be a paralogism if presented as a *demonstration*—may well meet the standard that applies to topic. Whereas demon-strative inference works out the exact implications of definitions, topical inference is based on presumptions and conjectures. In *presumptions*

> the proposed statement necessarily follows from what is established as true, without any other requirements than negative ones, namely, that there should exist no im-pediment. Therefore, it is always to be decided in favor of the party who has the pre-sumption unless the other party proves the contrary.
>
> (A VI iv C 2789)

In *conjectures*, on the other hand, "some positive elements are required to prove ex-actly either of the opposites, but if it is not estahlished that such elements are true it is pronounced for that opposite which is easier, having less requirements or inferior requirements of the same kind (A VI iv C 2789).

Presumptions and conjectures support defeasible or nonmonotonic reasoning be-cause they lead to provisional conclusions that may have to be abandoned should a

---

[14] Ibid., 79–92.

presumption be defeated by the proof of an impediment, or a conjecture by the exact proof of the opposite. Such nondemonstrative (nondeductive) patterns of reasoning are paramount in the law considering that, in "moral matters most inferences are indeed presumptive." Leibniz's considerations on defeasible legal reasoning clearly identify those nondeductive patterns of reasoning that only in recent decades have been studied in philosophy (Rescher 2006) and formalized in logic and artificial intelligence (Pollock 1989) and, in particular, in the logical analysis of legal argument (Prakken and Sartor 2015).

For systematization in law, a solution is provided that exploits the presumptive nature of legal reasoning in such a way as to reconcile the opposite requirements of coverage and conciseness in the representation of legal content, avoiding the combinatorial explosion that would result from an explicit specification of all possible cases. It consists in modeling legal systems as multilayered combinations of rules and exceptions. In this way, a few general rules combined with the exceptions limiting them under particular conditions "could cover countless cases." In such a system

> every law has a presumption, and applies in any given case, unless it is proved that some impediment or contradiction has emerged, which would generate an exception extracted from another law. But in that case the charge of proof is transferred to the person who adduces the exception.
>
> (A VI iv C 2791)

This way of dealing with legal complexity illustrates Leibniz's approach to the law. His aim is not to impose a single "scientific" model on the law but rather to complement the law with whatever useful tools can be extracted from science (logic, mathematics, physics, etc.: see the section "Leibniz's Early Legal Works"), as well as to expand the forms of rationality embedded in legal practice, thus giving them a precise form. He is not afraid to depart from his preferred deductive-axiomatic approach when that is needed for the purposes of the law (on Leibniz's approach to axiomatization, see Brewer 2013). This explains his pragmatic approach to legal interpretation (which, in conferring meaning on the legislator's statements, also takes account of the social and psychological context of their utterance), as well as his presumptive approach to legal reasoning and his proposal to model the law as a system of rules and exceptions, rather than through axioms for deduction.

CONCLUSION

Leibniz's involvement with the law is a key aspect of his intellectual development. He was educated as a lawyer and devoted most of his early works to the law. Although the focus of his inquiries shifted over time from law to mathematics, science, and metaphysics, he continued to study legal issues and to value the law not only as a necessary social practice but also as an intellectual endeavor. Indeed, he believed that both Roman law and traditional methods for the interpretation and application of law, for all their faults and limitations, embodied fundamental patterns of rationality that needed to be captured, developed, and integrated with those emerging from philosophy and science. Some of his considerations and results are amazingly ahead of their time and have yet to be fully understood and developed in mainstream legal theory: notably, his development of deontic logic; the connection he established between aretaic, axiological, and deontological notions; his combinatorial analysis of cases; and his rigorous characterization of the presumptive nature of legal reasoning.

We hope that the present work—while inevitably failing to do full justice to the extraordinary richness of Leibniz's legal corpus—may illustrate his main achievements in law and legal theory as well as the significance of his legal interests for his professional and scholarly life.

REFERENCES

Anderson, A. R. 1958. "A reduction of deontic logic to alethic modal logic." *Mind* 67: 100–103.

Antognazza, M. R. 2009. *Leibniz: An Intellectual Bibliography*. Cambridge: Cambridge University Press.

Armgardt, M. 2001. *Das rechtslogische System der "Doctrina Conditionum" von Gottfried Wilhelm Leibniz*. Marburg: Elwert.

Armgardt, M. 2014. "Leibniz as legal scholar." *Fundamina*, Special issue 1 (*Meditationes de iure et historia. Essays in honour of Laurens Winkel*): 27–38.

Armgardt, M. 2015a. "Presumptions and conjectures in Leibniz's legal theory." In M. Armgardt, P. Canivez, and S. Chassagnard-Pinet (eds.), *Legal Reasoning and Logic—Past and Present Interactions*. Dordrecht: Springer, pp. 51–69.

Armgardt, M. 2015b. "Die Rechstheorie von Leibniz im Licht seiner Kritik an Hobbes und Pufendorf." In L. H Wenchao (ed.), *Das Recht kann nicht ungerecht sein, Beitrage zu Leibniz' Philosophie der Gerechtigkeit, Studia Leibnitiana Supplementa, Sonderherft 44*. Stuttgart: Steiner, pp. 13–27.

Artosi, A., Pieri, B., and Sartor, G. (eds.). 2013. *Leibniz: Logico-Philosophical Puzzles in the Law. Philosophical Questions and Perplexing Cases in the Law*. Dordrecht: Springer.

Boucher, P. 2008. "Leibniz: What kind of legal rationalism?" In M. Dascal (ed.), *Leibniz: What Kind of Rationalist?* Dordrecht: Springer, pp. 231–249.

Brewer, S. 2013. "Law, logic, and Leibniz. A contemporary perspective." In A. Artosi, B. Pieri, and G. Sartor (eds.), *Leibniz: Logico-Philosophical Puzzles in the Law. Philosophical Questions and Perplexing Cases in the Law*. Dordrecht: Springer, pp. 199–226.

Brown, G. 2011. "Disinterested love: Understanding Leibniz's reconciliation of self- and other-regarding motives." *British Journal for the History of Philosophy* 19: 265–303.

Dascal, M. 2004. "Language as a cognitive technology." In B. Gorayska and J. L. May (ed.), *Cognition and technology: Co-existence, convergence and co-evolution*. Amsterdam: Benjamins, pp. 37–62.

Dascal, M. 2006. "Introductory Essay." In M. Dascal (ed.), *G. W. Leibniz: The Art of Controversies*. Dordrecht: Springer, pp. i–xix.

Hilpinen, R. 2001. "Deontic Logic." in L. Goble (ed.), *The Blackwell Guide to Philosophical Logic*. London: Blackwell, pp. 159–182.

Johns, C. L. 2013. *The Science of Right in Leibniz's Moral and Political Philosophy*. London: Bloomsbury.

Kalinowski, G., and Gardies, J. -L. 1974. "Un logicien déontique avant la lettre: Gottfried Wilhelm Leibniz." *Archiv für Rechts- und Sozialphilosophie* 60: 79–112.

Kanger, S. 1957/1971. "New foundations for ethical theory." In R. Hilpinen (ed.), *Deontic Logic*. Dordrecht: Reidel, pp. 36–58.

Leibniz, G. W. 1965. *Scritti politici e di diritto naturale*, V. Mathieu (ed.). Turin: Utet.

Leibniz, G. W. 2002. *De Conditionibus/des conditions*, P. Boucher (ed.). Paris: Vrin.

Leibniz, G. W. 2009. *Des cas perplexes en droit (De casibus perplexis in jure)*, P. Boucher (ed.). Paris: Vrin.

Leibniz, G. W. 2012. *Il nuovo metodo di apprendere ed insegnare la giurisprudenza*, C. M. De Iuliis (ed.). Milan: Giuffrè.

Leibniz, G. W. 2014. *I casi perplessi in diritto (De casibus perplexis in iure)*, M. De Iuliis (ed.). Milan: Giuffrè.

Leibniz, G. W. 2015. *Saggio di questioni filosofiche estratte dalla giusrisprudenza e Dissertazione sui casi perplessi in diritto*, A. Artosi, B. Pieri, and G. Sartor, (eds.). Turin: Giappichelli.

Lenzen, W. 2005. "Leibniz on alethic and deontic modal logic." In D. Berlioz and F. Nef (eds.), *Leibniz et les puissances du langage*. Paris: Vrin, pp. 341–362.

Magnier, S. 2015. "Suspensive condition and dynamic epistemic logic: A Leibnizian survey." In M. Armgardt, P. Canivez, and S. Chassagnard-Pinet (eds.), *Legal Reasoning and Logic—Past and Present Interactions*. Dordrecht: Springer, pp. 71–94.

Mulvaney, R. J. 1994. "Divine justice in Leibniz's 'Discourse on Metaphysics.'" In R. S. Woolhouse (ed.), *Gottfried Wilhelm Leibniz: Critical Assessments*, vol. 4. London: Routledge, pp. 413–432.

Pollock, John L. 1989. *How to Build a Person: A Prolegomenon*. Cambridge, MA: Cambridge University Press.

Prakken, H., and Sartor, G. 2015. "Law and logic: A review from an argumentation perspective." *Artificial Intelligence* 227: 214–245.

Rahman, S. 2015. "On hypothetical judgements and Leibniz's notion of conditional right." In M. Armgardt, P. Canivez, and S. Chassagnard-Pinet (eds.), *Legal Reasoning and Logic—Past and Present Interactions*. Dordrecht: Springer, pp. 109–167.

Rescher, N. 2006. *Presumption and the Practices of Tentative Cognition*. Cambridge: Cambridge University Press.

Riley, P. 1996. *Leibniz' Universal Jurisprudence: Justice as the Charity of the Wise*. Cambridge, MA: Harvard University Press.

CHAPTER 37

LEIBNIZ'S POLITICAL VISION FOR EUROPE

FRIEDRICH BEIDERBECK

LEIBNIZ ON THE HOLY ROMAN EMPIRE: IMPERIAL REFORM

IN Leibniz's political thought, the Holy Roman Empire of the German Nation constituted the conceptual framework most familiar to him. He regarded the Empire as Europe's center, viewing the continent and its state system as dependent on the Reich's strength and stability.[1] The significance of Germany's political and cultural structures in the seventeenth century for Leibniz's lifeworld, his hypotheses and fundamental convictions, his scientific and theoretical oeuvre, and his ethical orientation can hardly be rated highly enough. We find the political and social realities of his times reflected in central concepts and ideas such as unity in plurality, harmony, coexistence, and balance. His thoughts on order, security, and law are rooted in Germany's constitutional situation and in the seventeenth-century *Reichspublizistik* debate (the science of German polity and imperial law), to which Leibniz himself made a lasting contribution. It was the Peace of Westphalia in particular that determined how Germany and Europe appeared politically after 1648. This collection of treaties became the yardstick for ideas on public order that were the starting point for the Europeanization of the *Reichsverfassung* (imperial constitution) and a debate on the possibility of permanent peace among European states. Numerous examples can be cited as proof of Leibniz's deep-rooted political and cultural origins that prompted him throughout his life to champion the advancement of the concept of the Reich—from his early Mainz

---

[1] *Bedenken welchergestalt Securitas publica interna et externa und Status praesens im Reich auf festen Fuß zu stellen*; A IV i 166, 214.

writings on reform, through his submissions at the imperial court, to the later writings connected with the Utrecht negotiations.

Leibniz saw in the Holy Roman Empire the model for a body politic founded on balance and justice that ultimately had to orient itself toward the ideal of the *civitas dei*. This ideal would serve as the yardstick for all forms of human society seeking to bring about divine justice. In answer to the question as to the best political form of society—one that made well-being, peace, and security possible—Leibniz declared the *Reichsverfassung* to be exemplary. To continue to have a historical impact, the Reich's structure had to meet the great challenges of the Early Modern Age: a secular concept of state; the increasingly competitive European power system; and radical upheavals in the fields of ideology, economy, science, and society. In doing so, Leibniz based his political and constitutional ideas for imperial reform largely on the Peace of Westphalia. These ideas included the development of structures relating to the Estates and federal bodies in the framework of the *Reichsverfassung* and the right to enter alliances in both domestic and foreign policy. These alliances were not only to serve the territories, but, above all, to consolidate the Reich as a whole and its defense.

The spirit of optimism that ensued from Germany's restructuring in 1648 had also gripped the Electoral court in Mainz. Johann Philipp von Schönborn stood for a course of politics that emphasized the *Reichsverfassung*'s federal structures and culminated in the *Rheinbund* (1658). This alliance policy, practiced by the Imperial Estates as a means of maintaining balance and peace, constituted a starting point for Leibniz's own grand designs in his time at Mainz (1668–72). Defending the Reich effectively and establishing a reliably financed standing imperial army were just a few of the reform proposals that kept the *Reichspublizistik* occupied in connection with the debate on the *Reichsverfassung* and Pufendorf's hypotheses. Dissension among the Estates, the lack of strong imperial rule in domestic policy and of leadership in foreign affairs, the deficits in the legal and tax systems, and the consequences of the continuing religious schism and territorial particularism all provided fodder for a broad debate on reform. No one could escape the fact that France provided the model for the *raison d'État*; to the chagrin of the Empire, France, as a body politic ruled centrally and absolutely, proved its ability to act both in domestic and foreign policy. On the topic of imperial security, Leibniz penned *Sekuritäts-Bedencken*, a comprehensive political memorandum, at the peak of his activity in Mainz in 1670.[2] At the center of his reform ideas one finds the ambitious idea of consolidating the German constitutional structure by creating an alliance of the Estates with political and military powers. The context of this design resulted from his close collaboration with Boineburg, a politician from Mainz who was working on the *Fürstenbund* (Alliance of Princes) as a further development of the failed *Rheinbund*. The crucial goal was to succeed in keeping the

---

[2] *Bedenken*; A IV i 133–214.

Reich out of a war between France and Habsburg by strengthening its Estates' constitutional powers and its military strength. In the second part of *Sekuritäts-Bedenckens*,[3] however, Leibniz deviated from this goal and opined that only a collaboration among the militarily strong imperial princes and the emperor, the Netherlands, and England would meet the requirements for strengthening the dualist *Reichsverfassung* encompassing emperor, on the one hand, and Imperial Estates, on the other hand. These were precisely formulated ideas about how this German alliance of Estates was to look. Its most pressing task was to ensure the Reich's security, now increasingly threatened from outside, as made evident by Louis XIV's occupation of Lorraine. Improvement of its defenses was to be achieved by a corporative union of armed, powerful imperial princes, including the emperor, as an Imperial Estate ("*Teutscher Reichßbundt*"). A federal council led by people with far-reaching powers, a federal army 20,000–30,000 strong, and a federal treasury were to guarantee this imperial executive body's political viability.[4] Leibniz thus reverted to a federal tradition that reckoned the right of alliance or unification among the old rights of the Estates in the *Reichsherkommen* (Reich's law and conventions). Successful defense policies became the yardstick for the Reich's capacity to function and a precondition for guaranteeing political security, autonomy, and territorial integrity.

Accompanying Leibniz's plan for political and constitutional reform in the stricter sense were ideas that extended the concept of *Reichsreform* comprehensively to embrace social, economic, and cultural aspects. He was not only concerned with the Reich's political structure, but also more comprehensively with the *bonum commune*. In contrast to Pufendorf, who assessed the Reich primarily along lines of political and constitutional theory, Leibniz constructed his idea of the Reich altogether more universally: as a historical, political, legal, and social entity. His idea of *patria* goes beyond traditional aspects of political *securitas*—law, peace within, security without. Erecting a *societas perfecta* likewise means taking socioeconomic and culture factors into consideration. Leibniz designed a concept of society that included, alongside political rulers, all private individuals concerned with public welfare and envisaged them assuming appropriate responsibility. The approach Leibniz took in his concept of Reich—also the basis for his idea of a *respublica optima*—already hints at a distinction between state and society. However, he did not question the Early Modern state's wish to control all aspects of society. Working on these assumptions, Leibniz designs the general concept of how society in Germany—in his view really backward—should develop. This comprehensive approach to reform becomes more tangible in the institution of *Sozietät*.[5] It was to function as the "think-tank" and administrative body for

---

[3] *Bedenken*; A IV i 174–207, 211–214.

[4] *Bedenken*; A IV i 170–173, 207–211.

[5] See chapter 31. On the subject of concerns about *securitas*, we find other important schemes, too: *Grundriß eines Bedenkens* (A IV i 530–543); *Bedenken von Aufrichtung einer Akademie* (A IV i 543–552); *Societas philadelphica* (A IV i 552–557).

society's well-being: this included establishing a broad social space for communication by fostering culture in the native tongue and improving children's upbringing and education as crucial for society's general progress—socially, economically, scientifically, and legally.[6]

CAESARINUS FÜRSTENERIUS: IMPERIAL PUBLIC LAW

In the seventeenth century, there was controversial debate in the Reich about how to deal with the foreign philosophical concepts of *raison d'État* and *sovereignty* in the context of the German constitution. Leibniz belonged to those historians and constitutional law experts who, in grappling with the modern notion of state, contributed an independent theory. He did so by reconciling federalist principles with the concept of state and defending the *Reichsverfassung*'s dualism, showing the federation to be a genuinely German constitutional model.

After 1648, the *jus publicum* focused on how to interpret the Peace of Westphalia. The starting point for enquiring into state and constitution was dictated by Bodin's concept of sovereignty as statehood's main characteristic. Applying the concept to the Reich's constitutional reality became the great challenge for the *Reichspublizistik*. On the basis of being bound by the Reich's fundamental laws, among which the Peace of Westphalia ranked alongside electoral capitulations and imperial decrees (*Reichsabschiede*), the central theme was developed of a common responsibility shared by emperor and Imperial Estates. In territorial terms, the discussion of Bodin's idea nurtured the theory of *superioritas territorialis*. Here, too, Leibniz made an independent contribution. The full participation of the Imperial Estates, as determined in Article VIII paragraph 2 (IPO) of the Osnabrück Treaty, demanded of the *Reichspublizistik* that the question of the state system be clarified. There was general consensus that the debate on the *forma imperii* and the *status mixtus* theory would lead nowhere since it was not possible to characterize the Reich adequately with the Aristotelian doctrine on state systems. In fact, a definition developed by Christian Besold and Ludolph Hugo eventually prevailed—one that called the Reich a composite state. Leibniz also, in principle, shared this interpretation.

Pufendorf's attempt at describing the reality of the Reich let the debate intensify. Pufendorf's theoretical achievement consisted in detaching the theory of the Reich from Aristotelian and Bodin's terminology and redefining it with the help of the systems concept. Decisive for the reinterpretation was the theory's ambiguity. A less precise

---

[6] See chapters 35, 36, 38.

interpretation, in the sense of emphasizing the coherence of individual states within one whole structure, could thus stand in contrast to its interpretation as a system of alliances, which disputed the Reich's statehood. In grappling with the *Monzambano*, Leibniz defined his own position regarding the *forma imperii* more precisely. He rejected Pufendorf's main statement that the Reich was comparable with a system of allied states, arguing that the territories were *Reichslehen* (held in fealty) and that the sovereign princes were by no means generally independent and absolute rulers. Leibniz emphasized the personal element: the obligations of fealty made the Reich, as a political entity, a *persona civilis,* thereby possessing a single will and the *summa potestas*— preconditions for statehood.[7]

Leibniz valued the Reich's legal tradition more highly than the political structural weaknesses that resulted from particularism.

As embodied in the imperial overlordship, he argues, the *imperium,* consisting of the emperor and the entirety of the Imperial Estates, possessed supreme command. This entirety existed as *civitas imperans,* each individual Imperial Estate being itself part of the *persona civilis* to which it was subject.[8] On this condition, Leibniz also conceded in his Elementa juris naturalis: "And so the imperium is a system of allied civitates [Et ita esset imperium systema civitatum foederatarum]."[9] The Reich as a whole body possessed a different form of sovereignty compared to the highly independent territories. Basically, for Leibniz, the political nucleus of state development in the Reich consisted in the particularist territorial sovereignty. So, in contrast to Conring, who saw the origin of the territorial princes' rule in the gradual hereditary character of the Reich's offices of state, he was convinced that the oldest authority in the Reich had its origins in the independence of the lineages and their princes' power.[10]

In his treatise *De jure suprematus ac legationis principum Germaniae,* written under the pseudonym of *Caesarinus Fürstenerius* at the Nijmegen Peace Congress (1678/79), Leibniz developed his idea of a territorial power that had to prove its ability in international politics as a subject of laws of nations, above all through its capacity for war- and peace-making and participation in the business of diplomacy. The work's title itself is suggestive of innovation. Traditional public law did not know the term "supremacy." Leibniz sees this as a form of territorial rule that introduces a new interaction level, defined primarily by power-politics, that lay beyond legal concepts. Its basis is the *superioritas territorialis.* The territorial prince possesses a number of sovereign rights and absolute authority over his subjects and has, inter alia, the right to conduct war, forge alliances, and send legations. For his interpretation of territorial authority, Leibniz then refers to *souveraineté,* reverting to the terminology of the French draft

---

[7] *In Severinum de Monzambano;* A IV i 501.
[8] *Georgius Ulicovius Lithuanus;* A IV i 61.
[9] *Elementa juris naturalis;* A VI i 446.
[10] *Caesarini Fürstenerii de Jure Suprematus ac Legationis Principum Germaniae;* A IV ii 66–71.

contract of the Peace of Westphalia.[11] The actual power wielded by the individual imperial princes differed hugely, so that it was supremacy's mission to conceptualize these differences to the advantage of the Reich's powerful territories. This is one of the first times in German constitutional law that the concept of *souveraineté* is used to interpret territorial power; Leibniz does, however, distance himself from Bodin's idea of sovereignty: this supremacy was by no means synonymous with modern sovereignty; on the contrary, it corresponded rather to an extended form of *jus territoriale*. The basic concept that the Reich's territories were not independent state units was a conviction that Leibniz shared not only with the *Reichspublizistik*; it was also very much in line with the Peace of Westphalia.

A specific view of things that defined the state of the German constitution as one of balance went back to the later Hanoverian vice-chancellor Ludolph Hugo. Hugo presented to the theoretical debate the approach of a well-balanced division of responsibilities shared by emperor and Imperial Estates. Structuring the *summa potestas* in two types of tasks, he assigned the care for the general welfare to the Reich to the suzerain and the care for the special welfare of the territories to the Estates.[12] For his part, in *Caesarinus Fürstenerius*, Leibniz developed the idea of distinguishing different spheres of sovereignty and activity within the *summa potestas*. The assumption of a functional balance of power by a finer subdivision of sovereignty and state spheres of activity led him to endorse the principle of federation. In his desire to reconcile the concept of the Reich with modern ones of state, he developed the idea of an imperial state based on federalism. The territorial princes' independence would not preclude state cohesiveness within the Reich as a whole any more than the diversity in the *respublica christiana* would preclude a union of Christian churches. As a *systema foederatorum*, the Reich was in principle as much a state as the individual territories.

Leibniz's legal upgrading of princely sovereignty continued a line of argument that was able to appeal to the capacity for alliance as established in the Peace of Westphalia (IPO Article VIII paragraph 2) and institutionalized in international intercourse between states. Employing his supremacy, a prince with adequate means of power—Leibniz specifically had Braunschweig-Lüneburg in mind—should be able to use the prerogatives in foreign policy that accorded with his territorial and dynastic interests. His independence ended at the higher authority of the Reich as represented in the *Reichstag*.[13] The *Reichstag* was an institution that provided for a central and joint formulation of intent among all members of the Reich, thus constituting for Leibniz the Reich's character as a state regardless of territorial independence.

---

[11] *Caesarini Fürstenerii de Jure Suprematus*; A IV ii 55.

[12] Ludolph Hugo. *De statu regionum Germaniae et regimine principum summae Imperii reipublicae aemulo*, 1661.

[13] *Entretien de Philarete et d'Eugene*; A IV ii 303.

Defending the Reich Against Louis XIV: From the *Consilium Aegyptiacum* and *Mars Christianissimus* to the War of Spanish Succession and the Peace of Utrecht

Leibniz's political writings are characterized by a particular awareness of Central Europe's difficult geopolitical situation in the face of the danger emanating from France and the Ottoman Empire—a conjunction perceived by Leibniz as a constant state of threat. Thus, the desire for security without and stability within remained an important motive for him throughout his life as a political publicist and advisor.

While the Dutch War (1672–79) was approaching, Leibniz drew up his *Consilium Aegyptiacum* (1671/72).[14] This distinctive work enjoys a unique position among comparable seventeenth-century treatises on world politics on account of its great wealth of material and ideas. It offers a detailed analysis of the European power system and a vast global design for the future. Its immediate aim was to deter Louis XIV from a war of aggression against the Netherlands and thus to prevent a larger European war that would threaten the Reich's integrity. France is presented here as a model state.[15] It is shown to be a rich and autonomous country with a sophisticated society, the model of absolute monarchy, embodied by a wise, happy, and powerful king. Thus, true *raison d'État*, Leibniz argues, requires France to expand its power by conquering Egypt, thereby enlarging its own power resources and cutting the Netherlands off from their own, especially from trade with East Asia. He analyses the constellation of power in terms of trade relations and colonial expansion. He concludes: whoever possesses Egypt, the "*isthmus mundi principalis*," controls trade between Asia and Africa, between Orient and Occident.[16] Leibniz constructs a global West-East frame of reference, and comparisons are based on the criteria of power, trade, and geopolitics. He starts out from the basic idea that asserting oneself in the international power system depended on one's strength as a trade and colonial power. Regardless of France's supremacy, Habsburg's position had to be maintained as the leading power in Southeast Europe opposing the Turks. With his plan of an anti-Turkish alliance of all Christian powers, Leibniz is very close to sixteenth- and seventeenth-century crusade projects. It is worth noting that a power-political principle is elevated to the status of being crucial to international peace. Christian Europe was to be pacified by means of a common foreign policy of aggression and expansion. The Islamic sphere of power and area of culture and influence would become the victim

---

[14] A IV i N. V.
[15] A IV i 258–259.
[16] A IV i 274–275.

of large-scale colonial expansion. Leibniz promotes the idea that the expansion of a global Christian cultural system would ensue from the conquest of Islam Expanding the *Respublica Christiana*, he argues, would enable the emergence of a world system borne by education and culture and extending as far as Asia.

Leibniz viewed Strasbourg's annexation in 1681 by Louis XIV as a clear breach of the Peace of Westphalia. Once again, he states, the international binding force of the whole peace treaty was shown to be open to revision as long as the French king was appointed by the treaty to act as guarantor power for the German and European peace system.[17]

France's foreign policy, which in his eyes was a cynical breach of the law, provoked Leibniz into penning a correspondingly harsh response, his *Mars Christianissimus* (1683). This pamphlet numbers among the few of his works printed in his lifetime. The anonymously written, extremely witty polemic, characterized more or less throughout by the stylistic devices of irony and sarcasm, clearly did not attract much attention, either in the original Latin or in the subsequent French version. A faulty German translation was, however, in circulation—one that Leibniz undoubtedly did not arrange for.[18] With this treatise, the political publicist Leibniz left behind a piece of work that for him is singular in its passionate polemics, "Leibniz' most entertaining, and also most malicious, political work."[19] In view of the threat to Vienna by the advancing Ottoman Empire, he castigated France's alliance with the Turks. The scrupulousness with which the *Most Christian king* Louis XIV was taking advantage of the Habsburg monarchy's (and of the whole Reich's) predicament basically lets him appear as the ungodly enemy of Christendom.

The outbreak of the Palatine War in 1688 prompted Leibniz to again observe Louis XIV's European politics more closely, calling for power politics to be bound by agreements ratified by the law of nations. France itself had taken on supervising the Westphalian Peace Treaty's stipulations and had recently reconfirmed its universal validity in the Peace of Nijmegen.[20] The demand for legally binding relationships in international politics, repeatedly and vehemently formulated by Leibniz, agreed with his ideas of law and order centered on a universal Christian framework.[21] The fiercest reproach Leibniz could level at Louis XIV's politics from the angle of natural law and ethics was that of "*impiété*."[22] For a state's behavior to be legitimate without it being bound by natural law and thus ultimately by divine justice was unimaginable for Leibniz. He connected the imperative of *pietas*—the highest level of his natural law trilogy—with his verdict on a politics of aggression: a politics that, although supposedly for the good of Christendom, in fact ran counter to the fundamental interests of the Christian states, as evidenced by the French furtherance of aggressive Ottoman politics against the Reich.[23]

[17] *Mars Christianissimus*; A IV ii (2nd edn., 1984), N. 22, 473–474, 496–497.
[18] A IV ii, xxiii; English translation in PW, 121–145.
[19] Patrick Riley; PW 34.
[20] *Réflexions sur la déclaration de la guerre*; A IV iii 98–99, 102; A I xi 657–658.
[21] *Réflexions*, pp. 126–127.
[22] *Réflexions*, p. 99.
[23] *Réflexions*, p. 77.

The War of Spanish Succession (1701–13/14) also prompted Leibniz to take a critical look at Louis XIV's position of power, which seemed to be continuously growing. What directly triggered off this European crisis—one that had long been in the offing—was the death of Charles II of Spain (on November 1, 1700) and then, above all, his will. Contrary to the instructions of the Second Partition Treaty, the monarch named the Bourbon Philip of Anjou, Louis XIV's grandson, universal heir of the Spanish Empire as Philip V. The most contentious issue was the validity of the Infanta Maria Theresa's renunciation of the Spanish inheritance, which she had made on her marriage to Louis XIV. Leibniz in fact dismissed the restriction, expressed in Charles II's will, of the repudiation of the inheritance.

On the basis of a historical and legal analysis entitled *La justice encouragée* (1701),[24] he refuted the Bourbon claims. The differing rules of succession in the Spanish kingdoms of Castile and Aragon and the Reich's sovereignty in the Spanish Netherlands and Italian territories let Philip V's claims appear dubious, he argued. Leibniz offered the court in Vienna his knowledge of legal history and the law of nations, particularly for the defense of imperial claims to the Spanish territories in Italy. To this end, he also put his collections of historical sources at the Viennese court's service and backed up his polemics against the French legal interpretation with sound expertise and knowledge of sources. Leibniz referred to the succession crisis as "*la grande révolution d'Espagne.*" He feared the end of a well-balanced system of power founded on the Westphalian Peace and the erection of a "*Monarchie universelle des Bourbons.*" He saw political autonomy and religious freedom in Europe fundamentally threatened. Leibniz flanked Archduke Charles's proclamation as Spanish anti-king in 1703 with the anonymously published *Manifeste contenant les droits de Charles III roi d'Espagne.*[25] With this treatise, he not only emphatically spoke out again in favor of the imperial dynasty's rights to the Spanish crown, he also subtly made France out to be the bogeyman. Spain, Leibniz argues, had not been subjected to a greater threat since the Saracen invasion.

The contrast between these comments and the exemplary role that Leibniz attributed to France, for example in his *Consilium Aegyptiacum*, can only in part be explained by his comments' addressees. In later years, Leibniz was apparently more aware of the menacing aspect of French dominance. From being a political and cultural model, France had become the image of moral and religious decay. With appropriate vehemence, he railed against war-weariness and the Separate Peace of Utrecht (1713), which he called a "*paix inexcusable.*"[26] This critical attitude toward France corresponded to a noticeably pro-Habsburg position. The war against Louis XIV should, in his opinion, continue and be strengthened by an alliance between emperor and tsar.

---

[24] *La justice encouragée, contre les chicanes et les menaces d'un partisan des Bourbons,* 1701.
[25] FC, *Œuvres* 3, 1861, 360–431; translated in PW 146–163.
[26] *Paix d'Utrecht inexcusable*; FC, *Œuvres* 4, 1862, 1–140.

The European State System: Peace and Balance of Power. Leibniz's Dispute with Saint Pierre and the *Respublica Christiana*

Leibniz expressed his opinion on war and peace and on the European system of states in his correspondence and numerous memoranda. The international, legal, and philosophical aspects of his reflections manifested themselves both in his collections of sources, such as the *Codex juris gentium diplomaticus*,[27] and in occasional writings, such as *Justice encouragée*. The European peace system's anchorage in the law of nations was, for him, the Westphalian Peace Treaty as a whole, which had made the creation of stable German postwar rule into a European issue. The Osnabrück and Münster peace treaties linked Reich law to the law of nations and thus created a new legal and political framework for the European power system. The *Reichsverfassung* had become a constituent part of law among nations.

Leibniz favored the modern concept of state for a territorial state governed by a sovereign prince. Regarding the Reich as a whole and the European community of nations, however, he rejected the idea of an absolute, centralistic, and expansionist power structure. He preferred a polity that integrated particularist structures and traditional civil liberties and in which claims to power and sovereignty were interlocked with one another on different levels and complemented one another. Leibniz continued to be absorbed for a long time by the potential that resulted from making the *Reichsverfassung* more European. For him, maintaining the Reich's integrity in the center of the continent was crucially linked with Europe's stability. Only by consolidating the Reich, with its corporative and organic structure, as a strong European central power, not by destroying it, could stabilization of the international political system be ensured. Leibniz's formula of "unity in plurality" corresponds in its political application with the spirit of the multilateral agreement and of the rules for coexistence laid down in 1648. Leibniz resolutely countered the modern absolutist state's claim to unrestrained exercise of power and expansion—as embodied in exemplary fashion by Louis XIV's France—with his concept of law, which had to safeguard the existence of even the smallest political unit in the framework of the whole, as guaranteed by the *Reichsverfassung*. The secular concept of state—even though it had become the precondition for modern rule by sovereign princes—was limited and measured against the universal, Christian dimension of a concept of Reich that, even in the seventeenth century, Leibniz by no means found unattractive. Leibniz let his philosophical interpretation of the concept of Reich as a community of law and peace flow into the ideal of a state based on reason—one that was

---

[27] See chapter 36.

to promote the perfection of man and society and ultimately to pass into a global society united by culture. On this level, too, the concept of Reich could act as an intellectual symbol for a variform system that fostered education, law, and sciences.

France's aspiration to supremacy and the emerging European resistance to this made the leitmotif of a political power equilibrium very fashionable. Applying this idea of balance to the European community of states only became conceivable after the medieval Christian universality had grown weaker, as national territorial states were formed and the medieval concept of law began to be replaced by European natural law and law of nations. To be sure, the idea of equilibrium was only formulated in the Peace of Utrecht (1713) as a fundamental rule for the co-existence of European states, but, before this, it had already constituted an effective yardstick for political actions. One finds it in Leibniz early on as a means of interpreting the international system's dynamics of political power. It is this drive that pushes the Early Modern state to incessant growth and confronts it with the same power instinct in other states. Behind the menacing configuration sensed during the Reich's wars with Louis XIV and the Turks, the possibility of a European order of balance and coexistence seemed to open up for Leibniz. The idea of balance acted, so to speak, as a link between the concept of the Reich and that of Europe: the Reich's inner stability and political capacity to act and Europe's establishment of peace and security were inextricably linked. Every unilateral monopolization of power was contrary to his ideal of plurality and coexistence. So, for interrelations between peoples, the principle of balance seemed particularly suitable as a defense against the ascendancy of one single power.

The correspondence between Saint-Pierre and Leibniz documents the fertile meeting of two political schools of thought against the backdrop of a permanently changing Europe. Each grappled with the Early Modern organization of rule in the specific conditions of his own country and reflected on the possibility of states permanently coexisting in peace. It is of particular interest to see how awareness of the Holy Roman Empire, its history and political structures, played a model role in the discussion of the European system and of the establishment of peace there.

Saint-Pierre's idea of peace aimed at constructing a European Union that was in the position to ensure the existence of its member states but that also possessed the semiconstitutional authority to impose decisions and legal rulings on them. He was concerned with setting up supranational structures and institutions in a secularly defined power system. Saint-Pierre strove to break up the Holy Roman Empire's complex structures of fiefdoms and overlordships, thus letting completely new power relations emerge in Europe's center. However, this prospect provoked Leibniz's vehement protest.

The tendency, to be observed early in French political publications, toward secularization and rationalization in plans for Europe was reflected in how the Reich was perceived: from Sully to Rousseau, Germany became a symbolic stage for the controversy surrounding Europe's constitution, a field of experiment for forms of coexistence and for securing law and peace. For Saint-Pierre, the Reich represented a rational constitutional model. As the traditional and common-law justification for the *Reichsverfassung*, the Reich's customary and established law (*Reichsherkommen*) was of great significance to the *Reichspublizistik* and thus also to Leibniz. In contrast, Saint-Pierre made use of German history as a means of constructing the continent rationally. In his opinion, independent imperial princes had banded together of their own free will to convene a federal corporate body. Leibniz criticized this projection, which deprived the Reich of its historical singularity. In his observations on Saint-Pierre's *Projet de paix perpétuelle*, dated 1715, Leibniz interprets the *Reichsverfassung*'s development as a protracted dynamic process, nurtured by the contest, both cooperative and antagonistic, between monarchical power at the center and the Estates in the regions.[28] Leibniz explained the historical form of the German constitution as important for peace and equilibrium in Europe. The concept of the Reich had to be more than just an abstract model of coexistence, he argued; in its universalist and traditional meaning, it was the key to solving important tasks of the age. In contrast to Saint-Pierre, Leibniz's universality was of a deeply Christian nature. During the exchange with the Frenchman, he refers to the medieval concept of order—one that promoted close relations between clerical and secular authorities—and to the emperors' patronage of a crisis-ridden Christendom.[29] For Leibniz, the Christian concepts of order, oriented toward *pietas* and *caritas*, promised security and stability during society's shift to a modern pluralist system of states.

Leibniz's ideal of Europe as a community established on religion is already clearly tangible in his early writings. The *Demonstrationes Catholicae*, dated 1668/69, reveal this fundamental conviction. He describes Christianity as the link within the community of nations and formulates the philosophical, theological, and ecclesiastical conditions for a reunion of confessions and churches.[30] Deviating from the Peace of Westphalia's pluralist secular state system, Leibniz granted emperor and pope special roles as heads of Christendom.[31] Notwithstanding its sacred name, the Holy Roman Empire had developed into a multiconfessional and secular, primarily German, Reich. For Leibniz, however, it was completely correct that this federal structure retain both its name as well as its special role in the European conglomeration of states.[32] The claim appeared justified: when war commenced against the Ottoman Empire, there was a growth of imperial patriotism and a historical sense of mission derived from the old idea of emperor and Reich as the protectors of Christendom. "Roman" in the title stood for historical dignity, "Holy" characterized the *Reichsverfassung* safeguarding the nature of law and justice, security, and liberty. In Leibniz's ideal, the Reich's constitution best represented the form of state that allowed rights and political power to be separated in principle and in which the law acted as part of a comprehensive idea of justice that was ultimately bound

[28]   Robinet, André, ed. *Correspondance G. W. Leibniz—Ch. I. Castel de Saint-Pierre, éditée intégralement selon les manuscrits inédits des bibliothèques d'Hanovre et de Göttingen* (Paris: Centre de philosophie du droit, 1995), p. 40.

[29]   *Correspondance Leibniz—Saint-Pierre*, 36ff, 24f.

[30]   A VI i N. II. B.

[31]   *Caesarinus Fürstenerius*; A IV ii 15–17.

[32]   *Unvorgreiffliche Gedancken*; A IV vi 532.

by *justitia universalis*. The traditional occidental authorities, emperor and pope, were supposed to act as guarantors for this commitment.

Secular leadership of the *Respublica christiana* was the emperor's fundamental prerogative.[33] He was to assume central tasks for the protection of Christendom. Leibniz admittedly remained skeptical about the possibility of securing peace in Europe institutionally. In contrast to Saint-Pierre, he adhered to the principle of balance as a defensive weapon against the monopolization of power and supremacy. Leibniz did not favor an understanding of peace that conceived social peace and likewise peace between nations as a state of security founded only on treaties and guaranteed by institutions. Alluding to Aitzema's epitaph to *pax perpetua* used in the *Praefatio* of the *Codex juris gentium* of 1693, he states: "*les plus puissans ne respectent guères les tribunaux.*"[34]

CONFESSIONAL COEXISTENCE: PROTESTANTS AND CATHOLICS IN GERMANY

Religious peace formed one of the most important parts of the Peace of Westphalia (1648). The religious settlement was essentially political, and, although intended as an interim regulation, it eventually became permanently established, whereas the question of religious truth was postponed until a possible future reunification.

After 1648, the Reich's church law developed from being a system of conflict to one of balance. The *Reichsverfassung*'s particular achievement consisted in maintaining and securing each religious denomination's identity and autonomy without renouncing the traditional claim to clerical and secular unity. The secularized state church law, with parity between the churches, succeeded in serving the Reich politically as the basis for a supradenominational system of law and peace without affecting the denominations' own internal law and spiritual life. The denominations' political coexistence remained hedged in by the possibility of a religious reunion, so that—as Leibniz also demonstrated—it made sense holding a public debate on conditions for reunion. In his view, the state of the German constitution served as a good model for the reunion of the Christian churches. In parallel with the idea of the Reich, this process would even be conceivable under the legal and organizational leadership of the papacy. Leibniz can be reckoned among those of Germany's political thinkers who took the Peace of Westphalia's demand for reunion seriously. In his early years, he experienced a similar reconciliation policy on the Catholic side at Johann Philipp von Schönborn's court in Electoral Mainz. The University of Helmstedt, where Leibniz gained influence over the theological faculty, was also pursuing irenic tendencies at the time.

[33] *Ermahnung an die Teutsche*; A IV iii 801.
[34] *Correspondance Leibniz—Saint-Pierre*, p. 24.

Leibniz's statements on denominational issues and church politics do not present a uniform picture. Alongside a distinct concern for the continuing existence of European Protestantism was the idea of reunification. This aimed at transcending denominational differences within Latin Christendom and attributed traditional roles of leadership and patronage to papacy and imperial rule. A glance at Leibniz's activities illustrates to what extent denominational ideas of reunification were influenced by the prevailing political situation, specific circumstances, and attempts to promote pressure-group politics. This is true of his work at the courts, whether in Mainz, Hanover, or Vienna.

Elector Johann Philipp von Schönborn's court in Mainz set an example for the Reich's transdenominational policy. Since 1660, there had been a liberal debate there on what was needed to reunite the denominations, triggered off by Landgrave Ernst von Hessen-Rheinfels's conversion to Catholicism. Alongside plans for a synod, this also involved concessions to the Protestants (Mass in German, Communion under both kinds, abolition of auricular confession, celibacy only for monks and nuns). However, the plans for reunification discussed in a German context were met with fundamental reservations in Rome. During his time at Mainz (1667–72), Leibniz had close contact with the numerous converts supporting reunification. His idea of permitting the reunited German Protestants, similar to the united orthodox churches, to depart from rules appeared unrealistic, given the papacy's categorical refusal. The idea of suspending the Council of Trent's decrees and convening a new council also had little prospect of success.

At the royal court in Hanover, the underlying political motivation in the denomination debate appeared particularly obvious: it was hoped that efforts at reunification would be rewarded by the secularization of neighboring bishoprics such as Hildesheim and Osnabrück. Incidentally, Hanover's friendliness toward the Spanish Franciscan bishop Rojas y Spinola, who was serving the emperor, seemed very opportune, given that support was required from the Viennese court in obtaining the electoral title and introducing primogeniture.[35] The emperor backed the reunification negotiations led by Rojas y Spinola in the hope that they would strengthen his political authority and promote his efforts at reuniting the Reich to fend off the Turks and French. Leibniz's convictions, which were geared to consolidating the Reich, followed a similar direction. His appraisal of the religious aspect of the emperor's office was also strongly motivated by politics. Deviating from the 1648 system of peace, which was denominationally neutral, Leibniz supported the concept of office advanced by the Viennese court, which continued to define the emperor as protector of the church (*advocatia ecclesiae*) and secular head of occidental Christendom.[36] Leibniz can hardly have failed to realize that, for the imperial court—similarly to the conversion efforts at the Mainz court—reunification ultimately meant leading the Protestants back into the Church of Rome. Any ideas about concessions made to German Protestants on grounds of theology or church politics would have met with fierce resistance in Rome. As it was, the papacy feared the Reich's

[35] According to the rule of primogeniture, the oldest son inherited the undivided duchy; this ran against the well-established tradition of territorial subdivision among the male children of a duke.

[36] *Ermahnung an die Teutsche*; A IV iii 801.

church might want to adopt a special "Gallican" course, that is, a version of Catholicism modeled on the French church's attempt to limit papal authority. Leibniz's efforts at reunification show transdenominational tendencies, which clearly suited the imperial Catholic party. This is most evident in the ecclesiology: as a Christian who adhered to the "Augsburg Confession," Leibniz would have been prepared to recognize the pope's primacy.

ELECTORATE AND ENGLISH SUCCESSION: THE RISE OF THE HOUSE OF HANOVER

Leibniz worked for the Guelphs for four decades (1676–1716). Certain events fall within this period that fostered the rise of the House of Hanover. Among these were the award of the ninth Electoral title by Emperor Leopold I (1692) and, in particular, Georg Ludwig of Hanover's accession to the British throne (1714). In his capacity as legal expert and learned councilor, Leibniz also investigated problems of constitutional law and political issues and contributed toward scientific corroboration of the antiquity and dignity of the Guelph dynasty through historical research. For example, on the occasion of the marriage of Charlotte Felicitas, a niece of Ernst August, to the Duke of Modena (1695), he was able to present the first results of his genealogical research publicly in a festschrift that attracted much attention.[37] He had succeeded in proving the Guelphs' descent from the Este. Leibniz's expertise was also important in the run-up to the marriage of Wilhelmine Amalie to Joseph, King of the Romans, the later Emperor Joseph I, in 1699. His expert genealogical opinion removed any doubt as to the Hanoverian princess's impeccable descent.

The endeavor to move up into the illustrious circle of Electors by obtaining the ninth Electoral title was no insignificant matter at the Hanoverian court. After Duke Johann Friedrich, Ernst August also had a good mind to do this, demanding of Leibniz appropriate statements to this end.[38] This afforded Leibniz the opportunity to grapple with the issue and purpose of a Hanoverian Electorship, with all its implications regarding history, imperial law, and interest-driven politics. The constitutional rank of Elector would, in his view, symbolize the restoration of Braunschweig-Lüneburg to its former greatness. This had been lost with Henry the Lion's fall from power in 1180, but, by the beginning of the eighteenth century, it was being restored as the Guelphs gained ascendancy in northern Germany. The Elector's outstanding preeminence, measured in ceremony and prestige, was demonstrated not least by the exclusive right to dispatch an ambassador.

---

[37] *Lettre sur la connexion des maisons de Brunsvic et d'Este*; A IV vi N. 3.
[38] A I vii 62.

Elevation in rank would appropriately express the historical and political importance of the Guelph dukes, both in the Holy Roman Empire and among Europe's oldest and most powerful dynasties. Regarding Braunschweig-Lüneburg's interest-driven politics as a territorial state, Leibniz recommended using the constitutional privileges that the *Reichsverfassung* foresaw for electoral principalities: indivisibility, primogeniture, and unlimited jurisdictional authority. Leibniz particularly defended introducing the right of the firstborn, even vis-à-vis opposition within the Guelph dynasty.

In dealing with the electoral issue, Leibniz applied several principles of his own political thinking. He was concerned, in particular, with the question of the real benefit of this old and great traditional imperial dignity for the House of Hanover's advancement, but also, in general, with the College of Electors' importance for the crisis-ridden Reich. At the Mainz court of Elector Johann Philipp von Schönborn, imperial reform was defined primarily as an Elector's task—one that was also supposed to include forging a military alliance for the Reich's defense. As members of the *Reichstag's* highest college and of the association responsible for electing the emperor as well as mediating between emperor and Reich, the Electors could be the source of great impetus. In international circles, too, they were much in demand as allies. As an expert on the Reich's constitutional law and history, Leibniz belonged to the great thinkers who strove to preserve traditional offices, dignities, and structures while adopting them to modern functions and keeping an open mind on reform.

Fundamental was the question whether a traditional institution such as the Electoral title could still be reconciled with changing constitutional structures and Early Modern ideas of state. In accordance with the concept of supremacy, possession of the Electoral title was supposed to equate with a territory's political clout. It could not be reduced to a matter of protocol; as an expression of real power, it should give access to the elite inner circle that worked in close cooperation with emperor and Reich.[39] Accordingly, Leibniz's historical comments and remarks sound not only like work commissioned by the Guelphs, but also like a profession of loyalty to the efficiency of Germany's constitution in difficult times.[40]

Leibniz argued in favor of the ninth Electoral title in such a way as to bracket together a territorial prince's particularist interests with overall political responsibility for the functioning of the Reich and for a European system of equilibrium and peace. To this end, he used two lines of argument: a historical one and one relating to contemporary history and politics. First, he was concerned with the restitution claims, justified historically and relating to the losses of Guelph possessions and rank suffered by Henry the Lion. Second, Leibniz pointed to the services rendered by Hanover in the Ottoman War and in defending the Reich against Louis XIV.[41] The threat to the Rhenish Electoral principalities posed by Louis XIV's expansionist tendencies demanded a politically, economically, and militarily strong and independent north German Electoral

[39] *Ecrit . . . touchant la creation d'un Neuvième Electorat—Additions*; A I iv 232f.
[40] A IV v xxv–xxix; A IV vi xxviii–xxxi.
[41] *Ecrit . . . touchant la creation*; A I iv 229f; *Considerations sur les interests de Bronsvic*; A IV iv N. 70.

power—Hanover—as a counterbalance, Leibniz argued. Accordingly, the emperor's bestowal of the Electoral hat on Duke Ernst August on December 19, 1692, was also a personal success for Leibniz. His involvement with the Electoral title's acquisition can even be traced to the famous investiture speech that Otto Grote delivered on the occasion of the award of the Elector's hat on that day in Vienna in December 1692.[42]

Leibniz must have experienced obtaining the British Throne as the peak of the Guelph dynasty's greatness and fame and as the acknowledgment of his own purposeful endeavors. It is striking that Leibniz not only brought his historical and legal expertise into the issue of succession, but also employed means of political communication and propaganda.[43] For example, for a long time, he urged Electress Sophia, as heir presumptive (a fact that was almost ignored in England before 1700), to pursue her inheritance claims resolutely. A visit by William III of England to the Celle court in October 1698 offered Leibniz the opportunity to influence the future course of things. On his own initiative, he clearly succeeded in persuading Duchess Eleonore of Celle to approach William III on behalf of Sophia's hereditary claim.[44] Leibniz was concerned with safeguarding the dynastic legitimacy of the Guelph claims politically—not an easy task given Sophia's and Georg Ludwig's cautious attitude. The Electress considered, in fact her nephew, the Catholic Pretender James Stuart, likewise entitled to inherit, whereas her son disapproved of English parliamentarianism. To be sure, the *Bill of rights* (1689) had already excluded Catholics from the succession, but it had not taken the Guelphs into consideration at that point. After William's visit to Celle in 1698, things were to change. According to Leibniz's report, Eleonore succeeded in putting forward two basic proposals to the king: the Hanoverian succession was to be accepted constitutionally in the official rule of succession and the possible Guelph succession made more secure by marrying the Duke of Gloucester, the only son of the later Queen Anne, to the Hanoverian Electoral Princess, Sophia Dorothea.[45] Even though this was rendered impossible by the Duke of Gloucester's death (1700), the initiative took effect and the aspirations came to fruition when, finally, Sophia's claim to succession was recognized constitutionally. On William III's initiative, the English parliament reacted approvingly and, with the *Act of Settlement* (1701), regulated the succession in favor of Sophia and her descendants. Leibniz's influence on political developments was demonstrated not least by the personal influence he employed with determination and skill as Sophia's trusted advisor.[46] This is also evidenced by the high esteem in which Leibniz was held by the Hanover-friendly English faction. The Earl of Macclesfield delivered a testimonial from Bishop Gilbert Burnet in which Leibniz was praised as "the glory not only of the court of Brunswick but of the whole German Empire."[47]

---

[42] A I viii 21f; *Theatrum Europaeum*; edited by J. Ph. Abelin et al., vol. 14 (1702), p. 334.
[43] A I xiii N. 44 and N. 45.
[44] A I xvi N. 44, notes.
[45] A I xvi xxxii N. 44 and N. 52.
[46] A I xix xxxiv–xxxix.
[47] A I xx xli.

One finds both Leibniz's political thinking as well as his pragmatism as a political advisor reflected symbolically in the British succession.[48] Despite the reservations both he and the Guelphs had toward the limitations on monarchical power by the parliamentary system, he spoke out for the succession as imperative for the dynastic *"grandeur"* and *"gloire."* In Leibniz's eyes, achieving dynastic legitimacy also served to strengthen the monarchic principle that, in turn, in the shape of an enlightened absolutism guided by reason, was supposed to guarantee internal and external stability in Europe.[49]

No less important were considerations concerning the European order and its stability. For Leibniz, Great Britain played a key role in power-politics as a counterbalance to French hegemony.[50] This role was to take on more significance when the Bourbons succeeded to the Spanish inheritance. But, traditionally, England also took on an important role as the protector of European Protestantism. In Leibniz's opinion, the House of Hanover was admirably equipped to assume these tasks.

REFERENCES

Antognazza, Maria Rosa. 2002. "Leibniz and religious toleration: The correspondence with Paul Pellisson-Fontanier." *American Catholic Philosophical Quarterly* 76(4): 601–622.

Aretin, Karl Otmar von. 1997. *Das Alte Reich 1648–1806.* Vols. 1–2. Stuttgart: Klett-Cotta.

Beiderbeck, Friedrich. 2009. "Das Heilige Römische Reich als Modell europäischer Koexistenz bei Saint-Pierre und Leibniz." In Dominic Eggel and Brunhilde Wehinger (eds.), *Europavorstellungen des 18. Jahrhunderts. Imagining Europe in the 18th Century.* Hannover: Wehrhahn, pp. 47–61.

Beiderbeck, Friedrich. 2002. "Leibniz als politischer Berater des Welfenhauses am Beispiel der Neunten Kur." In *Nihil sine ratione. VII. Internationaler Leibniz-Kongreß, 2001.* Supplement, 142–149. Hannover: Gottfried-Wilhelm-Leibniz-Gesellschaft.

Beiderbeck, Friedrich. 2011. "Zur Bedeutung des Westfälischen Friedens für das politische Denken von G. W. Leibniz." In Friedrich Beiderbeck and Stephan Waldhoff (eds.), *Pluralität der Perspektiven und Einheit der Wahrheit im Werk von G. W. Leibniz. Beiträge zu seinem philosophischen, theologischen und politischen Denken.* Berlin: Akademie Verlag, pp. 155–173.

Burgdorf, Wolfgang. 1998. *Reichskonstitution und Nation. Verfassungsreformprojekte für das Heilige Römische Reich Deutscher Nation im politischen Schrifttum von 1648 bis 1806.* Mainz: Philipp von Zabern.

Dreitzel, Horst. 2005. "Zehn Jahre 'Patria' in der politischen Theorie in Deutschland: Prasch, Pufendorf, Leibniz, Becher 1662–1672." In Robert von Friedeburg (ed.), *'Patria' und, Patrioten' vor dem Patriotismus. Pflichten, Rechte, Glauben und die Rekonfigurierung europäischer Gemeinwesen im 17. Jahrhundert.* Wiesbaden: Harrassowitz, pp. 367–534.

Eisenkopf, Paul. 1975. *Leibniz und die Einigung der Christenheit. Überlegungen zur Reunion der evangelischen und katholischen Kirche.* München/Paderborn/Wien: Schöningh.

[48] A I xix N.18 and N. 24.
[49] A I iii N. 246; A I xx N. 185.
[50] A I xix 38.

Fricke, Waltraut. 1957. *Leibniz und die englische Sukzession des Hauses Hannover*. Hildesheim: Lax.

Gädeke, Nora. 2005. "Die Rolle des Historikers Gottfried Wilhelm Leibniz und der Aufstieg des Welfenhauses." In Heide Barmeyer (ed.), *Hannover und die englische Thronfolge*. Bielefeld: Verlag für Regionalgeschichte, pp. 157–178.

Gädeke, Nora. 2012. "Im Vorfeld des Spanischen Erbfolgekrieges. Leibniz bringt seine historischen Kollektaneen zum Einsatz." In Thomas Wallnig, Thomas Stockinger, Ines Peper, and Patrick Fiska (eds.), *Europäische Geschichtskulturen um 1700 zwischen Gelehrsamkeit, Politik und Konfession*. Berlin/Boston: De Gruyter, pp. 485–511.

Gollwitzer, Heinz. 1972. *Geschichte des weltpolitischen Denkens*. Vol. 1. Göttingen: Vandenhoeck und Ruprecht, pp. 184–193.

Gross, Hanns. 1973. *Empire and sovereignty: A history of the public law literature in the Holy Roman Empire, 1599–1804*. Chicago: University of Chicago Press.

Hammerstein, Notker. 1974. "Leibniz und das Heilige Römische Reich deutscher Nation." *Nassauische Annalen* 85: 87–102.

Herrmann, Karl. 1958. *Das Staatsdenken bei Leibniz*. Bonn: Bouvier.

Heuvel, Gerd van den. 2001. "Theorie ohne Praxis: Leibniz' Rolle in der Politik des Hauses Hannover." In *Ehrgeiz, Luxus und Fortune. Hannovers Weg zu Englands Krone*. Hannover: Historisches Museum, pp. 84–97.

Otte, Hans/Richard Schenk, ed. 1999. *Die Reunionsgespräche im Niedersachsen des 17. Jahrhunderts. Rojas y Spinola—Molan—Leibniz*. Göttingen: Vandenhoeck & Ruprecht.

Randelzhofer, Albrecht. 1967. *Völkerrechtliche Aspekte des Heiligen Römischen Reiches nach 1648*. Berlin: Duncker & Humblot.

Reese, Armin. 1967. *Die Rolle der Historie beim Aufstieg des Welfenhauses 1680–1714*. Hildesheim: Lax.

Riley, Patrick. 1976. "Three 17th century German theorists of federalism: Althusius, Hugo and Leibniz." *Publius: The Journal of Federalism* 6: 7–41.

Ritter, Paul. 1930. *Leibniz' Ägyptischer Plan*. Darmstadt: Otto Reichl.

Robinet, André, ed. 1995. *Correspondance G. W. Leibniz—Ch. I. Castel de Saint-Pierre, éditée intégralement selon les manuscrits inédits des bibliothèques d'Hanovre et de Göttingen*. Paris: Centre de philosophie du droit.

Robinet, André. 1994. *G. W. Leibniz: Le meilleur des mondes par la balance de l'Europe*. Paris: Presses Universitaires de France.

Roeck, Bernd. 1984. *Reichssystem und Reichsherkommen. Die Diskussion über die Staatlichkeit des Reiches in der politischen Publizistik des 17. und 18. Jahrhunderts*. Stuttgart: Franz Steiner Wiesbaden, pp. 24–74.

Roldán, Concha. 2004. "Leibniz' concept of Europe: between nationalism and universalism." In Manfred Buhr and Douglas Moggach (eds.), *Reason, universality, and history: standpoints on the European intellectual tradition*. New York: Legas, pp. 147–162.

Rudolph, Hartmut. 2000. "Bemerkungen zu Leibniz' Reunionskonzept." In Heinz Duchhardt and Gerhard May (eds.), *Union—Konversion—Toleranz. Dimensionen der Annäherung zwischen den christlichen Konfessionen im 17. und 18. Jahrhundert*. Mainz: Philipp von Zabern, pp. 227–242.

Scheel, Günter. 1999. "Leibniz als politischer Ratgeber des Welfenhauses." In Herbert Breger and Friedrich Niewöhner (eds.), *Leibniz und Niedersachsen*. Stuttgart: Steiner, pp. 35–52.

Schepers, Heinrich. 2011. "Demonstrationes Catholicae—Leibniz' großer Plan. Ein rationales Friedensprojekt für Europa." In Friedrich Beiderbeck and Stephan Waldhoff (eds.),

Pluralität der Perspektiven und Einheit der Wahrheit im Werk von G. W. Leibniz. Beiträge zu seinem philosophischen, theologischen und politischen Denken. Berlin: Akademie Verlag, pp. 3–14.

Schnath, Georg. 1938–82. *Geschichte Hannovers im Zeitalter der neunten Kur und der englischen Sukzession 1674–1714.* 4 vol. Hildesheim: Lax.

Schneider, Hans-Peter. 1995. "Gottfried Wilhelm Leibniz." In C. H. Beck (ed.), *Staatsdenker in der frühen Neuzeit.* München: C. H. Beck, pp. 197–226 at 205–209.

Schnettger, Matthias. 2000. "Kirchenadvokatie und Reichseinigungspläne. Kaiser Leopold I. und die Reunionsbestrebungen Rojas y Spinolas." In Heinz Duchhardt and Gerhard May (eds.), *Union—Konversion—Toleranz. Dimensionen der Annäherung zwischen den christlichen Konfessionen im 17. und 18. Jahrhundert.* Mainz: Philipp von Zabern, pp. 139–169.

Stolleis, Michael. 1988. *Geschichte des öffentlichen Rechts in Deutschland.* Vol. 1: *Reichspublizistik und Policeywissenschaft 1600–1800.* München: C. H. Beck, pp. 170–186.

Whaley, Joachim. 2012. *Germany and the Holy Roman Empire. Vol. 2: 1648–1806.* Oxford/ New York: Oxford University Press.

Wiedeburg, Paul. 1962–70. *Der junge Leibniz. Das Reich und Europa.* Wiesbaden: Steiner.

CHAPTER 38

PROPOSALS FOR POLITICAL, ADMINISTRATIVE, ECONOMIC, AND SOCIAL REFORM

STEPHAN WALDHOFF

As a political theorist, Gottfried Wilhelm Leibniz is difficult to pin down. His contributions to political theory cannot be neatly classified under a single subject heading such as "reason of state," "sovereignty," or "separation of powers." Even experts are hard-pressed to offer a concise answer if asked to name Leibniz's political magnum opus, to name *the* work that sums up his political thought. Three intertwined reasons may well explain this characteristic of Leibniz's political thought and writing.

First, Leibniz was not only a political theorist, but was also, above all, an administrative practitioner. Many of his political writings were commissioned. In other words, these were occasional writings that can only be understood within the context of the situation. With respect to general political theory, they are of interest only where they move beyond the question under discussion to fundamental political problems. Moreover, the majority of these writings were strictly intended for a small audience involved in administration. Consequently, they were not conceived with the idea of publication. And, even in those instances where Leibniz of his own volition wrote aides-mémoire, these were usually inspired by specific problems confronting the dynasty or territorial state.[1]

Second, Leibniz served as councilor in a principality of the Holy Roman Empire of the German Nation. Political discussions in the Holy Roman Empire primarily took place

---

[1] In this regard, clusters of aides-mémoire pertaining to specific biographical or political events can be identified: on the occasion of Duke Ernst August's accession to power in 1680 (cf. note 16); in preparation for the audience with Holy Roman Emperor Leopold I in 1688 (cf. note 14); in connection with the founding of the Berlin Academy and the Prussian coronation in 1700/1701; and Leibniz's final sojourn at the imperial court in 1712–14 (cf. note 37).

within the context of *Reichspublizistik*, the doctrine of the imperial constitutional law. This was strongly influenced by historical precedent, insofar as it was based on constitutional laws that had developed over the course of centuries, laws that, in their entirety, comprised the imperial constitution. As a result, political discourse had a markedly juridical aspect. The complex day-to-day reality of the Empire, as well as its theoretical incorporation into *Reichspublizistik,* informed the writings of Leibniz, who had earned a doctorate in law.[2]

Finally, there is good reason to assume that much of what Leibniz wrote was politically motivated. This is the spirit in which Heinrich Schepers recently states decisively: "There is no question that in terms of his entire approach and the focus of his life, Leibniz was an exceptionally political philosopher."[3] If one accepts this interpretation, the question of Leibniz's reform proposals must take into account many more excerpts from his works than those writings that can be specifically described as being political in nature.

The preceding remarks have not only attempted to explain some preconditions and distinctive features of Leibniz's political writings; at the same time, they reveal that the subject matter of this chapter harbors certain challenges as well. On the one hand, it is difficult to precisely narrow it down. It begins to unravel on all sides and encompasses aspects that have already been examined in greater detail and more knowledgeably in other contributions to this volume. In these cases, the pertinent aspect is mentioned here, but with a reference to the relevant chapter in lieu of a more detailed presentation. On the other hand, there is the problem of how to bring together this plethora of aspects in order to pose one overriding question, thus preventing the presentation from disintegrating into a mere sequence of individual topics and getting lost among the details.[4]

For this reason, the first section outlines some basic metaphysical principles of Leibniz's legal and political thought, his devotion to the Holy Roman Empire, and his position as a court councilor in Hanover. Apart from these principles and conditions

[2] In editions of selected works, specific legal references have been omitted in favor of philosophical statements, cf., for example, the excerpts from the preface to *Codex Juris Gentium* in Patrick Riley (trans.), *Leibniz: Political Writings* (Cambridge: Cambridge University Press, 2nd ed. 1988), pp. 165–176, with A IV v N. 7 or Grua 882–83, with A IV vi N. 2.

[3] Heinrich Schepers, "Demonstrationes Catholicae—Leibniz' großer Plan: Ein rationales Friedensprojekt für Europa," in Friedrich Beiderbeck and Stephan Waldhoff (eds.), *Pluralität der Perspektiven und Einheit der Wahrheit im Werk von G. W. Leibniz: Beiträge zu seinem philosophischen, theologischen und politischen Denken* (Berlin: Akademie Verlag, 2011), p. 3.

[4] Thus far, these topics have not been presented in relation to one another. Even the broadest, most well-balanced overview of Leibniz's political thought devotes just a few sentences to these subjects: Hans-Peter Schneider, "Gottfried Wilhelm Leibniz," in Michael Stolleis (ed.), *Staatsdenker in der frühen Neuzeit* (3rd edn. München: C. H. Beck, 1995), p. 220. A somewhat more thorough treatment, idem., "Praktische Philosophie," in Helmut Holzhey and Wilhelm Schmidt-Biggemann (eds.), *Die Philosophie des 17. Jahrhunderts, Band 4: Das Heilige Römische Reich Deutscher Nation, Nord- und Ostmitteleuropa (= Grundriss der Geschichte der Philosophie. Begründet von Friedrich Ueberweg* vol. 4/2 (Basel: Schwabe, 2001), chapter 9: "Gottfried Wilhelm Leibniz," paragraph 31: "Lehre und Wirkung," pp. 1123–27.

governing his reform proposals, the esteem enjoyed by science as the foundation of rational administration is a key feature of his political thinking. For Leibniz, administration becomes mainly information management (see the second section Administrative Information Management). In a manner of speaking, both sections create a framework for classifying Leibniz's specific political, administrative, economic, and social reform proposals, which is undertaken in the third (Public Finances and Economy) and fourth sections (Public Welfare).

BETWEEN THE CITY OF GOD, THE HOLY ROMAN EMPIRE, AND HANOVER

Although Leibniz was certainly a pragmatist in terms of his service to a sovereign, this should not be interpreted as meaning that his political, administrative, economic, and social reform proposals were merely a response to short-term political events and that, as a consequence, his metaphysical convictions are unable to contribute to the understanding of these reform proposals. Quite the opposite: "A narrower treatment, leaving his 'first philosophy' to one side, would inevitably ignore what is most distinctive in his political thought."[5] The basic principles of his moral philosophy will be presented in other contributions in this volume.[6] Here, they can only be sketched in brief, in the form of the intellectual premises behind his political reform proposals.

The close relationship between the metaphysical basic principles and practical proposals can be seen in Leibniz's early work "Outline of a Deliberation on the Establishment of an Academy or Society," penned in 1671.[7] This text comprises far more than what one would expect to see in a plan for a modern-day academy of sciences. Indeed, from Leibniz's perspective, the scholarly society could serve as a model for the ideal state. At the outset, the reasoning he uses in justification of his vision of a society is one that combines the three theological virtues of faith, hope, and love with divine knowledge, concluding: "The irrefutable consequence of this is that to practice charity, the love of God above all,. . . is in fact to love the common good (*bonum publicum*) and universal harmony; or, which is the same thing, the glory of God."[8] The text then ends with social and economic reform proposals in such areas as medicine, manufacture, and

---

[5] Patrick Riley, *Leibniz' Universal Jurisprudence: Justice as the Charity of the Wise* (Cambridge, Mass.: Harvard University Press, 1996), p. 21. For a critique of "Leibniz's political metaphysics," cf. Ian Hunter, *Rival Enlightenments: Civil and Metaphysical Philosophy in Early Modern Germany* (Cambridge: Cambridge University Press, 2001), pp. 95–147.

[6] Cf. especially chapter 35.

[7] A IV i N. 43; cf. chapter 31.

[8] A IV i 532.

coinage.[9] Leibniz saw charity as a "a benevolence which is general or universal." This "Leibnizian philanthropic benevolence is closer to policy than to passion."[10]

As a jurist, Leibniz interpreted God's dominion over the world as a kind of state as well. The universe, or at least its spiritual beings, constitutes a City of God, with God as its absolute monarch. This City of God is both a universal political system (*civitas universalis*) as well as the best possible political system (*civitas optima*). "The factual existence of the City of God means a counterfactual standard,. . . a critical instance that invites the imitation of divine reason and the limitation of human unreasonableness."[11] However, Leibniz did not derive specific stipulations for the shape an earthly state should take.

Although the City of God does not offer a tangible expression of what form an earthly state should take, the universal and harmonious dominion of God comes closest to a political system that is itself characterized by universality and harmony. Leibniz believed that he could see this ideal in a politically and religiously unified Christianity as represented by the Middle Ages' two universal powers: the emperor and the pope. Whether it can be said that Leibniz was truly "the last thinker of great stature to defend the Empire as something more than a vestigial Gothic oddity"[12] is a different matter (the role of the emperor and empire was still of greater significance around 1700 than it was later depicted in nineteenth-century German historiography). At the same time, his esteem for emperor and Empire was unusual, particularly in comparison to fellow Protestants of that era. However, Samuel Pufendorf, for example, was not speaking for the majority of his contemporaries—and even less so for Leibniz—when, in 1667, he rejected the Empire's claim to be a true state, likening it to a monstrosity. Nonetheless, the structure of the Empire's constitution—no less cumbersome than its official name—could not be easily classified according to the categories used since antiquity, which is what Pufendorf had done. Neither could the Early Modern concept of sovereignty be applied without further ado to determine constitutional reality.

The principalities of the Holy Roman Empire were sovereign powers, even if their sovereignty was not absolute. Leibniz published a pamphlet redefining the principalities' sovereignty under a descriptive pseudonym clearly demonstrating that his loyalties were neither strictly to the emperor nor to his sovereign, but to both: *Caesarinus Fürstenerius* (Latin *Caesar* = emperor; German *Fürst* = prince).[13] His position as court councilor in the Guelph principality of Hanover provided the context for many of the reform proposals that will be introduced later. Even though the Holy Roman Empire was not as absurdly outdated and powerless as it was often portrayed, the most significant

---

[9] Ibid., 540–43.

[10] Riley, *Leibniz' Universal Jurisprudence*, p. 33.

[11] Werner Schneiders, "Vera Politica: Grundlagen der Politiktheorie bei G. W. Leibniz," in Friedrich Kaulbach and Werner Krawietz (eds.), *Recht und Gesellschaft: Festschrift für Helmut Schelsky zum 65. Geburtstag* (Berlin: Duncker & Humblot, 1978), p. 597.

[12] Riley, *Leibniz' Universal Jurisprudence*, p. 2.

[13] A IV ii N. 1–4.

developments on the road to the modern state took place in the territorial states. This is also true of many of the reform proposals that Leibniz wished to submit to the emperor: these were not in relation to his position as leader of the Holy Roman Empire, but rather in relation to the territories under his reign.

His aim at practical efficiency within the context of the complex constitutional arrangement among emperor, Holy Roman Empire, and prince determined the character of Leibniz's political writings. For him, the issue was not the theoretical foundation of the state, but rather the question of the reforms to be made within the scope of fundamental and customary laws forming the Empire's constitution. This is why his political beliefs are reflected in a multitude of specific political, administrative, economic, and social reform proposals.

ADMINISTRATIVE INFORMATION MANAGEMENT

With the hope of joining the emperor's service, Leibniz sought an entrée to the imperial court in 1688. As his notes attest, he made thorough preparations for his audience with the emperor.[14] These notes offer insight into his self-image, illuminate the situation of a scholar at court during the Baroque era, and provide an excellent roadmap to Leibniz's political, administrative, economic, and social reform proposals.

Leibniz begins the description of his ideas and projects with an affirmation that human welfare is based on science and its practical application (as well as on the Christian religion). He continues:

> Science is humanity's true treasure. . . . But this treasure is neither administrated as it deserves nor is it applied well, because its significance is not sufficiently heeded. It can be compared to possessing a large library that is never enlarged, taken care of, or properly inventoried, and that ultimately no one wants to use.[15]

The prominent position given to this statement in Leibniz's argumentation demonstrates the great significance that he attached to knowledge and science in ensuring a well-run state.

Admittedly, Leibniz was not alone in his assessment. Both civil servants and statesmen endeavored to collect as much information as possible—both on the domestic front as well as abroad—and theorists placed academic institutions at the center of their utopian plans: for example, Salomon's House in Francis Bacon's "New Atlantis." Moreover, this quotation points to a second aspect that is crucial to Leibniz's reform proposals.

---

[14] A I v N. 149; A IV iv N. 1–11.
[15] A IV iv 21–22.

Collection of data is worthless unless it is both easy to locate and manageable. Leibniz and his contemporaries were all too familiar with the problem of information overload. For this reason, he viewed the collection of data in connection with its organization, preparation, and then, finally, its reduction and concentration on a few key statements that could be managed as a basis for political decisions. The rigor of this concept is most evident if one looks at its culmination.

Upon Duke Ernst August's accession to power in 1680, Leibniz responded with a veritable flood of aides-mémoire.[16] The most noteworthy of these is his "Outline of Certain State Tables."[17] Here, he defines his proposals for an information management system that is precisely tailored to the Duke's own government. The purpose of the "state tables" is to consolidate the country's key facts in concentrated form and present them so that the information sought is not only easily accessible but so that correlations can be made "at a single glance."[18] In the sovereign's hands, the concentration of pertinent knowledge in this work could be likened to the tip of a pyramid whose foundation is comprised of depositories and archives (among other sources). It is, therefore, essential to harmonize its internal organization and align it with this work "so that everything converges in this state table as though it flows to a central point."[19]

Thus, it is no surprise that, this very same year, Leibniz devised reform proposals for the keeping of administrative records and the Duke's archives. His interest in archive management was not for historico-antiquarian reasons, as can be seen from his list of ten examples of the benefits of an archive. He doesn't mention its significance for dynastic historiography until he reaches the second-to-last item on the list.[20] To ensure that the archives could be exploited as completely as possible in terms of their political, legal, and economic benefit and then be made centrally accessible through the "state tables," the records stored at various institutions would need to be uniformly organized. This step should take place at the point of record creation in the depository. Thus, at the same time, Leibniz proposed the establishment of a *General Registratur-Amt* (General Depository) to implement standardization.[21] His plan for a library, dating back to November 1680, is made to measure for the Duke's information requirements.[22] Leibniz could thus characterize it as a "printed archive."[23]

---

[16] A I iii xxix–xxx; A IV iii N. 28–36.

[17] A IV iii N. 29. The cultural turn brought this text to prominence and rightly so. However, prominence is accompanied by problematic interpretations isolating the text from its immediate context. For example, Bernhard Siegert, "Analysis als Staatsmaschine: Die Evidenz der Zeichen und der Ausdruck des Infinitesimalen bei Leibniz," in Inge Baxmann et al. (eds.), *Das Laokoon-Paradigma: Zeichenregime im 18. Jahrhundert* (Berlin: Akademie Verlag, 2000) integrates the "state tables"—surely without justification—together with the *characteristica universalis* and infinitesimal calculus.

[18] A IV iii 345. For the significance of this wording, cf. Steffen Siegel, *Tabula: Figuren der Ordnung um 1600* (Berlin: Akademie Verlag, 2009), pp. 65–66.

[19] A IV iii 341.

[20] A IV iii N. 28.

[21] A IV iii N. 36.

[22] A IV iii N. 30; cf. chapter 34.

[23] A IV iii 350; cf. A I xiii 138, 140.

These depositories, archives, and libraries were all institutions that provided information in the form of written records, visual representations, and maps. However, his vision of what the state's information management framework should be did not stop there. By January 1680, Leibniz had drawn up a panorama of institutions that collected and organized knowledge and in which the construction of a princely *Kunstkammer*, or cabinet of curiosities, played a prominent role. This cabinet of curiosities was intended to collect machine models as well as rock samples and mineral ores from the Harz Mountains, and the plans called for a laboratory to be built adjacent to it.[24] Leibniz envisioned collecting information for each of these institutions by means of visual inspections and surveys.[25]

Not all findings are needed by the government, said Leibniz, but all knowledge benefits the common good.[26] He therefore recommended seeking and compiling information from a wide variety of areas. In this proposal, there is not a trace of academic pretentiousness: anything from folk remedies to the techniques specific to crafts was to be recorded, especially those crafts in danger of disappearing.[27] However, the significance of science for the common good also prompted Leibniz to draw up projects that cause perplexity today. Such projects included a plan to promote scientific literature and to suppress useless or dangerous books from being published or sold in Brandenburg-Prussia. This would be carried out under the oversight of the newly founded Academy. Leibniz definitely supported "disciplining the world of books"[28] if it would serve the common good.

Finally, Leibniz also included scholars themselves as instruments of information management. Just weeks after entering service in Hanover, he emphasized his connections in the Republic of Letters as "a qualification, so to speak, for his position at court."[29] In a letter to Johann Daniel Crafft, Leibniz explained that the exchange of information in the Republic of Letters should benefit the common good.[30] Although Leibniz would later move away from the utopian vision of an international government led by scholars, as depicted in the "Outline of a Deliberation," he adhered to his esteem for a need for experts to ensure good state administration. He accordingly advocated the establishment of a council for all questions regarding economic and social policy.[31]

---

[24] A I iii 17–18, 19.

[25] A IV iii N. 61 (c. 1682).

[26] A IV iii 342.

[27] A IV iv 22–23.

[28] Helmut Zedelmaier, "Zwischen Fortschrittsgeschichte und Erfindungskunst. Gottfried Wilhelm Leibniz und Christian Wolff über Historia literaria," in Frank Grunert and Friedrich Vollhardt (eds.), *Historia literaria: Neuordnungen des Wissens im 17. und 18. Jahrhundert* (Berlin: Akademie Verlag, 2007), p. 91.

[29] A I ii N. 7. Nora Gädeke, "Leibniz läßt sich informieren—Asymmetrien in seinen Korrespondenzbeziehungen," in Klaus-Dieter Herbst and Stefan Kratochwil (eds.), *Kommunikation in der Frühen Neuzeit* (Frankfurt: Peter Lang, 2009), p. 37.

[30] A III vi N. 138 (July 1695).

[31] The greatest detail is provided in an aide-mémoire written in early 1695 for the Brandenburg statesman Eberhard von Danckelman: A I xi N. 121.

The fact that Leibniz considered the scholar in his role as political adviser to have the most important function in administrative information management, whereas the prince's "basic job of importance is to provide financial and administrative support for great projects that intellectuals are involved in,"[32] may explain why he concerned himself to a far greater extent with ideas for administrative reform rather than with the education of princes. His "Letter on the Education of a Prince"[33] identifies three stages toward perfection: what is necessary, what is useful, and what is ornamental. Four virtues are essential: as a man of good will, the prince should be pious, just, charitable, and dutiful. As a man of courage, he should have a free spirit; as a man of judgment, he should act with discernment; and, as a *honnête homme*, he should show good manners. It is significant that Leibniz only mentions the formation of character as essential—not specialized knowledge. It is not until the second stage that he discusses political and military knowledge as being useful for the ruler-to-be. The third stage then rightly adds an encyclopedic education, as well as such aspects of court life as dancing, hunting, and knowledge of art and music.

From a modern perspective, it stands to reason to ask whether, in the implementation of Leibniz's plans, the state would have served science (or his personal scientific interests) or whether science would have served the state. However, this is not how Leibniz would have viewed it. He wanted to see both in close interaction with one another, in so far as science—at least if it hoped to be of practical benefit—was dependent on support from the state, just as the state for its part required science to carry out its functions and to expand its power. And because both ultimately were intended to serve the common good, this close relationship seemed unproblematic. Leibniz's tenacious belief in the importance of the sciences and their practical application for the common welfare is the shared principle behind each of his reform proposals.

PUBLIC FINANCES AND ECONOMY

Early Modern states primarily focused their attention on increasing their population and their economic power; these were viewed as the basis of their position of power. "Mercantilism" is the term used to refer to this economic theory and practice in the western European states. Its counterpart in German-speaking areas, in which state administration had a generally greater involvement, is described as "cameralism."[34]

---

[32] Douglas J. Den Uyl, "The aristocratic element in Leibniz's political thought," in *Journal of the History of Philosophy* 15 (1977), p. 290.

[33] A IV iii N. 68 (1685/86).

[34] Whereas this represents an attempt to place Leibniz in the economic discourse of his era, more recent studies are more interested in applying his philosophical principles to current economic thinking; cf. Peter Koslowski, "Economic principle, maximizing, and the co-ordination of individuals in economy and philosophy," in Peter Koslowski (ed.), *Economics and Philosophy* (Tübingen: Mohr, 1985) and the critique: Hans Albert, "On using Leibniz in economics: Comment on Peter Koslowski," in ibid. Even Jon Elster, *Leibniz et la formation de l'esprit capitaliste* (Paris: Aubier Montaigne, 1975) is more interested in

This term is derived from the princely financial administration (German: *Kammer*; Latin: *camera*) and plainly indicates not only the goal of its deliberations—to increase state revenue—but, at the same time, clearly shows that cameralistic reforms in the German principalities were not limited to economic policy in the narrow sense. In fact, cameralism comprises three areas: (1) state (financial) administration; (2) management of princely enterprises (e.g., domains, mines, and manufacture); and (3) the actual financial policy. The following statement applies to cameralism as well as to mercantilism:

> These economic principles never attained the status of a cohesive theory, but instead fell apart in the midst of an overwhelming variety of practical formulas and recommendations.[35]

In light of his convictions regarding economic policy, one can definitely describe Leibniz as a cameralist.[36] And, in Leibniz's economic writings, the "overwhelming variety of practical formulas and recommendation" just quoted can be classified according to the three fields of activity in cameralism.[37] The list he drew up for the emperor with proposals for tapping into new sources of revenue present an entire kaleidoscope of ideas, from increasing state revenue to augmenting the population and promoting the economy.[38] The proposals range from establishing a lottery to trade agreements and sale of offices and honors to recommendations for tolerance of Protestants and Jews for economic reasons. In a paper entitled *Kammergefälle* (not his own choice)—which does not do justice to the content—Leibniz attempted to organize and assess the princely revenue. He divided it into three groups: first the *Kammergefälle*, which primarily included earnings from princely domains; second, services that subjects were required to render; and third, the levies that they paid. Here, Leibniz differentiated between money and tangible goods.[39]

Leibniz's metaphysics than in his economic thought. In this regard, Joseph Vogl, "Leibniz, Kameralist," in Bernhard Siegert and Joseph Vogl (eds.), *Europa: Kultur der Sekretäre* (Zürich-Berlin: Diaphanes, 2003) is only rephrasing Elster's position in terms of "cultural turn."

[35] Rainer Gömmel, *Die Entwicklung der Wirtschaft im Zeitalter des Merkantilismus 1620–1800* (München: R. Oldenbourg, 1998), p. 41.

[36] Elster, *Leibniz*, p. 26, ascribes "a mercantilist theory of the economy, a capitalist theory of the universe" to Leibniz.

[37] Leibniz wrote numerous aides-mémoire on these issues in conjunction with his deliberations concerning the establishment of the Berlin Academy (1700/1701) as well as his last sojourn in Vienna (late 1712 until September 1714) (Bodemann, *Handschriften* 269–81). Many of these texts have yet to be edited. The older works: Eduard Bodemann, "Leibnizens volkswirthschaftliche Ansichten und Denkschriften," *Preußische Jahrbücher 53* (1884) and Arthur Salz, "Leibniz als Volkswirt. Ein Bild aus dem Zeitalter des deutschen Merkantilismus," *Jahrbuch für Gesetzgebung, Verwaltung und Volkswirtschaft im Deutschen Reich* [= *Schmollers Jahrbuch*] *34* (1910), offer comprehensive overviews with extensive citations and paraphrasing. This makes some material accessible that has not yet been edited; however, the quotes have not been sufficiently substantiated, which makes them difficult or impossible to verify without recourse to the manuscripts.

[38] A IV iv N. 10.

[39] A IV iii N. 31.

Taxes and levies were the state's primary means of funding. An example of how Leibniz envisioned the ideal form of taxation can be seen in a proposal for introducing a consumption tax on clothing (*Kleider-Accis*):[40] this was intended as a universal tax because everyone needed to wear clothes. The upper classes were exempt from certain other taxes, but, in this case, they would not only have been taxed, but at a higher rate than the poor. This was because Leibniz sought to levy a tax of one-twelfth on necessities but one-ninth on luxury items. On the other hand, this emphasized that any infraction of the sumptuary law—in other words, wearing clothing more luxurious than that permitted to one's estate—would be subject to tax sanctions. In so doing, an actual dress code could be dispensed with. Moreover, the tax fits in perfectly with cameralistic ideals: because such taxes would be paid by the consumer, not by the craftsmen or merchants, Leibniz saw no disadvantages for the economy. And, in the long run, he thought it appropriate to restrict the import of foreign luxury goods.

Above all, it is worth noting how Leibniz sought to link his proposals for establishing institutions for administrative information management with proposals for their finance. In October 1696, Leibniz suggested to Elector Ernst August that a stamped paper—a type of administrative fee—be introduced, "with the proceeds to be used for the library and archive," as well as for other purposes, since "it would be fitting that the proceeds for the stamped paper would be used for paper, books, writings, histories, and *res literaria*."[41] Shortly thereafter, he also suggested to the dukes of Wolfenbüttel that stamped paper should be introduced to finance the maintenance of their renowned library.[42] These proposals fell on deaf ears. Only one of his financing plans met with success: the Berlin Academy's monopoly on the sale of calendars.

What Leibniz had to say in *Kammergefälle* with regard to princely revenue was not orientated toward maximizing (short-term) princely income, but rather with the welfare of all in mind. He was, therefore, skeptical about an expansion of princely domanial economy: large estates prevented the population from increasing, the farm laborers working there lacked the industry of an owner or tenant, and the tenants exploited the land in search of short-term profits. At the same time, Leibniz saw potential dangers in fragmenting a landed estate too far and viewed the domains as a "safe foundation" for state power.[43]

Leibniz's position in this regard is cautious rather than decisive, which shows to what extent he felt the state should be involved in commercial enterprises. He advocated a broadly based middle class as opposed to an overly proactive state while simultaneously allowing for exceptions such as the adoption of capital-intensive new technologies, supporting domestic merchants, strategic military production, or to prevent famine.[44] Here, on the one hand, we see typical cameralistic positions. On the other, certain

---

[40] A I v N. 192 (autumn 1688).
[41] A I xiii 68, 69.
[42] A I xiii N. 86–87.
[43] A IV iii 354–55.
[44] Ibid., 355–57. A IV vii N. 25 (c. 1697).

statements reveal a traditional "moral economy," more oriented toward a livelihood rather than on maximizing profit. He thus exhorts the authorities to prevent poor farmers "from being coerced to work for a song and—contrary to good order—being compelled to sell the grain of their fields and the fruit of their vineyards [before the harvest] at too low a price."[45]

Apart from certain rather utopian considerations such as the concept of a collective organization of handiwork, which Leibniz had incorporated in his early Academy projects,[46] his proposals for economic policy fit within the scope of contemporary cameralistic discourse as well. On the one hand, he recommended continuing to strengthen those sectors of the economy that were flourishing thanks to favorable conditions. Again and again, Leibniz advocated the promotion of canvas manufacture and trade: in Hanover (c. 1680), in Vienna (1688), and in Berlin (c. 1695).[47] On the other hand, he preached the benefits of adopting new technologies and manufacturing sectors not only to dispense with costly import of foreign technology and luxury items, but so that Germany itself might become an exporter of highly sought products. He also wished to use technical improvements to advance mining in the Harz Mountains.[48]

Here, it will not be possible to discuss the details of Leibniz's technical ideas; instead, I provide a brief outline of his understanding of technology within the scope of his economic concepts. Plans of this type could be used beyond their intended economic purpose to serve power-political objectives. For example, the brandy distillery project begun in 1694, during the Nine Years' War, shows his intention to not only wean Germany from reliance on French exports but to economically weaken its wartime enemy as well. With this in mind, Leibniz even spoke of a "type of war that is permitted in times of peace."[49]

Where technology was concerned, Leibniz was an optimist—in contrast to the "moral economy" of the craft guilds—who, fearing the loss of employment opportunities, rejected technological rationalization. In his view, technology could not only potentially offer relief from difficult, monotonous work but, in addition, he was not persuaded that, by and large, technical progress would lead to unemployment.[50] Upon hearing of the invention of a threshing machine, he commented: "Some people object to the introduction of such machines—which could make work easier—by saying that this would take away poor people's livelihood. This was the motivation behind the prohibition of

---

[45] A IV iii 356.

[46] A IV i N. 47. Not surprisingly, these projects have caught the attention of Marxist interpreters; cf. Hans Heinz Holz, *Herr und Knecht bei Leibniz und Hegel: Zur Interpretation der Klassengesellschaft* (Neuwied-Berlin: Luchterhand, 1968), pp. 21–22. Ruth Milachowski, "Die Schrift 'Societät und Wirtschaft'—Ausdruck der Gleichwertigkeit von Theorie und Praxis im Werk von G. W. Leibniz," in *Gottfried Wilhelm Leibniz—wissenschaftliche Methoden heute* (Leipzig: Rosa-Luxemburg-Stiftung Sachsen e. V., 1997).

[47] A I iii N. 74–75; A IV iii N. 35; A IV iv N. 11; A I xi N. 123.

[48] Cf. chapter 30.

[49] A III vi N. 72, 74–75; A IV v N. 40–45. Quotation: A III vi 214.

[50] A IV iii N. 63 (c. 1687).

stocking and ribbon mills in Regensburg some years ago. Not only was this prohibition ineffective, I am of the opinion that there will always be some way of providing useful employment."[51]

Leibniz ultimately depicted and described this threshing machine in the first volume of the journal of the Berlin Academy.[52] The Academy, intended to combine pure and applied research, was admittedly not the only state-run information management institution to take technology and crafts into account. As mentioned earlier, the *Kunstkammer* was intended as a storehouse for both machine models and rock samples. With respect to the latter, Leibniz wanted miners to be required to regularly supply samples to the *Kunstkammer*.[53] Leibniz's perception of information management as a tool for promoting scientific findings and technical innovations was based on a concept of give-and-take: the information acquired from individual workshops and mines was to be centrally collected, examined, organized, and then ultimately distributed throughout the country in order to promote economic development.

PUBLIC WELFARE

Leibniz's proposals, whose objective was to increase administrative and economic efficiency to strengthen the state, are, however, just one side of the coin. The other side is concern for the welfare of the state's subjects. The text of *Kammergefälle*, which begins with the keynote statement: "The purpose of authority is to ensure the welfare of all" shows just how closely these two aspects are intertwined.[54] Werner Schneiders has taken Leibniz's scattered comments on what the ideal state should be and described it as "a welfare state driven by reason."[55] Leibniz was certainly not alone in this conviction. Concern for the welfare of one's subjects was integral to the image of the ideal paternalistic sovereign as traditionally viewed in the German principalities. Leibniz and his contemporaries spoke of *gute Policey* in reference to this policy. This term has a far wider reaching significance than the modern word "police." It was not restricted to the protection against threats to public safety, but encompassed every aspect of what we would now describe as domestic and social policy. In this respect, cameralism and *gute Policey* were inextricably allied. However, this care and assistance was linked to a tendency toward coercion, described by historians as "social disciplining." Paternalistic care and

---

[51] Quoted in Kurt Müller and Gisela Krönert, *Leben und Werk von Gottfried Wilhelm Leibniz. Eine Chronik* (Frankfurt: Vittorio Klostermann, 1969), p. 160 (November 1699).

[52] "Explicatio Machinae Trituratoriae (Dreschmuhle) Erzae inventae 1700," *Miscellanea Berolinensia* 1 (1710). This is the only article in this volume to offer a German translation for the scholarly Latin text.

[53] A I iii 18 (January 1680).

[54] A IV iii 354.

[55] Schneiders, "Vera Politica," p. 597.

caring discipline together created a paternalism that sought to intervene in all spheres of its subjects' lives.

This paternalism was not a foreign concept to Leibniz. In an unfinished manuscript written at the time of Duke Ernst August's ascent to the throne, Leibniz developed his thoughts on universal education, advancement, and welfare for the ruler's subjects—from the cradle to the grave, as it were—in order to make a moral people out of them. This was because, from his perspective, both the internal and external security of the state depended on the morality of its subjects.[56] Leibniz saw education as the surest way to achieve that: "This is because habits are another nature, and nature is, as it were, the first habit; thus, good habits and education are the natural antidote against original sin and a precursor or companion of grace."[57] For this reason, he placed great value on the importance of a well-educated population.[58] So great a value, in fact, that he envisioned state-appointed "guardians" for children—a distant reminder of the insistence on public education for children, a concept both widespread in the utopian tradition as well as in Leibniz's early writings.[59]

For Leibniz, the most essential aspects of education were morality and piety. In general, he rejected what he saw as too great an emphasis on higher education. In contrast, it was "essential to teach everyone—without distinction—godliness and morality, then reading, writing, and arithmetic, and worldly subjects as well."[60] Here, it would seem that Leibniz is putting a case for differentiating between classes. But, in fact, his advice regarding the education of princes varies only slightly from the statements here. There, too, the formation of character takes precedence. Leibniz not only criticized the domination of a Latin-based education, but also placed greater value on a future sovereign having a knowledge of modern languages. Above all, he did not alter his pedagogical proposals according to the social status of his addressee. He emphasized the importance of clarity in teaching and called for playful learning at the same time.[61]

His interest in combining amusement, play, and playful learning also led Leibniz to an astonishing proposal: to establish a kind of popular cabinet of curiosities. This would be a public institution offering a variety of annual fair-type amusements: re-enacted experiments, a casino, shadow puppetry, and other attractions, more to instruct the common folk in an entertaining manner and—if possible—to earn revenue toward financing an academy. He himself described this as a "funny thought," adding as a gloss: "in fact, an academy of games."[62]

Leibniz not only wanted to see the state assume responsibility for the upbringing and education of children. In addition, the state should be concerned with discipline and

---

[56] A IV iii N. 33.
[57] Ibid., 369.
[58] Cf. also A IV iii N. 32 (1680).
[59] A IV iii 366; cf. A IV i 560 (c. 1671).
[60] A IV iii 364.
[61] Compare A IV iii 364 with ibid., 549–55.
[62] A IV i N. 49 (1675).

occupational advancement for young people and assist them when they began their working lives. Moreover, the state should protect everyone from envy, crime, and violence, and assist in times of adversity.[63] He viewed poverty as a source of lethargy, crime, and disease. He therefore sought to prevent its emergence:

> Above everything else, one must seek means of obviating public misery. . . . For extreme poverty is the mother of crimes and also the source of sicknesses:. . . From which it follows that one must furnish the poor with the means of earning their livelihood, not only by using charity and [charitable] foundations to this end, but also by taking an interest in agriculture, by furnishing to artisans materials and a market, by educating them to make their productions better, and finally, by putting an end to idleness and to abusive practices in manufactures and in commerce.[64]

As noted earlier, to combat the causes of poverty rather than to mitigate their effects through charity was primarily the responsibility of economic policy. In addition, Leibniz concerned himself with specific proposals and institutions intended to prevent, battle, or ease poverty. These included both thoroughly traditional concepts such as the *Monti di Pietà*, public lending institutions that offered loans without excessive interest to those in need,[65] as well as typical institutions of "social disciplining" such as jails and workhouses.[66]

However, Leibniz's most innovative reform proposals are in the area of public assistance, namely, his thoughts on insurance.[67] Leibniz summarized his ideas in his aide-mémoire on *Öffentliche Assekuranzen* (public insurance).[68] In order to prevent people from falling into poverty through no fault of their own—with the consequences already described—Leibniz called for compulsory public insurance, in particular fire and water insurance. Insurance funds should be kept completely separate from the treasury to avoid any suspicion that insurance contributions were nothing more than taxes in disguise. Instead, contributions should help finance preventive measure ("*real-assecuratio*") as well as to assist the person suffering damages ("*verbal assecuration*"). In general, prevention is a critical aspect in this project. The insurance was intended to be combined with a fire ordinance and the purchase of fire extinguishers. This demonstrates the plan's cameralistic and social disciplining character. The insurance projects are closely tied to Leibniz's writings on demography, (medical) statistics, and public health, which will not be discussed here.[69] These projects also show the reciprocity of administrative information management: the official duty of physicians to collect data for medical statistics

---

[63] A IV iii N. 33.

[64] FC, *Oeuvres* IV, 150–51 (1714); translated in Riley, *Leibniz: Political Writings*, pp. 106–107, note 2.

[65] A IV iii N. 60 (c. 1680).

[66] A I ii 76 (1678).

[67] His seminal writings on actuarial theory cannot be discussed here; cf. chapter 14.

[68] A IV iii N. 49 (c. 1680).

[69] Cf. chapters 14 and 27.

should provide the foundation for empirically firm medicine, which in turn promised these physicians a higher rate of successful cures.[70]

Conclusion

In the preceding sections, we have not short-circuited Leibniz's political, administrative, economic, and social reform proposals with his infinitesimal calculus; constructed parallels between his economic thought and theodicy; or derived solutions for modern-day economic issues from his metaphysics. Instead, we have attempted to interpret his thinking within its historical context. From this angle, Leibniz proves himself true to the leading political-economic convictions of his day, described as cameralism and *gute Policey*. This thinking seems foreign and obsolete to us, no less foreign and obsolete than the Holy Roman Empire of the German Nation, the historical area in which and for which Leibniz designed his projects. "In this sense, political philosophy as a politically committed philosophy is not a *philosophia perennis*. It has a currency that vanishes together with the circumstances upon which it was based."[71]

What, then, remains? Surely the high estimation of knowledge and science and their application as a foundation and frame of reference of his reform proposals. On the one hand, this means that, theoretically, Leibniz's reform proposals are firmly rooted in his metaphysics. On the other hand, they aimed to be a practical means of helping humankind—as citizens of the City of God—toward perfecting themselves. On this more abstract level, Leibniz's political, administrative, economic, and social ideas transcend the close ties to the specific problems of the Holy Roman Empire or its principalities and take on universal validity. Thus, in January 1712, Leibniz could repeat to Peter the Great—whose vast but scarcely developed Russian Empire seemed to be a *tabula rasa* ready to accept his reform proposals—what he had tried to explain to the Holy Roman Emperor more than twenty years earlier: "the arts and sciences are also the true treasure of humankind; this is what gives art power over nature and separates civilized peoples from barbarians."[72]

---

[70] A IV v N. 82 (1694).

[71] Hermann Lübbe, *Politische Philosophie in Deutschland: Studien zu ihrer Geschichte* (Basel: Schwabe, 1963), p. 9.

[72] Woldemar Guerrier, *Leibniz in seinen Beziehungen zu Russland und Peter dem Grossen* (St. Petersburg and Leipzig: Commissionäre der Kaiserlichen Akademie der Wissenschaften, 1873), p. 207; cf. A IV iv 21–22.

PART VIII

NATURAL AND REVEALED RELIGION

CHAPTER 39

··

ARGUMENTS FOR THE
EXISTENCE OF GOD

··

BRANDON C. LOOK

WRITING to Elizabeth von der Pfalz in 1678, Leibniz says:

> there is nothing more clichéd today than demonstrations of the existence of God. I observe that it is almost like proofs for squaring the circle and perpetual motion: the least student of mathematics and mechanics lays claim to these sublime problems. . . . Similarly, all those who have learned a little metaphysics begin first with the demonstration of God's existence and the immortality of our souls, which, in my opinion, are the fruits of all our studies, since they constitute the foundation of our greatest hopes.
>
> (A II.1².660–661/AG 235*)[1]

Yet twenty-five years later, Leibniz presents a less supercilious mien: "I believe indeed that almost all the methods which have been used to prove the existence of God are good, and could serve the purpose if they were perfected" (A VI.6.438/RB 438*). The constant in both these reflections is that Leibniz believes that the existence of God can be demonstrated but that most efforts have been in vain. He, on the other hand, is the man for the job. While the subsequent history of philosophy, leading through the critical philosophy of Kant, may call into question the very possibility of such demonstrations, there can be no doubt that Leibniz made greater and deeper contributions to natural theology than any of his fellow early modern philosophers. And while we may be justified in treating these arguments now with skepticism Leibniz's reflections on the nature of God, existence, modality and truth which form the basis of his argument still have much to teach us.

Leibniz adopted a number of different argumentative strategies for proving the existence of God. In this essay, I shall concentrate on just three: the ontological argument,

---

[1] An asterisk (*) denotes that I have altered the standard English-language translation.

the cosmological argument, and the argument from eternal truths.[2] Each of Leibniz's argumentative strategies has particular virtues and rewards study, and each has had more recent advocates. One version of Leibniz's ontological argument, for example, is echoed in the twentieth century by Kurt Gödel; the cosmological argument responds to what Martin Heidegger has called the "fundamental question of metaphysics," and Leibniz's formulation of the argument can be seen as the template for all later cosmological arguments; and the argument from the existence of eternal truths has been called by one of Leibniz's most acute interpreters his most forceful and convincing.[3] Now, Kant famously claimed that the ontological argument lay at the foundation of all other arguments for the existence of God.[4] But in ways he could never have known, this is not true in the case of Leibniz's reflections on philosophical theology and natural religion. Nevertheless, because of the intrinsic interest in the ontological argument and because Leibniz thought perhaps most deeply about this form of argument, it is where we shall begin.

THE ONTOLOGICAL ARGUMENT

Anselm of Canterbury was, of course, the first philosopher to offer an argument for the existence of God, the characteristic feature of which is the explicit appeal to our idea or definition of God. But it was the version given by Descartes in his *Meditations* that occasioned Leibniz's reflections while in Paris in the mid-1670s. As Leibniz thinks of it, the basic form of the argument is that "whatever follows from the idea or definition of anything can be predicated of that thing" (A 6.4.588/ AG 25). It is, therefore, an a priori argument for the existence of God, from causes to effects or from definitions to consequences. Now, for Descartes, since the idea or definition of God is that of the most perfect being and since existence must be a perfection, existence follows from the idea of God, and therefore God exists. Let us call this the "Cartesian Ontological Argument," which in its purest form is just the following.

---

[2] Leibniz also claims that the preestablished harmony of mind and body provides an argument for the existence of God (see *New System* 16: GP IV 486/AG 145), but I shall not consider that argument here. Leibniz's arguments for the existence of God have, of course, been treated elsewhere; most notable are the discussions of Adams 1994, Blumenfeld 1995, Jalabert 1960, Parkinson 1965, and Russell 1937.

[3] See Gödel's "Ontological proof" in *Gödel* 1995, 403–404. (The first publication of this argument, along with commentary, is in Sobel 1987.) For the affinities between Gödel and Leibniz, see Adams's introductory note in Gödel 1995 and Look 2006. For the notion of the fundamental metaphysical question, see Heidegger 1953 and 1957. The claim that Leibniz's version of the cosmological argument is the "basic form" of all subsequent cosmological arguments is to be found in Craig 1980, 257. Finally, it is Robert Merrihew Adams who is sympathetic to Leibniz's argument from eternal truths (1994, 177).

[4] *Critique of Pure Reason* A 607/B 635.

(1)   God has all perfections (or is the *ens perfectissimum*).

(2)   Existence is a perfection.

(3)   Therefore, God exists.[5]

On first glance, this argument, like other versions of the ontological argument, appears formally valid—much to the consternation of atheists and sceptics. Even at the time of the publication of the *Meditations*, however, there was resistance. For example, in his Objections, Pierre Gassendi denied premise (2), arguing that existence is not a perfection, long before Kant made his celebrated charge that existence is not a real predicate.[6]

According to Leibniz, on the other hand, the Cartesian ontological argument is to be faulted mainly for being incomplete—something he mentions whenever he can. [7] It assumes as true something that needs to be proven, namely, that an *ens perfectissimum* is possible. There are, after all, ideas or definitions that actually contain contradictions and are, therefore, impossible. For example, the ideas of *the greatest number* or *the fastest motion* seem to make sense; we can utter the words and think the thoughts. But closer inspection shows them to be impossible. The ontological argument is especially difficult on this score because, strictly speaking, "we do not have the idea of God, however we define him" (A 6.3.462/Parkinson 5).[8] We are working solely with the definition of God as the *ens perfectissimum*, the most perfect being (or being having all perfections). As Leibniz says in one of his first philosophical publications, *Meditations on Knowledge, Truth and Ideas*, the Cartesian Ontological Argument only licenses the conclusion "if God is possible, then it follows that he exists" (A 6.4.588/AG 25). We must be sure that we are using a "real definition"—that is, a definition that contains within it a proof of the possibility of the *definiendum*. In other words, if we can prove that the concept for the *definiendum* contains no contradiction, then the being that instantiates that concept is possible.

To fill the gap in the Cartesian ontological argument, therefore, it must be shown that it is possible for all perfections to be instantiated by the same object. In a number of texts from 1676, Leibniz gives us arguments that demonstrate precisely this possibility.

---

[5]   For Descartes's actual argument in the fifth of the *Meditations*, see AT VII 65–68/CSM II 45–46; it is also given in the First Set of Replies at AT VII 118–119/CSM II 84–85.

[6]   For Gassendi, see AT VII 322–325/CSM II 224–226; for Kant, see the *Critique of Pure Reason* (A 598–599/B 626–627) but also *The Only Possible Argument in Support of a Demonstration of the Existence of God* (Ak. 2.72, Ak. 2.156–157).

[7]   See, for example, A 6.3.395/Parkinson 47–49; A 6.3.511/Parkinson 63; A 6.3.579/Parkinson 103; A 2.1².725–26/L 211; GP IV 405; A 6.6.437/NE 437.

[8]   In this piece, from December 1675, Leibniz argues that we have only ideas of "simples" and symbols of composites (for example, definitions in words). In a letter most likely written to Elizabeth von der Pfalz three years later, Leibniz says: "I do not question the idea of God any more than I do his existence. . . . [But] we must prove with the greatest imaginable exactness that there is an idea of a completely perfect being, that is, an idea of God" (A 2.1².663–664/ AG 237–238) Much later in his career, Leibniz will say that the idea of God is innate in us (see, for example, A 6.6. 76, 96, 225; NE 76, 96, 225). How exactly to weigh these competing claims is difficult. Not only is there a temporal difference for these pronouncements, there is also a difference of intended audience. Nevertheless, I believe that, speaking in metaphysical and epistemological rigor, Leibniz thinks we do not have *an idea* of God.

According to him, "perfections, or simple forms, or absolute positive qualities, are indefinable or unanalyzable" (A 6.3.575/Parkinson 97); similarly, a perfection is a "simple quality which is positive and absolute, or, which expresses without any limits whatever it does express" (A VI iii 578/Parkinson 101). Now, for the sake of a *reductio ad absurdum* argument, suppose there are two perfections that cannot possibly belong to the same subject; that is, suppose the two perfections are necessarily incompatible. Call them A and B. If the proposition "A and B are incompatible" is necessarily true, then, according to Leibniz, it is either self-evident or demonstrable. Certainly, we cannot know by intuition that A and B are incompatible. But neither can we demonstrate the proposition "A and B are incompatible," for demonstration requires the analysis of concepts, and A and B are simple qualities, that is, unanalyzable. Therefore, it cannot be demonstrated that they are necessarily incompatible with each other. Since it cannot be shown that A and B cannot be in the same subject, it must be possible for them to be in the same subject. And since the same reasoning applies to any two or more simple, positive qualities, all perfections are compatible.[9] Therefore, a subject of all perfections, or an *ens perfectissimum*, is indeed possible, and we can rewrite the Cartesian ontological argument in the following way:

(1) God is the *ens perfectissimum*. (Definition)
(2) Existence is a perfection.
(3) If the *ens perfectissimum* is possible, it exists. (The intermediary conclusion from the Cartesian ontological argument, according to Leibniz.)
(4) The *ens perfectissimum* is possible. (The result of the foregoing ancillary argument.)
(5) Therefore, God exists.

Leibniz was particularly proud of this argument, writing: "I am perhaps the first to have shown that a being to which all affirmative attributes belong is possible" (A 6.3.395–96/Parkinson 47–49). Indeed, even Spinoza seems to have liked the argument.[10]

There are nevertheless two possible objections at this point. The first we have already seen expressed by Gassendi in his response to Descartes's *Meditations*: existence is not a perfection; the crucial premise is false; and so the *ens perfectissimum* simply does not exist. While Leibniz's considered view is, of course, that existence is a perfection, he does address the issue of the existence predicate, primarily in his correspondence with

---

[9] A 6.3.578–579/Parkinson 101–103 (= L 167). A similar argument is given at A 6.3.575–576/Parkinson 97–99. It should be noted that if God is to be conceived simply as a being that contains all primitive, positive qualities, then we have a clear case of "the God of the philosophers" and not "the God of Abraham." How to make *this* God, the God of pure perfections, capable of uttering, for example, "Vengeance *belongeth* unto me" (Heb. 10:30) is a separate matter. It is also worth noting that this separate subargument for the possibility of all perfections inhering in one subject actually revolves around *a proposition concerning* this set of perfections (Fichant 1998, 104–105).

[10] "I showed this argument to Mr. Spinoza when I was at the Hague, and he thought it to be sound" (A 6.3.579/Parkinson 103).

Arnold Eckhard in 1677 and in other texts from the same time. In a letter of the spring of that year, Leibniz recounts an earlier conversation with Eckhard and distinguishes two issues: "one is whether the *ens perfectissimum* does not imply a contradiction, the other is whether, once it is posited that an *ens perfectissimum* does not imply a contradiction, existence is among the perfections." We have reason to doubt this after all, "for perfections seem to be certain qualities of the sort that existence is not" (A 2.1².488). Writing in the summer, however, Leibniz says explicitly: "as I prefer to define it, *perfection* is a degree or quantity of reality or essence, as *intensity* is a degree of quality and *force* is a degree of action. It is also clear that existence is a perfection, or increases reality, that is, when an existing A is conceived, more reality is conceived than when a possible A is conceived" (A II, I², 543). While this passage shows that Leibniz is committed to the thesis that existence is a perfection, it shows at the same time that Leibniz does not exactly treat existence as a property on a par with other properties. Indeed, it seems that existence is almost treated as if it were a second-order property, for it can be predicated of ordinary positive properties or perfections and thereby add reality to the essence of a thing. In other words, one might naturally conclude that some individual, A, can have a fully determined essence, containing all its predicates, and that existence adds reality to that essence. In short, existence is a property of the concept of A.[11] In still another text that the Akademie editors date to the same period, Leibniz rejects entirely the idea that existence is a perfection: "existence is not any degree of reality, for of any degree of reality both the possibility and the existence can be understood. . . . Therefore it is true that what exists is more perfect than what is non-existent, but it is not true that existence itself is a perfection since it is only a certain comparison of perfections among themselves" (A 6.4.1354). By saying that what exists is more perfect than what does not, Leibniz appeals to the idea present in Anselm's argument that an actually existent being is greater (that is, has more perfection) than a nonexistent being without at the same time saying that existence is a perfection per se. These passages demonstrate that Leibniz is not consistent in his writing about the nature of existence. There are in fact three distinct positions represented here: (i) existence is a perfection, that is, a first-order divine property like all other simple, positive, and absolute qualities that are mutually consistent within the divine essence; (ii) existence is akin to a second-order property that can be thought to increase the degree of reality of a thing; (iii) existence is not a perfection at all. Leibniz's revised ontological argument, which he presented throughout the rest of his career and of which he was clearly proud, requires (i), that existence be considered a perfection, and we ought to conclude that he thought it so. Nevertheless, it should be clear that Leibniz was aware of this potential objection and even considered ways to blunt it.

While the first objection centered around existence, the second possible objection focuses attention on modality. Perhaps, the objection goes, it is just a contingent fact

[11] In Look 2011 I argue that Leibniz's reflections on the existence predicate bring him close to insights made later by Kant and Frege. Though he does not discuss Leibniz, on the issue of the existence predicate see also Forgie 1972 and 1974.

that the *ens perfectissimum* exists.[12] The ontological argument is not sufficient to determine that God exists *necessarily*, that the being having all perfections is exemplified necessarily, or that God's essence contains *necessary* existence. How is it, after all, that we move from the *possibility* of God's existence—proven by the in-principle compatibility of all positive qualities—to the *actuality* or even *necessity* of God's existence? More exactly, we can ask whether the conclusion given above is

(5*) Therefore, necessarily, God exists

or

(5**) Therefore, God necessarily exists.

The distinction is, of course, the standard distinction between *de dicto* (5*) and *de re* (5**) modality. In this case, the question becomes whether the necessity of God's existence is a function of the deduction or follows from the nature of God himself. The argument that was presented earlier most naturally should be read with a *de dicto* conclusion. But for someone working in philosophical theology, it might seem desirable to be making a *de re* claim about God. Thus, Leibniz needs to show not only that the *ens perfectissimum* is *possible* but also that God's very nature contains necessary existence and thus that God could not not exist. In another piece from the period, he attempts to do precisely this by first offering a more precise definition of a necessary being: "a necessary being is the same as a being from whose essence existence follows. For a necessary being is one which necessarily exists, such that for it not to exist would imply a contradiction, and so would conflict with the concept or essence of this being" (A 6.3.583/Parkinson 107). If a being having all perfections is possible and if existence is a perfection, then existence belongs to the essence of the *ens perfectissimum*. And if existence belongs to the essence of the *ens perfectissimum*, then, by Leibniz's new definition, the *ens perfectissimum* is a necessary being. But this also means that there is at least a conceptual difference between God as *ens perfectissimum* and God as *ens necessarium*—a difference Leibniz will exploit.

We can now reformulate the ontological argument without reference to an "ens perfectissimum," simply in terms of a "necessary being." If a necessary being is, by definition, a being whose essence entails existence, Leibniz believes "we have a splendid theorem, which is the pinnacle [fastigium] of modal theory and by which one moves in a wonderful way from potentiality to act: If a necessary being is possible, it follows that it exists actually, or, that such a being is actually found in the universe" (A 6.3.583/ Parkinson107).[13] What exactly is this "pinnacle of modal theory"? One might take the theorem to be "if possibly p, then p," the converse of the Axiom of Possibility ($p \rightarrow \Diamond p$); but this is generally regarded as invalid and is surely not what Leibniz meant.

---

[12] Adams makes this point in his introductory note to Gödel's ontological proof. See Gödel 1995, 394–395.

[13] Leibniz repeats this idea and terminology throughout his career, writing in 1688 (?) again of the "pinnacle of modal theory [fastigium doctrinae modalis]" (A 6.4.1617/MP 76) and after 1700 of "a modal

Alternatively, Leibniz could mean what will come to be an important axiom in modal logic B, "if possibly necessarily p, then p" ($\Diamond\Box p \to p$).[14] But this does not get us the *necessary* existence of God. No, what Leibniz means by the "pinnacle of modal theory" is one of the notorious axioms of the modal logic S5: "if possibly necessarily p, then necessarily p" ($\Diamond\Box p \to \Box p$).[15] In the case of the argument for the existence of God, we would seem to have this proposition working as a premise: "if it is possible that God necessarily exists, then God necessarily exists."[16] Leibniz is clear, however, that this is a "privilege" of the necessary being, for only it has such a nature that, given its possibility, it exists.[17]

In making this move, however, Leibniz has taken us beyond the rather simple version of the ontological argument—based on the mere definition of God as an *ens perfectissimum*—to what is usually termed nowadays a "modal ontological argument."[18] To a careful reader of Anselm, this is what one finds in the move from the argument of chapter 2 of the *Proslogion* to its supposed restatement in chapter 3. Leibniz was aware of the fact that he was presenting a different version and preferred this second, modal version of the ontological argument. As Leibniz puts it in his correspondence with Eckhard, this argument is "more advantageous" (*compendiosus*) (A 2.1².486). Perhaps the clearest version of this argument is on display in a letter written in January 1678 and most likely intended for Henning Huthmann.[19] He writes the following.

Proof of the Existence of God From His Essence

(1) The possible existence or the possibility of any thing and the essence of that same thing are inseparable (that is, if there is one of them in the region of ideas or truths or realities, then there is the other. That is, with the truth of one of them, the other is true, for truths exist even if things do not exist and are not thought by anyone . . .) Therefore, by subsumption

proposition which would be one of the greatest fruits of all of Logic [une proposition modale qui seroit un des meilleurs fruits de toute la Logique]" (GP IV 406).

[14] This is a point made in Adams 1971.

[15] The S5 axiom, as presented in most textbooks, is $\Diamond p \to \Box\Diamond p$, but this is logically equivalent to the formula shown above. To see this, recall first the equivalencies of the modal operators: $\Diamond p \equiv \neg\Box\neg p$ and $\Box p \equiv \neg\Diamond\neg p$. Now take the textbook S5 axiom $\Diamond p \to \Box\Diamond p$, but with the propositional variable negated: $\Diamond\neg p \to \Box\Diamond\neg p$. By transposition, this in turn is equivalent to $\neg\Box\Diamond\neg p \to \neg\Diamond\neg p$. Now, substituting modal equivalencies on the consequent, we get this: $\neg\Box\Diamond\neg p \to \Box p$. Focusing now on the antecedent, and again substituting modal operators, we get $\neg\neg\Diamond\neg\neg\Box\neg\neg p \to \Box p$; and removing the double negations, we have our desired formula: $\Diamond\Box p \to \Box p$.

[16] There is the potential for *de re/de dicto* confusion here as well, for we are left to ask whether the necessity is located in our relation to the proposition ("*p*") or in the nature of the being ("*P*"?). Still, I think it is important to see that Leibniz's "pinnacle of modal theory" belongs to the most powerful of our modal logics, in which any world is accessible from any other world. This is exactly what one would expect from Leibniz.

[17] See, for example, A 6.4.542/MP 13; A 6.6.438/NE 438; GP IV 359; GP IV 402; GP VI 614/AG 218 (*Monadology* 45).

[18] For the classic presentation of this second kind of ontological argument, see Malcolm 1960; see also Oppy 1995 and Harrelson 2008.

[19] While Adams (1994, 136–137) and Janke (1963, 284–287) reproduce this argument, it is generally not well known among students of Leibniz's thought. I therefore quote the argument in its entirety.

(2) The possible existence or the possibility of God and the essence of God are inseparable (for the essence of the thing is the particular reason [*specialis ratio*] of its
possibility).But

(3) The essence of God and his actual existence are inseparable. (See the proof of this
[below].)Therefore, by way of conclusion,

(4) The possible existence or the possibility of God and his actual existence are
inseparable.Or, which is the same thing,

(5) If it is supposed that God is possible, it follows that God exists in actuality (A
$2.1^2 2.588-89$).

This argument is formally valid. It does require, however, some further clarification.
What does it mean to say, as Leibniz does in premise (1), that the possible existence
of a thing and its essence are inseparable? His parenthetical remark offers the crucial
clue: something possibly exists just in case there is a complete essence of it in the divine
understanding. Moreover, when one thinks of other aspects of Leibniz's philosophy,
one could add that the existence of x in world w is possible if and only if there is some
fully determinate concept (essence) of x that is compatible with all other individuals
in world w. Premise (2) simply instantiates the universal claim of (1) with God. But, as
Leibniz notes himself, it is the third premise that requires additional support, and he
gives two separate arguments that are to buttress it. The first is as follows:

(1) The essence of God and the highest perfection are inseparable (by hypothesis, for
we suppose that the essence of God contains the highest perfection).

(2) The highest perfection and any perfection in kind [*quaevis perfectio in specie*] are
inseparable.

(3) Actual existence is some perfection in kind.

Therefore,

The essence of God and his actual existence are inseparable.
And the second runs thus:

(1) The essence of God involves the necessity of existing (for we understand by the
name of God a certain necessary being).

(2) If the essence of a thing involves the necessity of existing, its essence is inseparable from existence (for otherwise some thing is only possible or contingent).

Therefore,

The essence of God and existence are inseparable

(A $2.1^2.589$).[20]

---

[20] I have kept Leibniz's numbering of the premises of the argument and subarguments.

Leibniz concludes this discussion with his now familiar claim that, if God is possible, God actually exists. It is important to see at this point, however, that the crucial difference represented by this second form of ontological argument is in its explicit appeal to the inseparability of actual or necessary existence from the divine essence. As Leibniz explains in his notes to this letter, essences do not depend on the existence of the subjects or on our thought; for even if no one were to think the essences or if they were not exemplified in the world, still essences would exist in the realm of ideas.[21] But, again, if the essence of God cannot be thought except as containing necessary existence, then if the essence is possible (that is, internally consistent), then God exists.

We saw one argument already for the possibility of the concept or essence of God, which involved showing that it is possible for any and all positive qualities or perfections to exist in the same subject. Leibniz offers another argument as well. Writing much later in his career, he begins the argument by invoking the pinnacle of modal theory: if the necessary being is possible, it exists. The necessary being is, however, equivalent to the "being by its essence" or the "being in itself [l'Estre de soy]." If the being in itself were impossible, all beings by another ("estres par autruy") are impossible as well, for they derive their existence ultimately through the being in itself. Thus, nothing could exist. Since, of course, something *does* exist, it cannot be the case that the being in itself is impossible. Therefore, according to Leibniz, "this reasoning leads us to another important modal proposition equal to the preceding one, and which combined with it completes the demonstration. One could express it thus: if the necessary being does not exist, there is no being possible" (GP IV 406). The interesting feature of this second argument for the possibility of God is that it freely invokes argumentative impulses from the cosmological argument. Insofar as it does so, it would appear to undercut Kant's claim, mentioned in the introduction, that the cosmological argument makes implicit appeal to the ontological argument, for something like the cosmological argument refers to the obvious experience of contingent beings in the world and thus provides us with a proof of the possibility of God, which we need to complete the ontological argument. If the ontological argument is supposed to be purely a priori, move from our ideas or definitions, and arrive at the existence of God without any appeal to experience, then clearly this is not a pure form of the ontological argument. It does however lead us naturally into our next class of argument.

THE COSMOLOGICAL ARGUMENT

Whereas the ontological argument is an a priori argument for the existence of God, the cosmological argument is an a posteriori argument, one that moves from effects

---

[21] See point 3 at A 2.1^2.590—though this is a restatement and elaboration of the parenthetical remark in premise (1) of the main argument.

to the cause and depends on one of the fundamental principles of Leibniz's philosophy: the principle of sufficient reason, according to which there is nothing without a cause or a reason sufficient to determine why it is so and not otherwise. Leibniz is explicit in his popular *Principles of Nature and Grace*, writing that we must make use of "the *great principle*, little used, commonly, that *nothing takes place without sufficient reason.*. . . Assuming this principle, the first question we have the right to ask will be, *why is there something rather than nothing?*" (GP VI 602/AG 209–210: PNG 7).[22] The answer to this question leads us to an extramundane cause, God. In a rather truncated version, the cosmological argument is found in the *Monadology*, where Leibniz claims that truths are either necessary truths (truths of reason) or contingent truths (truths of fact) and that in the case of contingent truths there must be a sufficient reason why they are so (*Monadology* 36). But, Leibniz argues, since each particular truth of fact is contingent on some other (prior) truth of fact, the reason for the entire series of truths must be located outside the series, and this ultimate reason is in a necessary being, that is, God (*Monadology* 37–38). It is this last move that requires some explanation, and Leibniz unfortunately does not give us this in the *Monadology*.

A richer version of the cosmological argument is found in Leibniz's 1697 essay *On the Ultimate Origination of Things*. His fundamental question from the *Principles of Nature and Grace*—why is there something rather than nothing?—is, of course, a demand for a reason for the existence of the entire world, but "a sufficient reason for existence can be discovered in no individual thing nor in the entire collection and series of things" (GP VII 302/AG 149*). After all, any state of the world is explicable in terms of a preceding state of the world, but neither a particular state of the world nor the entire series of states explains why there is a world at all. One natural objection at this point is that the world might simply be eternal, and each world-state is explained by a prior world-state (together with laws of nature) *ad infinitum*. But, for Leibniz, this just shows that, if we accept the principle of sufficient reason, we must seek the reason elsewhere; for "in eternal things, even if there is no cause [*causa*], we must still understand there to be a reason [*ratio*]" (GP VII 302/AG 149).[23] In other words, even if the series of world-states were eternal, it would still only be a succession of states, each of which was necessitated or determined by

---

[22] Leibniz goes on immediately to say that "nothing is simpler and easier than something," suggesting that nothingness is, as it were, the default state of being that can only be overcome and explained through the necessary being. There is, I believe, some tension between this claim and the claim found elsewhere in Leibniz's writings that there is a striving toward existence and that whatever can exist does exist. (A 6.3.581–582/Parkinson 103–105; A 6.4.1444/AG 20; GP VII 303/AG 150) Space constraints prevent me from exploring this in detail.

[23] Leibniz's move here makes clear that his argument, focused on a *reason* (*ratio*) for the world, differs from the Thomistic a posteriori arguments that demand a first mover or a first (efficient) cause (*causa*) (i.e., the "first way" and the "second way"). See *Summa Theologiae*, Ia.2.3.

the prior state, which Leibniz terms the "physical or hypothetical necessity" of the world. While the world is thus physically or hypothetically necessary, it is not "absolutely or metaphysically necessary," for it might not have existed at all. Therefore, Leibniz concludes,

> [i] since the ultimate ground [*ultima radix*] must be in something which is of metaphysical necessity, and [ii] since the reason for an existing thing must come from something that actually exists, [iii] it follows that there must exist some one entity of metaphysical necessity, that is, there must be an entity whose essence is existence, and therefore something must exist which differs from the plurality of things, which differs from the world, which we have granted and shown is not of metaphysical necessity.
>
> (GP VII 303/AG 150)[24]

It is premise (i) that carries this argument and that calls for some explanation. Why should the "ultimate ground" of a thing be in something that is of metaphysical necessity? On Leibniz's view, something is metaphysically necessary if and only if the reason for its existence comes from itself, that is, it is its own ground or its essence includes existence. If the ultimate ground were *not* metaphysically necessary, then it would have its ground or explanation outside itself, which would be self-contradictory. In saying that the ultimate ground must be in something metaphysically necessary, Leibniz is therefore saying that explanations have to end somewhere. In our series of contingent things or world-states, the reasons are always found in a prior state; everything is physically or hypothetically necessary; and the world as a whole was itself seen as a contingent thing, which could not have within it its own reason for existence. Therefore, the ultimate ground is a being "for which a reason cannot be given" (GP VII 303/AG 150), which is to say a being whose essence is existence or whose reason is through itself: God.

Leibniz uses a slightly different version of the cosmological argument in the *Theodicy* to explicate the divine essence. First, insofar as the first cause of the entire series must have been able to survey all other possible worlds, it has understanding. Second, insofar as it was able to select one world among the infinity of possible worlds, it has a will. Third, insofar as it was able to bring about this world, it has power. (Leibniz adds here that "power relates to *being*, wisdom or understanding to *truth*, and will to *good*.") Fourth, insofar as the first cause relates to all possibles, its understanding, will, and power are infinite. And, fifth, insofar as everything is connected together, there is no reason to

---

[24] In AG, one finds "ultima radix" translated as "ultimate ground," which is perfectly acceptable. But it should not lead an unsuspecting reader to think that "ground" translates "ratio," which is more common. On the other hand, it would not be surprising if what Gerhardt has as "radix" should really be "ratio," either by virtue of a mistake on Gerhardt's part or a slip of the pen on Leibniz's part. Compare this with *A Specimen of Discoveries about Marvelous Secrets*, where the same kind of argument is given and Leibniz writes of the "ultima ratio rerum" (A 6.4.1618/MP 77); the same is true in 3 of *A Resumé of Metaphysics* (GP VII 299/MP 145).

suppose more than one God. In other words, Leibniz demonstrates the uniqueness, omniscience, omnipotence, and benevolence of God from the twin assumptions of the contingency of the world and the principle of sufficient reason (GP VI 106–107/H 127–128: *Theodicy* 7).

One of the most famous critiques of a generalized cosmological argument comes from Bertrand Russell, and it is worth noting why Leibniz's argument is perhaps resistant to his critique. According to Russell, if everything must have a cause except for one self-caused cause (*causa sui*), then one might as well consider the world itself as this self-caused cause rather than God.[25] Leaving aside the fact that Leibniz expresses his argument in terms of "ultimate reasons" or "ultimate grounds" rather than "ultimate causes," it is important to see that, for Leibniz, the *world* is not, as it were, a single thing or an individual, which could have an essence that contained existence. The world is simply a collection of genuine individuals and a series of states of their being; it cannot be said to have an essence *simpliciter*, nor could it be said to ever be a *causa sui*.[26] On the other hand, one could, in the spirit of Russell, press Leibniz on this score by denying the principle of sufficient reason when applied to the cosmos itself: it is simply a brute fact that it exists; no reason is required. Similarly, one might reject the thesis that nothingness is genuinely possible. In other words, it is not possible that the world did not exist or, alternatively, the world necessarily exists.

The Argument from Eternal Truths

According to Leibniz, we can also know that God exists because only a God-like mind can make the eternal truths possible. As he writes in 1686, "If there were no eternal substance, there would be no eternal truths; so this too affords a proof of God, who is the root [*radix*] of possibility, for his mind is the very region of ideas or truths" (A 6.4.1618/ MP 77). By "eternal truths" we mean, of course, the truths of mathematics and logic, which are necessary and true in all possible worlds. But Leibniz's argument actually has a broader scope that includes possibilities or essences as well.[27] On Leibniz's view,

---

[25]   See Russell 1957, 6–7. In his Leibniz book, Russell hints at the fact that this critique pushes an advocate of the cosmological argument toward Spinozism (Russell 1937, 177).

[26]   In a recent article, Mogens Laerke (2011) argues that Leibniz's cosmological argument differs from that of Spinoza because Leibniz rejects the Spinozistic idea of God as a *causa sui* and holds rather that God is an *ens a se* or *ens per se*—a being whose existence is simply to be understood through its own essence and through which all other beings are to be conceived. Insofar as this is the case, it would be difficult for Russell to run his argument against the Leibnizian cosmological argument.

[27]   It was claimed in the section on the ontological argument that Leibniz's "pinnacle of modal theory" is the S5 theorem $\Diamond \Box p \to \Box p$, and in a footnote it was pointed out that this is equivalent to the textbook S5 theorem $\Diamond p \to \Box \Diamond p$. Informally, the latter theorem can be expressed as the following: "if p is possible, then p is necessarily possible." For our purposes, however, it shows that possibilities (or essences) are themselves eternal truths. As this is Leibniz's considered position on the nature of essences and possibilities, we have separate confirmation that the "pinnacle of modal theory" is to be found in S5.

there must be a reason why a true proposition is true—that is, every truth requires a "truthmaker"—and there must be something that explains not only the truth of the proposition but also its *reality*. As we saw in his cosmological argument for the existence of God, Leibniz believes that "all reality must be grounded [*fondée*] in something existent" (GP VI 226/H 243*: *Theodicy* 184). Or, as he puts it in *Monadology* 44, "if there is reality in essences or possibles, or indeed, in eternal truths, this reality must be grounded [*fondée*] in something existent and actual" (GP VI 614/AG 218). Since, in one sense, all truths are true by virtue of the relations between the concepts of subject and predicate, one might naturally conclude that the truths of mathematics are simply true by definition; they are analytic truths, and the grounds for their existence and truth are merely human conventions. But Leibniz rejects this kind of Hobbesian nominalist position, according to which the propositions of mathematics are true merely by virtue of definitions and human conventions.[28] On the other hand, one might give a Platonist explanation of the truths and realities of mathematics, according to which the abstract objects of mathematics exist or subsist independently of anything else and propositions are true or false independent of subjective or mental features.[29] Leibniz rejects this option as well, for he believes that the objects of logic and mathematics are not the kinds of things that can subsist by themselves. On his view, only substances can truly be said to exist, and essences, possibilities, or truths require a mind. Therefore, Leibniz believes, it is "the divine understanding which gives reality to the eternal truths" (GP VI 226/ H 243: *Theodicy* 184).

The picture of God that comes out of Leibniz's argument is important. While he locates the reason or ground for the eternal truths in the divine understanding, he is explicitly opposed to the Cartesian position that the eternal truths owe their existence to the divine will.[30] "It is highly erroneous," he writes,

> to suppose that eternal truths and the goodness of things depend on the divine will; for every act of will presupposes a judgement of the intellect about goodness—unless by a change of names one transfers all judgements from the intellect to the will; and even then it cannot be said that the will is a cause of truths, since the judgement is not such a cause. The reason for truths lies in the ideas of things, which are involved in the divine essence itself.
>
> (A 6.4.1618/MP 77)

This last line—that the ideas of things are involved in the divine essence itself—carries a great deal of weight and brings out a certainly anti-Cartesian but still very strong conception of the dependence of truths, essences, and *possibilia* on God. We can see this

---

[28] Leibniz wrote a short and very instructive debate on this subject in 1677. See A 6.4.20–25/AG 268–272.

[29] Dummett (1991, 301) gives a similar definition.

[30] This is one of the most notorious and striking positions of Descartes, whose voluntarism rendered God capable of freely decreeing that, for example, 2 + 2 = 5. (See, for example, his letter to Mersenne of April 15, 1630: AT I 145/CSMK III 23.)

even more clearly in Leibniz's comments on Wachter's *Elucidarius cabalisticus*: "The very reality of the essences, indeed, that by which they flow into existence, is from God. The essences of things are coeternal with God like numbers. And the very essence of God comprehends all other essences, to the extent that God cannot be perfectly conceived without them."[31] But not only is it the case that essences in general and the eternal truths of mathematics and logic in particular are comprehended by or contained within the essence of God but it is also the case that our knowledge of essences and truths brings us into connection with God. According to Leibniz,

> God is the only immediate external object of souls, since there is nothing except him outside of the soul which acts immediately upon it. Our thoughts with all that is in us, insofar as it includes some perfection, are produced without interruption by his continuous operation. . . . And it is thus that our mind is affected immediately by the eternal ideas which are in God, since our mind has thoughts which are in correspondence with them and participate in them. It is in this sense that we can say that our mind sees all things in God.
>
> (GP VI 593–594/L 627)

Thus, the fascinating part of Leibniz's argument and conception of God is that he rejects Hobbesian conventionalist nominalism and Platonist realism in mathematics, while still maintaining a form of nominalism—insofar as only genuine individuals exist, not *abstracta*, as proposed by Platonists—as well as a form of Platonism, insofar as the divine mind illuminates our own souls and understanding and is the ground of all truth.

CONCLUSION

In the end, how successful are Leibniz's arguments for the existence of God? I suspect that none will produce conviction in those who are not theistically inclined. Nevertheless, I do think that Leibniz's arguments should lead us to reflect further on the very issues at hand. Is a necessary being possible? Is the fundamental question of metaphysics—why is there something rather than nothing?—a well-formed question, and if so, do we need to seek the ground of existence outside the world itself? If God does not make the eternal truths of mathematics possible, by virtue of what are mathematical truths true? In what sense do mathematical objects exist? Naturally, Leibniz has a coherent and powerful story to tell that answers such questions, and all students of philosophy must themselves address these questions and see if they can do better.[32]

---

[31] Beeley 2002, 5/AG 273*.
[32] Thanks to Maria Rosa Antognazza for very helpful comments on an earlier draft.

REFERENCES

Adams, Robert Merrihew. 1971. "The Logical Structure of Anselm's Arguments." *Philosophical Review 80*: 28–54.

Adams, Robert Merrihew. 1994. *Leibniz: Determinist, Theist, Idealist*. Oxford: Oxford University Press.

Anselm of Canterbury. 1998. *The Major Works*. Translated by Brian Davies and G. R. Evans. Oxford: Oxford University Press.

Beeley, Philip. 2002. "Leibniz on Wachter's Elucidarius Cabalisticus: A Critical Edition of the So-Called 'Refutation of Spinoza.'" *Leibniz Review 12*: 1–14.

Blumenfeld, David. 1995. "Leibniz's Ontological and Cosmological Arguments." In *The Cambridge Companion to Leibniz*, edited by Nicholas Jolley, 353–381. Cambridge: Cambridge University Press.

Craig, William. 1980. *The Cosmological Argument from Plato to Leibniz*. London: MacMillan.

Descartes, René. 1985–91. *The Philosophical Writings of Descartes*. Translated by John Cottingham, Robert Stoothoff, Dugald Murdoch, and Anthony Kenny. 3 vols. Cambridge: Cambridge University Press. [= CSM followed by volume and page number for vols. 1 and 2; = CSMK III for volume 3.]

Descartes, René. 1996. *Œuvres de Descartes*. Edited by Charles Adam and Paul Tannery. 11 vols. Paris: J. Vrin. [= AT followed by volume and page number]

Dummett, Michael. 1991. *Frege: Philosophy of Mathematics*. Cambridge, Mass.: Harvard University Press.

Fichant, Michel. 1998. "L'Origine de la négation." In *Science et métaphysique dans Descartes et Leibniz*, 85–119. Paris: Presses Universitaires de France.

Forgie, J. William. 1972. "Frege's Objection to the Ontological Argument." *Noûs 6*: 251–265.

Forgie, J. W. 1974. "Existence Assertions and the Ontological Argument." *Mind 73*: 260–262.

Gödel, Kurt. 1995. *Collected Works*. Vol. 3. *Unpublished Essays and Lectures*. Edited by S. Feferman, J. W. Dawson, Jr., W. Goldfarb, C. Parsons and R. N. Solovay Oxford: Oxford University Press.

Harrelson, Kevin. 2008. *The Ontological Argument from Descartes to Hegel*. Amherst, N.Y.: Humanity Books.

Heidegger, Martin. 1953. *Einführung in die Metaphysik*. Tübingen: Max Niemeyer.

Heidegger, Martin. 1957. *Der Satz vom Grund*. Stuttgart: Klett-Cotta.

Jalabert, Jacques. 1960. *Le dieu de Leibniz*. Paris: Presses Universitaires de France.

Janke, Wolfgang. 1963. "Das Ontologische Argument in der Frühzeit des Leibnizschen Denkens (1676–78)." *Kant-Studien 54*: 259–287.

Kant, Immanuel. 1781/1787. *Kritik der reinen Vernunft*. Riga: Hartknoch. [Cited according to the usual A (1781)/B (1787) eds.]

Kant, Immanuel. 1902–. *Immanuel Kants gesammelte Schriften*. 29 vols. Edited by the Royal Prussian Akademie of Sciences. Berlin: Georg Reimer (later Walter de Gruyter). [= Ak. followed by volume and page number]

Laerke, Mogens. 2011. "Leibniz's Cosmological Argument for the Existence of God." *Archiv für Geschichte der Philosophie 93*: 58–84.

Look, Brandon. 2006. "Some Remarks on the Ontological Arguments of Gödel and Leibniz." In *Einheit in der Vielheit: Akten des VIII. Internationalen Leibniz-Kongresses*, edited by H. Breger and S. Erdner 510–517. Hanover: Hartmann.

Look, Brandon. 2011. "Leibniz, Kant and Frege on the Existence Predicate." In *Natur und Subjekt: Akten des IX. Internationalen Leibniz-Kongresses*, edited by H. Breger, J. Herbst and S. Erdner 616–624. Hanover: Hartmann.

Malcolm, Norman. 1960. "Anselm's Ontological Arguments." *Philosophical Review* 69: 41–62.

Oppy, Graham. 1995. *Ontological Arguments and Belief in God*. Cambridge: Cambridge University Press.

Parkinson, G. H. R. 1965. *Logic and Reality in Leibniz's Metaphysics*. Oxford: Clarendon Press.

Russell, Bertrand. 1937. *A Critical Exposition of the Philosophy of Leibniz*. 2nd ed. London: Allen and Unwin.

Russell, Bertrand. 1957. *Why I Am Not a Christian and Other Essays on Religion and Related Subjects*. London: Allen and Unwin.

Sobel, Justin Howard. 1987. "Gödel's Ontological Proof." In *On Being and Saying: Essays for Richard Cartwright*, edited by J. J. Thomson, 241–261. Cambridge, Mass.: MIT Press.

Sobel, Justin Howard. 2004. *Logic and Theism: Arguments for and against the Existence of God*. Cambridge: Cambridge University Press.

St. Thomas Aquinas. 1955–58. *Summa Theologiae*. 5 vols. Madrid: Biblioteca de Autores Christianos. [Cited by part, question, and article.]

CHAPTER 40

∙∙∙

FAITH AND REASON

∙∙∙

MARIA ROSA ANTOGNAZZA

IN the *Rectoratsrede* held on February 28, 1888, at the University of Rostock, the Lutheran theologian and university rector, August Wilhelm Dieckhoff (1823–94), launched a critical assault on "Leibniz's position on revelation."[1] Although nominally a Lutheran, Dieckhoff scoffed, Leibniz did not really follow Luther at all. Instead, in direct contrast to the teaching of the Reformation, he sided with the medieval Scholastics and the "fundamental Pelagian mistake of the Roman-medieval Church" according to which "the natural man can love God above all things."[2] Instead of acknowledging that "faith finds its firm ground only in God's revelation, not in the discernment of reason," Dieckhoff opined, Leibniz reduced revealed theology to natural theology and subordinated revelation to reason. In so doing, the Rostock rector concluded, he paved the way to pantheism and materialism.[3]

Dieckhoff's assessment was far from unusual: it was a standard interpretation of Leibniz which is still reflected in recent literature. Leibniz, to quote recent examples, should be saluted as an Enlightenment hero who fought the good fight of "introducing rationality" into religious questions. The *Theodicy* should be regarded as one of the works in which he appears most explicitly "rationalist" in his defense of the "supremacy of reason"[4] and in his "choice of a strong theological rationalism" or "an extreme rationalism of faith."[5] Leibniz's theological rationalism, however, should be interpreted as an "overturning of Thomism and of scholasticism in general" due to its "apology of

---

[1] August Wilhelm Dieckhoff, *Leibnitz Stellung zur Offenbarung* (Rostock: Stiller, 1888). Unless otherwise stated, translations are my own. My thanks to Howard Hotson and Lucy Sheaf for helpful comments on a draft of this chapter.

[2] Dieckhoff, *Leibnitz Stellung zur Offenbarung*, p. 15.

[3] Idem, esp. pp. 17–19.

[4] Juan Antonio Nicolás, "Le mal comme limite du Principe de raison," in *Lectures et interprétations des Essais de théodicée de G. W. Leibniz*, edited by P. Rateau (Stuttgart: Steiner, 2011), pp. 211–227 (here pp. 226–227).

[5] Michel Fichant, "Vérité, foi et raison dans la Théodicée," *Lectures et interprétations des Essais de théodicée de G. W. Leibniz*, edited by P. Rateau (Stuttgart: Steiner, 2011), pp. 247–262 (here pp. 248–249).

reason,"[6] contrary to Dieckhoff's diagnosis of its being the result of "Pelagian" scholastic tendencies.

At the opposite end of the spectrum, other recent contributions detect instead in Leibniz a "moderate fideism" anticipating contemporary "Reformed Epistemology."[7] Leibniz's position, they claim, is similar to "Reformed Epistemology" insofar as it views religious beliefs as "properly basic." According to this alternative interpretation, Leibniz "assigns to faith the role of a primary truth. For Leibniz, some religious propositions can be believed immediately and without an additional examination and evaluation by reason."[8] Unlike Locke, who requires that we should carefully examine and evaluate not only the religious experience of others but also our own religious experiences, Leibniz is read as granting "immunity" "from further justificatory requirements" to first-person religious experiences.[9] These direct religious experiences would ground, for Leibniz, first-person religious beliefs that can be held in an epistemically justified manner without any further evidence or rational evaluation.

In contrast to these two opposite interpretations, this chapter will argue that Leibniz is neither a proto-Deist who subordinates revelation to reason, nor a Reformed Epistemologist ante-litteram who borders on fideism. Instead, Leibniz develops a "middle way" between a theological rationalism which denies any genuine epistemic space to truths above reason and a fideism which denies the need for religious belief to be rationally justified.[10] This middle way is deeply indebted to the scholastic tradition of philosophical theology—both the classic medieval tradition and the Protestant Scholastics of Leibniz's own time. While remarkably close to the Thomist conception of the epistemic space proper to faith, it is at the same time firmly anchored in Leibniz's Protestant background. Notably, it significantly diverges from the intellectualistic conception of theology characteristic of the Thomist tradition by regarding theology as ultimately practical.[11]

---

[6] Fichant, "Vérité, foi et raison dans la Théodicée," pp. 261–262.

[7] Cf. Vincent Delecroix, "Comment ne pas faire taire la raison après l'avoir fait trop parler: premisses de la philosophie de la religion," in C. Leduc, P. Rateau, J.-L. Solère (eds.), *Leibniz et Bayle* (Stuttgart: Steiner, 2015), pp. 269–286 (see pp. 276–281, comparing Leibniz's position to Alvin Plantinga's proposal in "Reason and belief in God," in *Faith and Rationality*, edited by A. Plantinga and N. Wolterstorff (Notre Dame, IN: University of Notre Dame Press, 1983), pp. 29–34).

[8] Michael Losonski, "Locke and Leibniz on religious faith," in *British Journal for the History of Philosophy* 20/4 (2012), pp. 703–721 (here p. 703).

[9] Losonski, "Locke and Leibniz on religious faith," pp. 718–719.

[10] I have argued for this interpretation in a number of publications, notably *Leibniz on the Trinity and the Incarnation: Reason and Revelation in the Seventeenth Century* (New Haven: Yale, 2007). A similar line of interpretation is defended, for instance, by Paul Rateau, "Sur la conformité de la foi avec la raison: Leibniz contre Bayle," in *Revue philosophique de la France et de l'étranger* 136/4 (2011), pp. 467–485.

[11] According to Aquinas, although "sacred doctrine" encompasses both speculative and practical aspects, it is speculative rather than practical. Cf. Thomas Aquinas, *Summa Theologiae, Textum Leoninum* (Rome 1886–87; now available online in *Corpus Thomisticum*), I, q. 1 a. 4 (hereafter *ST*). On Leibniz's view of theology as ultimately practical, see the last section of the chapter on "Philosophical Theology and Christian Doctrines."

WHAT IS FAITH?

Before embarking in a discussion of the relationship between faith and reason, it is helpful to consider what Leibniz means by "faith" and by "reason." Leibniz's conception of faith is richer than one might expect. It embraces both cognitive and noncognitive dimensions, involving intellectual apprehension and rational appetite, intellect and will.[12]

As it is generally the case with the intellect (the first of the two main faculties of our mental life), the cognitive or intellective element of faith has truth as its object. This is, however, a specific kind of truth: not the truth that the human intellect can reach in a natural way without the help of the supernatural light of faith, but "the truth which God has revealed in an extraordinary way."[13] The proper objects of faith are therefore truths "above reason," that is, revealed truths that surpass the ability of the human intellect to discover and fully comprehend.[14]

In turn, considering not the object or content of faith but the ground or reason for assenting to this content, faith "can be compared to experience." Faith, "as regards the motives which verify it," depends "on the experience of those who have seen the miracles, on which revelation is founded, and on the Tradition worthy of credibility, which has transmitted them to us, both through the Scriptures, and through the report of those who have preserved them." This is similar, Leibniz continues, to any belief based on testimony. For instance, we ground our beliefs about China "on the *experience* of those who have seen China, and on the *credibility* of their report, when we give credence [*ajoutons foy*] to the wonders which are narrated to us of that distant country."[15] This second aspect of faith captures faith as trust—more specifically, faith as trust in testimony that mediates divine testimony (or divine revelation) itself.

There is, however, a third component of faith, one that concerns the appetitive aspect of the human soul. As is generally the case with the volitional element of human life, its object is the good. The third aspect of faith is constituted by a longing for the good, which is desired and loved as our fulfilment and happiness. This striving for the good is informed by charity (the highest kind of love) rather than by rational arguments, and it is the fruit of the "internal movement of the Holy Spirit who takes possession of souls,

---

[12] Paul Lodge and Ben Crowe, "Leibniz, Bayle, and Locke on faith and reason," in *American Catholic Philosophical Quarterly* 76/4 (2002), pp. 575–600, show that Leibniz's account of faith is not deflationary. Although faith, for Leibniz, must be grounded in reason, in its full sense it is not reduced to reasonable belief but also requires a supernatural infusion of grace.

[13] *Theodicy*, "Preliminary Discourse," §1 (GP VI 49).

[14] See, e.g., *Theodicy*, "Preliminary Discourse," §23 (GP VI 64).

[15] *Theodicy*, "Preliminary Discourse," § 1 (GP VI 49–50). See the section on "Motives of Credibility" for a more detailed discussion of this passage.

and persuades them and brings them to the good, that is to say, to faith and charity, without always having need of motives."[16]

In sum, Leibniz's conception seems to capture the three traditional aspects of the act of faith expressed by the Thomist formula *credere Deum* (to believe "that God" or to believe some content about God); *credere Deo* (to believe God; that is, trust revelation); *credere in Deum* (to believe in God as fulling one's life, leading to happiness, and so on).[17] Moreover, Leibniz stresses another traditional component of orthodox accounts of faith: namely, the role of divine grace. This is a role acknowledged by all main Christian confessions but especially emphasized by Protestants, who perceived the Roman Catholic Church as inclining instead toward Pelagianism. More specifically, Leibniz distinguishes between "human faith" and "divine faith": "human faith" is grounded in "explicable" reasons or rational "motives of credibility"; "divine faith," or faith in the full sense of the term, is grounded in "inexplicable reasons," that is, in a direct religious experience which comes from grace.

> The reasons of our persuasion are of two kinds, those of one kind are explicable; those of the other kind are inexplicable. Those which I call explicable can be proposed to other people by distinct reasoning; but inexplicable reasons consist only in our conscience or perception, and in an experience of an interior feeling into which others cannot enter, if one does not find a way to make them feel the same things in the same manner. . . . Now, those who say that they find in themselves a divine internal light, or a ray [of light] which makes them feel some truth, base themselves on some inexplicable reasons. And I see that not only the Protestants but also the Roman Catholic use this ray [of light]: since—in addition to the motives of belief or of credibility (as they call them), that is to say, in addition to the explicable reasons of our Faith, which are nothing else than a collection of arguments of different degrees of force, and which even taken all together can only ground a human faith—they demand a light of grace from heaven capable of producing a full conviction, and which forms what is called divine Faith.[18]

In his virtual discussion with Locke in the *Nouveaux Essais*, Leibniz's spokesman (Theophilus) agrees with Locke's representative (Philalethes) that faith must be

---

[16] *Theodicy*, "Preliminary Discourse," §1 (GP VI 50). T. Allam Hillman, "Leibniz and Luther on the non-cognitive component of faith," in *Sophia* 52/2 (2013), pp. 219–234, notes that Leibniz follows the Thomist tradition rather than Luther in emphasizing love (*caritas*) as the noncognitive element of faith par excellence. According to Luther, the key noncognitive component of faith is trust in God's promise of mercy. Although trust is also present as an element of Leibniz's account of faith, it seems to be mainly intended as trust in human testimony mediating divine revelation.

[17] *ST* II–II, q. 2 a. 2.

[18] A I vi 76. Leibniz's use of this distinction is found in the context of his exchange with Paul Pellisson-Fontanier of 1690–91. The distinction is found also in the *Examen Religionis Christianae (Systema Theologicum)*, c. April–October 1686 (A VI iv 2362); the *Nouveaux Essais* (book IV, chap. xviii, §9; A VI vi 497); and the *Theodicy* ("Preliminary Discourse," §29; GP VI 67–98).

grounded in reason[19] but is keen to underscore that there is more to it than reasonable belief:

> If you take faith to be only what rests on motives of credibility (as they are called) and detach it from the inward grace which immediately moulds our spirit to faith, all that you say, sir, is incontestable. It must be acknowledged that there are many judgements which are more evident than those which depend on these motives. Some people have advanced toward them more than others, and indeed there are plenty of people who have never known such motives, and even less weighed them, and therefore do not even have what could be regarded as a motive of probability. But the inward grace of the Holy Spirit makes up for this immediately in a supernatural manner, and this is what theologians call divine faith. It is true that God never bestows it unless what he is making one believe is grounded in reason—otherwise he would destroy the means of knowing the truth, and would open the door to Enthusiasm—but it is not necessary that all those who have this divine faith know these reasons, and even less that they have them always before their eyes. Otherwise simple people and the feeble-minded, at least now, would never have the true faith, and the most enlightened people would not have it when they might need it most, since they cannot always remember the reasons for believing.[20]

Leibniz's claim is not that there is no need for religious belief to be supported by rational arguments[21] but that not everyone needs to know what these arguments are, and no one is required to remember them at all times in order to hold a rationally justified religious belief. Whether or not one knows or remembers them, the important point is that there *are* (and there must be) such arguments and that they can be recalled by someone in the community if and when faith is challenged:

> there can be faith even when one does not think, or perhaps never thought, of the grounds of persuasion sought from human reason. Indeed, the analysis of faith is neither always necessary, nor required from all, nor does everyone's condition bear the difficulty of this examination. In virtue of the very nature of true faith, however, it is necessary [*necesse est*] that those who, in the fear of God, examine the truth more attentively, should be able to put in place an analysis of its motives, when occasion

---

[19] *Nouveaux Essais*, book IV, chap. xvii, §24; A VI vi 494.

[20] *Nouveaux Essais*, book IV, chap. xviii, §9; A VI vi 497. See also *Theodicy*, "Preliminary Discourse," §§40 and 52 (GP VI 73, 79).

[21] See, e.g., *Nouveaux Essais*, book IV, chap. xvii, §24; A VI vi 494: "wise people have always been suspicious of those who have maintained that there is no need to trouble with reasons and proofs when it is a question of believing—something which is indeed impossible unless 'believe' is taken to mean 'recite,' or repeat and let it pass without taking any trouble over it"; *Examen Religionis Christianae*, A VI vi 2361: "In turn, revelation must be distinguished by certain marks (commonly called motives of credibility) from which it can be established that what is contained in it, and is shown to us, is God's will and not the illusion of an evil demon, or our sinister interpretation. And indeed, if any revelation is destitute of such marks, there is no obligation to submit to it."

requires. If it were not so, the Christian religion would have nothing to distinguish it from a false religion.

(Examen Religionis Christianae, A VI iv 2362)

In other words, the ability to produce rational arguments in support of the Christian religion is not needed for *salvation*. This fact, however, does not eliminate the need for reasons of credibility that can be presented to those who ask for them. Answering the objection that the "internal declaration of God is sufficient without rational arguments, for many people believe in accordance with the simplicity of their own heart, even if they know no rational reasons for believing," Leibniz writes:

> I agree that many people, with the singular benevolence of God adapting itself to the capacity of all, possess a true faith without having any convincing reasons for it, and that these people can be saved. But our religion would be wretched if it lacked persuasive arguments, and it would not be preferable to that of the Mohammedans or the pagans since no reason could be given to those who asked for one, nor could the faith be defended against impiety or even against the doubts which often make pious men anxious.[22]

Thus, to the objection that "we can be saved without logic," Leibniz replies decisively: "I agree, for we can also be saved without reasoning. . . . Yet we are unable to grasp and uphold the foundations of faith without reasoning."[23] In fact, according to Leibniz's psychology of belief, *any* belief must be based on some reasons, although these reasons may well fall short of watertight formal arguments: "it is obvious that nothing can be believed if one does not think that one has some proof or ground for it. Therefore it must be acknowledged that we all have need of some examination, otherwise religion would be arbitrary." "In order to believe, faith must be presented in a credible way: otherwise there is no obligation to believe."[24] Moreover, rational motives of credibility that support faith are important due to the very fact that they are "explicable"; that is, they can be communicated and shared with others. They constitute "public" as opposed to "private" marks of truth that are needed in religion as in philosophy.[25]

On the other hand, these rational arguments do not provide the full foundation on which the Christian faith rests.[26] Rather, they constitute the preliminary checks on the trustworthiness of a witness or a messenger whose testimony defies appearances and common experience:

---

[22] *Dialogus inter Theologum et Misosophum* (A VI iv 2215). Trans. by Lloyd Strickland in *Leibniz on God and Religion* (London: Bloomsbury, 2016), p. 98.

[23] *Dialogus inter Theologum et Misosophum* (A VI iv 2217). Trans. by Strickland in *Leibniz on God and Religion*, p. 101 (slightly modified).

[24] Respectively, A I vi 76 and 145. See also A VI vi 494.

[25] Cf. *Specimen Demonstrationum Catholicarum seu Apologia Fidei ex Ratione* (A VI iv 2323, 2327).

[26] Cf. A VI iv 2323.

the *motives of credibility* justify, once and for all, the authority of the Holy Scripture before the Tribunal of Reason, so that afterwards Reason surrenders to it, as to a new light, and sacrifices to it all its likelihoods. It is a bit like a new president sent by the Prince, who must show his Letters Patent in the Assembly where he will later have to preside.[27]

Moreover, rational arguments are not sufficient to convince on their own. For the "full conviction" of true faith (i.e., "divine" as opposed to merely "human" faith), the divine illumination of grace is needed. "Contrary to the Pelagians," Leibniz writes in the *Nouveaux Essais*, "all three of the accepted confessions[28] . . . agree in teaching that there is a supernatural grace in all who have faith" (A VI vi 502). Thus, "aside from human reasons for faith, or motives of credibility, a certain inward operation of the Holy Spirit is required to yield what is called divine faith, and to secure the mind in truth" (*Examen Religionis Christianae*, A VI iv 2362).

Most importantly, faith is not merely a cognitive state involving belief and the intellect. True faith involves also the will and our affective states ("the heart"):

Divine Faith itself, when it is kindled in the soul, is something more than an opinion, and does not depend upon the occasions or the motives that have given it birth; it goes beyond the intellect, and takes possession of the will and of the heart, to make us act with warmth and pleasure, as the law of God commands, without further need to think of reasons, or stop at argumentative difficulties that the mind may envisage.[29]

WHAT IS REASON?

Reason, in turn, is defined by Leibniz (at least in this context) as the "concatenation of truths, but especially (when it is compared with faith) of those truths that the human mind can attain naturally without being helped by the lights of faith."[30] Defined in this way, Leibniz continues, reason cannot be faulted, contrary to those who argue (like Pierre Bayle) that human reason is a fallible instrument that often deceives us and that, therefore, cannot be trusted. To be sure, understood as the faculty of reasoning correctly, reason is not infallible. There are indeed plenty of cases in which we are deceived by the false appearance of sound reasoning as much as we are deceived by the appearances

---

[27] *Theodicy*, "Preliminary Discourse," §29; GP VI 67. See also *Examen Religionis Christianae* (A VI vi 2362).

[28] Leibniz is referring to the Evangelical (or Lutheran), the Reformed (or Calvinist), and the Roman Catholic confessions.

[29] *Theodicy*, "Preliminary Discourse," §29; GP VI 67–68.

[30] *Theodicy*, "Preliminary Discourse," §1; GP VI 49.

of the senses.[31] The point is, however, that when the reasoning *is* sound—that is, when there is a sound "concatenation of truths and objections in due form"[32]—"it is impossible for reason to deceive us" (GP VI 87). In this sense of a concatenation of truths, human reason is as certain as God's reason.

According to Leibniz, it is therefore mistaken to maintain, like Bayle, that revealed doctrines conform to the "supreme and universal reason which is in the divine intellect, or to reason in general" but do not conform "to the portion of reason of which humankind makes use to judge of things."[33]

> This portion of reason which we possess is a gift of God, and consists in the natural light which has remained in us in the midst of corruption. This portion is conform to the whole, and differs from the reason which is in God only as a drop of water differs from the Ocean, or rather as the finite differs from the infinite. Therefore mysteries may surpass it, but they cannot be contrary to it. Something could not be contrary to a part without being contrary to the whole. That which contradicts a proposition of Euclid, is contrary to the *Elements* of Euclid. (GP VI 84)

In brief, divine reason and human reason are in conformity. What is contradictory for one is contradictory (and therefore necessarily false) for the other. On the other hand, due to the limitation of human reason, there are infinitely many truths which God's reason embraces but which surpass human comprehension.

Leibniz fully endorses, therefore, the traditional distinction between "contrary to reason" and "above reason."[34] A truth can never be contrary to reason (whether divine reason or human reason), but it can be above *human* reason. "Contrary to reason" is that which implies contradiction and is therefore logically and metaphysically impossible; that is, absolutely impossible. "Above reason" is what goes against mere "physical necessity"; that is, against the necessity of the contingent laws of nature which God has chosen but which admit exceptions for reasons of superior order. Physical necessity amounts, for Leibniz, to mere "moral necessity" or "hypothetical necessity"; that is, the necessity of a choice determined by perfect wisdom and goodness or the necessity that results from a set of preconditions that are not in themselves logically or metaphysically necessary. Thus, truths above reason may clash with our experience, with likelihood, and with appearances, but can never imply contradiction:

> The distinction that one commonly makes between what is *above reason*, and what is *against reason*, agrees quite well with the distinction that we just made between the

---

[31] *Theodicy*, "Preliminary Discourse," §65; GP VI 87: "If by Reason we mean in general the faculty to reason well or badly, I grant that this faculty could deceive us, and in fact it deceives us, and that the appearances of our understanding are often as deceptive as those of the senses."

[32] "A correct reasoning is nothing else than a concatenation of truths" (GP VI 86).

[33] *Theodicy*, "Preliminary Discourse," §61; GP VI 84.

[34] See *Theodicy*, "Preliminary Discourse," §§17, 23, 60, 63; *Nouveaux Essais*, book IV, chap. xviii, §9; A VI vi 498–499.

two types of necessity [metaphysical necessity and physical necessity].[35] For what is against reason is against the absolutely certain and indispensable truths; and what is above reason, is only against what one commonly experiences or comprehends. That is why I am amazed to see that there are people of spirit who fight against this distinction, and that Mr. Bayle is among these. This distinction is certainly well founded. A truth is above reason when our spirit (or even every created spirit) cannot comprehend it: and such is, in my opinion, the Holy Trinity; such are the miracles reserved to God alone, as, for example, the Creation; such is the choice of the order of the Universe, which depends on the Universal Harmony, and on the distinct knowledge of an infinite number of things at once. But a truth will never be against reason, and in the case of a dogma fought and refuted by reason, very far from being incomprehensible, one can say that nothing is easier to comprehend nor more manifest than its absurdity. (GP VI 64)

As indicated in this passage, "above reason" is (more generally) what cannot be comprehended by human reason because its explanation implies an infinite chain of reasons. In this general sense, not only the mysteries of faith are above (human) reason but also the comprehension of any individual substance or the perfect explanation of any truth of fact: "the comprehension itself of individual substances is impossible to the created mind because they involve the infinite. For this reason it is impossible to provide a perfect explanation of the things of the universe [*Unde fit ut rerum universi perfecta ratio reddi non possit*]. And nothing prevents certain divinely revealed dogmas from being so."[36]

Moreover, "comprehension" is for Leibniz a technical term to be read against the backdrop of his account of the degrees of knowledge.[37] Our knowledge has increasing degrees of perfection depending on the extent to which we are able to know the properties or requisites that enter into the notion of something. "Knowledge is *clear*, therefore, when I have that from which I can recognise the thing represented, and this [clear knowledge] is in turn either confused or distinct. It is *confused* when I cannot enumerate one by one the marks which are sufficient to distinguish the thing from others." On the other hand, it is *distinct* when I am able to distinguish something from everything else by the enumeration of sufficient marks or requisites; that is, when I have a definition. When "all that enters into a distinct notion is in turn known distinctly, that is, when the analysis is carried through to the end, knowledge is *adequate*."[38]

Comprehension implies adequate knowledge and adequate notions (or "ideas"). "I call comprehension," Leibniz writes, "not merely when distinct ideas are involved, but when there are adequate ideas, that is, when we have not only a definition or analysis of the terms proposed, but any term involved in the definition is in turn analysed until we

---

[35] *Theodicy*, "Preliminary Discourse," §21; GP VI 63.
[36] *Annotatiunculae subitaneae ad Tolandi Librum De Christianismo Mysteriis carente* (1701); Dutens V 147.
[37] See *Meditationes de Cognitione, Veritate et Ideis* (1684), A VI iv 585–592.
[38] *Meditationes de Cognitione, Veritate et Ideis* (1684), A VI iv 585–592 (here 586–587).

reach primitive terms, as in the case of numbers."[39] Thus, as he explains in the *Theodicy*, "to *comprehend* something, it is not enough to have some ideas of it, but it is necessary to have all the ideas of everything that goes into its make-up, and all these ideas must be clear, distinct and *adequate*" (GP VI 92). In the case of individual substances and contingent truths (or "truths of fact"), however, such an analysis involves an infinite process in which there is no end. Hence, in these cases, there is no possibility of adequate knowledge for the discursive reasoning of limited human beings (as opposed to the intuitive, nonanalytical science of vision proper only to God). Most of our cognition is in fact confused cognition or (at best) distinct but not adequate cognition; that is, cognition in which we have achieved an explanation and some degree of understanding, but these are far from perfect. "It is not necessary," Leibniz concludes, "to require always what I call *adequate notions*, which contain nothing that has not been explained, since even sensible qualities such as heat, light, sweetness, do not supply us with such notions. So we agree that the mysteries receive an explanation, but this explanation is imperfect" (GP VI 80).

THE CONFORMITY OF FAITH WITH REASON

Truths of faith, or true revealed doctrines, as any other truths, can therefore be "above reason" but can never be "against reason."[40] They can and should receive an explanation, but this explanation falls well short of comprehension. In brief, true faith, based on a genuine divine revelation, can only be in conformity with reason. Both reason and revelation are gifts of God: "their fight would be a fight of God against himself."[41]

Granted that truths of faith must be free of contradiction as a condition sine qua non of their truth, the problem which confronts Leibniz at this point is how human beings can determine that this condition is met by the mysteries of the Christian revelation. How can human reason determine whether a certain doctrine is or is not free of contradiction if this doctrine is by definition above human reason? For religious truths above reason, a positive proof of possibility does not seem achievable. According to Leibniz, there are in fact two ways of knowing the possibility of something: a priori and a posteriori. An a priori proof would require an analysis "carried through to the end." If the notions in question are completely analyzed into all their elements and no contradiction has appeared, their possibility is proved. As we have seen, such an analysis would

---

[39] *Annotatiunculae subitaneae*; Dutens V 147.

[40] Note that this is a view already supported by Thomas Aquinas, who writes in the *Summa contra Gentiles* 1, 7: "The truth of reason is not contrary to the truth of the Christian faith. Although the truth of the Christian faith which we have discussed surpasses the capacity of human reason, nevertheless what reason is naturally endowed with cannot be contrary to that truth." Leibniz is fond of mentioning the recommendation of the Fifth Lateran Council (1512–17) "to illuminate the truth of faith through sound reason" (A VI iv 2324). Cf. Grua 67 and GP VI 56.

[41] GP VI 73; see also GP VI 67.

correspond to adequate knowledge or comprehension. Adequate knowledge, however, is not possible in the case of truths above reason since, by definition, they are beyond human comprehension. An a posteriori proof, on the other hand, is based on experience since what we experience as existing is also certainly possible.[42] Yet, as Leibniz admits, truths above reason such as the Christian mysteries clash with our experience.

In order to tackle these problems, Leibniz develops a "strategy of defense" in which the notion of "presumption" plays a central role. Inspired by juridical practice and by procedures well-established within the *ars disputandi*, he points out that for something that has not been (or cannot be) positively demonstrated to be possible (i.e., noncontradictory), one can invoke a presumption of possibility that remains valid until the opposite (i.e., contradictoriness) is proved. In other words, a thesis is innocent (i.e., a presumption of possibility can be claimed in its favor) until proven guilty. Or, as Leibniz puts it in the *Nouveaux Essais*, "every time logical necessity is not demonstrated, one can presume in a proposition only physical necessity" (A VI vi 499). People, therefore, should not be too quick "to reject everything that does not conform to the order of nature, even when they cannot prove its absolute impossibility" (A VI vi 498). The burden of proof is on those attacking the thesis, not on those defending it. It is up to the attacker to prove that the thesis in question is contradictory; the defender of the thesis has merely the task of showing that the arguments presented by her adversary are not conclusive. As long as there is no demonstration of contradictoriness, something can legitimately be presumed possible.

This notion of presumption is introduced by Leibniz in defense of the Christian mysteries as early as his *Defensio Trinitatis* of 1669. In this youthful text, after his response to the charges of contradiction raised by the anti-Trinitarian Andreas Wissowatius, Leibniz writes: "Until the contrary has been more adequately proved, we will continue to maintain this statement: that the Son and the Holy Spirit are he who is the one God" (A VI i 520); "Anything is presumed [to be] possible until the contrary is proved" (A VI i 522). Toward the end of his life, in a text of 1702, Leibniz advances a similar claim as a general metaphysical thesis according to which presumption favors possibility, and the burden of proof therefore falls on those who deny this possibility:

> any being must be judged possible, *donec probetur contrarium* [until the contrary has been proved], until it is shown that it is not [possible]. This is what is called *presumption*, which is incomparably more than a simple *supposition*, since the majority of suppositions should not be admitted unless they are proved: but all that has presumption on its side must be taken as true until it is refuted. . . . [P]ossibility is always presumed and must be held as true until impossibility is proved. Thus this argument has the power to shift the *onus probandi in adversarium*, or of charging the opponent with the burden of proof.[43]

---

[42] *Meditationes de Cognitione, Veritate et Ideis* (A VI iv 589).

[43] *Raisons que M. Jaquelot m'a envoyées pour justifier l'Argument contesté de des-Cartes qui doit prouver l'existence de Dieu, avec mes reponses*, November 20, 1702; GP III 444.

The thought that presumption is stronger than supposition or conjecture is echoed both in the *Nouveaux Essais* and in the *Theodicy*, where Leibniz clarifies that "to presume" is not to accept without proof but to accept provisionally until a proof to the contrary is forthcoming:

> As for "presumption," which is a jurists' term, good usage by them distinguishes it from "conjecture." It is something more than that, and which should be accepted provisionally as true until there is a proof to the contrary. . . . In this sense, therefore, to *presume* is not *to accept before* the proof, which is not at all permitted, but *to accept in advance* but not without foundation, while waiting for a proof to the contrary.
> Amongst lawyers that is called "presumption" which must provisionally pass for truth in case the contrary is not proved; and it says more than "conjecture."[44]

In the case of the mysteries, a believer is epistemically justified "*to accept in advance* but not without foundation" (i.e., for Leibniz, on the basis of motives of credibility) their possibility until the contrary is proved. Thus, "*to presume* is . . . to hold something as certain until the opposite is proved" (A VI ii 567).

Moreover, Leibniz stresses that improbability must be sharply distinguished from impossibility. Mysteries are improbable according to reason.[45] "At first glance," they may even seem impossible.[46] It is granted from the very beginning that, precisely in so far as they are "mysteries," they are against appearances and contrary to the verisimilitudes of reason. It is enough, however, that they are not absurd, and any alleged absurdity requires a positive demonstration of contradictoriness.[47] From their contrariety to experience follows, in fact, only improbability, not impossibility:

> Merely the improbability of a thing is proved by induction from other examples, as when the Socinians say that in all of nature there is to be found no Being that is one in number which has three Subsistences; from this impossibility is not inferred, only improbability. Induction infers improbability, Demonstration impossibility. (A VI vi 553)

In sum, the problem of how human reason can check the contradictoriness or noncontradictoriness of a doctrine above its comprehension is solved by shifting from a positive argument to a negative argument; that is, from a proof of the possibility of the mysteries to a proof that their impossibility has not been proved. If a doctrine is a genuine divine revelation, it will always be possible to defend it against the charge of contradiction since no true revelation could be against reason.[48]

---

[44] Respectively, *Nouveaux Essais*, book IV, chap. xiv, §4; A VI vi 457, and *Theodicy*, "Preliminary Discourse," §33; GP VI 69.

[45] Cf. *Commentatiuncula de Judice Controversiarum*, §§33–34 (A VI i 552–3).

[46] Cf. *De Demonstratione Possibilitatis Mysteriorum Eucharistiae* (A VI i 515).

[47] Cf., e.g., *Theodicy*, "Preliminary Discourse," §28.

[48] See, e.g., *Theodicy*, "Preliminary Discourse," §§22–25. The Latin translation of the *Theodicy* (revised by Leibniz) adds to §58 of the "Preliminary Discourse" a reference to *ST* I, q. I, a. 8, where Thomas

The next step of the "strategy of defense" proposed by Leibniz is therefore to respond to objections against the mysteries. Leibniz is very clear that the burden of proof is on those who attack the mysteries, not on those who defend them.[49] It is up to the attacker to prove that a doctrine presumed true on the basis of a long ecclesiastical tradition is in fact false because it implies contradiction. The defender can limit herself to showing that the arguments presented by the objector are not conclusive (e.g., it is sufficient "to deny the universality of some proposition of the objection or to criticize its form")[50] without this involving any positive argument in favor of the thesis that is attacked. Those who uphold the mysteries grant in fact from the outset that, being above human reason, their truth cannot be demonstrated.[51] On the other hand, human reason can attain what is superior to it not by "penetrating it" but by supporting its possibility, "as we can attain the sky by sight, and not by touch."[52]

MOTIVES OF CREDIBILITY

Presumption, however, does not discriminate on its own between competing and opposed religious doctrines which could also claim for themselves a presumption of possibility. In order to establish the greater credibility of its doctrines over competing religions, a religion must support such a claim in some other way. This is the role of the "motives of credibility"; that is, the motives or reasons that can be produced to uphold the *credibility* of a putative divine revelation.

As we have already seen, the condition sine qua non of the credibility of any doctrine is, first of all, the lack of any proven contradiction. Polytheism, for instance, would not have for Leibniz any credibility since its falsity follows from the uniqueness of God, for which Leibniz argues, in turn, on the basis of the principle of identity of indiscernibles.[53] Second, in order for any religious doctrine to be credible, we must be able to grasp to some extent the meaning of the words that express this doctrine. "Faith," Leibniz writes, "is believing. Believing is holding something to be true. Truth is not of words but of things; for whoever holds something to be true, holds that the thing is such as the words signify [*Fides est credere. Credere est verum putare. Veritas est non verborum sed rerum;*

Aquinas writes: "since faith is based on infallible truth, and it is impossible to demonstrate the contrary of truth, it is evident that arguments brought against faith are not demonstrations but arguments that can be answered."

[49] Cf., e.g., *Theodicy*, "Preliminary Discourse," §58 (GP VI 82); §73 (GP VI 93); §77 (GP VI 95–6); §78 (GP VI 96).

[50] *Theodicy*, "Preliminary Discourse," §72 (GP VI 92).

[51] Cf., e.g., *Theodicy*, "Preliminary Discourse," §75 (GP VI 94).

[52] *Theodicy*, "Preliminary Discourse," §72 (GP VI 91).

[53] See A VI iii 396 and R. M. Adams, *Leibniz: Determinist, Theist, Idealist* (Oxford: Oxford University Press, 1994), p. 153. Cf. also *Il n'y a qu'un seul Dieu* (A VI iv 2211–12).

nam qui verum putat, putat sic rem se habere, ut verba significant], but no one can do this, unless he knows what the words mean or at least thinks about their meaning."[54]

Crucially, however, a confused degree of knowledge is sufficient. Most of our cognition is indeed of this kind. It would be unreasonable to expect higher epistemic standards for the supernatural realm than those routinely accepted in our grasp of the natural world or of many theoretical matters:

> it is not always necessary for faith to know what sense of the words is true as long as we understand it, nor do we positively reject it, but rather leave it in doubt even though we might be inclined towards some other [sense]. Indeed, it suffices that we believe in the first place that whatever sense is contained in the words, is true, and this first and foremost in the mysteries in which the practice does not change, whatever the meaning may finally be [§22]. Nonetheless, it is necessary that the intellect should not fall nakedly over the words, like a parrot,[55] but that some sense should appear before it, albeit a general and confused one, and almost disjunctive, as the country fellow, or other common man, has of nearly all theoretical things. . . . [S]o this faith will be disjunctive, inclining nevertheless to one side. And this is in fact, if you pay attention, what many Christians do in practice.[56]

Leibniz is keen to stress that this kind of "blind thinking [*cogitatio caeca*]" is sufficient to guide reasonable action. We rely on it in all sort of contexts, including in theoretical discussions in which (for instance) philosophers speak confidently of "matter," "form," and "cause."[57] His conclusion is that, a fortiori, in matters concerning the supernatural realm, such confused cognition ought to be sufficient for the most important of all practical purposes, namely, salvation:

> To anyone who maintains that a distinct cognition of the meaning of the mysteries of faith is necessary to Salvation, it will be demonstrated by me that hardly the thousandth of Christians . . . ever have had it. And as a consequence, it suffices for Salvation to hold onto the formula expressed in the Holy Scripture, with a confused cognition of the meaning by the intellect, and with a kind of disjunctive assent or opinion. (A VI i 552)

---

[54] *Commentatiuncula de Judice Controversiarum*, §20; A VI i 550.

[55] Ursula Goldenbaum, "Die Commentatiuncula de judice als Leibnizens erste philosophische Auseinandersetzung mit Spinoza nebst der Mitteilung über ein neuaufgefundenes Leibnizstück," in *Labora Diligenter*, edited by M. Fontius et al. (Stuttgart: Steiner, 1999), pp. 61–107, shows that Leibniz is directing here his criticism against Spinoza (see esp. pp. 80, 90–93; the comparison with the parrot is found in chapter XIII of Spinoza's *Tractatus Theologico-Politicus*). See also Ursula Goldenbaum, "Spinoza's parrot, Socinian syllogism and Leibniz's metaphysics: Leibniz's three strategies for defending Christian mysteries," in *American Catholic Philosophical Quarterly* 76/4 (2002), pp. 551–574.

[56] *Commentatiuncula de Judice Controversiarum*, §§21–22; A VI i 550–1.

[57] A VI i 551–2. The parallel between our cognition of the natural world and our cognition of supernatural matters is especially emphasized in Leibniz's *Annotatiunculae subitaneae ad Tolandi Librum De Christianismo Mysteriis carente* (August 8, 1701); Dutens V 142–9.

Equally importantly, "as regards the motives which verify it," the Christian faith depends "on the experience of those who have seen the miracles, on which revelation is founded, and on the Tradition worthy of credibility, which has transmitted them to us" (GP VI 49–50). Before any assessment of the *content* of Scripture, Leibniz is well aware of the need to verify the authenticity and antiquity of the texts using the philological and historical tools that would be employed for any other historical work. It is through these texts that the testimony about a putative divine revelation has reached us. As in any other case, their trustworthiness needs to be established "through reason and history," independently of what the texts say of themselves since a self-testimony of authenticity would not do.[58] In clear terms, Leibniz states on October 18, 1678, in a letter to Pierre-Daniel Huet:

> It must be demonstrated first of all that the sacred books we have are genuine and have come down to us uncorrupted in substance. No one can do this satisfactorily unless he understands the mysteries of the art of textual criticism and can explore the reliability of the manuscripts and unless he is familiar with the linguistic particularities, with the spirit of that epoch and with its chronology.[59]

Far from fearing such a historical investigation, Leibniz is confident that "history renders service to piety and it is from history that the truth of our religion can be demonstrated, for it is in history that it is adumbrated in no uncertain way."[60] Indeed, the recovery of a long and shared ecclesiastical tradition, attested not only in Scripture but also in the writings of the Church Fathers and authors acknowledged by all main Christian confessions, plays for Leibniz a fundamental role in the establishment of the truth of the Christian religion.

Ensuring that Scriptures "have come down to us uncorrupted in substance" is, however, only a first step. The question is still open on what we should make of the testimony about miracles and exceptional events contained in them. After all, even among those who witnessed the same events, some believed in them as signs of a divine revelation and some did not. Moreover, as Scripture itself warns, exceptional events of a miraculous kind are not by themselves signs of a divine origin.

On the whole, Leibniz seems to want to minimize reliance on miracles.[61] For him, the excellence of the doctrine and the test of charity take precedence as signs of genuine

---

[58] See *Commentatiuncula de Judice Controversiarum*, §16; A VI i 549–50. On Leibniz's concept of Sacred History and his claim that it should be studied with the same acumen and tools employed in the study of any other kind of history, see Irena Backus, *Leibniz: Protestant Theologian* (Oxford: Oxford University Press, 2016), pp. 155–178. Cf. also Daniel Cook, "Leibniz: Biblical historian and exegete," in *Leibniz' Auseinandersetzung mit Vorgängern und Zeitgenossen*, edited by Ingrid Marchlewitz (Stuttgart: Steiner, 1990), pp. 267–276.

[59] A II i 641. Trans. by Backus in *Leibniz: Protestant Theologian*, p. 170.

[60] *Contemplatio de Historia Literaria Statuque Praesenti Eruditionis*, 1682 (A VI iv 468). Trans. by Backus in *Leibniz: Protestant Theologian*, p. 166.

[61] This approach tallies, for instance, with Leibniz's eagerness to stress that his doctrine of pre-established harmony explains naturally what occasionalism explains in a miraculous way, as well as his contempt for Newtonian theories requiring (in his view) miracles to explain natural events.

divine illumination over miracles, which appear to play at best a confirmatory role. In 1678–79, for instance, he argues:

> A great deal of reasoning is required to prove miracles we have not seen; indeed, even if we see them with our own eyes, we still need to do a lot of weighing up to ensure we are not deceived. Besides, you know that the miracles of Scripture need another criterion in turn, namely doctrine, since the Antichrist too will conjure up signs which will deceive even the elect (if that were possible) [cf. Matthew 24:24]. Moses said that a prophet who teaches contrary to the law must not be believed, even if he give signs [cf. Deuteronomy 13:2–4].[62]

In turn, on December 20, 1696, he notes: "the touchstone of true illumination is a great eagerness for contributing to the general good."[63]

On the other hand, the possibility of miracles is not denied. In particular, there is a kind of miraculous event that Leibniz regards as, in principle, trustworthy as a sign of divine inspiration: prophesy.[64] Prophesy has the peculiarity of being capable of authentication by history. "As *prophecy* is in effect the *history of the future*," Leibniz writes to Sophie, "I believe that every prophet who could truly give us the history of the forthcoming century would without doubt be inspired by God."[65] "It is true," he notes in 1680,

> that the devil can mimic some miracles. But there is a kind of miracle that the devil could not imitate, all powerful and all enlightened as he is, which is prophecy. For if a person can tell me many particular truths about general affairs which are due to happen, for example in a year here, I will hold it as certain that it is God who enlightens him. For it is impossible to anyone aside from God to see the general chain of causes which have to come together in the production of contingent things.[66]

Notwithstanding this (parsimonious) endorsement of miracles, it is still necessary to ask in which sense there could be a miracle in the Leibnizian universe, given Leibniz's complete-concept theory and his conception of pre-established harmony.[67]

Leibniz defines a miracle, strictly speaking, as something which "could not be explained by the natures of created things."[68] The exceptionality or rarity of an event is

---

[62] *Dialogus inter Theologum et Misosophum*, A VI iv 2213–14. Trans. by Strickland in *Leibniz on God and Religion*, p. 97.

[63] A I xiii 399–400. Trans. by Howard Hotson in "Leibniz and millenarianism," in *Alsted and Leibniz on God, the Magistrate and the Millennium*, texts edited with introduction and commentary by Maria Rosa Antognazza and Howard Hotson (Wiesbaden: Harrassowitz, 1999), pp. 187–188.

[64] See Daniel Cook, "Leibniz on 'prophets', prophecy, and revelation," in *Religious Studies* 45 (2009), pp. 269–287.

[65] A I vii 36. Trans. by Cook in "Leibniz on 'prophets,'" p. 276.

[66] A I iii 356. Trans. by Strickland in *Leibniz on God and Religion*, p. 195, slightly modified.

[67] An illuminating discussion of miracles is offered by Adams, *Leibniz*, pp. 81–102. See also Frédéric de Buzon, "Les miracles dans la *Théodicée*," in *Lectures et interprétations des Essais de théodicée de G. W. Leibniz*, edited by Paul Rateau (Stuttgart: Steiner, 2011), pp. 263–281.

[68] *Theodicy* §207 (GP VI 241).

not in itself proof of its being miraculous, just as the generality of some kind of event is not in itself a proof of its being natural.[69] Furthermore, a miracle is not some event that does not follow order or does not follow any law.[70] Rather, a miracle is an event that does not follow a *natural* law, that is, one of the contingent laws of nature which God has chosen but which admit exceptions due to some reason which conforms to a superior order. Thus, miracles "are always in conformity with the universal law of the general order, although they are above subordinate maxims" or laws of nature.[71]

It is in this sense that a miracle "could not be explained by the natures of created things," that is, through natural laws which normally regulate created things and which provide the framework of what is "natural" to them. The "nature" of a created thing, intended instead as its individual essence, cannot but contain in itself also the explanation of any miracle which may affect that substance; that is, the explanation of any fact which does not follow a subordinate law of nature. This fact will still follow "the universal law of the general order" and will still be eternally included with its sufficient reason in the complete concept of that individual substance. Moreover, it will be mirrored in the essences of all the individuals that constitute the same possible world. Thus, Leibniz writes that "the primitive laws essential to the series, true without exception," "contain the whole purpose of God in choosing the universe," including "miracles."[72] In the *Theodicy*, he concludes:

> It will also be said that, if everything is governed by rules, God could not make miracles. But one should know that the miracles which happen in the world were also included and represented as possible in this same world, considered at the stage of pure possibility; and God, who has since performed them, had decided to perform them when he has chosen this world. (GP VI 132)

By making space for miracles in this limited and distinctive way, Leibniz is able to include them among the "motives of credibility" that the Christian revelation must have to be distinguished from "those believing without foundation that their [spiritual] movements come from God."[73]

To conclude, paragraph 5 of the "Preliminary Discourse" of the *Theodicy* offers a clear summary of Leibniz's position on "the use of Reason and Philosophy with regard to religion." People should not "confuse *explain, comprehend, prove* and *support*":

> The Mysteries can be *explained* as much as is needed in order to believe them; but one cannot *comprehend* them, nor show *how* they arise; even in physics we explain

---

[69] See *Theodicy* §207 (GP VI 241) in which Leibniz refers to gravitation and occasionalism as theories that would require "perpetual miracles." The generality of a theory does not ensure that it proposes a natural explanation.

[70] GP VI 241.

[71] *Discourse on Metaphysics* §16; A VI iv 1554.

[72] *De natura veritatis, contingentiae et indifferentiae*, 1685–86; A VI iv 1518.

[73] *Nouveaux Essais*, book IV, chap. xix ("Of Enthusiasm"), §16; A VI vi 505.

several sensible qualities up to a certain point, but in an imperfect manner, for we do not comprehend them. Nor is it possible for us, either, to *prove* the Mysteries by reason: for everything that can be proved *a priori,* or by pure reason, can be comprehended. All that remains for us to do, therefore, after having given faith to the Mysteries on the basis of the proofs of the truth of Religion (what one calls the *motives of credibility*), is to be able to *support* them against objections; without which we would have no grounds for believing them." (GP VI 52)

For Leibniz, faith must be grounded in reason, not in the sense that it should be subjected to reason but in the sense that it cannot be irrational. Faith, however, is not merely a matter of believing true doctrines. For the purpose of salvation, the greatest sign of true faith remains for him "the love of God above all things."[74]

---

[74] Cf. the final section of the chapter on "Philosophical Theology and Christian Doctrines."

CHAPTER 41

PHILOSOPHICAL THEOLOGY AND CHRISTIAN DOCTRINES

MARIA ROSA ANTOGNAZZA

IN paragraph 5 of the "Preliminary Discourse" of the *Theodicy*, Leibniz writes that "Mysteries can be *explained* as much as is needed in order to believe them." That is to say, in order for revealed doctrines to be the object of belief, there must be at least a confused grasp of what they mean. Moreover, we must "be able to *support* them against objections; without which we would have no grounds for believing them" (GP VI 52).[1] Throughout his life, Leibniz engages in a project of philosophical theology aimed at fulfilling these two conditions, focusing on some of the distinctive doctrines of Christianity. On the one hand, he rejects specific charges of contradiction as a necessary condition for continuing to be epistemically justified in holding these doctrines as true; on the other hand, he explores some metaphysical models capacious enough to accommodate the claims of revealed theology.

TRINITY AND INCARNATION

Among the doctrines of Christianity, it would be hard to find one more central and distinctive than the dogma of the Trinity, according to which there is only one God in three persons equal and distinct: the Father, the Son, and the Holy Spirit. Directly connected with the dogma of the Trinity is the dogma of the Incarnation, according to which Jesus Christ is true man and true God. In the early modern period, these two fundamental dogmas of Christianity, embraced by the main Christian confessions, came under sustained attack from a rapidly spreading anti-Trinitarian movement that rejected them

---

[1] See chapter on "Faith and Reason" for a discussion of these points. Unless otherwise stated, translations are my own.

as irrational. For his part, Leibniz endorses these doctrines as truths above reason, endeavoring to defend them against charges of contradiction while proposing his own possible explanations.[2]

Leibniz's defense of the doctrine of the Trinity intends to show that arguments attempting to prove its contradictoriness are not conclusive. It is crucial to note that his aim is purely to demonstrate that anti-Trinitarian arguments fail, not to provide positive arguments in support of the possibility of the Trinity. According to him, this defensive strategy is sufficient to allow the claim that the Trinity can legitimately be presumed to be possible (i.e., not irrational, not contradictory) until the contrary is proved. More specifically, Leibniz defends the Trinity from the charge of inconsistency with the logical principle *quae eadem sunt eidem tertio sunt eadem inter se* (those which are identical to a third are identical to each other)—a principle directly derived from the principle of noncontradiction and which, therefore, cannot admit any exception.

In *De Trinitate*, a text penned around 1685, Leibniz explains:

> That principle that those which are identical to a third are identical to each other, if identity is taken with the greatest rigor, has a place in divine matters no less than in natural affairs. When we say "the father is God" and "the son is God," and "God is One [*Unus est Deus*]," both father and son, surely the father and the son are identical, unless "God" in the first two propositions is understood as a person of the Godhead and in the last one as the divine nature or the absolute singular substance that we call God. (A VI iv 2346)

The logical problem Leibniz is referring to in this passage is the formally valid expository syllogism: "This God is the Father; this God is the Son; therefore the Father is the Son"—a syllogism that was routinely mentioned in Trinitarian discussions from John Duns Scotus to the sixteenth century.[3] Leibniz's strategy is to show that once the logical structure of the premises is properly exposed, the syllogism fails.

This result is achieved through a fine-grained analysis of a proposition such as "an *A* is *B*." Already in one of his earliest texts, the *Defensio Trinitatis* of 1669, Leibniz endorses the analysis proposed by the German logician Johannes Raue.[4] According to Raue, in propositions of ordinary language such as *Homo est animal*, the proper or formal copula—formed by *est*, a demonstrative pronoun (*ille, id, . . .*), and a relative pronoun (*qui, quod . . .*)—is omitted. The *est* that appears in the proposition is in fact a material (as opposed to a formal) part of the proposition, belonging to the predicate term (*est*

---

[2] See, e.g., *De Deo Trino*, A VI iv 2291: "There are three persons of the Divinity, of whom there is one essence in number. We do not demonstrate this Mystery of faith by reason, but we only illustrate it and defend it against objections."

[3] See Simo Knuuttila, "Trinitarian fallacies, identity and predication," in *Trinitarian Theology in the Medieval West*, edited by Pekka Kärkkäinen (Helsinki: Luther-Agricola-Society, 2007), pp. 72–87.

[4] See *Defensio Trinitatis*, A VI i 518–30, and Johannes Raue, *Subita et Necessaria Defensio adversus Sex Primas Lectiones V. Cl. Joh. Scharfii* (Rostock, 1636); *Prior Fundamentalis Controversia pro Logica Novissima* (Rostock, 1638).

animal). Logical analysis shows that the proposition should be read as having two terms (or material parts)—*Homo* or the subject term; *est animal* or the predicate term—which are both predicated of a common third term (*commune tertium*).[5] This *commune tertium* is the subject of both the subject term and the predicate term. The function of the pronouns (*ille, qui* . . .) is to refer to the common third term. The formal copula is the logical operator that unites the subject term and the predicate term precisely by stating the sameness of the subject of the subject term and the subject of the predicate term.[6]

Moreover, Raue notes that quantitative signs (*signa quantitativa*) such as *omnis* (all, every), *quicunque* (whoever), and *nullus* (none) include the demonstrative pronouns *ille, is,* . . . which are also formal parts of the proposition omitted in ordinary language.[7] Finally, in syllogistic propositions, singular propositions should be analyzed as universal. As Leibniz puts it in the *Defensio Trinitatis*: "all singular propositions are, by virtue of a hidden sign [e.g. *omnis*], universal . . . for example, if the signs and copula are rightly placed, this proposition, Peter the Apostle was the first Roman Bishop, is formulated thus: Everyone who is Peter the Apostle was [the first] Roman Bishop" (A VI i 520).[8]

Once the proposition *Homo est animal* is formally analyzed, it will be reformulated as follows (using bars to separate the proposition's parts): *Omnis qui | est homo | est is, qui | est animal*. The logical copula that appears in this formulation expresses the extensional sameness of the subject of predication. In other words, the sameness of A and B expressed by the proposition "an A is B" means that A is said of a thing and B is said of the same thing (the *commune tertium*); both A and B are predicated of the same subject or *commune tertium*.[9]

Leibniz applies this analysis to Trinitarian formulations,[10] noting, for instance, in *De lingua philosophica*: "in the Trinity these two are different: 'to be God the father,' and 'to be he who is [*illum qui est*] God the father.' For God the son is not God the father,

---

[5] Raue, *Subita et Necessaria Defensio*, pp. 125–126 and *Prior Fundamentalis Controversia pro Logica Novissima*, pp. 385–387.

[6] Raue, *Prior Fundamentalis Controversia pro Logica Novissima*, pp. 166–167: "Every one to whom *being a philosopher* is attributed, is the same one to whom *being a student of nature* is attributed. Here those things which are attributed are two terms and that to which they are attributed is the *common Third Term*. To this common third term the *Term of the Predicate* is therefore attributed because indeed the *Term of the Subject* is attributed to it." See also Knuuttila, "Trinitarian fallacies, identity and predication," pp. 71–72.

[7] Raue, *Prior Fundamentalis Controversia pro Logica Novissima*, pp. 403–404.

[8] Cf. Raue, *Subita et Necessaria Defensio*, p. 154: "*When it is commonly said*, He who [*Ille, qui*] redeems us is our Messiah. *This means:* Everyone who [*Omnis Ille, qui*] redeems us, *etc. Indeed it means that the Universal sign is omitted.*"

[9] See Knuuttila, "Trinitarian fallacies, identity and predication," pp. 72–74, who notes a precedent in Peter Aberlard. Intensional sameness would mean, instead, that A and B are synonyms standing for the same thing (idem, p. 74).

[10] See Leibniz's reformulations of the syllogisms proposed by a leading anti-Trinitarian of the day, Andreas Wissowatius, throughout the *Defensio Trinitatis*. For a detailed comment, see Maria Rosa Antognazza, *Leibniz on the Trinity and the Incarnation: Reason and Revelation in the Seventeenth Century* (New Haven, CT: Yale University Press, 2007), esp. pp. 20–30.

and yet he is the very one who is [*est ille ipse qui est*] God the father, namely the one most high God" (A VI iv 889). The same type of analysis is behind Leibniz's claims in *De Trinitate*: "When it is said that 'the same one who is [*idem ille qui est*] the father is also the son,' the meaning is that in the same absolute substance of God there are two relative substances differing in number from one another" (A VI iv 2346). Likewise, in *De Deo Trino* (1680–84), he explains:

> The most powerful of the objections is this: if three [entities] are different from one another, and any one of them is God, it follows that there are three Gods. For if the father is God, and the son is God, and the Holy Spirit is God, and the father is not the son, nor the Holy Spirit; and the Son is not the father or the Holy Spirit, and lastly the Holy Spirit is not the father or the son; either it will have to be said that there are three gods or that we do not know what one and many mean, and therefore in just such a manner it may even be denied that father, son, and grandson are three men; or, the reason will have to be adduced as to why we call these three men, and deny that those are three gods. We shall reply, although the father is not the son, yet the father is he who is [*est is qui est*] the son, namely, the one God in number. This cannot be said of two men, father and son, and this is the real reason for the difference. (A VI iv 2291–2)

In other texts, Leibniz claims that the apparent contradiction of Trinitarian formulations "is taken away by a distinction"[11]; namely, the distinction (common in Protestant scholastic theology) between *Deus absolute seu essentialiter sumtus* ("God" taken in an absolute or in an essential sense) and *Deus relative seu personaliter sumtus* ("God" taken in a relative or a personal sense).[12] Leibniz notes that in the propositions "the Father is God, the son is God, the Holy Spirit is God," the word "God" has a different sense than does the word "God" that appears in the proposition "only one is God [*Unus est Deus*]." The former means *Deus relative seu personaliter sumtus*; the latter means *Deus absolute seu essentialiter sumtus*. Although *Deus relative seu personaliter sumtus* and *Deus absolute seu essentialiter sumtus* refer really to the same entity, they cannot be substituted for one another *salva veritate* because they appear in contexts that "concern not the thing but the mode of conceiving it" (*non de re sed modo concipiendi agitur*).[13] Similarly, in his defence of the mystery of the Incarnation from the charge of contradiction, Leibniz employs reduplicative operators (*quatenus, qua*) to distinguish between the different senses in which the term "Christ" is used. What is said of Christ qua God

---

[11] *Circa Geometrica Generalia*, in Massimo Mugnai, *Leibniz' Theory of Relations* (Stuttgart: Steiner, 1992), p. 147. Cf. also *Origo Animarum et Mentium* (A VI iv 1461): "There is no contradiction in these matters, because men do not sufficiently consider what is identity and diversity [*idem et diversum*]."

[12] See *Notationes Generales*, A VI iv 552–3; *De Trinitate*, A VI iv 2346; *Circa Geometrica Generalia*, in Mugnai, *Leibniz' Theory of Relations*, p. 147; *Remarques sur le livre d'un Antitrinitaire Anglois*, A IV v 51; *Nouveaux Essais*, A VI vi 498; *Theodicy*, GP VI 63–4. For a discussion of the main texts see Antognazza, *Leibniz on the Trinity and the Incarnation*, pp. 71–73.

[13] See *Notationes Generales*, A VI iv 552–3.

cannot be substituted *salva veritate* to what is said of Christ qua man and vice versa.[14] As Leibniz clarifies in *De Persona Christi*:

> it can be said that a man is omnipresent in the same way as it can be said that a poet treats diseases, if the same man is also a doctor. Let it be understood in a sound way, that is, that he who is [*eum qui est*] a man, though not qua man, but qua God, is omnipresent, and that he who is [*eum qui est*] God was born of a virgin, but not inasmuch as he is God [*non qua est Deus*]. For we speak of the Divine or human nature in Christ according as Divine or human attributes are ascribed to the Christ.[15]

It should be noted that when Leibniz uses reduplicative operators in Trinitarian contexts[16] or writes of "God" taken absolutely versus "God" taken relatively, no modalism is implied. The point he is making is a purely defensive one: namely, that the Trinitarian formulations under scrutiny are not formally inconsistent when read in opaque contexts. He is not making substantive metaphysical claims about reducing the Trinity to different modes of presentation of God (i.e., as Father, as Son, as Holy Spirit).

Assuming Leibniz is successful in clearing the Trinity and the Incarnation of charges of contradiction, how does he propose to explain these two mysteries "as much as is needed in order to believe them?" As any Christian thinker wishing to remain within the boundaries of orthodoxy, Leibniz is well aware of the need to avoid the two opposite dangers of modalism and tritheism. Orthodoxy requires a combination of monotheism with some real subsistence of the divine persons. Leibniz's distinctive proposal is to talk of three relative substances constituting—"so to speak" (*ut sic dicam*)—one absolute substance. In the *Examen Religionis Christianae*, written in 1686, he states: "They are therefore three related singular substances, one absolute [substance] which contains them [all] and the same individual nature of which is communicated to the singular substances" (A VI iv 2365). To prevent suspicions of tritheism, he is eager to add that each divine person "essentially involves relation." No divine person could exist on its own, and together they constitute "an absolute substance single in number."[17]

Pressed some years later by his nephew (a student of theology in Leipzig) about the tritheistic flavor of defining the divine persons as "essentially relative intelligent singular substances," Leibniz resorts to a more prudent formulation, shifting from an account of what the persons *are* to an account of how they *are understood by us*: "they are understood through incommunicable relative modes of subsisting [*per modos subsistendi relativos incommunicabiles*]."[18] Notwithstanding this concession, it is apparent that Leibniz regards a more traditional conception of the divine persons as "subsisting

---

[14] Cf. *Defensio Trinitatis*, A VI i 521.

[15] A VI iv 2296. Note that also in this case Leibniz employs the analysis which refers to a *commune tertium*.

[16] Cf. *Defensio Trinitatis*, A VI i N. 16; *De Persona Christi*, A VI iv N. 405; *Examen Religionis Christianae*, A VI iv 2364, 2368.

[17] See *Examen Religionis Christianae* (A VI iv 2365) and *De Scriptura, Ecclesia, Trinitate* (A VI iv 2289).

[18] See A I xi 228, 234, and 312.

relations" as inadequate to account for the robust subsistence required by orthodoxy.[19] Indeed, he pushes back on his nephew's proposal to describe a divine person as a "mode of subsisting." If one wants to avoid the term "substance," Leibniz insists, it should at least be clear that "modes of subsisting" or "relations" are not the persons themselves but that through which ("per quid") the persons are constituted.[20] This is consistent with the weak ontological status of relations in Leibniz's metaphysical thought. In his framework, as a purely mental entity, a relation could hardly have the ontological status required by an orthodox reading of the Trinity. It is a measure of the earnestness of his engagement with Trinitarian theology that Leibniz is not simply prepared to endorse more traditional formulations to avoid trouble, but continues to labor at a model which would, by his own lights, genuinely preserve the dogmatic requirements.

The risk of tritheism, however, can also hardly be denied in a model envisaging three relative substances. In 1708, responding to the attacks of an anti-Trinitarian, Leibniz stresses that only the *subsistens absolutum* (absolute subsistent) can properly be called substance.[21] The divine persons, therefore, are said to be substances only in a loose sense of the word. The difference between absolute substance and relative substance seems to be that the latter cannot exist on its own due to its "essential relation" to the other persons. The Trinity seems, therefore, to be conceived as a concrete, complex system, implying constituents but not parts.[22]

But what should one make of these notions of relative versus absolute substance in the context of Leibniz's metaphysics? If we turn to the notion of a possible world, it seems that also in this case we have a complex system the strong unity of which results from essential relations of everything to everything. Leibniz even uses strikingly Trinitarian language to describe this universal harmony, calling it on occasion the "*perichōrēsis* of all things."[23] Such an analogy between a possible world and the individual substances

---

[19] Cf. Thomas Aquinas, *Summa Theologiae, Textum Leoninum* (Rome 1886–87; now available online in *Corpus Thomisticum*), I, q. 29. a. 4: "a divine person signifies a relation as subsisting."

[20] See, e.g., A I xi 311: "But since in divine matters these things are distinguished better by our mode of understanding than by the thing itself, perhaps you could abstain from both and say: several persons in the same absolute singular substance in number are understood by means of several relative incommunicable modes of subsisting in it [*per plures in ea modos subsistendi relativos incommunicabiles*]. I willingly add the mention of relative and absolute, on account of the reasons which are there manifest. Moreover, in my opinion it would be more cautious to say so, than if you say that the persons [of the Trinity] are modes, making of them modal or incomplete entities, and at the same time you will also avoid formulations which may seem too concrete and still obtain the thing itself, when you express all that through which [*per quid*] a person is constituted." In 1708, Leibniz writes that the divine persons are constituted *per relationes* ("through relations") (*Ad Christophori Stegmanni Metaphysicam Unitariorum*, in Nicholas Jolley, "An unpublished Leibniz MS on metaphysics," *Studia Leibnitiana* 7/2 (1975), pp. 161–189, at 188).

[21] See *Ad Christophori Stegmanni Metaphysicam Unitariorum*, p. 188.

[22] See R. M. Adams, "Review of Maria Rosa Antognazza's *Trinità e Incarnazione*," in *The Leibniz Review* 10 (2000): 53–59, at p. 57.

[23] See *Tractatio de Deo et Homine* (1702), GP III 34–35, and Look-Rutherford 188. Traditional Trinitarian theology employs the notion of *perichōrēsis* to indicate the reciprocal inexistence and compenetration of the divine persons.

that constitute it, on the one hand, and the absolute versus relative substances of which Leibniz speaks in the case of the Trinity, on the other, seems to yield (at least prima facie) a frankly Spinozistic picture.

The difference between the two cases, however, is significant. In the case of an individual substance, there is no metaphysical impossibility preventing it existing on its own as a "world apart." The fact that there is no solitary monad is down to moral necessity rather than metaphysical necessity. Metaphysically, the proper substance remains the individual substance rather than the world. In the case of the Trinity, Leibniz seems to indicate (in line with orthodoxy) that the impossibility for each person to exist without the others is instead metaphysical. Hence, it is only the *subsistens absolutum* which is properly a substance—namely, the "absolute substance which is only one in number, but which involves [complectitur] three persons of the Godhead" (A VI iv 2364).

The same balancing act between the requirements of orthodoxy and the attempt to provide a metaphysically consistent model is apparent in Leibniz's account of the mystery of the Incarnation. Throughout his life, Leibniz endorses the traditional analogy between the union in Christ of divine and human natures and the union in a human being of mind and body. Likewise, he constantly endorses the orthodox requirement of a substantial union of the two natures into one single person; that is, one subsistence (hypostasis) or one substantial being. Conversely, together with a range of traditionally heterodox ways of explaining this union, Leibniz rejects the doctrine of the *communicatio idiomatum*; that is, the communication of properties between the human and the divine nature of Christ. Despite its favor with Lutheran theologians, Leibniz is adamant that a *communicatio idiomatum* cannot be accepted because, in his view, it implies contradiction. True to his claim that a contradictory doctrine can only be false, he does not hesitate to part company on this point with many of his fellow Lutherans.[24]

Among his own attempts to provide an explanation of the Incarnation, the most ambitious goes back to his early years. In a writing of 1669–70, *De Incarnatione Dei*, the young Leibniz proposes to interpret in terms of a hypostatic union both the union of divine and human natures in Christ and the union of mind and body in human beings.[25] With the evolution of his metaphysics, this ingenious youthful model is abandoned. What is never abandoned, however, is the orthodox requirement driving the model: namely, the need for a substantial union. Leibniz constantly maintains that Christ is not an "*Ens per aggregationem* [Being by aggregation]"[26] but enjoys a true unity, the unity of the

---

[24] See, e.g., *De Persona Christi* (A VI iv 2296): "*the attributes and operations of one Nature are not to be attributed to the other nature* . . . and certainly it seems contradictory to attribute the things that are proper to one nature to the other."

[25] The theological doctrine of the hypostatic union, according to which two natures—human and divine—are substantially united in Christ in one single person or subsistence (*hypostasis*), was established by the Council of Chalcedon (451 CE). In *De Incarnatione Dei*, Leibniz defines the hypostatical union as "the action of a thing having in itself the principle of action immediately through another thing [*actio rei principium actus in se habentis immediatè per rem aliam*]" (A VI i 534). For a detailed discussion of *De Incarnatione Dei*, see Antognazza, *Leibniz on the Trinity and the Incarnation*, pp. 35–41.

[26] See *De Persona Christi* (A VI iv 2295).

person—that is to say, the intrinsic unity of a substantial being.[27] On the other hand, especially in his later years and in the correspondence with Bartholomew Des Bosses, it becomes increasingly doubtful whether his mature metaphysics has the resources to fulfill this requirement. Finally giving up his exploration with Des Bosses of a *vinculum substantiale*, or substantial bond, superadded to monads, Leibniz candidly admits: "Nor do we need any other thing besides Monads and their modifications, for Philosophy as opposed to the supernatural. But I fear that we cannot explain the mystery of the Incarnation, and other things, unless real bonds or unions are added."[28]

The problem Leibniz is grappling with is whether, in the framework of his monadology, *any* composite being could be granted, with metaphysical rigor, the status of substance. Of course, he often writes of corporeal substances; but can aggregates of monads unified by a dominating monad really be regarded as endowed with the in-trinsic unity needed for substantiality? In so far as Christ is an even more complex composite being, the problem is exacerbated. This is not, however, a problem unique to the Incarnation. Quite the opposite: it affects all the traditional primary substances of a broadly Aristotelian metaphysics. Leibniz seems to remain conspicuously uncon-cerned about ensuring that his metaphysical system has the resources for granting the status of substances to plants, animals, and embodied human beings. He seems, in fact, content with the thought that the dominating monad of these composite beings *is* a substance, without any pressing need to account for a substantial union with the changing body (i.e., aggregate of subordinate monads) that always accompanies it. In the case of the Incarnation, however, there is a requirement for substantial union that his monadological model cannot explain. Leibniz does not deny the possibility of such a stronger union as a truth above reason, but he finally retreats from his youthful ambition of providing a positive metaphysical model (however imperfect) of the Incarnation.[29]

RESURRECTION AND EUCHARIST

Two further core doctrines of the Christian tradition directly connected with the metaphysics of bodies are the resurrection and the Eucharist. In the framework of Leibniz's philosophy, the resurrection of bodies turns out to be remarkably easy to explain and, at the same time, remarkably at odds with the intentions of this

---

[27] See *Symbole et Antisymbole des Apostres*, in Maria Rosa Antognazza, "Inediti leibniziani sulle polemiche trinitarie," in *Rivista di filosofia neo-scolastica* 83/4 (1991): 525–550, at 538; *Il n'y a qu'un seul Dieu*, A VI iv 2211; *De Scriptura, Ecclesia, Trinitate*, A VI iv 2291; *De Persona Christi*, A VI iv 2294–7.

[28] Look-Rutherford 276–8. Trans. by R. M. Adams in *Leibniz: Determinist, Theist, Idealist* (Oxford: Oxford University Press, 1994), p. 304.

[29] For a more detailed discussion of this issue, see Maria Rosa Antognazza, "Leibniz's theory of substance and his metaphysics of the Incarnation," in *Locke and Leibniz on Substance and Identity*, edited by Paul Lodge and T. W. C. Stoneham (Abingdon/New York: Routledge, 2015), pp. 231–252 (esp. pp. 238–245).

traditional doctrine. According to tradition, the dead will be resurrected on the day of the Last Judgment, when our immortal souls will be reunited with our bodies. Underpinning this doctrine is a philosophical anthropology according to which the human being is not merely an immortal soul accidentally united to a mortal body for a limited period of time. If this were the case, the immortality of the soul would be sufficient to account for human beings' everlasting life without needing the postulation of a bodily resurrection bound to arouse all sorts of awkward philosophical problems. Instead, deeply ingrained in the Christian tradition is the view that embodiment is an essential constituent of human beings. The immortal soul that continues to live while our mortal earthly body decays does not constitute, on its own, our human nature. Therefore, the soul's immortality is not sufficient to ensure the preservation of our full identity. The nature and identity of a human being can be fully restored only through her or his resurrection as an embodied being. A crucial consequence of this view is that our earthly death is a real death, a real dissolution of a human being, as opposed to a transformation (however drastic) of the way of life of an immortal self. Furthermore, a proper resurrection (as opposed to a reincarnation) requires that human beings "will rise again with their own bodies which they now bear," as opposed to any odd body.[30]

While Scripture does not enter into much detail as to how one might think of this bodily resurrection, from early on the challenge for philosophical theology has been to provide an account that can answer (at the least to some extent) some obvious philosophical questions. The Apostolic Creed's formulation, according to which there will be a "resurrection of the flesh," has traditionally been taken as a claim that also the mortal aspects of our nature ("the flesh") will come to life again. Already Paul clarifies, however, that the resurrected body will be a "transfigurated" body, namely a "glorious" or even a "spiritual" body[31] that, unlike our earthly, corruptible, coarse body of flesh and bones, will be endowed with immortality. To those who ask: "How are the dead raised? With what kind of body do they come?" Paul replies:

> What you sow does not come to life unless it dies and what you sow is not the body which is to be, but a bare kernel . . . what is sown is perishable, what is raised is imperishable . . . the dead will be raised imperishable. . . . For this perishable nature must put on the imperishable, and this mortal nature must put on immortality. (1 Cor. 15:35–37, 42, 53)

Needless to say, this Pauline doctrine leaves plenty of open questions for the scores of theologians of all stripes who tackled them down the centuries.

---

[30] Cf. Lateran Council IV (1215) in Denz-Schönm, 801 (*Enchiridion symbolorum*, edited by H. Denzinger, revised by A. Schönmetzer. Online at Catho.Org: http://catho.org/9.php?d=g1).

[31] Cf. Phil 3:21: "Dominum Iesum Christum, qui transfigurabit corpus humilitatis nostrae, ut illud conforme faciat corpori gloriae suae" and 1 Cor 15:44: "seminatur corpus animale, resurgit corpus spirituale."

Leibniz bravely enters the fray as early as May 1671, with a letter to Duke Johann Friedrich and a brief essay sent with it on the resurrection of bodies (*De Resurrectione Corporum*).[32] In both the letter and the essay, Leibniz seems to take his cue from Paul's notion of "a bare kernel" to speculate about a metaphysical model according to which in "everything" (i.e., not only in human beings and animals, but also in vegetables and minerals) there is a "kernel of substance [*Kern der substantz*]" (A II² i 175) or a "certain self-diffusing seminal centre" (A II² i 185). This kernel is "so subtle, that it remains also in the ashes of burned things, and can, as it were, draw itself into an invisible centre" (A II² i 175).[33] In the course of his letter and essay, Leibniz employs also the expressions *punctum saliens*, "fountain of life," and "flower of substance" to indicate the survival of a subtle, indestructible bodily kernel or bodily essence capable of retreating into a point (A II² i 184–5; A II² i 175).[34] In turn, this point is further qualified in his letter to the duke as a "physical point" serving as "an instrument and as though a vehicle of the soul," which is "constituted in a mathematical point" (A II² i 176). From this point—in which also the soul is supposed to be somehow "implanted" (A II² i 184)—a human being can unfold again at the moment of the resurrection.

The metaphysical picture painted by Leibniz in these youthful texts is heavily in-debted to alchemical notions and far from straightforward. However, despite its imma-turity and strange details, the thought behind this model seems to be clear enough. Our earthly visible bodies, Leibniz reasons, "are in perpetual flux" (A II² i 184). Even here on earth, our identity therefore does not depend on the preservation of the same coarse matter. Given that, following Paul's teaching, the body is due to be resurrected as a "spir-itual body," the restoration of the same gross body is not a requirement for our bodily resurrection.[35] The survival of an indestructible kernel or flower of bodily essence, united in an invisible point with our soul and capable of unfolding again, is therefore sufficient to preserve the identity of a human being and to explain the resurrection.

During the following years, the evolution of Leibniz's metaphysics of bodies leaves behind the musings about alchemical bodily spirits and essences that characterize these early pieces. Rather than fully abandoning his youthful model, however, Leibniz's ma-ture metaphysics seems to breathe new life into the idea of a constant flux of the body and of its withdrawal into an involute minimal state from which it can unfold and

---

[32] A II i 108–9, 115–16 (pp. 175, 183–5 of the new edition).

[33] See also A II² i 185.

[34] Lloyd Strickland's careful discussion in "Leibniz, the 'flower of substance', and the resurrection of the same body," *The Philosophical Forum* 40/3 (2009): 391–410, traces these notions to the alchemical tradition. See also his helpful study on "The doctrine of 'the resurrection of the same body' in early modern thought," in *Religious Studies* 46 (2010): 163–183. A discussion of Leibniz's early pieces on the resurrection is offered by Christia Mercer in *Leibniz's Metaphysics: Its Origins and Development* (Oxford: Oxford University Press, 2001), pp. 284–288, and "Leibniz, matter, and the metaphysics of the resurrection," in *Einheit in der Vielheit. VIII. Internationaler Leibniz-Kongress*, edited by H. Breger, J. Herbst, and S. Erdner, vols. 1–2 (Hanover: Leibniz-Gesellschaft, 2006), vol. 2, pp. 601–605.

[35] Leibniz's phrase *"corpus spirituale resurgere debet"* (A II² i 184) echoes 1 Cor 15:44: *"resurgit corpus spirituale."*

develop again at the resurrection. By 1703, Leibniz thinks of the body as an aggregate of indestructible, mindlike, simple substances or monads, unified by a dominant monad (i.e., in human beings, the mind).[36] In created beings, this dominant monad is always "embodied," namely, it is always accompanied by a changing aggregate of monads represented by the dominant monad as its body.[37] Death is merely a regression into a state of stupor or unconsciousness similar to the state of all "bare" monads, which enjoy no apperception or distinct representations.[38] It is easy enough to see how monads can be awoken from this slumber. At the resurrection, they will resume (and presumably greatly improve) their distinct perceptions: they will even grow their bodies again—that is to say, they will perceive more distinctly the changing aggregate of mindlike simple substances that they represent as their bodies.

In his final years, Leibniz is explicit in linking his views on the constant "embodiment" of created simple substances with the "glorious body" envisaged by the Christian tradition:

> why could not the soul always keep a subtle body, organized in its own way, which could even one day resume what is needed of its visible body in the resurrection, since a glorious body is granted to the blessed, and since the ancient fathers have granted a subtle body to angels. . . . Because, as regards the beatific vision of the blessed souls, this is compatible with the functions of their glorified bodies, which will not fail to be organic in their own way.[39]

At the same time, he claims to see "no reason why some particular secondary matter should be perpetually attached to [the soul] until the resurrection" (Look-Rutherford 78–9)—by which he seems to mean that there is no reason for the aggregate of monads that the soul represents as its body to remain the same, as opposed to being in constant flux.

In sum, Leibniz's mature metaphysics appears to be uniquely well-placed to give content to Paul's claim that our resurrected bodies will be "spiritual bodies." In Leibniz's monadological framework, all bodies ultimately reduce to "spiritual" bodies; that is, to

---

[36] Cf. the fivefold ontological scheme presented by Leibniz in his letter to De Volder of June 20, 1703 (GP II 252; trans. by Adams in *Leibniz*, p. 265): "I distinguish therefore (1) the primitive Entelechy or Soul, (2) Matter, i. e. primary matter, or primitive passive power, (3) the Monad completed by these two, (4) the Mass [*Massa*] or secondary matter, or organic machine, for which countless subordinate Monads come together, (5) the Animal or corporeal substance, which is made One by the Monad dominating the Machine."

[37] Cf. *Principles of Nature and of Grace* (GP VI 598–9): "each distinct simple substance or monad, which forms the centre of a composite substance (for example, of an animal) and the principle of its oneness, is surrounded by a *mass* composed of an infinity of other monads, which constitute the body belonging to this central monad." In his fifth piece for Samuel Clarke, Leibniz writes: "there are no created substances entirely destitute of matter. Because I hold, in agreement with the Ancients and with reason, that the angels or Intelligences, and the souls separated from a gross body, have always subtle bodies despite their being themselves incorporeal" (GP VII 406).

[38] Cf. *Monadology* §§ 21, 23–24 (GP VI 610–1).

[39] *Considerations sur la doctrine d'un Esprit Universel Unique*, 1702 (GP VI 529–38, here pp. 533, 536).

aggregates of mindlike simple substances. Claiming that they can rise again no longer seems to pose a problem. The price to be paid for such a neat picture is, however, very high—indeed, so high that it arguably does away with the very doctrine that is supposed to be neatly explained. As Leibniz himself proudly notes in some remarks of 1712, among the accomplishments of his theory of substance there is the "banishment of death."[40] Unfortunately for him, it was not long before other thinkers pointed out the "scandalous" nature of this very "banishment."[41] If all substances are ultimately indestructible and hence immortal, one can hardly envisage a genuine resurrection—at any rate, not the robust kind of resurrection which presupposes (as in the traditional Christian doctrine) the reality of death as the dissolution of a human being not reducible to her or his immortal soul. The closest substitute Leibniz offers for the notion of natural mortality is the mere metaphysical possibility of a supernatural annihilation of created monads by God. Moreover, in Leibniz's monadological framework, there seem to be no resources for turning the ideal unification of an aggregate of simple substances into a substantial union constituting a being one per se. Although also for Leibniz a human being is not merely a disembodied soul or mind, it is this soul or mind which, strictly speaking, qualifies as a substance. Since there is no real metaphysical union with the changing aggregate of monads that always accompanies it, the soul or mind is also, arguably, our true (and immortal) self.

A related set of problems challenges Leibniz's reflection on the mystery of the Eucharist, for the explanation of which he experiments with the controversial notion of *vinculum substantiale* briefly mentioned earlier. Rather than a late entry into his own metaphysical toolkit, the *vinculum substantiale* is a metaphysical hypothesis that Leibniz considers offering to his Catholic friend, Des Bosses, as an addition to the theory of monads. The need for such an addition is precipitated by Leibniz's eventual acknowledgment that monads and monadic domination are insufficient for a satisfactory account of theological doctrines such as Eucharistic transubstantiation. Given that, as a Lutheran, Leibniz was not committed to transubstantiation (i.e., to a change of substance while the appearances of bread and wine remain unchanged), one may think that the problem was confined to maintaining the good will of the Catholic side toward his metaphysical theories rather than being an issue that really demanded, in his view, a satisfactory solution. Accordingly, Leibniz frankly points out to his friend that Lutherans only need to account for the real presence of Christ's body, not for transubstantiation.[42] On closer

---

[40] GP III 430. On August 23, 1713, Leibniz writes to Des Bosses: "as you know, I deny that not only the soul but also the animal dies" (Look-Rutherford 318–19).

[41] These later debates are discussed in Matteo Favaretti Camposampiero, "The Ban of Death: Leibniz's Scandalous Immortalism" (forthcoming). Favaretti Camposampiero identifies the dissertation by Elias Camerarius (1673–1734) *De morte in exilium acta* as the work introducing the phrase *exilium mortis Leibnitianum* ("the Leibnizian banishment of death") used to indicate Leibniz's controversial views on death. I am grateful to Favaretti Camposampiero for sharing with me a draft of his illuminating study.

[42] Leibniz to Des Bosses, September 8, 1709 (Look-Rutherford 152–3): "for us there is no place for either transubstantiation or consubstantiation of the bread, but only that Christ's body is perceived at the same time that the bread is received, so that the presence alone of Christ's body must be explained." For an insigthful and detailed discussion of transubstantiation and the *vinculum substantiale* in the context

inspection, however, the problems raised by transubstantiation expose more general problems about the ability of Leibniz's theory of monads to account for the existence of genuine corporeal substances, as well as for mysteries to which he was committed (such as the Incarnation).

Leibniz's first stab at explaining to Des Bosses how his monadology could accommodate transubstantiation is to suggest that "when the monads constituting the bread are destroyed with respect to their primitive active and passive powers, and the presence of the monads constituting Christ's body is substituted for them, there remain only the derivative forces that were in the bread exhibiting the same phenomena that the monads of the bread had exhibited" (Look-Rutherford 152–3). Des Bosses appreciates the similarity of this proposal to the doctrine of "real accidents" employed by Catholic theologians to explain transubstantiation; namely, the claim that there can be "absolute" or nonmodal accidents that remain in the Eucharist without a subject. He questions, however, the consistency of this view with Leibniz's metaphysical system. Since derivative forces are conceived as modifications of primitive forces, how can they remain when the latter are destroyed (Look-Rutherford 158–9)?

Leibniz is quick to see the point. He abandons the suggestion of a destruction of monads and their primitive forces, trying instead a different tack. In his letter to Des Bosses of February 15, 1712, the hypothesis of a "real unifier superadded to monads by God" is introduced. This first version of the *vinculum substantiale* appears to envisage some kind of bond holding together the simple substances that compose a corporeal substance, thereby bestowing the unity a corporeal substance would require if it has to be "something real over and above monads" (Look-Rutherford 224–5). The idea is that transubstantiation no longer rests on the destruction of monads. Since a corporeal substance depends on the presence of this substantial bond, in order to create a new corporeal substance it is enough for God to substitute one vinculum with another.[43] Leibniz's problems, however, are far from over. The vinculum cannot be merely a relation, given that relations for him are mental entities, namely, second-order truths resulting from the simultaneous consideration of two or more individuals with their properties. The bond envisaged by Leibniz's proposal clearly needs to have some substantial status of its own: it needs to be, in Leibniz's own phrase, a *substantial* bond or a "unifying reality, which adds *something absolute* (and therefore substantial), albeit impermanent, to the things to be unified" (Look-Rutherford 226–7).

In later letters, the character of substance (as opposed to relation) of the vinculum takes over,[44] until his final account of the substantial bond suggests a conception of corporeal substance much closer to the model of traditional Aristotelian substances than his theory of monads and monadic domination would allow. Corporeal substance is now identified with the substantial bond itself. Writing on January 13, 1716, Leibniz

of Leibniz's metaphysics of bodies, see the introduction by B. Look and D. Rutherford to their edition of the Leibniz–Des Bosses correspondence (Look-Rutherford lvii–lxxii).

[43]   Cf. Look-Rutherford 226–7 and lxiii.

[44]   Cf. the letter to Des Bosses of September 20, 1712, and Look-Rutherford lxviii.

notes that the "primary matter and substantial form" of the Scholastics, "namely the primitive active and passive powers of the composite, and the complete thing resulting from these, are really that substantial bond that I am urging." His reasoning seems to be that *if* there has to be composite *substances*, they must contain "something substantial beside monads; otherwise . . . composites will be mere phenomena" (Look-Rutherford 364–5). In other words, to be genuine substances, corporeal substances would need to be "substantial bonds" resulting from primary matter and substantial form as in the Aristotelian-Scholastic model. "Therefore," Leibniz concludes, "my doctrine of composite substance seems to be the very doctrine of the Peripatetic school, except that their doctrine does not recognize monads. But I add them" (Look-Rutherford 365). The problem is, however, that the model of monads and monadic domination "does not cohere well enough" with the real or metaphysical unification required for "the raising of phenomena to reality, that is, composite substances" (Look-Rutherford 340–1) and needed in turn to explain transubstantiation. So much Leibniz himself confesses to Des Bosses in a letter of June 30, 1715.

All in all, Leibniz's attempt to explain transubstantiation within his monadological framework seems to end in failure. His metaphysical theories meet, however, with greater success in accounting for the versions of the Eucharistic doctrine that matter to Lutherans: namely, the real presence, and the multipresence in different places, of Christ's body. The doctrine of real presence agrees with transubstantiation in maintaining that the body of Christ is substantially present in the Eucharistic, but does not claim that only the "accidents" of bread and wine, and not the substance, are left. In his own words, what Leibniz needs to explain is how "one and the same Body of Christ . . . is really present, by its substance, wherever the Eucharistic sacrificial offering [*Hostia*] is."[45]

Leibniz's solution hinges on the application to the specific case of the Eucharist of his general conception of the substance of a body as consisting in a force, or a principle of action, as opposed to extension.[46] In a letter of January 1692 to the Catholic convert, Paul Pellisson-Fontanier, he maintains that "it is not only in the Eucharist but everywhere else, that bodies are present only by this application of primitive force to the place."[47] That is, according to Leibniz, the local presence of a substance consists in some sort of immediate operation. A substance is present where it operates immediately. Although this operation, and therefore presence, is naturally limited to one place, there is no reason why a substance could not supernaturally operate immediately, and therefore be present, in many places. Substantial presence by operation is the way in which Christ is really multipresent in all the places in which the Eucharist is celebrated.[48]

---

[45] *De Demonstratione possibilitatis Mysteriorum Eucharistiae*, c. autumn 1671; A VI i 515. Trans. by Adams in *Leibniz*, p. 353.

[46] See the excellent discussion by Adams, *Leibniz*, pp. 349–360, from which I am drawing.

[47] A I vii 249.

[48] Adams, *Leibniz*, esp. pp. 358–360, shows that this same fundamental strategy was employed by Leibniz for some forty years and that it is already to be found in its key elements as early as 1668 in *De Transsubstantiatione* (A VI i N. 15/2). For the historical and theological background to Leibniz's

PREDESTINATION, GRACE, SALVATION, AND DAMNATION

Another central debate characterizing Christian theology from Luther's reformation onward is the issue of predestination. The doctrine of predestination stands at the intersection of a number of key Christian doctrines, notably, the notion, role, and distribution of divine grace as regards salvation and damnation; the concept of election; and the issue of justification and its relationship to faith and good works. Controversies *de auxiliis* (i.e., regarding the divine aids available to humankind) became a *locus classicus* of seventeenth-century theology, marking sharp divisions not only between Catholic, Lutheran (or Evangelical), and Reformed churches, but also inside these Christian denominations.[49] The distinction between alternative positions could be typically drawn along the lines of a different balance between two competing concerns of Christian theology: on the one hand, the fundamental role played in salvation by God's grace (blocking the Pelagian view that human beings can redeem themselves by dint of good works); on the other hand, the role of human beings' response to God's grace (blocking worries about God's arbitrariness and injustice in saving some but not others independently of a human response to His offer of redemption).

Among the most harshly contested issues in the Protestant camp was the so-called doctrine of double predestination, espoused by Calvinists following the teaching of Calvin's successor in Geneva, Theodor Beza (1519–1605). According to Beza, from all eternity, God has decreed not only who will be saved but also who will be damned, in contrast to the common view held by Lutheran churches according to which there is predestination to salvation but not to damnation. By the early seventeenth century, the Calvinist or Reformed churches further divided themselves between those denying any role to human beings' response to grace in determining their salvation and those upholding the role of human free will in resisting a salvific grace that is offered to all. Whereas for the former God saves only those he has elected independently of their merits or demerits, for the latter God wants the salvation of all but some human beings condemn themselves but refusing God's grace. The Synod of Dordrecht (1618–19) sealed the victory of hardline Calvinists who endorsed double predestination through an absolute decree issued by God after the Fall, against the universalist position on grace held

---

discussions of the Eucharist see Irena Backus, *Leibniz Protestant Theologian* (Oxford: Oxford University Press, 2016), pp. 9–54. On *De Transsubstantiatione* cf. also Christia Mercer, *Leibniz's Metaphysics: Its Origins and Development* (Cambridge: Cambridge University Press, 2001), pp. 82–89.

[49] On these debates see, e.g., Agustín Echavarría, "Leibniz on the efficacy and economy of divine grace," in *Tercentenary Essays on the Philosophy and Science of Leibniz*, edited by L. Strickland, E. Vynckier, and J. Weckend (Palgrave Macmillan, 2016), pp. 279–300 and Backus, *Leibniz Protestant Theologian*, esp. pp. 57–73. Leibniz strongly prefers to refer to his own denomination as "Evangelical" rather than "Lutheran," to avoid any perceived sectarianism.

by the opposing party, the Arminians, named after the Dutch Reformed theologian, Jacobus Arminius (1560–1609).

Leibniz engages intensively with the issue of predestination, especially in the late 1690s and early 1700s, in the context of the negotiations for the unification of the Lutheran church of Hanover with the Reformed church of Brandenburg.[50] In the same period, he also comments extensively on Gilbert Burnet's exposition of article 17 of the *Thirty-Nine Articles of the Church of England*, devoted to "Predestination and Election."[51] Leibniz's focal point is an attempt at mediation, in the framework of his philosophy, between those stressing the absolute decree of God in freely determining election versus those stressing God's consideration of human beings' responses to grace. In his view, these positions can be to some extent harmonized by maintaining that God's decree to create the world eternally entails the *simultaneous* considerations of all the factors that enter into the best of all possible worlds, including the interconnection between God's free election and the response of individuals to grace.

At any rate, Leibniz aligns himself with the view of all Christian denominations in regarding grace as an essential factor in salvation. More specifically, already in the *Discourse on Metaphysics* of 1686, he follows tradition in distinguishing between different types of grace.[52] This taxonomy is further clarified in his later comments on Burnet:

> Aids of grace are either efficacious (i.e., absolutely effective [*Effectricia*]) or merely sufficient. Effective aids are effective infallibly, but the considerations of efficacity and infallibility are distinct. Sometimes aids have efficacy per se and in virtue of their own nature. And aids have efficacy that is either *complete*, so that they cannot be thwarted by contrary circumstances (as they appear to have been in the miraculous conversion of Paul), or *sub modo*, because they are not in fact impeded by

[50] See Antognazza, *Leibniz*, pp. 308–406 and Backus, *Leibniz Protestant Theologian*, pp. 61–68. Of special importance is an extensive text of 1699 written by Leibniz in collaboration with the Lutheran abbot of Luccum, Gerhard Wolter Molanus (*Unforgreiffliches Bedencken über eine Schrifft genandt "Kurtze Vorstellung"*; A IV vii N. 79).

[51] Gilbert Burnet (1643–1715), Bishop of Salisbury and leading representative of theological latitudinarianism, published in 1699 an *Exposition of the Thirty-Nine Articles of the Church of England*; that is, a detailed commentary on the official doctrine of the Anglican Church summarized in the Thirty-Nine Articles promulgated in 1571 by the Archbishop of Canterbury and Queen Elisabeth I. Leibniz's own commentary on Article 17 was finished by 1705 but remained unpublished during his lifetime. It is edited, translated, and introduced by Michael J. Murray in G. W. Leibniz, *Dissertation on Predestination and Grace* (New Haven: Yale University Press, 2011) (hereafter DPG, followed by page).

[52] See Echavarría's illuminating discussion in "Leibniz on the efficacy and economy of divine grace," to which I am indebted. In the *Discourse on Metaphysics*, Leibniz writes (A VI iv 1577–8; AG 62): "This grace of God, whether ordinary or extraordinary, has its degrees and its measures; in itself, it is always efficacious in producing a certain proportionate effect, and, further, it is always sufficient, not only to secure us from sin, but even to produce salvation, assuming that man unites himself to it by what derives from him. But it is not always sufficient to overcome man's inclinations, for otherwise he would have nothing more to strive for; this is reserved solely for the absolutely efficacious grace which is always victorious, whether it is so by itself or by way of appropriate circumstances."

contrary circumstances. By contrast, aids have efficacity *per accidens* (so to speak) if they derive it from assisting circumstances. Only those that have complete per se efficaciousness have per se infallibility. Others derive their *infallibility* from the circumstances, which either do not impede, or, in general, assist and thus are *per accidens* (so to speak) (not with respect to God, but with respect to the thing). And finally, certain [aids] are not efficacious, but merely sufficient, for concerning the one who wills, an outcome is lacking where the will fails. (DPG, 46–9; trans. modified)

The main distinction here, endorsed also by Leibniz, is the well-established one between (objective) sufficient grace and (subjective) efficacious grace. Leibniz embraces a universalist position according to which sufficient grace is given to all.[53] That is to say, with his antecedent or absolute will, God wants all to be saved and gives to all sufficient grace to resist sin. This grace, however, does not obtain in all the same effects due to the different circumstances in which human beings find themselves and their response to these circumstances. In theological terms, although all are granted sufficient grace, whether this grace is efficacious in leading to salvation depends also on human beings' responses to their varying circumstances. It remains open to God, however, to bestow a special type of efficacious grace that is always per se infallible.[54]

Given that the efficacy of grace normally depends, for Leibniz, also on the circumstances dictated by the order which governs the best of all possible worlds, it hardly needs to be said that, in the context of his strict determinism, the usual problems raised by the relationship between grace and human responsibility become particularly acute. In his early *Confessio Philosophi* (1672–73) Leibniz shows himself intensely aware of the pressure put by the "lament of the damned" on his theodicy project:

> this inexorable difficulty is placed before us, whatever sophistry we may employ: the apparent justice of the lament of the damned, that they were born in such a way, sent into the world in such a way, came upon such times, persons, and occasions that they were not able not to perish; their minds, occupied prematurely by vicious thoughts, existed in circumstances that favored evil, that stimulated evil; they lacked circumstances that would have released them, that would have restrained them, as if the fates conspired in the ruin of the wretched . . . they curse the series of the universe, which also involves them.[55]

---

[53] *Theodicy* §95 (GP VI 155).

[54] Donald Rutherford proposes a naturalized conception of grace according to which God's grace, for Leibniz, "may be nothing more than his choice of external circumstances" (see Donald Rutherford, "Leibniz and the 'religion of reason,'" in *Für unser Glück oder das Glück anderer*, edited by Wenchao Li (Hildesheim: Olms, 2016), vol. 3, pp. 365–376 (here p. 373) and "Justice and circumstances: Theodicy as universal religion," in *New Essays on Leibniz's Theodicy*, edited by Larry M. Jorgensen and Samuel Newlands (Oxford: Oxford University Press, 2014), pp. 71–91). Although acknowledging the key role played by circumstances in Leibniz's account of grace, Echavarría resists identification (see "Leibniz on the efficacy and economy of divine grace").

[55] A VI iii 136–7; Sleigh 77. I am grateful to Lucy Sheaf for drawing my attention to this passage. The importance of the issue of eternal damnation for Leibniz's theodicy is lucidly highlighted in Lucy Sheaf, *Eternal Damnation in Leibniz's Early Theodicy* (King's College London, 2013; MPhilSt thesis).

A central plank of Leibniz's defense of God's justice is the claim that He loves everyone. But how can this claim be maintained if there are people who are eternally damned? A possible reply is that "of course evil men damn themselves . . . since they are forever impenitent and turn away from God."[56] Damnation is conceived by Leibniz as a persistent dissatisfaction with the state of things, a dissatisfaction which is in turn identified with "a burning hatred of God . . . in which consists the nature of despair" (A VI 3, 118; Sleigh 35):

> Whoever dies malcontent dies a hater of God. And now he follows along the road on which he began, as if he were headed for the precipice; and not being held back by external things, since access to his senses has been closed off, he nourishes his soul, which has withdrawn into itself, with that hatred of things already begun, and with that misery and disdain, and with indignation, envy, and displeasure, all of them increasing more and more. (A VI iii 142; Sleigh 91)

Leibniz is careful to stress that punishment consists in nothing else than this very hatred of God persistently chosen by the sinner. Moreover, the infinity of the sinner's punishment is justified by the perpetual continuation of his sinning:

> even if we should concede that no sin is infinite in itself, it can still be said that the sins of the damned are infinite in number, because they persist in sin throughout all eternity. Therefore if sins are eternal, it is just that the punishments should be eternal too.[57]

And yet the eternally damned seem to have a point in continuing to blame their circumstances. Had circumstances been significantly different, they, too, would not have sinned. In a text of 1689–90, Leibniz squarely faces this complain (A VI, 4, 1639): "You will insist that you can complain. Why did God not give you more strength? I reply, If He had done that, you would not exist, for He would have produced not you but another creature."[58] Fair enough, one could see the damned replying, but it would still have been better not to exist at all than enduring eternal misery. How can one claim that God loves also me in particular if I exist in the series of things which cannot but include my infinite unhappiness?

There can be little doubt that the doctrine of eternal damnation poses (to use his own phrase) an "inexorable difficulty" to Leibniz. However, it is debatable whether Leibniz

---

[56] *Preface to Ernst Soner's book on eternal punishment* (1708), LH 1, 20 Bl. 194 (draft); trans. by Lloyd Strickland in *Leibniz on God and Religion* (London: Bloomsbury, 2016), p. 326.

[57] Ibid. Interestingly, despite the rejection of purgatory typical of Protestants, Leibniz shows sympathy for this doctrine, involving a limited period of after-death punishment that leads, eventually, to eternal happiness (see Lloyd Strickland, "Leibniz's philosophy of purgatory," in *American Catholic Philosophical Quarterly* 84/3 (2010), pp. 531–548).

[58] *Mentes ipsae per se dissimiles sunt inter se* (c. March 1689–March 1690); Sleigh xl.

was really committed to it.[59] To be sure, there are numerous passages in which the doctrine is endorsed, but it has been noted that this endorsement stems from a pragmatic approach to revealed theology rather than from an explicit commitment to the truth of eternal damnation: it is *safer*, Leibniz suggests, to continue to maintain this traditional doctrine since it can serve to deter people from sinning.[60] On the other hand, he also expresses doubts about the actual usefulness of this doctrine in preventing sin as well as dismay at the readiness with which some theologians regard the damnation of others as an edifying thought:

> Mr Arnauld . . . finds it strange that so many millions of pagans have not been condemned; I would find it much stranger if they had been: I don't know why we are so inclined to believe that people are damned or sunk in eternal miseries, even if they could not help it; but this leads to thoughts hardly compatible with the goodness and justice of God. . . . I don't believe that the opinion of the eternal damnation of so many virtually innocent people is so edifying and so useful in preventing sin as is imagined. It leads to thoughts hardly compatible with the love of God. (A I vi 107–8)

Certainly, in his own positive account of salvation, Leibniz takes a remarkably liberal view on whom can be saved, extending this possibility to people of all religions, including pagans. For the salvation of an individual, he writes in 1690–91, "no revealed article is absolutely necessary, and therefore *it is possible to be saved* in every Religion, *provided that one truly loves God above all things.*"[61] In the earlier *Dialogue entre Poliandre and Theophile*, written in the mid-1679, he claims that "those who love God above all things are in a condition [*en estat*] to be saved." In the *Propositiones Theologicae*

---

[59] The controversy goes all the way back to the eighteenth century, when Johann August Eberhard argued in his *Neue Apologie des Sokrates* (1772) that Leibniz secretly embraced universal salvation while Gotthold Ephraim Lessing maintained that Leibniz was an advocate of eternal punishment (*Leibniz von den Ewigen Strafen*, 1773). This debate has been rejuvenated by Lloyd Strickland, "Leibniz on eternal punishment," in *British Journal for the History of Philosophy* 17/2 (2009), 307–331; Robert M. Adams, "Justice, happiness, and perfection in Leibniz's City of God," in *New Essays on Leibniz's Theodicy*, pp. 197–217 (see esp. pp. 207–213); and Paul Lodge, "Eternal punishment, universal salvation and pragmatic theology in Leibniz," in *Tercentenary Essays on the Philosophy and Science of Leibniz*, pp. 301–324.

[60] See Leibniz to Lorenz Hertel (January 1695), A I xi 21 (cited by Adams, "Justice, happiness, and perfection in Leibniz's City of God," see esp. pp. 216–217).

[61] A I vi 78–79. Cf. also Leibniz's marginal note on his copy of the fourth part of Paul Pellisson-Fontanier's *Réflexions sur les différends de la religion* (Paris, 1691) (A I vi 101). Leibniz is keen to stress that this is also the view held by many Roman Catholic theologians, notably the Jesuits. Cf. *Theodicy* §96 (GP VI 156): "the Roman Church, going further than the Protestants, does not absolutely damn those who are outside its communion, and even outside Christianity. . . . I will content myself with naming Father Friedrich Spee, the Jesuit, one of the most excellent men of his Society, who was also of this common view regarding the efficacy of the love of God"; NE 500: "many eminent doctors of the Roman Church, far from damning lax Protestants, have been willing to save even pagans"; A I vi 94: "The Jesuits have maintained that invincible ignorance excuses, and that therefore the sincere conscience of anyone is always the last judge down here, *in conscientiae foro.*" See also *Theodicy* §95 (GP VI 156), quoted later.

of 1685–86, he explains that: "No one can be justified without a true love of God."[62] "Nor," Leibniz clarifies in the *Nouveaux Essais*,

> are those who accord salvation to pagans, or to others who lack the ordinary aids, thereby obliged to rely for this on natural processes alone. . . . One can, after all, maintain that, when God gives them grace sufficient to call forth an act of contrition, he also gives them before their death, even if only in the final moments, all the light of faith and all the fervour of love which they need for salvation; this being given to them either explicitly or dispositionally, but in any case supernaturally.[63]

It is true that in *De Salvatione Ethnicorum*, written by 1698, he maintains that pagans cannot be saved without Christ "because no one is able to love God above all things except he who understands that this is the greatest good to him, but no one understands this except a Christian." Even in this text, however, he goes on to note that "if we imagine that there has been a love of God above all things in any of the pagans," the person who loved in this way would be saved—albeit not merely through natural powers. Leibniz's point is not that pagans cannot be saved at all but that anyone who loves God above all things (and is therefore saved) can do so only through grace mediated by Christ.[64] At the beginning of the text, he affirms in fact that in some cases pagans can be "granted pure grace through Christ."[65] As the passage from the *Nouveaux Essais* suggests, divine grace works in mysterious ways. For all that we know, it could be given at death, including to pagans.[66]

Grace is thus necessary for salvation, but the key point is, for Leibniz, that "God never refuses his grace to those who seek it with a good heart."[67] In support of this thesis, he quotes the sentence, "*facienti quod in se est Deus non denegat gratiam* [God does not deny grace to those who do their best],"[68] calling on the authority of

[62]   Respectively, A VI iv 2220 and A VI iv 2355. Trans. by Adams, "Justice, happiness, and perfection in Leibniz's City of God," p. 205.

[63]   *Nouveaux Essais*, book IV, chap. xviii, §9; NE 502. See also NE 500 and *Dialogue entre Poliandre and Theophile*, c. mid-1679 (A VI iv 2220–1) and *Theodicy* §95 (GP VI 155–6).

[64]   A IV vii 666: "Any one is able to fear God by his natural powers, but no one can love him except by grace through Christ." However, it should be noted that in *Dialogue entre Poliandre et Theophile* Leibniz does not object to Poliandre's claim that "a pagan philosopher can love God above all things, since reason can teach him that God is infinitely perfect and a supremely lovable being" (A VI iv 2220; trans. by Strickland in *Leibniz on God*, p. 142).

[65]   A IV vii 666–7; trans. by Strickland in *Leibniz on God*, pp. 323–324.

[66]   See also *Dialogue entre Poliandre et Theophile* (A VI iv 2220–2, 2226).

[67]   *Mémoire pour des Personnes éclairées* (A IV iv 615; PW 105).

[68]   See Leibniz's marginal note on his copy of the fourth part of Pellisson's *Réflexions* (A I vi 144); *Theodicy* §95 (GP VI 155); and *Dialogue entre Poliandre et Theophile* (A VI iv 2221). Trans. by Alister E. McGrath in *Iustitia Dei: A History of the Christian Doctrine of Justification* (Cambridge: Cambridge University Press, 2005), p. 107 (cf. pp. 107–117 for a helpful history of this "axiom"; I am grateful to Lucy Sheaf for drawing my attention to McGrath's work).

many theologians strongly approved in the Roman Church itself who taught that a sincere Act of love of God above all things suffices for salvation, when it is aroused by the grace of Jesus Christ. Father Francis Xavier replied to the Japanese that if their ancestors had used well their natural lights, God would have given them the necessary graces to be saved, and the Bishop of Geneva, Francis of Sales, strongly approves this reply (Book 4 of the love of God chap. 5). (*Theodicy* §95; GP VI 156)

In sum, salvation for Leibniz does not ultimately depend on believing a set of true doctrines, but on a practical attitude: the love of God above all things. To be sure, the best way to achieve this aim is to reach a true knowledge of God since truly knowing God can only lead to loving him. But also those whose knowledge is very imperfect can be saved since a sincere love of God is sufficient for salvation.[69] Leibniz acknowledges that the ability to love in this way requires the support of divine grace and the mediation of Christ. But he also maintains, most importantly, that such grace is given in a mysterious manner to all those who search God with a sincere heart,[70] whether or not they realize its being mediated through Christ and the Holy Spirit. Leibniz's theology is thus fundamentally a theology of love that is ultimately practical[71] and tries to be both universalist and Christian. Overall, it is strongly driven by soteriological considerations. What really matters is to be saved; that is, to achieve the dynamic state of eternal happiness or beatitude that consists in contemplating, and therefore loving, God's perfection.

[69] Cf., e.g., *Dialogue entre Poliandre et Theophile* (A VI iv 2226): "Let us return to what is more certain, namely, that we must love God above all things, and our neighbour as ourselves. It is in this that the law consists. It is in this, with the addition of the doctrine of Jesus Christ, that the true active faith also consists . . . let us agree with the Evangelist and Apostle St. John, who does not preach anything other than this charity full of faith and this divine love which shines out through good works, and we will have done enough to be saved."

[70] Cf. *Theodicy* §95 (GP VI 155-6): "I would be rather in favour of those who grant to all human beings a sufficient grace . . . for how do we know whether they do not receive ordinary or extraordinary aids which are unknown to us?"

[71] Leibniz's conception of theology as a theology of love, and its practical nature, are stressed by Robert M. Adams in "Justice, happiness, and perfection in Leibniz's City of God"; "Leibniz's conception of religion," in *The Proceedings of the Twentieth World Congress of Philosophy*, edited by Mark D. Gedney, vol. 7: Modern Philosophy (Philosophy Documentation Center, 2000), pp. 57-70; and "Leibniz's examination of the Christian religion," in *Faith and Philosophy* 11/4 (1994), pp. 517-546. See also Maria Rosa Antognazza, "Theory and praxis in Leibniz's theological thought," in *G. W. Leibniz im Lichte der Theologien*, edited by Wenchao Li and Hartmut Rudolph (Stuttgart: Steiner, 2017), pp. 35-57.

CHAPTER 42

ECCLESIOLOGY, ECUMENISM, AND TOLERATION

MARIA ROSA ANTOGNAZZA

LEIBNIZ'S conception of the Christian church, his life-long ecumenical efforts, and his stance toward religious toleration were shaped by the extraordinarily complex confessional and political situation of the Holy Roman Empire. At the time of Leibniz's birth in 1646, the belligerent European powers that had confronted one another on the battlefield since 1618 were in the process of hammering out the conditions of the peace eventually signed at Westphalia in 1648. A central provision of the peace was permanently to recognize the legitimacy of the three main Christian confessions—Roman Catholic, Evangelical or Lutheran, and Reformed or Calvinist—within the hundreds of semi-autonomous imperial estates under the loose authority of the Emperor and imperial diet. Flanked as it was by two aggressive and more religiously unified neighbors—Louis XIV's France to the West and the Ottoman Empire to the East—the Empire was inevitably weakened by its confessional fragmentation. At the same time, the necessity of cooperation within its borders for its very survival resulted in a political model in which the main Christian denominations could co-exist more or less peacefully. The officially sanctioned toleration of different denominations within the Empire as a whole and within some of its cities and principalities paved the way for a series of negotiations for church reunification sponsored at various points by various princes, not least by the Emperor himself.

Leibniz's own background was Lutheran. Leipzig, where he was born and raised in an extended family of staunch Lutherans, understood itself as a bastion of Lutheranism against the creeping dangers of Calvinism.[1] He moved away as a young man, but not without having first equipped himself with much broader religious views through the

---

[1] For a discussion of Leibniz's background and formative years, see Maria Rosa Antognazza, *Leibniz: An Intellectual Biography* (Cambridge: Cambridge University Press, 2009), chaps 1–3. Unless otherwise stated, translations are my own.

independent reading of irenical literature from all main Christian denominations.[2] After a formative period at the Catholic court of the tolerant Archbishop of Mainz, Johann Philipp von Schönborn, and four years in Paris, he settled in the Duchy of Hanover, a northern principality which, although Lutheran for more than a century, was ruled at the time of his arrival by a Catholic convert, Duke Johann Friedrich. An analogous situation had prevailed in the neighboring electoral principality of Brandenburg since 1613, when the solidly Lutheran estates had refused to follow the ruling dynasty in its conversion from Evangelical to Reformed. Such complex arrangements became increasingly commonplace after Westphalia. The heir to Brandenburg, for instance, married a Lutheran Hanoverian princess, Sophie Charlotte, herself the daughter of a Reformed princess, Sophie von der Pfalz, presumptive heir to the English crown and, as such, presumptive head of the Anglican church. Mirroring these increasingly intricate relations, the balance of power in the imperial diet maintained a precarious equilibrium between a mix of Lutheran, Reformed, and Catholic Electors under the rule of a Roman Catholic Emperor. Leibniz's life itself was interspersed with both deep friendship and tense relationships with Roman Catholics (not least a number of Jesuits), Lutheran, and Reformed women and men. It was against this variegated backdrop that his ecclesiastical views developed.

ECCLESIOLOGY

Leibniz remained a Lutheran all his life. Yet, as early as his departure from Leipzig for Mainz, his relatives were gripped by fears for the safety of his soul due to the perceived danger of an imminent conversion to Catholicism or (even worse, in their view) Calvinism.[3] To his half-brother, who fulminated against the theological "syncretism" of irenical theologians such as Helmstedt's Georg Calixt (1586–1656), Leibniz replied in 1669: "I hold and with God's help will continue to hold fast to the Evangelical truth as long as I live, but I am deterred from condemning others both by my own personal inclination and by the stern command of Christ: 'Judge not, that ye be not judged' [Matthew 7:1]."[4]

---

[2] On the complexity of irenicism within the Empire see Howard Hotson, "Irenicism in the Confessional Age: the Holy Roman Empire, 1563–1648," in *Conciliation and Confession: Struggling for Unity in the Age of Reform, 1415–1648*, edited by Howard Louthan and Randall Zachman (Notre Dame: University of Notre Dame Press, 2004), pp. 228–285.

[3] See Leibniz's response of October 5, 1669 to his half-brother's accusation that he was near to becoming a Calvinist (in Paul Schrecker, "G.-W. Leibniz. Lettres et fragments inédits," in *Revue philosophique de la France et de l'Étranger* 118 (1934), pp. 5–134, here p. 67) and the letter of January 22, 1672 written to him by his sister, Anna Catharina, while he was employed at the Catholic court of Mainz (A I i N. 157).

[4] In Schrecker, "G.-W. Leibniz. Lettres et fragments inédits," p. 82.

For their part, his Catholic friends were repeatedly puzzled and disappointed by his refusal to convert, given the closeness of many of his views to Catholicism. They were not mistaken in detecting this proximity: Leibniz went as far as drafting an entire theological system of markedly Roman Catholic flavor.[5] The main objections he had to the Roman church regarded its practices rather than its theology.[6] When it came to the issue of reunification, Leibniz openly accepted the idea of papal authority.[7] Remarkably, in a marginal note to one of his private papers of 1680–84, he wrote:

> However often I consider in my own mind which dogmas I would myself propose if I were granted the supreme power of deciding, all things considered I would be inclined to preserve the dogmas of the Roman church, and I would correct merely certain practices which have been disapproved of by pious and prudent men of that [the Catholic] side for some time now, [but] which until now have generally been tolerated in the Roman church due to the failings of times and men. If I had been born in the Roman church I would certainly not have abandoned it, and yet I would believe all the things which I now believe. The authority of the pope which frightens off many people above all, in fact deters me least of all, since I believe that nothing can be understood as more useful to the Church than its correct use.[8]

Yet, even when a conversion might have been to his immediate personal advantage, he resisted it. In 1687, while visiting Landgraf Ernst von Hessen-Rheinfels, another Catholic convert and close friend, he declined to pursue a candidacy for the position of chancellor of the Catholic bishopric of Hildesheim in view of his Lutheran commitments.[9] Although greatly desiring a move to Paris, in 1692, he refused an invitation to join the service of Louis XIV, which would in all probability have required conversion to Catholicism.[10] In early 1695, he renounced the possibility of "the post of *primus custos* of the Vatican library" as well as "many other advantages" due to their being conditional upon his willingness "to rejoin the Church."[11]

---

[5] *Examen Religionis Christianae*, 1686; A VI iv N. 420. A number of his theological sketches would also have pleased the Roman church (see for instance *De Schismate*, second half of 1683; A IV iii 236–7).

[6] In a letter of November 3, 1682, to Landgraf Ernst (A I iii 272), Leibniz writes: "Most of the objections which can be raised against Rome are rather against the practices of people than against dogmas. Were those practices to be publicly disavowed, these objections would cease." See also A I iii 246–7; A I iii 272; A I vi 165–6; A I vi 148; A VI iv 2286–7.

[7] Cf. for instance A VI i 499–500.

[8] *De Scriptura, Ecclesia, Trinitate*; A VI iv 2286–7. See also the letter to Landgraf Ernst of January 11, 1684, where Leibniz declares, "if I were born in the Roman church I would not leave it" (A I iv 321).

[9] Cf. A I iv N. 2 and N. 4.

[10] The invitation was conveyed by Jacob Auguste Barnabas Comte Des Viviers, to whom Leibniz replied in May 1692 (see A I viii N. 158).

[11] Letter of February 5, 1695 of Antonio Alberti (alias Amable de Tourreil) to Rudolf Christian von Bodenhausen (A II iii 19). Cf. Leibniz to Spanheim, end of July 1695 (A I ix 598); Leibniz to Bodenhausen (FC, *Oeuvres* II 79; quoted by André Robinet, *G. W. Leibniz. Iter Italicum* (Florence: Olschki, 1988) p. 180); Leibniz to Le Thorel, December 5, 1698 (A I xvi 306).

The Catholic hopefuls who mooted these offers may well have underestimated the extent to which he disagreed with some aspects of the Roman church.[12] Notwithstanding the importance of any such disagreement, however, his faithfulness to the confession of his birth does not appear to have been based on the conviction of its superiority to other Christian denominations. On the contrary, it seems to have stemmed from his belief that no particular Christian denomination is superior to the others. Hence, in his view, it would have been wrong to abandon one church to join another, as if the latter had a significantly greater claim to the status of true representative of Christianity. Already in 1669, he rebuked his half-brother's charge that he was one step from abandoning Lutheranism by noting that "it is foolish to flee from one fortress to the other" when "there is no difference regarding the foundation of salvation."[13] Rather than switching allegiances, Leibniz recommended remaining in one's confession and working instead for ecclesiastical reconciliation. He regarded, in fact, the main Christian denominations as particular churches constituting the only one truly catholic or universal church whose authority went back to apostolic times and whose theology was to be traced back to the entire ecclesiastical tradition.

He wrote, for instance, in private notes of 1690–1: "the churches of Italy or of France have no advantage over those of Germany or of England, and have no reason to believe themselves more in the Church than the latter. . . . The dogmas of Trent have no greater claim to be attributed to the Church than those of Augsburg or of Dordrecht. It is merely the dogmas of particular churches which will be reformed."[14] Against the denial by a prominent French Catholic convert, Paul Pellisson-Fontanier, that the truth might be distributed among the Christian churches, Leibniz replied in no uncertain terms: "this is possible."[15]

Nevertheless, ideally Leibniz envisaged a return of all Christian churches into the fold of a reformed Rome. This vision was driven by a conception of the relationship between temporal and spiritual powers informed by the medieval ideal of "two heads" of Christendom, the Holy Roman Emperor and the Pope, both invested with supranational authority: the emperor as the "secular arm of the Universal church," the pope as the spiritual authority who reserved the right to "curb tyranny."[16]

[12] See, e.g., in A II i 750–1, Leibniz's reservations about "three or four places of the Council of Trent" which, in his view, had to be interpreted "in a way rather distant from the common opinions of Scholastic theologians and, especially, of monks" in order to avoid contradiction. Cf. also A II i 758 and Leibniz to Landgraf Ernst, January 11, 1684 (A I iv 321).

[13] Leibniz to Johann Friedrich Leibniz, October 5, 1669 (in Schrecker, "G.-W. Leibniz. Lettres et fragments inédits," p. 67).

[14] A I vi 147–8. Leibniz is referring, respectively, to the Council of Trent (held in three parts, from 1545 to 1563, by the Roman Catholic church in response to the Reformation), the Confession of Augsburg (the twenty-eight articles presented in 1530 to the Diet of Augsburg as the basic confession of the Lutheran churches), and the Synod of Dordrecht (the assembly of Reformed churches held in 1618–19, marking the victory of strict Calvinists over the Arminians or Remonstrants).

[15] See Leibniz's marginal note on his copy of the fourth part of Pellisson's Réflexions sur les différends de la religion (Paris, 1691) (A I vi 141).

[16] See Caesarini Fürstenerii De Jure Suprematus, 1677 (A IV ii 15–17). Cf. also Leibniz to Duke Johann Friedrich, autumn 1679 (A II i 752, 756–7).

Ecumenism

This is the ecclesiology that underpins Leibniz's dogged efforts to advance church re-unification.[17] In all probability, Leibniz's first direct contacts with the ecclesiastical negotiations promoted by some German princes took place at the court of the arch-bishop of Mainz whose representatives (notably, the Catholic theologian Peter van Walenburch) were engaged in ecumenical colloquia.[18] Once in Hanover, Leibniz found in Duke Johann Friedrich a Catholic convert who chose not to exercise his right to impose his religion on his Lutheran subjects and fostered instead talks aimed at the reunification of Catholic and Lutheran churches. In 1676, the same year in which Leibniz took up his official duties, Johann Friedrich welcomed in Hanover the Franciscan Cristobal de Rojas y Spinola (c. 1626–95), entrusted by the emperor with the task of taking soundings among German princes of Protestant territories on the issue of church reunification. Central to the talks with Rojas (which resumed in 1679 and 1683) was Gerhard Wolter Molanus (1633–1722), the Lutheran abbot of Luccum in charge of Hanoverian ecclesiastical affairs. Over the years, Leibniz developed a close collaboration with Molanus, working with him at some important ecumenical schemes.

Although he did not have an official role in the talks held in Hanover in 1683 under Duke Ernst August, Leibniz regarded them as a turning point, lending his full support to the strategy devised by the chief negotiators, Rojas and Molanus.[19] This strategy envisaged a preliminary reunion of the Protestant and Roman Catholic churches before agreement on controversial issues had been reached. On the basis of this reunion, a properly representative ecumenical council would be called. This council, having been recognized at the outset by all parties as legitimate, would have the authority of settling the points under contention.[20] In practice, the proposal amounted to setting aside the decisions of the controversial Council of Trent in favor of a truly ecumenical council in which Protestant views would be taken fully into account. As Molanus crisply summarized the key principle, the reunion would have taken place *salvis*

---

[17] A more detailed discussion of Leibniz's participation in ecumenical efforts throughout his life is offered by Antognazza, *Leibniz: An Intellectual Biography*, from which I am drawing. On Leibniz's work toward the reunification of the Catholic and Lutheran churches, the classic volume by Paul Eisenkopf is still valuable (*Leibniz und die Einigung der Christenheit. Überlegungen zur Reunion der evangelischen und katholischen Kirche*. München-Paderbon-Wien: Schöningh, 1975). For recent work on Leibniz's ecumenism see *Leibniz und die Ökumene*, edited by Wenchao Li, Hans Poser, and Hartmut Rudolph (Stuttgart: Steiner 2013) and D. E. Jablonski and G. W. Leibniz, *Negotium Irenicum*, edited by C. Rösler-Le Van (Paris: Garnier, 2013).

[18] Cf. *Theodicy*, "Preface" (GP VI 43).

[19] See, e.g., A I v N. 6, a long memo prepared by Leibniz in 1687 for Landgraf Ernst, in which he endorsed the reunion strategy which emerged in the talks of 1683.

[20] Cf. A I v 19, in which Leibniz identifies the convocation of this "free and ecumenical Council" as the "nodal point of the business."

principiis utriusque partis; that is, preserving the principles of both parties.[21] Regrettably but perhaps not surprisingly, this ambitious plan did not meet with success. Lutheran theologians involved in the negotiations greeted the proposal with a distinct lack of enthusiasm. Even more importantly, the strength of Rojas's mandate as papal representative was far from clear. Although Pope Innocent XI regarded Rojas's endeavors toward reconciliation sympathetically, the extent of the pope's support for this specific reunion strategy was at best uncertain.

Meanwhile, Leibniz penned a number of sketches exploring the possibility of church reunification[22] and corresponded intermittently on church reunification with one of the chief theological authorities of France, the bishop of Meaux and preceptor to the Dauphin, Jacques Bénigne Bossuet (1627–1704). As a leading architect of Gallicanism (the French way to Catholicism), Bossuet theorized a limitation of papal authority through appeal to the authority of the universal church.[23] Leibniz saw the relative autonomy of the French church from Rome as an encouraging model for a flexible Catholic communion in which local churches operated with a degree of self-determination. His exchanges with Bossuet, however, never achieved the level of sympathy he enjoyed with other Catholic correspondents. To start with, Bossuet was closely involved in the court of Louis XIV, whose revocation of the Edict of Nantes in 1685 caused waves of Huguenots to seek refuge in Germany, the Dutch Republic, and England[24]—hardly a promising path to church reunification. More specifically, Bossuet's uncompromising insistence on the binding authority of the Council of Trent proved an insurmountable obstacle. After the death of Bossuet on April 12, 1704, Leibniz confided to his trusted correspondent, Thomas Burnett of Kemney: "the Bishop of Meaux . . . assumed too decisive a tone, and wanted to push things too far, advancing doctrines which I could not at all let pass without betraying my conscience and the truth. For these reasons I answered him vigorously and firmly, and adopted a tone as lofty as his to show him that, however great a controversialist he might be, I knew his subtleties too well to be taken by surprise" (Klopp IX, 182).

The mid-1690s constituted in many ways a watershed in the course of Leibniz's ecumenical efforts due to the alignment of his own personal circumstances with the shifting balance of power in the Empire. By 1695, all his closest Catholic discussion partners and supporters—Baron Johann Christian von Boineburg, Archbishop Johann Philipp von Schönborn, Duke Johann Friedrich, Paul Pellisson-Fontanier, Ernst von Hessen-Rheinfels, and Bishop Rojas—had passed away. In 1697, the conversion to Catholicism

---

[21] Cf. the two key documents prepared, respectively, by Rojas (*Regulae circa christianorum omnium Ecclesiasticam Reunionem*, 1682–3) and by Molanus and his Hanoverian colleague, Hermann Barckhausen (*Methodus reducendae Unionis Ecclesiasticae inter Romanenses et Protestantes*, 1683).

[22] See, e.g., four texts written in the second half of 1683 (A IV iii N. 16–19): *De unitate Ecclesiae; Apologia fidei Catholicae ex recta ratione; De Schismate;* and *Reunion der Kirchen.*

[23] Cf. the fourth article of the *Declaratio cleri Gallicani de ecclesiastica potestate* (March 19, 1682), penned by Bossuet.

[24] With the Edict of Nantes (April 13, 1598), Henry IV granted toleration to the French Calvinists, the Huguenots.

of the Duke of Saxony and the unfavorable conditions for Protestants contained in the Treaty of Ryswick suggested a reorientation of priorities away from a reunification between Catholics and Lutherans and toward an intra-protestant ecumenical project instead. Around the same time, the two northern Protestant electorates of Hanover and Berlin—the first once again ruled by a Lutheran, the second containing a Lutheran population still ruled by a Reformed dynasty that had welcomed a significant number of Reformed refugees from France—began earnest talks of church union between their Lutheran and Reformed confessions under the common denomination of *ecclesia evangelica et reformata*. Leibniz was at the forefront of the *negotium irenicum* launched by Berlin and led by Daniel Ernst Jablonski (1660–1741), court preacher in Berlin and grandson of a leading irenical thinker of the previous generation, Jan Amos Comenius (1592–1670).

Jablonski's preparatory document, the *Kurtze Vorstellung der Einigkeit und des Unterscheides, im Glauben beyder Evangelischen so genandten Lutherischen und Reformirten Kirchen* (1697), identified three main points of disagreement between the Lutheran and the Reformed churches: namely, the communication of attributes (*communicatio idiomatum*) between the natures of Christ, the real presence of Christ in the Eucharist, and the issues of election and predestination.[25] None of these, Jablonski opined, was an insuperable hurdle—a view shared by Leibniz.[26] In close collaboration with Molanus, he penned an extensive reply to Jablonski, the *Unvorgreiffliches Bedencken über eine Schrifft genandt "Kurtze Vorstellung"* (1698–99),[27] in which a cluster of philosophical issues raised especially by the doctrine of predestination and by Eucharistic real presence were tackled in an attempt to mediate differences between Lutheran and Calvinist positions.

Despite these sustained efforts and some half-backed attempts (criticized by Leibniz) to call a pan-protestant conference and enforce unification within Brandenburg-Prussia, agreement could not be found. Fresh hopes were subsequently pinned on the mediation of the Anglican church.[28] Leibniz regarded the theological and liturgical positions of the Church of England as a middle-ground between the Lutheran and Reformed confessions. For instance, on the occasion of the accession to the throne of England of the Hanoverian elector, Georg Ludwig (officially a Lutheran), Leibniz reasoned that his entrance into the Church of England as its head without a change of religion demonstrated that differences between the Lutheran and Anglican denominations were either merely liturgical or concerned nonessential theological matters.[29]

---

[25] Leibniz's position on these points is discussed in the chapter on "Philosophical Theology and Christian Doctrines."

[26] Cf. Leibniz's *Tentamen Expositionis irenicae trium potissimarum inter protestante controversiarum* (October–December 1698; A IV vii N. 62) and *Judicium de annotatis Placidis ad Tentamen expositionis irenicae* (written by February 11, 1699; A IV viii N. 56).

[27] A IV vii N. 79. See also the important series of texts relating to ecumenical efforts and discussing key theological issues, published in A IV vii N. 45–78 and A IV viii N. 44–65.

[28] On Leibniz's engagement with Gilbert Burnet's *Exposition of the Thirty-Nine Articles of the Church of England*, see chapter on "Philosophical Theology and Christian Doctrines."

[29] Cf. Leibniz to Caroline, undated (Klopp XI 20–21).

Moreover, since (on the one hand) the Church of England was evidently not opposed to Lutheranism and (on the other hand) considered itself as basically aligned with the international Reformed communities, it constituted the missing link that could unite the main Protestant denominations on the continent.[30] Needless to say, countless theologians and clergymen of all three parties saw matters differently.

While focusing on intra-protestant unification, Leibniz never abandoned hopes for broader ecclesiastical reunification. He continued to negotiate with Roman Catholics, answering, for instance, a direct summons to Vienna from the emperor who, in May 1700, requested Georg Ludwig to dispatch his "highly experienced, discreet, and qualified" counsellor for further talks on the reunification of the Catholic and Protestant churches.[31] Toward the end of his life, he cast his net even wider, envisaging a world-wide ecumenical council under the patronage of the Russian czar, Peter the Great.[32] This council should have prepared the eventual reunification of all main Christian traditions: the Greek, the Latin, and the Germanic. Leibniz had in fact long regarded the continuous tradition of the Eastern (or Greek) Christian church, arcing back to apostolic times, as a unique antidote with which to purge Christianity of dubious innovations introduced by the Latin church. In his view, the restoration of the true teaching of the catholic or universal church needed a truly ecumenical general council encompassing all Christian churches (Orthodox, Catholic, and Protestant):

> Nowadays one can divide Christians who acknowledge the ancient councils into three nations: the Greek nation (within which I would like to include some other eastern nations and the Muscovites); the Latin nation, within which I include the Italians, French, and Spaniards; and the German nation which includes the Germans, English, Danes, and Swedes. And I believe that all three are needed to form a General Council, which could make the views of the Church known to us.[33]

Realizing a plan of such breathtaking ambition was scarcely on the cards in the extremely fragile and intricate confessional situation of the late seventeenth and early eighteenth centuries. After decades of frustrating negotiations, even the most inveterate optimist could not have been unimpressed by its complexity. Leibniz was well aware of the need to proceed pragmatically and step by step, achieving what was possible and

[30] Cf. Leibniz to Caroline, undated (Klopp XI 85–90).

[31] See Klopp VIII xxx. This summons resulted in a sojourn in Vienna from the end of October to mid-December 1700, during which Leibniz met with Franz Anton von Buchhaim (the successor of Rojas on the episcopal seat of Wiener-Neustadt) and the apostolic nuncio in Vienna.

[32] See Ernst Benz, "Leibniz und Peter der Grosse," 1947, pp. 1–88 (here pp. 30–38), installment 2 in *Leibniz. Zu seinem 300. Geburtstage 1646–1946*, edited by Erich Hochstetter (Berlin: W. de Gruyter, 1946–52), installments 1–8; Franz Xaver Kiefl, *Der Friedensplan des Leibniz* (Paderborn: Schöningh, 1903), pp. lxxxvii–lxxxx; and Eisenkopf, *Leibniz und die Einigung der Christenheit*, p. 58.

[33] Leibniz to Landgraf Ernst, December 1692 (A I viii 210). On the possible role of mediation of the Greek Orthodox church, cf. also *Réponse de Leibniz au mémoire de l'Abbé Pirot*, in FC, *Oeuvres*, I 380–410 (see pp. 398–399, 405); Leibniz to Landgraf Ernst, March 14, 1685 (A I iv 356); Leibniz to Bossuet, May 14, 1700 (A I xviii N. 368, esp. pp. 636, 638–639).

leaving the rest as a regulative ideal. Already within the more limited project of intra-protestant unification, he lucidly identified three progressively difficult degrees: a political unity or "a good civic understanding," ecclesiastical toleration, and, finally, theological agreement or "concord of views." "The first and the second degree," Leibniz concluded,

> seem to me necessary and achievable, and sufficient. The first degree is necessary on political grounds for the conservation of both parties. The second degree is necessitated by the principle of Christian charity, and in consequence is more than feasible. The third degree does not seem attainable, but it is also not necessary. It would nevertheless be good if some able theologians were to work at it at least as regards certain points where, I believe, the disputes consist in fact more in formulations than in realities. (A I xiv 690–1)

TOLERATION

As shown by the passage just quoted, religious toleration among Christians was, for Leibniz, the preliminary condition of any further project of fuller ecclesiastical unification based on theological agreement. It is true that on several occasions he wrote dismissively of toleration as a cure targeting "the most pressing symptoms" of the illness but not its cause.[34] But these statements should be read in the context of his work for the actual unification or reunification of the Christian churches. Having his sight on the higher prize, he resisted calls to settle for mere toleration.[35]

When it comes to toleration as willingness to accept and respect irreducible differences in religious belief even on points of importance, Leibniz's support is clear. Although he never wrote a systematic treatise on the matter, a remarkably inclusive conception of toleration can be gleaned from a broad sample of his writings and correspondence.[36] Arguably, its most interesting aspects are the philosophical and theological

---

[34] Leibniz for Landgraf Ernst, November 1687 (A I v 11). However, also in this memo, Leibniz affirms that the starting point should always be "mutual Tolerance" (A v 11).

[35] See, e.g., the negotiations between Hanover and Berlin for intra-protestant unification.

[36] Most of the texts mentioned here are identified and discussed in Maria Rosa Antognazza, "Leibniz and religious toleration: The correspondence with Paul Pellisson-Fontanier," in *American Catholic Philosophical Quarterly* 76/4 (2002), pp. 601–622, and Maria Rosa Antognazza, "Leibniz's doctrine of toleration: philosophical, theological, and pragmatic reasons," in *Natural Law and Toleration in the Early Enlightenment*, edited by J. Parkin and T. Stanton (Oxford: Oxford University Press, 2013), pp. 139–164. On Leibniz and religious toleration see also Nicholas Jolley, "Leibniz, Locke, and the epistemology of toleration," in *Leibniz and the English—speaking world*, edited by Pauline Phemister and Stuart Brown (Dordrecht: Springer, 2007), pp. 133–143; Ursula Goldenbaum, "Leibniz über Toleranz und Wahrheit," in *Leibniz neu denken*, edited by Erich Barke, Rolf Wernstedt, and Herbert Breger (Stuttgart: Steiner, 2009), pp. 37–61; and Mariangela Priarolo, "Individual certainty and common truth: Leibniz's philosophical grounds for toleration," in *Society and Politics* 8/1 (2014), pp. 25–40.

grounds of Leibniz's stance. As Pellisson crisply frames the issue in his discussions with Leibniz, the matter at hand is not so much the question of

> whether the Prince should tolerate a plurality of Religions inside his State; this depends on one hundred thousand circumstances. . . . Here . . . we are only concerned with tolerance or intolerance of the Church. It is not a question of knowing, for instance, whether we should let the Socinian live, but whether we should promise eternal life to him.[37]

In other words, the question of religious toleration, as tackled by Leibniz, is not merely or even primarily a political issue concerning the conditions under which a state can and should allow different religions in order to promote its own security. It is first and foremost a philosophical and a theological issue concerning the nature of belief and the nature of salvation, from which important political consequences also follow.

For Leibniz, as for Locke, belief is not voluntary. To believe or not to believe something does not depend on the will but on the intellect. Responding in 1690 to Pellisson's *Réflexions sur les différends de la religion* (Paris 1686), Leibniz notes: "Opinions are not voluntary, and are not dismissed at will; this is why (absolutely speaking) they are not subject to orders."[38] Although (as Leibniz acknowledges in the *Nouveaux Essais*) belief can be obliquely influenced by the will, this is an *indirect* influence by which we "turn our attention" to think further about reasons in favor of a certain side of the issue. It is on these *reasons* that belief depends since "what we believe is never just what we want to believe but rather what we see as most likely."[39]

Moreover, unlike Descartes, Leibniz does not think that the root of error—that is, the source of a false belief—is ultimately to be located in the will.[40] Appealing (rightly or wrongly) to Cartesian epistemology, some authors concluded that to embrace a religious or theological error is a voluntary fault and should not, therefore, be tolerated.[41] Leibniz, on the contrary, is firm in sharply distinguishing error from voluntary action. The latter is punishable, the former is not: "one does not have a belief at will," he writes around 1711, "but acts as one wills; it is not the lack of belief which deserves properly to be punished, but malice and obstinacy."[42] "The penalty for the errant," he states, "is to be

---

[37] Pellisson to Marie de Brinon for Leibniz, September 4, 1690 (A I vi 92–3).

[38] A I vi 117. See also A I iv 320; A I ix 192; Grua 216.

[39] *Nouveaux Essais*, book IV, chap. xx, §16 (NE 517).

[40] In the *Fourth Meditation*, Descartes gives the following diagnosis of the source of error: "the scope of the will is wider than that of the intellect; but instead of restricting it within the same limits, I extend its use to matters which I do not understand. Since the will is indifferent in such cases, it easily turns aside from what is true and good, and this is the source of my error and sin." René Descartes, *Oeuvres de Descartes*, 12 vols., edited by C. Adam and P. Tannery (Paris: Léopold Cerf, 1897–1910), vol. VII, p. 58 (trans. by John Cottingham, Robert Stoothoff, and Dugald Murdoch, in *The Philosophical Writings of Descartes*, 3 vols. Cambridge: Cambridge University Press, 1984–91, vol. 2, pp. 40–41). Basically, the source of error is located in the fact that the will assents also to what is not seen clearly and distinctly.

[41] See Priarolo, "Individual certainty and common truth," pp. 25–26.

[42] *Remarques sur un petit livre traduit de l'Anglois, intitulé Lettre sur l'enthousiasme* [Shaftesbury's *Letter concerning enthusiasm* (London 1708)]; GP III 415. See also Leibniz to Johann Friedrich Leibniz,

taught."[43] Indeed, since it is "a natural right [*droit naturelle*] to express what one believes to be the truth," Leibniz questions the "right to proceed . . . to the ultimate punishment" (A II 1 535).

According to this view, those who hold some objectively false religious belief are merely material (as opposed to formal) heretics. In accordance with many Roman Catholic theologians, Leibniz notes, only formal heretics—that is, those who *knowingly* reject a true doctrine—are excluded from salvation.[44] Already in 1679, he writes to Duke Johann Friedrich: "if by chance a man believed to see clearly a contradiction in what it is ordered him to believe, it would be impossible for him to give it credence; he would be a heretic but only a material one, and that would not keep him from being saved."[45]

For Leibniz, salvation does not depend, in fact, on believing or not believing certain doctrines (even if these were objectively true ones) but on a practical attitude: the love of God above all things. This love requires the aid of God's grace, but Leibniz is confident that sufficient grace is granted to all.[46] Indeed, he writes to Landgraf Ernst in 1690, "to believe that people are damned or sunk in eternal miseries, even if they could not help it . . . leads to thoughts hardly compatible with the goodness and justice of God" (A I vi 107–8). In the *Nouveaux Essais*, referring to his exchange with Pellisson of 1690, he recalls:

> I once showed M. Pellisson that many eminent doctors of the Roman church, far from damning lax Protestants, have been willing to save even pagans and to maintain that the people in question may have been saved by an act of contrition, i.e. of penitence resting on a *love of benevolence*—leading to a love of God above all other things, since his perfections make him supremely worth of love. This leads one to the whole-hearted endeavour to conform to God's will and to imitate his perfections, the better to be united with him, since it appears just that God should not withhold his grace from those who are in this state of mind. . . . I adduced the view of a Portuguese teacher, Diego Payva de Andrada, who was very famous in his day and had been one of the theologians at the Council of Trent. He went so far as to say that those who

October 5, 1669, in Schrecker, "G.-W. Leibniz. Lettres et fragments inédits," pp. 68–69, where the young Leibniz maintains that "to err against conscience [*Errare contra conscientiam*] implies contradiction. In fact, from the beginning of the world, nobody has erred against conscience. Someone errs who believes as true that which is false [*Errat qui putat verum esse quod falsum est*]. Whoever believes, this person is not otherwise convinced; whoever is not otherwise convinced, does not know better; who does not know better, does not feel against conscience. . . . We can act against conscience but we cannot believe [*sentire non possumus*] against conscience. So you see that, if only those who err against conscience are to be damned, nobody is to be damned for his error."

[43]   See Dutens V 483; A II i 535.

[44]   See in particular A I vi 117 and 119–20; A I vi 79–80; A I vi 164; *De Haeresi Formali et Materiali*, A IV vi 337.

[45]   A II i 752. In 1703, Leibniz reiterates: "to believe or not to believe is not a voluntary thing. If I believe I see a manifest error, all the authority of the world could not change my view if this [authority] is not accompanied by some reasons capable of satisfying my difficulties or of overcoming them" (Grua 216).

[46]   On Leibniz's conception of salvation and its relation to grace (and, in particular, on the notion of sufficient grace) see chapter on "Philosophical Theology and Christian Doctrines."

took the opposite view of the matter were making God supremely cruel—"For," he said, "there can be no worse cruelty."[47]

Citing with approbation the Jesuit's view that "invincible ignorance excuses, and that therefore the sincere conscience of anyone is always the last judge down here, *in conscientiae foro*" (A I vi 94), Leibniz maintains that it is not the objective truth of what one believes, but the sincerity of conscience with which one holds this belief—and behaves in consequence—that matters for salvation: "One can be of bad faith and obstinate even if he asserts the truth, that is to say when this is maintained without foundation on the basis of a bad principle" (A I vi 141). Indeed, Leibniz goes so far as to maintain that "if someone were to embrace truth in bad conscience, he could be said a formal, and not a material heretic; and would be worthy of punishment although he did not err." A bad conscience [*malum animum*] is in fact what "constitutes the formal nature of heresy."[48]

It follows that coercion in matters of religion, far from being justified in view of the eternal life of those coerced, endangers their very salvation. Thus, "it is necessary to be very careful in matters of retractations to avoid forcing people to act against their conscience" (A I v 182). Writing in 1685 to Landgraf Ernst (himself a Catholic convert from Calvinism), Leibniz claims: "One should not create hypocrites, since a true Huguenot is incomparably more worthy than a false Catholic and will sooner be saved without any doubt" (A I iv 352). In another letter of the same year, he adds: "according to what I have been told, the King said that he makes bad converts to the truth but that their children will be good Catholics. However, I doubt this is worthy of approval since it amounts to wanting to cause the damnation of some in order to save some others" (A I iv 341). Thus, "those who are correctly persuaded that someone else is on path to perdition have the right and even the obligation to try to rescue them: but this must be done through permitted means . . . coercion is the enemy of truth."[49] In short, false beliefs must be combated with persuasion and arguments, not with violence. "Let them write, let them defend their opinions," Leibniz urges. "Their errors should be overturned with equal arms, not by force and fear . . . It is extremely harmful that freedom of thinking [*sentiendi libertatem*] be restrained from day to day within unnecessary limits" (Look-Rutherford 94–7).

More generally, Leibniz regards toleration as the path suggested by the core teaching of Christianity itself. Toleration is "necessary on account of the principle of Christian charity" (A I xiv 691). Persecution and condemnation are against the spirit of Christianity since "it is clear that the spirit of Christianity should lead to mildness" (A I iv 341).

Finally, even from a pragmatic point of view, persecution tends to be ineffective and is potentially counterproductive.[50] Around 1711, Leibniz notes that "in general persecution

---

[47] *Nouveaux Essais*, book IV, chap. xviii, §9 (NE 500–1). Cf. Diego Payva Andradius, *Orthodoxarum explicationum libri decem* (Köln, 1564).

[48] *De Haeresi Formali et Materiali*, c. 1695 (A IV vi 337).

[49] *Remarques sur un petit livre traduit de l'Anglois, intitulé Lettre sur l'enthousiasme*; GP III 410.

[50] Cf. A I v 11.

is not at all desirable, and that it has wronged the faith of many people but gives relief to that of some others: more zeal is never noted than in these occasions of trial, and greater examples of a great conviction are never found" (GP III 413–4). "Under the pretext of preventing heresies," he writes to Sophie on October 26, 1691, heresies "have been engendered."

> Normally these things fade away on their own when they lose the attraction of novelty; but when one wants to suppress them with noisy denunciations, persecutions, and refutations, it is like wanting to extinguish a fire with a pair of bellows. . . . For fear of being short of heretics, Messieurs the theologians sometimes do everything they can to find some. (A I vii 38)

Commenting on the burning in England of a heretical pamphlet, Leibniz notes that those promoting the pamphlet could reasonably retort that " 'it is easier to burn such things than to refute them: the truth, indeed, cannot be burned" (A I 11 123). In his view, false beliefs that lead to good actions, or which are at least harmless from a practical point of view, should definitely be tolerated. "What I find worst of all," he writes to Bartholomew Des Bosses on July 21, 1707, "is persecution on account of opinions that do not encourage criminal acts, a practice from which honorable men should not only refrain, but which we should also abhor and work against so that others, over whom we have some authority, are discouraged from it."[51]

The limits of toleration are in fact set by unacceptable actions rather than unacceptable beliefs. As Leibniz remarks in 1683:

> it is against natural right to punish someone because he is of some opinion, no matter which, as opposed to punishing someone for some actions; *for the penalty for one who is mistaken is to be taught.* And again, I do not believe that we have the right to punish someone with corporal pains for actions which he undertakes in accordance with his opinion, and which he believes his conscience obligates him to perform, apart from the case in which these actions are evil in themselves, manifestly contrary to natural right. As if someone wanted to trouble the State and use violence and poison for a religious principle. (A II i 535; A II^2 i 843; see also NE 463)

However, even though one could readily agree that violent actions cannot be tolerated and must be punished, the problem still remains of how to deal with *doctrines* that can lead to punishable actions. Leibniz warns that "in matter of Tolerance, one should not be prone to condemn, although one should not be negligent either when a doctrine is

---

[51] Look-Rutherford 94–5. See also Leibniz to Thomas Burnett of Kemney, April 8/18, 1698 (A I xv 489): "I am delighted that authors whose views are dangerous are refuted but I am not sure it is appropriate to establish against them a kind of inquisition when their false opinions have no influence on morals; and although I am very far from the views of the Socinians, I don't believe it is right to treat them as criminals."

dangerous."[52] His preferred solution is the use of moderate censorship and, in some cases, the ban of those spreading dangerous views; but recourse to such instruments should be limited. "One has some right to take measures to prevent the propagation of a pernicious error," he acknowledges in 1706, "but that is also all one has a right to do, and these measures must be the mildest possible" (Dutens V 483). The ban, for instance, should not be universal since a universal ban would amount to sentencing people to death.

In sum, religious toleration does not follow, in Leibniz's thought, from a deflationary account of religious truth or from indifference toward the content of revealed religion.[53] According to Leibniz, there is an objective truth also for religious matters. However, "not everything which is true is always necessary," and some views which are not true can be tolerated (A I vi 118). Thus, "there is no right to condemn all errors, or always to force people to disavow them" (A I v 182). Neither does toleration rest for him on a separation between church and state, as for some of his contemporaries.[54] Rather, religious toleration is grounded on the nature of belief and on the nature of salvation. Last, but not least, it is grounded on what Leibniz takes to be the central message of Christianity: namely, charity. It is thanks to these philosophical and theological foundations that, for Leibniz, toleration can be extended in principle to all men and women of good will.[55]

---

[52] *Réflexions de Leibniz sur un Écrit Irénique de Fétizon* (August 1700), in Schrecker, "G.-W. Leibniz. Lettres et fragments inédits," p. 107.

[53] The issue of indifference is discussed in particular in Antognazza, "Leibniz and religious toleration."

[54] For a brief comparison with Locke, see Antognazza, "Leibniz's doctrine of toleration," pp. 163–164.

[55] My thanks to Howard Hotson for helpful comments on a draft of this chapter.

Index

Printed in Dunstable, United Kingdom